ECONOMICS

Ninth edition

John Sloman

The Economics Network, University of Bristol
Visiting Professor, University of the West of England

Alison Wride

Provost and Professor of Economics, GSM London
(formerly Greenwich School of Management)

Dean Garratt

Principal Teaching Fellow, University of Warwick

PEARSON

Harlow, England • London • New York • Boston • San Francisco • Toronto • Sydney
Auckland • Singapore • Hong Kong • Tokyo • Seoul • Taipei • New Delhi
Cape Town • São Paulo • Mexico City • Madrid • Amsterdam • Munich • Paris • Milan

Pearson Education Limited
Edinburgh Gate
Harlow CM20 2JE
United Kingdom
Tel: +44 (0)1279 623623
Web: www.pearson.com/uk

First edition published 1991 (print)
Second edition published 1994 (print)
Updated second edition published 1995 (print)
Third edition published 1997 (print)
Updated third edition published 1998 (print)
Fourth edition published 2000 (print)
Fifth edition published 2003 (print)
Sixth edition published 2006 (print)
Seventh edition published 2009 (print)
Eighth edition published 2012 (print and electronic)
Ninth edition 2015 (print and electronic)

Pearson Education is not responsible for the content of third-party internet sites

ISBN: 978-1-292-06477-2 (print)
      978-1-292-06484-0 (PDF)
      978-1-292-06478-9 (eText)

British Library Cataloguing-in-Publication Data
A catalogue record for this book is available from the British Library

Library of Congress Cataloguing-in-Publication Data
Sloman, John, 1947-
  Economics / John Sloman, Alison Wride, Dean Garratt. -- Ninth edition.
    pages cm
  ISBN 978-1-292-06477-2
  1. Economics. I. Wride, Alison. II. Garratt, Dean, 1970- III. Title.
  HB171.5.S635 2015
  330--dc23

                                              2014042517

10 9 8 7 6 5 4 3 2 1
14 13 12 11 10

Front cover images: John Sloman

Typeset in 8/12pt Stone Serif ITC Pro by 35
Printed and bound in Slovakia by Neografia

NOTE THAT ANY PAGE CROSS REFERENCES REFER TO THE PRINT EDITION

ECONOMICS

About the authors

John Sloman is Visiting Fellow at the University of Bristol and Associate of the Economics Network (www.economicsnetwork. ac.uk) a UK-wide organisation, where, until his retirement in 2012, he was Director. The Economics Network is based at the University of Bristol and provides a range of services designed to promote and share good practice in learning and teaching economics. The Network is supported by grants from the Royal Economic Society, the Scottish Economic Society and university economic departments and units from across the UK.

John is also Visiting Professor at the University of the West of England, Bristol, where, from 1992 to 1999, he was Head of School of Economics. He taught at UWE until 2007.

John has taught a range of courses, including economic principles on social science and business studies degrees, development economics, comparative economic systems, intermediate macroeconomics and managerial economics. He has also taught economics on various professional courses.

John is the co author with Dean Garratt of *Essentials of Economics* (Pearson Education, 6th edition 2013) and, with Kevin Hinde from the University of Durham and Dean Garratt, of *Economics for Business* (Pearson Education, 6th edition 2013) and with Elizabeth Jones of the University of Warwick of *Essential Economics for Business* (Pearson Education, 4th edition 2014). Translations or editions of the various books are available for a number of different countries with the help of co-authors around the world.

John is very interested in promoting new methods of teaching economics, including group exercises, experiments, role playing, computer-aided learning and use of audience response systems and podcasting in teaching. He has organised and spoken at conferences for both lecturers and students of economics throughout the UK and in many other countries.

As part of his work with the Economics Network he has contributed to its two sites for students and prospective students of economics: Study Economics (www.study economics.org) and Why Study Economics? (www. whystudyeconomics.ac.uk).

From March to June 1997, John was a visiting lecturer at the University of Western Australia. In July and August 2000, he was again a visiting lecturer at the University of Western Australia and also at Murdoch University in Perth.

In 2007, John received a Lifetime Achievement Award as 'outstanding teacher and ambassador of economics' presented jointly by the Higher Education Academy, the Government Economic Service and the Scottish Economic Society.

Alison Wride is Provost of GSM London and a Professor of Economics. Prior to her appointment at GSM London she was Head of the College of Business, Economics and Law at Swansea University, and before that she spent her early career at the University of Exeter. Her areas of interest include the student experience and the relationship between skills, employability and education. She is acknowledged as having expertise in understanding the factors that influence student satisfaction and has always endeavoured to bring a sense of engagement to her teaching. In 2006 Alison received the Student Nominated Award for Teaching Excellence from the Economics Network of the UK Higher Education Academy. This was followed by the University of Exeter Vice Chancellor's Award for Excellence in 2007, in recognition of both her role in leading the transformation of the student experience in the Business School and her own teaching. In 2009 Alison was awarded a National Teaching Fellowship.

Alison believes that 'good' teaching depends on great communication. She sees that her job, as a teacher and author, is to take relatively complex ideas and to explain them in a way that is accessible and that inspires the reader, leaving them wanting to know more. She has taught economics to A level students, undergraduates and to those who are already out in the world of work. Her teaching ethos is based on enthusing students, bringing economics to life and setting the theory in context. She still believes that 'the best decision I ever made – in terms of my career – was choosing to take A-level economics. I fell in love with the subject within an hour and that was entirely due to the excellence and enthusiasm of my teacher.'

Alison's external interests include work with the Treasury and Government Economic Service on economics training for non-economists working in government; she is currently involved in a similar initiative with the Department for Business, Innovation and Skills. This work focuses on furnishing those at the cutting edge of developing policy with the tools and economic understanding to ensure that both the formulation of aims and the choice of methods result in coherent strategies that enhance efficiency and equity.

Dean Garratt is a Principal Teaching Fellow in the Department of Economics at the University of Warwick. Prior to joining Warwick in 2014, Dean was a principal lecturer and course leader of the undergraduate economics portfolio at Nottingham Business School. Dean teaches economics at a variety of levels, both to students on economics courses and to those taking economics on other degree courses.

Earlier in his career Dean worked as an economic assistant at both HM Treasury and at the Council of Mortgage Lenders. While at these institutions Dean was researching and briefing on a variety of issues relating to the household sector and to the housing and mortgage markets.

His time as an economic assistant has significantly influenced Dean's approach towards the teaching of economics. This has seen Dean frequently adopt a problem or issues-based approach in his teaching of economics. Dean believes that a deeper understanding of what it means to think like an economist is achieved when students are encouraged to see the relevance and application of economic ideas and principles.

In 2006 Dean received an Outstanding Teaching Award from the Economics Network of the Higher Education Academy. The award is given to an academic who demonstrates excellence in course structure, delivery, student response, student performance and peer recognition.

Subsequently, Dean became an Associate of the Economics Network helping to promote quality teaching practices through presentations and workshops. Dean has been involved in projects to develop problem-based learning and teaching resources for economists, including resources for use on level 1 quantitative methods and data analysis modules.

Dean is an academic assessor for the Government Economic Service (GES). In this role he helps to assess potential recruits to the GES with particular focus on the ability of candidates to articulate their understanding of economics and its applications.

Outside of work, Dean is an avid watcher of most sports. He is a season ticket holder at both Leicester City Football Club and Leicestershire County Cricket Club.

Brief Contents

Custom Publishing   *xv*

Preface   *xvi*

Student Resources Flowchart   *xx*

Lecturer Resources Flowchart   *xxi*

Acknowledgements   *xxii*

Publisher's Acknowledgements   *xxiii*

Part A   **INTRODUCTION**

     Why Economics is Good for You   2

1   Economics and Economies   6

Part B   **FOUNDATIONS OF MICROECONOMICS**

2   Supply and Demand   34

3   Markets in Action   60

Part C   **MICROECONOMIC THEORY**

4   Background to Demand   100

5   Background to Supply   132

6   Profit Maximising under Perfect Competition and Monopoly   170

7   Profit Maximising under Imperfect Competition   193

8   Alternative Theories of the Firm   221

9   The Theory of Distribution of Income   246

Part D   **MICROECONOMIC POLICY**

10   Inequality, Poverty and Policies to Redistribute Income   284

11   Markets, Efficiency and the Public Interest   314

12   Environmental Policy   353

13   Government Policy towards Business   381

Part E	FOUNDATIONS OF MACROECONOMICS	
14	The National Economy	400
15	Macroeconomic Issues and Analysis: An Overview	430
16	Macroeconomic Issues, Debates and Controversies	463

Part F	MACROECONOMIC MODELS, THEORIES AND POLICY	
17	Short-run Macroeconomic Equilibrium	494
18	Banking, Money and Interest Rates	523
19	The Relationship between the Money and Goods Markets	560
20	Aggregate Supply, Unemployment and Inflation	593
21	Fiscal and Monetary Policy	625
22	Long-term Economic Growth	669
23	Supply-side Policies	684

Part G	THE WORLD ECONOMY	
24	International Trade	706
25	The Balance of Payments and Exchange Rates	741
26	Global and Regional Interdependence	778
27	Economics of Developing Countries	799
	Postscript: The Castaways or Vote for Caliban	832
	Appendix 1: Some Techniques of Economic Analysis	A:1
	Appendix 2: Websites	A:15
	Threshold Concepts and Key Ideas	T:1
	Glossary	G:1
	Index	I:1

Contents

Custom Publishing		xv
Preface		xvi
Student Resources Flowchart		xx
Lecturer Resources Flowchart		xxi
Acknowledgements		xxii
Publisher's Acknowledgements		xxiii

Part A   INTRODUCTION

Why Economics is Good for You — 2
What is economics?	3
Puzzles and stories	4
Applying the principles	5

1 Economics and Economies — 6
1.1	What do economists study?	7
1.2	Different economic systems	18
1.3	The nature of economic reasoning	27

Boxes
1.1	What's the latest economics news?	8
1.2	Looking at macroeconomic data	10
1.3	The opportunity costs of studying	14
1.4	Scarcity and abundance	16
1.5	Command economies	22
1.6	Adam Smith (1723–90)	24
1.7	Ceteris paribus	28

Part B   FOUNDATIONS OF MICROECONOMICS

2 Supply and Demand — 34
2.1	Demand	35
2.2	Supply	42
2.3	Price and output determination	45
2.4	The control of prices	55

Boxes
*2.1	The demand for lamb	40
2.2	UK house prices	50
2.3	Stock market prices	52
2.4	Underground (or shadow) markets	57

3 Markets in Action — 60
3.1	Elasticity	61
3.2	The time dimension	74
3.3	Indirect taxes	80
3.4	Government rejection of market allocation	84
3.5	Agriculture and agricultural policy	86

Boxes
3.1	Advertising and its effect on demand curves	66
3.2	Any more fares?	67
*3.3	Using calculus to calculate the price elasticity of demand	69
3.4	Short selling	78
3.5	Dealing in futures markets	79
3.6	Ashes to ashes?	82
3.7	The fallacy of composition	88
3.8	Feed the world	94

Part C   MICROECONOMIC THEORY

4 Background to Demand — 100
4.1	Marginal utility theory	101
*4.2	Indifference analysis	109
4.3	Demand under conditions of risk and uncertainty	120
4.4	Behavioural economics	125

Boxes
*4.1	Using calculus to derive a marginal utility function	103
4.2	The marginal utility revolution: Jevons, Menger, Walras	107
4.3	Taking account of time	108
*4.4	Love and caring	114
*4.5	Consumer theory a further approach	119
4.6	Problems with insurance markets	124
4.7	Nudging people	127
4.8	Is economics the study of selfish behaviour?	129

5 Background to Supply — 132
5.1	The short-run theory of production	133
5.2	Costs in the short run	139

5.3 The long-run theory of production 144
5.4 Costs in the long run 154
5.5 Revenue 158
5.6 Profit maximisation 162

Boxes

5.1 Malthus and the dismal science of economics 134
5.2 Diminishing returns in the bread shop 137
5.3 The relationship between averages and marginals 138
*5.4 The relationship between TPP, MPP and APP 138
5.5 The fallacy of using historic costs 140
5.6 Cost curves in practice 143
*5.7 The Cobb–Douglas production function 149
5.8 Minimum efficient scale 156
*5.9 Using calculus to find the maximum profit output 165
5.10 The logic of logistics 167

6 Profit Maximising under Perfect Competition and Monopoly 170
6.1 Alternative market structures 171
6.2 Perfect competition 172
6.3 Monopoly 181
6.4 The theory of contestable markets 188

Boxes

6.1 Concentration ratios 173
6.2 Is perfect best? 174
6.3 E-commerce and market structure 178
6.4 Breaking Sky's monopoly on live football coverage 185
6.5 X inefficiency 186
6.6 Cut-throat competition 187
6.7 Airline deregulation in the USA and Europe 190

7 Profit Maximising under Imperfect Competition 193
7.1 Monopolistic competition 194
7.2 Oligopoly 197
7.3 Game theory 209
7.4 Price discrimination 214

Boxes

7.1 Selling ice cream as a student 195
7.2 Increasing concentration 199
7.3 OPEC 202
7.4 Buying power 208
7.5 The prisoners' dilemma 211
7.6 What's the train fare to London? 215
7.7 Peak-load pricing 215
7.8 Just the ticket? 218

8 Alternative Theories of the Firm 221
8.1 Problems with traditional theory 222
8.2 Behavioural theories 224
8.3 Alternative maximising theories 228
8.4 Multiple aims 238
8.5 Pricing in practice 240

Boxes

8.1 What do you maximise? 223
8.2 The US sub-prime hosing crisis 226
8.3 When is a theory not a theory? 228
8.4 Enron 234
8.5 Merger activity 236
8.6 Stakeholder power? 238
8.7 How do companies set prices? 242
8.8 How firms increase profits by understanding 'irrational' consumers 244

9 The Theory of Distribution of Income 246
9.1 Wage determination under perfect competition 247
9.2 Wage determination in imperfect markets 256
9.3 Capital and profit 268
9.4 Land and rent 278

Boxes

9.1 Labour as a factor of production 248
*9.2 Using indifference curve analysis to derive the individual's supply curve of labour 250
9.3 Immigration and the UK labour market 251
9.4 Life at the mill 257
9.5 The rise and decline of the labour movement in the UK 260
9.6 How useful is marginal productivity theory? 261
9.7 Equal pay for equal work? 262
9.8 Flexible labour markets and the flexible firm 264
9.9 Behaviour at work 266
9.10 Stocks and flows 271
9.11 The economics of non-renewable resources 280

Part D **MICROECONOMIC POLICY**

10 Inequality, Poverty and Policies to Redistribute Income 284
10.1 Inequality and poverty 285
10.2 Taxes, benefits and the redistribution of income 296

Boxes

10.1 Poverty in the past 293
10.2 Minimum wage legislation 295
10.3 The Laffer curve 303
*10.4 Tax cuts and incentives 304
10.5 UK tax credits 309
10.6 Reducing inequality 310
10.7 What the future holds 311

11 Markets, Efficiency and the Public Interest 314
11.1 Efficiency under perfect competition 315
11.2 The case for government intervention 323
11.3 Forms of government intervention 333
*11.4 Cost–benefit analysis 340
11.5 Government failure and the case for the market 348

Boxes

11.1	The police as a public service	326
11.2	A commons solution	328
11.3	Should health-care provision be left to the market?	332
11.4	Deadweight loss from taxes on goods and services	335
11.5	Putting the 'personal' into personal services	339
*11.6	What price a human life?	343
*11.7	HS2: is it really worth it?	344
11.8	Mises, Hayek and the Mont Pelerin Society	348

12   Environmental Policy   353

12.1	Economics of the environment	354
12.2	Policies to tackle pollution and its effects	359
12.3	The economics of traffic congestion	369
12.4	Urban transport policies	373

Boxes

12.1	A Stern warning	356
12.2	Green taxes	362
12.3	Are we all green now?	364
12.4	International co-ordination on climate change	364
12.5	Trading our way out of climate change	366
12.6	Restricting car access to Athens	375
12.7	Road pricing in Singapore	377
12.8	The economy and the environment	378

13   Government Policy towards Business   381

13.1	Competition policy	382
13.2	Privatisation and regulation	389

Boxes

13.1	Squeaky clean competition?	384
13.2	More than a coincidence?	386
13.3	Buy now, pay (a great deal more) later	388
13.4	Selling power to the people	394

Part E   FOUNDATIONS OF MACROECONOMICS

14   The National Economy   400

14.1	The scope of macroeconomics	401
14.2	The circular flow of income	405
14.3	Measuring national income and output	408
14.4	Short-term economic growth and the business cycle	414
14.5	Long-term economic growth	419
	Appendix: Calculating GDP	425

Boxes

14.1	Which country is better off?	411
14.2	Can GDP measure national happiness?	413
14.3	Output gaps	414
14.4	Is stability always desirable?	418
14.5	Theories of growth	421
14.6	The costs of economic growth	422

15   Macroeconomic Issues and Analysis: An Overview   430

15.1	The key issues: a recap	431
15.2	Unemployment	431
15.3	Aggregate demand and supply and the level of prices	441
15.4	Inflation	444
15.5	The balance of payments and exchange rates	453

Boxes

15.1	The costs of unemployment	436
15.2	Cost-push illusion	448
15.3	Inflation or deflation?	449
15.4	The Phillips curve	450
15.5	Dealing in foreign exchange	459

16   Macroeconomic Issues, Debates and Controversies   463

16.1	The macroeconomic environment and debates	464
16.2	Setting the scene: four key controversies	465
16.3	Classical macroeconomics	468
16.4	The Keynesian revolution	473
16.5	The rise of the monetarist and new classical schools	477
16.6	The Keynesian response	481
16.7	An emerging consensus up to the crisis of 2008	484
16.8	The financial crisis and the search for a new consensus	486

Boxes

16.1	Balance the budget at all costs	471
16.2	The crowding-out effect	472
16.3	Will wage cuts cure unemployment?	474
16.4	The paradox of thrift	489

Part F   MACROECONOMIC MODELS, THEORIES AND POLICY

17   Short-run Macroeconomic Equilibrium   494

17.1	Background to the theory	495
17.2	The determination of national income	507
17.3	The simple Keynesian analysis of unemployment and inflation	513
17.4	The Keynesian analysis of the business cycle	516

Boxes

*17.1	Using calculus to derive the MPC	500
17.2	The household sector balance sheets	502
17.3	Sentiment and spending	504
17.4	Deriving the multiplier formula	511
17.5	Has there been an acceleration effect in the UK?	519

18 Banking, Money and Interest Rates 523

18.1 The meaning and functions of money 524
18.2 The financial system 525
18.3 The supply of money 543
18.4 The demand for money 553
18.5 Equilibrium 557

Boxes

18.1 Money supply, national income and national
wealth 524
18.2 The growth of banks' balance sheets 530
18.3 The rise of securitisation 534
18.4 UK and eurozone monetary aggregates 544
*18.5 Calculating the money multiplier 547
18.6 Credit, the money supply and Minsky's financial
instability hypothesis 550

**19 The Relationship between the Money and
Goods Markets** 560

19.1 The effects of monetary changes on national
income 561
19.2 The monetary effects of changes in the goods
market 572
19.3 The interaction of monetary policy and the
goods market 575
19.4 ADI/ASI model 582
*Appendix: The IS/LM model 585

Boxes

19.1 Choosing the exchange rate or the money supply 566
19.2 Party games and the velocity of money 568
19.3 The stability of the velocity of circulation 570
19.4 Crowding out in an open economy 574
19.5 The financial accelerator 580

**20 Aggregate Supply, Unemployment and
Inflation** 593

20.1 Aggregate supply 594
20.2 The expectations-augmented Phillips curve 602
20.3 Inflation and unemployment: the new classical
position 609
20.4 Inflation and unemployment: the modern
Keynesian position 615
*20.5 Output inflation and expectations:
an integrated model 618
20.6 Postscript: the state of macroeconomic
thinking post-crisis 622

Boxes

20.1 Cost-push inflation and supply shocks 600
*20.2 Analysing demand-pull and cost-push
inflation using the ADI/ASI model 601
*20.3 Basing expectations on the past 604
20.4 The political business cycle 608
20.5 The rational expectations revolution 610
20.6 Forecasting the weather 612
20.7 The boy who cried 'Wolf' 614

21 Fiscal and Monetary Policy 625

21.1 Fiscal policy 626
21.2 Monetary policy 640
21.3 The policy-making environment 656
*Appendix: IS/LM analysis of fiscal and
monetary policy 665

Boxes

21.1 UK and US fiscal policy during and after the
financial crisis 632
21.2 Riding a switchback 636
21.3 The evolving fiscal frameworks in the UK and
eurozone 637
21.4 The operation of monetary policy in the UK 644
21.5 Central banking and monetary policy in the USA 646
21.6 Monetary policy in the eurozone 650
21.7 Goodhart's law 653
21.8 Using interest rates to control both aggregate
demand and the exchange rate 654
21.9 Quantitative easing 655
21.10 Inflation targeting 658
21.11 Interest rate responses and the financial crisis
of 2007–9 660
*21.12 How do inflation targets work in practice? 662

22 Long-term Economic Growth 669

22.1 Long-run economic growth in industrialised
countries 670
22.2 Economic growth without technological progress 673
22.3 Economic growth with technological progress 678

Boxes

22.1 Getting intensive with capital 676
22.2 Labour productivity 680

23 Supply-side Policies 684

23.1 Supply-side policies and the macroeconomy 685
23.2 Approaches to supply-side policy 686
23.3 Market-orientated supply-side policies 687
23.4 Interventionist supply-side policy 695

Boxes

23.1 The supply-side revolution in the USA 689
23.2 Assessing PFI 692
23.3 A new approach to industrial policy 697
23.4 Alternative approaches to training and education 700
23.5 Unemployment and supply-side policies 703

Part G   THE WORLD ECONOMY

24 International Trade 706

24.1 The advantages of trade 707
24.2 Arguments for restricting trade 719
24.3 Preferential trading 729
24.4 The European Union 733

Boxes

24.1	Trading places	708
24.2	Sharing out the jobs	711
24.3	Trade as exploitation?	713
24.4	Free trade and the environment	720
24.5	Strategic trade theory	722
*24.6	The optimum tariff or export tax	724
24.7	Giving trade a bad name	725
24.8	The Doha development agenda	726
24.9	Mutual recognition: the Cassis de Dijon case	735
24.10	Features of the single market	736
24.11	The Internal Market Scoreboard	738

25 The Balance of Payments and Exchange Rates 741

25.1	Alternative exchange rate regimes	742
25.2	Fixed exchange rates	752
25.3	Free-floating exchange rates	757
25.4	Exchange rate systems in practice	765
	*Appendix: The open economy IS/LM analysis	772

Boxes

25.1	Balance of trade and the public finances	744
25.2	The UK's balance of payments deficit	746
25.3	The effectiveness of fiscal and monetary policies under fixed exchange rates	755
25.4	The price of a Big Mac	758
25.5	The euro/dollar seesaw	762
25.6	The effectiveness of monetary and fiscal policies under floating exchange rates	764
25.7	Sterling in the 1990s and 2000s	768
25.8	Do inflation rates explain longer-term exchange rate movements?	771

26 Global and Regional Interdependence 778

26.1	Globalisation and the problem of instability	779
26.2	European economic and monetary union (EMU)	788
26.3	Achieving greater currency stability	793

Boxes

26.1	Globalisation and the US trade imbalance	782
26.2	Doctor, the world has caught a cold	786
26.3	Optimal currency areas	792
26.4	The Tobin tax	796

27 Economics of Developing Countries 799

27.1	The problem of underdevelopment	800
27.2	International trade and development	805
27.3	Structural problems within developing countries	817
27.4	The problem of debt	823

Boxes

27.1	The Human Development Index	804
27.2	When driving and alcohol do mix	811
27.3	The Chinese economic miracle	814
*27.4	Unemployment in developing countries	820
27.5	The building BRICs of development	822
27.6	'Ecocide'	826
27.7	Swapping debt	828

Postscript: The Castaways or Vote for Caliban	832
Appendix 1: Some Techniques of Economic Analysis	A:1
Appendix 2: Websites	A:15
Threshold Concepts and Key Ideas	T:1
Glossary	G:1
Index	I:1

Supporting Resources

You can use the power of MyEconLab to accelerate your learning. You need both an access card and a course ID to access MyEconLab. Students, is your lecturer using MyEconLab? If so, ask your lecturer for your course ID.

Has an access card been included with the book? Check the inside back cover of the book.

If you have a course ID but no access card, go to: www.myeconlab.com to buy access to this interactive study programme.

MyEconLab

MyEconLab for *Economics*, 9th edition enables you to assess your learning and provides you with a personalised Study Plan, which identifies areas you need to concentrate on to improve your grades. Specific tools are provided to direct your study in the most efficient way.

You can register at www.MyEconLab.com to find essential learning material such as:

- a personalised Study Plan, with extensive self-testing material and homework that can be set by your tutor;
- a complete online workbook for use alongside the textbook as you learn;
- multiple-choice questions to test your learning;
- extra case studies with questions per chapter;
- maths cases with exercises, related to the Looking at the Maths boxes in the book;
- answers to all in-chapter questions;
- an economics news blog updated several times per month – (each news item has an introduction, links to a range of news articles, questions and references to the relevant chapter of the book);
- animations of all key models with audio explanations, which can be downloaded to your iPod, iPad, iPhone or MP4 player;
- extensive annotated Hotlinks to relevant sites on the Internet, regularly updated;
- an online glossary to explain key terms with flashcards to test your knowledge;

MyEconLab for lecturers

- MyEconLab's gradebook which automatically records each student's time spent and performance on the tests and Study Plan and generates reports you can use to monitor your students' progress;
- using MyEconLab to build your own tests, assessments and homework assignments from the question base provided;
- questions generated algorithmically so that they use different values each time they are used;
- creation, if desired, of your own exercises by using the econ exercise builder.

For lecturers wanting more information about the MyEconLab product, please contact your local Pearson sales representative at www.pearsoned.co.uk/replocator or visit www.myeconlab.com.
Additional lecturer resources:

- tutor guide to using chapters and discussion of learning/teaching issues;
- customisable lecture plans in PowerPoint with questions for use in lectures with or without an audience response system;
- key models animated as full-colour PowerPoint slide shows;
- downloadable PowerPoint slides of all figures and tables from the book;
- a range of teaching and learning case studies;
- workshops with answers;
- answers to end-of-chapter questions;
- answers to the case studies found in MyEconLab.

These lecturer resources can be downloaded from the lecturer website at www.pearsoned.co.uk/sloman. Click on the *Economics*, 9th edition cover and select lecturer resources.

Custom Publishing

Custom publishing allows academics to pick and choose content from one or more textbooks for their course and combine it into a definitive course text.

Here are some common examples of custom solutions which have helped over 1000 courses across Europe:

- different chapters from across our publishing imprints combined into one book;
- lecturer's own material combined together with textbook chapters or published in a separate booklet;
- third-party cases and articles that you are keen for your students to read as part of the course;
- any combination of the above.

The Pearson Education custom text published for your course is professionally produced and bound – just as you would expect from any Pearson Education text. Since many of our titles have online resources accompanying them we can even build a Custom website that matches your course text.

If you are teaching a first year Economics course you may have a large teaching team with different lecturers teaching the micro and macroeconomics sections. Do you find that it can be difficult to agree on one textbook? If you do, you might find combining the macro and micro halves from different Pearson textbooks a useful solution. You may teach a mixed ability class and would like to be able to provide some advanced material from Sloman's larger economics text or perhaps you take more of a business focus where chapters from Sloman's *Essential Economics for Business* might be useful.

Custom publishing has enabled adopters of this text to employ these different solutions.

If, once you have had time to review this title, you feel Custom publishing might benefit you and your course, please do get in contact. However minor, or major the change – we can help you out.

For more details on how to make your chapter selection for your course please go to www.pearsoned.co.uk/sloman and select the custom publishing link.

You can contact us at: **www.pearsoncustom.co.uk** or via your local representative at: **www.pearsoned.co.uk/replocator**.

Preface

Economics affects all our lives. As consumers we try to make the best of our limited incomes. As workers – or future workers – we take our place in the job market. As citizens of a country our lives are affected by the decisions of our government and other policy-makers: decisions over taxes, decisions over spending on health and education, decisions on interest rates, decisions that affect unemployment, inflation and growth. As dwellers on the planet Earth we are affected by the economic decisions of each other: the air we breathe, the water we drink and the environment we leave to our children are all affected by the economic decisions taken by the human race.

Economics thus deals with some of the most challenging issues we face. It is this that still excites us about economics after many years of teaching the subject. We hope that some of this excitement rubs off on you.

The first eight editions of *Economics* have been widely used in the UK and throughout the world. Like them, this new edition is suitable for all students of economics at first-year degree level, A-level or on various professional courses where a broad grounding in both principles and applications is required. It is structured to be easily understood by those of you who are new to the subject, with various sections and boxes that can be left out on first reading or on shorter courses; yet it also has sufficient depth to challenge those of you who have studied the subject before, with starred sections (appearing on a grey background) and starred case studies that will provide much that is new. There are also optional short mathematical sections for those of you studying a more quantitatively-focused course.

The book gives a self-contained introduction to the world of economics and is thus ideal for those who will not study the subject beyond introductory level. But by carefully laying a comprehensive foundation and by the inclusion of certain materials in starred sections that bridge the gap between introductory and second-level economics, it provides the necessary coverage for those of you going on to specialise in economics.

The book looks at the world of the early twenty-first century. Despite huge advances in technology and despite the comfortable lives led by many people in the industrialised world, we still suffer from unemployment, poverty and inequality, and in many countries (the UK included) the gap between rich and poor has grown much wider; our environment is polluted; our economy still goes through periodic recessions; conflict and disagreement often dominate over peace and harmony.

What is more, the world order has been changing. With a growing interdependence of the economies of the world; with an inexorable process of 'globalisation', which links us all through a web of telecommunications and international trade into a world of Coca-Cola, Nike trainers, Microsoft, football and American TV shows; with repeated bouts of turmoil on international financial markets culminating in the banking crisis of 2008–9, the effects of which are still being felt today; with evidence that economic problems spread like a contagion around the world, tying domestic economic growth to global events; with Chinese economic growth increasingly becoming the powerhouse of the global economy; with the move away from the ideological simplicity of a 'free-market' solution to all economic problems; with a powerful but economically sluggish eurozone; with concerns over levels of indebtedness and financial resilience in the public and private sectors in many economies; and with an ever-deepening crisis for many of the poorest developing countries, often ravaged by disease, conflict and famine; so there are many new economic challenges that face us. Economists are called on to offer solutions.

But despite our changing environment, there are certain economic fundamentals that do not change. Despite disagreements among economists – and there are plenty – there is a wide measure of agreement on how to analyse these fundamentals.

We hope that this book will give you an enjoyable introduction to the economist's world and that it will equip you with the tools to understand and criticise the economic policies that others pursue.

Good luck and have fun.

John, Alison and Dean

TO LECTURERS AND TUTORS

In the light of the financial crisis, there has been much soul searching amongst economists about the appropriateness of the models we use and what should be taught to our students. These concerns were debated at an international conference at the Bank of England in 2012. One outcome of this was the publication of a book, *What's the Use of Economics*[1]. This considers how undergraduate courses could be reformed to meet the needs of employers and how economic models and syllabuses could be revised to reflect the real world and to provide a foundation for devising effective economic policy.

We attempted to address these concerns in the eight edition of this book and have gone further in this new edition. In particular, we have incorporated recent developments in macroeconomics, including stressing the importance of balance sheets and systemic risk. We have also given much more weight to behavioural economics and to the importance of institutional structures and culture.

In addition we show how many of the theories have developed to explain the problems that existed at the time. We have thus continued to emphasise the link between the history of economic thought and economic history.

This new edition also retains many of the popular features of the previous edition:

- A style that is direct and to the point, with the aim all the time to provide maximum clarity. There are numerous examples to aid comprehension.
- All economic terms highlighted in the text where they first appear and defined at the foot of that page. Each term is also highlighted in the index, so that the student can simply look up a given definition as required. By defining them on the page where they appear, the student can also see the terms used in context in the text.
- Key ideas highlighted and explained when they first appear. There are 39 of these ideas, which are fundamental to the study of economics. Students can see them recurring throughout the book, and an icon appears in the margin to refer back to the page where the idea first appears.
- Fifteen 'threshold concepts'. Understanding and being able to relate and apply these core economic concepts helps students to 'think like an economist' and to relate the different parts of the subject to each other. Again, an icon appears in the margin wherever the concept recurs.
- A wealth of applied material in boxes (185 in all), making learning more interesting for students and, by relating economics to the real world, bringing the subject alive. The boxes allow the book to be comprehensive without the text becoming daunting and allow more advanced material to be introduced where appropriate. Many of the boxes can be used as class exercises and virtually all have questions at the end.
- Full-page chapter introductions. These set the scene for the chapter by introducing the students to the topics covered and relating them to the everyday world. The introductions also include a 'chapter map'. This provides a detailed contents listing, helping students to see how the chapter is structured and how the various topics relate to each other.
- A consistent use of colour in graphs and diagrams, with explanations in panels where appropriate. These features make them easier to comprehend and more appealing.
- Starred sections and boxes for more advanced material (appearing with a grey background). These can be omitted without interrupting the flow of the argument. This allows the book to be used by students with different abilities and experience, and on courses of different levels of difficulty.
- 'Looking at the maths' sections. These short sections express a topic mathematically. Some use calculus; some do not. They are designed to be used on more quantitatively focused courses and go further than other textbooks at introductory level in meeting the needs of students on such courses. Most refer students to worked examples in Maths Cases in MyEconLab. Some of these use simultaneous equations; some use simple unconstrained optimisation techniques; others use constrained optimisation, using both substitution and Lagrange multipliers. The 'Looking at the maths' sections are short and can be omitted by students on non-mathematical courses without any loss of continuity.
- An open learning approach, with questions incorporated into the text so as to test and reinforce students' understanding as they progress. This makes learning a much more active process.
- End of chapter questions. These can be set as work for students to do in class or at home. Alternatively, students can simply use them to check their comprehension at the end of a topic.
- Summaries given at the end of each section, thus providing a point for reflection and checking on comprehension at reasonably frequent intervals.
- An even micro/macro split.
- The book is divided into seven parts. This makes the structure transparent and makes it easier for the student to navigate.
- Despite retaining these popular features, there have been many changes to this eighth edition.

Extensive revision

Economics (9th edition) uses a lot of applied material, both to illustrate theory and policy, and to bring the subject

[1] Diane Coyle (ed.), *What's the Use of Economics?* (London Publishing Partnership, 2012).

alive for students by relating it to contemporary issues. This has meant that, as with the previous edition, much of the book has had to be rewritten to reflect contemporary issues. Specifically this means that:

- Many of the boxes are new or extensively revised.
- There are many new examples given in the text.
- Theoretical coverage has been strengthened at various points in the book. This includes:
  - an increased emphasis on the role of borrowing, debt, balance sheets and risk at the government, corporate and household levels;
  - the development of macroeconomic models, including the interaction between the *IS/MP* model and the *ADI/ASI* model;
  - increased emphasis on behavioural economics.
- The text provides extensive coverage of the recent developments in money and banking and their impact on economies.

- All policy sections reflect the changes that have taken place since the last edition, including changes to the regulation of businesses and the protection of the environment, and international responses to the financial crisis and policies adopted in various countries to reduce levels of public-sector deficits and debt. The text enables students to see how they can apply fundamental economic concepts to gain a better understanding of these important issues and, as a result, analyse the actual responses of policy makers as well as the alternatives that could perhaps have been pursued.
- All tables and charts have been updated, as have factual references in the text.
- Most importantly, every single section and every single sentence of the book have been carefully considered, and if necessary redrafted, to ensure both maximum clarity and contemporary relevance. The result, we hope, is a text that your students will find exciting and relevant to today's world.

SUGGESTIONS FOR SHORTER OR LESS ADVANCED COURSES

The book is designed to be used on a number of different types of course. Because of its comprehensive nature, the inclusion of a lot of optional material and the self-contained nature of many of the chapters and sections, it can be used very flexibly.

It is suitable for one-year principles courses at first-year degree level, two-year economics courses on non-economics degrees, A-level, HND and professional courses. It is also highly suitable for single-semester courses, either with a micro or a macro focus, or giving a broad outline of the subject.

The following suggests chapters which are appropriate to different types of course and gives some guidance on chapters that can be omitted while retaining continuity:

Alternative 1: Less advanced but comprehensive courses

Omit all starred sections, starred sub-sections and starred boxes.

Example of a comprehensive course, omitting some of these chapters: Chapters 1–7, 9, 11–13, 14, 15, 17–22, 24–25.

Alternative 2: Economics for Business courses

Chapters 1–3, 5–9, 12–15, 18, 21, 23–26.

Example of an Economics for Business course, omitting some of these chapters: Chapters 1–3, 5–9, 13, 14, 15, 18, 21, 24–25.

Alternative 3: Introduction to microeconomics

Chapters 1–13, 24. The level of difficulty can be varied by including or omitting starred sections and boxes from these chapters.

Example of an Introduction to Microeconomics course, omitting some of these chapters: Chapters 1–7, 9, 11–13, 24.

Alternative 4: Introduction to macroeconomics

Chapters 1, 2, 14–26. The level of difficulty can be varied by including or omitting starred sections and boxes from these chapters.

Example of an Introduction to Macroeconomics course, omitting some of these chapters: Chapters 1, 2 (if microeconomics has not previously been covered), 14, 15, 17–23, 25.

Alternative 5: Outline courses

Chapters 1, 2, 5, 6, 14, 15, 17, 18, 24, 25 (section 25.1). Omit boxes at will.

Alternative 6: Courses with a theory bias

Chapters 1, 2, 4–9, 11, 14–19, 20, 22, 24, 25. The level of difficulty can be varied by including or omitting starred sections and boxes from these chapters.

Alternative 7: Courses with a policy bias (and only basic theory)

Chapters 1–3, 5, 6, 10–15, (17), 21, 23–26.

COMPANION RESOURCES

MyEconLab (for students)

MyEconLab is a comprehensive set of online resources developed for the 9th edition of *Economics*.

It provides a variety of tools to enable students to assess their own learning, including exercises, quizzes and tests, arranged chapter by chapter. There are many new questions in this edition and each question has been carefully considered to reflect the learning objectives of the chapter. A personalised Study Plan identifies areas to concentrate on to improve grades, and specific tools are provided to each student to direct their studies in the most efficient way.

In addition, a large range of other resources are available in MyEconLab, including:

- Animations of key models with audio explanations. These can be watched online or downloaded to a computer, MP4 player, smart phone, etc.
- A news blog with news items added several times each month.
- A comprehensive glossary with flashcards to check students' knowledge.
- 193 case studies with questions for self-study, ordered chapter by chapter and referred to in the text.
- Maths cases with exercises, related to the 'Looking at the Maths' sections in the book.
- Updated list of over 290 hotlinks to sites of use for economics.
- Answers to all in-chapter questions.
- Learning objectives for each chapter written in 'student-friendly' language.

Note that the news blog and hotlinks can also be accessed directly from www.pearsoned.co.uk/sloman.

MyEconLab (for lecturers)

You can register online at www.myeconlab.com to use MyEconLab, which is a complete virtual learning environment for your course or embedded into Blackboard, WebCT or Moodle. You can customise its look and feel and its availability to students. You can use it to provide support to your students in the following ways:

- MyEconLab's gradebook automatically records each student's time spent and performance on the tests and Study Plan. It also generates reports you can use to monitor your students' progress.
- You can use MyEconLab to build your own tests, quizzes and homework assignments from the question base provided to set for your students' assessment.
- Questions are generated algorithmically so that they use different values each time they are used.
- You can create your own exercises by using the econ exercise builder.

Additional resources for lecturers

There are also many additional resources for lecturers and tutors that can be downloaded from the lecturer section of MyEconLab. These have been thoroughly revised from the 8th edition. These include:

- PowerPoint® slideshows in full colour for use with a data projector in lectures and classes. These can also be made available to students by loading them on to a local network. Suggestions for use are given in an accompanying Word® file. There are several types of these slideshows:
  - All figures from the book and most of the tables. Each figure is built up in a logical sequence, thereby allowing them to be shown in lectures in an animated form. They are also available in a simple version suitable for printing onto acetate for OHPs.
  - A range of models. There are 37 files, each containing one of the key models from the book, developed in an animated sequence of between 20 and 80 screens.
  - Customisable lecture slideshows. These are a series of bullet-point screens. There is one for each chapter of the book. Each one can be easily edited, with points added, deleted or moved, so as to suit particular lectures. A consistent use of colour is made to show how the points tie together. They come in various versions:
    o Lecture slideshows with integrated diagrams. These lecture plans include animated diagrams, charts and tables at the appropriate points.
    o Lecture slideshows with integrated diagrams and questions. These include multiple-choice questions to allow lectures to become more interactive and can be used with or without an audience response system (ARS). ARS versions are available for InterWrite PRS® and for TurningPoint® and are ready to use with the appropriate 'clickers'.
    o Lecture slideshows without the diagrams. These allow you to construct your own on the blackboard or whiteboard or use an OHP.
- Tutor's Guide in Word®. This contains suggestions on how to use the text. It also contains learning objectives that can be used for syllabus design and course planning.
- Answers to all questions in *Economics* (9th edition): i.e. questions embedded in the text, box questions and end-of-chapter questions. These can be edited as desired and distributed to students.
- Answers to the case studies and maths cases found in MyEconLab.
- Case studies. These 193 cases, also available to students in MyEconLab, can be reproduced and used for classroom exercises or for student assignments. Most cases have questions, to which answers are also provided (not available to students).
- Maths cases. These 27 maths cases with exercises, also available to students in MyEconLab, relate to the 'Looking at the Maths' sections in the book. Answers to the exercises are also provided (not available to students).
- Workshops. There are 20 of these (10 micro and 10 macro/international). They are in Word® and can be reproduced for use with large groups of students (up to 200). They can also be amended to suit your course. Suggestions for use are given in an accompanying file. Answers to all workshop questions are given in separate Word® files.
- Teaching/learning case studies. These 20 case studies examine various ways to improve student learning of introductory economics. They have been completely revised with new hyperlinks where appropriate.

The following two pages show in diagrammatic form all the student and lecturer resources.

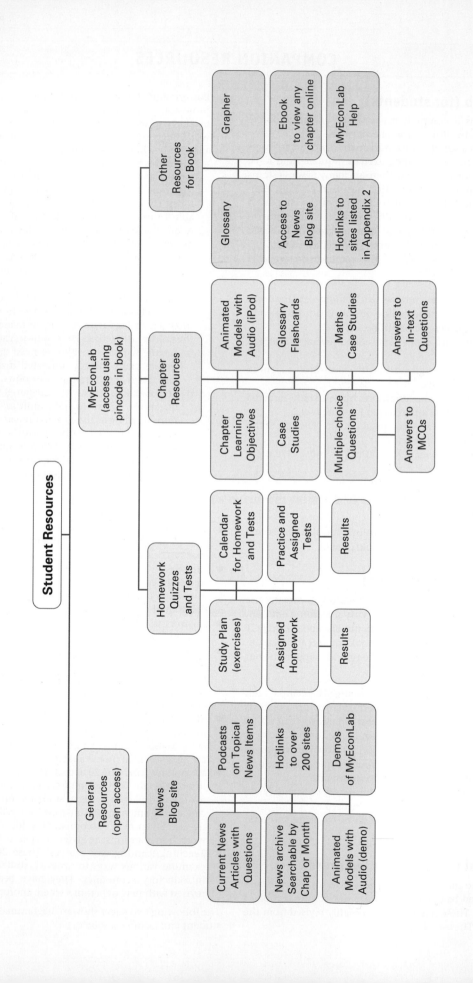

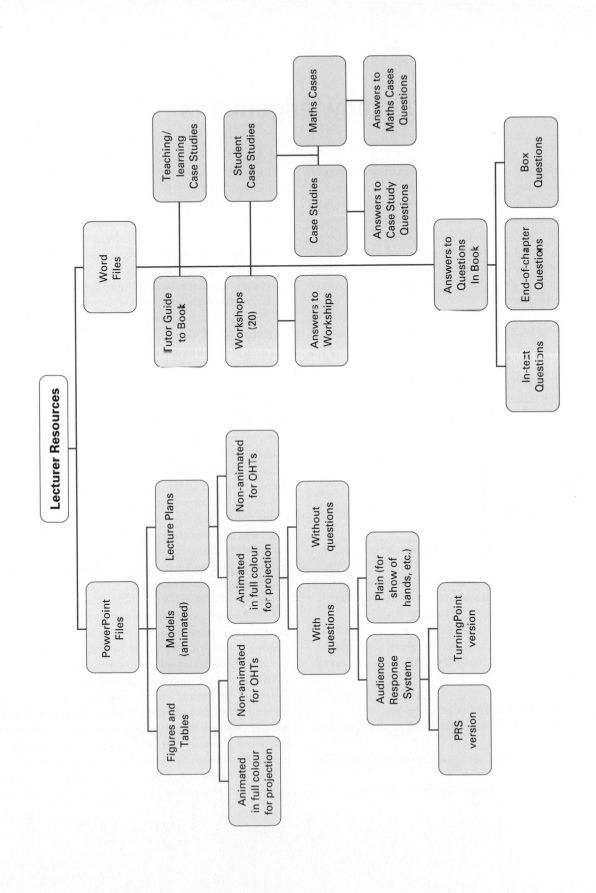

Acknowledgements

As with previous editions, we owe a debt to various people. The whole team from Pearson has, as always, been very helpful and supportive. Thanks in particular to Kate Brewin, the editor, who has been of tremendous help and support at every stage of revising the book, and to Tim Parker who has steered the book smoothly through production. Thanks also to Joan Dale Lace, who meticulously copy-edited the manuscript, Neville Hankins, proofreader, and Jane Ashley who prepared the Index.

Particular thanks go to Elizabeth Jones from the University of Warwick who has contributed to this edition and its supplements. She is also is a regular blogger on the Sloman Economics News site. Her ideas and input have been really valuable.

Thanks too to colleagues and students from many universities who have been helpful and encouraging and, as in previous editions, have made useful suggestions for improvement. We have attempted to incorporate their ideas wherever possible. Please do write or email if you have any suggestions. Especially we should like to thank the following reviewers of the current and previous editions. Their analysis and comments have helped to shape this new edition.

Dr Kent Springdal, Kingston Business School, Kingston University, UK

Professor Caroline Elliott, University of Huddersfield, UK

Paul Bullock, London Metropolitan University, UK

Dr Michail Karoglou, Aston Business School, UK

Dr Hui-Fai Shing, Royal Holloway, University of London

Dr Ian Elliott, Queen Margaret University, Edinburgh, UK

Dr Christopher J. Gerry, University College London SSESS, UK

David Ho

Ian Jackson, Staffordshire University, UK

Lars Bach, The International Business Academy, Kolding, Denmark

Leslie Christensen, Copenhagen Business School (CBS), Denmark

Professor Mark J. Holmes, University of Waikato, New Zealand

Pamela Siler, University of Abertay Dundee, UK

Richard O'Doherty, University of Gloucestershire, UK

Roy Bailey, University of Essex, UK

Stuart Sayer, University of Edinburgh, UK

Professor Sue Bowden, University of York, UK

Tony McGough, Course Director, Cass Business School, City University London, UK

Walter Vanthielen, Hasselt University, Belgium

Wilfried Pauwels, University of Antwerp, Belgium

Timothy Hinks, University of West of England

Bibhas Saha, University of East Anglia

Graham Cookson, King's College London

Gonzalo Varela, University of Sussex

A special thanks to Peter Smith from the University of Southampton who has thoroughly revised and updated the MyEconLab online course. It's great to have his input and ideas for improvements to the books and supplements.

A special thanks too to Mark Sutcliffe from the Cardiff School of Management. Mark provided considerable help and support on earlier editions and it's still much appreciated.

John: As with previous editions, my biggest thanks go to all my family, and especially to Alison, my wife and soulmate, and to all our children, the youngest of whom, Ellie, has just started university. As always they have been patient and supportive and have made the task of writing and updating books much more fun.

Alison: For this edition, I'd like to thank my colleagues at GSM London. Many of you have let me bounce ideas off you, made suggestions, and offered advice. Others have simply put up with my juggling writing and the 'day-job'. Of course most thanks are due to my husband, Chris, without whom none of this would (probably) have happened.

Dean: First, I would like to thank John and the Pearson team for once again inviting me to be part of this project. Second, I owe my parents so much, not least for the emotional and financial support over many years, including my time at university. Finally, an enormous thank you to Pat. She has been so supportive and incredibly tolerant and patient. Pat, you are very special; my Warwickshire bear.

Publisher's Acknowledgements

We are grateful to the following for permission to reproduce copyright material:

Figures

Figures on pages 236 and 237 after *World Investment Report 2014*, June, UNCTAD (2014) Annex Tables 9 and 11; Figure on page 264 from *Flexibility, Uncertainty and Manpower Management*, Institute of Manpower Studies (Atkinson, J. 1984) IMS Report No. 89, Institute for Employment Studies (IES); Figure 10.9 after *UK Personal Wealth Statistics* September 2012, HMRC (2012) Table 13.1, contains public sector information licensed under the Open Government Licence (OGL) v2.0. http://www.nationalarchives.gov.uk/doc/open-government-licence; Figure on page 356 from *Stern Review on the Economics of Climate Change*, Office of Climate Change (OCC), Stern Review, 2006 (Executive Summary, Figure 1, based on data drawn from World Resources Institute Climate Analysis Indicators Tool (CAIT) online database version 3.0), contains public sector information licensed under the Open Government Licence (OGL) v2.0. http://www.nationalarchives.gov.uk/doc/open-government-licence; Figure 12.4 adapted from *Family Spending 2012* National Statistics (2013) Table 3.2, Office for National Statistics licensed under the Open Government Licence v.2.0; Figure 12.5 adapted from *Statistical Pocketbook 2013* European Commission (2013) Table 2.6.2, © European Union, 1995–2014; Figure on page 394 from Electricity supply: re-organisation and privatisation, *The Economic Review*, March, Vol. 7, No. 4 (Green, R. 1991), Philip Allan Updates/Hodder Education, reproduced by permission of Hodder Education; Figures on pages 414 and 633 and Figure 14.6 after AMECO database, European Commission, DGECFIN, © European Union, 1995–2014; Figure on page 662 after *Inflation Report*, February, Bank of England (2014); Figure 24.8 from *The Competitive Advantage of Nations* The Free Press (Porter, M.E. 1998) p. 127, with the permission of The Free Press, a Division of Simon & Schuster, Inc. Copyright © 1998 by M.E. Porter. All rights reserved; Figure on page 822 from Building BRICs of growth, *The Economist*, © The Economist Newspaper Limited, London, 05/06/2008; Figure 27.2 after *World Economic Outlook* April 2014 database, International Monetary Fund.

Tables

Table A1.3 from *The Effects of Taxes and Benefits on Household Income, 2012/13* National Statistics (2014), Office for National Statistics licensed under the Open Government Licence v.2.0; Table on page 134 from *World Population Prospects: The 2012 Revision* United Nations, Department of Economic and Social Affairs; Table on page 156 from A survey of the economies of scale, *Research into the 'Costs of Non-Europe'*, Volume 2 (Pratten, C.F. 1988), Commission of the European Communities; Table on page 157 from Economies of Scale, *The Single Market Review*, Subseries V, Volume 4 (European Commission/Economists Advisory Group Ltd 1997), Commission of the European Communities, © European Union, 1995–2014; Tables on pages 173 and 199 after *United Kingdom Input–Output Analyses, 2006 Edition* (2006) Table 8.31, National Statistics, Office for National Statistics licensed under the Open Government Licence v.2.0; Tables on page 242 from How do UK companies set prices?, *Bank of England Quarterly Bulletin*, May, Table D, p. 188 (Hall, S., Walsh, M. and Yates, T. 1996); Table on page 243 from New insights into price-setting behaviour in the United Kingdom, *Bank of England Working Paper No. 395*, July (Greenslade, J. and Parker, M. 2010); Tables on page 262 after *Annual Survey of Hours and Earnings*, National Statistics (2013), Office for National Statistics licensed under the Open Government Licence v.2.0; Table 10.1 from *Family Spending* National Statistics (2013), Office for National Statistics licensed under the Open Government Licence v.2.0; Table on page 345 from *Economic Case for HS2*, February, Table 2 (Department for Transport 2011), contains public sector information licensed under the Open Government Licence (OGL) v2.0. http://www.nationalarchives.gov.uk/doc/open-government-licence; Table 12.2 after *Transport Statistics of Great Britain Database 2013*, December, Table TSGB0101 (2013), contains public sector information licensed under the Open Government Licence (OGL) v2.0. http://www.nationalarchives.gov.uk/doc/open-government-licence; Tables on pages 411, 415 and 429 and Table 15.1 after AMECO database, European Commission, DGECFIN, © European Union, 1995–2014; Tables 14.2 and 14.3 adapted from *Blue Book Tables* National Statistics (2013), Office for National Statistics licensed under the Open Government Licence v.2.0; Table 15.4 from *Balance of Payments quarterly First Release*, Office for National Statistics licensed under the Open Government Licence v.2.0; Table 15.6 from Bank of England; Tables on page 544 after *Bankstats*, January, Bank of England (2014) Tables A1.1.1, A2.2.1 and A2.3; Table 18.6 after *Bankstats*, January, Bank of England (2014) Table A3.2;

Table 18.7 after *Statistical Interactive Database* January, Bank of England (2014); Table 24.5 from The competition effects of the single market in Europe, *Economic Policy* (Allen, C., Gasiorek, M. and Smith, A. 1998), John Wiley & Sons Ltd; Table on page 804 after *2013 Human Development Report* United Nations Development Programme (2014); Table on page 822 and Table 27.3 after *World Development Indicators* The World Bank (2014); Table 27.1 after *World DataBank, World Development Indicators* The World Bank; Table 27.4 after *HIPC At-A-Glance Guide* Autumn, The World Bank (2013).

Text

Extract on page 243 from Sticky situations, *The Economist*, © The Economist Newspaper Limited, London, 09/11/2006; Extract on page 328 from Commons sense, *The Economist*, © The Economist Newspaper Limited, London, 31/07/2008; Extract on page 662 from Talk is expensive, *The Economist*, © The Economist Newspaper Limited, London, 18/10/2007; Extract on page 703 from Intricate workings, *The Economist*, © The Economist Newspaper Limited, London, 17/06/2006; Extract on page 759 from *The Economist*, © The Economist Newspaper Limited, London, 30/07/2011; Extract on page 822 from Building BRICs of growth, *The Economist*, © The Economist Newspaper Limited, London, 05/06/2008; Poetry on page 832 from *Adrian Mitchell's Greatest Hits, 1991*, Adrian Mitchell, reprinted by permission of United Agents on behalf of The Estate of the Late Adrian Mitchell.

In some instances we have been unable to trace the owners of copyright material, and we would appreciate any information that would enable us to do so.

Introduction

Why Economics is Good for You   2

 Economics and Economies   6

This opening part of the book introduces you to economics – what it is, some of the fundamental concepts and, most of all, why it is a great subject to study. Economics is not a set of facts or theories to be memorised, it is both more interesting and more useful than that. Studying economics enables you to think about the world in a different way; it helps you to make sense of the decisions people make: decisions about what to buy or what job to do; decisions governments make about how much to tax or what to spend those taxes on; decisions businesses make about what to produce, what prices to charge and what wages to pay. This makes economics relevant for everyone, not only those who are going on to further study.

After studying economics you will be able to apply this 'way of thinking' to your life both now and in the future. You will be able to think more analytically and problem-solve more effectively; this helps explain why studying economics can lead to a better career. We start you off in Chapter 0, with some puzzling ideas that should make you think. By the time you have studied, you'll be able to answer these and more.

Economics contains some simple core ideas which can be applied to a wide range of economic problems. We will start examining these ideas in Chapter 1. In 'Why Economics is Good for You' we start with a look at some interesting questions and puzzles that make the subject such a rich one.

Welcome

Welcome to the **Sloman Economics News Site**. This blog contains links to topical stories in the news discussing key economic issues and concepts.

Each news item starts with an introduction to the issue. This is followed by several links to relevant news articles – some to videos or podcasts. The item finishes with discussion questions that can be used either for self-testing or for use in class.

Scroll down below to read the latest articles posted, or use the search facilities on the left-hand side to search the articles by date, keyword and your chosen textbook.

Why Economics is Good for You

CHAPTER MAP

What is economics?	**3**
An island economy	3
Books and media	3
Puzzles and stories	**4**
A pay-rise, how exciting	4
Of course I want to know	4
We need to save more; we need to spend more	4
Applying the principles	**5**
Thinking like an economist – a word of warning	5

You may never have studied economics before, and yet when you open a newspaper what do you read? – a report from 'our economics correspondent'. Turn on the television news and what do you see? – an item on the state of the economy. Talk to friends and often the topic will turn to the price of this or that product, or whether you have got enough money to afford to do this or that.

The fact is that economics affects our daily lives. We are continually being made aware of local, national and international economic issues, whether price increases, interest rate changes, fluctuations in exchange rates, unemployment, economic recessions or the effects of globalisation.

We are also continually faced with economic problems and decisions of our own. What should I buy for supper? Should I save up for a summer holiday, or spend more on day-to-day living? Should I go to university, or should I try to find a job now? If I go to university, should I work part time?

This 'mini chapter' is an easy read, to get you started on the road to thinking like an economist.

WHAT IS ECONOMICS?

If we told you that economics is a problem of maximisation subject to constraints, you'd probably stop reading and find something else to do. So let's put it a different way. Economics is a way of answering some of the most important questions societies face. It's also a way of answering much 'smaller' questions: ones that affect all of us. We are going to set out some of these questions, and start you off on your economics journey. But be warned – once you start thinking like an economist, you probably won't be able to stop.

An island economy

In Chapter 1 we will introduce various core economic concepts and some formal definitions of the economic problems faced by individuals and society. But let's start with a flight of fancy.

Let's suppose that we wake up tomorrow and find ourselves in charge of an island economy. Who is 'we' in this case? Well perhaps it is the authors, plus the reader. Or perhaps it is your economics tutorial group, or a group of random strangers. It really doesn't matter, since it *is* just an imaginary problem.

Once we got over the excitement of being in charge of a whole economy, we might begin to appreciate it's not going to be all palm trees and days by the pool. An economy has people who need to eat, be housed and will need access to health care. It may have other islands, nearby, who are friendly and want to trade – or who are not friendly and may want to invade.

Being in charge suddenly seems to involve quite a few decisions. What is this island going to produce so that people can live? Is it going to be self-sufficient, or to 'swap' goods with other countries? How are people going to know what to produce? How will the products be shared out? Will they be allocated to everyone, even those who do not work? What will we do if some people are too old to work and haven't got savings or families? What should we do if the island bank runs out of money? How can we be sure that we will have enough resources to support the people next year, as well as this?

At the end of the text (page 832) you will see a poem about people cast away on a desert island. Hopefully, after reading this text, you will understand their plight better. But you might find it interesting to read it now before embarking on your studies.

Of course, we are never actually going to be parachuted in to be in charge of an island, although some of you reading this text may aspire to go into politics. But the questions we have posed above are a reflection of the real challenges countries face. We will look at the role of government throughout this text: decisions that need to be taken, different approaches, and what happens when governments need to work together.

Books and media

Economics has undergone something of a makeover in the past few years. There are two main reasons.

In 2007–8 there was a major financial crisis, which led to the collapse of banks across the world and a downturn in the global economy. It also led to a close scrutiny of why economists had not predicted the crisis. The outcome was a great deal more coverage of economics and economists than had been seen previously – an interesting example of the Oscar Wilde saying, 'There is only one thing worse than being talked about, and that is not being talked about.' Indeed, it stimulated a lot of interest in studying economics at university!

The second reason has less to do with actual economics and more to do with the way it has been written about. The first decade of the century saw the publication of a number of books which presented economics as a series of thought-provoking puzzles, rather than a purely academic subject. These included *The Undercover Economist*[1] by Tim Harford and the *Freakonomics*[2] titles, which resulted from collaboration between University of Chicago economist Steven Levitt and *New York Times* journalist Stephen J. Dubner.

Today, coverage of economics is widespread: in papers, on the Internet, in blogs and radio and television programmes. If you are reading this book because you are studying for a degree or other qualification, you may feel that you are just too busy to read more than the recommended reading list. But try to think more broadly than that. You will find that you can develop your 'economics' brain by spotting the issues. Whether you read papers, or look at news sites online, if you get into the habit of identifying economics issues and puzzles, you will be going a long way towards being an economist.

You could start by Googling the Sloman Economics News site.[3] This not only gives you links to up-to-date articles and some analysis. It also links through to chapters in this book.

---

[1] Tim Harford, *The Undercover Economist* (Little, Brown Book Group, 2005).
[2] Steven D. Levitt and Stephen J. Dubner, *Freakonomics: A Rogue Economist Explores the Hidden Side of Everything* (William Morrow and Company, 2005).
[3] www.pearsoned.co.uk/sloman

PUZZLES AND STORIES

Let's look at some examples of economic puzzles and ideas. The ones we discuss below are just a few that you might find interesting.

A pay-rise, how exciting

Do you work? By which we mean, do you work for money? If so, make a note of your hourly pay and how many hours you work per week.

Let's assume you are earning £7.50 per hour. Would you like a pay-rise to £15 per hour? You would? And what will you do with the extra money you earn? You might go on holiday, save more, or perhaps you'll simply go out for an extra evening per week, or buy nicer food when you go shopping.

But before we start talking about that, we need to go back to that note of yours. If your rate of pay doubled, how many hours would you work now? You might work the same number of hours; you might think it's worth working more hours; or you might decide that you can work fewer hours and have more time for other things. It's an interesting puzzle for you to think about. You could ask your friends how they might react in this situation. Perhaps you, or some of your friends, aren't working at the moment, but might do so if higher rates of pay were on offer.

We've thought about this from your point of view. Who else might be interested in the puzzle? Employers are obviously involved. If they want people to do more work, they might consider whether offering higher hourly rates will achieve that. Imagine how annoying it would be if instead people want to work fewer hours, not more. We will see in Chapter 9 that governments might be interested too.

Of course I want to know

One thing that economists spend a lot of time talking and thinking about is information. We will see in the rest of this text how important it is when making decisions. And as you've already seen, most of economics is about looking at decisions. How can you decide whether you work? You need to have all sorts of information: rates of pay, what hours are offered, what the job is actually like, what you'll have to wear. You can probably think of at least three or four other things just on this decision. If you are going to make a 'good' decision you need 'good' information. So if we can offer you some important information now, would you like it?

Of course, having information is going to affect your decision making: that's the whole point. So let's imagine you are trying to decide whether to see a film that's just been released. You can get information about the plot, the actors, the special effects, the rating, etc. You can also read opinions of critics and reviewers on the quality of the film. Hopefully all this information will help you decide whether

to spend money and time going to see it. Similarly, you can get information about many of the other goods and services you might want to buy, by talking to friends or family, researching on the Internet or browsing in shops.

What about a bigger piece of information? Suppose someone could tell you exactly how long you will live? Would that be a useful piece of information? How would it change your decisions every day? Would you behave differently right away? Does your answer depend on who gives the information? You might be more inclined to believe a scientist than an astrologer!

In practice, no one is going to be able to tell you your exact life expectancy (to the day). Accidents can happen and medicine moves on. So the best you could currently expect is an informed prediction based, usually, on statistical probability. But such informed predictions about life expectancy are crucial for insurance companies deciding on premiums.

Information is all around us – in fact, we are said to live in the information age. So the problem is often not one of a lack of information, but one of too much and what information is reliable. We hope, by reading this book, you will be better able to assess information and its usefulness for making economic decisions.

We need to save more; we need to spend more

Puzzles like the two above are looking at individual decisions and these are probably the easiest type to identify. But there are some which apply to a whole economy or country. The second half of this text (Chapters 14 onwards) looks at 'whole economy' economics, so let's identify an issue in that area.

How much do you save? The answer will depend on your income, your spending habits and probably on something that's hard to pin down, but really is about how 'good' you are at saving.

Now let's think about saving on a national basis. You may have heard people say that we need to save more. There are all sorts of reasons why saving is a 'good thing'. We are living longer and, unless we save more, we may not have enough to be comfortable in our old age. When we save, we have a buffer against emergencies. When we save, we are not (generally) borrowing, so we don't have to pay interest; instead we receive interest, so our income is higher.

All of these reasons can be scaled up to the whole economy. You have probably heard politicians say that the country needs to save for the future, especially if we all are going to live longer. The nation, they argue, needs to reduce its debts so that we can reduce the interest we have to pay, leaving more for the things people want, such as a better health service and better education. And if emergencies arise (the financial crisis of 2007–8 is a really good example) the country will be in a better position if banks have plenty of money. It's also true that saving by individuals provides a source of funds for businesses that want and need to borrow for investment.

You might be wondering why this is a puzzle, since it seems pretty straightforward.

Let's think about the opposite of saving. If you don't save, what do you do with your money? You spend it and, hopefully, enjoy it. Imagine the opposite – that you saved a lot of your income, much more than you do now. Imagine that you only bought the barest of necessities, grew your own food, wore the same clothes for years and didn't buy

any new technology, or even have an occasional night out. You might have a pretty miserable life.

Now scale this up to the whole economy again. If no one is spending much, what will happen? Businesses will very quickly be in trouble. The banks will be full of our savings, but no one will be borrowing. Spending will therefore be low and firms won't be able to make profits. We will have lots of security in the form of future spending, but an economy that is in recession and very soon could be in crisis.

Of course this is an exaggerated example. But you can see the puzzle, can't you? Saving is good, but so is spending. What should we do? What should the government encourage us to do?

APPLYING THE PRINCIPLES

Thinking like an economist – a word of warning

As you go through the rest of this text, whether you study all of it or just some sections, try to spot the puzzles we have talked about above. And look out for others. You can do this outside formal study. Economics is about people and society. It isn't a dry subject; it is something that is all around us. Try to get into the habit of thinking like an economist on a daily basis. If there's a decision to be made, there's an economic way of thinking about it.

Where will this approach take you? It will make you more analytical, it will help you make better decisions.

There's evidence that it can get you a better job and it will certainly make you better at a job.

We'd like to offer one word of warning though. Once you're thinking like an economist, there's no turning back. It's a skill that will be with you for life. Just bear in mind that the non-economists around you may need convincing about the beauty of the subject. One of the authors of this book has a story to relate on this. On her wedding anniversary one year, she presented her (non-economist) husband with an analysis of the costs and benefits of both marriage in general, and anniversaries in particular. Luckily he saw the funny side.

Enjoy the book, but, more importantly, enjoy your journey through economics.

MyEconLab

This book can be supported by MyEconLab, which contains a range of additional resources, including an online homework and tutorial system designed to test and build your understanding.

You need both an access card and a course ID to access MyEconLab:

1. Is your lecturer using MyEconLab? Ask your lecturer for your course ID.

2. Has an access card been included with the book at a reduced cost? Check the inside back cover of the book.

3. If you have a course ID but no access card, go to: http://www.myeconlab.com/ to buy access to this interactive study programme.

Economics and Economies

CHAPTER MAP

1.1 What do economists study?	**7**
The problem of scarcity	7
Demand and supply	8
Dividing up the subject	8
Macroeconomics	9
Microeconomics	10
Illustrating economic issues: the production possibility curve	13
Illustrating economic issues: the circular flow of goods and incomes	17
1.2 Different economic systems	**18**
The classification of economic systems	18
The command economy	20
Assessment of the command economy	20
The free-market economy	21
Assessment of the free-market economy	24
The mixed economy	26
1.3 The nature of economic reasoning	**27**
Economics as a science	27
Economics as a social science	28
Economics and policy	29

In the introductory chapter we introduced some of the questions and puzzles that make economics such an interesting subject to study. Now we turn to explaining those ideas in a bit more detail. We also introduce some of the tools you will need to help you analyse the puzzles posed and answer the questions.

Economics contains some core ideas. These ideas are simple, but can be applied to a wide range of economic problems. We start examining these ideas in Chapter 1. We begin on the journey to help you to 'think like an economist' – a journey that we hope you will find fascinating and will give you a sound foundation for many possible future careers.

In the introductory chapter, we asked what economics is about. In this chapter we will attempt to answer this question and give you greater insight into the subject that you are studying. We will see how the subject is divided up and we will distinguish between the two major branches of economics: microeconomics and macroeconomics.

We will also look at the ways in which different types of economy operate, from the centrally planned economies of the former communist countries to the more free-market economies of most of the world today. We will ask just how 'markets' work.

1.1 WHAT DO ECONOMISTS STUDY?

Many people think that economics is about *money*. Well, to some extent this is true. Economics has a lot to do with money: with how much money people earn; how much they spend; what various items cost; how much money firms make; the total amount of money there is in the economy. But as we will see later in the book, money is only important because of what it allows us to do; money is a tool and economics is more than just the study of money.

It is concerned with the following:

- The *production* of goods and services: how much an economy produces, both in total and of individual items; how much each firm or person produces; what techniques of production are used; how many people are employed.
- The *consumption* of goods and services: how much people spend (and how much they save); how much people buy of particular items; what individuals choose to buy; how consumption is affected by prices, advertising, fashion and other factors.

 Could production and consumption take place without money? If you think they could, give some examples.

But we still have not got to the bottom of what economics is about. Is there one crucial ingredient that makes a problem an economic one? The answer is that there is a central problem faced by all individuals and all countries, no matter how rich. It is the problem of scarcity; and scarcity underlies all other economic problems. For an economist, scarcity has a very specific definition.

 Before reading on, how would you define 'scarcity'? Must goods be at least temporarily unattainable to be scarce?

The problem of scarcity

Ask people if they would like more money, and the vast majority would answer 'Yes'. But they don't want more money for its own sake. Rather they want to be able to buy more goods and services, either today or in the future. These 'wants' will vary according to income levels and tastes. In a poor country 'wants' might include clean water, education and safe housing. In richer nations 'wants' might involve a second car, longer holidays and more time with friends and family. As countries get richer, human wants may change but they don't disappear. Wants are virtually unlimited.

Yet the means of fulfilling wants are limited. At any point the world can only produce a finite amount of goods and services because the world has a limited amount of *resources*. These resources, or *factors of production* as they are often called, are of three broad types:

- Human resources: *labour*. The labour force is limited in number, but also in skills. This limits the productivity of labour, the amount labour can produce.
- Natural resources: *land and raw materials*. The world's land area is limited, as are its raw materials.
- Manufactured resources: *capital*. Capital consists of all those inputs that have themselves had to be produced. The world has a limited stock of factories, machines, transportation and other equipment. The productivity of this capital is limited by the current state of technology.

 Could each of these types of resources be increased in quantity or quality? Is there a time dimension to your answer?

So this is the fundamental economic problem: human wants are virtually unlimited, whereas the resources available to meet those wants are limited. We can thus define scarcity as follows:

> **KEY IDEA 1** **Scarcity** is the excess of human wants over what can actually be produced. Because of scarcity, various choices have to be made between alternatives.

 If we would all like more money, why does the government not print a lot more? Could it not thereby solve the problem of scarcity 'at a stroke'?

Definitions

Production The transformation of inputs into outputs by firms in order to earn profit (or to meet some other objective).

Consumption The act of using goods and services to satisfy wants. This will normally involve purchasing the goods and services.

Factors of production (or resources) The inputs into the production of goods and services: labour, land and raw materials, and capital.

Labour All forms of human input, both physical and mental, into current production.

Land and raw materials Inputs into production that are provided by nature: e.g. unimproved land and mineral deposits in the ground.

Capital All inputs into production that have themselves been produced: e.g. factories, machines and tools.

- There are calls for access to the benefit system to be restricted for those arriving in the UK, from Romania and other EU countries.
- House prices are rising sharply in London and the South-East, with commentators expressing concern about the impact of the 'Help to Buy' scheme.
- Severe flooding hits parts of the UK for the third consecutive winter.
- There is widespread criticism of President Obama, as his proposed health care reforms stutter.
- Unemployment falls, leading to expectations of higher interest rates.
- The age at which UK workers can draw their state pension is raised further. Many predict that those currently under 30 will be working until at least the age of 70.

- The Chancellor of the Exchequer announces that undergraduate student numbers will no longer be capped in the UK higher education sector.
- A report suggests that the UK's energy security is at risk due to the slow pace of fracking.
- There is criticism following the privatisation of Royal Mail, as the share price rose strongly on the first day of trading.

1. What is it that makes each one of the above news items an economics item?
2. In each case identify two different individuals or groups who might be affected by the news item.

Of course, we do not all face the problem of *scarcity* to the same degree. A poor family who may not be able to afford enough to eat, or a decent place to live, will hardly see it as a 'problem' that a rich family cannot afford a second skiing holiday. But economists do not claim that we all face an equal problem of scarcity. In fact this is one of the major issues economists study: how resources are distributed, whether between different individuals, different regions of a country or different countries of the world.

This economic problem – limited resources but limitless wants – makes people, both rich and poor, behave in certain ways. Economics studies that behaviour. It studies people at work, producing goods that people want. It studies people as consumers, buying the goods that they want. It studies governments influencing the level and pattern of production and consumption. In short, it studies anything to do with the process of satisfying human wants.

Demand and supply

We have said that economics is concerned with consumption and production. Another way of looking at this is in terms of *demand* and *supply*. Demand and supply and the relationship between them lie at the very centre of economics. How does this relate to the problem of scarcity?

Demand is related to wants. If every good and service were free, people would simply demand whatever they wanted. In total such wants are likely to be virtually boundless, perhaps only limited by people's imagination. *Supply*,

on the other hand, is limited. It is related to resources. The amount that firms can supply depends on the resources and technology available.

Given the problem of scarcity – that human wants exceed what can actually be produced – *potential* demands will exceed *potential* supplies. Society has to find some way of dealing with this problem, to try to match demand with supply. This applies at the level of the economy overall: total or '*aggregate*' demand needs to be balanced against total or *aggregate* supply. In other words, total spending in the economy should balance total production. It also applies at the level of individual goods and services. The demand and supply of cabbages should balance, and so should the demand and supply of cars, houses, tablets and holidays.

But if potential demand exceeds potential supply, how are *actual* demand and supply made equal? Either demand has to be reduced, or supply has to be increased, or a combination of the two. Economics studies this process. It studies how demand adjusts to available supplies, and how supply adjusts to consumer demands.

Dividing up the subject

Economics is traditionally divided into two main branches – *macroeconomics* and *microeconomics*, where 'macro' means big and 'micro' means small.

Macroeconomics is concerned with the economy as a whole. It is concerned with **aggregate demand** and **aggregate supply**. By 'aggregate demand' we mean the total amount of

Definitions

Scarcity The excess of human wants over what can actually be produced to fulfil these wants.

Macroeconomics The branch of economics that studies economic aggregates (grand totals): e.g. the overall level of prices, output and employment in the economy.

Aggregate demand The total level of spending in the economy.

Aggregate supply The total amount of output in the economy.

spending in the economy, whether by consumers, by customers outside the country for our exports, by the government, or by firms when they buy capital equipment or stock up on raw materials. By 'aggregate supply' we mean the total national output of goods and services.

Microeconomics is concerned with the individual parts of the economy. It is concerned with the demand and supply of particular goods, services and resources such as cars, butter, clothes, haircuts, plumbers, accountants, blast furnaces, computers and oil.

Which of the following are macroeconomic issues, which are microeconomic ones and which could be either depending on the context?
(a) Inflation.
(b) Low wages in certain sectors.
(c) The rate of exchange between the pound and the euro.
(d) Why the price of cabbages fluctuates more than that of cars.
(e) The rate of economic growth this year compared with last year.
(f) The decline of traditional manufacturing industries.
(g) The influx of workers from eastern Europe.

Macroeconomics

Because scarcity exists, societies are concerned that their resources should be used *as fully as possible* and that over time their national output should grow.

Why should resources be used as fully as possible? If resources are 'saved' in one time period surely they can be used in the next time period? The answer is that not all resources can be saved. For example, if a worker doesn't go to work one week then that resource is lost: labour can't be saved up for the future.

Why do societies want growth? To understand this, think back to the discussion of endless wants: if our output grows, then more of our wants can be satisfied. Individuals and society can be made better off.

The achievement of growth and the full use of resources are not easy. This is demonstrated by periods of high unemployment and stagnation that have occurred from time to time throughout the world (e.g. in the 1930s, the early 1980s and the recent turndown that started in 2008). Furthermore, attempts by governments to stimulate growth and employment can result in inflation and rising imports. Economies have often experienced cycles where periods of growth alternate with periods of recession, such periods varying from a few months to a few years. This is known as the 'business cycle'.

Macroeconomic problems are closely related to the balance between aggregate demand and aggregate supply.

If aggregate demand is too *high* relative to aggregate supply, inflation and trade deficits are likely to result.

■ *Inflation* refers to a general rise in the level of prices throughout the economy. If aggregate demand rises substantially, firms are likely to respond by raising their prices. If demand is high, they can probably still sell as much as before (if not more) even at the higher prices,

and make higher profits. If firms in general put up their prices, inflation results.

■ *Balance of trade* deficits are the excess of imports over exports. If aggregate demand rises, people are likely to buy more imports. So part of the extra spending will go on goods from overseas, such as Japanese TVs, Chinese computers, etc. Also, if inflation is high, home-produced goods will become uncompetitive with foreign goods. We are likely to buy more foreign imports and people abroad are likely to buy fewer of our exports. If aggregate demand is too low relative to aggregate supply, unemployment and recession may well result.

■ *Recession* is where output in the economy declines: in other words, growth becomes negative. A recession is associated with a low level of consumer spending. If people spend less, shops are likely to find themselves with unsold stock. Then they will buy less from the manufacturers; they will cut down on production; and they will buy fewer capital goods such as machinery.

■ *Unemployment* is likely to result from cutbacks in production. If firms are producing less, they will need to employ fewer people.

Macroeconomic policy, therefore, tends to focus on the balance of aggregate demand and aggregate supply. It can be *demand-side policy*, which seeks to influence the level of spending in the economy. This in turn will affect the level of production, prices and employment. Or it can be *supply-side policy*. This is designed to influence the level of production directly: for example, by trying to create more incentives for firms to innovate.

Definitions

Microeconomics The branch of economics that studies individual units: e.g. households, firms and industries. It studies the interrelationships between these units in determining the pattern of production and distribution of goods and services.

Rate of inflation The percentage increase in the level of prices over a 12-month period.

Balance of trade Exports of goods and services minus imports of goods and services. If exports exceed imports, there is a 'balance of trade surplus' (a positive figure). If imports exceed exports, there is a 'balance of trade deficit' (a negative figure).

Recession A period where national output falls for six months or more.

Unemployment The number of people who are actively looking for work but are currently without a job. (Note that there is much debate as to who should officially be counted as unemployed.)

Demand-side policy Government policy designed to alter the level of aggregate demand, and thereby the level of output, employment and prices.

Supply-side policy Government policy that attempts to alter the level of aggregate supply directly.

BOX 1.2   LOOKING AT MACROECONOMIC DATA

Assessing different countries' macroeconomic performance

Rapid economic growth, low unemployment, low inflation and the avoidance of current account deficits[1] are major macroeconomic policy objectives of most governments around the world. To help them achieve these objectives they employ economic advisers. But when we look at the performance of various economies, the success of government macroeconomic policies seems decidedly 'mixed'.

The table shows data for the USA, Japan, Germany[2] and the UK from 1961 to 2015.

Macroeconomic performance of four industrialised economies (average annual figures)

	Unemployment (% of workforce)				Inflation (%)				Economic growth (%)				Balance on current account (% of national income)			
	USA	Japan	Germany	UK	USA	Japan	Germany	UK	USA	Japan	Germany	UK	USA	Japan	Germany	UK
1961–70	4.8	1.3	0.6	1.7	2.4	5.6	2.7	3.9	4.2	10.1	4.4	3.0	0.5	0.6	0.7	0.2
1971–80	6.4	1.8	2.2	3.8	7.0	8.8	5.1	13.2	3.2	4.4	2.8	2.0	0.9	0.5	1.1	−0.7
1981–90	2.5	2.5	6.0	9.6	4.5	2.2	2.5	6.2	3.2	3.9	2.3	2.6	−1.7	2.3	2.6	−1.4
1991–2000	3.3	3.3	7.9	7.9	2.2	0.4	2.3	3.3	3.3	1.5	1.9	2.4	−1.6	2.5	−0.7	−1.5
2001–6	5.3	4.8	9.2	5.1	2.7	−0.4	1.6	1.6	2.4	1.4	1.1	2.5	−5.0	3.3	3.3	−2.2
2007–15	7.7	4.1	6.3	7.0	1.5	0.3	1.2	2.3	1.2	0.2	1.2	1.2	−3.2	1.2	6.7	−2.1

Note: Years 2014 and 2015 forecasts.

Source: Statistical Annex of the European Economy (Commission of the European Communities), various tables and years.

1. *Has the UK generally fared better or worse than the other three countries?*
2. *Was there a common pattern in the macroeconomic performance of each of the four countries over these 55 years?*

If the government does not have much success in managing the economy, it could be for the following reasons:

- Economists have incorrectly analysed the problems and hence have given the wrong advice.
- Economists disagree and hence have given conflicting advice.

- Economists have based their advice on inaccurate statistics or incorrect forecasts.
- Governments have not listened to the advice of economists. This could be for political reasons, such as the electoral cycle.
- There is little else that governments could have done: the problems were insoluble or could not have been predicted.

[1] The current account balance is the trade balance plus any incomes earned from abroad minus any incomes paid abroad. These incomes could be wages, investment incomes or government revenues (see section 15.5 for details).

[2] West Germany from 1961 to 1991.

Microeconomics

Microeconomics and choice

Because resources are scarce, choices have to be made. There are three main categories of choice that must be made in any society:

- *What* goods and services are going to be produced and in what quantities, since there are not enough resources to produce everything people want? How many cars, how much wheat, how much insurance, how many iPhones, etc., will be produced?
- *How* are things going to be produced? What resources are going to be used and in what quantities? What techniques of production are going to be adopted? Will cars be produced by robots or by assembly line workers? Will electricity be produced from coal, oil, gas, nuclear fission, renewable resources such as wind-farms or a mixture of these?

- *For whom* are things going to be produced? In other words, how will the country's income be distributed? After all, the higher your income, the more you can consume of the total output. What will be the wages of shop workers, MPs, footballers and accountants? How much will pensioners receive? How much of the country's income will go to shareholders or landowners?

All societies have to make these choices, whether they are made by individuals, groups or the government. They can be seen as microeconomic choices, since they are concerned not with the total amount of national output, but with the individual goods and services that make it up: what they are, how they are made and who gets to consume them.

Choice and opportunity cost

Choice involves sacrifice. The more food you choose to buy, the less money you will have to spend on other goods. The more food a nation produces, the fewer resources will there be for producing other goods. In other words, the production or consumption of one thing involves the sacrifice of alternatives. This sacrifice of alternatives in the production (or consumption) of a good is known as its *opportunity cost*.

> **KEY IDEA 2**
>
> The *opportunity cost* of any activity is the sacrifice made to do it. It is the best thing that could have been done as an alternative.

If the workers on a farm can produce either 1000 tonnes of wheat or 2000 tonnes of barley, then the opportunity cost of producing 1 tonne of wheat is the 2 tonnes of barley forgone. The opportunity cost of buying a textbook is the new pair of jeans that you have had to go without. The opportunity cost of saving for your old age is the consumption you sacrifice while younger.

Opportunity cost as the basis for choice is the first of our 'Threshold Concepts' (see below). There are 15 of these threshold concepts, which we shall be exploring throughout the book. Once you have grasped these concepts and

seen their significance, they will affect the way that you understand and analyse economic problems. They will help you to 'think like an economist'.

Rational choices

Economists often refer to **rational choices**. This simply means the weighing up of the *costs* and *benefits* of any activity, whether it be firms choosing what and how much to produce, workers choosing whether to take a particular job or to work extra hours, or consumers choosing what to buy.

Imagine you are doing your shopping in a supermarket and you want to buy a chicken. Do you spend a lot of money and buy a free-range organic chicken, or do you buy a cheap bird instead? To make a rational (i.e. sensible)

> **Definitions**
>
> **Opportunity cost** The cost of any activity measured in terms of the best alternative forgone.
>
> **Rational choices** Choices that involve weighing up the benefit of any activity against its opportunity cost.

THRESHOLD CONCEPT 1 CHOICE AND OPPORTUNITY COST

THINKING LIKE AN ECONOMIST

Scarcity, as we have seen, is at the heart of economics.

We all face scarcity. With a limited income we cannot buy everything we want. And even if we had the money, with only 24 hours in a day, we would not have time to enjoy all the things we would like to consume. The same applies at a national level. A country has limited resources and so cannot produce everything people would like. Of course, this is also true on a global scale: our planet has finite resources, and the technology and our abilities to exploit these resources are also limited.

With limited resources and endless wants, we have to make choices. In fact, virtually every time we do something, we are making a choice between alternatives. If you choose to watch television, you are choosing not to go out. If you buy a pair of trainers for £60, you are choosing not to spend that £60 on something else. Likewise, if a country devotes more of its resources to producing manufactured goods, there will be less to devote to the provision of services. If we devote more resources to producing a cleaner environment, we may have to produce less of the material goods that people want to consume.

What we give up in order to do something is known as its *opportunity cost*. Opportunity cost is the cost of doing something measured in terms of the best alternative forgone. It's what you would have chosen to do with your time or money if you had not made the choice you did. This is one of the most fundamental concepts in economics. It is a threshold concept: once you have seen its importance, it affects the way you look at economic problems. When you use the concept of opportunity cost, you are thinking like an economist. And this may

be different from thinking like an accountant or from the way you thought before. We will come across this concept many times throughout this book.

By looking at opportunity cost we are recognising that we face trade-offs. To do more of one thing involves doing less of something else. For example, we trade off work and leisure. The more we work, the less leisure time we will have. In other words, the opportunity cost of working is the leisure we have sacrificed. Nations trade off producing one good against others. The more a country spends on defence, the less it will have to spend on consumer goods and services. This has become known as the 'guns versus butter' trade-off. In other words, if a country decides to use more of its resources for defence, the opportunity cost is the consumer goods sacrificed. (We examine such trade-offs at a national level on pages 13–17, when we look at the 'production possibility curve'.)

We therefore have to make decisions between alternatives. To make sensible decisions we must weigh up the benefits of doing something against its opportunity cost. This is known in economics as 'rational decision making'. It is another of our threshold concepts: No. 8 (see page 105).

1. *Think of three things you did last week. What was the opportunity cost of each one?*
2. *Assume that a supermarket has some fish that has reached its sell-by date. It was originally priced at £10, but yesterday was marked down to £5 'for quick sale'. It is now the end of the day and it still has not been sold. The supermarket is about to close and there is no one in the store who wants fish. What is the opportunity cost for the store of throwing the fish away?*

decision, you will need to weigh up the costs and benefits of each alternative. The free-range chicken may taste better and it may meet your concerns about animal welfare, but it has a high opportunity cost: because it is expensive, you will need to sacrifice quite a lot of consumption of other goods if you decide to buy it. If you buy the intensively farmed chicken, however, although you will not enjoy it so much, you will have more money left over to buy other things: it has a lower opportunity cost.

Thus rational decision making, as far as consumers are concerned, involves choosing those items that give you the best value for money: i.e. the *greatest benefit relative to cost*.

The same principles apply to firms when deciding what to produce. For example, should a car firm open up another production line? A rational decision will again involve weighing up the benefits and costs. The benefits are the revenues the firm will earn from selling the extra cars. The costs will include the extra labour costs, raw material costs, costs of component parts, etc. It will be profitable to open up the new production line only if the revenues earned exceed the costs entailed: in other words, if it increases profits.

In the more complex situation of deciding which model of car to produce, or how many of each model, the firm must weigh up the relative benefits and costs of each: i.e. it will want to produce the most profitable product mix.

 Assume that you are looking for a job and are offered two. One is more enjoyable, but pays less. How would you make a rational choice between the two jobs?

Marginal costs and benefits

In economics we argue that rational choices involve weighing up **marginal costs** and **marginal benefits**. These are the costs and benefits of doing a little bit more or a little bit less of a specific activity. They can be contrasted with the total costs and benefits of the activity.

Take a familiar example. What time will you set your alarm to go off tomorrow morning? Let us say that you have to leave home at 8.30. Perhaps you will set the alarm for 7.00. That will give you plenty of time to get ready, but it will mean less sleep. Perhaps you will decide to set it for 8.00. That will give you a longer lie-in, but more of a rush in the morning to get ready.

So how do you make a rational decision about when the alarm should go off? What you have to do is to weigh up the costs and benefits of *additional* sleep. Each extra minute in bed gives you more sleep (the marginal benefit), but means you'll be more rushed when you get up (the marginal cost). The decision is therefore based on the costs and benefits of *extra* sleep, not on the total costs and benefits of a whole night's sleep.

This same principle applies to rational decisions made by consumers, workers and firms. For example, the car firm we were considering just now will weigh up the marginal costs and benefits of producing cars: in other words, it will compare the costs and revenue of producing *additional* cars. If additional cars add more to the firm's revenue than to its costs, it will be profitable to produce them.

Rational decision making, then, involves weighing up the marginal benefit and marginal cost of any activity. If the marginal benefit exceeds the marginal cost, it is rational to do the activity (or to do more of it). If the marginal cost exceeds the marginal benefit, it is rational not to do it (or to do less of it).

Rational decision making is Threshold Concept 8 and this is examined in Chapter 4 (page 105).

 How would the principle of weighing up marginal costs and benefits apply to a worker deciding how much overtime to work in a given week?

Microeconomic objectives

Microeconomics is concerned with the allocation of scarce resources: with the answering of the *what*, *how* and *for whom* questions. But how satisfactorily will these questions be answered? Clearly this depends on society's objectives. There are two major objectives that we can identify: *efficiency* and *equity*.

Efficiency. If altering what was produced or how it was produced could make us all better off (or at least make some of us better off without anyone losing), then it would be efficient to do so. For a society to achieve full *economic efficiency*, three conditions must be met:

■ Efficiency in production (**productive efficiency**). This is where production of each item is at minimum cost. Producing any other way would cost more.

Definitions

Marginal cost The additional cost of doing a little bit more (or 1 unit more if a unit can be measured) of an activity.

Marginal benefit The additional benefit of doing a little bit more (or 1 unit more if a unit can be measured) of an activity.

Rational decision making Doing more of an activity if its marginal benefit exceeds its marginal cost and doing less if its marginal cost exceeds its marginal benefit.

Economic efficiency A situation where each good is produced at the minimum cost and where individual people and firms get the maximum benefit from their resources.

Productive efficiency A situation where firms are producing the maximum output for a given amount of inputs, or producing a given output at the least cost.

- Efficiency in consumption. This is where consumers allocate their expenditures so as to get maximum satisfaction from their income. Any other pattern of consumption would make people feel worse off.
- Efficiency in specialisation and exchange. This is where firms specialise in producing goods for sale to consumers, and where individuals specialise in doing jobs in order to buy goods, so that everyone maximises the benefits they achieve relative to the costs of achieving them.

These last two are collectively known as *allocative efficiency*. In any economic activity, allocative efficiency will be increased as long as doing more of that activity (and hence less of an alternative) involves a greater marginal benefit than marginal cost. Full efficiency will be achieved when all such improvements have been made.

> **KEY IDEA 3**
>
> *Economic efficiency* is achieved when each good is produced at the minimum cost and where individual people and firms get the maximum benefit from their resources.

Equity. Even though the current levels of production and consumption might be efficient, they might be regarded as unfair, if some people are rich while others are poor. Another microeconomic goal, therefore, is that of *equity*. Income distribution is regarded as equitable if it is considered to be fair or just. The problem with this objective, however, is that people have different notions of fairness. A rich person may well favour a much higher degree of inequality than will a poor person. Likewise socialist governments will generally be in favour of a larger redistribution of income from the rich to the poor than will conservative governments. Equity is therefore described as a value judgement: notions of equity will depend on the values of individuals or society.

> **KEY IDEA 4**
>
> *Equity* is where income is distributed in a way that is considered to be fair or just. Note that an equitable distribution is not the same as an equal distribution and that different people have different views on what is equitable.

Would it be desirable to have total equality in an economy, so that everyone receives the same share of resources?

The social implications of choice

In practice, the choices that people make may be neither efficient nor equitable. Firms may use inefficient techniques or be poorly managed; people often make wrong decisions about what to buy or what job to take; governments may be wasteful or inefficient in their use of tax revenues; there may be considerable inequality and injustice.

What is more, the effects of people's choices often spill over to other people. Take the case of pollution. It might be profitable for a firm to tip toxic waste into a river. But what is profitable for the firm will not necessarily be 'profitable' for society. Such an action may have serious environmental consequences.

Throughout the book we will be considering how well the economy meets various economic and social objectives, whether micro or macro. We will examine why problems occur and what can be done about them.

Illustrating economic issues: the production possibility curve

Economics books and articles frequently contain diagrams. The reason is that diagrams are very useful for illustrating economic relationships. Ideas and arguments that might take a long time to explain in words can often be expressed clearly and simply in a diagram.

Two of the most common types of diagram used in economics are graphs and flow diagrams. In this and the next section we will look at one example of each. These examples are chosen to illustrate the distinction between microeconomic and macroeconomic issues.

We start by having a look at a *production possibility curve*. This diagram is a graph. Like many diagrams in economics it shows a simplified picture of reality – a picture stripped of all details that are unnecessary to illustrate the points being made. Of course, there are dangers in this. In the attempt to make a diagram simple enough to understand, we run the risk of oversimplifying. If this is the case, the diagram may be misleading.

A production possibility curve is shown in Figure 1.1. The graph is based on the data shown in Table 1.1.

Assume that some imaginary nation devotes all its resources – land, labour and capital – to producing just two goods, food and clothing. Various possible combinations that could be produced over a given period of time (e.g. a year) are shown in the table. Thus the country, by devoting

> ## Definitions
>
> **Allocative efficiency** A situation where the current combination of goods produced and sold gives the maximum satisfaction for each consumer at their current levels of income. Note that a redistribution of income would lead to a different combination of goods that was allocatively efficient.
>
> **Equity** A distribution of income that is considered to be fair or just. Note that an equitable distribution is not the same as an equal distribution and that different people have different views on what is equitable.
>
> **Production possibility curve** A curve showing all the possible combinations of two goods that a country can produce within a specified time period with all its resources fully and efficiently employed.

BOX 1.3   THE OPPORTUNITY COSTS OF STUDYING

What are you sacrificing?

You may not have realised it, but you probably consider opportunity costs many times a day. We are constantly making choices: what to buy, what to eat, what to wear, whether to go out, how much to study, and so on. Each time we make a choice to do something, we are in effect rejecting doing some alternative. This alternative forgone is the opportunity cost of the action we choose.

Sometimes the opportunity costs of our actions are the direct monetary costs we incur. Sometimes it is more complicated.

Take the opportunity costs of your choices as a student.

Buying a textbook costing £59.99

This choice does involve a direct money payment. What you have to consider are the alternatives you could have bought with the £59.99. You then have to weigh up the benefit from the best alternative against the benefit of the textbook.

 What might prevent you from making the best decision?

Coming to lectures

Even though students now pay fees for their degrees in many countries, there is no extra (marginal) monetary cost in coming to classes once the fees have been paid. You will not get a refund by missing a lecture.

So are the opportunity costs zero? No: by coming to a lecture you are not working in the library; you are not sleeping; you are not undertaking paid work during that time. If you are making a rational decision to come to classes, then you will consider such possible alternatives.

Choosing to study at university or college

What are the opportunity costs of being a student in higher education?

1. *If there are several other things you could have done, is the opportunity cost the sum of all of them?*
2. *What is the opportunity cost of spending an evening revising for an economics exam? What would you need to know in order to make a sensible decision about what to do that evening?*

At first it might seem that the costs of higher education would include the following:

- Tuition fees.
- Books, stationery, etc.
- Accommodation, food, entertainment, travel and other living expenses.

But adding these up does not give the opportunity cost. The opportunity cost is the *sacrifice* entailed by going to university or college *rather than* doing something else. Let us assume that the alternative is to take a job that has been offered. The correct list of opportunity costs of higher education would include:

- Books, stationery, etc.
- Additional accommodation and travel expenses over what would have been incurred by taking the job.
- Wages that would have been earned in the job, less any income received as a student.
- The tuition fees paid by the student.

1. *Why is the cost of food not included? Should the cost of clothing be included?*
2. *Make a list of the benefits of higher education.*
3. *Is the opportunity cost to the individual of attending higher education different from the opportunity costs to society as a whole? Do the benefits of higher education for society differ from those for the individual?*

Figure 1.1   A production possibility curve

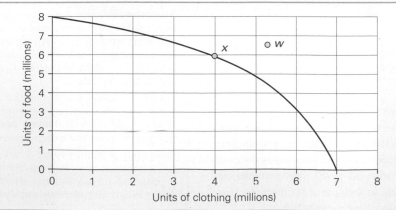

Table 1.1	Maximum possible combinations of food and clothing that can be produced in a given time period

Units of food (millions)	Units of clothing (millions)
8.0	0.0
7.0	2.2
6.0	4.0
5.0	5.0
4.0	5.6
3.0	6.0
2.0	6.4
1.0	6.7
0.0	7.0

all its resources to producing food, could produce 8 million units of food but no clothing. Alternatively by producing, say, 7 million units of food it could release enough resources – land, labour and capital – to produce 2.2 million units of clothing. At the other extreme, it could produce 7 million units of clothing with no resources at all being used to produce food.

The information in the table can be transferred to a graph (Figure 1.1). We measure units of food on one axis (in this case the vertical axis) and units of clothing on the other. The curve shows all the combinations of the two goods that can be produced with all the nation's resources fully and efficiently employed. For example, production could take place at point *x*, with 6 million units of food and 4 million units of clothing being produced. Production cannot take place beyond the curve. For example, production is not possible at point *w*: the nation does not have enough resources to do this.

Note that there are two simplifying assumptions in this diagram. First, it is assumed that there are just two types of good that can be produced. We have to assume this because we only have two axes on our graph. The other assumption is that there is only one type of food and one type of clothing. This is implied by measuring their output in particular units (e.g. tonnes). If food differed in type, it would be

possible to produce a greater tonnage of food for a given amount of clothing simply by switching production from one foodstuff to another.

These two assumptions are obviously enormous simplifications when we consider the modern complex economies of the real world. But despite this, the diagram still allows important principles to be illustrated simply. In fact, this is one of the key advantages of using diagrams.

Microeconomics and the production possibility curve

A production possibility curve illustrates the microeconomic issues of choice and opportunity cost.

If the country chose to produce more clothing, it would have to sacrifice the production of some food. This sacrifice of food is the opportunity cost of the extra clothing.

The fact that to produce more of one good involves producing less of the other is illustrated by the downward-sloping nature of the curve. For example, the country could move from point *x* to point *y* in Figure 1.2. In doing so it would be producing an extra 1 million units of clothing, but 1 million units less of food. Thus the opportunity cost of the 1 million extra units of clothing would be the 1 million units of food forgone.

It is because opportunity costs increase that the production possibility curve is bowed outwards rather than being a straight line. Thus in Figure 1.2 as production moves from point *x* to *y* to *z*, so the amount of food sacrificed rises for each additional unit of clothing produced. The opportunity cost of the fifth million units of clothing is 1 million units of food. The opportunity cost of the sixth million units of clothing is 2 million units of food.

KI 2
p11

1. *What is the opportunity cost of the seventh million units of clothing?*
2. *If the country moves upwards along the curve and produces more food, does this also involve increasing opportunity costs?*
3. *Under what circumstances would the production possibility curve be (a) a straight line; (b) bowed in towards the origin? Are these circumstances ever likely?*

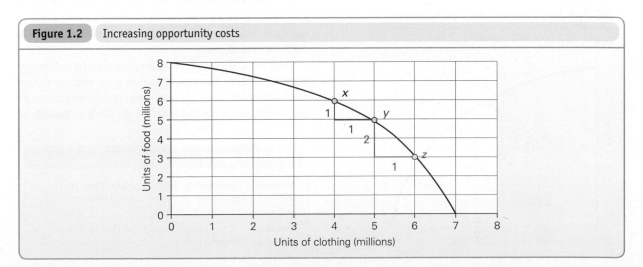

Figure 1.2	Increasing opportunity costs

KI 1
p7

> **BOX 1.4** **SCARCITY AND ABUNDANCE**
>
> ## Is lunch ever free?
>
> The central economic problem is scarcity. But are *all* goods and services scarce? Is anything we desire truly abundant?
>
> First, what do we mean by *abundance*? In the economic sense we mean something where supply exceeds demand at a *zero* price. In other words, even if it is free, there is no shortage. What is more, there must be no opportunity cost in supplying it. For example, if the government supplies health care free to the sick, it is still scarce in the economic sense because there is a cost to the government (and hence the taxpayer).
>
> Two things that might seem to be abundant are air and water.
>
> ### Air
>
> In one sense air *is* abundant. There is no shortage of air to breathe for most people for most of the time. But if we define air as clean, unpolluted air, then in some parts of the world it is scarce. It costs money to clean polluted air. We may not pay directly – the cleaned-up air may be free to the 'consumer' – but the taxpayer or industry (and hence its customers) will have to pay.
>
> Even if you live in a non-polluted part of the country, you may well have spent money moving there to escape the pollution. Again there is an opportunity cost to obtain the clean air.
>
> ### Water
>
> Whether water is abundant depends again on where you live. It also depends on what the water is used for.
>
> Water for growing crops in a country with plentiful rain *is* abundant. In drier countries, resources have to be spent on irrigation. Water for drinking is not abundant. Reservoirs have to be built. The water has to be piped, purified and pumped.
>
>
>
> 1. There is a saying in economics, 'There is no such thing as a free lunch' (hence the sub-title for this box). What does this mean?
> 2. Are any other (desirable) goods or services truly abundant?
>
> It also illustrates the phenomenon of *increasing opportunity costs*. By this we mean that as a country produces more of one good it has to sacrifice ever-increasing amounts of the other. The reason for this is that different factors of production have different properties. People have different skills; land varies across different parts of the country; raw materials differ one from another; and so on. Thus as a country concentrates more on the production of one good, it has to start using resources that are less suitable – resources that would have been better suited to producing other goods. In our example, then, the production of more and more clothing will involve a growing *marginal cost*: ever-increasing amounts of food have to be sacrificed for each additional unit of clothing produced.

Macroeconomics and the production possibility curve

There is no guarantee that resources will be fully employed, or that they will be used in the most efficient way possible. The nation may thus be producing at a point inside the curve: for example, point *v* in Figure 1.3.

What we are saying here is that the economy is producing less of both goods than it is possible for it to produce, either because some resources are not being used (e.g. workers may be unemployed), or because it is not using the most efficient methods of production possible, or a combination of the two. By using its resources to the full, the nation could move out onto the curve: to point *x* or *y*, for example. It could produce more clothing *and* more food.

Here we are concerned not with the combination of goods produced (a microeconomic issue), but with whether the total amount produced is as much as it could be (a macroeconomic issue).

Over time, the production possibilities of a nation are likely to increase. ***Investment*** in new plant and machinery will increase the stock of capital; new raw materials may be discovered; technological advances are likely to take place;

> **Figure 1.3** Making a fuller use of resources
>
>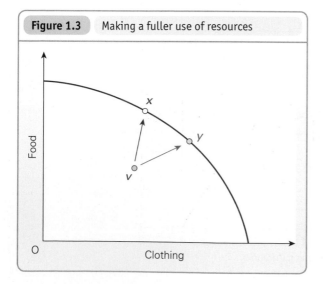

> **Definitions**
>
> **Increasing opportunity costs of production** When additional production of one good involves ever-increasing sacrifices of another.
>
> **Investment** The production of items that are not for immediate consumption.

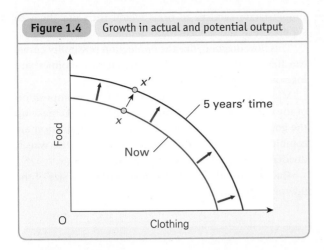

Figure 1.4 Growth in actual and potential output

through education and training, labour is likely to become more productive. This growth in potential output is illustrated by an outward shift in the production possibility curve. This will then allow actual output to increase: for example, from point x to point x' in Figure 1.4.

 Will economic growth always involve a parallel outward shift of the production possibility curve?

Illustrating economic issues: the circular flow of goods and incomes

The process of satisfying human wants involves producers and consumers. The relationship between them is two-sided and can be represented in a flow diagram (see Figure 1.5).

The consumers of goods and services are labelled 'households'. Some members of households, of course, are also workers, and in some cases are the owners of other factors of

production too, such as land. The producers of goods and services are labelled 'firms'.[1]

Firms and households are in a twin 'demand and supply' relationship with each other.

First, in the top part of the diagram, households demand goods and services, and firms supply goods and services. In the process, exchange takes place. In a money economy (as opposed to a ***barter economy***), firms exchange goods and services for money. In other words, money flows from households to firms in the form of consumer expenditure, while goods and services flow the other way – from firms to households.

This coming together of buyers and sellers is known as a ***market*** – it could be a street market, a shop or a website offering online shopping. Thus we talk about the market for apples, for oil, for houses, for televisions, and so on.

Second, firms and households come together in the market for factors of production. This is illustrated in the bottom half of Figure 1.5. This time the demand and

Definitions

Barter economy An economy where people exchange goods and services directly with one another without any payment of money. Workers would be paid with bundles of goods.

Market The interaction between buyers and sellers.

---

[1] In practice, much of society's production takes place within the household for its members' own consumption. Examples include cooking, cleaning, growing vegetables, decorating and childcare. Also, firms buy from and sell to each other – whether it be raw materials, capital goods or semi-finished goods. Nevertheless, it is still useful to depict the flows of goods and services and money between households and firms when explaining the operation of markets.

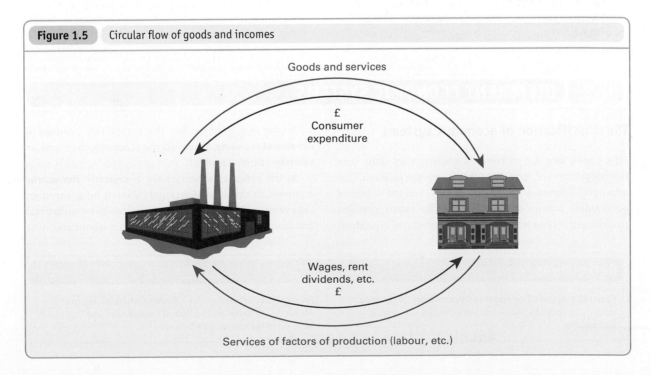

Figure 1.5 Circular flow of goods and incomes

Goods and services

£
Consumer
expenditure

Wages, rent
dividends, etc.
£

Services of factors of production (labour, etc.)

supply roles are reversed. Firms demand the use of factors of production owned by households – labour, land and capital. Households supply them. Thus the services of labour and other factors flow from households to firms, and in exchange firms pay households money – namely, wages, rent, dividends and interest. Just as we referred to particular goods markets, so we can also refer to particular factor markets – the market for bricklayers, for footballers, for land, and so on.

So there is a circular flow of incomes. Households earn incomes from firms and firms earn incomes from households. The money circulates. There is also a circular flow of goods and services, but in the opposite direction. Households

supply factor services to firms which then use them to supply goods and services to households.

This flow diagram, like the production possibility curve, can help us to distinguish between microeconomics and macroeconomics.

Microeconomics is concerned with the composition of the circular flow: what combinations of goods make up the goods flow; how the various factors of production are combined to produce these goods; for whom the wages, dividends, rent and interest are paid out.

Macroeconomics is concerned with the total size of the flow and what causes it to expand and contract.

Section summary

1. The central economic problem is that of scarcity. Given that there is a limited supply of factors of production (labour, land and capital), it is impossible to provide everybody with everything they want. Potential demands exceed potential supplies.

2. The subject of economics is usually divided into two main branches, macroeconomics and microeconomics.

3. Macroeconomics deals with aggregates such as the overall levels of unemployment, output, growth and prices in the economy.

4. Microeconomics deals with the activities of individual units within the economy: firms, industries, consumers, workers, etc. Because resources are scarce, people have to make choices. Society has to choose by some means or other *what* goods and services to produce, *how* to produce them and *for whom* to produce them. Microeconomics studies these choices.

5. Rational choices involve weighing up the marginal benefits of each activity against its marginal opportunity costs. If the marginal benefits exceed the marginal costs, it is rational to choose to do more of that activity.

6. The production possibility curve shows the possible combinations of two goods that a country can produce in a given period of time. Assuming that the country is already producing on the curve, the production of more of one good will involve producing less of the other. This opportunity cost is illustrated by the slope of the curve. If the economy is producing within the curve as a result of idle resources or inefficiency, it can produce more of both goods by taking up this slack. In the longer term it can only produce more of both by shifting the curve outwards through investment, technological progress, etc.

7. The circular flow of goods and incomes shows the interrelationships between firms and households in a money economy. Firms and households come together in markets. In goods markets, firms supply goods and households demand goods. In the process, money flows from households to firms in return for the goods and services that the firms supply. In factor markets, firms demand factors of production and households supply them. In the process, money flows from firms to households in return for the services of the factors that households supply.

1.2 DIFFERENT ECONOMIC SYSTEMS

The classification of economic systems

KI 1
p7

All societies face the problem of scarcity. They differ considerably, however, in the way they tackle the problem. One important difference between societies is in the degree of government control of the economy: the extent to which government decides 'what', 'how' and 'for whom' to produce.

At the one extreme lies the completely *planned or command economy*, where all the economic decisions are taken by the government.

At the other extreme lies the completely *free-market economy*. In this type of economy there is no government intervention at all. All decisions are taken by individuals and firms. Households decide how much labour and other

Definitions

Centrally planned or command economy An economy where all economic decisions are taken by the central authorities.

Free-market economy An economy where all economic decisions are taken by individual households and firms and with no government intervention.

Figure 1.6	Classifying economic systems

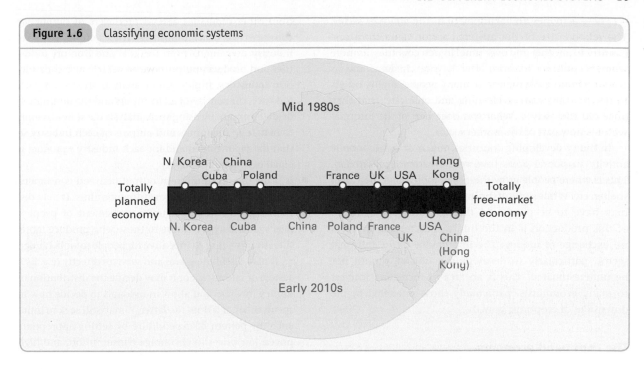

factors to supply, and what goods to consume. Firms decide what goods to produce and what factors to employ. The pattern of production and consumption that results depends on the interactions of all these individual demand and supply decisions in free markets.

In practice, all economies are a mixture of the two; it is the *degree* of government intervention that distinguishes different economic systems. The government plays a large role in China, whereas in the USA the government plays a much smaller role.

It is still useful to analyse the extremes, in order to put the different **mixed economies** of the real world into perspective. The mixture of government and the market can be shown by the use of a spectrum diagram such as Figure 1.6. It shows where particular economies of the real world lie along the spectrum between the two extremes.

The diagram is useful in that it provides a simple picture of the mixture of government and the market that exists in various economies. It can also be used to show changes in the mixture over time.

The problem with this type of classification is that it is one-dimensional and oversimplified. Countries differ in the *type* of government intervention as well as the level.

For example, governments can intervene through planning, public ownership, regulation, taxes and subsidies, partnership schemes with private industry, and so on. Two countries could be in a similar position along the spectrum but have very different types of government intervention.

Notice that there has been a general movement to the right along the spectrum since the 1980s. In former communist countries this has been a result of the abandonment of central planning and the adoption of private enterprise. In western economies it has been a result of deregulation of private industry and privatisation (the selling of nationalised industries to the private sector).

 How do you think the positions of these eight countries will change over the next decade?

The informal sector: a third dimension

In all societies, many economic decisions are made, whether individually or in groups, which involve neither the government nor the market. For example, many of the activities taking place in the home, such as cooking, cleaning, gardening and care for children or the elderly, can be seen as 'economic' activities. There is an output (such as a meal or a service provided) and there is an opportunity cost to the provider (in terms of alternative activities forgone). And yet no money changes hands. Similarly, many of the activities done in groups, such as clubs and charities, involve the provision of goods and/or services, but, again, no money changes hands.

Definition

Mixed economy An economy where economic decisions are made partly by the government and partly through the market. In practice all economies are mixed.

These activities are taking place in the *informal sector*. The relative size of the informal sector varies from one country to another and over time. In rich countries, as more women continue to work after having children, and as working hours have increased, many people employ others to do the jobs, such as cleaning and childcare, that they once did themselves. What was once part of the informal sector is now part of the market sector.

In many developing countries, much of the economic activity in poorer areas involves *subsistence production*. This is where people grow their own food, build their own shelter, etc. While some of the inputs (e.g. building materials) may have to be purchased through the market, much of this production is in the informal sector and involves no exchange of money. The importance of the informal sector, particularly to developing countries, should not be underestimated. This is an area of increasing interest to many economists, particularly those interested in the downsides of economic growth.

The command economy

The command economy is usually associated with a socialist or communist economic system, where land and capital are collectively owned. The state plans the allocation of resources at three levels:

- It plans the allocation of resources between current consumption and investment for the future. By sacrificing some present consumption and diverting resources into investment, it could increase the economy's growth rate.

  The amount of resources it chooses to devote to investment will depend on its broad macroeconomic strategy: the importance it attaches to growth as opposed to current consumption.

  TC 1
  p11
- At a microeconomic level, it plans the output of each industry and firm, the techniques that will be used, and the labour and other resources required by each industry and firm.

  In order to ensure that the required inputs are available, the state would probably conduct some form of *input–output analysis*. All industries are seen as users of inputs

from other industries and as producers of output for consumers or other industries. For example, the steel industry uses inputs from the coal and iron-ore industries and produces output for the vehicle and construction industries. Input–output analysis shows, for each industry, the sources of all its inputs and the destination of all its output. By using such analysis the state attempts to match up the inputs and outputs of each industry so that the planned demand for each industry's product is equal to its planned supply.

- It plans the distribution of output between consumers. This will depend on the government's aims. It may distribute goods according to its judgement of people's needs; or it may give more to those who produce more, thereby providing an incentive for people to work harder.

  It may distribute goods and services directly (e.g. by a system of rationing); or it may decide the distribution of money incomes and allow individuals to decide how to spend them. If it does the latter, it may still seek to influence the pattern of expenditure by setting appropriate prices: low prices to encourage consumption, and high prices to discourage consumption.

Assessment of the command economy

With central planning, the government could take an overall view of the economy. It could direct the nation's resources in accordance with specific national goals.

High growth rates could be achieved if the government directed large amounts of resources into investment. Unemployment could be largely avoided if the government carefully planned the allocation of labour in accordance with production requirements and labour skills. National income could be distributed more equally or in accordance with needs. The social repercussions of production and consumption (e.g. the effects on the environment) could be taken into account, provided the government was able to predict these effects and chose to take them into account.

In practice, a command economy could achieve these goals only at considerable social and economic cost. The reasons are as follows:

- The larger and more complex the economy, the greater the task of collecting and analysing the information essential to planning, and the more complex the plan. Complicated plans are likely to be costly to administer and involve cumbersome bureaucracy.
- If there is no system of prices, or if prices are set arbitrarily by the state, planning is likely to involve the inefficient use of resources. It is difficult to assess the relative efficiency of two alternative techniques that use different inputs, if there is no way in which the value of those inputs can be ascertained. For example, how can a rational decision be made between an oil-fired and a coal-fired furnace if the prices of oil and coal do not reflect their relative scarcity?

Definitions

Informal sector The parts of the economy that involve production and/or exchange, but where there are no money payments.

Subsistence production Where people produce things for their own consumption.

Input–output analysis This involves dividing the economy into sectors where each sector is a user of inputs from and a supplier of outputs to other sectors. The technique examines how these inputs and outputs can be matched to the total resources available in the economy.

- It is difficult to devise appropriate incentives to encourage workers and managers to be more productive without a reduction in quality. For example, if bonuses are given according to the quantity of output produced, a factory might produce shoddy goods, since it can probably produce a larger quantity of goods by cutting quality. To avoid this problem, a large number of officials may have to be employed to check quality.
- Complete state control over resource allocation would involve a considerable loss of individual liberty. Workers would have no choice where to work; consumers would have no choice what to buy.
- If production is planned, but consumers are free to spend money incomes as they wish, there will be a problem if the wishes of consumers change. Shortages will occur if consumers decide to buy more; surpluses will occur if they decide to buy less.

Most of these problems were experienced in the former Soviet Union and the other Eastern bloc countries, and were part of the reason for the overthrow of their communist regimes (see Box 1.5).

The free-market economy

Free decision making by individuals

In a free market, individuals are free to make their own economic decisions. Consumers are free to decide what to buy with their incomes: free to make demand decisions. Firms are free to choose what to sell and what production methods to use: free to make supply decisions. The demand and supply decisions of consumers and firms are transmitted to each other through their effect on prices: through the **price mechanism**. The prices that result are the prices that firms and consumers have to accept.

The price mechanism

The price mechanism works as follows. Prices respond to shortages and surpluses. Shortages result in prices rising. Surpluses result in prices falling. Let us take each in turn.

If consumers want more of a good (or if producers decide to cut back supply), demand will exceed supply. The resulting shortage will cause the price of the good to rise. This will act as an incentive to producers to supply more, since production will now be more profitable. At the same time it will discourage consumers from buying so much. *The price will continue rising until the shortage has been eliminated.*

If, on the other hand, consumers decide they want less of a good (or if producers decide to produce more), supply will exceed demand. The resulting surplus will cause the price of the good to fall. This will act as a disincentive to producers, who will supply less, since production will now be less profitable. It will encourage consumers to buy more. *The price will continue falling until the surplus has been eliminated.*

This price, where demand equals supply, is called the **equilibrium price**. By **equilibrium** we mean a point of balance or a point of rest: in other words, a point towards which there is a tendency to move.

1. Try using the same type of analysis in the labour market to show what will happen if there is an increase in demand for labour. What is the 'price' of labour?

2. Can you think of any examples where prices and wages do not adjust very rapidly to a shortage or surplus? For what reasons might they not do so?

The response of demand and supply to changes in price illustrates a very important feature of how economies work: *people respond to incentives*. It is important, therefore, that incentives are appropriate and have the desired effect. This is the fifth of our 15 threshold concepts (see Chapter 2, page 54).

The effect of changes in demand and supply

How will the price mechanism respond to changes in consumer demand or producer supply? Patterns of consumer demand will change over time: for example, people may decide they want more fixed-gear bikes and fewer mountain bikes. Likewise, the pattern of supply changes: for example, changes in technology may allow the mass production of microchips at lower cost, while the production of hand-built furniture becomes relatively expensive.

In all cases of changes in demand and supply, the resulting changes in price act as both signals and incentives.

A change in demand. A rise in demand is signalled by a rise in price, which then acts as an incentive for supply to rise. The high price of these goods relative to their costs of production signals that consumers are willing to see resources diverted from other uses. This is just what firms do. They divert resources from goods with lower prices relative to costs (and hence lower profits) to those goods that are more profitable.

A fall in demand is signalled by a fall in price. This then acts as an incentive for supply to fall. The goods are now less profitable to produce.

A change in supply. A rise in supply is signalled by a fall in price. This then acts as an incentive for demand to rise. A fall in supply is signalled by a rise in price. This then acts as an incentive for demand to fall.

Definitions

Price mechanism The system in a market economy whereby changes in price in response to changes in demand and supply have the effect of making demand equal to supply.

Equilibrium price The price where the quantity demanded equals the quantity supplied: the price where there is no shortage or surplus.

Equilibrium A position of balance. A position from which there is no inherent tendency to move away.

BOX 1.5   COMMAND ECONOMIES

The rise and fall of planning

Russia

The Bolsheviks under the leadership of Lenin came to power in Russia with the October Revolution of 1917. Communism was introduced and the market economy abolished. Industries were nationalised; workers were told what jobs to do; food was taken from peasants to feed the towns; workers were allocated goods from distribution depots.

With the ending of the civil war in 1921, the economy was in bad shape and Lenin embarked on the New Economic Policy. This involved a return to the use of markets. Smaller businesses were returned to private hands and peasants were able to sell their crops. The economy began to recover; however, Lenin died in 1924 and Stalin came to power.

The Russian economy underwent a radical transformation from 1928 onwards. The key features of the Stalinist approach were collectivisation, industrialisation and central planning. Peasant farms were abolished and replaced by large-scale collective farms where land was collectively owned and worked, and by state farms, owned by the state and run by managers. This caused disruption and famine, with peasants slaughtering their animals rather than giving them up. However, in the longer term more food was produced. Both collective and state farms were given quotas of output that they were supposed to deliver, for which the state would pay a fixed price.

Alongside the agricultural reforms a drive to industrialisation took place and a vast planning apparatus was developed. At the top was *Gosplan*, the central planning agency. This prepared five-year plans, which specified the general direction in which the economy was to move, and annual plans, which gave details of what was to be produced and with what resources for some 200 or so key products. The system operated without either the price mechanism or the profit motive, although incentives existed with bonuses paid to managers and workers if targets were achieved.

Stalin died in 1953, but the planning system remained largely unchanged throughout the Soviet Union until the late 1980s. Initially, high growth rates had been achieved, though at a cost of low efficiency. Poor flow of information led to inconsistencies in the plans. Targets were often unrealistic, and as a result there were frequent shortages and sometimes surpluses. There was little product innovation and goods were frequently of poor quality. A large 'underground economy' flourished in which goods were sold on the illegal market and in which people did second 'unofficial' jobs.

Moves to the market

By the time Gorbachev came to power in 1985 many people were pressing for economic reform. Gorbachev responded with his policy of *perestroika* (economic reconstruction), which involved managers preparing their own plans and managers and workers being rewarded for becoming more efficient. Under the new system, one-person businesses and larger co-operatives were allowed, while the price mechanism was reintroduced with the state raising prices if there were substantial shortages.

These reforms, however, did not halt the economic decline. Managers resented the extra responsibilities and people were unclear as to what to expect from the state. Queues lengthened in the shops and people became disillusioned with *perestroika*.

Communism fell apart in 1989 and both the Soviet Union and the system of central planning came to an end. Russia embarked upon a radical programme of market reforms in which competition and enterprise were intended to replace state central planning (see Case Studies 1.6, Free-market medicine in Russia, 13.6, Privatisation in transition economies, and 13.7, Forms of transition in transition countries, in MyEconLab).

Initially, the disruption of the move to the market led to a sharp decline in the Russian economy. GDP fell by an average of 5.5 per cent per annum between 1993 and 1998. This was followed by a period of rapid economic growth, which averaged 7 per cent from 2000 to 2008. But the economy declined by nearly 8 per cent in the 2009 recession.

 KEY IDEA 5 *Changes in demand or supply cause markets to adjust.* Whenever such changes occur, the resulting 'disequilibrium' will bring an automatic change in prices, thereby restoring equilibrium (i.e. a balance of demand and supply).

The fact that markets adjust so as to equate demand and supply is our fourth 'Threshold Concept', which is discussed in Chapter 2 (page 47).

 TC 4 p47

 1. *Why do the prices of fresh vegetables fall when they are in season? Could an individual farmer prevent the price falling?*

2. *If you were the manager of a supermarket, how would you set about deciding what prices to charge for food approaching its sell-by date?*
3. *Demand for downloaded music has grown rapidly, yet the prices of downloads have fallen. Why?*

The interdependence of markets

The interdependence of goods and factor markets. A rise in demand for a good will raise its price and profitability. Firms will respond by supplying more. But to do this they will need more inputs. Thus the demand for the inputs will rise, which in turn will raise the price of the inputs. The suppliers of inputs will respond to this incentive by supplying more. This can be summarised as follows:

KI 5 p22

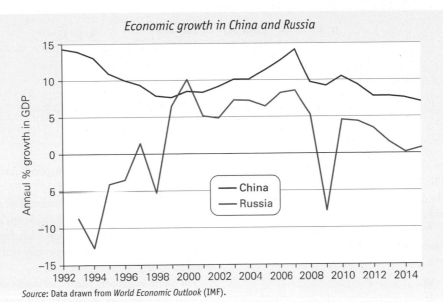

Economic growth in China and Russia

Source: Data drawn from *World Economic Outlook* (IMF).

Although this was followed by growth rates of 4.5 and 4.3 per cent in 2010 and 2011, since then growth has declined. Many commentators point to decades of underinvestment in industry and in road and rail infrastructure, corruption, disillusionment and continuing political uncertainty as root causes of this sluggish growth rate. From 2014, the economy was further dampened by Western economic sanctions in response to the crisis in Ukraine.

China

In contrast to the Soviet Union, China's move towards a more market-based economy has been carefully managed by the ruling Communist Party. From the 1940s to the 1970s central planning, combined with the removal of all property rights, resulted in low productivity, a creaking infrastructure and famine.

But after the death of Party Chairman Mao Zedong in 1976, a new breed of Chinese leaders came to power, and they were increasingly pragmatic. There was a focus on making use of aspects of capitalism alongside government control of the economy. Productivity was valued equally with political stability, while consumer welfare was considered as important as the elimination of unemployment. Economic zones were set up, where foreign investment was encouraged, and laws on patents and other intellectual property encouraged innovation. This approach was developed further over the following decades and from 1992 to 2010 China averaged growth of 10.5 per cent per annum – the highest in the world.

Today China is the world's second largest economy and, although growth has slowed somewhat to around 7.5 per cent, is poised to overtake the USA by 2020 (see Box 27.3), albeit with much lower output *per head*. Yet its human rights record remains a concern to many around the world; economic liberalisation and growth have not been accompanied by political freedom. Furthermore, it is experiencing some of the problems of capitalism: pollution, income inequality and potential instability of the financial system. It remains unclear how long the combination of capitalist economics alongside tight political control can continue to deliver.

1. Goods market
   - Demand for the good rises.
   - This creates a shortage.
   - This causes the price of the good to rise.
   - This eliminates the shortage by reducing demand and encouraging firms to produce more.
2. Factor market
   - The increased supply of the good causes an increase in the demand for factors of production (i.e. inputs) used in making it.
   - This causes a shortage of those inputs.
   - This causes their prices to rise.
   - This eliminates their shortage by reducing demand and encouraging the suppliers of inputs to supply more.

So changes in goods markets will lead to changes in factor markets. Figure 1.7 summarises this sequence of events. (It is common in economics to summarise an argument like this by using symbols.)

Interdependence exists in the other direction too: factor markets affect goods markets. For example, the discovery of raw materials will lower their price. This will lower the costs of production of firms using these raw materials and will increase the supply of the finished goods. The resulting surplus will lower the price of the good, which will encourage consumers to buy more.

Summarise this last paragraph using symbols like those in Figure 1.7.

Figure 1.7   The price mechanism: the effect of a rise in demand

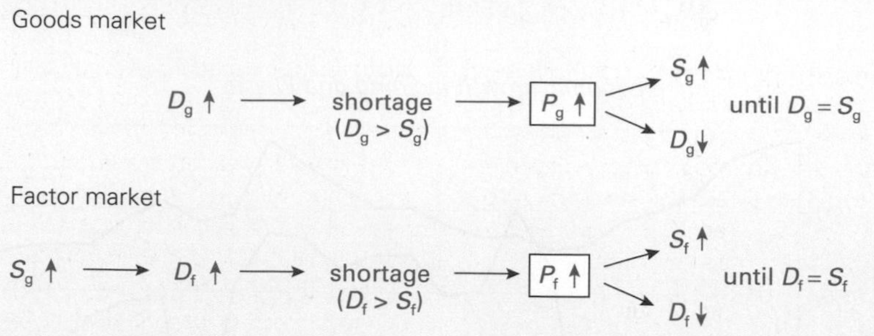

Goods market

$$D_g \uparrow \longrightarrow \text{shortage} \atop (D_g > S_g) \longrightarrow \boxed{P_g \uparrow} \quad \nearrow S_g \uparrow \atop \searrow D_g \downarrow \quad \text{until } D_g = S_g$$

Factor market

$$S_g \uparrow \longrightarrow D_f \uparrow \longrightarrow \text{shortage} \atop (D_f > S_f) \longrightarrow \boxed{P_f \uparrow} \quad \nearrow S_f \uparrow \atop \searrow D_f \downarrow \quad \text{until } D_f = S_f$$

The interdependence of different goods markets.   A rise in the price of one good will encourage consumers to buy alternatives. This will drive up the price of alternatives. This in turn will encourage producers to supply more of the alternatives.

 Are different factor markets similarly interdependent? What would happen if the price of capital equipment rose?

Conclusion

Even though all individuals are merely looking to their own self-interest in the free-market economy, they are in fact being encouraged to respond to the wishes of others through the incentive of the price mechanism. (See Case Study 1.4, The interdependence of markets, in MyEconLab; see also Box 1.6.)

Assessment of the free-market economy

The fact that a free-market economy functions automatically is one of its major advantages. There is no need for costly and complex bureaucracies to co-ordinate economic decisions. The economy can respond quickly to changing demand and supply conditions.

When markets are highly competitive, no one has great power. Competition between firms keeps prices down and acts as an incentive for efficiency. The more firms there are competing, the more responsive they will be to consumer wishes.

The more efficiently firms can combine their factors of production, the more profit they will make. The more efficiently workers work, the more secure will be their jobs and the higher their wages. The more carefully consumers decide what to buy, the greater the value for money they will receive.

Thus people pursuing their own self-interest through buying and selling in competitive markets helps to minimise the central economic problem of scarcity, by encouraging the efficient use of society's resources in line with consumer wishes. From this type of argument, the following conclusion is often drawn by defenders of the free market: 'The pursuit of private gain results in the social good.' This claim is the subject of much debate and has profound moral implications (see Threshold Concept 2).

BOX 1.6 **ADAM SMITH (1723–90)**

And the 'invisible hand' of the market

Many economists would argue that modern economics dates from 1776, the year in which Adam Smith's *An Inquiry into the Nature and Causes of the Wealth of Nations* was published – one of the most important books on economics ever written.

The work, in five books, is very wide-ranging, but the central argument is that market economies generally serve the public interest well. Markets guide production and consumption like an *invisible hand*. Even though everyone is looking after their own private self-interest, their interaction in the market will lead to the social good.

In book I, chapter 2, Smith writes:

Man has almost constant occasion for the help of his brethren and it is in vain for him to expect it from their benevolence only . . . It is not from the benevolence of the butcher, the brewer, or the baker that we expect our dinner, but from their regard to their own interest. We

address ourselves, not to their humanity but to their self-love, and never talk to them of our own necessities, but of their advantages.

Later, in book IV, chapter 2, he continues:

Every individual is continually exerting himself to find out the most advantageous employment of whatever capital he can command. It is his own advantage, indeed, and not that of the society, which he has in view. But the study of his own advantage naturally, or rather necessarily, leads him to prefer that employment which is most advantageous to the society . . . he intends only his own gain, and he is in this, as in many other cases, led by an invisible hand to promote an end which was no part of his intention. Nor is it always the worse for the society that it was no part of it. By pursuing his own interest he

THRESHOLD CONCEPT 2   PEOPLE GAIN FROM VOLUNTARY ECONOMIC INTERACTION

Economic interaction between people can take a number of different forms. Sometimes it takes place in markets. For example, when goods are exchanged, there is interaction between the consumer and the shop. When someone is employed, there is interaction between the employer and the employee. When a firm buys raw materials, there is interaction between the purchasing firm and the selling firm.

In each case there is expected to be a mutual gain. If there wasn't, the interaction would not take place. If you go on a holiday costing £400, then assuming the holiday turns out as you expected, you will have gained. You would rather have the holiday than spend the £400 on something else. The marginal benefit to you exceeds the marginal cost. The travel agent and tour operator also gain. They make a profit on selling you the holiday. It is a 'win–win situation'. This is sometimes called a *positive sum game*: an interaction where there is a positive net gain.

Another example is international trade (the subject of Chapter 24). If two countries trade with each other, there will be a net gain to both of them. If there wasn't, they would not trade. Both countries will end up consuming a greater value of products than they could without trade. The reason is that each country can specialise in the products it is relatively good at producing (compared with the other country) and export them, and import from the other country the goods it is relatively poor at producing.

That there is a net gain from voluntary interaction is a *threshold concept* because realising this tends to change the way we look at economic activity. Often it is important to identify what these overall gains are so that we can compare them with alternative forms of interaction. For example, even though both workers and their employer respectively gain from the wages currently paid and the output currently produced, it might still be possible to reorganise the workforce in a way that increases production. This could allow the employer to pay higher wages and still gain an increase in profits. Both sides could thus gain from constructive negotiation about wages and new work practices.

Sometimes it may appear that voluntary interaction results in one side gaining and the other losing. For example, a firm may raise its price. It gains and the consumer loses. But is this strictly true? Consumers are certainly worse off than before, but as long as they are still prepared to buy the product, they must consider that they are still gaining more by buying it than by not. There is still a gain to both sides: it's just that the firm is gaining more and the consumer is gaining less.

1. *Would you ever swap things with friends if both of you did not gain? Explain your answer.*
2. *Give one or two examples of involuntary (i.e. compulsory) economic interaction, where one side gains but the other loses.*

In practice, however, markets do not achieve maximum efficiency in the allocation of scarce resources, and governments therefore feel it necessary to intervene to rectify this and other problems of the free market. The problems of a free market include the following:

- Competition between firms is often limited. A few firms may dominate an industry, charging high prices and making large profits.
- Rather than responding to consumer wishes, firms may attempt to persuade consumers by advertising.

frequently promotes that of society more effectually than when he really intends to promote it.

He argued, therefore, with one or two exceptions, that the state should not interfere with the functioning of the economy. It should adopt a laissez-faire or 'hands-off' policy. It should allow free enterprise for firms and free trade between countries.

This praise of the free market has led many on the political right to regard him as the father of the 'libertarian movement' – the movement that advocates the absolute minimum amount of state intervention in the economy (see Box 11.8 on page 348). In fact one of the most famous of the libertarian societies is called the Adam Smith Institute.

But Smith was not blind to the drawbacks of unregulated markets. In book I, chapter 7, he looks at the problem of monopoly:

A monopoly granted either to an individual or to a trading company has the same effect as a secret in trade or manufactures. The monopolists, by keeping the market constantly under-stocked, by never fully supplying the effectual demand, sell their commodities much above the natural price, and raise their emoluments, whether they consist in wages or profit, greatly above their natural rate.

Later on he looks at the dangers of firms getting together to pursue their mutual interest:

People of the same trade seldom meet together, even for merriment or diversion, but the conversation ends in a conspiracy against the public or in some contrivance to raise prices.

THRESHOLD CONCEPT 3   MARKETS MAY FAIL TO MEET SOCIAL OBJECTIVES   THINKING LIKE AN ECONOMIST

We have seen that market forces can automatically equate demand and supply. The outcomes of the process may be desirable, but they are by no means always so. Unrestrained market forces can result in severe problems for individuals, society and the environment.

Markets tend to reflect the combined actions of individual consumers and firms. But when consumers and firms make their decisions, they may act selfishly and fail to take account of the broader effects of their actions. If people want to buy guns, market forces will make their supply profitable. If people want to drive fuel-hungry cars, then this will create the market for firms to supply them. Market forces are not kind and caring. They mechanically reflect human behaviour.

And it's not just selfish behaviour that markets reflect; it's ignorance too. You may be unaware that a toy that you buy for a child is dangerous, but by doing so, you encourage unscrupulous firms to supply them. A firm may not realise that a piece of machinery it uses is dangerous until an accident happens. In the meantime, it continues using it because it is profitable to do so.

If wages are determined purely by demand and supply, then some people, such as footballers and bankers, may be very well paid. Others, such as cleaners and shop workers, may be very poorly paid. Even if the resulting inequality is seen as unfair, market forces alone will not be enough to achieve a fair society.

Recognising the limitations and failings of markets is a *threshold concept*. It helps us to understand how laws or taxes or subsidies could be framed to counteract such failings. It helps us to relate the mechanical operation of demand and supply to a whole range of social objectives and ask whether the market system is the best way of meeting such objectives.

But to recognise market failures is only part of the way to finding a solution. Can the government put things right, and if so, how? Or do the limitations of government mean that the solution is sometimes worse than the problem? We examine these issues in many parts of the text. We set the scene in Threshold Concept 6 (page 55).

1. *If global warming affects all of us adversely, why in a purely market economy would individuals and firms continue with activities that contribute towards global warming?*
2. *In what ways do your own consumption patterns adversely affect other people?*

- Lack of competition and high profits may remove the incentive for firms to be efficient.

- Power and property may be unequally distributed. Those who have power and/or property (e.g. big business, unions and landlords) will gain at the expense of those without power and property.
- Consumers and firms may not have full information about the costs and benefits associated with different goods and factor inputs and may thus make the wrong decisions.
- The practices of some firms may be socially undesirable. For example, a chemical works may pollute the environment.
- Some socially desirable goods would simply not be produced by private enterprise. Who would carry out counter-terrorism activities if these were not funded by governments?
- A free-market economy may lead to macroeconomic instability. There may be periods of recession with high unemployment and falling output, and other periods of rising prices.
- Finally, there is the ethical objection, that a free-market economy, by rewarding self-interested behaviour, may encourage selfishness, greed, materialism and the acquisition of power.

The fact that free markets may fail to meet various social objectives is Threshold Concept 3.

The mixed economy

Because of the problems of both free-market and command economies, all real-world economies are a mixture of the two systems.

In *mixed market economies*, the government may control the following:

- *Relative prices* of goods and inputs, by taxing or subsidising them or by direct price controls.
- Relative incomes, by the use of income taxes, welfare payments or direct controls over wages, profits, rents, etc.
- The pattern of production and consumption, by the use of legislation (e.g. making it illegal to produce unsafe goods), by direct provision of goods and services (e.g. education and defence) or by taxes and subsidies.
- The macroeconomic problems of unemployment, inflation, lack of growth, balance of trade deficits and exchange rate fluctuations, by the use of taxes and government expenditure, the control of bank lending and interest rates, the direct control of prices and the control of the foreign exchange rate.

Definitions

Mixed market economy A market economy where there is some government intervention.

Relative price The price of one good compared with another (e.g. good X is twice the price of good Y).

The fact that government intervention can be used to rectify various failings of the market is Threshold Concept 6 (see Chapter 2, page 55). It is important to realise, however,

TC 6
p55

that government actions may bring adverse as well as beneficial consequences. For more on government intervention in the mixed economy see Chapters 10 to 13.

Section summary

1. The economic systems of different countries vary according to the extent to which they rely on the market or the government to allocate resources.

2. At the one extreme, in a command economy, the state makes all the economic decisions. It plans amounts of resources to allocate for present consumption and amounts for investment for future output. It plans the output of each industry, the methods of production it will use and the amount of resources it will be allocated. It plans the distribution of output between consumers.

3. A command economy has the advantage of being able to address directly various national economic goals, such as rapid growth and the avoidance of unemployment and inequality. A command economy, however, is likely to be inefficient and bureaucratic; prices and the choice of production methods are likely to be arbitrary; incentives may be inappropriate; shortages and surpluses may result

4. At the other extreme is the free-market economy. In this economy, decisions are made by the interaction of demand and supply. Price changes act as the mechanism whereby demand and supply are balanced. If there is a shortage, price will rise until the shortage is eliminated. If there is a surplus, price will fall until that is eliminated.

5. A free-market economy functions automatically and if there is plenty of competition between producers this can help to protect consumers' interests. In practice, however, competition may be limited; there may be great inequality; there may be adverse social and environmental consequences; there may be macroeconomic instability.

6. In practice, all economies are some mixture of the market and government intervention. It is the degree and form of government intervention that distinguishes one type of economy from another.

1.3 THE NATURE OF ECONOMIC REASONING

Economics is one of the social sciences. So in what sense is it a *science*? Is it like the natural sciences such as physics and astronomy? What is the significance of the word 'social' in social science? What can economists do, and what is their role in helping governments devise economic policy?

Economics as a science

The methodology employed by economists has a lot in common with that employed by natural scientists. Both attempt to construct theories or *models* which are then used to *explain* and *predict*. An astronomer, for example, constructs models of planetary movements to *explain* why planets are in the position they are and to *predict* their position in the future.

Models in economics

In order to explain and predict, the economist constructs models which show simplified relationships between various economic phenomena. For example, a model of a market shows the relationships between demand, supply and price. Although most models can be described verbally, they can normally be represented more precisely in graphical or mathematical form.

Building models

Models are constructed by making general hypotheses about the causes of economic phenomena: for example,

that consumer demand will rise when consumer incomes rise. These hypotheses will often be based on observations. This process of making general statements from particular observations is known as **induction**.

Using models

Explanation. Models explain by showing how things are caused: what the causes of inflation are, why workers in some industries earn more than others, and so on.

Prediction. Models are sometimes used to make simple forecasts: for example, inflation will be below 5 per cent next year. Usually, however, predictions are of the 'If . . . then . . .' variety: for example, if demand for good x rises, its price will rise. This process of drawing conclusions from models is known as **deduction**.

When making such deductions it has to be assumed that nothing else that can influence the outcome has changed in

---

Definitions

Economic model A formal presentation of an economic theory.

Induction Constructing general theories on the basis of specific observations.

Deduction Using a theory to draw conclusions about specific circumstances.

BOX 1.7 *CETERIS PARIBUS*

Because of the complexities of the real world, economic models have to make various simplifying assumptions. Sometimes, however, economists are criticised for making unrealistic assumptions, assumptions that make their models irrelevant. The following joke illustrates the point.

There were three people cast away on a desert island: a chemist, an engineer and an economist. There was no food on the island and their plight seemed desperate.

Then they discovered a crate of canned food that had been washed up on the island. When they realised that they had no means of opening the cans, they decided that each of them should use their expertise to find a solution.

The chemist searched around for various minerals that could be heated up to produce a compound that would burn through the lids of the cans.

The engineer hunted around for rocks and then worked out what height of tree they would have to be dropped from in order to smash open the cans.

Meanwhile the economist sat down and thought 'Assuming we had a can opener . . . '.

---

the meantime. For example, if demand for good *x* rises, its price will rise *assuming* the cost of producing good *x* has not fallen. This is known as the **ceteris paribus** assumption. *Ceteris paribus* is Latin for 'other things being equal'.

Assessing models

Models can be judged according to how successful they are in explaining and predicting.

If the predictions are wrong, the first thing to do is to check whether the deductions were correctly made. If they were, the model must be either adapted or abandoned in favour of an alternative model with better predictive ability. But in economics, as with many other disciplines, academics are often unwilling to abandon their models. Instead they prefer the minimum adaptation necessary. This can lead to lively debates between different 'schools of thought', each claiming that their models paint a more accurate picture of the economy.

There has been a great deal of debate recently about why economic models failed to forecast the financial crisis of 2007–8. In September 2010, Ben Bernanke, the then Federal Reserve Board Chairman, said the failure of the economic models did not mean that they were irrelevant or significantly flawed. Rather than throwing out the models, more work was needed to capture how the financial system impacts on growth and stability.

Others disagreed. They claimed that many of the main models that had failed to predict the crisis were fundamentally flawed and needed replacing with other models – perhaps amended versions of older ones; perhaps new ones.

(We look at these debates in Parts E and F of the text.)

Economists as detectives

Because of a lack of conclusive evidence about just how many parts of the economy function, economists also need the skills of detectives. This involves a third type of reasoning (in addition to induction and deduction), known as **abduction**. This involves making informed guesses or estimates from limited evidence. It is using the scraps of evidence as clues as to what might be really going on. It is

how many initial hypotheses are formed. Then the researcher (or detective) will use the clues to search for more evidence that can be used for induction that will yield a more robust theory. The clues may lead to a false trail, but sometimes they may allow the researcher to develop a new theory or amend an existing one. A good researcher will be alert to clues; to seeing patterns in details that might previously have been dismissed or gone unnoticed.

Before the banking crisis of 2007–8 and the subsequent credit crunch and recession in the developed world, many economists were picking up clues and trying to use them to develop a theory of systemic risk in financial markets. They were using the skills of an economic detective to try to discover not only what was currently going on, but also what might be the consequences for the future. Some used abductive reasoning successfully to predict the impending crisis; most did not.

Economics as a social science

Economics concerns human behaviour. One problem here is that individuals often behave in very different ways. People have different tastes and different attitudes. This problem, however, is not as serious as it may seem at first sight. The reason is that people *on average* are likely to behave more predictably. For example, if the price of a product goes up by 5 per cent, we might be able to predict, *ceteris paribus*, that the quantity demanded will fall by approximately 10 per cent. This does not mean that every single individual's demand

---

Definitions

Ceteris paribus Latin for 'other things being equal'. This assumption has to be made when making deductions from theories.

Abduction Using pieces of evidence to develop a plausible explanation. This can then be tested by gathering more evidence.

will fall by 10 per cent, only that *total* demand will. Some people may demand a lot less; others may demand the same as before.

Even so, there are still things about human behaviour that are very difficult to predict, even when we are talking about whole groups of people. How, for example, will firms react to a rise in interest rates when making their investment decisions? This will depend on things such as the state of business confidence, something that is notoriously difficult to predict. How will a business respond to price changes by its rivals? This will often depend on how it thinks its rivals themselves will react to its own response. How will people respond to a crisis, such as the global banking and credit crisis of 2007–8? This depends very much on the mood of financial and other companies and individuals. A mood of pessimism (or optimism for that matter) can quickly spread, but not to a degree that is easily predictable.

For these reasons there is plenty of scope for competing models in economics, each making different assumptions and leading to different policy conclusions. As a result, economics can often be highly controversial. As we shall see later on in the book, different political parties may adhere to different schools of economic thought. Thus the political left may adhere to a model which implies that governments must intervene if unemployment is to be cured, whereas the political right may adhere to a model which implies that unemployment will be reduced if the government intervenes less and relies more on the free market.

One branch of economics that has seen considerable growth in recent years is behavioural economics, which adds elements of psychology to traditional models in an attempt to gain a better understanding of decision making by investors, consumers and other economic participants. Behavioural economists set up experiments and simulations to see how people respond to various sets of circumstances. For more on behavioural economics see Chapters 4, 8, 12 and 13.

The fact that there are different economic theories does not mean that economists always disagree. Despite the popular belief that 'if you laid all the economists of the world end to end they would still not reach a conclusion', there is in fact a large measure of agreement between economists about how to analyse the world and what conclusions to draw.

Economics and policy

Economists play a major role in helping governments to devise economic policy. In order to understand this role, it is necessary to distinguish between positive and normative statements.

A *positive statement* is a statement of fact. It may be right or wrong, but its accuracy can be tested by appealing to the facts. 'Unemployment is rising', 'Inflation will be over 6 per cent by next year' and 'If the government cuts taxes, imports will rise' are all examples of positive statements.

A *normative statement* is a statement of value: a statement about what ought or ought not to be, about whether something is good or bad, desirable or undesirable. 'It is right to tax the rich more than the poor', 'The government ought to reduce inflation' and 'Old-age pensions ought to be increased' are all examples of normative statements. They cannot be proved or disproved by a simple appeal to the facts.

Economists can only contribute to questions of policy in a positive way. That is, they can analyse the consequences of following certain policies. They can say which of two policies is more likely to achieve a given aim, but they should not, as economists, say whether the aims of the policy are desirable. For example, economists may argue that a policy of increasing government expenditure will reduce unemployment and raise inflation, but they cannot, as economists, decide whether such a policy is desirable.

 The importance of the positive/normative distinction. Economics can only contribute to policy issues in a positive way. Economists, as scientists, should not make normative judgements. They can make them only as individual people, with no more moral right than any other individual.

 Which of the following are positive statements and which are normative?
(a) Cutting the higher rates of income tax will redistribute incomes from the poor to the rich.
(b) It is wrong that inflation should be targeted if the consequence is higher unemployment.
(c) It is incorrect to state that putting up interest rates will reduce inflation.
(d) The government should introduce road pricing to address the issue of congestion.
(e) Current government policies should be aimed at reducing the deficit rather than stimulating growth.

Definitions

Positive statement A value-free statement which can be tested by an appeal to the facts.

Normative statement A value judgement.

Section summary

1. The methodology used by economists is similar to that used by natural scientists. Economists construct models which they use to explain and predict economic phenomena. These models can be tested by appealing to facts and seeing how successfully they have been predicted or explained by the model. Unsuccessful models can be either abandoned or amended.

2. Being a social science, economics is concerned with human actions. Making accurate predictions in economics is very difficult given that economics has to deal with a constantly changing environment.

3. Economists can help governments to devise policy by examining the consequences of alternative courses of action. In doing this, it is important to separate positive questions about what the effects of the policies are from normative ones as to what the goals of policy should be. Economists in their role as economists have no superior right to make normative judgements. They do, however, play a major role in assessing whether a policy meets the political objectives of government (or opposition).

END OF CHAPTER QUESTIONS

1. Imagine that a country can produce just two things: goods and services. Assume that over a given period it could produce any of the following combinations:

Units of goods

| 0 | 10 | 20 | 30 | 40 | 50 | 60 | 70 | 80 | 90 | 100 |

Units of services

| 80 | 79 | 77 | 74 | 70 | 65 | 58 | 48 | 35 | 19 | 0 |

   (a) Draw the country's production possibility curve.

   (b) Assuming that the country is currently producing 40 units of goods and 70 units of services, what is the opportunity cost of producing another 10 units of goods?

   (c) Explain how the figures illustrate the principle of increasing opportunity cost.

   (d) Now assume that technical progress leads to a 10 per cent increase in the output of goods for any given amount of resources. Draw the new production possibility curve. How has the opportunity cost of producing extra units of services altered?

2. Imagine that you won millions of pounds on the National Lottery. Would your 'economic problem' be solved?

3. Assume that in a household one parent currently works full time and the other stays at home to look after the family. How would you set about identifying and calculating the opportunity costs of the second parent now taking a full-time job? How would such calculations be relevant in deciding whether it is worth taking that job?

4. When you made the decision to study economics, was it a 'rational' decision (albeit based on the limited information you had available at the time)? What additional information would you like to have had in order to ensure that your decision was the right one?

5. In what way does specialisation reduce the problem of scarcity?

6. Would redistributing incomes from the rich to the poor reduce the overall problem of scarcity?

7. Assume that fracking becomes common across the UK. The result is that supplies of shale gas and oil increase sharply. Trace through the effects of this on the market for oil and gas and the market for other fuels.

8. Give two examples of positive statements about the economy, and two examples of normative ones. Now give two examples that are seemingly positive, but which have normative implications or undertones.

Online resources

Additional case studies in MyEconLab

1.1 **Buddhist economics.** A different perspective on economic problems and economic activity.

1.2 **Green economics.** This examines some of the environmental costs that society faces today. It also looks at the role of economics in analysing these costs and how the problems can be tackled.

1.3 **Global economics.** This examines how macroeconomics and microeconomics apply at the global level and identifies some key issues.

1.4 **The interdependence of markets.** A case study in the operation of markets, examining the effects on a local economy of the discovery of a large coal deposit.

1.5 **Free-market medicine in Russia.** This examines the operating of the fledgling market economy in Russia and the successes and difficulties in moving from a planned to a market economy.

1.6 **Alternative measures of well-being.** This case study takes a preliminary look at how we measure the well-being of society. Should we use output (GDP) per head or some other measure?

Websites relevant to this chapter

Numbers and sections refer to websites listed in the Web Appendix and hotlinked from this book's website at **www.pearsoned.co.uk/sloman**.

- For news articles relevant to this chapter, see the *Sloman Economics News* site link from the book's website or the *Economic News* section in MyEconLab.

- For a tutorial on finding the best economics websites, see site C8 (*Internet for Economics*)

- For general economics news sources, see websites in section A of the Web Appendix at the end of the book, and particularly A1–9, 24, 38, 39. See also A39–44 for links to newspapers worldwide.

- For sources of economic data, see sites in section B and particularly B1–5, 21, 33, 34, 38, 48, 49.

- For general sites for students of economics, see sites in section C and particularly C1–7.

- For sites giving links to relevant economics websites, organised by topic, see sites 4, 7, 8, 11, 12, 17, 18.

- For news on the Russian economy (Box 1.5 and Case Study 1.5 in MyEconLab), see sites A14, 15. See also the *Economic Systems and Theories* sections of sites 7 and 11.

- For an excellent site giving details of the lives, works and theories of famous economists from the history of economic thought (including Adam Smith from Box 1.6), see C18.

MyEconLab

This book can be supported by MyEconLab, which contains a range of additional resources, including an online homework and tutorial system designed to test and build your understanding.

You need both an access card and a course ID to access MyEconLab:

1. Is your lecturer using MyEconLab? Ask your lecturer for your course ID.

2. Has an access card been included with the book at a reduced cost? Check the inside back cover of the book.

3. If you have a course ID but no access card, go to: http://www.myeconlab.com/ to buy access to this interactive study programme.

SUOMALAINEN SIPULI 2 50 € NIPPU · SUOMALAINEN PUNASIPULI 2 50 € NIPPU · SUOMAL... · B Part

Foundations of Microeconomics

2   Supply and Demand   34

3   Markets in Action   60

In the first half of the book, we focus on microeconomics. Despite being 'small economics' – in other words, the economics of the individual parts of the economy, rather than the economy as a whole – it is still concerned with many of the big issues of today. To understand how the economy works at this micro level, we must understand how markets work. This involves an understanding of demand and supply.

In Chapter 2, we look at how demand and supply interact to determine prices (and so allocate resources) in a free-market economy. Markets, however, are not always free: governments frequently intervene in markets and Chapter 2 goes on to consider the impact of some forms of government intervention. In Chapter 3, we take the analysis of markets further to look at markets in action. We will see just how responsive they are to changing circumstances and look at how governments may choose to reject market allocations.

Supply and Demand

CHAPTER MAP

2.1 Demand	35
The relationship between demand and price	35
The demand curve	36
Other determinants of demand	37
Movements along and shifts in the demand curve	38

2.2 Supply	42
Supply and price	42
The supply curve	42
Other determinants of supply	43
Movements along and shifts in the supply curve	44

2.3 Price and output determination	45
Equilibrium price and output	45
Movement to a new equilibrium	47
Incentives in markets	49
*Identifying the position of demand and supply curves	49

2.4 The control of prices	55
Setting a minimum (high) price	56
Setting a maximum (low) price	56

As we saw in Chapter 1, in a free-market economy prices play a key role in transmitting information from buyers to sellers and from sellers to buyers. This chapter examines this 'price mechanism' in more detail.

We examine what determines demand, what determines supply and what the relationship is between demand, supply and price. We see how the price mechanism transmits information both from consumers to producers, and from producers to consumers; and how prices act as incentives – for example, if consumers want more European city breaks, how this increased demand leads to an increase in their price and hence to an incentive for firms to increase their production.

What we will see is just how the free market responds to changes in demand or supply – and responds in a way that balances demand and supply at a position of 'equilibrium'.

In practice, not all prices are determined in the free market. After all, we live in a mixed economy. Sometimes the government or some other agency attempts to control prices. In the final section of this chapter, we see what would happen if the government sets about *controlling* prices. Why will shortages occur if it sets a low price or surpluses if it sets a high one? When might governments feel that it is a good idea to fix prices, despite this?

The markets we will be examining are highly competitive ones, with many firms competing against each other. In economics we call this *perfect competition*. This is where consumers and producers are too numerous to have any control over prices: they are *price takers*.

In the case of consumers, this means that they have to accept the prices as given for the things that they buy. On most occasions this is true; when you get to the supermarket checkout you cannot start haggling with the checkout operator over the price of a can of beans or a tub of ice cream.

In the case of firms, perfect competition means that producers are small and face too much competition from other firms to be able to raise prices. Take the case of farmers selling wheat. They have to sell it at the current market price. If individually they try to sell at a higher price, no one will buy, since purchasers of wheat (e.g. flour millers) can get all the wheat they want at the market price.

Of course, many firms *do* have the power to choose their prices. This does not mean that they can simply charge whatever they like. They will still have to take account of overall consumer demand and their competitors' prices. Ford, when setting the price of its Focus cars, will have to ensure that they remain competitive with Astras, Golfs, etc. Nevertheless, most firms have some flexibility in setting their prices: they have a degree of 'market power'.

If this is the case, then why do we study *perfect* markets, where firms are price takers? One reason is that they provide a useful approximation to the real world and give us many insights into how a market economy works. Many markets do function very similarly to the markets we shall be describing.

Another is that perfect markets provide an ideal against which to compare the real world, since in perfect markets we see resources being used and allocated efficiently. Economists can therefore use them as a benchmark when comparing the prices, output, profit, etc., in different types of market. For example, will the consumer end up paying higher prices in a market dominated by just a few firms than in one operating under perfect competition? Will Sky respond to an increase in demand for television services in the same way as a farmer does to an increase in the demand for cauliflowers?

Markets with powerful firms are examined in Chapters 6 and 7. For now we concentrate on price takers.

2.1 DEMAND

The relationship between demand and price

The headlines announce 'Major crop failures in Brazil and East Africa: coffee prices soar'. Shortly afterwards you find that coffee prices have increased sharply in the shops. What do you do? You will probably cut back on the amount of coffee you drink. Perhaps you will reduce it from, say, six cups per day to four. Perhaps you will give up drinking coffee altogether.

This is simply an illustration of the general relationship between price and consumption: *when the price of a good rises, the quantity demanded will fall*. This relationship is known as the *law of demand*. There are two reasons for this law:

- People will feel poorer. They will not be able to afford to buy as much of the good with their money. The purchasing power of their income (their *real income*) has fallen. This is called the *income effect* of a price rise.
- The good will now cost more than alternative or 'substitute' goods, and people will switch to these. This is called the *substitution effect* of a price rise.

Similarly, when the price of a good falls, the quantity demanded will rise. People can afford to buy more (the income effect), and they will switch away from consuming alternative goods (the substitution effect).

Therefore, returning to our example of the increase in the price of coffee, we will not be able to afford to buy as

---

Definitions

Perfect competition (preliminary definition) A situation where the consumers and producers of a product are price takers. (There are other features of a perfectly competitive market; these are examined in Chapter 6.)

Price taker A person or firm with no power to be able to influence the market price.

Law of demand The quantity of a good demanded per period of time will fall as price rises and will rise as price falls, other things being equal (*ceteris paribus*).

Income effect The effect of a change in price on quantity demanded arising from the consumer becoming better or worse off as a result of the price change.

Substitution effect The effect of a change in price on quantity demanded arising from the consumer switching to or from alternative (substitute) products.

much as before, and we will probably drink more tea, cola, fruit juices or even water instead.

The income and substitution effects are useful concepts as they help to explain why people react to a price rise by buying less. The size of these effects depends on a range of factors. These factors determine the shape of the demand curve.

A word of warning: be careful about the meaning of the words *quantity demanded*. They refer to the amount that consumers are willing and able to purchase at a given price over a given period (e.g. a week, or a month, or a year). They do not refer to what people would simply *like* to consume. You might like to own a luxury yacht, but your demand for luxury yachts will almost certainly be zero at the current price.

The demand curve

Consider the hypothetical data in Table 2.1, which shows how many kilograms of potatoes per month would be purchased at various prices.

Columns (2) and (3) show the *demand schedules* for two individuals, Kate and Simon. Column (4) shows the total *market demand schedule*. This is the total demand by all consumers. To obtain the market demand schedule for potatoes, we simply add up the quantities demanded at each price by *all* consumers: i.e. Kate, Simon and everyone

else who demands potatoes. Notice that we are talking about demand *over a period of time* (not at *a point* in time). Thus we could talk about daily demand or weekly demand or annual demand.

Assume that there are 200 consumers in the market. Of these, 100 have schedules like Kate's and 100 have schedules like Simon's. What would be the total market demand schedule for potatoes now?

The demand schedule can be represented graphically as a *demand curve*. Figure 2.1 shows the market demand curve for potatoes corresponding to the schedule in Table 2.1. The price of potatoes is plotted on the vertical axis. The quantity demanded is plotted on the horizontal axis.

Point *E* shows that at a price of 100p per kilo, 100 000 tonnes of potatoes are demanded each month. When the price falls to 80p we move down the curve to point *D*. This shows that the quantity demanded has now risen to 200 000 tonnes per month. Similarly, if the price falls to 60p we move down the curve again to point *C*: 350 000 tonnes are now demanded. The five points on the graph (*A–E*) correspond to the figures in columns (1) and (4) of Table 2.1. The graph also enables us to read off the likely quantities demanded at prices other than those in the table.

1. *How much would be demanded at a price of 30p per kilogram?*
2. *Assuming that demand does not change from month to month, plot the annual market demand for potatoes.*

Table 2.1	The demand for potatoes (monthly)			
	Price (pence per kg) (1)	Kate's demand (kg) (2)	Simon's demand (kg) (3)	Total market demand (tonnes: 000s) (4)
A	20	28	16	700
B	40	15	11	500
C	60	5	9	350
D	80	1	7	200
E	100	0	6	100

Definitions

Quantity demanded The amount of a good that a consumer is willing and able to buy at a given price over a given period of time.

Demand schedule for an individual A table showing the different quantities of a good that a person is willing and able to buy at various prices over a given period of time.

Demand schedule (market) A table showing the different total quantities of a good that consumers are willing and able to buy at various prices over a given period of time.

Demand curve A graph showing the relationship between the price of a good and the quantity of the good demanded over a given time period. Price is measured on the vertical axis; quantity demanded is measured on the horizontal axis. A demand curve can be for an individual consumer or group of consumers, or more usually for the whole market.

Figure 2.1   Market demand curve for potatoes (monthly)

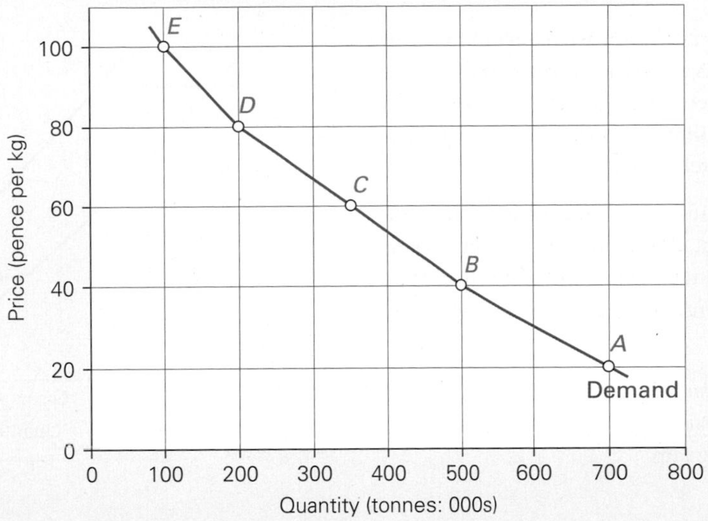

A demand curve could also be drawn for an individual consumer. Like market demand curves, individuals' demand curves generally slope downwards from left to right: they have negative slope. The lower the price of the product, the more a person is likely to buy.

1. *Draw Kate's and Simon's demand curves for potatoes on one diagram. Note that you will use the same vertical scale as in Figure 2.1, but you will need a quite different horizontal scale.*
2. *At what price is their demand the same?*
3. *What explanations could there be for the quite different shapes of their two demand curves? (This question is explored in section 3.1 below.)*

Two points should be noted at this stage:

■ In textbooks, demand curves (and other curves too) are only occasionally used to plot specific data. More frequently they are used to illustrate general theoretical arguments. In such cases the axes will simply be price and quantity, with the units unspecified.
■ The term 'curve' is used even when the graph is a straight line. In fact when using demand curves to illustrate arguments we frequently draw them as straight lines – it's easier.

Other determinants of demand

Price is not the only factor that determines how much of a good people will buy. Demand is also affected by the following.

Tastes.   The more desirable people find the good, the more they will demand. Tastes are affected by advertising, by trends and fashion, by observing other consumers, by considerations of health and by the experience of consuming the good on previous occasions.

The number and price of substitute goods (i.e. competitive goods). The higher the price of **substitute goods**, the higher will be the demand for this good as people switch from the substitutes. For example, the demand for coffee will depend on the price of tea. If tea goes up in price, the demand for coffee will rise.

The number and price of complementary goods. **Complementary goods** are those that are consumed together: cars and petrol, paper and ink cartridges, fish and chips. The higher the price of complementary goods, the fewer of them will be bought and hence the less will be the demand for the good under consideration. For example, the demand for inner

TC 1
p11

Definitions

Substitute goods A pair of goods which are considered by consumers to be alternatives to each other. As the price of one goes up, the demand for the other rises.

Complementary goods A pair of goods consumed together. As the price of one goes up, the demand for both goods will fall.

tubes will depend on the price of bicycles. If the price of bikes comes down, so that more are bought, the demand for inner tubes will rise.

Income. As people's incomes rise, their demand for most goods will rise. Such goods are called **normal goods**. There are exceptions to this general rule, however. As people get richer, they spend less on **inferior goods**, such as supermarket 'value' ranges, and switch to better quality goods.

Distribution of income. If national income were redistributed from the poor to the rich, the demand for luxury goods would rise. At the same time, as the poor got poorer they might have to buy more inferior goods; demand for these would rise too.

Expectations of future price changes. If people think that prices are going to rise in the future, they are likely to buy more now before the price does go up.

Movements along and shifts in the demand curve

A demand curve is constructed on the assumption that 'other things remain equal' (*ceteris paribus*). In other words, it is assumed that, apart from price, none of the determinants of demand change. The effect of a change in price is then simply illustrated by a movement along the demand curve: for example, from point B to point D in Figure 2.1 when the price of potatoes rises from 40p to 80p per kilo.

What happens, then, when one of these other determinants does change? The answer is that we have to construct a whole new demand curve: the curve shifts. If a change in one of the other determinants causes demand to rise – say, income rises – the whole curve will shift to the right. This shows that at each price more will be demanded than before. Thus, in Figure 2.2, at a price of P, a quantity of Q_0 was originally demanded. But now, after the increase in demand, Q_1 is demanded. (Note that D_1 is not necessarily parallel to D_0.)

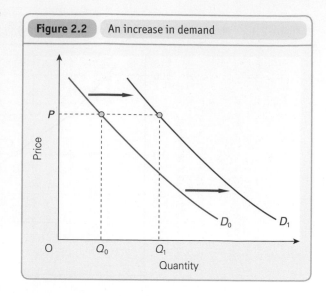

Figure 2.2   An increase in demand

If a change in a determinant other than price causes demand to fall, the whole curve will shift to the left.

To distinguish between shifts in and movements along demand curves, it is usual to distinguish between a change in *demand* and a change in the *quantity demanded*. A shift in the demand curve is referred to as a **change in demand**, whereas a movement along the demand curve as a result of a change in price is referred to as a **change in the quantity demanded**.

1. *Assume that in Table 2.1 the total market demand for potatoes increases by 20 per cent at each price – due, say, to substantial increases in the prices of bread and rice. Plot the old and the new demand curves for potatoes. Is the new curve parallel to the old one?*
2. *The price of blueberries rises and yet it is observed that the sales of blueberries increase. Does this mean that the demand curve for blueberries is upward sloping? Explain.*

Definitions

Normal good A good whose demand rises as people's incomes rise.

Inferior good A good whose demand falls as people's incomes rise.

Change in demand The term used for a shift in the demand curve. It occurs when a determinant of demand other than price changes.

Change in the quantity demanded The term used for a movement along the demand curve to a new point. It occurs when there is a change in price.

*LOOKING AT THE MATHS

We can represent the relationship between the market demand for a good and the determinants of demand in the form of an equation. This is called a **demand function**. It can be expressed either in general terms or with specific values attached to the determinants.

Simple demand functions

Demand equations are often used to relate quantity demanded to just one determinant. Thus an equation relating quantity demanded to price could be in the form

$$Q_d = a - bP \qquad (1)$$

For example, the actual equation might be

$$Q_d = 10\,000 - 200P \qquad (2)$$

From this a complete demand schedule or demand curve can be calculated, as shown in the table and diagram. As price (P) changes, the equation tells us how much the quantity demanded (Q_d) changes.

Demand schedule for equation (2)

P	Q_d
5	9000
10	8000
15	7000
20	6000
25	5000

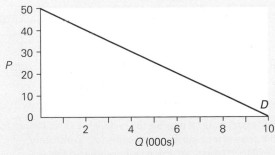

Demand curve for equation (2)

1. Complete the demand schedule in the table up to a price of 50.
2. What is it about equation (2) that makes the demand curve (a) downward sloping; (b) a straight line?

Definitions

Demand function An equation which shows the mathematical relationship between the quantity demanded of a good and the values of the various determinants of demand.

Regression analysis A statistical technique which allows a functional relationship between two or more variables to be estimated.

Econometrics The science of applying statistical techniques to economic data in order to identify and test economic relationships.

This equation is based on a *ceteris paribus* assumption: it is assumed that all the other determinants of demand remain constant. If one of these other determinants changed, the equation itself would change. There would be a shift in the curve: a change in demand. If the a term alone changed, there would be a parallel shift in the curve. If the b term changed, the slope of the curve would change.

Simple equations can be used to relate demand to other determinants too. For example, an equation relating quantity demanded to income would be in the form

$$Q_d = a + bY \qquad (3)$$

1. Referring to equation (3), if the term 'a' has a value of –50 000 and the term 'b' a value of 0.001, construct a demand schedule with respect to total income (Y). Do this for incomes between £100 million and £300 million at £50 million intervals.
2. Now use this schedule to plot a demand curve with respect to income. Comment on its shape.

More complex demand functions

In a similar way, we can relate the quantity demanded to two or more determinants. For example, a demand function could be of the form

$$Q_d = a - bP + cY + dP_s - eP_c \qquad (4)$$

This equation says that the quantity demanded (Q_d) will fall as the price of the good (P) rises, will rise as the level of consumer incomes (Y) rises, will rise as the price of a particular substitute (P_s) rises and will fall as the price of a particular complement (P_c) rises, by amounts b, c, d and e respectively.

Estimated demand equations

Surveys can be conducted to show how demand depends on each one of a number of determinants, while the rest are held constant. Using statistical techniques called **regression analysis**, a demand equation can be estimated.

For example, assume that it was observed that the demand for butter (measured in 250 g units) depended on its price (P_b), the price of margarine (P_m) and total annual consumer incomes (Y). The estimated weekly demand equation may then be something like

$$Q_d = 2\,000\,000 - 50\,000P_b + 20\,000P_m + 0.01Y \qquad (5)$$

Thus if the price of butter were 50p, the price of margarine were 35p and consumer incomes were £200 million, and if P_b and P_m were measured in pence and Y was measured in pounds, then the demand for butter would be 2 200 000 units. This is calculated as follows:

$$\begin{aligned}
Q_d &= 2\,000\,000 - (50\,000 \times 50) + (20\,000 \times 35) \\
&\quad + (0.01 \times 200\,000\,000) \\
&= 2\,000\,000 - 2\,500\,000 + 700\,000 + 2\,000\,000 \\
&= 2\,200\,000
\end{aligned}$$

The branch of economics that applies statistical techniques to economic data is known as **econometrics**. Econometrics is beyond the scope of this book. It is worth noting, however, that econometrics, like other branches of statistics, cannot produce equations and graphs that allow totally reliable predictions to be made. The data on which the equations are based are often incomplete or unreliable, and the underlying relationships on which they are based (often ones of human behaviour) may well change over time.

*BOX 2.1 **THE DEMAND FOR LAMB**

A real-world demand function[1]

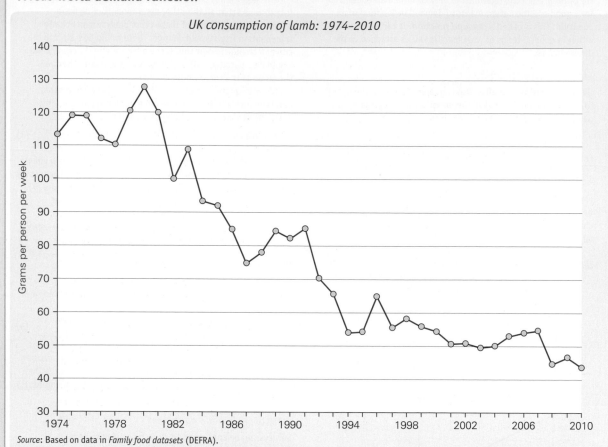

UK consumption of lamb: 1974–2010

Source: Based on data in *Family food datasets* (DEFRA).

The diagram shows what happened to the consumption of lamb in the UK over the period 1974–2010. How can we explain this dramatic fall in consumption? One way of exploring this issue is to make use of a regression model, which should help us to see which variables are relevant and how they are likely to affect demand.

The following is an initial model fitted (using *Gretl*, a free, open source, statistical software package) to annual data for the years 1974–2010:

$$Q_L = 144.0 - 0.137P_L - 0.034P_B + 0.214P_P - 0.005\,13Y \quad \textbf{(1)}$$

where:

Q_L is the quantity of lamb sold in grams per person per week;

P_L is the 'real' price of lamb (in pence per kg, 2000 prices);

P_B is the 'real' price of beef (in pence per kg, 2000 prices);

P_P is the 'real' price of pork (in pence per kg, 2000 prices);

Y is households' real disposable income per head (£ per year, 2000 prices).

This model makes it possible to predict what would happen to the demand for lamb if any one of the four explanatory variables changed, assuming that the other variables remained constant.

Using equation (1), calculate what would happen – ceteris paribus – to the demand for lamb if:

(a) the real price of lamb went up by 10p per kg;
(b) the real price of beef went up by 10p per kg;
(c) the real price of pork fell by 10p per kg;
(d) real disposable income per head rose by £100 per annum?
Are the results as you would expect?

There is a serious problem with estimated demand functions like these: they assume that *other* determinants of demand (i.e. those not included in the model) have not changed. In the case of this demand-for-lamb function, one of the other determinants *did* change. This was tastes – during the 37-year period there was a shift in demand away from lamb and other meats, partly for health reasons, and partly because of an expansion in the availability of and demand for vegetarian and low-meat alternatives.

On the assumption that this shift in taste took place steadily over time, a new demand equation was estimated for the same years:

$$Q_L = 121.4 - 0.151P_L - 0.0213P_B + 0.180P_P \\ - 0.000391Y - 1.728TIME \tag{2}$$

where $TIME = 1$ in 1974, 2 in 1975, 3 in 1976, etc.

1. How does the introduction of the variable *TIME* affect the relationship between the demand for lamb and (a) its real price; (b) real disposable income per head?
2. Does lamb appear to be a normal good or an inferior good?
3. What does the negative coefficient of P_B indicate?

Model (2) is a better model than model (1) in two major respects. The first point is that it has a better 'goodness of fit'. This can be shown by the 'R-squared'. $R^2 = 1$ represents a perfect fit, whereas $R^2 = 0$ shows that the model has no explanatory power whatsoever. In model (2), $R^2 = 0.913$ compared with 0.908 for model (1). This means that model (2) can explain 91.3 per cent of the variation in the consumption of lamb during the period 1974 to 2010, whereas model (1) can explain 90.8 per cent.

Whilst model (2) is clearly an improvement on model (1), it is by no means perfect. The second model still has problems. For example, the coefficient of Y remains positive. The estimated coefficient is much smaller and very close to zero, suggesting that household income has little effect on demand. Is this realistic?

Another problem is that P_B should have a positive coefficient, since beef is surely a substitute for lamb. More importantly, the model takes no account of the fact that consumers' purchases of lamb this year are likely to be strongly influenced by what they were consuming last year. Finally, whilst the model includes the real prices of two substitutes for lamb, it does not include the real prices of any complements. By omitting these variables from model (1) and (2) we mis-specified the models and introduced a bias

into the estimated coefficients. By including *all* variables that we believe are relevant we hope to remove this bias.

To take the above points into account, the following third model was estimated, using data for 1975 to 2010:

$$Q_L = -37.520 - 0.128P_L + 0.0757P_B + 0.122P_P + 0.00415Y \\ - 1.529TIME + 0.679LQ_L - 0.0519P_C \tag{3}$$

where LQ_L is the lagged consumption of lamb (i.e. consumption in the previous year) and P_C is the real price of a complement (potatoes). $R^2 = 0.958$.

1. To what extent is model (3) an improvement on model (2)? (Hint: is lamb now a normal or inferior good?)
2. Use the three equations and also the data given in the table below to estimate the demand for lamb in 2000 and 2010. Which model works the best in each case? Why? Explain why the models are all subject to error in their predictions.
3. Use model (3) and the data given in the table to explain why the demand for lamb fell so dramatically between 1980 and 2010.
4. The formula for the elasticity of demand (price elasticity, income elasticity or cross elasticity) can be written as $dQ/dX \div Q/X$, where dQ/dX represents the coefficient for a given variable, X. For example, in equation (3), 0.0757 gives the value of the term dQL/dP_B when working out the cross-price elasticity of demand for lamb with respect to changes in the price of beef. Using equation (3) and the table below work out the following for 2010:
   (a) the price elasticity of demand for lamb;
   (b) the income elasticity of demand for lamb;
   (c) the cross-price elasticity of demand for lamb with respect to (i) beef, (ii) pork, (iii) potatoes.

	Q_L	LQ_L	P_L	P_B	P_P	Y	$TIME$	P_C
1980	128	121	421.7	546.0	414.6	10 498	7	26.7
2000	54	56	467.0	480.5	381.1	17 797	27	44.9
2010	44	46	506.2	470.1	381.1	19 776	37	53.5

Nominal food prices were calculated by dividing expenditure by consumption. These nominal prices in pence per kg were then adjusted to 'real' prices by dividing by the RPI (retail price index) for total food (2000 = 100) and multiplying by 100.
Sources: www.defra.gov.uk/statistics/foodfarm/food/familyfood/datasets/ (expenditure and consumption)
www.ons.gov.uk/ (income and RPI food)

[1] Thanks to Tony Flegg, John's 'office mate' at UWE, for contributing to this box and to Andrew Hunt from Plymouth University for updating the figures.

Section summary

1. When the price of a good rises, the quantity demanded per period of time will fall. This is known as the 'law of demand'. It applies both to individuals' demand and to the whole market demand.

2. The law of demand is explained by the income and substitution effects of a price change.

3. The relationship between price and quantity demanded per period of time can be shown in a table (or 'schedule') or as a graph. On the graph, price is plotted on the vertical axis and quantity demanded per period of time on the horizontal axis. The resulting demand curve is downward sloping (negatively sloped).

4. Other determinants of demand include tastes, the number and price of substitute goods, the number and price of complementary goods, income, distribution of income and expectations of future price changes.

5. If price changes, the effect is shown by a movement along the demand curve. We call this effect 'a change in the quantity demanded'.

6. If any other determinant of demand changes, the whole curve will shift. We call this effect 'a change in demand'. A rightward shift represents an increase in demand; a leftward shift represents a decrease in demand.

7. *The relationship between the quantity demanded and the various determinants of demand (including price) can be expressed as an equation.

2.2 SUPPLY

Supply and price

Imagine you are a farmer deciding what to do with your land. Part of your land is in a fertile valley, while part is on a hillside where the soil is poor. Perhaps, then, you will consider growing vegetables in the valley and keeping sheep on the hillside.

Your decision will depend to a large extent on the price that various vegetables will fetch in the market and the price you can expect to get for meat and wool. As far as the valley is concerned, you will plant the vegetables that give the best return. If, for example, the price of potatoes is high, you might use a lot of the valley for growing potatoes. If the price gets higher, you may well use the whole of the valley. If the price is very high indeed, you may even consider growing potatoes on the hillside, even though the yield per acre is much lower there.

In other words, the higher the price of a particular farm output, the more land will be devoted to it. This illustrates the general relationship between supply and price: *when the price of a good rises, the quantity supplied will also rise.* There are three reasons for this:

- As firms supply more, they are likely to find that beyond a certain level of output, costs rise more and more rapidly. In the case of the farm just considered, if more and more potatoes are grown, then the land which is less suitable for potato cultivation has to be used. This raises the cost of producing extra potatoes. It is the same for manufacturers. Beyond a certain level of output, costs are likely to rise rapidly as workers have to be paid overtime and as machines approach capacity working. If higher output involves higher costs of producing each unit, producers will need to get a higher price if they are to be persuaded to produce extra output.

- The higher the price of the good, the more profitable it becomes to produce. Firms will thus be encouraged to produce more of it by switching from producing less profitable goods.

- Given time, if the price of a good remains high, new producers will be encouraged to enter the industry. Total market supply thus rises.

The first two determinants affect supply in the short run. The third affects supply in the long run. (We distinguish between short-run and long-run supply in section 3.2 on page 74.)

The supply curve

The amount that producers would like to supply at various prices can be shown in a *supply schedule*. Table 2.2 shows a monthly supply schedule for potatoes, both for an individual farmer (farmer X) and for all farmers together (the whole market).

Definition

Supply schedule A table showing the different quantities of a good that producers are willing and able to supply at various prices over a given time period. A supply schedule can be for an individual producer or group of producers, or for all producers (the market supply schedule).

Table 2.2	The supply of potatoes (monthly)		
	Price of potatoes (pence per kg)	Farmer X's supply (tonnes)	Total market supply (tonnes: 000s)
a	20	50	100
b	40	70	200
c	60	100	350
d	80	120	530
e	100	130	700

The supply schedule can be represented graphically as a *supply curve*. A supply curve may be an individual firm's supply curve or a market curve (i.e. that of the whole industry).

Figure 2.3 shows the *market* supply curve of potatoes. As with demand curves, price is plotted on the vertical axis and quantity on the horizontal axis. Each of the points *a–e* corresponds to a figure in Table 2.2. Thus, for example, a price rise from 60p per kilogram to 80p per kilogram will cause a movement along the supply curve from point *c* to point *d*: total market supply will rise from 350 000 tonnes per month to 530 000 tonnes per month.

1. *How much would be supplied at a price of 70p per kilo?*
2. *Draw a supply curve for farmer X. Are the axes drawn to the same scale as in Figure 2.3?*

Not all supply curves will be upward sloping (positively sloped). Sometimes they will be vertical, or horizontal, or even downward sloping. This will depend largely on the time period over which firms' response to price changes is considered. This question is examined in the section on the elasticity of supply (see section 3:1 below) and in more detail in Chapters 5 and 6.

Other determinants of supply

Like demand, supply is not simply determined by price. The other determinants of supply are as follows.

The costs of production. The higher the costs of production, the less profit will be made at any price. As costs rise, firms will cut back on production, probably switching to alternative products whose costs have not risen so much.

The main reasons for a change in costs are as follows:

■ Change in input prices: costs of production will rise if wages, raw material prices, rents, interest rates or any other input prices rise.
■ Change in technology: technological advances can fundamentally alter the costs of production. Consider, for example, how the microchip revolution has changed production methods and information handling in virtually every industry in the world.
■ Organisational changes: various cost savings can be made in many firms by reorganising production.
■ Government policy: costs will be lowered by government subsidies and raised by various taxes.

Definition

Supply curve A graph showing the relationship between the price of a good and the quantity of the good supplied over a given period of time.

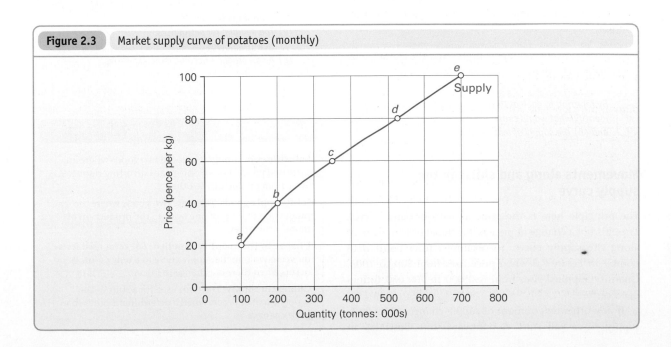

Figure 2.3 Market supply curve of potatoes (monthly)

The profitability of alternative products (substitutes in supply). If a product which is a **substitute in supply** becomes more profitable to supply than before, producers are likely to switch from the first good to this alternative. Supply of the first good falls. Other goods are likely to become more profitable if their prices rise and/or their costs of production fall. For example, if the price of carrots goes up, or the cost of producing carrots comes down, farmers may decide to cut down potato production in order to produce more carrots.

The profitability of goods in joint supply. Sometimes when one good is produced, another good is also produced at the same time. These are said to be **goods in joint supply**. An example is the refining of crude oil to produce petrol. Other grade fuels will be produced as well, such as diesel and paraffin. If more petrol is produced due to a rise in demand and hence its price, then the supply of these other fuels will rise too.

Nature, 'random shocks' and other unpredictable events. In this category we would include the weather and diseases affecting farm output, wars affecting the supply of imported raw materials, the breakdown of machinery, industrial disputes, earthquakes, floods and fire, etc.

The aims of producers. A profit-maximising firm will supply a different quantity from a firm that has a different aim, such as maximising sales. For most of the time we shall assume that firms are profit maximisers. In Chapter 8, however, we consider alternative aims.

Expectations of future price changes. If price is expected to rise, producers may temporarily reduce the amount they sell. They may build up their stocks and only release them onto the market when the price does rise. At the same time they may install new machines or take on more labour, so that they can be ready to supply more when the price has risen.

The number of suppliers. If new firms enter the market, supply is likely to increase.

 By referring to each of the above determinants of supply, identify what would cause (a) the supply of potatoes to fall and (b) the supply of leather to rise.

Movements along and shifts in the supply curve

The principle here is the same as with demand curves. The effect of a change in price is illustrated by a movement along the supply curve: for example, from point *d* to point *e* in Figure 2.3 when price rises from 80p to 100p. Quantity supplied rises from 530 000 to 700 000 tonnes per month.

If any other determinant of supply changes, the whole supply curve will shift. A rightward shift illustrates an

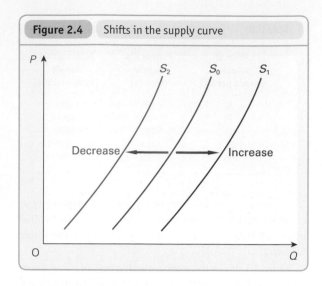

Figure 2.4 Shifts in the supply curve

increase in supply. A leftward shift illustrates a decrease in supply. Thus in Figure 2.4, if the original curve is S_0, the curve S_1 represents an increase in supply (more is supplied at each price), whereas the curve S_2 represents a decrease in supply (less is supplied at each price).

A movement along a supply curve is often referred to as a **change in the quantity supplied**, whereas a shift in the supply curve is simply referred to as a **change in supply**.

 This question is concerned with the supply of oil for central heating. In each case consider whether there is a movement along the supply curve (and in which direction) or a shift in it (and whether left or right).
(a) New oil fields start up in production.
(b) The demand for central heating rises.
(c) The price of gas falls.
(d) Oil companies anticipate an upsurge in demand for central-heating oil.
(e) The demand for petrol rises.
(f) New technology decreases the costs of oil refining.
(g) All oil products become more expensive.

Definitions

Substitutes in supply These are two goods where an increased production of one means diverting resources away from producing the other.

Joint supply goods These are two goods where the production of more of one leads to the production of more of the other.

Change in the quantity supplied The term used for a movement along the supply curve to a new point. It occurs when there is a change in price.

Change in supply The term used for a shift in the supply curve. It occurs when a determinant other than price changes.

*LOOKING AT THE MATHS

Using survey data and regression analysis, equations can be estimated relating supply to some of its determinants. Note that not all determinants can be easily quantified (e.g. nature and the aims of firms), and they may thus be left out of the equation.

The simplest form of supply equation relates supply to just one determinant. Thus a function relating supply to price would be of the form

$$Q_s = c + dP \qquad (1)$$

Using regression analysis, values can be estimated for c and d. Thus an actual supply equation might be something like

$$Q_s = 500 + 1000P \qquad (2)$$

1. If P was originally measured in pounds, what would happen to the value of the d term in equation (2) if P were now measured in pence?
2. Draw the schedule (table) and graph for equation (2) for prices from £1 to £10. What is it in the equation that determines the slope of the supply 'curve'?

If any determinant other than price changed, a new equation would result. For example, if costs of production fell, the equation might then be

$$Q_s = 1000 + 1500P \qquad (3)$$

More complex supply equations would relate supply to more than one determinant. For example,

$$Q_s = 200 + 80P - 20a_1 - 15a_2 + 30j \qquad (4)$$

where P is the price of the good, a_1 and a_2 are the profitability of two alternative goods that could be supplied instead, and j is the profitability of a good in joint supply.

Explain why the P and j terms have a positive sign, whereas the a_1 and a_2 terms have a negative sign.

Section summary

1. When the price of a good rises, the quantity supplied per period of time will usually also rise. This applies both to individual producers' supply and to the whole market supply.

2. There are two reasons in the short run why a higher price encourages producers to supply more: (a) they are now willing to incur the higher costs per unit associated with producing more; (b) they will switch to producing this product and away from products that are now less profitable. In the long run, there is a third reason: new producers will be attracted into the market.

3. The relationship between price and quantity supplied per period of time can be shown in a table (or schedule) or as a graph. As with a demand curve, price is plotted on the vertical axis and quantity per period of time on the horizontal axis. The resulting supply curve is upward sloping (positively sloped).

4. Other determinants of supply include the costs of production, the profitability of alternative products, the profitability of goods in joint supply, random shocks and expectations of future price changes.

5. If price changes, the effect is shown by a movement along the supply curve. We call this effect 'a change in the quantity supplied'.

6. If any determinant *other* than price changes, the effect is shown by a shift in the whole supply curve. We call this effect 'a change in supply'. A rightward shift represents an increase in supply; a leftward shift represents a decrease in supply.

7. *The relationship between the quantity supplied and the various determinants of supply can be expressed in the form of an equation.

2.3 PRICE AND OUTPUT DETERMINATION

Equilibrium price and output

We can now combine our analysis of demand and supply. This will show how the actual price of a product and the actual quantity bought and sold are determined in a free and competitive market.

Let us return to the example of the market demand and market supply of potatoes, and use the data from Tables 2.1 and 2.2. These figures are given again in Table 2.3.

What will be the actual price and output? If the price started at 20p per kilogram, demand would exceed supply by 600 000 tonnes ($A - a$). Consumers would be unable to obtain all they wanted and would thus be willing to pay a higher price. Producers, unable or unwilling to supply enough to meet the demand, will be only too happy to accept a higher price. The effect of the shortage, then, will be to drive up the price. The same would happen at a price of 40p per kilogram. There would still be a shortage;

Table 2.3	The market demand and supply of potatoes (monthly)	
Price of potatoes (pence per kg)	Total market demand (tonnes: 000s)	Total market supply (tonnes: 000s)
20	700 (*A*)	100 (*a*)
40	500 (*B*)	200 (*b*)
60	350 (*C*)	350 (*c*)
80	200 (*D*)	530 (*d*)
100	100 (*E*)	700 (*e*)

price would still rise. But as the price rises, the quantity demanded falls and the quantity supplied rises. The shortage is progressively eliminated.

 Explain the process by which the price of houses would rise if there were a shortage.

What would happen if the price of potatoes started at a much higher level: say, at 100p per kilogram? In this case supply would exceed demand by 600 000 tonnes (*e – E*). The effect of this surplus would be to drive the price down as farmers competed against each other to sell their excess supplies. The same would happen at a price of 80p per kilogram. There would still be a surplus; price would still fall.

In fact, only one price is sustainable – the price where demand equals supply: namely, 60p per kilogram, where both demand and supply are 350 000 tonnes. When supply matches demand the market is said to *clear*. There is no shortage and no surplus.

TC 4 **p47**

As we have already seen in section 1.2, The price where demand equals supply is called the *equilibrium price* and we

return to this in more detail in Threshold Concept 4 (on page 47). In Table 2.3, if the price starts at anything other than 60p per kilogram, it will tend to move towards 60p. The equilibrium price is the only price at which producers' and consumers' wishes are mutually reconciled: where the producers' plans to supply exactly match the consumers' plans to buy.

 KEY IDEA 8 — *Equilibrium is the point where conflicting interests are balanced.* Only at this point is the amount that demanders are willing to purchase the same as the amount that suppliers are willing to supply. It is a point that will be automatically reached in a free market through the operation of the price mechanism.

Demand and supply curves

The determination of equilibrium price and output can be shown using demand and supply curves. Equilibrium is where the two curves intersect.

Figure 2.5 shows the demand and supply curves of potatoes corresponding to the data in Table 2.3. Equilibrium price is P_e (60p) and equilibrium quantity is Q_e (350 000 tonnes).

At any price above 60p, there would be a surplus. Thus at 80p there is a surplus of 330 000 tonnes (*d – D*). More is supplied than consumers are willing and able to purchase at

Definition

Market clearing A market clears when supply matches demand, leaving no shortage or surplus.

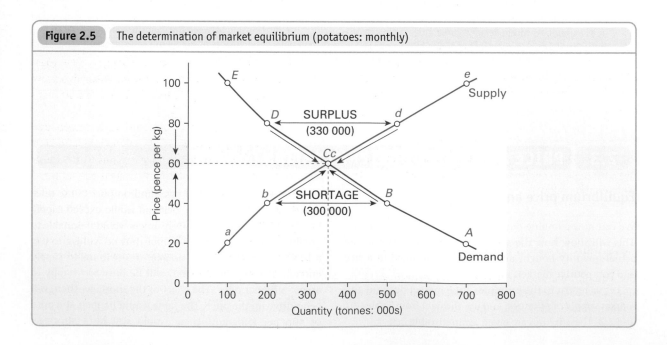

Figure 2.5	The determination of market equilibrium (potatoes: monthly)

THRESHOLD CONCEPT 4   MARKETS EQUATE DEMAND AND SUPPLY   THINKING LIKE AN ECONOMIST

'Let the market decide.' 'Market forces will dictate.' 'You can't buck the market.'

These sayings about the market emphasise the power of market forces and how they affect our lives. Markets affect the prices of the things we buy and the incomes we earn. Even governments find it difficult to control many key markets. Governments might not like it when stock market prices plummet or when oil prices soar, but there is little they can do about it.

In many ways a market is like a democracy. People, by choosing to buy goods, are voting for them to be produced. Firms finding 'a market' for their products are happy to oblige and produce them. The way it works is simple. If people want more of a product, they buy more and thereby 'cast their votes' (i.e. their money) in favour of more being produced. The resulting shortage drives up the price, which gives firms the incentive to produce more of the product. In other words, firms are doing what consumers want – not because of any 'love' for consumers, or because they are being told to produce more by the government – but because it is in their own self-interest. They supply more because the higher price has made it profitable to do so.

This is a *threshold concept* because to understand market forces – the forces of demand and supply – is to go straight to the heart of a market economy. And in this process, prices are the key. It is changes in price that balance demand and supply. If demand exceeds supply, price will rise. This will choke off some of the demand and encourage more supply until demand equals supply – until an equilibrium has been reached. If supply exceeds demand, price will fall. This will discourage firms from supplying so much and encourage consumers to buy more, until, once more, an equilibrium has been reached.

In this process, markets act like an 'invisible hand' – a term coined by the famous economist Adam Smith (see Box 1.6 on page 24). Market prices guide both producers to respond to consumer demand and consumers to respond to changes in producer supply.

In many circumstances, markets bring outcomes that people want. As we have seen, if consumers want more, then market forces will lead to more being produced. Sometimes, however, market forces can bring adverse effects. We explore these at various parts of the book. It is important, at this stage, however, to recognise that markets are rarely perfect. Market failures, from pollution to the domination of our lives by big business, are very real. Understanding this brings us to Threshold Concept 6 (see page 55).

Partial equilibrium

The type of equilibrium we will be examining for the next few chapters is known as 'partial equilibrium'. It is partial because what we are doing is examining just one tiny bit of the economy at a time: just one market (e.g. that for eggs). It is even partial within the market for eggs because we are assuming that price is the *only* thing that changes to balance demand and supply – that nothing else changes. In other words, when we refer to equilibrium price and quantity, we are assuming that all the other determinants of both demand and supply are held constant.

If another determinant of demand or supply *does* change, there would then be a new partial equilibrium as price adjusts and both demanders and suppliers respond. For example, if a health scare connected with egg consumption causes the demand for eggs to fall, the resulting surplus will lead to a fall in the equilibrium price and quantity.

1. *If there is a shortage of certain skilled workers in the economy, how will market forces lead to an elimination of the skills shortage?*
2. *If consumers want more of a product, is it always desirable that market forces result in more being produced?*

---

that price. Thus a price of 80p fails to clear the market. Price will fall to the equilibrium price of 60p. As it does so, there will be a movement along the demand curve from point *D* to point *C*, and a movement along the supply curve from point *d* to point *c*.

At any price below 60p, there would be a shortage. Thus at 40p there is a shortage of 300 000 tonnes (*B* – *b*). Price will rise to 60p. This will cause a movement along the supply curve from point *b* to point *c* and along the demand curve from point *B* to point *C*.

Point *Cc* is the equilibrium: where demand equals supply.

Movement to a new equilibrium

The equilibrium price will remain unchanged only so long as the demand and supply curves remain unchanged. If either of the curves shifts, a new equilibrium will be formed.

A change in demand

If one of the determinants of demand changes (other than price), the whole demand curve will shift. This will lead to a movement *along* the *supply* curve to the new intersection point.

For example, in Figure 2.6, if a rise in consumer incomes led to the demand curve shifting to D_2, there would be a shortage of $h - g$ at the original price P_{e_1}. This would cause price to rise to the new equilibrium P_{e_1}. As it did so, there would be a movement along the supply curve from point *g* to point *i*, and along the new demand curve (D_2) from point *h* to point *i*. Equilibrium quantity would rise from Q_{e_1} to Q_{e_2}.

The effect of the shift in demand, therefore, has been a movement *along* the supply curve from the old equilibrium to the new: from point *g* to point *i*.

What would happen to price and quantity if the demand curve shifted to the left? Draw a diagram to illustrate your answer.

KI 5
p22

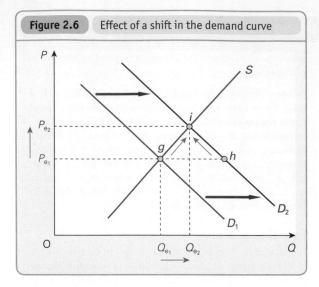

Figure 2.6   Effect of a shift in the demand curve

What will happen to the equilibrium price and quantity of butter in each of the following cases? You should state whether demand or supply (or both) have shifted and in which direction. (In each case assume ceteris paribus.)

(a) A rise in the price of non-dairy spread.
(b) A rise in the demand for cream.
(c) A rise in the price of bread.
(d) A rise in the demand for bread.
(e) An expected rise in the price of butter in the near future.
(f) A tax on butter production.
(g) The invention of a new, but expensive, process for removing all saturated fat from butter, alongside the passing of a law which states that all butter producers must use this process.

A change in supply

Likewise, if one of the determinants of supply changes (other than price), the whole supply curve will shift. This will lead to a movement *along* the *demand* curve to the new intersection point.

For example, in Figure 2.7, if costs of production rose, the supply curve would shift to the left: to S_2. There would be a shortage of $g - j$ at the old price of P_{e_1}. Price would rise from P_{e_1} to P_{e_3}. Quantity would fall from Q_{e_1} to Q_{e_3}. In other words, there would be a movement along the demand curve from point g to point k, and along the new supply curve (S_2) from point j to point k.

To summarise: a shift in one curve leads to a movement along the other curve to the new intersection point.

Sometimes a number of determinants might change. This might lead to a shift in *both* curves. When this happens, equilibrium simply moves from the point where the old curves intersected to the point where the new ones intersect.

Figure 2.7   Effect of a shift in the supply curve

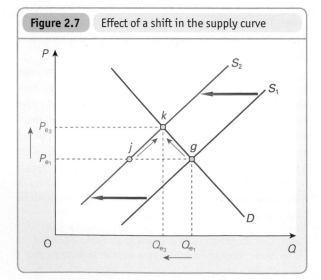

*LOOKING AT THE MATHS

We saw above (on pages 39 and 45) how demand and supply curves can be represented by equations. Assume that the equations for the supply and demand curves in a particular market are as follows:

$$Q_D = a - bP \tag{1}$$
$$Q_s = c + dP \tag{2}$$

We can find the market equilibrium price by setting the two equations equal to each other, since, in equilibrium, the quantity supplied (Q_s) equals the quantity demanded (Q_D). Thus

$$c + dP = a - bP$$

Subtracting c from and adding bP to both sides gives

$$dP + bP = a - c$$
$$\therefore (d + b)P = a - c$$
$$\therefore P = \frac{a - c}{d + b} \tag{3}$$

We can then solve for equilibrium quantity (Q_e) by substituting equation (3) in either equation (1) or (2) (since $Q_D = Q_s$). Thus, from equation (1),

$$Q_e = a - b\left(\frac{a - c}{d + b}\right)$$
$$= \frac{a(d + b) - b(a - c)}{d + b}$$
$$= \frac{ad + ab - ba + bc}{d + b} = \frac{ad + bc}{d + b} \tag{4}$$

or, from equation (2),

$$Q_e = c + d\left(\frac{a - c}{d + b}\right)$$
$$= \frac{cd + cb + da - dc}{d + b} = \frac{cb + da}{d + b} \tag{5}$$

Thus

$$Q_e = \frac{ad + bc}{d + b} \text{ (equation (4))} = \frac{cb + da}{d + b} \text{ (equation (5))}$$

A worked example is given in Maths Case 2.1 in MyEconLab.

Incentives in markets

Throughout this chapter we have seen that people and firms respond to incentives. In all cases of changes in demand and supply, the resulting changes in price act as both signals and incentives. This is Threshold Concept 5.

*Identifying the position of demand and supply curves

Both demand and supply depend on price, and yet their interaction determines price. For this reason it is difficult to identify just what is going on when price and quantity change, and to identify just what the demand and supply curves look like.

Let us say that we want to identify the demand curve for good X. We observe that when the price was 20p, 1000 units were purchased. At a later date the price has risen to 30p and 800 units are now purchased. What can we conclude from this about the demand curve? The answer is that without further information we can conclude very little. Consider Figures 2.8 and 2.9. Both are consistent with the facts.

In Figure 2.8 the demand curve has not shifted. The rise in price and the fall in sales are due entirely to a shift in the supply curve. The movement from point *a* to point *b* is thus a movement along the demand curve. If we can be certain that the demand curve has not shifted, then the evidence allows us to identify its position (or, at least, two points on it).

In Figure 2.9, however, not only has the supply curve shifted, but so also has the demand curve. Let us assume that people's tastes for the product have increased. In this case a movement from *a* to *b* does *not* trace out the demand curve. We cannot derive the demand curve(s) from the evidence of price and quantity alone.

The problem is that when the supply curve shifts, we often cannot know whether or not the demand curve has shifted, and if so by how much. How would we know, for example, just how much people's tastes have changed?

The problem works the other way round too. It is difficult to identify a supply curve when the demand curve shifts. Is the change in price and quantity entirely due to the shift in the demand curve, or has the supply curve shifted too?

This is known as the *identification problem*. It is difficult to identify just what is causing the change in price and quantity.

> ## Definition
>
> **Identification problem** The problem of identifying the relationship between two variables (e.g. price and quantity demanded) from the evidence when it is not known whether or how the variables have been affected by other determinants. For example, it is difficult to identify the shape of a demand curve simply by observing price and quantity when it is not known whether changes in other determinants have shifted the demand curve.

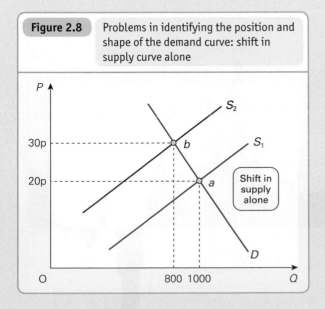

Figure 2.8 Problems in identifying the position and shape of the demand curve: shift in supply curve alone

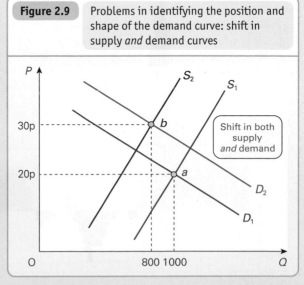

Figure 2.9 Problems in identifying the position and shape of the demand curve: shift in supply *and* demand curves

BOX 2.2   UK HOUSE PRICES

The ups and downs (and ups again) of the housing market

Housing is one of the most important markets in the UK; households spend a higher proportion of their income on housing than on any other good; nearly 40 per cent of personal wealth is held in housing equity and house prices are linked to both consumer confidence and the willingness of banks to lend to small businesses. It is therefore not surprising that government, businesses and individuals all have a keen interest in both house prices and the outlook for the market.

If we look back at the history of housing markets in the UK, we can identify a pattern of periods when prices have risen sharply, followed by times when they have fallen. This happened in the 1970s, the late 1980s/early 1990s and the 2000s. It is often described as a house price 'bubble', which then bursts.

The diagram shows what happened to house prices in the period 1984 to 2014. The vertical axis measures the annual percentage increase in average house prices. The figures are adjusted quarterly. In the UK, between 1984 and 1989 house prices *doubled*, but then fell in the early 1990s; there was another boom from 1996 to 2007, with house prices rising by 26 per cent in 2003. Then in 2008, house prices plummeted once again, falling by 19 per cent over the following year. They remained flat for several years, mirroring the lack of growth in the economy, but by late 2013 prices were rising once again, particularly in south-east England.

The determinants of house prices

House prices are determined by demand and supply. If demand rises (i.e. shifts to the right) or if supply falls (i.e. shifts to the left), the equilibrium price of houses will rise. Similarly, if demand falls or supply rises, the equilibrium price will fall.

So why did house prices rise so rapidly in the 1980s and again in the late 1990s and 2000s, but fall in the early 1990s and from 2008? The answer lies primarily in changes in the *demand* for housing. Let us examine the various factors that affected the demand for houses.

Incomes (actual and anticipated).   The second half of the 1980s and the years from 1997 to 2007 were periods of economic 'boom' with rapidly rising incomes. People wanted to spend much of their extra income on housing: either buying a house for the first time, or moving to a better one. They were confident that incomes would continue to grow and were prepared to stretch themselves financially in the short term by buying an expensive house, assuming that their mortgage payments would become more affordable over time.

The early 1990s and the years from 2008 to 2009 and 2011 to 2012, by contrast, were periods of recession, with rising unemployment and falling incomes. People had much less confidence about their ability to afford large mortgages;

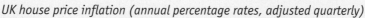

UK house price inflation (annual percentage rates, adjusted quarterly)

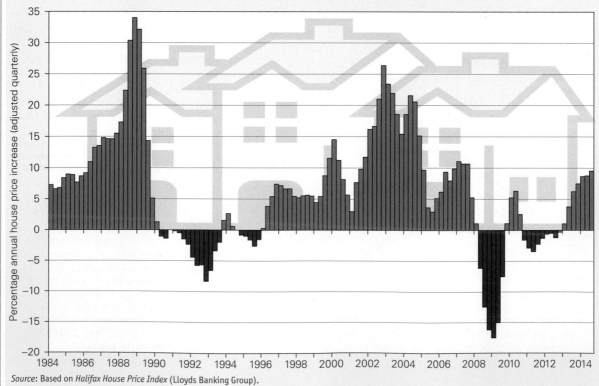

Source: Based on *Halifax House Price Index* (Lloyds Banking Group).

fewer entered the market, many existing owners deferred plans to buy larger houses, while others sold their properties and moved into rented accommodation.

The number of households. Social and demographic changes have resulted in a sharp increase in the number of households over the past 30 years. In 1981 there were 20.18 million households in Great Britain; by 2014 this had increased to 26.34 million. Reasons include more lone parents, increased life expectancy and flows of workers from EU countries. Average household size was lower, but even so the overall impact was an increase in demand for housing.

The cost of mortgages. During the second half of the 1980s, mortgage interest rates were generally falling. This meant that people could afford larger mortgages, and thus afford to buy more expensive houses. In 1989, however, this trend was reversed. Mortgage interest rates went up sharply and this deterred buyers from entering the market or from buying a larger property. This helps explain the sharp fall in demand seen in 1989 and 1990.

From 1996 to 2003 mortgage rates generally fell, once more fuelling the demand for houses. Even when interest rates rose gradually over the period from 2004 to 2007 they didn't come close to the rates reached in the early 1990s.

Many people with existing mortgages experienced very low rates in the period from 2008, mirroring the low bank base rate. However, this was not the case for those seeking new loans.

The availability of mortgages. In the housing boom periods of the late 1980s and from 1997 to 2007, mortgages were readily available. With house prices rising, banks and building societies were prepared to accept smaller (or no) deposits on houses and to lend a larger multiple of people's income. After all, if borrowers were to default, lenders would still have a very good chance of getting all their money back. This approach was to have some unintended consequences as lenders relaxed their requirements further, the faster prices grew. By the mid-2000s many lenders were allowing borrowers to self-certificate their income and were prepared to lend to those with a poor credit history. The same policies were adopted by lenders in the USA, where these 'sub-prime' loans became a key contributory factor in the financial crisis of 2007–8.

In the early 1990s, however, and again from 2008, banks and building societies were much more cautious about granting mortgages. With falling house prices, rising unemployment and the growing problem of *negative equity*, where people find themselves in a position where the size of their mortgage is greater than the value of their house, there was an increased danger that borrowers would default on payments and that banks would lose money. In 2008–9 this problem was compounded by the credit crunch, meaning that banks had less money to lend. However, even an increase in credit in the following years did little to ease the situation; by 2010 many mortgage lenders were effectively asking for deposits of at least 25 per cent, over £40 000 for an average house in the UK.

By early 2014, there had been a relaxation in this requirement; the government-backed 'Help to Buy' schemes allowed borrowers to get a mortgage with a 5 per cent deposit, and some banks offered similar schemes independently. This helped to fuel an acceleration of house price rises.

Speculation. Unlike many other goods, expenditure on housing is not only for consumption purposes (i.e. providing households with somewhere to live; housing is also a way of holding household wealth), but also an asset. In both the 1980s and 1997–2007, and again from late 2103, people generally believed that house prices would continue rising. This encouraged them to buy as soon as possible, and to take out the biggest mortgage possible, before prices went up any further. There was also an effect on supply. Those with houses to sell held back until the last possible moment in the hope of getting a higher price. The net effect was a rightward shift in the demand curve for houses and a leftward shift in the supply curve. The effect of this speculation, therefore, was to help bring about the very effect that people were predicting (for more on speculation see section 3.2).

In the early 1990s, and again in 2008 and 2009, the opposite occurred. People thinking of buying houses held back, hoping to buy at a lower price. People with houses to sell tried to sell as quickly as possible before prices fell any further. Again the effect of this speculation was to aggravate the change in prices – this time a fall in prices.

Speculation in recent years has been compounded by the growth in the 'buy-to-let' industry, with mortgage lenders entering this market in large numbers and a huge amount of media attention focused on the possibilities for individuals to make very high returns.

What of the future?

In 2014 a recovery in the UK housing market was taking place in some areas, while others remained relatively flat. In London and the South-East, house prices had risen to above their 2007–8 highs. A continued shortage of supply, coupled with rising demand and more easily available credit, combined to push up prices. In contrast, much of the rest of the country was still experiencing flat prices, with concerns being expressed about widening regional gaps. There is little doubt that we will continue to see house prices rise, initially in London and then more widely, as long as demand increases while supply is constrained.

1. *Draw supply and demand diagrams to illustrate what was happening to house prices (a) in the second half of the 1980s and the period from 1997 to 2007; (b) in the early 1990s and the period from 2008; (c) in 2014 in London, and in a region outside SE England.*
2. *What determines the supply of housing? How will factors on the supply side influence house prices?*
3. *What is the role of the prices of 'other goods' in determining the demand for housing?*
4. *Find out what forecasters are predicting for house prices over the next year and attempt to explain their views.*

BOX 2.3	STOCK MARKET PRICES

Demand and supply in action

Firms that are quoted on the stock market can raise money by issuing shares. These are sold on the 'primary stock market'. People who own the shares receive a 'dividend' on them, normally paid six-monthly. The amount varies with the profitability of the company. People or institutions that buy these shares, however, may not wish to hold onto them for ever. This is where the 'secondary stock market' comes in. It is where existing shares are bought and sold. There are stock markets, primary and secondary, in all the major countries of the world.

There are some 2400 shares and other securities listed on the London Stock Exchange and trading in them takes place each Monday to Friday. The prices of shares depend on demand and supply; if the demand for Tesco shares at any one time exceeds the supply on offer, the price will rise until demand and supply are equal. Share prices fluctuate throughout the trading day and sometimes price changes can be substantial.

To give an overall impression of share price movements, stock exchanges publish share price indices. The best known one in the UK is the FTSE ('footsie') 100, which stands for the 'Financial Times Stock Exchange' index of the 100 largest companies' shares. The index represents an average price of these 100 shares. The chart shows movements in the FTSE 100 from 1995 to 2014. The index was first calculated on 3 January 1984 with a base level of 1000 points. It reached

a peak of 6930 points on 30 December 1999 and fell to 3287 on 12 March 2003. By February 2011 it had moved back up above 6000, and by March 2014 it had come close to reaching the 1999 peak (see chart).

But what causes share prices to change? Why were they so high in 1999, but only just over half that value just three years later? The answer lies in the determinants of the demand and supply of shares.

Demand

There are five main factors that affect the demand for shares.

The dividend yield. This is the dividend on a share as a percentage of its price. The higher the dividend yields on shares, the more attractive they are as a form of saving. One of the main explanations of rising stock market prices from 2003 to 2007 was high profits and resulting high dividends. Similarly, the slowdown in the world economy from late 2007 led to falling profits and falling dividends. As the world emerged from the global downturn, profits rose and so did share prices.

The price of and/or return on substitutes. The main substitutes for shares in specific companies are other shares. Thus if, in comparison with other shares, Tesco shares are

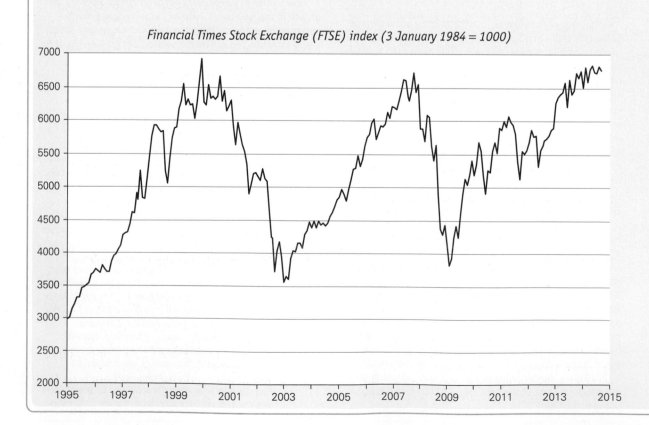

Financial Times Stock Exchange (FTSE) index (3 January 1984 = 1000)

expected to pay high dividends relative to the share price, people will buy Tesco shares. As far as shares in general are concerned, the main substitutes are other forms of saving. Thus if the interest rate on savings accounts in banks and building societies fell, people with such accounts would be tempted to take their money out and buy shares instead.

Another major substitute is property. If house prices rise rapidly, as they did in 2002 and 2003, this will reduce the demand for shares as many people switch to buying property in anticipation of even higher prices. If house prices level off, as they did in 2005–6, this makes shares relatively more attractive as an investment and can boost the demand for them.

Of course, other factors may affect *both* house prices *and* shares in the same way. Thus the 'credit crunch' that started in 2007, when finance became both harder to obtain and more expensive, resulted in both falling house prices *and* falling share prices as the economy slowed down and profits fell.

In the years from 2011 to 2013, property prices remained flat, but crucially so did interest rates. As savers became increasingly disillusioned by the return on cash savings, they moved into shares, seeking a return that would at least offset inflation.

Incomes. If the economy is growing rapidly and people's incomes are thus rising rapidly, they are likely to save some of their extra income and therefore to buy more shares. Thus in the mid-to-late 1990s, when UK incomes were rising at an average annual rate of over 3 per cent, share prices rose rapidly (see chart). As the economy slowed in 2008, so share prices fell.

Wealth. 'Wealth' is people's accumulated savings and property. Wealth rose in the 1990s and many people used their increased wealth to buy shares. It was a similar picture in the mid-2000s.

Expectations. In the mid-to-late 1990s, people expected share prices to go on rising. They were optimistic about continued growth in the economy and that certain sectors, such as leisure and high-tech industries, would grow particularly strongly. And as people bought shares, this pushed their prices up even more, thereby fuelling further speculation that they would go on rising and encouraging further share buying.

In the early 2000s, by contrast, confidence was shaken. Most countries experienced a slowing down in economic growth, or even a recession (a fall in national output). This, combined with other negative factors, such as the 11 September 2001 attack on the World Trade Center and various corporate scandals such as the accounting fraud concerning the giant US company Enron, caused share prices to plummet. As people anticipated further price falls, so they held back from buying, thereby pushing prices even lower. Conversely, as share prices began rising again from 2003

onwards, so this boosted the demand for shares, thereby fuelling the surge in share prices. The rise and fall in share prices associated with expectations mirror those seen in the housing market and discussed in Box 2.2.

Then with the credit crunch and falling profits from 2007, share prices fell, with the falls resulting in further selling and further falls as confidence waned. Things reached crisis point in October 2008, as people feared banking collapses and the onset of recession. On 10 October the FTSE fell as low as 3874, 31 per cent down on early September and 42 per cent down from October of the previous year. However, with a bank rescue plan announced by governments around the world (see Box 18.3), expectations became more positive and the FTSE rose by 17 per cent in just two days.

As recession deepened and as more news about banks' bad debts emerged, so share prices remained volatile, until a rising trend was established once the worst of the downturn was over. (We examine speculation in detail in section 3.2.)

Supply

The factors affecting supply are largely the same as those affecting demand, but in the opposite direction.

If the return on alternative forms of saving falls, people with shares are likely to hold onto them, as they represent a better form of saving. The supply of shares to the market will fall. If incomes or wealth rise, people again are likely to want to hold onto their shares.

As far as expectations are concerned, if people believe that share prices will rise, they will hold onto the shares they have. Supply to the market will fall, thereby pushing up prices. If, however, they believe that prices will fall, they will sell their shares now before prices do fall. Supply will increase, driving down the price.

Share prices and business

Companies are crucially affected by their share price. If a company's share price falls, this is taken as a sign that 'the market' is losing confidence in the company. This will make it more difficult to raise finance, not only by issuing additional shares in the primary market, but also from banks. It will also make the company more vulnerable to a takeover bid. This is where one company seeks to buy out another by offering to buy all its shares. A takeover will succeed if the owners of more than half of the company's shares vote to accept the offered price. Shareholders are more likely to agree to the takeover if the company's shares have not being doing very well recently.

1. *If the rate of economic growth in the economy is 3 per cent in a particular year, why are share prices likely to rise by more than 3 per cent that year?*
2. *Find out what has happened to the FTSE 100 index over the past 12 months and explain why (see site B27 on the hotlinks part of the website).*
3. *Why would you expect the return on shares to be greater than that offered by a bank savings account?*

So it's important to get them right

What gets you out of bed and into an economics lecture on time? What helps decide whether you wear a cycle helmet when out for a bike ride? What motivates a firm to invest in extra training for its workforce? Incentives drive the way individuals and businesses behave – even when we don't see that the incentive exists.

Financial and non-financial incentives

When there is a shortage of a good, its market price will rise, the opportunity cost goes up and there is an incentive for us to consume less. Similarly there is an incentive for firms to produce more. After all, the good is now more profitable to produce. This is an example of a financial incentive, for both buyers and producers. Other financial incentives include wages (i.e. being paid to work), bursaries for students and tax relief on investment for businesses.

But when we look at what motivates people making decisions, we see that non-financial incentives also play an important role. When we give to charity, support a football team, buy presents for our family or decide to run across a busy road rather than use a crossing, we are reacting to non-financial incentives.

Do incentives lead to desirable outcomes?

Let us return to the example of a shortage of a good, leading to a price rise. The resulting incentives could be seen as desirable, the shortage is eliminated and consumers are able to buy more of a good where demand initially exceeds supply.

However, there are plenty of instances where incentives may be 'perverse'. In other words, they could have undesirable effects. For example, if a particular course or module on your degree is assessed by two pieces of coursework, this may act as an incentive for you to concentrate solely on these two pieces and do little work on the rest of the syllabus.

There are plenty of other examples where incentives can be perverse. Making cars safer may encourage people to drive faster. Increasing top rates of income tax may encourage high earners to work less or to evade paying taxes by not declaring income – tax revenues may end up falling.

If an economic system is to work well, it is important, therefore, that the incentives are appropriate and do not bring about undesirable side effects. This is a *threshold concept*

because virtually every action taken by households or firms is influenced by incentives. We need to understand just what the incentives are, what their effects are likely to be, and how the incentives could be improved.

We can see the outcome of inappropriate incentives, when we look at what happened in the former Soviet Union in the days of central planning. The targets given to factory managers (see Box 1.5 on pages 22) were often inappropriate. For example, if targets were specified in tonnes, the incentive was to produce heavy products. Soviet furniture and cooking utensils tended to be very heavy! If targets were set in area (e.g. sheet glass), then the incentive was to produce thin products. If targets were set simply in terms of number of units, then the incentive was to produce shoddy products.

Despite the lessons that should have been learnt from the failures of Soviet planning, we still see a lack of real understanding of incentives and the role they can play. If banks are told to increase the amount of financial capital they hold, they may reduce lending to small businesses. If a university's quality is measured by how many first and upper second class degrees it awards, then there is an incentive to make it easier for students to get high marks.

We will examine the role of incentives in more detail later in the text, particularly when we look at behavioural economics. One crucial incentive is that of profit. In a competitive environment, firms striving for increased profit may result in better products and a lower price for consumers as firms seek to undercut each other. In other cases, however, firms may be able to make bigger profits by controlling the market and keeping competitors out or by colluding with them. Here the profit incentive has a perverse effect: it leads to higher prices for consumers and less choice.

1. Give two other examples of perverse incentives. How could the incentives be improved?
2. Suppose that the kitchen is very untidy – what are the incentives for you to address this? What incentives could you use to get someone else to do it for you?
3. Many students undertake voluntary work while at university. What do you think the incentives are for this? Identify any perverse incentives associated with volunteering and how they could be addressed.

Section summary

1. If the demand for a good exceeds the supply, there will be a shortage. This will lead to a rise in the price of the good.

2. If the supply of a good exceeds the demand, there will be a surplus. This will lead to a fall in the price.

3. Price will settle at the equilibrium. The equilibrium price is the one that clears the market: the price where demand equals supply.

4. If the demand or supply curve shifts, this will lead either to a shortage or to a surplus. Price will therefore either rise or fall until a new equilibrium is reached at the position where the supply and demand curves now intersect.

5. It is difficult to identify the position of a real-world supply (or demand) curve simply by looking at the relationship between price and quantity at different points in time. The problem is that the other curve may have shifted (by an unknown amount).

2.4 THE CONTROL OF PRICES

 TC 3 p26

 TC 6 p55

At the equilibrium price, there will be no shortage or surplus. The equilibrium price, however, may not be the most desirable price. The government, therefore, may prefer to keep prices above or below the equilibrium price.

If the government sets a ***minimum price*** above the equilibrium (a price floor), there will be a surplus: $Q_s - Q_d$ in Figure 2.10. Price will not be allowed to fall to eliminate this surplus.

If the government sets a ***maximum price*** below the equilibrium (a price ceiling), there will be a shortage: $Q_d - Q_s$ in Figure 2.11. Price will not be allowed to rise to eliminate this shortage.

| THRESHOLD CONCEPT 6 | GOVERNMENTS CAN SOMETIMES IMPROVE MARKET OUTCOMES | THINKING LIKE AN ECONOMIST |

Threshold Concept 3 was that markets may fail to meet social objectives; this implies that there may be a need for government intervention. Governments have a number of policy instruments that they can use, either to influence markets or to replace them altogether. These policy instruments include taxation, benefits and subsidies, laws and regulations, licences and permits, and direct provision by government departments or agencies (such as the National Health Service).

The threshold concept here is not merely that governments intervene, but that they can correct, or at least lessen, market failures. Once we have understood the nature of a market failure, we can then set about designing a policy to correct it. For example, if we could identify that the cost to society of producing a product in a way which created pollution was £20 per unit more than the benefit that society gained from the product, then the government could tax the producer £20 per unit.

In Chapters 10 to 13 we consider a number of these policy instruments and seek to identify the optimum level of government intervention to meet social objectives. In this chapter and the next we have a preliminary look at some of these instruments.

Governments themselves, however, are imperfect organisations with a number of different motivations. For an economic adviser to recommend a particular policy as the best means of correcting a market failure does not mean that the government will carry it out efficiently or, indeed, carry it out at all. In fact, sometimes, intervention can make things worse rather than better.

1. *What market failures could be corrected by the use of welfare benefits? Does the payment of such benefits create any problems for society?*
2. *Assume that the government sees litter as a market failure that requires government action. Give some examples of policies it could adopt to reduce litter.*

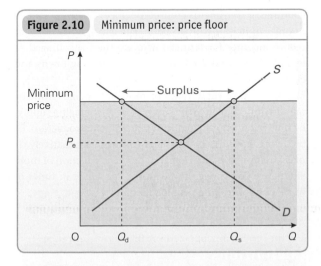

Figure 2.10   Minimum price: price floor

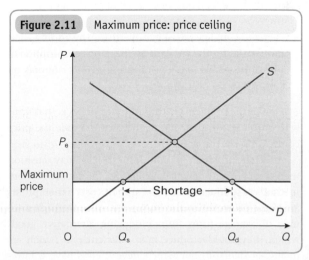

Figure 2.11   Maximum price: price ceiling

Definitions

Minimum price A price floor set by the government or some other agency. The price is not allowed to fall below this level (although it is allowed to rise above it).

Maximum price A price ceiling set by the government or some other agency. The price is not allowed to rise above this level (although it is allowed to fall below it).

Setting a minimum (high) price

The government sets minimum prices to prevent them from falling below a certain level. It may do this for various reasons:

- To protect producers' incomes. If the industry is subject to supply fluctuations (e.g. fluctuations in weather affecting crops), prices are likely to fluctuate severely. Minimum prices will prevent the fall in producers' incomes that would accompany periods of low prices. (This is examined further in section 3.5.)
- To create a surplus (e.g. of grains) – particularly in times of plenty – which can be stored in preparation for possible future shortages.
- In the case of wages (the price of labour), minimum wage legislation can be used to prevent workers' wage rates from falling below a certain level. This may form part of a government policy on poverty and inequality (see Box 10.3).

 Draw a supply and demand diagram with the price of labour (the wage rate) on the vertical axis and the quantity of labour (the number of workers) on the horizontal axis. What will happen to employment if the government raises wages from the equilibrium to some minimum wage above the equilibrium?

The government can use various methods to deal with the surpluses associated with minimum prices:

- The government could buy the surplus and store it, destroy it or sell it abroad in other markets.
- Supply could be artificially lowered by restricting producers to particular quotas. In Figure 2.10, supply could therefore be reduced to Q_d.
- Demand could be raised by advertising, by finding alternative uses for the good, or by reducing consumption of substitute goods (e.g. by imposing taxes or quotas on substitutes, such as imports).

One of the problems with minimum prices is that firms with surpluses on their hands may try to evade the price control and cut their prices.

Another problem is that high prices may cushion inefficiency. Firms may feel less need to find more efficient methods of production and to cut their costs if their profits are being protected by the high price. Also, the high price may discourage firms from producing alternative goods which they could produce more efficiently or which are in higher demand, but which nevertheless have a lower (free-market) price.

Setting a maximum (low) price

The government may set maximum prices to prevent them from rising above a certain level. This will normally be done for reasons of fairness. In wartime, or times of famine, the

government may set maximum prices for basic goods so that poor people can afford to buy them.

The resulting shortages, however, create further problems. If the government merely sets prices and does not intervene further, the shortages will lead to the following:

- Allocation on a 'first come, first served' basis. This is likely to lead to queues developing, or firms adopting waiting lists. Queues were a common feature of life in the former communist east European countries where governments kept prices below the level necessary to equate demand and supply. In the 1990s, as part of their economic reforms, they lifted price controls; this had the obvious benefit of reducing or eliminating queues. However, the consequential sharp increase in food prices made life very hard for those on low incomes.
- Firms deciding which customers should be allowed to buy: for example, giving preference to regular customers.

Neither of the above may be considered fair since some people in need may be forced to go without. Therefore, the government may adopt a system of **rationing**. People could be issued with a set number of coupons for each item rationed.

A major problem with maximum prices is likely to be the emergence of **underground (or shadow) markets**, where customers, unable to buy enough in legal markets, may well be prepared to pay very high prices: prices above P_e in Figure 2.11 (see Box 2.4).

Another problem is that the maximum prices reduce the quantity produced of an already scarce commodity. For example, artificially low prices in a famine are likely to reduce food supplies: if not immediately, then at the next harvest, because of less being grown. In many developing countries, governments control the price of basic foodstuffs in order to help the urban poor. The effect, however, is to reduce incomes for farmers, who are then encouraged to leave the land and flock into the ever-growing towns and cities.

To minimise these types of problems the government may attempt to reduce the shortage by encouraging supply: by drawing on stores, by direct government production, or by giving subsidies or tax relief to firms. Alternatively, it may attempt to reduce demand: by the production of more alternative goods (e.g. home-grown vegetables in times of war) or by controlling people's incomes.

Definitions

Rationing Where the government restricts the amount of a good that people are allowed to buy.

Underground or shadow markets Where people ignore the government's price and/or quantity controls and sell illegally at whatever price equates illegal demand and supply.

BOX 2.4 **UNDERGROUND (OR SHADOW) MARKETS**

A consequence of low fixed prices

When the government sets maximum prices, an 'underground' or 'shadow' market[1] is likely to result. An underground market is one where sellers ignore the government's price restrictions. But why is it in their interest to do so, given that they probably run the risk of fines or even imprisonment?

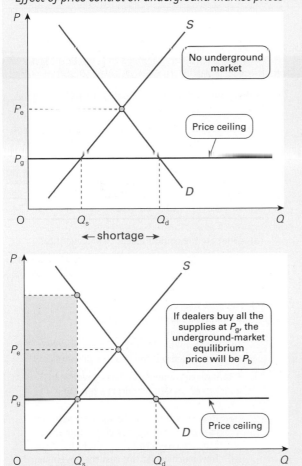

Effect of price control on underground-market prices

Take the case of price controls used in the Second World War. The government set maximum prices for many essential items that were in short supply. This is illustrated in the diagram.

The unacceptably high equilibrium price is P_e. The price fixed by the government is P_g. But at P_g there is a shortage of $Q_d - Q_s$. To deal with the shortage, either the government will have to accept queues or shops selling only to 'regular' customers; or alternatively a system of rationing will have to be introduced.

But whichever system is adopted, one thing is clear: many consumers would be prepared to pay a price considerably above P_g in order to get hold of the good. The demand curve shows this: the less the supply, the higher up the demand curve will the equilibrium price be.

This is where people dealing in the underground market come in. Provided they can get supplies (maybe by some shady dealing), provided they can have access to consumers, provided consumers are willing to break the law, and provided they can escape detection, dealers can charge a price considerably above P_g. But what price can they charge?

Take the extreme case. Assume that the dealers buy up all the supply (Q_s) from the producers at the official price and then sell it at a price that clears the market. The underground-market price will be P_b: at that price, demand is equal to Q_s. The dealers gain the extra revenue shown by the shaded area.

In practice, of course, many people will get their supplies from official sources, and pay only P_g. On the other hand, if dealers are few in number and have only limited supplies, they could sell them at very high prices, above P_b.

During the Second World War, 'spivs' (as these dealers were called) could often charge extortionately high prices for such items as nylon stockings and coffee.

1. *What would be the effect on underground-market prices of a rise in the official price?*
2. *Will a system of low official prices plus an underground market be more equitable or less equitable than a system of free markets?*

[1] In the past they were known as 'black markets'.

Another example of maximum prices is where the government imposes rent controls in an attempt to make rented accommodation more affordable. Here the 'price' is the rent people are charged. The danger of this policy is that it will create a shortage of rental property. (The policy is examined in Case Study 2.4 in MyEconLab.)

Think of some examples where the price of a good or service is kept below the equilibrium (e.g. rent controls). In each case, consider the advantages and disadvantages of the policy.

Section summary

1. There are several ways in which the government intervenes in the operation of markets. It can fix prices, tax or subsidise products, regulate production, or produce goods directly itself.

2. The government may fix minimum or maximum prices. If a minimum price is set above the equilibrium, a surplus will result. If a maximum price is set below the equilibrium price, a shortage will result.

3. Minimum prices are set as a means of protecting the incomes of suppliers or creating a surplus for storage in case of future reductions in supply. If the government is not deliberately trying to create a surplus, it must decide what to do with it.

4. Maximum prices are set as a means of keeping prices down for the consumer. The resulting shortage will cause queues, waiting lists or the restriction of sales by firms to favoured customers. Alternatively, the government could introduce a system of rationing. With maximum prices, underground markets are likely to arise. This is where goods are sold illegally above the maximum price.

END OF CHAPTER QUESTIONS

1. The weekly demand and supply schedules for T-shirts (in millions) in a free market are as follows:

Price (£)	8	7	6	5	4	3	2	1
Quantity demanded	6	8	10	12	14	16	18	20
Quantity supplied	18	16	14	12	10	8	6	4

   (a) What are the equilibrium price and quantity?

   (b) Assume that changes in fashion cause the demand for T-shirts to rise by 4 million at each price. What will be the new equilibrium price and quantity? Has equilibrium quantity risen as much as the rise in demand? Explain why or why not.

   (c) Now plot the data in the table and mark the equilibrium. Also plot the new data corresponding to (b).

2. On separate demand and supply diagrams for bread, sketch the effects of the following: (a) a rise in the price of wheat; (b) a rise in the price of butter and margarine; (c) a rise in the price of rice, pasta and potatoes. In each case, state your assumptions.

3. For what reasons might the price of overseas holidays rise? In each case, identify whether these are reasons affecting demand, supply, or both.

4. If both demand and supply change, and if we know which direction they have shifted but not how much, why is it that we will be able to predict the direction in which *either* price *or* quantity will change, but not both? (Clue: consider the four possible combinations and sketch them if necessary: (a) *D* left, *S* left; (b) *D* right, *S* right; (c) *D* left, *S* right; (d) *D* right, *S* left.)

5. If you were the owner of a clothes shop, how would you set about deciding what prices to charge for each garment at the end-of-season sale?

6. Is there any truth in the saying that the price of a good is a reflection of its quality?

7. Assume that the (weekly) market demand and supply of tomatoes are given by the following figures:

Price (£ per kilo)	4.00	3.50	3.00	2.50	2.00	1.50	1.00
Q_d (000 kilos)	30	35	40	45	50	55	60
Q_s (000 kilos)	80	68	62	55	50	45	38

   (a) What are the equilibrium price and quantity?

   (b) What will be the effect of the government fixing a *minimum* price of (i) £3 per kilo; (ii) £1.50 per kilo?

   (c) Suppose that the government paid tomato producers a subsidy of £1 per kilo.
   (i) Give the new supply schedule.
   (ii) What will be the new equilibrium price?
   (iii) How much will this cost the government?

   (d) Alternatively, suppose that the government guaranteed tomato producers a price of £2.50 per kilo.
   (i) How many tomatoes would it have to buy in order to ensure that all the tomatoes produced were sold?
   (ii) How much would this cost the government?

   (e) Alternatively, suppose it bought *all* the tomatoes produced at £2.50.
   (i) At what single price would it have to sell them in order to dispose of the lot?
   (ii) What would be the net cost of this action?

8. Assume that oil begins to run out and that extraction becomes more expensive. Trace through the effects of this on the market for oil and the market for other fuels.

Online resources

Additional case studies in MyEconLab

2.1 **Adjusting to oil price shocks.** A case study showing how demand and supply analysis can be used to examine the price changes in the oil market since 1973.

2.2 **Coffee prices.** An examination of the coffee market and the implications of fluctuations in the coffee harvest for growers and coffee drinkers.

2.3 **Rationing.** A case study in the use of rationing as an alternative to the price mechanism. In particular, it looks at the use of rationing in the UK during the Second World War.

2.4 **Rent control.** The effect of government control of rents on the market for rental property.

Maths Case 2.1 Finding equilibrium price and quantity using algebra. This gives an example of solving equilibrium price and quantity from a demand and a supply equation using the method of simultaneous equations.

Websites relevant to this chapter

Numbers and sections refer to websites listed in the Web Appendix and hotlinked from this book's website at **www.pearsoned.co.uk/sloman**.

- For news articles relevant to this chapter, see the *Economic News* section in MyEconLab.
- For general news on markets, see websites in section A, and particularly A2, 3, 4, 5, 8, 9, 18, 22, 25, 26, 36. See also links to newspapers worldwide in A38, 39, 43 and 44, and the news search feature in Google at A41.
- For links to sites on markets, see the relevant sections of I4, 7, 11, 17.
- For data on the housing market (Box 2.2), see sites B7–11.
- For sites favouring the free market, see C17 and E34.
- For student resources relevant to this chapter, see sites C1–7, 9, 10, 19.
- For a range of classroom games and simulations of markets, see sites C23 and also C24 (computer-based) and C20 (non-computer-based).

MyEconLab

This book can be supported by MyEconLab, which contains a range of additional resources, including an online homework and tutorial system designed to test and build your understanding.

You need both an access card and a course ID to access MyEconLab:

1. Is your lecturer using MyEconLab? Ask your lecturer for your course ID.

2. Has an access card been included with the book at a reduced cost? Check the inside back cover of the book.

3. If you have a course ID but no access card, go to: http://www.myeconlab.com/ to buy access to this interactive study programme.

Markets in Action

CHAPTER MAP

3.1 Elasticity   61
Price elasticity of demand   61
Measuring the price elasticity of demand   61
Interpreting the figure for elasticity   62
Determinants of price elasticity of demand   62
Price elasticity of demand and consumer
   expenditure   63
The measurement of elasticity: arc elasticity   65
*The measurement of elasticity: point elasticity   67
Price elasticity of supply   69
Income elasticity of demand   71
Cross-price elasticity of demand   73

3.2 The time dimension   74
Short-run and long-run adjustment   74
Price expectations and speculation   75
Dealing with uncertainty and risk   77

3.3 Indirect taxes   80
The effect of imposing taxes on goods   80
Elasticity and the incidence of taxation   82

3.4 Government rejection of market
allocation   84
Providing goods and services free at the point of
   delivery: the case of hospital treatment   84
Prohibiting the sale of certain goods and
   services: the case of illegal drugs   85

3.5 Agriculture and agricultural policy   86
Why intervene?   86
Government intervention   89
The Common Agricultural Policy of the EU   91
Criticisms of the former CAP system of price
   support   92
Reforming the CAP   93

In Chapters 1 and 2 we demonstrated that changes in price affect the quantity demanded and supplied. But how much? How much will the demand for DVDs go up if the price of DVDs comes down? How much will the supply of new houses go up if the price of houses rises? In Chapter 3 we develop the concept of *elasticity* of demand and supply to examine this responsiveness.

We then look at how quickly markets adjust and also examine how people's expectations of price changes affect what actually happens to prices. In particular, we look at speculation – people attempting to gain from anticipated price changes.

In Chapter 1 we identified that the real world is one of mixed economies. The government intervenes in many markets, even highly competitive ones. This intervention can take a number of forms:

- Fixing prices, either above or below the free-market equilibrium. We looked at this in Chapter 2.
- Taxing the production or sale of various goods, such as petrol.
- Subsidising the production or sale of various goods, such as public transport.
- Producing goods or services directly (e.g. defence and health care).
- Regulation. Various laws could be passed to regulate the behaviour of firms. For example, some activities, such as the dumping of toxic waste, could be made illegal; or licences or official permission might have to be obtained to produce certain goods; or a regulatory body could supervise the activities of various firms and prevent any that it felt to be against the public interest (e.g. the production of unsafe toys).

Supply and demand analysis is a useful tool for examining the effects of government intervention. First we examine what could happen if a government seeks to do away with a market system of allocation, either by providing things free to consumers, or by banning certain harmful activities. We then examine government intervention in agriculture – a sector that has received massive government support in many countries of the world. We look at the economic arguments for such intervention and then examine some specific measures that governments have taken.

The role of government in the economy is examined further in Chapters 10 to 13.

Price elasticity of demand

When the price of a good rises, the quantity demanded will fall. But in most cases we will want to know more than this. We will want to know by just *how much* the quantity demanded will fall. In other words, we will want to know how *responsive* demand is to a rise in price.

Take the case of two products: oil and cabbages. In the case of oil, a rise in price is likely to result in a relatively small fall in the quantity demanded. If people want to continue driving, they have to pay the higher prices for fuel. A few may turn to riding bicycles, and some people may make fewer journeys, but for most people, a rise in the price of petrol and diesel will make little difference in the short term to how much they use their cars.

In the case of cabbages, however, a rise in price may lead to a substantial fall in the quantity demanded. The reason is that there are alternative vegetables that people can buy. Many people, when buying vegetables, will buy whatever is reasonably priced.

We call the responsiveness of demand to a change in price the *price elasticity of demand*, and it is one of the most important concepts in economics. For example, if we know the price elasticity of demand for a product, we can predict the effect on price and quantity of a shift in the *supply* curve for that product.

Figure 3.1 shows the effect of a shift in supply with two quite different demand curves (*D* and *D′*). Curve *D′* is more elastic than curve *D* over any given price range. In other words, for any given change in price, there will be a larger

change in quantity demanded along curve *D′* than along curve *D*.

Assume that initially the supply curve is S_1, and that it intersects with both demand curves at point *a*, at a price of P_1 and a quantity of Q_1. Now supply shifts to S_2. What will happen to price and quantity? In the case of the less elastic demand curve *D*, there is a relatively large rise in price (to P_2) and a relatively small fall in quantity (to Q_2): equilibrium is at point *b*. In the case of the more elastic demand curve *D′*, however, there is only a relatively small rise in price (to P_3), but a relatively large fall in quantity (to Q_3): equilibrium is at point *c*.

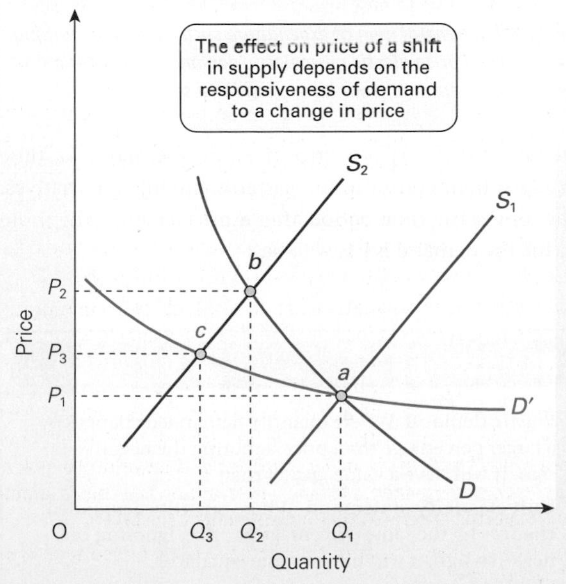

Measuring the price elasticity of demand

What we want to compare is the size of the change in quantity demanded with the size of the change in price. But since price and quantity are measured in different units, the only sensible way we can do this is to use percentage or proportionate changes. This gives us the following *formula for the price elasticity of demand* ($P\epsilon_D$) for a product: percentage (or proportionate) change in quantity demanded divided by the percentage (or proportionate) change in price. Putting this in symbols gives

$$P\epsilon_D = \frac{\%\Delta Q_D}{\%\Delta P}$$

where ϵ (the Greek epsilon) is the symbol we use for elasticity, and Δ (the capital Greek delta) is the symbol we use for a 'change in'.

Thus, if a 40 per cent rise in the price of oil caused the quantity demanded to fall by a mere 10 per cent, the price elasticity of oil over this range will be

$$-10\%/40\% = -0.25$$

whereas, if a 5 per cent fall in the price of cabbages caused a 15 per cent rise in the quantity demanded, the price elasticity of demand for cabbages over this range would be

$$15\%/-5\% = -3$$

Cabbages have a more elastic demand than oil, and this is shown by the figures. But just what do these two figures show? What is the significance of minus 0.25 and minus 3?

Figure 3.1 Market supply and demand

The effect on price of a shift in supply depends on the responsiveness of demand to a change in price

Definitions

Price elasticity of demand The responsiveness of quantity demanded to a change in price.

Price elasticity of demand (formula) ($P\epsilon_D$) The percentage (or proportionate) change in quantity demanded divided by the percentage (or proportionate) change in price: $\%\Delta Q_D \div \%\Delta P$.

Interpreting the figure for elasticity

The use of proportionate or percentage measures

Elasticity is measured in proportionate or percentage terms for the following reasons:

- It allows comparison of changes in two qualitatively different things, which are thus measured in two different types of unit: i.e. it allows comparison of *quantity* changes with *monetary* changes.
- It is the only sensible way of deciding *how big* a change in price or quantity is. Take a simple example. An item goes up in price by £1. Is this a big increase or a small increase? We can answer this only if we know what the original price was. If a can of beans goes up in price by £1 that is a huge price increase. If, however, the price of a house goes up by £1 that is a tiny price increase. In other words, it is the percentage or proportionate increase in price that determines how big a price rise is.

The sign (positive or negative)

Demand curves are generally downward sloping. This means that price and quantity change in opposite directions. A *rise* in price (a positive figure) will cause a *fall* in the quantity demanded (a negative figure). Similarly a *fall* in price will cause a *rise* in the quantity demanded. Thus when working out price elasticity of demand, we divide either a negative figure by a positive figure, or a positive figure by a negative. Either way, we end up with a negative figure.

The value (greater or less than 1)

If we now ignore the negative sign and just concentrate on the value of the figure, this tells us whether demand is **elastic** or **inelastic**.

Elastic (ε > 1). This is where a change in price causes a proportionately larger change in the quantity demanded. In this case the value of elasticity will be greater than 1, since we are dividing a larger figure by a smaller figure.

Inelastic (ε < 1). This is where a change in a price causes a proportionately smaller change in the quantity demanded. In this case elasticity will be less than 1, since we are dividing a smaller figure by a larger figure.

Unit elastic (ε = 1). **Unit elasticity of demand** occurs where price and quantity demanded change by the same proportion. This will give an elasticity equal to 1, since we are dividing a figure by itself.

Determinants of price elasticity of demand

 KI 9
p71

The price elasticity of demand varies enormously from one product to another. For example, the demand for a holiday in any given resort typically has a price elasticity greater than 5, whereas the demand for electricity has a price elasticity less than 0.5 (ignoring the negative signs). But why do some products have a highly elastic demand,

whereas others have a highly *in*elastic demand? What determines price elasticity of demand?

The number and closeness of substitute goods. This is the most important determinant. The more substitutes there are for a good and the more similar they are to the good, the more people will switch to these alternatives when the price of the good rises: the greater, therefore, will be the price elasticity of demand.

Returning to our examples of oil and cabbages, there is no close substitute for oil and thus demand is relatively inelastic. There are plenty of alternatives to cabbages, however, and thus demand is relatively elastic.

 Why will the price elasticity of demand for holidays in Crete be greater than that for holidays in general? Is this difference the result of a difference in the size of the income effect or the substitution effect? Is there anything the suppliers of holidays in Crete can do to reduce this higher price elasticity?

The proportion of income spent on the good. The higher the proportion of our income we spend on a good, the more we will be forced to cut consumption when its price rises: the bigger will be the income effect and the more elastic will be the demand.

Thus salt has a very low price elasticity of demand. Part of the reason is that there is no close substitute. But part is that we spend such a tiny fraction of our income on salt that we would find little difficulty in paying a relatively large percentage increase in its price: the income effect of a price rise would be very small. By contrast, there will be a much bigger income effect when a major item of expenditure rises in price. For example, if mortgage interest rates rise (the 'price' of loans for house purchase), people may have to cut down substantially on their demand for housing – being forced to buy somewhere much smaller and cheaper, or to live in rented accommodation.

 Will a general item of expenditure such as food or clothing have a price-elastic or -inelastic demand? (Consider both the determinants we have considered so far.)

The time period. When price rises, people may take time to adjust their consumption patterns and find alternatives. The longer the time period after a price change, the more elastic the demand is likely to be.

Definitions

Elastic demand Where quantity demanded changes by a larger percentage than price. Ignoring the negative sign, it will have a value greater than 1.

Unit elasticity of demand Where quantity demanded changes by the same percentage as price. Ignoring the negative sign, it will have a value equal to 1.

To illustrate this, let us return to our example of oil. Between December 1973 and June 1974 the price of crude oil quadrupled, which led to large increases in the prices of petrol and central-heating oil. Over the next few months, there was only a very small reduction in the consumption of oil products. Demand was highly inelastic. The reason was that people still wanted to drive their cars and heat their houses.

Over time, however, as the higher oil prices persisted, new fuel-efficient cars were developed and many people switched to smaller cars or moved closer to their work. Similarly, people switched to gas or solid fuel central heating, and spent more money insulating their houses to save on fuel bills. Demand was thus much more elastic in the long run.

In 2007 and 2008 oil prices again were increasing very sharply (see Box 7.3 on page 202). If the high oil price had persisted, we might have expected to see patterns of demand changing over the next few years as consumers adjusted to these higher prices. In fact, within months there were signs of these effects beginning to occur as demand for large fuel-hungry cars in the USA (such as Hummers and other SUVs) fell and demand for smaller European and Japanese models rose. But as recession swept the world, so the oil price rapidly fell. We would have to wait for recovery to see soaring oil prices again.

 Demand for oil might be relatively elastic over the longer term, and yet it could still be observed that over time people consume more oil (or only very slightly less) despite rising oil prices. How can this apparent contradiction be explained?

Price elasticity of demand and consumer expenditure

One of the most important applications of price elasticity of demand concerns its relationship with the total amount of money consumers spend on a product. **Total consumer expenditure (TE)** is simply price multiplied by quantity purchased:

$$TE = P \times Q$$

For example, if consumers buy 3 million units (Q) at a price of £2 per unit (P), they will spend a total of £6 million (TE).

Total consumer expenditure will be the same as the **total revenue (TR)** received by firms from the sale of the product (before any taxes or other deductions).

What will happen to consumer expenditure (and hence firms' revenue) if there is a change in price? The answer depends on the price elasticity of demand.

Elastic demand

As price rises, so quantity demanded falls and vice versa. When demand is elastic, quantity demanded changes proportionately more than price. Thus the change in quantity

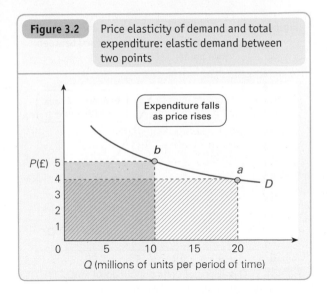

Figure 3.2 Price elasticity of demand and total expenditure: elastic demand between two points

has a bigger effect on total consumer expenditure than does the change in price. For example, when the price rises, there will be such a large fall in consumer demand that *less* will be spent than before. This can be summarised as follows:

- P rises; Q falls proportionately more; thus TE falls.
- P falls; Q rises proportionately more; thus TE rises.

In other words, total expenditure changes in the same direction as *quantity*.

This is illustrated in Figure 3.2. The areas of the rectangles in the diagram represent total expenditure. Why? The area of a rectangle is its height multiplied by its length. In this case, this is price multiplied by quantity bought, which is total expenditure. Demand is elastic between points *a* and *b*. A rise in price from £4 to £5 causes a proportionately larger fall in quantity demanded: from 20 million to 10 million. Total expenditure *falls* from £80 million (the striped area) to £50 million (the pink area).

When demand is elastic, then, a rise in price will cause a fall in total consumer expenditure and thus a fall in the total revenue that firms selling the product receive. A reduction in price, however, will result in consumers spending more, and hence firms earning more.

Definitions

Total consumer expenditure on a product (TE) (per period of time) The price of the product multiplied by the quantity purchased: $TE = P \times Q$.

Total revenue (TR) (per period of time) The total amount received by firms from the sale of a product, before the deduction of taxes or any other costs. The price multiplied by the quantity sold: $TR = P \times Q$.

Figure 3.3 Price elasticity of demand and total expenditure: inelastic demand between two points

Expenditure rises as price rises

P(£)

Q (millions of units per period of time)

Inelastic demand

When demand is **inelastic**, it is the other way around. Price changes proportionately more than quantity. Thus the change in price has a bigger effect on total consumer expenditure than does the change in quantity. To summarise the effects:

- *P* rises; *Q* falls proportionately less; *TE* rises.
- *P* falls; *Q* rises proportionately less; *TE* falls.

In other words, total consumer expenditure changes in the same direction as *price*.

This is illustrated in Figure 3.3. Demand is inelastic between points *a* and *c*. A rise in price from £4 to £8 causes a proportionately smaller fall in quantity demanded: from 20 million to 15 million. Total expenditure *rises* from £80 million (the striped area) to £120 million (the pink area).

Definition

Inelastic demand Where quantity demanded changes by a smaller percentage than price. Ignoring the negative sign, it will have a value less than 1.

In this case, firms' revenue will increase if there is a rise in price and fall if there is a fall in price.

 Assume that demand for a product is inelastic. Will consumer expenditure go on increasing as price rises? Would there be any limit?

Special cases

Figure 3.4 shows three special cases: (a) a totally inelastic demand ($P\epsilon_D = 0$), (b) an infinitely elastic demand ($P\epsilon_D = -\infty$) and (c) a unit elastic demand ($P\epsilon_D = -1$).

Totally inelastic demand. This is shown by a vertical straight line. No matter what happens to price, quantity demanded remains the same. It is obvious that the more the price rises, the bigger will be the level of consumer expenditure. Thus in Figure 3.4(a), consumer expenditure will be higher at P_2 than at P_1.

 Can you think of any examples of goods which have a totally inelastic demand (a) at all prices; (b) over a particular price range?

Infinitely elastic demand. This is shown by a horizontal straight line. At any price above P_1 in Figure 3.4(b), demand is zero. But at P_1 (or any price below) demand is 'infinitely' large.

This seemingly unlikely demand curve is in fact relatively common for an *individual producer*. In a perfect market, as we have seen, firms are small relative to the whole market (like the small-scale grain farmer). They have to accept the price as given by supply and demand in the *whole market*, but at that price they can sell as much as they produce. (Demand is not *literally* infinite, but as far as the firm is concerned it is.) In this case, the more the individual firm produces, the more revenue will be earned. In Figure 3.4(b), more revenue is earned at Q_2 than at Q_1.

Unit elastic demand. This is where price and quantity change in exactly the same proportion. Any rise in price will be exactly offset by a fall in quantity, leaving total consumer

Figure 3.4 Price elasticity of demand: special cases

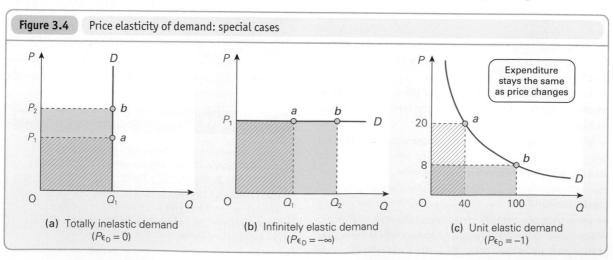

(a) Totally inelastic demand ($P\epsilon_D = 0$)

(b) Infinitely elastic demand ($P\epsilon_D = -\infty$)

(c) Unit elastic demand ($P\epsilon_D = -1$)

Expenditure stays the same as price changes

expenditure unchanged. In Figure 3.4(c), the striped area is exactly equal to the pink area: in both cases, total expenditure is £800.

You might have thought that a demand curve with unit elasticity would be a straight line at 45° to the axes. Instead it is a curve called a *rectangular hyperbola*. The reason for its shape is that the proportionate *rise* in quantity must equal the proportionate *fall* in price (and vice versa). As we move down the demand curve, in order for the *proportionate* change in both price and quantity to remain constant there must be a bigger and bigger *absolute* rise in quantity and a smaller and smaller absolute fall in price. For example, a rise in quantity from 200 to 400 is the same proportionate change as a rise from 100 to 200, but its absolute size is double. A fall in price from £5 to £2.50 is the same percentage as a fall from £10 to £5, but its absolute size is only half.

 To illustrate these figures, draw the demand curve corresponding to the following table.

P	Q	TE
£2.50	400	£1000
£5	200	£1000
£10	100	£1000
£20	50	£1000
£40	25	£1000

If the curve had an elasticity of −1 throughout its length, what would be the quantity demanded (a) at a price of £1; (b) at a price of 10p; (c) if the good were free?

The measurement of elasticity: arc elasticity

We have defined price elasticity as the percentage or proportionate change in quantity demanded divided by the percentage or proportionate change in price. But how, in practice, do we measure these changes for a specific demand curve? We shall examine two methods. The first is called the *arc method*. The second (in an optional section) is called the *point method*.

A common mistake that students make is to think that you can talk about the elasticity of a *whole curve*. In fact in most cases the elasticity will vary along the length of the curve.

Take the case of the demand curve illustrated in Figure 3.5. Between points *a* and *b*, total expenditure rises ($P_2Q_2 > P_1Q_1$): demand is thus elastic between these two points. Between points *b* and *c*, however, total expenditure falls ($P_3Q_3 < P_2Q_2$). Demand here is inelastic.

Normally, then, we can only refer to the elasticity of a *portion* of the demand curve, not of the *whole* curve. There are, however, two exceptions to this rule.

The first is when the elasticity just so happens to be the same all the way along a curve, as in the three special cases illustrated in Figure 3.4. The second is where two curves are drawn on the same diagram, as in Figure 3.1. Here we can say that demand curve D is less elastic than demand curve D' at any given price. Note, however, that each of

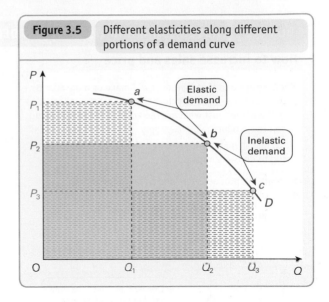

Figure 3.5 Different elasticities along different portions of a demand curve

these two curves will still have different elasticities along its length.

Although we cannot normally talk about the elasticity of a whole curve, we can nevertheless talk about the elasticity between any two points on it. This is known as **arc elasticity**. In fact the formula for price elasticity of demand that we have used so far is the formula for arc elasticity. Let us examine it more closely. Remember the formula we used was

$$\frac{\text{Proportionate } \Delta Q}{\text{Proportionate } \Delta P} \text{ (where } \Delta \text{ means 'change in')}$$

The way we measure a proportionate change in quantity is to divide that change by the level of Q: $\Delta Q/Q$. Similarly, we measure a proportionate change in price by dividing that change by the level of P: $\Delta P/P$. Price elasticity of demand can thus now be rewritten as

$$\frac{\Delta Q}{Q} \div \frac{\Delta P}{P}$$

But just what value do we give to P and Q? Consider the demand curve in Figure 3.6. What is the elasticity of demand between points *m* and *n*? Price has fallen by £2 (from £8 to £6), but what is the proportionate change? Is it $-2/8$ or $-2/6$? The convention is to express the change as a proportion of the average of the two prices, £8 and £6: in other words, to take the midpoint price, £7. Thus the proportionate change is $-2/7$.

Similarly, the proportionate change in quantity between points *m* and *n* is $10/15$, since 15 is midway between 10 and 20.

> ### Definition
>
> **Arc elasticity** The measurement of elasticity between two points on a curve.

BOX 3.1 ADVERTISING AND ITS EFFECT ON DEMAND CURVES

How to increase sales and price

When we are told that a product will make us more attractive, enrich our lives, make our clothes smell great or allow us to save the planet, just what are the advertisers up to? 'Trying to sell the product', you may reply.

In fact there is a bit more to it than this. Advertisers are trying to do two things:

- Shift the product's demand curve to the right.
- Make it less price elastic.

This is illustrated in the diagram.

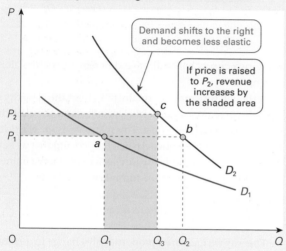

Effect of advertising on the demand curve

D_1 shows the original demand curve with price at P_1 and sales at Q_1. D_2 shows the curve after an advertising campaign. The rightward shift allows an increased quantity (Q_2) to be sold at the original price. If the demand is also made highly inelastic, the firm can also raise its price and still have a substantial increase in sales. Thus in the

diagram, price can be raised to P_2 and sales will be Q_3 – still substantially above Q_1. The total gain in revenue is shown by the shaded area.

How can advertising bring about this new demand curve?

Shifting the demand curve to the right

This can occur in two ways. First, if advertising brings the product to more people's attention, then the market for the good grows and the demand curve shifts to the right. Second, if the advertising increases people's desire for the product, they will be prepared to pay a higher price for each unit purchased.

Making the demand curve less elastic

This will occur if the advertising creates greater brand loyalty. People must be led to believe (rightly or wrongly) that competitors' brands are inferior. This can be done directly by comparing the brand being advertised with a competitor's product. Alternatively, the adverts may concentrate on making the product seem so special that it implies that no other product can compete. These approaches will allow the firm to raise its price above that of its rivals with no significant fall in sales. The substitution effect will have been lessened because consumers have been led to believe that there are no close substitutes.

1. *Think of some advertisements which deliberately seek to make demand less elastic.*
2. *Imagine that 'Sunshine' sunflower spread, a well-known brand, is advertised with the slogan 'It helps you live longer'. What do you think would happen to the demand curve for a supermarket's own brand of sunflower spread? Consider both the direction of shift and the effect on elasticity. Will the elasticity differ markedly at different prices? How will this affect the pricing policy and sales of the supermarket's own brand? What do you think might be the response of government to the slogan?*

Thus using the **average (or 'midpoint') formula**, elasticity between *m* and *n* is given by

$$\frac{\Delta Q}{\text{average } Q} \div \frac{\Delta P}{\text{average } P} = \frac{10}{15} \div \frac{-2}{7} = 2.33$$

Since 2.33 is greater than 1, demand is elastic between *m* and *n*.

Referring to Figure 3.6, use the midpoint formula to calculate the price elasticity of demand between (a) P = 6 and P = 4; (b) P = 4 and P = 2. What do you conclude about the elasticity of a straight-line demand curve as you move down it?

Figure 3.6 Measuring elasticity

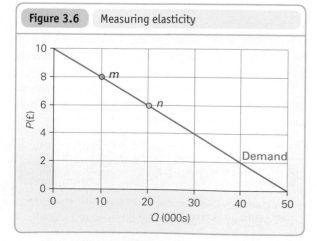

Definition

Average (or 'midpoint') formula for price elasticity of demand ΔQ_D/average $Q_D \div \Delta P$/average *P*.

BOX 3.2 ANY MORE FARES?

Pricing on the buses

Imagine that a local bus company is faced with increased costs and fears that it will make a loss. What should it do?

The most likely response of the company will be to raise its fares. But this may be the wrong policy, especially if existing services are underutilised. To help it decide what to do, it commissions a survey to estimate passenger demand at three different fares: the current fare of 50p per mile, a higher fare of 60p and a lower fare of 40p. The results of the survey are shown in the first two columns of the table.

Demand turns out to be elastic. This is because of the existence of alternative means of transport. As a result of the elastic demand, total revenue can be increased by reducing the fare from the current 50p to 40p. Revenue would rise from £2 million to £2.4 million per annum.

But what will happen to the company's profits? Its profit is the difference between the total revenue from passengers and its total costs of operating the service. If buses are

currently underutilised, it is likely that the extra passengers can be carried without the need for extra buses, and hence at no extra cost.

At a fare of 50p, the old profit was £0.2 million (£2.0m – £1.8m). After the increase in costs, a 50p fare now gives a loss of £0.2 million (£2.0m – £2.2m).

By raising the fare to 60p, the loss is increased to £0.4 million. But by lowering the fare to 40p, a profit of £0.2 million can again be made.

1. *Estimate the price elasticity of demand between 40p and 50p and between 50p and 60p.*
2. *Was the 50p fare the best fare originally?*
3. *The company considers lowering the fare to 30p, and estimates that demand will be 8.5 million passenger miles. It will have to put on extra buses, however. How should it decide?*

Fare (£ per mile)	Estimated demand (passenger miles per year: millions)	Total revenue (£ millions per year)	Old total cost (£ millions per year)	New total cost (£ millions per year)
(1)	(2)	(3)	(4)	(5)
0.40	6	2.4	1.8	2.2
0.50	4	2.0	1.8	2.2
0.60	3	1.8	1.8	2.2

*The measurement of elasticity: point elasticity

Rather than measuring elasticity between two points on a demand curve, we may want to measure it at a single point: for example, point *r* in Figure 3.7. In order to measure *point elasticity* we must first rearrange the terms in the formula $\Delta Q/Q \div \Delta P/P$. By doing so we can rewrite the formula for price elasticity of demand as

$$\frac{\Delta Q}{\Delta P} \times \frac{P}{Q}$$

Since we want to measure price elasticity at a *point* on the demand curve, rather than between two points, it is

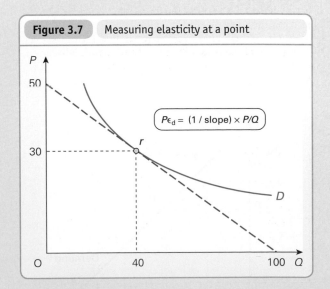

Figure 3.7 Measuring elasticity at a point

$P\epsilon_d = (1 \text{ / slope}) \times P/Q$

Definition

Point elasticity The measurement of elasticity at a point on a curve. The formula for price elasticity of demand using the point elasticity method is $dQ/dP \times P/Q$, where dQ/dP is the inverse of the slope of the tangent to the demand curve at the point in question.

necessary to know how quantity demanded would react to an *infinitesimally small* change in price. In the case of point *r* in Figure 3.7, we want to know how the quantity demanded would react to an infinitesimally small change from a price of 30.

An infinitesimally small change is signified by the letter *d*. The formula for price elasticity of demand thus becomes

$$\frac{dQ}{dP} \times \frac{P}{Q}$$

where *dQ/dP* is the differential calculus term for the rate of change of quantity with respect to a change in price (see Appendix 1). And conversely, *dP/dQ* is the rate of change of price with respect to a change in quantity demanded. At any given point on the demand curve, *dP/dQ* is given by the *slope* of the curve (its rate of change). The slope is found by drawing a tangent to the curve at that point and finding the slope of the tangent.

The tangent to the demand curve at point *r* is shown in Figure 3.7. Its slope is −50/100. Thus, *dP/dQ* is −50/100 and *dQ/dP* is the inverse of this, −100/50 = −2.

Returning to the formula *dQ/dP* × *P/Q*, elasticity at point *r* equals

$$-2 \times 30/40 = -1.5$$

Rather than having to draw the graph and measure the slope of the tangent, the technique of differentiation can be used to work out point elasticity as long as the equation for the demand curve is known. An example of the use of this technique is given in Box 3.3 (on page 69).

*LOOKING AT THE MATHS

Elasticity of a straight-line demand curve

A straight-line demand curve has a different elasticity at each point on it. The only exceptions are a vertical demand curve ($P\epsilon_D = 0$) and a horizontal demand curve ($P\epsilon_D = \infty$). The reason for this differing elasticity can be demonstrated using the equation for a straight-line demand curve:

$$Q = a - bP$$

The term '−*b*' would give the slope of the demand curve if we were to plot *Q* on the vertical axis and *P* on the horizontal. Since we plot them the other way around,[1] the term '*b*' gives the inverse of the slope as plotted. The slope of the curve as plotted is given by *dP/dQ*; the inverse of the slope is given by *dQ/dP* = −*b*.

The formula for price elasticity of demand (using the point elasticity method) is

$$P\epsilon_D = \frac{dQ}{dP} \cdot \frac{P}{Q}$$

This can thus be rewritten as

$$P\epsilon_D = -b\frac{P}{Q}$$

This is illustrated in the diagram, which plots the following demand curve:

$$Q = 50 - 5P$$

The slope of the demand curve (*dP/dQ*) is constant (i.e. −10/50 or −0.2). The inverse of the slope (*dQ/dP*) is thus −5, where 5 is the '*b*' term in the equation. In this example, therefore, price elasticity of demand is given by

$$P\epsilon_D = -5\frac{P}{Q}$$

The value of *P/Q*, however, differs along the length of the demand curve. At point *n*, *P/Q* = 8/10. Thus

$$P\epsilon_D = -5(8/10) = -4$$

At point *m*, however, *P/Q* = 6/20. Thus

$$P\epsilon_D = -5(6/20) = -1.5$$

These questions refer to the diagram.
1. *What is the price elasticity of demand at points l and k?*
2. *What is the price elasticity of demand at the point (a) where the demand curve crosses the vertical axis; (b) where it crosses the horizontal axis?*
3. *As you move down a straight-line demand curve, what happens to elasticity? Why?*
4. *Calculate price elasticity of demand between points n and l using the arc method. Does this give the same answer as the point method? Would it if the demand curve were actually curved?*

[1] It is contrary to normal convention to plot the independent variable (*P*) on the vertical axis and the dependent variable (*Q*) on the horizontal axis. The reason why we do this is because there are many other diagrams in economics where *Q* is the independent variable. Such diagrams include cost curves and revenue curves, which we will consider in Chapter 5. As you will see, it is much easier if we always plot *Q* on the horizontal axis even when, as in the case of demand curves, *Q* is the dependent variable.

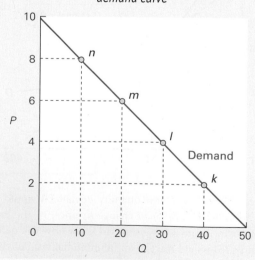

Different elasticities along a straight-line demand curve

Price elasticity of supply ($P\epsilon_s$)

When price changes, there will be not only a change in the quantity demanded, but also a change in the quantity supplied. Frequently we will want to know just how responsive quantity supplied is to a change in price. The measure we use is the *price elasticity of supply*.

Figure 3.8 shows two supply curves. Curve S_2 is more elastic between any two prices than curve S_1. Thus, when price rises from P_1 to P_2 there is a larger increase in quantity supplied with S_2 (namely, Q_1 to Q_3) than there is with S_1

Definition

Price elasticity of supply The responsiveness of quantity supplied to a change in price.

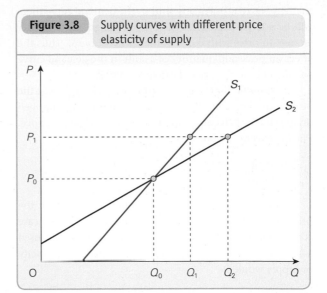

Figure 3.8 Supply curves with different price elasticity of supply

---

*BOX 3.3 USING CALCULUS TO CALCULATE THE PRICE ELASTICITY OF DEMAND

(A knowledge of the rules of differentiation is necessary to understand this box. See Appendix 1.)

The following is an example of an equation for a demand curve:

$$Q_d = 60 - 15P + P^2$$

(where Q_d is measured in thousands of units). From this the following table and the graph can be constructed.

P	60	$-15P$	$+P^2$	$=$	Q_d (000s)
0	60	-0	$+0$	$=$	60
1	60	-15	$+1$	$=$	46
2	60	-30	$+4$	$=$	34
3	60	-45	$+9$	$=$	24
4	60	-60	$+16$	$=$	16
5	60	-75	$+25$	$=$	10
6	60	-90	$+36$	$=$	6

Point elasticity can be easily calculated from such a demand equation using calculus. To do this you will need to know the rules of differentiation (see pages A:10–13). Remember the formula for point elasticity:

$$P\epsilon_D = dQ/dP \times P/Q$$

The term dQ/dP can be calculated by differentiating the demand equation:

Given $Q_d = 60 - 15P + P^2$
then $dQ/dP = -15 + 2P$

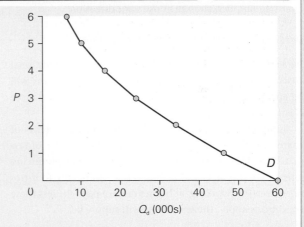

Thus at a price of 3, for example,

$$dQ/dP = -15 + (2 \times 3)$$
$$= -9$$

Thus price elasticity of demand at a price of 3

$$= -9 \times P/Q$$
$$= -9 \times 3/24$$
$$= -9/8 \text{ (which is elastic)}$$

Calculate the price elasticity of demand on this demand curve at a price of (a) 5; (b) 2; (c) 0.

(namely, Q_1 to Q_2). For any shift in the demand curve there will be a larger change in quantity supplied and a smaller change in price with curve S_2 than with curve S_1. Thus the effect on price and quantity of a shift in the demand curve will depend on the price elasticity of supply.

The *formula for the price elasticity of supply* ($P\epsilon_s$) is: the percentage (or proportionate) change in quantity supplied divided by the percentage (or proportionate) change in price. Putting this in symbols gives

$$P\epsilon_s = \frac{\%\Delta Q_s}{\%\Delta P}$$

In other words, the formula is identical to that for the price elasticity of demand, except that quantity in this case is quantity *supplied*. Thus if a 10 per cent rise in price caused a 25 per cent rise in the quantity supplied, the price elasticity of supply would be

25%/10% = 2.5

and if a 10 per cent rise in price caused only a 5 per cent rise in the quantity, the price elasticity of supply would be

5%/10% = 0.5

In the first case, supply is elastic ($P\epsilon_s > 1$); in the second it is inelastic ($P\epsilon_s < 1$). Notice that, unlike the price elasticity of demand, the figure is positive. This is because price and quantity supplied change in the *same* direction.

Determinants of price elasticity of supply

The amount that costs rise as output rises. The less the additional costs of producing additional output, the more firms will be encouraged to produce for a given price rise: the more elastic will supply be.

Supply is thus likely to be elastic if firms have plenty of spare capacity, if they can readily get extra supplies of raw materials, if they can easily switch away from producing alternative products and if they can avoid having to introduce overtime working, at higher rates of pay. The less these conditions apply, the less elastic will supply be.

Time period.

- Immediate time period. Firms are unlikely to be able to increase supply by much immediately. Supply is virtually fixed, or can only vary according to available stocks. Supply is highly inelastic.
- Short run. If a slightly longer period of time is allowed to elapse, some inputs can be increased (e.g. raw materials) while others will remain fixed (e.g. heavy machinery). Supply can increase somewhat.
- Long run. In the long run, there will be sufficient time for all inputs to be increased and for new firms to enter the industry. Supply, therefore, is likely to be highly elastic in many cases. In some circumstances the long-run supply curve may even slope downwards. (See the section on economies of scale in Chapter 5, pages 145–6.)

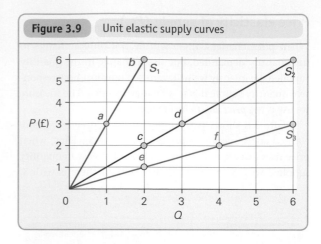

| Figure 3.9 | Unit elastic supply curves |

The measurement of price elasticity of supply

A vertical supply has zero elasticity. It is totally unresponsive to a change in price. A horizontal supply curve has infinite elasticity. There is no limit to the amount supplied at the price where the curve crosses the vertical axis.

When two supply curves cross, the steeper one will have the lower price elasticity of supply (e.g. curve S_1 in Figure 3.8). Any straight-line supply curve starting at the origin, however, will have an elasticity equal to 1 throughout its length, *irrespective of its slope*. This perhaps rather surprising result is illustrated in Figure 3.9. This shows three supply curves, each with a different slope, but each starting from the origin. On each curve two points are marked. In each case there is the *same* proportionate rise in Q as in P. For example, with curve S_1 a doubling in price from £3 to £6 leads to a doubling of output from 1 unit to 2 units.

This demonstrates nicely that it is not the *slope* of a curve that determines its elasticity, but its proportionate change.

Other supply curves' elasticities will vary along their length. In such cases we have to refer to the elasticity either between two points on the curve, or at a specific point. Calculating elasticity between two points will involve the *arc method*. Calculating elasticity at a point will involve the point method. These two methods are just the same for supply curves as for demand curves: the formulae are the same, only the term Q now refers to quantity supplied rather than quantity demanded.

Definitions

Price elasticity of supply (formula) ($P\epsilon_s$) The percentage (or proportionate) change in quantity supplied divided by the percentage (or proportionate) change in price: $\%\Delta Q_s \div \%\Delta P$.

Price elasticity of supply (arc formula) ΔQ_s/average $Q_s \div \Delta P$/average P.

We can use a supply equation to demonstrate why a straight-line supply curve through the origin has an elasticity equal to 1. Assume that the supply equation is

$$Q_s = a + bP \qquad (1)$$

If the supply curve passes through the origin, the value of $a = 0$. Thus

$$Q_s = bP \qquad (2)$$

The point elasticity formula for price elasticity of supply is similar to that for price elasticity of demand (see pages 67–8) and is given by

$$P\epsilon_s = \frac{dQ_s}{dP} \cdot \frac{P}{Q_s} \qquad (3)$$

But

$$b = \frac{dQ_s}{dP} \qquad (4)$$

since this is the slope of the equation (the inverse of the slope of the curve). Substituting equation (4) in equation (3) gives

$$P\epsilon_s = b \cdot \frac{P}{Q_s}$$

Substituting equation (2) in equation (5) gives

$$P\epsilon_s = b \cdot \frac{P}{bP} = \frac{hP}{bP} = 1$$

Given the following supply schedule:

P	2	4	6	8	10
Q	0	10	20	30	40

(a) *Draw the supply curve.*
(b) *Using the arc method, calculate price elasticity of supply (i) between P = 2 and P = 4; (ii) between P = 8 and P = 10.*
(c) **Using the point method, calculate price elasticity of supply at P = 6.*
(d) *Does the elasticity of the supply curve increase or decrease as P and Q increase? Why?*
(e) *What would be the answer to (d) if the supply curve were a straight line but intersecting the horizontal axis to the right of the origin?*

Income elasticity of demand

So far we have looked at the responsiveness of demand and supply to a change in price. But price is just one of the determinants of demand and supply. In theory, we could look at the responsiveness of demand or supply to a change in *any* one of their determinants. We could have a whole range of different types of elasticity of demand and supply.

KEY IDEA 9

Elasticity. The responsiveness of one variable (e.g. demand) to a change in another (e.g. price). This concept is fundamental to understanding how markets work. The more elastic variables are, the more responsive is the market to changing circumstances.

In practice there are just two other elasticities that are particularly useful to us, and both are demand elasticities.

The first is the *income elasticity of demand* ($Y\epsilon_D$). This measures the responsiveness of demand to a change in consumer incomes (Y). It enables us to predict how much the demand curve will shift for a given change in income. The *formula for the income elasticity of demand* is: the percentage (or proportionate) change in demand divided by the percentage (or proportionate) change in income. Putting this in symbols gives

$$Y\epsilon_D = \frac{\%\Delta Q_D}{\%\Delta Y}$$

In other words, the formula is identical to that for the price elasticity of demand, except that we are dividing the change in demand by the change in income that caused it rather than by a change in price. Thus if a 2 per cent rise in income caused an 8 per cent rise in a product's demand, then its income elasticity of demand would be

$$8\%/2\% = 4$$

The major determinant of income elasticity of demand is the degree of 'necessity' of the good. In a developed country, the demand for luxury goods expands rapidly as people's incomes rise, whereas the demand for basic goods rises only a little. Thus items such as designer handbags and foreign holidays have a high income elasticity of demand, whereas items such as vegetables and socks have a low income elasticity of demand.

The demand for some goods actually *decreases* as people's incomes rise beyond a certain level. These are inferior goods such as supermarkets' 'value lines' and bus journeys. As people earn more, so they switch to better quality products. Unlike *normal goods*, which have a positive income elasticity of demand, *inferior goods* have a negative income elasticity of demand.

Look ahead to Table 3.1 (page 87). It shows the income elasticity of demand for various foodstuffs. Explain the difference in the figures for milk, bread and fresh fish.

Definitions

Income elasticity of demand The responsiveness of demand to a change in consumer incomes.

Income elasticity of demand (formula) ($Y\epsilon_D$) The percentage (or proportionate) change in demand divided by the percentage (or proportionate) change in income: $\%\Delta Q_D \div \%\Delta Y$.

Normal goods Goods whose demand increases as consumer incomes increase. They have a positive income elasticity of demand. Luxury goods will have a higher income elasticity of demand than more basic goods.

Inferior goods Goods whose demand decreases as consumer incomes increase. Such goods have a negative income elasticity of demand.

THRESHOLD CONCEPT 7 — ELASTICITY: OF A VARIABLE TO A CHANGE IN A DETERMINANT

As we have seen in the case of price elasticity of demand, elasticity measures the responsiveness of one variable (e.g. quantity demanded) to change in another (e.g. price). This concept is fundamental to understanding how markets work. The more elastic variables are, the more responsive is the market to changing circumstances.

Elasticity is more than just a technical term. It's not difficult to learn the formula

$$P\epsilon_D = \frac{\%\Delta Q_D}{\%\Delta P}$$

in the case of price elasticity of demand, and then to interpret this as

$$P\epsilon_D = \frac{\Delta Q_D}{\text{average } Q_D} \div \frac{\Delta P}{\text{average } P}$$

using the arc elasticity method, or as

$$P\epsilon_D = \frac{dQ_D}{dP} \times \frac{P}{Q}$$

using the point elasticity method.

We can also very simply state the general formula for any elasticity as

$$\epsilon_{XY} = \frac{\%\Delta X}{\%\Delta Y}$$

where the formula refers to the responsiveness of variable X to a change in variable Y (where X could be quantity supplied or demanded, and Y could be price, income, the price of substitutes, or any other determinant of demand or supply). Again, we could use the arc or point elasticity methods. Although students often find it hard at first to use the formulae, it's largely a question of practice in mastering them.

What makes elasticity a *threshold concept* is that it lies at the heart of how economic systems operate. In a market economy, prices act as signals that demand or supply has changed. They also act as an incentive for people to respond to the new circumstances. The greater the elasticity of demand, the bigger will be the response to a change in supply; the greater the elasticity of supply, the bigger will be the response to a change in demand.

Understanding elasticity and what determines its magnitude helps us understand how an economy is likely to respond to the ever-changing circumstances of the real world.

In a perfect market economy, firms face an infinitely elastic (horizontal) demand curve: they are price takers (see page 64 and Figure 3.4(b)). What this means is that they have no power to affect prices: they are highly dependent on market forces.

By contrast, big businesses (and some small ones too) are in a very different position. If there are only one or two firms in a market, each is likely to face a relatively inelastic demand. This gives them the power to raise prices and make more profit. As we have seen, if demand is price inelastic, then raising prices will increase the firm's revenue (see Figure 3.4(b)). Even if demand is elastic (but still downward sloping) the firm could still increase profit by raising prices, provided that the fall in revenue was less than the reduction in costs from producing less. The general point here is that the less elastic is the firm's demand curve, the greater will be its power to raise prices and make a bigger profit.

It's not just price elasticity of demand that helps us understand how market economies operate. In a perfect market, market supply is likely to be highly elastic, especially in the long run after firms have had time to enter the industry. Thus if a new lower cost technique is discovered, which increases profits in an industry, new firms will enter the market, attracted by the higher profits. This increased supply will then have the effect of driving prices down and hence profit rates will fall back. What this means is that in highly competitive industries firms are very responsive to changing economic circumstances. If they are not, they are likely to be forced out of business; it's a question of survival of the fittest. We explore this process in more detail in section 6.2.

If there is less competition, firms have an easier life. But what is good for them may be bad for us as consumers. We may end up paying higher prices and having poorer quality goods – although not necessarily. We explore this in sections 6.3 and 6.4 and in Chapter 7.

So, getting to grips with elasticity is not just about doing calculations. It's about understanding the very essence of how economies operate.

1. *What would you understand by the 'wage elasticity of demand for labour'? How would the magnitude of this elasticity affect the working of the market for (a) plumbers and (b) footballers?*
2. *How can income elasticity of demand help explain how the structure of economies changes over the years?*

Income elasticity of demand is an important concept to firms considering the future size of the market for their product. If the product has a high income elasticity of demand, sales are likely to expand rapidly as national income rises, but may also fall significantly if the economy moves into recession. (See Case Study 3.2, Income elasticity of demand and the balance of payments, in MyEconLab: this shows how the concept of income elasticity of demand can help us understand why so many developing countries have chronic balance of payments problems.)

Cross-price elasticity of demand ($C\epsilon_{D_{AB}}$)

This is often known by its less cumbersome title of *cross elasticity of demand*. It is a measure of the responsiveness of demand for one product to a change in the price of another (either a substitute or a complement). It enables us to predict how much the demand curve for the first product will shift when the price of the second product changes.

The *formula for the cross-price elasticity of demand* ($C\epsilon_{D_{AB}}$) is: the percentage (or proportionate) change in demand for good A divided by the percentage (or proportionate) change in price of good B. Putting this in symbols gives

$$C\epsilon_{D_{AB}} = \frac{\%\Delta Q_{D_A}}{\%\Delta P_B}$$

If good B is a *substitute* for good A, A's demand will *rise* as B's price rises. In this case, cross elasticity will be a positive figure. For example, if the demand for butter rose by 2 per cent when the price of margarine (a substitute) rose by 8 per cent, then the cross elasticity of demand for butter with respect to margarine would be

2%/8% = 0.25

If good B is *complementary* to good A, however, A's demand will *fall* as B's price rises and thus as the quantity of B demanded falls. In this case, cross elasticity of demand will be a negative figure. For example, if a 4 per cent rise in the price of bread led to a 3 per cent fall in demand for butter, the cross elasticity of demand for butter with respect to bread would be

–3%/4% = –0.75

The major determinant of cross elasticity of demand is the closeness of the substitute or complement. The closer it is, the bigger will be the effect on the first good of a change in the price of the substitute or complement, and hence the greater the cross elasticity – either positive or negative.

Firms need to know the cross elasticity of demand for their product when considering the effect on the demand for their product of a change in the price of a rival's product or of a complementary product. These are vital pieces of information for firms when making their production plans.

Another application of the concept of cross elasticity of demand is in the field of international trade and the balance of payments. How does a change in the price of domestic goods affect the demand for imports? If there is a high cross elasticity of demand for imports (because they are close substitutes for home-produced goods), and if prices at home rise due to inflation, the demand for imports will rise substantially, thus worsening the balance of trade.

 Which are likely to have the highest cross elasticity of demand: two brands of coffee, or coffee and tea?

Definitions

Cross-price elasticity of demand The responsiveness of demand for one good to a change in the price of another.

Cross-price elasticity of demand (formula) ($C\epsilon_{D_{AB}}$) The percentage (or proportionate) change in demand for good A divided by the percentage (or proportionate) change in price of good B: $\%\Delta Q_{D_A} \div \%\Delta P_B$.

---

*LOOKING AT THE MATHS

Calculating income and cross-price elasticities from a demand equation

The following demand equation relates quantity demanded (Q_A) for good A to its own price (P_A), consumer income (Y) and the price of a substitute good B (P_B):

$$Q_A = a - bP_A + cY + eP_B$$

Note that this is a 'linear' equation because it has no power terms, such as P^2 or Y^2. The formula[1] for income elasticity of demand for good A will be

$$Y\epsilon_\Delta = \frac{\partial Q_A}{\partial Y} \cdot \frac{Y}{Q_A}$$

But since the term $\partial Q_A/\partial Y$ represents the amount that Q_A will change for a given change in Y (i.e. the value of c), then

$$Y\epsilon_D = c\frac{Y}{Q_A}$$

Similarly, the formula for cross-price elasticity of demand for good A with respect to good B will be

$$C\epsilon_{D_{AB}} = \frac{\partial Q_A}{\partial P_B} \cdot \frac{P_B}{Q_A} = e\frac{P_B}{Q_A}$$

A worked example of these two formulae is given in Maths Case 3.1 in MyEconLab. We can also use calculus to work out the two elasticities for both linear and non-linear demand equations. A worked example of this is given in Maths Case 3.2 in MyEconLab.

[1] Note that in this case we use the symbol '∂' rather than 'd' to represent an infinitely small change. This is the convention when the equation contains more than one independent variable (in this case P_A, Y and P_B). The term $\partial Q_A/\partial Y$ is the 'partial derivative' (see page A:13) and refers to the rate of change of Q_A to just one of the three variables (in this case Y).

Section summary

1. Elasticity is a measure of the responsiveness of demand (or supply) to a change in one of the determinants.

2. It is defined as the proportionate change in quantity demanded (or supplied) divided by the proportionate change in the determinant.

3. If quantity changes proportionately more than the determinant, the figure for elasticity will be greater than 1 (ignoring the sign): it is elastic. If the quantity changes proportionately less than the determinant, the figure for elasticity will be less than 1: it is inelastic. If they change by the same proportion, the elasticity has a value of 1: it is unit elastic.

4. Price elasticity of demand measures the responsiveness of demand to a change in price. Given that demand curves are downward sloping, price elasticity of demand will have a negative value. Demand will be more elastic the greater the number and closeness of substitute goods, the higher the proportion of income spent on the good and the longer the time period that elapses after the change in price.

5. When demand is price elastic, a rise in price will lead to a reduction in total expenditure on the good and hence a reduction in the total revenue of producers.

6. Demand curves normally have different elasticities along their length. We can thus normally refer only to the specific value for elasticity between two points on the curve or at a single point.

7. Elasticity measured between two points is known as arc elasticity. When applied to price elasticity of demand the formula is

$$\frac{\Delta Q_d}{\text{average } Q_d} \div \frac{\Delta P}{\text{average } P}$$

*8. Elasticity measured at a point is known as *point elasticity*. When applied to price elasticity of demand the formula is

$$\frac{dQ}{dP} \times \frac{P}{Q}$$

where dQ/dP is the inverse of the slope of the tangent to the demand curve at the point in question.

9. Price elasticity of supply measures the responsiveness of supply to a change in price. It has a positive value. Supply will be more elastic the less costs per unit rise as output rises and the longer the time period.

10. Income elasticity of demand measures the responsiveness of demand to a change in income. For normal goods it has a positive value. Demand will be more income elastic the more luxurious the good and the less rapidly demand is satisfied as consumption increases. For inferior goods, income elasticity has a negative value.

11. Cross-price elasticity of demand measures the responsiveness of demand for one good to a change in the price of another. For substitute goods the value will be positive; for complements it will be negative. The cross-price elasticity will be higher, the closer the two goods are as substitutes or complements.

3.2 THE TIME DIMENSION

The full adjustment of price, demand and supply to a situation of disequilibrium will not be instantaneous. It is necessary, therefore, to analyse the time path which supply takes in responding to changes in demand, and which demand takes in responding to changes in supply.

Short-run and long-run adjustment

As we saw in the previous section, elasticity varies with the time period under consideration. The reason is that producers and consumers take time to respond to a change in price. The longer the time period, the bigger the response, and thus the greater the elasticity of supply and demand.

This is illustrated in Figures 3.10 and 3.11. In both cases, as equilibrium moves from points a to b to c, there is a large short-run price change (P_1 to P_2) and a small short-run quantity change (Q_1 to Q_2), but a small long-run price change (P_1 to P_3) and a large long-run quantity change (Q_1 to Q_3).

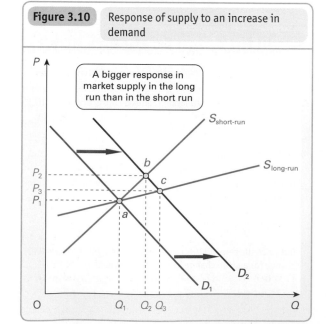

Figure 3.10 Response of supply to an increase in demand

A bigger response in market supply in the long run than in the short run

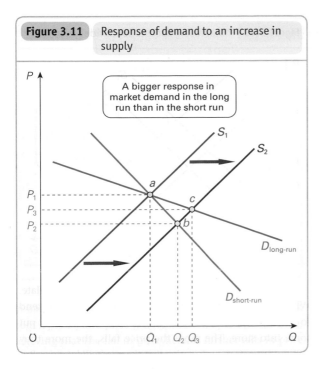

Figure 3.11 Response of demand to an increase in supply

A bigger response in market demand in the long run than in the short run

Price expectations and speculation

In a world of shifting demand and supply curves, prices do not stay the same. Sometimes they go up; sometimes they come down.

If people think prices are likely to change in the foreseeable future, this will affect the behaviour of buyers and sellers *now*. If, for example, it is now December and you are thinking of buying a new television, you might decide to wait until the January sales, and in the meantime make do with your existing set. If, on the other hand, in December you see a summer holiday advertised that you like, you might well book it then and not wait until nearer the summer for fear that the price will have gone up by then. Thus a belief that prices will go up will cause people to buy now; a belief that prices will come down will cause them to wait.

The reverse applies to sellers. If you are thinking of selling your house and prices are falling, you will want to sell it as quickly as possible. If, on the other hand, prices are rising sharply, you will wait as long as possible so as to get the highest price. Thus a belief that prices will come down will cause people to sell now; a belief that prices will go up will cause them to wait.

 KEY IDEA 10

People's actions are influenced by their expectations. People respond not just to what is happening now (such as a change in price), but to what they anticipate will happen in the future.

This behaviour of looking into the future and making buying and selling decisions based on your predictions is called *speculation*. Speculation is often based on current trends in prices. If prices are currently rising, people may try to decide whether they are about to peak and go back down again, or whether they are likely to go on rising. Having made their prediction, they will then act on it. Their actions will then affect demand and supply, which in turn will affect price. Speculation is commonplace in many markets: the stock exchange, the foreign exchange market and the housing market are three examples.

Sometimes people will take advantage of expected price rises purely to make money and have no intention of keeping the item they have bought. For example, if shares in a particular company are expected to rise in price, people may buy them now while they are cheap and sell them later when the price has risen, thereby making a profit from the difference in price.

Similarly, people will sometimes take advantage of expected price reductions by selling something now only to buy it back later. For example, if you own shares and expect their price to fall, you may sell them now and buy them back later when their price has fallen. Again, you make a profit from the difference in price.

Sometimes the term *speculation* is used in this narrower sense of buying (or selling) commodities or financial assets simply to make money from later selling them (or buying them back) again at a higher (or lower) price. The term *speculators* usually refers to people engaged in such activities.

In the extreme case, speculators need not part with any money. If they buy an item and sell it back fairly soon at a higher price, they may be able to use the money from the sale to pay the original seller: just pocketing the difference. Alternatively, speculators may sell an item they do not even possess, as long as they can buy it back in time (at a lower price) to hand it over to the original purchaser. Again, they simply pocket the difference in price.

It may sound as if speculators are on to a good thing, and often they are, but speculation does carry risks: the predictions of individual speculators may turn out to be wrong, and then they could make losses rather than profits.

Nevertheless, speculators on average tend to gain rather than lose. The reason is that speculation tends to be *self-fulfilling*. In other words, the actions of speculators tend to bring about the very effect on prices that they had anticipated. For example, if speculators believe that the price of Barclays

Definitions

Speculation Where people make buying or selling decisions based on their anticipations of future prices.

Speculators People who buy (or sell) commodities or financial assets with the intention of profiting by selling them (or buying them back) at a later date at a higher (lower) price.

Self-fulfilling speculation The actions of speculators tend to cause the very effect that they had anticipated.

BOX 3.4   SHORT SELLING

Gambling on a fall in share prices

A form of speculation that can be very damaging to stock markets is the practice of *short selling*. This is where people take advantage of anticipated falls in share prices by selling shares they do not possess. How does this work?

Assume that a share price is currently £10 per share and traders on the stock market believe that the price is about to fall. They want to take advantage of this but don't possess any shares. What they do is borrow shares from dealers who do own some and agree to return them on a specified date. They pay a fee for doing this. In the meantime they sell the shares on the market at the current price of £10 and wait for it to fall. They are now 'short' of the shares (i.e. they don't possess them but still owe them).

Assume that just before the agreed time comes for returning the shares the price has fallen to £8. The trader then buys the shares, returns them to the dealer who had lent them and pockets the difference of £2 (minus the fee).

Although anyone can short sell shares, it is largely traders from various financial institutions who engage in this practice. Huge bonuses can be earned from their employers if the short selling is profitable. This encourages an atmosphere of risk taking and looking to short-term gains rather than providing long-term capital to firms.

Short selling in the banking crisis of 2008

The practice of short selling had become rife in recent years and added to the instability of markets, driving share prices down that were anticipated to fall. This was a particular problem in 2008, when worries about bad debts and losses in the banking sector led many traders to short-sell the shares of banks and other financial institutions felt to be most at risk.

The short selling of Halifax Bank of Scotland (HBOS) shares in September 2008 was a major contributing factor to the collapse in its share price. HBOS, the UK's largest mortgage lender, had been suffering losses as a result of falling house prices and difficulties of many house owners in keeping up with their monthly mortgage payments. The share price plummeted by over 70 per cent in the space of a few days. The fall was driven on by speculation, much of it short selling. On 17 September it was announced that HBOS would be taken over by Lloyds TSB.

Concerns about the practice of short selling driving instability in financial markets have led a number of governments – or agencies acting on their behalf – to ban the practice. In September 2008 the Financial Services Authority, the UK industry's regulator at the time, announced a four-month ban on the practice. At the same time, the US financial regulator, the Securities and Exchange Commission, announced a similar move. Both these bans were imposed for a matter of months, but Denmark held a similar policy for more than two years.

In May 2010 the German government put in place a ban on short selling all EU government debt and bank shares and, in August 2011, various European countries banned the short selling of bank shares following dramatic falls in bank share prices.

Is short selling always profitable?

Short selling, as with other forms of speculation, is a form of gambling. If you gamble on a price fall and the price does fall, your gamble pays off and you make a profit. If you get it wrong, however, and the price rises, you will make a loss. In the case of short selling, you would have to buy the shares (to give back to the lender) at a higher price than you sold them.

This is just what happened in September 2008. With central banks around the world supporting markets, with the US government announcing that it would take over the bad debts of banks and with future short selling temporarily banned, share prices rapidly increased. The FTSE rose by a record 8.8 per cent on 19 September. Those with 'short positions' (i.e. those who had sold shares they had borrowed) then had to buy them back at a much higher price. Losses of hundreds of millions of pounds were made by short sellers. But they gained little sympathy from the general public, who blamed their 'greed' for much of the falls in share prices of the previous weeks.

 Why would owners of shares, such as pension funds, lend them to short sellers rather than selling the shares themselves and then buying them back later?

---

outcome is known. Risk itself is a measure of the *variability* of an outcome. For example, if you bet £1 on the toss of a coin, such that heads you win £1 and tails you lose £1, then the variability is –£1 to +£1.

The second form of gamble is the more usual. This is where the odds are not known or are known only roughly. Gambling on the stock exchange is like this. You may have a good idea that a share will go up in price, but is it a 90 per cent chance, an 80 per cent chance or what? You are not certain. Gambling under this sort of condition is known as operating under **uncertainty**. *This is when the probability of an outcome is not known.*

Definitions

Short selling (or **shorting**) Where investors borrow an asset, such as shares, oil contracts or foreign currency; sell the asset, hoping the price will soon fall; then buy it back later and return it to the lender. Assuming the price has fallen, the short seller will make a profit of the difference (minus any fees). There is always the danger, however, that the price may have risen, in which case the short seller will make a loss.

Uncertainty When an outcome may or may not occur and its probability of occurring is not known.

BOX 3.5 DEALING IN FUTURES MARKETS

A way of reducing uncertainty

One way of reducing or even eliminating uncertainty is by dealing in *futures* or *forward markets*. Let us examine first the activities of sellers and then those of buyers.

Sellers

Suppose you are a farmer and want to store grain to sell at some time in the future, expecting to get a better price then than now. The trouble is that there is a chance that the price will go down. Given this uncertainty, you may be unwilling to take a gamble.

An answer to your problem is provided by the *commodity futures market*. This is a market where prices are agreed between sellers and buyers today for delivery at some specified date in the future.

For example, if it is 20 October today, you could be quoted a price today for delivery in six months' time (i.e. on 20 April). This is known as the six-month *future price*. Assume that the six-month future price is £160 per tonne. If you agree to this price and make a six-month forward contract, you are agreeing to sell a specified amount of wheat at £160 on 20 April. No matter what happens to the *spot price* (i.e. the current market price) in the meantime, your selling price has been agreed. The spot price could have fallen to £140 (or risen to £180) by April, but your selling price when 20 April arrives is fixed at £160. There is thus *no risk to you whatsoever of the price going down*. You will, of course, have lost out if the spot price is *more* than £160 in April.

Buyers

Now suppose that you are a flour miller. In order to plan your expenditures, you would like to know the price you will have to pay for wheat, not just today, but also at various future dates. In other words, if you want to take delivery of wheat at some time in the future, you would like a price quoted *now*. You would like the risks removed of prices going *up*.

Let us assume that today (20 October) you want to *buy* the same amount of wheat on 20 April that a farmer wishes to sell on that same date. If you agree to the £160 future price, a future contract can be made with the farmer. You are then guaranteed that purchase price, no matter what happens to the spot price in the meantime. There is thus *no risk to you whatsoever of the price going up*. You will, of course, have lost out if the spot price is *less* than £160 in April.

The determination of the future price

Prices in the futures market are determined in the same way as in other markets: by demand and supply. For example, the six-month wheat price or the three-month coffee price will be that which equates the demand for those futures with the supply. If the five-month sugar price is currently £220 per tonne and people expect by then, because of an anticipated good beet harvest, that the spot price for sugar will be £170 per tonne, there will be few who want to buy the futures at £220 (and many who want to sell). This excess of supply of futures over demand will push the price down.

Speculators

Many people operate in the futures market who never actually handle the commodities themselves. They are neither producers nor users of the commodities. They merely speculate. Such speculators may be individuals, but they are more likely to be financial institutions.

Let us take a simple example. Suppose that the six-month (April) coffee price is £1300 per tonne and that you, as a speculator, believe that the spot price of coffee is likely to rise above that level between now (October) and six months' time. You thus decide to buy 20 tonnes of April coffee futures now.

But you have no intention of taking delivery. After four months, let us say, true to your prediction, the spot price (February) has risen and as a result the April price (and other future prices) have risen too. You thus decide to *sell* 20 tonnes of April (two-month) coffee futures, whose price, let us say, is £1500. You are now 'covered'.

When April comes, what happens? You have agreed to buy 20 tonnes of coffee at £1300 per tonne and to sell 20 tonnes of coffee at £1500 per tonne. All you do is to hand the futures contract to buy to the person to whom you agreed to sell. They sort out delivery between them and you make £200 per tonne profit.

If, however, your prediction had been wrong and the price had *fallen*, you would have made a loss. You would have been forced to sell coffee contracts at a lower price than you bought them.

Speculators in the futures market thus incur risks, unlike the sellers and buyers of the commodities, for whom the futures market eliminates risk. Financial institutions offering futures contracts will charge for the service: for taking on the risks.

 If speculators believed that the price of cocoa in six months was going to be below the six-month future price quoted today, how would they act?

Definitions

Futures or forward market A market in which contracts are made to buy or sell at some future date at a price agreed today.

Future price A price agreed today at which an item (e.g. commodities) will be exchanged at some set date in the future.

Spot price The current market price.

You may well disapprove of gambling and want to dismiss people who engage in it as foolish or morally wrong. But 'gambling' is not just confined to horses, cards, roulette and the like. Risk and uncertainty pervade the whole of economic life, and decisions are constantly having to be made whose outcome cannot be known for certain. Even the most morally upright person will still have to decide which career to go into, whether and when to buy a house, or even something as trivial as whether or not to take an umbrella when going out. Each of these decisions and thousands of others are made under conditions of uncertainty (or occasionally risk).

KEY IDEA 11

People's actions are influenced by their attitudes towards risk. Many decisions are taken under conditions of risk or uncertainty. Generally, the lower the probability of (or the more uncertain) the desired outcome of an action, the less likely people will be to undertake the action.

Give some examples of decisions you have taken recently that were made under conditions of uncertainty. With hindsight do you think you made the right decisions?

We shall be examining how risk and uncertainty affect economic decisions on several occasions throughout the text. For example, in Chapter 4 we will see how it affects people's attitudes and actions as consumers and how taking out insurance can help to reduce their uncertainty. At this point, however, let us focus on firms' attitudes when supplying goods.

Stock holding as a way of reducing the problem of uncertainty

A simple way that suppliers can reduce the problem of uncertainty is by holding stocks. Take the case of the wheat farmers we saw in the previous section. At the time when they are planting the wheat in the spring, they are uncertain as to what the price of wheat will be when they bring it to market. If they keep no stores of wheat, they will just have to accept whatever the market price happens to be at harvest time. If, however, they have storage facilities, they can put the wheat into store if the price is low and then wait until the price goes up. Alternatively, if the price of wheat is high at harvest time, they can sell the wheat straight away. In other words, they can choose the time to sell.

Section summary

1. A complete understanding of markets must take into account the time dimension.

2. Given that producers and consumers take time to respond fully to price changes, we can identify different equilibria after the lapse of different lengths of time. Generally, short-run supply and demand tend to be less price elastic than long-run supply and demand. As a result, any shifts in *D* or *S* curves tend to have a relatively bigger effect on price in the short run and a relatively bigger effect on quantity in the long run.

3. People often anticipate price changes and this will affect the amount they demand or supply. This

   speculation will tend to stabilise price fluctuations if people believe that the price changes are only temporary. However, speculation will tend to destabilise these fluctuations (i.e. make them more severe) if people believe that prices are likely to continue to move in the same direction as at present (at least for some time).

4. Many economic decisions are taken under conditions of risk or uncertainty. Uncertainty over future prices can be tackled by holding stocks. When prices are low, the stocks can be built up. When they are high, stocks can be sold.

3.3 INDIRECT TAXES

The effect of imposing taxes on goods

In section 2.4 we started looking at government intervention in markets and considered the impact of setting maximum and minimum prices. We now turn to another example of government intervention – the imposition of taxes on goods.

TC 6 p55

These *indirect taxes*, as they are called, include taxes such as value added tax (VAT) and excise duties on cigarettes, petrol and alcoholic drinks.

These taxes can be a fixed amount per unit sold – a *specific tax*. An example is the tax per litre of petrol.

Definitions

Indirect tax A tax on the expenditure on goods. Indirect taxes include value added tax (VAT) and duties on tobacco, alcoholic drinks and petrol. These taxes are not paid directly by the consumer, but indirectly via the sellers of the good. Indirect taxes contrast with direct taxes (such as income tax) which are paid directly out of people's incomes.

Specific tax An indirect tax of a fixed sum per unit sold.

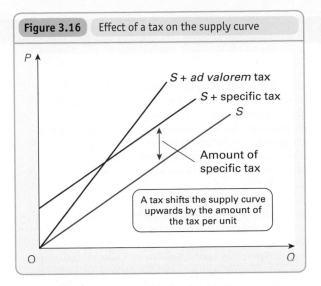
Alternatively, they can be a percentage of the price or value added at each stage of production – an **ad valorem tax**. An example is VAT.

When a tax is levied on a good, this has the effect of shifting the supply curve upwards by the amount of the tax (see Figure 3.16). In the case of a specific tax, it will be a parallel shift, since the amount of the tax is the same at all prices. In the case of an *ad valorem* tax, the curve will *swing* upwards. At a zero price there would be no tax and hence no shift in the supply curve. As price rises, so the gap between the original and new supply curves will widen, since a given *percentage* tax will be a larger *absolute* amount the higher the price.

But why does the supply curve shift upwards by the amount of the tax? This is illustrated in Figure 3.17. To be persuaded to produce the same quantity as before the imposition of the tax (i.e. Q_1), firms must now receive a price which allows them fully to recoup the tax they have to pay (i.e. $P_1 + \text{tax}$).

Figure 3.17 Effect of a tax on price and quantity

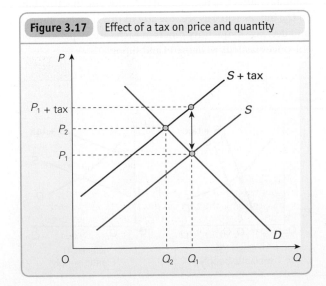

*LOOKING AT THE MATHS

Assume that a specific tax per unit of t is imposed on producers of a good. This is then added to the pre-tax price of P_1. The price paid by consumers is thus $P_1 + t$.

Assuming linear demand and supply equations (see page 48), these can be written as

$$Q_D = a - b(P_1 + t) \tag{1}$$

$$Q_S = c + dP_1 \tag{2}$$

In equilibrium, $Q_D = Q_S$. Thus

$$a - b(P_1 + t) = c + dP_1$$

We can rearrange this equation to give

$$bP_1 + dP_1 = a - c - bt$$

Thus

$$P_1 = \frac{a - c - bt}{b + d} \tag{3}$$

Take the following example. If the demand and supply equations were

$$Q_D = 120 - 10(P_1 + t) \tag{4}$$

and

$$Q_S = 10 + 5P_1 \tag{5}$$

and $t = 2$, then from equation (3)

$$P_1 = \frac{120 - 10 - (10 \times 2)}{10 + 5} = 6$$

and from equations (4) and (5)

$$Q_D = 120 - 80 = Q_S = 10 + 30 = 40$$

The market price will be

$$P_1 + t = 6 + 2 = 8$$

 Assuming that the pre-tax equations were

$$Q_D = 120 + 10P$$

and

$$Q_S = 10 - 5P$$

what is (a) the consumer share of the tax and (b) the producer share?

The effect of the tax is to raise price and reduce quantity. Price will not rise by the full amount of the tax, however, because the demand curve is downward sloping. In Figure 3.17, price rises only to P_2. Thus the burden or **incidence** of such taxes is distributed between consumers and producers. Consumers

KI 5
p22

Definitions

Ad valorem tax An indirect tax of a certain percentage of the price of the good.

Incidence of tax The distribution of the burden of tax between sellers and buyers.

BOX 3.6 ASHES TO ASHES?

A moral dilemma of tobacco taxes

Revenue from tobacco taxes

Consider the following dilemma. Cigarettes have a fairly price-inelastic demand (approximately −0.6: see below), and thus placing a tax on them is an effective means of generating revenue. In the UK in 2013/14 tobacco duties raised £9.7 billion or 1.7 per cent of total tax revenue. This compares with 4.6 per cent for fuel duties and 1.8 per cent for alcohol duties. (Note that these figures exclude the additional revenue raised through VAT.)

Clearly, then, tobacco duties are a major source of revenue for the government. The less people are put off smoking by the tax, the more revenue will be raised. In fact, if the government were to encourage people to smoke, it would raise more revenue. The dilemma is that there is strong pressure on governments around the world to discourage people from smoking and the more governments succeed in this, the less will be their tax revenue.

This is not a new problem. Cabinet papers released in May 2008 revealed that in 1956 the Chancellor, Harold Macmillan, argued against issuing a government health warning about cigarettes, despite being presented with statistical evidence that it was harmful. He was concerned that an official warning would lead to reduced tax revenue from tobacco.

The costs of smoking

But would a reduction in smoking represent a cost to the government? Clearly it would represent a cut in tax revenue, but it would also reduce spending on smoking-related diseases. According to estimates by the Department of Public Health at Oxford University,[1] the amount spent by the National Health Service on smoking-related illness is over £5 billion per year. This, however, is less than the

£9.7 billion revenue raised from tobacco taxes. Clearly smokers more than pay for their own treatment. Indeed, the state and the NHS may acquire further financial benefit from smokers. The benefits stem from the fact that smokers die younger. The NHS gains from avoiding many of the high-cost treatments required by elderly patients and the state gains from having to pay out less in pensions and other benefits.

The costs of smoking, however, are not limited to health-care costs and other costs to the Exchequer. There are also costs in terms of lost output as a result of smoking-related illnesses. Then there are the human costs from suffering and deaths. Smoking kills over 100 000 people per year in the UK, with an additional 3000 or more killed by the effects of passive smoking. More than 17 000 children each year are admitted to hospital because of the effects of passive smoking.

The effects of raising tobacco taxes

So perhaps raising tobacco taxes would be doubly beneficial. Not only would it raise revenue, but also it would help to back up other anti-smoking measures. There are, however, three problems with this.

The first concerns smuggling and tobacco-related crime. Smuggled cigarettes account for around 12 per cent of the UK market. Not only is the high price differential between tobacco prices in the UK and abroad encouraging criminality, but estimates suggest that smuggled tobacco products are losing the government around £2 billion each year in tax revenue.

Another issue concerns the poorest households. The poorer people are, the larger the proportion of their income

pay to the extent that price rises. Producers pay to the extent that this rise in price is not sufficient to cover the tax.

Elasticity and the incidence of taxation

TC 7 **p72** The incidence of indirect taxes depends on the elasticity of demand and supply of the commodity in question.

Consider cases (1)–(4) in Figure 3.18. In each of the diagrams (which are all drawn to the same scale), the size of the tax is the same: the supply curve shifts upwards by the same amount. Price rises to P_2 in each case and quantity falls to Q_2; but, as you can see, the size of this increase in price and decrease in quantity differs in each case, depending on the price elasticity of demand and supply.

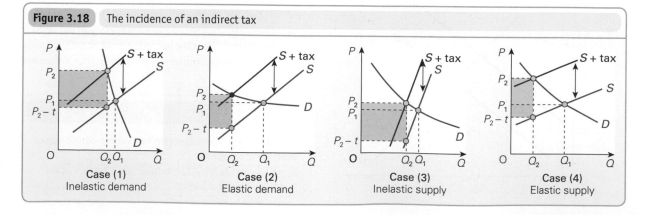

Figure 3.18   The incidence of an indirect tax

Case (1) Inelastic demand   Case (2) Elastic demand   Case (3) Inelastic supply   Case (4) Elastic supply

is spent on tobacco (and hence tobacco taxes). The poorest 10 per cent of the population spend approximately 15 per cent of their disposable income on tobacco. This compares with a figure of just 2 per cent for the population as a whole. As such, the higher the tax on tobacco, the more it redistributes incomes from the poor to the rich.

The third problem is that raising tobacco taxes does *not* have a very marked effect on the consumption of cigarettes; taxes are an ineffective way of discouraging smoking. Why is this? Think back to the discussion on elasticity in section 3.1; demand for cigarettes is inelastic because there are few substitutes and cigarette smokers are often addicted to their habit. A study by HM Revenue and Customs in December 2010[2] estimated the short-run elasticity of demand at approximately −0.57, with long-run elasticity of −1.05. The work suggests that, with the long-run elasticity figure, a 1 per cent increase in specific duty will raise an extra £25 million each year.

Thus when taxes on tobacco are raised there are three consequences: smuggling is more profitable; low-income households are affected more than high-income households; and, finally, tax revenues go up substantially while smoking is reduced only a little.

The use of alternative policies

This dilemma helps explain the move away from using taxes as a method of reducing smoking and towards policies that more directly impact on smokers' behaviour. In 2006 and 2007 legislation came into force in the UK banning smoking in workplaces and public places such as shops, bars and restaurants. This followed similar moves in other countries and was supported by an earlier report by the Chief Medical Officer,[3] which suggested that such a ban would save up to £2.7 billion from a healthier workforce. More recently there have been moves to ban smoking in cars and the use of e-cigarettes in public places.

Early indications are that the ban has had some impact on the numbers of smokers, but that a substantial minority continue to smoke. In 2013 just under 20 per cent of all adults were smokers. If smokers were to give up in substantial numbers then the government would find itself having to look elsewhere for a source of replacement tax revenue.

1. *You are a government minister. What arguments might you put forward in favour of maximising the revenue from cigarette taxation?*
2. *What has been the likely impact on businesses and individuals of the ban on smoking in public places?*
3. *A 2010 HMRC study on smoking estimates the long-term elasticity of demand as −1.05, with a short-term elasticity of −0.57. Explain these figures.*
4. *Many people think that if tobacco were to be discovered today it would be an illegal substance, as is the case with cannabis. What problems would face a government trying to ban smoking completely (see section 3.4)?*

[1] S. Allender, R. Balakrishnan, P. Scarborough, P. Webster and M. Rayne, 'The burden of smoking-related ill health in the United Kingdom', *Tobacco Control*, 2009; 0: 1–7 (BMJ).
[2] Magdalena Cuzbek and Surjinder Johal, *Econometric Analysis of Cigarette Consumption in the UK* (HMRC Working Paper, 2010).
[3] Annual Report of the Chief Medical Officer 2003 (www.publications.doh. gov.uk/cmo/annualreport2003/smokefree.htm).

The total tax revenue is given by the amount of tax per unit (the vertical difference between the two supply curves) multiplied by the new amount sold (Q_2). This is shown as the total shaded area in each case in Figure 3.18.

The rise in price from P_1 to P_2 multiplied by the number of goods sold (Q_2) (the pink area) is the amount of the tax passed on to consumers and thus represents the **consumers' share** of the tax. The remainder (the green area) is the **producers' share**. This is the amount by which the producers' net price ($P_2 - t$) is below the original price (P_1) multiplied by Q_2.

The following conclusions can be drawn:

- Quantity will fall less, and hence tax revenue for the government will be greater, the less elastic are demand and supply (cases (1) and (3)).
- Price will rise more, and hence the consumers' share of the tax will be larger, the less elastic is demand and the more elastic is supply (cases (1) and (4)).
- Price will rise less, and hence the producers' share will be larger, the more elastic is demand and the less elastic is supply (cases (2) and (3)).

Cigarettes, petrol and alcohol have been major targets for indirect taxes. Demand for each of them is high and fairly inelastic. Thus the tax will not curb demand greatly. They are good sources, therefore, of tax revenue to the government (see Box 3.6).

Supply tends to be more elastic in the long run than in the short run. Assume that a tax is imposed on a good that was previously untaxed. How will the incidence of this tax change as time passes? How will the incidence be affected if demand too becomes more elastic over time?

Definitions

Consumers' share of a tax on a good The proportion of the revenue from a tax on a good that arises from an increase in the price of the good.

Producers' share of a tax on a good The proportion of the revenue from a tax on a good that arises from a reduction in the price to the producer (after the payment of the tax).

goes with illegal products (such as drugs gangs, violence and money laundering) and the resulting costs of law enforcement. It would also bring in tax revenue for the government.

The reason given by governments for keeping drugs illegal is that it sends out important messages to society and reflects what the majority wants. Taxing something, by contrast, implies that the product is acceptable. Also, if taxes were to be set high enough to reduce legal consumption to a politically acceptable level, there would then develop a large illegal market in the drugs as people sought to evade the tax.

What are the arguments for and against making the sale of alcoholic drinks illegal? To what extent can an economist help to resolve the issue?

Section summary

1. Sometimes the government will want to avoid allocation by the market for a particular good or service. Examples include things provided free at the point of use and products that are prohibited by the government.

2. If products are provided free to consumers, demand is likely to exceed supply. This is a particular problem in the case of health care, where demand is growing rapidly.

3. If products such as drugs are prohibited, an illegal market is likely to develop. Demand and supply would be less than in a free market. The price could be either higher or lower, depending on who faces the harshest penalties and the greatest likelihood of being caught – suppliers or users.

4. A similar reduction in consumption could be achieved by using taxation. Other effects, however, such as on the price, on allied crime and on public perceptions of the acceptability of the product, will be different.

3.5 AGRICULTURE AND AGRICULTURAL POLICY

If markets for agricultural products were free from government intervention, they would be about as close as one could get to perfect competition in the real world. There are thousands of farmers, each insignificantly small relative to the total market. As a result, farmers are price takers.

Yet despite this high degree of competition, there is more government intervention in agriculture throughout the world than in virtually any other industry. For example, nearly half of the EU budget is spent on agricultural support. Agricultural markets therefore pose something of a paradox. If they are so perfect, why is there so much government intervention?

Why intervene?

The following are the most commonly cited problems of a free market in agricultural products.

Agricultural prices are subject to considerable fluctuations. This has a number of effects:

- Fluctuating prices cause fluctuating farm incomes. In some years, farm incomes may be very low.
- In other years, the consumer will suffer by having to pay very high prices.
- Fluctuating prices make the prediction of future prices very difficult. This in turn makes rational economic decision making very difficult. How is a farmer to choose which of two or more crops to plant if their prices cannot be predicted?

- This uncertainty may discourage farmers from making long-term investment plans. A farmer may be reluctant to invest in, say, a new milking parlour if in a couple of years it might be more profitable to switch to arable farming. A lack of investment by farmers will reduce the growth of efficiency in agriculture.

Low incomes for those in farming. Over the years, farm incomes have tended to decline relative to those in other sectors of the economy. What is more, farmers have very little market power. A particular complaint of farmers is that they have to buy their inputs (tractors, fertilisers, etc.) from non-competitive suppliers who charge high prices. Then they often have to sell their produce at very low prices to food processors, packers, distributors and supermarkets. Farmers thus feel squeezed from both directions.

Traditional rural ways of life may be destroyed. The pressure on farm incomes may cause unemployment and bankruptcies; smaller farms may be taken over by larger ones; village life may be threatened – with the break-up of communities and the closure of schools, shops and other amenities.

Competition from abroad. Farming may well be threatened by cheap food imports from abroad. This may drive farmers out of business.

Against all these arguments must be set the argument that intervention involves economic costs. These may be costs to the taxpayer in providing financial support to farmers, or costs to the consumer in higher prices of foodstuffs, or costs to the economy as a whole by keeping resources locked into agriculture that could have been more efficiently used elsewhere.

Then there is the question of recent trends in food prices. With the rise in demand for food from rapidly growing countries, such as China and India, and with the increased use of land for growing biofuels rather than food crops, world food prices have risen. Farming in many parts of the world is becoming more profitable.

Causes of short-term price fluctuations

Supply problems.   A field is not like a machine. It cannot produce a precisely predictable amount of output according to the inputs fed in. The harvest is affected by a number of unpredictable factors such as the weather, pests and diseases. Fluctuating harvests mean that farmers' incomes will fluctuate.

Demand problems.   Food, being a basic necessity of life, has no substitute. If the price of food in general goes up, people cannot switch to an alternative: they have either to pay the higher price or to consume less food. They might consume a bit less, but not much! The price elasticity for food in general, therefore, is very low, as Table 3.1 shows.

It is not quite so low for individual foodstuffs because, if the price of one goes up, people can always switch to an alternative. If beef goes up in price, people can buy pork or lamb instead. Nevertheless, certain foodstuffs still have a low price elasticity, especially if they are considered to be basic foods rather than luxuries, there are no close

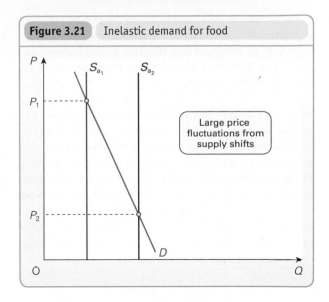

Figure 3.21   Inelastic demand for food

substitutes, or they account for a relatively small portion of consumers' income.

With an inelastic demand curve, any fluctuations in supply will cause large fluctuations in price. This is illustrated in Figure 3.21.

 Why is the supply curve drawn as a vertical straight line in Figure 3.21?

Causes of declining farm incomes

Demand problems.   There is a limit to the amount people wish to eat. As people get richer, they might buy better cuts of meat, or more convenience foods, but they will spend very little extra on basic foodstuffs. Their income elasticity of demand for basic foods is very low (see Table 3.1).

 Why don't farmers benefit from a high income elasticity of demand for convenience foods?

This very low income elasticity of demand has a crucial effect on farm incomes. It means that a rise in national income of 1 per cent leads to a rise in food consumption of considerably less than 1 per cent. As a result, total farm incomes will grow much more slowly than the incomes of other sectors, farmers' incomes will grow less rapidly than those of the owners of other businesses, and farm workers' wages will grow less rapidly than those of other workers.

Supply problems.   Farming productivity has grown dramatically over the years as farmers have invested in new technology and improved farming methods. (Increases in crop yields in various EU countries are shown in Table 3.2 on page 92.) But, given the price-inelastic demand for food, increased supply will have the effect of driving down agricultural prices, thus largely offsetting any reduction in costs. And given the income-inelastic demand for food, the long-term rise in demand will be less than the long-term rise in supply.

Table 3.1	Price and income elasticities of demand in the UK for various foodstuffs	
Foodstuff	**Price elasticity of demand (average 2001–9)**	**Income elasticity of demand (1998–2000)**
Milk	−0.70	−0.17
Cheese	−0.60	0.23
Poultry	−0.94	0.16
Lamb	−0.59	0.15
Pork	−0.77	0.13
Fish	−0.36	0.27
Eggs	−0.57	−0.01
Fresh vegetables	−1.00	0.22
Potatoes	−0.51	0.09
Fresh fruit	−0.99	0.30
Bananas	−0.62	0.12
Canned and dried fruit	−0.78	0.37
Fruit juice	−0.79	0.45
All foods	−0.07	0.20

Sources: Price elasticity data: Based on and averaged from multiple tables by JS in Richard Tiffin, Kelvin Balcombe, Matthew Salois and Ariane Kehlbacher, *Estimating Food and Drink Elasticities* (University of Reading, 2011); Income elasticity data: *National Food Survey 2000* (*National Statistics*, 2001), extracted by JS from Tables 6.3 and 6.5.

KI 9
p71

TC 7
p72

Figure 3.22 shows a basic foodstuff like potatoes or other vegetables. Rising productivity leads to an increase in supply from S_1 to S_2. But given that demand is price inelastic and shifts only slightly to the right over time, from D_1 to D_2, price falls from P_1 to P_2.

As we saw above, this national effect of low price and income elasticities of demand and rising supply has been offset in recent years by growing *world* demand for food and problems with world supply, such as poor harvests, rising input costs (such as diesel and fertilisers) and the diversion of land to growing biofuels – in 2013, some 35 per cent of the US maize (corn) crop was being used for ethanol production. The effect of all this is a substantial increase in the prices of many foodstuffs, and in particular wheat, rice, maize and soya.

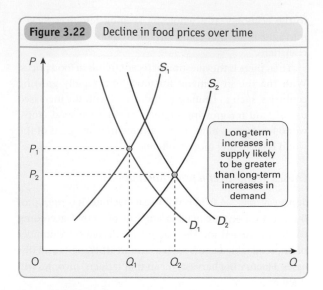

Figure 3.22　Decline in food prices over time

Long-term increases in supply likely to be greater than long-term increases in demand

---

BOX 3.7　THE FALLACY OF COMPOSITION

Or when good is bad

Ask farmers whether they would like a good crop of potatoes this year, or whether they would rather their fields be ravaged by pests and disease, and the answer is obvious. After all, who would wish disaster upon themselves!

And yet what applies to an individual farmer does not apply to farmers as a whole. Disaster for all may turn out not to be disaster at all.

Why should this be? The answer has to do with price elasticity. The demand for food is highly price inelastic. A fall in supply, due to a poor harvest, will therefore cause a proportionately larger rise in price. Farmers' incomes will therefore rise, not fall.

Look at diagram (a). Farmer Giles is a price taker. If he alone has a bad harvest, price will not change. He simply sells less (Q_2) and thus earns less. His revenue falls by the amount of the shaded area. But if all farmers have a bad harvest the picture is quite different, as shown in diagram (b). Supply falls from Q_1 to Q_2, and consequently price rises from P_1 to P_2. Revenue thus rises from areas (1 + 2) to areas (1 + 3).

(b) *All farmers*

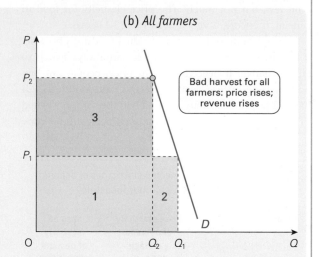

Bad harvest for all farmers: price rises; revenue rises

And so what applies to a single farmer in isolation (a fall in revenue) does not apply to farmers in general. This is known as the 'fallacy of composition'.

KEY IDEA 12　*The fallacy of composition.* What applies in one case will not necessarily apply when repeated in all cases.

(a) *Farmer Giles*

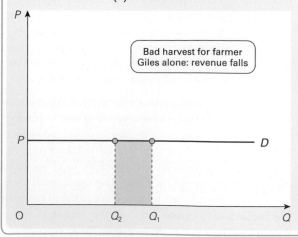

Bad harvest for farmer Giles alone: revenue falls

? 　1.　Can you think of any other (non-farming) examples of the fallacy of composition?
　　2.　Would the above arguments apply in the case of foodstuffs that can be imported as well as being produced at home?

Government intervention

There are five main types of government intervention that can be used to ease the problems for farmers.

Buffer stocks

Buffer stocks involve the government buying food and placing it in store when harvests are good, and then releasing the food back onto the market when harvests are bad. They can thus only be used with food that can be stored: non-perishable foods, such as grain; or food that can be put into frozen storage, such as butter. The idea of buffer stocks is a very ancient one, as Case Study 3.6 in MyEconLab, Seven years of plenty and seven years of famine, demonstrates.

What the government does is to fix a price. Assume that this is P_g in Figure 3.23. At this price demand is Q_{d_1}. If there is a good harvest (S_{a_1}), the government buys up the surplus, $Q_{s_1} - Q_d$, and puts it into store. If there is a bad harvest (S_{a_2}), it releases $Q_d - Q_{s_2}$ from the store onto the market.

This system clearly stabilises price, at P_g. At this price, though, farm incomes will still fluctuate with the size of the harvest. It is possible, however, to have a buffer stock system that stabilises *incomes*. Such a system is examined in Case Study 3.6 in MyEconLab, Buffer stocks to stabilise farm incomes.

To prevent stores mounting over time, the government price will have to be the one that balances demand and supply over the years. Surpluses in good years will have to match shortages in bad years. Buffer stocks, therefore, can only *stabilise* prices or incomes; they do not *increase* farm incomes over the long term.

Subsidies

The government can pay subsidies or grant tax relief to farmers to compensate for low market prices. Subsidies can be used to increase farm incomes as well as to stabilise them. The simplest form of subsidy is one known as **direct income support** or **direct aid**. Here farmers are paid a fixed sum of

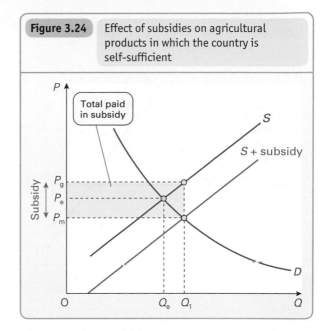

Figure 3.24 Effect of subsidies on agricultural products in which the country is self-sufficient

money irrespective of output. Given that such subsidies are unrelated to output, they do not provide an incentive to produce more.

An alternative system is to pay a subsidy *per unit of output*. This, of course, will encourage farmers to produce more, which in turn will depress the market price.

Figure 3.24 illustrates the case of an agricultural product in which the country is self-sufficient. Without a subsidy the market price would be P_e, where supply equals demand.

Assume now that the government wishes farmers to receive a price of P_g. If farmers do receive this price, they will plan to increase production to Q_1, which will push the market price down to P_m. The size of the subsidy that the government must pay, therefore, will be $P_g - P_m$. The total amount of taxpayers' money spent will be the shaded area. The effect of the subsidy is to shift the effective supply curve downwards by the amount of the subsidy, to $S +$ subsidy.

When some of the product is imported, the effect is slightly different. Let us assume, for simplicity, that a country is a price taker in world markets. It will face a horizontal world supply curve of the product at the world price. In other words, consumers can buy all they want at the world price. In Figure 3.25 the world price is P_w. Without a subsidy, domestic supply is Q_{s_1}. Domestic demand is Q_d. Imports are therefore the difference: $Q_d - Q_{s_1}$.

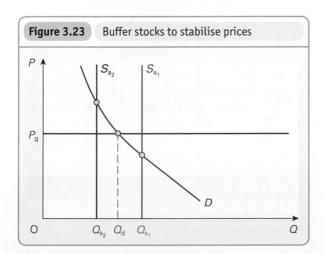

Figure 3.23 Buffer stocks to stabilise prices

Definitions

Buffer stocks Stocks of a product used to stabilise its price. In years of abundance, the stocks are built up. In years of low supply, stocks are released onto the market.

Direct income support or **direct aid** A fixed grant to farmers that does not vary with current output. It may be based on acreage, number of livestock or past output.

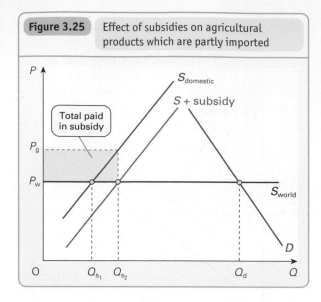

Figure 3.25 Effect of subsidies on agricultural products which are partly imported

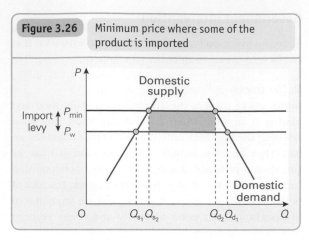

Figure 3.26 Minimum price where some of the product is imported

Assume now that the government wants farmers to receive a price of P_g. At that price, domestic supply increases to Q_{s_2}, but the price paid by the consumer does not fall. It remains at P_w. The subsidy paid per unit is $P_g - P_w$. The cost to the taxpayer is again shown by the shaded area.

A problem with subsidies of a fixed amount per unit is that the price the farmer receives will fluctuate along with the market price. An alternative, therefore, would be to let the size of the subsidy vary with the market price. The lower the price, the bigger the subsidy.

An advantage of subsidies is that they result in lower prices for the consumer. On the other hand, they have to be paid from tax revenues and therefore result in higher taxes.

High minimum prices

If the government considers agricultural prices to be too low, it can set a minimum price for each product above the free-market level. This was the traditional approach adopted in the EU. In recent years, however, forms of intervention in the EU have become more diverse.

The effect of high minimum prices will vary between products, depending on whether the country is a net importer or self-sufficient. Let us consider each case in turn.

Agricultural products where the country is a net importer. Assuming that the minimum price is above the world price, the government will need to impose customs duties (known alternatively as *tariffs* or *import levies*) on imported products to bring them up to the required price. Given that the world price will fluctuate, these import levies would need to be variable.

The effects of this system are illustrated in Figure 3.26. If trade took place freely at the world price P_w, Q_{d_1} would be demanded and Q_{s_1} supplied domestically. The difference $(Q_{d_1} - Q_{s_1})$ would be imported.

If a minimum price P_{min} is now set and a levy imposed on imports to raise their price to P_{min}, domestic prices will also rise to this level. Demand will fall to Q_{d_2}. Domestic supply will rise to Q_{s_2}. Imports will fall to $Q_{d_2} - Q_{s_2}$. The amount paid in import levies is shown by the shaded area.

Agricultural products where the country is self-sufficient. The effects of a minimum price in this situation are illustrated in Figure 3.27. Assume that the world price is P_w. This will be the equilibrium price, since any domestic surplus at P_w (i.e. $b - a$) will be exported at that price.

Now assume that the government sets a minimum price of P_{min}. Given that this is above the equilibrium (world) price, there will be an unsold surplus of $d - e$ (i.e. $Q_{s_2} - Q_{d_2}$).

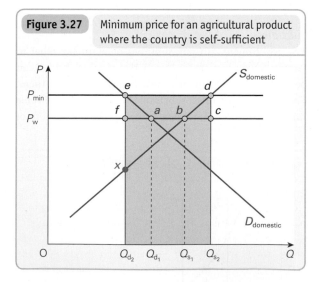

Figure 3.27 Minimum price for an agricultural product where the country is self-sufficient

Definition

Tariffs or **import levies** Taxes on imported products: i.e. customs duties.

But what will happen to this surplus? If farmers are to be helped, and not merely find that they cannot sell all they produce, the government will have to buy up this surplus. This is what happens in the EU. 'Intervention Boards' buy up the surpluses and in most cases (e.g. grains, milk powder and beef) put them into storage. In Figure 3.27, the cost to the government of buying the surplus is shown by the total shaded area ($edQ_{s_2}Q_{d_2}$). Unless the food is thrown away or otherwise disposed of, there will obviously then be the additional costs of storing this food – costs that could be very high over time, especially if the food has to be frozen.

An alternative to storing the food is for the government to sell the surpluses on the world market. In this case, the net cost would only be area *edcf*.

What would be the amount paid in Figure 3.27 if instead of the government buying the surpluses, export subsidies were given to farmers so as to guarantee them a price (plus subsidy) of P_{min}?

Reductions in supply

An alternative approach would be to find some way of reducing supply. This would lead to a higher market price and could avoid the cost to the taxpayer of buying surpluses or paying subsidies.

In open markets, however, a reduction in domestic supply could simply lead to an increase in imports, with the result that the price would not rise to the desired level. In such a case, a combination of a reduction in domestic supply and import levies (or other import restrictions) would be required. This can be illustrated using Figure 3.27. First, by the use of various restrictions on output, the domestic supply curve could be shifted to the left, so that it intersected the demand curve at point *e*. Second, an import levy of $P_{min} - P_w$ would need to be imposed to bring the price up to the desired level.

But how could supply be reduced to Q_{d_2}? The simplest way would be to give farmers a quota of how much each was allowed to produce. The effect would be to make the domestic supply curve vertical above point *x*. Milk quotas, which have been in force in the EU since 1984, are an example of this system.

Alternatively, farmers could be required to limit the amount of *land* they use for a particular product. The problem with this is that supply, and hence price, would still vary according to the yield. Another alternative would be to require farmers to withdraw a certain percentage of their land from agricultural use. This would shift supply curves for food to the left generally, but they would still be upward sloping because farmers could still switch from one product to another on their remaining land, according to which products gave the best price.

Compare the relative merits of (a) quotas on output, (b) limits to the amount of land used for a particular product and (c) farmers being required to take land out of food production.

Structural policies

The government could provide retraining or financial help for people to leave agriculture. It could provide grants or other incentives for farmers to diversify into forestry, tourism, rural industry or different types of food, such as organically grown crops, or other foods with a high income elasticity of demand.

The Common Agricultural Policy of the EU

Imagine public reaction if the government decided that the car industry needed protection from foreign competition and as a result decided to fix car prices some 20 per cent above current levels, and also agreed to buy up any unsold cars and put them into giant car parks, selling some of them off later on world markets at a knock-down price. There would be public uproar. And yet this is very similar to the type of support that was, until relatively recently, the main one given to farmers under the EU's Common Agricultural Policy (CAP).

It involved setting an intervention price for each product above the free-market equilibrium, with any surpluses being bought by Intervention Boards and then either stored or sold on world markets. If products were exported, then export subsidies were paid to make up the difference between export prices and the intervention price. In addition to high minimum prices, the CAP has involved various subsidies, primarily in the beef and sheep sectors but also in the arable sector.

The objectives of the CAP were set out in 1957 in Article 39 of the Treaty of Rome. They included the following:

- Assured supplies of food.
- A fair standard of living for those working in agriculture.
- A growth in agricultural productivity.
- Stable prices.
- Reasonable prices for consumers.

How successful has the CAP been in meeting these objectives? It has certainly helped to increase the self-sufficiency of the EU in many agricultural products, which could be valuable if world food prices were to rise. Also, by fixing prices that did not fluctuate with demand and supply, stable prices were guaranteed – at least for a year. It has also directly increased farm incomes. Indeed, some larger farmers have benefited greatly from the CAP. Nevertheless, average incomes in farming have continued to lag behind those of other sectors of the economy, and many farmers face periodic losses.

Agricultural productivity has grown rapidly, as illustrated by Table 3.2. This has been in large part the result of technological improvements and a greater use of chemicals. It is difficult, however, to judge the extent to which this has resulted directly from higher food prices or subsidies rather than the simple availability of new techniques, or competition from other farmers.

Table 3.2	Yields of selected crops (average annual, 100 kg/hectare)			
	Year	**Wheat**	**Barley**	**Potatoes**
Belgium	1970	39.0	31.0	293
	2008–11	88.5	82.6	471
France	1970	34.5	27.8	223
	2008–11	72.4	64.2	441
Germany	1970	37.9	32.2	272
	2008–11	75.4	61.0	434
Netherlands	1970	45.0	31.9	354
	2008–11	87.0	62.4	455
UK	1970	42.0	33.6	276
	2008–11	79.1	57.9	431

Source: Data from *Agriculture in the EU* (Commission of the European Communities, DG for Agriculture and Rural Development, 2014), selected tables.

What of the final objective: 'reasonable prices for consumers'? In the short run, a policy of high prices is inconsistent with reasonable prices for consumers (if 'reasonable' is defined as 'low' or at any rate 'not high'). This was one of the main reasons for the replacement of the system (see below). In the long run, however, it can be argued that, if prices above the market equilibrium encourage investment and productivity increases, then after a number of years they will end up lower than they would have been without the policy.

Criticisms of the former CAP system of price support

If the arguments in favour of price support are questionable, the arguments against are substantial.

Agricultural surpluses (not sold on world markets)

The costs of any surpluses were borne by consumers and taxpayers. They can be illustrated by referring back to Figure 3.27. Assume that the intervention is P_{min}.

- The cost to the taxpayer is shown by the shaded area.
- The cost to the consumer arises from having to pay the higher price P_{min}.
- There is a gain to farmers, however, from the extra profits resulting from the rise in price.

The costs and benefits of this system of high minimum prices are compared with those of a system of per-unit subsidies in Case Study 3.7 in MyEconLab.

Over the longer term, surpluses were increasing. The reason is that higher prices encouraged more investment in farming and therefore greater increases in long-run supply. The attendant costs to taxpayers therefore tended to rise over time.

By the early 1990s, European butter, grain and beef 'mountains' and wine 'lakes' had become symbols of a failed policy.

Inequity

The system of high support prices as it operated in the EU was inequitable at three levels.

Increase in inequalities in agriculture. The degree of price support varied enormously from one product to another and tended to favour farmers in the richer northern countries of the EU – those producing arable crops and those with the largest farms.

Increase in inequalities generally. Poor people spend a larger proportion of their income on food than the rich, but pay a lower proportion of their income in taxes than the rich. A system of high prices for food therefore directly penalises the poor and reduces the burden on richer taxpayers.

A system of subsidies, on the other hand, leads to lower prices for the consumer, the cost being borne entirely by the taxpayer. It therefore leads to greater equality.

Inequity between member countries of the EU. Countries that import the most food from outside the EU – countries like the UK – paid the most in import levies into the EAGGF (European Agricultural Guidance and Guarantee Fund). The countries with the greatest food surpluses drew most from the EAGGF.

Harmful effects on the environment

By encouraging increased output, the CAP encouraged the destruction of hedgerows, and the increased use of chemical fertilisers and pesticides. Many of these chemicals have caused pollution. This issue is examined in Case Study 3.8 in MyEconLab.

Effects on the rest of the world

The CAP has had a very damaging effect on agriculture in non-EU countries in two ways.

Import levies. Levies on imported food substantially reduced the amount of food that other countries could export to the EU. For example, Australia, a low-cost producer of butter, and once a major exporter to the UK, found it impossible to export any butter at all to the EU.

'Dumping' surpluses on world markets. Export subsidies have allowed EU surpluses to be sold at very low prices on world markets. This has a doubly damaging effect on agriculture in developing countries: (a) exporters of foodstuffs find it very difficult to compete with subsidised EU exports; (b) farmers in developing countries who are producing for their domestic market find that they cannot compete with cheap imports of food.

Agriculture in the developing world thus declines. Farmers' incomes are too low to invest in the land. Many migrate to the overcrowded cities and become slum dwellers in shanty towns, with little or no paid employment (see Chapter 27). The neglect of agriculture can then lead to famines if there is poor rainfall in any year.

One of the major sticking points in the protracted international trade talks under the so-called 'Doha round'[1] has been the insistence of developing countries that Europe and North America abandon their policies of protecting their farmers.

Reforming the CAP

Proposals for reforming the CAP have been debated within the EU for a number of years. Most have focused on the high costs of the CAP and on the resulting demands made on the EU budget. Reforms can be grouped into two broad categories: those that seek to lower prices and those that seek to reduce supply.

Early reforms
Early reforms focused on reductions in supply. There were two main reforms.

Production quotas. These were introduced in the mid-1980s for sugar and milk. They involve imposing limits (or 'quotas') on the amount that farmers are permitted to produce. It is not practical, however, to have a quota system for grains and vegetables where yields fluctuate with the harvest. But if quotas are applied only to a limited range of products, this merely encourages farmers to switch to other products which may already be in surplus.

Acreage controls (set-aside). Another way of reducing cereal production has been to pay subsidies to farmers to leave their land fallow. Under a *set-aside* scheme, which began in 1988, farmers were required to withdraw part of their arable land from production, and in return were paid compensation. From 2000 to 2001 farmers were required to set aside 10 per cent of their land. This land, however, could be used for products not intended for human or animal consumption (e.g. biofuels).

A problem with set-aside was that farmers tended to set aside their least productive land, thereby making little difference to total output. Another problem was that farmers tended to put in extra effort on the remaining land, and use more fertilisers, again hoping to maintain total output. Supply was reduced little, if at all, while pollution levels rose.

With rising world food prices, the EU announced in 2008 that it would abolish set-aside.

The MacSharry reforms
In 1992 a major reform package was introduced. These 'MacSharry reforms' (named after the EU agriculture commissioner) included a substantial cut in intervention prices, including a 29 per cent cut in cereal prices, phased in over three years. There was also a corresponding cut in export subsidies. (Intervention prices were still somewhat above world prices.)

Farmers were then paid compensation for their resulting loss of income. Since this income support (or 'direct aid', as it is known) was based on average historical yields in each farming region, it was independent of any changes in production by individual farmers. It thus provided no direct incentive to increase production. In order to receive direct aid, all except small farmers had to abide by the set-aside system and incentives were paid for farmers to switch to less intensive farming methods, with less use of chemical pesticides and fertilisers, and less livestock per hectare.

The effect of these measures was to reduce farm surpluses and in the first three years after these reforms, annual cereal output fell from 180 million tonnes to 160 million tonnes, and intervention stocks all but disappeared.

The 2003 package
In June 2003, EU farm ministers adopted fundamental reforms. It had been proposed to abolish all production-related subsidies and replace them with direct aid, but in the end a compromise deal was reached. This allowed countries to retain up to 25 per cent of support linked to production for cereals, 50 per cent for sheep and 100 per cent for beef.

Most countries, however, moved to a system of direct aid, which involved making annual 'single farm payments'. Payments to each farm were based on the average funds it had received in the previous three years and were conditional on farmers making environmental improvements. Funding was also gradually diverted away from large farms towards rural development.

The gradual shift from price support to direct aid did reduce food prices and hence helped EU consumers. What is more, low-income families benefited relatively more than high-income ones as poor people spend a higher proportion of their income on food. Taxpayers still had to finance the direct aid to farmers, but, with less incentive to expand production, this was less of a burden than paying high intervention prices for large food surpluses.

The 2008 'Health Check'
In 2008 some additional reforms were made to the CAP. These included further decoupling of financial support from output, phasing out milk quotas, increased investment aid for young farmers and the ending of set-aside. They reinforced a shift towards viewing agriculture as part of the

---

[1] The Doha round of trade talks began in Doha, Qatar, in 2001 and continued without agreement for the next 11 years. Developing countries wanted substantial reductions in agricultural support by the USA and the EU in order to allow greater access to these markets. They also wanted to retain the right to levy substantial tariffs on food imports from the rich world. In December 2013 agreement was reached on a number of areas; this was known as the Bali Package.

Definition

Set-aside A system in the EU of paying farmers not to use a certain proportion of their land.

BOX 3.8 | **FEED THE WORLD**

Rising populations, diminishing returns

The population of the world is currently 7 billion and is projected to increase to 8 billion by 2030 and over 9 billion by 2050. What does this mean for food supply and prices? Are we facing a catastrophe? (See Box 5.1 on page 134 for detailed discussion of this issue.) Governments around the world are certainly concerned about this issue and have responded with a number of reports and initiatives.

Food price inflation

Real food prices fell between 1990 and 2003, despite over 1 billion more people in the world. However, since then they have risen substantially, with particularly sharp increases experienced in 2007/8 and 2010/11. In the six years from 2005 to 2011, global food prices doubled (see the chart).

Contributing factors have been: a steady increase in global demand, in particular due to population growth in low-income countries and economic growth in middle-income countries; an increase in energy prices and changes encouraging the conversion of agricultural land to the production of biofuels; a series of poor wheat harvests in agriculturally important regions such as Australia; an

increase in the number of 'natural disasters' such as floods and earthquakes; and a general rundown in commodity stocks. The height of the spike in 2008 was exacerbated by the introduction or tightening of export restrictions by governments in some important producer countries.

The Foresight project

The Foresight project, *Global Food and Farming Futures*, sponsored by the UK government and involving some 400 leading experts and stakeholders from about 35 countries across the world, was set up to help governments think systematically about the future. It analysed trends in food demand and supply and considered long-term risks and threats, some 50 to 80 years ahead.

Its final report[1] highlights the decisions that policy makers need to take today, and in the years ahead, to ensure that a global population rising to 9 billion or more can be fed sustainably and equitably. It makes a compelling case for urgent action to redesign the global food system to meet the challenge of feeding the world over the next 40 years.

World food prices: 2005 = 100

Note: Price indices calculated by JS.
Source: Based on data in Index Mundi.

whole rural environment, increasing the grants available for setting up alternative rural industries and 'environmentally friendly' farm activities.

The sharp increases in food prices seen in 2007 and early 2008 raised the whole question of the need for agricultural support in times of high free-market prices for food. With the onset of recession from mid-2008, however, food prices

fell rapidly. There were calls from many parts of agriculture for additional support from the EU. The EU responded in various ways. For example, in the dairy sector, export subsidies for butter, cheese and whole and skimmed milk powder were reintroduced in January 2009; and in March 2009, the EU resumed intervention buying of butter and skimmed milk powder.

The report analysed five key challenges for the future:

- Balancing future demand and supply sustainably – to ensure that food supplies are affordable.
- Ensuring that there is adequate stability in food prices – and protecting the most vulnerable from the volatility that does occur.
- Achieving global access to food and ending hunger – this recognises that producing enough food in the world so that everyone can potentially be fed is not the same thing as ensuring food security for all.
- Managing the contribution of the food system to the mitigation of climate change.
- Maintaining biodiversity and ecosystem services while feeding the world.

The report identified a number of policy responses. These include producing more, controlling demand, reducing waste and increasing productivity and sustainability. However, it also recognised that there may be conflicts between maintaining food supplies and addressing climate change; these need to be treated as twin imperatives.

A global response

The United Nations has long recognised that global hunger represents a threat to world security and to the future prosperity of all countries. The Food and Agriculture Organization of the UN (FAO) has the stated aim of leading international efforts to defeat hunger. It undertakes activities to share information and knowledge and to bring together countries, both rich and poor.

In its 2010 report, *Growing Food for Nine Billion*,[2] the FAO identified the major issue we face:

> Food production will have to increase by 70 per cent to feed a population of nine billion people by 2050 . . . In order to intensify production by that much on our finite earth, immense effort will have to go into new, better and more intensive ways of producing our food. We will have to reflect on the wise way forward and what needs to be done.
>
> The trends in food production are in fact worrisome. For example, globally the rate of growth in yields of the major cereal crops has been declining steadily. The rate of growth in global cereal yields dropped from 3.2 per cent per year in 1960 to 1.5 per cent in 2000. The challenge is to reverse this decline.

Is there any cause for optimism?

Despite serious concerns, the *Global Food and Farming Futures* report was not wholly pessimistic. It identified a number of ways in which technology and research could improve current predictions. There is unlikely to be any one solution, but each of the following may play a role:

- The development of new varieties or breeds of crops, livestock and aquatic organisms, including those that have been genetically modified.
- Technological advances in soil science.
- Extending best practice across the global supply chain, to reduce waste.
- The use of environmentally friendly energy to produce foodstuffs, thus increasing sustainability.

Many of these advances will require global initiatives, with developed countries investing in research and being prepared to share existing knowledge and technology.

A further cause for optimism lies in the fact that population growth is predicted to tail off as low-income countries develop further. There of course remains a great deal of uncertainty about final figures, but many commentators predict that world population will peak at between 8 and 10 billion. So, perhaps, possible catastrophe can be averted.

1. Why do increasing food prices impact most sharply on low-income households and the poorest countries?
2. Why might there be a conflict between increasing food supplies and addressing climate change? Which of these issues are likely to be prioritised by governments?
3. Explain why it is in the interests of all countries to share knowledge and to work together to resolve this issue.

---

[1] *Foresight: The Future of Food and Farming (2011), Final Project Report* (www.gov.uk/government/collections/global-food-and-farming-futures) (The Government Office for Science, London).
[2] *Growing Food for Nine Billion: FAO at Work 2009–10* (www.fao.org/docrep/013/am023e/am023e00.pdf) (Food and Agriculture Organization of the United Nations, 2010).

'The CAP towards 2020'

In late 2010 the Commission published a set of policy options for future reforms of the CAP,[1] entitled 'The CAP towards 2020'. There was widespread recognition that change

was still needed, given the very volatile global conditions since 2003, the expansion of the EU and the continued pressure on the EU budget. However, Agriculture Commissioner Dacian Ciolos stressed the continuing importance of the CAP for ensuring food supply, for contribution to growth and employment, and for the building of sustainable economies across Europe.

[1] See http://ec.europa.eu/agriculture/cap-post-2013/communication/index_en.htm

Websites relevant to this chapter

Numbers and sections refer to websites listed in the Web Appendix and hotlinked from this book's website at
www.pearsoned.co.uk/sloman.

- For news articles relevant to this chapter, see the *Economic News* section in MyEconLab.
- For general news on markets and market intervention, see websites in section A, and particularly A1–5, 7–9, 18, 22, 25, 26, 33, 36. See also A38, 39, 42, 43 and 44 for links to newspapers worldwide; and A40 and 41 for links to economics news articles from newspapers worldwide.
- For information on taxes in the UK, see sites E25, 30 and 36.
- For information on agriculture and the Common Agricultural Policy, see sites E14 and G9.
- For sites favouring the free market, see C17 and E34.
- For student resources relevant to this chapter, see sites C1–7, 10, 19.
- For a simulation of running a farm, see site D3.
- For a range of classroom games and simulations of markets and market intervention, see sites C23 and also C24 (computer-based) and C20 (non-computer-based).
- Site D3 contains simulations on elasticity, house prices and the relationships between markets.

MyEconLab

This book can be supported by MyEconLab, which contains a range of additional resources, including an online homework and tutorial system designed to test and build your understanding.

You need both an access card and a course ID to access MyEconLab:

1. Is your lecturer using MyEconLab? Ask your lecturer for your course ID.
2. Has an access card been included with the book at a reduced cost? Check the inside back cover of the book.
3. If you have a course ID but no access card, go to: http://www.myeconlab.com/ to buy access to this interactive study programme.

Microeconomic Theory

4   **Background to Demand**   100

5   **Background to Supply**   132

6   **Profit Maximising under Perfect Competition and Monopoly**   170

7   **Profit Maximising under Imperfect Competition**   193

8   **Alternative Theories of the Firm**   221

9   **The Theory of Distribution of Income**   246

We now examine in more detail how economies function at a micro level. In doing so, we look at some of the big questions of our time. How do consumers choose between different goods? Why do some firms make such large profits? Why is there such a gap between the rich and the poor?

Chapters 4 and 5 examine demand and supply in more detail. Then in Chapters 6 to 8 we look at how the degree of competition a firm faces affects its prices and profits. Finally, in Chapter 9 we look at the distribution of income: why some people are rich while others are poor.

Background to Demand

CHAPTER MAP

4.1 Marginal utility theory   101
Total and marginal utility   101
The optimum level of consumption:
    the simplest case – one commodity   103
Marginal utility and the demand curve for a good   105
The optimum combination of goods consumed   106
The multi-commodity version of marginal utility
    and the demand curve   107

*4.2 Indifference analysis   109
The limitations of the marginal utility approach
    to demand   109
Indifference curves   109
The budget line   111
The optimum consumption point   112
The effect of changes in income   113
The effect of changes in price   115
Deriving the individual's demand curve   116
The income and substitution effects of a
    price change   116
The usefulness of indifference analysis   118

4.3 Demand under conditions of risk and
    uncertainty   120
The problem of imperfect information   120
Attitudes towards risk and uncertainty   121
Diminishing marginal utility of income and
    attitudes towards risk taking   122
Insurance: a way of removing risks   122

4.4 Behavioural economics   125
What is behavioural economics?   125
The role of experiments   125
Explaining 'irrational' behaviour   126
What does this mean for economic theory?   128

In this chapter we take a more detailed look at consumer demand. If we had unlimited income and time we would not have to be careful with our money. In the real world, however, given limited incomes and the problem of scarcity, we have to make choices about what to buy. You may have to choose between buying textbooks and going to a festival, between a new pair of jeans and a meal out, between saving for a car and having more money to spend on everyday items.

We start by assuming in this chapter that consumers behave 'rationally'. Remember in Chapter 1 we defined rational choices, those that involve the weighing up of the costs and benefits of our actions. As far as consumption is concerned, rational action involves considering the relative costs and benefits to us of the alternatives we could spend our money on. We do this in order to gain the maximum satisfaction possible from our limited incomes.

Of course this does not mean that you look at every item on the supermarket shelf and weigh up the satisfaction you think you would get from it against the price on the label. Nevertheless, you have probably learnt over time the sort of things you like and what they cost and can make out a 'rational' shopping list quite quickly.

There are two main approaches to analysing consumer behaviour: the marginal utility approach and the indifference approach. We examine both of them in this chapter. We also look at the problem of making rational choices when we have only limited information.

We also consider an area of economics that has received increasing attention since the financial crisis of 2007–8: behavioural economics. This does not assume rationality on the part of consumers; instead it looks at how we actually behave when faced with decisions and choices.

As we start by examining the **rational consumer**, it is important to understand what we mean by the term. It means a person who attempts to get the best value for money from his or her purchases, given a limited income. Thus the rational consumer tries to ensure that the benefits of a purchase are worth the expense.

Sometimes we may act 'irrationally'. We may buy goods impetuously or out of habit. In general, however, economists believe that it is reasonable to assume that people behave rationally.

1. *Do you ever purchase things irrationally? If so, what are they and why is your behaviour irrational?*
2. *If you buy something in the shop on the corner when you know that the same item could have been bought more cheaply two miles up the road in the supermarket, is your behaviour irrational? Explain.*

Two words of warning before we go on. First, don't confuse irrationality and ignorance. In the first three parts of this chapter we assume that consumers behave rationally, but that does not mean that they have perfect information. Have you ever been disappointed after buying something? Perhaps it was not as good as you had expected from an advert? Or perhaps you found later that you could have bought an alternative more cheaply? Perhaps a holiday may not turn out to be as good as the website led you to believe. This is a problem of ignorance rather than irrationality.

Second, the term 'rational' does not imply any approval of the decision involved. It is simply referring to behaviour that is consistent with your own particular goals: behaviour directed to getting the most out of your limited income. People may disapprove of the things that others buy – their clothes, junk food, lottery tickets – but as economists we should not make judgements about people's goals. We can, however, look at the implications of people behaving rationally in pursuit of those goals. This is what we are doing when we examine rational consumer behaviour: we are looking at its implications for consumer demand.

4.1 MARGINAL UTILITY THEORY

Total and marginal utility

People buy goods and services because they get satisfaction from them. Economists call this satisfaction 'utility'.

An important distinction must be made between *total utility* and *marginal utility*.

Total utility (*TU*) is the total satisfaction a person gains from all those units of a commodity consumed within a given time period. If Lucy drinks 10 cups of tea a day, her daily total utility from tea is the satisfaction derived from those 10 cups.

Marginal utility (*MU*) is the additional satisfaction gained from consuming one *extra* unit within a given period of time. Thus we might refer to the marginal utility that Lucy gains from her third cup of tea of the day or her eleventh cup.

A difficulty arises with the utility approach to explaining demand: how do you measure utility? Utility is subjective. There is no way of knowing what another person's experiences are really like. How satisfying does Nick find his first cup of tea in the morning? How does his utility compare with Lucy's?

For the moment, we will assume that a person's utility *can be measured*. We use an imaginary measure called utils, where a *util* is one unit of satisfaction.

Diminishing marginal utility

Up to a point, the more of a commodity you consume, the greater will be your total utility. However, as you become more satisfied, each extra unit that you consume will probably give you less additional utility than previous units. In other words, your marginal utility falls, the more you consume. This is known as the **principle of diminishing marginal utility**.

> **KEY IDEA 13**
>
> **The principle of diminishing marginal utility.** The more of a product a person consumes, the less will be the additional utility gained from one more unit.

For example, the second cup of tea in the morning gives you less additional satisfaction than the first cup. The third cup gives less satisfaction still.

At some level of consumption, your total utility will be at a maximum. No extra satisfaction can be gained by the consumption of further units within that period of time. Thus marginal utility will be zero. Your desire for tea may be fully

Definitions

Rational consumer A person who weighs up the costs and benefits to him or her of each additional unit of a good purchased.

Total utility The total satisfaction a consumer gets from the consumption of all the units of a good consumed within a given time period.

Marginal utility The extra satisfaction gained from consuming one extra unit of a good within a given time period.

Util An imaginary unit of satisfaction from the consumption of a good.

Diminishing marginal utility As more units of a good are consumed, additional units will provide less additional satisfaction than previous units.

satisfied at seven cups per day. An eighth cup will yield no extra utility. It may even give you displeasure (i.e. negative marginal utility).

 Are there any goods or services where consumers do not experience diminishing marginal utility?

Total and marginal utility curves

If we could measure utility, we could construct a table showing how much total and marginal utility a person would gain at different levels of consumption of a particular commodity. This information could then be transferred to a graph. Table 4.1 and Figure 4.1 do just this. They show the imaginary utility that Ollie gets from consuming packets of crisps.

Referring first to the table, if Ollie consumes no crisps, he obviously gets no satisfaction from crisps: his total utility is zero. If he now consumes one packet a day, he gets 7 utils of satisfaction. (Sorry if this sounds silly, but we will tackle this question of measurement later.) His total utility is 7, and his marginal utility is also 7. They must be equal if only one unit is consumed.

Table 4.1	Ollie's utility from consuming crisps (daily)	
Packets of crisps consumed	**TU in utils**	**MU in utils**
0	0	–
1	7	7
2	11	4
3	13	2
4	14	1
5	14	0
6	13	–1

If he now consumes a second packet, he gains an extra 4 utils (*MU*), giving him a total utility of 11 utils (i.e. 7 + 4). His marginal utility has fallen because, having already eaten one packet, he has less craving for a second. A third packet gives him less extra utility still: marginal utility has fallen to 2 utils, giving a total utility of 13 utils (i.e. 11 + 2).

By the time he has eaten five packets, he would rather not eat any more. A sixth actually reduces his utility (from 14 utils to 13): its marginal utility is negative.

The information in Table 4.1 is plotted in Figure 4.1. Notice the following points about the two curves:

- The *MU* curve slopes downwards. This is simply illustrating the principle of diminishing marginal utility.
- The *TU* curve starts at the origin. Zero consumption yields zero utility.
- The *TU* curve reaches a peak when marginal utility is zero. When marginal utility is zero (at five packets of crisps), there is no addition to total utility. Total utility must be at the maximum – the peak of the curve.
- Marginal utility can be derived from the *TU* curve. It is the slope of the line joining two adjacent quantities on the curve. For example, the marginal utility of the third packet of crisps is the slope of the line joining points *a* and *b*. The slope of such a line is given by the formula

$$\frac{\Delta TU}{\Delta Q}(= MU)$$

In our example $\Delta TU = 2$ (total utility has risen from 11 to 13 utils), and $\Delta Q = 1$ (one more packet of crisps has been consumed). Thus $MU = 2$.

 If Ollie were to consume more and more crisps, would his total utility ever (a) fall to zero; (b) become negative? Explain.

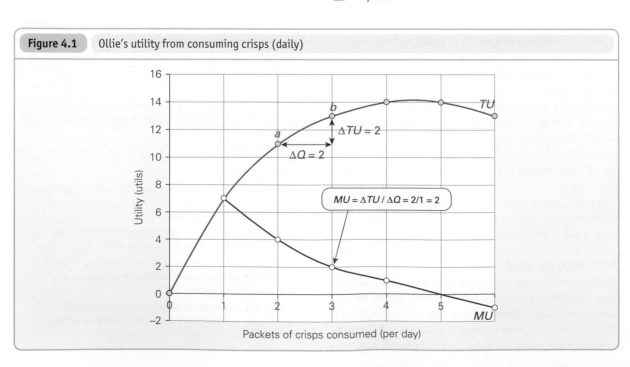

Figure 4.1   Ollie's utility from consuming crisps (daily)

*BOX 4.1   USING CALCULUS TO DERIVE A MARGINAL UTILITY FUNCTION

The relationship between total utility and marginal utility can be shown using calculus. If you are not familiar with the rules of calculus, ignore this box (or see Appendix 1, pages A:10–13).

A consumer's typical utility function for a good might be of the form

$$TU = 600Q - 4Q_2$$

where Q is the quantity of the good consumed. This would give the figures shown in the following table.

Q	60Q	$-4Q^2$	=	TU
1	60	−4	=	56
2	120	−16	=	104
3	180	−36	=	144
4	240	−64	=	176
.	.	.		.

Complete this table to the level of consumption at which TU is at a maximum.

Marginal utility is the first derivative of total utility. In other words, it is the rate of change of total utility. Differentiating the *TU* function gives

$$MU = \frac{dTU}{dQ} = 60 - 8Q$$

This gives the figures shown in the following table.

Q	60	−8Q	=	MU
1	60	−8	=	52
2	60	−16	=	44
3	60	−24	=	36
4	60	−32	=	28
.	.	.		.

Note that the marginal utility diminishes.

The *MU* function we have derived is a straight-line function. If, however, the *TU* function contained a cubed term (Q^3), the *MU* function would be a curve.

Derive the MU function from the following TU function:

$$TU = 200Q - 25Q^2 + Q^3$$

From this MU function, draw up a table (like the one above) up to the level of Q where MU becomes negative. Graph these figures.

The ceteris paribus assumption

The table and graph we have drawn are based on the assumption that other things do not change.

In practice, other things *do* change – and frequently. The utility that Ollie gets from crisps depends on what else he eats. If on Saturday he has a lot to eat he will get little satisfaction from crisps. If on Monday, however, he is too busy to eat proper meals, he would probably welcome one or more packets of crisps.

Each time the consumption of *other* goods changed – whether substitutes or complements – a new utility schedule would have to be drawn up. The curves would shift. Remember, utility is not a property of the goods themselves. Utility is in the mind of the consumer, and consumers change their minds. Their tastes change; their circumstances change; their consumption patterns change.

The optimum level of consumption: the simplest case – one commodity

Just how much of a good should people consume if they are to make the best use of their limited income? To answer this question we must tackle the problem of how to measure utility, given that in practice we cannot measure 'utils'.

One solution to the problem is to measure utility with money. In this case, utility becomes the value that people place on their consumption. Marginal utility thus becomes the amount of money a person would be prepared to pay to obtain one more unit: in other words, what that extra unit is worth to that person. If Ollie is prepared to pay 45p to obtain an extra packet of crisps, then we can say that packet yields him 45p worth of utility: $MU = 45p$.

So how many packets should he consume if he is to act rationally? To answer this we need to introduce the concept of *consumer surplus*.

Marginal consumer surplus

Marginal consumer surplus (*MCS*) is the difference between what you are willing to pay for one more unit of a good and what you are actually charged. If Ollie were willing to pay 45p for another packet of crisps which in fact only cost him 40p, he would be getting a marginal consumer surplus of 5p.

$$MCS = MU - P$$

Definitions

Consumer surplus The excess of what a person would have been prepared to pay for a good (i.e. the utility) over what that person actually pays.

Marginal consumer surplus The excess of utility from the consumption of one more unit of a good (*MU*) over the price paid: $MCS = MU - P$.

Total consumer surplus

Total consumer surplus (*TCS*) is the sum of all the marginal consumer surpluses that you have obtained from all the units of a good you have consumed. It is the difference between the total utility from all the units and your expenditure on them. If Ollie consumes four packets of crisps, and if he would have been prepared to spend £1.60 on them and only had to spend £1.20, then his total consumer surplus is 40p.

$$TCS = TU - TE$$

where *TE* is the total expenditure on a good: i.e. $P \times Q$.

Let us define **rational consumer behaviour** as the attempt to maximise consumer surplus. How do people set about doing this?

People will go on purchasing additional units as long as they gain additional consumer surplus: in other words, as long as the price they are prepared to pay exceeds the price they are charged ($MU > P$). But as more is purchased, so they will experience diminishing marginal utility. They will be prepared to pay less for each additional unit. Their marginal utility will go on falling until $MU = P$: i.e. until no further consumer surplus can be gained. At that point, they will stop purchasing additional units. Their optimum level of consumption has been reached: consumer surplus has been maximised. If they continue to purchase beyond this point, *MU* would be less than *P*, and thus they would be paying more for the last units than they were worth to them.

The process of maximising consumer surplus can be shown graphically. Let us take the case of Tanya's annual purchases of petrol. Tanya has her own car, but as an alternative she can use public transport or walk. To keep the analysis simple, let us assume that Tanya's parents bought her the car and pay the licence duty, and that Tanya does not have the option of selling the car. She does, however, have to buy the petrol. The current price is £1.30 per litre. Figure 4.2 shows her consumer surplus.

If she were to use just a few litres per year, she would use them for very important journeys for which no convenient alternative exists. For such trips she may be prepared to pay up to £1.60 per litre. For the first few litres, then, she is getting a marginal utility of around £1.60 per litre, and hence a marginal consumer surplus of around 30p (i.e. £1.60 – £1.30).

By the time her annual purchase is around 200 litres, she would be prepared to pay only around £1.50 for additional litres. The additional journeys, although still important, would be less vital. Perhaps these are journeys where she could have taken public transport, albeit at some inconvenience. Her marginal consumer surplus at 200 litres is 20p (i.e. £1.50 – £1.30).

Gradually, additional litres give less and less additional utility as less important journeys are undertaken. The 500th litre yields £1.40 worth of extra utility. Marginal consumer surplus is now 10p (i.e. £1.40 – £1.30).

By the time she gets to the 900th litre, Tanya's marginal utility has fallen to £1.30. There is no additional consumer

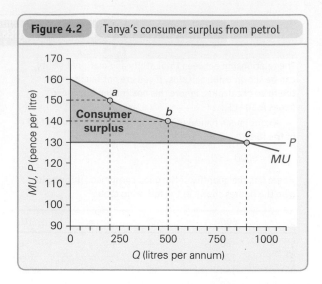

Figure 4.2   Tanya's consumer surplus from petrol

surplus to be gained. Her total consumer surplus is at a maximum. She thus buys 900 litres, where $P = MU$.

Her total consumer surplus is the sum of all the marginal consumer surpluses: the sum of all the 900 vertical lines between the price and the *MU* curve. This is shown by the total *area* between *P* and *MU* up to 900 litres (i.e. the pink shaded area in Figure 4.2).

This analysis can be expressed in general terms. In Figure 4.3, if the price of a commodity is P_1, the consumer will consume Q_1. The person's total expenditure (*TE*) is

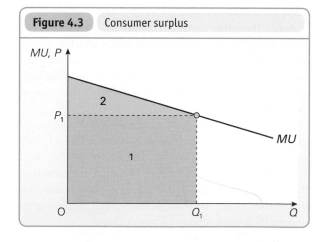

Figure 4.3   Consumer surplus

Definitions

Total consumer surplus The excess of a person's total utility from the consumption of a good (*TU*) over the total amount that person spends on it (*TE*): $TCS = TU - TE$.

Rational consumer behaviour The attempt to maximise total consumer surplus.

THRESHOLD CONCEPT 8 **RATIONAL DECISION MAKING INVOLVES CHOICES AT THE MARGIN** **THINKING LIKE AN ECONOMIST**

Rational decision making involves weighing up the marginal benefit and marginal cost of any activity. If the marginal benefit exceeds the marginal cost, it is rational to do the activity (or to do more of it). If the marginal cost exceeds the marginal benefit, it is rational not to do it (or to do less of it).

Let's take the case of when you go to the supermarket to do shopping for the week. Assume that you have £50 to spend. Clearly, you will want to spend it wisely. With each item you consider buying, you should ask yourself what its marginal benefit is to you: in other words, how much you would be prepared to spend on it. This will depend on the prices and benefits of alternatives. Thus if you were considering spending £3 from the £50 on wholemeal bread, you should ask yourself whether the £3 would be better spent on some alternative, such as white bread, rolls or crackers. The *best* alternative (which might be a combination of products) is the marginal opportunity cost. If the answer is that you feel you are getting better value for money by spending it on the wholemeal bread, then you are saying that the marginal benefit exceeds the marginal opportunity cost. It is an efficient use of your money to buy the wholemeal bread and forgo the alternatives.

Most decisions are more complex than this, as they involve buying a whole range of products. In fact, that is what you are doing in the supermarket. But the principle is still the same. In each case, a rational decision involves weighing up marginal benefits and marginal costs.

This is another example of a *threshold concept* because it is a way of thinking about economic problems. It is a general principle that can be applied in a whole host of contexts: whether it is individuals deciding what to buy, how much to work, what job to apply for, or whether to study for a degree or take a job; or firms deciding how much to produce, whether to invest in new capacity or new products, or what type of people to employ and how many; or governments deciding how much to spend on various projects, such as roads, hospitals and schools, or what rates of tax to impose on companies that pollute the environment.

In each case, better decisions will be made by weighing up marginal costs and marginal benefits.

1. Assume that a firm is selling 1000 units of a product at £20 each and that each unit on average costs £15 to produce. Assume also that to produce additional units will cost the firm £19 each and that the price will remain at £20. To produce additional products will therefore reduce the average profit per unit. Should the firm expand production? Explain.
2. Assume that a ferry has capacity for 500 passengers. Its operator predicts that it will typically have only 200 passengers on each of its midweek sailings over the winter. Assume also that each sailing costs the company £10 000. This means that midweek winter sailings cost the company an average of £10 000/200 = £50 per passenger. Currently tickets cost £60. Should the company consider selling stand-by tickets during the winter for (a) less than £60; (b) less than £50? (Clue: think about the marginal cost of taking additional passengers.)

P_1Q_1, shown by area 1. Total utility (*TU*) is the area under the marginal utility curve: i.e. areas 1 + 2. Total consumer surplus (*TU − TE*) is shown by area 2.

 If a good were free, why would total consumer surplus equal total utility? What would be the level of marginal utility at the equilibrium level of consumption?

Marginal utility and the demand curve for a good

An individual's demand curve

Individual people's demand curve for any good will be the same as their marginal utility curve for that good, where utility is measured in money.

This is demonstrated in Figure 4.4, which shows the marginal utility curve for a particular person and a particular good. If the price of the good were P_1, the person would consume Q_1, where $MU = P_1$. Thus point *a* would be one point on that person's demand curve. If the price fell to P_2, consumption would rise to Q_2, since this is where $MU = P_2$. Thus point *b* is a second point on the demand curve.

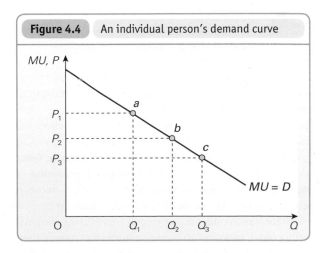

Figure 4.4 An individual person's demand curve

Likewise if the price fell to P_3, Q_3 would be consumed. Point *c* is a third point on the demand curve.

Thus as long as individuals seek to maximise consumer surplus and hence consume where $P = MU$, their demand curve will be along the same line as their marginal utility curve.

The market demand curve

The market demand curve will simply be the (horizontal) sum of all individuals' demand curves and hence *MU* curves.

The shape of the demand curve. The price elasticity of demand will reflect the rate at which *MU* diminishes. If there are close substitutes for a good, it is likely to have an elastic demand, and its *MU* will diminish slowly as consumption increases. The reason is that increased consumption of this product will be accompanied by decreased consumption of the alternative product(s). Since total consumption of this product plus the alternatives has increased only slightly (if at all), the marginal utility will fall only slowly.

For example, the demand for a certain brand of petrol is likely to have a fairly high price elasticity, since other brands are substitutes. If there is a cut in the price of Texaco petrol (assuming the prices of other brands stay constant), consumption of Texaco petrol will increase a lot. The *MU* of Texaco petrol will fall slowly, since people consume less of other brands. Petrol consumption *in total* may be only slightly greater, and hence the *MU* of petrol only slightly lower.

> ? Why do we get less total consumer surplus from goods where our demand is relatively elastic?

Shifts in the demand curve. How do shifts in demand relate to marginal utility? For example, how would the marginal utility of (and hence demand for) tea be affected by a rise in the price of coffee? The higher price of coffee would cause less coffee to be consumed. This would increase the marginal utility of tea since if people are drinking less coffee, their desire for tea is higher. The *MU* curve (and hence the demand curve) for tea thus shifts to the right.

> ? How would marginal utility and market demand be affected by a rise in the price of a complementary good?

Weaknesses of the one-commodity version of marginal utility theory

A change in the consumption of one good will affect the marginal utility of substitute and complementary goods. It will also affect the amount of income left over to be spent on other goods. Thus a more satisfactory explanation of demand would involve an analysis of choices between goods, rather than looking at one good in isolation.

What is more, deriving a demand curve from a marginal utility curve measured in money assumes that money itself has a constant marginal utility. The trouble is that it does not. If people have a rise in income, they will consume more. Other things being equal, the marginal utility of the goods that they consume will diminish. Thus an extra £1 of consumption will bring less satisfaction than previously. In other words, it is likely that the *marginal utility of money diminishes as income rises*.

Unless a good occupies only a tiny fraction of people's expenditure, a fall in its price will mean that their real income has increased: i.e. they can afford to purchase more goods in general. As they do so, the marginal utility of their money will fall. We cannot, therefore, legitimately use money to measure utility in an absolute sense. We can, however, still talk about the relative utility that we get from various goods for a given increase in expenditure.

The following sections thus look at the choice between goods, and how it relates to marginal utility.

The optimum combination of goods consumed

We can use marginal utility analysis to show how a rational person decides what combination of goods to buy. Given that we have limited incomes, we have to make choices. It is not just a question of choosing between two obvious substitutes, like a holiday in Greece and one in Spain, but about allocating our incomes between all the goods and services we might like to consume. If you have, say, an income of £20 000 per year, what is the optimum 'bundle' of goods and services for you to spend it on?

The rule for rational consumer behaviour is known as the *equi-marginal principle*. This states that a consumer will get the highest utility from a given level of income when the ratio of the marginal utilities is equal to the ratio of the prices. Algebraically, this is when, for any pair of goods, A and B, that are consumed

$$\frac{MU_A}{MU_B} = \frac{P_A}{P_B} \tag{1}$$

To understand this, suppose that the last unit of good A you consumed gave three times as much utility as the last unit of B. Yet good A only cost twice as much as good B. You would obviously gain by increasing your consumption of A and cutting your purchases of B. But as you switched from B to A, the marginal utility of A would fall due to diminishing marginal utility, and conversely the marginal utility of B would rise. To maximise utility you would continue this substitution of A for B until the ratios of the marginal utilities (MU_A/MU_B) equalled the ratio of the prices of the two goods (P_A/P_B). At this point, no further gain can be made by switching from one good to another. This is the optimum combination of goods to consume.

Equation (1) is a specific example of the general equi-marginal principle in economics, which applies to all rational

> **Definition**
>
> **Equi-marginal principle (in consumption)** Consumers will maximise total utility from their incomes by consuming that combination of goods where
>
> $$\frac{MU_A}{MU_B} = \frac{P_A}{P_B}$$

THE MARGINAL UTILITY REVOLUTION: JEVONS, MENGER, WALRAS

Solving the diamonds–water paradox

What determines the market value of a good? We already know the answer: demand and supply. So if we find out what determines the position of the demand and supply curves, we will at the same time be finding out what determines a good's market value.

This might seem obvious. Yet for years economists puzzled over just what determines a good's value.

Some economists like Karl Marx and David Ricardo concentrated on the supply side. For them, value depended on the amount of resources used in producing a good. This could be further reduced to the amount of labour time embodied in the good. Thus, according to the labour theory of value, the more labour that was directly involved in producing the good, or indirectly in producing the capital equipment used to make the good, the more valuable the good would be.

Other economists looked at the demand side. But here they came across a paradox.

Adam Smith in the 1760s gave the example of water and diamonds. 'How is it', he asked, 'that water which is so essential to human life, and thus has such a high "value-in-use", has such a low market value (or "value-in-exchange")? And how is it that diamonds which are relatively so trivial have such a high market value?' The answer to this paradox had to wait over a hundred years until the marginal utility revolution of the 1870s. William Stanley Jevons (1835–82) in England, Carl Menger (1840–1921) in Austria, and Léon Walras (1834–1910) in Switzerland all independently claimed that the source of the market value of a good was its marginal utility, not its total utility.

This was the solution to the diamonds–water paradox. Water, being so essential, has a high total utility: a high 'value in use'. But for most of us, given that we consume so much already, it has a very low marginal utility. Do you leave the cold tap running when you clean your teeth? If you do, it shows just how trivial water is to you at the margin.

Diamonds, on the other hand, although they have a much lower total utility, have a much higher marginal utility. There are so few diamonds in the world, and thus people have so few of them, that they are very valuable at the margin. If, however, a new technique were to be discovered of producing diamonds cheaply from coal, their market value would fall rapidly. As people had more of them, so their marginal utility would rapidly diminish.

Marginal utility still only gives the demand side of the story. The reason why the marginal utility of water is so low is that supply is so plentiful. Water is very expensive in Saudi Arabia! In other words, the full explanation of value must take into account both demand and supply.

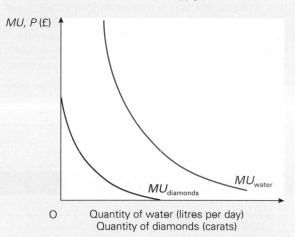

 The diagram illustrates a person's MU curves of water and diamonds. Assume that diamonds are more expensive than water. Show how the MU of diamonds will be greater than the MU of water. Show also how the TU of diamonds will be less than the TU of water. (Remember: TU is the area under the MU curve.)

---

choices between two alternatives, whether in production, consumption, employment or whatever.

The multi-commodity version of marginal utility and the demand curve

How can we derive a demand curve from the above analysis?

Let us simply reinterpret equation (1) so that it relates the *MU* and *P* of good A to the *MU* and *P* of *any* other good.

 KEY IDEA 14 *The equi-marginal principle.* The optimum amount of two alternatives consumed (or produced) will be where the marginal benefit ratios of the two alternatives are equal to their marginal cost ratios:

$$\frac{MB_A}{MB_B} = \frac{MC_A}{MC_B}$$

In other words, the equation would be the same for goods B, C, D, E and any other good. For any given income, and given prices for good A and all other goods, the quantity a person will demand of good A will be that which satisfies equation (1). One point on the individual's demand curve for good A has been determined.

If the price of good A now falls, such that

$$\frac{MU_A}{MU_B} > \frac{P_A}{P_B} \quad \text{(and similarly for goods C, D, E, etc.)}$$

the person would buy more of good A and less of all other goods (B, C, D, E, etc.), until equation (1) is once more satisfied. A second point on the individual's demand curve for good A has been determined.

Further changes in the price of good A would bring further changes in the quantity demanded, in order to satisfy equation (1). Further points on the individual's demand curve would thereby be derived.

If the price of *another* good changed, or if the marginal utility of any good changed (including good A), then again the quantity demanded of good A (and other goods) would change, until again equation (1) were satisfied. These changes in demand will be represented by a *shift* in the demand curve for good A.

BOX 4.3   TAKING ACCOUNT OF TIME

CASE STUDIES AND APPLICATIONS

Do you take a taxi or go by bus? How long do you spend soaking in the bath? Do you cook a meal from scratch, or will you get a take-away?

We have argued that if decisions are to be rational, they should involve weighing up the relative marginal utilities of these activities against their relative marginal costs. As economists, of course we are interested in considering all costs, including time. One of the opportunity costs of doing any activity is the sacrifice of time.

A take-away meal may be more expensive than one cooked at home, but it saves you time. Part of the cost of the home-cooked meal, therefore, is the sacrifice of time involved. The full cost is therefore not just the cost of the ingredients and the fuel used, but also the opportunity cost of the alternative activities you have sacrificed while you were cooking.

Given the busy lives many people lead in affluent countries, they often put a high value on time. Increased sales of ready meals and the employment of home cleaners are consequences of this valuation.

Of course, leisure activities also involve a time cost. The longer you spend doing pleasurable activity 'a', the less time you will have for doing pleasurable activity 'b'. The longer you laze in the bath, the less TV you will be able to watch (unless you have a TV in the bathroom).

1. We have identified that consumers face limits on their income and time. Can you think of any other constraints that we face when making consumption decisions?
2. Give some examples of business opportunities that could arise as a consequence of people being 'cash-rich, but time-poor'.
3. If someone hires a cleaner, does this imply that they are 'cash-rich, but time-poor'? How about hiring a personal trainer?

Section summary

1. The satisfaction people get from consuming a good is called 'utility'. Total utility is the satisfaction gained from the total consumption of a particular good over a given period of time. Marginal utility is the extra satisfaction gained from consuming one more unit of the good.

2. The marginal utility tends to fall the more that people consume. This is known as the 'principle of diminishing marginal utility'.

3. The utility that people get from consuming a good will depend on the amount of other goods they consume. A change in the amount of other goods consumed, whether substitutes or complements, will shift the total and marginal utility curves.

4. 'Rational' consumers will attempt to maximise their consumer surplus. Consumer surplus is the excess of people's utility (measured in money terms) over their expenditure on the good. This will be maximised by purchasing at the point where the *MU* of a good is equal to its price.

5. In the simple case where the price and consumption of other goods are held constant, a person's *MU* curve will lie along the same line as that person's demand curve.

6. The market demand curve is merely the horizontal sum of the demand curves of all the individual consumers. The elasticity of the market demand curve will depend on the rate at which marginal utility diminishes as more is consumed. This in turn depends on the number and closeness of substitute goods. If there are close substitutes, people will readily switch to this good if its price falls, and thus marginal utility will fall only slowly. The demand will be elastic.

7. Measuring the marginal utility of a good in money avoids the problem of using some imaginary unit such as utils, but it assumes that money has a constant utility. In reality, the marginal utility of money is likely to decrease as income rises.

8. A more satisfactory way of analysing the demand for goods is to look at people's choices between goods. A consumer will maximise utility from a given income by consuming according to the 'equi-marginal principle'. This states that goods should be consumed in that combination which equates the *MU/P* ratio for each good.

*4.2   INDIFFERENCE ANALYSIS

The limitations of the marginal utility approach to demand

Even though the multi-commodity version of marginal utility theory is useful in demonstrating the underlying logic of consumer choice, it still has a major weakness. Utility cannot be measured in any absolute sense. We cannot really say, therefore, by how much the marginal utility of one good exceeds another.

An alternative approach is to use *indifference analysis*. This does not involve measuring the *amount* of utility a person gains, but merely *ranking* various combinations of goods in order of preference. In other words, it assumes that consumers can decide whether they prefer one combination of goods to another. For example, if you were asked to choose between two baskets of fruit, one containing four oranges and three pears and the other containing two oranges and five pears, you could say which you prefer or whether you are indifferent between them. It does not assume that you can decide just *how much* you prefer one basket to another or just how much you like either.

The aim of indifference analysis, then, is to analyse, *without having to measure utility*, how a rational consumer chooses between two goods. As we shall see, it can be used to show the effect on this choice of (a) a change in the consumer's income and (b) a change in the price of one or both goods. It can also be used to analyse the income and substitution effects of a change in price.

Indifference analysis involves the use of *indifference curves* and *budget lines*.

Indifference curves

An *indifference curve* shows all the various combinations of two goods that give an equal amount of satisfaction or utility to a consumer.

To show how one can be constructed, consider the following example. Imagine that a supermarket is conducting a survey about the preferences of its customers for different types of fruit. One of the respondents is Ali, a student who likes a healthy diet and regularly buys fresh fruit. He is asked his views about various combinations of oranges and pears. Starting with the combination of 10 pears and 13 oranges, he is asked what other combinations he would like the same amount as this one. From his answers a table is constructed (Table 4.2). What we are saying here is that Ali would be equally happy to have any one of the combinations shown in the table.

This table is known as an *indifference set*. It shows alternative combinations of two goods that yield the same level of satisfaction. From this we can plot an indifference curve. We measure units of one good on one axis and units of the other good on the other axis. Thus in Figure 4.5, which is

Table 4.2 Combinations of pears and oranges that Ali likes the same amount as 10 pears and 13 oranges

Pears	Oranges	Point in Figure 4.5
30	6	a
24	7	b
20	8	c
14	10	d
10	13	e
8	15	f
6	20	g

based on Table 4.2, pears and oranges are measured on the two axes. The curve shows that Ali is indifferent as to whether he consumes 30 pears and 6 oranges (point *a*) or 24 pears and 7 oranges (point *b*) or any other combination of pears and oranges along the curve.

Notice that we are not saying *how much* Ali likes pears and oranges; merely that he likes all the combinations along the indifference curve the same amount. All the combinations thus yield the same (unspecified) utility.

The shape of the indifference curve

As you can see, the indifference curve we have drawn is not a straight line. It is bowed in towards the origin. In other words, its slope gets shallower as we move down the curve. Indifference curves are normally drawn this shape. But why?

Let us see what the slope of the curve shows us. It shows the rate at which the consumer is willing to exchange one good for the other, holding his or her level of satisfaction the same. For example, consider the move from point *a* to point *b* in Figure 4.5. Ali gives up 6 units of pears and requires 1 orange to compensate for the loss. The slope of the indifference curve is thus −6/1 = −6. Ignoring the negative sign, the slope of the indifference curve (i.e. the rate at which the consumer is willing to substitute one good for the other) is known as the *marginal rate of substitution* (MRS). In this case, therefore, the MRS = 6.

Definitions

Indifference curve A line showing all those combinations of two goods between which a consumer is indifferent: i.e. those combinations that give the same level of utility.

Indifference set A table showing the same information as an indifference curve.

Marginal rate of substitution (between two goods in consumption) The amount of one good (Y) that a consumer is prepared to give up in order to obtain one extra unit of another good (X): i.e. ΔY/ΔX.

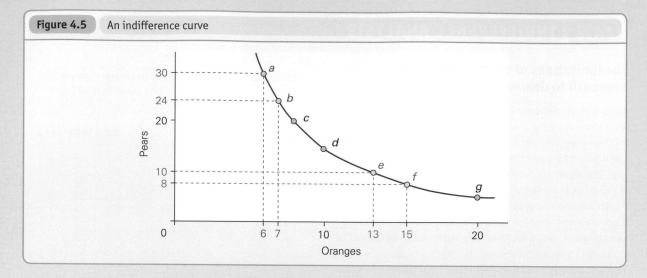

Figure 4.5 An indifference curve

Pears / Oranges

Note that as we move down the curve, the marginal rate of substitution diminishes as the slope of the curve gets less. For example, look at the move from point *e* to point *f*. Here the consumer gives up 2 pears and requires 2 oranges to compensate. Thus along this section of the curve, the slope is −2/2 = −1 (and hence the *MRS* = 1).

The reason for a ***diminishing marginal rate of substitution*** is related to the *principle of diminishing marginal utility* that we looked at in section 4.1. This stated that individuals will gain less and less additional satisfaction the more of a good that they consume. This principle, however, is based on the assumption that the consumption of other goods is held *constant*. In the case of an indifference curve, this is not true. As we move down the curve, more of one good is consumed but *less* of the other. Nevertheless the effect on consumer satisfaction is similar. As Ali consumes more pears and fewer oranges, his marginal utility from pears will diminish, while that from oranges will increase. He will thus be prepared to give up fewer and fewer pears for each additional orange. *MRS* diminishes.

The relationship between the marginal rate of substitution and marginal utility

In Figure 4.5, consumption at point *a* yields equal satisfaction with consumption at point *b*. Thus the utility sacrificed by giving up six pears must be equal to the utility gained by consuming one more orange. In other words, the marginal utility of an orange must be six times as great as that of a pear. Therefore, $MU_{oranges}/MU_{pears} = 6$. But this is the same as the marginal rate of substitution. With *X* measured on the horizontal axis and *Y* on the vertical axis, then

$$MRS = \frac{MU_X}{MU_Y} = \frac{\text{slope of indifference curve}}{\text{(ignoring negative sign)}}$$

 Although indifference curves will normally be bowed in towards the origin, on odd occasions they might not be. Which of the following diagrams correspond to which of the following? Explain the shape of each curve.

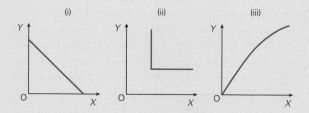

(a) *X* and *Y* are left shoes and right shoes.
(b) *X* and *Y* are two brands of the same product, and the consumer cannot tell them apart.
(c) *X* is a good but *Y* is a 'bad' – like household refuse.

An indifference map

More than one indifference curve can be drawn. For example, referring back to Table 4.2, Ali could give another set of combinations of pears and oranges that all give him a higher (but equal) level of utility than the set shown in the table. This could then be plotted in Figure 4.5 as another indifference curve.

Although the actual amount of utility corresponding to each curve is not specified, indifference curves further out to the right would show combinations of the two goods that yield a higher utility, and curves further in to the left would show combinations yielding a lower utility.

In fact, a whole ***indifference map*** can be drawn, with each successive indifference curve showing a higher level of utility. Combinations of goods along I_2 in Figure 4.6 give a

---

Definitions

Diminishing marginal rate of substitution The more a person consumes of good X and the less of good Y, the less additional Y will that person be prepared to give up in order to obtain an extra unit of X: i.e. $\Delta Y/\Delta X$ diminishes.

Indifference map A graph showing a whole set of indifference curves. The further away a particular curve is from the origin, the higher the level of satisfaction it represents.

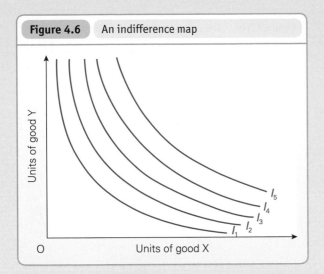

Figure 4.6 An indifference map

Units of good Y

I_5
I_4
I_3
I_2
I_1

O   Units of good X

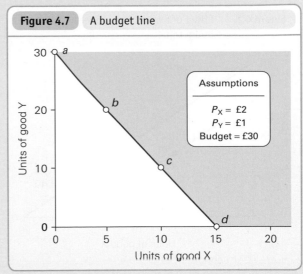

Figure 4.7 A budget line

Units of good Y

Assumptions

P_X = £2
P_Y = £1
Budget = £30

Units of good X

higher utility to the consumer than those along I_1. Those along I_3 give a higher utility than those along I_2, and so on. The term 'map' is appropriate here, because the indifference curves are rather like contours on a real map. Just as a contour joins all those points of a particular height, so an indifference curve shows all those combinations yielding a particular level of utility.

 Draw another two indifference curves on Figure 4.5, one outward from and one inward from the original curve. Read off various combinations of pears and oranges along these two new curves and enter them on a table like Table 4.2.

The budget line

We turn now to the ***budget line***. This is the other important element in the analysis of consumer behaviour. Whereas indifference maps illustrate people's preferences, the actual choices they make will depend on their incomes. The budget line shows what combinations of two goods you are able to buy, given (a) your income available to spend on them and (b) their prices.

Just as we did with an indifference curve, we can construct a budget line from a table. The first two columns of Table 4.3 show various combinations of two goods X and Y

that can be purchased assuming that (a) the price of X is £2 and the price of Y is £1 and (b) the consumer has a budget of £30 to be divided between the two goods.

In Figure 4.7, then, if you are limited to a budget of £30, you can consume any combination of X and Y along the line (or inside it). You cannot, however, afford to buy combinations that lie outside it (i.e. in the darker shaded area). This area is known as the *unfeasible region* for the given budget.

We have said that the amount people can afford to buy will depend on (a) their budget and (b) the prices of the two goods. We can show how a change in either of these two determinants will affect the budget line.

A change in income

If the consumer's income (and hence budget) increases, the budget line will shift outwards, parallel to the old one. This is illustrated in the last two columns of Table 4.3 and in Figure 4.8, which show the effect of a rise in the consumer's budget from £30 to £40. (Note that there is no change in the prices of X and Y, which remain at £2 and £1 respectively.)

More can now be purchased. For example, if the consumer was originally purchasing 7 units of X and 16 units of Y (point *m*), this could be increased, with the new budget of £40, to 10 units of X and 20 units of Y (point *n*) or any other combination of X and Y along the new higher budget line.

A change in price

The relative prices of the two goods are given by the slope of the budget line. The slope of the budget line in Figure 4.7 is 30/15 = 2. (We are ignoring the negative sign: strictly speaking, the slope should be −2.) Similarly, the slope of the new

Table 4.3	Consumption possibilities for budgets of £30 and £40				
	Budget of £30			**Budget of £40**	
Units of good X	Units of good Y	Point on budget line in Figure 4.7		Units of good X	Units of good Y
0	30	A		0	40
5	20	B		5	30
10	10	C		10	20
15	0	D		15	10
				20	0

Note: It is assumed that P_X = £2, P_Y = £1.

Definition

Budget line A graph showing all the possible combinations of two goods that can be purchased at given prices and for a given budget.

Figure 4.8   Effect of an increase in income on the budget line

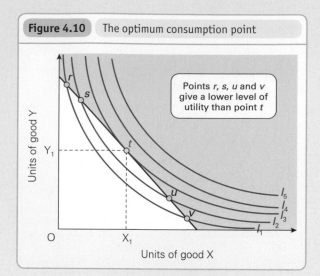

Figure 4.10   The optimum consumption point

higher budget line in Figure 4.8 is 40/20 = 2. But in each case this is simply the ratio of the price of X (£2) to the price of Y (£1).

Thus the slope of the budget line equals

$$\frac{P_X}{P_Y}$$

If the price of either good changes, the slope of the budget line will change. This is illustrated in Figure 4.9, which, like Figure 4.7, assumes a budget of £30 and an initial price of X of £2 and a price of Y of £1. The initial budget line is B_1.

Now let us assume that the price of X falls to £1 but that the price of Y remains the same (£1). The new budget line will join 30 on the Y axis with 30 on the X axis. In other words, the line pivots outwards on point a. If, instead, the price of Y changed, the line would pivot on point b.

1. *Assume that the budget remains at £30 and the price of X stays at £2, but that Y rises in price to £3. Draw the new budget line.*
2. *What will happen to the budget line if the consumer's income doubles and the prices of both X and Y double?*

Figure 4.9   Effect on the budget line of a fall in the price of good X

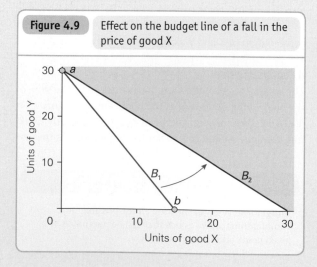

The optimum consumption point

We are now in a position to put the two elements of the analysis together: the indifference map and a budget line. This will enable us to show how much of each of the two goods the 'rational' consumer will buy from a given budget. Let us examine Figure 4.10.

The consumer would like to consume along the highest possible indifference curve. This is curve I_3 at point t. Higher indifference curves, such as I_4 and I_5, although representing higher utility than curve I_3, are in the unfeasible region: they represent combinations of X and Y that cannot be afforded with the current budget. The consumer *could* consume along curves I_1 and I_2, between points r and v, and s and u respectively, but they give a lower level of utility than consuming at point t.

The optimum consumption point for the consumer, then, is where the budget line touches (is 'tangential to') the highest possible indifference curve. If the budget line is tangential to an indifference curve, they will have the same slope. (The slope of a curve is the slope of the tangent to it at the point in question.) But as we have seen, the slope of the budget line is

$$\frac{P_X}{P_Y}$$

and the slope of the indifference curve is

$$MRS = \frac{MU_X}{MU_Y}$$

Therefore, at the optimum consumption point

$$\frac{P_X}{P_Y} = \frac{MU_X}{MU_Y}$$

But this is the *equi-marginal principle* that we established in the first part of this chapter; only this time, using the indifference curve approach, there has been no need to measure utility. All we have needed to do is to observe, for any two combinations of goods, whether the consumer preferred one to the other or was indifferent between them.

*LOOKING AT THE MATHS

We can express the optimum consumption point algebraically. With a limited budget of B, the objective is to maximise utility subject to this budget constraint. This can be expressed as

Max $TU(X,Y)$ (1)

subject to the budget constraint that

$P_X X + P_Y Y = B$ (2)

Equation (1) is known as the 'objective function' and says that the objective is to maximise utility, which depends on the consumption of two goods, X and Y. For example, assume that the utility function is

$TU = X^{3/4}Y^{1/4}$

This is known as a 'Cobb–Douglas utility function' and will give smooth convex indifference curves. Assume also that the price of X is 4, the price of Y is 2 and the budget is 64. Thus

$4X + 2Y = 64$

Rearranging this constraint to express X in terms of Y gives

$X = 16 - \dfrac{Y}{2}$

By first substituting this value of X into the utility function (so that it is expressed purely in terms of Y) and then differentiating the resulting equation and setting it equal to zero, we can solve for the value of Y and then X that yields the maximum utility for the given budget. The answer is

$X = 12$ and $Y = 8$

The workings of this are given in Maths Case 4.1 in MyEconLab.

An alternative method, which is slightly longer but is likely to involve simpler calculations, involves the use of 'Lagrangian multipliers'. This method is explained, along with a worked example, in Maths Case 4.2.

The effect of changes in income

As we have seen, an increase in income is represented by a parallel shift outwards of the budget line (assuming no change in the price of X and Y). This will then lead to a new optimum consumption point on a higher indifference curve. A different consumption point will be found for each different level of income.

In Figure 4.11 a series of budget lines are drawn representing different levels of consumer income. The corresponding optimum consumption points (*r*, *s*, *t*, *u*) are shown. Each point is where the new higher budget line just touches the highest possible indifference curve.[1] The line

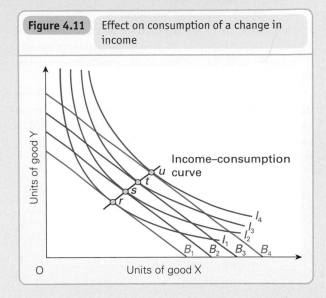

Figure 4.11 Effect on consumption of a change in income

joining these points is known as the *income-consumption curve*.

If your money income goes up and the price of goods does not change, we say that your *real income* has risen. In other words, you can buy more than you did before. But your real income can also rise even if you do not earn any more money. This will happen if prices fall. For the same amount of money, you can buy more goods than previously. We analyse the effect of a rise in real income caused by a fall in prices in just the same way as we did when money income rose and prices stayed the same. Provided the *relative* prices of the two goods stay the same (i.e. provided they fall by the same percentage), the budget line will shift outwards parallel to the old one.

Income elasticity of demand and the income–consumption curve

The income-consumption curve in Figure 4.11 shows that the demand for both goods rises as income rises. Thus both goods have a positive income elasticity of demand: they are both normal goods.

Definitions

Income–consumption curve A line showing how a person's optimum level of consumption of two goods changes as income changes (assuming the prices of the goods remain constant).

Real income Income measured in terms of how much it can buy. If your *money* income rises by 10 per cent, but prices rise by 8 per cent, you can buy only 2 per cent more goods than before. Your *real* income has risen by 2 per cent.

---

[1] We can always draw in an indifference curve that will be tangential to a given budget line. Just because we only draw a few indifference curves on a diagram, it does not mean that there are only a few possible ones. We could draw as many as we liked. Again it is rather like the contours on a real map. They may be drawn at, say, 10 metre intervals. We could, however, if we liked, draw them at 1 metre or even 1 cm intervals, or at whatever height was suitable to our purpose. For example, if the maximum height of a lake were 32.45 metres above sea level, it might be useful to draw a contour at that height to show what land might be liable to flooding.

Now let us focus just on good X. If the income–consumption curve became flatter at higher levels of income, it would show an increasing proportion of income being spent on X. The flatter it became, the higher would be the income elasticity of demand for X.

If, by contrast, X were an inferior good, such as cheap margarine, its demand would fall as income rose; its income elasticity of demand would be negative. This is illustrated in Figure 4.12. Point *b* is to the left of point *a*, showing that at the higher income B_2, less X is purchased.

1. *The income–consumption curve in Figure 4.12 is drawn as positively sloped at low levels of income. Why?*
2. *Show the effect of a rise in income on the demand for X and Y, where this time Y is the inferior good and X is the normal good. Is the income–consumption curve positively or negatively sloped?*

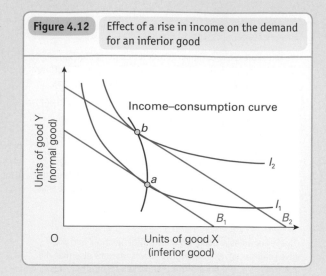

Figure 4.12   Effect of a rise in income on the demand for an inferior good

---

LOVE AND CARING

An economic approach to family behaviour

We have been using indifference analysis to analyse a single individual's choices between two goods. The principles of rational choice, however, can be extended to many other fields of human behaviour. These include situations where people are members of groups and where one person's behaviour affects another. Examples include how friends treat each other, how sexual partners interrelate, how parents treat children, how chores are shared out in a family, how teams are organised, how people behave to each other at work, and so on.

In all these cases, decisions constantly have to be made. Generally people try to make the 'best' decisions, decisions which will maximise the interests of the individual or the members of the group, decisions that are 'rational'. This will involve weighing up (consciously or subconsciously) the costs and benefits of alternative courses of action to find out which is in the individual's or group's best interests.

One of the pioneers of this approach has been Gary Becker (1930–). Becker has been a professor at Chicago University since 1970 and is a member of the 'Chicago school', a group of economists from the university who advocate the market as the best means of solving economic problems.

Gary Becker has attempted to apply simple economic principles of rational choice to a whole range of human activities, including racial and sexual discrimination, competition in politics, and criminal behaviour. Much of his work, however, has focused on the family, a field previously thought to be the domain of sociologists, anthropologists and psychologists. Even when family members are behaving lovingly and unselfishly, they nevertheless, according to Becker, tend to behave 'rationally' in the economists' sense of trying to maximise their interests, only in this case their

'interests' include the welfare of the other members of their family.

A simple illustration of this approach is given in the diagram below. It assumes, for simplicity, that there are just two members of the family, Judy and Warren. Warren's consumption is measured on the horizontal axis; Judy's on the vertical. Their total joint income is given by Y_T. The line $Y_T Y_T$ represents their consumption possibilities. If Warren were to spend their entire joint income on himself, he would consume at point *g*. If Judy were to spend their entire joint income on herself, she would consume at point *f*.

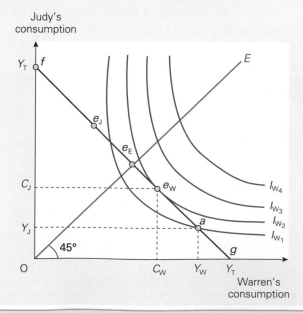

The effect of changes in price

If either X or Y changes in price, the budget line will 'pivot'. Take the case of a reduction in the price of X (but no change in the price of Y). If this happens, the budget line will swing outwards. We saw this effect in Figure 4.9 (on page 112). These same budget lines are reproduced in Figure 4.13, but this time we have added indifference curves.

The old optimum consumption point was at *j*. After the reduction in the price of good X, a new optimum consumption point is found at *k*.

 Illustrate on an indifference diagram the effects of the following:
(a) A rise in the price of good X (assuming no change in the price of Y).
(b) A fall in the price of good Y (assuming no change in the price of X).

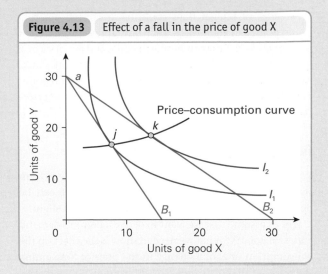

Figure 4.13 Effect of a fall in the price of good X

Let us assume that Warren works full time and Judy works part time. As a result Warren earns more than Judy. He earns Y_W; she earns Y_J. If each spent their own incomes on themselves alone, they would consume at point *a*.

But now let us assume that Warren loves Judy, and that he would prefer to consume less than Y_W to allow her to consume more than Y_J. His preferences are shown by the indifference curves. Each curve shows all the various combinations of consumption between Warren and Judy that give Warren equal satisfaction. (Note that because he loves Judy, he gets satisfaction from her consumption: her happiness gives him pleasure.)

Warren's optimum distribution of consumption between himself and Judy is at point e_W. This is the highest of his indifference curves that can be reached with a joint income of Y_T. At this point he consumes C_W; she consumes C_J.

If he loved Judy 'as himself' and wanted to share their income out equally, then the indifference curves would be shallower. The tangency point to the highest indifference curve would be on the 45° line *OE*. Consumption would be at point e_E.

Similar indifference curves could be drawn for Judy. Her optimum consumption point might be at point e_J. But if she loved Warren 'as herself', her optimum point would then be at point e_E.

Some interesting conclusions can be drawn from this analysis:

■ Income redistribution (i.e. consumption redistribution) within the family can be to the benefit of all the members. In the case we have been considering, both Warren and Judy gain from a redistribution of income from point *a* to

point e_W. The only area of contention is between points e_W and e_J. Here negotiation would have to take place. This might be in return for some favour. 'If you'll let me have the money I need for that new coat, I'll do the washing up for a whole month.'

■ In the case of each one loving the other as him- or herself, there is no area of contention. They are both happiest with consumption at point e_E.

■ In the case of 'extreme love', where each partner would prefer the other to have more than him- or herself, point e_W would be above point e_E, and point e_J would be below point e_E. In this case, each would be trying to persuade the other to have more than he or she wanted. Here a different type of negotiation would be needed. 'I'll only let you buy me that coat if you let me do the washing up for a whole month.'

■ Some forms of consumption benefit both partners. Household furniture or a new car would be cases in point. Any such purchases would have the effect of shifting the consumption point out beyond line Y_TY_T, and could lead to both partners consuming on a higher indifference curve. This shows the 'economic' advantages of the collective consumption that can be experienced in households or other groups (such as clubs).

 1. If Judy earned more than Warren, show how much income she would redistribute to him if (a) she cared somewhat for him; (b) she loved him 'as herself'. Draw her indifference curves in each of these two cases.
2. In the case where they both love each other 'as themselves', will their two sets of indifference curves be identical?

A series of budget lines could be drawn, all pivoting round point *a* in Figure 4.13. Each one represents a different price of good X, but with money income and the price of Y held constant. The flatter the curve, the lower the price of X. At each price, there will be an optimum consumption point. The line that connects these points is known as the *price-consumption curve*.

Deriving the individual's demand curve

We can use the analysis of price changes to show how in theory a person's demand curve for a product can be derived. To do this we need to modify the diagram slightly.

Let us assume that we want to derive a person's demand curve for good X. What we need to show is the effect on the consumption of X of a change in the price of X assuming the prices of all other goods are held constant. To do this we need to redefine good Y. Instead of being a *single* good, Y becomes the total of *all other* goods. But what units are we to put on the vertical axis? Each of these other goods will be in different units: litres of petrol, loaves of bread, kilograms of cheese, numbers of haircuts, etc. We cannot add them all up unless we first convert them to a common unit. The answer is to measure them as the total amount of money spent on them: i.e. what is *not* spent on good X.

With expenditure on all other goods plotted on the vertical axis and with income, tastes and the price of all other goods held constant, we can now derive the demand curve for X. This is demonstrated in Figure 4.14.

We illustrate the changes in the price of X by pivoting the budget line on the point where it intersects the vertical axis. It is then possible, by drawing a price–consumption line, to show the amount of X demanded at each price. It is then a simple matter of transferring these price–quantity relationships onto a demand curve. In Figure 4.14, each of the points *a*, *b*, *c* and *d* on the demand curve in the lower part of the diagram corresponds to one of the four points on the price–consumption curve. (Note that P_2 is half of P_1, P_3 is one-third of P_1 and P_4 is one-quarter of P_1.)

As quantity demanded increases from Q_1 to Q_2 in Figure 4.14, the expenditure on all other goods decreases. (Point b is lower than point a.) This means, therefore, that the person's total expenditure on X has correspondingly increased. What, then, can we say about the person's price elasticity of demand for X between points a and b? What can we say about the price elasticity of demand between points b and c, and between points c and d?

The income and substitution effects of a price change

In Chapter 2 we argued that when the price of a good rises, consumers will purchase less of it for two reasons:

■ They cannot afford to buy so much. This is the *income effect*.

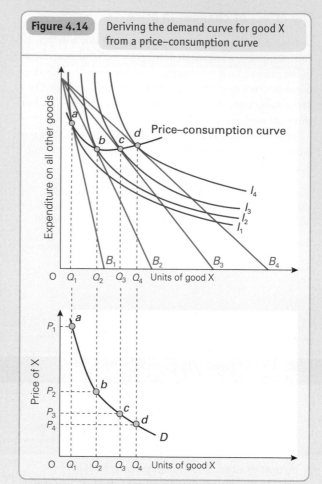

Figure 4.14 Deriving the demand curve for good X from a price–consumption curve

■ The good is now more expensive relative to other goods. Therefore consumers substitute alternatives for it. This is the *substitution effect*.

We can extend our arguments from Chapter 2 by demonstrating the income and substitution effects with the use of indifference analysis. Let us start with the case of a normal good and show what happens when its price changes.

Definitions

Price–consumption curve A line showing how a person's optimum level of consumption of two goods changes as the price of one of the two goods changes (assuming that income and the price of the other good remain constant).

Income effect of a price change That portion of the change in quantity demanded that results from the change in real income.

Substitution effect of a price change That portion of the change in quantity demanded that results from the change in the relative price of the good.

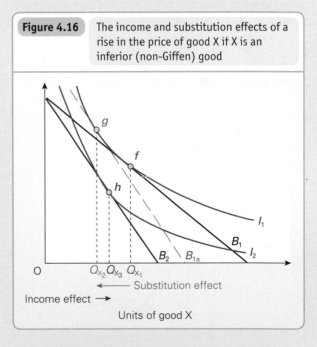

Figure 4.15 The income and substitution effects of a rise in the price of good X if X is a normal good

The bigger the income and substitution effects, the higher will be the price elasticity of demand for good X.

Illustrate on two separate indifference diagrams the income and substitution effects of the following:
(a) A decrease in the price of good X (and no change in the price of good Y).
(b) An increase in the price of good Y (and no change in the price of good X).

An inferior good

As we saw above, when people's incomes rise, they will buy less of **inferior goods** such as poor-quality margarine and cheap powdered instant coffee, since they will now be able to afford better quality goods instead. Conversely, when their income falls, they will have to reduce their living standards: their consumption of inferior goods will thus rise.

The substitution effect. If the price of an inferior good (good X) rises, the substitution effect will be in the same direction as for a normal good (i.e. it will be negative). People will consume less X relative to Y, since X is now more expensive relative to Y. For example, if the price of inferior-quality margarine (good X) went up, people would tend to use better quality margarine or butter (good Y) instead. This is illustrated in Figure 4.16 by a movement along the original indifference curve (I_1) from point f to point g. The quantity of X demanded falls from Q_{X_1} to Q_{X_2}.

A normal good

In Figure 4.15 the price of **normal good** X has risen and the budget line has pivoted inwards from B_1 to B_2. The consumption point has moved from point f to point h. Part of this shift in consumption is due to the substitution effect and part is due to the income effect.

The substitution effect. To separate these two effects a new budget line is drawn, parallel to B_2 but tangential to the original indifference curve I_1. This is the line B_{1a}. Being parallel to B_2, it represents the new price ratio (i.e. the higher price of X). Being tangential to I_1, however, it enables the consumer to obtain the same utility as before: in other words, there is no loss in real income to the consumer. By focusing, then, on B_{1a}, which represents no change in real income, we have excluded the income effect. The movement from point f to point g is due purely to a change in the relative prices of X and Y. The movement from Q_{X_1} to Q_{X_2} is the substitution effect.

The income effect. In reality, the budget line has shifted to B_2 and the consumer is forced to consume on a lower indifference curve I_2: real income has fallen. Thus the movement from Q_{X_2} to Q_{X_3} is the income effect.

In the case of a normal good, therefore, the income and substitution effects of a price change reinforce each other. They are both negative: they *both* involve a *reduction* in the quantity demanded as price *rises* (and vice versa).[1]

Figure 4.16 The income and substitution effects of a rise in the price of good X if X is an inferior (non-Giffen) good

[1] It is important not to confuse the income effect of a price change with the simple effect on demand of an increase in income. In the latter case, a rise in income will cause a rise in demand for a normal good – a positive effect (and hence there will be a positive income elasticity of demand). In the case of a price reduction, although for a normal good the resulting rise in real income will still cause a rise in demand, it is in the opposite direction from the change in price – a negative effect with respect to price (and hence there will be a negative price elasticity of demand).

Definitions

Normal good A good whose demand increases as income increases.

Inferior good A good whose demand decreases as income increases.

The income effect. The income effect of the price rise, however, will be the opposite of that for a normal good: it will be positive. The reduction in real income from the rise in price of X will tend to increase the consumption of X, since with a fall in real income more inferior goods will now be purchased – including more X. Thus point h is to the right of point g: the income effect increases quantity back from Q_{X_2} to Q_{X_3}.

A Giffen good: a particular type of inferior good

If the inferior good were to account for a very large proportion of a consumer's expenditure, a change in its price would have a significant effect on the consumer's real income, resulting in a large income effect. It is conceivable, therefore, that this large abnormal income effect could outweigh the normal substitution effect. In such a case, a rise in the price of X would lead to more X being consumed!

This is illustrated in Figure 4.17, where point h is to the *right* of point f. In other words, the fall in consumption (Q_{X_1} to Q_{X_2}) as a result of the substitution effect is more than offset by the rise in consumption (Q_{X_2} to Q_{X_3}) as a result of the large positive income effect.

Such a good is known as a ***Giffen good***, after Sir Robert Giffen (1837–1910), who is alleged to have claimed that the consumption of bread by the poor rose when its price rose. Bread formed such a large proportion of poor people's consumption that, if its price went up, the poor could not afford to buy so much meat, vegetables, etc., and had to buy more bread instead. It is possible that in countries in Africa today with very low incomes, staple foods such as manioc and maize are Giffen goods. Naturally, such cases must be very rare indeed and some economists remain unconvinced of their existence, except as a theoretical possibility.

 Could you conceive of any circumstances in which one or more items of your expenditure would become Giffen goods? Apply the same analysis to an elderly couple on a state pension.

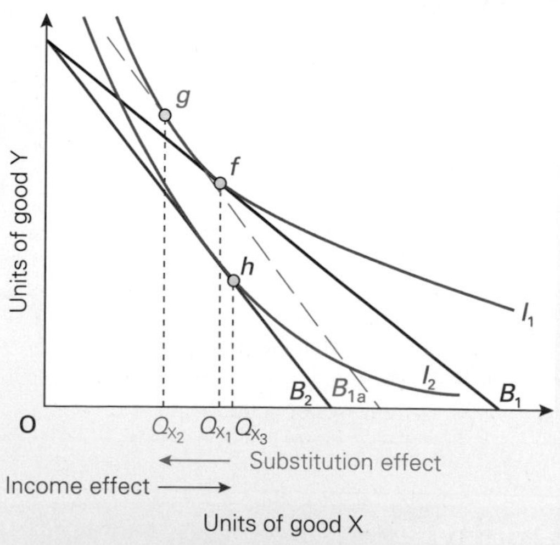

The usefulness of indifference analysis

Indifference analysis has made it possible to demonstrate the logic of 'rational' consumer choice, the derivation of the individual's demand curve, and the income and substitution effects of a price change. All this has been done without having to measure utility.

Nevertheless there are limitations to the usefulness of indifference analysis:

- In practice it is virtually impossible to derive indifference curves, since it would involve a consumer having to imagine a whole series of different combinations of goods and deciding in each case whether a given combination gave more, equal or less satisfaction than other combinations.
- Consumers may not behave 'rationally', and hence may not give careful consideration to the satisfaction they believe they will gain from consuming goods. They may behave impetuously.
- Indifference curves are based on the satisfaction that consumers believe they will gain from a good. This belief may well be influenced by advertising. Consumers may be disappointed or pleasantly surprised, however, when they actually consume the good. In other words, consumers are not perfectly knowledgeable. Thus the 'optimum consumption' point may not in practice give consumers maximum satisfaction for their money.
- Certain goods are purchased only now and again, and then only one at a time. Examples would include consumer durables such as cars, televisions and washing machines. Indifference curves are based on the assumption that marginal increases in one good can be traded off against marginal decreases in another. This will not be the case with consumer durables.

TC 9 p121

Figure 4.17 | The income and substitution effects of a rise in the price of good X if X is a Giffen good

Units of good Y

g
f
h
I_1
I_2
B_2 B_{1a} B_1
O Q_{X_2} Q_{X_1} Q_{X_3}
← Substitution effect →
Income effect →
Units of good X

Definition

Giffen good An inferior good whose demand increases as its price increases as a result of a positive income effect larger than the normal negative substitution effect.

*BOX 4.5 CONSUMER THEORY: A FURTHER APPROACH   EXPLORING ECONOMICS

Characteristics theory

Characteristics theory was developed in the mid-1960s by Kelvin Lancaster. He argued that people demand goods not for their own sake, but for the characteristics they possess.

Take cars, for example. When choosing between the different makes, consumers do not just consider their relative prices, they also consider their attributes: comfort, style, performance, durability, reliability, fuel consumption, etc. It is these characteristics that give rise to utility.

Characteristics theory, then, is based on four crucial assumptions:

- All goods possess various characteristics.
- Different brands possess them in different proportions.
- The characteristics are measurable: they are 'objective'.
- The characteristics (along with price and income) determine consumer choice.

Let us assume that you are choosing between three different goods or brands of a good (e.g. a foodstuff). Each one has a different combination of two characteristics (e.g. protein and calories). Your choices can be shown graphically.

The choice between brands of a product: each brand has different characteristics

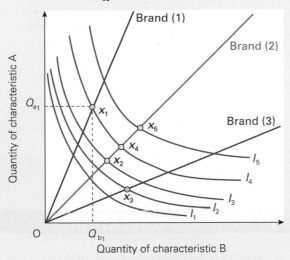

The levels of two characteristics are shown on the two axes. An indifference map can be constructed, showing the different combinations of the two characteristics that yield given levels of utility. Thus any combination of the two characteristics along indifference curve I_4 in the diagram gives a higher level of utility than those along I_3, and so on. The shape of the indifference curves (bowed in) illustrates a diminishing marginal rate of substitution between the two characteristics.

The amounts of the two characteristics given by the three brands are shown by the three rays. The more that is consumed of each brand, the further up the respective ray will the consumer be. Thus at x_1, the consumer is gaining Q_{a1} of characteristic A and Q_{b1} of characteristic B.

Assume that, for the same money, the consumer could consume at x_1 with brand (1), x_2 with brand (2) and x_3 with brand (3). The consumer will consume brand (1): x_1 is on a higher indifference curve than x_2 or x_3.

Now assume that the price of brand (2) falls. For a given expenditure, the consumer can now move up the brand (2) ray. But not until the price has fallen enough to allow consumption at point x_4 will the consumer consider switching from brand (1). If price falls enough for consumption to be at point x_5, clearly the consumer will switch.

The characteristics approach has a number of advantages over conventional indifference curve analysis in explaining consumer behaviour:

- It helps to explain brand loyalty. When price changes, people will not necessarily gradually move from one brand to another. Rather they will stick with a brand until a critical price is reached. Then they will switch brands all at once.
- It allows the choice between several goods to be shown on the same diagram. Each good or brand has its own ray.
- It helps to explain the nature of substitute goods. The closer substitutes are, the more similar will be their characteristics and hence the closer will be their rays. The closer the rays, the more likely it is that there will be a shift in consumption to one good when the price of the other good changes.
- A change in the quality of a good can be shown by rotating its ray.

There are weaknesses with the approach, however:

- Some characteristics cannot be measured. Such characteristics as beauty, taste and entertainment value are subjective: they are in the mind of the consumer.
- Only two characteristics can be plotted. Most goods have several characteristics.

1. *Make a list of the characteristics of shoes. Which are 'objective' and which are 'subjective'?*
2. *If two houses had identical characteristics, except that one was near a noisy airport and the other was in a quiet location, and if the market price of the first house were £180 000 and that of the second £200 000, how would that help us to put a value on the characteristic of peace and quiet?*

Characteristics theory is examined in more detail in Case Study 4.6 in MyEconLab.

Section summary

1. The indifference approach to analysing consumer demand avoids having to measure utility.

2. An indifference curve shows all those combinations of two goods that give an equal amount of satisfaction to a consumer. An indifference map can be drawn with indifference curves further to the north-east representing higher (but still unspecified) levels of satisfaction.

3. Indifference curves are usually drawn convex to the origin. This is because of a diminishing marginal rate of substitution between the two goods. As more of one good is purchased, the consumer is willing to give up less and less of the other for each additional unit of the first. The marginal rate of substitution is given by the slope of the indifference curve, which equals MU_X/MU_Y.

4. A budget line can be drawn on an indifference diagram. A budget line shows all those combinations of the two goods that can be purchased for a given amount of money, assuming a constant price of the two goods. The slope of the budget line depends on the relative price of the two goods. The slope is equal to P_X/P_Y.

5. The consumer will achieve the maximum level of satisfaction for a given income (budget) by consuming at the point where the budget line just touches the highest possible indifference curve. At this point of tangency, the budget line and the indifference curve have the same slope. Thus $MU_X/MU_Y = P_X/P_Y$, which is the 'equi-marginal principle' for maximising utility from a given income that was established in section 4.1.

6. If the consumer's real income (and hence budget) rises, there will be a parallel outward shift of the budget line. The 'rational' consumer will move to the point of tangency of this new budget line with the highest indifference curve. The line that traces out these optimum positions for different levels of income is known as the 'income–consumption curve'.

7. If the price of one of the two goods changes, the budget line will pivot on the axis of the other good. An outward pivot represents a fall in price; an inward pivot represents an increase in price. The line that traces the tangency points of these budget lines with the appropriate indifference curves is called a 'price–consumption curve'.

8. By measuring the expenditure on all other goods on the vertical axis and by holding their price constant and money income constant, a demand curve can be derived for the good measured on the horizontal axis. Changes in its price can be represented by pivoting the budget line. The effect on the quantity demanded can be found from the resulting price–consumption curve.

9. The effect of a change in price on quantity demanded can be divided into an income and a substitution effect. The substitution effect is the result of a change in relative prices alone. The income effect is the result of the change in real income alone.

10. For a normal good, the income and substitution effects of a price rise will both be negative and will reinforce each other. With an inferior good, the substitution effect will still be negative but the income effect will be positive and thus will to some extent offset the substitution effect. If the good is 'very' inferior and the (positive) income effect is bigger than the (negative) substitution effect, it is called a Giffen good. A rise in the price of a Giffen good will thus cause a rise in the quantity demanded.

11. Indifference analysis, although avoiding having to measure utility, nevertheless has limitations. Indifference curves are difficult to derive in practice; consumers may not behave rationally; the 'optimum' consumption point may not be optimum if the consumer lacks knowledge of the good; indifference curves will not be smooth for items where single units each account for a large proportion of income.

4.3 DEMAND UNDER CONDITIONS OF RISK AND UNCERTAINTY

The problem of imperfect information

So far we have assumed that when people buy goods and services, they know what price they will pay and how much utility they will gain. In many cases this is a reasonable assumption. When you buy a bar of chocolate, you know how much you are paying for it and have a good idea how much you will like it. But what about a mobile phone, or a car, or a laptop, or any other *consumer durable*? In each of these cases you are buying something that will last you a long time, and the further into the future you look, the less certain you can be of its costs and benefits to you.

Take the case of a washing machine costing you £300. If you pay cash, your immediate outlay involves no uncertainty: it is £300. But washing machines can break down. In

two years' time you could face a repair bill of £100. In other words, when you buy the washing machine, you are uncertain as to the full 'price' it will entail over its lifetime.

If the costs of the washing machine are uncertain, so too are the benefits. You might have been attracted in the first place by the description in the shop, or by an advert in a magazine. When you have used it for a while, however, you might discover things you had not anticipated. Perhaps

Definition

Consumer durable A consumer good that lasts a period of time, during which the consumer can continue gaining utility from it.

THRESHOLD CONCEPT 9   PEOPLE'S ACTIONS DEPEND ON THEIR EXPECTATIONS   THINKING LIKE AN ECONOMIST

Many, if not most, economic actions are taken before the benefits are enjoyed. You work first and get paid at the end of the month; you buy something in a shop today, and consume it later. In the case of a bar of chocolate, you may consume it fairly soon and pretty well all at once; in the case of many 'consumer durables', such as electrical goods, you will enjoy them over a much longer period.

It is the same with firms. What they produce today will be sold at some point in the future. In other words, firms typically incur costs first and receive revenues later. In the case of investing in new buildings or equipment, it may be a very long time before the firm starts seeing profits from the investment.

In each of these cases, then, the decision is made to do something now in anticipation of what will happen in the future. The threshold concept here is that decision making is only as good as the information on which it is based. If your expectations turn out to be wrong, a seemingly good decision may turn out disastrously. Part of what we do as economists is to examine how people get information and on what basis they form their expectations; part of what we do is to forecast the future.

When information about the future is imperfect, as it nearly always will be, there are risks involved in basing decisions on such information. Businesses constantly have to live with risk: risk that market prices will decline, that costs will rise, that machinery will break down, that competitors will launch new products, and so on. But in our everyday lives, we too face risks because of poor information about the future. Do you spend money on a holiday in this country and risk having a wet week? Do you go to the cinema to see a film, only to find out that you don't enjoy it?

Sometimes you lack information simply because you have not taken the time or paid the money to acquire it. This could apply to the specifications of a product. A little research could give you the information you require. Sometimes, however, the information is simply not available – at least not in the form that will give you certainty. A firm may do market research to find out what consumers want, but until a product is launched, it will not be certain how much will be sold. A market analyst may give you a forecast of what will happen to stock market prices or to the dollar/euro exchange rate, but analysts frequently get it wrong.

1. *What risks are involved in buying the latest version of the iPhone? Compare these with the risks of buying a house.*
2. *Give some examples of ways in which it is possible to buy better information. Your answer should suggest that there is profitable business to be made in supplying information.*
3. *Is there a role for government intervention in the provision of information? (We return to this in Chapter 11.)*

---

the cycle takes longer than you had hoped or the machine is noisy.

Buying consumer durables thus involves uncertainty. So too does the purchase of assets, whether a physical asset such as a house or financial assets such as shares. In the case of assets, the uncertainty is over their future *price*. If you buy shares in a company, what will happen to their price? Will it shoot up, thus enabling you to sell them at a large profit, or will it fall? You cannot know for certain.

KEY IDEA 15 *Good decision making requires good information.* Where information is poor, decisions and their outcomes are also likely to be poor.

The problems surrounding making decisions today based on expectations of the future are explored in Threshold Concept 9.

Attitudes towards risk and uncertainty

So how will uncertainty affect people's behaviour? The answer is that it depends on their attitudes towards taking a gamble. To examine these attitudes let us assume that a person does at least know the odds of the gamble. In other words, the person is operating under conditions of risk rather than uncertainty.

KI 11 p80

 Define 'risk' and 'uncertainty' (see Chapter 3, pages 71–80).

To illustrate different attitudes towards risk, consider the case of gambling that a particular number will come up on the throw of a dice. There is a one in six chance of this happening. Would you gamble? It depends on what odds you were offered and on your attitude to risk.

Odds can be of three types. They can be *favourable* odds. This is where on average you will gain. If, for example, you were offered odds of 10 to 1 on the throw of a dice, then for a £1 bet you would get nothing if you lost, but you would get £10 (plus your £1 stake) if your number came up. Since your number should come up on average one time in every six, on average you will gain. The longer you go on playing, the more money you are likely to win. If the odds were 5 to 1 (i.e. you win £5 plus get your £1 stake back), they would be *fair* odds. On average you would break even. If, however, they were less than 5 to 1, they would be described as *unfavourable*. On average you would lose.

Give some examples of gambling (or risk taking in general) where the odds are (a) unfavourable; (b) fair; (c) favourable.

There are three possible categories of attitude towards risk.

Risk neutral. This is where a person will take a gamble if the odds are favourable; not take a gamble if the odds are unfavourable; and be indifferent about taking a gamble if the odds are fair.

Risk loving. Such a person is prepared to take a gamble even if the odds are unfavourable. The more risk loving a person is, the worse the odds he or she will be prepared to accept.

Risk averse. Such a person may not be prepared to take a gamble even if the odds are favourable. The more risk averse people are, the better the odds would have to be to entice them to take a gamble. Few people are totally risk averse and thus totally unwilling to take a gamble. If I offered people a bet on the toss of a coin such that tails they pay me 10p and heads I pay them £100, few would refuse (unless on moral grounds).

Diminishing marginal utility of income and attitudes towards risk taking

Avid gamblers may be risk lovers. People who spend hours in the betting shop or at the race track may enjoy the risks, knowing that there is always the chance that they might win. On average, however, such people will lose. After all, the bookmakers have to take their cut and thus the odds are generally unfavourable.

Most people, however, for most of the time are risk averse. We prefer to avoid insecurity. But is there a simple reason for this? Economists use marginal utility analysis to explain why.

They argue that the gain in utility to people from an extra £100 is less than the loss of utility from forgoing £100. Imagine your own position. You have probably adjusted your standard of living to your income, or are trying to do so. If you unexpectedly gained £100 that would be very nice: you could buy some new clothes or have a meal out. But if you lost £100, you might have serious difficulties in making ends meet. Thus if you were offered the gamble of a 50:50 chance of winning or losing £100, you might well decline the gamble.

 Which gamble would you be more likely to accept, a 60:40 chance of gaining or losing £10 000, or a 50:50 chance of gaining or losing £1? Explain why.

This risk-averse behaviour accords with the principle of *diminishing marginal utility*. Up to now in this chapter we have been focusing on the utility from the consumption of individual goods: Lucy and her cups of tea; Ollie and his packets of crisps. In the case of each individual good, the more we consume, the less satisfaction we gain from each additional unit: the marginal utility falls. But the same principle applies if we look at our *total* consumption. The higher our level of total consumption, the less additional satisfaction will be gained from each additional £1 spent. What we are saying here is that there is a *diminishing marginal utility of income*. The more you earn, the lower will be the utility gained from each *extra* £1. If people on low incomes earn an extra £100, they will feel a lot better off: their marginal utility from that income will be very high. If rich people earn an extra £100, however, their gain in utility will be less.

 Do you think that this provides a moral argument for redistributing income from the rich to the poor? Does it prove that income should be so redistributed?

Why, then, does a diminishing marginal utility of income make us risk averse? The answer is illustrated in Figure 4.18, which shows the *total* utility you get from your income.

The slope of this curve gives the *marginal* utility of your income. As the marginal utility of income diminishes, so the curve gets flatter. A rise in income from £5000 to £10 000 will cause a movement along the curve from point *a* to point *b*. Total utility rises from U_1 to U_2. A similar rise in income from £10 000 to £15 000, however, will lead to a move from point *b* to point *c*, and hence a *smaller* rise in total utility from U_2 to U_3.

Now assume that your income is £10 000 and you are offered a chance of gambling £5000 of it. You are offered the fair odds of a 50:50 chance of gaining an extra £5000 (i.e. doubling it) or losing it. Effectively, then, you have an equal chance of your income rising to £15 000 or falling to £5000.

At an income of £10 000, your total utility is U_2. If your gamble pays off and raises your income to £15 000, your total utility will rise to U_3. If it does not pay off, you will be left with only £5000 and a utility of U_1. Given that you have a 50:50 chance of winning, your *average* expected utility will be midway between U_1 and U_3 (i.e. U_4). But this is the utility that would be gained from an income of £8000. Given that you would prefer U_2 to U_4 you will choose not to take the gamble.

Thus risk aversion is part of rational utility-maximising behaviour.

 If people are generally risk averse, why do so many around the world take part in national lotteries?

In fact most of the time we do not know the odds of taking a gamble. In other words, we operate under conditions of *uncertainty*. This could make us very cautious indeed. The more pessimistic we are, the more cautious we are.

Insurance: a way of removing risks

Insurance is the opposite of gambling. It removes the risk. If, for example, you risk losing your job if you are injured, you can remove the risk of loss of income by taking out an appropriate insurance policy.

Since people are generally risk averse, they will be prepared to pay a premium even though it is more than their expected loss – in other words, they are accepting 'unfair odds'. The total premiums paid to an insurance company

> **Definition**
>
> **Diminishing marginal utility of income** Where each additional pound earned yields less additional utility.

Figure 4.18 The total utility of income

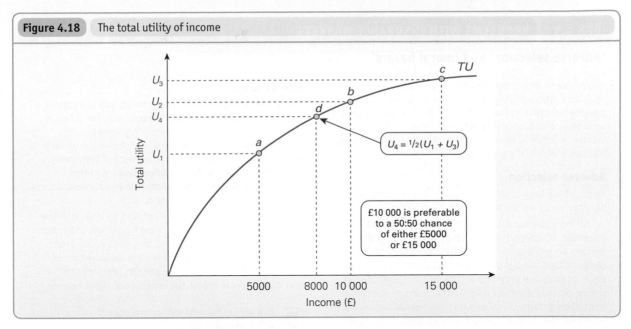

$U_4 = \frac{1}{2}(U_1 + U_3)$

£10 000 is preferable
to a 50:50 chance
of either £5000
or £15 000

will be *more* than the amount it pays out; that is how such companies make a profit.

But does this mean that an insurance company is less risk averse than its customers? Why is it prepared to shoulder the risks that its customers were not? The answer is that the insurance company is able to *pool its risks*.

The pooling of risks

Suppose that each year there is a one in a hundred chance of your house burning down. Although this is only a small chance, it would be so disastrous that you are simply not prepared to take the risk. You thus take out house insurance and are prepared to pay a premium of more than 1 per cent (one in a hundred).

The insurance company, however, is not just insuring you. It is insuring thousands of others at the same time. If your house burns down, there will be approximately 99 others that do not. The premiums the insurance company has collected will be more than enough to cover its payments. The more houses it insures, the smaller will be the variation in the proportion that actually burn down each year.

This is an application of the *law of large numbers*. What is unpredictable for an individual becomes highly predictable in the mass. The more people the insurance company insures, the more predictable is the total outcome.

What is more, the insurance company is in a position to estimate just what the risks are. It can thus work out what premiums it must charge in order to make a profit. Insurance companies even share data amongst themselves to make the estimation of such risk more accurate. With individuals, however, the precise risk is rarely known. You probably do not know your chances of living to 80. But a life assurance company has the statistical data to work out precisely the chances of a person of your age, gender and occupation living to 80. It can convert your *uncertainty* into the company's *risk*.

The pooling of risks does not just require a large number of policies. It also requires the risks to be *independent*. If an insurance company insured 1000 houses *all in the same neighbourhood*, and then there were a major fire in the area, the claims would be enormous. The risks of fire were not independent. The company would, in fact, have been taking a gamble on a single event. If, however, it provides fire insurance for houses scattered all over the country, the risks *are* independent.

1. Why are insurance companies unwilling to provide insurance against losses arising from war or 'civil insurrection'?
2. Name some other events where it would be impossible to obtain insurance.
3. Explain why an insurance company could not pool the risk of flooding in a particular part of a country. Does your answer imply that insurance against flooding is unobtainable?

Another way in which insurance companies can spread their risks is by *diversification*. The more types of insurance a company offers (car, house, life, health, etc.), the greater is likely to be the independence of the risks.

Definitions

Pooling risks (for an insurance company) The more policies an insurance company issues and the more independent the risks of claims from these policies are, the more predictable will be the number of claims.

Law of large numbers The larger the number of events of a particular type, the more predictable will be their average outcome.

Independent risks Where two risky events are unconnected. The occurrence of one will not affect the likelihood of the occurrence of the other.

Diversification Where a firm expands into new types of business.

BOX 4.6   PROBLEMS WITH INSURANCE MARKETS

'Adverse selection' and 'moral hazard'

Two problems encountered by insurance companies in setting insurance premiums (the price of insurance) are termed *adverse selection* and *moral hazard*. Both these problems arise as a consequence of asymmetric information, when the insurance company knows less about the individual seeking insurance than that person does.

Adverse selection

This is where the people who take out insurance are likely to be those who have the highest risk.

For example, suppose that a company offers health-care insurance. It surveys the population and works out that the average person requires £200 of treatment per year. The company thus sets the premium at £250 (the extra £50 to cover its costs and provide a profit). But it is probable that the people most likely to take out the insurance are those most likely to fall sick: those who have been ill before, those whose families have a history of illness, those in jobs that are hazardous to health, etc. These people on average may require £500 of treatment per year. The insurance company would soon make a loss.

But could the company then simply raise premiums to £550 or £600? It could, but the problem is that the higher premiums will only be attractive to the high-risk individuals. If the company raises the premium it will thereby be depriving the person of average health of reasonably priced insurance and reducing the potential to sell insurance to people who value it.

The answer is for the company to obtain information that will allow it to identify the risk different people face. This process is known as 'screening'. There are several methods that the company can adopt. It can ask for personal information; for example, if you are applying for health-care insurance, you may have to fill out a questionnaire giving details of your lifestyle and family history or undergo a medical so that the company can have an expert opinion on your level of risk and set an appropriate premium.

The second form of screening occurs when an insurance company makes use of market data to assess risk. For example, companies offering life insurance can make use of life expectancy tables produced annually by the National Office of Statistics.

1. *What details does an insurance company require to know before it will insure a person to drive a car?*
2. *In 2011 the European Court ruled that from December 2012 insurance companies would not be able to vary premiums according to gender. What would you expect the impact of this legislation to have been? Find out what did happen in the market for motor insurance.*

Moral hazard

This occurs when having insurance makes you less careful and thus increases your risk to the company. For example, if your bicycle is insured against theft, you may be less concerned to go through the hassle of chaining it up each time you leave it. Again this is an example of asymmetric information, because the insurance company cannot determine for any individual whether taking out insurance will make him or her more careless.

If insurance companies work out risks by looking at the total number of bicycle thefts, these figures will understate the risks to the company because they will include thefts from uninsured people who are likely to be more careful. One solution is for insurance companies to write contracts that allow them to reduce the incidence of moral hazard.

How will the following reduce moral hazard?
(a) A no-claims bonus.
(b) An excess, which means that the claimant has to pay the first part of any claim.
(c) Offering lower premiums to those less likely to claim (e.g. lower house contents premiums for those with burglar alarms).

The problem of moral hazard occurs in many other walks of life. A good example is that of debt. If someone else is willing to pay your debts (e.g. your parents), it is likely to make you less careful in your spending. If a bank knows that it will be bailed out by a government and not allowed to fail, it is likely to take more risks in seeking profits. This type of argument has been used by some rich countries as a reason for not cancelling the debts of poor countries (see section 27.4).

Insurance market failure

If the problems of adverse selection and moral hazard cannot be overcome by screening and carefully written contracts, then this is not a problem for them alone. Most people in society are risk averse and are willing to pay others to reduce the risk that they face. Insurance markets have grown up in response to this. If insurance markets fail, then society suffers as a consequence. If individuals cannot get insurance at a 'fair' price, their utility will be lower and so will that of society.

Definitions

Adverse selection The tendency of those who are at greatest risk to take out insurance.

Moral hazard The temptation to take more risk when you know that other people (e.g. insurers) will cover the risks.

Section summary

1. When people buy consumer durables, they may be uncertain of their benefits and any future costs. When they buy financial assets, they may be uncertain of what will happen to their price in the future. Buying under these conditions of imperfect knowledge is therefore a form of gambling. If we know the odds of such gambles we are said to be operating under conditions of risk. If we do not know the odds, we are said to be operating under conditions of uncertainty.

2. People can be divided into risk lovers, those who are risk averse and those who are risk neutral. Because of the diminishing marginal utility of income, it is rational for people to be risk averse (unless gambling is itself pleasurable).

3. Insurance is a way of eliminating risks for policy holders. If people are risk averse they will be prepared to pay premiums in order to obtain insurance. Insurance companies, on the other hand, are prepared to take on these risks because they can pool risk by selling a large number of policies. According to the law of large numbers, what is unpredictable for a single policy holder becomes highly predictable for a large number of them provided that their risks are independent of each other.

4. Insurance markets arise as an institutional response to risk aversion. Their existence makes society 'better off' since they increase individual utility. Insurance market failure may arise as a result of asymmetric information, through either adverse selection or moral hazard.

4.4 BEHAVIOURAL ECONOMICS

What is behavioural economics?

Behavioural economics is the study of how society answers the 'What', 'How' and 'For whom' questions that we looked at in Chapter 1. In other words, it looks at the choices people make, the decisions of firms, the way governments can use information and incentives.

At this point you may be thinking there is something wrong here – surely we have just described traditional economics, so what is different about behavioural economics? The answer lies in the assumptions made; traditional economics assumes that people behave rationally. Behavioural economics relaxes this assumption and looks at the way people actually behave. Individuals are subject to emotions and impulses, which can result in 'errors' and biases in decision making; recognising this can lead to greater understanding of economic systems and agents' behaviour.

Why is everyone talking about behavioural economics?

Until relatively recently there was general agreement amongst economists about how economies worked. It was assumed that people ('agents') were rational and that markets balanced supply and demand. At a macro level there were fluctuations associated with the business cycle, but these had become smaller than in the past and some believed that we had seen the end of 'boom and bust'. Although it was recognised by many economists that people did not behave rationally all the time, it was still assumed that any mistakes resulting from irrational choices and decisions would 'balance out' on average.

However, when the financial crisis occurred in 2007–8, it quickly became clear that agents had made the same mistakes over and over. (See Case Study 18.7 in MyEconLab for a look at the sub-prime housing market.) This has provoked a great deal of discussion about how economists should model the financial crisis and subsequent recession and whether assumptions of rationality have resulted in inaccurate models and forecasts. The broader question for economists and policy makers is whether the failures of financial markets can be incorporated into standard economics, or whether we need a new paradigm that emphasises people's behaviour and examines in detail how people act when they have less than perfect information.

The role of experiments

In Chapter 1 (see pages 28–9) we explained that economics is a social science, with methodologies in common with the natural sciences; both construct models which can be used to explain and predict. In the natural sciences it is common to use experiments to test models or to drive their construction. This, however, was generally not the case with economics. However, with the rise of behavioural economics, the use of experiments has become increasingly popular, for both research and teaching purposes.

Economists can study how people behave under a range of conditions, changing one variable at a time. In an experiment the *ceteris paribus* principle can be put into practice. Experiments are now a well-established method of looking at consumer behaviour, but are also increasingly being used by policy makers to understand outcomes that traditional theory might not predict.

It is important to realise that experiments do not always suggest that rationality is a mistaken assumption. In many circumstances individuals do behave in exactly the way that traditional theory would suggest.

Explaining 'irrational' behaviour

Of course, identifying that individuals do not always behave in a rational manner is only part of the task facing behavioural economists. They also need to explain *why* people behave in the way that they do. This is the subject of a rich and growing literature, but some of the main ideas are described below.

Framing options will affect choice

In traditional models of consumer choice, individuals aim to maximise their utility when choosing between goods, or bundles of goods. The context in which the choices are offered is not considered. Yet, in real life, we see that context is important; people will often make different choices when they are presented, or framed, in different ways. For example, people will buy more of a good when it is flagged up as a special offer than they would if there is no mention of an offer, *even though the price is the same*. This principle has led to the development of 'nudge' theory, which underpins many marketing techniques. We will look at it in more detail in Chapter 8 and in Box 4.7 below.

Too much choice

Choice is a good thing; well that is certainly what economists thought for a long time. Choice allows us to maximise our utility by making 'better' decisions. Yet this does not always seem to be the case. A well-known experiment conducted by Sheena Iyengar and Mark Lepper suggested that in some circumstances choice may be bad for consumers. They set up stalls offering shoppers the chance to sample a number of jams. They showed that while shoppers were most attracted to the stall that offered 24 samples, they were in fact 10 times more likely actually to buy when offered only six varieties. Too much choice appeared to hinder decision making and so to reduce consumers' utility.

Bounded rationality

A person might in principle want to maximise utility, but faces complex choices and imperfect information. Sometimes it *would* be possible to obtain better information, but the person decides it is not worth the time and effort, and perhaps expense, of getting more information. Their ability to be 'rational' is thus limited or '**bounded**' by the situation in which they find themselves. So they resort to making the best guess, or to drawing on past experiences of similar choices that turned out to be good or bad. For example, people may have found that a particular brand of products is to their liking. When they want a new type of product, they may thus decide to use the same brand, even though they have never bought that particular product before. This 'brand loyalty' is something that companies recognise and strive to develop in their customers.

Sometimes, when people are likely to face similar choices again, they resort to trial and error. They try a product. If they like it, they buy it again; if not, they don't.

This use of past experience, or rules of thumb or trial and error is known as *heuristics*. The decision is not guaranteed to be optimal, but it might be the best bet given the limited information or time available.

Where behavioural economics comes in is that different people may respond differently from each other in otherwise similar circumstances. These differences may relate to their risk attitudes (how willing they are to 'get it wrong') or to their overall degree of optimism or pessimism. Or they may relate to how similar the present choice is to previous ones. Behavioural economists seek to understand the different assumptions people make and their different responses in situations of bounded rationality. Such an understanding is also important to those working in the advertising and marketing industry: they want to know the most effective ways of influencing people's spending decisions.

Relativity matters

If I am making a choice about buying a car, traditional economics says my demand will derive from a number of factors: my income, my tastes for driving and for particular cars; the price of the car I am considering, and of the alternatives; and the associated costs of motoring. Yet I might be also highly influenced by the car my brother drives; if he chooses an Audi, perhaps I would like a more expensive car, a Mercedes possibly. If he switches to a Jaguar, then perhaps I will opt for a Porsche. I want a better (or faster or more expensive) car than my brother; I am concerned not only with my choice of car but with my *relative* choice.

This does not disprove that choice depends on perceived utility. But it does demonstrate that utility often depends on your consumption relative to that of other people. Again, this is something that the advertising industry is only too well aware of. Adverts often try to encourage you to buy a product by showing that *other* people are buying it.

Herding and 'groupthink'

Being influenced by what other people buy, and thus making relative choices, can lead to herd behaviour. A fashion might catch on; people might grab an item in a sale because other people seem to be grabbing it as well; people might buy a particular share on the stock market because other people are buying it.

Definitions

Bounded rationality When the ability to make rational decisions is limited by lack of information or the time necessary to obtain such information or by a lack of understanding of complex situations.

Heuristics The use of strategies that draw on simple lessons from past experience when faced with similar, although not identical, choices.

BOX 4.7 NUDGING PEOPLE

How to change behaviour without taking away choice

One observation of behavioural economists is that people make many decisions out of habit. They use simple rules, such as: 'I'll buy the more expensive item because it's bound to be better'; or 'I'll buy this item because it's on offer'; or 'I always take the car to work, so I don't need to consider alternatives'; or 'Other people are buying this, so it must be worth having'.

Given people behave like this, how might they be persuaded to change their behaviour? Governments might want to know this. Are there 'nudges' which will encourage people to stop smoking, or save energy, or take more exercise, or eat more healthy food? Firms too will want to know how to sell more of their products or to motivate their workforce. Even parents might want to make use of behavioural economics.

In a 2008 book by Richard Thaler and Cass Sunstein.[1] They identify how people can be 'nudged' to change their behaviour. They use the expression 'choice architecture' – the deliberate framing of choices to 'nudge' people to make the preferred decision. For example, healthy food can be placed in a prominent position in a school cafeteria or healthy snacks at the supermarket checkout. Traditionally, sweets and other unhealthy, but tasty, snacks were found by the checkout. If fashion houses ceased to use ultra-thin models, it could reduce the incentive for teenage girls to under-eat. If schoolchildren are given stars or smiley faces for turning off lights or picking up litter, they might be more inclined to do so.

Another example concerns 'opting in' versus 'opting out'. With organ donor cards, or many company pension schemes, or charitable giving, people have to opt in. In other words, they have to make the decision to take part. Many as a result do not, partly because they never seem to find the time to do so, even though they might quite like to. With the busy lives people lead, it's too easy to think, 'Yes, I'll do that some time', but never actually get round to doing it.

With an 'opt-out' system, people are automatically signed up to the scheme, but can freely choose to opt out. Thus it would be assumed that organs from people killed in an accident who had not opted out could be used for transplants. If you did not want your organs to be used, you would have to join a register. It could be the same with charitable giving. Some firms add a small charitable contribution to the price of their products (e.g. airline tickets or utility bills), unless people opt out. Similarly, under pension arrangements introduced from 2012, firms automatically deduct pension contributions from employees' wages unless they opt out of the scheme.

Opt-in schemes have participation rates of around 60 per cent, while otherwise identical opt-out funds retain between 90 and 95 per cent of employees. It is no wonder that Adair Turner, in his report on pensions, urged legislation to push pension schemes to an opt-in default position and that policy is moving in this direction.[2]

Understanding people's behaviour and then adjusting incentives, often only very slightly, can nudge people to behave differently. The Coalition government adopted an enthusiastic approach to policy making informed by 'nudge' theory from the time they took office in 2010. They set up a dedicated 'nudge' unit, officially known as the Behavioural Insights Team. This looks at policy mechanisms to nudge people to behave in ways that the government perceives as better, whether socially, environmentally or simply personally.

The approach has been called 'soft paternalism'; there remains choice, but this choice is framed in such a way that policy aims are more likely to be achieved. The effects that underpin behaviour have been summarised by the unit in an acronym, MINDSPACE.[3]

Messenger	We are heavily influenced by the person or agency that communicates information.
Incentives	Our responses to incentives are by predictable mental shortcuts, such as strongly avoiding losses.
Norms	We are strongly influenced by what others do.
Defaults	We 'go with the flow' of pre-set options.
Salience	Our attention is drawn to what is novel and seems relevant to us.
Priming	Our acts are often influenced by subconscious cues.
Affect	Our emotional associations can powerfully shape our actions.
Commitments	We seek to be consistent with our public promises and to reciprocate acts.
Ego	We act in ways which make us feel better about ourselves.

Some examples of the way the unit has influenced policy certainly appear impressive. A trial with HMRC was carried out, telling late taxpayers that most people in their towns had already paid their tax. This increased payment rates by 15 percentage points, which could generate £30 million of extra revenue to the Exchequer annually if repeated nationally.

1. How would you nudge members of a student household to be more economical in the use of electricity?
2. How could the government nudge people to stop dropping litter?
3. In the 2011 Budget, George Osborne announced that charitable giving in wills would be exempt from inheritance tax. Do you think this will be an effective way of encouraging more charitable donations?

[1] Richard H. Thaler and Cass R. Sunstein, *Nudge: Improving Decisions about Health, Wealth, and Happiness* (Yale University Press, 2008).
[2] Richard Reeves, 'Why a nudge from the state beats a slap', *Observer*, 20 July 2008.
[3] *MINDSPACE: A Practical Guide* (Institute for Government, 2010).

Now part of this may simply be bounded rationality. Sometimes it may be a good rule of thumb to buy something that other people want, as they might know more about it than you do. But there is a danger in such behaviour: other people may also be buying it because other people are buying it, and this builds a momentum. Sales may soar and the price may be driven well above a level that reflects the utility that people will end up gaining. People have been persuaded to buy various risky financial assets because other people have been buying them and hence their price has been rising. This type of behaviour helps to understand some of the aspects of destabilising speculation that we examined in section 3.2 (pages 76–7).

Sunk costs

Think back to our definition of rational decision making; consumers will weigh up the marginal costs and benefits of any action. This must imply that costs already incurred in the past are irrelevant. These are called sunk costs. (The same principle applies to firms: see Key Idea 18 on page 139 and Box 5.5 on page 140.) Yet when we look at how people actually behave, they do seem to be influenced by sunk costs. An example of this arises if you find yourself reading a novel, but not enjoying it. What should you do? The answer is that, unless you believe that you will start enjoying the story soon, you should stop reading it. Many people would argue that they have paid for the book and so should carry on to the end. But this is not rational. It doesn't matter whether the book cost £5 or £25, the decision to read on should only take the future (opportunity) costs and future benefits into account.

Economic policy

Governments, in designing policy, will normally attempt to change people's behaviour. They might want to encourage people to work harder, to save more, to recycle rubbish, to use their cars less, to eat more healthily, and so on. If the policy is to be successful, it is vital for the policy measures to contain appropriate incentives: whether it be a tax rise, a grant or subsidy, a new law or regulation, an advertising campaign or direct help.

But whether the incentives are appropriate depends on how people will respond to them, and to know that, the policy makers will need to understand people's behaviour. This is where behavioural economics comes in. People might respond as rational maximisers; but they may not. It is thus important to understand how context affects behaviour and adjust policy incentives appropriately.

 Remember the question we asked at the beginning of this chapter: 'Do you ever purchase things irrationally? If so, what are they and why is your behaviour irrational?' Can you better explain this behaviour in the light of behavioural economics?

What does this mean for economic theory?

We have seen that behavioural economics can identify and explain situations where traditional economic models fail to predict outcomes. But should we go further than this? If the rational consumer lies at the heart of economic theory, and if we can show that individuals frequently behave irrationally, does this mean all economic reasoning is invalid? Well, as we have shown in this chapter, we can't know what the future will bring. However, it seems more likely that economists will adapt existing theories, using behavioural economics to enhance what we have previously understood. The aim should be for more flexible and robust models, which will not fail to anticipate problems in the way that happened in 2007.

Section summary

1. Traditional economics is based on the premise that consumers act rationally, weighing up the costs and benefits of the choices open to them. Behavioural economics acknowledges that real-world decisions do not always appear rational; it seeks to understand and explain what economic agents actually do. Although much of this work was started more than 10 years ago, the financial crisis of 2007/8 focused attention on the systematic failure of existing models.

2. Experiments provide useful insights into the way individuals act when faced with choices and decisions. They allow economists to test existing models and theories, but also provide motivation for the construction of new theories of human behaviour.

3. A number of effects can explain why rational decision making may fail to predict actual behaviour. These include: the roles of framing and relativity; individuals failing to disregard sunk costs and being confused by too many choices. Research undertaken by behavioural economists is bringing together aspects of psychology and economics, in order to understand fully how we behave.

4. The question of how valid is the assumption of rationality remains. Is behavioural economics a refinement of traditional economics, or a new paradigm, which will eventually result in the reworking of existing theories and models?

| BOX 4.8 | IS ECONOMICS THE STUDY OF SELFISH BEHAVIOUR? | CASE STUDIES AND APPLICATIONS |

Is what's best for the individual, best for others?

Many of the choices we make are not made as individuals purely for ourselves. If you are a member of a family or living with friends, many of your 'consumption' decisions will affect the other members of the household and many of their decisions will affect you.

Some things will be decided jointly: what to have for dinner, what colour to paint the hall, whether to have a party. Put it another way: when you gain utility, the other members of the household will often gain too (e.g. from things 'jointly' consumed, such as central heating).

Sometimes, however, it is the other way round. When things are jointly purchased, such as food, then one person's consumption will often be at the expense of other members of the household. 'Who's finished all the milk?' 'I want to watch a different television programme.'

What we are saying is that when individuals are in a group, such as a family, a club or an outing with a group of friends, their behaviour will affect and be affected by the other members of the group. For this reason, we have to amend our simple analysis of 'rational' choice. Let us consider two situations. The first is where people are trying to maximise their own self-interest within the group. The second is where people are genuinely motivated by the interests of the other members – whether from feelings of love, friendship, moral duty or whatever. We will consider these two situations within a family.

Self-interested behaviour

If you do not consider the other members of the family, this could rebound on you. For example, if you do not clean out the bath after yourself, or do not do your share of the washing up, then you may have to 'pay the price'. Other family members may get cross with you, or behave equally selfishly themselves.

When considering doing things for their own benefit, therefore, the 'rational' person would at the very least consider the reactions of the other members of the family. We could still use the concept of marginal utility, however, to examine such behaviour. If marginal utility were greater than the price ($MU > P$), it would be 'rational' to do more of any given activity. Here, though, marginal utility would include utility not only from directly consuming goods or services within the household, but also from the favourable reactions to you from other family members. Likewise, marginal utility would be reduced if there were any unfavourable reaction from other family members. The 'price' (i.e. the marginal cost to you) would include not only the monetary costs to you of consuming something, but also any other sacrifice you make in order to consume it. In other words, the price would be the full opportunity cost.

Take first the case of goods or services jointly consumed, such as a family meal. Do you offer to cook dinner? If you were motivated purely by self-interest, you would do so if the marginal benefit (i.e. marginal utility) to you exceeded the marginal cost to you. The marginal benefit would include the benefit to you of consuming the meal, plus any pleasure you got from the approval of other family members, plus any entitlement to being let off other chores. The marginal cost to you would include any monetary costs to you (e.g. of purchasing the ingredients) and the sacrifice of any alternative pleasurable activities that you had to forgo (such as watching television). Whether the actual preparation of the meal was regarded as a marginal benefit or a marginal cost would depend on whether the individual saw it as a pleasure or a chore.

Clearly, these benefits and costs are highly subjective: they are as you perceive them. But the principle is simple: if you were behaving purely out of self-interest, you would cook the meal if you felt that you would gain more from doing so than it cost you.

Now take the case of consuming something individually where it deprives another household member of consuming it (such as taking the last yoghurt from the fridge). Again, if you were behaving purely out of self-interest, you would have to weigh up the pleasure from that yoghurt against the cost to you of incurring the irritation of other family members.

Behaviour in the interests of the family as a whole

However, most people are not totally selfish, especially when it comes to relating to other members of their family. In fact, family members are often willing to make personal sacrifices or put in considerable effort (e.g. with household chores or child rearing) for the sake of other family members, without being motivated by what they individually can get out of it.

In such cases, consumption decisions can be examined at two levels: that of the individual and that of the whole family.

As far as individuals are concerned, analysis in terms of their own marginal benefit and marginal cost would be too simplistic. Often it is a more accurate picture to see household members, rather than behaving selfishly, instead behaving in the self-interest of the whole household. So a decision about what food to buy for the family at the supermarket, if taken by an individual member, is likely to take into account the likes and dislikes of other family members, and the costs to the whole household budget. In other words, it is the whole family's marginal benefits and marginal costs that the individual family member is considering.

Other forms of altruism

It can be argued that unselfish behaviour within a family, or social circle, is not truly altruistic. After all, it is not unreasonable to suppose that others will treat you better as a consequence. But outside the circle of family and friends we do see behaviour that does appear to be altruistic. Individuals choose to give money to charity, to return other people's property when they find it and to give blood that will help save strangers. This is a further area of economic theory that behavioural economists find interesting and it is providing a focus for economic research. The apparent contradiction between utility maximisation and the actions of individuals provides an opportunity to gain further understanding about motivation and utility.

1. *Imagine that you are going out for the evening with a group of friends. How would you decide where to go? Would this decision-making process be described as 'rational' behaviour?*

2. *Think of some examples of altruistic behaviour towards strangers. In each case list some of the reasons why individuals might behave 'unselfishly'.*

END OF CHAPTER QUESTIONS

1. Imagine that you had £10 per month to allocate between two goods, A and B. Imagine that good A cost £2 per unit and good B cost £1 per unit. Imagine also that the utilities of the two goods are those set out in the table below. (Note that the two goods are not substitutes for each other, so that the consumption of one does not affect the utility gained from the other.)

   (a) What would be the marginal utility ratio (MU_A/MU_B) for the following combinations of the two goods: (i) 1A, 8B; (ii) 2A, 6B; (iii) 3A, 4B; (iv) 4A, 2B? (Each combination would cost £10.)

   (b) Show that where the marginal utility ratio (MU_A/MU_B) equals the price ratio (P_A/P_B), total utility is maximised.

   (c) If the two goods were substitutes for each other, why would it not be possible to construct a table like the one given here?

The utility gained by a person from various quantities of two goods: A and B

Good A			Good B		
Units per month	MU (utils)	TU (utils)	Units per month	MU (utils)	TU (utils)
0	–	0.0	0	–	0.0
1	11.0	11.0	1	8.0	8.0
2	8.0	19.0	2	7.0	15.0
3	6.0	25.0	3	6.5	21.5
4	4.5	29.5	4	5.0	26.5
5	3.0	32.5	5	4.5	31.0
			6	4.0	35.0
			7	3.5	38.5
			8	3.0	41.5
			9	2.6	44.1
			10	2.3	46.4

2. Is it reasonable to assume that people seek to equate the marginal utility/price ratios of the goods that they purchase, if (a) they have never heard of 'utility', let alone 'marginal utility'; (b) marginal utility cannot be measured in any absolute way?

3. Consider situations where you might consider swapping items with someone. Why are such situations relatively rare? Can you think of circumstances in which this might be more common?

4. Explain why the price of a good is no reflection of the total value that consumers put on it.

*5. Sketch a person's indifference map for two goods X and Y. Mark the optimum consumption point. Now illustrate the following (you might need to draw a separate diagram for each):

   (a) A rise in the price of good X, but no change in the price of good Y.

   (b) A shift in the person's tastes from good Y to good X.

   (c) A fall in the person's income and a fall in the price of good Y, with the result that the consumption of Y remains constant (but that of X falls).

*6. Distinguish between a normal good, an inferior good and a Giffen good. Use indifference curves to illustrate your answer.

*7. Assume that commuters regard bus journeys as an inferior good and car journeys as a normal good. Using indifference curves, show how (a) a rise in incomes and (b) a fall in bus fares will affect the use of these two modes of transport. How could people's tastes be altered so that bus journeys were no longer regarded as an inferior good? If tastes were altered in this way, what effect would it have on the indifference curves?

8. A country's central bank (e.g. the Bank of England or the US Federal Reserve Bank) has a key role in ensuring the stability of the banking system. In many countries the central bank is prepared to bail banks out which find themselves in financial difficulties. Although this has the benefit of reducing the chance of banks going bankrupt and depositors losing their money, it can create a moral hazard. Explain why.

9. Consider the EU ruling that gender may not be used to differentiate insurance premiums. Which insurance markets would be affected by outlawing age 'discrimination' in a similar manner? What would be the impact?

10. How does economics predict rational consumers will treat spending on credit cards compared with spending cash? Do you think that there are likely to be differences in the way people spend by each? If so, can you explain why?

11. Many European countries operate organ donor schemes, some with schemes requiring that potential donors opt in, others with a system of opting out, or presumed consent. Explain why a system of presumed consent is likely to result in much higher numbers of donors. Does your answer suggest that we should move to presumed consent for organ donors in the UK?

Online resources

Additional case studies in MyEconLab

4.1   Bentham and the philosophy of utilitarianism. This looks at the historical and philosophical underpinning of the ideas of utility maximisation.

4.2   Utility under attack. This looks at the birth of indifference analysis, which was seen as a means of overcoming the shortcomings of marginal utility analysis.

4.3   Applying indifference curve analysis to taxes on goods. Assume that the government wants to raise extra revenue from an expenditure tax. Should it put a relatively small extra tax on all goods, or a relatively large one on just certain selected goods?

4.4   Income and substitution effects: the Slutsky approach. This looks at an alternative way of using indifference analysis to analyse income and substitution effects.

4.5   Deriving an Engel curve. Income elasticity of demand and the income–consumption curve.

4.6   The characteristics approach to analysing consumer demand. This is an extension of the analysis of Box 4.5.

Maths Case 4.1 Finding the optimum consumption point: Part 1. This case looks at how the utility maximisation point can be discovered with a Cobb–Douglas utility function with given prices and a given budget constraint.

Maths Case 4.2 Finding the optimum consumption point: Part 2. This case uses the Lagrange method to solve the same problem as in Maths Case 4.1

Websites relevant to this chapter

Numbers and sections refer to websites listed in the Web Appendix and hotlinked from this book's website at **www.pearsoned.co.uk/sloman.**

- For news articles relevant to this chapter, see the *Economic News* section in MyEconLab.

- For general news on demand and consumers, see websites in section A, and particularly A2, 3, 4, 8, 9, 11, 12, 23, 25, 36. See also site A41 for links to economics news articles on particular search topics (e.g. consumer demand and advertising).

- For data, information and sites on products and marketing, see sites B2, 3, 17, 11, 13, 17.

- For student resources relevant to Part C, see sites C1–7, 19.

- For more on behavioural economics, see sites C1, 6, 7, 23.

MyEconLab

This book can be supported by MyEconLab, which contains a range of additional resources, including an online homework and tutorial system designed to test and build your understanding.

You need both an access card and a course ID to access MyEconLab:

1. Is your lecturer using MyEconLab? Ask your lecturer for your course ID.

2. Has an access card been included with the book at a reduced cost? Check the inside back cover of the book.

3. If you have a course ID but no access card, go to: http://www.myeconlab.com/ to buy access to this interactive study programme.

Background to Supply

CHAPTER MAP

5.1 The short-run theory of production   **133**
Short- and long-run changes in production   133
The law of diminishing returns   135
The short-run production function: total product   135
The short-run production function: average and
    marginal product   136

5.2 Costs in the short run   **139**
Measuring costs of production   139
Costs and inputs   139
Total cost   140
Average and marginal costs   141

5.3 The long-run theory of production   **144**
The scale of production   144
Location   146
The size of the whole industry   146
The optimum combination of factors: the
    marginal product approach   147
*The optimum combination of factors: the
    isoquant/isocost approach   148
Postscript: decision making in different
    time periods   152

5.4 Costs in the long run   **154**
Long-run average costs   154
Long-run marginal costs   155
The relationship between long-run and short-run
    average cost curves   155
Long-run cost curves in practice   156
*Derivation of long-run costs from an isoquant map 157

5.5 Revenue   **158**
Total, average and marginal revenue   158
Revenue curves when price is not affected by the
    firm's output   159
Revenue curves when price varies with output   160
Shifts in revenue curves   162

5.6 Profit maximisation   **162**
Short-run profit maximisation: using total curves   163
Short-run profit maximisation: using average and
    marginal curves   163
Some qualifications   164

So far we have assumed that supply curves are upward sloping: that a higher price will encourage firms to supply more. But just how much will firms choose to supply at each price? It depends largely on the amount of profit they will make. If a firm can increase its profits by producing more, it will normally do so.

Profit is made by firms earning more from the sale of goods than they cost to produce. A firm's total profit ($T\Pi$) is thus the difference between its total sales revenue (TR) and its total costs of production (TC):

$$T\Pi = TR - TC$$

In order then to discover how a firm can maximise its profit or even get a sufficient level of profit, we must first consider what determines costs and revenue.

The first four sections build up a theory of short-run and long-run costs. They show how output depends on the inputs used, and how costs depend on the amount of output produced. Section 5.5 then looks at revenue. Finally, in section 5.6, we bring cost and revenue together to see how profit is determined. In particular, we shall see how profit varies with output and how the point of maximum profit is found.

Chapter 4 went behind the demand curve. It saw how the 'rational' consumer weighs up the *benefits* (utility) of consuming various amounts of goods or combinations of goods against their *costs* (their price).

We now need to go behind the supply curve and find out just how the **rational producer** (or 'firm' as we call all producers) will behave.

In this case, we shall be looking at the benefits and costs to the firm of producing various quantities of goods and using various alternative methods of production. We shall be asking:

- How much will be produced?
- What combination of inputs will be used?
- How much profit will be made?

Profit and the aims of a firm

The traditional theory of supply, or **theory of the firm**, assumes that firms aim to maximise profit; this is a realistic assumption in many cases. The traditional profit-maximising theory of the firm is examined in this and the following two chapters. First we examine the general principles that govern how much a firm supplies. Then, in Chapters 6 and 7, we look at how supply is affected by the amount of competition a firm faces.

In some circumstances, however, firms may not seek to maximise profits. Instead they may seek to maximise sales, or the rate of growth of sales. Alternatively, they may have no *single* aim, but rather a series of potentially conflicting aims held by different managers in different departments of the firm. Sometimes there may be a conflict between the owners of the firm and those running it. Not surprisingly, a firm's behaviour will depend on just what its aims are. Chapter 8 looks at various **alternative theories** to profit maximisation, each theory depending on the particular aims of the firm.

5.1   THE SHORT-RUN THEORY OF PRODUCTION

The cost of producing any level of output will depend on the amount of inputs (or 'factors of production') used and the price the firm must pay for them. Let us first focus on the quantity of factors used.

 KEY IDEA 16

Output depends on the amount of resources and how they are used. Different amounts and combinations of inputs will lead to different amounts of output. If output is to be produced efficiently, then inputs should be combined in the optimum proportions.

Short- and long-run changes in production

If a firm wants to increase production, it will take time to acquire a greater quantity of certain inputs. For example, a manufacturer can use more electricity by turning on switches, but it might take a while to obtain and install more machines, and longer still to build a bigger, or a second, factory.

If the firm wants to increase output in a hurry, it will only be able to increase the quantity of certain inputs. It can use more raw materials and more fuel. It may be able to use more labour by offering overtime to its existing workforce, or by recruiting extra workers if they are available. But it will have to make do with its existing buildings and most of its machinery.

The distinction we are making here is between *fixed factors* and *variable factors*. A *fixed* factor is an input that cannot be increased within a given time period (e.g. buildings). A *variable* factor is one that can.

The distinction between fixed and variable factors allows us to distinguish between the **short run** and the **long run**.

The short run is a time period during which at least one factor of production is fixed. Output can be increased only by using more variable factors. For example, if an airline wanted to carry more passengers it could do so on existing

---

BOX 5.1 MALTHUS AND THE DISMAL SCIENCE OF ECONOMICS

EXPLORING ECONOMICS

Population growth + diminishing returns = starvation

The law of diminishing returns has potentially cataclysmic implications for the future populations of the world.

If the population of the world grows rapidly, then food output may not keep pace with it. There could be diminishing returns to labour as more and more people crowd onto the limited amount of land available.

This is already a problem in some of the poorest countries of the world, especially in sub-Saharan Africa. The land is barely able to support current population levels. Only one or two bad harvests are needed to cause mass starvation – witness the appalling famines in recent years in Ethiopia and Sudan.

The relationship between population and food output was analysed as long ago as 1798 by the Reverend Thomas Robert Malthus (1766–1834) in his *Essay on the Principle of Population*. This book was a bestseller and made Robert Malthus perhaps the best known of all social scientists of his day.

Malthus argued as follows:

I say that the power of population is indefinitely greater than the power in the earth to produce subsistence for man.

Population when unchecked, increases in a geometrical ratio. Subsistence increases only in an arithmetical ratio. A slight acquaintance with numbers will show the immensity of the first power in comparison with the second.[1]

What Malthus was saying is that world population tends to double about every 25 years or so if unchecked. It grows geometrically, like the series 1, 2, 4, 8, 16, 32, 64, etc. But food output, because of diminishing returns, cannot keep pace with this. It is likely to grow at only an arithmetical rate, like the series 1, 2, 3, 4, 5, 6, 7, etc. It is clear that population, if unchecked, will soon outstrip food supply.

So what is the check on population growth? According to Malthus, it is starvation. As population grows, so food output per head will fall until, with more and more people starving, the death rate will rise. Only then will population growth stabilise at the rate of growth of food output.

Have Malthus's predictions been borne out by events? Two factors have mitigated the forces that Malthus described:

■ The rate of population growth tends to slow down as countries become more developed. Although improved health prolongs life, this tends to be more than offset by a decline in the birth rate as people choose to have smaller families. This is illustrated in the table below. Population growth peaked in the 1960s, has fallen substantially since then and is projected to fall further in future decades.
■ Technological improvements in farming have greatly increased food output per hectare. These include better fertilisers and the development of genetically modified crops. (See Case Study 5.1 in MyEconLab for an example.)

The growth in food output has thus exceeded the rate of population growth in developed countries and in some developing countries too. Nevertheless, the Malthusian spectre is very real for some of the poorest developing countries, which are simply unable to feed their populations satisfactorily. It is these poorest countries of the world which have some of the highest rates of population growth – around 3 per cent per annum in many African countries.

A further cause for concern arises from the move in Asia towards a westernised diet, with meat and dairy products playing a larger part. This further increases pressure on the land, since cattle require considerably more grain to produce meat than would be needed to feed humans a vegetarian diet.

A third factor is cited by some commentators, who remain unconvinced of the strength of Malthus's gloomy prognostication for the world. They believe that he seriously underestimated humankind's capacity to innovate; perhaps human ingenuity is one resource that doesn't suffer from diminishing returns.

1. Why might it be possible for there to be a zero marginal productivity of labour on many family farms in poor countries and yet just enough food for all the members of the family to survive? (Illustrate using MPP and APP curves.)
2. The figures in the following table are based on the assumption that birth rates will fall faster than death rates. Under what circumstances might these forecasts underestimate the rate of growth of world population?

World population levels and growth: actual and projected

		Average annual rate of increase (%)		
Year	World population (billions)	World	More developed regions	Less developed regions
1950	2.5			
1960	3.0	1.8	1.2	2.1
1970	3.7	2.0	1.0	2.4
1980	4.5	1.9	0.7	2.2
1990	5.3	1.7	0.6	2.1
2000	6.1	1.4	0.3	1.7
2010	6.9	1.2	0.3	1.4
2020	7.7	1.1	0.3	1.3
2030	8.4	0.9	0.1	1.0
2040	9.0	0.7	0.1	0.8
2050	9.6	0.6	0.0	0.6

Source: *World Population Prospects: The 2012 Revision* (United Nations, Department of Economic and Social Affairs).

[1] T. R. Malthus, *First Essay on Population* (Macmillan, 1926), pp. 13–14.

flights, if there was space. It could possibly increase the number of flights with its existing fleet, by hiring more crew and using more fuel. But in the short run it could not buy more aircraft: there would not be time for them to be built.

The long run is a time period long enough for all inputs to be varied. Given enough time, a firm can build additional factories and install new machines; an airline can have more aircraft built.

The actual length of the short run will differ from firm to firm and industry to industry. It is not a fixed period of time. It might take a farmer a year to obtain new land, buildings and equipment; if so, the short run is any time period up to a year and the long run is any time period longer than a year. If it takes an airline two years to obtain an extra aircraft, the short run is any period up to two years and the long run is any period longer than two years.

1. How will the length of the short run for the airline depend on the state of the aerospace industry?
2. Up to roughly how long is the short run in the following cases?
    (a) A firm supplying DJs for clubs and parties.
    (b) Nuclear power generation.
    (c) A street food wagon.
    (d) 'Superstore Hypermarkets Ltd.'
    In each case specify your assumptions.

For the remainder of this section we will concentrate on short-run production.

The law of diminishing returns

Production in the short run is subject to *diminishing returns*. You may well have heard of 'the law of diminishing returns': it is one of the most famous of all 'laws' of economics. To illustrate how this law underlies short-run production let us take the simplest possible case where there are just two factors: one fixed and one variable.

Take the case of a farm. Assume the fixed factor is land and the variable factor is labour. Since the land is fixed in supply, output per period of time can be increased only by increasing the number of workers employed. But imagine what would happen as more and more workers crowd onto a fixed area of land. The land cannot go on yielding more and more output indefinitely. After a point the additions to output from each extra worker will begin to diminish.

We can now state the law of diminishing (marginal) returns.

KEY IDEA 17
The law of diminishing marginal returns states that when increasing amounts of a variable factor are used with a given amount of a fixed factor, there will come a point when each extra unit of the variable factor will produce less extra output than the previous unit.

A good example of the law of diminishing returns is given in Case Study 5.1 in MyEconLab. It looks at diminishing returns to the application of nitrogen fertiliser on farmland.

The short-run production function: total product

Let us now see how the law of diminishing returns affects total output, or *total physical product* (TPP) as it is sometimes called.

The relationship between inputs and output is shown in a *production function*. In the simple case of the farm with only two factors – namely, a fixed supply of land ($\bar{L}n$) and a variable supply of farm workers (Lb) – the production function would be

$$TPP = f(\bar{L}n, Lb)$$

This states that total physical product (i.e. the output of the farm) over a given period of time is a function of (i.e. depends on) the quantity of land and labour employed. We could express the precise relationship using an equation (an example is given in Box 5.4).

Alternatively, the production function could be expressed in the form of a table or a graph. Table 5.1 and Figure 5.1 show a hypothetical production function for a farm producing wheat. The first two columns of Table 5.1 and the top diagram in Figure 5.1 show how total wheat output per year varies as extra workers are employed on a fixed amount of land.

With nobody working on the land, output will be zero (point *a*). As the first farm workers are taken on, wheat output initially rises more and more rapidly. The assumption behind this is that with only one or two workers efficiency is low, since the workers are spread too thinly. With more workers, however, they can work together – each, perhaps, doing some specialist job – and thus they can use the land more efficiently. In Table 5.1, output rises more and more rapidly up to the employment of the third worker (point *b*). In Figure 5.1 the *TPP* curve gets steeper up to point *b*.

Definitions

Law of diminishing (marginal) returns When one or more factors are held fixed, there will come a point beyond which the extra output from additional units of the variable factor will diminish.

Total physical product The total output of a product per period of time that is obtained from a given amount of inputs.

Production function The mathematical relationship between the output of a good and the inputs used to produce it. It shows how output will be affected by changes in the quantity of one or more of the inputs.

Table 5.1 Wheat production per year from a particular farm

	Number of workers (Lb)	TPP	APP (= TPP/Lb)	MPP (= ΔTPP/ΔLb)
a	0	0	–	
				3
	1	3	3	
				7
	2	10	5	
b				14
	3	24	8	
				12
c	4	36	9	
				4
	5	40	8	
				2
	6	42	7	
d				0
	7	42	6	
				–2
	8	40	5	

The short-run production function: average and marginal product

In addition to total physical product, two other important concepts are illustrated by a production function: namely, *average physical product* (*APP*) and *marginal physical product* (*MPP*).

Average physical product

This is output (*TPP*) per unit of the variable factor (Q_v). In the case of the farm, it is the output of wheat per worker:

$$APP = TPP/Q_v$$

After point *b*, however, diminishing marginal returns set in: output rises less and less rapidly, and the *TPP* curve correspondingly becomes less steeply sloped.

When point *d* is reached, wheat output is at a maximum: the land is yielding as much as it can. Any more workers employed after that are likely to get in each other's way. Thus beyond point *d*, output is likely to fall again: eight workers actually produce less than seven workers.

Definitions

Average physical product Total output (*TPP*) per unit of the variable factor in question: $APP = TPP/Q_v$.

Marginal physical product The extra output gained by the employment of one more unit of the variable factor: $MPP = \Delta TPP/\Delta Q_v$.

Figure 5.1 Wheat production per year (tonnes)

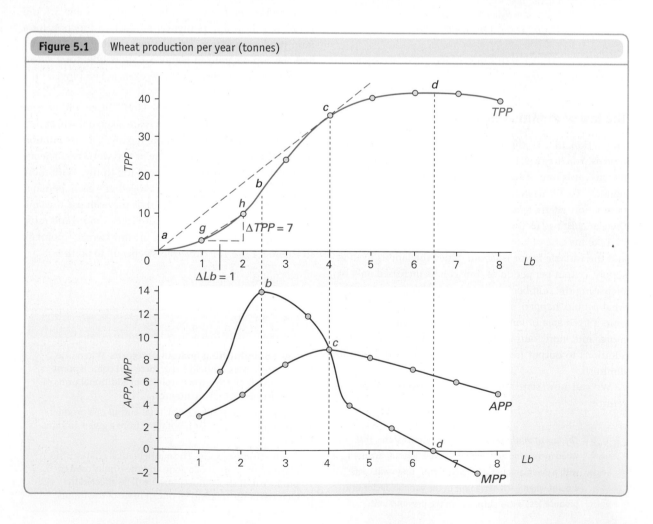

| BOX 5.2 | **DIMINISHING RETURNS IN THE BREAD SHOP** | CASE STUDIES AND APPLICATIONS |

Is the baker using his loaf?

Just up the road from where John lives is a bread shop. Like many others, he buys his bread there on a Saturday morning. Not surprisingly, Saturday morning is the busiest time of the week for the shop and as a result it takes on extra assistants.

During the week only one assistant serves the customers, but on a Saturday morning there used to be five serving. But could they serve five times as many customers? No, they could not. There were diminishing returns to labour.

The trouble is that certain factors of production in the shop are fixed:

- The shop is a fixed size. It gets very crowded on Saturday morning. Assistants sometimes had to wait while customers squeezed past each other to get to the counter, and with five serving, the assistants themselves used to get in each other's way.

- There is only one cash till. Assistants frequently had to wait while other assistants used it.
- There is only one pile of tissue paper for wrapping the bread. Again the assistants often had to wait.

The fifth and maybe even the fourth assistant ended up serving very few extra customers.

John is still going to the same bread shop and they still have only one till and one pile of tissue paper. But now only three assistants are employed on a Saturday! The shop, however, is just as busy.

 How would you advise the baker as to whether he should (a) employ four assistants on a Saturday; (b) extend his shop, thereby allowing more customers to be served on a Saturday morning; (c) extend his opening hours on a Saturday?

Thus in Table 5.1 the average physical product of labour when four workers are employed is 36/4 = 9 tonnes per year.

Marginal physical product

This is the *extra* output (ΔTPP) produced by employing *one more* unit of the variable factor.

Thus in Table 5.1 the marginal physical product of the fourth worker is 12 tonnes. The reason is that by employing the fourth worker, wheat output has risen from 24 tonnes to 36 tonnes: a rise of 12 tonnes.

In symbols, marginal physical product is given by

$$MPP = \Delta TPP / \Delta Q_v$$

Thus, in our example:

$$MPP = 12/1 = 12$$

The reason why we divide the increase in output (ΔTPP) by the increase in the quantity of the variable factor (ΔQ_v) is that some variable factors can be increased only in multiple units. For example, if we wanted to know the MPP of fertiliser and we found out how much extra wheat was produced by using an extra 20 kg bag, we would have to divide this output by 20 (ΔQ_v) to find the MPP of *one* more kilogram.

Note that in Table 5.1 the figures for MPP are entered in the spaces between the other figures. The reason is that MPP can be seen as the *difference* in output *between* one level of input and another. Thus in the table the difference in output between five and six workers is 2 tonnes.

The figures for APP and MPP are plotted in the lower diagram of Figure 5.1. We can draw a number of conclusions from these diagrams:

- The MPP between two points is equal to the slope of the TPP curve between those two points. For example, when the number of workers increases from 1 to 2 ($\Delta Lb = 1$), TPP rises from 3 to 10 tonnes ($\Delta TPP = 7$). MPP is thus 7: the slope of the line between points g and h.
- MPP rises at first: the slope of the TPP curve gets steeper.
- MPP reaches a maximum at point b. At that point the slope of the TPP curve is at its steepest.
- After point b, diminishing returns set in. MPP falls. TPP becomes less steep.
- APP rises at first. It continues rising as long as the addition to output from the last worker (MPP) is greater than the average output (APP): the MPP pulls the APP up (see Box 5.3). This continues beyond point b. Even though MPP is now falling, the APP *goes on* rising as long as the MPP is still above the APP. Thus APP goes on rising to point c.
- Beyond point c, MPP is below APP. New workers add less to output than the average. This pulls the average down: APP falls.
- As long as MPP is greater than zero, TPP will go on rising: new workers add to total output.
- At point d, TPP is at a maximum (its slope is zero). An additional worker will add nothing to output: MPP is zero.
- Beyond point d, TPP falls. MPP is negative.

KI 17
p135

 1. What is the significance of the slope of the line a–c in the top part of Figure 5.1?
2. Given that there is a fixed supply of land in the world, what implications can you draw from Figure 5.1 about the effects of an increase in world population for food output per head? (See Box 5.1.)

| BOX 5.3 | THE RELATIONSHIP BETWEEN AVERAGES AND MARGINALS | EXPLORING ECONOMICS |

In this chapter we have just examined the concepts of *average* and *marginal* physical product. We shall be coming across several other average and marginal concepts later on. It is useful at this stage to examine the general relationship between averages and marginals. In all cases there are three simple rules that relate them.

To illustrate these rules, consider the following example.

Imagine a room with 10 people in it. Assume that the *average* age of those present is 20.

Now if a 20-year-old enters the room (the *marginal* age), this will not affect the average age. It will remain at 20. If a 56-year-old now comes in, the average age will rise: not to 56, of course, but to 23. This is found by dividing the sum of everyone's ages (276) by the number of people (12). If then a child of 10 were to enter the room, this would pull the average age down.

From this example we can derive the three universal rules about averages and marginals:

- If the marginal equals the average, the average will not change.
- If the marginal is above the average, the average will rise.
- If the marginal is below the average, the average will fall.

A cricketer scores the following number of runs in five successive innings:

Innings:	1	2	3	4	5
Runs:	20	20	50	10	0

These can be seen as the marginal number of runs from each innings. Calculate the total and average number of runs after each innings. Show how the average and marginal scores illustrate the three rules above.

| *BOX 5.4 | THE RELATIONSHIP BETWEEN *TPP*, *MPP* AND *APP* | EXPLORING ECONOMICS |

Using calculus again

The total physical product of a variable factor (e.g. fertiliser) can be expressed as an equation. For example

$$TPP = 100 + 32Q_f + 10Q_f^2 - Q_f^3 \qquad (1)$$

where *TPP* is the output of grain in tonnes per hectare, and Q_f is the quantity of fertiliser applied in kilograms per hectare.

From this we can derive the *APP* function. *APP* is simply TPP/Q_f: i.e. output per kilogram of fertiliser. Thus

$$APP = \frac{100}{Q_f} + 32 + 10Q_f - Q_f^2 \qquad (2)$$

We can also derive the *MPP* function. *MPP* is the rate of increase in *TPP* as additional fertiliser is applied. It is thus the first derivative of *TPP*: $dTPP/dQ_f$. Thus

$$APP = 32 + 20Q_f - 3Q_f^2 \qquad (3)$$

From these three equations we can derive the table shown.

Check out some figures by substituting values of Q_f into each of the three equations.

Maximum output (484 tonnes) is achieved with 8 kg of fertiliser per hectare. At that level, *MPP* is zero: no additional output can be gained.

Q_f	*TPP*	*APP*	*MPP*
1	141	141	49
2	196	98	60
3	259	86	65
4	324	81	64
5	385	77	57
6	436	72	44
7	471	67	25
8	484	60	0
9	469	52	−31

This maximum level of *TPP* can be discovered from the equations by using a simple technique. If *MPP* is zero at this level, then simply find the value of Q_f where

$$MPP = 32 + 20Q_f - 3Q_f^2 = 0 \qquad (4)$$

Solving this equation[1] gives $Q_f = 8$.

[1] By applying the second derivative test (see Appendix 1) you can verify that $Q_f = 8$ gives the maximum *TPP* rather than the minimum. (Both the maximum and the minimum point of a curve have a slope equal to zero.)

Section summary

1. A production function shows the relationship between the amount of inputs used and the amount of output produced from them (per period of time).

2. In the short run it is assumed that one or more factors (inputs) are fixed in supply. The actual length of the short run will vary from industry to industry.

3. Production in the short run is subject to diminishing returns. As greater quantities of the variable factor(s) are used, so each additional unit of the variable factor will add less to output than previous units: marginal physical product will diminish and total physical product will rise less and less rapidly.

4. As long as marginal physical product is above average physical product, average physical product will rise. Once *MPP* has fallen below *APP*, however, *APP* will fall.

5.2 COSTS IN THE SHORT RUN

We have seen how output changes as inputs are varied in the short run. We now use this information to show how costs vary with the amount a firm produces. Obviously, before deciding how much to produce, it has to know the precise level of costs for each level of output.

But first we must be clear on just what we mean by the word 'costs'. The term is used differently by economists and accountants.

Measuring costs of production

When measuring costs, economists always use the concept of *opportunity cost*. Remember from Chapter 1 how we defined opportunity cost. It is the cost of any activity measured in terms of the *sacrifice* made in doing it: in other words, the cost measured in terms of the opportunities forgone.

How do we apply this principle of opportunity cost to a firm? First we must discover what factors of production it is using. Then we must measure the sacrifice involved. To do this it is necessary to put factors into two categories.

Factors not owned by the firm: explicit costs

The opportunity cost of using factors not already owned by the firm is simply the price that the firm has to pay for them. Thus if the firm uses £100 worth of electricity, the opportunity cost is £100. The firm has sacrificed £100 which could have been spent on something else. These costs are called *explicit costs* because they involve direct payment of money by firms.

Factors already owned by the firm: implicit costs

When the firm already owns factors (e.g. machinery), it does not as a rule have to pay out money to use them. Their opportunity costs are thus *implicit costs*. They are equal to what the factors could earn for the firm in some alternative use, either within the firm or hired out to some other firm.

Here are some examples of implicit costs:

- A firm owns some buildings. The opportunity cost of using them is the rent it could have received by letting them out to another firm.
- A firm draws £100 000 from the bank out of its savings in order to invest in new plant and equipment. The opportunity cost of this investment is not just the £100 000 (an explicit cost), but also the interest it thereby forgoes (an implicit cost).
- The owner of the firm could have earned £30 000 per annum by working for someone else. This £30 000 is then the opportunity cost of the owner's time.

If there is no alternative use for a factor of production, as in the case of a machine designed to produce a specific product, and if it has no scrap value, the opportunity cost of using it is *zero*. In such a case, if the output from the machine is worth more than the cost of all the *other* inputs involved, the firm might as well use the machine rather than let it stand idle.

What the firm paid for the machine – its *historic cost* – is irrelevant. Not using the machine will not bring that money back. It has been spent. These are sometimes referred to as 'sunk costs'.

 KEY IDEA 18 — *The 'bygones' principle* states that sunk (fixed) costs should be ignored when deciding whether to produce or sell more or less of a product. Only variable costs should be taken into account.

Likewise the *replacement cost* is irrelevant. That should be taken into account only when the firm is considering replacing the machine.

Costs and inputs

A firm's costs of production will depend on the factors of production it uses. The more factors it uses, the greater will its costs be. More precisely, this relationship depends on two elements:

- The productivity of the factors. The greater their physical productivity, the smaller will be the quantity of them required to produce a given level of output, and hence the lower will be the cost of that output. In other words, there is a direct link between *TPP*, *APP* and *MPP* and the costs of production.
- The price of the factors. The higher their price, the higher will be the costs of production.

In the short run, some factors are fixed in supply. Their total costs, therefore, are fixed, in the sense that they do not vary with output. Rent on land is a *fixed cost*. It is the same whether the firm produces a lot or a little.

Definitions

Opportunity cost Cost measured in terms of the next best alternative forgone.

Explicit costs The payments to outside suppliers of inputs.

Implicit costs Costs that do not involve a direct payment of money to a third party, but which nevertheless involve a sacrifice of some alternative.

Historic costs The original amounts the firm paid for factors it now owns.

Replacement costs What the firm would have to pay to replace factors it currently owns.

Fixed costs Total costs that do not vary with the amount of output produced.

BOX 5.5 — THE FALLACY OF USING HISTORIC COSTS

Or there's no point crying over spilt milk

If you fall over and break your leg, there is little point in saying 'If only I hadn't done that, I could have gone on that skiing holiday; I could have done so many other things (sigh).' Wishing things were different won't change history. You have to manage as well as you can with your broken leg.

It is the same for a firm. Once it has purchased some inputs, it is no good then wishing it hadn't. It has to accept that it has now got them, and make the best decisions about what to do with them.

Take a simple example. The local greengrocer decides in early December to buy 100 Christmas trees for £10 each. At the time of purchase, this represents an opportunity cost of £10 each, since the £10 could have been spent on something else. The greengrocer estimates that there is enough local demand to sell all 100 trees at £20 each, thereby making a reasonable profit.

But the estimate turns out to be wrong. On 23 December there are still 50 trees unsold. What should be done? At this stage the £10 that was paid for the trees is irrelevant. It is an historic cost. It cannot be recouped: the trees cannot be sold back to the wholesaler, nor can they be kept for next year.

In fact, the opportunity cost is now zero. It might even be negative if the greengrocer has to pay to dispose of any unsold trees. It might, therefore, be worth selling the trees at £10, £5 or even £1. Last thing on Christmas Eve it might even be worth giving away any unsold trees.

1. *Why is the correct price to charge (for the unsold trees) the one at which the price elasticity of demand equals −1? (Assume no disposal costs.)*
2. *Supermarkets have to pay for the rubbish they produce to be disposed of. Given this, what should they do with food that is approaching the sell-by date?*

The total cost of using variable factors, however, does vary with output. The cost of raw materials is a **variable cost**. The more that is produced, the more raw materials are used and therefore the higher is their total cost.

The following are some costs incurred by a shoe manufacturer. Decide whether each one is a fixed cost or a variable cost or has some element of both.

(a) The cost of leather.
(b) The fee paid to an advertising agency.
(c) Wear and tear on machinery.
(d) Business rates on the factory.
(e) Electricity for heating and lighting.
(f) Electricity for running the machines.
(g) Basic minimum wages agreed with the union.
(h) Overtime pay.
(i) Depreciation of machines as a result purely of their age (irrespective of their condition).

Total cost

The **total cost** (*TC*) of production is the sum of the *total variable costs* (*TVC*) and the *total fixed costs* (*TFC*) of production:

$$TC = TVC + TFC$$

Definitions

Variable costs Total costs that do vary with the amount of output produced.

Total cost The sum of total fixed costs and total variable costs: $TC = TFC + TVC$.

Table 5.2	Total costs for firm X		
Output (Q)	**TFC (£)**	**TVC (£)**	**TC (£)**
0	12	0	12
1	12	10	22
2	12	16	28
3	12	21	33
4	12	28	40
5	12	40	52
6	12	60	72
7	12	91	103
.	.	.	.

Consider Table 5.2 and Figure 5.2. They show the total costs for firm X of producing different levels of output (*Q*). Let us examine each of the three cost curves in turn.

Total fixed cost (TFC)

In our example, total fixed cost is assumed to be £12. Since this does not vary with output, it is shown by a horizontal straight line.

Total variable cost (TVC)

With a zero output, no variable factors will be used. Thus $TVC = 0$. The *TVC* curve, therefore, starts from the origin.

The shape of the *TVC* curve follows from the law of diminishing returns. Initially, *before* diminishing returns set in, *TVC* rises less and less rapidly as more variable factors are added. Take the case of a factory with a fixed supply of machinery: initially as more workers are taken on the workers can do increasingly specialist tasks and make a fuller use of the

KI 17
p135

Figure 5.2 Total costs for firm X

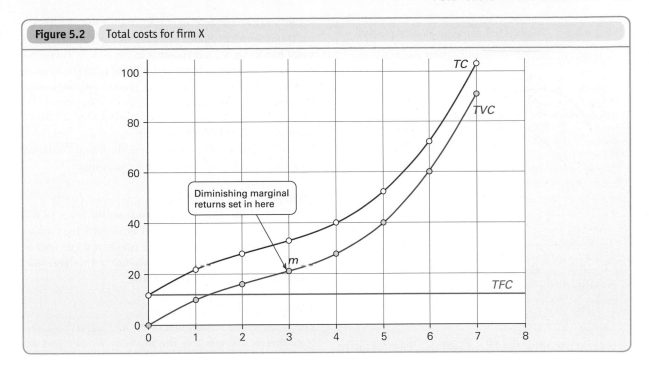

capital equipment. This corresponds to the portion of the *TPP* curve that rises more rapidly (up to point *b* in Figure 5.1 on page 136).

As output is increased beyond point *m* in Figure 5.2, diminishing returns set in. Since extra workers (the extra variable factors) are producing less and less extra output, the extra units of output they do produce will cost more and more in terms of wage costs. Thus *TVC* rises more and more rapidly. The *TVC* curve gets steeper. This corresponds to the portion of the *TPP* curve that rises less rapidly (between points *b* and *d* in Figure 5.1).

Total cost (TC)

Since *TC = TVC + TFC*, the *TC* curve is simply the *TVC* curve shifted vertically upwards by £12.

Average and marginal costs

Average cost (*AC*) is cost per unit of production:

$AC = TC/Q$

Thus if it cost a firm £2000 to produce 100 units of a product, the average cost would be £20 for each unit (£2000/100).

Like total cost, average cost can be divided into the two components, fixed and variable. In other words, average cost equals *average fixed cost* (*AFC = TFC/Q*) plus *average variable cost* (*AVC = TVC/Q*):

$AC = AFC + AVC$

Marginal cost (*MC*) is the *extra* cost of producing *one more unit*, that is the rise in total cost per one unit rise in output:

$$MC = \frac{\Delta TC}{\Delta Q}$$

For example, assume that a firm is currently producing 1 000 000 boxes of matches a month. It now increases output by 1000 boxes (another batch): $\Delta Q = 1000$. As a result, its total costs rise by £30: $\Delta TC = £30$. What is the cost of producing one more box of matches? It is

$$\frac{\Delta TC}{\Delta Q} = \frac{£30}{1000} = 3p$$

(Note that all marginal costs are variable, since, by definition, there can be no extra fixed costs as output rises.)

Given the *TFC*, *TVC* and *TC* for each output, it is possible to derive the *AFC*, *AVC*, *AC* and *MC* for each output using the above definitions.

Definitions

Average (total) cost Total cost (fixed plus variable) per unit of output: $AC = TC/Q = AFC + AVC$.

Average fixed cost Total fixed cost per unit of output: $AFC = TFC/Q$.

Average variable cost Total variable cost per unit of output: $AVC = TVC/Q$.

Marginal cost The extra cost of producing one more unit of output: $MC = \Delta TC/\Delta Q$.

Figure 5.3   Average and marginal physical product

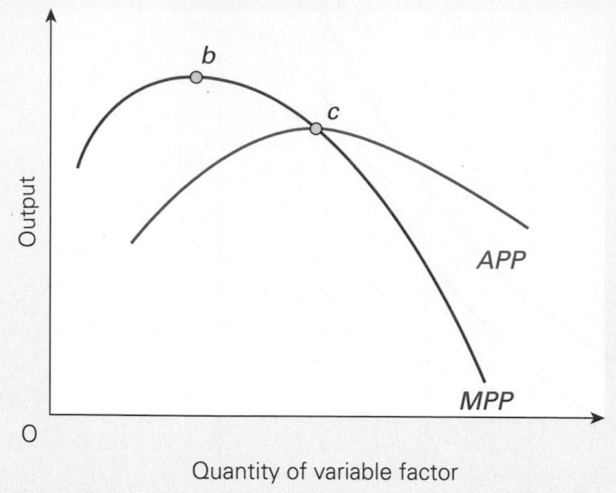

Beyond a certain level of output, diminishing returns set in. This is shown as point *x* in Figure 5.4 and corresponds to point *b* in Figure 5.3 (and point *m* in Figure 5.2). Thereafter *MC* rises as *MPP* falls. Additional units of output cost more and more to produce, since they require ever-increasing amounts of the variable factor.

Average fixed cost (AFC)

This falls continuously as output rises, since *total* fixed costs are being spread over a greater and greater output.

Average variable cost (AVC)

The shape of the *AVC* curve depends on the shape of the *APP* curve. As the average product of workers rises (up to point *c* in Figure 5.3), the average labour cost per unit of output (the *AVC*) falls: as far as point *y* in Figure 5.4. Thereafter, as *APP* falls, *AVC* must rise.

Average (total) cost (AC)

This is simply the vertical sum of the *AFC* and *AVC* curves. Note that as *AFC* gets less, the gap between *AVC* and *AC* narrows.

For example, using the data of Table 5.2, Table 5.3 can be constructed.

 Fill in the missing figures in Table 5.3. (Note that the figures for MC come in the spaces between each level of output.)

What will be the shapes of the *MC*, *AFC*, *AVC* and *AC* curves? These follow from the nature of the *MPP* and *APP* curves that we looked at in section 5.1 above. You may recall that the typical shapes of the *APP* and *MPP* curves are like those illustrated in Figure 5.3.

Marginal cost (MC)

The shape of the *MC* curve follows directly from the law of diminishing returns. Initially, in Figure 5.4, as more of the variable factor is used, extra units of output cost less than previous units. *MC* falls. This corresponds to the rising portion of the *MPP* curve in Figure 5.3 and the portion of the *TVC* curve in Figure 5.2 to the left of point *m*.

The relationship between average cost and marginal cost

This is simply another illustration of the relationship that applies between *all* averages and marginals (see Box 5.3).

As long as new units of output cost less than the average, their production must pull the average cost down. That is, if *MC* is less than *AC*, *AC* must be falling. Likewise, if new units cost more than the average, their production must drive the average up. That is, if *MC* is greater than *AC*, *AC* must be rising. Therefore, the *MC* crosses the *AC* at its minimum point (point *z* in Figure 5.4).

Since all marginal costs are variable, the same relationship holds between *MC* and *AVC*.

Why is the minimum point of the AVC curve at a lower level of output than the minimum point of the AC curve?

Table 5.3   Total, average and marginal costs for firm X

Output (Q) (units)	TFC (£)	AFC (TFC/Q) (£)	TVC (£)	AVC (TVC/Q) (£)	TC (TFC + TVC) (£)	AC (TC/Q) (£)	MC (ΔTC/ΔQ) (£)
0	12	–	0	–	12	–	
							10
1	12	12	10	10	22	22	
							. . .
2	12	6	16	. . .	28	14	
							5
3	. . .	. . .	21	7	. . .	. . .	
							7
4	. . .	3	28	. . .	40	. . .	
							12
5	. . .	2.4	. . .	8	52	10.4	
							. . .
6	. . .	. . .	. . .	10	. . .	12	
							31
7	. . .	1.7	91	13	103	14.7	

| Figure 5.4 | Average and marginal costs |

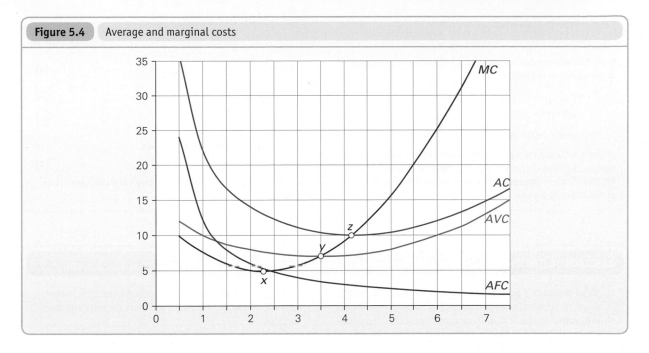

BOX 5.6   COST CURVES IN PRACTICE

When fixed factors are divisible

Are cost curves always the shape depicted in this chapter? The answer is no. Sometimes, rather than being U-shaped, the AVC and MC curves are flat-bottomed, like the curves in the diagram below. Indeed, they may be constant (and equal to each other) over a substantial range of output.

The reason for this is that fixed factors may sometimes not have to be in full use all the time. Take the case of a firm with 100 identical machines, each one requiring one person to operate it. Although the firm cannot use more than the 100 machines, it could use fewer: in other words, some of the machines could be left idle. Assume, for example, that instead of using 100 machines, the firm uses only 90. It

would need only 90 operatives and 90 per cent of the raw materials.

Similarly, if it used only 20 machines, its total variable costs (labour and raw materials) would be only 20 per cent. What we are saying here is that average variable cost remains constant – and over a very large range of output, using anything from 1 machine to 100 machines.

The reason for the constant AVC (and MC) is that by varying the amount of fixed capital used, the proportions used of capital, labour and raw materials can be kept the same and hence the average and marginal productivity of labour and raw materials will remain constant.

Only when all machines are in use (at Q_1) will AVC start to rise if output is further expanded. Machines may then have to work beyond their optimal speed, using more raw materials per unit of output (diminishing returns to raw materials), or workers may have to work longer shifts with higher (overtime) pay.

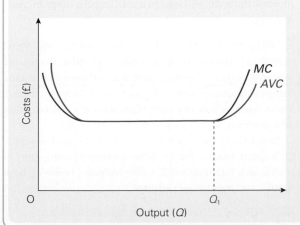

1. Assume that a firm has five identical machines, each operating independently. Assume that with all five machines operating normally, 100 units of output are produced each day. Below what level of output will AVC and MC rise?
2. Manufacturing firms like the one we have been describing will have other fixed costs (such as rent and managerial overheads). Does the existence of these affect the argument that the AVC curve will be flat-bottomed?

Section summary

1. When measuring costs of production, we should be careful to use the concept of opportunity cost. In the case of factors not owned by the firm, the opportunity cost is simply the explicit cost of purchasing or hiring them. It is the price paid for them. In the case of factors already owned by the firm, it is the implicit cost of what the factor could have earned for the firm in its next best alternative use.

2. In the short run, some factors are fixed in supply. Their total costs are thus fixed with respect to output. In the case of variable factors, their total cost will increase as more output is produced and hence as more of the variable factor is used.

3. Total cost can be divided into total fixed and total variable costs. Total variable cost will tend to increase less rapidly at first as more is produced, but then, when diminishing returns set in, it will increase more and more rapidly.

4. Marginal cost is the cost of producing one more unit of output. It will probably fall at first (corresponding to the part of the TVC curve where the slope is getting shallower), but will start to rise as soon as diminishing returns set in.

5. Average cost, like total cost, can be divided into fixed and variable costs. Average fixed cost will decline as more output is produced since total fixed cost is being spread over a greater and greater number of units of output. Average variable cost will tend to decline at first, but once the marginal cost has risen above it, it must then rise.

5.3 THE LONG-RUN THEORY OF PRODUCTION

In the long run, *all* factors of production are variable. There is time for the firm to build a new factory, to install new machines, to use different production techniques and to combine its inputs in whatever proportion and in whatever quantities it chooses.

KI 16
p133

In the long run, then, there are several decisions that a firm has to make: decisions about the scale and location of its operations and what techniques of production it should use. These decisions affect the costs of production. It is important, therefore, to get them right.

The scale of production

If a firm were to double all of its inputs – something it could do in the long run – would it double its output? Or will output more than double or less than double? We can distinguish three possible situations:

Constant returns to scale. This is where a given percentage increase in inputs will lead to the *same* percentage increase in output.

Increasing returns to scale. This is where a given percentage increase in inputs will lead to a *larger* percentage increase in output.

Decreasing returns to scale. This is where a given percentage increase in inputs will lead to a smaller percentage increase in output.

Notice the terminology here. The words 'to scale' mean that all inputs increase by the same proportion. Decreasing returns to scale are therefore quite different from diminishing marginal returns (where only the variable factor increases). The differences between marginal returns to a variable factor and returns to scale are illustrated in Table 5.4.

In the short run, input 1 is assumed to be fixed in supply (at 3 units). Output can be increased only by using more of the variable factor (input 2). In the long run, however, both input 1 and input 2 are variable.

 Referring still to Table 5.4, are there diminishing or increasing marginal returns, and are there decreasing or increasing returns to scale?

Table 5.4		Short-run and long-run increases in output			
Short run			**Long run**		
Input 1	Input 2	Output	Input 1	Input 2	Output
3	1	25	1	1	15
3	2	45	2	2	35
3	3	60	3	3	60
3	4	70	4	4	90
3	5	75	5	5	125

Economies of scale

The concept of increasing returns to scale is closely linked to that of *economies of scale*. A firm experiences economies of scale if costs per unit of output fall as the scale of production increases. Clearly, if a firm is getting increasing returns to scale from its factors of production, then as it produces more it will be using smaller and smaller amounts of factors per unit of output. Other things being equal, this means that it will be producing at a lower unit cost.

There are several reasons why firms are likely to experience economies of scale. Some are due to increasing returns to scale; some are not.

Specialisation and division of labour. In large-scale plants workers can often do simple, repetitive jobs. With this **specialisation and division of labour** less training is needed; workers can become highly efficient in their particular job, especially with long production runs; there is less time lost in workers switching from one operation to another; and supervision is easier. Workers and managers can be employed who have specific skills in specific areas.

Indivisibilities. Some inputs are of a minimum size: they are indivisible. The most obvious example is machinery. Take the case of a combine harvester. A small-scale farmer could not make full use of one. They only become economical to use, therefore, on farms above a certain size. The problem of **indivisibilities** is made worse when different machines, each of which is part of the production process, are of a different size. For example, if there are two types of machine, one producing 6 units a day, and the other packaging 4 units a day, a minimum of 12 units would have to be produced, involving two production machines and three packaging machines, if all machines are to be fully utilised.

The 'container principle'. Any capital equipment that contains things (blast furnaces, oil tankers, pipes, vats, etc.) tends to cost less per unit of output the larger its size. The reason has to do with the relationship between a container's volume and its *surface area*. A container's cost depends largely on the materials used to build it and hence roughly on its surface area. Its output depends largely on its *volume*. Large containers have a bigger volume relative to surface area than do small containers.

For example, a container with a bottom, top and four sides, with each side measuring 1 metre, has a volume of 1 cubic metre and a surface area of 6 square metres (six surfaces of 1 square metre each). If each side were now to be doubled in length to 2 metres, the volume would be 8 cubic metres and the surface area 24 square metres (six surfaces of 4 square metres each). Thus an eightfold increase in capacity has been gained at only a fourfold increase in the container's surface area, and hence an approximate fourfold increase in cost.

Greater efficiency of large machines. Large machines may be more efficient in the sense that more output can be gained for a given amount of inputs. For example, only one worker may be required to operate a machine whether it be large or small. Also, a large machine may make more efficient use of raw materials.

By-products. With production on a large scale, there may be sufficient waste products to enable some by-product or by-products to be made.

Multi-stage production. A large factory may be able to take a product through several stages in its manufacture. This saves time and cost in moving the semi-finished product from one firm or factory to another. For example, a large cardboard-manufacturing firm may be able to convert trees or waste paper into cardboard and then into cardboard boxes in a continuous sequence.

All the above are examples of **plant economies of scale**. They are due to an individual factory or workplace or machine being large. There are other economies of scale, however, that are associated with the *firm* being large – perhaps with many factories.

Organisational economies. With a large firm, individual plants can specialise in particular functions. There can also be centralised administration of the firm; for example, one human resources department could administer all the wages. Often, after a merger between two firms, savings can be made by **rationalising** their activities in this way.

Spreading overheads. Some expenditures are economic only when the *firm* is large: for example, research and development

---

Definitions

Economies of scale When increasing the scale of production leads to a lower cost per unit of output.

Specialisation and division of labour Where production is broken down into a number of simpler, more specialised tasks, thus allowing workers to acquire a high degree of efficiency.

Indivisibility The impossibility of dividing a factor into smaller units.

Plant economies of scale Economies of scale that arise because of the large size of a factory.

Rationalisation The reorganising of production (often after a merger) so as to cut out waste and duplication and generally to reduce costs.

– only a large firm can afford to set up a research laboratory. This is another example of indivisibilities, only this time at the level of the firm rather than the plant. The greater the firm's output, the more these **overhead** costs are spread.

Financial economies.   Large firms are often able to obtain finance at lower interest rates than small firms, since they are seen by banks to be lower risk. They may be able to obtain certain inputs cheaper by buying in bulk.

Economies of scope.   Often a firm is large because it produces a range of products. This can result in each individual product being produced more cheaply than if it was produced in a single-product firm. The reason for these *economies of scope* is that various overhead costs and financial and organisational economies can be shared among the products. For example, a firm that produces a whole range of DVD players, televisions and hard disc recorders can benefit from shared marketing and distribution costs and the bulk purchase of electronic components.

1. *Which of the economies of scale we have considered are due to increasing returns to scale and which are due to other factors?*
2. *What economies of scale is a large department store likely to experience?*

Diseconomies of scale

When firms get beyond a certain size, costs per unit of output may start to increase. There are several reasons for such **diseconomies of scale**:

- Management problems of co-ordination may increase as the firm becomes larger and more complex, and as lines of communication get longer. There may be a lack of personal involvement by management.
- Workers may feel 'alienated' if their jobs are boring and repetitive, and if they feel that they are an insignificantly small part of a large organisation. Small to medium-sized companies often report that workers feel they 'make a difference'; this may be lost in a large firm and as a consequence lower motivation may lead to shoddy work.
- Industrial relations may deteriorate as a result of these factors and also as a result of the more complex interrelationships between different categories of worker. More levels of 'people management' may therefore be required.
- Production-line processes and the complex interdependencies of mass production can lead to great disruption if there are hold-ups in any one part of the firm.

Whether firms experience economies or diseconomies of scale will depend on the conditions applying in each individual firm.

Why are firms likely to experience economies of scale up to a certain size and then diseconomies of scale after some point beyond that?

Location

In the long run, a firm can move to a different location. The location will affect the cost of production since locations differ in terms of the availability and cost of raw materials, suitable land and power supply, the qualifications, skills and experience of the labour force, wage rates, transport and communications networks, the cost of local services, and banking and financial facilities. In short, locations differ in terms of the availability, suitability and cost of the factors of production.

Transport costs will be an important influence on a firm's location. Ideally, a firm will wish to be as near as possible to both its raw materials and the market for its finished product. When market and raw materials are in different locations, the firm will minimise its transport costs by locating somewhere between the two.

In general, if the raw materials are more expensive to transport than the finished product, the firm should be located as near as possible to the raw materials. Thus heavy industry, which uses large quantities of coal and various ores, tends to be concentrated near the coal fields or near the ports. If, on the other hand, the finished product is more expensive to transport (e.g. bread and beer), the firm will probably be located as near as possible to its market.

When raw materials or markets are in many different locations, transport costs will be minimised at the 'centre of gravity'. This location will be nearer to those raw materials and markets whose transport costs are greater per mile.

How is the opening up of trade and investment between eastern and western Europe likely to affect the location of industries within Europe that have (a) substantial economies of scale; (b) little or no economies of scale?

The size of the whole industry

As an *industry* grows in size, this can lead to **external economies of scale** for its member firms. This is where a firm, whatever its own individual size, benefits from the *whole industry* being large. For example, the firm may benefit

---

Definitions

Overheads Costs arising from the general running of an organisation, and only indirectly related to the level of output.

Economies of scope When increasing the range of products produced by a firm reduces the cost of producing each one.

Diseconomies of scale Where costs per unit of output increase as the scale of production increases.

External economies of scale Where a firm's costs per unit of output decrease as the size of the whole industry grows.

from having access to specialist raw material or component suppliers, labour with specific skills, firms that specialise in marketing the finished product, and banks and other financial institutions with experience of the industry's requirements. What we are referring to here is the *industry's infrastructure*: the facilities, support services, skills and experience that can be shared by its members.

1. *Name some industries where external economies of scale are gained. What are the specific external economies in each case?*
2. *Would you expect external economies to be associated with the concentration of an industry in a particular region?*

The member firms of a particular industry might experience *external diseconomies of scale*. For example, as an industry grows larger, this may create a growing shortage of specific raw materials or skilled labour. This will push up their prices, and hence the firms' costs.

The optimum combination of factors: the marginal product approach

In the long run, all factors can be varied. The firm can thus choose what techniques of production to use: what design of factory to build, what types of machine to buy, how to organise the factory, whether to use highly automated processes or more labour-intensive techniques. It must be very careful in making these decisions. After all, once it has built a factory and installed machinery, these then become fixed factors of production, and the subsequent 'short-run' time period may in practice last a very long time.

For any given scale, how should the firm decide what technique to use? How should it decide the optimum 'mix' of factors of production?

The profit-maximising firm will obviously want to use the least costly combination of factors to produce any given output. It will therefore substitute factors, if by so doing it can reduce the cost of a given output. What then is the optimum combination of factors?

The simple two-factor case

Take first the simplest case where a firm uses just two factors: labour (L) and capital (K). The least-cost combination of the two will be where

$$\frac{MPP_L}{P_L} = \frac{MPP_K}{P_K}$$

in other words, where the extra product (*MPP*) from the last pound spent on each factor is equal. But why should this be so? The easiest way to answer this is to consider what would happen if they were not equal.

If they were not equal, it would be possible to reduce cost per unit of output, by using a different combination of labour and capital. For example, if

$$\frac{MPP_L}{P_L} > \frac{MPP_K}{P_K}$$

more labour should be used relative to capital, since the firm is getting a greater physical return for its money from extra workers than from extra capital. As more labour is used per unit of capital, however, diminishing returns to labour set in. Thus MPP_L will fall. Likewise, as less capital is used per unit of labour, MPP_K will rise. This will continue until

$$\frac{MPP_L}{P_L} = \frac{MPP_K}{P_K}$$

At this point, the firm will stop substituting labour for capital.

Since no further gain can be made by substituting one factor for another, this combination of factors or 'choice of technique' can be said to be the most efficient. It is the least-cost way of combining factors for any given output. Efficiency in this sense of using the optimum factor proportions is known as *productive efficiency*.

The multi-factor case

Where a firm uses many different factors, the least-cost combination of factors will be where

$$\frac{MPP_a}{P_a} = \frac{MPP_b}{P_b} = \frac{MPP_c}{P_c} = \cdots = \frac{MPP_n}{P_n}$$

where $a \ldots n$ are different factors. This is a variant of the equi-marginal principle (see page 106).

The reasons are the same as in the two-factor case. If any inequality exists between the *MPP/P* ratios, a firm will be able to reduce its costs by using more of those factors with a high *MPP/P* ratio and less of those with a low *MPP/P* ratio until they all become equal.

A major problem for a firm in choosing the least-cost technique is in predicting future factor price changes.

If the price of a factor were to change, the *MPP/P* ratios would cease to be equal. The firm, to minimise costs, would then like to alter its factor combinations until the *MPP/P* ratios once more became equal. The trouble is that, once it has committed itself to a particular technique, it may be several years before it can switch to an alternative one. Thus if a firm invests in labour-intensive methods of production and is then faced with an unexpected wage rise, it may regret not having chosen a more capital-intensive technique. While there is no simple solution to this issue, there are a number of companies that have made a business of

Definitions

Industry's infrastructure The network of supply agents, communications, skills, training facilities, distribution channels, specialised financial services, etc., that supports a particular industry.

External diseconomies of scale Where a firm's costs per unit of output increase as the size of the whole industry increases.

Productive efficiency The least-cost combination of factors for a given output.

predicting trends across different sectors to assist firms in their decision making.

 If factor X costs twice as much as factor Y ($P_X/P_Y = 2$), what can be said about the relationship between the MPPs of the two factors if the optimum combination of factors is used?

*LOOKING AT THE MATHS

We can express the long-run production function algebraically. In the simple two-factor model, where capital (K) and labour (L) are the two factors, the production function is

$$TPP = f(K, L)$$

A simple and widely used production function is the **Cobb–Douglas production function**. This takes the form

$$TPP = AK^\alpha L^\beta$$

Box 5.7 demonstrates that where $\alpha + \beta = 1$, there are constant returns to scale; where $\alpha + \beta > 1$, there are increasing returns to scale; and where $\alpha + \beta < 1$, there are decreasing returns to scale.

A multiple-factor Cobb–Douglas production function would take the form

$$TPP = AF_1^\alpha F_2^\beta F_3^\gamma \ldots F_n^\omega$$

where $F_1, F_2, F_3, \ldots, F_n$ are all the factors. For example, if there were six factors, n would be factor 6. Again, it can be shown that where $\alpha + \beta + \gamma + \ldots + \omega = 1$, there are constant returns to scale; where $\alpha + \beta + \gamma + \ldots + \omega > 1$, there are increasing returns to scale; and where $\alpha + \beta + \gamma + \ldots + \omega < 1$, there are decreasing returns to scale.

*The optimum combination of factors: the isoquant/isocost approach

This section is optional. You can skip straight to page 152 without loss of continuity.

A firm's choice of optimum technique can be shown graphically. This graphical analysis takes the simplest case of just two variable factors – for example, labour and capital.

The amount of labour used is measured on one axis and the amount of capital used is measured on the other.

The graph involves the construction of *isoquants* and *isocosts*.

Isoquants

Imagine that a firm wants to produce a certain level of output: say, 5000 units per year. Let us assume that it estimates all the possible combinations of labour and capital that could produce that level of output. Some of these estimates are shown in Table 5.5.

Technique *a* is a capital-intensive technique, using 40 units of capital and only five workers. As we move towards technique *e*, labour is substituted for capital. The techniques become more labour intensive.

These alternative techniques for producing a given level of output can be plotted on a graph. The points are joined to form an **isoquant**. Figure 5.5 shows the 5000 unit isoquant corresponding to Table 5.5.

Table 5.5 Various capital and labour combinations to produce 5000 units of output per year

	a	b	c	d	e
Units of capital (K)	40	20	10	6	4
Number of workers (L)	5	12	20	30	50

Definitions

Cobb–Douglas production function Like other production functions, this shows how output (TPP) varies with inputs of various factors (F_1, F_2, F_3, etc.). In the simple two-factor case it takes the following form:

$$TPP = f(F_1, F_2) = AF_1^\alpha F_2^\beta$$

If $\alpha + \beta = 1$, there are constant returns to scale; if $\alpha + \beta > 1$, there are increasing returns to scale; if $\alpha + \beta < 1$, there are decreasing returns to scale.

Isoquant A line showing all the alternative combinations of two factors that can produce a given level of output.

Figure 5.5 An isoquant

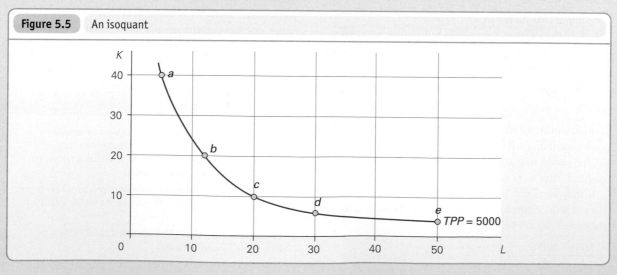

*BOX 5.7   THE COBB–DOUGLAS PRODUCTION FUNCTION

Exploring its properties

Let us take the simple Cobb–Douglas production function (see Looking at the Maths box on page 148):

$$TPP = AK^{\alpha}L^{\beta} \tag{1}$$

Returns to scale and the Cobb–Douglas production function

What would happen if you were to double the amount of both K and L used (in other words, the scale of production doubles)? If output doubles, there are constant returns to scale. If output more than doubles, there are increasing returns to scale; if it less than doubles, there are decreasing returns to scale. Let us see what happens when we double the amount of K and L in equation (1):

$$TPP = A(2K^{\alpha})(2L^{\beta})$$
$$= A2^{\alpha}K^{\alpha}\,2^{\beta}L^{\beta}$$
$$= A2^{\alpha+\beta}K^{\alpha}L^{\beta}$$

If $\alpha + \beta = 1$, then $2^{\alpha+\beta} = 2$. Thus

$$TPP = 2AK^{\alpha}L^{\beta}$$

In other words, doubling the amount of K and L used has doubled output: there are constant returns to scale.

If $\alpha + \beta > 1$, then $2^{\alpha+\beta} > 2$. In this case, doubling inputs will more than double output: there are increasing returns to scale. Similarly, if $\alpha + \beta < 1$, then $2^{\alpha+\beta} < 2$ and there are decreasing returns to scale.

Finding the marginal physical products of labour and capital

The marginal physical product (MPP) of a factor is the additional output obtained by employing one more unit of that factor, while holding other factors constant. The MPP of either factor in the above Cobb–Douglas production function can be found by differentiating the function with respect to that factor (see pages A:10–13 for the rules of partial differentiation). Thus

$$MPP_K = \frac{\partial(TPP)}{\partial K} = \alpha AK^{\alpha-1}L^{\beta} \tag{2}$$

and

$$MPP_L = \frac{\partial(TPP)}{\partial L} = \beta AK^{\alpha}L^{\beta-1} \tag{3}$$

For example, if the production function were

$$TPP = 4K^{3/4}L^{1/2} \tag{4}$$

and if $K = 81$ and $L = 36$, then, from equations (2) and (4),

$$MPP_K = \alpha AK^{\alpha-1}L^{\beta}$$

$$= \frac{3}{4} \times 4(81^{-1/4})(36^{1/2})$$

$$= 3 \times \frac{1}{3} \times 6 = 6$$

and $MPP_L = \beta AK^{\alpha}L^{\beta-1}$

$$= \frac{1}{2} \times 4(81^{3/4})(36^{-1/2})$$

$$= 2 \times 27 \times \frac{1}{6} = 9$$

In other words, an additional unit of capital will produce an extra 6 units of output and an additional unit of labour will produce an extra 9 units of output.

Assume that the production function is given by

$$TPP = 36K^{1/3}L^{1/2}R^{1/4}$$

where R is the quantity of a particular raw material used.

(a) Are there constant, increasing or decreasing returns to scale?

(b) What is the marginal productivity of the raw material if $K = 8$, $L = 16$ and $R = 81$?

KI 16
p133

The isoquant shows the whole *range* of alternative ways of producing a given output. Thus Figure 5.5 shows not only points *a* to *e* from the table, but all the intermediate points too.

Like an indifference curve, an isoquant is rather like a contour on a map. As with contours and indifference curves, a whole series of isoquants can be drawn, each one representing a different level of output (*TPP*). The higher the output, the further out to the right will the isoquant be. Thus in Figure 5.6, isoquant I_5 represents a higher level of output than I_4, and I_4 a higher output than I_3, and so on.

1. *Could isoquants ever cross?*
2. *Could they ever slope upwards to the right? Explain your answers.*

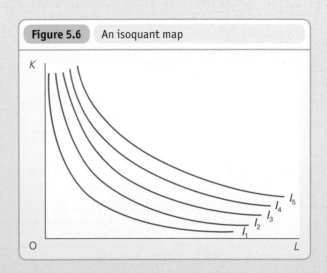

Figure 5.6   An isoquant map

The shape of the isoquant. Why is the isoquant 'bowed in' towards the origin? This illustrates a diminishing **marginal rate of factor substitution** (*MRS*). This, as we shall see very soon, is due to the law of diminishing returns.

The *MRS*[1] is the amount of one factor (e.g. *K*) that can be replaced by a 1 unit increase in the other factor (e.g. *L*), if output is to be held constant. So if 2 units of capital ($\Delta K = 2$) could be replaced by 1 unit of labour ($\Delta L = 1$) the *MRS* would be 2. Thus

$$MRS = \frac{\Delta K}{\Delta L} = \frac{2}{1} = 2$$

The *MRS* between two points on the isoquant will equal the slope of the line joining those two points. Thus in Figure 5.7, the *MRS* between points *g* and *h* is 2 ($\Delta K/\Delta L = 2/1$). But this is merely the slope of the line joining points *g* and *h* (ignoring the negative sign).

When the isoquant is bowed in towards the origin, the slope of the isoquant will diminish as one moves down the curve, and so too, therefore, will the *MRS* diminish. Referring again to Figure 5.7, between points *g* and *h* the *MRS* = 2. Lower down the curve between points *j* and *k*, it has fallen to 1.

 Calculate the MRS moving up the curve in Figure 5.5 between each pair of points: e–d, d–c, c–b and b–a. Does the MRS diminish moving in this direction?

The relationship between MRS and MPP. As one moves down the isoquant, total output, by definition, will remain the same. Thus the loss in output due to less capital being used (i.e. $MPP_K \times \Delta K$) must be exactly offset by the gain in output due to more labour being used (i.e. $MPP_L \times \Delta L$). Thus

$$MPP_L \times \Delta L = MPP_K \times \Delta K$$

This equation can be rearranged as follows:

$$\frac{MPP_L}{MPP_K} = \frac{\Delta K}{\Delta L} (= MRS)$$

Thus the *MRS* is equal to the inverse of the marginal productivity ratios of the two factors.

Diminishing MRS and the law of diminishing returns. The principle of diminishing *MRS* is related to the law of diminishing returns. As one moves down the isoquant, increasing amounts of labour are being used relative to capital. This, given diminishing returns, would lead the *MPP* of labour to fall relative to the *MPP* of capital. But since $MRS = MPP_L/MPP_K$, if MPP_L/MPP_K diminishes, then, by definition, so must *MRS*.

The less substitutable factors are for each other, the faster *MRS* will diminish, and therefore the more bowed in will be the isoquant.

Isocosts

We have seen how factors combine to produce different levels of output, but how do we choose the level of output? This will involve taking costs into account.

Assume that factor prices are fixed. A table can be constructed showing the various combinations of factors that a firm can use for a particular sum of money.

For example, assuming that P_K is £20 000 per unit per year and P_L is £10 000 per worker per year, Table 5.6 shows various combinations of capital and labour that would cost the firm £300 000 per year.

These figures are plotted in Figure 5.8. The line joining the points is called an **isocost**. It shows all the combinations of labour and capital that cost £300 000.

As with isoquants, a series of isocosts can be drawn. Each one represents a particular cost to the firm. The higher the cost, the further out to the right will the isocost be.

 1. *What will happen to an isocost if the prices of both factors rise by the same percentage?*
2. *What will happen to the isocost in Figure 5.8 if the wage rate rises to £15 000?*

Table 5.6	Combinations of capital and labour costing the firm £300 000 per year			
Units of capital (at £20 000 per unit)	0	5	10	15
No. of workers (at a wage of £10 000)	30	20	10	0

Definitions

Marginal rate of factor substitution The rate at which one factor can be substituted by another while holding the level of output constant:

$$MRS = \Delta F_1/\Delta F_2 = MPP_{F2}/MPP_{F1}$$

Isocost A line showing all the combinations of two factors that cost the same to employ.

Figure 5.7 Diminishing marginal rate of factor substitution

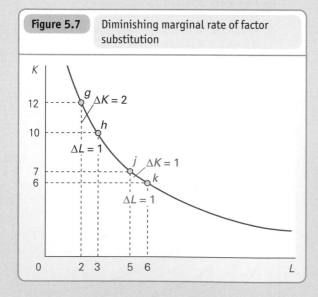

[1] Note that we use the same letters *MRS* to refer to the marginal rate of factor substitution as we did in the previous chapter to refer to the marginal rate of substitution in consumption. Sometimes we use the same words too – just 'marginal rate of substitution' rather than the longer title. In this case we must rely on the context in order to tell which is being referred to.

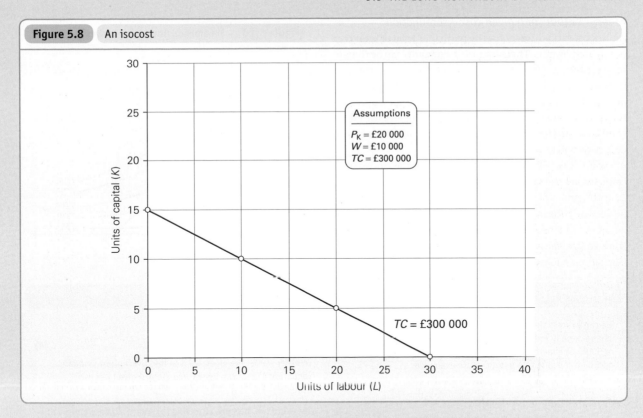

Figure 5.8 An isocost

The slope of the isocost equals

$$\frac{P_L}{P_K}$$

This can be shown in the above example. The slope of the isocost in Figure 5.8 is 15/30 = ½. But this is P_L/P_K (i.e. £10 000/£20 000).

Isoquants and isocosts can now be put on the same diagram. The diagram can be used to answer either of two questions: (a) What is the least-cost way of producing a particular level of output? (b) What is the highest output that can be achieved for a given cost of production?

These two questions are examined in turn.

The least-cost combination of factors to produce a given level of output

First the isoquant is drawn for the level of output in question: for example, the 5000 unit isoquant in Figure 5.5. This is reproduced in Figure 5.9.

Then a series of isocosts are drawn representing different levels of total cost. The higher the level of total cost, the further out will be the isocosts.

The least-cost combination of labour and capital is shown at point r, where $TC = £400\ 000$. This is where the isoquant just touches the lowest possible isocost. Any other point on the isoquant (e.g. s or t) would be on a higher isocost.

KI 3
p13

TC 8
p105 *Comparison with the marginal productivity approach.* We showed earlier that the least-cost combination of labour and capital was where

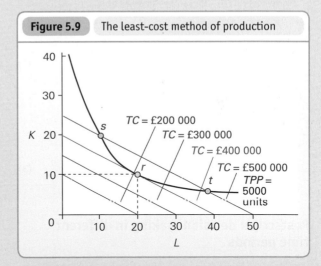

Figure 5.9 The least-cost method of production

$$\frac{MPP_L}{P_L} = \frac{MPP_K}{P_K}$$

In this section it has just been shown that the least-cost combination is where the isoquant is tangential to an isocost (i.e. point r in Figure 5.9). Thus their slope is the same. The slope of the isoquant equals *MRS*, which equals MPP_L/MPP_K; and the slope of the isocost equals P_L/P_K.

$$\therefore \quad \frac{MPP_L}{MPP_K} = \frac{P_L}{P_K}$$

$$\therefore \quad \frac{MPP_L}{P_L} = \frac{MPP_K}{P_K}$$

Thus, as one would expect, the two approaches yield the same result.

KI 14
p107

Highest output for a given cost of production

An isocost can be drawn for the particular level of total cost outlay in question. Then a series of isoquants can be drawn, representing different levels of output (*TPP*). This is shown in Figure 5.10. The higher the level of output, the further out will lie the corresponding isoquant. The point at which the isocost touches the highest isoquant will give the factor combination yielding the highest output for that level of cost. This will be at point *h* in Figure 5.10.

Again this will be where the slopes of the isocost and isoquant are the same: where $P_L/P_K = MRS$.

If the prices of factors change, new isocosts will have to be drawn. Thus in Figure 5.10, if the wage rate goes up, less labour can be used for a given sum of money. The isocost will swing inwards round point *x*. The isocost will get steeper. Less labour will now be used relative to capital.

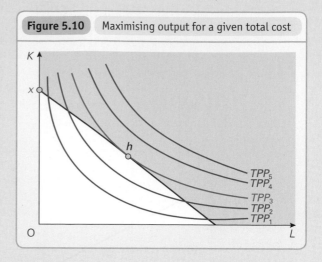

Figure 5.10 Maximising output for a given total cost

---

*LOOKING AT THE MATHS

We can express the optimum production point algebraically. This can be done in either of two ways, corresponding to Figures 5.9 or 5.10. (The method is similar to that used for finding the optimum consumption point that we examined on page 113.)

(a) Corresponding to Figure 5.9

The first way involves finding the least-cost method of producing a given output (*Q*). This can be expressed as

$$Min\ P_K K + P_L L \tag{1}$$

subject to the output constraint that

$$Q = Q(K,L) \tag{2}$$

In other words, the objective is to find the lowest isocost (equation 1) to produce on a given isoquant (equation 2).

(b) Corresponding to Figure 5.10

The second involves finding the highest output that can be produced for a given cost. This can be expressed as

$$Max\ Q(K,L) \tag{3}$$

subject to the cost constraint that

$$P_K K + P_L L = C \tag{4}$$

In other words, the objective is to find the highest isoquant (equation 3) that can be reached along a given isocost (equation 4).

There are two methods of solving (a) and (b) for any given value of P_K, P_L and either *Q* (in the case of (a)) or *C* (in the case of (b)). The first involves substituting the constraint equation into the objective function (to express *K* in terms of *L*) and then finding the value of *L* and then *K* that minimises the objective function in the case of (a) or maximises it in the case of (b). This involves differentiating the objective function and setting it equal to zero. A worked example of this method is given in Maths Case 5.2 in MyEconLab.

The second method, which is slightly longer but is likely to involve simpler calculations, involves the use of 'Lagrangian multipliers'. This method is explained, along with a worked example, in Maths Case 5.3. It is the same method as we used in Maths Case 4.2 when finding the optimal level of consumption of two products.

Postscript: decision making in different time periods

We have distinguished between the short run and the long run. Let us introduce two more time periods to complete the picture. The complete list then reads as follows.

Very short run (immediate run).   All factors are fixed. Output is fixed. The supply curve is vertical. On a day-to-day basis, a firm may not be able to vary output at all. For example, a flower seller, once the day's flowers have been purchased from the wholesaler, cannot alter the amount of flowers available for sale on that day. In the very short run, all that may remain for a producer to do is to sell an already produced good.

Why are Christmas trees and fresh foods often sold cheaply on Christmas Eve? (See Box 5.5.)

Short run.   At least one factor is fixed in supply. More can be produced, but the firm will come up against the law of diminishing returns as it tries to do so.

Long run.   All factors are variable. The firm may experience constant, increasing or decreasing returns to scale. But although all factors can be increased or decreased, they are of a fixed *quality*.

Very long run.   All factors are variable, *and* their quality and hence productivity can change. Labour productivity can increase as a result of education, training, experience and social factors. The productivity of capital can increase as a result of new inventions (new discoveries) and innovation (putting inventions into practice).

Improvements in factor quality will increase the output they produce: *TPP*, *APP* and *MPP* will rise. These curves will shift vertically upwards.

Just how long the 'very long run' is will vary from firm to firm. It will depend on how long it takes to develop new techniques, new skills or new work practices.

It is important to realise that decisions *for* all four time periods can be made *at* the same time. Firms do not make short-run decisions *in* the short run and long-run decisions *in* the long run. They can make both short-run and long-run decisions today. For example, assume that a firm experiences an increase in consumer demand and anticipates that it will continue into the foreseeable future. It thus wants to increase output. Consequently, it makes the following four decisions *today*:

- (*Very short run*) It accepts that for a few days it will not be able to increase output. It informs its customers that they will have to wait. In some markets the firm may temporarily raise prices to choke off some of the demand.
- (*Short run*) It negotiates with labour to introduce overtime working as soon as possible, to tide it over the next few weeks. It orders extra raw materials from its suppliers. It launches a recruitment drive for new labour so as to avoid paying overtime longer than is necessary.
- (*Long run*) It starts proceedings to build a new factory. What would this involve? In some cases the firm may talk to the bank directly about finance and start investigating

sites. A different approach might be to discuss requirements with a firm of consultants.

- (*Very long run*) It institutes a programme of research and development and/or training in an attempt to increase productivity.

1. *Could the long run and the very long run ever be the same length of time?*
2. *What will the long-run and very-long-run market supply curves for a product look like? How will the shape of the long-run curve depend on returns to scale?*
*3. *In the very long run, new isoquants will have to be drawn as factor productivity changes. An increase in productivity will shift the isoquants inwards towards the origin: less capital and labour will be required to produce any given level of output. Will this be a parallel inward shift of the isoquants? Explain.*

Although we distinguish these four time periods, it is the middle two we are primarily concerned with. The reason for this is that there is very little the firm can do in the *very* short run. And concerning the *very* long run, although the firm will obviously want to increase the productivity of its inputs, it will not be in a position to make precise calculations of how to do it. It will not know precisely what inventions will be made, or just what will be the results of its own research and development.

Section summary

1. In the long run, a firm is able to vary the quantity it uses of all factors of production. There are no fixed factors.

2. If it increases all factors by the same proportion, it may experience constant, increasing or decreasing returns to scale.

3. Economies of scale occur when costs per unit of output fall as the scale of production increases. This can be due to a number of factors, some of which result directly from increasing (physical) returns to scale. These include the benefits of specialisation and division of labour, the use of larger and more efficient machines, and the ability to have a more integrated system of production. Other economies of scale arise from the financial and administrative benefits of large-scale organisations.

4. Long-run costs are also influenced by a firm's location. The firm will have to balance the needs to be as near as possible both to the supply of its raw materials and to its market. The optimum balance will depend on the relative costs of transporting the inputs and the finished product.

5. To minimise costs per unit of output, a firm should choose that combination of factors which gives an equal marginal product for each factor relative to its price: i.e. $MPP_a/P_a = MPP_b/P_b = MPP_c/P_c$, etc. (where a, b and c are different factors). If the MPP/P ratio for one factor is greater than for another, more of the first should be used relative to the second.

*6. An isoquant shows the various combinations of two factors to produce a given output. A whole map of such

isoquants can be drawn with each isoquant representing a different level of output. The slope of the isoquant ($\Delta K/\Delta L$) gives the marginal rate of factor substitution (MPP_L/MPP_K). The bowed-in shape of isoquants illustrates a diminishing marginal rate of factor substitution, which in turn arises because of diminishing marginal returns.

*7. An isocost shows the various combinations of two factors that cost a given amount to employ. It will be a straight line. Its slope is equal to the price ratio of the two factors (P_L/P_K).

*8. The tangency point of an isocost with an isoquant represents the optimum factor combination. It is the point where MPP_L/MPP_K (the slope of the isoquant) $= P_L/P_K$ (the slope of the isocost). By drawing a single isoquant touching the lowest possible isocost, we can show the least-cost combination of factors for producing a given output. By drawing a single isocost touching the highest possible isoquant, we can show the highest output obtainable for a given cost of production.

9. Four distinct time periods can be distinguished. In addition to the short- and long-run periods, we can also distinguish the very-short- and very-long-run periods. The very short run is when all factors are fixed. The very long run is where not only the quantity of factors but also their quality is variable (as a result of changing technology etc.).

5.4 COSTS IN THE LONG RUN

We turn now to *long-run* cost curves. Since there are no fixed factors in the long run, there are no long-run fixed costs. For example, the firm may rent more land in order to expand its operations. Its rent bill therefore goes up as it expands its output. All costs, then, in the long run are variable costs.

 KEY IDEA 19 *Fixed costs and the time period.* Fixed costs occur only in the short run, since in the long run all inputs can be varied.

Long-run average costs

Long-run average cost (LRAC) curves can take various shapes, but a typical one is shown in Figure 5.11.

It is often assumed that as a firm expands, it will initially experience economies of scale and thus face a downward-sloping *LRAC* curve. After a point, however, all such economies will have been achieved and thus the curve will flatten out. Then (possibly after a period of constant *LRAC*) the firm will get so large that it will start experiencing diseconomies of scale and thus a rising *LRAC*. At this stage, production and financial economies will begin to be offset by the managerial problems of running a giant organisation.

 Given the LRAC curve in Figure 5.11, what would the firm's long-run total cost curve look like?

Assumptions behind the long-run average cost curve
We make three key assumptions when constructing long-run average cost curves.

Factor prices are given. At each level of output, it is assumed that a firm will be faced with a given set of factor prices. If factor prices *change*, therefore, both short- and long-run cost curves will shift. Thus an increase in nationally negotiated wage rates would shift the curves upwards.

However, factor prices might be different at *different* levels of output. For example, one of the economies of scale that many firms enjoy is the ability to obtain bulk discount on raw materials and other supplies. In such cases, the curve does *not* shift. The different factor prices are merely experienced at different points along the curve, and are reflected in the shape of the curve. Factor prices are still given for any particular level of output.

The state of technology and factor quality are given. These are assumed to change only in the *very* long run. If a firm gains economies of scale, it is because it is being able to exploit *existing* technologies and make better use of the existing availability of factors of production.

Firms choose the least-cost combination of factors for each output. The assumption here is that firms operate efficiently: that they choose the cheapest possible way of producing any level of output. In other words, at every point along the *LRAC* curve, the firm will adhere to the cost-minimising formula (see page 147):

$$\frac{MPP_a}{P_a} = \frac{MPP_b}{P_b} = \frac{MPP_c}{P_c} = \cdots = \frac{MPP_n}{P_n}$$

where *a . . . n* are the various factors the firm uses.

If the firm did not choose the optimum factor combination, it would be producing at a point above the *LRAC* curve.

Definition

Long-run average cost curve A curve that shows how average cost varies with output on the assumption that *all* factors are variable. (It is assumed that the least-cost method of production will be chosen for each output.)

Figure 5.11 A typical long-run average cost curve

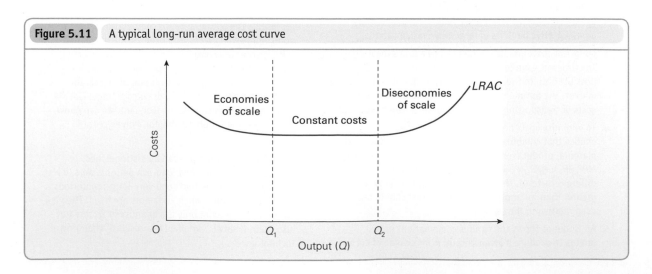

Long-run marginal costs

The relationship between long-run average and *long-run marginal cost* curves is just like that between any other averages and marginals (see Box 5.3). This is illustrated in Figure 5.12.

If there are economies of scale (diagram (a)), additional units of output will add less to costs than the average. The *LRMC* curve must be below the *LRAC* curve and thus pulling the average down as output increases. If there are diseconomies of scale (diagram (b)), additional units of output will cost more than the average. The *LRMC* curve must be above the *LRAC* curve, pulling it up. If there are no eco-

nomies or diseconomies of scale, so that the *LRAC* curve is horizontal, any additional units of output will cost the same as the average and thus leave the average unaffected (diagram (c)).

1. *Explain the shape of the LRMC curve in diagram (d) in Figure 5.12.*
2. *What would the LRMC curve look like if the LRAC curve were 'flat-bottomed', as in Figure 5.11?*

The relationship between long-run and short-run average cost curves

Take the case of a firm which has just one factory and faces a short-run average cost curve illustrated by $SRAC_1$ in Figure 5.13.

In the long run, it can build more factories. If it thereby experiences economies of scale (due, say, to savings on administration), each successive factory will allow it to produce with a new lower *SRAC* curve. Thus with two factories it will face $SRAC_2$, with three factories $SRAC_3$, and so on. Each *SRAC* curve corresponds to a particular amount of the

Definition

Long-run marginal cost The extra cost of producing one more unit of output assuming that all factors are variable. (It is assumed that the least-cost method of production will be chosen for this extra output.)

Figure 5.12 The relationship between long-run average and marginal costs

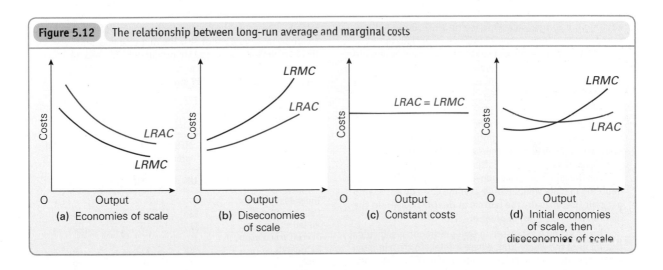

(a) Economies of scale
(b) Diseconomies of scale
(c) Constant costs
(d) Initial economies of scale, then diseconomies of scale

Figure 5.13 Constructing long-run average cost curves from short-run average cost curves

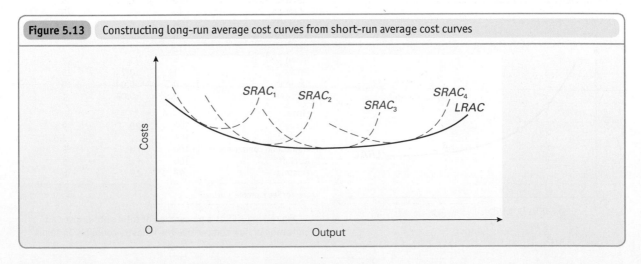

factor that is fixed in the short run: in this case, the factory. (There are many more *SRAC* curves that could be drawn between the ones shown, since factories of different sizes could be built or existing ones could be expanded.)

From this succession of short-run average cost curves we can construct a long-run average cost curve, as shown in Figure 5.13. This is known as the **envelope curve**, since it envelopes the short-run curves.

Definition

Envelope curve A long-run average cost curve drawn as the tangency points of a series of short-run average cost curves.

 Will the envelope curve be tangential to the bottom of each of the short-run average cost curves? Explain why it should or should not be.

Long-run cost curves in practice

Firms do experience economies of scale. Some experience continuously falling *LRAC* curves, as in Figure 5.12(a). Others experience economies of scale up to a certain output and thereafter constant returns to scale.

Evidence is inconclusive on the question of diseconomies of scale. There is little evidence to suggest the existence of *technical* diseconomies, but the possibility of diseconomies due to managerial and industrial relations problems cannot be ruled out.

Some evidence on economies of scale in the UK is considered in Box 5.8.

BOX 5.8	MINIMUM EFFICIENT SCALE

The extent of economies of scale in practice

Two of the most important studies of economies of scale are those made by C. F. Pratten[1] in the late 1980s and by a group advising the European Commission[2] in 1997. Both studies found strong evidence that many firms, especially in manufacturing, experienced substantial economies of scale.

In a few cases, long-run average costs fell continuously as output increased. For most firms, however, they fell up to a certain level of output and then remained constant.

The extent of economies of scale can be measured by looking at a firm's *minimum efficient scale* (*MES*). The *MES* is the size beyond which no significant additional economies of scale can be achieved: in other words, the point where the *LRAC* curve flattens off. In Pratten's studies, he defined this level as the minimum scale above which any possible doubling in scale would reduce average costs by less than 5 per cent (i.e. virtually the bottom of the *LRAC* curve). In the diagram, *MES* is shown at point *a*.

The *MES* can be expressed in terms either of an individual factory or of the whole firm. Where it refers to the minimum efficient scale of an individual factory, the *MES* is known as the *minimum efficient plant size* (*MEPS*).

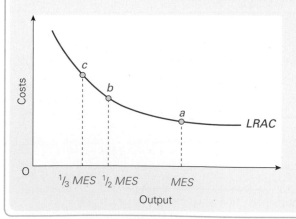

The *MES* can then be expressed as a percentage of the total size of the market or of total domestic production. Table (a), based on the Pratten study, shows *MES* for plants and firms in various industries. The first column shows *MES* as a percentage of total UK production. The second column shows *MES* as a percentage of total EU production. Table (b), based on the 1997 study, shows *MES* for various plants.

Table (a)

Product	MES as % of production		% additional cost at ½ MES
	UK	EU	
Individual plants			
Cellulose fibres	125	16	3
Rolled aluminium semi-manufactures	114	15	15
Refrigerators	85	11	4
Steel	72	10	6
Electric motors	60	6	15
TV sets	40	9	9
Cigarettes	24	6	1.4
Ball-bearings	20	2	6
Beer	12	3	7
Nylon	4	1	12
Bricks	1	0.2	25
Carpets	0.3	0.04	10
Footwear	0.3	0.03	1
Firms			
Cars	200	20	9
Lorries	104	21	7.5
Mainframe computers	> 100	n.a.	5
Aircraft	100	n.a.	5
Tractors	98	19	6

Source: See footnote 1 below.

Expressing *MES* as a percentage of total output gives an indication of how competitive the industry could be. In some

*Derivation of long-run costs from an isoquant map[1]

Cost curves are drawn on the assumption that, for any output, the least-cost combination of factors is used: that is, that production will take place at the tangency point of the isoquant and an isocost, where $MPP_L/MPP_K = P_L/P_K$: i.e. where $MPP_L/P_L = MPP_K/P_K$. By drawing a series of isoquants and isocosts, long-run costs can be derived for each output.

In Figure 5.14, isoquants are drawn for a hypothetical firm at 100 unit intervals. Up to 400 units of output, the isoquants are getting closer together. Thereafter, the gap between the isoquants widens again.

[1] This optional section is based on the material in the optional section on pages 148–52.

The line from *a* to *g* is known as the *expansion path*. It traces the tangency points of the isoquants and isocosts, and thus shows the minimum-cost combinations of labour and capital to produce each output: the (long-run) total cost being given by the isocost.

Up to point *d*, less and less *extra* capital (*K*) and labour (*L*) are required to produce each extra 100 units of output. Thus long-run marginal cost is falling. Above point *d*, more and more extra *K* and *L* are required and thus *LRMC* rises.

Definition

Expansion path The line on an isoquant map that traces the minimum-cost combinations of two factors as output increases. It is drawn on the assumption that both factors can be varied. It is thus a long-run path.

industries (such as footwear and carpets), economies of scale were exhausted (i.e. *MES* was reached) with plants or firms that were still small relative to total UK production and even smaller relative to total EU production. In such industries, there would be room for many firms and thus scope for considerable competition.

Table (b)

Plants	MES as % of total EU production
Aerospace	12.19
Agricultural machinery	6.57
Electric lighting	3.76
Steel tubes	2.42
Shipbuilding	1.63
Rubber	1.06
Radio and TV	0.69
Footwear	0.08
Carpets	0.03

Source: See footnote 2 below.

In other industries, however, even if a single plant or firm were large enough to produce the whole output of the industry in the UK, it would still not be large enough to experience the full potential economies of scale: the *MES* is greater than 100 per cent. Examples from Table (a) include factories producing cellulose fibres, and car manufacturers. In these industries, there is no possibility of competition from within the country. In fact, as long as the *MES* exceeds 50 per cent, there will not be room for more than one firm large enough to gain full economies of scale (unless they export). In this case, the industry is said to be a natural monopoly.

As we shall see in the next few chapters, when competition is lacking, consumers may suffer by firms charging prices considerably above costs.

A second way of measuring the extent of economies of scale is to see how much costs would increase if production were reduced to a certain fraction of *MES*. The normal fractions used are ½ or ⅓ *MES*. This is illustrated in the diagram. Point *b* corresponds to ½ *MES*; point *c* to ⅓ *MES*. The greater the percentage by which *LRAC* at point *b* or *c* is higher than at point a, the greater will be the economies of scale to be gained by producing at *MES* rather than at ½ *MES* or ⅓ *MES*. For example, in Table (a) there are greater economies of scale to be gained from moving from ½ *MES* to *MES* in the production of electric motors than in cigarettes.

The main purpose of the studies was to determine whether the single EU market is big enough to allow both economies of scale and competition. The tables suggest that in all cases, other things being equal, the EU market is indeed large enough for this to occur. The second study also found that 47 of the 53 manufacturing sectors analysed had scope for further exploitation of economies of scale.

In the 2007–13 research framework the European Commission agreed to fund a number of research projects, to conduct further investigations of *MES* across different industries and to consider the impact of the expansion of the EU.

1. *Why might a firm operating with one plant achieve MEPS and yet not be large enough to achieve MES? (Clue: are all economies of scale achieved at plant level?)*
2. *Why might a firm producing bricks have an MES which is only 0.2 per cent of total EU production and yet face little effective competition from other EU countries?*

[1] C. F. Pratten, 'A survey of the economies of scale', in *Research into the 'Costs of Non-Europe'*, Volume 2 (Commission of the European Communities, Luxembourg, 1988).
[2] European Commission/Economists Advisory Group Ltd, 'Economies of Scale', *The Single Market Review*, Subseries V, Volume 4 (Commission of the European Communities, Luxembourg, 1997).

Figure 5.14 Deriving an *LRAC* curve from an isoquant map

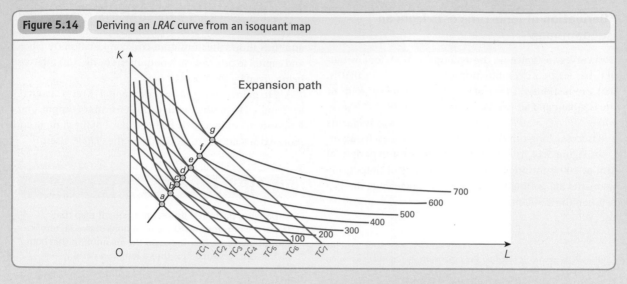

Thus the isoquant map of Figure 5.14 gives an *LRMC* curve that is ⌣-shaped. The *LRAC* curve will therefore also be ⌣-shaped (only shallower) with the *LRMC* coming up through the bottom of the *LRAC*.

 What would the isoquant map look like if there were (a) continuously increasing returns to scale; (b) continuously decreasing returns to scale?

Section summary

1. In the long run, all factors are variable. There are thus no long-run fixed costs.

2. When constructing long-run cost curves, it is assumed that factor prices are given, that the state of technology is given and that firms will choose the least-cost combination of factors for each given output.

3. The *LRAC* curve can be downward sloping, upward sloping or horizontal, depending in turn on whether there are economies of scale, diseconomies of scale or neither. Typically, *LRAC* curves are drawn saucer-shaped or ⌣-shaped. As output expands, initially there are economies of scale. When these are exhausted, the curve will become flat. When the firm becomes very large, it may begin to experience diseconomies of scale.

If this happens, the *LRAC* curve will begin to slope upwards again.

4. The long-run marginal cost curve will be below the *LRAC* curve when *LRAC* is falling, above it when *LRAC* is rising and equal to it when *LRAC* is neither rising nor falling.

5. An envelope curve can be drawn which shows the relationship between short-run and long-run average cost curves. The *LRAC* curve envelops the short-run *LRAC* curves: it is tangential to them.

*6. Costs can be derived from an isoquant map. Long-run total costs are found from the expansion path, which shows the least-cost combination of factors to produce any given output. It traces out the tangency points of the isocosts and isoquants.

5.5 REVENUE

Remember that we defined a firm's total profit as its total revenue minus its total costs of production. So far in this chapter we have examined costs. We now turn to revenue.

As with costs, we distinguish between three revenue concepts: total revenue (*TR*), average revenue (*AR*) and marginal revenue (*MR*).

Total, average and marginal revenue

Total revenue (TR)

Total revenue is the firm's total earnings per period of time from the sale of a particular amount of output (*Q*). For

example, if a firm sells 1000 units (*Q*) per month at a price of £5 each (*P*), then its monthly total revenue will be £5000: in other words, £5 × 1000 (*P* × *Q*). Thus

$$TR = P \times Q$$

Definition

Total revenue A firm's total earnings from a specified level of sales within a specified period: $TR = P \times Q$.

Average revenue (AR)

Average revenue is the amount the firm earns per unit sold. Thus

$$AR = TR/Q$$

So if the firm earns £5000 (*TR*) from selling 1000 units (*Q*), it will earn £5 per unit. But this is simply the price! Thus

$$AR = P$$

(The only exception to this is when the firm is selling its products at different prices to different consumers. In this case, *AR* is simply the (weighted) average price.)

Marginal revenue (MR)

Marginal revenue is the extra total revenue gained by selling one more unit (per time period). So if a firm sells an extra 20 units this month compared with what it expected to sell, and in the process earns an extra £100, then it is getting an extra £5 for each extra unit sold: *MR* = £5. Thus

$$MR = \Delta TR/\Delta Q$$

We now need to see how each of these three revenue concepts (*TR*, *AR* and *MR*) varies with output. We can show this graphically in the same way as we did with costs.

The relationships will depend on the market conditions under which a firm operates. A firm that is too small to be able to affect market price will have different-shaped revenue curves from a firm that is able to choose the price it charges. Let us examine each of these two situations in turn.

Revenue curves when price is not affected by the firm's output

Average revenue

If a firm is very small relative to the whole market, it is likely to be a *price taker*. That is, it has to accept the price given by the intersection of demand and supply in the whole market.

But, being so small, it can sell as much as it is capable of producing at that price. This is illustrated in Figure 5.15.

The left-hand part of the diagram shows market demand and supply. Equilibrium price is £5. The right-hand part of the diagram looks at the demand for an individual firm that is tiny relative to the whole market. (Look at the differences in the scale of the horizontal axes in the two parts of the diagram.)

Being so small, any change in its output will be too insignificant to affect the market price. It thus faces a horizontal demand 'curve' at the price. It can sell 200 units, 600 units, 1200 units or whatever without affecting this £5 price.

Average revenue is thus constant at £5. The firm's average revenue curve must therefore lie along exactly the same line as its demand curve.

Marginal revenue

In the case of a horizontal demand curve, the marginal revenue curve will be the same as the average revenue curve, since selling one more unit at a constant price (*AR*) merely adds that amount to total revenue. If an extra unit is sold at a constant price of £5, an extra £5 is earned.

Total revenue

Table 5.7 shows the effect on total revenue of different levels of sales with a constant price of £5 per unit. As price is

---

Definitions

Average revenue Total revenue per unit of output. When all output is sold at the same price, average revenue will be the same as price: $AR = TR/Q = P$.

Marginal revenue The extra revenue gained by selling one more unit per period of time: $MR = \Delta TR/\Delta Q$.

Price taker A firm that is too small to be able to influence the market price.

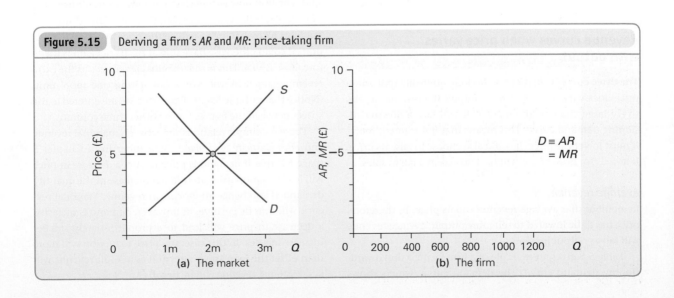

Figure 5.15 Deriving a firm's *AR* and *MR*: price-taking firm

(a) The market

(b) The firm

Table 5.7	Deriving total revenue for a price-taking firm		
Quantity (units)	**Price ≡ AR = MR (£)**		**TR (£)**
0	5		0
200	5		1000
400	5		2000
600	5		3000
800	5		4000
1000	5		5000
1200	5		6000
.	.		.

Table 5.8	Revenues for a firm facing a downward-sloping demand curve		
Q (units)	**P = AR (£)**	**TR (£)**	**MR (£)**
1	8	8	
			6
2	7	14	
			4
3	6	18	
			2
4	5	20	
			0
5	4	20	
			−2
6	3	18	
			−4
7	2	14	
.	.	.	

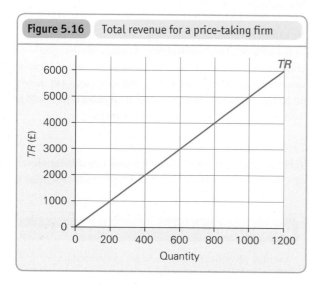

Figure 5.16   Total revenue for a price-taking firm

constant, total revenue will rise at a constant rate as more is sold. The *TR* 'curve' will therefore be a straight line through the origin, as in Figure 5.16.

 What would happen to the TR curve if the market price rose to £10? Try drawing it.

Revenue curves when price varies with output

The three curves (*TR*, *AR* and *MR*) look quite different when price does vary with the firm's output. If a firm has a relatively large share of the market, it will face a downward-sloping demand curve. This means that if it is to sell more, it must lower the price. It could also choose to raise its price. If it does so, however, it will have to accept a fall in sales.

Average revenue

Remember that average revenue equals price. If, therefore, price has to be lowered to sell more output, average revenue will fall as output increases.

Table 5.8 gives an example of a firm facing a downward-sloping demand curve. The demand curve (which shows how much is sold at each price) is given by the first two columns.

Note that, as in the case of a price-taking firm, the demand curve and the *AR* curve lie along exactly the same line. The reason for this is simple: *AR = P*, and thus the curve relating price to quantity (the demand curve) must be the same as that relating average revenue to quantity (the *AR* curve).

Marginal revenue

When a firm faces a downward-sloping demand curve, marginal revenue will be less than average revenue, and may even be negative. But why?

If a firm is to sell more per time period, it must lower its price (assuming it does not advertise). This will mean lowering the price not just for the extra units it hopes to sell, but also for those units it would have sold had it not lowered the price.

Thus the marginal revenue is the price at which it sells the last unit, *minus* the loss in revenue it has incurred by reducing the price on those units it could otherwise have sold at the higher price. This can be illustrated with Table 5.8.

Assume that the price is currently £7. Two units are thus sold. The firm now wishes to sell an extra unit. It lowers the price to £6. It thus gains £6 from the sale of the third unit, but loses £2 by having to reduce the price by £1 on the two units it could otherwise have sold at £7. Its net gain is therefore £6 − £2 = £4. This is the marginal revenue: it is the extra revenue gained by the firm from selling one more unit. (Notice that in Table 5.8 the figures for *MR* are entered in the spaces between the figures for the other three columns.)

There is a simple relationship between marginal revenue and *price elasticity of demand*. Remember from Chapter 3 (page 63) that if demand is price elastic, a *decrease* in price will lead to a proportionately larger increase in the quantity demanded and hence an *increase* in revenue. Marginal revenue will thus be positive. If, however, demand is inelastic, a decrease in price will lead to a proportionately smaller increase in sales. In this case, the price reduction will more than offset the increase in sales and as a result revenue will fall. Marginal revenue will be negative.

 KI 9 p71

Figure 5.17 *AR* and *MR* curves for a firm facing a downward-sloping demand curve

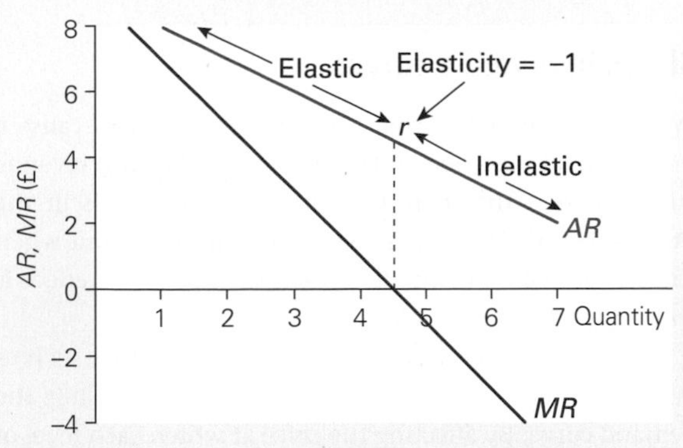

If, then, at a particular quantity sold marginal revenue is a positive figure (i.e. if sales per time period are 4 units or less in Figure 5.17), the demand curve will be elastic at that quantity, since a rise in quantity sold (as a result of a reduction in price) would lead to a rise in total revenue. If, on the other hand, marginal revenue is negative (i.e. at a level of sales of 5 or more units in Figure 5.17), the demand curve will be inelastic at that quantity, since a rise in quantity sold would lead to a *fall* in total revenue.

Thus the demand (*AR*) curve in Figure 5.17 is elastic to the left of point *r* and inelastic to the right.

Total revenue

Total revenue equals price times quantity. This is illustrated in Table 5.8. The *TR* column from Table 5.8 is plotted in Figure 5.18.

*LOOKING AT THE MATHS

As with cost curves (see page 144), we can express revenue curves algebraically.

Price-taking firms

Let us take *TR*, *AR* and *MR* in turn. They will take the following forms:

$$TR = bQ \tag{1}$$

This equation will give an upward-sloping straight-line *TR* 'curve', with a slope of *b*. Note that the absence of a constant (*a*) term means that the line passes through the origin. This is obviously the case, given that if sales (*Q*) are zero, total revenue will be zero.

$$AR = \frac{TR}{Q} = b \tag{2}$$

This will give a horizontal *AR* curve at an *AR* (i.e. price) of *b*.

$$MR = \frac{d(TR)}{dQ} = b \tag{3}$$

Differentiating the *TR* function gives a value of *b*. As we have seen, *AR* = *MR* when the firm is a price taker and faces a horizontal demand curve (at the market price).

Price-making firms: a straight-line demand 'curve'

'Price makers' face a downward-sloping demand curve. If this is a straight-line demand curve, the revenue equations will be as follows:

$$TR = bQ - cQ^2 \tag{4}$$

The negative cQ^2 term will give a revenue curve whose slope gets less until a peak is reached (see Figure 5.18). Thereafter, as the cQ^2 term becomes bigger than the bQ term, *TR* will fall.

$$AR = \frac{TR}{Q} = b - cQ \tag{5}$$

This gives a straight-line downward-sloping *AR* curve (demand curve) with a slope of −*c*, which crosses the horizontal axis when *cQ* becomes bigger than *b*.

$$MR = \frac{d(TR)}{dQ} = b - 2cQ \tag{6}$$

This again gives a straight downward-sloping line, this time with a slope of −2*c*. Note that this means that the slope of the *MR* curve is twice that of the *AR* curve.

But what if the demand curve is actually curved? What will the three revenue equations be then? We explore this in Maths Case 5.4 in MyEconLab and relate the equations to the relevant diagrams.

The relationship between marginal revenue and price elasticity of demand

You can see from Figure 5.17 how price elasticity of demand and marginal revenue are related. We can express this relationship algebraically as follows:

$$MR = P(1 + (1/P\epsilon_D)) \tag{7}$$

or

$$P = \frac{MR}{1 + (1/P\epsilon_D)}$$

Proof of this relationship is given in Maths Case 6.2 in MyEconLab, but for now we can see how equation (7) relates to Figure 5.17. The *P* term must be positive. If demand is elastic, then $P\epsilon_D$ must have a value less than −1 (i.e. the figure for elasticity, ignoring the negative sign, must be greater than 1). Thus the term $1/P\epsilon_D$ must have a negative value between 0 and −1. This means, therefore, that the term $(1 + (1/P\epsilon_D))$ must be positive, and hence *MR* must be positive.

If, however, demand is inelastic, then $P\epsilon_D$ must have a value between −1 and 0. Thus the term $1/P\epsilon_D$ must have a negative value less than −1 (i.e. an absolute value, ignoring the negative sign, that is greater than 1). This means, therefore, that the term $(1 + (1/P\epsilon_D))$ must be negative, and hence *MR* must be negative.

Finally, if demand is unit elastic, then the term $1/P\epsilon_D$ must have a value of −1 and hence the term $(1 + (1/P\epsilon_D))$ must have a value of 0. *MR* must be zero.

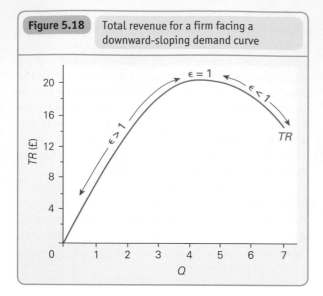

Figure 5.18 Total revenue for a firm facing a downward-sloping demand curve

(and hence demand is inelastic), total revenue will fall. The peak of the *TR* curve will be where *MR* = 0. At this point, the price elasticity of demand will be equal to 1.

Shifts in revenue curves

We saw in Chapter 2 that a change in *price* will cause a movement along a demand curve. It is similar with revenue curves, except that here the causal connection is in the other direction. Here we ask what happens to revenue when there is a change in the firm's *output*. Again the effect is shown by a movement along the curves.

A change in any *other* determinant of demand, such as tastes, income or the price of other goods, will shift the demand curve. By affecting the price at which each level of output can be sold, there will be a shift in all three revenue curves. An increase in revenue is shown by a shift upwards; a decrease by a shift downwards.

 Copy Figures 5.17 and 5.18 (which are based on Table 5.8). Now assume that incomes have risen and that, as a result, two more units per time period can be sold at each price. Draw a new table and plot the resulting new AR, MR and TR curves on your diagrams. Are the new curves parallel to the old ones? Explain.

Unlike the case of a price-taking firm, the *TR* curve is not a straight line. It is a curve that rises at first and then falls. But why? As long as marginal revenue is positive (and hence demand is price elastic), a rise in output will raise total revenue. However, once marginal revenue becomes negative

Section summary

1. Total revenue (*TR*) is the total amount a firm earns from its sales in a given time period. It is simply price times quantity: *TR* = *P* × *Q*.

2. Average revenue (*AR*) is total revenue per unit: *AR* = *TR/Q*. In other words, *AR* = *P*.

3. Marginal revenue is the extra revenue earned from the sale of one more unit per time period.

4. The *AR* curve will be the same as the demand curve for the firm's product. In the case of a price taker, the demand curve and hence the *AR* curve will be a horizontal straight line and will also be the same as the *MR* curve. The *TR* curve will be an upward-sloping straight line from the origin.

5. A firm that faces a downward-sloping demand curve must obviously also face the same downward-sloping *AR* curve. The *MR* curve will also slope downwards, but will be below the *AR* curve and steeper than it. The *TR* curve will be an arch shape starting from the origin.

6. When demand is price elastic, marginal revenue will be positive and the *TR* curve will be upward sloping. When demand is price inelastic, marginal revenue will be negative and the *TR* curve will be downward sloping.

7. A change in output is represented by a movement along the revenue curves. A change in any other determinant of revenue will shift the curves up or down.

5.6 PROFIT MAXIMISATION

We are now in a position to put costs and revenue together to find the output at which profit is maximised, and also to find out how much that profit will be.

There are two ways of doing this. The first and simpler method is to use total cost and total revenue curves. The second method is to use marginal and average cost and marginal and average revenue curves. Although this method is

a little more complicated (but only a little!), it is more useful when we come to compare profit maximising under different market conditions.

We will look at each method in turn. In both cases, we will concentrate on the short run – that period in which one or more factors are fixed in supply. In both cases, we take the instance of a firm facing a downward-sloping demand curve.

Table 5.9	Total revenue, total cost and total profit		
Q (units)	TR (£)	TC (£)	Π (£)
0	0	6	−6
1	8	10	−2
2	14	12	2
3	18	14	4
4	20	18	2
5	20	25	−5
6	18	36	−18
7	14	56	−42
.	.	.	.

Short-run profit maximisation: using total curves

Table 5.9 shows the total revenue figures from Table 5.8. It also shows figures for total cost. These figures have been chosen so as to produce a TC curve of a typical shape.

Total profit (TΠ) is found by subtracting TC from TR. Check this out by examining the table. Where TΠ is negative, the firm is making a loss. Total profit is maximised at an output of 3 units, where there is the greatest gap between total revenue and total costs. At this output, total profit is £4 (£18 − £14).

The TR, TC and TΠ curves are plotted in Figure 5.19. The size of the maximum profit is shown by the arrows.

 What can we say about the slope of the TR and TC curves at the maximum profit point? What does this tell us about marginal revenue and marginal cost?

Short-run profit maximisation: using average and marginal curves

Table 5.10 is based on the figures in Table 5.9.

1. *Fill in the missing figures (without referring to Table 5.8 or 5.9).*
2. *Why are the figures for MR and MC entered in the spaces between the lines in Table 5.10?*

Finding the maximum profit that a firm can make is a two-stage process. The first stage is to find the profit-maximising

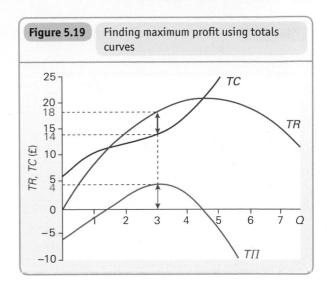

Figure 5.19 Finding maximum profit using totals curves

output. To do this we use the MC and MR curves. The second stage is to find out just how much profit is at this output. To do this we use the AR and AC curves.

Stage 1: Using marginal curves to arrive at the profit-maximising output

There is a very simple **profit-maximising rule**: if profits are to be maximised, MR must equal MC. From Table 5.10 it can be seen that MR = MC at an output of 3. This is shown as point e in Figure 5.20.

But why are profits maximised when MR = MC? The simplest way of answering this is to see what the position would be if MR did not equal MC.

Referring to Figure 5.20, at a level of output below 3, MR exceeds MC. This means that by producing more units there will be a bigger addition to revenue (MR) than to cost (MC). Total profit will *increase*. As long as MR exceeds MC, profit can *be increased by increasing production.*

> **Definition**
>
> **Profit-maximising rule** Profit is maximised where marginal revenue equals marginal cost.

Table 5.10	Revenue, cost and profit							
Q (units)	P = AR (£)	TR (£)	MR (£)	TC (£)	AC (£)	MC (£)	TΠ (£)	AΠ (£)
0	9	0		6	−		−6	−
			8			4		
1	8	8		10	10		. . .	−2
			. . .			2		
2	7	14		12	. . .		2	1
			4			2		
3	6	18		14	4²/₃		4	1¹/₃
			2			4		
4	5	20		18	4¹/₂		2	¹/₂
			0			7		
5	4	20		25	5		−5	−1
			−2			. . .		
6	3	18		36	. . .		. . .	. . .
			. . .			20		
7	2	14		56	8		−42	−6
.	.	.	.	.	.		.	.

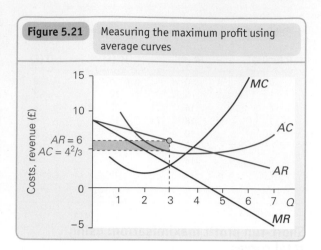

Figure 5.20   Finding the profit-maximising output using marginal curves

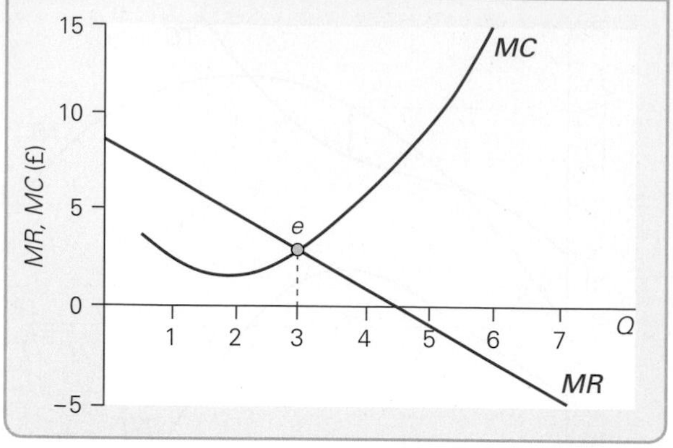

Figure 5.21   Measuring the maximum profit using average curves

At a level of output above 3, *MC* exceeds *MR*. All levels of output above 3 thus add more to cost than to revenue and hence *reduce* profit. *As long as MC exceeds MR, profit can be increased by cutting back on production.*

Profits are thus maximised where *MC* = *MR*: at an output of 3. This can be confirmed by reference to the *TΠ* column in Table 5.10.

Students worry sometimes about the argument that profits are maximised when *MR* = *MC*. Surely, they say, if the last unit is making no profit, how can profit be at a *maximum*? The answer is very simple. If you cannot *add* anything more to a total, the total must be at the maximum. Take the simple analogy of going up a hill. When you cannot go any higher, you must be at the top.

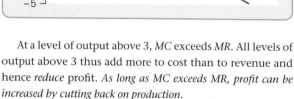

*LOOKING AT THE MATHS

As we have seen, the rule for profit maximisation is that firms should produce where *MC* = *MR*. This can be derived algebraically as follows. Profit is defined as

$$TΠ = TR − TC \tag{1}$$

Profit is maximised at the point where an additional unit of output will add no more to profit – that is, where

$$\frac{ΔTΠ}{ΔQ} = MΠ = 0 \tag{2}$$

or, from (1), where

$$\frac{ΔTR}{ΔQ} − \frac{ΔTC}{ΔQ} = 0 \tag{3}$$

or

$$\frac{ΔTR}{ΔQ} = \frac{ΔTC}{ΔQ} \tag{4}$$

that is, where *MR* = *MC*.

Equation (2) can be related to Figure 5.19. Profits are maximised at the highest point of the *TΠ* curve. At the top of any curve (or bottom for that matter), its slope is zero. Thus $ΔTΠ/Q = MΠ = 0$. Put another way, the tangent to the top of the *TΠ* curve is horizontal.

Stage 2: Using average curves to measure the size of the profit

Once the profit-maximising output has been discovered, we use the average curves to measure the *amount* of profit at the maximum. Both marginal and average curves corresponding to the data in Table 5.10 are plotted in Figure 5.21.

First, average profit (*AΠ*) is found. This is simply *AR* − *AC*. At the profit-maximising output of 3, this gives a figure for *AΠ* of £6 − £4²/₃ = £1¹/₃. Then total profit is obtained by multiplying average profit by output:

$$TΠ = AΠ × Q$$

This is shown as the shaded area. It equals £1¹/₃ × 3 = £4. This can again be confirmed by reference to the *TΠ* column in Table 5.10.

 From the information for a firm given in the table below, construct a table like Table 5.10.

Q	0	1	2	3	4	5	6	7
P	12	11	10	9	8	7	6	5
TC	2	6	9	12	16	21	28	38

Use your table to draw diagrams like Figures 5.19 and 5.21. Use these two diagrams to show the profit-maximising output and the level of maximum profit. Confirm your findings by reference to the table you have constructed.

Some qualifications

Long-run profit maximisation

Assuming that the *AR* and *MR* curves are the same in the long run as in the short run, long-run profits will be maximised at the output where *MR* equals the *long-run MC*. The reasoning is the same as with the short-run case.

The meaning of 'profit'

One element of cost is the opportunity cost to the owners of the firm of being in business. This is the minimum return

KI 2
p11

*BOX 5.9 — USING CALCULUS TO FIND THE MAXIMUM PROFIT OUTPUT

Imagine that a firm's total revenue and total cost functions were

$$TR = 48Q - Q^2$$
$$TC = 12 + 16Q + 3Q^2$$

From these two equations the following table can be derived.

Q	TR	TC	$T\Pi$ (= TR − TC)
0	0	12	−12
1	47	31	16
2	92	56	36
3	135	87	48
4	176	124	52
5	215	167	48
6	252	216	36
7	287	271	16
.	.	.	.

1. How much is total fixed cost?
2. Continue the table for $Q = 8$ and $Q = 9$.
3. Plot TR, TC and $T\Pi$ on a diagram like Figure 5.19.

It can clearly be seen from the table that profit is maximised at an output of 4, where $T\Pi = 52$.

This profit-maximising output and the level of profit can be calculated without drawing up a table. The calculation involves calculus. There are two methods that can be used.

Finding where $MR = MC$

Marginal revenue can be found by differentiating the total revenue function:

$$MR = dTR/dQ$$

The reason is that marginal revenue is the rate of change of total revenue. Differentiating a function gives its rate of change.

Similarly, marginal cost can be found by differentiating the total cost function:

$$MC = dTC/dQ$$

Differentiating TR and TC gives

$$dTR/dQ = 48 - 2Q = MR$$

and

$$dTR/dQ = 16 + 6Q = MC$$

Profit is maximised where $MR = MC$, in other words where

$$48 - 2Q = 16 + 6Q$$

Solving this for Q gives

$$32 = 80$$
$$\therefore Q = 4$$

The equation for total profit ($T\Pi$) is

$$T\Pi = TR - TC$$
$$= 48Q - Q^2 - (12 + 16Q + 3Q^2)$$
$$= -12 + 32Q - 4Q^2$$

Substituting $Q = 4$ into this equation gives

$$T\Pi = 12 + (32 \times 4) - (4 \times 4^2)$$
$$\therefore T\Pi = 52$$

These figures can be confirmed from the table.

Maximising the total profit equation

To maximise an equation we want to find the point where the slope of the curve derived from it is zero. In other words, we want to find the top of the $T\Pi$ curve.

The slope of a curve gives its rate of change and is found by differentiating the curve's equation. Thus to find maximum $T\Pi$ we differentiate it (to find the slope) and set it equal to zero (to find the top).

$$T\Pi = -12 + 32Q - 4Q^2 \text{ (see above)}$$
$$\therefore dT\Pi/dQ = 32 - 8Q$$

Setting this equal to zero gives

$$32 - 8Q = 0$$
$$\therefore 8Q = 32$$
$$\therefore Q = 4$$

This is the same result as was found by the first method. Again $Q = 4$ can be substituted into the $T\Pi$ equation to give

$$T\Pi = 52$$

Given the following equations:

$$TR = 72Q - 2Q^2; TC = 10 + 12Q + 4Q^2$$

calculate the maximum profit output and the amount of profit at that output using both methods.

---

the owners must make on their capital in order to prevent them from eventually deciding to close down and perhaps move into some alternative business. It is a *cost* because, just as with wages, rent, etc., it has to be covered if the firm is to continue producing. This opportunity cost to the owners is sometimes known as **normal profit**, and is *included in the cost curves.*

Definition

Normal profit The opportunity cost of being in business: the profit that could have been earned in the next best alternative business. It is counted as a cost of production.

What determines this normal rate of profit? It has two components. First, someone setting up in business invests capital in it. There is thus an opportunity cost. This is the interest that could have been earned by lending it in some riskless form (e.g. by putting it in a savings account in a bank). Nobody would set up a business unless they expected to earn at least this rate of profit. Running a business is far from riskless, however, and hence a second element is a return to compensate for risk. Thus

$$\text{normal profit (\%)} = \text{rate of interest on a riskless loan} + \text{a risk premium}$$

The risk premium varies according to the line of business. In those with fairly predictable patterns, such as food retailing, it is relatively low. Where outcomes are very uncertain, such as mineral exploration or the manufacture of fashion garments, it is relatively high.

Thus, if owners of a business earn normal profit, they will (just) be content to remain in that industry. If they earn more than normal profit, they will also (obviously) prefer to stay in this business. If they earn less than normal profit, then after a time they will consider leaving and using their capital for some other purpose. We will see in Chapter 6 that the level of profits that a firm can make plays a pivotal role in the way markets are structured.

How will the size of 'normal profit' vary with the general state of the economy?

Given that normal profits are included in costs, any profit that is shown diagrammatically (e.g. the shaded area in Figure 5.21) must therefore be over and above normal profit. It is known by several alternative names: *supernormal profit*, *pure profit*, *economic profit* or sometimes simply *profit*. They all mean the same thing: the excess of total profit over normal profit.

Loss minimising

It may be that there is no output at which the firm can make a profit. Such a situation is illustrated in Figure 5.22: the *AC* curve is above the *AR* curve at all levels of output.

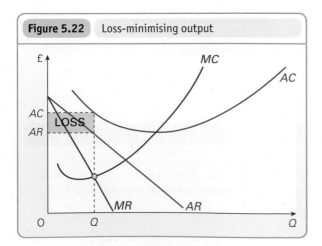

Figure 5.22   Loss-minimising output

In this case, the output where *MR* = *MC* will be the loss-minimising output. The amount of loss at the point where *MR* = *MC* is shown by the shaded area in Figure 5.22. Even though the firm is making losses, there is no 'better' level of output at this point.

Whether or not to produce at all

The short run.   Fixed costs have to be paid even if the firm is producing nothing at all. Rent and business rates have to be paid, etc. Providing, therefore, that the firm is able to cover its *variable* costs, it is no worse off and therefore will continue to produce. Of course, if the firm's revenues are more than its variable costs, then it is able to go some way to covering the fixed costs and again it will continue to produce.

KI 18
p139

What happens if the firm's revenue is not enough to cover its variable costs: that is, if the *AVC* curve is above, or the *AR* curve below, the position illustrated in Figure 5.23? In that case the firm is worse off than if it only has fixed costs and it will shut down production. This situation is known as the **short-run shut-down point**.

The long run.   All costs are variable in the long run. If, therefore, the firm cannot cover its long-run average costs (which include normal profit), it will close down. The **long-run shut-down point** will be where the *AR* curve is tangential to the *LRAC* curve.

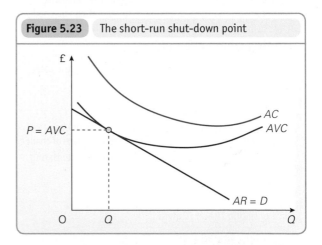

Figure 5.23   The short-run shut-down point

Definitions

Supernormal profit (also known as **pure profit**, **economic profit** or simply **profit**) The excess of total profit above normal profit.

Short-run shut-down point Where the *AR* curve is tangential to the *AVC* curve. The firm can only just cover its variable costs. Any fall in revenue below this level will cause a profit-maximising firm to shut down immediately.

Long-run shut-down point Where the *AR* curve is tangential to the *LRAC* curve. The firm can just make normal profits. Any fall in revenue below this level will cause a profit-maximising firm to shut down once all costs have become variable.

BOX 5.10	THE LOGIC OF LOGISTICS	CASE STUDIES AND APPLICATIONS

Driving up profits

One key to a company's success is the logistics of its operations. 'Logistics' refers to the management of the inflow of resources to a company and the outflow of finished goods from it; in other words, it refers to 'supply-chain management'. This includes the purchasing of raw materials, transporting them, production sequencing, stock control, delivery to wholesalers or retailers, and so on.

Logistics depends on the provision of high-quality and timely information. As IT systems have become increasingly sophisticated, they have enabled modern developments in logistics to transform the operation of many industries.

Driving down costs

With the widespread use of containerisation and development of giant distribution companies, such as UPS and DHL, transporting materials and goods around the world has become much faster and much cheaper. Instead of having to make parts in-house, companies can now use the logistics industry to obtain them at lower cost elsewhere, often from the other side of the world.

With improved systems for ordering materials, and deliveries becoming more and more reliable, firms no longer need keep large stocks of parts; they simply buy them as they need them. The same opportunity to save costs lies with the finished product: a company can keep lower levels of stocks when its own delivery mechanisms are more efficient.

The globalisation of logistics, with increasing use of the Internet, has resulted in a hugely complex logistics industry. Firms that were once solely concerned with delivery are now employed to manage companies' supply chains and achieve substantial cost savings for them.

Driving up revenues

Efficient logistics has not just resulted in lower costs. The flexibility it has given firms has allowed many to increase their sales.

Carrying lower levels of stocks and switching from supplier to supplier, with the process often being managed by a logistics company, can allow companies to change the products they offer more rapidly. They can be more responsive to consumer demand and thereby increase their sales.

A well-known example of a company benefiting from this approach is Primark. This low-cost fashion retailer focuses much more on buying, logistics and supply-chain management than on branding or advertising.

1. *What dangers are there in keeping stocks to a minimum and relying on complex supply chains?*
2. *Which industries do you think would benefit most from reduced transport times for their finished products? Think of an industry, other than low-cost fashion, which would benefit from the ability to switch rapidly the products offered.*

*LOOKING AT THE MATHS

We can state the short- and long-run shut-down points algebraically. Remember that total profit ($T\Pi$) is defined as

$$T\Pi = TR - TC = TR - (TFC + TVC) \qquad (1)$$

A negative value for $T\Pi$ means that the firm makes a loss. This will occur when

$$TR - (TFC + TVC) < 0$$

or

$$TR < (TFC + TVC)$$

But when should the firm shut down?

Short-run shut-down point

If the firm shuts down, TR and TVC will be zero, but in the short run it will still incur total fixed costs (TFC) and thus

$$T\Pi = -TFC \qquad (2)$$

In other words, it will make a loss equal to total fixed costs. From this it can be seen that the firm should close in the short run only if

$$T\Pi < -TFC$$

that is,

$$(TR - TFC - TVC) < -TFC \qquad (3)$$

In other words, the loss should not exceed fixed costs. Put another way (i.e. by rearranging (3)), it should continue in production as long as

$$TR \geq TVC \qquad (4)$$

or, dividing both sides of (4) by quantity, where

$$AR \geq AVC \qquad (5)$$

The firm, therefore, should shut down if

$$AR < AVC$$

This is shown in Figure 5.23.

Long-run shut-down point

In the long run, there are no fixed costs. Thus

$$T\Pi = TR - TVC = TR - TC \qquad (6)$$

If the firm shuts down, it will earn no revenue, but incur no costs. Thus

$$T\Pi = TR - TC = 0 - 0 = 0$$

The firm should therefore continue in production as long as

$$(TR - TC) \geq 0$$

that is,

$$TR \geq TC$$

or, dividing both sides by quantity, as long as

$$AR \geq AC$$

(where AC in this case is long-run average cost). The firm, therefore, should shut down if

$$AR < AC$$

Section summary

1. Total profit equals total revenue minus total cost. By definition, then, a firm's profits will be maximised at the point where there is the greatest gap between total revenue and total cost.

2. Another way of finding the maximum profit point is to find the output where marginal revenue equals marginal cost. Having found this output, the level of maximum profit can be found by finding the average profit ($AR - AC$) and then multiplying it by the level of output.

3. Normal profit is the minimum profit that must be made to persuade a firm to stay in business in the long run. It is counted as part of the firm's costs. Supernormal profit is any profit over and above normal profit.

4. For a firm that cannot make a profit at any level of output, the point where $MR = MC$ represents the loss-minimising output.

5. In the short run, a firm will close down if it cannot cover its variable costs. In the long run, it will close down if it cannot make normal profits.

END OF CHAPTER QUESTIONS

1. The following table shows the average cost and average revenue (price) for a firm at each level of output.

Output	1	2	3	4	5	6	7	8	9	10
AC (£)	7.00	5.00	4.00	3.30	3.00	3.10	3.50	4.20	5.00	6.00
AR (£)	10.00	9.50	9.00	8.50	8.00	7.50	7.00	6.50	6.00	5.50

   (a) Construct a table to show *TC, MC, TR* and *MR* at each level of output (put the figures for *MC* and *MR* midway between the output figures).

   (b) Using *MC* and *MR* figures, find the profit-maximising output.

   (c) Using *TC* and *TR* figures, check your answer to (b).

   (d) Plot the *AC, MC, AR* and *MR* figures on a graph.

   (e) Mark the profit-maximising output and the *AR* and *AC* at this output.

   (f) Shade in an area to represent the level of profits at this output.

*2. Draw the isoquant corresponding to the following table, which shows the alternative combinations of labour and capital required to produce 100 units of output per day of good X.

K	16	20	26⅔	40	60	80	100
L	200	160	120	80	53⅓	40	32

   (a) Assuming that capital costs are £20 per day and the wage rate is £10 per day, what is the least-cost method of producing 100 units? What will the daily total cost be? (Draw in a series of isocosts.)

   (b) Now assume that the wage rate rises to £20 per day. Draw a new set of isocosts. What will be the least-cost method of producing 100 units now? How much labour and capital will be used?

3. Choose two industries that you believe are very different. Identify factors used in those industries that in the short run are (a) fixed; (b) variable.

4. Taking the same industries, identify as many economies of scale as you can.

5. 'Both short-run and long-run average cost curves may be ⌣-shaped, but the explanations for their respective shapes are quite different.' Explain this statement.

6. Why do marginal cost curves intersect both the average variable cost curve and the average cost curve at their lowest point?

7. Draw a diagram like that in Figure 5.21. Now illustrate the effect of a rise in demand for the product. Mark the new profit-maximising price and output. Will the profit-maximising output, price, average cost and profit necessarily be higher than before?

8. Why might it make sense for a firm which cannot sell its output at a profit to continue in production for the time being? For how long should the firm continue to produce at a loss?

Online resources

Additional case studies in MyEconLab

5.1 **Diminishing returns to nitrogen fertiliser.** This case study provides a good illustration of diminishing returns in practice by showing the effects on grass yields of the application of increasing amounts of nitrogen fertiliser.

5.2 **Deriving cost curves from total physical product information.** This shows how total, average and marginal costs can be derived from total product information and the price of inputs.

5.3 **Division of labour in a pin factory.** This is the famous example of division of labour given by Adam Smith in his *Wealth of Nations* (1776).

5.4 **Followers of fashion.** This case study examines the effects of costs on prices of fashion-sensitive goods.

5.5 **Putting on a duplicate.** This examines the effects on marginal costs of additional passengers on a coach journey.

5.6 **Comparing the behaviour of long-run and short-run costs.** This is an application of isoquant analysis.

Maths Case 5.1 Total, average and marginal cost. Looking at the mathematical functions for these curves and deriving specific types of cost from a total cost equation.

Maths Case 5.2 Finding the optimum production point: Part 1. Examples using the method of substituting the constraint equation into the objective function.

Maths Case 5.3 Finding the optimum production point: Part 2. The same examples as in Maths Case 5.2, but this time using the Lagrangian methods.

Maths Case 5.4 Total, average and marginal revenue. Looking at the mathematical functions for these curves for both price-taking and price-making firms and relating them to revenue curves.

Websites relevant to this chapter

Numbers and sections refer to websites listed in the Web Appendix and hotlinked from this book's website at **www.pearsoned.co.uk/sloman**.

- For news articles relevant to this chapter, see the *Economic News* section in MyEconLab.
- For student resources relevant to this chapter, see sites C1–7, 9, 10, 14, 19, 20.
- For a case study examining costs, see site D2.
- For sites that look at companies, their scale of operation and market share, see B2 (third link); E4, 10; G7, 8.
- For links to sites on various aspects of production and costs, see the sections *Microeconomics* in sites I7 and 11.

MyEconLab

This book can be supported by MyEconLab, which contains a range of additional resources, including an online homework and tutorial system designed to test and build your understanding.

You need both an access card and a course ID to access MyEconLab:

1. Is your lecturer using MyEconLab? Ask your lecturer for your course ID.

2. Has an access card been included with the book at a reduced cost? Check the inside back cover of the book.

3. If you have a course ID but no access card, go to: http://www.myeconlab.com/ to buy access to this interactive study programme.

Profit Maximising under Perfect Competition and Monopoly

CHAPTER MAP

6.1 Alternative market structures   **171**

6.2 Perfect competition   **172**
Assumptions of perfect competition   172
The short run and the long run   172
The short-run equilibrium of the firm   174
The short-run supply curve   175
The long-run equilibrium of the firm   176
The long-run industry supply curve   176
The incompatibility of perfect competition and
   substantial economies of scale   177
Perfect competition and the public interest   177

6.3 Monopoly   **181**
What is a monopoly?   181
Barriers to entry   181
Equilibrium price and output   182
Monopoly and the public interest   184

6.4 The theory of contestable markets   **188**
Potential competition or monopoly?   188
The importance of costless exit   188
Assessment of the theory   189
Contestable markets and the public interest   189

As we saw in Chapter 5, a firm's profits are maximised where its marginal cost equals its marginal revenue: $MC = MR$. But we will want to know more than this.

- What determines the amount of profit that a firm will make? Will profits be large, or just enough for the firm to survive, or so low that it will be forced out of business?
- Will the firm produce a high level of output or a low level?
- Will it be producing efficiently, making best use of resources?
- Will the price charged to the consumer be high or low?
- More generally, will the consumer benefit from the decisions a firm makes? This is, of course, a normative question (see section 1.3). Nevertheless, economists can still identify and analyse the effects these decisions have on consumers.

The answers to these questions largely depend on the amount of competition that a firm faces. A firm in a highly competitive environment will behave quite differently from a firm facing little or no competition. In particular, a firm facing competition from many other firms will be forced to keep its prices down and be as efficient as possible, simply to survive. If, however, the firm faces little or no competition (like a local water company or a major pharmaceutical company), it may have considerable power over prices, and we may end up paying considerably more as a result.

In this chapter and the next, we consider different types of market structure. Here we focus on the extremes: perfect competition (very many firms competing) and monopoly (only one firm in the industry).

6.1 ALTERNATIVE MARKET STRUCTURES

It is traditional to divide industries into categories according to the degree of competition that exists between the firms within the industry. There are four such categories.

At one extreme is **perfect competition**, where there are very many firms competing. Each firm is so small relative to the whole industry that it has no power to influence price. It is a price taker. At the other extreme is **monopoly**, where there is just one firm in the industry, and hence no competition from within the industry. In the middle come **monopolistic competition**, which involves quite a lot of firms competing and where there is freedom for new firms to enter the industry, and **oligopoly**, which involves only a few firms and where entry of new firms is restricted.

To distinguish more precisely between these four categories, the following must be considered:

- How freely firms can enter the industry. Is entry free or restricted? If it is restricted, just how great are the barriers to the entry of new firms?
- The nature of the product. Do all firms produce an identical product, or do firms produce their own particular brand or model or variety?
- The firm's degree of control over price. Is the firm a price taker or can it choose its price, and if so, how will changing its price affect its profits? What we are talking about here is the nature of the demand curve it faces. How elastic is it? If the firm puts up its price, will it lose (a) all its sales (a horizontal demand curve), or (b) a large pro-

portion of its sales (a relatively elastic demand curve), or (c) just a small proportion of its sales (a relatively inelastic demand curve)?

KEY IDEA 20

Market power. When firms have market power over prices, they can use this to raise prices and profits above the perfectly competitive level. Other things being equal, the firm will gain at the expense of the consumer. Similarly, if consumers or workers have market power, they can use this to their own benefit.

Table 6.1 shows the differences between the four categories.

1. *Give two more examples in each category.*
2. *Would you expect builders and restaurateurs to have the same degree of control over price?*

The market structure under which a firm operates will determine its behaviour. Firms under perfect competition will behave quite differently from firms which are monopolists, which will behave differently again from firms under oligopoly or monopolistic competition.

TC 5 p54

This behaviour (or 'conduct') will in turn affect the firm's performance: its prices, profits, efficiency, etc. In many cases, it will also affect other firms' performance: *their* prices, profits, efficiency, etc. The collective conduct of all the firms in the industry will affect the whole industry's performance.

Economists thus see a causal chain running from market structure to the performance of that industry:

Structure → Conduct → Performance

First we shall look at the two extreme market structures: perfect competition and monopoly. Then in Chapter 7 we shall look at the two intermediate cases of monopolistic competition and oligopoly.

The two intermediate cases are sometimes referred to collectively as **imperfect competition**. The vast majority of firms in the real world operate under imperfect competition. It is still worth studying the two extreme cases, however, because they provide a framework within which to understand the real world. Some industries tend more to the competitive extreme, and thus their performance corresponds to some extent to perfect competition. Other industries tend more to the other extreme: for example, when there is one dominant firm and a few much smaller firms. In such cases, their performance corresponds more to monopoly.

Chapters 6 and 7 assume that firms, under whatever market structure, are attempting to maximise profits. Chapter 8 questions this assumption. It looks at alternative theories of the firm: theories based on assumptions other than profit maximising.

KI 9 p71

Definitions

Perfect competition A market structure where there are many firms, none of which is large; where there is freedom of entry into the industry; where all firms produce an identical product; and where all firms are price takers.

Monopoly A market structure where there is only one firm in the industry. (Note that this is the economic definition of a pure monopoly. In UK competition law, the part that applies to the abuse of monopoly power covers firms that are in a position of 'market dominance'. Such firms will have a large share, but not necessarily a 100 per cent share, of the market. See Chapter 13 for more on this.)

Monopolistic competition A market structure where, as with perfect competition, there are many firms and freedom of entry into the industry, but where each firm produces a differentiated product and thus has some control over its price.

Oligopoly A market structure where there are few enough firms to enable barriers to be erected against the entry of new firms.

Imperfect competition The collective name for monopolistic competition and oligopoly.

Table 6.1	Features of the four market structures					
Type of market	**Number of firms**	**Freedom of entry**	**Nature of product**	**Examples**	**Implication for demand curve for firm**	
Perfect competition	Very many	Unrestricted	Homogeneous (undifferentiated)	Cabbages, carrots (these approximate to perfect competition)	Horizontal. The firm is a price taker	
Monopolistic competition	Many/several	Unrestricted	Differentiated	Builders, restaurants	Downward sloping, but relatively elastic. The firm has some control over price	
Oligopoly	Few	Restricted	1. Undifferentiated 2. Differentiated	1. Petrol 2. Cars, electrical appliances	Downward sloping, relatively inelastic but depends on reactions of rivals to a price change	
Monopoly	One	Restricted or completely blocked	Unique	Prescription drugs produced under a patent, local water companies	Downward sloping, more inelastic than oligopoly. The firm has considerable control over price	

6.2 PERFECT COMPETITION

Assumptions of perfect competition

The model of perfect competition is built on four assumptions:

- Firms are *price takers*. There are so many firms in the industry that each one produces an insignificantly small portion of total industry supply, and therefore has no power whatsoever to affect the price of the product. It faces a horizontal demand 'curve' at the market price: the price determined by the interaction of demand and supply in the whole market.

- There is complete *freedom of entry* into the industry for new firms. Existing firms are unable to stop new firms setting up in business. Setting up a business takes time, however. Freedom of entry, therefore, applies in the long run.

- All firms produce an *identical product*. (The product is 'homogeneous'.) There is therefore no branding and no advertising, since there would be no point in the firm incurring this cost.

- Producers and consumers have *perfect knowledge* of the market. Producers are fully aware of prices, costs and market opportunities. Consumers are fully aware of the price, quality and availability of the product.

These assumptions are very strict. Few, if any, industries in the real world meet these conditions. Certain agricultural markets are perhaps closest to perfect competition. The market for fresh vegetables is an example.

Nevertheless, despite the lack of real-world cases, the model of perfect competition plays a very important role in economic analysis and policy. Its major relevance is as an 'ideal type' and many argue that achieving perfect competi-

tion would bring a number of important advantages, such as keeping prices down to marginal cost and preventing firms from making supernormal profit over the long run. The model can thus be used as a standard against which to judge the shortcomings of real-world industries. However, we will also see that it has disadvantages, when compared with other market structures.

1. *It is sometimes claimed that the market for various stocks and shares is perfectly competitive, or nearly so. Take the case of the market for shares in a large company like Ford. Go through each of the four assumptions above and see if they apply in this case. (Don't be misled by the first assumption. The 'firm' in this case is not Ford itself.)*
2. *Is the market for gold perfectly competitive?*

The short run and the long run

Before we can examine what price, output and profits will be, we must first distinguish between the short run and the long run as they apply to perfect competition.

In the ***short run***, the number of firms is fixed. Depending on its costs and revenue, a firm might be making large profits, small profits, no profits or a loss; and in the short run, it may continue to do so.

> **Definition**
>
> **Short run under perfect competition** The period during which there is insufficient time for new firms to enter the industry.

BOX 6.1 **CONCENTRATION RATIOS**   EXPLORING ECONOMICS

Measuring the degree of competition

We can get some indication of how competitive a market is by observing the number of firms: the more the firms, the more competitive the market would seem to be. However, this does not tell us anything about how *concentrated* the market might be. There may be *many* firms (suggesting a situation of perfect competition or monopolistic competition), but the largest two firms might produce 95 per cent of total output. This would make these two firms more like oligopolists.

Thus, even though a large number of producers may make the market *seem* highly competitive, this could be deceiving. Another approach, therefore, to measuring the degree of competition is to focus on the level of concentration of firms.

Five-firm concentration ratios for various industries (by output)

Industry	5-firm ratio	15-firm ratio
Sugar	99	99
Tobacco products	99	99
Oils and fats	88	95
Confectionery	81	91
Gas distribution	82	87
Soft drinks, mineral water	75	93
Postal/courier services	65	75
Telecommunications	61	75
Inorganic chemicals	57	80
Pharmaceuticals	57	74
Alcoholic beverages	50	78
Soap and toiletries	40	64
Accountancy services	36	47
Motor vehicles	34	54
Glass and glass products	26	49
Fishing	16	19
Advertising	10	20
Wholesale distribution	6	11
Furniture	5	13
Construction	5	9

Source: Based on data in *United Kingdom Input–Output Analyses*, 2006 Edition (National Statistics, 2006), Table 8.31.

The simplest measure of industrial concentration involves adding together the market share of the largest so many firms: e.g. the largest 3, 5 or 15. This would give what is known as the '3-firm', '5-firm' or '15-firm' 'concentration ratio'. There are different ways of estimating market share: by revenue, by output, by profit, etc.

The table shows the 5-firm and 15-firm concentration ratios of selected industries in the UK by output. As you can see, there is an enormous variation in the degree of concentration from one industry to another.

One of the main reasons for this is differences in the percentage of total industry output at which economies of scale are exhausted. If this occurs at a low level of output, there will be room for several firms in the industry which are all benefiting from the maximum economies of scale.

The degree of concentration will also depend on the barriers to entry of other firms into the industry (see pages 159–60) and on various factors such as transport costs and historical accident. It will also depend on how varied the products are within any one industrial category. For example, in categories as large as furniture and construction there is room for many firms, each producing a specialised range of products.

So is the degree of concentration a good guide to the degree of competitiveness of the industry? The answer is that it is *some* guide, but on its own it can be misleading. In particular, it ignores the degree of competition from abroad.

1. *What are the advantages and disadvantages of using a 5-firm concentration ratio rather than a 15-firm, a 3-firm or even a 1-firm ratio?*
2. *Why are some industries, such as bread baking and brewing, relatively concentrated, in that a few firms produce a large proportion of total output (see Box 7.2 and Case Study 7.4 in MyEconLab), and yet there are also many small producers?*

In the **long run**, however, the level of profits affects entry and exit from the industry. If supernormal profits are made (see page 166), new firms will be attracted into the industry, whereas if losses are being made, firms will leave.

Note that although we shall be talking about the *level* of profit (since that makes our analysis of pricing and output decisions simpler to understand), in practice it is usually the *rate* of profit that determines whether a firm stays in the industry or leaves. The **rate of profit** (*r*) is the level of profit (*TΠ*) as *a proportion of the level of capital (K) employed*: $r = T\Pi/K$. As you would expect, larger firms will need to make a larger *total* profit to persuade them to stay in an industry. Total normal profit is thus larger for them than for a small firm. The *rate* of normal profit, however, will probably be similar.

Definitions

Long run under perfect competition The period of time that is long enough for new firms to enter the industry.

Rate of profit Total profit (*TΠ*) as a proportion of the capital employed (*K*): $r = T\Pi/K$.

KI 6
p29

BOX 6.2	IS PERFECT BEST?	EXPLORING ECONOMICS

Be careful of the word 'perfect'.

'Perfect competition' refers to competition that is complete. Perhaps 'complete competition' would be a better term. There is a complete absence of power, a complete absence of entry barriers, a complete absence of product differentiation between producers, and complete information for producers and consumers on the market. It is thus useful for understanding the effects of power, barriers, product differentiation and lack of information.

Perfect does not mean 'best', however.

Just because it is at the extreme end of the competition spectrum, it does not follow that perfect competition is desirable. After all, you could have a perfect killer virus: i.e. one that is totally immune to drugs, and against which

humans have no natural protection at all. Such a thing, though perfect, is hardly desirable.

To say that perfect competition is desirable and that it is a goal towards which government policy should be directed are normative statements. Economists, in their role as economists, cannot make such statements.

This does not mean, of course, that economists cannot identify the effects of perfect competition, but whether these effects are *desirable* or not is an ethical question.

The danger is that by using perfect competition as a yardstick, and by using the word 'perfect' rather than 'complete', economists may be surreptitiously persuading their audience that perfect competition is a goal we *ought* to be striving to achieve.

1. *Why do economists treat normal profit as a cost of production?*
2. *What determines (a) the level and (b) the rate of normal profit for a particular firm?*

Thus whether the industry expands or contracts in the long run will depend on the rate of profit. Naturally, since the time a firm takes to set up in business varies from industry to industry, the length of time before the long run is reached also varies from industry to industry.

The short-run equilibrium of the firm

TC 4
p47

The determination of price, output and profit in the short run under perfect competition can best be shown in a diagram.

Figure 6.1 shows a short-run equilibrium for both an industry and a firm under perfect competition. Both parts of the diagram have the same scale for the vertical axis. The

horizontal axes have totally different scales, however. For example, if the horizontal axis for the firm were measured in, say, thousands of units, the horizontal axis for the whole industry might be measured in millions or tens of millions of units, depending on the number of firms in the industry.

Let us examine the determination of price, output and profit in turn.

Price

The price is determined in the industry by the intersection of demand and supply. The firm faces a horizontal demand (or average revenue) 'curve' at this price. It can sell all it can produce at the market price (P_e), but nothing at a price above P_e.

Output

The firm will maximise profit where marginal cost equals marginal revenue ($MR = MC$), at an output of Q_e. Note that,

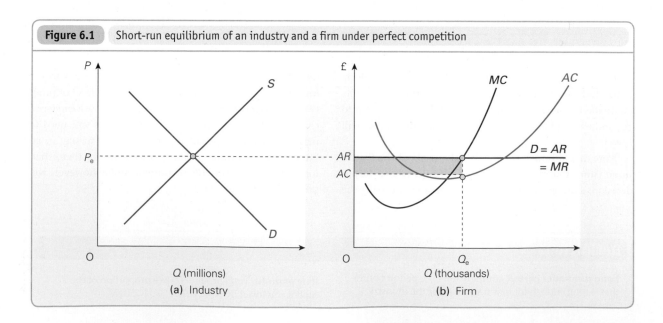

Figure 6.1 Short-run equilibrium of an industry and a firm under perfect competition

(a) Industry

(b) Firm

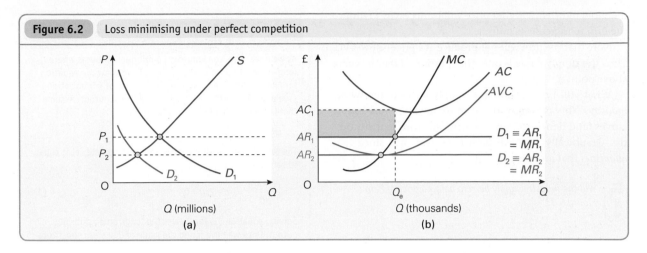

Figure 6.2 Loss minimising under perfect competition

since the price is not affected by the firm's output, marginal revenue will equal price (see pages 159–60 and Figure 5.15).

Profit

If the average cost (*AC*) curve (which includes normal profit) dips below the average revenue (*AR*) 'curve', the firm will earn supernormal profit. Supernormal profit *per unit* at Q_e is the vertical difference between *AR* and *AC* at Q_e. *Total* supernormal profit is the shaded rectangle in Figure 6.1.

What happens if the firm cannot make a profit at *any* level of output? This situation would occur if the *AC* curve were above the *AR* curve at all points. This is illustrated in Figure 6.2, where the market price is P_1. In this case, the point where *MC = MR* represents the *loss-minimising* point (where loss is defined as anything less than normal profit). The amount of the loss is represented by the shaded rectangle.

As we saw in section 5.6, whether the firm is prepared to continue making a loss in the short run or whether it will close down immediately depends on whether it can cover its *variable* costs.

Provided price is above average variable cost (*AVC*), the firm will still continue producing in the short run: it can pay

its variable costs and go some way to paying its fixed costs. It will shut down in the short run only if the market price falls below P_2 in Figure 6.2.

The short-run supply curve

The firm's short-run supply curve will be its (short-run) marginal cost curve.

A supply curve shows how much will be supplied at each price: it relates quantity to price. The marginal cost curve relates quantity to marginal cost. But under perfect competition, given that *P = MR*, and *MR = MC*, *P* must equal *MC*. Thus the supply curve and the *MC* curve will follow the same line.

For example, in Figure 6.3(b), if price were P_1, profits would be maximised at Q_1 where $P_1 = MC$. Thus point *a* is one point on the supply curve. At a price of P_2, Q_2 would be produced. Thus point *b* is another point on the supply curve, and so on.

So, under perfect competition, the firm's supply curve is entirely dependent on costs of production. This demonstrates why the firm's supply curve is upward sloping. Given that marginal costs rise as output rises (due to diminishing

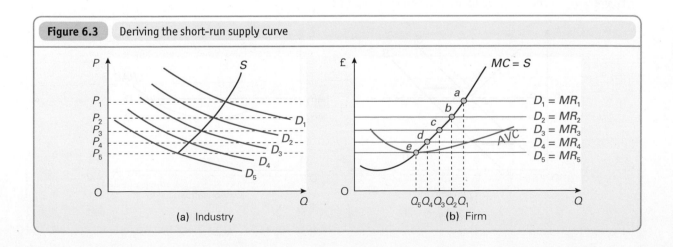

Figure 6.3 Deriving the short-run supply curve

marginal returns), a higher price will be necessary to induce the firm to increase its output.

Note that the firm will not produce at a price below *AVC*. Thus the supply curve is only that portion of the *MC* curve above point *e*.

What will be the short-run supply curve of the whole *industry*? This is simply the sum of the short-run supply curves (and hence *MC* curves) of all the firms in the industry. Graphically this will be a *horizontal* sum, since it is *quantities* that are being added.

 Will the industry supply be zero below a price of P_5 in Figure 6.3?

The long-run equilibrium of the firm

In the long run, if typical firms are making supernormal profits, new firms will be attracted into the industry. Likewise, if established firms can make supernormal profits by increasing the scale of their operations, they will do so, since all factors of production are variable in the long run.

The effect of the entry of new firms and/or the expansion of existing firms is to increase industry supply. This is illustrated in Figure 6.4. At a price of P_1 supernormal profits are earned. This causes industry supply to expand (the industry supply curve shifts to the right). This in turn leads to a fall in price. Supply will go on increasing and price falling until firms are making only normal profits. This will be when price has fallen to the point where the demand 'curve' for the firm just touches the bottom of its long-run average cost curve. Q_L is thus the long-run equilibrium output of the firm, with P_L the long-run equilibrium price.

 Illustrate on a diagram similar to Figure 6.4 what would happen in the long run if price were initially below P_L.

As we have seen, the long-run equilibrium output is where long-run average cost is minimised. If we know the equation for *LRAC*, we can simply use the techniques of minimisation (see pages A:11–14) to find the equilibrium output. Assume that the long-run average cost function is

$$LRAC = a - bQ + cQ^2$$

The technique is to differentiate this function and set it equal to zero: i.e.

$$\frac{d(LRAC)}{dQ} = -b + 2cQ = 0 \tag{1}$$

Solving equation (1) for Q gives the long-run equilibrium output. Once we have found the value of Q, we can substitute it back into equation (1) to find the value of *LRAC* and hence the equilibrium price (since $P = LRAC$).

We can then use the second derivative test (see page A:11) to check that this indeed does represent a minimum, not a maximum, *LRAC*. An example of this is given in Maths Case 6.1 in MyEconLab.

Since the *LRAC* curve is tangential to all possible short-run *AC* curves (see section 5.4), the full long-run equilibrium will be as shown in Figure 6.5 where

$$LRAC = AC = MC = MR = AR$$

The long-run industry supply curve

If industry demand increased, what would happen to industry price and output in the long run? The long-run supply curve gives the answer.

Each of the diagrams in Figure 6.6 shows an increase in demand. The demand curve shifts from D_1 to D_2. Equilibrium in the short run moves from point *a* to point *b*, where D_2 and S_1 intersect. After the initial rise in price, the resulting supernormal profit attracts new firms into the industry. The short-run supply curve shifts to S_2 and equilibrium moves to point *c*. Thus the long-run effect of the increase in demand

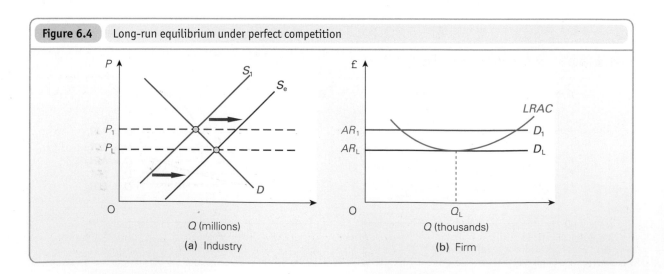

Figure 6.4 Long-run equilibrium under perfect competition

(a) Industry

(b) Firm

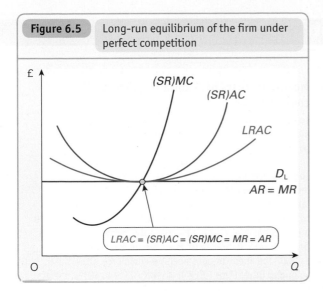

Figure 6.5   Long-run equilibrium of the firm under perfect competition

$LRAC = (SR)AC = (SR)MC = MR = AR$

---

has been to move the equilibrium from point *a* to point *c*. This means, therefore, that the *long-run* supply curve will pass through points *a* and *c*. This is illustrated in each of the three diagrams.

If price falls back to its original level (i.e. points *a* and *c* are at the *same* price) the *long-run* supply curve will be horizontal (see diagram (a) in Figure 6.6). This would occur if there were no change in firms' average cost curves. Price would simply return to the bottom of firms' *LRAC* curve.

If, however, the entry of new firms creates a shortage of factors of production, this will bid up factor prices. Firms' *LRAC* curve will shift vertically upwards, and so the long-run equilibrium price will be higher. The long-run supply curve of the industry, therefore, will slope upwards, as in diagram (b) in Figure 6.6. This is the case of *increasing industry costs* or *external diseconomies of scale*: i.e. diseconomies external to the firm (see section 5.3).

If the expansion of the industry lowers firms' *LRAC* curve, due, say, to the building up of an industrial infrastructure

(distribution channels, specialist suppliers, banks, communications, etc.), the long-run supply curve will slope downwards, as in diagram (c) in Figure 6.6. This is the case of *decreasing industry costs* or *external economies of scale*.

The incompatibility of perfect competition and substantial economies of scale

Why is perfect competition so rare in the real world – if it even exists at all? One important reason for this has to do with economies of scale.

In many industries, firms may have to be quite large if they are to experience the full potential economies of scale. But perfect competition requires there to be *many* firms and that each one is a price taker. Firms must therefore be small under perfect competition – too small in most cases for economies of scale.

Once a firm expands sufficiently to achieve economies of scale, it will usually gain market power. It will be able to undercut the prices of smaller firms, which will thus be driven out of business. Perfect competition is destroyed.

Perfect competition could only exist in any industry, therefore, if there were no (or virtually no) economies of scale.

1. *What other reasons can you think of why perfect competition is so rare?*
2. *Why does the market for fresh vegetables approximate to perfect competition, whereas that for aircraft does not?*

Perfect competition and the public interest

There are a number of features of perfect competition which, it could be argued, benefit society:

- Price equals marginal cost. As we shall see in Chapter 11, this has important implications for the allocation of resources between alternative products. Given that price equals marginal utility (see Chapter 4), marginal utility will equal marginal cost. This is argued to be an *optimal* position.

TC 8
p 105

Figure 6.6   Various long-run industry supply curves under perfect competition

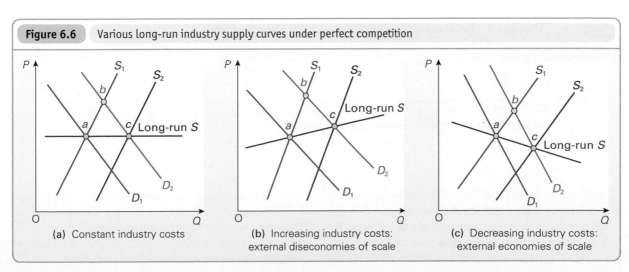

(a) Constant industry costs

(b) Increasing industry costs: external diseconomies of scale

(c) Decreasing industry costs: external economies of scale

BOX 6.3	E-COMMERCE AND MARKET STRUCTURE

Has technology shifted market power?

The relentless drive towards big business in recent decades saw many markets become more concentrated and dominated by large producers. And yet there are forces that undermine this dominance, bringing more competition to markets. One of these forces is *e-commerce*.

In this case study, we will consider the impact of e-commerce on market structures and power.

What do we mean by e-commerce?

E-commerce is a shorthand term for buying and selling products through electronic means, in most cases through the Internet. It involves a number of processes including marketing, purchase transactions and payments. This is a fast-moving sector; only a decade ago, buying something online might have involved sending an email order via your computer. Now we are genuinely surprised if even small firms don't have straightforward online processes, including a variety of payment mechanisms.

The growth in online shopping has been spectacular and shows no sign of slowing down. The chart shows the rise in online retail sales as a proportion of all retail sales in the UK between 2007 and 2014. Note that the proportion of Internet sales rises each year in the run-up to Christmas as many people buy gifts online.

Moving markets back towards perfect competition?

To see the extent to which e-commerce is making markets more competitive, let's look at the assumptions of perfect competition.

Large number of firms. The growth of e-commerce has led to many new firms starting up in business. It's not just large firms like Amazon.com that are providing increased competition for established firms, but the thousands of small online companies that are being established. Many of these firms are selling directly to us as consumers. This is known as 'B2C' (business-to-consumers) e-commerce. Others are selling to other firms ('B2B').

The reach of the Web is global. This means that all firms are able to keep an eye on the prices and products of competitors and suppliers across the world. Firms' demand curves have become more price elastic, regardless of whether they sell to consumers or other businesses. This is especially so for goods that are cheap to transport, or for services such as insurance and banking where no transport is required.

Perfect knowledge. There are various ways in which e-commerce is adding to the consumer's knowledge.

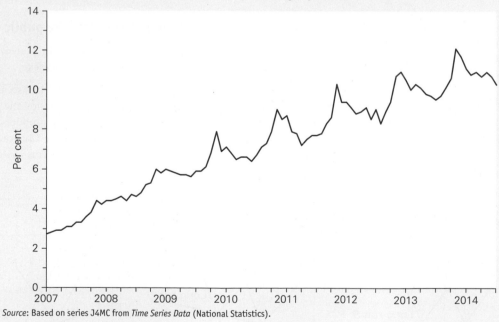

Value of Internet retail sales as a percentage of total retail sales

Source: Based on series J4MC from *Time Series Data* (National Statistics).

To demonstrate why, consider what would happen if they were not equal. If price were greater than marginal cost, this would mean that consumers were putting a higher value ($P = MU$) on the production of extra units than they cost to produce (MC). Therefore more ought to be produced. If price were less than marginal cost, consumers would be putting a lower value on extra units than they cost to produce. Therefore less ought to be produced. When they are equal, therefore, production levels are just right. But, as we shall see later, it is only under perfect competition that $MC = P$.

KI 3
p13

There is greater price transparency, with consumers able to compare prices online. Online shopping agents, such as Kelkoo, BizRate and Google Shopping, can quickly locate a list of alternative suppliers. There is greater information on product availability and quality and this information is available at very little cost to the consumer. It is common to see people in shops (physical shops in this case) browsing competitors' prices on their mobile phones. This places the high street retailer under intense competitive pressure.

The pressure is even greater in the market for intermediate products. Many firms are constantly searching for cheaper sources of supply, and the Internet provides a cheap and easy means of conducting such searches.

Freedom of entry. Internet companies often have lower start-up costs than their conventional rivals. Their premises are generally much smaller, with no 'shop-front' costs and lower levels of stockholding; in fact many of these businesses are initially operated from their owners' homes. Marketing costs can also be relatively low, especially given the ease with which companies can be located with search engines. Internet companies are often smaller and more specialist, relying on Internet 'outsourcing' (buying parts, equipment and other supplies through the Internet), rather than making everything themselves. They are also more likely to use delivery firms rather than having their own transport fleet. All this makes it relatively cheap for new firms to set up and begin trading over the Internet.

One consequence of the rise of e-commerce is that the distinction between firms and consumers is becoming increasingly blurred. With the rise of eBay, more and more people have found going into business incredibly easy. Some people sell products they produce at home, while others specialise in selling on products using the marketing power of eBay. There are some 128 million active eBay users worldwide, and hundreds of thousands of them make a full-time living from buying and selling on eBay.

Not only do these factors make markets more price competitive, they also bring other benefits. Costs are driven down, as firms economise on stockholding, rely more on outsourcing and develop more efficient relationships with suppliers. 'Procurement hubs', online exchanges and trading communities are now well established in many industries. The competition also encourages innovation, which improves quality and the range of products.

What are the limits to e-commerce?

In 20 years, will we be doing all our shopping on the Internet? Will the only shopping malls be virtual ones? Although e-commerce is revolutionising markets, it is unlikely that things will go that far.

The benefits of 'shop shopping' are that you get to see the good and touch it before buying. Many people like wandering round the shops, meeting friends, trying on clothes, browsing through DVDs, and so on. Equally you can take possession immediately, while online shopping does require that you have to wait for goods to be delivered.

However, a new style of shopping is becoming increasingly popular. Increasing numbers of us go onto the high street, try on clothes or look at gadgets; we then go home and order them on the Internet. This allows us to get the best price possible and saves us the effort of taking the item home.

There has been concern that e-commerce can itself result in substantial monopoly power. As the leading 'marketplace' platform, bringing together buyers and sellers, eBay has the advantages of a well-known brand and market dominance. The consequence is that it can extract surplus from the traders who use its services. In 2008 eBay sellers called for a boycott of the site, following changes in the fees being charged and the removal of their ability to leave feedback on buyers. However, the profits eBay makes have attracted other firms into this area. Amazon Marketplace, ASOS and Not on the High Street are giving independent traders the opportunity to sell through well-known companies and providing competition to eBay.

There is no doubt that e-commerce is here to stay in all sectors. The supermarket chain Morrisons held off entering the online grocery arena for years. But after falling sales and profit warnings it had to reverse that decision. Many large companies recognise that their retail outlets have effectively become display space for their online activities. Meanwhile, thousands of small, new companies have transformed markets across the world.

1. *Why may the Internet work better for replacement buys than for new purchases?*
2. *Give three examples of products that are particularly suitable for selling over the Internet and three that are not. Explain your answer.*
3. *As eBay has grown in size it has acquired substantial monopoly power. What are the barriers to entry for other companies wishing to act as a marketplace for B2C and B2B business?*

- Long-run equilibrium is at the bottom of the firm's long-run *AC* curve. That is, for any *given* technology, the firm, in the long run, will produce at the least-cost output.
- Perfect competition is a case of 'survival of the fittest'. Inefficient firms will be driven out of business, since they will not be able to make even normal profits. This encourages firms to be as efficient as possible.
- The combination of (long-run) production being at minimum average cost and the firm making only normal profit keeps prices at a minimum.

■ If consumer tastes change, the resulting price change will lead firms to respond (purely out of self-interest). An increased consumer demand will result in extra supply with only a short-run increase in profit.

Because of these last two points, perfect competition is said to lead to *consumer sovereignty*. Consumers, through the market, determine what and how much is to be produced. Firms have no power to manipulate the market. They cannot control price. The only thing they can do to increase profit is to become more efficient, and that benefits the consumer too.

Even under perfect competition, however, the free market has various limitations. For example, there is no guarantee that the goods produced will be distributed to the members of society in the *fairest* proportions. There may be considerable inequality of income. (We examine this issue in Chapter 10.) What is more, a redistribution of income would lead to a different pattern of consumption and hence production. Thus there is no guarantee that perfect competition will lead to the optimum combination of goods

being produced when society's views on equity are taken into account.

Another limitation is that the production of certain goods may lead to various undesirable side effects, such as pollution. Perfect competition cannot safeguard against this either.

What is more, perfect competition may be less desirable than other market structures such as monopoly:

■ Even though firms under perfect competition may seem to have an incentive to develop new technology (in order to gain supernormal profits, albeit temporarily), the long-run normal profits they make may not be sufficient to fund the necessary research and development. Also, with complete information available, if they did develop new, more efficient methods of production, their rivals would merely copy them, in which case the investment would have been a waste of money.

■ Perfectly competitive industries produce undifferentiated products. This lack of variety might be seen as a disadvantage to the consumer. Under monopolistic competition and oligopoly there is often intense competition over the quality and design of the product. This can lead to innovation and improvements that would not exist under perfect competition.

The issue of the efficiency or otherwise of perfect markets and the various failings of real-world markets is examined in more detail in Chapters 11 to 13.

Definition

Consumer sovereignty A situation where firms respond to changes in consumer demand without being in a position in the long run to charge a price above average cost.

Section summary

1. The assumptions of perfect competition are: a very large number of firms, complete freedom of entry, a homogeneous product and perfect knowledge of the good and its market on the part of both producers and consumers.

2. In the short run, there is not time for new firms to enter the market, and thus supernormal profits can persist. In the long run, however, any supernormal profits will be competed away by the entry of new firms.

3. The short-run equilibrium for the firm will be where the price, as determined by demand and supply in the market, is equal to marginal cost. At this output, the firm will be maximising profit. The firm's short-run supply curve is the same as its marginal cost curve (that portion of it above the *AVC* curve).

4. The long-run equilibrium will be where the market price is just equal to firms' long-run average cost. The long-run industry supply curve will thus depend on what happens to firms' *LRAC* curves as industry output expands. If their *LRAC* curves shift upwards (due to external diseconomies of scale), the long-run industry supply curve will slope

upwards. If their *LRAC* curves shift downwards (due to external economies of scale), the long-run industry supply curve will slope downwards.

5. There are no substantial (internal) economies of scale to be gained by perfectly competitive firms. If there were, the industry would cease to be perfectly competitive as the large, low-cost firms drove the small, high-cost ones out of business.

6. Under perfect competition, production will be at the point where $P = MC$. This can be argued to be optimal. Perfect competition can act as a spur to efficiency and bring benefits to the consumer in terms of low costs and low prices.

7. On the other hand, perfectly competitive firms may be unwilling to invest in research and development or may have insufficient funds to do so. They may also produce a lack of variety of goods. Finally, perfect competition does not necessarily lead to a fair distribution of income or guarantee an absence of harmful side effects of production.

What is a monopoly?

This may seem a strange question because the answer seems obvious. A monopoly exists when there is only one firm in the industry.

But whether an industry can be classed as a monopoly is not always clear. It depends how narrowly the industry is defined. For example, a confectionary company may have a monopoly on certain chocolate bars, but it does not have a monopoly on chocolate in general. A pharmaceutical company may have a monopoly of a certain drug, but there may be alternative drugs for treating a particular illness.

To some extent, the boundaries of an industry are arbitrary. What is more important for a firm is the amount of monopoly *power* it has, and that depends on the closeness of substitutes produced by rival industries. A train company may have a monopoly over railway journeys between two towns, but it faces competition in transport from cars and coaches.

 As an illustration of the difficulty in identifying monopolies, try to decide which of the following are monopolies: BT; a local evening newspaper; a rail company; food sold in a university outlet; a village post office; Interflora; the London Underground; ice creams in the cinema; Guinness; the board game 'Monopoly'. (As you will quickly realise in each case, it depends how you define the industry.)

Barriers to entry

For a firm to maintain its monopoly position, there must be **barriers to entry** of new firms. Barriers also exist under oligopoly, but in the case of monopoly they must be high enough to block the entry of new firms. Barriers can be of various forms.

Economies of scale. If a monopoly experiences substantial economies of scale, the industry may not be able to support more than one producer. In Figure 6.7, D_1 represents the industry demand curve, and hence the demand curve for the firm under monopoly. The monopolist can gain supernormal profit at any output between points a and b. If there were two firms, however, each charging the same price and supplying half the industry output, they would both face the demand curve D_2. There is no price that would allow them to cover costs.

This case is known as **natural monopoly**. It is particularly likely if the market is small or if the costs of capital required are very high. For example, two bus companies might find it unprofitable to serve the same routes, each running with perhaps only half-full buses, whereas one company with a monopoly of the routes could make a profit. Electricity transmission via a national grid is another example of a natural monopoly.

Even if a market could support more than one firm, a new entrant is unlikely to be able to start up on a very large scale. Thus a monopolist already experiencing economies of scale can charge a price below the cost of the new entrant and drive it out of business. There are, however, some circumstances where a new entrant may be able to survive this competition – if, for example, it is a firm already established in another industry.

Network economies. When a product or service is used by everyone in the market, there are benefits to all users from having access to other users. Thus eBay, by providing such large **network economies**, makes it very difficult for other online auction houses to compete. Similar network economies apply to Microsoft's Windows (see Case Study 6.4 in MyEconLab), Adobe's Acrobat (for PDF files) and airlines operating interconnecting routes (see Box 6.7).

Economies of scope. A firm that produces a range of products is also likely to experience a lower average cost of production. For example, a large pharmaceutical company producing a range of drugs and toiletries can use shared research,

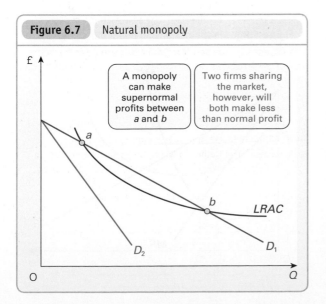

Figure 6.7 Natural monopoly

> A monopoly can make supernormal profits between *a* and *b*

> Two firms sharing the market, however, will both make less than normal profit

Definitions

Barrier to entry Anything that prevents or impedes the entry of firms into an industry and thereby limits the amount of competition faced by existing firms.

Natural monopoly A situation where long-run average costs would be lower if an industry were under monopoly than if it were shared between two or more competitors.

Network economies The benefits to consumers of having a network of other people using the same product or service.

marketing, storage and transport facilities across its range of products. These lower costs make it difficult for a new single-product entrant to the market, since the large firm could undercut its price to drive it out of the market.

 Under what circumstances might a new entrant succeed in the market for a product, despite existing firms benefiting from economies of scale?

Product differentiation and brand loyalty. If a firm produces a clearly differentiated product, where the consumer associates the product with the brand, it will be very difficult for a new firm to break into that market.

In 1908 James Spengler invented, and patented, the electric vacuum cleaner. Later that year he sold the patent to his cousin's husband, William Hoover, who set about putting mass production in place. Decades after their legal monopoly (see below) ran out, people still associate vacuum-cleaning with Hoover and many of us would say that we are going to 'Hoover the carpet', despite using a Dyson, or other machine.

Other examples of strong brand image include Guinness, Kellogg's Cornflakes, Coca-Cola, Nescafé and Sellotape. In many cases, strong brand presence would not be enough to *block* entry, but it might well reinforce other barriers.

Lower costs for an established firm. An established monopoly may have developed specialised production and marketing skills. It is more likely to be aware of the most efficient techniques and the most reliable and/or cheapest suppliers and to have access to cheaper finance. Thus it could be operating on a lower cost curve. New firms would therefore find it hard to compete.

Ownership of, or control over, key inputs. In some markets a firm may govern the supply of vital inputs, say, by owning the sole supplier of some component part. In this instance it can deny access to these inputs to potential rivals. On a world scale, the de Beers company has a monopoly in fine diamonds because all diamond producers market their diamonds through de Beers.

Ownership of, or control over, wholesale or retail outlets. Similarly, it may be in a firm's interest to gain control over the outlets through which the product is sold. If it does so, it can hinder potential rivals from gaining access to consumers. For example, Coca-Cola supplies chilled display units free of charge to shops on the condition that they stock only Coca-Cola's range of drinks in them.

Legal protection. The firm's monopoly position may be protected by patents on essential processes, by copyright, by various forms of licensing (allowing, say, only one firm to operate in a particular area) and by tariffs (i.e. customs duties) and other trade restrictions to keep out foreign competitors. Examples of monopolies protected by patents include most new medicines developed by pharmaceutical

companies, Microsoft's Windows operating systems, and agro-chemical companies, such as Monsanto, with various genetically modified plant varieties and pesticides.

Mergers and takeovers. The monopolist can put in a takeover bid for any new entrant. The mere threat of takeovers may discourage new entrants.

Aggressive tactics. An established monopolist can probably sustain losses for longer than a new entrant. Thus it can start a price war, mount massive advertising campaigns, offer an attractive after-sales service, introduce new brands to compete with new entrants, and so on.

Intimidation. The monopolist may resort to various forms of harassment, legal or illegal, to drive a new entrant out of business.

Equilibrium price and output

Since there is, by definition, only one firm in the industry, the firm's demand curve is also the industry demand curve.

Compared with other market structures, demand under monopoly will be relatively inelastic at each price. The monopolist can raise its price and consumers have no alternative firm in the industry to turn to. They either pay the higher price or go without the good altogether. TC 7 p72

Unlike the firm under perfect competition, the monopoly firm is a 'price maker'. It can choose what price to charge. Nevertheless, it is still constrained by its demand curve. A rise in price will lower the quantity demanded. Be careful not to fall into the trap of thinking that a monopoly can control both price *and* output simultaneously.

As with firms in other market structures, a monopolist will maximise profit where $MR = MC$. In Figure 6.8, profit is maximised at Q_m. The supernormal profit obtained is shown by the shaded area.

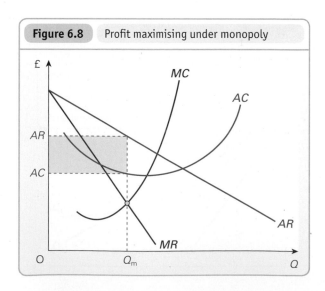

Figure 6.8 Profit maximising under monopoly

These profits will tend to be larger the less elastic is the demand curve (and hence the steeper is the *MR* curve), and thus the bigger is the gap between *MR* and price (*AR*). The actual elasticity will depend on whether reasonably close substitutes are available in *other* industries. The demand for a rail service will be much less elastic (and the potential for profit greater) if there is no bus service to the same destination.

Since there are barriers to the entry of new firms, these supernormal profits will not be competed away in the long run. The only difference, therefore, between short-run and long-run equilibrium is that in the long run the firm will produce where *MR = long-run MC*.

Try this brain teaser. A monopoly would be expected to face an inelastic demand. After all, there are no direct substitutes. And yet, if it produces where MR = MC, MR must be positive and demand must therefore be elastic. Therefore the monopolist must face an elastic demand! Can you solve this conundrum?

Limit pricing

If the barriers to the entry of new firms are not total, and if the monopolist is making very large supernormal profits, there may be a danger in the long run of potential rivals breaking into the industry. In such cases, the monopolist may keep its price down and thereby deliberately restrict the size of its profits so as not to attract new entrants. This practice is known as ***limit pricing***.

---

*LOOKING AT THE MATHS

From Figure 6.8, it can be seen that the less elastic the demand at the output where *MC = MR*, the greater will be the gap between *AR* and *MR*, and hence the further above *MR* will the price be. The relationship between price, *MR* (or *MC*) and price elasticity of demand ($P\epsilon_D$) is given by the following formula:

$$P = \frac{MR}{1 + (1/P\epsilon_D)}$$

Thus if *MR = MC = £12* and $P\epsilon_D = -4$, the profit-maximising price would be

$$\frac{£12}{1 + (1/-4)} = \frac{£12}{1 - 1/4} = \frac{£12}{0.75} = £16$$

Proof of this rule is given in Maths Case 6.2 in MyEconLab. You can see simply by examining the formula, however, that the lower the elasticity, the greater will be the price relative to *MR* or *MC*.[1]

What is the profit-maximising price if MR = MC = £12 and $P\epsilon_D = -2$?

[1] Note that this formula works only if demand is elastic, as it must be if *MR* is positive (which it will be, since *MC* must be positive).

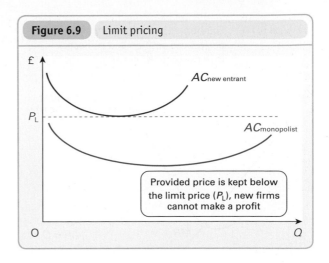

Figure 6.9   Limit pricing

Provided price is kept below the limit price (P_L), new firms cannot make a profit

In Figure 6.9, two *AC* curves are drawn: one for the monopolist and one for a potential entrant. The monopolist, being established, has a lower *AC* curve. The new entrant, if it is to compete successfully with the monopolist, must charge the same price or a lower one. Thus, provided the monopolist does not raise price above P_L, the other firm, unable to make supernormal profits will not be attracted into the industry.

P_L may well be below the monopolist's short-run profit-maximising price, but the monopolist may prefer to limit its price to P_L to protect its long-run profits from damage by competition.

Fear of government intervention to curb the monopolist's practices may have a similar restraining effect on the price that the monopolist charges. In the UK the Competition and Markets Authority may undertake an investigation (see section 13.1 for more on this).

1. *On a diagram like Figure 6.9, by drawing in MR and MC curves, demonstrate that P_L could be below the short-run profit-maximising price.*
2. *What does this analysis assume about the price elasticity of demand for the new entrant (a) above P_L; (b) below P_L?*

Definition

Limit pricing Where a monopolist (or oligopolist) charges a price below the short-run profit-maximising level in order to deter new entrants.

| **Figure 6.10** | Equilibrium of the industry under perfect competition and monopoly: with the same *MC* curve |

Monopoly and the public interest

Disadvantages of monopoly

There are several reasons why monopolies may be against the public interest. As we shall see in Chapter 13, these have given rise to legislation to regulate monopoly power and/or behaviour.

Higher price and lower output than under perfect competition (short run). Figure 6.10 compares the profit-maximising position for an industry under monopoly with that under perfect competition. The monopolist will produce Q_1 at a price of P_1. This is where $MC = MR$.

If the same industry operated under perfect competition, however, it would produce at Q_2 and P_2 – a higher output and a lower price. This is where industry supply under perfect competition equals industry demand. (Remember, we showed in section 6.2 that the firm's supply curve under perfect competition is its MC curve and thus the industry's supply curve is simply the *industry MC* curve: the *MC* curve shown in Figure 6.10.)

This analysis is based on the assumption that the industry has the *same AC* and *MC* curves whether under perfect competition or run as a monopoly. For example, suppose some potato farmers initially operate under perfect competition. The market price is P_2 in Figure 6.10. Then they set up a marketing agency through which they all sell their potatoes. The agency therefore acts as a monopoly supplier to the market and charges a price of P_1. Since it is the same farmers before and after, production costs are unlikely to have changed much. But, as we shall see below, even if an industry has *lower AC* and *MC* curves under monopoly than under perfect competition, it is still likely to charge a higher price and produce a lower output.

When we were looking at the advantages of perfect competition, we said that the level where $P = MC$ could be argued to be the *optimum* level of production. Clearly, if

a monopolist is producing below this level (e.g. at Q_1 in Figure 6.10 – where $P > MC$), the monopolist can be argued to be producing at *less* than optimal output. Consumers would be prepared to pay more for additional units than they cost to produce.

Higher price and lower output than under perfect competition (long run). Under perfect competition, freedom of entry eliminates supernormal profit and forces firms to produce at the bottom of their *LRAC* curve. The effect, therefore, is to keep long-run prices down. Under monopoly, however, barriers to entry allow profits to remain supernormal in the long run. The monopolist is not forced to operate at the bottom of the *AC* curve. Thus, other things being equal, long-run prices will tend to be higher, and hence output lower, under monopoly.

Possibility of higher cost curves due to lack of competition. The sheer survival of a firm in the long run under perfect competition requires that it uses the most efficient known technique, and develops new techniques wherever possible. The monopolist, however, sheltered by barriers to entry, can still make large profits even if it is not using the most efficient technique. It has less incentive, therefore, to be efficient (see Box 6.4).

On the other hand, if it can lower its costs by using and developing more efficient techniques, it can gain extra supernormal profits which will not be competed away.

Unequal distribution of income. The high profits of monopolists may be considered unfair, especially by competing firms, or anyone on low incomes for that matter. The scale of this problem obviously depends on the size of the monopoly and the degree of its power. The monopoly profits of the village store may seem of little consequence when compared with the profits of a giant national or international company.

> *If the shares in a monopoly (such as a water company) were very widely distributed among the population, would the shareholders necessarily want the firm to use its monopoly power to make larger profits?*

In addition to these problems, monopolies may lack the incentive to introduce new product varieties, and large monopolies may be able to exert political pressure and thereby get favourable treatment from governments.

Advantages of monopoly

Despite these arguments, monopolies can have some advantages.

Economies of scale. The monopoly may be able to achieve substantial economies of scale due to larger plant, centralised administration and the avoidance of unnecessary duplication (e.g. a monopoly water company would eliminate the need for several sets of rival water mains under

BOX 6.4 BREAKING SKY'S MONOPOLY ON LIVE FOOTBALL COVERAGE

The impact of opening up the market

The early days of Sky

The structure of English football was changed with the formation of the FA Premier League for the 1992/3 football season. One justification for this was the promise of higher payments by TV companies. Live league football had been shown on free-to-air television throughout the 1980s and the clubs were very aware that this was potentially a very lucrative source of revenue.

The first contract to acquire the live and exclusive FA Premier League football broadcasting rights for the United Kingdom and the Republic of Ireland was worth £191 million over five seasons. A consequence of Sky being awarded the contract was that live top-flight English league football was no longer available on terrestrial and free-to-air television. Those who wanted to watch live football matches on television had to sign up with Sky, buying both a basic package and the additional Sky sports channels; Sky thus had a monopoly.

Attempts to reduce monopoly power

Both the Premier League and Sky's coverage proved to be hugely successful with viewers and advertisers and this was reflected in the price paid for subsequent packages. The one starting in 1997 cost Sky £670 million for four seasons, while in 2003 BSkyB, as the company was now formally known, paid over £1 billion for exclusive rights for three seasons.

However, over this period the European Commission was expressing increasing concern about the extent of Sky's monopoly. The Commission started legal proceedings in 2002, filing a statement of objections, but was thwarted when the League agreed a new contract with Sky before ironing out an EC-approved deal.

At this time Sky did agree to sub-license up to eight 'top quality Premier League matches' each season to another broadcaster in order to win European approval. The Commission trumpeted this pledge as meaning 'that for the first time in the history of the Premier League free to-air television will have a realistic opportunity to show live Premier League matches'. These hopes were dashed, however, when no rival broadcaster met the asking price set by Sky.

In 2005 the European Commission announced that Sky's monopoly would be broken. From 2007, the next set of rights, for a three-season period, would be sold in six 'balanced' packages of 23 games per season, with no broadcaster allowed more than five packages.

The Commission claimed that the deal would give fans 'greater choice and better value'.

However, concern was expressed about the impact on the incomes of the Premiership clubs. While some commentators expected a more competitive process to result in roughly the same total income as was paid by Sky in 2003, just over £1 billion, others suggested that Sky paid a premium for the guarantee that it would be the sole broadcaster. Thus one effect of the new process might be reduced revenues for the clubs.

The outcome of the EC ruling

In May 2006 the bidding process for the rights for 2007–10 was completed. The outcome was that Sky won four of the six available packages and would show 92 live Premiership matches per season, while Setanta, an Irish-based satellite broadcaster, won the remaining two packages and would have 46 games. The same process was undertaken in 2009, and in 2012 for the 2013–16 seasons. By now Setanta had folded, with BT entering this market in 2012.

Despite the opening up of 'competition', the total amount paid under the 'non-monopoly' schemes exceeded the previous contracts. In 2012, the agreed payment from BT and Sky combined was over £3 billion for three seasons, a 70 per cent increase on the previous contracts. This was clearly good news for the Premier League, but less so for the fans in 2010. There were more live games shown than prior to the breaking of BSB's monopoly, but fans found themselves having to commit to two contracts with broadcasters.

BT's entry into the market did, however, have an impact on prices. It conducted a fairly aggressive pricing strategy, undercutting Sky and offering live football 'free' to those taking phone and broadband packages. This provides a clue to the increasing prices broadcasters are willing to pay. If switching to Sky or BT for broadband services – which are highly profitable to them – brings cheaper live football, many fans will be willing to do so.

1. *What other examples of monopoly power exist in football? Could this power be reduced?*
2. *Assess the impact of the pay broadcasters' emergence over the past 20 years on (a) football fans, (b) other viewers.*
3. *What are the challenges that would face a new broadband company wishing to enter the market?*

each street). If this results in an *MC* curve substantially below that of the same industry under perfect competition, the monopoly will produce a *higher* output at a *lower* price. In Figure 6.11, the monopoly produces Q_1 at a price of P_1, whereas the perfectly competitive industry produces Q_2 at the higher price P_2.

Note that this result follows only if the monopoly *MC* curve is below point *x* in Figure 6.11. Note also that

since an industry cannot exist under perfect competition if substantial economies of scale can be gained, it is somewhat hypothetical to make the comparison between a monopoly and an alternative situation that could not exist. What is more, were the monopolist to follow the $P = MC$ rule observed by perfectly competitive firms, it would charge an even lower price (P_3) and produce an even higher output (Q_3).

Possibility of lower cost curves due to more research and development and more investment. Although the monopolist's sheer survival does not depend on its finding evermore efficient methods of production, it can use part of its supernormal profits for research and development and investment. It thus has a greater ability to become efficient than has the small firm with limited funds.

KI 3
p13

Competition for corporate control. Although a monopoly faces no competition in the goods market, it may face an alternative form of competition in financial markets. A monopoly, with potentially low costs, which is currently run inefficiently, is likely to be subject to a takeover bid from another company. This **competition for corporate control** may thus force the monopoly to be efficient in order to avoid being taken over.

KI 3
p13

Innovation and new products. The promise of supernormal profits, protected perhaps by patents, may encourage the development of new (monopoly) industries producing new products.

KI 10
p75

TC 5
p54

Definition

Competition for corporate control The competition for the control of companies through takeovers.

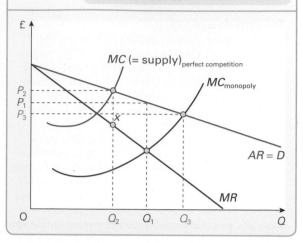

Figure 6.11 Equilibrium of the industry under perfect competition and monopoly: with different *MC* curves

Monopoly and price discrimination

One further characteristic of monopoly is that it allows firms to price discriminate: to charge different prices either to all customers or to different groups of customers. Firms undertake this as a way of further increasing profits. The ability to price-discriminate rests on the firm having some monopoly power, although this need not be a complete monopoly. (Price discrimination is discussed in more detail in section 7.4, pages 214–18.)

BOX 6.5 | **X INEFFICIENCY** | **EXPLORING ECONOMICS**

The cost of a quiet life

The major criticism of monopoly has traditionally been that of the monopoly's power in selling the good. The firm charges a price above *MC* (see Figure 6.10). This is seen as *allocatively inefficient* because at the margin consumers are willing to pay more than it is costing to produce (*P > MC*); and yet the monopolist is deliberately holding back, so as to keep its profits up. (Allocative inefficiency is examined in detail in section 11.1.)

KI 31
p13

But monopolies may also be inefficient for another reason: they may have higher costs. Why is this?

Higher costs may be the result of *X inefficiency*[1] (sometimes known as *technical inefficiency*). Without competitive pressure on profit margins, cost control may become lax. The firm may employ too many staff and spend on prestigious buildings and equipment. There may be less effort to keep technologically up to date, to research new products, or to develop new domestic and export markets.

The more comfortable the situation, the less may be the effort which is expended to improve it. The effect of this X inefficiency is to make the *AC* and *MC* curves higher than they would otherwise be. The outcome is that consumers pay higher prices and the firm moves even further away from the efficient, competitive, outcome.

Following the financial crisis in 2007–8 and subsequent recession, there were significant reductions in X inefficiency in many countries. To cope with falling sales, and a fall in both sales and profits, many firms embarked on cost-cutting programmes. Much out-of-date plant was closed down, and employment was reduced. Those firms that survived the recession (and many did not) tended to emerge both more competitive and more efficient.

A further factor in the reduction in X inefficiency has been the growth in international competition. Even if a firm has monopoly power at home, the growth in global markets and e-commerce (see Box 6.3), and reductions in customs duties and other barriers to trade (see section 24.2), provide fiercer competition from abroad.

1. *How might you measure X inefficiency?*
2. *Another type of inefficiency is productive inefficiency. What do you think this is? (Clue: it has to do with the proportions in which factors are used.)*
3. *Explain why X inefficiency might be more common in state monopolies than those owned by shareholders.*

---

[1] This term was coined by Harvey Leibenstein, 'Allocative efficiency or X efficiency', *American Economic Review*, June 1966.

BOX 6.6   CUT-THROAT COMPETITION

The UK razor market

The market for wet razors and their blades is worth approximately £400 million in the UK. It was traditionally dominated by two producers, Gillette and Procter & Gamble, with more than two-thirds of sales between them. When they merged in 2007, the result was very substantial monopoly power. Wilkinson Sword was the next largest manufacturer, with around 18 per cent of sales.

The market displays many of the characteristics we would expect of an oligopoly with high levels of advertising and strong branding. There is also evidence of on going innovation; where once the twin-blade razor was a novelty, now five blades are the norm.

Yet, despite the barriers to entry presented by this dominance, a new player entered in 2008. The King of Shaves razor was launched onto the market, with a view to building on the success of the brand's shaving gels and foams. The company, KMI, worked for five years to develop a lower-cost, lighter-weight alternative to the products offered by Gillette and Wilkinson Sword.

It wasn't only its design that challenged the existing companies; its approach to marketing also differed somewhat. KMI has made much greater use of online advertising, email and social media than the incumbent firms. It launched an iPhone app in 2011 and has a website with hundreds of thousands of hits every month. It offers a number of innovations, such as a monthly subscription service, halving the price of blades. It has also worked very closely with large retailers on special offers from launch onwards, sacrificing early profits to build market share.

KMI's stated intention was to take 25 per cent of market share within five years of launch. This was described as highly ambitious by commentators at the time and proved to be the case. In that period it had to spend over £1 million in legal fights over patents, and suffered an abortive launch in the USA.

By the end of 2013, Gillette had an 84 per cent share of the market for razors, whilst KMI had just 3 per cent, with sales of around £10 million. It did, however, have 9 per cent of the shaving products market, reflecting its origins in gels and foams. Given that, it is perhaps surprising that in January 2014 it announced that its new foam-free Hyperblade was to be launched.

It has proved tough to break Gillette's monopoly power, but KMI is not giving up yet.

1. *What are the characteristics of the razor market that present barriers to entry for new firms? How has KMI sought to overcome these?*
2. *High levels of innovation have been seen in the market for wet razors. Do these always benefit the consumer?*
3. *It has been estimated that Gillette makes a profit of 3000 per cent on each razor blade sold. Explain how this figure might have arisen.*

Section summary

1. A monopoly is where there is only one firm in an industry. In practice, it is difficult to determine that a monopoly exists because it depends on how narrowly an industry is defined.

2. Barriers to the entry of new firms are usually necessary to protect a monopoly from competition. Such barriers include economies of scale (making the firm a natural monopoly or at least giving it a cost advantage over new – small – competitors), control over supplies of inputs or over outlets, patents or copyright, and tactics to eliminate competition (such as takeovers or aggressive advertising).

3. Profits for the monopolist (as for other firms) will be maximised where $MC = MR$. In the case of monopoly, this will probably be at a higher price relative to marginal cost than for other firms, due to the less elastic nature of its demand at any given price.

4. Monopolies may be against the public interest to the extent that they charge a higher price relative to cost than do competitive firms; if they cause a less desirable distribution of income; if a lack of competition removes the incentive to be efficient and innovative; and if they exert undesirable political pressures on governments.

5. On the other hand, any economies of scale will in part be passed on to consumers in lower prices, and the monopolist's high profits may be used for research and development and investment, which in turn may lead to better products at possibly lower prices.

6.4 THE THEORY OF CONTESTABLE MARKETS

Potential competition or monopoly?

In recent years, economists have developed the theory of contestable markets. This theory argues that what is crucial in determining price and output is not whether an industry is *actually* a monopoly or competitive, but whether there is the real *threat* of competition.

If a monopoly is protected by high barriers to entry – if, for example, it owns all the relevant raw materials – then it will be able to make supernormal profits with no fear of competition.

If, however, another firm *could* take over from it with little difficulty, it will behave much more like a competitive firm. The threat of competition has a similar effect to actual competition.

As an example, consider a catering company engaged by a factory to run its canteen. The catering company has a monopoly over the supply of food to the workers in that factory. If, however, it starts charging high prices or providing a poor service, the factory could offer the running of the canteen to an alternative catering company. This threat may force the original catering company to charge 'reasonable' prices and offer a good service.

Perfectly contestable markets

A market is **perfectly contestable** when the costs of entry and exit by potential rivals are zero, and when such entry can be made very rapidly. In such cases, the moment it becomes possible to earn supernormal profits, new firms will enter, thus driving profits down to a normal level. The sheer threat of this happening, so the theory goes, will ensure that the firm already in the market will (a) keep its prices down, so that it just makes normal profits, and (b) produce as efficiently as possible, taking advantage of any economies of scale and any new technology. If it did not do this, rivals would enter, and potential competition would become actual competition.

This is illustrated in Figure 6.12. Assume that there is only one firm in the industry, which faces a long-run average cost curve given by *LRAC*. Assume that profits are maximised at a price of P_1, with supernormal profits being shown by the shaded area. If entry and exit costs are high, the price will remain at this level. If entry and exit costs are low, however, rival firms may be tempted to enter and take over the monopoly. To avert this, the existing firm will have to lower its price. In the case of zero entry and exit costs, the

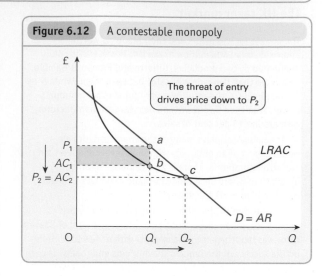

Figure 6.12 A contestable monopoly

The threat of entry drives price down to P_2

monopolist will have to lower its price to P_2, where price equals *LRAC*, and where, therefore, profits are normal and would not attract rival firms to enter. At the same time, the monopolist will have to ensure that its *LRAC* curve is as low as possible (i.e. that it avoids any X inefficiency (see Box 6.5)).

Contestable markets and natural monopolies

So why in such cases are the markets not *actually* perfectly competitive? Why do they remain monopolies?

The most likely reason has to do with economies of scale and the size of the market. To operate on a minimum efficient scale, the firm may have to be so large relative to the market that there is only room for one such firm in the industry. If a new firm does come into the market, then one or other of the two firms will not survive the competition. The market is simply not big enough for both of them. This is the case in Figure 6.12. The industry is a natural monopoly, given that the *LRAC* curve is downward sloping even at output *c*.

If, however, there are no entry or exit costs, new firms will be perfectly willing to enter even though there is only room for one firm, provided they believe that they are more efficient than the established firm. The established firm, knowing this, will be forced to produce as efficiently as possible and with only normal profit.

The importance of costless exit

Setting up in a new business usually involves large expenditures on plant and machinery. Once this money has been spent, it becomes fixed costs. If these fixed costs are no higher than those of the existing firm, then the new firm could win the battle. But, of course, there is always the risk that it might lose.

Definition

Perfectly contestable market A market where there is free and costless entry and exit.

But does losing the battle really matter? Can the firm not simply move to another market?

It does matter if there are substantial costs of exit. This will be the case if the capital equipment cannot be transferred to other uses, as would be the case, for example, with a power station. In this case, these fixed costs are known as *sunk costs*. The losing firm is left with capital equipment that it cannot use. The firm may therefore be put off entering in the first place. The market is not perfectly contestable, and the established firm can make supernormal profits.

If, however, the capital equipment can be transferred, the exit costs will be zero (or at least very low), and new firms will be more willing to take the risks of entry. For example, a rival coach company may open up a service on a route previously operated by only one company, and where there is still only room for one operator. If the new firm loses the resulting battle, it can still use the coaches it has purchased. It simply uses them for a different route. The cost of the coaches is not a sunk cost.

Costless exit, therefore, encourages firms to enter an industry, knowing that, if unsuccessful, they can always transfer their capital elsewhere.

The lower the exit costs, the more contestable the market. This implies that firms already established in other similar markets may provide more effective competition against monopolists, since they can simply transfer capital from one market to another. For example, studies of airlines in the USA show that entry to a particular route may be much easier for an established airline, which can simply transfer aircraft from one route to another (see Box 6.7).

 In which of the following industries are exit costs likely to be low: (a) steel production; (b) market gardening; (c) nuclear power generation; (d) specialist financial advisory services; (e) production of a new drug; (f) street food; (g) car ferry operators? Do these exit costs depend on how narrowly the industry is defined?

> ### Definition
>
> **Sunk costs** Costs that cannot be recouped (e.g. by transferring assets to other uses). Examples include specialised machinery or the costs of an advertising campaign.

Assessment of the theory

The theory of contestable markets is an improvement on simple monopoly theory, which merely focuses on the existing structure of the industry and makes no allowance for potential competition: no allowance for the size of the barriers to entry and the costs of exit.

Perfectly contestable markets may exist only rarely. But like perfect competition they provide an *ideal type* against which to judge the real world. It can be argued that they provide a more useful ideal type than perfect competition, since they provide a better means of predicting firms' price and output behaviour than does the simple portion of the market currently supplied by the existing firm.

One criticism of the theory, however, is that it does not take sufficient account of the possible reactions of the established firm. There could be a perfectly contestable market, with no cost barriers to entry or exit, but the established firm may let it be known that any firm that dares to enter will face all-out war! This could well act as a deterrent to entry and allow the established firm to continue charging high prices and making supernormal profits.

Contestable markets and the public interest

If a monopoly operates in a perfectly contestable market, it might bring the 'best of both worlds'. Not only will it be able to achieve low costs through economies of scale, but also the potential competition will keep profits and hence prices down.

For this reason, the theory has been seized on by politicians on the political right to justify a policy of laissez-faire (non-intervention) and deregulation (e.g. coach and air routes). They argue that the theory vindicates the free market. There are two points in reply to this:

- Few markets are *perfectly* contestable. If entry and exit are not costless, a monopoly can still make supernormal profits in the long run.
- There are other possible failings of the market beside monopoly power: e.g. inequality, pollution. (These failings are examined in Chapters 10 and 11.)

Nevertheless the theory of contestable markets has highlighted the importance of entry barriers in determining monopoly behaviour. The size of the barriers has therefore become the focus of attention of many politicians and academics when considering anti-monopoly policy.

KI 11
p80

BOX 6.7	AIRLINE DEREGULATION IN THE USA AND EUROPE

A case study of contestable markets

If a market is highly contestable, the mere threat of competition may be successful in keeping prices and profits down. Of course, established firms would be keen to erect barriers to entry and to make exit more costly for any firm that did enter.

Governments around the world are generally in favour of increased competition and frown on the erection of entry barriers (see section 13.1). This means that they generally prefer not to intervene if markets are competitive or highly contestable, but may attempt to regulate the prices, profits or behaviour of firms where competition or contestability is limited. Conversely, if markets have been regulated and yet are potentially competitive, many governments have then deregulated them (i.e. removed regulations).

A good case study of deregulation and contestability (or lack of it) is the airline industry. Here the reduction of regulations over decades has allowed low-cost airlines to build market share and challenge the large network carriers.

The USA

The airline industry in the USA was deregulated in 1978. Prior to that, air routes were allocated by the government, with the result that many airlines operated as monopolies or shared the route with just one other airline. Now there exists a policy of 'open skies'.

Initially the consequences were dramatic, with lower fares and, over many routes, a greater choice of airlines. The Brookings Institution calculated that, in the first 10 years of deregulation, the lower fares saved consumers some $100 billion. One consequence of the increased competition was that many long-established US airlines went out of business.

Even where routes continued to be operated by just one or two airlines, fares still fell if the route was *contestable*: if the entry and exit costs remained low. In 1992, despite the bankruptcies, 23 new carriers were established in North America, and many routes were taken over by existing carriers.

But deregulation did not make all routes more contestable. In some cases the reverse happened. In a situation of rising costs and falling revenues, there were mergers and takeovers of the vulnerable airlines. By 2000 just seven airlines accounted for over 90 per cent of American domestic air travel, compared with 15 in 1984. With this move towards greater monopolisation, some airlines managed to make their routes *less* contestable. The result was that air fares over the 1990s rose faster than prices in general.

A key ingredient in making routes less contestable was the development of a system of air routes radiating out from about 30 key or 'hub' airports. With waves of flights scheduled to arrive and depart within a short space of time, passengers can make easy connections at these hub airports.

The problem is that several of these hub airports became dominated by single airlines which, through economies of scale and the ownership or control of various airport facilities, such as boarding gates or check-in areas, could effectively keep out potential entrants. By 2002, at 15 of the hub airports, including some of the busiest, the dominant airline had a market share in excess of 70 per cent.

The airlines also used measures to increase 'customer loyalty' and thereby make entry barriers higher. These measures include frequent flier rewards, deals with travel agents and code sharing with 'partner' airlines.

The rise of the low-cost airlines. In the 2000s, however, the domestic US airlines market became more competitive again, thanks to the growth of low-cost carriers (LCCs), the largest being Southwest Airlines. These accounted for just 7 per cent of US domestic passengers in 1990; by 2009 this had risen to 34 per cent and in 2013, for the first time, LCCs had a greater market share than the network carriers. The response of the major airlines was to create their own low-cost carriers, such as Delta's 'Song' in 2004 and United's 'Ted' in 2004.

A danger here is that big airlines may use their LCCs to undercut the prices of small new entrants so as to drive them out of the market. Such 'predatory pricing' (see pages 217 and 387) is illegal, and the Department of Justice investigated several cases. However, observing predatory practices is much easier than proving them. Thus cases have been consistently dismissed by juries, who have concluded that there was insufficient proof that the big airlines were breaking the law. This issue re-emerged in 2011, when Delta Airlines was criticised for adopting predatory practices in order to maintain a monopoly position at Minneapolis St Paul Airport.

With the rise in fuel prices in 2006–8 and lower passenger numbers from 2007, resulting from the global recession, some of these new LCCs went out of business. Delta shut its Song division in 2006 and United shut Ted in 2008. Southwest continued in its position of market dominance, with over 20 per cent of domestic passengers carried in 2013.

Europe

Until the early 1990s, the European air transport industry was highly regulated, with governments controlling routes. National routes were often licensed to the national airline and international routes to the two respective national airlines. Since 1993, the industry has been progressively deregulated and competition has increased, with a growing availability of discount fares. Now, within the EU, airlines are free to charge whatever they like, and any EU airline can fly on any route it wants, providing it can get the slots at the airports at either end.

As in the USA, however, whilst increased competition has benefited passengers, many of the airlines have tried to make their routes less contestable by erecting entry barriers. Predatory pricing occurred, as the established airlines tried to drive out new competitors. The proliferation of fare categories made it hard for consumers to compare prices, and established carriers' highly publicised fares often had many restrictions, with most people having to pay considerably higher fares. As in the USA, code sharing and airline alliances have reduced competition. Finally, at busy airports, such as Heathrow, the shortage of check-in and boarding gates, runways and airspace provided a major barrier to new entrants.

Nevertheless, new low-cost airlines, such as easyJet, Ryanair and Flybe, provided effective competition for the established national and short-haul international carriers, which were forced to cut fares on routes where they directly competed. British Airways went as far as re-badging its loss-making subsidiary regional airline as BA Connect in 2006, adopting a low-cost model and pledging to 'cut one third from standard domestic fares'. However, the company accrued further losses that year and was sold to Flybe in early 2007.

Low-cost airlines have been able to enter the market by using other airports, such as Stansted and Luton in the case of London, and various regional airports throughout Europe. Many passengers showed themselves willing to travel further at the beginning and end of their journey if the overall cost remained much lower. Ryanair, in particular, has made use of smaller airports located some way from major cities.

Lower costs

How do the LCCs compete? The airline industry does not on the face of it seem to be a highly contestable one. Apart from anything else, aircraft would appear to be a high-cost input.

The answer lies in a variety of cost-saving opportunities. The LCCs are able to lease aircraft rather than buy them; even when they own their own, the aircraft are generally older and more basic, offering a standard accommodation rather than different classes. The result is reduced exit costs, increasing contestability. In addition, by charging extra for each item of luggage, they reduce the amount they carry, thus saving fuel.

There is also evidence of lower staff costs. Initially, LCCs paid less than the traditional airlines; however, this is no longer the case. Peter Belobaba, of MIT, has reported that since 2006 salaries and benefits for LCC employees have equalled those available to employees of the larger carriers. Yet productivity is measurably higher, with 15 per cent more available seat miles per employee.

The large hub-and-spoke carriers have also found that the very nature of their operations constricts their ability to compete with the LCCs on city-to-city routes. Not only are the hubs themselves expensive, but the movement of passengers in and out of the terminals takes longer than with smaller airports. Thus the LCCs, with operating costs some 25 to 50 per cent lower than the traditional carriers, have become a highly effective competitive force on these routes between various city pairs and have forced down prices.

Despite these successes, a period of increasing fuel prices and falling consumer demand from 2008 led some commentators to suggest that the LCCs were unlikely to survive. The past decade has certainly proved tough for some carriers, with Flybe making losses and Ryanair issuing several profit warnings in 2013. However others, such as easyJet, have grown increasingly successful, while in China and South Africa there have been a number of new entrants. It seems likely that the global airline market will remain highly contestable.

1. Make a list of those factors that determine the contestability of a particular air route.
2. In the UK, train operators compete for franchises to run services on a particular route. The franchises are normally for 7, 10, 12 or 15 years. The franchise specifies prices and minimum levels of services (frequency, timing and quality). Would this be a good system to adopt in the airline market over particular routes? How is the airline market similar to/different from the rail market in this regard?
3. In a period of rising fuel prices, and thus higher airfares, do you think that the low-cost carriers are more or less vulnerable than the traditional carriers in the short term? Would your answer differ when we look at the longer-term decisions of passengers?
4. In a recession, do you think that the low-cost carriers are more or less vulnerable than the traditional carriers? And in a boom?

Section summary

1. Potential competition may be as important as actual competition in determining a firm's price and output strategy.

2. The threat of this competition increases as entry and exit costs to and from the industry diminish. If the entry and exit costs are zero, the market is said to be *perfectly* contestable. Under such circumstances, an existing

monopolist will be forced to keep its profits down to the normal level if it is to resist entry by new firms. Exit costs will be lower, the lower are the sunk costs of the firm.

3. The theory of contestable markets provides a more realistic analysis of firms' behaviour than theories based simply on the *existing* number of firms in the industry.

END OF CHAPTER QUESTIONS

1. A perfectly competitive firm faces a price of £14 per unit. It has the following short-run cost schedule:

Output	0	1	2	3	4	5	6	7	8
TC (£)	10	18	24	30	38	50	66	91	120

   (a) Copy the table and put in additional rows for average cost and marginal cost at each level of output. (Enter the figures for marginal cost in the space between each column.)

   (b) Plot *AC*, *MC* and *MR* on a diagram.

   (c) Mark the profit-maximising output.

   (d) How much (supernormal) profit is made at this output?

   (e) What would happen to the price in the long run if this firm were typical of others in the industry? Why would we need to know information about long-run average cost in order to give a precise answer to this question?

2. If the industry under perfect competition faces a downward-sloping demand curve, why does an individual firm face a horizontal demand curve?

3. If supernormal profits are competed away under perfect competition, why will firms have an incentive to become more efficient?

4. Is it a valid criticism of perfect competition to argue that it is incompatible with economies of scale?

5. On a diagram similar to Figure 6.4, show the long-run equilibrium for both firm and industry under perfect competition. Now assume that the demand for the product falls. Show the short-run and long-run effects.

6. Why is the profit-maximising price under monopoly greater than marginal cost? In what way can this be seen as inefficient?

7. On three diagrams like Figure 6.8, illustrate the effect on price, quantity and profit of each of the following: (a) a rise in demand; (b) a rise in fixed costs; (c) a rise in variable costs. In each case, show only the *AR*, *MR*, *AC* and *MC* curves.

8. Think of three examples of monopolies (local or national) and consider how contestable their markets are.

Online resources

Additional case studies in MyEconLab

6.1 **B2B electronic marketplaces.** This case study examines the growth of firms trading with each other (business to business or 'B2B') over the Internet and considers the effects on competition.

6.2 **Measuring monopoly power.** This case study examines how the degree of monopoly power possessed by a firm can be measured.

6.3 **Windows cleaning.** This discusses the examination of Microsoft's market dominance by the US Justice Department and the European Commission.

Maths Case 6.1 Long-run equilibrium under perfect competition. Using calculus to find equilibrium output and price.

Maths Case 6.2 Price elasticity of demand and the profit-maximising price. A proof of the profit-maximising rule relating price elasticity of demand, price and marginal revenue.

Websites relevant to this chapter

See sites listed at the end of Chapter 7 on page 220.

MyEconLab

This book can be supported by MyEconLab, which contains a range of additional resources, including an online homework and tutorial system designed to test and build your understanding.

You need both an access card and a course ID to access MyEconLab:

1. Is your lecturer using MyEconLab? Ask your lecturer for your course ID.

2. Has an access card been included with the book at a reduced cost? Check the inside back cover of the book.

3. If you have a course ID but no access card, go to: http://www.myeconlab.com/ to buy access to this interactive study programme.

Profit Maximising under Imperfect Competition

CHAPTER MAP

7.1 Monopolistic competition   194
Assumptions of monopolistic competition   194
Equilibrium of the firm   194
Limitations of the model   195
Non-price competition   196
Monopolistic competition and the public interest   196

7.2 Oligopoly   197
The two key features of oligopoly   197
Competition and collusion   198
Industry equilibrium under collusive oligopoly   198
Tacit collusion: price leadership   200
Tacit collusion: rules of thumb   201
Factors favouring collusion   201
Non-collusive oligopoly: the breakdown
  of collusion   204
Non-collusive oligopoly: assumptions about
  rivals' behaviour   204
Oligopoly and the public interest   207

7.3 Game theory   209
Single-move games   209
Multiple-move games   212
The importance of threats and promises   212
The importance of timing   212
Assessing the theory of games   213

7.4 Price discrimination   214
Conditions necessary for price discrimination
  to operate   214
Advantages to the firm   216
Profit-maximising prices and output   216
Price discrimination and the public interest   217

Very few markets in practice can be classified as perfectly competitive or as a pure monopoly. The vast majority of firms do compete with other firms, often quite aggressively, and yet they are not price takers: they do have some degree of market power. Most markets, therefore, lie between the two extremes of monopoly and perfect competition, in the realm of 'imperfect competition'.

There are two types of imperfect competition: monopolistic competition and oligopoly.

Under monopolistic competition, there will normally be quite a large number of relatively small firms. Think of the number of car repair garages, builders, hairdressers, restaurants and other small traders that you get in any large town or city. They are in fierce competition with each other, and yet competition is not perfect. They are all trying to produce a product that is different from their rivals.

Under oligopoly, there will be only a few firms competing. Most of the best-known companies, such as Ford, Coca-Cola, Nike, BP and Apple, are oligopolists. Sometimes oligopolists will attempt to collude with each other to keep prices up. On other occasions, competition will be intense, with rival firms trying to undercut each other's prices, or developing new or better products in order to gain a larger share of the market. We will examine both collusion and competition between oligopolists and show when each is more likely to occur.

7.1   MONOPOLISTIC COMPETITION

We will start by looking at monopolistic competition. This was a theory developed in the 1930s by the American economist Edward Chamberlin. Monopolistic competition is nearer to the competitive end of the spectrum. It can best be understood as a situation where there are a lot of firms competing, but where each firm does nevertheless have some degree of market power (hence the term 'monopolistic' competition): each firm has some choice over what price to charge for its products.

Assumptions of monopolistic competition

- There are *quite a large number of firms*. As a result, each firm has an insignificantly small share of the market, and therefore its actions are unlikely to affect its rivals to any great extent. This means that when each firm makes its decisions it does not have to worry how its rivals will react. It assumes that what its rivals choose to do will *not* be influenced by what it does.

    This is known as the assumption of **independence**. (As we shall see later, this is not the case under oligopoly. There we assume that firms believe that their decisions *do* affect their rivals, and that their rivals' decisions will affect them. Under oligopoly, we assume that firms are *inter*dependent.)

- There is *freedom of entry* of new firms into the industry. If any firm wants to set up in business in this market, it is free to do so.

In these two respects, therefore, monopolistic competition is like perfect competition.

- The situation differs from perfect competition, however, in that each firm produces a product or provides a service in some way different from those of its rivals. As a result, it can raise its price without losing all its customers. Thus its demand curve is downward sloping, although it will be relatively elastic given the large number of competitors to whom customers can turn. This is known as the assumption of **product differentiation**.

Restaurants, hairdressers and builders are all examples of monopolistic competition.

 Give some other examples of monopolistic competition. (Try looking at www.yell.com if you are stuck.)

Equilibrium of the firm

Short run

As with other market structures, profits are maximised at the output where $MC = MR$. The diagram will be the same as for the monopolist, except that the AR and MR curves will be more elastic. This is illustrated in Figure 7.1(a). As with perfect competition, it is possible for the monopolistically competitive firm to make supernormal profits in the short run. This is shown as the shaded area.

Just how much profit the firm will make in the short run depends on the strength of demand: the position and elasticity of the demand curve. The further to the right the demand curve is relative to the average cost curve, and the less elastic the demand curve is, the greater will be the firm's short-run profit. Thus a firm facing little competition and whose product is considerably differentiated from that of its rivals may be able to earn considerable short-run profits.

1. *Why may a food shop charge higher prices than supermarkets for 'essential items' and yet very similar prices for delicatessen items?*
2. *Which of these two items is a petrol station more likely to sell at a discount: (a) oil; (b) sweets? Why?*

Long run

If typical firms are earning supernormal profits, new firms will enter the industry in the long run. As they do, they will take some of the customers away from established firms. The demand for the established firms will therefore fall. Their demand (AR) curve will shift to the left, and will continue doing so as long as supernormal profits remain and thus new firms continue entering.

Long-run equilibrium is reached when only normal profits remain: when there is no further incentive for new firms to enter. This is illustrated in Figure 7.1(b). The firm's demand curve settles at D_L, where it is tangential to the firm's $LRAC$ curve. Output will be Q_L: where $AR_L = LRAC$. (At any other output, $LRAC$ is greater than AR and thus less than normal profit would be made.)

1. *Why does the LRMC curve cross the MR_L curve directly below the tangency point of the LRAC and AR_L curves?*
2. *Assuming that supernormal profits can be made in the short run, will there be any difference in the long-run and short-run elasticity of demand? Explain.*

Definitions

Independence (of firms in a market) Where the decisions of one firm in a market will not have any significant effect on the demand curves of its rivals.

Product differentiation Where one firm's product is sufficiently different from its rivals' to allow it to raise the price of the product without customers all switching to the rivals' products. A situation where a firm faces a downward-sloping demand curve.

Figure 7.1 Equilibrium of the firm under monopolistic competition

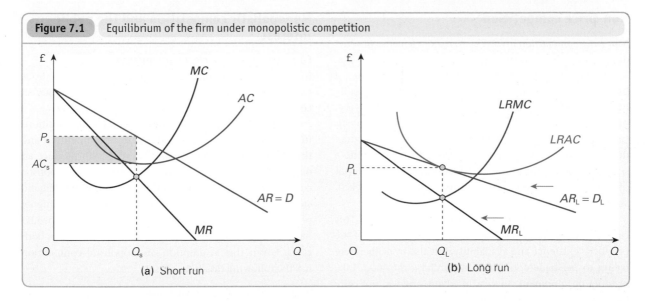

(a) Short run

(b) Long run

Limitations of the model

There are various problems in applying the model of monopolistic competition to the real world:

- Information may be imperfect. Firms will not enter an industry if they are unaware of what supernormal profits are being made, or if they underestimate the demand for the particular product they are considering selling.

- Given that the firms in the industry produce different products, it is difficult if not impossible to derive a demand curve for the industry as a whole. Thus the analysis has to be confined to the level of the firm.

- Firms are likely to differ from each other not only in the product they produce or the service they offer, but also in their size and cost structure. What is more,

entry may not be *completely* unrestricted. Two petrol stations could not set up in exactly the same place – on a busy crossroads, say. Thus, although the typical or 'representative' firm may earn only normal profit in the long run, other firms may be able to earn long-run supernormal profit. They may have some cost advantage or produce something that is impossible to duplicate perfectly.

- One of the biggest problems with the simple model shown in Figure 7.1 is that it concentrates on price and output decisions. In practice, the profit-maximising firm under monopolistic competition also has to decide the exact variety of product to produce and how much to spend on advertising it. This will lead the firm to take part in non-price competition.

BOX 7.1 **SELLING ICE CREAM AS A STUDENT**

CASE STUDIES AND APPLICATIONS

John's experience of monopolistic competition

When I was a student, my parents lived in Exeter in Devon, and at that time the city's bypass became completely jammed on a summer Saturday as holidaymakers made their way to the coast. Traffic queues were several miles long.

For a summer job, I drove a small ice-cream van. Early on, I had the idea of selling ice cream from a tray to the people queuing in their cars. I made more money on a Saturday than the rest of the week put together. I thought I was on to a good thing.

But news of this lucrative market soon spread, and each week new ice-cream sellers appeared – each one reducing my earnings! By the middle of August there were over 30 ice-cream sellers from five different ice-cream companies. Most tried to get to the beginning of the queue, to get ahead of their rivals.

Imagine the scene. A family driving to the coast rounds a bend and is suddenly met by a traffic jam and several ice-cream sellers all jostling to sell them an ice cream. It was quite surreal. Not surprisingly, many of the potential customers refused to buy, feeling somewhat intimidated by the spectacle. It was not long before most of us realised that it was best to disperse and find a section of the road where there were no other sellers.

But with so many ice-cream sellers, no one made much money. My supernormal earnings had been reduced to a normal level. I made about the same on Saturday to people stuck in queues as I would have done if I had driven my van around the streets.

1. *Was there totally free entry to this market?*
2. *What forms of product differentiation were there?*

Non-price competition

Non-price competition involves two major elements: product development and advertising.

The major aims of *product development* are to produce a product that will sell well (i.e. one in high or potentially high demand) and that is different from rivals' products (i.e. has a relatively inelastic demand due to lack of close substitutes). For shops or other firms providing a service, 'product development' takes the form of attempting to provide a service which is better than, or at least different from, that of rivals: personal service, late opening, certain lines stocked, and so on.

The major aim of *advertising* is to sell the product. This can be achieved not only by informing the consumer of the product's existence and availability, but also by deliberately trying to persuade consumers to purchase the good. Like product development, successful advertising will not only increase demand, but also make the firm's demand curve less elastic since it stresses the specific qualities of this firm's product over its rivals' (see Box 3.1 on page 66).

Product development and advertising not only increase a firm's demand and hence revenue, they also involve increased costs. So how much should a firm advertise to maximise profits?

For any given price and product, the optimal amount of advertising is where the revenue from *additional* advertising (MR_A) is equal to its cost (MC_A). As long as $MR_A > MC_A$, additional advertising will add to profit. But extra amounts spent on advertising are likely to lead to smaller and smaller increases in sales. Thus MR_A falls, until $MR_A = MC_A$. At that point, no further profit can be made. It is at a maximum.

> *Why will additional advertising lead to smaller and smaller increases in sales?*

Two problems arise with this analysis:

- The effect of product development and advertising on demand will be difficult for a firm to forecast.
- Product development and advertising are likely to have different effects at different prices. Profit maximisation, therefore, will involve the more complex choice of the optimum combination of price, type of product, and level and variety of advertising.

Definitions

Non-price competition Competition in terms of product promotion (advertising, packaging, etc.) or product development.

Excess capacity (under monopolistic competition) In the long run, firms under monopolistic competition will produce at an output below their minimum-cost point.

Monopolistic competition and the public interest

Comparison with perfect competition

It is often argued that monopolistic competition leads to a less efficient allocation of resources than perfect competition.

Figure 7.2 compares the long-run equilibrium positions for two firms. One firm is under perfect competition and thus faces a horizontal demand curve. It will produce an output of Q_1 at a price of P_1. The other is under monopolistic competition and thus faces a downward-sloping demand curve. It will produce the lower output of Q_2 at the higher price of P_2. A crucial assumption here is that a firm would have the *same* long-run average cost (*LRAC*) curve in both cases. Given this assumption, monopolistic competition has the following disadvantages:

- Less will be sold and at a higher price.
- Firms will not be producing at the least-cost point.

By producing more, firms would move to a lower point on their *LRAC* curve. Thus firms under monopolistic competition are said to have ***excess capacity***. In Figure 7.2 this excess capacity is shown as $Q_1 - Q_2$. In other words, monopolistic competition is typified by quite a large number of firms (e.g. petrol stations), all operating at an output less than that necessary to achieve minimum cost, and thus being forced to charge a price above that which they could charge if they had a bigger turnover. How often have you been to a petrol station and had to queue for the pumps?

> *Does this imply that if, say, half of the petrol stations were closed down, the consumer would benefit? (Clue: what would happen to the demand curves of the remaining stations?)*

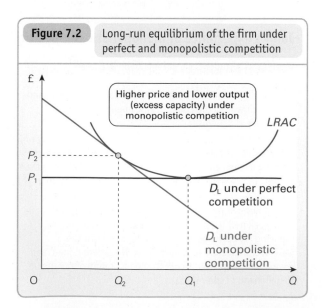

Figure 7.2 Long-run equilibrium of the firm under perfect and monopolistic competition

On the other hand, it is often argued that these wastes of monopolistic competition may be insignificant. In the first place, although the firm's demand curve is downward sloping, it is still likely to be highly elastic due to the large number of substitutes. In the second place, although the firm under monopolistic competition will not be operating quite at the bottom of its *LRAC* curve, the nature of the industry may allow some economies of scale to be gained. The *LRAC* curve would thus be lower than in the case of the larger number of smaller firms that would be necessary to keep the industry perfectly competitive. The size of the economies of scale, if any, will obviously vary from industry to industry.

Perhaps more importantly, consumers are likely to benefit from monopolistic competition by having a greater variety of products to choose from. Given that we all have individual tastes and preferences, our utility will be higher with choice.

 Which would you rather have: five restaurants to choose from, each with very different menus and each having spare tables so that you could always guarantee getting one; or just two restaurants to choose from, charging less but with less choice and making it necessary to book well in advance?

Comparison with monopoly

The arguments here are very similar to those comparing perfect competition and monopoly.

On the one hand, freedom of entry for new firms and hence the lack of long-run supernormal profits under monopolistic competition are likely to help keep prices down for the consumer and encourage cost saving. On the other hand, monopolies are likely to achieve greater economies of scale and have more funds for investment and research and development.

Section summary

1. Monopolistic competition occurs where there is free entry to the industry and quite a large number of firms operating independently of each other, but where each firm has some market power as a result of producing differentiated products or services.

2. In the short run, firms can make supernormal profits. In the long run, however, freedom of entry will drive profits down to the normal level. The long-run equilibrium of the firm is where the (downward-sloping) demand curve is tangential to the long-run average cost curve.

3. The long-run equilibrium is one of excess capacity. Given that the demand curve is downward sloping, its tangency point with the *LRAC* curve will not be at the bottom of the *LRAC* curve. Increased production would thus be possible at *lower* average cost.

4. In practice, supernormal profits may persist into the long run: firms have imperfect information; entry may not be completely unrestricted; firms may use non-price competition to maintain an advantage over their rivals.

5. Non-price competition may take the form of product development or product promotion (advertising etc.).

6. Monopolistically competitive firms, because of excess capacity, may have higher costs than perfectly competitive firms, but consumers may gain from a greater diversity of products.

7. Monopolistically competitive firms may have fewer economies of scale than monopolies and conduct less research and development, but the competition may keep prices lower than under monopoly.

7.2 OLIGOPOLY

Oligopoly occurs when just a few firms between them share a large proportion of the industry.

There are, however, significant differences in the structure of industries under oligopoly and similarly significant differences in the behaviour of firms. The firms may produce a virtually identical product (e.g. metals, chemicals, sugar, petrol). Most oligopolists, however, produce differentiated products (e.g. cars, soap powder, soft drinks, electrical appliances). Much of the competition between such oligopolists is in terms of the marketing of their particular brand. Marketing practices may differ considerably from one industry to another.

The two key features of oligopoly

Despite the differences between oligopolies, two crucial features distinguish oligopoly from other market structures.

Barriers to entry

In contrast to the situation under monopolistic competition, there are various barriers to the entry of new firms. These are similar to those under monopoly (see pages 181–2). The size of the barriers, however, varies from industry to industry. In some cases entry is relatively easy, whereas in others it is virtually impossible.

Interdependence of the firms

Because there are only a few firms under oligopoly, each has to take account of the others. This means that they are mutually dependent: they are **interdependent**. Each firm is affected by its rivals' actions. If a firm changes the price or specification of its product, for example, or the amount of its advertising, the sales of its rivals will be affected. The rivals may then respond by changing their price, specification or advertising. No firm can afford to ignore the actions and reactions of other firms in the industry.

> **KEY IDEA 21**
>
> **People often think and behave strategically.** How you think others will respond to your actions is likely to influence your own behaviour. Firms, for example, when considering a price or product change will often take into account the likely reactions of their rivals.

 KI 10 p75

It is impossible, therefore, to predict the effect on a firm's sales of, say, a change in its price without first making some assumption about the reactions of other firms. Different assumptions yield different predictions. For this reason there is no one single theory of oligopoly. Firms may react differently and unpredictably.

Competition and collusion

Oligopolists are pulled in two different directions:

- The interdependence of firms may make them wish to *collude* with each other. If they could club together and act as if they were a monopoly, they could jointly maximise industry profits.
- On the other hand, they will be tempted to *compete* with their rivals to gain a bigger share of industry profits for themselves.

These two policies are incompatible. The more fiercely firms compete to gain a bigger share of industry profits, the smaller these industry profits will become. For example, price competition will drive down the average industry price, while competition through advertising will raise industry costs. Either way, industry profits will fall.

Sometimes firms collude, sometimes not. The following sections examine first *collusive oligopoly* (both open and tacit) and then *non-collusive oligopoly*.

Industry equilibrium under collusive oligopoly

When firms under oligopoly engage in collusion, they may agree on output, prices, market share, advertising expenditure, etc. Such collusion reduces the uncertainty they face. It reduces the fear of engaging in competitive price cutting or retaliatory advertising, both of which could reduce total industry profits.

A formal collusive agreement is called a **cartel**. The cartel will maximise profits if it acts like a monopoly: if the members behave as if they were a single firm. This is illustrated in Figure 7.3.

The total market demand curve is shown with the corresponding market *MR* curve. The cartel's *MC* curve is the *horizontal* sum of the *MC* curves of its members (since we are adding the *output* of each of the cartel members at each level of marginal cost). Profits are maximised at Q_1 where $MC = MR$. The cartel must therefore set a price of P_1 (at which Q_1 will be demanded). TC 8 p105

Having agreed on the cartel price, the members may then compete against each other using *non-price competition*, to gain as big a share of resulting sales (Q_1) as they can. KI 20 p171

 How will advertising affect the cartel's MC and AR curves? How will this affect the profit-maximising output? Is there any problem here for the cartel in fixing the price?

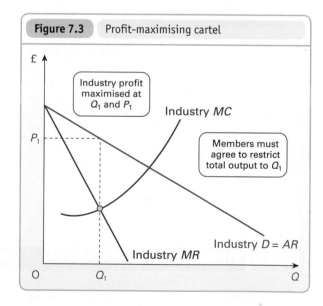

Figure 7.3 Profit-maximising cartel

Definitions

Interdependence (under oligopoly) One of the two key features of oligopoly. Each firm will be affected by its rivals' decisions. Likewise its decisions will affect its rivals. Firms recognise this interdependence. This recognition will affect their decisions.

Collusive oligopoly Where oligopolists agree (formally or informally) to limit competition between themselves.

They may set output quotas, fix prices, limit product promotion or development, or agree not to 'poach' each other's markets.

Non-collusive oligopoly Where oligopolists have no agreement between themselves, formal, informal or tacit.

Cartel A formal collusive agreement.

BOX 7.2   INCREASING CONCENTRATION

Losing innocence

We have identified barriers to entry under oligopoly as a factor in keeping the number of firms low. But why does market power grow in some oligopolies, with the number of firms decreasing? The answer can be found in mergers and acquisitions, tough economic conditions and increasing brand loyalty, all of which can reduce competition.

As we saw in Box 6.1, one of the simplest ways of assessing the extent of market power is to look at concentration ratios – the market share of the leading firms. The table below gives some extracts of the table in that box.

Five-firm concentration ratios for various industries (by output)

Industry	Five-firm ratio	Industry	Five-firm ratio
Sugar	99	Fishing	16
Tobacco products	99	Advertising	10
Confectionary	81	Wholesale distribution	6
Soft drinks, mineral water	75	Furniture	6
Motor vehicles	34	Construction	5

Source: Based on data in *United Kingdom Input–Output Analyses*, 2006 Edition (Office of National Statistics), Table 8.31.

1. *Can you identify which firms make up the majority of the soft drinks industry?*
2. *What are the characteristics that make fishing so 'unconcentrated'?*
3. *Does the relatively low concentration in the car industry surprise you? Explain your answer.*

Unsurprisingly the industries with the highest concentration ratios display a number of varying characteristics. They often involve high capital costs, allowing firms to benefit from economies of scale.

Alternatively a small number of firms have control of the required resources; sugar is a good example here.

In industries with differentiated products, such as confectionary, there are high levels of branding and advertising. On the other hand, the industries with the lowest ratios tend to have lower costs of entry. In many cases their advertising spend is likely to be local, if it exists at all.

Innocent

But why do concentration ratios change over time? One factor is mergers and takeovers. Take the case of Innocent. In 1999 three friends set up the Innocent Drinks Company. Specialising in smoothies, it was a new entrant to the soft drinks industry, one which is dominated by Coca-Cola, Pepsi and Cadbury Schweppes (now the Dr Pepper Snapple Group).

Over the next decade the company grew, from 3 employees to more than 250, achieving a market share of over 77 per cent by 2007. (By 'market' here we are referring to smoothies and yoghurt drinks rather than all soft drinks.) Making good profits and with a reputation for outstanding corporate social responsibility, life seemed good for the three entrepreneurs.

However, even the most successful of firms is vulnerable to takeover and in 2009 it was announced that Coca-Cola had acquired an 18 per cent stake in Innocent. By 2013, this had increased to 90 per cent, with Coca-Cola taking full control. The outcome was uproar from those who had 'bought-in' to the Innocent mission, and of course an increase in the concentration ratio of the soft drinks industry.

1. *Are there any advantages to consumers in a highly concentrated industry?*
2. *Explain why the measurement of the concentration ratio will be dependent on the definition of the market, referring to the Innocent story.*
3. *Do small independent burger companies have any market advantages over global firms such as McDonald's and Burger King?*

Alternatively, the cartel members may somehow agree to divide the market between them. Each member would be given a *quota*. The sum of all the quotas must add up to Q_1. If the quotas exceeded Q_1, either there would be output unsold if price remained fixed at P_1, or the price would fall.

But if quotas are to be set by the cartel, how will it decide the level of each individual member's quota? The most likely method is for the cartel to divide the market between the members according to their current market share. This is the solution most likely to be accepted as 'fair'.

If this 'fair' solution were adopted, what effect would it have on the industry MC curve in Figure 7.3?

In many countries, cartels are illegal – being seen by the government as a means of driving up prices and profits, and thereby as being against the public interest (see section 13.1). Where open collusion is illegal, however, firms may simply break the law, or get round it. Alternatively, firms may stay within the law, but still *tacitly* collude by watching each other's prices and keeping theirs similar. Firms may tacitly 'agree' to avoid price wars or aggressive advertising campaigns.

Definition

Quota (set by a cartel) The output that a given member of a cartel is allowed to produce (production quota) or sell (sales quota).

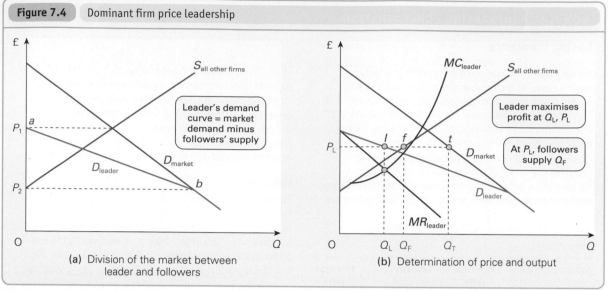

Figure 7.4 Dominant firm price leadership

(a) Division of the market between leader and followers

(b) Determination of price and output

Tacit collusion: price leadership

One form of **tacit collusion** is where firms keep to the price set by an established leader. The leader may be the largest firm, the one dominating the industry. This is known as **dominant firm price leadership**. Alternatively, the price leader may simply be the one that has proved to be the most reliable one to follow, the one that is the best barometer of market conditions. This is known as **barometric firm price leadership**. Let us examine each of these two types of price leadership in turn.

Dominant firm price leadership

How in theory does the leader set the price? The leader will maximise profits where its marginal revenue is equal to its marginal cost. Figure 7.4(a) shows the total market demand curve and the supply curve of all followers. These firms, like perfectly competitive firms, accept the price as given, only in this case it is the price set by the leader, and thus their joint supply curve is simply the sum of their MC curves – the same as under perfect competition.

The leader's demand curve can be seen as that portion of market demand unfilled by the other firms. In other words, it is market demand minus other firms' supply. At P_1 the whole of market demand is satisfied by the other firms, and so the demand for the leader is zero (point a). At P_2 the other firms' supply is zero, and so the leader faces the full market demand (point b). The leader's demand curve thus connects points a and b.

The leader's profit will be maximised where its marginal cost equals its marginal revenue. This is shown in Figure 7.4(b). The diagram is the same as Figure 7.4(a) but with the addition of MC and MR curves for the leader. The leader's marginal cost equals its marginal revenue at an output of Q_L (giving a point l on its demand curve). The leader thus sets a price of P_L, which the other firms then duly follow. They supply Q_F (i.e. at point f on their supply curve). Total market demand at P_L is Q_T (i.e. point t on the market demand curve), which must add up to the output of both leader and followers (i.e. $Q_L + Q_F$).

Draw a pair of diagrams like those in Figure 7.4. Illustrate what would happen if market demand rose but the costs of neither leader nor followers rose. Would there be an equal percentage increase in the output of both leader and followers?

Definitions

Tacit collusion Where oligopolists take care not to engage in price cutting, excessive advertising or other forms of competition. There may be unwritten 'rules' of collusive behaviour such as price leadership.

Dominant firm price leadership Where firms (the followers) choose the same price as that set by a dominant firm in the industry (the leader).

Barometric firm price leadership Where the price leader is the one whose prices are believed to reflect market conditions in the most satisfactory way.

*LOOKING AT THE MATHS

In Figure 7.4, the various curves can be represented by equations and this would allow us to solve for P_L, Q_L, Q_F and Q_T. An example of this is given in Maths Case 7.1 in MyEconLab.

Note that we derived all the curves in Figure 7.4 from just three: the market demand curve, the followers' supply curve and the leader's MC curve. It follows that, if we know the functions for these three curves, we can derive the functions for the remainder.

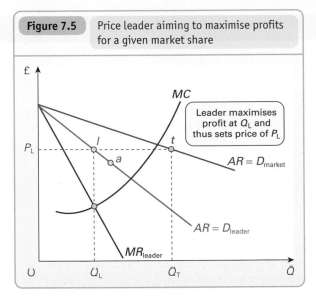

Figure 7.5 Price leader aiming to maximise profits for a given market share

Leader maximises profit at Q_L and thus sets price of P_L

In practice, which firm is taken as the barometer may frequently change. Whether we are talking about oil companies, car producers or banks, any firm may take the initiative in raising prices. Then, if the other firms are merely waiting for someone to take the lead – say, because costs have risen – they will all quickly follow suit. For example, if one of the banks raises its mortgage rates by 1 per cent, then this is likely to stimulate the others to follow suit.

Tacit collusion: rules of thumb

An alternative to following an established leader is to follow an established set of simple 'rules of thumb'. These rules do not involve setting *MC* equal to *MR*, and thus may involve an immediate loss of profit. They do, however, help to prevent an outbreak of competition, and thus help to maintain profits into the longer term.

One example of a rule of thumb is *average cost pricing*. Here, producers simply add a certain percentage for profit on top of average costs. Thus, if average costs rise by 10 per cent, prices will automatically be raised by 10 per cent. This is a particularly useful rule of thumb in times of inflation, when all firms will be experiencing similar cost increases

 If a firm has a typically shaped average cost curve and sets prices 10 per cent above average cost, what will its supply curve look like?

In practice, however, it is very difficult for the leader to apply this theory. The leader's demand and *MR* curves depend on the followers' supply curve – something the leader will find virtually impossible to estimate with any degree of accuracy. The leader will thus have to make a rough estimate of what its profit-maximising price and output will be, and simply choose that. That is the best it can do!

 A simpler model is where the leader assumes that it will maintain a constant *market share* (say, 50 per cent). It makes this assumption because it also assumes that all other firms will follow its price up and down. This is illustrated in Figure 7.5. It knows its current position on its demand curve (say, point *a*). It then estimates how responsive its demand will be to industry-wide price changes and thus constructs its demand and *MR* curves accordingly. It then chooses to produce Q_L at a price of P_L: at point *l* on its demand curve (where $MC = MR$). Other firms then follow that price. Total market demand will be Q_T, with followers supplying that portion of the market not supplied by the leader, namely $Q_T - Q_L$.

There is one problem with this model: the assumption that the followers will want to maintain a constant market share. If the leader raises its price, the followers may want to supply more, given that the new price (= *MR* for a price-taking follower) may well be above their marginal cost. On the other hand, the followers may decide merely to maintain their market share for fear of retaliation from the leader, in the form of price cuts or an aggressive advertising campaign.

Barometric firm price leadership

A similar exercise can be conducted by a barometric firm. Although such a firm does not dominate the industry, its price will be followed by the others. It merely tries to estimate its demand and *MR* curves – assuming, again, a constant market share – and then produces where $MR = MC$ and sets price accordingly.

Another rule of thumb is to have certain *price benchmarks*. Thus clothes may sell for £19.95, £24.95 or £49.95 (but not £18.31 or £36.42). If costs rise, then firms simply raise their price to the next benchmark, knowing that other firms will do the same.

Rules of thumb can also be applied to advertising (e.g. you do not criticise other firms' products, only praise your own); or to the design of the product (e.g. lighting manufacturers tacitly agreeing not to bring out an everlasting light bulb).

Factors favouring collusion

Collusion between firms, whether formal or tacit, is more likely when firms can clearly identify with each other or some leader and when they trust each other not to break agreements. It will be easier for firms to collude if the following conditions apply:

| BOX 7.3 | OPEC |

The history of the world's most famous cartel

OPEC is probably the best known of all cartels. It was set up in 1960 by the five major oil-exporting countries: Saudi Arabia, Iran, Iraq, Kuwait and Venezuela. Today it has 12 members, including Nigeria, Angola, Libya and Ecuador. Its stated objectives were as follows:

- The co-ordination and unification of the petroleum policies of member countries.
- The organisation of means to ensure the stabilisation of prices, eliminating harmful and unnecessary fluctuations.

The years leading up to 1960 had seen the oil-producing countries increasingly in conflict with the international oil companies, which extracted oil under 'concessionary agreement'. The oil-producing countries had little say over output and price levels.

The early years

Despite the formation of OPEC in 1960, it was not until 1973 that control of oil production was effectively transferred from the oil companies to the oil countries, with OPEC making the decisions on how much oil to produce and thereby determining its oil revenue. By this time OPEC consisted of 13 members.

OPEC's pricing policy during the 1970s consisted of setting a market price for Saudi Arabian crude (the market leader), and leaving other OPEC members to set their prices in line with this. This was a form of dominant 'firm' price leadership.

As long as demand remained buoyant, and was price inelastic, this policy allowed large price increases with consequent large revenue increases. In 1973/4, after the Arab–Israeli War, OPEC raised the price of oil from around $3 per barrel to over $12. The price was kept at roughly this level until 1979. And yet the sales of oil did not fall significantly.

 Illustrate what was happening here on a demand and supply diagram. Remember that demand was highly inelastic and was increasing over time.

After 1979, however, following a further increase in the price of oil from around $15 to $40 per barrel, demand did fall. This was largely due to the recession of the early 1980s (although, as we shall see later on when we look at macroeconomics, this recession was in turn largely caused by governments' responses to the oil price increases).

The use of quotas

Faced by declining demand, OPEC after 1982 agreed to limit output and allocate production quotas in an attempt to keep the price up. A production ceiling of 16 million barrels per day was agreed in 1984.

The cartel was beginning to break down, however, due to the following:

- The world recession and the resulting fall in the demand for oil.

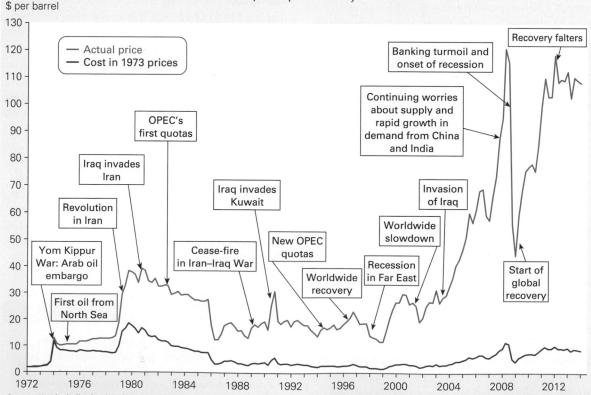

Oil prices (Brent Crude)

Sources: Nominal oil price data from Energy Informational Administration database (http:tonto.eia.doe.gov/dnav/pet/hist/rbrteM.htm); Price data from *World Economic Outlook* (IMF).

- Growing output from non-OPEC members.
- 'Cheating' by some OPEC members who exceeded their quota limits.

With a glut of oil, OPEC could no longer maintain the price. The 'spot' price of oil (the day-to-day price at which oil was trading on the open market) was falling, as the graph shows.

The trend of lower oil prices was reversed in the late 1980s. With the world economy booming, the demand for oil rose and along with it the price. Then in 1990 Iraq invaded Kuwait and the Gulf War ensued. With supplies from Kuwait and Iraq cut off, the supply of oil fell and there was a sharp rise in its price.

But with the ending of the war and the recession of the early 1990s, the price rapidly fell again and only recovered slowly as the world economy started expanding once more.

On the demand side, the development of energy-saving technology plus increases in fuel taxes led to a relatively slow growth in consumption. On the supply side, the growing proportion of output supplied by non-OPEC members, plus the adoption in 1994 of a relatively high OPEC production ceiling of 24.5 million barrels per day, meant that supply more than kept pace with demand.

The situation for OPEC deteriorated further in the late 1990s, following the recession in the Far East. Oil demand fell by some 2 million barrels per day. By early 1999, the price had fallen to around $10 per barrel – a mere $2.70 in 1973 prices! In response, OPEC members agreed to cut production by 4.3 million barrels per day. The objective was to push the price back up to around $18–20 per barrel. But, with the Asian economy recovering and the world generally experiencing more rapid economic growth, the price rose rapidly and soon overshot the $20 mark. By early 2000 it had reached $30: a tripling in price in just 12 months. With the world economy then slowing down, however, the price rapidly fell back, reaching $18 in November 2001.

However, in late 2001 the relationship between OPEC and non-OPEC oil producers changed. The 10 members of the OPEC cartel decided to cut production by 1.5 million barrels a day. This followed an agreement with five of the major oil producers outside of the cartel to reduce their output too, the aim being to push oil prices upwards and then stabilise them at around $25 per barrel. The alliance between OPEC and non-OPEC oil producers is the first such instance of its kind in the oil industry. As a result, it seemed that OPEC might now once again be able to control the market for oil.

The price surge of 2003–8

But how successfully could this alliance cope with crisis? With worries over an impending war with Iraq and a strike in Venezuela, the oil price rose again in late 2002, passing the $30 mark in early 2003. In 2004 the situation worsened with supply concerns related to the situation in Iraq, Saudi Arabia, Russia and Nigeria, and the oil price rose to over $50 in October 2004. OPEC tried to relax the quotas, but found it difficult to adjust supply sufficiently quickly to make any real difference to the price.

From 2006, oil prices increased more sharply than they ever had before and, for the first time in years, the real price of oil exceeded that seen in the 1970s. The major cause of the increases was very substantial increases in demand, particularly from India and China, coupled with continuing concerns about supply. The implications of the sharp price increases were substantial: inflationary pressures built up across the world, while the income of OPEC nations doubled in the first half of 2008.

By July 2008 the price reached $147. Some analysts were predicting a price of over $200 per barrel by the end of the year.

. . . and then the fall

But then, with the growing banking turmoil and fears of a recession, the price began to fall – and rapidly so. When the price dropped below $100 in September 2008 the majority of the world breathed a sigh of relief. But as the economic outlook became gloomier and the demand for oil fell, so the price plummeted, reaching $34 by the end of the year – less than a quarter of the price just five months previously. While this was good news for the consumer, it was potentially damaging for investment in oil exploration and development and also for investment in alternative energy supplies.

OPEC responded to the falling price by announcing cuts in production, totalling some 14 per cent between August 2008 and January 2009. But with OPEC producing less than a third of global oil output, this represented less than 5 per cent of global production. It was a recovery in global demand during 2009 and 2010 that was largely responsible for the rise in price.

Increasingly OPEC's activities appear irrelevant in stabilising prices, which continue to fluctuate with demand, expectations and supply factors. With the increasing discovery in non-OPEC countries of non-conventional deposits, such as in shale formations, OPEC's market share has waned. Proven oil reserves are now at an historic high, with some 20 per cent in non-OPEC countries, although some estimates put the figure as high as 31 per cent.

The recent history of OPEC illustrates the difficulty of using supply quotas to achieve a particular price. With demand being price inelastic but income elastic (responsive to changes in world income, such as rising demand from China), and with considerable speculative movements in demand, the equilibrium price for a given supply quota can fluctuate wildly.

1. *What conditions facilitate the formation of a cartel? Which of these conditions were to be found in the oil market in (a) the early 1970s; (b) the mid-1980s; (c) the mid-2000s; (d) 2015?*
2. *Could OPEC have done anything to prevent the long-term decline in real oil prices seen from 1981 to 2002?*
3. *Does the increased demand seen from China and India imply that the era of cheap energy is over? What impact could technology have in the long run on (a) demand; (b) supply?*

- There are only very few firms, all well known to each other.
- They are not secretive with each other about costs and production methods.
- They have similar production methods and average costs, and are thus likely to want to change prices at the same time and by the same percentage.
- They produce similar products and can thus more easily reach agreements on price.
- There is a dominant firm.
- There are significant barriers to entry and therefore little fear of disruption by new firms.
- The market is stable. If industry demand or production costs fluctuate wildly, it will be difficult to make agreements, partly due to difficulties in predicting and partly because agreements may frequently have to be amended. There is a particular problem in a declining market where firms may be tempted to undercut each other's prices in order to maintain their sales.
- There are no government measures to curb collusion.

 In which of the following industries is collusion likely to occur: bricks, beer, margarine, cement, crisps, washing powder, blank DVDs, carpets?

Non-collusive oligopoly: the breakdown of collusion

In some oligopolies, there may only be a few (if any) factors favouring collusion. In such cases, the likelihood of price competition is greater.

Even if there is collusion, there will always be the temptation for individual oligopolists to 'cheat', by cutting prices or by selling more than their allotted quota.

Let us take the case of a cartel consisting of five equal-sized firms. The whole cartel is illustrated in Figure 7.6(a).

Assume that the cartel sets the industry profit-maximising price of £10. This will give an industry output of 1000 units, which the cartel divides equally between its five members: i.e. each member is assigned a quota of 200 units.

Now consider Figure 7.6(b). This shows the position for one of the members of the cartel, firm A. Provided the cartel's price remains fixed at £10, then £10 would also be the marginal revenue for the individual firm. This will create an incentive for cartel members to cheat: to sell more than their allotted quota. Firm A would maximise its own profits by selling 600 units, where $MC = P (= MR)$, provided it could do this by taking market share off the other members, and thus leaving total industry output (and hence price) unaffected.

Alternatively, individual members might be tempted to undercut the cartel's price. Again, provided the rest of the cartel maintained its price at £10, firm A would face a relatively elastic demand curve (shown by *AR* in Figure 7.6(b)). A modest cut in its price would attract considerable custom away from the other members of the cartel. Firm A would maximise its profit by cutting its price to £8 and thereby increasing its sales to 400 units.

The danger, of course, with either selling above quota or cutting price is that this would invite retaliation from the other members of the cartel, with a resulting price war. Price would then fall and the cartel could well break up in disarray.

Non-collusive oligopoly: assumptions about rivals' behaviour

Even though oligopolists might not collude, they will still need to take account of rivals' likely behaviour when deciding their own strategy. In doing so, they will probably look at rivals' past behaviour and make assumptions based on it. There are three well-known models, each based on a different set of assumptions.

Figure 7.6   The incentive for a firm to produce more than its quota, or undercut the cartel's price

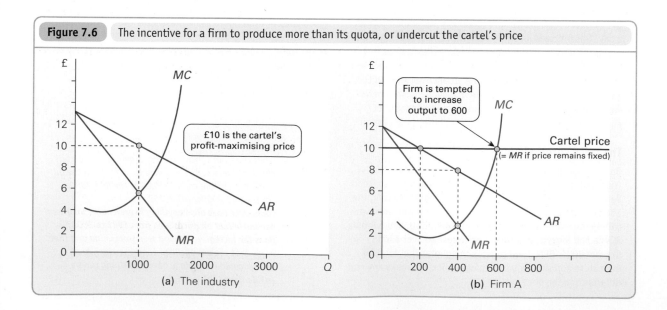

(a) The industry

(b) Firm A

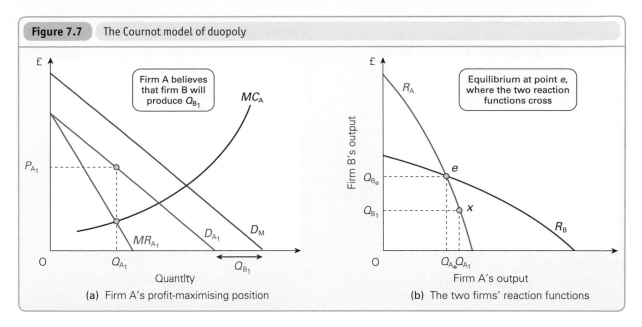

Figure 7.7   The Cournot model of duopoly

(a)   Firm A's profit-maximising position

(b)   The two firms' reaction functions

Assumption that rivals produce a given quantity: the Cournot model

One assumption is that rivals will produce a particular quantity. This is most likely when the market is stable and the rivals have been producing a relatively constant quantity for some time. The task, then, for the individual oligopolist is to decide its own price and quantity given the presumed output of its competitors.

The earliest model based on this assumption was developed by the French economist Augustin Cournot[1] in 1838. The *Cournot model* takes the simple case of just two firms (a *duopoly*) producing an identical product: for example, two electricity generating companies supplying the whole country.

This is illustrated in Figure 7.7(a), which shows the profit-maximising price and output for firm A. The total market demand curve is shown as D_M. Assume that firm A believes that its rival, firm B, will produce Q_{B_1} units. Thus firm A perceives its own demand curve (D_{A_1}) to be Q_{B_1} units less than total market demand. In other words, the horizontal gap between D_M and D_{A_1} is Q_{B_1} units. Given its perceived demand curve of D_{A_1}, its marginal revenue curve will be MR_{A_1} and the profit-maximising output will be Q_{A_1}, where $MR_{A_1} = MC_A$. The profit-maximising price will be P_{A_1}.

If firm A believed that firm B would produce *more* than Q_{B_1}, its perceived demand and *MR* curves would be further to the left and the profit-maximising quantity and price would both be lower.

Figure 7.7(b) illustrates the *reaction functions* of firm A and firm B. Each curve shows the amount of output the respective firm will produce in the light of how much it perceives the other firm will produce. Take the reaction curve for firm A. If it assumes that firm B will produce Q_{B_1}

(as in Figure 7.7(a)) it will choose to produce Q_{A_1}, at point x on its reaction curve.

We can now conduct a similar analysis for firm B, again using a diagram like Figure 7.7(a). If it assumes that firm A will produce a particular level of output, it will then decide its profit-maximising price and output in the light of this. Firm B's reaction curve in Figure 7.7(b) shows all the profit-maximising outputs for firm B for each output of firm A.

What will the market equilibrium be? This will be at point e in Figure 7.7(b). It is known as the **Cournot equilibrium**. Only at this point will neither firm choose to adjust its output. How will the equilibrium be reached if production is currently *not* at equilibrium?

Assume that production is at point x. Although firm A is on its reaction curve, firm B is not. Given production of Q_{A_1} by firm A, firm B will produce at a point on its reaction curve vertically above this (i.e. an output *greater* than Q_{B_1}). This will cause firm A to move up its reaction curve. The process will continue until point e is reached.

Profits in the Cournot model.   Industry profits will be *less* than under a monopoly or a cartel. The reason is that price will

TC 8
p 105

Definitions

Cournot model   A model of duopoly where each firm makes its price and output decisions on the assumption that its rival will produce a particular quantity.

Duopoly   An oligopoly where there are just two firms in the market.

Reaction function (or curve)   This shows how a firm's optimal output varies according to the output chosen by its rival (or rivals).

Cournot equilibrium   Where the outputs chosen by each firm are consistent with each other: where the two firms' reaction curves cross.

---

[1] See http://cepa.newschool.edu/het/profiles/cournot.htm for a profile of Cournot and his work.

be lower than the monopoly price. This can be seen from Figure 7.7(a). If this were a monopoly, then to find the profit-maximising output we would need to construct an *MR* curve corresponding to the market demand curve (D_M). This would intersect with the *MC* curve at a higher output than Q_{A_1} and a *higher* price (given by D_M).

Nevertheless, profits in the Cournot model will be higher than under perfect competition, since price is still above marginal cost.

Maths Case 7.2 in MyEconLab shows how the Cournot equilibrium can be derived algebraically from the market demand function and the cost functions of the two firms.

Assumption that rivals set a particular price: the Bertrand model

An alternative assumption is that rival firms set a particular price and stick to it. This scenario is more realistic when firms do not want to upset customers by frequent price changes or when they want to produce catalogues which specify prices. The task, then, for a given oligopolist is to choose its own price and quantity in the light of the prices set by rivals.

The most famous model based on this assumption was developed by another French economist, Joseph Bertrand, in 1883. Bertrand again took the simple case of a duopoly, but its conclusions apply equally to oligopolies with three or more firms.

The outcome is one of price cutting until all supernormal profits are competed away. The reason is simple. If firm A assumes that its rival, firm B, will hold price constant, then firm A should undercut this price by a small amount and as a result gain a large share of the market. At this point, firm B will be forced to respond by cutting its price. What we end up with is a price war until price is forced down to the level of average cost, with only normal profits remaining. This is discussed in more detail in section 7.3 below.

Nash equilibrium. The equilibrium outcome in either the Cournot or Bertrand models is not in the *joint* interests of the firms. In each case, total profits are less than under a monopoly or cartel. But, in the absence of collusion, the outcome is the result of each firm doing the best it can, given its assumptions about what its rivals are doing. The resulting equilibrium is known as a **Nash equilibrium**, after John Nash, a US mathematician (and subject of the film *A Beautiful Mind*) who introduced the concept in 1951.

In practice, when competition is intense, as in the Bertrand model, the firms may seek to collude long before profits have been reduced to a normal level. Alternatively, firms may put in a **takeover bid** for their rival(s).

The kinked demand curve assumption

In 1939 a theory of non-collusive oligopoly was developed simultaneously on both sides of the Atlantic: in the USA by

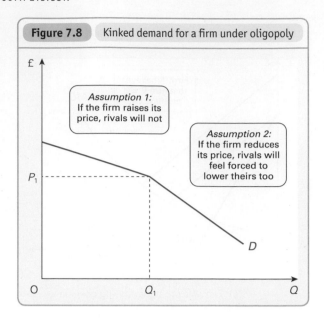

Figure 7.8 Kinked demand for a firm under oligopoly

Assumption 1: If the firm raises its price, rivals will not

Assumption 2: If the firm reduces its price, rivals will feel forced to lower theirs too

Paul Sweezy and in the UK by R. L. Hall and C. J. Hitch. This **kinked demand theory** has since become perhaps the most famous of all theories of oligopoly. The model seeks to explain how it is that, even when there is no collusion at all between oligopolists, prices can nevertheless remain stable.

The theory is based on two asymmetrical assumptions:

- If an oligopolist cuts its price, its rivals will feel forced to follow suit and cut theirs, to prevent losing customers to the first firm.
- If an oligopolist raises its price, however, its rivals will *not* follow suit since, by keeping their prices the same, they will thereby gain customers from the first firm.

On these assumptions, each oligopolist will face a demand curve that is *kinked* at the current price and output (see Figure 7.8). A rise in price will lead to a large fall in sales as customers switch to the now relatively lower-priced rivals. The firm will thus be reluctant to raise its price.

Definitions

Nash equilibrium The position resulting from everyone making their optimal decision based on their assumptions about their rivals' decisions. Without collusion, there is no incentive for any firm to move from this position.

Takeover bid Where one firm attempts to purchase another by offering to buy the shares of that company from its shareholders.

Kinked demand theory The theory that oligopolists face a demand curve that is kinked at the current price, demand being significantly more elastic above the current price than below. The effect of this is to create a situation of price stability.

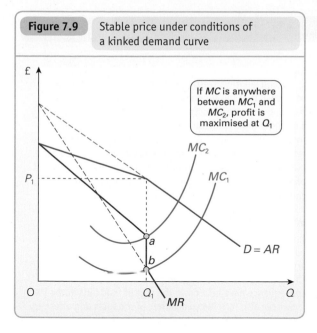

Figure 7.9 Stable price under conditions of a kinked demand curve

If *MC* is anywhere between MC_1 and MC_2, profit is maximised at Q_1

Demand is relatively elastic above the kink. On the other hand, a fall in price will bring only a modest increase in sales, since rivals lower their prices too and therefore customers do not switch. The firm will thus also be reluctant to lower its price. Demand is relatively inelastic below the kink. Thus oligopolists will be reluctant to change prices at all.

This price stability can be shown formally by drawing in the firm's marginal revenue curve, as in Figure 7.9.

To see how this is done, imagine dividing the diagram into two parts, one on either side of Q_1. At quantities less than Q_1 (the left-hand part of the diagram), the *MR* curve will correspond to the shallow part of the *AR* curve. At quantities greater than Q_1 (the right-hand part), the *MR* curve will correspond to the steep part of the *AR* curve. To see how this part of the *MR* curve is constructed, imagine extending the steep part of the *AR* curve back to the vertical axis. This and the corresponding *MR* curve are shown by the dashed lines in Figure 7.9.

As you can see, there will be a gap between points *a* and *b*. In other words, there is a vertical section of the *MR* curve between these two points.

Profits are maximised where *MC* = *MR*. Thus, if the *MC* curve lies anywhere between MC_1 and MC_2 (i.e. between points *a* and *b*), the profit-maximising price and output will be P_1 and Q_1. Thus prices will remain stable *even with a considerable change in costs*.

Despite its simple demonstration of the real-world phenomenon of price stability, the model does have two major limitations:

- Price stability may be due to *other* factors. Firms may not want to change prices too frequently as this involves modifying price lists, working out new revenue predictions and revaluing stocks of finished goods, and it may upset customers. Price stability, therefore, is not proof of the accuracy of the model.
- Although the model can help to explain price stability, it does not explain how prices are set in the first place. To do this, some other model would be required. This is a serious limitation in times of inflation, when oligopolists, like other firms, raise prices in response to higher costs and higher demand. What the model does predict, however, is that the price will be raised only after marginal cost has risen above MC_2 in Figure 7.9, and that once it has been raised, a new kink will form at that price. Price will then remain fixed at that level until higher costs once more force a further price rise.

Oligopoly and the public interest

If oligopolists act collusively and jointly maximise industry profits, they will in effect be acting together as a monopoly. In such cases, the disadvantages to society experienced under monopoly will also be experienced under oligopoly (see section 6.3).

Furthermore, in two respects, oligopoly may be more disadvantageous than monopoly:

- Depending on the size of the individual oligopolists, there may be less scope for economies of scale to mitigate the effects of market power.
- Oligopolists are likely to engage in much more extensive advertising than a monopolist (see Case Study 7.9 in MyEconLab).

These problems will be less, however, if oligopolists do not collude, if there is some degree of price competition and if barriers to entry are weak.

Also, the power of oligopolists in certain markets may to some extent be offset if they sell their product to other powerful firms. Thus oligopolistic producers of baked beans sell a large proportion of their output to giant supermarket chains, which can use their market power to keep down the price at which they purchase the beans. This phenomenon is known as ***countervailing power***.

 Which of the following are examples of effective countervailing power?
(a) Tour operators purchasing seats on charter flights.
(b) A large office hiring a photocopier from Xerox.
(c) Marks & Spencer buying clothes from a garment manufacturer.
(d) A small village store (but the only one for miles around) buying food from a wholesaler.

Definition

Countervailing power Where the power of a monopolistic/oligopolistic seller is offset by powerful buyers who can prevent the price from being pushed up.

BOX 7.4 **BUYING POWER**

The UK grocery sector

Over the past few years there has been increasing concern about the power of large supermarket chains in the UK. This has resulted in a number of Competition Commission investigations. Many of these have focused on anti-competitive practices such as rival chains agreeing not to set up in the same town and price collusion on some staple products. (For more on government competition policy, see Chapter 13, pages 385–7.)

However, more recently, focus has turned to the supermarkets' power not as sellers, but as buyers. If a wholesale manufacturer of ready-meals, or a supplier of sausages, wants to reach a wide customer base, it will need to deal with the four largest supermarket chains, which control over 75 per cent of the market. A market like this, where there are a few large purchasers of goods and services, is known as an *oligopsony*. (A single large buyer of goods, services or factors of production is known as a monopsony and we look at this in Chapter 9, page 256.)

Market power

Over the years a number of unfair practices by the supermarkets towards their suppliers have been identified. These include retrospectively changing contracts and forcing suppliers to fund special offers such as 'buy one, get one free'. Furthermore, there is evidence that firms are regularly asked for very substantial payments in order to be included on 'preferred supplier' lists.

After a lengthy investigation, the Competition Commission concluded that the supermarkets were passing on excessive risks and unexpected costs to their suppliers. As a consequence, a stronger Grocery Supplies Code of Practice was introduced in 2010. This recognised the power that large grocery retailers wield over their smaller suppliers and outlawed the practices detailed above. It also set in train the appointment of an independent adjudicator, allowing suppliers to bring confidential complaints against the supermarkets.

Who benefits?

It would be easy to conclude that the power of supermarkets, both as purchasers and as retailers, is so great that they are a 'bad thing'. However, that would be overly simplistic. There is evidence that they compete on price and that as a consequence have held down the cost of food bills in the UK. They have also introduced a variety of products and offer very convenient shopping for many people, particularly those who work full time. The grocery market is a good example of a sector where growth and market power can be identified as both beneficial and harmful to other economic agents.

1. *Explain why manufacturers of food products continue to supply supermarkets, despite concerns that they are not always treated fairly.*
2. *Is the supermarket sector an oligopoly or monopolistically competitive, in your opinion? Justify your answer.*

The power of oligopolists will also be reduced if the market in which they operate is contestable (see section 6.4). The lower the entry and exit costs for new firms, the more difficult it will be for oligopolists to collude and make supernormal profits.

 Which of the following markets do you think are contestable: (a) credit cards; (b) brewing; (c) petrol retailing; (d) insurance services; (e) compact discs?

In some respects, oligopoly may have *advantages* to society over other market structures:

- Oligopolists, like monopolists, can use part of their supernormal profit for research and development. Unlike monopolists, however, oligopolists will have a considerable *incentive* to do so. If the product design is improved, this may allow the firm to capture a larger share of the market, and it may be some time before rivals can respond with a similarly improved product. If, in addition, costs are lowered by technological improvement, the resulting higher profits will improve the firm's capacity to withstand any price war.

- Non-price competition through product differentiation may result in greater choice for the consumer. Take the case of stereo equipment. Non-price competition has led to a huge range of different products of many different specifications, each meeting the specific requirements of different consumers.

It is difficult, however, to draw any general conclusions, since oligopolies differ so much in their performance.

Definition

Oligopsony A goods market with just a few buyers (or employers in the case of labour markets).

Section summary

1. An oligopoly is where there are just a few firms in the industry with barriers to the entry of new firms. Firms recognise their mutual dependence.

2. Oligopolists will want to maximise their joint profits. This will tend to make them collude to keep prices high. On the other hand, they will want the biggest share of industry profits for themselves. This will tend to make them compete.

3. They are more likely to collude if there are few of them; if they are open with each other; if they have similar products and cost structures; if there is a dominant firm; if there are significant entry barriers; if the market is stable; and if there is no government legislation to prevent collusion.

4. Collusion can be open or tacit.

5. A formal collusive agreement is called a 'cartel'. A cartel aims to act as a monopoly. It can set prices and leave the members to compete for market share, or it can assign quotas. There is always a temptation for cartel members to 'cheat' by undercutting the cartel price if they think they can get away with it and not trigger a price war.

6. Tacit collusion can take the form of price leadership. This is where firms follow the price set by either a dominant firm in the industry or a firm seen as a reliable 'barometer' of market conditions. Alternatively, tacit collusion can simply involve following various rules of thumb such as average cost pricing and benchmark pricing.

7. Even when firms do not collude, they will still have to take into account their rivals' behaviour. In the Cournot model, firms assume that their rivals' output is given and then choose the profit-maximising price and output in the light of this assumption. The resulting price and profit are lower than under monopoly, but still higher than under perfect competition.

8. In the Bertrand model, firms assume that their rivals' price is given. This will result in prices being competed down until only normal profits remain.

9. In the kinked demand curve model, firms are likely to keep their prices stable unless there is a large shift in costs or demand.

10. Whether oligopoly behaviour is in the public interest depends on the particular oligopoly and how competitive it is; whether there is any countervailing power; whether the firms engage in extensive advertising and of what type; whether product differentiation results in a wide range of choice for the consumer; how much of the profits are ploughed back into research and development; and how contestable the market is. Since these conditions vary substantially from oligopoly to oligopoly, it is impossible to state just how well or how badly oligopoly in general serves the public interest.

7.3 GAME THEORY

As we have seen, the behaviour of a firm under non-collusive oligopoly will depend on how it thinks its rivals will react to its policies. When considering whether to cut prices in order to gain a larger market share, a firm will ask itself two key questions: first, how much it can get away with, without inciting retaliation; second, if its rivals do retaliate and a price war ensues, whether it will be able to 'see off' some or all of its rivals, while surviving itself.

It is not unreasonable to compare rival firms in an oligopoly with the players in a game or generals in a battle. They will need to choose the appropriate strategy with respect to price, advertising and product development. The firm's choice of strategy will depend both on how it thinks its rivals will react and on how willing it is to take risks.

Economists have developed *game theory* to look at this strategic approach in more depth. It examines the best strategy that each firm can adopt for each assumption about its rivals' behaviour.

Single-move games

The simplest type of 'game' is a single-move or single-period game. This involves just one 'move' by each firm involved. For example, if two or more firms are bidding for a contract which will be awarded to the lowest bidder, each firm will consider the likely bids that its rivals will make, when setting out their own. Once the bids are all made the contract will be awarded to the lowest bidder: the 'game' is over.

Simple dominant-strategy games

Many single-period games have predictable outcomes, no matter what assumptions each firm makes about its rivals' behaviour. Such games are known as *dominant-strategy games*.

Definitions

Game theory A mathematical method of decision making in which alternative strategies are analysed to determine the optimal course of action for the interested party, depending on assumptions about rivals' behaviour. Widely used in economics, game theory is also used as a tool in biology, psychology and politics.

Dominant-strategy game Where different assumptions about rivals' behaviour lead to the adoption of the same strategy.

TC 9
p121

KI 21
p198

Table 7.1	Profits for firms X and Y at different prices		
		X's price	
		£2	**£1.80**
Y's price	**£2**	A £10m each	B £5m for Y £12m for X
	£1.80	C £12m for Y £5m for X	D £8m each

The simplest case is where there are just two firms with identical costs, products and demand. They are both considering which of two alternative prices to charge. Table 7.1 shows typical profits they could each make.

Let us assume that at present both firms (X and Y) are charging a price of £2 and that they are each making a profit of £10 million, giving a total industry profit of £20 million. This is shown in cell A in Table 7.1.

Now assume they are both (independently) considering reducing their price to £1.80. First they must take into account what their rival might do, and how this will affect them. Let us consider X's position. In our simple example, we assume that there are just two things that its rival, firm Y, might do. Either Y could cut its price to £1.80, or it could leave its price at £2. What should X do?

To answer this question we need to take each of firm Y's two possible actions and look at firm X's best response to each. If we assume that firm Y chooses a price of £2, firm X could decide to keep its price at £2 giving it £10 million in profit. This is shown by cell A. Alternatively, firm X could cut its price to £1.80 and earn £12 million in profit, in cell B. Firm X's best response is therefore to cut price to £1.80, preferring a profit of £12 million to one of £10 million.

What about if we now assume that firm Y charges £1.80 – how should firm X best respond? If firm X charged £2, we would end up in cell C and firm X would earn only £5 million in profits. On the other hand, firm X could also cut its price to £1.80, moving us to cell D and it would earn £8 million in profits. By comparing these two profit outcomes, we can see that firm X's best response is to cut price to £1.80, preferring a profit of £8 million to a profit of £5 million. Note that firm Y will argue along similar lines, cutting price to £1.80 as well.

Therefore, no matter what price firm X assumes firm Y will charge, firm X's best response is always to charge £1.80, as this will yield the highest possible profits. As the decision for firm Y is identical to that of firm X, firm Y's best response will be the same: always charge £1.80. With both firms X and Y best responding to each other by charging £1.80 no matter what its rival does, the firms will end up in cell D. Both charge £1.80 and they each earn £8 million in profit.

TC 9
p121

This game is a dominant-strategy game, since the firm's best response is always to play the same (dominant) strategy (namely, cutting price to £1.80). Both firms do what is best for them, given their assumptions about their rivals' behaviour. The result is that the firms will end up in cell D, earning a lower profit (£8 million each) than if they had charged the higher price (£10 million each in cell A).

As we saw above, the equilibrium outcome of a game where there is no collusion between the players is known as a *Nash equilibrium*. The Nash equilibrium in this game is cell D.

But, given that both X and Y will be tempted to lower prices, they will both end up earning a lower profit (£8 million profit each in cell D) than if they had charged the higher price (£10 million profit each in cell A). Thus collusion, rather than a price war, would have benefited both, and yet both would be tempted to cheat and cut prices. This is known as the *prisoners' dilemma* (see Box 7.4).

More complex games

More complex 'games' can be devised with more than two firms, many alternative prices, differentiated products and various forms of non-price competition (e.g. advertising). Table 7.2 illustrates a more complex game.

It shows the profits that will result from three alternative strategies that firm X can pursue (e.g. price cut, advertising campaign, new model) and six possible responses from rivals (e.g. all rivals cutting price, some cutting price, all increasing advertising). It is assumed that firm X can calculate the effects on its profits of these various reactions.

Which strategy will X choose? It may go for the safe strategy. Here it will choose strategy 2. The worst outcome from strategy 2 (response c) will still give a profit of £20 million, whereas the worst outcome from strategy 3 (response b) is a profit of only £15 million, and the worst outcome from strategy 1 (response c) is a loss of £20 million.

Alternatively, firm X may go for a high-risk strategy: the one with highest maximum profit. Here it would choose strategy 1. This has a potential maximum profit of £100 million (response a), whereas the best outcome from strategy 3 is only £90 million (response a), and for strategy 2 only £60 million (response f).

Alternatively, it may go for a *compromise strategy* and choose strategy 3. The best outcome from strategy 3

Definitions

Prisoners' dilemma Where two or more firms (or people), by attempting independently to choose the best strategy, think about what their rivals are likely to do, and end up in a worse position than if they had co-operated in the first place.

Compromise strategy A strategy whose worst outcome is better than under a high-risk strategy and whose best outcome is better than under a low-risk strategy.

Table 7.2 Profit possibilities for firm X (£m)

		Other firms' responses					
		a	b	c	d	e	f
Strategies for firm X	1	100	60	−20	10	30	80
	2	40	50	20	30	25	60
	3	90	15	30	25	20	50

BOX 7.5 THE PRISONERS' DILEMMA

Game theory is not just relevant to economics. A famous non-economic example is the prisoners' dilemma.

Nigel and Amanda have been arrested for a joint crime of serious fraud. Each is interviewed separately and given the following alternatives:

- First, if they say nothing, the court has enough evidence to sentence both to a year's imprisonment.
- Second, if either Nigel or Amanda *alone* confesses, he or she is likely to get only a three-month sentence but the partner could get up to 10 years.
- Third, if both confess, they are likely to get three years each.
- What should Nigel and Amanda do?

		Amanda's alternatives	
		Not confess	Confess
Nigel's alternatives	Not confess	**A** Each gets 1 year	**C** Nigel gets 10 years / Amanda gets 3 months
	Confess	**B** Nigel gets 3 months / Amanda gets 10 years	**D** Each gets 3 years

Let us consider Nigel's dilemma. Should he confess in order to get the short sentence? This is better than the year he would get for not confessing. There is, however, an even better reason for confessing. Suppose Nigel doesn't confess but, unknown to him, Amanda does confess. Then Nigel ends up with the long sentence. Better than this is to confess and to get no more than three years. Nigel's best response is always to confess.

Amanda is in exactly the same dilemma, so the result is simple. When both prisoners act in their own self-interest by confessing, they both end up with relatively long prison terms. Only when they collude will they end up with relatively short prison terms, the best combined solution.

Of course, the police know this and will do their best to prevent any collusion. They will keep Nigel and Amanda in separate prison cells and try to persuade each of them that the other is bound to confess.

Thus the choice of strategy depends on:

- Nigel's and Amanda's risk attitudes – are they 'risk-lovers' or 'risk averse'?
- Nigel's and Amanda's estimates of how likely the other is to own up.

1. Why is this a dominant-strategy 'game'?
2. How would Nigel's choice of strategy be affected if he had instead been involved in a joint crime with Bilal, Kate, Anna and Dave, and they had all been caught?

The prisoners' dilemma is a good illustration of *the fallacy of composition* (see Box 3.7, page 88). What applies at the level of the individual does not apply to the group as a whole. It might be in the individual's interests to confess. It is clearly not in the interests of both, however, for both to confess.

Let us now look at two real-world examples of the prisoners' dilemma.

Standing at football

When people go to some public event, such as a football match, they often stand in order to get a better view. But once people start standing, everyone is likely to do so: after all, if they stayed sitting, they would not see at all. If everyone stands, no one has an incentive to sit down, since they would then see nothing. In this Nash equilibrium, most people are worse off, since, except for tall people, their view is likely to be worse and they lose the comfort of sitting down.

Too much advertising

Why do firms spend so much on advertising? If they are aggressive, they do so to get ahead of their rivals. If they are cautious, they do so in case their rivals increase their advertising. Although in both cases it may be in the individual firm's best interests to increase advertising, the resulting Nash equilibrium is likely to be one of excessive advertising: the total spent on advertising (by all firms) is not recouped in additional sales.

1. Give some other non-economic examples of the prisoners' dilemma.
2. Can collusion by firms overcome the prisoners' dilemma?

(response a) is only slightly lower than strategy 1 (response a) – £90 million compared with £100 million. The worst outcome (response b) is only slightly lower than strategy 2 (response c) – £15 million compared with £20 million.

It is also likely to weigh up the *likelihood* of each outcome occurring. For example, in Table 7.2, firm X is much more likely to adopt the high-risk solution if the chances of response a occurring are very high and the chances of outcome c occurring are very low.

Multiple-move games

In many situations firms will *react* to what their rivals do; their rivals, in turn, will react to what they do. In other words, the game moves back and forth from one 'player' to the other like a game of chess or cards. Firms will still have to think strategically (as you do in chess), considering the likely responses of their rivals to their own actions. These multiple-move games are known as *repeated* or *sequential games*.

One of the simplest repeated games is the *tit-for-tat*. This is where a firm will *only* cut prices, or make some other aggressive move, if the rival does so first. To illustrate this in a multiple-move situation let us look again at the example we considered in Table 7.1, but this time we will extend it beyond one time period.

Assume that firm X is adopting the tit-for-tat strategy. If firm Y cuts its price from £2.00 to £1.80, then firm X will respond in round 2 by also cutting its price. The two firms will end up in cell D – worse off than if neither had cut their price. If, however, firm Y had left its price at £2.00 then firm X would respond by leaving its price unchanged too. Both firms would remain in cell A with a higher profit than in cell D.

As long as firm Y knows that firm X will respond in this way, it has an incentive not to cut its price. Thus it is in X's interests to make sure that Y clearly 'understands' how X will react to any price cut. In other words, X will make a threat.

The importance of threats and promises

In many situations, an oligopolist will make a threat or promise that it will act in a certain way. As long as the threat or promise is *credible* (i.e. its competitors believe it), the firm can gain and it will influence its rivals' behaviour.

Take the simple situation where a large oil company, such as Esso, states that it will match the price charged by any competitor within a given radius. Assume that competitors believe this 'price promise' but also that Esso will not try to *undercut* their price. In the simple situation where there is only one other filling station in the area, what price should it charge? Clearly it should charge the price that would maximise its profits, assuming that Esso will charge the *same* price. In the absence of other filling stations in the area, this is likely to be a relatively high price.

Now assume that there are several filling stations in the area. What should the company do now? Its best bet

is probably to charge the same price as Esso and hope that no other company charges a lower price and forces Esso to cut its price. Assuming that Esso's threat is credible, other companies are likely to reason in a similar way.

Assume that there are two major oil companies operating filling stations in an area. The first promises to match the other's prices. The other promises always to sell at 1p per litre cheaper than the first. Describe the likely sequence of events in this 'game' and the likely eventual outcome. Could the promise of the second company be seen as credible?

The importance of timing

Most decisions by oligopolists are made by one firm at a time rather than simultaneously by all firms. Sometimes a firm will take the initiative. At other times it will respond to decisions taken by other firms.

Take the case of a new generation of large passenger aircraft that can fly further without refuelling. Assume that there is a market for a 500-seater version of this type of aircraft and a 400-seater version, but that the market for each size of aircraft is not big enough for the two manufacturers, Boeing and Airbus, to share it profitably. Let us also assume that the 400-seater market would give an annual profit of £50 million to a single manufacturer and the 500-seater would give an annual profit of £30 million, but that if both manufacturers produced the same version, they would each make an annual loss of £10 million.

Assume that Boeing announces that it is building the 400-seater plane. What should Airbus do? The choice is illustrated in Figure 7.10. This diagram is called a **decision tree** and shows the sequence of events. The small square at the left of the diagram is Boeing's decision point (point A). If it decided to build the 500-seater plane, we would move up the top branch. Airbus would now have to make a decision (point B_1). If it too built the 500-seater plane, we would move to outcome 1: a loss of £10 million for both manufacturers. Clearly, with Boeing building a 500-seater plane, Airbus would choose the 400-seater plane: we would move to outcome 2, with Boeing making a profit of £30 million and Airbus a profit of £50 million. Airbus would be very pleased!

Boeing's best strategy at point A, however, would be to build the 400-seater plane. We would then move to

---

Definitions

Credible threat (or promise) One that is believable to rivals because it is in the threatener's interests to carry it out.

Decision tree (or game tree) A diagram showing the sequence of possible decisions by competitor firms and the outcome of each combination of decisions.

Figure 7.10   A decision tree

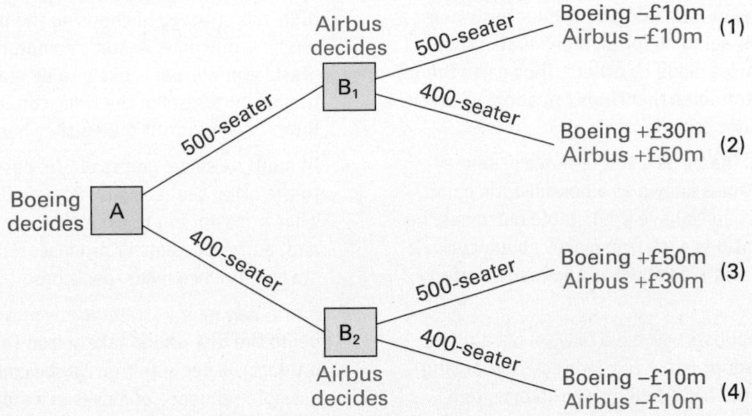

Airbus decides

Boeing decides   A

B₁   Airbus decides

500-seater

400-seater

500-seater
Boeing −£10m
Airbus −£10m   (1)

400-seater
Boeing +£30m
Airbus +£50m   (2)

B₂   Airbus decides

500-seater
Boeing +£50m
Airbus +£30m   (3)

400-seater
Boeing −£10m
Airbus −£10m   (4)

Airbus's decision point B_2. In this case, it is in Airbus's interests to build the 500-seater plane. Its profit would be only £30 million (outcome 3), but this is better than a £10 million loss if it too built the 400-seater plane (outcome 4). With Boeing deciding first, the Nash equilibrium will thus be outcome 3.

There is clearly a **_first-mover advantage_** here. Once Boeing has decided to build the more profitable version of the plane, Airbus is forced to build the less profitable one. Naturally, Airbus would like to build the more profitable one and be the first mover. Which company succeeds in going first depends on how advanced they are in their research and development and in their production capacity.

More complex decision trees

The aircraft example is the simplest version of a decision tree, with just two companies and each one making only one key decision. In many business situations, much more complex trees could be constructed. The 'game' would be more like one of chess, with many moves and several options on each move. If there were more than two companies, the decision tree would be more complex still.

 Give an example of decisions, other than those about pricing, which two firms could make in sequence, each one affecting the other's next decision.

Definition

First-mover advantage When a firm gains from being the first one to take action.

Assessing the theory of games

The advantage of the game theory approach is that the firm does not need to know which response its rivals will make. However, it must be able to measure the effect of each possible response. This will be virtually impossible to do with many firms competing and many different possible responses. The approach is useful, therefore, only in relatively simple cases, and even here the estimates of profit from each outcome may amount to no more than a rough guess.

It is thus difficult for an economist to predict with any accuracy what price, output and level of advertising the firm will choose. This problem is compounded by the difficulty in predicting the type of strategy – safe, high-risk, compromise – that the firm will adopt.

In some cases, firms may compete hard for a time (in price or non-price terms) and then realise that maybe no one is winning. Firms may then start to collude and jointly raise prices and reduce advertising. Later, after a period of tacit collusion, competition may break out again. This may be sparked off by the entry of a new firm, by the development of a new product design, by a change in market demand, or simply by one or more firms no longer being able to resist the temptation to 'cheat'. In short, the behaviour of particular oligopolists may change quite radically over time.

Finally, we have been assuming that people behave selfishly. In reality, people's actions are likely to be influenced by their moral values. Businesspeople may be unwilling to behave ruthlessly or dishonestly, or to undertake profitable activities that they regard as unfair. In Chapter 8 we examine some of the consequences of pursuing goals other than ruthless profit maximisation.

Section summary

1. Game theory is a way of modelling behaviour in strategic situations where the outcome for an individual or firm depends on the choices made by others. Thus game theory examines various strategies that firms can adopt when the outcome of each is not certain.

2. The simplest type of 'game' is a single-move or single-period game, sometimes known as a normal-form game. Many single-period games have predictable outcomes, no matter what assumptions each firm makes about its rivals' behaviour. Such games are known as dominant-strategy games.

3. Non-collusive oligopolists will have to work out a price strategy. They can adopt a low-risk strategy of choosing the policy that has the least-bad worst outcome, or a high-risk strategy of choosing the policy with the best possible outcome, or some compromise. Either way, a 'Nash' equilibrium is likely to be reached which is not in the best interests of the firms collectively. It will entail a lower level of profit than if they had colluded.

4. In multiple-move games play is passed from one 'player' to the other sequentially. Firms will respond not only to what firms do, but to what they say they will do. To this end, a firm's threats or promises must be credible if they are to influence rivals' decisions.

5. A firm may gain a strategic advantage over its rivals by being the first one to take action (e.g. launch a new product). A decision tree can be constructed to show the possible sequence of moves in a multiple-move game.

7.4 PRICE DISCRIMINATION

Up to now we have assumed that a firm will sell its output at a single price. Sometimes, however, firms may practise *price discrimination*. This is where a firm sells the same product to different consumers at different prices *even though production costs are the same*. There are three major varieties of price discrimination:

- *First-degree price discrimination* is where the firm charges each consumer the maximum price he or she is prepared to pay for each unit. For example, stallholders in a street market will attempt to do this when bartering with their customers.

- *Second-degree price discrimination* is where the firm charges customers different prices according to how much they purchase. It may charge a high price for the first so many units, a lower price for the next so many units, a lower price again for the next, and so on. For example, electricity companies in some countries charge a high price for the first so many kilowatts. This is the amount of electricity that would typically be used for lighting and running appliances: in other words, the uses for which there is no substitute fuel. Additional kilowatts are charged at a much lower rate. This is electricity that is typically used for heating and cooking, where there are alternative fuels.

- *Third-degree price discrimination* is where consumers are grouped into two or more independent markets and a separate price is charged in each market. Examples include different bus fares for adults and children, and different prices charged by a firm for the same product in different countries. Third-degree price discrimination is much more common than first- or second-degree discrimination.

Conditions necessary for price discrimination to operate

As we shall see, a firm will be able to increase its profits if it can engage in price discrimination. But under what circumstances will it be able to charge discriminatory prices? There are three conditions that must be met:

- The firm must be able to set its price. Thus price discrimination will be impossible under perfect competition, where firms are price takers. In other words, firms practising price discrimination must have some monopoly power.

- The markets must be separable. Consumers in the low-priced market must not be able to resell the product in the high-priced market. For example, children must not be able to resell a half-priced child's cinema ticket for use by an adult.

Definitions

Price discrimination Where a firm sells the same product at different prices.

First-degree price discrimination Where a firm charges each consumer for each unit the maximum price which that consumer is willing to pay for that unit.

Second-degree price discrimination Where a firm charges a consumer so much for the first so many units purchased, a different price for the next so many units purchased, and so on.

Third-degree price discrimination Where a firm divides consumers into different groups and charges a different price to consumers in different groups, but the same price to all the consumers within a group.

BOX 7.6 **WHAT'S THE TRAIN FARE TO LONDON?**

Price discrimination on the trains

Ask the question 'What's the fare to London?' at ticket enquiries, and you may receive any of the following replies:

- Do you want first or standard class?
- Do you want single or return?
- How old are you?
- Do you have a railcard (family & friends, 16–25, disabled adult or child, senior, two together)?
- Will you be travelling on a weekday?
- Will you be travelling out before 9.30 a.m.?
- Will you be leaving London between 4 p.m. and 6.30 p.m.?
- Are you able to book your ticket in advance?

- Do you need to be flexible about the time and date of your journeys, or are you willing to pre-commit to a specific train?

1. *Look at each of the above questions. In each case, decide whether price discrimination is being practised. If it is, is it sensible for train operators to practise it? How are the train operators able to identify travellers with different price elasticities of demand?*
2. *Are these various forms of price discrimination in the traveller's interest?*

You can check out the range of ticket types and prices by going to the National Rail website at www.nationalrail.co.uk and selecting a journey.

BOX 7.7 **PEAK-LOAD PRICING**

Charging more when it costs more to produce

A common form of price discrimination is *peak-load pricing*. This is where people are charged more at times of peak demand and less at off-peak times. Take the case of a holiday. If you look through the brochures or online, you will see that high-season prices are often considerably higher than low-season prices. Similarly, call charges for telephones are often much higher during weekdays than in the evenings and weekends. Other examples of peak-load (or 'peak-period') pricing are rail and airfares, prices in cinemas and restaurants (higher in the evenings) and charges made by health and sports clubs (higher at weekends and in the evenings).

The reason for the higher prices charged at peak times has partly to do with elasticity of demand. Demand is less elastic at peak times. For example, many commuters have little option but to pay higher rail fares at peak times. This is genuine price discrimination.

But often the higher charges also have to do with higher marginal costs incurred at peak times and, as such, are not true price discrimination. With various fixed factors (such as plant and equipment), marginal costs are likely to rise as output expands to meet higher demand. This could be due to diminishing returns to the variable factors; or it could be due to having to use additional equipment with higher operating costs.

Take the case of electricity. At off-peak times, the power stations with the lowest operating costs will be used. These are normally the wind, nuclear and coal-fired stations. At periods of peak demand, however, stations with higher operating costs, such as oil-fired and gas-fired stations, will have to be brought on line. (Both oil- and gas-fired stations are relatively cheap to build, but have higher running costs, largely because of the more expensive fuel.) As a result, the marginal cost of generating electricity is higher at peak times than at off-peak times.

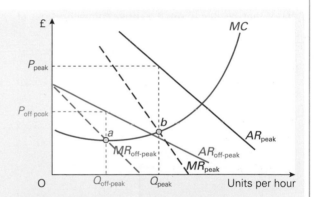

But what are the profit-maximising peak and off-peak prices? These are illustrated in the diagram, which shows units per hour (e.g. of electricity). There are two demand (*AR*) curves – peak and off-peak – and their corresponding marginal revenue (*MR*) curves. Profit is maximised in either period at the output where $MR = MC$ (points *a* and *b* respectively). In the peak period, this will be at the higher price P_{peak}. There are two reasons why the price is higher. First, demand is less elastic. This is demonstrated by the fact that price is a higher percentage above *MR* in the peak period than in the off-peak period. Second, marginal cost is higher in the peak period.

1. *How likely is it that domestic customers will be able to switch consumption of electricity to off-peak periods? How likely is it that businesses will be able to do so?*
2. *If, over time, consumers are encouraged to switch their consumption to off-peak periods, what will happen to peak and off-peak prices?*
3. *To what extent is peak-load pricing in the interests of consumers?*
4. *Is total consumption likely to be higher or lower with a system of peak and off-peak prices as opposed to a uniform price at all times?*

- Demand elasticity must differ in each market. The firm will charge the higher price in the market where demand is less elastic, and thus less sensitive to a price rise.

Advantages to the firm

Price discrimination allows the firm to earn a higher revenue from any given level of sales. Let us examine the case of third-degree price discrimination.

Figure 7.11 represents a firm's demand curve. If the firm is to sell 200 units without price discrimination, it must charge a price of P_1. The total revenue it earns is shown by the green area. If, however, it can practise third-degree price discrimination by selling 150 of those 200 units at the higher price of P_2, it will gain the pink area in addition to the green area in Figure 7.11.

Explain why, if the firm can practise first-degree price discrimination by selling every unit at the maximum price each consumer is prepared to pay, its revenue from selling 200 units will be the green area plus the pink area in Figure 7.12.

Another advantage to the firm of price discrimination is that it may be able to use it to drive competitors out of

business. If a firm has a monopoly in one market (e.g. the home market), it may be able to charge a high price due to relatively inelastic demand, and thus make high profits. If it is under oligopoly in another market (e.g. the export market), it may use the high profits in the first market to subsidise a very low price in the oligopolistic market, thus forcing its competitors out of business.

Profit-maximising prices and output

Assuming that the firm wishes to maximise profits, what discriminatory prices should it charge and how much should it produce? Let us first consider the case of first-degree price discrimination.

First-degree price discrimination

Since an increase in sales does not involve lowering the price for any unit save the *extra* one sold, the extra revenue gained from the last unit (MR) will be its price. Thus profit is maximised at Q_1 in Figure 7.13, where $MC = MR$ ($= P$ of the *last* unit).

Third-degree price discrimination

Assume that a firm sells an identical product in two separate markets X and Y with demand and MR curves as shown in Figure 7.14.

Diagram (c) shows the MC and MR curves for the firm as a whole. This MR curve is found by adding the amounts sold in the two markets at each level of MR (in other words, the horizontal addition of the two MR curves). Thus, for example, with output of 1000 units in market X and 2000 in market Y, making 3000 in total, revenue would increase by £5 if one extra unit were sold, whether in market X or Y.

Total profit is maximised where $MC = MR$: i.e. at an output of 3000 units in total. This output must then be divided between the two markets so that MC is equal to MR in each market: i.e. $MC = MR = £5$ in each market. MR must be the same in both markets, otherwise revenue could be increased by switching output to the market with the higher MR.

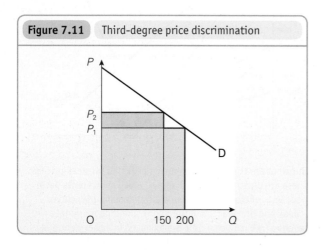

Figure 7.11 Third-degree price discrimination

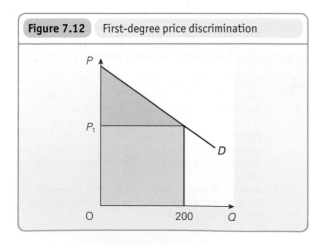

Figure 7.12 First-degree price discrimination

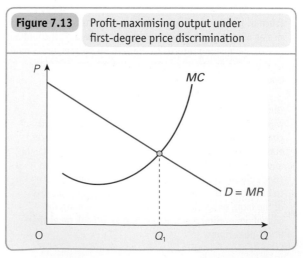

Figure 7.13 Profit-maximising output under first-degree price discrimination

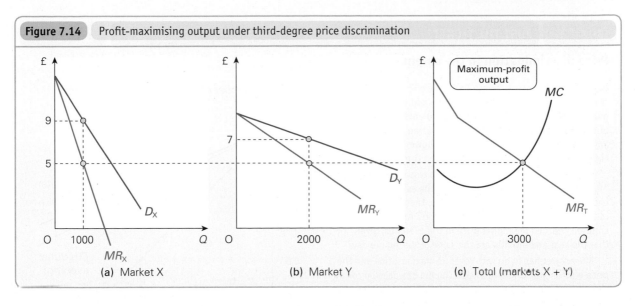

Figure 7.14 Profit-maximising output under third-degree price discrimination

(a) Market X (b) Market Y (c) Total (markets X + Y)

The profit-maximising price in each market is given by the relevant demand curve. Thus, in market X, 1000 units will be sold at £9 each, and in market Y, 2000 units will be sold at £7 each. Note that the higher price is charged in the market with the less elastic demand curve.

TC 7
p72

>
>
> *How would profit-maximising output and price be determined under third-degree price discrimination if there were three separate markets? Draw a diagram to illustrate your answer.*

*LOOKING AT THE MATHS

We can use calculus to work out the profit-maximising prices and outputs in each of the two markets X and Y in Figure 7.14. If we know the demand functions in each of the two markets, X and Y, we can derive the total revenue functions in each market (TR_X and TR_Y) and hence in the two markets together ($TR = TR_X + TR_Y$). Total profit is given by

$$T\Pi = TR_X + TR_Y - TC$$

To find the maximum-profit output in each market, we (partially) differentiate the total profit equation with respect to output in each of X and Y and set each equal to zero and solve for Q_X and Q_Y (see page A:11 for how calculus is used to find a maximum value). We can then substitute these values of Q_X and Q_Y in the respective demand functions to work out P_X and P_Y.

Maths Case 7.3 in MyEconLab shows how this is done by using a worked example.

Price discrimination and the public interest

It is tempting to think that anything that increases firms' profits must be at the expense of consumers' welfare. However, this is not necessarily the case and no clear-cut decision can be made over the social desirability of price discrimination. Some people benefit from it; others lose. This can be illustrated by considering the effects of price discrimination on the following aspects of the market.

TC 3
p26

Distribution

Those paying the higher price will certainly have a lower consumer surplus and may well feel that price discrimination is unfair to them. On the other hand, those charged the lower price will have a greater consumer surplus than they would have had otherwise. They will consume more of the good and in some cases they may be able to obtain a good or service they could not otherwise afford, as with, for example, concessionary rail fares for pensioners. Price discrimination is likely to increase output and make the good or service available to more people.

KI 4
p13

Competition

As explained above, a firm may use price discrimination to drive competitors out of business. This is known as **predatory pricing**. For example, in many towns, large bus companies have used profits they make in *other* towns where they have a monopoly to subsidise their bus fares and thereby drive competitors out of business, only then to raise prices above those that the competitors had been charging. On the other hand, a firm might use the profits from its high-priced market to break into another market and withstand a possible price war. Competition is thereby increased.

Profits

Price discrimination raises a firm's profits. This could be seen as an undesirable redistribution of income in society, especially if the average price of the product is raised. On the other hand, the higher profits may be reinvested and lead to innovation or lower costs in the future.

Definition

Predatory pricing Where a firm sets its prices below average cost in order to drive competitors out of business.

| BOX 7.8 | JUST THE TICKET? | CASE STUDIES AND APPLICATIONS |

Price discrimination in the cinema

One of the commonest forms of price discrimination is where children are charged a lower price than adults, whether on public transport or for public entertainment. Take the case of cinema tickets. In most cinemas, children pay less than adults during the day. In the evening, however, many cinemas charge both adults and children the same price.

But why do cinemas charge children less during the day? After all, the child is seeing the same film as the adult and occupying a whole seat. In other words, there is no difference in the 'product' that they are 'consuming'. And why are children charged the higher price in the evenings, given that the seat and the film are the same as during the day?

The answer has to do with revenue maximisation and the price elasticity of demand. Once a cinema has decided to show a film, the marginal costs of an additional customer are zero. There are no additional staffing, film-hire, electricity or other costs. With marginal costs equal to zero, profits will be maximised where marginal revenue is also equal to zero: in other words, where total revenue is maximised.

Take the case of a cinema with 500 seats. This is illustrated in the diagrams, which show the demand and marginal revenue curves for both adults and children. It is assumed that the elasticity of demand for children's tickets is greater than that for adults' tickets. Diagram (a) shows demand during the late afternoon (i.e. after school). Here the demand by children is relatively high compared with adults, but the overall demand is low. Diagram (b) shows demand during the evening. Here there is a higher overall level of demand, especially by adults, many of whom work during the day.

For the afternoon screening (diagram (a)), revenue is maximised from children by charging them a price of £4.00:

(a) Number of tickets (afternoon)

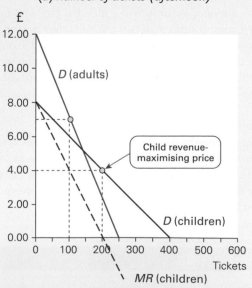

(b) *Number of tickets (evening and total)*

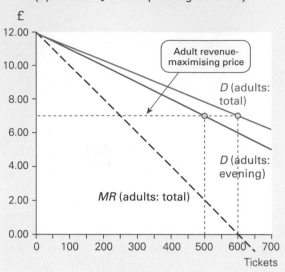

i.e. at the point on the demand curve where $MR = 0$. At this price, 200 child tickets will be sold.

Assuming that the same adult price is charged in both the afternoon and the evening, we need to look at the *total* demand for full-priced tickets (i.e. for both afternoon and evening screenings) in order to ascertain the revenue-maximising price. This will be a price of £7.00, where total adult $MR = 0$ (see diagram (b)). This will lead to 100 adult tickets being sold in the afternoon and 500 in the evening.

But why are reduced-price tickets not available for children in the evening? In diagram (b), the sale of low-priced tickets for children would lead to demand exceeding the 500-seat capacity of the cinema. Each time an adult was turned away because the seat had already been sold to a child, the cinema would lose.

1. *Which type of price discrimination is the cinema pursuing: first, second or third degree? Could it pursue either of the other two types?*
2. *If all cinema seats could be sold to adults in the evenings at the end of the week, but only a few on Mondays and Tuesdays, what price discrimination policy would you recommend to the cinema in order for it to maximise its weekly revenue?*
3. *Would the cinema make more profit if it could charge adults a different price in the afternoon and the evenings?*
4. *Would you advise that the cinema extend its practice of price discrimination to include other groups? If so, which groups should be targeted?*
5. *Are there any other advantages, beyond the additional revenues generated, to having more people in the cinema? Are there any disadvantages?*

Section summary

1. Price discrimination is where a firm sells the same product at different prices even though costs are the same. It can be first-degree, second-degree or third-degree price discrimination.

2. Price discrimination allows the firm to earn a higher revenue from a given level of sales.

3. Under first-degree price discrimination, the profit-maximising output is where $MC = P$. Under third-degree price discrimination, profit-maximising output is where the firm's MC is equal to the overall MR (found by adding horizontally the MR curves in each of the separate markets). This is then divided between the markets by selling that amount in each market where $MC = MR$, at a price given by the demand curve in each market.

4. Some people will gain from price discrimination; others will lose.

END OF CHAPTER QUESTIONS

1. Assume that firm X is considering four possible strategies: 1, 2, 3 and 4. Assume that firm X estimates that there are five possible responses (a, b, c, d and e) that its rivals might make to its actions. It estimates the effects on its profits in the case of each of these five responses to each of its four strategies. Its estimates are given in the following table.

Profit possibilities for firm X (£m)

		Rivals' responses				
		a	b	c	d	e
	1	30	20	80	−10	100
Alternative strategies	2	−5	105	40	100	30
for firm X	3	90	0	50	45	60
	4	30	15	10	20	25

(a) Which of the strategies (1, 2, 3 or 4) should it adopt if it is hoping to make the maximum possible profit and willing to take a gamble?

(b) Which of the strategies should it adopt if it is very cautious and decides to assume that the worst will happen?

(c) Which of the strategies might be the best compromise between these two extreme positions? Explain.

2. Assume that a monopolistically competitive industry is in long-run equilibrium. On a diagram like Figure 7.1(b), show the effect of a fall in demand on a firm's price and profit in (a) the short run and (b) the long run.

3. In what ways is a monopolistically competitive firm likely to be less efficient than one under perfect competition?

4. Are there any shops in your area that stay open later than others? If so, does this affect the prices they charge? Why do you think this is?

5. Give three examples of oligopolistic industries. In what ways do the firms in each of these industries compete? Why do they choose to compete in the way that they do?

6. Why, under oligopoly, might a particular industry be collusive at one time and yet highly price competitive at another?

7. What is meant by the *prisoners' dilemma game* when applied to the behaviour of oligopolists? What will determine the outcome of the game?

8. Think of two examples of price discrimination. In what ways do the consumers gain or lose? What information would you need to be certain in your answer?

Online resources

Additional case studies in MyEconLab

7.1 **Edward Chamberlin and Joan Robinson.** A portrait of the two economists who developed the model of monopolistic competition.

7.2 **The motor vehicle repair and servicing industry.** A case study of monopolistic competition.

7.3 **The corner shop and the superstore.** A case study in non-price competition: how the corner shop can survive competition from the big supermarkets.

7.4 **Curry wars.** Monopolistic competition in the take-away food market.

7.5 **Bakeries: oligopoly or monopolistic competition.** A case study on the bread industry, showing that small-scale local bakeries can exist alongside giant national bakeries.

7.6 **Is beer becoming more concentrated?** A study of oligopoly in the brewing industry. There have been mergers between large brewers, but a rise in small breweries.

7.7 **'Rip-off Britain'.** This examines the evidence for oligopolistic collusion in the car, supermarket and banking industries.

7.8 **Fair wars in the skies?** The effect of the entry of low-cost airlines on airfares.

7.9 **A product's life cycle.** How market conditions vary at different stages in a product's life.

7.10 **Advertising and the public interest.** Does the consumer benefit from advertising?

Maths Case 7.1 Calculating the profit-maximising price of a price leader. Using equations for demand, revenue and cost curves.

Maths Case 7.2 Deriving the Cournot equilibrium. An algebraic example.

Maths Case 7.3 Calculating the profit-maximising prices under third-degree price discrimination. Using calculus to find the profit-maximising output and price in each market and to compare the profit with and without price discrimination.

Websites relevant to Chapters 6 and 7

Numbers and sections refer to websites listed in the Web Appendix and hotlinked from this book's website at **www.pearsoned.co.uk/sloman**.

- For news articles relevant to this and the previous chapter, see the *Economic News* section in MyEconLab.
- For general news on companies and markets, see websites in section A, and particularly A2, 3, 4, 5, 8, 9, 18, 24, 25, 26, 36. See also A38, 39, 42, 43 and 44 for links to newspapers worldwide; and A40 and 41 for links to economics news articles from newspapers worldwide.
- For sites that look at competition and market power, see B2 (third link); E4, 10, 18; G7, 8. See also links in I7, 11, 14 and 17.
- For information on OPEC (Box 7.3), see site H6.
- For sites with resources on game theory, see C23; I11; D4; C20.
- For a site that contains a number of open-access computer-based games on oligopoly and game theory that can be played between students, see sites D13–19.
- For a simulation of running a farm (under perfect competition), see site D3.
- For a simulation on third-degree price discrimination, see again site D3.

MyEconLab

This book can be supported by MyEconLab, which contains a range of additional resources, including an online homework and tutorial system designed to test and build your understanding.

You need both an access card and a course ID to access MyEconLab:

1. Is your lecturer using MyEconLab? Ask your lecturer for your course ID.

2. Has an access card been included with the book at a reduced cost? Check the inside back cover of the book.

3. If you have a course ID but no access card, go to: http://www.myeconlab.com/ to buy access to this interactive study programme.

Alternative Theories of the Firm

CHAPTER MAP

8.1 Problems with traditional theory 222
Difficulties in maximising profit 222
Alternative aims 222

8.2 Behavioural theories 224
Are firms rational? 224
Revenge is sweet 224
Asymmetric information and the principal–agent
    problem 224
Survival and attitudes towards risk 225
Can firms make use of behavioural economics? 226

8.3 Alternative maximising theories 228
Long-run profit maximisation 228
Managerial utility maximisation 228
Sales revenue maximisation (short run) 229
Growth maximisation 230
Growth by internal expansion 231
Growth by merger 231
Growth through strategic alliances 233
Growth through going global 234
Equilibrium for a growth-maximising firm 235
Alternative maximising theories and the public
    interest 235

8.4 Multiple aims 238
Satisficing and the setting of targets 238
Organisational slack 239
Multiple goals: predictions of behaviour 239
Satisficing and the public interest 239

8.5 Pricing in practice 240
Cost-based pricing 240

The traditional theories of the firm that we have been looking at in the previous three chapters assume that firms aim to maximise profits. Although this is an accurate assumption for many firms, for many it is not.

Some firms would *like* to maximise profits, but have insufficient information to enable them to do so. Others do not even want to maximise profits if that means sacrificing achieving some other aim, such as rapid growth or increased market share.

In this chapter, we focus on the behaviour of decision makers in firms. We look at various aims they might pursue as an alternative to maximum profits: aims such as maximum sales revenue or maximum growth. We also examine the implications of pursuing alternative aims for the profitability of the firm and for the prices paid by the consumer.

Many firms, especially larger ones, are complex organisations, with different individuals and departments pursuing their own agenda. What happens when these various goals come into conflict? How does conflict get resolved? What are the implications for consumers and other 'stakeholders'? We examine these issues in section 8.4.

Finally we ask how prices are determined in practice. If firms do not use marginal revenue and marginal cost concepts in setting their prices, or if they are not aiming to achieve maximum profits, how do they choose the price to charge? As we shall see, firms often base their prices on average cost.

8.2 BEHAVIOURAL THEORIES

Are firms rational?

In section 4.4 we considered why consumers do not always behave 'rationally', in the sense of trying to maximise their consumer surplus. We studied the behaviour of consumers in practice when faced with limited information and a range of incentives. In this chapter we consider why firms also may deviate from 'rationality'; why they may not always attempt to maximise profit.

As we have already suggested, one reason is that individual managers may be pursuing their own interests rather than those of their employer. In addition, firms operate in complex environments, dealing with imperfect information and uncertainty about both the present and the future. As a consequence managers may resort to using rules of thumb or other shortcuts when making decisions.

Since the late 1950s a number of alternative theories have been developed that focus on the actual behaviour of key decision makers within the firm. The most influential early exponents of this approach were Richard Cyert and James March[1] (see section 8.4). Their research made use of case studies of four multinational firms. They used the observations obtained to develop models of the firm, where decisions resulted from sequences of behaviours. Their work highlighted the limitations of the neoclassical assumption of profit maximisation and proved to be highly influential in two ways. First, it led to the study of behaviour, both of firms and of the individual decision makers within them. Second, the research methods used have been adopted by experimentalists, not only in economics, but across the social sciences.

There are a number of topics of interest to behavioural economists when considering the actions of firms. These include behaviour towards competitors, the role of asymmetric information and attitudes to risk.

Revenge is sweet

As we saw in Chapter 7, in non-collusive oligopoly the behaviour of a firm will depend on how it thinks its rivals will react. In collusive oligopoly firms agree to limit competition in order to maximise joint profits. Game theory allows us to examine these strategic decisions in more depth. A consistent assumption is that firms are attempting to maximise profits (or achieve some alternative aim) in a rational and neutral manner. Yet is this always a reasonable assumption?

If firms – or the managers of firms – have interacted over a number of years, there may be a 'history between them'. This may influence subsequent decisions.

Perhaps Firm A suffered from the effects of a predatory pricing policy by Firm B. Possibly Firms C and D colluded over output or prices, but one of them failed to keep to the agreement. It is possible that the firms, or the managers who are now working for other companies, have held a grudge ever since. Next time they interact, the strategy may be coloured by a desire for revenge. Experiments have demonstrated that in repeated games, individuals are willing to give up winnings if they can see their opponents punished for previous 'bad behaviour'.

Asymmetric information and the principal–agent problem

Can the owners of a firm ever be sure that their managers will pursue the business strategy most appropriate to achieving the owners' goals (i.e. maximisation of profit)? This is an example of what is known in economics as the *principal–agent problem*. One of the features of a complex modern economy is that people (principals) have to employ others (agents) to carry out their wishes. If you want to go on holiday, it is easier to go to a travel agent to sort out the arrangements than to do it all yourself. Likewise, if you want to buy a house, it is more convenient to go to an estate agent. The point is that these agents have specialist knowledge and can save you, the principal, a great deal of time and effort. It is merely an example of the benefits of the specialisation and division of labour.

It is the same with firms. They employ people with specialist knowledge and skills to carry out specific tasks. Companies frequently employ consultants to give them advice or engage the services of specialist firms such as an advertising agency. Even employees of a company can be seen as 'agents' of their employer. In the case of workers, they can be seen as the agents of management. Junior managers are the agents of senior management. Senior managers are the agents of the directors, who are themselves agents of the shareholders. Thus in large firms there is often a complex chain of principal–agent relationships.

---

[1] *A Behavioural Theory of the Firm* (Blackwell, 1963).

Definition

Principal–agent problem Where people (principals), as a result of lack of knowledge, cannot ensure that their best interests are served by their agents.

But these relationships have an inherent danger for the principal: there is *asymmetric information* between the two sides.

The agent knows more about the situation than the principal – of course, this is part of the reason why the principal employs the agent in the first place. The danger is that the agent may well not act in the principal's best interests, and may be able to get away with it because of the principal's imperfect knowledge. The estate agent may try to convince the vendor that it is necessary to accept a lower price, while the real reason is to save the agent time, effort and expense.

In firms, too, agents may not act in the best interests of their principals. For example, workers may be able to get away with not working very hard, preferring instead an easy life. Similarly, given the divorce between the ownership and control of a company, managers (agents) may pursue goals different from those of shareholders (principals). Thus *X inefficiency* is likely to occur (see Box 6.5).

KEY IDEA 23

The principal–agent problem. Where people (principals), as a result of a lack of knowledge, cannot ensure that their best interests are served by their agents. Agents may take advantage of this situation to the disadvantage of the principals.

So how can principals tackle the problem? There are two elements in the solution:

KI 15 p121

- The principals must have some way of *monitoring* the performance of their agents. For example, a company might employ efficiency experts to examine the operation of its management.

TC 5 p54

- Second, there must be *incentives* for agents to behave in the principals' interests. For example, managers' salaries could be closely linked to the firm's profitability.

Alternative theories of the firm therefore place considerable emphasis on incentive mechanisms in explaining the behaviour of managers and the resulting performance of their companies.

In a competitive market, managers' and shareholders' interests are more likely to coincide. Managers have to ensure that the company remains efficient or it may not survive the competition and they might lose their jobs. In monopolies and oligopolies, however, where supernormal profits can often be relatively easily earned, the interests of shareholders and managers are likely to diverge. Here it

Definition

Asymmetric information Where one party in an economic relationship (e.g. an agent) has more information than another (e.g. the principal).

will be in shareholders' interests to institute incentive mechanisms that ensure that their agents, the managers, are motivated to strive for profitability.

The adverse impact of asymmetric information

Asymmetric information is likely to prevent efficient outcomes for firms. Consider the example of a small business seeking finance for investment purposes. Banks and financial institutions are unlikely to have full access to information about the business or the individuals who own it. Since investment opportunities often also involve some uncertainty about the future, the likely outcome is a lower level of lending than is desirable.

Explain why the existence of asymmetric information may be damaging for both parties in an economic exchange, not only for the one who has incomplete information.

Firms also face asymmetric information about the quality of supplies and the ability of customers to pay; the latter may be a particular issue for transactions that take place between firms and where credit is extended. If firms recognise these issues when writing contracts, they may be able to address the problem and achieve better outcomes. But often the problem only becomes apparent when it is too late.

On occasion the impact of asymmetric information can be so serious that the consequences are devastating, not only for the individual market, but also for the wider economy. One example of this is examined in Box 8.2.

Survival and attitudes towards risk

Aiming for profits, sales, salaries, power, etc., will be useless if the firm does not survive. Trying to *maximise* any of the various objectives may be risky. For example, if a firm tries to maximise its market share by aggressive advertising or price cutting, it might invoke a strong response from its rivals. The resulting price war may drive it out of business. Concern with survival, therefore, may make firms cautious.

Not all firms, however, make survival the top priority. Some are adventurous and are prepared to take risks. Adventurous firms may be dominated by a powerful and ambitious individual – an individual who is risk loving and therefore prepared to take gambles. Indeed, a willingness to take risks is a noticeable characteristic of successful entrepreneurs.

KI 11 p80

Economists have long identified overoptimism as a trait seen in many people. Adam Smith commented that 'the chance of gain is by every man, more or less over-valued, and the chance of loss is by most men under-valued'.

Why might it present problems for a firm if managers are overconfident? Can you think of any reason why CEOs might be more inclined to optimism than the population average?

BOX 8.2 THE US SUB-PRIME HOUSING CRISIS

Obvious in hindsight

The causes of the financial crisis of 2007–8, and of the subsequent global recession, are numerous and complex. However, there was one factor which made a major contribution to the collapse of confidence in the banking sector – the increased rate of mortgage defaults in the US housing market.

Background to the crisis

Up to 2006, the USA had experienced over a decade of sharply increasing house prices alongside growth in the number of homeowners, attracted by the promise of high returns. Over this period the US financial system was awash with funds flowing in from growing economies in Asia, and interest rates were low. The result was an easing of credit conditions and a sharp increase in the availability of mortgages. Home ownership was approaching 70 per cent, an historic high and an increase of around 7 per cent on the previous decade. Many of these new buyers were on low incomes, or had poor credit ratings – collectively they are known as *sub-prime borrowers*.

In 2006 the housing market in the USA peaked and values started to fall. This had an immediate effect on consumer confidence and demand for owner-occupied housing fell sharply, leading to a collapse in house prices. The 'house price bubble' had burst.

As the world moved into a recession, many borrowers found it hard to maintain their mortgage payments, particularly those on low incomes who had borrowed large amounts. The resulting high level of defaults and foreclosures (or repossessions) had an immediate and serious impact on the value of financial institutions across the world.

Sub-prime borrowers

Why was the sub-prime market so vulnerable to falling house prices? The answer lies in both the amount of lending that took place and the type of mortgages that were taken out by these borrowers. The role of mortgage brokers, who acted as agents, also proved to be crucial.

Borrowers with low incomes were mostly sold adjustable rate mortgages, which left them vulnerable to future interest rate rises. In addition, they were encouraged to accept deals that fixed lower payments in the first few years, with planned increases after that, regardless of interest rate adjustments. The result was that they would often see mortgage payments double, or even treble, after a couple of years. For most this would present a major problem, since their wages were unlikely to have risen that fast.

However, the brokers had a solution: over the period of increasing house prices sub-prime borrowers were easily able to refinance their housing loans when the time came for higher payments. This ensured that the sub-prime borrowers could retain their properties while the brokers generated further transactions fees. But once prices started to fall, this option disappeared and so the numbers defaulting on their mortgages increased sharply.

Securitisation of sub-prime debt

Since the mid-1990s many financial institutions have chosen not to hold mortgages through to the end of their term, retaining the associated risk. Instead, they have sold them on to other investors in the form of mortgage-backed securities (MBSs). This practice increased the incentives for banks to offer mortgages to sub-prime borrowers, since now

The more dispersed the decision-making power is in the firm, however, and the more worried managers are about their own survival, the more cautious are their policies likely to be. They may prefer collusion to competition, to stick with popular products, and to expand steadily. If a firm is too cautious, however, it may not survive. It may find that it loses markets to more aggressive competitors.

Can firms make use of behavioural economics?

Behavioural economics is a relatively new area of study for economists; yet when we look at what firms actually do, it would appear that they have been taking some of the principles on board for years. For example, they develop marketing strategies that do not concentrate solely on price, but are tailored to consumers' (sometimes irrational) preferences. Examples include offering 'buy one, get one free' and loyalty points. In Box 8.8 at the end of this chapter we look at some examples of how businesses can bring the lessons of behavioural economics into their pricing and marketing.

Of course there are other aspects to running a business than understanding consumer behaviour. Since for most firms labour is a major input, it will be important to account for the motivation of employees – to ensure that they work hard and that their actions are aligned with the interests of the firm. Mechanisms of reward (and possibly punishment) may be most effective if the behaviour of workers is fully understood. (This is considered in more detail in Chapter 9.)

 Are there other points in the supply chain/production process where firms could make use of better understanding of behavioural economics?

KI 22
p 223

they did not have to bear the full risk of default throughout a 20- or 25-year term.

The rate of securitisation increased sharply between 1997 and 2007, with 75 per cent of sub-prime mortgages being sold on to third parties by 2006. It played a pivotal role in the financial crisis (see pages 530–6). Once the US housing market collapsed, the effect was felt not only by American mortgage lenders, but also by financial institutions and investors across the world, all of whom had bought mortgage-backed securities or similar financial instruments.

The role of asymmetric information

One question of interest is what light can behavioural economics and the role of asymmetric information shed on the sub-prime market and the broader financial crisis? There is little doubt that throughout the market, economic principals were not in possession of complete information (nor, for that matter, were agents) and thus were unable to make rational decisions in the way that traditional theory would predict.

The opportunity for asymmetric information arose, in part, because mortgage brokers acted as agents for the principals. Since they were paid by transaction fees, their incentive was to complete as many mortgages as possible, regardless of the possibility of future default; this is an example of *moral hazard* (see Box 4.6 on page 124).

In particular:

■ Sub-prime borrowers were permitted to self-certify their incomes; this provided them with a mechanism to conceal full information about their earnings/debts.

■ There is evidence that many borrowers were not given full, or clear, information about the escalating payments that

they would face under their payment plans. As a result they could not anticipate the problems they would face after two or three years.

■ The commissions received by brokers were not transparent; thus borrowers could not readily identify the motives that lay behind being sold products that would require refinancing after some years.

■ The financial institutions that bought mortgage-backed securities relied on credit ratings agencies to verify the risks involved. These agencies consistently rated the instruments as lower risk than they turned out to be. It is a matter of debate as to whether this was done deliberately, or as a consequence of overreliance on risk-reducing practices. No matter, the result was that high-risk, sub-prime mortgages ended up in the portfolios of investors who would not have bought them given full information.

1. *Why was the market for sub-prime mortgages sustainable from 1996 to 2005? Explain how this changed in 2006.*
2. *The credit ratings agencies were paid by the companies who had been heavily involved in the market for sub-prime mortgages. Explain why this presents a moral hazard.*
3. *Financial regulation has endowed the judgements of the three credit ratings agencies with legal backing and has protected them from competition. Explain why this presented a problem in the process of securitisation.*
4. *If you were set the task of preventing similar sub-prime issues in the future, what regulations would you put in place?*

Section summary

1. Behavioural economics is relevant for understanding why and how the aims and strategies of firms deviate from traditional profit maximisation. This deviation is in part explained by the role of agents, particularly when there is a separation of management and ownership. Uncertainty and poor-quality information also play a part.

2. Since firms are managed by individuals, who are motivated by a number of possible factors, we should not be surprised if companies do not always appear to adopt 'rational' strategies.

3. The problem of managers not pursuing the same goals as the owners is an example of the *principal–agent problem*. Agents (in this case the managers) may not always carry out the wishes of their principals (in this case the owners).

4. Because of asymmetric information, managers are able to pursue their own aims, just so long as they produce results that will satisfy the owners. The solution for owners is to monitor the performance of managers, and create incentives for managers to behave in the owners' interests.

5. Asymmetric information is likely to prevent efficient outcomes for firms in a number of circumstances. This may arise as a result of the principal–agent problem, or because the relevant information is either unavailable to economic agents, or confusing if it is available.

6. Some alternative theories assume that there is a single alternative aim that firms seek to maximise. Others assume that managers have a series of (possibly conflicting) aims.

7. Firms can make use of the principles identified in behavioural economics to increase profits. Opportunities may arise in the relationship with consumers, particularly when looking at marketing and pricing. There may also be examples where greater understanding of behaviour can be used to inform contracts with employees, or with suppliers.

8. Levels of optimism and attitudes to risk will vary amongst owners and managers. If a firm is unwilling to make bold decisions it may increase its chances of survival, but will pay for this with lower profits. Overcautious strategies may also leave a firm vulnerable, if its competitors are able to gain market share by being bold.

8.3 ALTERNATIVE MAXIMISING THEORIES

Long-run profit maximisation

The traditional theory of the firm is based on the assumption of *short-run* profit maximisation. Many actions of firms may be seen to conflict with this aim and yet could be consistent with the aim of **long-run profit maximisation**. For example, policies to increase the size of the firm or the firm's share of the market may involve heavy advertising or low prices to the detriment of short-run profits. But if this results in a larger market share, the resulting economic power may enable the firm to make larger profits in the long run.

At first sight, a theory of long-run profit maximisation would seem to be a realistic alternative to the traditional short-run profit-maximisation theory. In practice, however, the theory is not a very useful predictor of firms' behaviour and is very difficult to test.

A claim by managers that they were attempting to maximise long-run profits could be an excuse for virtually any policy. When challenged as to why the firms had, say, undertaken expensive research or high-cost investment, or had engaged in a damaging price war, the managers could reply 'Ah, yes, but in the long run it will pay off.' This is very difficult for shareholders to refute (until it is too late!).

Even if long-run profit maximisation *is* the prime aim, the means of achieving it are extremely complex. The firm will need a plan of action for prices, output, investment, etc., stretching from now into the future. But today's pricing and marketing decisions affect tomorrow's demand. Therefore, future demand curves cannot be taken as given. Today's investment decisions will affect tomorrow's costs. Therefore, future cost curves cannot be taken as given either. These shifts in demand and cost curves will be very difficult to estimate with any precision. Quite apart from this, the actions of competitors, suppliers, unions, the future state of the economy, and so on, are difficult to predict. Thus the picture of firms making precise calculations of long-run profit-maximising prices and outputs is an unrealistic one.

It may be useful, however, simply to observe that firms, when making current price, output and investment decisions, try to judge the approximate effect on new entrants, consumer demand, future costs, etc., and try to avoid decisions that would appear to conflict with long-run profits. Often this will simply involve avoiding making decisions (e.g. cutting price) that may stimulate an unfavourable result from rivals (e.g. rivals cutting their price).

TC 9 p121

Managerial utility maximisation

One of the most influential of the alternative theories of the firm has been that developed by O. E. Williamson[1] in the 1960s. Williamson argued that, provided satisfactory levels of profit are achieved, managers often have the discretion to choose what policies to pursue. In other words, they are free to pursue their *own* interests. And what are the managers' interests? To maximise their own utility, argued Williamson.

[1] *The Economics of Discretionary Behaviour* (Prentice Hall, 1964), p. 3.

> ### Definition
>
> **Long-run profit maximisation** An alternative theory which assumes that managers aim to shift cost and revenue curves so as to maximise profits over some longer time period.

BOX 8.3 WHEN IS A THEORY NOT A THEORY?

EXPLORING ECONOMICS

Have you heard the joke about the man sitting in a railway carriage who was throwing pieces of paper out of the window? A fellow traveller was curious and asked him why he kept doing this.

'It keeps the elephants down', was the reply.

'But', said the other man, 'there are no elephants around here.'

'I know', said the first man. 'Effective, isn't it?'

Let's reformulate this joke.

Once upon a time there was this boss of a company who kept doing strange things. First he would spend a massive amount of money on advertising, and then stop. Then he would pay a huge wage increase 'to keep his workforce happy'. Then he would close the factory for two months to give everyone a break. Then he would move the business, lock, stock and barrel, to a new location.

One day he was talking to an accountant friend, who asked, 'Why do you keep doing these strange things?'

'I have to do them to make the business profitable', was the reply.

'But your business is profitable', said the accountant.

'I know. It just goes to show how effective my policies are.'

1. *Why might it be difficult to refute a theory of long-run profit maximisation?*
2. *If a theory cannot in principle be refuted, is it a useful theory?*

Williamson identified a number of factors that affect a manager's utility. The four main ones were salary, job security, dominance (including status, power and prestige) and professional excellence.

Of these only salary is *directly* measurable. The rest have to be measured indirectly. One way of doing this is to examine managers' expenditure on various items, and in particular on *staff*, on *perks* (such as a company car) and on *discretionary investment*. The greater the level of expenditure by managers on these items, the greater is likely to be their status, power, prestige, professional excellence and job security, and hence utility.

Having identified the factors that influence a manager's utility, Williamson developed several models in which managers seek to maximise their utility. He used these to predict managerial behaviour under various conditions and argued that they performed better than traditional profit-maximising theory.

One important conclusion was that average costs are likely to be higher when managers have the discretion to pursue their own utility. For example, perks and unnecessarily high staffing levels add to costs. On the other hand, the resulting 'slack' allows managers to rein in these costs in times of low demand (see page 239). This enables them to maintain their profit levels. To support these claims he conducted a number of case studies. These did indeed show that staff and perks were cut during recessions and expanded during booms, and that new managers were frequently able to cut staff without influencing the productivity of firms.

Sales revenue maximisation (short run)

Perhaps the most famous of all alternative theories of the firm is that developed by William Baumol in the late 1950s. This is the theory of *sales revenue maximisation*. Unlike the theories of long-run profit maximisation and managerial utility maximisation, it is easy to identify the price and output that meet this aim – at least in the short run.

So why would managers want to maximise their firm's sales revenue? The answer is that the success of managers, and in particular sales managers, may be judged according to the level of the firm's sales. Sales figures are an obvious barometer of the firm's health. Managers' salaries, power and prestige may depend directly on sales revenue. The firm's sales representatives may be paid commission on their sales. Thus sales revenue maximisation may be a more dominant aim in the firm than profit maximisation, particularly if it has a dominant sales department.

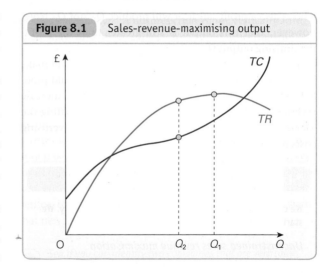

Figure 8.1 Sales-revenue-maximising output

Sales revenue will be maximised at the top of the *TR* curve at output Q_1 in Figure 8.1. Profits, by contrast, would be maximised at Q_2. Thus, for given total revenue and total cost curves, sales revenue maximisation will tend to lead to a higher output and a lower price than profit maximisation.

Draw a diagram with MC and MR curves. Mark the output (a) at which profits are maximised; (b) at which sales revenue is maximised.

The firm will still have to make sufficient profits, however, to keep the shareholders happy. Thus firms can be seen to be operating with a profit constraint. They are *profit satisficers*.

The effect of this profit constraint is illustrated in Figure 8.2. The diagram shows a total profit (*TΠ*) curve. (This is found by simply taking the difference between *TR* and *TC* at each output.) Assume that the minimum acceptable profit is $Π$ (whatever the output). Any output greater than Q_3 will give a profit less than $Π$. Thus the sales revenue maximiser

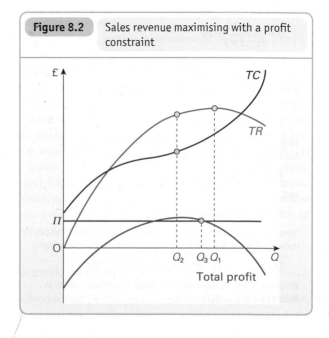

Figure 8.2 Sales revenue maximising with a profit constraint

KI 22
p223

Definition

Sales revenue maximisation An alternative theory which assumes that managers aim to maximise the firm's short-run total revenue.

takeover bid for another. This involves the first firm offering to buy the shares of the second for cash, to swap them for shares in the acquiring company, or to issue fixed-interest securities (debentures). The shareholders of the second firm then vote on whether to accept the offer. (Technically this is an 'acquisition' or 'takeover' rather than a merger, but the term 'merger' is generally used to include both mutual agreements and acquisitions.)

There are three types of merger:

- A **horizontal merger** is where firms in the same industry and at the same stage of production merge: e.g. two car manufacturers.
- A **vertical merger** is where firms in the same industry but at different stages in the production of a good merge: e.g. a car manufacturer with a car component parts producer.
- A **conglomerate merger** is where firms in different industries merge: e.g. when British Aerospace acquired Austin Rover.

Motives for merger

But why do firms want to take over others? Economists have identified a number of possible motives.

Merger for growth. Merger provides a much quicker means to growth than does internal expansion. Not only does the firm acquire new capacity, but also it acquires additional consumer demand. There is a danger for growth-maximising firms, however, of being taken over themselves. If they are growing rapidly and yet have a relatively low profit and a low stock market value, they will be attractive to predators.

Merger for economies of scale. Once the merger has taken place, the constituent parts can be reorganised through a process of 'rationalisation'. The result can be a reduction in costs. For example, only one head office will now be needed. Reduced costs are a way of increasing profits and thereby increasing the rate of growth.

In fact the evidence suggests that most mergers result in few if any cost savings: either potential economies of scale are not exploited due to a lack of rationalisation, or diseconomies result from the disruptions of reorganisation. New managers installed by the parent company are often seen as unsympathetic, and morale may go down.

Merger for monopoly power. Here the motive is to reduce competition and thereby gain greater market power and larger

profits. With less competition, the firm will face a less elastic demand and will be able to charge a higher percentage above marginal cost. This obviously fits well with the traditional theory of the firm.

 Which of the three types of merger (horizontal, vertical and conglomerate) are most likely to lead to (a) reductions in average costs; (b) increased market power?

Merger for increased market valuation. A merger can benefit shareholders of *both* firms by leading to a potential increase in the stock market valuation of the merged firm. If both sets of shareholders believe that they will make a capital gain, then they are more likely to give the go-ahead to the merger.

In practice, however, there is little evidence to suggest that mergers lead to a capital gain. In the early stages of a merger boom, as in 2005–6, when some good deals may be had, the share price of acquiring firms may rise. But as the merger boom develops, more marginal firms are acquired. Take the merger boom of the late 1990s. In some 80 per cent of cases, there was a significant fall in the share value of the acquiring firm.

Merger to reduce uncertainty. There are two major sources of uncertainty for firms. The first is the behaviour of rivals. Mergers, by reducing the number of rivals, can correspondingly reduce uncertainty. At the same time they can reduce the costs of competition (e.g. by reducing advertising). The second source of uncertainty is the economic environment. In a period of rapid change, such as often accompanies a boom, firms may seek to protect themselves by merging with others.

Merger due to opportunity. Sometimes mergers occur simply as a consequence of opportunities that suddenly and unexpectedly arise. Such mergers are largely unplanned and thus virtually impossible to predict. Dynamic business organisations are constantly on the lookout for such opportunities.

Other motives. Other motives for mergers include:

- Getting bigger so as to become less likely to be taken over oneself.
- Merging with another firm to prevent its being taken over by an unwanted predator (the 'White Knight' strategy).
- Asset stripping. This is where a firm buys another and then breaks it up, selling off the profitable bits and probably closing down the remainder.
- Empire building. This is where owners or managers like the power or prestige of owning or controlling several (preferably well-known) companies.
- Broadening the geographical base of the company by merging with a firm in a different part of the country or the world.

These theories, alongside the general area of mergers and acquisitions, are the subject of ongoing research, but most are in need of greater empirical investigation and support.

Definitions

Horizontal merger Where two firms in the same industry at the same stage in the production process merge.

Vertical merger Where two firms in the same industry at different stages in the production process merge.

Conglomerate merger Where two firms in different industries merge.

1. *Which of the above theories overlap and in what way?*
2. *Why do you think it is difficult to find adequate empirical support for any of them?*

Mergers and the relationship between growth and profit

In order for a firm to be successful in a takeover bid, it must be sufficiently profitable to finance the takeover. Thus the faster it tries to grow and the more takeovers it attempts, the higher must be its profitability.

In addition to being an obvious means to the growth of the firm, mergers may be a means of increasing profits, since mergers can lead to both lower average costs through economies of scale and higher average revenue through increased market power over prices. These profits in turn may be seen as a means of financing further growth.

It can therefore be seen that, whichever way it is financed, growth is closely linked to profits. High profits can help a firm grow. Rapid growth can lead to a rapid growth in profits.

These are not inevitable links, however. For example, long-run profits may not increase if a firm invests in risky projects or projects with a low rate of return. Expansion alone is no guarantee of profits. Also, high profits will not necessarily lead to growth if a large proportion is distributed to shareholders and only a small proportion is reinvested. High profits may help growth, but they do not guarantee it.

Growth through strategic alliances

One means of achieving growth is through the formation of *strategic alliances* with other firms. They are a means whereby business operations can be expanded relatively quickly and at relatively low cost, and are a common way in which firms can deepen their involvement in global markets.

There are many types of strategic alliance between businesses, covering a wide range of alternative collaborative arrangements.

Joint ventures. A **joint venture** is where two or more firms decide to create, and jointly own, a new independent organisation. The creation of O_2, originally called Cellnet, by BT and Securicor is an example of such a strategy.

Consortia. In recent years, many consortia have been created. Camelot, the company that runs the UK National Lottery, and Trans Manche Link, the company that built the Channel Tunnel, are two examples. A **consortium** is usually created for very specific projects, such as a large civil engineering work. As such they have a focused objective, and once the project is completed, the consortium is usually dissolved.

Franchising. A less formal strategic alliance is where a business agrees to **franchise** its operations to third parties. McDonald's and Coca-Cola are good examples of businesses that use a franchise network. In such a relationship, the franchisee is responsible for manufacturing and/or selling, and the franchiser retains responsibility for branding and marketing.

Subcontracting. Like franchising, **subcontracting** is a less formal source of strategic alliance, where companies maintain their independence. When a business subcontracts, it employs an independent business to manufacture or supply some service rather than conduct the activity itself. Car manufacturers are major subcontractors. Given the multitude and complexity of components that are required to manufacture a car, the use of subcontractors to supply specialist items, such as brakes and lights, seems a logical way to organise the business.

Networks. **Networks** are less formal than any of the above alliances. A network is where two or more businesses work collaboratively but without any formal relationship binding one to the other. Such a form of collaboration is highly prevalent in Japan. Rather than a formal contract regulating the behaviour of the partners to the agreement, their relationship is based upon an understanding of trust and loyalty.

Why form strategic alliances? As a business expands, possibly internationally, it may well be advantageous to join with an existing player in the market. Such a business would have local knowledge and an established network of suppliers and distributors.

In addition, strategic alliances allow firms to share risk. The Channel Tunnel and the consortium of firms that built

---

Definitions

Strategic alliance Where two firms work together, formally or informally, to achieve a mutually desirable goal.

Joint venture Where two or more firms set up and jointly own a new independent firm.

Consortium Where two or more firms work together on a specific project and create a separate company to run the project.

Franchise A formal agreement whereby a company uses another company to produce or sell some or all of its product.

Subcontracting Where a firm employs another firm to produce part of its output or some of its input(s).

Network An informal arrangement between businesses to work together towards some common goal.

> **BOX 8.4** **ENRON**
>
>
> ### A cautionary tale of business growth
>
> Not many companies come bigger than Enron did, and none bigger has ever filed for bankruptcy, as Enron did on 1 December 2001.
>
> Enron seemed to have everything going for it, being the largest energy trader in the USA with 25 per cent of the market. In 2000, Enron earned $100 billion in revenue and turned a profit of $1 billion. But by the time it filed for bankruptcy, the seventh largest company in the USA had seen its market value collapse from $80 billion to less than $400 million. Its shares fell from a high of $89.50 in the previous year to a meagre 26 cents. How did it all go so wrong so quickly?
>
> Enron was created in 1986, following the merger of two gas pipeline companies, Houston Natural Gas and InterNorth. As US energy and utility markets were deregulated, Enron diversified rapidly into alternative sources of energy supply such as electricity, and established interests in areas such as water. This diversification in Enron's interests was not restricted to the US market. Enron embarked upon a global growth strategy, which involved its acquiring interests in utilities throughout the world.
>
> As Enron grew, it also shifted its business focus. It gradually reduced its role in gas and oil production, its traditional core business activities, and moved into the new world of online energy trading. This appeared to have been a wise move, as by November 1999 it had traded more than $1 trillion of electricity and gas online. Enron was, at this time, the largest business on the Internet. So what went wrong?
>
> The weaknesses in Enron's growth strategy lay both in the speed of its expansion and, most crucially, in how its growth was financed. On declaring bankruptcy in December 2001, the scale of Enron's debts was revealed to be both massive and global. Creditors were estimated to be owed some $18.7 billion.
>
> Clearly, Enron had financed an overwhelming part of its growth through borrowing. As a source of finance for business growth, this only becomes a problem if revenue begins to fall and you are unable to meet the payments on the money owed. Given the public picture presented by Enron, and its apparent success, revenue and profits seemed to be guaranteed. The business was a clear winner. Such a picture would certainly have helped Enron to attract significant amounts of capital to fund its expansion plans.
>
> However, everything was not as it seemed. Enron's financial position was precarious. In October 2001, Enron announced unexpected losses, which led it to reduce capital by $1.2 billion. A series of bad investments overseas were held to be the main reason for this decision. The announcement of losses was swiftly followed by the revelation that Enron was to be investigated by the US Securities and Exchange Commission for financial irregularities. It was subsequently revealed that through some accounting loophole Enron had been overstating its earnings since 1997 to the value of some $600 million. Predictably many of Enron's trading partners had by this stage begun to lose confidence in the business and started to pull out of deals.
>
> At this point Dynegy, one of Enron's smaller rivals, agreed to buy the company for $9 billion in stock. However, as more losses were disclosed, and the need to get regulatory approval for the acquisition was established, Dynegy pulled out of the deal. Shareholder confidence had by this point totally collapsed and Enron's credit rating plummeted.
>
> Enron's rise and fall reveals a tale of unsustainable growth and expansion that was bought on debt. It reveals not only the folly of such a strategy, but the need to have a strong system of financial regulation to ensure that a business's true financial position is reflected in its balance sheet.
>
>
>
> 1. *Why might a business favour borrowing, as a means of financing growth, over other sources of finance?*
> 2. *What are the strengths and weaknesses of diversification as a business growth strategy?*

it is one such example. The construction of the Channel Tunnel was a massive undertaking and far too risky for any single firm to embark upon. With the creation of a consortium, risk was spread and the various consortium members were able to specialise in their areas of expertise.

Projects that might have prohibitively high start-up costs, or running costs, may become feasible if firms co-operate and pool their capital. In addition, an alliance of firms, with their combined assets and credibility, may find it easier to generate finance, whether from investors in the stock market or from the banking sector.

The past 30 years have seen a flourishing of strategic alliances. They have become a key growth strategy for business both domestically and internationally. They are seen as a way of expanding business operations quickly without the difficulties associated with the more aggressive approach of acquisition or the more lengthy process of merger.

Growth through going global

In many respects, a firm's global strategy is simply an extension of its strategy within its own domestic market. However, opening up to global markets can provide an obvious means for a business to expand its markets and spread its risks. It is also a means of reducing costs, whether through economies of scale or from accessing cheap sources of supply or low-wage production facilities.

A firm's global growth strategy may involve simply exporting or opening up factories abroad, or it may involve merging with businesses abroad or forming strategic alliances.

As barriers to trade and to the international flow of capital have reduced, so more and more businesses have sought to become multinational. The result is that the global business environment has tended to become more and more competitive.

Equilibrium for a growth-maximising firm

What will a growth-maximising firm's price and output be? Unfortunately there is no simple formula for predicting this.

In the short run, the firm may choose the profit-maximising price and output – so as to provide the greatest funds for investment. On the other hand, it may be prepared to sacrifice some short-term profits in order to mount an advertising campaign. It all depends on the strategy it considers most suitable to achieve growth.

In the long run, prediction is more difficult still. The policies that a firm adopts will depend crucially on the assessments of market opportunities made by managers. But this involves judgement, not fine calculation. Different managers will judge a situation differently.

One prediction can be made: growth-maximising firms are likely to diversify into different products, especially as they approach the limits to expansion in existing markets.

TC 9
p121

Alternative maximising theories and the public interest

It is difficult to draw firm conclusions about the public interest.

In the case of sales revenue maximisation, a higher output will be produced than under profit maximisation, but the consumers will not necessarily benefit from lower prices, since more will be spent on advertising – costs that will be reflected in a higher price.

In the case of growth and long-run profit maximisation, there are many possible policies that a firm could pursue. To the extent that a concern for the long run encourages firms to look to improved products, new products and new techniques, the consumer may benefit from such a concern. To the extent, however, that growth encourages a greater level of industrial concentration through merger, the consumer may lose from the resulting greater level of monopoly power.

As with the traditional theory of the firm, the degree of competition a firm faces is a crucial factor in determining just how responsive it will be to the wishes of the consumer.

How will competition between growth-maximising firms benefit the consumer?

Section summary

1. Rather than seeking to maximise short-run profits, a firm may take a longer-term perspective. It is very difficult, however, to predict the behaviour of a long-run profit-maximising firm, since (a) different managers are likely to make different judgements about how to achieve maximum profits and (b) demand and cost curves may shift unpredictably both in response to the firm's own policies and as a result of external factors.

2. Managers may seek to maximise their own utility, which, in turn, will depend on factors such as salary, job security and power within the organisation. Given, however, that managerial utility depends on a range of variables, it is difficult to use the theory to make general predictions of firms' behaviour.

3. Managers may gain utility from maximising sales revenue. They will, however, still have to ensure that a satisfactory level of profit is achieved. The output of a firm which seeks to maximise sales revenue will be higher than that for a profit-maximising firm. Its level of advertising will also tend to be higher. Whether price will be higher or lower depends on the relative effects on demand and cost of the additional advertising.

4. Many managers aim for maximum growth of their organisation, believing that this will help their salaries, power, prestige, etc.

5. Growth may be by internal expansion. This can be financed by ploughing back profits, by share issue, or by borrowing. Whichever method a firm uses, it will require

sufficient profits to avoid becoming vulnerable to a takeover.

6. Vertical integration can reduce a firm's costs through various economies of scale. It can also help to reduce uncertainty, as the vertically integrated business can hopefully secure supply routes and/or retail outlets.

7. Growth may be by merger. Mergers can be horizontal, vertical or conglomerate. Merger activity tends to occur in waves. Various motives have been suggested for mergers, including growth, economies of scale, market power, increased share values, reduction in uncertainty, and simply taking advantage of opportunities as they occur.

8. One means of achieving growth is through the formation of strategic alliances with other firms. They have the advantage of allowing easier access to new markets, risk sharing and capital pooling.

9. Many firms' growth strategy includes expansion abroad.

10. As with long-run profit-maximising theories, it is difficult to predict the price and output strategies of a growth-maximising firm. Much depends on the judgements of particular managers about growth opportunities.

11. Alternative aims will benefit the consumer to the extent that they encourage firms to develop new products and to find more efficient methods of production. They may be against the consumer's interest to the extent that they lead firms to engage in extensive advertising or to merge with a resulting increased concentration of market power.

BOX 8.5 | **MERGER ACTIVITY**

A worldwide perspective

What have been the trends, patterns and driving factors in mergers and acquisitions[1] (M&A) around the world over the past 20 years? An overview is given in Chart (a). The 1990s saw a rapid growth in M&A as the world economy boomed. Then with a slowing down in economic growth after 2000, M&A activity declined, both in value and in the number of deals, only to pick up again after 2003 as the world economy surged ahead again. By 2007, the annual value of M&A had reached a record $4 trillion, of which just over $1 trillion was of cross-border M&A. A further fall was seen with the financial crisis of 2008–9, but as confidence grew in 2010, so did the level of M&A.

The 1990s

The early 1990s saw relatively low M&A activity as the world was in recession, but as world economic growth picked up, so worldwide M&A activity increased. Economic growth was particularly rapid in the USA, which became the major target for acquisitions.

There was also an acceleration in the process of 'globalisation'. With the dismantling of trade barriers around the world and increasing financial deregulation, international competition increased. Companies felt the need to become bigger in order to compete more effectively.

In Europe, M&A activity was boosted by the development of the Single Market, which came into being in January 1993. Companies took advantage of the abolition of trade barriers in the EU, which made it easier for them to operate on an EU-wide basis. As 1999 approached, and with it the arrival of the euro, so European merger activity reached fever pitch, stimulated also by the strong economic growth experienced throughout the EU.

By the end of the 1990s, annual worldwide M&A activity was three times the level of the beginning of the decade. At this time there were some very large mergers indeed. These included a €29.4 billion marriage of pharmaceutical companies Zeneca of the UK and Astra of Sweden in 1998, a €205 billion takeover of telecoms giant

Mannesmann of Germany by Vodafone of the UK in 1999 and a €50.8 billion takeover of Orange of the UK by France Telecom in 2000.

Other sectors in which merger activity was rife included financial services and the privatised utilities sector. In the UK, in particular, most of the privatised water and electricity companies were taken over, with buyers attracted by the sector's monopoly profits. French and US buyers were prominent.

2000–7

With a worldwide economic slowdown after 2000, there was a fall in both the number and value of mergers throughout most of the world. But as the world economy grew rapidly from 2003 to 2007, so M&A grew rapidly too. What is more, the worldwide pattern of M&A activity was changing. Increasingly, both European and US companies were looking to other parts of the world to expand their activities. This is illustrated in Chart (b).

The two major target regions were (a) the rest of Europe, especially the 10 countries joining the EU in 2004 plus Russia, and (b) Asian countries, especially India and China. These new markets have the twin attractions of rapidly growing demand and low costs, including cheap skilled labour and low tax rates.

M&A activity was becoming more widespread across industrial sectors. In the 1997–2000 boom, the companies targeted were predominantly in the telecoms and media sectors. The boom of the mid-2000s, by contrast, saw companies involved in M&A from across the range of industries. According to a 2006 survey of Chief Executive Officers around the world,[2] 47 per cent were actively engaged to some degree in M&A activity. The figure rises to 61 per cent for CEOs of large companies (those with revenue of more than $10 billion).

Overwhelmingly, gaining access to new markets and customers is the main purpose given for cross-border M&A, cited by nearly two-thirds of CEOs. However, CEOs do not underestimate the

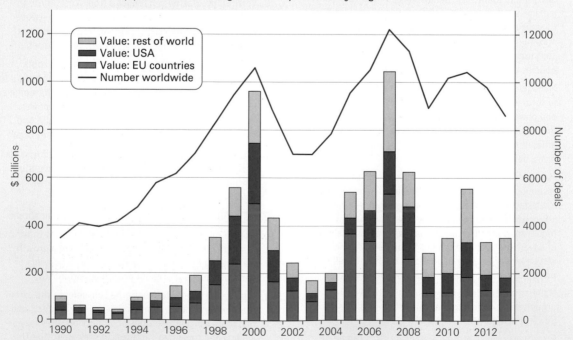

(a) *Cross-border mergers and acquisitions by target: 1990–2013*

Note: The data cover only those deals that involve an acquisition of an equity of more than 10%.
Source: *World Investment Report 2014*, Annex Tables 9 and 11 (UNCTAD, June 2014).

(b) *Cross-border mergers and acquisitions by target region (% of total number and value)*

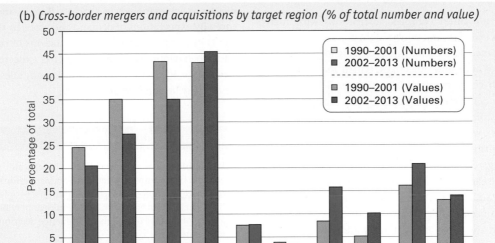

Note: The data cover only those deals that involve an acquisition of an equity of more than 10%.
Source: *World Investment Report 2014*, Annex Tables 9 and 11 (UNCTAD, June 2014).

difficulties faced in cross-border acquisition and integration. Cultural issues and conflicts, differences in regulations and unexpected costs are the main obstacles to cross-border M&A activity cited by CEOs . . . The global winners of tomorrow are those that can change their outlook from local to global in the true sense, and learn to operate in a world now subject to far more influences from a wider array of sources than ever before.[3]

From 2008 onwards

In 2008, as the world economy slid into recession, so M&A activity slowed. Over the period 2008–9 global M&A activity was substantially lower than in the first years of the decade, with figures for 2009 at a six-year low. Firms hoarded cash, deterred by high levels of uncertainty about future stock values and interest rates. Banks were also reluctant to fund takeover activity.

This situation was reversed in 2010 and 2011, with sharp increases on 2009. Interest rates remained low and finance became more readily available. Share prices had risen since the low of 2008, increasing corporate confidence. Yet many companies were still seen as 'good value', with expectations growing about the global recovery. The result was some very large deals. Examples included the $7.7 billion takeover of the Internet security company, McAfee, by chip manufacturer Intel, and the $20.1 billion acquisition of the US biotech company, Genzyme, by the French health-care products company, Sanofi-Aventis, in 2011.

However, the following years saw a slide back to lower global activity levels. Uncertainty around the eurozone and slower growth in China both contributed to this, although the technology sector remained buoyant, as the influence and marketing power of social media continued to grow.

A report by Credit-Suisse, in February 2014, assessed that 2013 activity levels remained 8 per cent lower than those of 2008, albeit 13 per cent up on 2012. With stock markets up substantially and many businesses holding record levels of cash, it forecast a forthcoming boom.

However, not all sectors are likely to see equally high levels of M&A activity. Pound stores (and dollar stores in the USA) and food retailers were identified as industries where consolidation would benefit firms.

Meanwhile, Google continues to acquire businesses at a voracious rate, spending over $4 billion in January 2014 alone. The majority of this went on Nest labs, which produced home automation technology,

while Deepmind, a UK artificial intelligence company, also became part of the Google stable.

Types of M&A activity

There is evidence that the proportion of M&A deals that are 'hostile' has continued to increase over the past decade. In other words, the company being taken over does not want to be. The deals are often concluded after prolonged boardroom battles, with bosses of the target company attempting all sorts of manoeuvres to avoid being taken over. This may involve their seeking deals with alternative, more 'friendly' companies. Generally companies are increasingly using the services of investment banks to help them in the process of making or warding off deals.

Despite the growing number of horizontal mergers, there has also been a tendency for companies to become more focused, by selling off parts of their business that are not seen as 'core activities'. For example, not long after its takeover of Wellcome, Glaxo decided to concentrate on the production of prescription drugs and, as a consequence, to sell its share of Warner Wellcome, which produced non-prescription drugs.

This trend of horizontal mergers and conglomerate and vertical de-mergers has allowed companies to increase their market power in those specific sectors where they have expertise. Consumers may gain from lower costs, but the motives of the companies are largely to gain increased market power – something of dubious benefit to consumers.

1. *Are the motives for merger likely to be different in a recession from those in a period of rapid economic growth? What would you predict about the pattern of mergers over the next few years, given the current state of the economy?*
2. *Between March 2011 and April 2014 Google acquired nearly 100 companies. Find out how many it has acquired since. What is Google's motivation for this activity?*

---

[1] By 'acquisitions' we mean takeovers or the acquiring of at least 5 per cent of a company's shares.
[2] *Global CEO Survey 2006*, PricewaterhouseCoopers.
[3] 'Global CEOs' business confidence reaches record levels', PricewaterhouseCoopers Press Release, 24 January 2007.
[4] 'Mergers and acquisitions: the long awaited boom is coming', Credit Suisse Global Equity Strategy Team, February 2014.

8.4   MULTIPLE AIMS

Satisficing and the setting of targets

Large firms are often complex institutions with many departments (sales, production, design, purchasing, personnel, finance, etc.). Each department is likely to have its own specific set of aims and objectives, which may come into conflict with those of other departments. These aims in turn will be constrained by the interests of shareholders, workers, customers and creditors (collectively known as *stakeholders*), who will need to be kept sufficiently happy.

In many firms, targets are set for production, sales, profit, stockholding, etc. If, in practice, target levels are not achieved, a 'search' procedure will be started to find what went wrong and how to rectify it. If the problem cannot be rectified, managers will probably adjust the target downwards. If, on the other hand, targets are easily achieved, managers may adjust them upwards. Thus the targets to

which managers aspire depend to a large extent on the success in achieving *previous* targets. Targets are also influenced by expectations of demand and costs, by the achievements of competitors and by expectations of competitors' future behaviour. For example, if it is expected that the economy is likely to move into recession, sales and profit targets may be adjusted downwards.

> ### Definition
>
> **Stakeholders (in a company)** People who are affected by a company's activities and/or performance (customers, employees, owners, creditors, people living in the neighbourhood, etc.). They may or may not be in a position to take decisions, or influence decision taking, in the firm.

KI 22
p 223

TC 9
p 121

BOX 8.6   STAKEHOLDER POWER?

CASE STUDIES AND APPLICATIONS

Who governs the firm?

The concept of the 'stakeholder economy' became fashionable in the late 1990s. Rather than the economy being governed by big business, and rather than businesses being governed in the interests of shareholders (many of whom are big institutions, such as insurance companies and pension funds), the economy should serve the interests of everyone. But what does this mean for the governance of firms?

The stakeholders of a firm include customers, employees (from senior managers to the lowest-paid workers), shareholders, suppliers, lenders and the local and national communities.

The supporters of a stakeholding economy argue that *all* these interest groups ought to have a say in the decisions of the firm. Trade unions or workers' councils ought to be included in decisions affecting the workforce, or indeed all company decisions. They could be represented on decision-making bodies and perhaps have seats on the board of directors. Alternatively, the workforce might be given the power to elect managers.

Banks or other institutions lending to firms ought to be included in investment decisions. In Germany, where banks finance a large proportion of investment, banks are represented on the boards of most large companies.

Local communities ought to have a say in any projects (such as new buildings or the discharge of effluent) that affect the local environment. Customers ought to have more say in the quality of products being produced: for example, by being given legal protection against the production of shoddy or unsafe goods.

Where interest groups cannot be directly represented in decision making, companies ought to be regulated by the government in order to protect the interests of the various groups. For example, if farmers and other suppliers to supermarkets are paid very low prices, then the purchasing behaviour of the supermarkets could be regulated by some government agency.

But is this vision of a stakeholder economy likely to become reality? Trends in the international economy suggest that the opposite might be occurring. The growth of multinational corporations, with their ability to move finance and production to wherever it is most profitable, has weakened the power of employees, local interest groups and even national governments.

Employees in one part of the multinational may have little in the way of common interests with employees in another. In fact, they may vie with each other – for example, over which plant should be expanded or closed down. With new 'flexible labour markets', firms are making more use of casual, part-time, temporary or agency workers. These employees are generally 'outsiders' to decision making within the firm (see Box 9.8).

Also, the widespread introduction of share incentive schemes for managers has increasingly made profits their driving goal. Finally, the policies of opening up markets and deregulation – policies that have been adopted by many governments round the world in recent years – have again weakened the power of many stakeholders.

Nevertheless, many firms in recent years have put greater emphasis on 'corporate social responsibility' (CSR), seeing it as important to have an ethical dimension to their business practices. Whether this is a genuine commitment to the interests of society, or simply an attempt to win a larger market by gaining a good public image, clearly varies from firm to firm. CSR and business ethics are explored in Case Study 8.4 in MyEconLab.

 Are customers' interests best served by profit-maximising firms, answerable primarily to shareholders, or by firms where various stakeholder groups are represented in decision taking?

If targets conflict, the conflict could be settled by a bargaining process between managers. In this case, the outcome of the bargaining will depend on the power and ability of the individual managers concerned and the governance structure in which they operate. Thus a similar set of conflicting targets may be resolved differently in different firms.

Organisational slack

Since changing targets often involves search procedures and bargaining processes and is therefore time consuming, and since many managers prefer to avoid conflict, targets tend to be changed fairly infrequently. Business conditions, however, often change rapidly. To avoid the need to change targets, therefore, managers will tend to be fairly conservative in their aspirations. This leads to the phenomenon known as *organisational slack* — a term coined by Cyert and March (see above, page 224).

When the firm does better than planned, it will allow slack to develop. This slack can then be taken up if the firm does worse than planned. For example, if the firm produces more than it planned, it will build stocks of finished goods and draw on them if subsequently production falls. It would not, in the meantime, increase its sales target or reduce its production target. If it did, and production then fell below target, the production department might not be able to supply the sales department with its full requirement.

Thus keeping targets fairly low and allowing slack to develop allows all targets to be met with minimum conflict.

Organisational slack, however, adds to a firm's costs. If firms are operating in a competitive environment, they may be forced to cut slack in order to survive. In the 1970s, many Japanese firms succeeded in cutting slack by using *just-in-time* methods of production. These involve keeping stocks to a minimum and ensuring that inputs are delivered as required. Clearly, this requires that production is tightly controlled and that suppliers are reliable. Many firms today have successfully cut their warehouse costs by using such methods. (These methods are examined in Box 9.8.)

Multiple goals: predictions of behaviour

Conservatism

Some firms may be wary of change, seeing it as risky. They may prefer to stick with current practices. This could apply to pricing policies, marketing techniques, product design and range, internal organisation of the firm, etc.

If something does not work, managers will probably change it, but again they may be cautious, perhaps imitating successful competitors.

This safe, satisficing approach makes prediction of any given firm's behaviour relatively straightforward. You simply examine its past behaviour. Making generalisations about all such cautious firms, however, is more difficult. Different firms will have established different rules of behaviour depending on their experiences of their own particular market.

Comparison with other firms

Managers may judge their success by comparing their firm's performance with that of rivals. For example, growing market share may be seen as a more important indicator of 'success' than simple growth in sales. Similarly, they may compare their profits, their product design, their technology or their industrial relations with those of rivals. To many managers it is *relative* performance that matters, rather than absolute performance.

What predictions can be made if this is how managers behave? The answer is that it depends on the nature of competition in the industry. The more profitable, innovative and efficient are the competitors, the more profitable, innovative and efficient will managers try to make their particular firm.

The further ahead of their rivals firms try to stay, the more likely it is that there will be a 'snowballing' effect, with each firm trying to outdo the other.

 Will this type of behaviour tend to lead to profit maximisation?

Satisficing and the public interest

Firms with multiple goals will be satisficers. The greater the number of goals of the different managers, the greater is the chance of conflict, and the more likely it is that organisational slack will develop. Satisficing firms are therefore likely to be less responsive to changes in consumer demand and changes in costs than profit-maximising firms. They may thus be less efficient.

On the other hand, such firms may be less eager to exploit their economic power by charging high prices, or to use aggressive advertising, or to pay low wages.

The extent to which satisficing firms do act in the public interest will, as in the case of other types of firm, depend to a large extent on the amount and type of competition they face, and their attitudes towards this competition. Firms that compare their performance with that of their rivals are more likely to be responsive to consumer wishes than firms that prefer to stick to well-established practices. On the other hand, they may be more concerned to 'manipulate' consumer tastes than the more traditional firm.

 Are satisficing firms more likely to suffer from X inefficiency (see Box 6.5) than firms which seek to maximise profit or sales revenue?

> ## Definitions
>
> **Organisational slack** Where managers allow spare capacity to exist, thereby enabling them to respond more easily to changed circumstances.
>
> **Just-in-time methods** Where a firm purchases supplies and produces both components and finished products as they are required. This minimises stockholding and its associated costs. It does, however, put pressure on the supply chain and increases the probability that on occasion firms may not be able to meet demand – for example, in times of bad weather.

Section summary

1. In large firms, decisions are taken by or influenced by a number of different people, including various managers, shareholders, workers, customers, suppliers and creditors. If these different people have different aims, a conflict between them is likely to arise. A firm cannot maximise more than one of these conflicting aims. The alternative is to seek to achieve a satisfactory target level of a number of aims.

2. If targets were easily achieved last year, they are likely to be made more ambitious next year. If they were not achieved, a search procedure will be conducted to identify how to rectify the problem. This may mean adjusting targets downwards, in which case there will be some form of bargaining process between managers.

3. Life is made easier for managers if conflict can be avoided. This will be possible if slack is allowed to develop in various parts of the firm. If targets are not being met, the slack can then be taken up without requiring adjustments in other targets.

4. Satisficing firms may be less innovative, less aggressive and less willing to initiate change. If they do change, it is more likely to be in response to changes made by their competitors. Managers may judge their performance by comparing it with that of rivals.

5. Satisficing firms may be less aggressive in exploiting a position of market power. On the other hand, they may suffer from greater X inefficiency.

8.5 PRICING IN PRACTICE

What is the typical procedure by which firms set prices? Do they construct marginal cost and marginal revenue curves (or equations) and find the output where they are equal? Do they then use an average revenue curve (or equation) to work out the price at that output?

As we saw in section 8.1, firms often do not have the information to do so, even if they wanted to. In practice, firms look for rules of pricing that are relatively simple to apply.

Cost-based pricing

One approach is *average cost* or *mark-up pricing*. Here producers work out the price by simply adding a certain percentage (mark-up) for profit on top of average costs (average fixed costs plus average variable costs):

$$P = AFC + AVC + \text{profit mark-up}$$

Choosing the mark-up

The level of profit mark-up on top of average cost will depend on the firm's aims: whether it is aiming for high or even maximum profits, or merely a target based on previous profit. It will also depend on the likely actions of rivals and their responses to changes in this firm's price and how these responses will affect demand.

If a firm could estimate its demand curve, it could then set its output and profit mark-up at levels that will avoid a shortage or surplus. Thus in Figure 8.3 it could choose a lower output (Q_1) with a higher mark-up (fg) or a higher output (Q_2) with a lower mark-up (hj), depending on its aims. If the firm could not estimate its demand curve, it could adjust its mark-up and output over time by a process of trial and error, according to its success in meeting profit and sales aims.

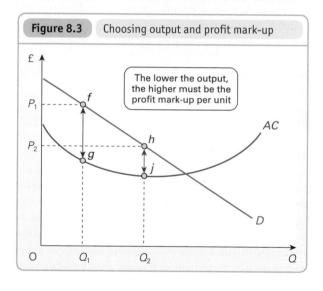

Figure 8.3 Choosing output and profit mark-up

The lower the output, the higher must be the profit mark-up per unit

The equilibrium price and output

Is it possible to identify an equilibrium price and output for the firm that sets its prices by adding a mark-up to average cost? To answer this we can identify a supply curve for the firm.

If a firm is aiming for a particular profit *per unit* of output and does not adjust this target, the firm's supply curve is derived by adding the mark-up to the *AC* curve. This is shown by curve S_1 in Figure 8.4. If, however, a firm is aiming

Definition

Average cost or **mark-up pricing** Where firms set the price by adding a profit mark-up to average cost.

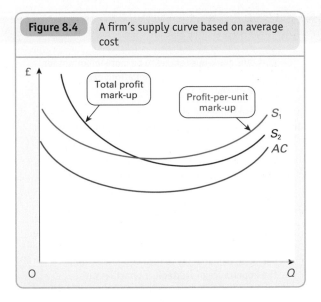

Figure 8.4 A firm's supply curve based on average cost

The firm is likely to take account of the actions and possible reactions of its competitors. It may well be unwilling to change prices when costs or demand change, for fear of the reactions of competitors (see the discussion of kinked demand curve theory on pages 206–7). If prices are kept constant but costs change, either due to a movement along the *AC* curve in response to a change in demand, or due to a shift in the *AC* curve, the firm must necessarily change the size of the mark-up.

All this suggests that, whereas the mark-up may well be based on a target profit, firms are often prepared to change their target and hence their mark-up, according to market conditions.

1. *If the firm adjusts the size of its mark-up according to changes in demand and the actions of competitors, could its actions approximate to setting price and output where MC = MR?*
2. *Some firms set their prices by adding a mark-up to average variable cost (the mark-up would be larger to include an element to cover fixed cost). Why might this make pricing easier for the firm? (See Box 5.6.)*

for a particular level of *total* profit, and does not adjust this target, its supply curve will be like curve S_2. The greater the output, the less the profit per unit needs to be (and hence the less the mark-up) to give a particular level of total profit.

In either case, price and quantity can be derived from the intersection of demand and supply. Price and output will change if the demand or cost (and hence supply) curve shifts.

The main problem here is in predicting the demand curve, since it depends not only on consumer tastes but on the prices and behaviour of competitors. In practice, firms will usually base their assumptions about future sales on current figures, add a certain percentage to allow for growth in demand and then finally adjust this up or down if they decide to change the mark-up.

Variations in the mark-up

In most firms, the mark-up is not rigid. In expanding markets, or markets where firms have monopoly/oligopoly power, the size of the mark-up is likely to be greater. In contracting markets, or under conditions of rising costs and constant demand, a firm may well be forced to accept lower profits and thus reduce the mark-up.

Multi-product firms often have different mark-ups for their different products depending on their various market conditions. Such firms will often distribute their overhead costs unequally between their products. The potentially most profitable products, often those with the least elastic demands, will probably be required to make the greatest contribution to overheads.

BOX 8.7　HOW DO COMPANIES SET PRICES?

In 1996 the Bank of England published a survey of price-setting behaviour in 654 UK companies.[1] Among other things, the survey sought to establish what factors influenced companies' pricing decisions. The results are shown in table (a).

Companies were asked to rank alternative methods of pricing of their main product . . . The most popular response was that prices were set with respect to market conditions. The top preference[2] for almost 40 per cent of respondents was that prices were set at the highest level that the market could bear. An additional 25 per cent of respondents stated that they set prices in relation to their competitors – this was the second choice most popular among companies . . .

The survey also confirmed the importance of company-specific factors. The first preference of about 20 per cent of respondents was that price was made up of a direct cost per unit plus a variable percentage mark-up . . . A further 17 per cent of companies, particularly retailing companies, stated that they priced on the basis of costs plus a fixed percentage mark-up.

Cost plus mark-ups tended to be more important for small companies . . . which cannot afford expensive market research.

The survey also sought to establish those factors which could cause prices to change – either up or down (see table (b)).

The Bank survey asked companies to rank those factors most likely to push prices up or down. It found that there were substantial differences between the factors that influenced price increases and those that influenced price decreases. First, many more companies said that cost rises were likely to push prices up than said that cost reductions were likely to push prices down. Second, a rise in demand seemed less likely to lead to a price increase than a fall in demand was to lead to a price cut . . .

The importance of strategic interaction with competitors suggests that when contemplating a price cut, companies need to consider the chance of sparking off a price war . . . The finding that companies were much more likely to match rival price falls than they are to follow rival price rises appears to support the importance of strategic behaviour.

(a) How are prices determined?

	1st	%	2nd	%	3rd	%
Market level	257	39	140	21	78	12
Competitors' prices	161	25	229	35	100	15
Direct cost plus variable mark-up	131	20	115	18	88	14
Direct cost plus fixed mark-up	108	17	49	8	42	6
Set by customer	33	5	52	8	47	7
Regulatory agency	11	2	3	1	5	1

Source: S. Hall, M. Walsh and T. Yates, 'How do UK companies set prices?', Bank of England Quarterly Bulletin, May 1996, Table D, p. 188.

(b) Factors leading to a rise or fall in price

Rise	Number[a]	%	Fall	Number[a]	%
Increase in material costs	421	64	Decrease in material costs	186	28
Rival price rise	105	16	Rival price fall	235	36
Rise in demand	101	15	Fall in demand	146	22
Prices never rise	26	4	Prices never fall	75	12
Increase in interest rates	18	3	Decrease in interest rates	8	1
Higher market share	14	2	Lower market share	69	11
Fall in productivity	5	1	Rise in productivity	22	3

[a] Numbers citing a scenario as most important.

Note: Top preferences only.

Source: S. Hall, M. Walsh and T. Yates, 'How do UK companies set prices?', Bank of England Quarterly Bulletin, May 1996, Table D, p. 188.

More recent surveys

Europe-wide survey.　A European study of 2006 reported similar results to the 1996 UK survey. This European study brought together surveys conducted by nine Eurosystem national central banks on the price-setting behaviour of over 11 000 European firms.[3]

The research found that price-setting behaviour is consistent across Europe, with mark-up pricing the dominant strategy in the eurozone and price discrimination widely practised. The asymmetries noted above with respect to price increases and decreases were also seen.

Further Bank of England survey.　In 2008, the Bank of England conducted another survey of price-setting behaviour. This time 693 firms responded, with a spread across industry consistent with shares in UK GDP. The findings broadly supported those of the 1996 survey.

KI 22
p 223

KI 21
p 198

(c) *Most important factors leading to a rise or fall in price*

Price rise	Rank	Price reduction	Rank
Increase in cost of labour	1	Actual decline in demand	1
Increase in the prices of fuel, raw materials or other inputs	2	Actual price reduction by domestic competitor(s)	2
Actual rise in demand	3	Expected decline in demand	3
Increasing costs arising out of regulation	4	Significant reduction in market share	4
Actual price increase by domestic competitor(s)	5	Expected price reduction by domestic competitor(s)	5
Expected rise in demand	6	Decrease in the prices of fuel, raw materials or other inputs	6
Increase in financing costs	7	Decrease in cost of labour	7
Expected price increase by one or more of your domestic rivals	8	Decrease in costs arising out of regulation	8

Source: Jennifer Greenslade and Miles Parker, 'New insights into price-setting behaviour in the United Kingdom', *Bank of England Working Paper No. 395* (Bank of England, July 2010).

The survey revealed that different factors influence price rises and price falls. Higher costs – in particular, labour costs and raw materials – are the most important driver behind price rises, whereas lower demand and competitors' prices are the main factor resulting in price falls.[4]

Companies were asked to rank the importance of 11 factors in determining both price rises and price reductions. Table (c) shows the most important eight in determining price changes (based on share of companies responding 'important' or 'very important').

Unlike the 1996 survey, companies were asked about *expected* changes in key variables, including demand, costs and rivals' prices. These were important determinants for many companies.

The survey confirmed that a majority of firms use mark-up pricing, with 58 per cent describing it as 'very important'. More than half of these firms *adjust* their mark-up according to market conditions. Competitors' prices and market demand are the two most important factors leading to a fall in price. The increase in the cost of labour and prices of fuel and raw materials are the two most important factors leading to a price rise.

Price flexibility

Evidence from the USA[5] and the eurozone study suggests that the frequency and magnitude of price changes varies enormously from product to product.

Generally speaking, the greater the share of raw materials in a product, the more often its price moves: petrol prices change, on average, in five months out of six in both America and Europe; the prices of fresh food are altered far more frequently than those of processed food. The prices of services are stickier than those of goods. This may be because services tend to be more labour-intensive than goods, and because wages are stickier (downwards, anyway) than other prices.[6]

For most products, prices change relatively infrequently in Europe, with retail prices changing on average just over once per year. In the USA, sales are much more common, especially with clothes, furniture and processed food. The

prices of services also change more frequently in the USA. In Europe services are more regulated and wages (a large proportion of the cost of most services) are less flexible.

How often individual prices move is an important question. Shifts in prices are like the traffic lights of an economy, signalling to people to buy more of this and less of that, to spend or to save, or to find new jobs. If the lights change readily, resources can be redirected smoothly; if they get stuck, so does the economy. In particular, if neither prices nor wages fall easily, the cost in output and jobs of reducing inflation can be high. Sticky prices also mean that an inflationary shock – an increase in oil prices, say – can take a long time to work its way through the system.[7]

As far as the magnitude of price changes is concerned, in both the USA and Europe, price changes are typically much bigger than the rate of inflation. In Europe, average price increases are 8 per cent and average price reductions 10 per cent.

1. *Which of the following is more likely to be consistent with the aim of maximising profits: pricing on the basis of (a) cost per unit plus a variable percentage mark-up; (b) cost per unit plus a fixed percentage mark-up?*
2. *Explain the differences between the importance attached to the different factors leading to price increases and those leading to price reductions.*
3. *Why do you think percentage price changes are bigger than the rate of inflation?*

[1] Simon Hall, Mark Walsh and Tony Yates, 'How do UK companies set prices?', *Bank of England Quarterly Bulletin*, May 1996.
[2] Companies were able to show more than one response as their top preference. This means the total percentage of companies expressing first preferences for all of the explanations of price determination exceeds 100%.
[3] Silvia Fabiani *et al.*, 'What firms' surveys tell us about price-setting behaviour in the euro area', *International Journal of Central Banking*, September 2006.
[4] Jennifer Greenslade and Miles Parker, 'Price-setting behaviour in the United Kingdom', *Bank of England Quarterly Bulletin*, 2008 Q4.
[5] Emi Nakamura and Jón Steinsson, 'Five facts about prices: a re-evaluation of menu cost models', Harvard University, May 2007.
[6] 'Sticky situations', *The Economist*, 9 November 2006.
[7] Ibid.

BOX 8.8 HOW FIRMS INCREASE PROFITS BY UNDERSTANDING 'IRRATIONAL' CONSUMERS

In section 4.4 we looked at behavioural economics and at some of the reasons why people might not always act in the way that traditional economics predicts. This suggests that there may be an opportunity for business to increase profits by taking this 'irrationality' into account.

The role of 'special offers'

We all love a bargain and firms know this. If you walk around any supermarket, or look at online shopping sites, you will notice how many special deals are offered to entice us. 'Sale price'; 'Reduced'; '15% off'; 'Free delivery'; 'Everything must go'.

One thing that these all have in common is that they are only available for a limited time. Behavioural economists suggest that the combination of a special offer and a looming deadline pushes us into a state of excitement. We buy in a frenzy and fail to compute whether the benefits are worth the cost. In particular, there is evidence that we spend money on items that we would not have bought at the same price if there wasn't a special offer involved. We see the original price as a signal of quality and the reduced price as an unmissable opportunity.

The cost of inaction

Have you ever joined a gym? Every January thousands of people do, when they make New Year's resolutions to get fit and lose weight. By March most of them have stopped going. A report published in January 2011 suggested that Britons are wasting millions of pounds each year on unused memberships.[1] We could argue that this is a result of poor information (we underestimate the effort required and overestimate the pleasure involved) or of uncertainty (we can't anticipate how we will feel about visiting the gym later in the year). However, neither of these factors explains why we fail to cancel unused gym memberships once the contract allows us to do so.

The answer lies in our tendency to inertia and procrastination; we intend to cancel the membership and the associated direct debit, yet we fail to do so. This inertia is demonstrated in a number of other markets – households have a legal right to switch energy suppliers, yet the majority fail to do so unless they are targeted by salespeople. Many people take out savings accounts which offer high interest rates for a limited period – but then forget, or can't be bothered, to switch to other accounts at the end of the introductory period. As with the failure to cancel gym

membership, the intention may be there, but our inertia leads to failure to maximise our utility.

Alternative contracts

If firms make profits from our inertia, they may also vary contracts to respond to our own understanding of our failure to behave rationally. There is an argument that suggests that at least some consumers will recognise the irrational behaviour that is costing them money. Does this mean that fitness clubs face losing members and lower profits? Not necessarily; some companies seek to appeal to the 'informed consumer' and to extend their customer base by offering rolling contracts, and by offering a 'no-frills' experience.

In 2010, two Harvard graduates set up a business, Gym-Pact, which bought group gym memberships from a number of existing gyms. Gym-Pact then sold on these memberships; but rather than a regular deal, they offered 'motivational' contracts to individuals, who pay more if they miss their regular workouts. The pair came up with this idea after studying behavioural economics as part of their degree; they learnt that people react more strongly to immediate certainties than to future possibilities.

This business model turned out to be short-lived. However, the founders did not give up on the principle. By 2014 Gym-Pact had become Pact, a business that brings together members who commit to working out, to logging their food intake and to eating vegetables. Those who succeed are rewarded with small cash sums, of up to £5 per day. Those who fail are charged for their lack of willpower. Pact makes money as the intermediary.

1. Insurance companies are keen to offer their customers ongoing renewal, where the annual premium is automatically charged to a credit card. Explain the advantages to the company. Are there benefits to the customers in this arrangement?
2. UK consumer protection laws require that goods offered at 'sale prices' have previously been offered at the higher price for at least 28 days. Why is this in the customer's interest?
3. Think of two or three things that you intend to do when you 'get around to it'? Are there any business opportunities that might arise from this type of procrastination?

[1] www.dailymail.co.uk/femail/article-1345759/Britons-spend-37m-year-wasted-gym-memberships-slimming-classes.html?ITO=1490

KI 15 p121

Section summary

1. Many firms set prices by adding a profit mark-up to average cost. This cost-plus pricing is most likely when firms are profit satisficers or when they do not have the information to find the price that will equate marginal cost and marginal revenue.

2. The mark-up could be based on achieving a target level of either *total* profit or profit per unit. In either case, a supply curve can be derived by adding the corresponding mark-up to the average cost curve.

3. For firms keen to increase profit, the size of the mark-up can be varied as market conditions permit the target profit to be increased.

END OF CHAPTER QUESTIONS

1. Assume that a firm faces a downward-sloping demand curve. Draw a diagram showing the firm's *AR*, *MR*, *AC* and *MC* curves. (Draw them in such a way that the firm can make supernormal profits.) Mark the following on the diagram:

   (a) The firm's profit-maximising output and price.

   (b) Its sales-revenue-maximising output and price.

   (c) Its sales-maximising output and price (subject to earning at least normal profit).
   Could the answer to (a) and (b) ever be the same?
   Could the answer to (b) and (c) ever be the same?

2. Would it be possible for firms to calculate their maximum-profit output if they did not use marginal cost and marginal revenue concepts?

3. What is meant by the principal–agent problem? Give two examples of this problem that you have come across in your own experience.

4. 'A firm will always prefer to make more profit rather than less.' Do you agree with this statement? Is it compatible with alternatives to the profit-maximising theory of the firm?

5. A firm under monopoly or oligopoly that aims to maximise sales revenue will tend to produce more than a firm that aims to maximise profits. Does this conclusion also apply under (a) perfect competition and (b) monopolistic competition, given that there is freedom of entry?

6. What are the potential costs and benefits of mergers to (a) shareholders; (b) managers; (c) customers?

7. Why is it difficult to test the assumption that firms seek to maximise *long-run* profits?

8. Do behavioural theories of the firm allow us to make any predictions about firms' prices and output?

9. Are 'special offers' likely to benefit consumers?

Online resources

Additional case studies in MyEconLab

8.1 The legal structure of firms. A study of the different types of legal identity that a firm can take – from the sole proprietor to the partnership to the limited company.

8.2 Inside the firm. An examination of alternative organisation structures of firms.

8.3 The Body Shop. A case study of 'alternative business values'.

8.4 Corporate social responsibility. An examination of social responsibility as a goal of firms and its effect on business performance.

8.5 The global information economy and strategic alliances. The way forward for companies such as America Online?

8.6 Downsizing and business organisation. The historical case of IBM.

8.7 Vouchers and discounts. This case examines the rise of Groupon and looks at its business practices.

8.8 J. K. Galbraith. A portrait of this pioneer of alternative theories of the firm and critic of traditional neoclassical analysis and free-market capitalism.

Maths Case 8.1 Sales revenue maximising with a profit constraint. Part 1: Using simple algebra to find the sales-revenue-maximising output.

Maths Case 8.2 Sales revenue maximising with a profit constraint. Part 2: Using the Lagrangian approach.

Websites relevant to this chapter

Numbers and sections refer to websites listed in the Web Appendix and hotlinked from this book's website at **www.pearsoned.co.uk/sloman**.

- For news articles relevant to this chapter, see the Economic News section in MyEconLab.
- For general news relevant to alternative strategies, see websites in section A, and particularly A2, 3, 8, 9, 23, 25, 26, 35, 36. See also A38, 39, 42, 43 and 44 for links to newspapers worldwide, and A40 and 41 for links to economics news articles on particular search topics from newspapers worldwide.
- For student resources relevant to this chapter, see sites C1–7, 9, 10, 19.
- For information on mergers, see sites B3, 43; E4, 10, 18, 20; G1 and 8.
- For data on small and medium-sized enterprises, see the database in B3 or E10.
- For information on pricing, see site E10 and the sites of the regulators of the privatised industries: E15, 16, 19, 22.
- Sites I7 and 11 in the Business and Management section contain links to *Management*.
- Site D3 has a simulation on sales revenue versus profit maximisation.

MyEconLab

This book can be supported by MyEconLab, which contains a range of additional resources, including an online homework and tutorial system designed to test and build your understanding.

You need both an access card and a course ID to access MyEconLab:

1. Is your lecturer using MyEconLab? Ask your lecturer for your course ID.

2. Has an access card been included with the book at a reduced cost? Check the inside back cover of the book.

3. If you have a course ID but no access card, go to: http://www.myeconlab.com/ to buy access to this interactive study programme.

The Theory of Distribution of Income

Why do film stars, footballers and investment bankers earn such large incomes? Why, on the other hand, do cleaners, hospital porters and workers in clothing factories earn very low incomes? These are the types of question that the theory of distribution seeks to answer. It attempts to explain why some people are rich and others poor.

The explanation for differences in wages lies in the working of labour markets. In sections 9.1 and 9.2, we will consider how labour markets operate. In particular, we will focus on the determination of wage rates in different types of market: ones where employers are wage takers, ones where they can choose the wage rate, and ones where wage rates are determined by a process of collective bargaining. In the final two sections, we turn to capital and land and ask what determines the rewards that their owners receive.

This chapter examines the theory of income distribution by showing how the rewards to factors of production (labour, capital and land) depend on market conditions. Chapter 10, on the other hand, looks at income distribution in practice. It looks at inequality and poverty and at government policies to tackle the problem.

CHAPTER MAP

9.1 Wage determination under perfect competition   **247**
Perfect labour markets   247
The supply of labour   248
The demand for labour: the marginal productivity theory   252
Wages and profits under perfect competition   254
Equality and inequality under perfect competition   254
Who are the poor? Who are the rich?   255

9.2 Wage determination in imperfect markets   **256**
Firms with market power in employing labour   256
Labour with market power (union monopoly or oligopoly)   257
Firms and labour with market power (bilateral monopoly)   258
Collective bargaining   258
The efficiency wage hypothesis   259
Other labour market imperfections   263
Discrimination   263
Who are the poor? Who are the rich?   268

9.3 Capital and profit   **268**
The non-human factors of production   268
The demand for capital services   269
The supply of capital services   270
Determination of the price of capital services   271
*Demand for and supply of capital for purchase   272
*Determination of the rate of interest   274
Capital and profit   274
Financing investment   275
The role of the stock market   275

9.4 Land and rent   **278**
Rent: the reward to landowners   278
The price of land   279
Who are the poor? Who are the rich?   281

9.1   WAGE DETERMINATION UNDER PERFECT COMPETITION

Perfect labour markets

When looking at the market for labour, it is useful to distinguish between perfect and imperfect markets. Although in practice few labour markets are totally perfect, many are at least approximately so.

The assumptions of perfect labour markets are similar to those of perfect goods markets. The main one is that everyone is a **wage taker**. In other words, neither employers nor employees have any economic power to affect wage rates. This situation is not uncommon. Small employers are likely to have to pay the 'going wage rate' to their employees, especially when the employee is of a clearly defined type, such as an electrician, a bar worker, a data analyst or a porter. As far as employees are concerned, being a wage taker means competing with other identical (or very similar) workers. It also means not being a member of a union and therefore not being able to use collective bargaining to push up the wage rate.

The other assumptions of a perfect labour market are as follows:

Freedom of entry.   There are no restrictions on the movement of labour. Workers are free to move to different jobs or to areas of the country where wages are higher. There are no barriers erected by, say, unions, professional associations or the government. Of course, it takes time for workers to change jobs and maybe to retrain. This assumption therefore applies only in the long run.

Perfect knowledge.   Workers are fully aware of what jobs are available at what wages and with what conditions of employment. Likewise, employers know what labour is available and how productive that labour is.

Homogeneous labour.   It is usually assumed that, in perfect markets, workers of a given category are identical in terms of productivity. For example, it would be assumed that all bricklayers are equally skilled and motivated.

Which of the above assumptions do you think would be correct in each of the following cases?
(a) Supermarket checkout operators.
(b) Agricultural workers.
(c) Crane operators.
(d) Economics teachers.
(e) Call-centre workers.
(f) Professional footballers.
(g) Bar workers.

Wage rates and employment under perfect competition are determined by the interaction of the market demand and supply of labour. This is illustrated in Figure 9.1(a).

Generally it would be expected that the supply and demand curves slope the same way as in goods markets. The higher the wage paid for a certain type of job, the more workers will want to do that job and, generally, the more hours each will be willing to work. This gives an upward-sloping supply curve of labour. On the other hand, the higher the wage that employers have to pay, the less labour they will employ. They may produce less, or they may substitute other factors of production, like machinery, for labour. Thus the demand curve for labour slopes downwards.

Figure 9.1(b) shows how an individual employer has to accept this wage. The supply of labour to that employer is infinitely elastic. In other words, at the market wage W_m, there is no limit to the number of workers available to that employer (but no workers at all will be available below it: they will all be working elsewhere). At the market wage W_m, the employer will employ Q_1 hours of labour.

TF 4
p47

Definition

Wage taker An employer or employee who has no power to influence the market wage rate.

Figure 9.1	A perfectly competitive labour market

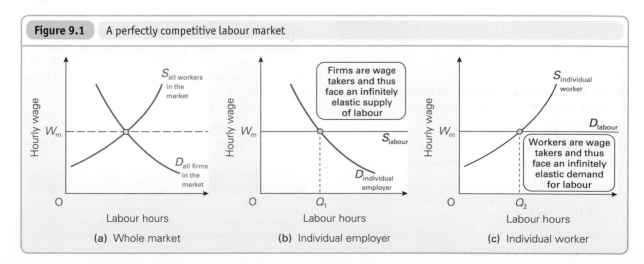

(a) Whole market   (b) Individual employer   (c) Individual worker

---

BOX 9.1 LABOUR AS A FACTOR OF PRODUCTION

Is this any way to treat a worker?

The theory that wages depend on demand and supply is often referred to as the 'neoclassical' theory of wages. Treated as pure theory it is value free and does not involve moral judgements. It does not say, for example, whether the resulting distribution of income is fair or just.

In practice, however, the neoclassical theory is often used in such a way as to imply moral judgements. It is a theory that tends to be associated with the political right and centre: those who are generally in favour of markets and the capitalist system. Many on the political left are critical of its implied morality. They make the following points:

- By treating labour as a 'factor of production', it demeans labour. Labour is not the same as a piece of land or a machine.
- It legitimises the capitalist system, where some people own land and capital while others have only their own labour. It implies that people have a right to income from their property even if that property is unequally distributed among the population.
- It implies that labour has no rights to the goods that it produces. These goods are entirely the property of the employer, even though it is the workers who made them.

Karl Marx (1818–83) was highly critical of these values and the way that the capitalist system led to extremes of wealth and poverty. He argued that labour was the only true source of value. After all, it is labour that makes machines, labour that works the land, labour that mines coal and other natural resources. Property, he argued, is therefore a form of theft. When capitalists extract profits from their enterprises, he continued, they are stealing part of the value produced by labour.

Neoclassical economists defend their position against the Marxist 'labour theory of value' by arguing the following:

- They are merely describing the world. If people want to draw pro-capitalist conclusions from their theory, then that is up to them.
- If the labour theory of value is used in any practical way to evaluate costs and output, it will lead to a misallocation of resources. Labour is not the only scarce resource. Land, for example, is also scarce and needs to be included in calculations of costs, otherwise it will be used wastefully.

 Assume that it is agreed by everyone that it is morally wrong to treat labour as a mere 'factor of production', with no rights over the goods produced. Does this make the neoclassical theory wrong?

Figure 9.1(c) shows how an individual worker also has to accept this wage. In this case it is the demand curve for that worker that is infinitely elastic. In other words, there is as much work as the worker chooses to do at this wage, but none at all above it.

We now turn to look at the supply and demand for labour in more detail.

The supply of labour

We can look at the supply of labour at three levels: the supply of hours by an individual worker, the supply of workers to an individual employer, and the total market supply of a given category of labour. Let us examine each in turn.

The supply of hours by an individual worker

Work involves two major costs (or 'disutilities') to the worker:

- When people work they sacrifice leisure.
- The work itself may be unpleasant or tedious.

Each extra hour worked will involve additional disutility. This **marginal disutility of work** (*MDU*) will tend to *increase* as people work more hours. There are two reasons for this. First, the less leisure they have left, the greater is the disutility they experience in sacrificing a further hour of leisure.

Second, any unpleasantness they experience in doing the job tends to increase due to boredom, tiredness or frustration.

 Re-word the explanation of marginal disutility of work in terms of the marginal utility of leisure.

This increasing marginal disutility (see Figure 9.2(a)) will tend to give an upward-sloping supply curve of hours by an individual worker (see Figure 9.2(b)). The reason is that, in order to persuade people to work more hours, a higher hourly wage must be paid to compensate for the higher marginal disutility incurred. This helps to explain why overtime rates are higher than standard rates.

TC 8 p105

Under certain circumstances, however, the supply of hours curve might bend backwards (see Figure 9.3). The reason is that when wage rates go up, two opposing forces operate on the individual's labour supply.

On one hand, with higher wage rates people tend to work more hours, since time taken in leisure now involves a greater sacrifice of income and hence consumption. They

---

Definition

Marginal disutility of work The extra sacrifice/hardship to a worker of working an extra unit of time in any given time period (e.g. an extra hour per day).

Figure 9.2   Marginal disutility of work and an individual's supply of labour

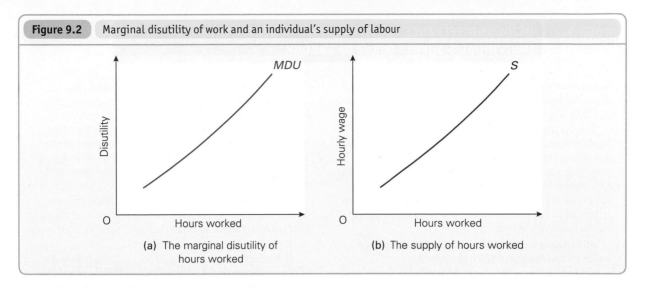

(a) The marginal disutility of
hours worked

(b) The supply of hours worked

Figure 9.3   Backward-bending supply curve of labour

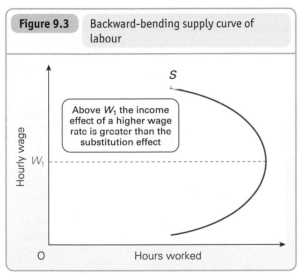

thus substitute income (i.e. work) for leisure. This is called the **substitution effect** of the increase in wage rates.

On the other hand, people may feel that with higher wage rates they can afford to work less and have more leisure. This is called the **income effect**. It reflects the fact that leisure is a *normal good*, one which is consumed in greater quantities as incomes rise.

With two effects working in opposite directions, the relative size of the effects determines the slope of the individual's supply curve. At lower wage rates, it is generally assumed that the substitution effect outweighs the income effect. A rise in the wage rate acts as an incentive and encourages a

person to work more hours. At higher wage rates, however, the income effect might outweigh the substitution effect. As wages rise, people may feel they can afford to give up some consumption in exchange for more leisure time.

If the wage rate becomes high enough for the income effect to outweigh the substitution effect, the supply curve will begin to slope backwards. This occurs above a wage rate of W_1 in Figure 9.3.

These considerations are particularly important for a government when thinking about policies on income tax. Conservative governments have often argued that cuts in income tax are the equivalent of giving people a pay rise, and that they provide an incentive for people to work harder. This analysis is only correct, however, if the substitution effect dominates. If the income effect dominates, people will work less after the tax cut. These questions are examined in Chapter 10.

The supply of labour to an individual employer

Under perfect competition, the supply of labour to a particular firm will be perfectly elastic, as in Figure 9.1(b). The firm is a 'wage taker' and thus has no power to influence wages. Take the case of a small firm that wishes to employ a temporary receptionist via an agency. It has to pay the 'going rate', and presumably will be able to employ as many receptionists as it likes (within reason) at that wage rate.

The market supply of a given type of labour

This will typically be upward sloping, as in Figure 9.1(a). The higher the wage rate offered in a particular type of job, the more people will want to do that job.

Definitions

Substitution effect of a rise in wage rates Workers will tend to substitute income for leisure as leisure now has a higher opportunity cost. This effect leads to *more* hours being worked as wage rates rise.

Income effect of a rise in wage rates Workers get a higher income for a given number of hours worked and may thus feel they need to work *fewer* hours as wage rates rise.

*BOX 9.2 USING INDIFFERENCE CURVE ANALYSIS TO DERIVE THE INDIVIDUAL'S SUPPLY CURVE OF LABOUR

Indifference curve analysis (see section 4.2) can be used to derive the individual's supply curve of labour. The analysis can show why the supply curve may be backward bending.

Assume that an individual can choose the number of hours to work and has 12 hours a day to divide between work and leisure (the remaining 12 being for sleep, shopping, travelling, etc.). In the diagram, with an hourly wage rate of £10, budget line B_1 shows all the possible combinations of daily income and leisure hours. For example, at point x the individual has an income of £80 by working eight hours and having four hours of leisure.

At an hourly wage of £20, the budget line becomes B_2, and at an hourly wage of £25 it becomes B_3.

The choice of hours worked at different wage rates

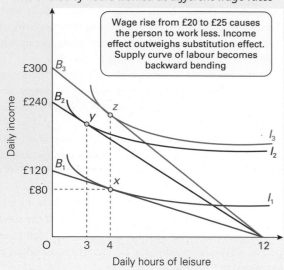

Wage rise from £20 to £25 causes the person to work less. Income effect outweighs substitution effect. Supply curve of labour becomes backward bending

The diagram also shows three indifference curves. Each indifference curve shows all those combinations of income and leisure that give the individual a particular level of utility. The curves are bowed in towards the origin, showing that increasingly higher incomes are necessary to compensate for each hour of leisure sacrificed. Curve I_3 shows a higher level of utility than I_2, and I_2 a higher level than I_1.

At a wage rate of £10 per hour, the individual can move along budget line B_1. Point x shows the highest level of utility that can be achieved. The individual thus supplies eight hours of labour (and has four hours of leisure).

At the higher wage rate of £20 per hour, the individual is now on budget line B_2 and maximises utility at point y by working nine hours. Thus the higher wage has encouraged the individual to work one more hour. So far, then, the individual's supply curve would be upward sloping: a higher wage rate leads to more labour hours supplied.

At the still higher wage rate of £25 per hour, the individual is on budget line B_3, and now maximises utility at point z. But this means that only eight hours are now worked. The supply curve has begun to bend backwards. In other words, the individual is now in a position to be able to afford to take more time off in leisure. The income effect has begun to offset the substitution effect.

1. *Using the analysis developed in Chapter 4, try to show the size of the income and substitution effects when moving from point x to point y and from point y to point z.*
2. *Illustrate on an indifference diagram the effect on the hours a person works of (a) a cut in the rate of income tax; (b) the introduction of a weekly tax credit, worth £30 to all adults irrespective of income.*

KI 7 p36

The *position* of the market supply curve of labour depends on the number of people willing and able to do the job at each given wage rate. This depends on three things:

- The number of qualified people. Of course if the job is unskilled then a large number of people will be 'qualified'.
- The non-wage benefits or costs of the job, such as the pleasantness of the working environment, job satisfaction or dissatisfaction, status, the degree of job security, pensions and other fringe benefits.
- The wages and non-wage benefits in alternative jobs.

A change in the wage rate will cause a movement along the supply curve. A change in any of these other three determinants will shift the whole curve.

Which way will the supply curve shift if the wage rates in alternative jobs rise?

The elasticity of the market supply of labour

How responsive will the supply of labour be to a change in the wage rate? If the market wage rate goes up, will a lot more labour become available or only a little? We looked at elasticity of demand and supply in Chapter 3; a similar analysis is used for the labour market. Thus the responsiveness (elasticity) depends on (a) the difficulties and costs of changing jobs and (b) the time period under consideration.

Another way of looking at the elasticity of supply of labour is in terms of the **mobility of labour**: the willingness and ability of labour to move to another job, whether in a

Definition

Mobility of labour The willingness and ability of labour to move to another job.

different location (geographical mobility) or in a different industry (occupational mobility). The mobility of labour (and hence the elasticity of supply of labour) will be higher when there are alternative jobs in the same location, when alternative jobs require similar skills, and when people have good information about these jobs. It is also much higher in the long run, when people have the time to move or to acquire new skills and when the education system has time to adapt to the changing demands of industry.

1. *Assume that there is a growing demand for computer programmers. As a result more people train to become programmers. Does this represent a rightward shift in the supply curve of programmers, or merely the supply curve becoming more elastic in the long run, or both? Explain.*
2. *Which is likely to be more elastic, the supply of coal miners or the supply of shop assistants? Explain.*

If the demand for a particular category of worker increases, the wage rate will rise. The more inelastic the supply of labour, the higher the rise will be. Workers already employed in that industry will get the benefit of that rise, even though they are doing the same job as before. They are now earning a premium above the wage that was necessary to attract them into the industry in the first place. This premium is called *economic rent*. Case Study 9.1 in MyEconLab explores this concept and its relationship with the elasticity of supply of labour.

Definition

Economic rent The excess that a factor of production is paid over the amount necessary to keep it in its current employment.

| BOX 9.3 | IMMIGRATION AND THE UK LABOUR MARKET | CASE STUDIES AND APPLICATIONS |

Free movement of people and the single European market

Ten countries, including eight former communist states, joined the European Union in May 2004. Many of the existing members decided not to open up their labour markets fully for fear of being overwhelmed by an inflow of economic migrants. But the UK chose to adopt an open borders policy, allowing workers from the new accession countries, including Poland and the Czech Republic, to take up jobs.

The expansion of the EU raised questions about the impact on the UK labour market, and concerns were raised by those who predicted that an inflow of workers would result in increased unemployment and lower wages.

Those in favour of allowing eastern European workers free access pointed to the buoyant state of the UK economy at the time, with low levels of unemployment and a growing number of unfilled job vacancies. The UK, like other western European countries, was facing an ageing population, with the ratio of workers to pensioners predicted to fall sharply over the following two decades. Immigration was seen as one solution to this problem.

In the three years following the accession of the new member countries, the UK saw very substantial inflows of workers; over 750 000 by 2007. The UK responded by placing restrictions on workers from the next two countries to join the EU – Bulgaria and Romania in January 2007. Workers from these countries were granted work permits only in sectors where there was a skills shortage. However, by then higher inflation, increasing wages in eastern Europe and the weakening value of the pound combined to make the UK less attractive, and the numbers arriving started to fall.

European rules allow restrictions on workers from the accession countries to be put in place for seven years; so restrictions on Bulgarian and Romanian workers were lifted in 2014.

There have been several studies attempting to quantify the impact of immigration on the economy. At the microeconomic level we would expect an increase both in

labour supply and in the elasticity of supply as the pool of available workers expands to include those across Europe. At a macroeconomic level, we would also expect a general increase in demand, as the new workers would also be new consumers. A 2007 Ernst & Young study,[1] suggested that there had been a positive effect on growth, with resulting lower inflation and interest rates.

However, immigration has remained a politically contentious issue, in part because there is a widespread perception that it reduces employment of UK workers, particularly in times of recession. Government sources have been quoted as saying that 'for every 100 additional immigrants . . . 23 British workers would not be employed'.

In March 2014, a government report[2] was published which synthesised the research to date. It concluded that there was little evidence of long-term damage to UK workers' prospects, with the labour market adjusting in both booms and times of recession, albeit more slowly in the latter. What is more, according to a University College London study,[3] since 2000, immigrants to the UK from the rest of the EU have made a substantial net contribution to UK finances, paying considerably more in taxes than claiming in benefits.

Draw a diagram illustrating the UK's decision to open up labour markets to workers from the accession countries. Show the situation both before and after. Consider both the position and slope of the labour supply curve and the impact on the number employed and on wages. Would you expect there to be any movement in the demand for labour?

[1] 'Migration and the UK Economy', Ernst & Young ITEM Club, December 2007.
[2] 'Impacts of Migration on UK Native Employment', Home Office and Department for Business, Innovation and Skills, March 2014.
[3] Christian Dustmann and Tommaso Frattini, 'The Fiscal Effects of Immigration to the UK', Centre for Research and Analysis of Migration, University College London, November 2013.

The demand for labour: the marginal productivity theory

The traditional 'neoclassical' theory of the firm assumes that firms aim to maximise profits. The same assumption is made in the neoclassical theory of labour demand. This theory is generally known as the ***marginal productivity theory***.

The profit-maximising approach

How many workers will a profit-maximising firm want to employ? The firm will answer this question by weighing up the costs of employing extra labour against the benefits. It will use exactly the same principles as in deciding how much output to produce.

In the goods market, the firm will maximise profits where the marginal cost of an extra unit of *goods* produced equals the marginal revenue from selling it: $MC = MR$.

In the labour market, the firm will maximise profits where the marginal cost of employing an extra *worker* equals the marginal revenue that the worker's output earns for the firm: MC of labour = MR of labour. The reasoning is simple. If an extra worker adds more to a firm's revenue than to its costs, the firm's profits will increase. It will be worth employing that worker. But as more workers are employed, diminishing returns to labour will set in (see page 135). Each extra worker will produce less than the previous one, and thus bring in less revenue for the firm. Eventually the marginal revenue from extra workers will fall to the level of their marginal cost. At that point, the firm will stop employing extra workers. There are no additional profits to be gained from employing further workers. Profits are at a maximum.

Measuring the marginal cost and revenue of labour

Marginal cost of labour (MCL). This is the extra cost of employing one more worker. Under perfect competition, the firm is too small to affect the market wage. It faces a horizontal supply curve (see Figure 9.1(b) on page 247). Thus the additional cost of employing one more person will simply be the wage: $MC_L = W$.

Marginal revenue of labour (MRPL). The marginal revenue that the firm gains from employing one more worker is called the ***marginal revenue product*** of labour. The MRP_L is found by multiplying two elements – the *marginal physical product* of labour (MPP_L) and the marginal revenue gained by selling one more unit of output (MR):

$$MRP_L = MPP_L \times MR$$

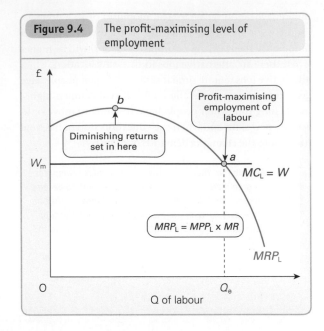

Figure 9.4 The profit-maximising level of employment

The MPP_L is the extra output produced by the last worker. Thus if the last worker produces 100 tonnes of output per week (MPP_L), and if the firm earns an extra £4 for each additional tonne sold (MR), then the worker's MRP is £400. This extra worker is adding £400 to the firm's revenue.

The profit-maximising level of employment for a firm

The MPP curve was illustrated in Figure 5.3 (see page 142). As more workers are employed, there will come a point when diminishing returns set in (point b). The MPP_L curve thus slopes down after this point. The MRP_L curve will be a similar shape to the MPP_L curve, since it is merely being multiplied by a constant figure, MR. (Under perfect competition MR equals P and does not vary with output.) The MRP_L curve is illustrated in Figure 9.4, along with the MC_L 'curve'.

 Why is the MC$_L$ curve horizontal?

Profits will be maximised at an employment level of Q_e, where MC_L (i.e. W) = MRP_L. Why? At levels of employment below Q_e, MRP_L exceeds MC_L. The firm will increase profits by employing more labour. At levels of employment above Q_e, MC_L exceeds MRP_L. In this case, the firm will increase profits by reducing employment.

Definitions

Marginal productivity theory The theory that the demand for a factor depends on its marginal revenue product.

Marginal revenue product (of a factor) The extra revenue that a firm earns from employing one more unit of a variable factor: $MRP_{factor} = MPP_{factor} \times MR_{good}$

*LOOKING AT THE MATHS

The marginal product of labour can be expressed using calculus. It is the rate of increase in output of good X with respect to changes in the quantity of labour:

$$MPP_L = \frac{\partial X}{\partial L}$$

The marginal revenue product of labour is thus given by

$$MRP_L = MR \frac{\partial X}{\partial L}$$

Profits are maximised at the level of employment (L) where $W = MRP_L$: i.e. where

$$W = MR \frac{\partial X}{\partial L} \qquad (1)$$

We can easily move from this to the level of profit-maximising output of good X (where $MC = MR$). Rearranging equation (1), we get

$$\frac{W}{\partial X/\partial L} = MR \qquad (2)$$

But, assuming that labour is the only variable factor, marginal cost (of output) is the extra cost of employing labour (the only extra cost) per unit of output. In other words,

$$MC = \frac{W}{\partial X/\partial L} \qquad (3)$$

that is

$$MC = MR$$

Thus, not surprisingly, the profit-maximising employment of labour (where $W = MRP_L$) will yield the profit-maximising output (where $MC = MR$).

Derivation of the firm's demand curve for labour

No matter what the wage rate, the quantity of labour demanded will be found from the intersection of W and MRP_L (see Figure 9.5). At a wage rate of W_1, Q_1 labour is demanded; at W_2, Q_2 is demanded; at W_3, Q_3 is demanded.

Thus the MRP_L curve will show the quantity of labour employed at each wage rate. But this is just what the demand curve for labour shows. Thus the MRP_L curve is the demand curve for labour.

There are three determinants of the demand for labour:

- The wage rate. This determines the position *on* the demand curve: i.e. the quantity demanded.
- The productivity of labour (MPP_L). This determines the position *of* the demand curve.
- The demand for the good being produced. The higher the demand for the good, the higher its price, and hence the higher will be the MR, and the MRP_L. This too determines the position of the demand curve. It shows how the demand for labour (and other factors) is a ***derived demand***: i.e. derived from the demand for the good. For example, the higher the demand for houses, and hence

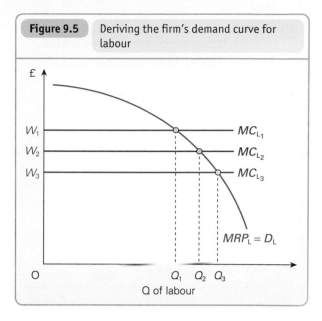

Figure 9.5   Deriving the firm's demand curve for labour

the higher their price, the higher will be the demand for bricklayers.

A change in the wage rate is represented by a movement *along* the demand curve for labour. A change in the productivity of labour or the demand for the good *shifts* the curve.

Derivation of the industry demand curve for labour

This is not simply the sum of the demand curves of the individual firms. The firm's demand curve is based on a constant P and MR, no matter how many workers the firm employs (this is one of the assumptions of perfect competition). In Figure 9.6, when the wage rate falls from W_1 to W_2 the firm will employ more labour by moving from *a* to *b* along its demand curve MRP_1.

The trouble with this analysis is that when the wage rate falls, it will affect *all* employers. They will all want to employ more labour. But when they do, the total industry output will increase, and hence P (and MR) will be pushed down. This will shift the firm's MRP curve to the left and lead to a lower level of employment at point *c*. Therefore, when we allow for the effect of lower wages on the market price of the good, the firm's demand curve for labour will be the *green* line passing through points *a* and *c*.

Thus the *industry* demand curve for labour is the (horizontal) sum of the *green* lines for each firm, and is therefore less elastic than the firm's MRP curve.

 What will determine the elasticity of this curve?

Definition

Derived demand Demand for a factor of production that depends on the demand for the good that uses it.

The industry demand curve for labour is derived from the line connecting points *a* and *c*

The elasticity of demand for labour

The elasticity of demand for labour (with respect to changes in the wage rate) will be greater:

- The greater the price elasticity of demand for the good. A fall in *W* leads to higher employment and more output. This will drive *P* down. If the market demand for the good is elastic, this fall in *P* will lead to a lot more being sold and hence to a lot more people being employed.

- The easier it is to substitute labour for other factors and vice versa. If labour can be readily substituted for other factors, then a reduction in *W* will lead to a large increase in labour used to replace these other factors.

- The greater the elasticity of supply of complementary factors. If the wage rate falls, a lot more labour will be demanded if plenty of complementary factors can be obtained at little increase in their price.

- The greater the elasticity of supply of substitute factors. If the wage rate falls and more labour is used, fewer substitute factors will be demanded and their price will fall. If their supply is elastic, a lot less will be supplied and therefore a lot more labour will be used instead.

- The greater the wage cost as a proportion of total costs. If wages are a large proportion of total costs and the wage rate falls, total costs will fall significantly; therefore production will increase significantly, and so too will the demand for labour.

- The longer the time period. Given sufficient time, firms can respond to a fall in wage rates by reorganising their production processes to make use of the now relatively cheap labour.

 For each of the following jobs, check through the above list of determinants (excluding the last), and try to decide whether demand would be relatively elastic or inelastic: firefighters; telesales operators; app developers; bus drivers; accountants; farm workers; car workers.

Wages and profits under perfect competition

The wage rate (*W*) is determined by the interaction of demand and supply in the labour market. It will be equal to the value of the output that the last person produces (MRP_L).

Profits to the individual firm arise from the fact that the MRP_L curve slopes downwards (diminishing returns). Thus the last worker adds less to the revenue of firms than was added previously by workers already employed.

If *all* workers in the firm receive a wage equal to the *MRP* of the *last* worker, everyone but the last worker will receive a wage less than their *MRP*. This excess of MRP_L over *W* of previous workers provides a surplus to the firm over its wages bill (see Figure 9.7). Part of this will be required for paying non-wage costs; part will be profits for the firm.

Perfect competition between firms ensures that profits are kept down to *normal* profits. If the surplus over wages is such that *supernormal* profits are made, new firms will enter the industry. The price of the good (and hence MRP_L) will fall, and the wage rate will be bid up, until only normal profits remain.

Equality and inequality under perfect competition

The mythical world of perfect wage equality

Under certain very strict assumptions, a perfectly competitive market will lead to perfect equality of wage rates. All workers will earn exactly the same. These strict assumptions are as follows:

- All workers have identical abilities.
- There is perfect mobility of labour.
- All jobs are equally attractive to all workers.
- All workers and employers have perfect knowledge.
- Wages are determined entirely by demand and supply.

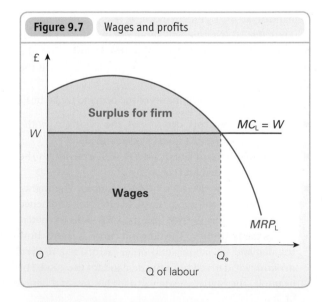

Figure 9.7 Wages and profits

Given these assumptions, if consumer demand rose in any industry, the demand for labour would rise. As a result, wage rates would begin to rise. Immediately workers would flood into this industry, attracted by the higher wages. Very quickly, then, wage rates would be competed back down to the level in the rest of the economy. Likewise if wage rates began to fall in any industry, workers would leave, thereby eliminating any labour surplus and preventing the fall in wage rates.

Under these conditions, therefore, not only would the labour supply curve to a *firm* be infinitely elastic, but so too would the labour supply curve to each *industry* at the universal wage rate.

TC 7
p72

Of course, in the real world these conditions do not hold and we do not see perfectly competitive labour markets. Huge inequalities of wages exist. But even if markets *were* perfect, inequality would be expected to persist.

Causes of inequality under perfect competition

In the short run, inequality will exist under perfect competition because it takes time for changes in demand and supply conditions to bring new long-run equilibria. Thus expanding industries will tend to pay higher wage rates than contracting industries.

KI 4
p13

But even after enough time has elapsed for all adjustments to be made to changes in demand and supply, long-run wage differentials will still exist for the following reasons:

- Workers do not have identical abilities.
- Workers are not perfectly mobile, even in the long run. People have different preferences about where they want to live and the jobs they like to do. They may not have access to training or may be unable to afford to retrain. Workers may not have the innate talent to do particular jobs, even if they did retrain.

- Jobs differ enormously in terms of the skills they require and in terms of their pleasantness or unpleasantness.

What is more, since demand and supply conditions are constantly changing, long-run general equilibrium throughout the economy will never be reached.

Who are the poor? Who are the rich?

The lowest paid will be those whose labour is in low demand or high supply. Low demand will be due to low demand for the good or low labour productivity. High supply will be due to low mobility out of industries in decline or to a surplus of people with the same skills or qualifications. Thus, for example, workers who possess few skills, are working in contracting industries, do not want to move from the area and will not or cannot retrain will be low paid.

KI 4
p13

The highly paid will be those whose labour is in high demand or low supply. Thus workers who possess skills or talents that are in short supply, especially if those skills take a long time for others to acquire, and those who are working in expanding industries, will tend to earn high wages.

Although the movement of labour from low-paid to high-paid jobs will tend to reduce wage differentials, considerable inequality will persist even under perfect competition. It is, therefore, not possible to eliminate poverty and inequality by 'freeing up' markets and encouraging workers to 'stand on their own feet' or 'get on their bikes'.

Furthermore, in the real world there exist many market imperfections, which tend to make inequality greater. These imperfections are examined in the next section.

TC 3
p26

Finally, income inequality under capitalism will also arise from the unequal distribution of the ownership of land and capital. Even under perfect competition, considerable inequality will therefore exist if wealth is concentrated in the hands of the few.

Section summary

1. Wages in a perfect market are determined by supply and demand.

2. The supply curve of hours by an individual worker reflects the increasing marginal disutility of work. Its shape depends on the relative sizes of the substitution and income effects of a wage change. The substitution effect is positive: higher wages encourage people to work more by substituting wages for leisure. The income effect, however, is negative: higher wages make people feel that they can afford to enjoy more leisure. If the income effect is bigger than the substitution effect, the supply curve for labour hours will bend backwards.

3. The supply of labour to a particular employer under perfect competition is infinitely elastic.

4. The market supply is typically upward sloping. Its elasticity depends on labour mobility.

5. The demand for labour depends on a worker's marginal revenue product. This is the extra revenue that a firm will gain from the output of an extra worker. The profit-maximising firm will continue taking on extra workers until MRP_L is equal to MC_L (= W under perfect competition).

6. The elasticity of demand for labour depends on the elasticity of demand for the good being produced, the ease of substituting labour for other factors and vice versa, the elasticity of supply of substitute and complementary factors, wages as a proportion of total costs, and the time period involved.

7. Although market forces will tend to lead to the elimination of differentials as workers move from low-paid to high-paid jobs, nevertheless inequality can persist even under perfect competition. People have different abilities and skills; people are not perfectly mobile; and jobs differ in their labour requirements.

8. Inequality is also caused by market imperfections and by unequal ownership of land and capital.

9.2 WAGE DETERMINATION IN IMPERFECT MARKETS

In the real world, firms and/or workers are likely to have the power to influence wage rates: they are not wage takers. This is one of the major types of labour market imperfection.

When a firm is the only employer of a certain type of labour, this situation is called a **monopsony**. A monopsony may arise in a market for particular types of labour; Royal Mail is a monopsony employer of postal workers. Alternatively, and more commonly, it may arise in a local market. Thus a factory may be the only employer of certain types of labour in that district. When there are just a few employers, this is called **oligopsony**. Oligopsony is much more common than monopsony, just as in goods markets oligopoly is much more common than monopoly.

In monopsonistic or oligopsonistic labour markets the employers have market power. Workers too may have market power as members of unions. When a single union bargains on behalf of a certain type of labour, it is acting as a monopolist. When there is more than one union, they are oligopolists.

When a monopsonist employer faces a monopolist union, the situation is called **bilateral monopoly**.

Firms with market power in employing labour (monopsony etc.)

Monopsonists (and oligopsonists too) are 'wage setters', not 'wage takers'. A large employer in a small town, for example, may have considerable power to resist wage increases or even to force wage rates down. The National Health Service has considerable power in setting wages for health workers in the UK.

Such firms face an upward-sloping supply curve of labour. This is illustrated in Figure 9.8. If the firm wants to take on more labour, it will have to pay a higher wage rate to attract workers away from other industries. But conversely, when employing less labour it will be able to pay a lower wage rate.

The supply curve shows the wage rate that must be paid to attract a given quantity of labour. The wage it pays is the *average cost* to the firm of employing labour (AC_L). The supply curve is also therefore the AC_L curve.

The *marginal cost* of employing one more worker (MC_L) will be above the wage (AC_L). The reason is that the wage rate has to be raised to attract extra workers. The MC_L will thus be the new higher wage paid to the new employee *plus* the small rise in the total wages bill for existing employees: after all, they will have to be paid the higher wage too.

The profit-maximising employment of labour would be at Q_1, where $MC_L = MRP_L$. The wage paid would thus be W_1.

If this had been a perfectly competitive labour market, equilibrium employment would have been at the higher level Q_2, with the wage rate at the higher level W_2, where $W = MRP_L$. The monopsonist is therefore forcing the wage rate down by restricting the number of workers employed.

1. The following table shows data for a monopsonist employer. Fill in the missing figures. How many workers should the firm employ if it wishes to maximise profits?

Number of workers	Wage rate (£)	Total cost of labour (£)	Marginal cost of labour (£)	Marginal revenue product (£)
1	100	100		
2	105	210	110	230
3	110	330	120	240
4	115	...	...	240
5	120	...	...	230
6	125	...	...	210
7	130	...	...	190
8	135	...	...	170
9	140	...	...	150

2. Will a monopsony typically also be a monopoly? Give examples of monopsonists that are not monopolists, and monopolists that are not monopsonists.

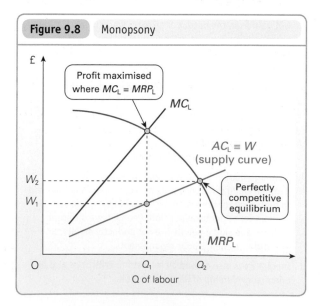

Figure 9.8 Monopsony

Profit maximised where $MC_L = MRP_L$

MC_L

$AC_L \equiv W$ (supply curve)

W_2

W_1

Perfectly competitive equilibrium

MRP_L

O Q_1 Q_2

Q of labour

Definitions

Monopsony A market with a single buyer or employer.

Oligopsony A market with just a few buyers or employers.

Bilateral monopoly Where a monopsony buyer faces a monopoly seller.

| BOX 9.4 | LIFE AT THE MILL | | CASE STUDIES AND APPLICATIONS |

Monopsony in Victorian times

A dramatic illustration of the effects of extreme monopsony power is that of the textile mill in nineteenth-century England. When a mill was the only employer in a small town, or when factory owners colluded as oligopsonists, things could be very bad for the workers. Very low pay would be combined with often appalling working conditions.

Friedrich Engels described the life of the textile factory worker as follows:

> The factory worker is condemned to allow his physical and mental powers to become atrophied. From the age of eight he enters an occupation which bores him all day long. And there is no respite from this boredom. The machine works ceaselessly. Its wheels, belts and spindles

hum and rattle ceaselessly in his ears, and if he thinks of taking even a moment's rest, the overlooker is always there to punish him with a fine. It is nothing less than torture of the severest kind to which the workers are subjected by being condemned to a life-sentence in the factory, in the service of a machine which never stops.[1]

1. *Why did competition between employers not force up wages and improve working conditions?*
2. *Were the workers making a 'rational economic decision' when they chose to work in such factories?*

[1] F. Engels, *The Condition of the Working Class in England*, translated by W. O. Henderson and W. H. Chaloner (Basil Blackwell, 1971), pp. 199–200.

Labour with market power (union monopoly or oligopoly)

The extent to which unions will succeed in achieving higher wage rates depends on their power and willingness to take action. It also depends on the power of firms to resist and on their ability to pay higher wages. In particular, the scope for unions to gain a better deal for their members depends on the sort of market in which the employers are producing.

If the employers are producing under perfect or monopolistic competition, wage rates will only rise at the expense of employment. Firms are earning only normal profit. Thus if unions force up wage rates, the marginal firms will make losses and eventually leave the industry. Fewer workers will be employed. The fall in output will lead to higher prices. This will enable the remaining firms to pay a higher wage rate.

Figure 9.9 illustrates these effects. If unions succeed in raising the wage from W_1 to W_2, employment will fall from

Q_1 to Q_2. There will be a surplus of people ($Q_3 - Q_2$) wishing to work in this industry for whom no jobs are available.

The union faces a second effect. Not only will jobs be lost as a result of the higher wage rate, but there is also a danger that those who are unemployed as a result might undercut the union wage.

In a competitive goods market, wage rates can only be increased without a reduction in the level of employment if, as part of the bargain, the productivity of labour is increased. This is called a **productivity deal**. The *MRP* curve, and hence the demand curve in Figure 9.9, shifts to the right.

Which of the following unions find themselves in a weak bargaining position for the above reasons?
(a) *The shopworkers' union (USDAW).*
(b) *The tube and train drivers' union (ASLEF).*
(c) *The farm workers' union (part of Unite).*

In a competitive market, then, the union is faced with the choice between wages and jobs. Its actions will thus depend on its objectives.

If it wants to *maximise employment*, it will have to content itself with a wage of W_1 in Figure 9.9, unless productivity deals can be negotiated. At W_1, Q_1 workers will be employed. Above W_1 fewer than Q_1 workers will be *demanded*. Below W_1 fewer than Q_1 workers will be *supplied*.

If the union is more concerned with securing a higher wage rate, it may be prepared to push for a wage rate above W_1 and accept some reduction in employment. This is more likely if the reduction can be achieved through

| Figure 9.9 | Monopoly union facing producers under perfect competition |

Definition

Productivity deal Where a union agrees to changes in working practices that will increase output per worker. This may be in return for a rise in the wage rate.

natural wastage. This is where people retire, or take voluntary redundancy, or simply leave for another job.

Firms and labour with market power (bilateral monopoly)

It is common to find the strongest unions where there is a monopsonistic labour market. In these circumstances we can think of the union monopoly as a counterweight to the power of a monopsony employer. What will the wage rate be under these circumstances? What will the level of employment be? Unfortunately, economic theory cannot give a precise answer. There is no 'equilibrium' level as such. Ultimately, the wage rate and the level of employment will depend on the relative bargaining strengths and skills of unions and management.

Strange as it may seem, unions may be in a stronger position to make substantial gains for their members when they are facing a powerful employer. There is often considerable scope for them to increase wage rates *without* this leading to a reduction in employment, or even for them to increase both the wage rate *and* employment. Figure 9.10 shows how this can be so.

Assume first that there is no union. The monopsonist will maximise profits by employing Q_1 workers at a wage rate of W_1. (Q_1 is where $MRP_L = MC_L$.)

What happens when a union is introduced into this situation? Wage rates will now be set by negotiation between unions and management. Once the wage rate has been agreed, the employer can no longer drive the wage rate down by employing fewer workers. If it tries to pay less than the agreed wage, it may well be faced by a strike, and thus have a zero supply of labour.

Similarly, if the employer decides to take on *more* workers, it will not have to *increase* the wage rate, as long as the negotiated wage is above the free-market wage: as long as the wage rate is above that given by the supply curve S_1.

The effect of this is to give a new supply curve that is horizontal up to the point where it meets the original supply curve. Assume that the union succeeds in negotiating a wage rate of W_2 in Figure 9.10. The supply curve will be horizontal at this level to the left of point *x*. To the right of this point it will follow the original supply curve S_1, since to acquire more than Q_3 workers the employer would have to raise the wage rate above W_2.

If the supply curve is horizontal to the left of point *x* at a level of W_2, so too will be the MC_L curve. The reason is simply that the extra cost to the employer of taking on an extra worker (up to Q_3) is merely the wage rate: no rise has to be given to existing employees. If MC_L is equal to the wage, the profit-maximising level of employment ($MC_L = MRP_L$) will now be where $W = MRP_L$. At a negotiated wage rate of W_2, the firm will therefore choose to employ Q_1 workers.

What this means is that even if the union succeeds in negotiating a wage rise from W_1 to W_2, the firm will still

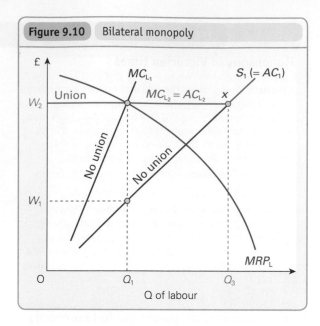

Figure 9.10 Bilateral monopoly

want to employ Q_1. In other words, a wage rise can be obtained *without* a reduction in employment.

 If the negotiated wage rate were somewhere between W_1 and W_2, what would happen to employment?

The union could go further still. It may be able to achieve a wage rate above W_2 and still insist that Q_1 workers are employed (i.e. no redundancies). The firm may be prepared to see profits drop right down to the normal level rather than face a strike or other industrial action and risk losses. The absolute upper limit to wages will be that at which the firm is forced to close down.

Collective bargaining

Sometimes when unions and management negotiate, *both* sides can gain from the resulting agreement. For example, the introduction of new technology may allow higher wages, improved working conditions and higher profits. Usually, however, one side's gain is the other's loss. Higher wages mean lower profits.

In collective bargaining, there are various 'threats' or 'promises' that either side can make. Union *threats* might include strike action, **picketing**, **working to rule** or refusing

Definitions

Natural wastage Where a firm wishing to reduce its workforce does so by not replacing those who leave or retire.

Picketing Where people on strike gather at the entrance to the firm and attempt to dissuade workers or delivery vehicles from entering.

Working to rule Workers do the bare minimum they have to, as set out in their job descriptions.

to co-operate with management, for example in the introduction of new technology. Alternatively, in return for higher wages or better working conditions, unions might *offer* no-strike agreements, increased productivity or long-term deals over pay.

In turn, employers might *threaten* employees with redundancies or reduced benefits. Alternatively, they might *offer*, in return for lower wage increases, better rewards such as productivity bonuses, profit-sharing schemes, more holidays or greater job security.

The outcome of negotiations. The success of a union in achieving its goals depends on its financial strength, the determination of its members and the level of support from the public in general. It also depends on the willingness of the firm to make concessions and on its profitability. Firms earning substantial profits are in a much better position to pay wage increases than firms operating in a highly competitive environment.

The wage settlement may be higher if the union represents only *core workers*. It may be able to secure a higher wage rate at the expense of non-members, who might lose their jobs or be replaced by part-time or temporary workers. The core workers can be seen as *insiders*. Their union(s) can prevent the unemployed – the *outsiders* – from competing wages down.

Industrial action imposes costs on both unions and firms. Union members lose pay. Firms lose revenue. It is usually in both sides' interests, therefore, to settle by negotiation. Nevertheless, to gain the maximum advantage, each side must persuade the other that it will carry out its threats if pushed.

The approach described so far has essentially been one of confrontation. The alternative is for both sides to concentrate on increasing the total net income of the firm by co-operating on ways to increase efficiency or the quality of the product. This approach is more likely when unions and management have built up an atmosphere of trust over time.

 Recall the various strategies that rival oligopolists can adopt. What parallels are there in union and management strategies?

The role of government in collective bargaining

The government can influence the outcome of collective bargaining in a number of ways. One is to try to set an example. It may take a tough line in resisting wage demands by public-sector workers, hoping thereby to persuade employers in the private sector to do likewise.

Additionally, it could set up mechanisms to assist in arbitration or conciliation. For example, in the UK, the Advisory, Conciliation and Arbitration Service (ACAS) is largely funded by the Department of Business, Innovation & Skills (BIS) and conciliates in over a thousand disputes each year.

Another approach is to use legislation. The government could pass laws that restrict the behaviour of employers or unions; that set a minimum wage rate (see Box 10.3); that prevent discrimination against workers on various grounds. The UK Conservative governments between 1979 and 1997 put considerable emphasis on reducing the power of trade unions and making labour markets more 'flexible'. Several Acts of Parliament were passed. These effectively ended *closed-shop* agreements, made secret ballots mandatory and outlawed political strikes and secondary action. It was also made unlawful for employers to deny employment on the grounds that an applicant does not belong to a union, or indeed to penalise the applicant for joining a union.

The effect of these measures was to weaken the power of trade unions in the UK considerably.

The efficiency wage hypothesis

We have seen that a union may be able to force an employer to pay a wage above the market-clearing rate. But it may well be in firms' interests to pay higher wage rates, even in non-unionised sectors.

One explanation for this is the *efficiency wage hypothesis*. This states that the productivity of workers rises as the wage rate rises. As a result, employers may be willing to offer wage rates above the market-clearing level, attempting to balance increased wage costs against gains in productivity. But why might higher wage rates lead to higher productivity? There are three main explanations.

Definitions

Core workers Workers, normally with specific skills, who are employed on a permanent or long-term basis.

Insiders Those in employment who can use their privileged position (either as members of unions or because of specific skills) to secure pay rises.

Outsiders Those out of work or employed on a casual, part-time or short-term basis, who have little or no power to influence wages or employment.

Closed shop Where a firm agrees to employ only union members.

Secondary action Industrial action taken against a company not directly involved in a dispute (e.g. a supplier of raw materials to a firm whose employees are on strike).

Efficiency wage hypothesis The hypothesis that the productivity of workers is affected by the wage rate that they receive.

BOX 9.5   THE RISE AND DECLINE OF THE LABOUR MOVEMENT IN THE UK

Modern trade unionism had its birth with the Industrial Revolution of the eighteenth and nineteenth centuries. Unions were seen as a means of improving the lot of industrial workers, most of whom suffered low pay and poor working conditions. But, with great hostility from employers, membership grew slowly. By the end of the nineteenth century, only just over 10 per cent of manual workers were in an effective union.

The big change came after the First World War, when returning troops demanded that the sacrifices made should be rewarded. Membership of trade unions increased sharply as workers sought to improve wages and working conditions. By 1920, 45 per cent of the total labour force (8.3 million workers) were in trade unions.

But it was after the Second World War that the trade union movement in the UK really became established as a substantial economic and political force. This can be explained by three crucial trends:

- The growth in the public sector meant that government was itself becoming increasingly responsible for determining wages and conditions of service for many workers.
- In their attempt to control inflation in the 1960s and 1970s, governments sought to impose an 'incomes policy' constraining wage increases. To be successful, this required acceptance by the trade union movement.
- The philosophy of many post-war governments was to govern by consent. Social contracts and discussions between government, employers and unions gave the union movement considerable influence over economic decision making.

Union power grew steadily during the 1950s and 1960s, so much so that attempts were made by successive governments to curb its influence. However, such moves attracted fierce and widespread opposition, and legislation was in many cases abandoned. The trade union movement had become very powerful by the late 1970s with over 13 million members.

The election of the Conservative government in 1979 ushered in a new wave of trade union reform, eroding and removing many rights and privileges acquired by unions over the years.

Trade union membership stood at about 6.5 million in 2012, around half of that seen in the late 1970s. This can be explained by a number of factors: the shift to a service-based economy; continued privatisation and the introduction of private-sector management practices, such as local pay bargaining; and contracted-out services in many of the remaining parts of the public sector. More women working and more part-time and casual work, with many people having no guaranteed hours (so-called 'zero-hours contracts'), are also contributory factors, as are the attitudes of many firms to union recognition. In many cases an aggressive management style and a highly competitive environment have made it virtually impossible for unions to gain bargaining rights in the private sector.

Union membership remains highest in areas of the public sector with high levels of monopsony power, such as education, but there is no doubt that, even here, union power has declined.

In the light of these changes, many unions have adopted a 'new realism', accepting single-union agreements and supporting flexible working practices and individualised pay packets based on performance (see Box 9.8).

However, not all the unions have lost their power. The British Medical Association is an example of a union (although it doesn't choose to use that title), which has protected the pay and power of doctors against a very large employer.

The RMT Union, which represents workers on London Underground, has been consistently recognised as highly successful in protecting jobs and securing pay-rises. Working closely with two other unions, ASLEF and TSSA, it has achieved above-inflationary pay deals, improved working conditions and shorter hours for tube staff. Critics point out that this has been at the expense of inconvenience to other workers, with regular tube strikes taking place. However, others would cite it as an example of the benefits of a strong union, protecting its members from monopsony power.

 What factors, other than the ones identified above, could account for the decline in union membership in recent years?

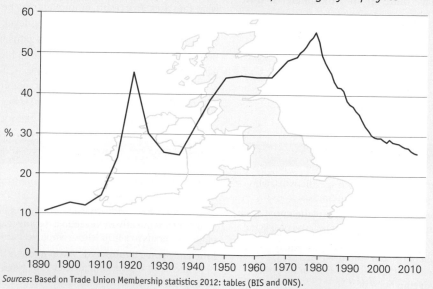

Trade union membership in Great Britain as a percentage of employees

Sources: Based on Trade Union Membership statistics 2012: tables (BIS and ONS).

BOX 9.6 HOW USEFUL IS MARGINAL PRODUCTIVITY THEORY?

Reality or the fantasy world of economists?

The marginal productivity theory of income distribution has come in for a number of criticisms. Are they justified?

To start with, marginal productivity theory has been criticised for assuming perfect competition. It doesn't! Rather, it merely states that to maximise profits an employer will employ workers up to the point where the worker's marginal cost equals the extra revenue added by that worker: $MC_L = MRP_L$. This applies equally under perfect competition, monopsony and oligopsony.

What it does say is that, if there is perfect competition, then the worker's wage will equal MRP_L. It certainly does not say that $W = MRP_L$ in other market structures.

A second criticism is that employers do not behave in this 'marginal way', weighing up each additional worker's costs and revenues for the firm. There are three possible reasons for this.

Ignorance of the theory of profit maximisation. The employer may use some rule of thumb, but nevertheless is attempting to maximise profits.

This is a criticism of the theory only if the theory is supposed to describe how employers actually behave. It does not. It merely states that, if firms are attempting to maximise profits, they will in fact be equating MC_L and MRP_L, whether they realise it or not!

A worker's marginal productivity cannot be calculated. When workers are part of a team, it is not usually possible to separate out the contribution to output of each individual. What is the marginal productivity of a cleaner, a porter or even a member of a production line? Similarly, it may not be possible to separate the contribution of workers from that of their tools. A lathe operator is useless without a lathe, as is a lathe without a lathe operator.

This is a more fundamental criticism. Nevertheless it is possible to amend the theory to take this into account. First,

an employer can look at the composition of the team, or the partnership of worker and tools, and decide whether any reorganisations or alternative production methods will increase the firm's profitability (i.e. increase revenue more than costs). Second, the employer can decide whether to expand or contract the overall size of the team, or the number of workers plus machines. Here the whole team or the worker plus machine is the 'factor of production' whose marginal productivity must be weighed against its costs.

Firms are not always profit maximisers. This is a criticism only if the theory states that firms are. As long as the theory is merely used to describe what would happen if firms maximised profits, there is no problem.

This criticism, then, is really one of how the theory is used. And even if it is used to predict what will actually happen in the real world, it is still relatively accurate in the large number of cases where firms' behaviour diverges only slightly from profit maximising. It is clearly wrong in other cases.

Moral issues. A final criticism is the moral one. If economists focus their attention exclusively on how to maximise profits, it might be concluded that they are putting their seal of approval on this sort of behaviour. Of course, economists will respond by saying that they are doing no such thing: they are confining themselves to positive economics. Nevertheless the criticism has some force. What an economist chooses to study is in part a normative decision.

 Do any of the following contradict marginal productivity theory: (a) wage scales related to length of service (incremental scales); (b) nationally negotiated wage rates; (c) discrimination; (d) firms taking the lead from other firms in determining this year's pay increase?

Less 'shirking'

In many jobs it is difficult to monitor the effort individuals put into their work. Workers may thus get away with shirking or careless behaviour. This is an example of the principal–agent problem (see page 225 and Box 9.9). The worker, as an agent of the employer (the principal), is not necessarily going to act in the principal's interest.

KI 23
p225

The business could attempt to reduce shirking by imposing a series of sanctions, the most serious of which would be dismissal. The greater the wage rate, the greater will be the cost to the individual of dismissal, and the less likely it is, therefore, that workers will shirk. The business will benefit not only from the additional output but also from a reduction in the costs of having to monitor workers' performance. As a consequence the *efficiency wage rate* for the business will lie above the market-determined wage rate.

Reduced labour turnover

If workers receive on-the-job training or retraining, then to lose a worker once the training has been completed is a significant cost to the business. Labour turnover, and hence its associated costs, can be reduced by paying a wage above the market-clearing rate. By paying such a wage rate the business is seeking a degree of loyalty from its employees.

Definition

Efficiency wage rate The profit-maximising wage rate for the firm after taking into account the effects of wage rates on worker motivation, turnover and recruitment.

BOX 9.7   EQUAL PAY FOR EQUAL WORK?

(a) *Average hourly pay, excluding overtime, for full-time UK employees, aged 18 and over, 1970–2013 (£ per hour)*

	1970	1974	1978	1982	1986	1990	1994	1998	2002	2006	2010	2013
Men	0.67	1.05	2.00	3.55	4.82	6.89	8.65	10.65	12.92	14.64	16.27	16.91
Women	0.42	0.71	1.48	2.62	3.58	5.28	6.88	8.39	10.32	12.10	13.74	14.25
Women's pay as % of men's	63.1	67.4	73.9	73.9	74.3	76.6	79.5	78.8	79.9	82.7	84.5	84.3

Source: Annual Survey of Hours and Earnings (National Statistics, various years).

(b) *Average hourly pay, excluding overtime, for selected occupations, full-time UK employees on adult rates, 2013 (£ per hour)*

Occupation	Men	Women	Women's pay as % of men's
Nurses	17.14	16.84	98.2
Call-centre workers	9.02	8.71	96.6
Social workers	17.31	16.61	96.0
Chefs	8.82	8.43	95.6
Secondary school teachers	22.28	21.22	95.2
Police officers (sergeant and below)	18.53	17.36	93.7
Bar staff	7.02	6.55	93.3
Sales and retail assistants	8.73	7.96	91.2
Librarians	15.62	13.98	89.5
Hairdressers, barbers	8.60	7.53	87.6
Laboratory technicians	12.88	11.17	86.7
Solicitors, lawyers and judges	32.11	25.48	79.4
Human resource managers/directors	31.81	25.12	79.0
Economists and statisticians	29.30	22.84	78.0
Medical practitioners	36.02	27.85	77.3
Assemblers and routine operatives	11.39	8.60	75.5
Chief executives and senior officials	58.27	38.10	65.4
All occupations	16.91	14.25	84.3
Average *gross weekly* pay (incl. overtime)	676.70	532.90	78.7
Average weekly hours worked (incl. overtime)	40.2	37.4	
Average weekly overtime	1.5	0.5	

Source: Annual Survey of Hours and Earnings (National Statistics, 2013).

Women earn less than men. How much less depends on how earnings are measured, but on the most widely used definition, earnings per hour, women on average earn about 16 per cent less than men. The gender wage gap narrowed gradually over the years. In 1970, it was 37 per cent (see table (a) above). Since 2010, however, it has remained roughly constant.

A similar picture of gender inequality in pay can be seen throughout the EU. In 2012, women's average hourly pay was 83.6 per cent of men's. The gender pay gap varies from one country to another. In Germany and Austria it was over 20 per cent, whereas in Italy and Slovenia it was less than 10 per cent.

The inequality between male and female earnings can in part be explained by the fact that men and women are occupationally segregated. Seeing that women predominate in poorly paid occupations, the difference in earnings is somewhat to be expected. But if you consider table (b), you can see that quite substantial earnings differentials persist within particular occupations.

1. *If we were to look at weekly rather than hourly pay and included the effects of overtime, what do you think would happen to the pay differentials in table (a)?*
2. *In table (b), which of the occupations have a largely female workforce?*

Morale

A simple reason for offering wage rates above the market-clearing level is to motivate the workforce – to create the feeling that the firm is a 'good' employer that cares about its employees. As a consequence, workers might be more industrious and more willing to accept the introduction of new technology (with the reorganisation and retraining that it involves).

The paying of efficiency wages above the market-clearing wage will depend upon the type of work involved. Workers

who occupy skilled positions, especially where the business has invested time in their training (thus making them costly to replace) are likely to receive efficiency wages considerably above the market wage. By contrast, workers in unskilled positions, where shirking can be easily monitored, where little training takes place and where workers can be easily replaced, are unlikely to command an 'efficiency wage premium'. In such situations, rather than keeping wage rates high, the business will probably try to pay as little as possible.

TC 5
p54

So why has this inequality persisted? There are a number of possible reasons:

- The marginal productivity of labour in typically female occupations may be lower than in typically male occupations. This may in part be due to simple questions of physical strength. Very often, however, it is due to the fact that women tend to work in more labour-intensive occupations. If there is less capital equipment per female worker than there is per male worker, then it would be expected that the marginal product of a woman would be less than that of a man. Evidence from the EU as a whole suggests that occupational segregation is a significant factor in explaining pay differences.
- Many women take career breaks to have children. For this reason, employers are sometimes more willing to invest money in training men (thereby increasing their marginal productivity), and more willing to promote men.
- Women tend to be less geographically mobile than men. If social norms are such that the man's job is seen as somehow more 'important' than the woman's, then a couple will often move if necessary for the man to get promotion. The woman, however, will have to settle for whatever job she can get in the same locality as her partner. This may also reduce a woman's bargaining power when negotiating for wage increases in her current job. A smaller proportion of women workers are members of unions than men. Even when they are members of unions, these are often in jobs where unions are weak (e.g. clothing industry workers and shop assistants).
- Part-time workers (mainly women) have less bargaining power, less influence and less chance of obtaining promotion.
- Custom and practice. Despite equal pay legislation, many jobs done wholly or mainly by women continue to be low paid, irrespective of productivity.
- Prejudice. In many jobs women are discriminated against when it comes to promotion, especially to senior positions. A report published in 2011 for the UK government[1] confirmed that women remain seriously underrepresented in boardrooms. This phenomenon is known as the 'glass ceiling' and it is very difficult to legislate against. Businesses can simply claim that the 'better' person was promoted or that women do not put themselves forward. The report recommended a number of

initiatives for businesses to improve this situation, and set a target of 25 per cent by 2015. By 2014 progress had been made with just over 20 per cent of board positions going to women.

Which of the above reasons could be counted as economically 'irrational' (i.e. paying different wage rates to women and men for other than purely economic reasons)? Certainly the last two would classify. Paying different wage rates on these grounds would not be in the profit interests of the employer.

Some of the others, however, are more difficult to classify. The causes of the inequality in wage rates may be traced back beyond the workplace: perhaps to the educational system or to a culture that discourages women from being assertive in seeking promotion.

It is interesting to consider the role that maternity pay and leave may have played in the continuation of unequal incomes between women and men. In July 2008 Nicola Brewer, Chief Executive of the Equality and Human Rights Commission, gave a speech in which she suggested that overgenerous treatment of mothers, compared with fathers, was a contributory factor in continuing inequality. Ms Brewer argued that the UK's approach perpetuated the view that childcare was a women's issue rather than a parental one.

Her views, and those of others, have influenced recent developments in 'family-friendly' policies and from 2014 both parents have the right to share up to a year of parental leave. However, until this is widely accepted as the 'norm' and is used equally by men and women, employers may retain the view that women are less valuable and productive employees.

1. *If employers were forced to give genuinely equal pay for equal work, how would this affect the employment of women and men? What would determine the magnitude of these effects?*
2. *How could family policy ensure that parents are able to work, while reducing pay differentials?*
3. *What measures could a government introduce to increase the number of women getting higher-paid jobs?*

[1] www.bis.gov.uk/assets/biscore/business-law/docs/w/ 11-745-women-on-boards.pdf

Other labour market imperfections

The possession of power by unions and/or firms is not the only way in which real-world labour markets diverge from the perfectly competitive model:

- Workers or employers may have imperfect information.
- Wages may respond very slowly to changes in demand and supply, causing disequilibrium in labour markets to persist.
- Firms may not be profit maximisers. Likewise workers may not seek to maximise their 'worker surplus' – the excess

of benefits from working (i.e. wages) over the disutility of working (displeasure in doing the job and lost leisure).

Some of the forms and effects of these three imperfections are examined in Case Study 9.3. in MyEconLab.

Discrimination

Discrimination can be another major factor in determining wages. It can take many forms: it can be by race, gender, sexual orientation, age, class, religion, etc.; it can occur in

BOX 9.8 FLEXIBLE LABOUR MARKETS AND THE FLEXIBLE FIRM

New work practices for old?

KI 22
p223

The past 35 years have seen sweeping changes in the ways that firms organise their workforce. Global recessions combined with rapid changes in technology led many firms to question the wisdom of appointing workers on a permanent basis to specific jobs. Instead, they want the flexibility to respond to changing situations. If demand falls, they want to be able to reduce labour without facing large redundancy costs. If demand rises, they want rapid access to additional labour. If technology changes they want to have the flexibility to move workers around, or to take on new workers in some areas and lose workers in others.

What many firms seek, therefore, is flexibility in employing and allocating labour. What countries are experiencing is an increasingly flexible labour market, as workers and employment agencies respond to the new 'flexible firm'.

There are three main types of flexibility in the use of labour:

- *Functional flexibility*. This is where an employer is able to transfer labour between different tasks within the production process. It contrasts with traditional forms of organisation where people were employed to do a specific job, and then stuck to it. A functionally flexible labour force will tend to be multi-skilled and relatively highly trained.
- *Numerical flexibility*. This is where the firm is able to adjust the size and composition of its workforce according to changing market conditions. To achieve this, the firm is likely to employ a proportion of its labour on a part-time or casual basis, or even subcontract specialist requirements. An increasingly common practice is for workers to be on 'zero-hours contracts', where the employee has no guaranteed hours at all and where actual hours may vary on a weekly basis.
- *Financial flexibility*. This is where the firm has flexibility in its wage costs. In large part it is a result of functional and numerical flexibility. Financial flexibility can be achieved by rewarding individual effort and productivity rather than paying a given rate for a particular job. Such rates of pay are increasingly negotiated at the local level rather than being nationally set. The result is not only

a widening of pay differentials between skilled and unskilled workers, but also growing differentials in pay between workers within the same industry but in different parts of the country.

The diagram shows how these three forms of flexibility are reflected in the organisation of a *flexible firm*, an organisation quite different from that of the traditional firm. The most significant difference is that the labour force is segmented. The core group, drawn from the *primary labour market*, will be composed of functionally flexible workers, who are generally on secure full-time permanent contracts. Such workers will be relatively well paid and receive wages reflecting their scarce skills.

The periphery, drawn from the *secondary labour market*, is more fragmented than the core, and can be subdivided into a first and a second peripheral group. The first peripheral group

The flexible firm

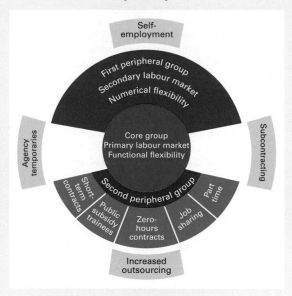

Source: J. Atkinson, *Flexibility, Uncertainty and Manpower Management* (Institute of Manpower Studies, 1984), IMS Report No. 89.

Definitions

Functional flexibility Where employers can switch workers from job to job as requirements change.

Numerical flexibility Where employers can change the size of their workforce as their labour requirements change.

Financial flexibility Where employers can vary their wage costs by changing the composition of their workforce or the terms on which workers are employed.

Flexible firm A firm that has the flexibility to respond to changing market conditions by changing the composition of its workforce.

Primary labour market The market for permanent full-time core workers.

Secondary labour market The market for peripheral workers, usually employed on a temporary or part-time basis, or a less secure 'permanent' basis.

is composed of workers with a lower level of skill than those in the core, skills that tend to be general rather than firm-specific. Thus workers in this group can be drawn from the external labour market, often through agencies. Such workers may be employed on full-time contracts, but they will generally face less secure employment than those workers in the core.

The business gains a greater level of numerical flexibility by drawing labour from the second peripheral group. Here workers are employed on a variety of short-term, part-time contracts, often again through agencies. Some of these workers may be working from home, or online from another country, such as India, where wage rates are much lower. Workers in this group have little job security.

As well as supplementing labour in the first peripheral group, the second periphery can also provide high-level specialist skills. In this instance the business can subcontract or hire self-employed labour, minimising its commitment to such workers. The business thereby gains both functional and numerical flexibility simultaneously.

The Japanese model

The application of new flexible working patterns is becoming more prevalent in businesses in the UK and elsewhere in Europe and North America. In Japan, flexibility has been part of the business way of life for many years and was crucial in shaping the country's economic success in the 1970s and 1980s. In fact we now talk of a Japanese model of business organisation, which many of its competitors seek to emulate.

The model is based around four principles:

- *Total quality management (TQM).* This involves all employees working towards continuously improving all aspects of quality, both of the finished product and of methods of production.
- *Elimination of waste.* According to the 'just-in-time' (JIT) principle, businesses should take delivery of just sufficient quantities of raw materials and parts, at the right time and place. Stocks are kept to a minimum and hence the whole system of production runs with little, if any, slack. For example, supermarkets today have much smaller storerooms relative to the total shopping area than they did in the past, and take more frequent deliveries.

- *A belief in the superiority of team work.* Collective effort is a vital element in Japanese working practices. Team work is seen not only to enhance individual performance, but also to involve the individual in the running of the business and thus to create a sense of commitment.
- *Functional and numerical flexibility.* Both are seen as vital components in maintaining high levels of productivity.

The principles of this model are now widely accepted as being important in creating and maintaining a competitive business in a competitive marketplace.

Recent UK experience

Within the EU, prior to the recession of 2008–9, the UK was one of the most successful countries in cutting unemployment and creating jobs. Much of this has been attributed to increased labour market flexibility.

One of the puzzles of the downturn that took place from 2008 is how 'little' unemployment occurred in the UK. Of course if you were one of the 2.7 million people unemployed in 2011, then the use of this term may stick in your throat. However, it remains a fact that relative to output, fewer people were out of work than economic models predicted. One argument is that this happened because of the flexibility of reducing hours per worker or pay per hour rather than laying workers off. As a result, other EU member states, such as Italy and Germany, have sought to emulate many of the measures the UK has adopted.

1. *Is a flexible firm more likely or less likely to employ workers up to the point where their $MRP = MC_L$?*
2. *Would you expect the advent of flexible firms to alter the gender balance of employment and unemployment?*
3. *If a firm is trying to achieve flexibility in its use of labour, do you think this would be harder or easier in a period of recession? Explain why.*
4. *Assume workers in a firm are allowed to choose between a 20 per cent reduction in pay, or 20 per cent of the workforce being laid off. What factors would influence the workers' choice?*

many different aspects of society. This section is concerned with *economic discrimination*, where workers of identical ability receive different pay for doing the same job, or are given different chances of employment or promotion.

Definition

Economic discrimination Where workers of identical *ability* are paid different wages or are otherwise discriminated against because of race, age, sex, etc.

Take the case of racial discrimination by employers. Figure 9.11 illustrates the wages and employment of both black and white workers by a firm with monopsony power which practises racial discrimination against black workers. Let us assume that there is no difference in the productivity of black and white workers. Let us also assume for simplicity that there is an equal number of black workers and white workers available at any given wage rate. Finally, let us assume that there are no laws to prevent the firm discriminating in terms of either wages or employment.

BEHAVIOUR AT WORK

What motivates employees?

Much of the work of behavioural economists concentrates on how rational we are in our role as consumers. Do we weigh up the costs and benefits of purchases? Do we ignore sunk costs? Do we get excited by special offers? These are all interesting questions. Yet, most of us spend as much as 25 per cent of our lives as workers and thus this also merits attention.

Dan Ariely, Professor of Psychology and Behavioural Economics at Duke University, is one of the best-known researchers on the subject. In his second book, *The Upside of Irrationality*,[1] he looks at our behaviour at the world of work and identifies a number of areas where experimental findings appear to contradict the predictions of economic theory.

We care about what we produce

One area that Ariely looked at was how we feel both about what we produce, and about what happens to it. Economic theory suggests workers will be motivated by the rewards they receive for their work and the associated costs. It doesn't ascribe emotions to the outcome of our labour.

Ariely set up an experiment where participants built Lego models; they were paid for each model – at a diminishing rate – and could choose how many to build. There were two sets of participants. Each knew that the models would eventually be disassembled, but for the first set this happened out of their sight after they had finished building. The second set saw the models broken up in front of them, almost immediately.

How did the 'workers' react to these different circumstances? Those who saw their models remain in a valuable state built an average of more than 10 models each, and 68 per cent of them continued to produce when the price of their labour fell below a dollar. In contrast those whose models were destroyed in front of them built an average of just over seven models and only 20 per cent were prepared to work for less than a dollar per model. Ariely concludes from this and other experiments that we are more productive when our labour has meaning; when the outputs are valued.

Bonuses and incentives

There has been a great deal of discussion about bankers' bonuses in the past few years; hardly surprising given the number of banks that taxpayers around the world have bailed out. The response from financial institutions has been predictable: if they are to retain their best staff and get them to perform in the best possible way, they have to offer large bonuses.

It may be true that bonuses are an important part of recruitment and retention, but is it true that they increase productivity? Ariely and his colleagues tested this in a series of experiments, offering participants a variety of bonuses to reward achievement in a series of tasks. By doing this in India, where average incomes are very low, they were able to offer bonuses ranging from a day's wage through to the equivalent of five months' earnings.

Their findings were striking; those offered low and medium bonuses performed at about the same level, with a 'very good' performance on the tasks set around 30 per cent of the time. What about those who stood to gain more? Surely very large bonuses would concentrate the mind (and body, for some of the tasks were physical) and induce better performance? Well large bonuses certainly did have a noticeable effect and the results were striking. Those who could get up to five months' pay achieved a 'very good' performance less than 10 per cent of the time!

What happened? It seems that very large bonuses can lead to considerably worse performance. The pressure and the fear of not achieving the bonus combine to give a level of stress that diminishes performance, rather than enhances it.

Dan Ariely's experiment suggests that large bonuses are counter-productive. But do bonuses work at all? A research project led by Roland Fryer at Harvard University suggests not. In a study of a pay-for-performance programme in more than 200 schools in New York City, he looked at the impact of providing incentives to teachers. He found that offering bonuses to staff did not increase student achievement; furthermore there was no impact on teacher absences or on staff retention. So, in the real world, as in the laboratory, it seems that incentivising staff may not be a simple matter of offering cash, despite what the banks claim.

Lessons for employers

Academics believe that studying behaviour is inherently valuable and, of course, writers like Dan Ariely can also excite the attention and interest of a wider audience. Yet there is also an opportunity for employers to make use of these findings. Staff surveys often highlight concern about quality of outputs, in-house communications and the need to feel part of decision making. If firms are able to gain a better understanding of workers' motivation and to set rewards and incentives that account for this, the outcome may be higher productivity and a happier workforce.

1. *Dan Ariely suggests that bonuses should be based on an average of the previous five years' performance. Explain why this might lead to better performance than a simple annual bonus.*
2. *In Chapter 5 we identified specialisation and division of labour as a source of economies of scale. How might this principle be altered if we care about the finished product of our labour?*

[1] Dan Ariely, *The Upside of Irrationality* (Harper Collins, 2010).

Figure 9.11(a) shows the *MC* and *MRP* curves for black workers. If there were no discrimination, employment of black workers would be at Q_{B_1}, where $MRP_B = MC_B$. The wage rate paid to black workers would be W_{B_1}.

Figure 9.11(b) shows the position for white workers. Again, if there were no discrimination, Q_{W_1} white workers would be employed at a wage of W_{W_1}: the same wage as black workers. (Note that in each case the *MRP* curve is

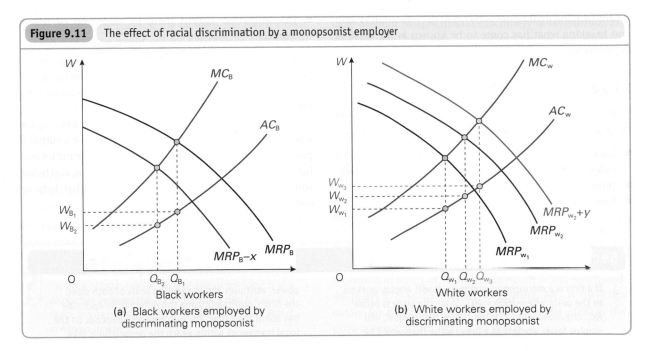

Figure 9.11   The effect of racial discrimination by a monopsonist employer

(a) Black workers employed by discriminating monopsonist

(b) White workers employed by discriminating monopsonist

drawn on the assumption that the number of workers employed from the other ethnic group is constant.)

If the firm now discriminates against black workers, it will employ workers along a lower curve, $MRP_B - x$ (where x can be seen as the discriminatory factor). Employment of black workers will thus be at the lower level of Q_{B_2} and the wage they receive will be at the lower level of W_{B_2}.

How will discrimination against black workers affect the wages and employment of white workers? Let us consider two cases.

In the first case, assume that the employer practises economic discrimination purely in the negative sense: i.e. it discriminates against black workers but employs white workers on profit-maximising principles. Thus white workers would be employed up to that point where their MC equals their MRP. But the fact that fewer black workers are now being employed will mean that for any given quantity of white workers there will be fewer workers employed in total, and therefore the MRP of white workers will have increased. In Figure 9.11(b) the white workers' MRP curve has shifted to MRP_{W_2}. This has the effect of raising employment of white workers to Q_{W_2} and the wage rate to W_{W_2}.

Firms may, however, also practise economic discrimination *in favour* of certain groups. Figure 9.11(b) also illustrates this second case, where the employer practises economic discrimination in favour of white workers. Here the firm will employ workers along a higher curve, $MRP_{W_2} + y$, where y is the discriminatory factor. The effect is further to increase the wage rate and level of employment of white workers, to W_{W_3} and Q_{W_3} respectively.

What effect will the discrimination by the firm have on the wages and employment of black workers in other firms in the area if (a) these other firms discriminate against black workers; (b) they do not discriminate?

If the government now legislates for equal pay for equal work, then employers that discriminate will respond by further cutting back on black workers. The answer to *this* problem would seem to be for the government to pass laws that insist not only that black workers be paid the same as white workers for doing the same job, but also that they be treated equally when applying for jobs.

The type of discrimination considered so far can be seen as 'irrational' if the firm wants to maximise profits. After all, to produce a given amount of output, it would be paying out more in wages to employ white workers than black workers. In a competitive market environment, such firms may be forced to end discrimination simply to survive the competition from non-discriminating rivals. If, however, the firm has market power, it will probably be making sufficient profits to allow it to continue discriminating. The main pressure to end discrimination is then likely to come from unions, customers, shareholders or race relations organisations.

Other examples of non-economic discrimination stem from unequal educational opportunities. If the educational system discriminates against black children, they are likely to end up with poorer qualifications. They have less **human capital** invested in them. Under these circumstances, employers, preferring to employ the best-qualified applicants, are likely to choose white people. This is particularly so in the more highly paid jobs that require a higher level of educational attainment. Tackling this problem at source

Definition

Human capital The qualifications, skills and expertise that contribute to a worker's productivity.

days. If it hires it for a second day, it can perhaps save another one or two days. Hiring it for additional days may save extra still. But diminishing returns are occurring: the longer the scaffolding is up, the less intensively it will be used, and the less additional time it will save. Perhaps for some of the time it will be used when ladders could have been used equally easily.

The time saved allows the firm to take on extra work. Thus each extra day the scaffolding is hired gives the firm extra revenue. This is the scaffolding's marginal revenue product of capital (MRP_K). Diminishing returns mean that it has the normal downward-sloping shape (see Figure 9.12).

Market demand

The market demand for capital services is derived in exactly the same way as the market demand for labour (see Figure 9.6 on page 254). It is the horizontal sum of the MRP_K curves of the individual firms, corrected for the fact that increased use of capital will increase output, drive down the price of the good and hence reduce MRP. This means that the market demand curve for capital is steeper than the horizontal sum of the demand curves (MRP_K) of all the firms in the market.

 Under what circumstances would the market demand for renting a type of capital equipment be (a) elastic; (b) inelastic? (Clue: turn back to page 62 and see what determines the elasticity of demand for labour.)

The supply of capital services

It is necessary to distinguish (a) the supply *to* a single firm, (b) the supply *by* a single firm and (c) the market supply.

Supply to a single firm

This is illustrated in Figure 9.13(a). The small firm renting capital equipment is probably a price taker. If so, it faces a horizontal supply curve at the going rental rate (R_e). If, however, it has monopsony power, it will face an upward-sloping supply curve as in Figure 9.12(b).

Supply by a single firm

This is illustrated in Figure 9.13(b). On the demand side, the firm is likely to be a price taker. It has to accept the going rental rate (R_e) established in the market. If it tries to charge more, then customers are likely to turn to rival suppliers.

But what will the individual supplier's *supply* curve look like? The theory here has a lot in common with perfect competition in the goods market (see pages 175–6): the supply curve is the firm's MC curve, only here the MC is the extra cost of supplying one more unit of capital equipment for rent over a given time period.

The problem with working out the marginal cost of renting out capital equipment is that the equipment probably cost a lot to buy in the first place, but lasts a long time. How then are these large costs to be apportioned to each new rental? The answer is that it depends on the time period under consideration.

The short run. In the short run, the hire company is not buying any new equipment: it is simply hiring out its existing stock of equipment. In the case of the scaffolding hire firm, the marginal costs of doing this will be as follows:

■ Depreciation. Scaffolding has second-hand value. Each time the scaffolding is hired out it deteriorates, and thus its second-hand value falls. This loss in value is called 'depreciation'.
■ Maintenance and handling. Hiring out equipment involves labour time (e.g. in the office) and possibly transport costs; the equipment may need servicing after being hired out.

These marginal costs are likely to rise relatively slowly. For each extra day a piece of equipment is hired out, the

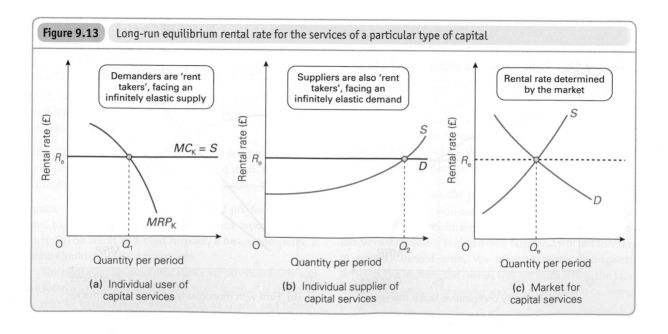

Figure 9.13　Long-run equilibrium rental rate for the services of a particular type of capital

(a) Individual user of capital services

(b) Individual supplier of capital services

(c) Market for capital services

company will incur the same or only slightly higher additional costs. This gives a relatively flat supply curve of capital services in Figure 9.13(b) up to the hire company's maximum capacity. Once the scaffolding firm is hiring out all its scaffolding, the supply curve becomes vertical.

 Assume now that the firm has monopoly power in hiring out equipment, and thus faces a downward-sloping demand curve. Draw in two such demand curves on a diagram like Figure 9.13(b), one crossing the MC curve in the horizontal section, and one in the vertical section. How much will the firm supply in each case and at what price? (You will need to draw in MR curves too.) Is the MC curve still the supply curve?

The long run. In the long run, the hire company will consider purchasing additional equipment. It can therefore supply as much as it likes in the long run. The supply curve will be relatively elastic, or if it is a price taker itself (i.e. if the scaffolding firm simply buys scaffolding at the market price), the supply curve will be horizontal. This long-run supply curve will be vertically higher than the short-run curve, since the long-run *MC* includes the cost of purchasing each additional piece of equipment.

Maths Case 9.1 in MyEconLab shows how this marginal cost can be calculated.

Market supply

This is illustrated in Figure 9.13(c). The market supply curve of a particular type of capital service is the sum of the quantities supplied by all the individual firms.

In the short run, the market supply will be relatively inelastic, given that it takes time to manufacture new equipment

and that stocks of equipment currently held by manufacturers are likely to be relatively small. Also, capital is *heterogeneous* (i.e. one piece of capital equipment is not the same as another). If there is a shortage of scaffolding, you cannot use a cement mixer instead; people would fall off! Finally, hire companies may be unwilling to purchase (expensive) new equipment immediately there is a rise in demand; after all, the upsurge in demand may turn out to be short-lived.

 If supply is totally inelastic, what determines the rental value of capital equipment in the short run?

In the *long run*, the supply curve of capital services will be more elastic because extra capital equipment can be produced. It will not be horizontal, however, but upward sloping. Its elasticity will depend on the elasticity of supply of capital equipment to the hire companies.

Determination of the price of capital services

As Figure 9.13(c) shows, in a perfect market the market rental rate for capital services will be determined by the interaction of market demand and supply. Note that the analysis here parallels that of the determination of the equilibrium wage in a given labour market (see Figure 9.1 on page 247).

 What will happen to the demand for capital services and the equilibrium rental if the price of some other factor, say labour, changes? Assume that wage rates fall. Trace through the effects on a three-section diagram like Figure 9.13. (Clue: a fall in wages will reduce costs and hence the price of the product, so that more will be sold; and it will make labour cheaper relative to capital.)

BOX 9.10 STOCKS AND FLOWS   EXPLORING ECONOMICS

The discussion of the rewards to capital and land leads to a very important distinction: that between stocks and flows.

A stock is a quantity of something held. A landowner may own 200 hectares. A farmer may have a barn with 500 tonnes of grain. You may have £1000 in a savings account. These are all stocks: they are all quantities held at a given point in time.

A flow is an increase or decrease in quantity over a specified period. The landowner may buy another 10 hectares during the year. The farmer may use 10 tonnes of grain from the barn each week as animal feed. You may save £10 per month.

Wages, rent and interest are all rewards to flows. Wages are the amount paid for the services of a person's labour for a week or month. Rent is the amount paid per period of time to use the services of land. Likewise interest is the reward paid to people per year for the use of their money.

If an asset is sold, its value is the value of the stock. It is a simple payment at a single point in time for the transfer of a whole asset. Thus the price of land and the price of capital are stock concepts.

An important example of stocks and flows arises with capital and investment. If a firm has 100 machines, that is a stock of capital. It may choose to build up its stock by investing. Investment is a flow concept. The firm may choose to invest in 10 new machines each year. This may not add 10 to the stock of machines, however, as some may be wearing out (a negative flow).

KEY IDEA 24 ***Stocks and flows.*** A stock is a quantity of something at a given point in time. A flow is an increase or decrease in something over a specified period of time. This is an important distinction and a common cause of confusion.

 Which of the following are stocks and which are flows?
(a) Unemployment.
(b) Redundancies.
(c) Profits.
(d) A firm's stock market valuation.
(e) The value of property after a period of inflation.

If there is monopsony power on the part of the users of hired capital, this will have the effect of depressing the rental rate below the MRP_K (see Figure 9.12(b)). If, on the other hand, there is monopoly power on the part of hire companies, the analysis is similar to that of monopoly in the goods market (see Figure 6.8 on page 182). The firm, by reducing the supply of capital for hire, can drive up the rental rate. It will maximise profit where the marginal revenue from hiring out the equipment is equal to the marginal cost of so doing: at a rental rate (price) *above* the marginal cost.

*Demand for and supply of capital for purchase

The alternative to hiring capital is to buy it outright. This section examines the demand and supply of capital for purchase.

The demand for capital: investment

How many computers will an engineering firm want to buy? Should a steelworks install another blast furnace? Should a removal firm buy another furniture lorry? These are all **investment** decisions. Investment involves purchasing of additional capital.

The demand for capital, or 'investment demand', by a profit-maximising firm is based on exactly the same principles as the demand for labour or the demand for capital services. The firm must weigh up the marginal revenue product of that investment (i.e. the money it will earn for the firm) against its marginal cost.

TC 8
p105

The problem is that capital is durable. It goes on producing goods, and hence yielding revenue for the firm, for a considerable period of time. Calculating these benefits therefore involves taking account of their timing.

There are two ways of approaching the problem: the *present value* approach and the *rate of return* approach. In both cases, the firm is comparing the marginal benefits with the marginal costs of the investment.

Present value approach.   To work out the benefit of an investment (its *MRP*), the firm must estimate all the future earnings it will bring and then convert them to a **present value**. It can then compare this with the cost of the investment. Let us take a simple example.

Assume that a firm is considering buying a machine. It will produce £1000 per year (net of operating costs) for four years and then wear out and sell for £1000 as scrap. What is

the benefit of this machine to the firm? At first sight the answer would seem to be £5000. This, after all, is the total income earned from the machine. Unfortunately, it is not as simple as this. The reason is that money earned in the future is less beneficial to the firm than having the same amount of money today: if the firm has the money today, it can earn interest on it by putting it in the bank or reinvesting it in some other project.

To illustrate this, assume that you have £100 today and can earn 10 per cent interest by putting it in a bank. In one year's time that £100 will have grown to £110, in two years' time to £121, in three years' time to £133.10, and so on. This process is known as *compounding*.

It follows that if someone offered to give you £121 in two years' time, that would be no better than giving you £100 today, since, with interest, £100 would grow to £121 in two years. What we say, then, is that, with a 10 per cent interest rate, £121 in two years' time has a *present value* of £100.

The procedure of reducing future value back to a present value is known as *discounting*.

 KEY IDEA 25

The principle of discounting. People generally prefer to have benefits today rather than in the future. Thus future benefits have to be reduced (discounted) to give them a present value.

When we do discounting, the rate we use is called the *rate of discount*: in this case, 10 per cent. The formula for discounting is as follows:

$$PV = \sum \frac{R_t}{(1 + r)^t}$$

where *PV* is the present value, R_t is the revenue from the investment in year *t*, *r* is the rate of discount (expressed as a decimal: e.g. 10% = 0.1) and $\sum$ is the sum of each of the years' discounted earnings.

So what is the present value of the investment in the machine that produced £1000 for four years and then is sold as scrap for £1000 at the end of the four years? According to the formula it is

$$\begin{array}{cccc} \text{Year 1} & \text{Year 2} & \text{Year 3} & \text{Year 4} \end{array}$$
$$= \frac{£1000}{1.1} + \frac{£1000}{(1.1)^2} + \frac{£1000}{(1.1)^3} + \frac{£2000}{(1.1)^4}$$
$$= £909 + £829 + £751 + £1366$$
$$= £3852$$

Definitions

Investment The purchase by the firm of equipment or materials that will add to its stock of capital.

Present value approach to appraising investment This involves estimating the value *now* of a flow of future benefits (or costs).

Compounding The process of adding interest each year to an initial capital sum.

Discounting The process of reducing the value of future flows to give them a present valuation.

Rate of discount The rate that is used to reduce future values to present values.

Thus the present value of the investment (i.e. its *MRP*) is £3852, *not* £5000 as it might seem at first sight. In other words, if the firm had £3852 today and deposited it in a bank at a 10 per cent interest rate, the firm would earn exactly the same as it would by investing in the machine.

So is the investment worthwhile? It is now simply a question of comparing the £3852 benefit with the cost of buying the machine. If the machine costs less than £3852, it will be worth buying. If it costs more, the firm would be better off keeping its money in the bank.

The difference between the present value of the benefits (PV_b) of the investment and its cost (C) is known as the **net present value** (*NPV*):

$$NPV = PV_b - c$$

If the *NPV* is positive, the investment is worthwhile.

 What is the present value of a machine that lasts three years, earns £100 in year 1, £200 in year 2 and £200 in year 3, and then has a scrap value of £100? Assume that the rate of discount is 5 per cent. If the machine costs £500, is the investment worthwhile? Would it be worthwhile if the rate of discount were 10 per cent?

Rate of return approach. The alternative approach when estimating whether an investment is worthwhile is to calculate the investment's *rate of return*. This rate of return is known as the firm's **marginal efficiency of capital** (*MEC*) or **internal rate of return** (*IRR*).

We use the same formula as for calculating present value:

$$PV = \sum \frac{R_t}{(1+r)^t}$$

and then calculate what value of *r* would make the *PV* equal to the cost of investment: in other words, the rate of discount that would make the investment just break even. Say this worked out at 20 per cent. What we would be saying is that the investment would just cover its costs if the current rate of interest (rate of discount) were 20 per cent. In other words, this investment is equivalent to receiving 20 per cent interest: it has a 20 per cent rate of return (*MEC*).

Details of how to calculate the internal rate of return, along with a worked example, are given in Maths Case 9.2 in MyEconLab.

So should the investment go ahead? Yes, if the actual rate of interest (*i*) is less than 20 per cent. The firm is better

KI 25
p272

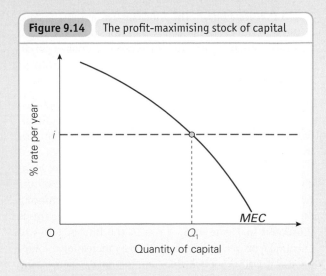

Figure 9.14 The profit-maximising stock of capital

off investing its money in this project than keeping it in the bank: i.e. if *MEC* > *i* the investment should proceed.

This is just one more application of the general rule that if $MRP_f > MC_f$ then more of the factor should be used: only in this case, *MRP* is expressed as a rate of return (*MEC*), and *MC* is expressed as a rate of interest (*i*).

The profit-maximising position is illustrated in Figure 9.14. As the firm invests more, and thus builds up its stock of capital, so *MEC* will fall due to diminishing returns. As long as *MEC* is greater than *i*, the firm should invest more. It should stop when the stock of capital has reached Q_1. Thereafter it should cut investment to a level just sufficient to replace worn-out machines, and thus keep the capital stock at Q_1.

TC 8
p105

KI 17
p135

The risks of investment. One of the problems with investment is that the future is uncertain. The return on an investment will depend on the value of the goods it produces, which will depend on the goods market. But future markets depend on consumer tastes, the actions of rivals and the whole state of the economy, none of which can be known with certainty. Investment is thus risky.

Risk may also be incurred in terms of the output from an investment. Take the case of prospecting for oil. An oil company may have a major strike, but it may simply drill dry well after dry well. If it does get a major strike, and hence earn a large return on its investment, these profits will not be competed away by competitors prospecting in other fields, because they too still run the risk of drilling dry holes.

How is this risk accounted for when calculating the benefits of an investment? The answer is to use a higher rate of discount. The higher the risk, the bigger the risk premium that must be added to the rate.

KI 11
p80

The supply of capital

It is necessary to distinguish the supply of *physical* capital from the supply of *finance* to be used by firms for the purchase of capital.

Supply of physical capital. The principles here are just the same as those in the goods market. It does not matter whether a firm is supplying lorries (capital) or cars (a consumer good), it will still produce up to the point where *MC = MR* if it wishes to maximise profits.

Supply of finance. An economy will have a stock of financial capital (or 'loanable funds') held in banks and other financial institutions. These funds can be borrowed by firms for investment in new physical capital.

When people save, this will build up the stock of loanable funds. This flow of saving represents the resources released when people refrain from consumption. Among other things, saving depends on the rate of interest. This is illustrated in Figure 9.15. A rise in the interest rate will encourage people to save more, thereby increasing the supply (i.e. the stock) of loanable funds (a movement up along the supply curve).

This supply curve will be relatively inelastic in the short run, since the flow of saving over a short time period (say, a month) will have only a relatively small effect on the total stock of funds. Over a year, however, the effect would be 12 times bigger. The longer the time period, therefore, the more elastic the supply curve.

Saving also depends on the level of people's incomes, their expectations of future price changes, and their willingness to sacrifice present consumption in order to be able to have more in the future. A change in any of these other determinants will shift the supply curve.

*Determination of the rate of interest

The rate of interest is determined by the interaction of supply and demand in the market for loanable funds. This is illustrated in Figure 9.15. As we have seen, supply represents accumulated savings.

The demand curve includes the demand by households for credit and the demand by firms for funds to finance their investment. The curve slopes downwards for two reasons.

First, households will borrow more at lower rates of interest. It effectively makes goods cheaper for them to buy. Second, it reflects the falling rate of return on investment as investment increases. This is simply due to diminishing returns to investment. As rates of interest fall, it will become profitable for firms to invest in projects that have a lower rate of return: the quantity of loanable funds demanded thus rises.

Equilibrium will be achieved where demand equals supply at an interest rate of i_e and a quantity of loanable funds $£_e$.

How will this market adjust to a change in demand or supply? Assume that there is a rise in demand for capital equipment, due, say, to an improvement in technology that increases the productivity of capital. There is thus an increase in demand for loanable funds. The demand curve shifts to the right in Figure 9.15. The equilibrium rate of interest will rise and this will encourage more savings. The end result is that more money will be spent on capital equipment.

Capital and profit

What does the analysis so far tell us about the amount of profit that firms will earn? After all, profit is the reward that the owners of firms get from owning and using capital.

Remember from Chapter 6 the distinction between normal and supernormal profit. In a perfectly competitive world, all supernormal profits will be competed away in the long run.

Another way of putting this is that a perfectly competitive firm in the long run will earn only a **normal rate of return** on capital. This means that the return on capital (after taking risk into account) will be the same as if the owners of capital had simply deposited their money in a bank instead. If a firm's capital yields a higher rate of return than this normal level (i.e. supernormal returns), other firms will be attracted to invest in similar capital. The resulting increased level of capital will increase the supply of goods. This in turn will lower the price of the goods and hence lower the rate of return on capital until it has fallen back to the normal level.

 Can a perfectly competitive firm earn a supernormal rate of return on capital if it continuously innovates?

If, however, capital owners have monopoly/oligopoly power and can thus restrict the entry of new firms or the copying of innovations – for example, by having a patent on a particular process – they can continue to get a supernormal return on their capital.

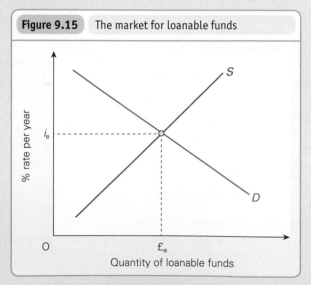

Figure 9.15 The market for loanable funds

Definition

Normal rate of return The rate of return (after taking risks into account) that could be earned elsewhere.

Financing investment

Sources of business finance

A firm can finance capital investment in one of three major ways:

- Internal funds (i.e. retained profits).
- Borrowing from the banking sector.
- Issuing new shares (equities) or debentures (fixed-interest loan stock).

The largest source of finance for investment in the UK is firms' own internal funds (i.e. ploughed-back profits). Given, however, that business profitability depends in large part on the general state of the economy, internal funds as a source of business finance are likely to vary considerably across the business cycle. When profits are squeezed in a recession, this source of investment will decline.

Other sources of finance, which include borrowing and the issue of shares and debentures, are known as 'external funds'. These are then categorised as short-term, medium-term or long-term sources of finance:

- Short-term finance is usually in the form of a short-term bank loan or overdraft facility, and is used by business as a form of working capital to aid it in its day-to-day business operations.
- Medium-term finance, again provided largely by banks, is usually in the form of a loan with set repayment targets. It is common for such loans to be made at a fixed rate of interest, with repayments being designed to fit in with the business's expected cash flow. Bank lending has been the most volatile source of business finance, and has been particularly sensitive to the state of the economy. While part of the reason is the lower demand for loans during a recession, another part of the reason is the caution of banks in granting loans if prospects for the economy are poor. In 2008 there was a reduction in the willingness of banks to grant loans to businesses following the credit crunch. (This is examined in more detail in sections 18.2 and 21.2.)
- Long-term finance, especially in the UK, tends to be acquired through the stock market. It will usually be in the form of *shares* (or *equities*). This is where members of the public or institutions (such as pension funds) buy a part ownership in the company and, as a result, receive dividends on those shares. The dividends depend on the amount of profit the company makes and distributes to shareholders. The proportion of business financing from this source clearly depends on the state of the stock market.

In the late 1990s, with a buoyant stock market, the proportion of funds obtained through share issue increased. Then with a decline in stock market prices from 2000 to 2003, this proportion fell. In 2008 there were very substantial falls in the values of shares, further reducing the ability of firms to raise finance. The recovery in share prices seen in 2013 gave rise to hope that firms would be able to fund the investment needed to increase growth back to pre-recession levels.

Alternatively, firms can issue *debentures* (or *company bonds*). These securities are fixed-interest loans to firms. Debenture holders have a prior claim on company shares. Their interest must be paid in full before shareholders can receive any dividends.

Despite the traditional reliance on the stock market for external long-term sources of finance, there has been a growing involvement of banks in recent years. Prior to the credit crunch in 2008, banks had become more willing to provide finance for business start-ups and for diversification. This has been less apparent since, and there is a concern that banks are inherently cautious. This risk aversion results in a problem of 'short-termism', with bankers often demanding a quick return on their money or charging high interest rates, and being less concerned to finance long-term investment.

Comparison of the UK with other European countries. In other European countries, notably Germany and France, the attitude towards business funding is quite different from that in the UK. In these countries banks provide a significant amount of long-term, fixed-rate finance. This provides a much more stable source of finance and creates an environment where banks are much more committed to the long-run health of companies.

The role of the stock market

The London Stock Exchange operates as both a primary and secondary market in capital.

As a *primary market*, it is where public limited companies (see Case Study 8.1 in MyEconLab) can raise finance by issuing new shares, whether to new shareholders or to existing ones. To raise finance on the Stock Exchange a business must be 'listed'. The Listing Agreement involves directors agreeing to abide by a strict set of rules governing behaviour and levels of reporting to shareholders. Companies must have at least three years' trading experience and make at

---

Definitions

Shares (equities) A part ownership of a company. Companies' distributed profits are paid to shareholders in the form of dividends according to the number of shares held.

Debentures (company bonds) Fixed-interest loans to firms. These assets can be traded on the stock market and their market price is determined by demand and supply.

Primary market in capital Where shares are sold by the issuer of the shares (i.e. the firm) and where, therefore, finance is channelled directly from the purchasers (i.e. the shareholders) to the firm.

least 25 per cent of their shares available to the public. In March 2014, there were 881 UK and 480 international companies on the Official List.

As well as those on the Official List, there are nearly 1100 companies on what is known as the Alternative Investment Market (AIM). Companies listed here tend to be young but with growth potential, and do not have to meet the strict criteria or pay such high costs as companies on the Official List. In 2013, 105 companies joined the London Stock Exchange, the highest number for six years. As a consequence, new capital worth over £15.7 billion was raised through 43 main market listings and 62 AIM IPOs.

As a *secondary market*, the Stock Exchange enables investors to sell *existing* shares and debentures to one another. In March 2014, on an average day's trading, trading in UK equities worth £5.5 billion took place.

The advantages and disadvantages of using the stock market to raise capital

As a market for raising capital, the stock market has a number of advantages:

- It brings together those that wish to invest and companies that seek investment, and does so in a relatively low-cost way. It thus represents a way that savings can be mobilised to generate output.
- Firms that are listed on the Stock Exchange are subject to strict regulations. This is likely to stimulate investor confidence, making it easier for business to raise finance.
- The process of merger and acquisition is facilitated by having a share system, which in turn increases competition for corporate control (see page 186).

The main weaknesses of the stock market for raising capital are as follows:

- The cost to a business of getting listed can be immense, not only in a financial sense, but also in being open to public scrutiny. Directors' and senior managers' decisions will often be driven by how the market is likely to react, rather than by what they perceive to be in the business's best interests. They always have to think about the reactions of those large shareholders in the City that control a large proportion of their shares.
- In the UK, it is often claimed that the market suffers from *short-termism*. Investors on the Stock Exchange are mainly concerned with a company's short-term performance

and its share value. In responding to this, the business might neglect its long-term performance and potential.

Is the stock market efficient?

One of the arguments made in favour of the stock market is that it acts as an arena within which share values can be accurately or efficiently priced. If new information comes onto the market concerning a business and its performance, this will be quickly and rationally transferred into the business's share value. This is known as the *efficient market hypothesis*. So, for example, if an investment analyst found that, in terms of its actual and expected dividends, a particular share was underpriced and thus represented a 'bargain', the analyst would advise investors to buy. As people then bought the shares, their price would rise, pushing their value up to their full worth. Thus by attempting to gain from inefficiently priced securities, investors will encourage the market to become more efficient.

So how efficient is the stock market in pricing securities? Is information rationally and quickly conveyed into the share's price? Or are investors able to prosper from the stock market's inefficiencies?

We can identify three levels of efficiency.

The weak form of efficiency. Share prices often move in cycles that do not reflect the underlying performance of the firm. If information is imperfect, those with a better understanding of such cycles gain from buying shares at the trough and selling them at the peak of the cycles. They are taking advantage of the market's inefficiency.

Increasing numbers of investment analysts are using technical models to track share cycles. As they do so and knowledge becomes more perfect, so the market will become more efficient and the cycles will tend to disappear. But why?

As more people buy a company's shares as the price falls towards its trough, extra demand will prevent the price falling so far. Similarly, as people sell as the price rises towards its peak, so this extra supply will prevent the price rising so far. This is an example of stabilising speculation (see page 76). As more and more people react in this way, so the cycle all but disappears. When this happens, *weak efficiency* has been achieved.

The semi-strong form of efficiency. Semi-strong efficiency is when share prices adjust fully to publicly available information. In practice, not all investors will interpret such information correctly: their knowledge is imperfect. But increasingly more

---

Definitions

Secondary market in capital Where shareholders sell shares to others. This is thus a market in 'second-hand' shares.

Short-termism Where firms and investors take decisions based on the likely short-term performance of a company, rather than on its long-term prospects. Firms may thus sacrifice long-term profits and growth for the sake of a quick return.

Efficient (capital) market hypothesis The hypothesis that new information about a company's current or future performance will be quickly and accurately reflected in its share price.

Weak efficiency (of share markets) Where share dealing prevents cyclical movements in shares.

advice is available to shareholders (through stockbrokers, newspapers, online commentators, published accounts, etc.), and more shares are purchased by professional fund managers. The result is that the interpretation of public information becomes more perfect and the market shows more **semi-strong efficiency**.

If the market were efficient in the semi-strong sense, then no gain could be made from studying a company's performance and prospects, as this information would *already* be included in the current share price. In selecting shares, you would do just as well by pinning the financial pages of a newspaper on the wall, throwing darts at them, and buying the shares the darts hit!

The strong form of efficiency.   If the stock market showed the **strong form of efficiency**, then share prices would fully reflect *all* available information – whether public or not. For this to be so, all 'inside' information would have to be reflected in the share price the moment the information became available.

If the market is *not* efficient at this level, then people who have access to privileged information will be able to make large returns from their investments by acting on such information. For example, directors of a company would know if the company was soon to announce better-than-expected profits. In the meantime, they could gain by buying shares in the company, knowing that the share price would rise when the information about the profits became public. Gains made from such 'insider dealing' are illegal. However, proving whether individuals are engaging in it is very difficult. By the time of its replacement by the Financial Conduct Authority in April 2013, the Financial Services Authority had secured just 23 convictions for insider dealing, prompting criticism that it was toothless.

Given the penalties for insider dealing and the amount of private information that firms possess, it is unlikely that all such information will be reflected in share prices. Thus the strong form of stock market efficiency is unlikely to hold.

 Would the stock market be more efficient if insider dealing were made legal?

If stock markets were fully efficient, the expected returns from every share would be the same. The return is referred to as the *yield*: this is measured as the dividends paid on the

share as a percentage of the share's market price. For example, if you hold shares whose market price is £1 per share and you receive an annual dividend of 3p per share, then the yield on the shares is 3 per cent. But why should the expected returns on shares be the same? If any share was expected to yield a higher-than-average return, people would buy it; its price would rise and its yield would correspondingly fall.

It would only be unanticipated information, therefore, that would cause share prices to deviate from that which reflected expected average yields. Such information must, by its nature, be random, and as such would cause share prices to deviate randomly from their expected price, or follow what we call a **random walk**. Evidence suggests that share prices do tend to follow random patterns.

Challenging the efficient market hypothesis

The efficient market hypothesis has been challenged by critics who laid the blame for the financial crisis in 2007–8 on unfounded belief in rational markets. They argued that regulators failed to understand the role that exuberance plays in financial markets. If investors are 'caught up' in the belief that share prices (or property values) will continue to increase in value, regardless of underlying information, then the result will be a bubble – a situation where assets are traded above their fundamental value.

According to behavioural economists, bubbles can be explained by a number of psychological factors. Among these are paying too little attention to the past, over confidence, overoptimism and herding. In short, people pay too much for assets because they remember recent returns more than historical averages, because they take more notice of economic good news than bad and because everyone else is doing it. Asset bubbles are vulnerable to breaking on the basis of changes in beliefs, as we saw in the collapse of the US housing market from 2006 and the subsequent stock market crash.

What does this imply for policy makers? The argument might be made that an asset bubble is simply a magnification of any market, with both losers and winners; this does not suggest a need for intervention. However, this ignores the macroeconomic consequences of the bubble, consequences which were clearly seen from 2007 on. Behaviourists therefore believe that effective financial regulation must take account of irrationality.

TC 5
p54

Definitions

Semi-strong efficiency (of share markets) Where share prices adjust quickly, fully and accurately to publicly available information.

Strong efficiency (of share markets) Where share prices adjust quickly, fully and accurately to all available information, both public and that only available to insiders.

Yield on a share The dividend received per share expressed as a percentage of the current market price of the share.

Random walk Where fluctuations in the value of a share away from its 'correct' value are random: i.e. have no systematic pattern. When charted over time, these share price movements would appear like a 'random walk': like the path of someone staggering along drunk!

Section summary

1. It is necessary to distinguish between buying the services of land (by renting) or capital (by hiring) and buying them outright.

2. The profit-maximising employment of land and capital services will be where the factor's *MRP* is equal to its price (under perfect competition) or its *MC* (where firms have monopsony power).

3. The demand for capital services will be equal to MRP_K. Due to diminishing returns, this will decline as more capital is used.

4. The supply of capital services to a firm will be horizontal or upward sloping depending on whether the firm is perfectly competitive or has monopsony power. The supply of capital services by a firm in the short run is likely to be relatively elastic up to its maximum use, and then totally inelastic. In the long run, the supplying firm can purchase additional capital equipment for hiring out. The long-run supply curve will therefore be very elastic, but at a higher rental rate than in the short run, given that the cost of purchasing the equipment must be taken into account in the rental rate.

5. The market supply of capital services is likely to be highly inelastic in the short run, given that capital equipment tends to have very specific uses and cannot normally be transferred from one use to another. In the long run, it will be more elastic.

6. The price of capital services is determined by the interaction of demand and supply.

*7. The demand for capital for purchase will depend on the return it earns for the firm. To calculate this return, all future earnings from the investment have to be reduced to a present value by discounting at a market rate of interest (discount). If the present value exceeds the cost of the investment, the investment is worthwhile. Alternatively, a rate of return from the investment can be calculated and then this can be compared with the return that the firm could have earned by investing elsewhere.

8. The supply of finance for investment depends on the supply of loanable funds, which in turn depends on the rate of interest, on the general level of thriftiness and on expectations about future price levels and incomes.

9. The rate of interest will be determined by the demand and supply of loanable funds. When deciding whether to make an investment, a firm will use this rate for discounting purposes. If, however, an investment involves risks, the firm will require a higher rate of return on the investment than current market interest rates.

10. Business finance can come from internal sources (ploughed-back profits) or from external ones. External sources of finance include borrowing and the issue of shares.

11. The stock market operates as both a primary and a secondary market in capital. As a primary market it channels finance to companies as people purchase new shares and debentures. It is also a market for existing shares and debentures.

12. The stock market helps to stimulate growth and investment by bringing together companies and people who want to invest in them. By regulating firms and by keeping transaction costs of investment low, it helps to ensure that investment is efficient.

13. The stock market does impose costs on firms, however. It is expensive for firms to be listed and the public exposure may make them too keen to 'please' the market. It can also foster short-termism.

14. The stock market is relatively efficient. It achieves weak efficiency by reducing cyclical movements in share prices. It achieves semi-strong efficiency by allowing share prices to respond quickly and fully to publicly available information. Whether it achieves strong efficiency by adjusting quickly and fully to all information (both public and insider), however, is more doubtful.

9.4 LAND AND RENT

Rent: the reward to landowners

We turn now to land. The income it earns for landowners is the *rent* charged to the users of the land. This rent, like the rewards to other factors, is determined by demand and supply.

What makes land different from other factors of production is that it has an inelastic supply. In one sense, this is obvious. The total supply of land in any area is fixed.

In another sense, supply is not *totally* inelastic. Land can be improved. It can be cleared, levelled, drained, fertilised, etc. Thus the supply of a certain type of land can be increased by expending human effort on improving it. The question is whether *land* has thereby increased, or whether

the improvements constitute *capital* invested in land, and if so whether the higher rents that such land can earn really amount to a return on the capital invested in it.

To keep the analysis simple, let us assume that land *is* fixed. Let us take the case of an area of 10 000 hectares surrounding the village of Oakleigh. This is shown as a vertical supply 'curve' in Figure 9.16. The demand curve for that land will be like the demand curve for other factors of production. It is the *MRP* curve and slopes down due to diminishing returns from land. The equilibrium rent is r_e, where demand and supply intersect.

Notice that the level of this rent depends entirely on *demand*. If a new housing development takes place in Oakleigh, due perhaps to a growth in employment in a

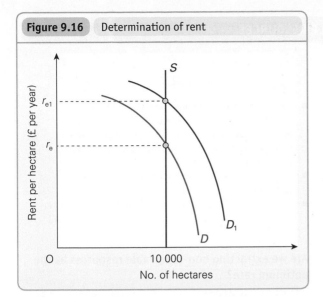

Figure 9.16 Determination of rent

1. We defined the factor of production 'land' to include raw materials. Does the analysis of rent that we have just been looking at apply to raw materials?
2. The supply of land in a particular area may be totally inelastic, but the supply of land in that area for a specific purpose (e.g. growing wheat) will be upward sloping: the higher the price of wheat and thus the higher the rent that wheat producers are prepared to pay, the more will be made available for wheat production. What will determine the elasticity of supply of land for any particular purpose?

The price of land

Not all land is rented: much of it is bought and sold outright. Its price will depend on what the purchaser is prepared to pay, and this will depend on the land's rental value.

Let us say that a piece of land can earn £1000 per year. What would a person be prepared to pay for it? There is a simple formula for working this out:

$$P = \frac{R}{i} \qquad (1)$$

where P is the price of the land, R is the rent per year and i is the market rate of interest.

Let us assume that the market rate of interest is 10 per cent (i.e. 0.1). Then according to the formula, a purchaser would be prepared to pay

$$\frac{£1000}{0.1} = £10\,000$$

Why should this be so? If a person deposits £10 000 in the bank, with an interest rate of 10 per cent this will earn that person £1000 per year. Assuming our piece of land is guaranteed to earn a rent of £1000 per year, then provided it costs less than £10 000 to buy, it is a better investment than putting money in the bank. The competition between people to buy this land will drive its price up until it reaches £10 000.

This is just another example of equilibrium being where marginal cost equals marginal benefit. This can be demonstrated by rearranging equation (1) to give

$$Pi = R$$

Remember that the equilibrium price of the land (P) is £10 000 and that the rate of interest (i) is 0.1. If you borrow the £10 000 to buy the land, it will cost you £1000 per year in interest payments (i.e. Pi). This is your annual marginal cost. The annual marginal benefit will be the rent (R) you will earn from the land.

1. What price would the same piece of land sell for if it still earned £1000 rent per year, but if the rate of interest were now (a) 5 per cent; (b) 20 per cent?
2. What does this tell us about the relationship between the price of an asset (like land) and the rate of interest?

---

nearby town, the demand curve will shift to D_1 and the equilibrium rent will rise to r_{e1}. But the supply of land remains fixed at 10 000 hectares. Landowners will earn more rent, but they themselves have done nothing: the higher rent is a pure windfall gain.

So why are rents in the centre of London many times higher per hectare than they are in the north of Scotland? The answer is that demand is very much higher in London.

Demand for land depends on its marginal revenue product. Thus it is differences in the *MRP* of land that explain the differences in rent from one area to another. There are two reasons for differences in *MRP*. Remember that *MRP* = *MPP* (marginal physical product of the factor) × *MR* (marginal revenue of the good produced by that factor).

Differences in MPP. Land differs in productivity. Fertile land will produce a higher output than deserts or moorland. Similarly, land near centres of population will be of much more use to industry than land in the middle of nowhere.

What other factors will determine the MPP of land for industry?

Differences in MR. The higher the demand for a particular good, the higher its price and marginal revenue, and hence the higher the demand and rent for the land on which that good is produced. Thus if the demand for housing rises relative to the demand for food, the rent on land suitable for house building will rise relative to the rent on agricultural land.

To summarise: rents will be high on land that is physically productive (high *MPP*) and produces goods in high demand (high *MR*).

| BOX 9.11 | THE ECONOMICS OF NON-RENEWABLE RESOURCES | EXPLORING ECONOMICS |

What happens as stocks diminish?

As world population rises, so the demands on resources continue to grow. Some of these resources are renewable. Water resources are replenished by rain. The soil, if properly managed, can continue to grow crops. Felled forests can be replanted. Of course, if we use these resources more rapidly than they are replenished, stocks will run down. We are all aware of the problems of seas that are overfished, or rainforests that are cleared, or reservoirs that are inadequate to meet our growing demand for water.

But whereas these resources can be replenished, others cannot. These are known as non-renewable resources. What determines the price of such resources and their rate of depletion? Will we eventually run out of resources such as oil, coal, gas and various minerals? To answer these questions, we need to distinguish between the available stock of such resources, and their use (a flow). The greater their use, the faster the stocks will run down.

Price increases over time

As stocks run down, so the price of the resources will tend to increase. Thus we can all expect to pay more for fossil fuels as remaining reserves are depleted. Owners of the reserves (e.g. mine owners and owners of oil wells) will thus find the value of their assets increasing. But how quickly will prices rise? In a perfect market, they will rise at the market rate of return on other assets (of equivalent risk). This is known as the Hotelling rule, named after Harold Hotelling who developed the argument in the early 1930s.

To understand why this is so, consider what would happen if the price of oil rose more slowly than the rate of return on other assets. People who owned oil wells would find that the value of their oil reserves was increasing less rapidly than the value of other assets. They might as well sell more oil now and invest the money in other assets, thereby getting a higher return. The extra oil coming to the market would depress the current oil price, but also reduce reserves, thereby creating a bigger shortage for the future and hence a higher future price. This would cause oil prices to rise more quickly over time (from the new lower base). Once the rate of price increase has risen to equal the rate of return on other assets, equilibrium has occurred. There will no longer be an incentive for the oil to be extracted faster.

The current price

But what determines the current price level (as opposed to its rate of increase)? This will be determined by supply and demand for the extracted resource (its flow).

In the case of a resource used by households, demand will depend on consumer tastes, the price of other goods, income, etc. Thus the greater the desire for using private cars, the greater the demand for petrol. In the case of minerals used by firms, demand will depend on the marginal revenue product of the resources. In either case, a rise in demand will cause a rise in the resource's price.

Supply will depend on three things:

- The rate of interest on other assets. As we have seen, the higher the rate of interest, the faster will the resource be extracted, in order that the mine owners (or well owners) can reinvest their profits at these higher rates of interest.
- The stock of known reserves. As new reserves are discovered, this will push down the price.
- The costs of extraction. The lower the costs, the greater will be the amount extracted, and hence the lower will be the market price of the resource.

Are we extracting non-renewable resources at the optimum rate?

If there are limited reserves of fossil fuels and other minerals, are we in danger that they will soon run out? Should we be more concerned with conservation?

In fact, the market provides an incentive to conserve such resources. As reserves run down, so the price of non-renewable resources will rise. This will create an incentive to discover alternatives. For example, as fossil fuels become more expensive, so renewable sources of energy, such as solar power, wind power and wave power, will become more economical. There will also be a greater incentive to discover new techniques of power generation and to conserve energy.

Markets, however, are imperfect. As we shall see in Chapter 11, when we consume natural resources, we do not take into account the full costs. For example, the burning of fossil fuels creates harmful environmental effects in the form of acid rain and the greenhouse effect, but these 'external' costs are not included in the price we pay.

Then there is the question of the distribution of income between present and future generations. If non-renewable resources are going to be expensive in the future, should we not be conserving these resources today in order to help our descendants? The problem is that consumers may well act totally selfishly, saying, 'Why should we conserve resources? By the time they run out, we will be dead.' We almost certainly do care about the welfare of our children and grandchildren, but what about our great-great-grandchildren, whom we will never meet?

1. Will the market provide incentives for firms to research into energy-conserving techniques, if energy prices at present are not high enough to make the use of such techniques profitable?
2. How will the existence of monopoly power in the supply of resources influence their rate of depletion?
3. If the current generation wants to consume all non-renewable resources, is there any market solution to prevent this happening? (We will come back to this in Chapter 12.)

Who are the poor? Who are the rich?

We have been building up an answer to these questions as this chapter has progressed. The final part of the answer concerns the ownership of land and capital. Many people own no land or capital at all. These people will therefore earn no profit, rent or interest.

For those who are fortunate enough to own productive assets, their income from them will depend on (a) the quantity they own and (b) their rental value.

The quantity of assets owned

This will depend on the following:

- Inheritance. Some people have rich parents who leave them substantial amounts of land and capital.
- Past income and savings. If people have high incomes and save a large proportion of them, this helps them to build up a stock of assets.
- Skill in investment (entrepreneurial skill). The more skilful people are in investing and in organising production, the more rapidly will their stock of assets grow.
- Luck. When people open up a business, there are usually substantial risks. The business might flourish or fail.

The rental value

This is the income earned per unit of land and capital. It will depend on the following:

- The level of demand for the factor. This depends on the factor's *MRP*, which in turn depends on its physical productivity (*MPP*) and the demand for the good it produces and hence the good's *MR*.
- The elasticity of demand for the good. The greater the monopoly power that capital owners have in the goods market, the less elastic will be the demand for the product and the greater will be the supernormal returns they can earn on their capital.
- The elasticity of supply of the factor. The less elastic its supply, the more factor owners can gain from a high demand. The high demand will simply push up the level of economic rent that the factor will earn.
- The total factor supply by other factor owners. The further to the left the total factor supply curve, the higher the level of economic rent that each unit of the factor can earn for any given level of demand.

Thus if you are lucky enough to have rich parents who leave you a lot of money when you are relatively young; if you are a skilful investor and save and reinvest a large proportion of your earnings; if you own assets that few other people own, and which produce goods in high demand: then you may end up very rich.

If you have no assets, you will have no property income at all. If at the same time you are on a low wage or are unemployed, then you may be very poor indeed.

Section summary

1. Rent on land, like the price of other factor services, is determined by the interaction of demand and supply. Its supply is totally inelastic (or nearly so). Its demand curve is downward sloping and will equal the *MRP* of land.

2. The price of land depends on its potential rental value (its marginal benefit) and the repayment costs of borrowing to pay for the land (its marginal cost). Equilibrium is where the two are equal.

3. People's income depends not only on their wages but on whether they own any land or capital, and, if they do, the rental value of these assets. This is the final element in determining the distribution of income in the economy.

END OF CHAPTER QUESTIONS

1. The wage rate that a firm has to pay and the output it can produce vary with the number of workers as follows (all figures are hourly):

Number of workers	1	2	3	4	5	6	7	8
Wage rate (AC_L) (£)	3	4	5	6	7	8	9	10
Total output (TPP_L)	10	22	32	40	46	50	52	52

Assume that output sells at £2 per unit.

(a) Copy the table and add additional rows for TC_L, MC_L, TRP_L and MRP_L. Put the figures for MC_L and MRP_L in the spaces between the columns.

(b) How many workers will the firm employ in order to maximise profits?

(c) What will be its hourly wage bill at this level of employment?

(d) How much hourly revenue will it earn at this level of employment?

(e) Assuming that the firm faces other (fixed) costs of £30 per hour, how much hourly profit will it make?

(f) Assume that the workers now formed a union and that the firm agreed to pay the negotiated wage rate to all employees. What is the maximum to which the hourly wage rate could rise without causing the firm to try to reduce employment below the level of (b) above? (See Figure 9.10.)

(g) What would be the firm's hourly profit now?

2. If a firm faces a shortage of workers with very specific skills, it may decide to undertake the necessary training

itself. If, on the other hand, it faces a shortage of unskilled workers, it may well offer a small wage increase in order to obtain the extra labour. In the first case, it is responding to an increase in demand for labour by attempting to shift the supply curve. In the second case, it is merely allowing a movement along the supply curve. Use a demand and supply diagram to illustrate each case. Given that elasticity of supply is different in each case, do you think that these are the best policies for the firm to follow? What would happen to wages and economic rent if it used the second policy in the first case?

3. Why do the world's top footballers earn millions of pounds per year, while the top lacrosse players are paid less than the equivalent of £30 000?

4. For what reasons is the median hourly wage rate of women some 16 per cent lower than of that of men in the UK, and the average gross weekly pay, including overtime, more than 21 per cent less?

5. Given the analysis of bilateral monopoly, if the passing of minimum wage legislation forces employers to pay higher wage rates to low-paid employees, will this necessarily cause a reduction in employment?

6. Using a diagram like Figure 9.13, demonstrate what will happen under perfect competition when there is an increase in the productivity of a particular type of capital. Consider the effects on the demand, price (rental rate) and quantity supplied of the services of this type of capital.

7. What factors could cause a rise in the market rate of interest?

8. How is the market price of land related to its productivity?

9. In recent years there have been a number of changes in planning laws to make it easier for commercial properties to be converted to housing. What would be the impact on property values?

Online resources

Additional case studies in MyEconLab

9.1 **Economic rent and transfer earnings.** This examines a way of classifying the earnings of a factor of production and shows how these earnings depend on the elasticity of supply of the factor.

9.2 **Telecommuters.** This case study looks at the rise of telecommuting, whereby people are able to work from home utilising modern technology.

9.3 **Other labour market imperfections.** This looks at three imperfections (see page 263): namely, imperfect information, persistent disequilibria in labour markets and non-maximising behaviour by firms or workers.

9.4 **Profit sharing.** An examination of the case for and against profit sharing as a means of rewarding workers.

9.5 **Holidays: good for workers; bad for employers?** An examination of holiday entitlements in the USA and Europe and their effects on workers and business.

Maths Case 9.1 Calculating the long-run cost of supplying additional equipment for rent. A worked example.

Maths Case 9.2 Calculating the internal rate of return. A worked example.

Websites relevant to this chapter

See sites listed at the end of Chapter 10 on page 313.

MyEconLab

This book can be supported by MyEconLab, which contains a range of additional resources, including an online homework and tutorial system designed to test and build your understanding.

You need both an access card and a course ID to access MyEconLab:

1. Is your lecturer using MyEconLab? Ask your lecturer for your course ID.

2. Has an access card been included with the book at a reduced cost? Check the inside back cover of the book.

3. If you have a course ID but no access card, go to: http://www.myeconlab.com/ to buy access to this interactive study programme.

Microeconomic Policy

10	Inequality, Poverty and Policies to Redistribute Income	284
11	Markets, Efficiency and the Public Interest	314
12	Environmental Policy	353
13	Government Policy towards Business	381

We now turn to the application of microeconomics and its role in government policy. In Part C we looked at *how* market economies function at a micro level. In Part D we examine the various policies that can be adopted to deal with shortcomings of the market system.

There are various questions that governments will ask. How much monopoly power is too much? How equal do we want the distribution of income to be? How can we make markets more efficient? How can we protect the environment and prevent the depletion of resources? How can we prevent climate change?

In Chapter 10 we look at policies that address the distribution of income. In Chapter 11 we examine the issue of market failure and consider the potential for government intervention. Finally in Chapters 12 and 13 we turn to government policies with respect to the environment and business.

Inequality, Poverty and Policies to Redistribute Income

CHAPTER MAP

10.1 Inequality and poverty	**285**
Types of inequality	285
The size distribution of income in the UK	286
Measuring the size distribution of income	286
The functional distribution of income in the UK	289
Other determinants of income inequality	290
The distribution of wealth	292
Causes of inequality	293
Government attitudes towards inequality	294
10.2 Taxes, benefits and the redistribution of income	**296**
The use of taxation and government expenditure to redistribute income	296
The requirements of a good tax system	296
Types of tax	297
Taxes as a means of redistributing income	300
Problems with using taxes to redistribute incomes	300
Taxation and incentives	303
Benefits	306
Benefits and the redistribution of income	308
The tax/benefit system and the problem of disincentives: the poverty trap	308
Conclusions	308

In Chapter 9 we saw that there are considerable differences in wage rates, and that these depend on market conditions. Similarly, we saw that differences in rewards to owners of capital and land also depend on their respective markets.

But differences in factor rewards are only part of the explanation of inequality. In this chapter, we open out the analysis. We take a more general look at why some people are rich while others are poor, and consider the overall degree of inequality in our society: a society that includes the super-rich, with their luxury yachts, and people living in slum conditions, with not enough to feed themselves or their children. We will see how the gap between rich and poor has tended to widen over time.

We will show how inequality can be measured so that we can make comparisons over time and between countries. We will also look at how incomes are distributed between particular groups, whether by occupation, age, sex, household composition or geographical area.

The second part of the chapter considers what can be done to reduce inequality. Is the solution to tax the rich heavily, so that the money can be redistributed to the poor? Or might this discourage people from working so hard? Would it be better, then, to focus on benefits and increase the support for the poor? Or might this discourage people from taking on work for fear of losing their benefits? We look at the attitudes of governments and at some of the debates taking place today over how to reduce inequality without discouraging effort or initiative.

10.1 INEQUALITY AND POVERTY

Inequality is one of the most contentious issues in the world of economics and politics. Some people have incomes far in excess of what they need to enjoy a luxurious lifestyle, while others struggle to purchase even necessities.

The need for some redistribution from rich to poor is broadly accepted across the political spectrum. Thus the government taxes the rich (and those who most would agree are not rich) and transfers some of the proceeds to the poor, either as cash benefits or as benefits in kind. Nevertheless there is considerable disagreement as to the appropriate *amount* of redistribution.

Whether the current distribution of income is desirable or not is a normative question. Economists therefore should not specify how much the government should redistribute incomes. Nevertheless economists do have a role to play in the analysis of inequality and in assessing the impact of policies. They can do the following:

- Identify the extent of inequality and analyse how it has changed over time.
- Explain why a particular level of income distribution occurs and what causes inequality to grow or to lessen.
- Examine the relationship between equality and other economic objectives such as efficiency.
- Identify various government policies to deal with problems of inequality and poverty.
- Examine the effects of these policies, both on inequality itself and on other questions such as efficiency, inflation and unemployment.
- Examine the effect of other policies, for example the reduction of the budget deficit, on inequality and poverty.

Types of inequality

There are a number of different ways of looking at the distribution of income and wealth.

The distribution of income

There are three broad ways of examining the distribution of income. First we can look at how evenly incomes are distributed among the population. This is known as the *size distribution of income*. It can be expressed between *households*, or between *individual earners*, or between *all individuals*. It can be expressed either *before* or *after* the deduction of taxes and the receipt of benefits. For example, we might want to know the proportion of pre-tax national income going to the richest 10 per cent of households.

Then there is distribution between different *factors of production*, known as the *functional distribution of income*. At the *broader* level, we could look at the distribution between the general factor categories: labour, land and capital. At a *narrower* level, we could look at distribution within the factor categories. Why are some jobs well paid

while others are badly paid? Why are rents higher in some areas than in others? We looked at this distribution in Chapter 9.

Finally there is the question of the *distribution of income by class of recipient*. This can be by *class of person*: women, men, single people, married people, people within a particular age group or ethnic group, and so on. Alternatively, it can be by *geographical area*. Typically, this is expressed in terms of differences in incomes between officially defined regions within a country.

The distribution of wealth

Income is a *flow*. It measures the receipt of money per period of time (e.g. £25 000 per year). Wealth, by contrast, is a stock (see Box 9.10). It measures the value of a person's assets at a particular point in time. The distribution of wealth can be measured as a size distribution (how evenly it is distributed among the population); as a functional distribution (the proportion of wealth held in various forms, such as dwellings, land, company shares, bank deposits, etc.), or according to the holders of wealth, classified by age, sex, geographical area, etc.

Analysis of incomes below a certain level: the analysis of poverty

A major problem here is in defining just what is meant by poverty. The dividing line between who is poor and who is not is necessarily arbitrary. Someone who is classed as poor in the UK may seem rich to an Ethiopian.

The extent and nature of poverty can be analysed in a number of ways:

- The number or proportion of people or households falling into the category.
- The occupational distribution of poverty.
- The geographical distribution of poverty.
- The distribution of poverty according to age, sex, ethnic origin, marital status, educational attainment, etc.

Definitions

Size distribution of income Measurement of the distribution of income according to the levels of income received by individuals (irrespective of source).

Functional distribution of income Measurement of the distribution of income according to the source of income (e.g. from employment, from profit, from rent, etc.).

Distribution of income by class of recipient Measurement of the distribution of income between the classes of person who receive it (e.g. homeowners and non-homeowners or those in the north and those in the south).

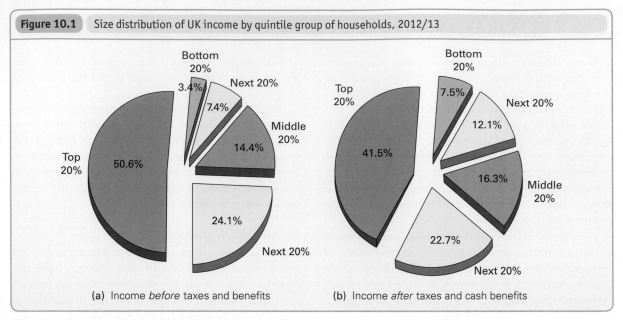

Figure 10.1 Size distribution of UK income by quintile group of households, 2012/13

(a) Income *before* taxes and benefits

(b) Income *after* taxes and cash benefits

Note: Figures do not necessarily add up to 100 due to rounding.
Source: Based on data in *The effects of taxes and benefits on household income, 2012/13* (National Statistics, June 2014).

It is not possible in this chapter to look at all aspects of inequality in the UK. Nevertheless some of the more important facts are considered, along with questions of their measurement and interpretation.

The size distribution of income in the UK

Figure 10.1 shows the size distribution of income in the UK. It covers income from all sources. In each chart, households are grouped into five equal-sized groups or *quintiles*, from the poorest 20 per cent of households up to the richest 20 per cent. (The general term for division into equal-sized groups is *quantiles*.) The following points can be drawn from these statistics:

- In 2012/13 the richest 20 per cent of households earned 50.6 per cent of national income, and even after the deduction of taxes this was still 41.5 per cent.
- The poorest 20 per cent, by contrast, earned a mere 3.4 per cent of national income, and even after the receipt of benefits this had risen to only 7.5 per cent.

Inequality grew dramatically in the 1980s and did not begin to reduce again until 2000, and then only very slightly. Between 1977 and 2012/13 the post-tax-and-benefits share of national income of the bottom 40 per cent of households fell from 23 per cent to 19.6 per cent, while the share of the top 20 per cent grew from 37 per cent to 41.5 per cent.

As we shall see in section 10.2, by taxing the rich proportionately more than the poor, taxes can be used as a means of reducing inequality. In the UK, however, indirect taxes (e.g. on tobacco and alcohol) are paid proportionately more by the poor and so have the opposite effect. In 2012/13, the lowest-earning 20 per cent of households paid 37.4 per cent of their gross income in taxes, while the highest-earning

20 per cent paid only 35.1 per cent. When we look at indirect taxes we see that the poorest quintile paid 27.5 per cent of their income while the richest quintile paid only 10.9 per cent. This more than offsets the redistributive effect from income tax being paid proportionately more by the rich.

Redistribution of income in the UK, therefore, is achieved mainly through the benefits system.

Measuring the size distribution of income

Apart from tables and charts, two of the most widely used methods for measuring inequality are the *Lorenz curve* and the *Gini coefficient*.

Lorenz curve

Figure 10.2 shows the **Lorenz curve** for the UK based on pre-tax (but post-benefit) incomes.

The horizontal axis measures percentages of the population from the poorest to the richest. Thus the 40 per cent point represents the poorest 40 per cent of the population. The vertical axis measures the percentage of national income they receive.

Definitions

Quintiles Divisions of the population into five equal-sized groups (an example of a quantile).

Quantiles Divisions of the population into equal-sized groups.

Lorenz curve A curve showing the proportion of national income earned by any given percentage of the population (measured from the poorest upwards).

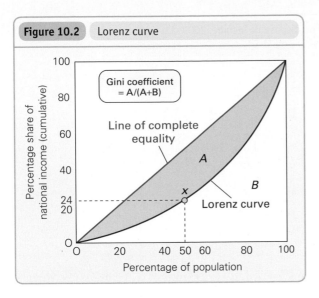

The curve starts at the origin: zero people earn zero incomes. If income were distributed totally equally, the Lorenz curve would be a straight 45° line. The 'poorest' 20 per cent of the population would earn 20 per cent of national income; the 'poorest' 60 per cent would earn 60 per cent; and so on. The curve ends up at the top right-hand corner, with 100 per cent of the population earning 100 per cent of national income.

In practice, the Lorenz curve will 'hang below' the 45° line. Point *x*, for example, shows a country where the poorest 50 per cent of households receive only 24 per cent of national income. The further the curve drops below the 45° line, the greater will be the level of inequality.

The Lorenz curve is quite useful for showing the change in income distribution over time. From 1949 to 1979 the curve for the UK moved inwards towards the 45° line, suggesting a lessening of inequality. Then from 1979 to 1990 it moved downwards away from the 45° line, suggesting a deepening of inequality. Since 1990 it has remained approximately the same.

The problem with simply comparing Lorenz curves by eye is that it is imprecise. This problem is overcome by using Gini coefficients.

Gini coefficient

The **Gini coefficient** is a precise way of measuring the position of the Lorenz curve. It is the ratio of the area between the Lorenz curve and the 45° line to the whole area below the 45° line. In Figure 10.2 this is the ratio of the shaded area *A* to the whole area (*A* + *B*), sometimes expressed as a percentage.

If income is totally equally distributed so that the Lorenz curve follows the 45° line, area *A* disappears and the Gini coefficient is 0. As inequality increases, so does area *A*. The Gini coefficient rises. In the extreme case of total inequality, where one person earns the whole of national income, area *B* would disappear and the Gini coefficient

would be 1. Thus the Gini coefficient will be between 0 and 1. The higher it is, the greater is the inequality. In 1979 the pre-tax Gini coefficient in the UK was 0.30. With the growth in inequality during the 1980s, the coefficient steadily increased and stood at 0.39 in 1990. Since then it has remained at approximately that level (fluctuating between 0.36 and 0.39). The post-tax coefficient rose even more dramatically – from 0.29 in 1979 to 0.41 in 1990. It was 0.37 in 2012/13.

Figure 10.3 shows the Gini coefficients for a selection of countries for 2009, 2010 or 2011. These are based on disposable income: that is, income after the deduction of taxes and the receipt of cash benefits (transfers). As you can see, northern European countries had the lowest Gini coefficients and hence were the most equal. The most unequal was South Africa, followed by Brazil and Chile. The average of the 34 developed countries that form the Organization for Economic Co-operation and Development (OECD) was 0.313, more equal than the USA (0.380) and slightly more than the UK (0.323).

Gini coefficients have the advantage of being relatively simple to understand and use. They provide a clear way of comparing income distribution either in the same country at different times, or between different countries.

However, they cannot take into account all the features of inequality. Take the case of the two countries illustrated in Figure 10.4. If area *X* is equal to area *Y*, they will have the same Gini coefficient, and yet the pattern of their income distribution is quite different.

Also it is important to note what statistics are used in the calculation. Are they pre-tax or post-tax; do they include benefits; do they include non-monetary incomes (such as food grown for own consumption, a major item in many developing countries); are they based on individuals, households or tax units?

 In which country in Figure 10.4 would you expect to find the highest number of poor people? Describe how income is distributed in the two cases.

Ratios of the shares in national income of two quantile groups

This is a very simple method of measuring income distribution. A ratio quite commonly used is that of the share of national income of the *bottom 40 per cent* of the population to that of the *top 20 per cent*. Thus if the bottom 40 per cent earned 15 per cent of national income and the top 20 per cent earned 50 per cent of national income, the ratio would be 15/50 = 0.3. The lower the ratio, therefore, the greater the inequality.

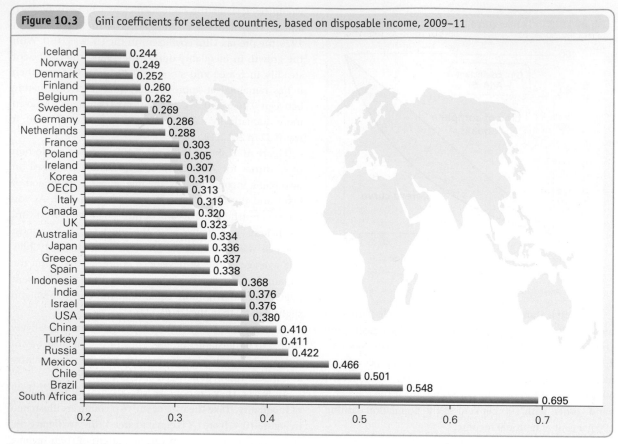

Figure 10.3 Gini coefficients for selected countries, based on disposable income, 2009–11

Source: Based on data in StatExtracts (OECD).

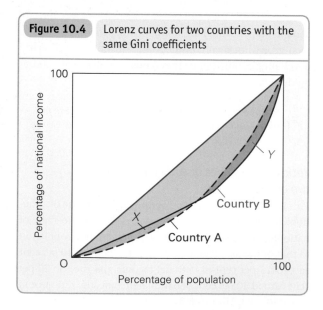

Figure 10.4 Lorenz curves for two countries with the same Gini coefficients

Romania of 0.62. Generally more advanced countries are more equal than developing countries. Western European countries typically have a ratio of between 0.4 and 0.65. The UK's is 0.41. The USA, however, is less equal, with a ratio of around 0.35. Note that all these ratios are drawn from the World Bank's database and refer to disposable income.

1. *Why do you think that the ratios for developing countries are lower than those for developed countries?*
2. *Make a list of reasons why the ratios of the bottom 40 per cent to the top 20 per cent may not give an accurate account of relative levels of inequality between countries.*
3. *What would the ratio be if national income were absolutely equally distributed?*

Do earnings statistics give a true representation of inequality?

Although the size distribution of income gives a good first indication of inequality, there are various factors that need to be taken into account when interpreting the statistics.

The first is the diminishing marginal utility of income. If a rich person spends twice as much as a poor person, does that mean that they get twice as much utility? The answer is probably no. The more you earn and spend, the

South Africa, the world's most unequal country, has a ratio of just 0.11. Zambia and Brazil, also highly unequal, have ratios of 0.16 and 0.17 respectively. By contrast, India and Pakistan are much more equal, with ratios of 0.48 and 0.56 respectively. Some of the former communist countries are much more equal still. Hungary has a ratio of 0.53 and

less additional utility you will get for each extra amount spent (see pages 101 and 122). Part of the reason is that you buy more luxurious versions of products. The argument here is that a car costing £40 000 will not give you four times as much utility as one costing £10 000.

The second factor concerns the interpretation of changes in inequality over time. The past 30 years have seen income increases skewed towards the rich, with the top 10 per cent of income earners getting a lot richer, while the incomes of the poor have risen very little. As we have seen, from 1979 to 2012/13 the Gini coefficient of post-tax income in the UK rose from 0.29 to 0.37.

Although it appears from these figures that inequality has grown rapidly, there may have been factors that mitigate against this. As people earn more, they spend proportionately more on services, such as childcare and personal trainers, and on luxury goods such as designer clothing and fast cars, and proportionately less on items such as basic foodstuffs and clothing. The argument here is that if the prices of these more luxurious goods and services rise faster than those of more basic goods, the poor will experience a lower inflation rate than the rich. This is what happened over the period 1990–2005, meaning that inequality did not rise as fast as the simple statistics would suggest.

More recently, however, the inflation rate of the poor has overtaken that of the rich. Prices of food and energy have risen faster than those of luxury goods. This would suggest that more recent statistics may have *understated* the growth in inequality.

The third factor that needs to be taken into account when assessing inequality is the distribution of *wealth*. We consider this below (pages 292–3).

The functional distribution of income in the UK

Distribution of income by source

Figure 10.5 shows the sources of household incomes in 1975 and 2012. Wages and salaries constitute by far the largest element. However, their share fell from 77 per cent to 65 per cent of national income between 1975 and 2012. Conversely, the share coming from social security benefits and pensions rose from 12 per cent to 23 per cent, reflecting the growing proportion of the population past retirement age and the stage of the economic cycle.

In contrast to wages and salaries, investment income (dividends, interest and rent) accounts for a relatively small percentage of household income – a mere 3 per cent in 2012. Nevertheless, some groups, typically elderly people, rely on savings interest as a key source of income. With the plummeting of interest rates in 2008 in response to the credit crunch, many of these people were badly hit. The problem worsened from 2009 to 2012 as nominal interest rates remained at historically low levels but inflation rose, meaning that for most savers real interest rates were negative. Conversely, those with large mortgages linked to the Bank of England's Bank Rate ('tracker mortgages'), found themselves with much smaller payments each month. There was thus a major redistributive effect away from net savers to net borrowers.

With the growth of small businesses and the increased numbers of people being 'employed' on a freelance basis, the proportion of incomes coming from self-employment has grown. It rose from 6 per cent in 1975 to 8 per cent in 2012, although this is lower than the 10 per cent seen in 2010.

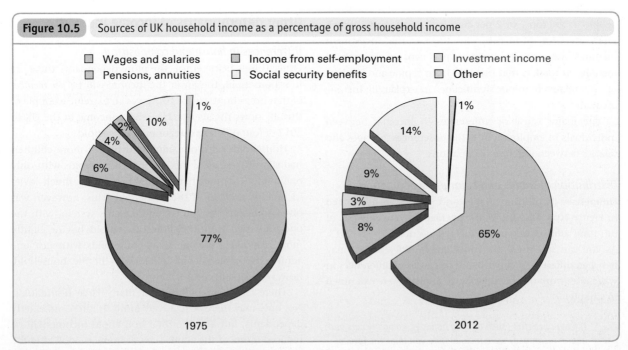

| Figure 10.5 | Sources of UK household income as a percentage of gross household income |

Source: Based on data in *Family Spending* (National Statistics, 2013).

Table 10.1   Sources of UK household income as a percentage of total household income by quintile groups: 2012

Gross household weekly incomes (quintiles)	Wages and salaries (1)	Income from self-employment (2)	Income from investments (3)	Pensions and annuities (4)	Social security benefits (5)	Other (6)	Total (7)
Lowest 20%	11	4	1	9	73	2	100
Next 20%	30	5	2	16	45	2	100
Middle 20%	53	7	2	14	21	2	100
Next 20%	71	6	2	10	9	2	100
Highest 20%	78	11	3	5	2	1	100
All households	65	8	3	9	14	1	100

Source: Family Spending (National Statistics, 2013).

The overall shares illustrated in Figure 10.5 hide the fact that the sources of income differ quite markedly between different income groups. These differences are shown in Table 10.1.

Column (1) shows that higher-income groups get a larger proportion of their income from wages and salaries than do lower-income groups. This can be largely explained by examining column (5). As would be expected, the poor tend to get a larger proportion of their incomes in social security benefits than do people further up the income scale.

It is interesting to note that the second poorest 20 per cent of households have a larger proportion of their income from pensions and annuities than any other group. Pensioners are clustered in this group because they tend to be fairly poor (pensions being less than wages), but not as poor as unemployed people or families on low incomes.

One feature to note is that the proportion of income coming from profits, rent and interest (column (3)) varies little between the income groups. In fact only for those people in the top 1 or 2 per cent is it significantly higher. The conclusion from this, plus the fact that investment incomes account for only 3 per cent of household incomes in total, is that incomes from capital and land are of only relatively minor significance in explaining income inequality.

The major cause of differences in incomes between individuals in employment is the differences in wages and salaries between different occupations.

Distribution of wages and salaries by occupation

Differences in full-time wages and salaries are illustrated in Figure 10.6. This shows the average gross weekly pay of full-time adult workers in selected occupations in 2013. As you can see, there are considerable differences in pay between different occupations. The causes of differences in wage rates from one occupation to another were examined in Chapter 9.

If fringe benefits (such as long holidays, company cars and health insurance) were included, do you think the level of inequality would increase or decrease? Explain why.

Since the late 1970s, wage differentials have widened. Part of the explanation lies in a shift in the demand for labour. Many firms have adopted new techniques which require a more highly educated workforce. Wage rates in some of these skilled occupations have increased substantially.

At the same time, there has been a decline in the number of unskilled jobs in industry and, along with it, a decline in the power of unions to represent such people. Where low-skilled jobs remain, there will be pressure on employers to reduce wage costs if they are competing with companies based in developing countries, where wage rates are much lower.

As prospects for unskilled people decline in industry, so people with few qualifications increasingly compete for low-paid, service-sector jobs (e.g. in supermarkets and fast-food outlets). The growth in people seeking part-time work has also kept wage rates down in this sector.

Other determinants of income inequality

Differences in household composition

Other things being equal, the more dependants there are in a household, the lower the income will be *per member* of that household. Figure 10.7 gives an extreme example of this. It shows the average household income in the UK in 2012 of four different categories of household.

Households with one adult and two or more children had slightly less gross income than households with only one adult. This means that they had a very much lower income *per member* of the household. This, however, was offset somewhat by the tax and benefits system, with the one-adult, two-or-more-children households having slightly more disposable income than households with just one adult. Disposable income *per member* of the household, however, was still considerably less.

There is a twin problem for many large households. Not only may there be relatively more children and elderly dependants, but also the total household income will be reduced if one of the adults stays at home to look after the family or works only part time.

Figure 10.6 Average gross weekly earnings (excluding overtime) of UK full-time adult employees (£): 2013

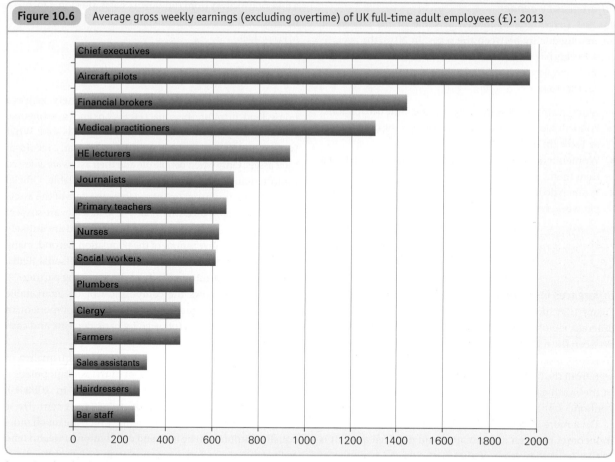

Source: Based on data in *Annual Survey of Hours and Earnings* (National Statistics, 2013).

Figure 10.7 Weekly income for different types of UK households (£), 2012

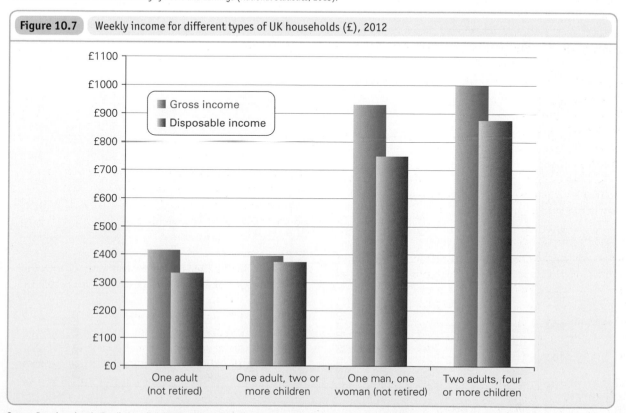

Source: Based on data in *Family Spending* (National Statistics, 2013).

Differences by gender

Box 9.7 (pages 262–3) looked at some of the aspects of income inequality between the sexes. In 2013, the average gross weekly pay for full-time female employees was £532.90. For male employees it was £676.70. There are three important factors to note:

- Women are paid less than men in the same occupations. You will see this if you compare some of the occupations in Table (b) in Box 9.7.
- Women tend to be employed in lower-paid occupations than men.
- Women do less overtime than men (on average, 0.5 hours per week, compared with 1.5 for men).

 List the reasons for each of the three factors above. (Reread section 9.2 and Box 9.7 if you need help.)

Differences in the geographical distribution of income

Figure 10.8 shows the gross weekly household incomes in different regions of the UK in 2012. Differences in incomes between the regions reflect regional differences in industrial structure, unemployment and the cost of living. As can be seen from the figure, average incomes are significantly lower in the north-east than in the south-east of England and in London.

On a more local level, there are considerable differences in incomes between affluent areas and deprived areas. It is at this level that some of the most extreme examples of inequality can be observed, with 'leafy' affluent suburbs only

a mile or two away from run-down estates. (Regional inequality and local inequality are explored in Case Study 23.10 in MyEconLab.)

The distribution of wealth

Wealth is difficult to measure. Being a *stock* of assets (such as a house, land, furniture, personal possessions and investments), it has an easily measurable value only when it is sold. What is more, individuals are not required to keep any record of their assets. Only when people die and their assets are assessed for inheritance tax does a record become available. Official statistics are thus based on Inland Revenue data of the assets of those who have died that year. These statistics are suspect for two reasons. First, the people who have died are unlikely to be a representative sample of the population. Second, many items are excluded, such as household and personal items, and items passed automatically to the surviving partner.

Figure 10.9 shows the composition of UK marketable wealth. Residential property is the largest component of wealth (50.8 per cent), followed by bank deposits and cash (15.6 per cent).

Inequality of wealth is far greater than inequality of income. The wealthiest 20 per cent of the adult population owned 59.6 per cent of marketable wealth in 2008–10, and the wealthiest 10 per cent owned 44.5 per cent. These figures do not include pension rights, which are much more equally distributed. The level and distribution of wealth tend to fluctuate somewhat in the short term with movements in share prices and house prices.

Figure 10.8 Gross weekly household income, selected UK regions (£), 2012

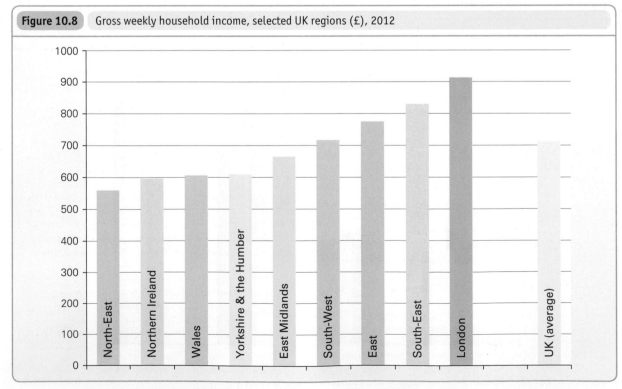

Source: Based on data in *Family Spending* (National Statistics, 2013).

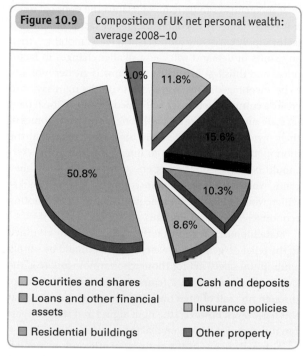

Figure 10.9 Composition of UK net personal wealth: average 2008–10

3.0%
11.8%
15.6%
10.3%
8.6%
50.8%

☐ Securities and shares
☐ Loans and other financial assets
☐ Residential buildings
■ Cash and deposits
☐ Insurance policies
☐ Other property

Source: After Table 13.1 of *UK Personal Wealth Statistics* (HMRC, September 2012).

The four major causes of inequality in the distribution of wealth are as follows:

- Inheritance. This allows inequality to be perpetuated from one generation to another.
- Income inequality. People with higher incomes can save more.
- Different propensities to save. People who save a larger proportion of their income will build up a bigger stock of wealth.

- Entrepreneurial and investment talent/luck. Some people are successful in investing their wealth and making it grow rapidly.

Even though wealth is still highly concentrated, there was a significant reduction in inequality of wealth up to the early 1990s. From 1971 to 1991 the Gini coefficient of wealth fell a full 16 percentage points from 0.80 to 0.64. A major reason for this was the increased taxation of inherited wealth. Since 1991, however, this reduction in inequality has been reversed somewhat. This can be explained by lower levels of inheritance tax and substantial rises in property prices and share values.

Causes of inequality

We turn now to identify the major causes of inequality. The problem has many dimensions and there are many factors that determine the pattern and depth of inequality. It is thus wrong to try to look for a single cause, or even the major one. The following are possible determinants of inequality:

- Inequality of wealth. People with wealth are able to obtain an income other than from their own labour.
- Differences in ability. People differ in intelligence, strength, etc. Some of these differences are innate and some are acquired through the process of 'socialisation' – education, home environment, etc.
- Differences in attitude. Some people are adventurous, willing to take risks, willing to move for better jobs, keen to push themselves forward. Others are much more cautious.
- Differences in qualifications. These are reflections of a number of things: ability, attitudes towards study, access to good education, income of parents, etc.
- Differences in hours worked. Some people do a full-time job plus overtime, or a second job; others work only part time.

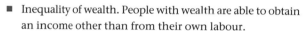

KT 4 p13

KI 11 p80

Consider from the following passage whether it is reasonable or even possible to compare poverty today with poverty in the 1800s:

> Every great city has one or more slums, where the working class is crowded together. True, poverty often dwells in hidden alleys close to the palaces of the rich; but, in general, a separate territory has been assigned to it, where, removed from the sight of the happier classes, it may struggle along as it can.
>
> The houses are occupied from cellar to garret, filthy within and without, and their appearance is such that no human being could possibly wish to live in them . . . the filth and tottering ruin surpass all description. Scarcely a whole window-pane can be found, the walls are crumbling, doorposts and window-frames loose and broken, doors of old boards nailed together, or altogether wanting in this thieves' quarter, where no doors are needed, there being

nothing to steal. Heaps of garbage and ashes lie in all directions, and the foul liquids emptied before the doors gather in stinking pools. Here live the poorest of the poor, the worst-paid workers with thieves and the victims of prostitution indiscriminately huddled together . . . and those who have not yet sunk in the whirlpool of moral ruin which surrounds them, sinking daily deeper, losing daily more and more of their power to resist the demoralising influence of want, filth, and evil surroundings.[1]

1. *If we were to measure poverty today and in the nineteenth century in absolute terms, in which would there be the greater number of poor?*
2. *If we measure poverty in relative terms, must a society inevitably have a problem of poverty, however rich it is?*

[1] F. Engels, *The Condition of the Working Class in England* (Progress Publishers, 1973), pp. 166–7.

- Differences in job utility/disutility. Other things being equal, unpleasant or dangerous jobs will need to pay higher wages.
- Differences in power. Monopoly power in the supply of factors or goods, and monopsony power in the demand for factors, are unequally distributed in the economy.
- Differences in the demand for goods. Factors employed in expanding industries will tend to have a higher marginal revenue product because their output has a higher market value.
- Differences in household composition. The greater the number of dependants relative to income earners, the poorer the average household member will be (other things being equal).
- Discrimination by race, sex, age, social background, etc.
- Degree of government support. The greater the support for the poor, the less will be the level of inequality in the economy.
- Unemployment. When unemployment levels are high, this is one of the major causes of poverty.

Which of the above causes are reflected in differences in the marginal revenue product of factors?

Government attitudes towards inequality

The political right sees inequality as having an important economic function. Factor price differences are an essential part of a dynamic market economy. They are the price signals that encourage resources to move to sectors of the economy where demand is growing, and away from sectors where demand is declining. If the government interferes with this process by taxing high incomes and subsidising low incomes, working people will not have the same incentive to gain better qualifications, to seek promotion, to do overtime, or to move for better jobs. Similarly, owners of capital will not have the same incentive to invest.

If inequality is to be reduced, claims the political right, it is better done by encouraging greater factor mobility. If factor supply curves are more elastic (greater mobility), then any shifts in demand will cause smaller changes in factor prices and thus less inequality. But how is greater mobility to be encouraged? The answer, those on the right say, is to create a culture of self-help: where people are not too reliant on state support; where they will look for higher incomes of their own volition. At the same time, they argue that the monopoly power of unions to interfere in labour markets should be curtailed. The net effect of these policies, they claim, would be to create a more competitive labour market which would help to reduce inequality as well as promoting economic growth and efficiency.

State support, say those on the right, should be confined to the relief of 'genuine' poverty. Benefits should be simply a minimum safety net for those who cannot work (e.g. the sick or disabled), or on a temporary basis for those who, through no fault of their own, have lost their jobs. Even at this basic level, however, the right argues that state support can discourage people from making more effort.

Although many in the political centre and on the left accept that there is a trade-off between equality and efficiency, they tend to see it as a far less serious problem. They claim that questions of efficiency and growth are best dealt with by encouraging investment. They argue that this can be achieved by creating an environment of industrial democracy where workers participate in investment decisions. This common purpose is in turn best achieved in a more equal and less individualistically competitive society. The left also sees a major role for government in providing support for investment: for example, through government-sponsored research, by investment grants or by encouraging firms to get together and plan a co-ordinated strategy.

These policies to achieve growth and efficiency, claims the left, will leave the government freer to pursue a much more active policy on redistribution.

Section summary

1. Inequality can be examined by looking at the size distribution of income, the functional distribution of income, the distribution of income by recipient, the distribution of wealth, or the extent and nature of poverty.

2. An analysiss of the size distribution of income in the UK shows that inequality has grown over the past 30 to 40 years.

3. The size distribution of income can be illustrated by means of a Lorenz curve. The greater the inequality, the more bowed the curve will be towards the bottom right-hand corner.

4. Size distribution can also be measured by a Gini coefficient. This will give a figure between 0 (total equality) and 1 (total inequality). Income distribution can also be measured as the ratio of the share of national income of a given lower-income quantile to that of a higher-income quantile.

5. Wages and salaries constitute by far the largest source of income, and thus inequality can be explained mainly in terms of differences in wages and salaries. Nevertheless state benefits are an important moderating influence on inequality and constitute the largest source of income for the poorest 20 per cent of households. Investment earnings are only a minor determinant of income except for the richest 1 or 2 per cent.

6. Other determinants of income inequality include differences in household composition, gender and where people live.

7. The distribution of wealth is less equal than the distribution of income.

8. Attitudes towards government redistribution of income vary among political parties. The political right stresses the danger that redistributive policies may destroy incentives. The best approach to inequality, according to the right, is to 'free up' markets so as to encourage greater mobility. The left, by contrast, sees fewer dangers in reducing incentives and stresses the moral and social importance of redistribution from rich to poor.

| BOX 10.2 | MINIMUM WAGE LEGISLATION | CASE STUDIES AND APPLICATIONS |

A way of helping the poor?

The Labour government introduced a statutory UK minimum wage in April 1999. The rate was £3.60 per hour for those aged 22 and over, and £3.00 for those between 18 and 21. In 2004 an additional rate was introduced for 16- and 17-year-olds. The rates have been increased every year and in 2013–14 were £6.31, £5.03 and £3.72. These compare with the following adult rates in Europe: Netherlands, €8.53; Belgium, €9.43; France, €9.12; Ireland, €8.65; Slovakia, €2.02. Spain froze its minimum wage in 2011, as a response to the euro crisis, and in 2014 it remained at €4.34. For comparison, the UK adult rate was €7.70 (at exchange rates as of April 2014).

The call for a minimum wage in the UK grew during the 1990s as the number of low-paid workers increased. There were many people working as cleaners, security guards and shop assistants who were receiving very low rates of pay, sometimes less than £2 per hour. Several factors explain the growth in the size of the low-pay sector:

- *Lower demand for unskilled labour.* Increased unemployment since the early 1980s had shifted the balance of power from workers to employers. Employers were able to force many wage rates downwards, especially those of unskilled workers.
- *Growth in part-time employment.* Changes in the structure of the UK economy, particularly the growth in the service sector and the growing proportion of women seeking work, had led to an increase in part-time employment and zero-hours contracts, with many part-time workers not receiving the same rights and hourly pay as their full-time equivalents until 2000.
- *Changes in labour laws.* The abolition of 'wages councils' in 1993, which had set legally enforceable minimum hourly rates in various low-paid industries, and the introduction of various new laws to reduce the power of labour (see page 259) had left low-paid workers with little protection.

Assessing the arguments

The principal argument against imposing a national minimum wage concerns its impact on employment. If you raise wage rates above the equilibrium level, there will be surplus labour: i.e. unemployment (see Figure 9.9 on page 257). However, the impact of a national minimum wage on employment is not so simple.

In the case of a firm operating in competitive labour and goods markets, the demand for low-skilled workers is relatively wage sensitive. Any rise in wage rates, and hence prices, by this firm alone would lead to a large fall in sales and hence to employment. But given that all firms face the minimum wage, individual employers are more able to pass on higher wages in higher prices, knowing that their competitors are doing the same.

When employers have a degree of monopsony power, however, it is not even certain that they would want to reduce employment. Remember what we argued in

Figure 9.10 (on page 258) when we were examining the effects of unions driving up wages. The argument is the same with a minimum wage. The minimum wage can be as high as W_2 and the firm will still want to employ as many workers as at W_1. The point is that the firm can no longer drive down the wage rate by employing fewer workers, so the incentive to cut its workforce has been removed.

In the long run, the effect on unemployment will depend on the extent to which the higher wages are compensated by higher labour productivity.

Evidence from the USA and other countries suggested that modest increases in the minimum wage had a neutral effect upon employment. Similarly in the UK, there is little evidence to suggest that from 1999 employers responded by employing fewer workers. In fact, until 2008 unemployment rates fell every year, due to the buoyant economy and increasing labour market flexibility (see Box 9.8).

Whether there would continue to be little effect if the minimum wage were to rise substantially is another matter. The question for policy makers, then, seems to be how high the minimum wage can be set before unemployment begins to rise.

Impact of the minimum wage in the UK

Around 1 million workers now earn the minimum wage, while another 1 million earn within 50p of that hourly rate. These figures include high numbers of female workers, part-time workers and people from ethnic minorities.

One concern for economists, when assessing the national minimum wage, is that living costs, and particularly housing costs, vary substantially across the economy. There have been suggestions that *local* minimum wages rates should be set, to ensure a more efficient outcome. However, a more vociferous campaign has been launched for a 'living wage' – one which would lift those working full time out of poverty. In London, where the cost of living is highest, this would have required an hourly rate of £8.80 in 2014.

Of course a weakness of using a minimum wage as a means of relieving poverty is that it only affects the employed; yet one of the main causes of poverty is unemployment. This, in part, explains the focus on getting adults into work as the major plank of poverty relief policy in the UK. It is apparent that a minimum wage rate cannot be the sole answer to poverty and must be considered in conjunction with benefits.

1. *If an increase in wage rates for low-paid workers leads to their being more motivated, how would this affect the marginal revenue product and the demand for such workers? What implications does your answer have for the effect on employment in such cases? (See pages 259–62 on the efficiency wage hypothesis.)*
2. *If a rise in the minimum wage encourages employers to substitute machines for workers, will this necessarily lead to higher long-term unemployment in (a) that industry and (b) the economy in general?*

The *average* rate is a person's total income tax as a fraction of total income. This will always be less than the marginal rate, since part of a person's income will be tax-free; and for higher tax rate payers, part will be taxed at lower rates.

Individuals' social security contributions. In the UK these are known as national insurance contributions (NICs). These are like income taxes in that they are generally charged as a percentage of a person's income, the marginal rate varying with income. Unlike other taxes, which are paid into a common fund to finance government expenditure, they are used to finance *specific* expenditure: namely, pensions and social security. Although they do not officially count as 'taxes', to all intents and purposes they are so. In the 2011 Budget the Chancellor announced that the UK government would consult on merging the income tax and national insurance systems. However, this does not seem to be a high priority.

Table 10.2 and Figure 10.10 show the marginal and average rates of income tax and social security contributions in the UK (in 2014–15). Notice that above £100 000, the personal allowance is reduced by £1 for each £2 earned. This is equivalent to an extra 20 per cent for the next £20 000 (i.e. £10 000 × 2).

Employers' social security contributions. Employers also have to pay social security contributions on behalf of their employees. These are paid per employee. In some countries, small firms pay reduced rates.

Tax on corporate income. In the UK this is known as corporation tax. It is a tax on the profits of limited companies. In

Table 10.2	UK marginal income tax and national insurance rates: 2014–15		
Income per annum **(£)**	**Marginal income tax rate** **(%)**	**Marginal NIC rate** **(%)**	**Marginal income tax plus NIC rate** **(%)**
0–7956	0	0	0
7957–10 000	0	12	12
10 001–41 865	20	12	32
41 866–100 000	40	2	42
100 001–120 000	40+20	2	62
120 001–150 000	40	2	42
Above 150 000	45	2	47

most countries, there are lower rates for small companies. Profits can usually be offset against capital expenditure and interest payments when working out the tax liability. This effectively means that profits that are reinvested are not taxed.

Tax on capital gains. This is a tax payable when a person sells assets, such as property or shares. It is payable on the gain in value of these assets since a set date in the past, or since they were purchased if this was after the set date.

Taxes on wealth. These are taxes on assets held or acquired by individuals. One form of wealth tax in most countries is that on inherited assets or assets transferred before a person's death. Another is taxes based on the value of a person's property. This is a particularly common form

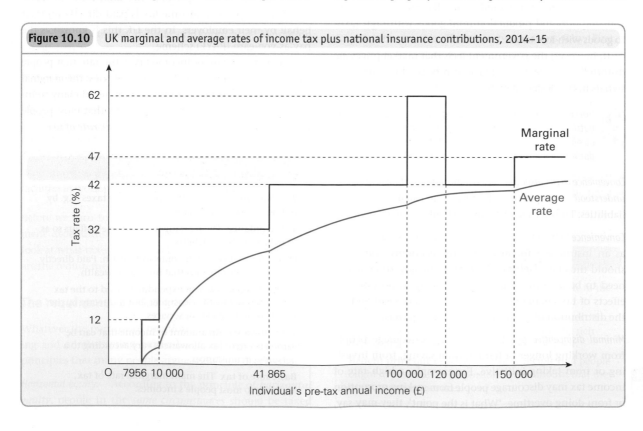

Figure 10.10 UK marginal and average rates of income tax plus national insurance contributions, 2014–15

Table 10.3	Calculating VAT: an example where the rate of VAT is 20%				
		Value added (1)	VAT (2)	Value added plus VAT (3)	Price sold to next stage (4)
Firm A sells raw materials to firm B for £12 000		£10 000	£2000	£12 000	£12 000
Firm B processes them and sells them to a manufacturer, firm C, for £21 600		£8 000	£1600	£9 600	£21 600
Firm C sells the manufactured goods to a wholesaler, firm D, for £30 000		£7 000	£1400	£8 400	£30 000
Firm D sells them to a retailer, firm E, for £36 000		£5 000	£1000	£6 000	£36 000
Firm E sells them to consumers for £48 000		£10 000	£2000	£12 000	£48 000
		£40 000 +	£8000 =	£48 000	

of local taxation (the others being local income tax, local business tax and local sales tax).

Poll taxes. These are fixed-sum charges per head of the population, irrespective of the person's income. Very few countries use such taxes as they are regarded as unfair. A poll tax (or 'community charge') was introduced in Scotland in 1989 and in England and Wales in 1990 as the new form of local tax, replacing the property tax called 'rates', which was based on property values. But it was massively unpopular with the electorate, leading to demonstrations and riots, and was replaced by 'council tax' (again based on property values) in 1993.

Indirect taxes

There are three main types of indirect tax, all of which are taxes on *expenditure*.

General expenditure taxes. An example of this is *value added tax (VAT)*. This is the main indirect tax throughout the EU. VAT is paid on the value that firms add to goods and services at each stage of their production and distribution. For example, if a firm purchases supplies costing £10 000 and with them produces goods that it sells for £15 000 (before VAT), it is liable to pay VAT on the £15 000 minus £10 000: in other words, on the £5000 value it has added. Suppliers must provide invoices to show that the VAT has already been paid on all the inputs.

The example in Table 10.3 can be used to show how the tax eventually gets passed on to the consumer. For simplicity's sake, assume that the rate of VAT is 20 per cent and that each firm uses only one supplier.

The value added at each stage plus VAT adds up to the total amount paid by the consumer: £48 000 in this case. The total VAT paid, therefore, amounts to a tax on the consumer. In the example, the £8000 VAT is 20 per cent of the (pre-tax) consumer price of £40 000.

The rates of VAT in the various EU countries are considered in Box 24.10. Each country has a standard rate and up to two lower rates for basic goods and services. Standard rates vary between 15 and 27 per cent, but are typically between 20 and 25 per cent.

Many other countries levy general expenditure taxes at a *single* stage (either wholesale or retail). These taxes are called *purchase taxes* and will normally be a percentage of the price of the good at that stage.

Excise duties. These are taxes on particular goods and services: for example, petrol and diesel, alcoholic drinks, tobacco products and gambling. They are a single-stage tax levied on the manufacturer. They are paid in addition to VAT.

VAT is an *ad valorem tax*. This means that the tax is levied at a *percentage* of the value of the good. The higher the value of the good, the higher the tax paid. Excise duties, by contrast, are a *specific tax*. This means that they are levied at a *fixed amount*, irrespective of the value of the good. Thus the duty on a litre of unleaded petrol is the same for a cut-price filling station as for a full-price one.

Customs duties. Economists normally refer to these as *tariffs*. They are duties on goods imported from outside the country.

 To what extent do (a) income tax, (b) VAT and (c) a poll tax meet the various requirements for a good tax system (see pages 296–7 above)? (Some of the answers to this question are given below.)

Details of tax rates in the UK are given in Case Study 10.3 in MyEconLab. This case study also examines how progressive or regressive the various types of tax are.

The balance of taxation

Table 10.4 shows the balance of the different types of tax in selected countries. Some striking differences can be seen between the countries. In France, income taxes account for

Definitions

Value added tax (VAT) A tax on goods and services, charged at each stage of production as a percentage of the value added at that stage.

Ad valorem tax A tax on a good levied as a percentage of its value. It can be a single-stage tax or a multi-stage tax (as with VAT).

Specific tax A tax on a good levied at a fixed amount per unit of the good, irrespective of the price of that unit.

Tariff A tax on imported goods.

Table 10.4	Balance of taxation in selected countries (2012)					
Types of tax as percentage of GDP	**France**	**Germany**	**Japan**	**Sweden**	**UK**	**USA**
Personal income tax and capital gains tax	8.2	9.6	5.4	12.5	9.7	8.9
Social security: employee and self-employed contributions	5.5	7.7	6.5[1]	2.6	2.9	2.3
Social security: employer contributions	11.5	6.7	5.4[1]	7.6	3.9	3.1
Corporate taxes	2.5	1.8	3.4	3.0	2.9	2.6
Payroll taxes	1.5	0.0	0.0	4.5	0.0	0.0
Taxes on property and wealth	3.9	0.9	2.7	1.0	4.2	3.0
Taxes on goods and services	11.0	10.7	5.2	12.8	11.6	4.4
Other taxes	1.2	0.2	0.0	0.3	0.0	0.0
Total taxes	45.3	37.6	28.6[1]	44.3	35.2	24.3

[1] 2011.
Source: Extracted from Revenue Statistics tables in *StatExtracts* (OECD).

only 18.1 per cent of tax revenue, whereas in the USA they account for 36.6 per cent. In the UK, social security contributions (national insurance) are a lower percentage of total taxes than in other countries, whereas taxes on property (mainly the council tax) are a higher percentage of total taxes.

There is also a big difference between countries in the proportion of taxes paid by companies and that paid by individuals. Corporate taxes, payroll taxes and employer social security contributions account for 34.2 per cent of taxes and 15.5 per cent of GDP[1] in France. In the USA they account for only 23.5 per cent of taxes and just 5.7 per cent of GDP.

In terms of total taxes, again there are large differences between countries. In France 45.3 per cent of GDP is paid in tax whereas in the USA the figure is only 24.3 per cent.

Taxes as a means of redistributing income

If taxes are to be used as a means of achieving greater equality, the rich must be taxed proportionately more than the poor. The degree of redistribution will depend on the degree of 'progressiveness' of the tax. In this context, taxes may be classified as follows:

- *Progressive tax*. As people's income (Y) rises, the percentage of their income paid in the tax (T) rises. In other words, the *average* rate of tax (T/Y) rises.
- *Regressive tax*. As people's income rises, the percentage of their income paid in the tax falls: T/Y falls.
- *Proportional tax*. As people's income rises, the percentage of their income paid in the tax stays the same: T/Y is constant.

In other words, progressiveness is defined in terms of what happens to the average rate of tax as incomes rise. (Note that it is not defined in terms of the *marginal* rate of tax.)

[1] GDP is a measure of the nation's income: we will be examining how it is measured in the appendix to Chapter 14.

1. *If a person earning £10 000 per year pays £1000 in a given tax and a person earning £20 000 per year pays £1600, is the tax progressive or regressive?*
2. *A proportional tax will leave the distribution of income unaffected. Why should this be so, given that a rich person will pay a larger absolute amount than a poor person?*

An extreme form of regressive tax is a lump-sum tax (e.g. a poll tax). This is levied at a fixed *amount* (not rate) irrespective of income.

Figure 10.11 illustrates these different categories of tax. Diagram (a) shows the total amount of tax that a person pays. With a progressive tax, the curve gets progressively steeper, showing that the average rate of tax (T/Y) rises. The marginal rate of tax ($\Delta T/\Delta Y$) is given by the slope. Thus between points x and y the marginal tax rate is 40 per cent.

Diagram (b) shows the average rates. With a proportional tax, a person pays the same amount of tax on each pound earned. With a progressive tax, a larger proportion is paid by a rich person than by a poor person, and vice versa with a regressive tax.

The more steeply upward sloping the average tax curve, the more progressive is the tax, and the more equal will be the post-tax incomes of the population.

Problems with using taxes to redistribute incomes

How successfully can taxes redistribute income, and at what economic cost?

Definitions

Progressive tax A tax whose average rate with respect to income rises as income rises.

Regressive tax A tax whose average rate with respect to income falls as income rises.

Proportional tax A tax whose average rate with respect to income stays the same as income rises.

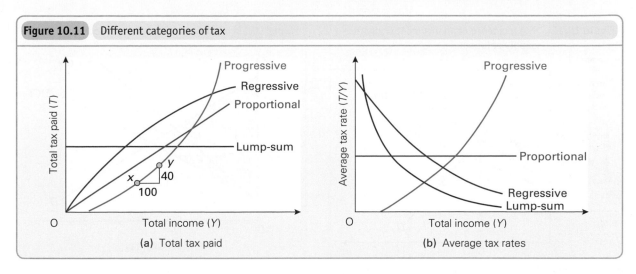

Figure 10.11 Different categories of tax

(a) Total tax paid

(b) Average tax rates

Problems in achieving redistribution

How to help the very poor. Taxation takes away income. It can thus reduce the incomes of the rich. But no taxes, however progressive, can *increase* the incomes of the poor. This will require subsidies (i.e. benefits).

But what about tax cuts? Can bigger tax cuts not be given to the poor? This is possible only if the poor are already paying taxes in the first place. Take the two cases of income tax and taxes on goods and services.

- Income tax. If the government cuts income tax, then anyone currently paying it will benefit. A cut in tax *rates* will give proportionately more to the rich, since they have a larger proportion of taxable income relative to total income. An increase in personal *allowances*, on the other hand, will give the same *absolute* amounts to everyone above the new tax threshold. This will therefore represent a smaller proportionate gain to the rich. In either case, however, there will be no gain at all to those people below the tax threshold. They paid no income tax in the first place and gain nothing at all from income tax cuts.
- Taxes on goods and services. Since these taxes are generally regressive, any cut in their rate will benefit the poor proportionately more than the rich. A more dramatic effect would be obtained by cutting the rate most on those goods consumed relatively more by the poor.

The government may not wish to cut the overall level of taxation, given its expenditure commitments. In this case, it can switch the burden from regressive to progressive taxes, if it wishes to benefit the very poor.

Tax evasion and tax avoidance. The higher the rates of tax, the more likely are people to try to escape paying some of their taxes.

People who are subject to higher rates of income tax will be more tempted not to declare all their income. This tax *evasion* will be much easier for people not paying all their taxes through a pay-as-you-earn (PAYE) scheme. This will

include the self-employed and people doing casual work on top of their normal job ('moonlighting'). Furthermore, richer people can often reduce their tax liability – engage in *tax avoidance* – by a careful use of various legal devices such as trusts and tax loopholes, for example being allowed to offset 'business expenses' against income.

Part of the government's justification for abolishing income tax rates above 40 per cent in 1988 was that many people escaped paying these higher taxes. Nevertheless, in 2009 the Labour Chancellor, Alistair Darling, announced that a new top rate of 50 per cent would be introduced in 2010–11. He forecast that this would bring an extra £3 billion per year in tax revenues. However, in 2011 the Office for Budget Responsibility suggested that the overall increases were likely to be much lower than this and HMRC figures suggested that £100 million a year would be lost in avoidance.

In 2013, the Coalition reduced the top rate to 45 per cent. It is difficult, if not impossible, to calculate the exact effect of these marginal changes.

 Why may a steeply progressive income tax which is designed to achieve greater vertical equity lead to a reduction in horizontal equity?

Undesired incidence of tax. High rates of income tax on high-wage earners may simply encourage employers to pay them higher wages. At the other end of the scale, tax cuts for low-paid workers may simply allow employers to cut wages. In other words, part of the incidence of income taxes will be borne by the employer and only part by the employee. Thus attempting to make taxes more 'progressive' will fail if employers simply adjust wages to compensate.

The incidence of income tax is determined by the elasticity of supply and demand for labour. In Figure 10.12, the initial supply and demand curves for labour (before the imposition of the tax) intersect at point (1), giving Q_1 labour employed at a wage of W_1. Now an income tax is imposed. This shifts the labour supply curve vertically upwards by

TC 5
p54

KI 9
p71

Figure 10.12 The incidence of an income tax: elastic supply of labour

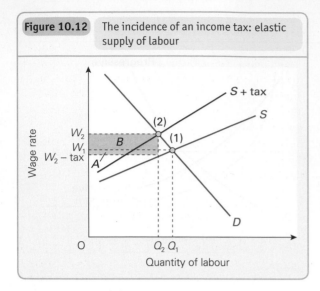

Figure 10.13 Indirect tax applied to good X

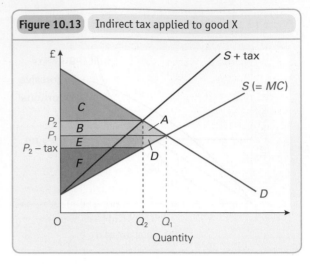

the amount of the tax, giving the new labour supply curve, $S + \text{tax}$. The new equilibrium is reached at point (2) with Q_2 labour employed at a (gross) wage of W_2.

The incidence of the tax is as follows:

- The total tax revenue for the government is shown by the total shaded area.
- Workers' take-home pay is cut from W_1 to $W_2 - \text{tax}$. Their share of the tax is thus area A.
- Employers have to pay workers a rise of $W_2 - W_1$. They pay area B.

If the supply curve of labour of well-paid workers is relatively elastic, as shown in Figure 10.12, there will only be a relatively slight fall in take-home pay (the workers' share of the tax is relatively small). The tax will, therefore, have only a relatively slight redistributive effect away from this group of workers.

1. *Do poor people gain more from a cut in income tax with an elastic or an inelastic supply of labour? Is the supply of unskilled workers likely to be elastic or inelastic?*
2. *Draw two diagrams like Figure 10.12, one with a steep demand curve and one with a shallow demand curve. How does the elasticity of demand affect the incidence of the income tax?*

Of course, income taxes are not imposed on workers in one industry alone. People, therefore, cannot move to another industry to avoid paying taxes. This fact will cause a relatively inelastic supply response to any rise in income tax, since the only alternative to paying the income tax is to work less. The less elastic this response, the more will the burden of the tax fall on the taxpayer and the more effectively can income taxes be used to redistribute incomes.

The economic costs of redistribution

If redistribution is to be achieved through *indirect* taxes, this can lead to market distortions.

Take first the case of an indirect tax applied to one good only. Assume for simplicity that there is universal perfect competition. Raising the price of this good relative to other goods will introduce a market distortion. Consumption will shift away from this good towards other goods that people preferred less at the original prices. What is more, the loss to consumers and producers (other things being equal) will be greater than the gain to the community from the tax revenue. This is illustrated in Figure 10.13.

With no tax, price will be at P_1 and output at Q_1, where demand equals supply. By imposing a tax on the good, the supply curve shifts upwards to $S + \text{tax}$. Price rises to P_2 and output falls to Q_2. Producers are left with $P_2 - \text{tax}$. What are the various losses and gains?

Consumers, by having to pay a higher price, lose consumer surplus (see section 4.1). Originally their consumer surplus was areas $A + B + C$. With the price now at P_2, the consumer surplus falls to area C alone. The loss to consumers is areas $A + B$.

Producers, by receiving a lower price after tax and selling fewer units, lose profits. In the simple case where there are no fixed costs of production, total profits are simply the sum of all the marginal profits ($P (= MR) - MC$) on each of the units sold. Thus before the tax is imposed, firms receive total profits of areas $D + E + F$. After the tax is imposed, they receive a profit of area F alone. The loss in profits to producers is therefore areas $D + E$.

The total loss to consumers and producers is areas $A + B + D + E$. The gain to the government in tax revenue is areas $B + E$: the tax rate times the number of units sold (Q_2). There is thus a net loss to the community of areas $A + D$. This is known as the *deadweight loss of the tax*.

Definition

Deadweight loss of an indirect tax The net loss of consumer plus producer surplus (after adding in the tax revenue) from the imposition of an indirect tax.

However, if the money raised from the tax is redistributed to the poor, their gain in welfare is likely to exceed the loss in welfare from the higher tax. The reason is that a pound sacrificed by the average consumer is probably of less value to him or her than a pound gained by a poor person.

What is more, if the tax is applied at a uniform rate to *all* goods, there is no distortion resulting from reallocation between goods. This is one of the major justifications for having a single rate of VAT.

Of course, in the real world, markets are highly imperfect and there is no reason why taxes will necessarily make these imperfections worse. In fact, it might be desirable on efficiency grounds to tax certain goods and services, such as cigarettes, alcohol, petrol and gambling, at higher rates than other goods and services. We will examine these arguments in the next chapter.

Although there are costs of redistribution, there are also benefits extending beyond those to whom income is redistributed. If redistribution to the poor reduces crime, vandalism and urban squalor, then it is not just the poor who gain: it is everyone, both financially in terms of reduced policing and social work costs, and more generally in terms of living in a happier and less divided society.

Taxation and incentives

Another possible economic cost of high tax rates is that they may act as a disincentive to work, thereby reducing national output and consumption. This whole question of incentives is highly charged politically. According to the political right, there is a trade-off between output and equity. High and progressive income taxes can lead to a more equal distribution of income, but a smaller national output. Alternatively, if taxes are cut there will be a bigger national output, but less equally divided. If many on the left are correct, however, we can have both a more equal society *and* a bigger national output: there is no trade-off.

The key to analysing these arguments is to distinguish between the *income effect* and the *substitution effect* of a tax rise. Raising taxes does two things:

- It reduces incomes. People may therefore work *more* in an attempt to maintain their consumption of goods and services. This is the **income effect**.
- It reduces the opportunity cost of leisure. An extra hour taken in leisure now involves a smaller sacrifice in consumption, since each hour less worked involves less sacrifice in after-tax income. Thus people may substitute leisure for consumption, and work *less*. This is the **substitution effect**.

Definitions

Income effect of a tax rise Tax increases reduce people's incomes and thus encourage people to work more.

Substitution effect of a tax rise Tax increases reduce the opportunity cost of leisure and thus encourage people to work less.

TC 5
p54

KI 7
p36

BOX 10.3   **THE LAFFER CURVE**   EXPLORING ECONOMICS

Having your cake and eating it

TC 5
p54

Professor Art Laffer was one of President Reagan's advisers during his first administration (1981–4). He was a strong advocate of income tax cuts, arguing that substantial increases in output would result.

He went further than this. He argued that tax cuts would actually increase the amount of tax revenue that the government earned.

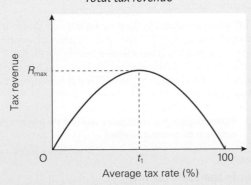

Total tax revenue

If tax cuts cause income to rise (due to incentives) proportionately more than the tax rate has fallen, then tax revenues will increase. These effects are illustrated by the now famous 'Laffer' curve.

If the average tax rate were zero, no revenue would be raised. As the tax rate is raised above zero, tax revenues will increase. The curve will be upwards sloping. Eventually, however, the curve will peak (at tax rate t_1). Thereafter tax rates become so high that the resulting fall in output more than offsets the rise in tax rate. When the tax rate reaches 100 per cent, the revenue will once more fall to zero, since no one will bother to work.

The curve may not be symmetrical. It may peak at a 40 per cent, 50 per cent, 60 per cent or even 90 per cent rate. Nevertheless, Laffer and others on the political right argued that tax rates were above t_1. In fact most evidence suggests that tax rates in most countries were well below t_1 in the 1980s and certainly are now, given the cuts in income tax rates that have been made around the world over the past 20 years.

1. *What is the elasticity of supply of output with respect to changes in tax rates at a tax rate of t_1? What is it below t_1? What is it above t_1?*
2. *If the substitution effect of a tax cut outweighs the income effect, does this necessarily mean that the economy is to the right of point t_1?*

The relative size of the income and substitution effects is likely to differ for different types of people and different types of tax change.

Different types of people

The *income* effect is likely to dominate for people with long-term commitments: for example, those with families, or those with mortgages and other debts. They may feel forced to work *more* to maintain their disposable income. Clearly, for such people higher taxes are *not* a disincentive to work. The income effect is also likely to be relatively large for people on higher incomes, for whom an increase in tax rates represents a substantial cut in income.

The *substitution* effect is likely to dominate for those with few commitments: those whose families have left home,

KI 7
p36

the single, and second-income earners in families where that second income is not relied on for 'essential' consumption. A rise in tax rates for these people is likely to encourage them to work less.

Although high-income earners may work more when there is a tax *rise*, they may still be discouraged by a steeply progressive tax *structure*. If they have to pay very high marginal rates of tax, it may simply not be worth their while seeking promotion or working harder (see Boxes 10.3 and 10.4).

1. *Who is likely to work harder as a result of a cut in income tax rates, a rich person or a poor person? Why? Would your answer be different if personal allowances were zero?*

2. *How will tax cuts affect the willingness of women to return to employment after having brought up a family?*

---

*BOX 10.4 TAX CUTS AND INCENTIVES

An application of indifference curve analysis[1]

Will tax cuts provide an incentive for people to work more? This question can be analysed using indifference curves (see section 4.2). The analysis is similar to that developed in Box 9.2. It is assumed that individuals can choose how many hours a day to work.

The position with no income tax

Diagram (a) shows the situation without income tax.

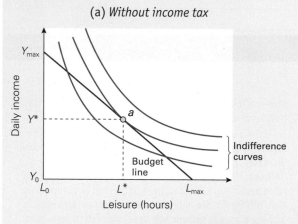

(a) *Without income tax*

The budget line shows the various combinations of leisure and income open to an individual at a given wage rate.

Why is the budget line straight? What would it look like if overtime were paid at higher rates per hour?

The indifference curves show all the combinations of income and leisure that give the person equal satisfaction. The optimum combination of income and leisure is at Y^* and L^* where the individual is on the highest possible indifference curve: point a.

The position with income tax

Now let us introduce a system of income taxes. This is illustrated in diagram (b).

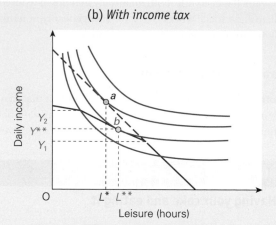

(b) *With income tax*

Assume that the tax has the following features:

■ Up to an income of Y_1 no tax is paid: Y_1 is the individual's personal allowance.

■ From Y_1 to Y_2 the basic rate of tax is paid. The budget line is flatter, since less extra income is earned for each extra hour of leisure sacrificed.

■ Above Y_2 the higher rate of tax is paid. The budget line becomes flatter still.

The individual illustrated in the diagram will now choose to earn a take-home pay of Y^{**} and have L^{**} hours of leisure: point b. Note that this is more leisure than in the no-tax situation (point a). In this diagram, then, the tax has acted as a disincentive. The substitution effect has outweighed the income effect.

Redraw diagram (b), but in such a way that the income effect outweighs the substitution effect.

A cut in the basic tax rate

We can now analyse the effects of tax cuts. A cut in the basic rate is shown in diagram (c).

Different types of tax change

A government may wish to raise income taxes in order to redistribute incomes through higher benefits. There are three main ways it can do so: raising the higher rates of tax; raising the basic rate; and reducing tax allowances.

Raising the higher rates of tax. This may seem the most effective way of redistributing incomes: after all, it is only the rich who will suffer. There are, however, serious problems:

- The income effect will be relatively small, since it is only that part of incomes subject to the higher rates that will be affected. The substitution effect, however, could be relatively high. Rich people are likely to put a higher premium on leisure, and may well feel that it is

not worth working so hard if a larger proportion of any increase in income is taken in taxes.

- It may discourage risk taking by businesspeople.
- The rich may be more mobile internationally, so there may be a 'brain drain'. This criticism was made by the Mayor of London, Boris Johnson, when discussing the effect of a 50 per cent tax rate on the financial sector.

Raising the basic rate of tax. As we have seen, the income effect is likely to be relatively large for those with higher incomes, especially if they have substantial commitments like a large mortgage. For such people, a rise in tax rates is likely to act as an incentive.

For those just above the tax threshold, there will be very little extra to pay on *existing* income, since most of it is

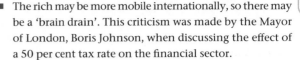

(c) Cut in the basic rate of tax

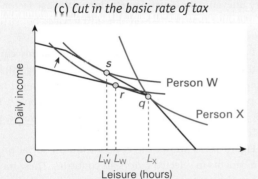

(d) Increase in the tax threshold

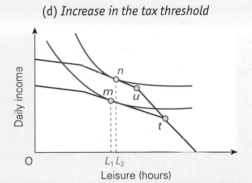

The tax cut makes the budget line steeper above point q (the tax threshold).

For people on the tax threshold – like person X – the cut in the basic rate makes no difference. Person X was originally taking L_X hours of leisure (point q) and will continue to do so.

For people above the tax threshold – like person W – the tax cut will enable them to move to a higher indifference curve. Person W will move from point r to point s. The way this diagram is drawn, point s is to the left of point r. This means that person W will work more: the substitution effect is greater than the income effect.

 Try drawing two or three diagrams like diagram (c), with the tangency point at different points along the budget line to the left of q. You will find that the further to the left you move, the less likely is the substitution effect to outweigh the income effect: i.e. the more likely are people to work less when given a tax cut.

A rise in the tax threshold

Diagram (d) shows a rise in personal allowances while the tax rates stay the same.

The point at which people start paying taxes rises from point t to point u. The slope of the budget line remains the same, however, since the tax rates have not changed.

For people paying taxes, the increase in allowances represents a lump-sum increase in income; there will thus be an income effect. But since tax rates have not changed, there is no substitution effect. People therefore work less. The person in the diagram moves from point m to point n, taking L_2 rather than L_1 hours in leisure.

 Will people actually on the old tax threshold (i.e. those whose indifference curve/budget line tangency point is at t) work more or less? Try drawing it.

A cut in the higher rate of tax

It is likely that the income effect of this will be quite small except for those on very high incomes. The substitution effect is therefore likely to outweigh the income effect, causing people to work more.

All the above analysis assumes that taxes will not affect people's gross wage rates. If part of the incidence of taxes is borne by the employer, so that gross wages fall, after-tax wages will fall less. There will therefore be a smaller shift in the budget line. How will this affect the argument for tax cuts?

[1] This box is based on D. Ulph, 'Tax cuts: will they work?', *Economic Review*, March 1987.

tax-free. However, each *extra* pound earned will be taxed at the new higher rate. The substitution effect, therefore, is likely to outweigh the income effect. For these people, a rise in tax rates will act as a disincentive.

For those below the tax threshold, the marginal rate remains at zero. A rise in the basic rate might nevertheless deter them from undertaking training in order to get a better wage.

For those people who are not employed, a rise in tax rates may make them feel that it is no longer worth looking for a job.

Reducing tax allowances.　For all those above the old tax threshold, there is no *substitution* effect at all. The rate of tax has not changed. However, there is an *income* effect. The effect is like a lump-sum tax. Everyone's take-home pay is cut by a fixed sum, and people will need to work harder to make up some of the shortfall. This type of tax change, however, is highly regressive. If everyone pays the same *amount* of extra tax, this represents a bigger percentage for poorer people than richer people. In other words, there may be no negative incentive effects, but it is not suitable as part of a policy to redistribute incomes more equally!

The conclusion from the theoretical arguments is that tax changes will have very different effects depending on (a) whom they affect and (b) the nature of the change.

1. *A key policy of the UK Coalition government, achieved in April 2014, was to raise the personal income tax allowance to £10 000. This was accompanied by the gradual removal of the same allowance from those earning over £100 000 (see Table 10.2 on page 298). Evaluate these policies.*
2. *What would the effects be of cuts in (i) the basic rate of tax (ii) the top rate of tax?*
3. *What tax changes (whether up or down) will have a positive incentive effect and also redistribute incomes more equally?*

One final point should be stressed. For many people, there is no choice in the amount they work. The job they do dictates the number of hours worked, irrespective of changes in taxation.

Evidence

All the available evidence suggests that the effects of tax changes on output are relatively small. Labour supply curves seem highly inelastic to tax changes.

Benefits

Benefits can be either cash benefits or benefits in kind.

Cash benefits

Means-tested benefits.　**Means-tested benefits** are available only to those whose incomes (and savings in some instances) fall below a certain level. To obtain such benefits, therefore, people must apply for them and declare their personal circumstances to the authorities. Examples include housing benefit and income support, the safety net that exists for all in the UK.

The benefits could be given as grants or merely as loans. They could be provided as general income support or for the meeting of specific needs, such as rents, fuel bills and household items.

Universal benefits.　**Universal benefits** are those that everyone is entitled to, irrespective of their income, if they fall into a certain category or fulfil certain conditions (these conditions might include a contributions record). Examples include state pensions, and certain unemployment, sickness and invalidity benefits.

Benefits in kind

Individuals receive other forms of benefit from the state, not as direct monetary payments, but in the form of the provision of free or subsidised goods or services. These are known as **benefits in kind**. The two largest items in most countries are health care and education. They are distributed very unevenly, however, largely due to the age factor. Old people use a large proportion of health services, but virtually no education services.

Benefits in kind tend to be consumed roughly equally by the different income groups. Nevertheless they still have some equalising effect, since they represent a much larger proportion of poor people's income than rich people's. They still have a far smaller redistributive effect, however, than cash benefits.

Figure 10.14 shows the expenditure on social protection benefits in selected European countries. These include unemployment, sickness, invalidity, maternity, family, survivors' and housing benefits and state pensions. They are mainly cash benefits, but do include some benefits in kind. They exclude health and education.

As you can see, the benefits vary significantly from one country to another. Part of the reason for this is that countries differ in their rates of unemployment and in the age structure of their population. Thus, compared with other countries in the EU, Ireland has a very low percentage of people over 65 and the smallest share of benefits devoted to pensions. Despite this, however, the generosity and coverage of benefits varies considerably from country to country, reflecting, in part, the level of income per head.

> ### Definitions
>
> **Means-tested benefits** Benefits whose amount depends on the recipient's income or assets.
>
> **Universal benefits** Benefits paid to everyone in a certain category irrespective of their income or assets.
>
> **Benefits in kind** Goods or services that the state provides directly to the recipient at no charge or at a subsidised price. Alternatively, the state can subsidise the private sector to provide them.

Figure 10.14 Social protection benefits in various European countries

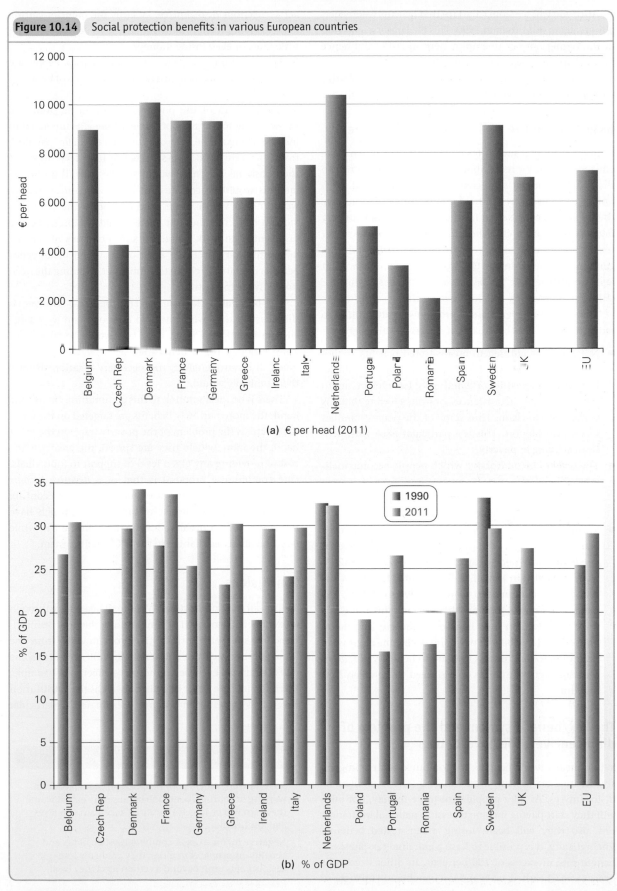

(a) € per head (2011)

(b) % of GDP

Source: Based on data in *Social Protection* tables (Eurostat, 2014).

Also, you will see from Chart (b) that benefits were generally greater in 2011 than in 1990. This is a largely a reflection of the higher rates of unemployment in 2011, and hence more people in receipt of unemployment benefits.

The system of benefits in the UK and their redistributive effects are examined in Case Study 10.5 in MyEconLab.

Benefits and the redistribution of income

It might seem that means-tested benefits are a much more efficient system for redistributing income from the rich to the poor: the money is directed to those most in need. With universal benefits, by contrast, many people may receive them who have little need for them. Do families with very high incomes need child benefit? Would it not be better for the government to redirect the money to those who are genuinely in need? In the UK, from 2012, families with at least one higher-rate taxpayer were no longer eligible for child benefit (see Box 10.6 for more on this).

There are, however, serious problems in attempting to redistribute incomes by the use of means-tested benefits:

■ Not everyone entitled to means-tested benefits applies for them, whether from ignorance of what is available, from the complexities of claiming, or from reluctance to reveal personal circumstances, or from a feeling that it is demeaning to claim. Thus some of the poorest families receive no support. This is a particular issue with pensioners living in poverty.

■ The level of income above which people become ineligible for benefits may be set too low. Even if it were raised, there will always be some people just above the level who will still find difficulties.

■ Means tests based purely on *income* (or even universal benefits based on broad categories) ignore the very special needs of many poor people. A person earning £120 a week and living in a small, well-appointed flat with a low rent and an allotment to grow vegetables will have less need of assistance than another person who also earns £120 per week but lives in a cold, draughty and damp house with large bills to meet and no means of growing their own food. If means tests are to be really fair, *all* of a person's circumstances would need to be taken into account.

The tax/benefit system and the problem of disincentives: the poverty trap

When means-tested benefits are combined with a progressive income tax system, there can be a serious problem of disincentives. As poor people earn more money, not only will they start paying income taxes and national insurance, but also they will begin losing means-tested benefits. Theoretically, it is possible to have a marginal tax-plus-lost-benefit rate in excess of 100 per cent. In other words, for every extra £1 earned, taxes and lost benefits add up to more than £1. High marginal tax-plus-lost-benefit rates obviously

act as a serious disincentive. What is the point of getting a job or trying to earn more money, if you end up earning little more or even losing money?

This situation is known as the *poverty trap*. People are trapped on low incomes with no realistic means of bettering their position.

The problem of the poverty trap could be overcome by switching to a system of universal benefits unrelated to income. For example, *everyone* could receive a flat payment from the state fixed at a sufficiently high level to cover their basic needs. There would still be *some* disincentive, but this would be confined to an income effect: people would not have the same need to work if the state provided a basic income. But there would no longer be the disincentive to work caused by a resulting *loss* of benefits (a substitution effect). In addition a system of universal benefits is relatively cheap to administer, avoiding the need for costly means-testing.

The big drawback with universal benefits, however, is their cost. If they were given to everyone and were large enough to help the poor, their cost would be enormous. Thus although the benefits themselves would not create much disincentive effect, the necessary taxation to fund them probably would.

There is no ideal solution to this conundrum. On the one hand, the more narrowly benefits are targeted on the poor, the greater is the problem of the poverty trap. On the other hand, the more widely they are spread, the greater is the cost of providing any given level of support to individuals. One compromise proposal is that of a *negative income tax*. This is examined in Case Study 10.6 in MyEconLab. Box 10.5 examines the use of tax credits – which have similarities with a negative income tax – in the UK, while Box 10.6 discusses changes to the UK benefits system.

Conclusions

Redistribution is not costless. Whether it takes place through taxes or benefits or both, it can pose a problem of disincentives. The size of the disincentive problem varies from one tax to another and from one benefit to another, and in some cases there may even be an incentive effect – for example, when the income effect of a tax outweighs the substitution effect. It is therefore important to estimate the particular

Definitions

Poverty trap Where poor people are discouraged from working or getting a better job because any extra income they earn will be largely or entirely taken away in taxes and lost benefits.

Negative income tax A combined system of tax and benefits. As people earn more, they gradually lose their benefits until beyond a certain level they begin paying taxes.

| BOX 10.5 | UK TAX CREDITS | | CASE STUDIES AND APPLICATIONS |

An escape from the poverty trap?

Tax credits (which share characteristics with negative income taxes) were introduced in the UK in 1999 in the form of Working Families Tax Credit, which was replaced in 2003 by Working Tax Credit (WTC) and Child Tax Credit (CTC). These credits are paid as a cash benefit.

Working Tax Credit was designed for working people on low incomes. To be eligible for the basic amount (£1940 in 2014–15), people without children must be aged 25 or over and work at least 30 hours per week. People with children, the over 50s returning to work, the over 60s and the disabled must work at least 16 hours per week. Couples and lone parents receive an additional amount (£1990 in 2014–15). There is a further addition for anyone with children who works at least 30 hours per week, or for couples who jointly work at least 30 hours per week. This is designed as an incentive for people to move from part-time to full-time work. Recipients of WTC also get paid 70 per cent of eligible childcare costs up to £175 per week for one child and £300 for two or more children (2014–15). For each pound earned above a threshold amount (£6420 in 2014–15), relief is reduced by 41p.

Child Tax Credit provides support to families with children, whether or not anyone in the family works. It is paid in addition to WTC and child benefit.

These tax credits were designed to improve incentives to work, by reducing the poverty trap (see page 308). In other words, the aim was to reduce the financial penalties for parents working by tapering off more slowly the rate at which benefits are lost. With a lost-benefit rate of 41 per cent, the combined marginal tax-plus-lost-benefit rate (the 'marginal deduction rate') is typically around 73 per cent.

Although the introduction of these tax credits did reduce the marginal deduction rate, it remained high. For many poor parents, therefore, the incentive to work was still relatively low. What is more, a lower taper rate brings *more* families into the tax credit system. While this is good, in terms of providing support for them, the result is more of a disincentive for parents in such families to work extra hours, or to take a better job, since the marginal deduction rate is now higher. In other words, although they are better off, they will take home less for each extra hour worked.

WTC and CTC illustrate the general problem of providing support to poor people which is affordable for taxpayers without creating disincentives to work. The more gently the support tapers off (and hence the less the disincentive to earn extra money), the more costly it is to finance, and hence higher tax rates are needed elsewhere. The problems with using negative income taxes are explored in Case Study 10.6 in MyEconLab.

A major criticism of tax credits lies in the complexity of the system. This has two consequences: first, it is estimated that of the 7 million households eligible for the benefits, around 2 million fail to claim them; second, the system is administratively costly and prone to errors.

A universal approach

In 2011 Ian Duncan Smith, the Secretary of State for Work and Pensions, announced plans fundamentally to reform the benefit system with the introduction of a new Universal Credit.

His intention was radically to simplify the system to make work pay and combat worklessness and poverty.[1] The new credit was described as an integrated working-age credit providing a basic allowance with additional elements for children, disability, housing and caring. It differs from the system that it will replace, in that it supports people both in and out of work, replacing Working Tax Credit, Child Tax Credit, Housing Benefit, Income Support, income-based Jobseeker's Allowance and income-related Employment and Support Allowance. (Note that although it is called Universal Credit, it is not a universal benefit and is means-tested.)

The design of the Universal Credit is intended to address the concerns tax credits raise:

- Smoother taper rates, lessening the impact of the poverty trap and ensuring work pays.
- Removing the distortions that over-reward individuals working a certain number of hours, notably 16 or 30 hours with Working Tax Credits.
- Bringing together of in-work and out-of-work benefits, reducing the risks and transactions costs for those moving into work.
- Lower administrative costs, with benefits being overseen by a single body, the Department for Work and Pensions.

However, the higher levels of support promised were accompanied by a warning to those out of work. The government would be applying a stronger level of conditionality: those who can work would be expected to do so.

Unfortunately, achieving simplicity in a benefits system has proved more complex than Ian Duncan Smith had anticipated. There have been setbacks in the implementation of the new system, which has been dogged by design errors and cost overruns. It is not expected to be rolled out fully until the end of 2017. Many people have experienced delays in receiving the benefit and have suffered considerable hardship in the meantime.

1. *Economists sometimes refer to an 'unemployment trap'. People are discouraged from taking work in the first place. Explain how such a 'trap' arises. Will the Universal Credit create an unemployment trap? What are the best ways of eliminating, or at least reducing, the unemployment trap?*
2. *Universal Credit involves a single monthly payment direct to the claimant's bank account. This replaces fortnightly payments, some in the form of cashable cheques, and rent payments direct to landlords. What additional support do you anticipate claimants would need?*

[1] White Paper *Universal Credit: Welfare that Works*, www.gov.uk/government/publications/universal-credit-welfare-that-works

TC 5
p54

BOX 10.6   REDUCING INEQUALITY

CASE STUDIES AND APPLICATIONS

Policies to address child poverty in the UK

In February 1995 the Joseph Rowntree Foundation published the results of a comprehensive inquiry into the UK's growing inequality since 1979.[1] The findings made grim reading. Inequalities in income had widened further and faster than in any other period in history. The rich had got substantially richer, while the poor had become not only relatively poorer, but absolutely poorer.

The report recommended various remedies. The thrust of them was to encourage employment and improve the lot of low-paid workers. Suggested measures included increased government expenditure on training schemes, top-up benefits for those on low wages and tax cuts targeted at the poor. These were seen as much better alternatives than simply increasing unemployment benefits, which could well make people more reluctant to get a job.

The response from 1997

Once elected in 1997, the Labour government put the reduction of poverty, especially child poverty, high on its agenda. In 1999 the Prime Minister, Tony Blair, pledged to halve child poverty by 2010–11 and eliminate it within a generation. The focus was on eliminating the 'cycle of deprivation', where children in poor households are more likely to leave school early, less likely to get good jobs and more likely to be unemployed themselves as adults, and thus to bring up their children in poverty.

A number of measures were taken, including making work more financially worthwhile for poor families by the use of tax credits (see Box 10.5) and increasing benefits for all families with children.

In 2005 the Joseph Rowntree Foundation was optimistic that the policy was proving effective and that the government had a good chance of hitting its 2004–5 targets.[2]

However, the rate of progress slowed and it soon became clear that the previous report had been too optimistic. In 2006 an independent report for the Department of Work and Pensions was published.[3] This identified a substantial number of children who remained in workless households, for whom there was no end to poverty in sight.

Following this, the Labour government continued to increase benefits and to offer further support to parents wishing to work by the extension of family policies, including parental leave and the right to request flexible working. However, the changing macroeconomic climate in the late 2000s, and the cuts in public-sector spending put in place by the incoming Coalition government from 2011, led campaigners to voice concerns about the prospects for children living in poverty.

Social mobility

As with the previous administration, the Coalition government pledged to reduce poverty and to increase equality and opportunity. One fundamental difference, however, was that it was now attempting to do this in a climate of lower public spending.

In the government's first year in office, a number of changes to benefits were announced, most notably the move to the Universal Credit (see Box 10.5). The government also announced the setting up of a new Social Mobility and Childhood Poverty Commission. This would make annual progress reports to Parliament on progress of the social mobility strategy. A number of key indicators were identified, including birth weight, readiness for school, educational achievement and entry to the 'most selective third' of universities and economic activity between the ages of 18 and 24.

Generally these measures were welcomed. However, the question of the relationship between poverty and inequality remains paramount. Social mobility may be a solution for some, increasing opportunities for children born into low-income households. But it does not reduce the gap that exists between the rich and the poor. A more equal society requires better opportunities *and* substantial redistribution.

Furthermore, there have been delays to the implementation of the government's proposed changes to definitions of poverty. In a time of austerity, even rewriting the question (of just who is poor) has proved too expensive.

1. *Suggest a range of 'direct' policies that the government might pursue in order to reduce child poverty within the UK. What will their impact be on social mobility?*
2. *If the government concentrates on eliminating child poverty, what is likely to happen to other vulnerable groups? Which groups might this include? How should the government prioritise which groups it will help?*
3. *The definition of child poverty in the UK is any child living in a household with income below 60 per cent of median household income. What are the disadvantages of such a definition? What are the advantages?*

---

[1] *Income and Wealth* (Joseph Rowntree Foundation, 1995).
[2] Policies towards poverty, inequality and exclusion since 1997, www.jrf. org.uk/knowledge/findings/socialpolicy/0015.asp. This report from the Joseph Rowntree Foundation summarises the findings of a book, *A More Equal Society? New Labour, Poverty, Inequality and Exclusion*, edited by John Hills and Kitty Stewart (The Policy Press, 2005).
[3] Lisa Harker for the Department of Work and Pensions, *Delivering on Child Poverty: What Would It Take?* (November 2006).

| BOX 10.7 | WHAT THE FUTURE HOLDS | CASE STUDIES AND APPLICATIONS |

Approaches to pensioner poverty in the UK

While much of the focus since 1997 has been on child poverty, politicians have also been concerned about the plight of pensioners. After all, unlike children, they have the vote. And with an ageing population, the numbers of pensioners are increasing.

For most of the first decade of this century, the analysis was relatively simple: many pensioners are poor and pensioner poverty needs to be addressed. Pensioner incomes had fallen relative to those of the working population, as pensions were uprated in line with prices rather than wages. Increasing life expectancy and changing labour markets combined to leave nearly 3 million pensioners living in poverty by 1998.

Policy responses included more generous means-tested benefits and the introduction of a number of universal benefits for pensioners, such as free bus travel and winter fuel allowances. The result was that by 2009 the number of pensioners living in poverty had fallen by one-third to around 2 million.

Intergenerational equity

More recently, the focus has moved to looking at the question of equity between different generations. With many reliant on incomes from savings and personal pensions, older people have suffered from low or even negative real interest rates since 2008. Younger people with mortgages and other debts, by contrast, have benefited from these low real interest rates. Then there is the question of the fruits of economic growth. Should only companies and wage earners benefit from economic growth, or should the retired benefit too?

Many people, however, are concerned that pensioners as a group are getting more than their fair share of national income. They argue that it is those under 30 who are worst off.

David Willetts, the Conservative Minister for Higher Education, discusses this issue in his book *The Pinch*,[1] published in 2010. He asserts that the generation born between the late 1940s and mid-1960s has benefited from an unprecedented combination of financial and social factors. This has left them considerably better off than later generations. They are the generation that had free health care from birth, free higher education and generous final salary pension schemes. They have built up substantial wealth in the form of housing equity, buying initially when prices were very low, and will be able to retire to enjoy a long and comfortable old age.

He contrasts this with the young: higher education fees of up to £9000, house prices so high that they remain unaffordable for many, final salary pension schemes closed

and retirement ages likely to increase beyond 70. What is more, they face higher taxes to pay for past spending, the effects of climate change and, of course, for the costs of the bank bailouts in 2008.

Willetts argues that we need a stronger social contract between generations; he approves of the way that Native American tribal councils used to take account of seven generations when making decisions. Whether this can be achieved by government is debatable, but what is clear is that this 'lucky' generation, now either retired or coming up for retirement, is unlikely to give up its good fortune willingly.

UK government policy

It is reasonable to assume that governments would prefer both child and pensioner poverty to be eliminated. The problem with the latter is that the opportunities are limited for the current generation of pensioners with few or no assets.

If we are to address the issue, we need to start now with those who are of working age. To that end the government has put in place new pension requirements. All employers must now offer a low-cost pension scheme, into which employees are automatically enrolled. Workers are encouraged to save more and to plan for a retirement that may last several decades.

To that end, in the 2014 Budget, the Chancellor announced that those reaching retirement would be given increased flexibility over their pension pots. They will even be able to draw the whole amount as a lump-sum. Despite this, there is little doubt that we persist in saving too little. In April 2014 Steve Webb, the Pensions Minister, announced that the government wanted to give people an indication of their life expectancy, presumably to concentrate their minds on saving for their old age.

1. Why has the government legislated for the new national pension scheme to involve auto-enrolment? (Hint: think back to section 4.4, page 127.)
2. The last two governments have used universal benefits, such as winter fuel allowances and free bus travel, as part of their approach to eliminating pensioner poverty. What are the advantages (and disadvantages) of this approach?
3. If you could find out, with some associated probability, when you might die, would you choose to do so? How might the answer affect the way you live today?

[1] David Willetts, *The Pinch: How the Baby Boomers Took their Children's Future – and Why They Should Give it Back* (Atlantic, 2010).

Markets, Efficiency and the Public Interest

CHAPTER MAP

11.1 Efficiency under perfect competition — 315
Social efficiency: 'Pareto optimality' — 315
The simple analysis of social efficiency: marginal
  benefit and marginal cost — 315
Achieving social efficiency through the market — 316
Interdependence, efficiency and the 'invisible hand':
  the simple analysis of general equilibrium — 318
*The intermediate analysis of social efficiency:
  marginal benefit and marginal cost ratios — 320
*Efficiency in the goods market (intermediate
  analysis) — 320
*Efficiency in the factor market (intermediate
  analysis) — 322
*The intermediate analysis of general equilibrium — 322

11.2 The case for government intervention — 323
Externalities — 323
Public goods — 325
Common resources — 326
Market power — 327
Other market failures — 330
Conclusions — 331

11.3 Forms of government intervention — 333
Taxes and subsidies — 333
Changes in property rights — 336
Laws prohibiting or regulating undesirable
  structures or behaviour — 337
Regulatory bodies — 337
Price controls — 338
Provision of information — 338
The direct provision of goods and services — 338
Public ownership — 338

***11.4 Cost–benefit analysis** — 340
The procedure — 340
Identifying the costs and benefits — 341
Measuring the costs and benefits — 341
Risk and uncertainty — 343
Discounting future costs and benefits — 346
CBA and the distribution of costs and benefits — 346

**11.5 Government failure and the case for
  the market** — 348
Drawbacks of government intervention — 348
Advantages of the free market — 350
Should there be more or less intervention? — 350

In Chapter 10 we examined the problem of inequality. In this chapter we turn to examine another major area of concern. This is the question of the efficiency (or inefficiency) of markets in allocating resources.

First we show how a perfect market economy could under certain conditions lead to 'social efficiency'. In section 11.2 we examine the real world and show how real-world markets fail to meet social goals. These failures provide the major arguments in favour of government intervention in a market economy. We then turn to discuss the alternative ways in which a government can intervene to correct these various market failings.

If the government is to replace the market and provide goods and services directly, it will need some way of establishing their costs and benefits. Section 11.4 looks at 'cost–benefit analysis'. This is a means of establishing the desirability of a public project such as a new motorway or a new hospital. Finally, in section 11.5, we look at the case for restricting government intervention. We examine the advantages of real-world markets and the drawbacks of government intervention.

11.1 EFFICIENCY UNDER PERFECT COMPETITION

Perfect competition has been used by many economists and policy makers as an ideal against which to compare the benefits and shortcomings of real-world markets.

As was shown in Chapter 6, perfect competition has various advantages for society. Under perfect competition, firms' supernormal profits are competed away in the long run by the entry of new competitors. As a result, firms are forced to produce at the bottom of their average cost curves. What is more, the fear of being driven out of business by the entry of new firms forces existing firms to try to find lower-cost methods of production, thus shifting their *AC* curves downwards.

 Perhaps the most wide-reaching claim for perfect competition is that under certain conditions it will lead to a *socially efficient* use of a nation's resources.

Social efficiency: 'Pareto optimality'

If it were possible to make changes in the economy – changes in the combination of goods produced or consumed, or changes in the combination of inputs used – and if these changes benefited some people without anyone else being made worse off, economists would describe this as an *improvement in social efficiency*, or a **Pareto improvement**, after Vilfredo Pareto, the Italian social scientist (for a profile of Pareto, see Case Study 11.1 in MyEconLab).

 Do you agree that, if some people gain and if no one loses, then this constitutes an 'improvement' in the well-being of society? Does it depend who gains? Would it be possible to improve the well-being of society without a Pareto improvement?

When all Pareto improvements have been made – in other words, when any additional changes in the economy would benefit some people only by making others worse off – the economy is said to be *socially efficient*, or Pareto optimal. What we shall show is that under certain conditions a perfect market will lead to *Pareto optimality*.

But a word of caution. Just because social efficiency is achieved in a particular market environment, it does not necessarily make that environment *ideal*. It may be a *necessary* condition for an ideal allocation of resources that all Pareto improvements are made. It is not *sufficient*, however. If, for example, the government redistributed income from the rich to the poor, there would be no Pareto improvement, since the rich would lose. Thus both an equal and a highly unequal distribution of income could be Pareto optimal, and yet it could be argued that a more equal distribution is socially more desirable. For the moment, however, we will ignore questions of fairness and just focus on social efficiency.

So why may a perfect market lead to social efficiency? The following sections explain.

The simple analysis of social efficiency: marginal benefit and marginal cost

Remember how we defined 'rational' choices. A rational person will choose to do an activity if the gain from so doing exceeds any sacrifice involved. In other words, whether as a producer, a consumer or a worker, a person will gain by expanding any activity whose marginal benefit (*MB*) exceeds its marginal cost (*MC*) and by contracting any activity whose marginal cost exceeds its marginal benefit. Remember that when economists use the term 'cost', they are referring to 'opportunity cost': in other words, the *sacrifice* of alternatives. Thus when we say that the marginal benefit of an activity is greater than its marginal cost, we mean that the additional benefit gained exceeds any sacrifice in terms of alternatives forgone.

Thus the economist's rule for *rational economic behaviour* is that a person should expand or contract the level of any activity until its marginal benefit is equal to its marginal cost. At that point, the person will be acting efficiently in his or her own private interest. Only when *MB* = *MC* can no further gain be made. This is known as a situation of *private efficiency*.

By analogy, *social* efficiency will be achieved where, for any activity, the marginal benefit to *society* (*MSB*) is equal to the marginal (opportunity) cost to *society* (*MSC*):

$$MSB = MSC$$

 KEY IDEA 26 *Allocative efficiency (simple formulation) in any activity is achieved where marginal benefit equals marginal cost.* Private efficiency is achieved where marginal private benefit equals marginal private cost (*MB* = *MC*). Social efficiency is achieved where marginal social benefit equals marginal social cost (*MSB* = *MSC*).

Definitions

Pareto improvement Where changes in production or consumption can make at least one person better off without making anyone worse off.

Social efficiency A situation of Pareto optimality.

Pareto optimality Where all possible Pareto improvements have been made; where, therefore, it is impossible to make anyone better off without making someone else worse off.

Rational economic behaviour Doing more of those activities whose marginal benefit exceeds their marginal cost and doing less of those activities whose marginal cost exceeds their marginal benefit.

Private efficiency Where a person's marginal benefit from a given activity equals the marginal cost.

THRESHOLD CONCEPT 11   ALLOCATIVE EFFICIENCY: PRIVATE AND SOCIAL   THINKING LIKE AN ECONOMIST

Economics is concerned with the allocation of scarce resources. Whenever choices are made, whether by consumers, firms, the government or any other agency, a choice is being made about the allocation of resources.

When you buy a T-shirt costing £10, you are choosing to allocate £10 of your money to the purchase – £10 that could have been spent on something else. But have you allocated your money in the best way?

Similarly, when a firm chooses to produce one product rather than another, or to use technique A rather than some alternative technique, it is choosing to allocate its resources in particular ways. But are these the best ways?

The question is whether the resources have been allocated *efficiently*. We define an efficient allocation of resources as one which brings the maximum benefit for that level of costs. In other words, no gain would be made by reallocating resources in some alternative way. Thus your decision to spend £10 on a T-shirt is an efficient allocation of your resources, if it brings you more benefit (i.e. utility) for the £10 than could any other purchase. The firm's decision to use technique A is an efficient one if it leads to a higher rate of profit: if the marginal benefit (i.e. marginal revenue) relative to the marginal cost is greater than for any other technique.

What we are talking about here is 'allocative efficiency'. It is a *threshold concept* because to understand it is to understand how to make the most of scarce resources: and scarcity is the core problem of economics for all of us. It is obvious that poor people on very limited incomes will want to spend their money as efficiently as possible. But even exceedingly rich people, who can buy anything they want, are still likely to have limited time or opportunities.

Allocative efficiency is a threshold concept for another reason. We need to see how it relates to *social* objectives. If people all individually achieve their own *private efficiency*, does this mean that society will have an efficient allocation of resources? The answer is no. The reason is that our decisions often have consequences for *other* people: our actions have external costs and/or benefits. These externalities mean that private efficiency and *social efficiency* diverge. We need to understand how and why, and how social efficiency can be achieved.

Then there is the question of equity. Just because everyone is allocating their resources in the best possible way for them, and even if there were no externalities, it does not follow that the allocation of resources is *fair*. However efficiently rich people spend their money, most people would still argue that it is socially desirable to redistribute part of rich people's income to the poor through the tax and benefit system.

1. *Why might consumers not always make efficient consumption decisions?*
2. *Explain the meaning of social efficiency using the concept of Pareto improvements.*

KI 4
p13

KI 14
p107

---

*The intermediate analysis of social efficiency: marginal benefit and marginal cost ratios

In practice, consumers do not consider just one good in isolation. They make choices between goods. Likewise firms make choices as to which goods to produce and which factors to employ. A more satisfactory analysis of social efficiency, therefore, considers the choices that firms and households make.

TC 11
p320

Whether as a producer, consumer or worker, a person will gain by expanding activity X relative to activity Y if

$$\frac{MB_X}{MB_Y} > \frac{MC_X}{MC_Y}$$

The reason is straightforward. Activity X is giving a greater benefit relative to its cost than is activity Y. Only when

KI 14
p107

$$\frac{MB_X}{MB_Y} = \frac{MC_X}{MC_Y}$$

can no further gain be made by switching from the one activity to the other. At this point, people will be acting efficiently in their own private interest.

By analogy, social efficiency is achieved where the social marginal benefit ratio of two goods is equal to the social marginal cost ratio.

KEY IDEA
27

Social efficiency (equi-marginal formulation) is achieved where the marginal social benefit ratios are equal to the marginal social cost ratios for any two alternatives. In the case of two alternatives X and Y, this will be where

$$\frac{MSB_X}{MSB_Y} = \frac{MSC_X}{MSC_Y}$$

As with the simple analysis of social efficiency, it can be shown that, provided there is perfect competition and no externalities, the achievement of private efficiency will result in social efficiency also. This will be demonstrated in the following sections.

*Efficiency in the goods market (intermediate analysis)

Private efficiency under perfect competition

Consumption.   The optimum combination of two goods X and Y consumed for any consumer is where

$$\frac{MU_X}{MU_Y} \text{ (i.e. } MRS) = \frac{P_X}{P_Y}$$

KI 14
p107

The *marginal rate of substitution in consumption (MRS)* (see page 109) is the amount of good Y that a consumer would be willing to sacrifice for an increase in consumption of good X (i.e. $\Delta Y / \Delta X$). $MRS = MU_X / MU_Y$ since, if X gave twice the marginal utility of Y, the consumer would be prepared to give up two of Y to obtain one of X (i.e. $MRS = 2/1$).

 If MU_X / MU_Y were greater than P_X / P_Y, how would consumers behave? What would bring consumption back to equilibrium where $MU_X / MU_Y = P_X / P_Y$?

Production. The optimum combination of two goods X and Y produced for any producer is where

$$\frac{MC_X}{MC_Y} \text{(i.e. } MRT) = \frac{P_X}{P_Y}$$

The *marginal rate of transformation in production (MRT)* is the amount of good Y that the producer will have to give up producing for an increase in production of good X (i.e. $\Delta Y / \Delta X$) if total costs of production are to remain unchanged. $MRT = MC_X / MC_Y$ since, if the marginal cost of good X were twice that of Y, the firm's costs would remain constant if it gave up producing two of Y in order to produce an extra X (i.e. $MRT = 2/1$).

 If MC_X / MC_Y were greater than P_X / P_Y, how would firms behave? What would bring production back into equilibrium where $MC_X / MC_Y = P_X / P_Y$?

Social efficiency under perfect competition

In each of the following three cases, it will be assumed that there are no externalities.

Social efficiency between consumers. If MU_X / MU_Y for person a is greater than MU_X / MU_Y for person b, *both* people would gain if person a gave person b some of good Y in exchange for some of good X. There would be a Pareto improvement. The Pareto optimal distribution of consumption will therefore be where

$$\frac{MU_X}{MU_Y} \text{person a} = \frac{MU_X}{MU_Y} \text{person b} = \frac{MU_X}{MU_Y} \text{person c} \cdots$$

i.e. *MRS* is the same for all consumers.

But this will be achieved *automatically* under perfect competition, since each consumer will consume that combination of goods where $MU_X / MU_Y = P_X / P_Y$ and all consumers face the *same* (market) prices and hence the *same* P_X / P_Y.

Social efficiency between producers. If MC_X / MC_Y for producer g is greater than MC_X / MC_Y for producer h, then if producer g produced relatively more Y and producer h produced relatively more X, the same output could be produced at a lower total cost (i.e. with less resources). There would be a Pareto improvement. The Pareto optimal distribution of production between firms is therefore where

$$\frac{MC_X}{MC_Y} \text{producer g} = \frac{MC_X}{MC_Y} \text{producer h} = \frac{MC_X}{MC_Y} \text{producer i} \cdots$$

i.e. *MRT* is the same for all producers.

This too will be achieved *automatically* under perfect competition, since each producer will maximise profits where $MC_X / MC_Y = P_X / P_Y$ and all producers face the *same* (market) prices and hence the *same* P_X / P_Y.

Social efficiency in exchange. If MU_X / MU_Y (i.e. *MRS*) for all consumers is greater than MC_X / MC_Y (i.e. *MRT*) for all producers, then there would be a Pareto improvement if resources were reallocated to produce relatively more X and less Y.

Assume *MRS* (i.e. $\Delta Y / \Delta X$) = 3/1 and *MRT* (i.e. $\Delta Y / \Delta X$) = 2/1. Consumers will be prepared to give up three units of Y to obtain one unit of X, and yet producers only have to sacrifice producing two units of Y to produce one unit of X. Thus consumers can pay producers in full for extra units of X they produce and there will still be a net gain to consumers. There has been a Pareto improvement.

The Pareto optimal allocation of resources is where

Social MRS (SMRS) = Social MRT (SMRT)

Assuming no externalities, this will be achieved automatically under perfect competition, since (a) with no externalities, social and private marginal rates of substitution will be the same, and similarly social and private marginal rates of transformation will be the same, and (b) P_X / P_Y is the same for all producers and consumers. In other words,

$$SMRS = MRS_{\text{all consumers}} = \frac{MU_X}{MU_Y}_{\text{all consumers}} = \frac{P_X}{P_Y}$$

and

$$SMRT = MRT_{\text{all producers}} = \frac{MC_X}{MC_Y}_{\text{all producers}} = \frac{P_X}{P_Y}$$

that is

SMRS = SMRT

Thus the pursuit of private gain, it is argued, has led to the achieving of social efficiency. This is an important conclusion. It is clearly very attractive to people (and to many politicians) to think that, simply by looking after their own interests, social efficiency will thereby be achieved!

This is illustrated graphically in Figure 11.3. A production possibility curve (the red line) shows the various combinations of two goods X and Y that can be produced (see pages 13–17). Its slope is given by $\Delta Y / \Delta X$ and shows how much Y must be given up to produce one more of X. Its slope, therefore, is the marginal rate of transformation (*MRT*).

Social indifference curves can be drawn showing the various combinations of X and Y that give particular levels of satisfaction to consumers as a whole. Their slope is given by $\Delta Y / \Delta X$ and shows how much Y consumers are prepared to give up to obtain one more unit of X. Their slope, therefore, is the marginal rate of substitution in consumption (*MRS*).

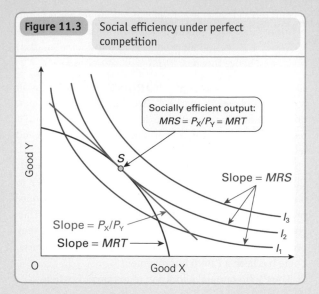

Figure 11.3   Social efficiency under perfect competition

Socially efficient output:
$MRS = P_X/P_Y = MRT$

Slope = MRS

Slope = P_X/P_Y

Slope = MRT

Good Y

Good X

I_3
I_2
I_1

The Pareto optimal combination of goods is at point *S*, where the production possibility curve is tangential to the highest possible indifference curve. At any other point on the production possibility curve, a lower level of consumer satisfaction is achieved. The slope of the tangent at *S* is equal to both *MRT* and *MRS*, and hence also to P_X/P_Y.

 If production were at a point on the production possibility curve below point S, describe the process whereby market forces would return the economy to point S.

*Efficiency in the factor market (intermediate analysis)

A similar analysis can be applied to factor markets, showing that perfect competition and the absence of externalities will lead to efficiency in the use of factors between firms. Assume that there are two factors: labour (*L*) and capital (*K*).

If MPP_L/MPP_K for firm g is greater than MPP_L/MPP_K for firm h, then if firm g were to use relatively more labour and firm h relatively more capital, more could be produced for the same total input. There would be a Pareto improvement.

The Pareto optimum distribution of factors between firms will therefore be where

$$\frac{MPP_L}{MPP_K}_{\text{firm g}} = \frac{MPP_L}{MPP_K}_{\text{firm h}} = \frac{MPP_L}{MPP_K}_{\text{firm i}} \cdots$$

But this will be achieved automatically under perfect competition since, as we saw in section 5.3, each producer will be producing where $MPP_L/MPP_K = P_L/P_K$ and each producer will face the same factor prices and hence P_L/P_K.

Provided there are no externalities, the marginal private benefit of labour to a firm (MPP_L) will equal the marginal social benefit of labour (MSB_L). The same applies to capital. Thus $MPP_L/MPP_K = MSB_L/MSB_K = P_L/P_K$. Similarly on the cost side, if there are no externalities, then $MC_L/MC_K = MSC_L/MSC_K = P_L/P_K$. Therefore,

$$\frac{MSB_L}{MSB_K} = \frac{MSC_L}{MSC_K}$$

*The intermediate analysis of general equilibrium

General equilibrium is where equilibrium exists in all markets (see Threshold Concept 10 on page 317). Under perfect competition and in the absence of externalities, general equilibrium will give Pareto optimality.

If any change in the conditions of demand or supply occurs, this disequilibrium will automatically create a whole series of interdependent reactions in various markets.

Assume, for example, that tastes change such that MU_X rises and MU_Y falls. This will lead to the following sequence of events in the goods market.

MU_X/MU_Y will now be greater than P_X/P_Y. Thus consumers buy more X relative to Y. This causes MU_X/MU_Y to fall (due to diminishing marginal utility) and P_X/P_Y to rise (due to a relative shortage of X and a surplus of Y), helping to restore equilibrium where $MU_X/MU_Y = P_X/P_Y$. The rise in P_X/P_Y causes P_X/P_Y to be greater than MC_X/MC_Y. Thus firms produce more X relative to Y. This causes MC_X/MC_Y to rise (due to diminishing returns), helping to restore equilibrium where $P_X/P_Y = MC_X/MC_Y$. This process of price and quantity adjustment thus continues until once more

$$\frac{MU_X}{MU_Y} = \frac{P_X}{P_Y} = \frac{MC_X}{MC_Y}$$

Similar adjustments will take place in the factor market. The price of those factors used in producing good X will be bid up and those used in producing Y will be bid down. This will encourage factors to move from industry Y and into industry X. The whole process of adjustment continues until equilibrium and Pareto optimality are restored in all goods and factor markets.

Definition

General equilibrium Where all the millions of markets throughout the economy are in a simultaneous state of equilibrium.

Section summary

1. Social efficiency (Pareto optimality) will be achieved when it is not possible to make anyone better off without making someone else worse off. This will be achieved if people behave 'rationally' under perfect competition providing there are no externalities.

2. Rational behaviour involves doing more of any activity whose marginal benefit (*MB*) exceeds its marginal cost (*MC*) and less of any activity whose marginal cost exceeds its marginal benefit. The optimum level of consumption or production for the individual consumer or firm will be where $MB = MC$. This is called a situation of 'private efficiency'.

3. In a perfectly competitive goods market, the consumer will achieve private efficiency where $MU = P$, and the producer where $P = MC$. Thus $MU = MC$. In the absence of externalities, private benefits and costs will equal social benefits and costs. Thus $MU = MSB$ and $MC = MSC$. Thus $MSB = MSC$: a situation of social efficiency (Pareto optimality).

4. Given perfect competition and an absence of externalities, if the equality of marginal benefit and marginal cost is destroyed in any market (by shifts in demand or supply), price adjustments will take place until general equilibrium is restored where $MSB = MSC$ in all markets: a situation of general Pareto optimality.

*5. The rational producer or consumer will choose the combination of any two pairs of goods where their marginal benefit ratio is equal to their marginal cost ratio. Consumers will achieve private efficiency where

$$\frac{MU_X}{MU_Y} \ (\text{i.e. } MRS) = \frac{P_X}{P_Y}$$

Producers will achieve private efficiency where

$$\frac{P_X}{P_Y} = \frac{MC_X}{MC_Y} \ (\text{i.e. } MRT)$$

Thus

$$\frac{MU_X}{MU_Y} = \frac{MC_X}{MC_Y}$$

In the absence of externalities, this will give a situation of social efficiency where

$$\frac{MSB_X}{MSB_Y} = \frac{MSC_X}{MSC_Y}$$

*6. Similarly, in factor markets, social efficiency will be achieved if there is perfect competition and an absence of externalities. This will be where the *MSB* ratio for any two factors is equal to their *MSC* ratio.

*7. Again assuming perfect competition and an absence of externalities, general equilibrium will be achieved where there is a socially efficient level of production, consumption and exchange in all markets: where the *MSB* ratio for any pair of goods or factors is equal to the *MSC* ratio.

11.2 THE CASE FOR GOVERNMENT INTERVENTION

The discussion above considered what happens 'under ideal conditions', but in the real world, markets fail to achieve social efficiency. Part of the problem is the existence of externalities, part is a lack of perfect competition. Even if those were not considerations, we are also faced with markets that may take a long time to adjust to any disequilibrium given short-run immobility of factors. What is more, social efficiency (i.e. Pareto optimality) is not the only economic goal of society. Markets may also fail to the extent that they fail to achieve other objectives such as greater equality and faster growth. In this section we explore the various categories of market failure.

KEY IDEA 28 *Markets generally fail to achieve social efficiency.* There are various types of market failure. Market failures provide one of the major justifications for government intervention in the economy.

Externalities

The market will not lead to social efficiency if the actions of producers or consumers affect people other than themselves: in other words, when there are *externalities* (side effects).

KEY IDEA 29 *Externalities are spill-over costs or benefits.* Where these exist, even an otherwise perfect market will fail to achieve social efficiency.

Whenever other people are affected beneficially, there are said to be *external benefits*. Whenever other people are affected adversely, there are said to be *external costs*.

Thus the full cost to society (the *social cost*) of the production of any good is the private cost faced by firms plus

Definitions

External benefits Benefits from production (or consumption) experienced by people *other* than the producer (or consumer).

External costs Costs of production (or consumption) borne by people *other* than the producer (or consumer).

Social cost Private cost plus externalities in production.

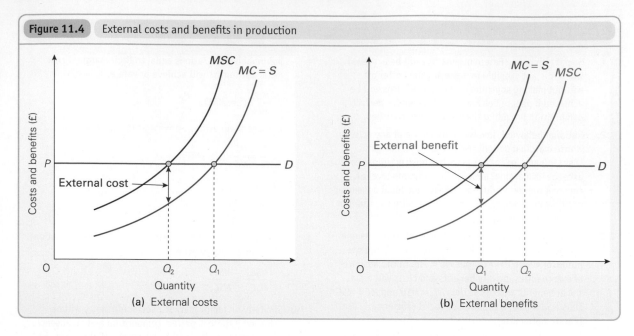

Figure 11.4 External costs and benefits in production

(a) External costs

(b) External benefits

any externalities of production. Likewise the full benefit to society (the **social benefit**) from the consumption of any good is the private benefit enjoyed by consumers plus any externalities of consumption.

There are four major types of externality. (In each case, we will assume that the market is in other respects perfect.)

External costs of production (MSC > MC)

When a chemical firm dumps waste in a river or pollutes the air, the community bears costs additional to those borne by the firm. The marginal *social* cost (*MSC*) of chemical production exceeds the marginal private cost (*MC*). Diagrammatically, the *MSC* curve is above the *MC* curve. This is shown in Figure 11.4(a), which assumes that the firm in other respects is operating in a perfect market, and is therefore a price taker (i.e. faces a horizontal demand curve).

The *socially* optimal output would be Q_2, where $P = MSC$. The firm, however, produces Q_1, which is more than the optimum. Thus external costs lead to overproduction from society's point of view.

The problem of external costs arises in a free-market economy where no one has legal ownership of the air or rivers and so no one can prevent or charge for their use as a dump for waste. The 'market' is missing and control must, therefore, be left to the government.

Other examples are intensive farming that destroys hedgerows and wildlife, and climate change caused by CO_2 emissions from power stations.

Definition

Social benefit Private benefit plus externalities in consumption.

External benefits of production (MSC < MC)

If a forestry company plants new woodlands, there is a benefit not only to the company itself, but also to the world through a reduction of CO_2 in the atmosphere (forests are a carbon sink). The marginal *social* cost of providing timber, therefore, is less than the marginal *private* cost.

In Figure 11.4(b), the *MSC* curve is *below* the *MC* curve. The level of output provided by the forestry company is Q_1, where $P = MC$, a *lower* level than the social optimum, Q_2, where $P = MSC$.

Another example of external benefits in production is that of research and development. If other firms have access to the results of the research, then clearly the benefits extend beyond the firm that finances it. Since the firm receives only the private benefits, it will conduct less than the socially optimal amount of research.

External costs of consumption (MSB < MB)

When people use their cars, other people suffer from their exhaust fumes, the added congestion, the noise, etc. These 'negative externalities' make the marginal social benefit of using cars less than the marginal private benefit (i.e. marginal utility).

Figure 11.5(a) shows the marginal utility and price to a consumer of using a car. The distance travelled by this motorist will be Q_1 miles: i.e. where $MU = P$ (where price is the cost of petrol, oil, wear and tear, etc., per mile). The *social* optimum, however, would be less than this, namely Q_2, where $MSB = P$.

Other examples are noisy radios in public places, the smoke from cigarettes, and litter.

Is it likely that the MSB curve will be parallel to the MU curve? Explain your reasoning.

Figure 11.5   External costs and benefits in consumption

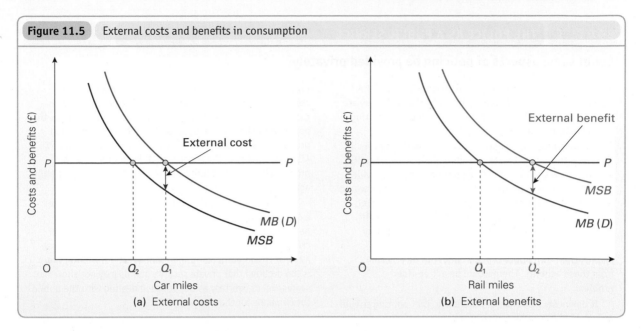

(a) External costs

(b) External benefits

External benefits of consumption (MSB > MB)

When people travel by train rather than by car, other people benefit by there being less congestion and exhaust fumes and fewer accidents on the roads. Thus the marginal social benefit of rail travel is *greater* than the marginal private benefit (i.e. marginal utility). There are external benefits from rail travel. In Figure 11.5(b), the *MSB* curve is *above* the private *MB* curve. The actual level of consumption (Q_1) is thus below the socially optimal level of consumption (Q_2).

Other examples include the beneficial effects for other people of deodorants, vaccinations and planting flowers in a front garden.

To summarise, whenever there are external benefits, there will be too little produced or consumed. Whenever there are external costs, there will be too much produced or consumed. The market will not equate *MSB* and *MSC*.

1. *Give other examples of each of the four types of externality.*
2. *Redraw Figures 11.4(a) and 11.5(a), only this time assume that the producer (in the first diagram) or the consumer (in the second) has economic power and is thus not a price taker. How does the existence of power affect the relationship between the private and the social optimum positions?*
3. *Do flowers in a back garden only give private benefits? What about house plants?*

Public goods

There is a category of goods where the positive externalities are so great that the free market, whether perfect or imperfect, may not produce at all. They are called ***public goods***. KI 28 p323 Examples include lighthouses, pavements, flood-control dams, public drainage, public services such as the police and even government itself.

Public goods have two important characteristics: *non-rivalry* and *non-excludability*:

■ If I consume a bar of chocolate, it cannot then be consumed by someone else. If, however, I walk along a pavement or enjoy the benefits of street lighting, it does not prevent you or anyone else doing the same. There is thus what we call ***non-rivalry*** in the consumption of such goods. These goods have large external benefits relative to private benefits. This makes them socially desirable, but privately unprofitable. No one person alone would pay to have a pavement built along his or her street. The private benefit would be too small relative to the cost. And yet the social benefit to all the other people using the pavement may far outweigh the cost.

Which of the following have the property of non-rivalry: (a) a can of drink; (b) public transport; (c) a radio broadcast; (d) a sea view?

■ If I spend money erecting a flood-control dam to protect my house, my neighbours will also be protected by the dam. I cannot prevent them enjoying the benefits of my expenditure. This feature of ***non-excludability*** means

Definitions

Public good A good or service that has the features of non-rivalry and non-excludability and as a result would not be provided by the free market.

Non-rivalry Where the consumption of a good or service by one person will not prevent others from enjoying it.

Non-excludability Where it is not possible to provide a good or service to one person without it thereby being available for others to enjoy.

BOX 11.1 | **THE POLICE AS A PUBLIC SERVICE** | CASE STUDIES AND APPLICATIONS

Could some aspects of policing be provided privately?

A good example of a public good or service is that of the police. Take the case of police officers on the beat. They are providing a general service to the community by deterring and detecting crime.

If individuals had to employ their own police officers privately, this would create considerable external benefits relative to private benefits. One police officer can provide protection to *many* individuals. But for most people it would be out of the question to employ their own police officer: the private cost would hugely exceed the private benefit. Also, once such privately employed police were on duty catching and deterring criminals, people who did not employ their own police officers could not be excluded from these benefits. There would be a 'free-rider' problem.

It obviously makes sense, therefore, that policing should be provided as a public service.

But do all aspects of policing come into this category? The answer is no. When there is a *specific* task of guarding specific property, policing could be provided by the market. This is in fact done by security firms. Security guards are employed by banks, shops, etc., to prevent theft or criminal damage to their property. In these cases, the private benefits are perceived to exceed the private costs.

Should such security services be provided privately or are they better provided by the police? Since the *private* benefits in such cases are large, there is a strong argument for charging the recipient. But why should the service be

provided by private security firms? Could the police not charge firms for specific guard duties? The problem here is that, if private security firms were not allowed to operate, the police would have a monopoly and could charge very high prices unless the prices were regulated by the government. Also, the quality of the service might be poorer than that provided by private security companies which were competing against each other for business.

On the other hand, the police are likely to bring greater expertise to the job. There are also economies of scale to be gained: for example, the police may have knowledge of criminal activities in other parts of the area which may pose a threat to the particular property in question. Finally, there is the problem that private security guards may not show the same level of courtesy as the police in dealing with the public (or criminals for that matter).

1. *The police charge football clubs for policing inside football grounds, but make no charge for policing outside the ground. Explain this approach.*
2. *Could other aspects of policing make use of market forces? Examine the case for charging to investigate the theft of a bicycle. Would your conclusion differ if the crime involved an attack on an individual rather than property?*
3. *Some roads could be regarded as a public good, but some could be provided by the market. Which types of road could be provided by the market? Why? Would it be a good idea?*

that they would get the benefits free, and would therefore have no incentive to pay themselves. This is known as the *free-rider problem*.

> **KEY IDEA 30**
>
> *The free-rider problem.* People are often unwilling to pay for things if they can make use of things other people have bought. This problem can lead to people not purchasing things that it would be to the benefit of them and other members of society to have.

When goods have these two features the free market will simply not provide them. Thus these public goods can be provided only by the government or by the government subsidising private firms. (Note that not all goods produced by the public sector are public goods.)

> ## Definition
>
> **Free-rider problem** When it is not possible to exclude other people from consuming a good that someone has bought.

1. *Give some other examples of public goods. Does the provider of these goods (the government or local authority) charge for their use? If so, is the method of charging based on the amount of the good that people use? Is it a good method of charging? Could you suggest a better method?*
2. *Name some goods or services provided by the government or local authorities that are not public goods.*
3. *Are there ways in which we could overcome the free-rider problem? Start by thinking about the provision of a public good amongst a group of friends or neighbours.*

Common resources

Common resources are not owned but are available free of charge to anyone. Examples include the air we breathe and the oceans for fishing. Like public goods, they are non-excludable. For example, in the absence of intervention, fishing boats can take as many fish as they are able from the open seas. There is no 'owner' of the fish to stop them. As long as there are plentiful stocks of fish, there is no problem.

But as more people fish the seas, so fish stocks are likely to run down. This is where common resources differ from public goods. There *is* rivalry. One person's use of a common resource diminishes the amount available for others.

This result is an overuse of common resources. This is why many fish stocks are severely depleted, why rainforests are disappearing (cut down for timber or firewood), why many roads are congested and why the atmosphere is so polluted (being used as a common 'dump' for emissions). In each case, a resource that is freely available is overused. This has become known as the *tragedy of the commons*.

How can we analyse the overuse of common resources? The simplest way is in terms of externalities. When I use a common resource, I am reducing the amount available for others. I am imposing a cost on other people: an external cost. If I am motivated by self-interest, I will not take these external costs into account. In terms of Figure 11.4(a), I will produce Q_1, which is above the socially optimal amount, Q_2. Overuse of the resource thus occurs.

Another way of analysing it is to examine the effect of one person's use of a resource on other people's output. Take the case of fishing grounds. In Figure 11.6 the horizontal axis measures the use of this common resource, say in terms of the number of fishing boats per day. The average cost of operating a boat (e.g. the wages of the crew and the fuel) is taken to be constant and is thus equal to the marginal cost. For the sake of simplicity, the price of fish is also assumed to be constant.

As the number of boats increases and fish stocks decline, so each extra boat entering will add less and less to the total catch. The revenue added by each extra boat – the marginal revenue product (*MRP*) – thus declines. Eventually, at point B_2, no more fish can be caught: $MRP = 0$. The catch is at the maximum. The average revenue product (*ARP*) is the revenue earned per boat: i.e. the total value of the catch divided by the number of boats.

The average and marginal revenue product curves have to be interpreted with care. Say one additional boat enters the fishing ground. The *MRP* curve shows the extra revenue accruing to the boat operators collectively. It does *not* show the revenue actually earned by the additional boat. The extra boat gets an average catch (which has been reduced somewhat because of the additional boat) and hence gains the average revenue product of all the boats.

What will be the equilibrium? Note first that the optimal number of boats for the boat operators collectively is B_1, where the marginal cost of an extra boat equals its marginal revenue product. In other words, this maximises the collective profit. At point B_1, however, there will be an incentive for extra boats to enter the fishery because the average revenue product (i.e. the return that an additional boat gets) is greater than the cost of operating the boat.

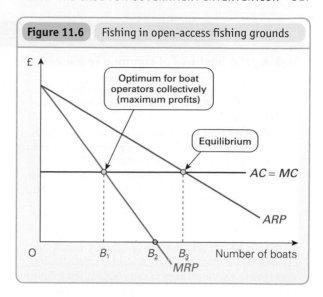

Figure 11.6 Fishing in open-access fishing grounds

More boats will enter as long as the value earned by each boat (*ARP*) is greater than the cost of operating it: as long as the *ARP* curve is above the $AC = MC$ line. Equilibrium is reached with B_3 boats considerably above the collective profit-maximising number. Note also that the way the diagram is drawn, marginal revenue product is negative. The last boat has *decreased* the total value of the catch.

In many parts of the world, fish stocks have become so severely depleted that governments, individually or collectively, have had to act. Measures have included quotas on catches or the number of boats, minimum net mesh sizes (to allow young fish to escape), or banning fishing altogether in certain areas or for certain species.

 To what extent can the following be regarded as common resources: (a) rainforests; (b) children's playgrounds in public parks; (c) silence in a library; (d) the Internet?

Market power

Lack of Pareto optimality

Whenever markets are imperfect, whether as pure monopoly or monopsony or as some form of imperfect competition, the market will fail to equate *MSB* and *MSC*. Pareto optimality will not be achieved.

This is illustrated in Figure 11.7, which shows revenue and cost curves for a monopolist. It assumes no externalities. The socially efficient (Pareto optimal) output is Q_2, where $MSB = MSC$. The monopolist, however, produces the lower output Q_1, where $MR = MC$.

 Referring back to Figure 9.8 (page 256), and assuming that the MRP_L curve represents the marginal social benefit from the employment of a factor, and that the price of the factor represents its marginal social cost (i.e. assuming no externalities), show that a monopsony will employ less than the Pareto optimal amount of factors.

 KI 20 p171

KI 29 p323

KI 2 p11

Definition

Tragedy of the commons When resources are commonly available at no charge, people are likely to overexploit them.

BOX 11.2   **A COMMONS SOLUTION**   EXPLORING
                                                              ECONOMICS

Making the best use of common resources

To avoid the tragedy of the commons, one solution is to change the status of such resources. There are two obvious ways of doing this.

The first is for the government or an intergovernmental agency either to take over the resources or to regulate their use. Thus a national or local government could pass laws preventing people from tipping waste onto common land or into rivers. Alternatively, groups of governments could act collectively to regulate activities. An example here is the EU's common fisheries policy or international agreements to ban whaling.

The second is to privatise such resources. Common land could be sold or given to private landowners. Such land would then have the property of excludability. This solution clearly raises questions of fairness. How should the land be divided up? If it is sold, how should the previous users of the resource be compensated – if at all? In the 'enclosure movement' in Britain in the eighteenth and nineteenth centuries, common lands were often acquired by wealthy aristocracy and hedges put around them. Poor peasants, who had previously used the land, either had to rent it from the landlords or left the land and were forced to take low-paid work in the cities.

But is there any way for resources to stay as common resources without their being overexploited? After all, economic theory would seem to suggest that the overexploitation of such resources is inevitable: that common ownership will end in tragedy.

Social attitudes towards common resources

In practice, many common resources are used sustainably without government regulation.

When economists began to look at how systems of commonly managed resources actually worked, they found to their surprise that they often worked quite well. Swiss Alpine pastures; Japanese forests; irrigation systems in Spain and the Philippines. All these were examples of commons that lasted for decades. Some irrigation networks held in common were more efficiently run than the public and private systems that worked alongside them. Though there were failures, too, it seemed as if good management could stave off the tragedy.[1]

The crucial factor here is whether a sense of individual responsibility can be fostered and whether mechanisms can be found for the users to act collectively to manage the resources – a form of quasi-government. Also there has to be some agreement about what is a fair use of such resources and, in many cases, rules will have to be developed.

In *Governing the Commons*, which was published in 1990, Elinor Ostrom of Indiana University described the rules needed to keep a commons going. She showed that there are almost always elaborate conventions over who can use resources and when. What you take out of a commons has to be proportional to what you put in. Usage has to be compatible with the commons' underlying health (i.e., you cannot just keep grazing your animals regardless). Everyone has to have some say in the rules. And people usually pay more attention to monitoring abuses and to conflict resolution than to sanctions and punishment.[2]

Sometimes the rules of behaviour can be deeply embedded in culture. Thus Indigenous peoples operating on marginal lands, such as the Aborigines in Australia or the San in the Kalahari, have a culture that respects common resources and puts sustainability at the heart of its philosophy.

Land is fundamental to the wellbeing of Aboriginal people. The land is not just soil or rocks or minerals, but a whole environment that sustains and is sustained by people and culture. For Indigenous Australians, the land is the core of all spirituality and this relationship and the spirit of 'country' is central to the issues that are important to Indigenous people today.[3]

But if rules are not embedded in culture, how can they be made to stick? One way is through the development of pressure groups, such as Friends of the Earth or local community action groups.

Mrs Ostrom suggests the so-called 'miracle of the Rhine' – the clean-up of Europe's busiest waterway – should be seen as an example of successful commons management because it was not until local pressure groups, city and regional governments and non-governmental organisations got involved that polluters were willing to recognise the costs they were imposing on others, and cut emissions. An inter-governmental body (the International Commission for the Protection of the Rhine) did not have the same effect.[4]

The importance of Elinor Ostrom's work was recognised when she was awarded the Nobel Prize in Economics Sciences in 2009.

1. *Is there any way in which people's behaviour towards the global commons can be changed so as to reduce the problem of climate change?*
2. *List some factors which would make successful management of common resources achievable. You might want to think about the number of people, the stability of the population and the role of traditions. What others can you identify?*

[1] 'Commons sense', *The Economist*, 31 July 2008.
[2] Ibid.
[3] Australian Indigenous cultural heritage (www.cultureandrecreation.gov.au/articles/indigenous/).
[4] 'Commons sense', *The Economist*, 31 July 2008.

KI 4
p13

KI 4
p13

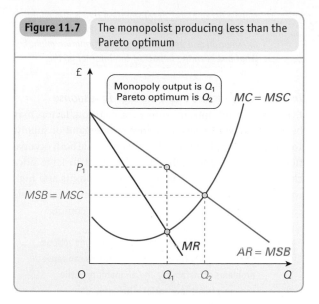

Figure 11.7   The monopolist producing less than the Pareto optimum

Monopoly output is Q_1
Pareto optimum is Q_2

competition (since area 2 is larger than area 5). The consumer surplus, however, will fall dramatically. With consumption at Q_m, total utility is given by areas $1 + 2 + 4 + 6$, whereas consumer expenditure is given by areas $2 + 4 + 6$. Consumer surplus, then, is simply area 1. (Note that area 2 has been transformed from consumer surplus to producer surplus.)

Total surplus under monopoly is therefore areas $1 + 2 + 4$: a smaller surplus than under perfect competition. 'Monopolisation' of the industry has resulted in a loss of total surplus of areas $3 + 5$. The producers' gain has been more than offset by the consumers' loss. This loss of surplus is known as the ***deadweight welfare loss*** of monopoly.

KI 28
p323

*LOOKING AT THE MATHS

Total consumer surplus (*TCS*) equals total utility minus total expenditure (i.e. total revenue). Total producer surplus (*TPS*) equals total revenue minus total variable cost. Thus total surplus (*TS*) is given by

$$TS = TCS + TPS = (TU - TR) + (TR - TVC) = TU - TVC$$

Assuming that the demand curve traces out the marginal utility curve (see pages 105–6), this allows us to derive the total utility function. To do this, you would need to use the technique of integration. Assuming that the total utility function is

$$TU = bQ - cQ^2$$

and that the total variable cost function is

$$TVC = jQ - kQ^2 + lQ^3$$

this will give a total surplus function of

$$TS = (bQ - cQ^2) - (jQ - kQ^2 + lQ^3) \qquad \textbf{(1)}$$

To find the level of deadweight welfare loss, we would then subtract total surplus under perfect competition from that under monopoly. To do this, we would solve equation (1) first for Q_{pc} and then for Q_m and then subtract the second from the first. A worked example of this is given in Maths Case 11.1 in MyEconLab.

Deadweight loss under monopoly

Another way of analysing the welfare loss that occurs under monopoly is to use the concepts of consumer and producer *surplus*. The two concepts are illustrated in Figure 11.8, which is similar to Figure 11.7. The diagram shows an industry that is initially under perfect competition and then becomes a monopoly (but faces the same revenue and cost curves).

Under *perfect competition* the industry will produce an output of Q_{pc} at a price of P_{pc}, where $MC (= S) = P (= AR)$: i.e. at point *a*. Consumer surplus is shown by areas $1 + 2 + 3$, and producer surplus by areas $4 + 5$. Total surplus (i.e. consumer plus producer surplus) is maximised at this output (see Figure 11.1 on page 316).

What happens when the industry is under *monopoly*? The firm will produce where $MC = MR$, at an output of Q_m and a price of P_m (at point *b* on the demand curve). Total revenue is $P_m \times Q_m$ (areas $2 + 4 + 6$). Total cost is the area under the MC curve (area 6). Thus the producer surplus is areas $2 + 4$. This is clearly a *larger* surplus than under perfect

Conclusions

The firm with market power uses fewer factors and produces less output than the Pareto optimum. It also causes deadweight welfare loss. To the extent, however, that the firm seeks aims *other* than profit maximisation and thus may produce more than the profit-maximising output, so these criticisms must be relaxed.

As was shown in Chapter 6, there are possible social *advantages* from powerful firms: advantages such as economies of scale and more research and development. These advantages may outweigh the lack of Pareto optimality. It can be argued that an ideal situation would be where firms

Definition

Deadweight welfare loss The loss of consumer plus producer surplus in imperfect markets (when compared with perfect competition).

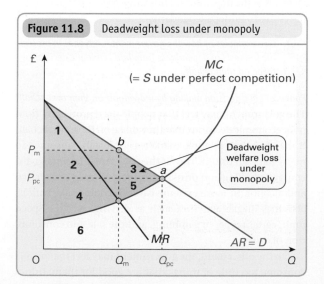

Figure 11.8   Deadweight loss under monopoly

MC (= S under perfect competition)

Deadweight welfare loss under monopoly

are large enough to gain economies of scale and yet are somehow persuaded or compelled to produce where $P = MC$ (assuming no externalities).

With oligopoly and monopolistic competition, further waste may occur because of possibly substantial resources involved in non-price competition. Advertising is the major example. It is difficult to predict just how much oligopolists will diverge from the Pareto optimum, since their pricing and output depend on their interpretation of the activities of their rivals.

 Why will Pareto optimality not be achieved in markets where there are substantial economies of scale in production?

Other market failures

Imperfect information

KI 15
p 121

Perfect competition assumes that consumers, firms and factor suppliers have perfect knowledge of costs and benefits. In the real world, there is often a great deal of ignorance and uncertainty. Thus people are unable to equate marginal benefit with marginal cost.

Consumers purchase many goods infrequently. Cars, washing machines and other consumer durables fall into this category, as do houses. Consumers may not be aware of the quality of such goods until they have purchased them, by which time it is too late. Advertising may contribute to people's ignorance by misleading them as to the benefits of a good.

Firms are often ignorant of market opportunities, prices, costs, the productivity of factors (especially white-collar workers), the activity of rivals, etc.

TC 9
p 121

Many economic decisions are based on expected future conditions. Since the future can never be known for certain, many decisions may turn out to be wrong.

In some cases, it may be possible to obtain the information through the market. There may be an agency that will sell you the information or a newspaper or magazine that contains the information. In this case, you will have to decide whether the cost to you of buying the information is worth the benefit it will provide you. A problem here is that you may not have sufficient information to judge how reliable the information is that you are buying!

1. Assume that you wanted the following information. In which cases might you (i) buy perfect information, (ii) buy imperfect information, (iii) be able to obtain information without paying for it, (iv) not be able to obtain information?
   (a) Which washing machine is the most reliable?
   (b) Which of two vacant jobs is more satisfying?
   (c) Which builder will repair my roof most cheaply?
   (d) Which builder is the best value for money?
   (e) How big a mortgage would it be wise for me to take out?
   (f) Should I take a degree or get a full-time job?
   (g) What brand of washing powder washes whiter?
   (h) Will a house need any work done on it over the next few years?

2. Make a list of pieces of information that a firm might want to know, and consider whether it could buy the information and how reliable that information might be.
3. What has been the impact of the Internet on the provision of information?

Immobility of factors and time lags in response

Even under conditions of perfect competition, factors may be very slow to respond to changes in demand or supply. Labour, for example, may be highly immobile both occupationally and geographically. This can lead to large price changes and hence to large supernormal profits and high wages for those in the sectors of rising demand or falling costs. The long run may be a very long time coming!

 The problem of time lags. Many economic actions can take a long time to take effect. This can cause problems of instability and an inability of the economy to achieve social efficiency.

KEY IDEA 31

In the meantime, there will be further changes in the conditions of demand and supply. Thus the economy is in a constant state of disequilibrium and the long run never comes. As firms and consumers respond to market signals and move towards equilibrium, so the equilibrium position moves and the social optimum is never achieved.

Whenever monopoly/monopsony power exists, the problem is made worse if firms or unions put up barriers to the entry of new firms or factors of production.

Protecting people's interests

Dependants. People do not always make their own economic decisions. They are often dependent on decisions made by others. Parents make decisions on behalf of their children; partners on each other's behalf; younger adults on behalf of old people; managers on behalf of shareholders; etc. This is the principal–agent issue that we looked at in section 8.1.

KI 23
p 225

A free market will respond to these decisions, however good or bad they may be, and whether or not they are in the interests of the dependant. Thus the government may feel it necessary to protect dependants.

 Give examples of how the government intervenes to protect the interests of dependants from bad economic decisions taken on their behalf.

Poor economic decision making by individuals on their own behalf. The government may feel that people need protecting from poor economic decisions that they make on their *own* behalf. It may feel that, in a free market, people will consume too many harmful things. Thus if the government wants to discourage smoking and drinking, it can put taxes on tobacco and alcohol. In more extreme cases, it could make various activities illegal: activities such as driving over the speed limit, certain types of gambling, and the sale and consumption of drugs.

On the other hand, the government may feel that people consume too little of things that are good for them: things such as education, preventative health care and sports facilities. Such goods are known as *merit goods*. The government could either provide them free or subsidise their production; it could also make their consumption compulsory (e.g. as with fluoride added to water in many areas).

 How do merit goods differ from public goods?

Other objectives

As we saw in Chapter 10, one of the major criticisms of the free market is the problem of *inequality*. The Pareto criterion gives no guidance, however, as to the most desirable distribution of income. A redistribution of income will benefit some and make others worse off. Thus Pareto optimality can be achieved for *any* distribution of income. Pareto optimality merely represents the efficient allocation of resources for any *given* distribution of income.

KI 4
p15

In addition to social efficiency and greater equality, we can identify other social goals: goals such as moral behaviour (however defined), enlightenment, social consciousness, co-operation, the development of culture, fulfilment, freedom from exploitation, and freedom to own, purchase and inherit property. The unfettered free market may not be very successful in achieving social efficiency. It may be even less successful in achieving many other social goals.

Finally, the free market is unlikely to achieve simultaneously the *macroeconomic objectives* of rapid economic growth, full employment, stable prices and a balance of international payments. These problems, and methods of government intervention that may be used to deal with them, are examined in later chapters.

Conclusions

It is not the role of economists to make judgements as to the relative importance of social goals. Economics can only consider the means to achieving stated goals. First, therefore, the goals have to be clearly stated by the policy makers. Second, they have to be quantifiable so that the effectiveness of different policies can be compared. Certain goals, such as growth in national income, changes in the distribution of income and greater efficiency, are relatively easy to quantify. Others, such as enlightenment, are virtually impossible to quantify. For this reason, economics tends to concentrate on the means to achieving a relatively narrow range of goals. The danger is that, by concentrating on a limited number of goals, economists may well influence policy makers into doing the same, and thus into neglecting other social goals.

KI 6
p29

Different objectives are likely to conflict. For example, economic growth may conflict with greater equality. In the case of such 'trade-offs', all the economist can do is to demonstrate the effects of a given policy, and leave the policy makers to decide whether the benefits in terms of one goal outweigh the costs in terms of another goal.

TC 1
p11

 How do the economic policies of the major political parties differ? How far can an economist go in assessing these policies?

> ## Definition
>
> **Merit goods** Goods that the government feels people will underconsume and which therefore ought to be subsidised or provided free.

Section summary

1. Real-world markets will fail to achieve Pareto optimality. What is more, there are objectives other than social efficiency, and real-world markets may fail to achieve these too.

2. Externalities are spill-over costs or benefits. Whenever there are external costs, the market will (other things being equal) lead to a level of production and consumption *above* the socially efficient level. Whenever there are external benefits, the market will (other things being equal) lead to a level of production and consumption *below* the socially efficient level.

3. Public goods will be underprovided by the market. They have large external benefits relative to private benefits, and without government intervention it would not be possible to prevent people having a 'free ride' and thereby escape contributing to their cost of production.

4. Common resources are likely to be overused, since people do not take into account the effect of their use of such resources on other people.

5. Monopoly power will (other things being equal) lead to a level of output below the socially efficient level. It will lead to a deadweight welfare loss: a loss of consumer plus producer surplus.

6. Ignorance and uncertainty may prevent people from consuming or producing at the levels they would otherwise choose. Information, however, may sometimes be provided (at a price) by the market.

7. Markets may respond sluggishly to changes in demand and supply. The time lags in adjustment can lead to a permanent state of disequilibrium and to problems of instability.

8. In a free market there may be inadequate provision for dependants and an inadequate output of merit goods; there are likely to be macroeconomic problems and problems of inequality and poverty; finally, there may be a whole series of social, moral, attitudinal and aesthetic problems arising from a market system.

9. These being normative questions, the economist cannot make ultimate pronouncements on the rights and wrongs of the market. The economist can, however, point out the consequences of the market and of various government policies, and also the trade-offs that exist between different objectives.

BOX 11.3   SHOULD HEALTH-CARE PROVISION BE LEFT TO THE MARKET?   CASE STUDIES AND APPLICATIONS

A case of multiple market failures

In the UK, the National Health Service provides free hospital treatment, a free general practitioner service, and free prescriptions for certain categories of people. Their marginal cost to the patient is thus zero. Of course, these services use resources and they thus have to be paid for out of taxes.

But why are these services not sold directly to the patient, thereby saving the taxpayer money? There are, in fact, a number of reasons why the market would fail to provide the optimum amount of health care.

TC 3
p26

The issue of equity

This is a problem connected with the distribution of income. Because income is unequally distributed, some people will be able to afford better treatment than others, and the poorest people may not be able to afford treatment at all. On grounds of equity, therefore, it is argued that health care should be provided free – at least for those on low incomes.

KI 4
p13

The concept of equity that is usually applied to health care is that individuals should be able to access treatment according to their medical need rather than according to their ability to pay.

?   *Does this argument also apply to food and housing?*

Difficulty of predicting future medical needs

If you were suddenly taken ill and required a major operation, it could be very expensive indeed for you if you had to pay. On the other hand, you may go through life requiring very little if any medical treatment. In other words, there is great uncertainty about your future medical needs. As a result it would be very difficult to plan your finances and budget for possible future medical expenses if you had to pay for treatment.

Medical insurance provides a solution to this problem, but there remains a problem of equity. Would the chronically sick or very old be able to obtain cover, and if so, would they be able to afford the premiums? This issue of 'gaps' in an insurance-based system means that some form of intervention on grounds of equity may be needed, even if most provision is private.

Externalities

Health care generates a number of benefits *external* to the patient. If you are cured of an infectious disease, for example, it is not just you who benefits but also others, since you will not infect them. In addition if you have a job you will be able to get back to work, thus reducing the disruption there. These external benefits of health care could be quite large.

KI 29
p323

If sick people have to pay the cost of their treatment, they may decide not to be treated – especially if they are poor. They will consider the costs and benefits they might experience, but will probably not take into account the effect that their illness has on other people. The market, by equating *private* benefits and costs, would produce too little health care.

Information problems and patient ignorance

Markets only function well to allocate resources efficiently if the consumer has the information to make informed decisions. For many products that we buy, we have a pretty good idea how

much we will like them. In the case of health care, however, 'consumers' (i.e. patients) may have very poor knowledge. If you have a pain in your chest, it may be simple muscular strain, or it may be a symptom of heart disease. You rely on the doctor (the *supplier* of the treatment) to give you the information: to diagnose your condition. Two problems could arise here with a market system of allocating health care.

The first is that unscrupulous doctors might advise more expensive treatment than is necessary; they might even have an agreement with certain drugs companies that they will try to persuade you to buy an expensive branded product rather than an identical cheaper version. This problem will also exist in an insurance-based system, where the doctor may be even more inclined to oversupply if the patient has sufficient cover.

KI 23
p225

The second is that patients suffering from the early stages of a serious disease might not consult their doctor until the symptoms become acute, by which time it might be too late to treat the disease, or very expensive to do so. With a health service that is free at the point of use, however, a person is likely to receive an earlier diagnosis of serious conditions.

Oligopoly

If doctors and hospitals operated in the free market as profit maximisers, it is unlikely that competition would drive down their prices. Instead they might collude to fix standard prices for treatment, so as to protect their incomes. Even if doctors did compete openly, it is unlikely that consumers would have enough information to enable them to 'shop around' for the best value.

We have to be careful: to argue that the market system will fail to provide an optimal allocation of health-care resources does not in itself prove that *free provision* will result in optimal provision. For example, with no charge for GP appointments it is likely that some patients will consult their doctors over trivial complaints. The result will be consumption beyond the socially efficient point.

In the USA there is much more reliance on *private medical insurance* with only very poor people getting free treatment. Alternatively, the government may simply *subsidise* health care, so as to make it cheaper rather than free. This is the case with prescriptions and dental treatment in the UK, where many people have to pay part of the cost of treatment. Also, the government can *regulate* the behaviour of the providers of health care, to prevent exploitation of the patient. Thus only people with certain qualifications are allowed to operate as doctors, nurses, pharmacists, etc.

1. *If health care is provided free at the point of consumption, the demand is likely to be high. How is this high demand likely to be dealt with? Is this a good way of dealing with the issue?*
2. *Go through each of the market failures identified in this box. In each case, consider what alternative policies are open to a government to tackle them. What are the advantages and disadvantages of these alternatives?*
3. *Does the provision of free health care mean that it needs to be publicly produced? What would be the advantages, and disadvantages, of private provision?*

Faced with all the problems of the free market, what is a government to do?

There are several policy instruments that a government can use. At one extreme, it can totally replace the market by providing goods and services itself. At the other extreme, it can merely seek to persuade producers, consumers or workers to act differently. Between the two extremes, the government has a number of instruments that it can use to change the way markets operate. These include taxes, subsidies, laws and regulatory bodies.

Before looking at different forms of government intervention and their relative merits, it is first necessary to look at a general problem concerned with all forms of intervention. This is known as the ***problem of the second best***.

In an ideal free market, where there are no market failures of any sort (the 'first-best' world), there would be no need for government intervention at all. If in this world there did then arise just one failure, in theory its correction would be simple. Say a monopoly arose, or some externality (e.g. pollution) was produced by a particular firm, with the result that the marginal social cost was no longer equal to the marginal social benefit. In theory, the government should simply intervene to restore production to the point where $MSC = MSB$. This is known as the ***first-best solution***.

Of course, the real world is not like this. It is full of imperfections. What this means is that, if one imperfection is 'corrected' (i.e. by making $MSB = MSC$), it might aggravate problems elsewhere. For example, if a local authority introduces residents-only parking in an inner city area to prevent commuters parking there, they may simply park just outside the area, thus imposing additional costs on people living there.

Give some examples of how correcting problems in one part of the economy will create problems elsewhere.

As the first-best solution of a perfectly efficient, distortion-free world is obviously not possible, the ***second-best solution***

needs to be adopted. Essentially this involves seeking the best compromises. This means attempting to minimise the *overall* distortionary effects of the policy measure. Some second-best *rules* can be applied in certain cases. We will examine these in the following sections as we look at specific policy measures.

Taxes and subsidies

A policy instrument particularly favoured by many economists is that of taxes and subsidies. They can be used for two main microeconomic purposes: (a) to promote greater social efficiency by altering the composition of production and consumption: and (b) to redistribute incomes. We examined their use for the second purpose in Chapter 10. Here we examine their use to achieve greater social efficiency.

When there are imperfections in the market (such as externalities or monopoly power), Pareto optimality will not be achieved. Taxes and subsidies can be used to correct these imperfections. Essentially the approach is to tax those goods or activities where the market produces too much, and subsidise those where the market produces too little.

Taxes and subsidies to correct externalities

Assume that a chemical works emits smoke from a chimney and thus pollutes the atmosphere. This creates external costs for the people who breathe in the smoke. The marginal social cost of producing the chemicals thus exceeds the marginal private cost to the firm: $MSC > MC$.

The first-best world.   In Figure 11.9, the firm is producing in an otherwise perfect world. It produces Q_1 where $P = MC$ (its profit-maximising output), but in doing so takes no account

Definitions

Problem of the second best The difficulty of working out the best way of correcting a specific market distortion if distortions in other parts of the market continue to exist.

First-best solution The solution of correcting a specific market distortion by ensuring that the whole economy operates under conditions of social efficiency (Pareto optimality).

Second-best solution The solution to a specific market distortion that recognises distortions elsewhere and seeks to minimise the overall distortionary effects to the economy of tackling this specific distortion.

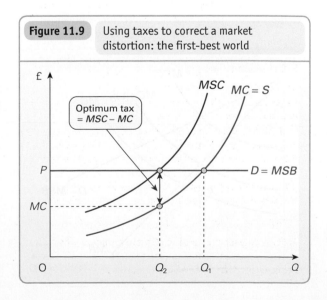

Figure 11.9   Using taxes to correct a market distortion: the first-best world

of the external pollution costs it imposes on society. If the government imposes a tax on production equal to the marginal pollution cost, it will effectively 'internalise' the externality. The firm will have to pay an amount equal to the external cost it creates. It will therefore now maximise profits at Q_2, which is the socially optimum output where $MSB = MSC$. In the first-best world, then, the optimum tax is equal to the marginal external cost.

By analogy, if a firm produced an external benefit, then in the first-best world it ought to be given a subsidy equal to that marginal external benefit.

Note that a tax or subsidy ought to be directed as closely as possible to the source of the externality. For example, if a firm trains labour, and that creates a benefit to society, then ideally it ought to be given a subsidy for each person trained, rather than a general output subsidy. After all, an output subsidy not only encourages the firm to train more people (the desired effect), but also encourages it to use more capital and raw materials (an undesired side effect). This is a general maxim of welfare economics: *a distortion should be corrected at source if side-effect problems are to be avoided.*

Second-best tax and subsidy policies. In reality, the government must tackle imperfections in a world that has many other imperfections. Figure 11.10 shows a firm that both produces an external cost ($MSC > MC$) and *also* has monopoly power. It will maximise profits at Q_1 where $MC = MR$ (point x).

The socially efficient level of output in this case is Q_2, where MSB equals MSC. To persuade the monopolist to produce at this level, a tax of $a - b$ must be imposed (since at point a, $MR = MC + \text{tax}$). This tax is *less* than the full amount of the externality because of the problem of monopoly power. Were the monopolist to be charged a tax *equal* to the externality (so that its $MC + \text{tax}$ curve was equal to the MSC curve), it would maximise profits at point y, at a price of P_3

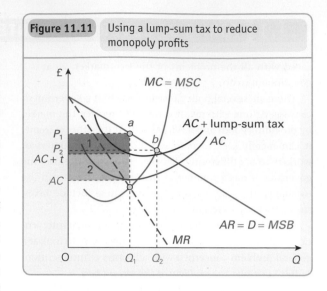

Figure 11.11   Using a lump-sum tax to reduce monopoly profits

and an output of Q_3. This would not be socially efficient, since MSB would now be *above MSC*.

Taxes to correct for monopoly

So far we have considered the use of taxes to correct for externalities. Taxes can also be used to regulate the behaviour of monopolies and oligopolies.

If the government wishes to tackle the problem of excessive monopoly profits, it can impose a *lump-sum* tax on the monopolist. The 'windfall tax', imposed in the UK in 1997 by the incoming Labour government on the profits of various privatised utilities, is an example of such a tax. The use of a lump-sum tax is illustrated in Figure 11.11.

Being of a fixed amount, a lump-sum tax is a fixed cost to the firm. It does not affect the firm's marginal cost. It shifts the AC curve upwards.

Profits continue to be maximised where $MC = MR$, at an output of Q_1 and a price of P_1. But profits are reduced from areas $1 + 2$ to area 1 alone. Area 2 now represents the amount of tax paid to the government. If the lump-sum tax were large enough to make the $AC + \text{lump-sum tax}$ curve cross the demand curve at point a, *all* the supernormal profits would be taken as tax.

If the government also wants to increase the monopolist's output to the socially efficient level of Q_2, and wants it to charge a price of P_2, it could do this with a careful combination of a per-unit subsidy (which will shift both the AC and the MC curves downwards) and a lump-sum tax. The required level of subsidy will be that which shifts the MC curve downwards to the point where it intersects MR at output Q_2. Then a lump-sum tax would be imposed that would be big enough to shift the AC curve back up again so that it crosses the demand curve at point b.

 What could we say about the necessary subsidy if the MR curve crossed the horizontal axis to the left of point b?

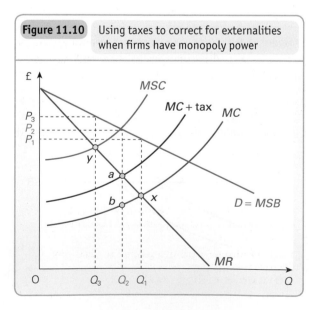

Figure 11.10   Using taxes to correct for externalities when firms have monopoly power

| BOX 11.4 | DEADWEIGHT LOSS FROM TAXES ON GOODS AND SERVICES | EXPLORING ECONOMICS |

The excess burden of taxes

Taxation can be used to correct market failures, but taxes can have adverse effects themselves. One such effect is the deadweight loss that results when taxes are imposed on goods and services (see page 302).

The diagram shows the demand and supply of a particular good. Equilibrium is initially at a price of P_1 and a level of sales of Q_1 (i.e. where $D = S$). Now an excise tax is imposed on the good. The supply curve shifts upwards by the amount of the tax, to S + tax. Equilibrium price rises to P_2 and equilibrium quantity falls to Q_2. Producers receive an after-tax price of P_2 – tax.

Consumer surplus falls from areas $1 + 2 + 3$, to area 1 (the green area). Producer surplus falls from areas $4 + 5 + 6$ to area 6 (the blue area). Does this mean, therefore, that

total surplus falls by areas $2 + 3 + 4 + 5$? The answer is no, because there is a gain to the government from the tax revenue (and hence a gain to the population from the resulting government expenditure). The revenue from the tax is known as the government surplus. It is given by areas $2 + 4$ (the pink area).

But, even after including *government surplus*, there is still a fall in total surplus of areas $3 + 5$. This is the deadweight loss of the tax. It is sometimes known as the *excess burden*.

Does this loss of total surplus from taxation imply that taxes on goods are always a 'bad thing'? The answer is no. This conclusion would follow only in a 'first-best' world where there were no market failures: where competition was perfect, where there were no externalities and where income distribution was optimum. In such a world, the loss of surplus from imposing a tax on a good would represent a reduction in welfare.

In the real world of imperfect markets and inequality, taxes can do more good than harm. As we have shown in this section, they can help to correct for externalities; and, as we showed in the previous chapter, they can be used as a means of redistributing incomes. Nevertheless, the excess burden of taxes is something that ideally ought to be considered when weighing up the desirability of imposing taxes on goods and services, or of increasing their rate.

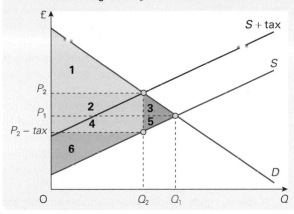

Deadweight loss from an indirect tax

1. *How far can an economist contribute to this normative debate over the desirability of an excise tax?*
2. *What is the excess burden of a lump-sum tax? (For a clue, see Figure 11.11.)*

Advantages of taxes and subsidies

Many economists favour the tax/subsidy solution to market imperfections (especially the problem of externalities) because it still allows the market to operate. It forces firms to take on board the full social costs and benefits of their actions; this is often described as *internalising the externality*. Furthermore, once the policy is in place, taxes and subsidies can be adjusted according to the magnitude of the problem.

Moreover, if firms are taxed for polluting, they are encouraged to find cleaner ways of producing. The tax acts as an incentive over the longer run to reduce pollution. Likewise, by subsidising *good* practices, firms are given the incentive to adopt more good practices.

The most suitable situation for imposing a pollution tax is when there is a clearly measurable emission, like a particular chemical waste. The government can then impose a tax per litre or per tonne of that waste.

Disadvantages of taxes and subsidies

Infeasibility of using different tax and subsidy rates. Each firm produces different levels and types of externality and operates

under different degrees of imperfect competition. It would be administratively very difficult and expensive to charge every offending firm its own particular tax rate (or grant every relevant firm its own particular rate of subsidy). Even in the case of pollution where it is possible to measure a firm's emissions, there would still have to be a different tax rate for each pollutant and even for each environment, depending on its ability to absorb the pollutant.

Lack of knowledge. Even if a government did decide to charge a tax equal to each offending firm's marginal external costs, it would still have the problem of measuring those costs and

Definitions

Government surplus (from a tax on a good) The total tax revenue earned by the government from sales of a good.

Excess burden (of a tax on a good) The amount by which the loss in consumer plus producer surplus exceeds the government surplus.

apportioning blame. The damage to lakes and forests from acid rain has been a major concern since the beginning of the 1980s. But just how serious is that damage? What is its current monetary cost? How long lasting is the damage? Just what and who are to blame? These questions cannot be answered precisely. It is thus impossible to fix the 'correct' pollution tax on, say, a particular coal-fired power station.

KI 15
p121

1. *Why is it easier to use taxes and subsidies to tackle the problem of car exhaust pollution than to tackle the problem of peak-time traffic congestion in cities?*
2. *CFCs in fridges were known to cause environmental damage and their use was banned in most countries over the last two decades. Why has this approach been adopted rather than the tax solution?*

Changes in property rights

One cause of market failure is the limited nature of property rights. If someone dumps a load of rubble in your garden, you can insist that it is removed. If, however, someone dumps a load of rubble in their *own* garden, which is next door to yours, what can you do? You can still see it from your window. It is still an eyesore. But you have no property rights over the next-door garden.

Property rights define who owns property, to what uses it can be put, the rights other people have over it and how it may be transferred. By *extending* these rights, individuals may be able to prevent other people from imposing costs on them or charge them for doing so.

The socially efficient level of charge would be one that was equal to the marginal external cost (and would have the same effect as the government charging a tax on the firm of that amount: see Figure 11.9). The **Coase theorem**[1] states that in an otherwise perfectly competitive market, the socially efficient charge *will* be levied. But why?

KI 26
p315

Let us take the case of river pollution by a chemical works that imposes a cost on people fishing in the river. If property rights to the river were now given to the fishing community, they could impose a charge on the chemical works per unit of output. If they charged *less* than the marginal external cost, they would suffer more from the last unit (in terms of lost fish) than they were being compensated. If they charged *more*, and thereby caused the firm to cut back its output below the socially efficient level, they would be sacrificing receiving charges that would be greater than the marginal suffering. It will be in the sufferers' best interests, therefore, to charge an amount *equal* to the marginal externality.

KI 29
p323

If the sufferers had no property rights, show how it would still be in their interests to 'bribe' the firm to produce the socially efficient level of output.

In most instances, however, this type of solution is totally impractical. It is impractical when *many* people are *slightly* inconvenienced, especially if there are many culprits imposing the costs. For example, if I were disturbed by noisy lorries passing by my house, it would not be practical to negotiate with every haulage company involved. What if I wanted to ban the lorries from the street but my next-door neighbour wanted to charge them 10p per journey? Who gets their way?

The extension of private property rights becomes more practical where the parties involved are few in number, are easily identifiable and where the costs are clearly defined. Thus a noise abatement Act could be passed which allowed me to prevent my neighbours from playing noisy radios, having noisy parties or otherwise disturbing the peace in my home. The onus would be on me to report them. Or I could agree not to report them if they paid me adequate compensation.

But even in cases where only a few people are involved, there may still be the problem of litigation. Justice may not be free, and thus there may be concerns about equity. The rich can afford 'better' justice. They can employ top lawyers. Even if I have a right to sue a large company for dumping toxic waste near me, I may not have the legal muscle to win.

Finally, the extension of private property rights may favour the rich (who tend to have more property) at the expense of the poor. Ramblers may get great pleasure from strolling across a great country estate, along public rights of way. If the owner's property rights were now extended to exclude the ramblers, would this be a social gain?

KI 4
p13

Of course, equity considerations can also be dealt with by altering property rights, but in a different way. *Public* property, like parks, open spaces, libraries and historic buildings, could be extended. Also, the property of the rich could be redistributed to the poor. Here it is less a question of the rights that ownership confers, and more a question of altering the ownership itself.

1. *To what extent could property rights (either public or private) be successfully extended and invoked to curb the problem of industrial pollution (a) of the atmosphere; (b) of rivers; (c) by the dumping of toxic waste; (d) by the erection of ugly buildings; (e) by the creation of high levels of noise?*
2. *What protection do private property rights in the real world give to sufferers of noise (a) from neighbours; (b) from traffic; (c) from MP3 players on public transport?*

> ### Definition
>
> **Coase theorem** By sufferers from externalities doing deals with perpetrators (by levying charges or offering bribes), the externality will be 'internalised' and the socially efficient level of output will be achieved.

---

[1] Named after Ronald Coase, who developed the theory. See his 'The problem of social cost', *Journal of Law and Economics*, 1960.

Laws prohibiting or regulating undesirable structures or behaviour

Laws are frequently used to correct market imperfections. This section examines three of the most common cases.

Laws prohibiting or regulating behaviour that imposes external costs

Laws can be applied both to individuals and to firms. In the case of individuals, it is illegal to drive when drunk. Drunk driving imposes costs on others in the form of accidents and death. Another example is the banning of smoking in public places.

In the case of firms, various polluting activities can be banned or restricted; safety standards can be imposed in the place of work; building houses or factories may be prohibited in green-belt areas.

In the case of common resources, restrictions can be placed on their use. For example, in the case of fishing grounds, governments can limit the size of fleets, impose quotas on catches or specify the types of net to be used. In extreme cases, they could ban fishing altogether for a period of time to allow fish stocks to recover. In order to be able to enforce restrictions, many governments have extended their 'territorial waters' to 200 miles from their coast.

Advantages of legal restrictions.

- They are simple and clear to understand and are often relatively easy to administer. Inspectors or the police can conduct spot checks to see that the law is being obeyed.
- When the danger is very great, it might be much safer to ban various practices altogether rather than to rely on taxes or on individuals attempting to assert their property rights through the civil courts.
- When a decision needs to be taken quickly, it might be possible to invoke emergency action. For example, in a city it would be simpler to ban or restrict the use of private cars during a chemical smog emergency than to tax their use (see Box 12.6).

Disadvantages of legal restrictions. The main problem is that legal restrictions tend to be a rather blunt weapon. If, for example, a firm were required to reduce the effluent of a toxic chemical to 20 tonnes per week, it would have no incentive to reduce it further. With a tax on the effluent, however, the more the firm reduced the effluent, the less tax it would pay. Thus with a system of taxes there is a *continuing* incentive to cut pollution.

Laws to prevent or regulate monopolies and oligopolies

Laws affecting structure. Various mergers or takeovers could be made illegal. The criterion would probably have to be the level of market concentration that results. For example,

the law could set a limit of 60 per cent of the market to be controlled by the five largest firms. Or it could require that merging firms have less than a certain percentage share of the market.

Laws affecting behaviour. Firms could be prohibited from engaging in various types of oligopolistic collusion, or various monopolistic practices. For example, manufacturers could be prevented from fixing the prices that retailers must charge, or from refusing to supply certain retailers.

Use of the law to regulate monopolies and oligopolies in the UK and the EU is examined in Chapter 13.

 How suitable are legal restrictions in the following cases: (a) ensuring adequate vehicle safety; (b) reducing traffic congestion; (c) preventing the abuse of monopoly power; (d) ensuring that mergers are in the public interest; (e) ensuring that firms charge a price equal to marginal cost?

Laws to prevent firms from exploiting people's ignorance

Given that consumers have imperfect information, consumer protection laws can make it illegal for firms to sell shoddy or dangerous goods, or to make false or misleading claims about their products.

The problem is that the firms most likely to exploit the consumer are often the ones that are most elusive when it comes to prosecuting them.

Regulatory bodies

A more subtle approach than banning or restricting various activities involves the use of regulatory bodies.

Having identified possible cases where action might be required (e.g. potential cases of pollution or the abuse of monopoly power), the regulatory body would probably conduct an investigation and then prepare a report containing its findings and recommendations. It might also have the power to enforce its decisions, or this might be up to some higher authority.

An example of such a body is the Competition and Markets Authority, the work of which is examined in section 13.1. Other examples are the bodies set up to regulate the privatised utilities: e.g. Ofwat, the Office of Water Services. These are examined in section 13.2.

The advantage of this approach is that a case-by-case method can be used and, as a result, the most appropriate solution adopted. However, investigations may be expensive and time consuming, only a few cases may be examined, and offending firms may make various promises of good behaviour which, if not followed up by the regulatory body, may not in fact be carried out.

 What other forms of intervention are likely to be necessary to back up the work of regulatory bodies?

Price controls

Price controls could be used to prevent a monopoly or oligopoly from charging excessive prices. Currently, sections of various privatised industries such as water and electricity are restricted in their ability to raise their prices (see section 13.2).

Price controls could also be used with the objective of redistributing incomes. Prices could be fixed either above or below equilibrium. Thus (high) minimum farm prices can be used to protect the incomes of farmers, and minimum wage legislation can help those on low incomes. On the consumption side, (low) maximum rents might be put in place with the intention of helping those on low incomes afford housing, and price ceilings on food or other essentials during a war or other emergency can ensure everyone can afford such items. However, as was argued in section 2.4, the problem with price controls is that they cause shortages (in the case of low prices) or surpluses (high prices).

Provision of information

When ignorance is a reason for market failure, the direct provision of information by the government or one of its agencies may help to correct that failure. An example is the information on jobs provided by job centres to those looking for work. This will speed up the 'matching process' between the unemployed and employers. It helps the labour market to work better and increases the elasticity of supply of labour.

Another example is the provision of consumer information – for example, on the effects of smoking, or of the benefits of eating vegetables. Another is the provision of government statistics on prices, costs, employment, sales trends, etc. This enables firms to plan with greater certainty.

> **?** *In what way is the provision of information a public good? Do all the examples above come into the category of public goods? Give some other examples of information that is a public good. (Clue: refer back to the characteristics of public goods in section 11.2 and do not confuse a public good with something merely provided by the government, which could also be provided by the private sector.)*

The direct provision of goods and services

In the case of public goods and services, such as streets, pavements, seaside illumination and national defence, the market may completely fail to provide. In this case, the government must take over the role of provision. Central government, local government or some other public agency could provide these goods and services directly. Alternatively, they could pay private firms to provide them.

But just what quantity of the public good should be provided? How can the level of public demand or public 'need'

be identified? Should any charge at all be made to consumers for each unit consumed?

With a pure public good, once it is provided the marginal cost of supplying one more consumer is zero. Take the case of a lighthouse. Once it is constructed and in operation, there is no extra cost of providing the service to additional passing ships. Even if it were *possible* to charge ships each time they make use of it, it would not be socially desirable. Assuming no external costs, MSC is zero. Thus $MSB = MSC$ at a price of zero. Zero is thus the socially efficient price.

But what about the construction of a new public good, like a new road or a new lighthouse? How can a rational decision be made by the government as to whether it should go ahead? This time the marginal cost is not zero: extra roads and lighthouses cost money to build. The solution is to identify all the costs and benefits to society from the project, and to weigh them up. This is where cost–benefit analysis comes in – the subject of section 11.4.

The government could also provide goods and services directly which are *not* public goods. Examples include health and education. There are four reasons why such things are provided free or well below cost.

Social justice. Society may feel that these things should not be provided according to ability to pay. Rather, as *merit goods*, they should be provided according to need.

Large positive externalities. People other than the consumer may benefit substantially. If a person decides to get treatment for an infectious disease, other people benefit by not being infected. A free health service thus helps to combat the spread of disease.

Dependants. If education were not free, and if the quality of education depended on the amount spent, and if parents could choose how much or little to buy, then the quality of children's education would depend not just on their parents' income, but also on how much they cared. A government may choose to provide such things free in order to protect children from 'bad' or 'foolish' parents. A similar argument is used for providing free prescriptions and dental treatment for all children.

Ignorance. Consumers may not realise how much they will benefit. If they had to pay, they might choose (unwisely) to go without. Providing health care free may persuade people to consult their doctors before a complaint becomes serious.

Public ownership

This is different from direct provision, in that the goods and services produced by publicly owned (nationalised) industries are sold in the market. The costs and benefits of public ownership are examined in detail in section 13.2.

| BOX 11.5 | PUTTING THE 'PERSONAL' INTO PUBLIC SERVICES | CASE STUDIES AND APPLICATIONS |

Criticisms of public provision of health care

For many years the National Health Service has been seen to be doing a good job by most people in the UK. An Ipsos MORI survey in June 2010 reported that 72 per cent of respondents were satisfied with the NHS,[1] a figure that at that point had been stable for several years. However, 75 per cent of respondents also believed that the NHS was 'characterised by waste and inefficiency', while 25 per cent felt that top-heavy management and bureaucracy was the biggest problem facing the NHS.

In March 2014, the outcomes of the repeated survey[2] were published and the overall satisfaction score had fallen to 66 per cent. This may not be surprising. The austerity agenda, in combination with a persistent downturn, had led to a reversal in the growth in NHS spending seen from 2000 to 2010.

However, one interesting section of the survey looked at attitudes to recent changes in the NHS. Here the picture was generally positive. Sixty per cent of those questioned felt that choice was increasing; 51 per cent that the NHS was already making changes to provide for the future; and 50 per cent that private-sector involvement in delivery resulted in better outcomes. All three figures had increased since the survey was previously conducted. One example of a policy that has increased choice and opened the door to private-sector delivery has been the introduction of 'personal budgets in social care'.

Choice in social care

For many years, criticisms had been levelled at the provision of social care services, such as support for the disabled and elderly, provided by local councils. A social worker would arrange a 'care package'; this might include visits to a day centre, help with physical needs or the provision of hot meals. The recipient (or his or her carer) might have some opportunity to negotiate the services, but often a standard package would be organised. This might take little account of individual preferences.

In order to address these concerns, personal budgets in social care were introduced. These offered an opportunity for individuals to buy support services themselves or to access services from their local council, or a mix of the two. The intention was to increase choice and autonomy, while reducing bureaucracy. Examples of their use include people paying for 'alert dogs' and for someone to accompany them to a football match. Neither of these would have been widely available under council-determined packages.

Personal budgets were introduced in 1996, but by 2008 they were not widely used, with only 13 per cent of those eligible using them. However, an increased focus on personalising services to improve welfare led to a commitment that all those eligible would be using them by 2013.

Assessing the success of the initiative is not straightforward. There is no doubt that those who have the resources to identify a suitable, individual package of care are more satisfied. However, there have been ongoing concerns that many of those who need social care do not have access to the information required to make effective choices. The introduction of Individual Service Funds for Homecare is intended to address this concern. Local authorities act as a go-between, paying the personal budgets on behalf of those requiring care and, in some instances, offering a choice of packages rather than free choice.

Personal budgets in health care

In 2009 the Labour government introduced proposals for NHS patients in England to buy health-care services such as physiotherapy and home nursing. The intention was that people with long-term medical conditions should have more control over the services to which they are entitled. According to the then Minster of Health, Alan Johnson, 'people can become experts at handling their illnesses and should be allowed to decide which therapy suits them, who should deliver it, and when'.[3]

This approach was supported by the Coalition in 2010 and pilots were run through 2010–12. From April 2014, all those receiving continuing care have the right to request a personal budget.

1. *What would be the advantages of giving those diagnosed with particular conditions a personal budget for their care? Would there be any disadvantages?*
2. *Should we each be given a personal budget for all our health-care needs at birth?*
*3. *Using indifference curve analysis (see section 4.2, page 109), draw a diagram illustrating how a move from a council-defined care package to a personal budget may increase utility.*

[1] Public Perceptions of the NHS and Social Care. A study conducted for the Department of Health, March 2010.
[2] Public Perceptions of the NHS and Social Care. A study conducted for the Department of Health, March 2014.
[3] 'NHS "personal budget" for patients outlined', *Guardian*, 1 January 2010.

Section summary

1. If there were a distortion in just one part of the economy, the 'first-best' solution would be possible. This would be to correct that one distortion. In the real world, where there are many distortions, the first-best solution will not be possible. The second-best solution will be to seek the best compromise that minimises the *relative* distortions between the industry in question and other parts of the economy.

2. Taxes and subsidies are one means of correcting market distortions. In the first-best world, externalities can be corrected by imposing tax rates equal to the size of marginal external costs, and granting rates of subsidy equal to marginal external benefits. In the second-best world, taxes and subsidies can be used to correct externalities that create *relative* distortions between this industry and others, or externalities that exist along with other distortions within this industry.

3. Taxes and subsidies can also be used to affect monopoly price, output and profit. Subsidies can be used to persuade a monopolist to increase output to the competitive level. Lump-sum taxes can be used to reduce monopoly profits without affecting price or output.

4. Taxes and subsidies have the advantages of 'internalising' externalities and of providing incentives to reduce external

costs. On the other hand, they may be impractical to use when different rates are required for each case, or when it is impossible to know the full effects of the activities that the taxes or subsidies are being used to correct.

5. An extension of property rights may allow individuals to prevent others from imposing costs on them. This is not practical, however, when many people are affected to a small degree, or where several people are affected but differ in their attitudes towards what they want doing about the 'problem'.

6. Laws can be used to tackle various market failures. Legal controls are often simpler and easier to operate than taxes, and are safer when the danger is potentially great. However, they tend to be rather a blunt weapon.

7. Regulatory bodies can be set up to monitor and control activities that are against the public interest (e.g. anti-competitive behaviour of oligopolists).

8. The government may provide information in cases where the private sector fails to provide an adequate level. It may also provide goods and services directly. These could be either public goods or other goods where the government feels that provision by the market is inadequate.

*11.4 COST–BENEFIT ANALYSIS

Cost-benefit analysis (CBA) is a technique used to help governments decide whether to go ahead with various projects such as a new motorway, a bypass, an Underground line, a hospital, a health-care programme, a dam, and so on. The analysis seeks to establish whether the benefits to society from the project outweigh the costs, in which case the project should go ahead; or whether the costs outweigh the benefits, in which case it should not.

CBAs are usually commissioned either by a government department or by a local authority. Unlike the techniques of project evaluation used by private firms, which take into account only *private monetary* costs and benefits, CBA takes into account *externalities* and private *non-monetary* costs and benefits as well. Thus a cost–benefit study of a proposed new road might attempt to assess the external costs of noise to local residents and destruction of wildlife as well as the direct costs and benefits to the travellers.

The procedure

The procedure at first sight seems fairly straightforward:

- All costs and benefits are identified. These include all private monetary and non-monetary costs and benefits and all externalities.

- A monetary value is assigned to each cost and benefit. This is essential if costs and benefits are to be added up: a common unit of measurement must be used. As might be expected, assigning monetary values to externalities like noise, pollution and the quality of life is fraught with difficulties and may involve subjective decisions.

- Account is taken of the likelihood of a cost or benefit occurring. The simplest way of doing this is to multiply the monetary value of a cost or benefit by the probability of its occurrence. This is called the *expected value*. So if there were a 60 per cent chance of a cost of £100 occurring, it would be valued at £60.

- Account is taken of the timing of the costs and benefits. £100 of benefits received today would be regarded as more desirable than having to wait, say, 10 years to receive the £100. Likewise it is a greater sacrifice to pay

Definitions

Cost–benefit analysis The identification, measurement and weighing up of the costs and benefits of a project in order to decide whether or not it should go ahead.

Expected value The value of a possible outcome multiplied by the probability of its occurrence.

£100 today than to have to pay it within 10 years. Thus future costs and benefits must be reduced in value to take this into account. Discounting techniques (similar to those we examined in section 9.3: see pages 272–3) are used for this purpose.

- Some account may also be taken of the distribution of the costs and benefits. Is it considered fair that, although some people will gain from the project, others will lose? Will the losers be compensated in any way?

- A recommendation is then made by weighing up the costs and benefits. In the simplest terms, if the benefits exceed the costs, it will be recommended that the project goes ahead.

- Each of these stages involves a number of difficulties. These are examined in the following sections.

Identifying the costs and benefits

Identifying costs and benefits is relatively easy, although there are some problems in predicting what types of external effect are likely to occur.

Costs

Direct (private) monetary costs. These include all the construction costs and the operating and maintenance costs.

External costs. These fall into two categories:

- *Monetary costs*, such as the loss of profits to competitors. Thus in the case of a CBA of a tunnel under a river, external monetary costs would include the loss of profits to ferry operators.

- *Non-monetary costs*, such as pollution, spoiling the landscape, noise and various other forms of inconvenience to local residents. In some projects, such as a tunnel, these costs will be largely confined to the construction phase. With other projects, however, like a new airport, there may be considerable externalities resulting from its operation (e.g. noise). These non-monetary externalities are usually the most difficult costs to identify.

Benefits

Direct (private) monetary benefits. These are also easy to identify. They consist of the revenues received from the users of the project. The direct monetary benefits of a toll bridge, for example, are the tolls paid.

Private non-monetary benefits. These are the benefits to consumers over and above what they actually pay: in other words, the consumer surplus. For example, if a bridge had a toll of £1.50, and yet a person was prepared to pay £3 if necessary to avoid the long trip round the estuary, then the person's consumer surplus is £1.50. Total consumer surplus is thus the area between the demand curve (which shows what people are willing to pay) and the price charged. This is illustrated in Figure 11.12.

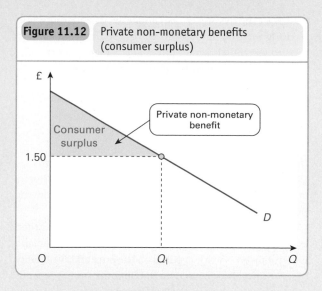

Figure 11.12 Private non-monetary benefits (consumer surplus)

External benefits. These are the benefits to the non-users of the project. For example, the Victoria Underground line CBA identified external benefits to road users in central London. The roads would become less congested as people used the new Underground line. Usually these benefits are non-monetary benefits, but sometimes they may result in direct financial gain (e.g. higher profits to companies from reduced transport costs on less crowded roads).

Measuring the costs and benefits

Identifying costs and benefits may be relatively easy; measuring them is another matter. Difficulties in measurement depend on the type of cost and benefit. There are four types.

Direct private monetary costs and benefits

These would seem to be the simplest to measure. Normally the simple financial costs and revenues are used. In the case of a new Underground line, for example, such costs would include excavation, construction and capital costs (such as new rolling stock) and the operating costs (such as labour, electricity and maintenance). Revenues would be the fares paid by travellers. There are two problems, nevertheless:

- What *will* these financial costs and revenues be? It is all very well using current prices, but prices rise over time, and at different and unpredictable rates. Also, it is difficult to forecast demand and hence revenues. There is thus a large element of *uncertainty*.

- The prices will often be distorted by the existence of monopoly power. Should this be taken into account? In an otherwise perfect world (the first-best situation), the answer would be yes. But in the real world, where price distortions exist throughout the economy, actual prices should normally be used. In the case of a proposed Undergound line, for example, it makes sense to use market prices, given that market prices are paid by car drivers and by users of taxis and buses (the alternatives to using the Underground). Thus the second-best solution is to use actual market prices *unless* there is a price distortion that applies only to the specific project.

 What price should be used when there is such a distortion?

Non-monetary private benefits: consumer surplus

Consumer surplus is a private benefit – it accrues to the users of the project – but is not part of the money earned from the project. There are two ways of estimating it.

The first way is to estimate the demand curve and then estimate the shaded area in Figure 11.12. Estimating demand is very difficult, since it depends on the price and availability of substitutes. The demand for the Channel Tunnel depends on the price, frequency and convenience of ferry crossings. It also depends on the overall level of activity in the economy and perhaps the world generally. Thus estimates of air traffic (essential information when deciding whether to build a new airport) have often been proved wrong as the world economy has grown more rapidly or less rapidly than previously forecast.

Another problem is that the consumer surplus gained from the project (e.g. the Channel Tunnel) may replace the albeit smaller consumer surplus from a competing service (e.g. cross-Channel ferries). In this case, the non-monetary private benefit is merely the *additional* consumer surplus of those who switch, but still the *full* consumer surplus of those who would not otherwise have crossed the Channel. This makes calculation less straightforward.

An alternative approach is to focus on specific non-monetary benefits to consumers. This approach is more useful when the service is to be provided free and thus no estimate of a demand curve can be made. Assume that a new motorway saves 20 000 hours of travelling time per week. (This, of course, will first have to be estimated, and again a prediction will have to be made of the number of people using the motorway.) How is this 20 000 hours to be evaluated? In the case of businesspeople and lorry drivers, the average hourly wage rate will be used to estimate the value of each labour hour saved. In the case of leisure time, there is less agreement on how to value an hour saved. Usually it is simply assumed to be some fraction of the average hourly wage. This method is somewhat arbitrary, however, and a better approach, though probably impractical, would be to attempt to measure how the travellers themselves evaluate their time.

Another way of measuring time saved would be to see how much money people would be prepared to spend to save travelling time. For example, how much extra would people be prepared to pay for a taxi that saved, say, 10 minutes over the bus journey? This method, however, has to take account of the fact that taxis may be more desirable for other reasons too, such as comfort.

 How would you attempt to value time that you yourself save (a) getting to work; (b) going on holiday; (c) going out in the evening?

Monetary externalities

These would normally be counted at face value. Thus the external monetary costs of a new Underground line would include the loss of profits to taxi and bus companies. The external monetary benefits of a new motorway would include the profits to be made by the owners of the motorway service stations.

Non-monetary externalities

These are likely to be the hardest to measure. The general principle employed is to try to find out how much people would be prepared to pay to obtain the benefits or avoid the costs, if they were able to do so. There are two approaches here.

Ask people (questionnaires).   Take the case of noise from an airport or motorway. People could be asked how much they would need to be compensated. There are two problems with this:

- *Ignorance.* People will not know just how much they will suffer *until* the airport or motorway is built.
- *Dishonesty.* People will tend to exaggerate the compensation they would need. After all, if compensation is actually going to be paid, people will want to get as much as possible. But even if it is not, the more people exaggerate the costs to themselves, the more likely it is that they can get the project stopped.

These problems can be lessened if people are questioned who have already experienced a similar project elsewhere. They have less to gain from being dishonest.

Make inferences from people's behaviour.   Take the case of noise again. In similar projects elsewhere, how have people actually reacted? How much have they spent on double glazing or other noise insulation? How much financial loss have they been prepared to suffer to move somewhere quieter? What needs to be measured, however, is not just the financial cost, but also the loss of consumer surplus. The Roskill Commission in 1968 examined the siting of a third London airport. It attempted to evaluate noise costs, and looked at the difference in value of house prices around Gatwick compared with elsewhere. A problem with this approach is in finding cases elsewhere that are directly comparable. Were the four potential sites for the third London airport directly comparable with Gatwick?

Another example of externalities would be a reduction in accidents from a safer road. How is this to be measured? Obviously there are the monetary benefits from reduced medical expenditures. But how would you value a life saved? This question is examined in Box 11.6.

 How would you evaluate (a) the external effects of building a reservoir in an area of outstanding natural beauty; (b) the external effects of acid rain pollution from a power station?

*BOX 11.6 WHAT PRICE A HUMAN LIFE?

A difficult question for cost–benefit analysis

Many projects involve saving lives, whether they be new hospitals or new transport systems. This is obviously a major benefit, but how is a life to be evaluated?

Some people argue 'You can't put a price on a human life: life is priceless.' But just what are they saying here? Are they saying that life has an *infinite* value? If so, this project must be carried out *whatever* the costs, and even if other benefits from it were zero! Clearly, when evaluating lives saved from the project, a value less than infinity must be given.

Other people might argue that human life cannot be treated like other costs and benefits and put into mathematical calculations. But what are these people saying? That the question of lives saved should be excluded from the cost–benefit study? If so, the implication is that life has a *zero* value! Again this is clearly not the case.

So if a value somewhere between zero and infinity should be used, what should it be?

Some economists have suggested that a life be valued in terms of a person's future earning potential. But this implies that the only value of a person is as a factor of production. Would the life of a disabled person, for example, who is unable to work and draws state benefit, be given a *negative* value? Again this is clearly not the solution. It would also value the life of a banker as worth considerably more than that of other workers; an approach that would be hard to justify politically!

Can any inferences be drawn from people's behaviour?

How much are people prepared to spend on safety: on making their car roadworthy, on buying crash helmets, etc.? This approach too has serious drawbacks. People are wishful thinkers. They obviously do not want to be killed, but simply believe that accidents happen to other people, not to them.

Then again, there are the problems of estimating the effects on other people: on family and friends. Can the amount that people are willing to spend on life insurance be a guide here? Again, people are optimists and in any case may be cash-constrained. Also, it is not the family and friends who buy the insurance; it is the victim, who may not take the effect on others fully into account.

The Department for Transport[1] puts a value of £1852483 on a life saved from a road safety project (in 2010 prices). This is based partly on the (discounted) average value of individuals' lost output for the rest of their lives (£613609), partly on emergency services and hospital costs (£22576), partly on the costs of insurance and damage to property (£11330) and partly on the human cost based on people's willingness to pay (if they had to) for the enjoyment of life over and above the consumption of goods and services plus costs to family and friends (£1204968). The US Department of Transportation reports an average valuation of just over $9 million.

1. *Can you think of any other ways of getting a more 'rational' evaluation of human life? Would the person's age make any difference?*
2. *If you had to decide whether more money from a hospital's budget were to be spent on hip replacements (which do not save lives, but do dramatically improve the quality of the patient's life), or on heart transplants (which do save lives, but are expensive), how would you set about making a rational decision?*
3. *If different values are used in different countries, does this have implications for policy makers? Does your answer change if different departments within a government use varying valuations?*

[1] 'WebTAG Table A 4.1.3, Accident Impacts', *Transport Analysis Guidance* (TAG): data book (DfT, January 2014).

Risk and uncertainty

Taking account of *risk* is relatively straightforward. The value of a cost or benefit is simply multiplied by the probability of its occurrence.

The problem is that *risk* is less frequent than *uncertainty*. As was explained in section 4.2, in the case of uncertainty all that is known is that an outcome *might* occur. The likelihood of its occurring, however, is uncertain.

How then can uncertainty be taken into account? The best approach is to use *sensitivity analysis*. Let us consider two cases.

Definition

Sensitivity analysis Where a range of possible values of uncertain costs and benefits are given to see whether the project's desirability is sensitive to these different values.

Individual uncertain outcomes

A range of possible values can be given to an uncertain item in the CBA: for example, damage from pollution. Table 11.1 illustrates two possible cases.

Table 11.1	Effect of different estimates of the costs of production on the viability of a project

	Total costs other than pollution (£m)	Total pollution cost (£m)	Total benefits (£m)	Net benefits (total benefits – total costs) (£m)
Case A	100	10	200	90
	100	20	200	80
	100	50	200	50
Case B	140	10	160	10
	140	20	160	0
	140	50	160	–30

BOX 11.7 HS2: IS IT REALLY WORTH IT?

The case for (and against) high-speed rail in the UK

In January 2009 the Department for Transport published a report[1] into various options for a new high-speed rail network in the UK. It concluded that an initial route between London and the West Midlands would be the best way forward. The then Labour government acted swiftly. It set up a company, High Speed Two Limited (HS2 Ltd), tasked with further investigating the proposals and providing advice on factors such as connection with the existing network, an extension beyond the East Midlands, financing and construction.

Following the 2010 general election, the incoming Coalition government reviewed the proposal and published a revised route to be put out to public consultation. In 2011 the first section of the route was confirmed as running from London to Birmingham. This first phase of construction would also include connection to the UK's only existing high-speed rail link, HS1, which links London St Pancras to the Channel Rail Tunnel. This section would open in around 2026. The second phase of the project was intended to include branches to Manchester and Leeds and a high-speed connection with Heathrow Airport. The government also confirmed that it intended that a third phase would see high-speed rail reach central Scotland at some point in the future.

An appetite for rail travel

From the early part of the nineteenth century, the rail network played a pivotal role in Britain's economic growth and industrial development. Yet by the end of the 1960s it would have been easy to conclude that the future of transport lay on the roads. Many railway branch lines had been closed, passenger numbers had fallen and freight was increasingly transported by lorry rather than by train. However, the introduction of the first 125 mph high-speed trains in the 1970s and sharp increases in the cost of petrol over that decade revived interest in train travel. It became clear that the railways remained an important part of the country's infrastructure.

Following privatisation of the system from 1993 onward, freight services became a commercial operation and passenger services were operated by a number of franchise holders, which continued to receive subsidies. By 2008 rail travel and freight carriage had once again soared in popularity with passenger numbers back to the highs last seen in the 1940s, while freight had increased by 40 per cent over the previous decade.

In this climate the Labour government set out a programme of investment for the next decade in the 2007 Rail White Paper, *Delivering a Sustainable Railway*.[2] This identified the immediate need for increased capacity, while also addressing long-term plans for new, faster rail lines. Analysis undertaken by Network Rail and the not-for-profit organisation Greengauge 21 led to the proposals for High Speed 2 and the setting up of HS2 Ltd.

The international picture

The proposals for increased investment in high-speed rail in the UK are set against an international picture of similar work already completed or currently underway. Japan has been the acknowledged world leader in this area since it opened the first 'bullet-train' between Tokyo and Osaka in 1964. In 2013 the first trials took place on a £40 billion scheme that uses magnetic levitation to allow trains running between Tokyo and Nagoya, the trains achieving speeds of 310 mph.

The USA, by contrast, has a history of underinvestment in rail, with passenger trains travelling at average speeds of less than 50 mph and, even more remarkably, freight trains averaging less than 30 mph. There are currently only two sections of high-speed rail track in the North East Corridor; proposals to extend these folded under political pressure from the airlines. However, the Obama administration put in place an investment programme of $53 billion aimed to bring high-speed rail within reach of 80 per cent of the population by 2025. Plans for routes from Dallas to Houston and from San Francisco to Los Angeles are progressing, albeit at a less than high-speed pace. However, it is unlikely that the USA will overtake other countries – high-speed rail is embedded across Europe; South American countries are investing heavily; and China is building as much as the rest of the world combined.

The rationale for HS2

The 2007 White Paper and 2009 DfT report identified a number of ways that new lines could deliver economic, environmental and social benefits:

- Providing additional capacity and reducing crowding.
- Reducing journey times and improving punctuality.
- Supporting expected housing and population growth and encouraging regeneration.
- Improving links to key international gateways.

Unsurprisingly this broad approach was insufficient to justify the spending involved in the project, particularly in an era of sustained public finance cuts. Therefore HS2 Ltd was tasked with undertaking detailed analysis of the benefits of the planned route to Birmingham, and of the proposal to extend HS2 to Scotland in the future. The Economic Case for HS2 was published in February 2011, concentrating on the Y-shaped network, with further analysis on the longer route published the following year.

> The economic appraisal of a transport scheme seeks to cover the full economic costs and full economic benefits of a scheme and to quantify these in monetary terms . . . We assess the direct impacts that HS2 would have on transport users through, for instance, journey time savings and reductions in crowding on trains. We also measure the impacts, both positive and negative, that HS2 would have on the classic rail network. Finally, we look at some of the wider economic impacts on the UK economy, using Department for Transport guidance to quantify and value these impacts. The appraisal of quantified benefits provides a numerical result, a 'Benefit Cost Ratio' or BCR. This ratio represents the level of benefit per pound (£) spent by Government (e.g. if a scheme generates £2 of benefit for every £1 spent this is presented as a BCR of 2.0).[3]

The following table summarises the costs and benefits of the Y network:

Quantified benefits and costs (£ billions) of the Y network (2009 PV/prices) and the resulting BCR

(1)	Transport User Benefits	Business £25.2bn
		Other £13.1bn
(2)	Other quantifiable benefits (excl. Carbon)	£0.4bn
(3)	Loss to Government of Indirect Taxes	−£2.7bn
(4)	Estimate of additional released capacity benefits facilitated by the Y network	£1.3bn (£0 to £2.6bn)
(5)	**Net Transport Benefits (PVB)** = (1) + (2) + (3) + (4)	**£37.3bn** (£36.0bn to £38.7bn)
(6)	Wider Economic Impacts (WEIs) (London to West Midlands only)	£4.0bn
(7)	Estimate of additional WEIs from the Y network	£2.3bn (£0bn to £4.7bn)
(8)	**Net Benefits including WEIs** = (5) + (6) + (7)	**£43.7bn** (£40.0bn to £47.4bn)
(9)	Capital Costs	£30.4bn
(10)	Operating Costs	£17.0bn
(11)	Estimate of additional classic line cost savings facilitated by the Y network	−£3.1bn (£0 to −£6.1bn)
(12)	**Total Costs** = (9) + (10) + (11)	**£44.3bn** (£47.4bn to £41.3bn)
(13)	Revenues	£27.2bn
(14)	**Net Costs to Government (PVC)** = (12) − (13)	**£17.1bn** (£20.2bn to £14.1bn)
(15)	BCR without WEIs (ratio) = (5)/(14)	2.2 (1.8 to 2.7)
(16)	**BCR with WEIs (ratio)** = (8)/(14)	**2.6** (2.0 to 3.4)

Source: 'Economic Case for HS2', Table 2 (Department for Transport, February 2011).

In order to appreciate the complexity of the economic assessment, it is interesting to look at just one component and consider how easily this can be measured. For HS2 any measure of the benefits requires *estimation of demand* for rail journeys on the network over the life of the project. (In practice this could be over 100 years, but government accounting conventions require that the analysis is undertaken for 60 years, plus the construction period.)

To estimate demand the report uses data and trends in rail and other journeys; forecasts for economic growth; forecasts for the cost of travel, population growth and employment rates; and lifestyle factors, looking at the impact of higher incomes and increased leisure time on demand for travel. Each of these factors will have some uncertainty associated with it; thus the analysis requires that this is accounted for and that the underlying assumptions are rigorously tested.

It is also complicated to estimate the benefits of HS2 that will derive from the resulting shorter journey times. Time saved by commuters, or leisure travellers, is assessed as being less valuable than that saved during working hours. Yet, in an age when technology allows use of train travel time

to check emails, write documents and do other work, the benefits of time saved may be less than in the past.

Overall the report assessed that the first stage of the HS2 scheme would offer economic benefits of £20.6 billion. Comparing this with estimated net costs (after revenues) of £10.3 billion, the result would be a BCR of 2.0, enough to recommend that the scheme go ahead. It should be noted that this *excludes* environmental impacts, which were assessed in a separate report.[4] The two stages together (see table) would bring economic benefits of around £43.7 billion. With net costs of around £17.1 billion, the BCR would be 2.6.

Opposition to HS2

HS2 has been subject to a great deal of opposition, particularly from those directly affected by the proposed route. Campaigning has focused on the uncertainty associated with the economic case.

These views were supported by a report for the Institute of Economic Affairs,[5] published in July 2011, which suggested that the costs were likely to rise, the benefits were uncertain and that environmental and social impacts were not fully included.

However, the government has remained committed to the general approach, although there have been some changes in the detail. The spur to Heathrow has been shelved as has some of the route through London.

In 2014 a further report[6] by David Higgins, the incoming Chairman of HS2 Ltd, reaffirmed the belief that high-speed rail was the best way to increase capacity and provide economic benefits to the country beyond London. This has provoked some interesting debate. The underlying premise for HS2 has been that cities outside the South-East will benefit from investment and skilled labour. However, if we turn this around, it may be that firms in London benefit most. Shorter travel times mean that their employees can live further away and benefit from lower house prices. Phase One is currently on track to be operational in 2026, with Phase Two due in 2033. With time-frames that stretch over two decades, it will be a long wait until we find out whose views were correct: those thinking the scheme will prove to be a driver for economic growth, or those who are convinced it will be an expensive white elephant.

1. *Why is this type of cost–benefit analysis so complex?*
2. *'The "losers" will be compensated, so there is no reason for them to protest.' Assess this statement with reference to HS2.*
3. *Explain why companies in London might benefit as much from HS2 as those in Manchester.*

[1] *Britain's Transport Infrastructure – High Speed Two* (Department for Transport, 2009).
[2] *Delivering a Sustainable Railway* (Department for Transport, 2007).
[3] *Economic Case for HS2 – the Y Network and London–West Midlands* (Department for Transport, 2011).
[4] *HS2 Appraisal of Sustainability – A Report for HS2 Ltd.* (Booz & Co and Temple, 2011).
[5] Kyn Aizlewood and Richard Wellings, *High Speed 2, the Next Government Project Disaster?* (IEA, 2011).
[6] *The Higgins Report – HS2 Plus* (Department for Transport, 2014).

The lowest estimate for pollution damage is £10 million; the highest is £50 million. In case A, given a very high margin of benefits over *other* costs, the project's desirability is *not* sensitive to different values for pollution damage. Even with the highest value (£50 million), the project still yields a net benefit.

In case B, however, the project's desirability *is* sensitive to pollution damage. If the damage exceeds £20 million, the project becomes undesirable. In this case, the government will have to decide whether it is prepared to take the gamble.

A number of uncertain outcomes

When there are several uncertain outcomes the typical approach is to do three cost–benefit calculations: the most optimistic (where all the best possible outcomes are estimated), the most pessimistic (where all the worst possible outcomes are estimated), and the most likely (where all the middle-of-the-range outcomes are estimated). This approach can give a good guide to just how 'borderline' the project is.

Discounting future costs and benefits

As we saw in section 9.3, discounting is a procedure for giving a present value to costs and benefits that will not occur until some time in the future.

Discounting in CBA

The procedure is as follows:

- Work out the costs and benefits for each year of the life of the project.
- Subtract the costs from the benefits for each year, to give a net benefit for each year.
- Discount each year's net benefit to give it a present value.
- Add up all of these present values. This gives a *net present value (NPV)*.
- If the *NPV* is greater than zero, the benefits exceed the costs: the project is worthwhile.

Maths Case 11.2 in MyEconLab gives a worked example.

Choosing the discount rate

Apart from the problems of measuring the costs and benefits, there is the problem of choosing the rate of interest/discount.

If it were a private-sector project, the firm would probably choose the market rate of interest as its rate of discount. This is the rate that it would have to pay to borrow money to finance the project.

In the case of CBA, however, it is argued that the government ought to use a *social rate of discount*. This rate should reflect society's preference for present benefits over future benefits. But just what is this rate? If a high rate is chosen, then future net benefits will be discounted more, and projects with a long life will appear less attractive than projects yielding a quick return. Since the government has a responsibility to future generations and not just to the present one, it is argued that a relatively low discount rate should be chosen.

 Imagine that a specific public project yields a return of 13 per cent (after taking into account all social costs and benefits), whereas a 15 per cent private return could typically be earned by projects in the private sector. How would you justify diverting resources from the private sector to this project?

Inevitably, the choice of discount rate is arbitrary. As a result, the analysis will normally be conducted using two or three alternative discount rates to see whether the outcome is sensitive to the choice of discount rate. If it is, then again the project will be seen as borderline.

CBA and the distribution of costs and benefits

Virtually all projects involve gainers and losers. For example, the majority may gain from the construction of a new motorway, but not those whose homes lie alongside it. So how is the distribution of costs and benefits to be taken into account?

The strict Pareto criterion

According to the strict Pareto criterion, a project is unequivocally desirable only if there are some gains and *no one* is made worse off. But are there likely to be any projects that fulfil this criterion? If there are always losers then let us think about a situation where the losers are compensated. Thus we can now state that a project would be accepted only if the gainers *fully* compensated the losers, with the gainers still being better off after doing so.

In practice, this never happens. Often compensation is simply not paid. Even when it is, the recipients rarely feel as well off as before, and there will still be many who do not get compensation. Also, the compensation is usually paid not by the project users, but by the general taxpayer (who will thus be *worse* off).

Definition

Social rate of discount A rate of discount that reflects society's preferences for present benefits over future ones.

The Hicks–Kaldor criterion

To get round this problem, J. R. Hicks and N. Kaldor suggested an alternative criterion. This states that a project is desirable if it leads to a *potential* Pareto improvement: in other words, if the gainers could *in principle* fully compensate the losers and still have a net gain, even though in practice they do not pay any compensation at all.

This criterion is what lies behind conventional CBA. If the benefits of a project are greater than the costs, then in principle the losers could be fully compensated with some net benefits left over.

But what is the justification for using this test? The losers, after all, will still lose. Its advocates argue that questions of *efficiency* should be kept separate from questions of *equity*. Projects, they argue, should be judged on efficiency grounds. They are efficient if their benefits exceed their costs. Questions of fairness in distribution, on the other hand, should be dealt with through the general system of taxation and welfare.

This is a 'useful' argument because it lets the proponents of the project off the hook. Nevertheless the problem still remains that some people will lose. People do not like living near a new motorway, airport or power station. These people cannot expect to receive special welfare benefits from general taxation.

Thus other economists have argued that more specific account should be taken of distributional effects when *measuring* costs and benefits.

Taking specific account of distributional consequences

One way this could be done would be to give a higher weighting to the costs of individual, as opposed to corporate, losers. The justification is simple. The pain for one person of losing £10 000 is greater than the collective pain of 10 000 people losing just £1 each. Just how much higher this weighting should be, however, is a matter of judgement, not of precise calculation.

Another way distribution can be taken into account is to give a higher weighting to the costs incurred by poor people than to those incurred by rich people. For example, assume that a new airport is built. As a result, house prices nearby fall by 10 per cent. A rich person's house price falls from £1 000 000 to £900 000 – a loss of £100 000. A poor person's house price falls from £125 000 to £112 500 – a loss of £12 500. Is the loss to the rich person eight times as painful as that to the poor person? Probably not. It is argued, therefore, that the poorer people are, the higher the weighting that should be given to each £1 lost. Just what this weighting should be, however, is controversial.

Section summary

1. Cost–benefit analysis (CBA) can help a government decide whether or not to go ahead with a particular public project, or which of alternative projects to choose. CBA involves a number of stages.

2. All costs and benefits must be identified. These include the direct costs of constructing and operating the project, the direct monetary benefits to the operators and the consumer surplus of the users. They also include external costs and benefits to non-users.

3. Direct monetary costs and benefits are relatively easy to measure. Nevertheless there is still uncertainty about their *future* values. Also, there is a problem if prices are distorted.

4. Non-monetary private benefit (consumer surplus) is difficult to estimate because of the difficulty of estimating the shape and position of the demand curve. The alternative approach is to focus on specific non-monetary benefits, such as journey time saved, and then to evaluate how much people would be prepared to pay for them if they could.

5. Monetary externalities would normally be counted at face value. Non-monetary externalities are much more difficult to estimate. The approach is to try to estimate the value that consumers would put on them in a market environment. Questionnaire techniques could be used, or inferences could be drawn from people's actual behaviour elsewhere.

6. Figures would then have to be adjusted for risk and uncertainty.

7. Discounting techniques would then have to be used to reduce future benefits and costs to a present value.

8. The study may also take distributional questions into account. The Hicks–Kaldor criterion suggests a compensation test for deciding whether a project is desirable. But given that in practice full compensation would be unlikely, the distributional questions may need to be taken into account more specifically.

9. Having adjusted the costs and benefits for risk and uncertainty, timing and distributional effects, a recommendation to go ahead with the project will probably be given if its net present value (*NPV*) is positive: in other words, if the discounted social benefits exceed the discounted social costs.

11.5 GOVERNMENT FAILURE AND THE CASE FOR THE MARKET

Government intervention in the market can itself lead to problems. The case for non-intervention (laissez-faire) or very limited intervention is not that the market is the *perfect* means of achieving given social goals, but rather that the problems created by intervention are greater than the problems overcome by that intervention.

Drawbacks of government intervention

Shortages and surpluses.   If the government intervenes by fixing prices at levels other than the equilibrium, this will create either shortages or surpluses (see section 2.4).

If the price is fixed *below* the equilibrium, there will be a shortage. For example, if the rent of social housing is fixed below the equilibrium in order to provide affordable housing for low-income households, demand will exceed supply. In the case of such shortages the government will have to adopt a system of waiting lists, or rationing, or giving certain people preferential treatment. Alternatively it will have to allow allocation to be on a first-come, first-served basis or allow queues to develop. Underground markets are also likely to develop (see page 56 and Box 2.4).

If the price is fixed *above* the equilibrium price, there will be a surplus. Such surpluses are wasteful, and high prices

---

BOX 11.8   MISES, HAYEK AND THE MONT PELERIN SOCIETY

The birth of post-war libertarianism

After the Second World War, governments in the western world were anxious to avoid a return to the high levels of unemployment and poverty experienced in the 1930s. The free market was seen to have failed. Governments, it was therefore argued, should take on the responsibility for correcting or counteracting these failings. This would involve various measures such as planning, nationalisation, the restriction of monopoly power, controls on prices, the macroeconomic management of the economy and the provision of a welfare state.

But this new spirit of intervention deeply troubled a group of economists and other social scientists who saw it leading to an erosion of freedom. In 1947 this group met in a hotel in the Swiss Alps. There they formed the Mont Pelerin Society: a society pledged to warn against the dangers of socialism and to advocate the freedom for individuals to make their own economic choices.

Two of the most influential figures in the society were the Austrians Ludwig von Mises (1881–1973) and Friedrich von Hayek (1899–1992). They were the intellectual descendants of the nineteenth-century 'Austrian school'. Carl Menger, the originator of the school, had (along with Jevons and Walras (see Box 4.2)) emphasised the importance of individuals' marginal utility as the basis of demand. The Austrian school of economists was famous for its stress on individual choice as the basis for rational economic calculation and also for its advocacy of the free market.

Mises and Hayek (the 'neo-Austrians' as they became known) provided both a critique of socialism and an advocacy of the free market. There were two main strands to their arguments.

The impossibility of rational calculation under socialism

In his famous book *Socialism* (1922), Mises argued that centrally planned socialism was logically incapable of achieving a rational allocation of resources. Given that scarcity is the fundamental economic problem, all societies, whether capitalist or socialist, will have to make choices. But rational choices must involve weighing up the costs and benefits of alternatives. Mises argued that this cannot be done in a centrally planned economy. The reason is that costs and benefits can be measured only in terms of money prices, prices which reflect demand and supply. But such prices can be established only in a market economy.

In a centrally planned economy, prices will be set by the state and no state will have sufficient information on demand and supply to set rational prices. Prices under centrally planned socialism will thus inevitably be arbitrary. Also, with no market for land or capital these factors may not be given a price at all. The use of land and capital, therefore, may be highly wasteful.

Many democratic socialists criticised Mises' arguments that rational prices *logically* cannot be established under socialism. In a centrally planned economy, the state can in theory, if it chooses, set prices so as to balance supply and demand. It can, if it chooses, set an interest rate for capital and a rent for land, even if capital and land are owned by the state. And certainly in a mixed market socialist economy, prices will merely reflect the forces of demand and supply that have been modified by the state in accordance with its various social goals.

Hayek modified Mises' arguments somewhat. He conceded that some imperfect form of pricing system could be established under socialism, even under centrally planned socialism. Hayek's point was that such a system would inevitably be inferior to capitalism. The problem was one of imperfect information under socialism.

Calculation of costs and benefits requires knowledge. But that knowledge is dispersed amongst the millions of consumers and producers throughout the economy. Each consumer possesses unique information about his or her own tastes; each manager or worker possesses unique information

may protect inefficient producers. (The problem of food surpluses in the EU was examined in section 3.5.)

 What are the possible arguments in favour of fixing prices (a) below and (b) above the equilibrium? Are there any means of achieving the same social goals without fixing prices?

 Poor information.   The government may not know the full costs and benefits of its policies. It may genuinely wish to pursue the interests of consumers or any other group, and yet may be unaware of people's wishes or misinterpret their behaviour.

Bureaucracy and inefficiency.   Government intervention involves administrative costs. The more wide-reaching and detailed the intervention, the greater the number of people and material resources that will be involved. These resources may be used wastefully and the effect on welfare may not be an improvement on the free-market situation. Think back to the problem of scarcity we discussed in Chapter 1; if we 'use up' resources on managing intervention, we need to be sure that the outcome is markedly better than without intervention.

Lack of market incentives.   If government intervention removes market forces or reduces their effect (by the use of subsidies, welfare provisions, minimum wages, etc.), it may remove certain useful incentives. Subsidies may allow inefficient firms to survive. Welfare payments may discourage people from working. The market may be imperfect, but it does tend to encourage efficiency by allowing the efficient to receive greater rewards.

EXPLORING ECONOMICS

about his or her own job. No government could hope to have this knowledge. Planning will inevitably, therefore, be based on highly imperfect information.

The market, by contrast, is a way of co-ordinating this dispersed information: it co-ordinates all the individual decisions of suppliers and demanders, decisions based on individuals' own information. And it does it all without the need for an army of bureaucrats.

> The economic problem of society is thus not merely a problem of how to allocate 'given' resources – if 'given' is taken to mean given to a single mind which deliberately solves the problem set by these 'data'. It is rather a problem of how to secure the best use of resources known to any of the members of society, for ends whose relative importance only these individuals know. Or, to put it briefly, it is a problem of the utilisation of knowledge not given to anyone in its totality.[1]

Lack of dynamic incentives under socialism

A planned socialist economy will, according to Mises and Hayek, lack the incentives for people to take risks. Even a 'market socialist' society, where prices are set so as to equate demand and supply, will still lack the crucial motivating force of the possibility of large personal economic gains. Under capitalism, by contrast, a firm that becomes more efficient or launches a new or improved product can gain huge profits. The prospect of such profits is a powerful motivator.

> Without the striving of entrepreneurs (including the shareholders) for profit, of the landlords for rent, of the capitalists for interest and the labourers for wages, the successful functioning of the whole mechanism is not to be thought of. It is only the prospect of profit which directs production into those channels in which the demands of the consumer are best satisfied at least cost. If the prospect of profit disappears the mechanism of the market loses its mainspring, for it is only this prospect

which sets it in motion and maintains it in operation. The market is thus the focal point of the capitalist order of society; it is the essence of capitalism. Only under capitalism, therefore, is it possible; it cannot be 'artificially' imitated under socialism.[2]

In addition to these economic criticisms of socialism, Mises and Hayek saw government intervention as leading down the road towards totalitarianism. The more governments intervened to correct the 'failings' of the market, the more this tended to erode people's liberties. But the more people saw the government intervening to help one group of people, the more help they would demand from the government for themselves. Thus inexorably the role of the state would grow and grow, and with it the size of the state bureaucracy.

In the early years after the war, the Mont Pelerin Society had little influence on government policy. Government intervention and the welfare state were politically popular.

In the late 1970s, however, the society, along with other similar libertarian groups, gained increasing influence as a new breed of politicians emerged who were wedded to the free market and were looking for an intellectual backing for their beliefs.

Libertarian thinkers such as Hayek and Milton Friedman (see Person Profiles in MyEconLab) had a profound effect on many right-wing politicians, and considerably influenced the economic programmes of the Thatcher, Reagan and both Bush (Snr and Jnr) administrations.

 Do the arguments of Mises and Hayek necessarily infer that a free market is the most desirable alternative to centrally planned socialism?

[1] F. von Hayek, 'The price system as a mechanism for using knowledge', *American Economic Review*, September 1945, p. 519.
[2] L. von Mises, *Socialism: An Economic and Sociological Analysis* (Jonathan Cape, 1936), p. 138.

Shifts in government policy. Industrial performance may suffer if government intervention changes too frequently. It makes it difficult for firms to plan if they cannot predict tax rates, subsidies, wage controls, etc. Shifts in policy are also likely to involve costs for both business and public-sector providers. This may result in wasted resources.

Lack of freedom for the individual. Government intervention may involve a loss of freedom for individuals to make economic choices. The argument is not just that the pursuit of individual gain is seen to lead to the social good, but that it is desirable in itself that individuals should be as free as possible to pursue their own interests with the minimum of government interference, and with that minimum being largely confined to the maintenance of laws consistent with the protection of life, liberty and property.

 Go through the above arguments and give a reply to the criticisms made of government intervention.

Advantages of the free market

Although markets in the real world are not perfect, even imperfect markets can be argued to have positive advantages over government provision or even government regulation.

Automatic adjustments. Government intervention requires administration. A free-market economy, on the other hand, leads to the automatic, albeit imperfect, adjustment to demand and supply changes.

TC 4
p47

Even under oligopoly, it is claimed, the competition between firms will be enough to encourage firms to produce goods that are desirable to consumers and at not excessively high prices, and will encourage more efficient production methods. Cases of pure monopoly with total barriers to entry are extremely rare.

Dynamic advantages of the free market. The chances of making high monopoly/oligopoly profits will encourage capitalists to invest in new products and new techniques. Prices may be high initially, but new firms will sooner or later break into the market and competition will ensue. If the government tries to correct the misallocation of resources under monopoly/oligopoly either by regulating monopoly power or by nationalisation, any resulting benefits could be outweighed by a loss in innovation and growth. This is one of the major arguments put forward by the neo-Austrian libertarian school – a school that passionately advocates the free market (see Box 11.7).

 Are there any features of free-market capitalism that would discourage innovation?

A high degree of competition even under monopoly/oligopoly. Even though an industry at first sight may seem to be highly monopolistic, competitive forces may still work for the following reasons:

- A fear that excessively high profits might encourage firms to attempt to break into the industry (assuming that the market is contestable).
- Competition from closely related industries (e.g. coach services for rail services, or electricity for gas).
- The threat of foreign competition. Additional competition was one of the main purposes behind the Single European Act which led to the abolition of trade barriers within the EU in 1993 (see section 24.4).
- Countervailing powers. Large powerful producers often sell to large powerful buyers. For example, the power of detergent manufacturers to drive up the price of washing powder is countered by the power of supermarket chains to drive down the price at which they purchase it. Thus power is to some extent neutralised.
- The competition for corporate control (see page 186).

Should there be more or less intervention in the market?

No firm conclusions can be drawn in the debate between those who favour more and those who favour less government intervention, for the following reasons:

- The debate involves normative issues that cannot be settled by economic analysis. For example, it could be argued that freedom to set up in business and freedom from government regulation are desirable *for their own sake*. As a fundamental ethical point of view, this can be disputed, but not disproved.

KI 6
p29

- In principle, the issue of whether a government ought to intervene in any situation could be settled by weighing up the costs and benefits of that intervention. Such costs and benefits, however, even if they could be identified, are extremely difficult, if not impossible, to measure, especially when the costs are borne by different people from those who receive the benefits and when externalities are involved.
- Often the effect of more or less intervention simply cannot be predicted: there are too many uncertainties.

Nevertheless, economists can make a considerable contribution to analysing problems of the market and the effects of government intervention. Chapters 12 and 13 illustrate this by examining specific problem areas.

Section summary

1. Government intervention in the market may lead to shortages or surpluses; it may be based on poor information; it may be costly in terms of administration; it may stifle incentives; it may be disruptive if government policies change too frequently; it may remove certain liberties.

2. By contrast, a free market leads to automatic adjustments to changes in economic conditions; the prospect of monopoly/oligopoly profits may stimulate risk taking and hence research and development and innovation;

there may still be a high degree of actual or potential competition under monopoly and oligopoly.

3. It is impossible to draw firm conclusions about the 'optimum' level of government intervention. This is partly due to the normative nature of the question, partly due to the difficulties of measuring costs and benefits of intervention/non-intervention, and partly due to the difficulties of predicting the effects of government policies, especially over the longer term.

END OF CHAPTER QUESTIONS

1. Assume that a firm discharges waste into a river. As a result, the marginal social costs (*MSC*) are greater than the firm's marginal (private) costs (*MC*). The following table shows how *MC*, *MSC*, *AR* and *MR* vary with output.

Output	1	2	3	4	5	6	7	8
MC (£)	23	21	23	25	27	30	35	42
MSC (£)	35	34	38	42	46	52	60	72
TR (£)	60	102	138	168	195	219	238	252
AR (£)	60	51	46	42	39	36.5	34	31.5
MR (£)	60	42	36	30	27	24	19	14

(a) How much will the firm produce if it seeks to maximise profits?

(b) What is the socially efficient level of output (assuming no externalities on the demand side)?

(c) How much is the marginal external cost at this level of output?

(d) What size tax would be necessary for the firm to reduce its output to the socially efficient level?

(e) Why is the tax less than the marginal externality?

(f) Why might it be equitable to impose a lump-sum tax on this firm?

(g) Why will a lump-sum tax not affect the firm's output (assuming that in the long run the firm can still make at least normal profit)?

2. Why might it be argued that a redistribution of consumption, while not involving a Pareto improvement, could still be desirable?

3. Assume that a country had no state education at all. For what reasons might the private education system not provide the optimal allocation of resources to and within education?

4. Why might it be better to ban certain activities that cause environmental damage rather than to tax them?

5. Distinguish between publicly provided goods, public goods and merit goods.

6. Consider the advantages and disadvantages of extending property rights so that everyone would have the right to prevent people imposing any costs on them whatsoever (or charging them to do so).

7. The food industry provides a great deal of information about its products. Why, despite this, does the government run various campaigns about healthy eating?

8. Should all investment be subject to a social cost–benefit appraisal?

9. Make out a case for (a) increasing and (b) decreasing the role of the government in the allocation of resources.

Online resources

Additional case studies in MyEconLab

11.1 **Vilfredo Pareto (1843–1923).** A profile of a key figure in the development of welfare economics.

11.2 **Can the market provide adequate protection for the environment?** This explains why markets generally fail to take into account environmental externalities.

11.3 **Catastrophic risk.** This examines how a cost–benefit study could put a monetary value on a remote chance of a catastrophe happening (such as an explosion at a nuclear power station).

11.4 **Evaluating the cost of aircraft noise.** This case study looks at the method used by the Roskill Commission, which in the 1960s investigated the siting of a third major London airport.

11.5 **CBA of the Glasgow canal project.** A cost–benefit study carried out in the late 1980s of the restoration of the Glasgow canal system.

11.6 **Meeting the Kyoto Protocol.** This examines the options open to the EU in meeting the targets set under international climate change agreements. It illustrates the use of cost–benefit analysis.

11.7 **Public choice theory.** This examines how economists have attempted to extend their analysis of markets to the field of political decision making.

Maths Case 11.1 Calculating deadweight welfare loss. A worked example.

Maths Case 11.2 Calculating net present value. The use of discounting techniques in CBA.

Websites relevant to this chapter

See sites listed at the end of Chapter 13 on page 398.

MyEconLab

This book can be supported by MyEconLab, which contains a range of additional resources, including an online homework and tutorial system designed to test and build your understanding.

You need both an access card and a course ID to access MyEconLab:

1. Is your lecturer using MyEconLab? Ask your lecturer for your course ID.

2. Has an access card been included with the book at a reduced cost? Check the inside back cover of the book.

3. If you have a course ID but no access card, go to: http://www.myeconlab.com/ to buy access to this interactive study programme.

Environmental Policy

> **CHAPTER MAP**
>
> **12.1 Economics of the environment** 354
> The environmental problem 354
> An optimum use of the environment 355
> Market failures 358
>
> **12.2 Policies to tackle pollution and its
> effects** 359
> Market-based policies 359
> Non-market-based policies 360
> Tradable permits 362
> How much can we rely on governments? 367
>
> **12.3 The economics of traffic congestion** 369
> The existing system of allocating road space 369
> Identifying a socially efficient level of road
> usage (short run) 371
> Identifying a socially optimum level of road
> space (long run) 373
>
> **12.4 Urban transport policies** 373
> Direct provision (supply-side solutions) 373
> Regulation and legislation 374
> Changing market signals 374
> Conclusions 378

Just how far should things be left to the market in practice? Just how much should a government intervene? These are clearly normative questions, and the answers to them may depend on a person's politics. Politicians on the right tend to favour a lesser degree of intervention while those on the left generally prefer more intervention.

In the final two chapters of Part D we examine some topics that illustrate well the possible strengths and weaknesses of both the market and government intervention. In Chapter 12 we look closely at the environment, an area where the existence of externalities results in substantial market failure. We start by considering the broader environmental issues and then turn to alternative policies for dealing with pollution and urban traffic congestion.

As we shall see, the economist's approach is to focus on both the costs and the benefits of various policies and how these costs and benefits can be weighed up. Scientists are the ones who need to assess whether global warming is a real phenomenon and to determine the physical consequences of our actions, such as the degree of warming that might result from a particular level of CO_2 emissions. But it is economists who must assess the implications for various policies to deal with the problems.

12.1 ECONOMICS OF THE ENVIRONMENT

Scarcely a day goes by without some environmental issue or other featuring in the news: another warning about global warming; a company fined for illegally dumping waste; a drought or flood blamed on pollution; smog in our major cities.

Ask virtually anyone if they would like a cleaner, more attractive environment and the answer would be yes. Ask them, however, what they would be prepared to pay for such improvements and there would be much more disagreement. Environmental improvement normally comes at a cost: whether that is a cost in cleaning up waste or pollution, or a cost in terms of the higher price we might need to pay for 'green' products, such as organic foods, low-emission cars and electricity from renewable sources.

Economists are concerned with choices, and rational choices involve weighing up costs and benefits. Increasingly, people are recognising that such costs and benefits ought to include the effects on the environment: the effects on the planet we share with each other and with future generations.

The environmental problem

Why do people misuse the environment? To answer this we have to understand the nature of the economic relationship between humans and the natural world. We all benefit from the environment in three ways: as an amenity to be enjoyed, as a source of primary products (food, raw materials and other resources) and as a place where we can dump waste.

The relationship between these uses of the environment and the rest of the economy is shown in Figure 12.1. These three uses, however, tend to conflict with each other:

- The use of the environment as a productive resource reduces its amenity value. Intensive agriculture, with hedges and woods removed, spoils the beauty of the countryside and can lead to a decline in animal and plant species. Mines and quarries are ugly. Commercial forestry is often at the expense of traditional broad-leaved forests.
- Similarly, the use of the environment as a dump for waste reduces its amenity value. The environment becomes dirtier and uglier.

 What are the conflicts between using the environment as a productive resource and as a dump?

These conflicts have always existed, but are they getting worse? Let us examine the arguments.

Population pressures and limited resources

As we saw in Box 5.1, as more people crowd onto the fixed supply of world land, so diminishing returns to labour will occur. If food output per head is to remain constant, let alone increase, land must be made to yield more and more. One answer has been to use increasing amounts of fertiliser and pesticides. Likewise, if the increasing world population is to have higher levels of material consumption, this will

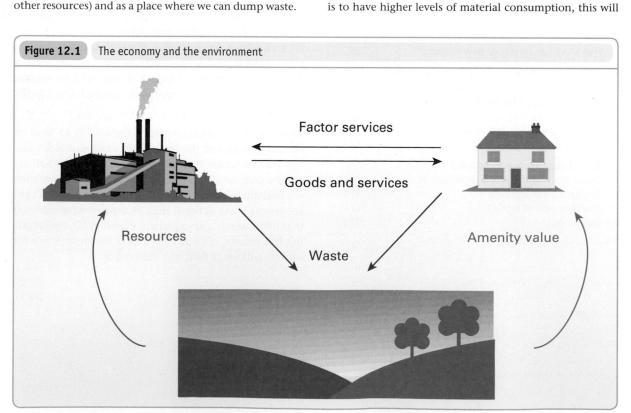

Figure 12.1 The economy and the environment

generate increased demands for natural resources, many of which are non-renewable and generate pollution. With the rapid growth of countries such as China and India, the pressures on the environment are already growing sharply.

The environment is able to absorb most types of waste up to certain levels of emission. Beyond such levels, however, environmental damage is likely to accelerate. Other things being equal, as population and waste grow, so environmental degradation is likely to grow at a faster rate.

Cause for optimism?

Despite population pressures, there are various factors that are helping to reduce environmental degradation.

Technological developments. Many newer industrial processes are cleaner and make a more efficient use of resources, leading to less waste and a slowdown in the rate of extraction of various minerals and fossil fuels. What is more, the production of less waste, or the recycling of waste, is often in the commercial interests of firms: it allows them to cut costs. In 2010, companies in the UK invested in excess of £650 million on initiatives to increase energy efficiency. This is projected to produce cost savings of around £1.2 billion. Firms thus have an incentive both to use such technology and to research into cleaner and more resource-efficient techniques. Similarly, in a competitive market firms have an incentive to produce products that save consumers money, such as fuel-efficient cars, domestic boilers, fires, cookers and electrical appliances.

Increased price of non-renewable resources. As we saw in Box 9.11 (see page 280), as resources become scarcer, so their prices rise. This encourages people to use less of them, either by using more efficient technology or by switching to renewable alternatives as they become available.

Public opinion. As knowledge about environmental damage has grown, so too has pressure from public opinion to do something about it. Many firms see the opportunity to gain commercially from having a 'green image' and to publicise their positive attitude towards corporate social responsibility. In addition governments see electoral advantage in policies to create a cleaner, greener environment.

Despite these developments, however, many aspects of environmental degradation continue to worsen.

In the past decade or so the OECD has produced three major reports. The first of these was the *OECD Environmental Outlook*, produced in 2001. This was followed in 2008 by the *OECD Environmental Outlook to 2030*. The latest, produced in 2012, is the *OECD Environmental Outlook to 2050: The Consequences of Inaction*. In these publications the main environmental issues for the next 40 years have been identified, and classified according to a traffic-light system as serious (red light), moderate (amber light) or satisfactory (green light). The two later reports have concentrated on the four key environmental challenges, identified as most urgent (and badged as red light): climate change, biodiversity, water and the health impacts of pollution.

An optimum use of the environment

If the current levels of pollution and environmental degradation are too high, then can we identify an optimum use of the environment? To do this, we have to go back to first principles of efficiency and also look at our attitudes towards *sustainability*.

Different approaches to sustainability

We can identify four different approaches to the environment and sustainability.

The free-market approach. At the one extreme, we could regard the world as there purely for ourselves: a resource that belongs to individual property owners to do with as they choose, or a 'common asset', such as the air and seas, for individuals to use for their own benefit. In this view of the world, we are entitled simply to weigh up the marginal costs and benefits to ourselves of any activity. Sustainability is achieved in this free-market world only to the extent that resource prices rise as they become scarce and to the extent that environmentally friendly technologies are in firms' (or consumers') private interests.

The social efficiency approach. A somewhat less extreme version of this view is one that takes the social costs and benefits of using the environment into account: i.e. the costs and benefits not only to the direct producer or consumer, but to people in general. Here we would apply the standard rules for social efficiency – that if marginal social benefit exceeds marginal social cost, we should do more of the activity, and if marginal social cost exceeds marginal social benefit, we should do less. Even though this approach does take into account environmental externalities (such as pollution), these environmental costs are costs only to the extent that they adversely affect *human beings*.

Within this general approach, however, more explicit account can be taken of sustainability, by including the costs of our use of the environment today to *future* generations. For example, we could take into account the effects of climate change not just on ourselves, but on our children and their descendants. Depending on people's views on 'intergenerational' equity, a higher or lower weighting could be given to future (as opposed to present) costs and benefits (see page 346 on the choice of a social discount rate).

The conservationist approach. Many environmentalists argue that our responsibilities should not be limited to each other, or even to future generations, but should include the environment for its own sake. Such a view would involve

TC 5	p54
TC 4	p47
TC 11	p320
KI 25	p272

Definition

Sustainability The ability of the environment to survive its use for economic activity.

BOX 12.1 A STERN WARNING

Economists can offer solutions, but they can't solve the problem

The analysis of global warming is not just for climate scientists. Economists have a major part to play in examining its causes and consequences and the possible solutions. And these solutions are likely to have a major impact on business.

Perhaps the most influential study of climate change in recent times was the Stern Review. This was an independent review led by Sir Nicholas Stern, the then head of the Government Economic Service and former chief economist of the World Bank. Here was an economist using the methods of economics to analyse perhaps the most serious problem facing the world.

Climate change presents a unique challenge for economics: it is the greatest and widest-ranging market failure ever seen. The economic analysis must therefore be global, deal with long time horizons, have the economics of risk and uncertainty at centre stage, and examine the possibility of major, non-marginal change.[1]

First the bad news . . .

According to the Stern Report, if no action were taken, global temperatures would rise by some 2–3°C within the next 50 years. As a result the world economy would shrink by an average of up to 20 per cent. The economies of the countries most seriously affected by floods, drought and crop failure could shrink by considerably more. Rising sea levels could displace some 200 million people; droughts could create tens or even hundreds of millions of 'climate refugees'.

. . . Then the good

However, Stern concluded that these consequences could be averted – and at relatively low cost – if action were taken early enough. According to the report, a sacrifice of just 1 per cent of global GDP (global income) could be enough to stabilise greenhouse gases to a sustainable level. To achieve this, action would need to be taken to cut emissions from their various sources (see the chart). This would involve a mixture of four things:

■ Reducing consumer demand for emissions-intensive goods and services.

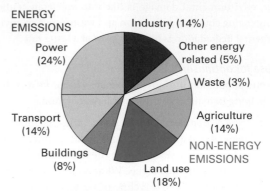

Greenhouse gas emissions in 2000, by source

Total emissions in 2000: 42 GtCO$_2$e.

Energy emissions are mostly CO$_2$ (some non-CO$_2$ in industry and other energy related).

Non-energy emissions are CO$_2$ (land use) and non-CO$_2$ (agriculture and waste).

Source: *Stern Review on the Economics of Climate Change*, Office of Climate Change (OCC) (Stern Review, 2006), Executive Summary, Figure 1 based on data drawn from World Resources Institute *Climate Analysis Indicators Tool* (CAIT) on-line database version 3.0.

■ Increased efficiency, which can save both money and emissions.
■ Action on non-energy emissions, such as avoiding deforestation.
■ Switching to lower-carbon technologies for power, heat and transport.

As one might expect from a report produced by an economist, the policy proposals focused on altering incentives. This could involve taxing polluting activities; subsidising green alternatives, including the development of green technology; establishing a price for carbon through trading carbon (see section on tradable permits on pages 362–7 below) and regulating its production; and encouraging behavioural change through education, better labelling of products and encouraging public debate.

downplaying the relative importance of material consumption and economic growth, and putting greater emphasis on the maintenance of ecosystems. Growth in consumption would be ethically acceptable only if it led to no (or only very minor) environmental degradation. Maintenance of the environment is thus seen as an ethical *constraint* on human activity.

The Gaia approach.   The strongest approach to sustainability involves a fundamentally different ethical standpoint. Here the Earth itself, and its various natural species of animals and

plants, have moral rights. According to this *Gaia philosophy*, people are seen as mere custodians of the planet: the planet

Definition

Gaia philosophy The respect for the rights of the environment to remain unharmed by human activity. Humans should live in harmony with the planet and other species. We have a duty to be stewards of the natural environment, so that it can continue to be a self-maintaining and self-regulating system.

Heeding the warnings?

So nearly 10 years after the Stern Report, how much progress has been made? We have already seen that the OECD is very concerned about the environmental impact on growth and is pressing for a global response (page 355). So are national governments therefore acting with urgency?

In 2014, the Intergovernmental Panel on Climate Change (IPCC) issued its Fifth Assessment Report[2] (AR5) – the first one had been published in 1990. This major document consists of three working group reports and an overarching synthesis. The first working group looked at the physical science. The second considered impacts, adaptation and vulnerability, while the third focused on mitigation of climate change. Economists contributed substantially to both the second and third groups.

The report on impact[3] confirmed that the effects of climate change are already occurring on all continents and across the oceans. It concluded that the world is ill-prepared for risks from a changing climate.

As with Stern, it stated that that there are currently opportunities to respond to such risks, though this will be difficult to manage with high levels of warming.

The report details the impacts of climate change to date, the future risks from a changing climate, and the opportunities for effective action to reduce risks. It identifies vulnerable people, industries and ecosystems around the world. It finds that risk from a changing climate comes from vulnerability (lack of preparedness) and exposure (people or assets in harm's way) overlapping with hazards (triggering climate events or trends). Each of these three components can be a target for smart actions to decrease risk.

Adaptation to reduce the risks from a changing climate is now starting to occur, but with a stronger focus on reacting to past events than on preparing for a changing future. According to Chris Field, the Co-Chair of Working Group II:

> Climate-change adaptation is not an exotic agenda that has never been tried. Governments, firms, and communities around the world are building experience

with adaptation. This experience forms a starting point for bolder, more ambitious adaptations that will be important, as climate and society continue to change.

Less than a month after this report, the working group on mitigation published its own findings.[4] It summarised the diverse options open to policy makers and reaffirmed the conclusion that the worst effects of climate can be prevented, if action is taken.

Part of the Mitigation report takes the form of a summary for policy makers. It acknowledges that substantial reductions in emissions will require major changes in investment patterns. The report finds that some progress in policy development has been achieved, particularly at a national level. These policies are often at sectoral level and involve the regulatory, financial and information measures that economists have recommended for some time.

There is, however, a substantial time lag between the implementation of policies and the impact on the environment. AR5 found that since 2008 emission growth has not yet deviated from the previous trend. Of course, a major characteristic of climate change is that it is not restricted by national boundaries. This highlights the potential for international co-operation and we look at this further in Box 12.4 (page 364).

1. *Would it be in the interests of a business to reduce its carbon emissions if this involved it in increased costs?*
2. *How is the concept of 'opportunity cost' relevant in analysing the impact of business decisions on the environment?*
3. *The Stern Report was produced in 2006. Why has progress to date been slow? Does this reflect a lack of political will or scepticism about the extent of climate change?*

[1] *Stern Review on the Economics of Climate Change*, Executive Summary (TSO, 2006).
[2] *The Fifth Assessment Report (AR5)* (IPCC, 2014).
[3] *Climate Change 2014: Impacts, Adaptation, and Vulnerability*, from Working Group II of the IPCC (IPCC, 2014).
[4] *Climate Change 2014: Mitigation from Climate Change*, from Working Group III of the IPCC (IPCC, 2014).

does not belong to them, any more than a dog belongs to the fleas on its back! This view of the environment is similar to that held by some Indigenous peoples living in marginal areas, such as the Aborigines in Australia and the San (Bushmen) of the Kalahari, and to various other 'hunter-gatherer' peoples in developing countries. Their ethic is that the land they leave their descendants should be as good as, if not better than, the land they inherited from their ancestors. Conservation is a 'prime directive'. This approach to the environment has been dubbed the 'deep green' approach.

Making optimum decisions concerning the environment
Choice between these four approaches is essentially normative, and therefore we cannot as economists stand in judgement between them. When anti-road protesters debate with commuters wanting a new bypass to be built across a site of outstanding natural beauty, there is little common ground between them. There is even less common ground between a multinational logging company and Indigenous rainforest dwellers.

Nevertheless, economists can help in identifying optimum decisions *within* a given set of values. Most environmental

KI 6
p 29

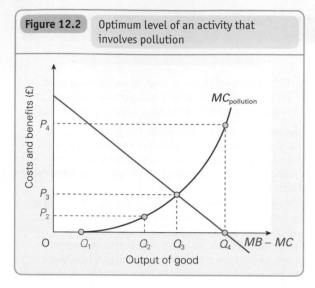

Figure 12.2 Optimum level of an activity that involves pollution

optimum output to Q_2. A Gaian approach would be to restrict output to Q_1 in order to prevent any pollution. Of course, as we move towards 'greener' approaches, so it becomes more important to look for less polluting methods for producing this good (causing the $MC_{pollution}$ curve to shift downwards), and for alternative goods that involve less pollution (thus reducing the need to consume this good).

Market failures

What is clear from all the attitudes towards sustainability, other than the free-market one, is that the market system will fail to provide adequate protection for the environment. In fact, the market fails for various reasons.

The environment as a common resource. The air, the seas and many other parts of the environment are not privately owned. They are a global 'commons', and thus have the characteristic of 'non-excludability' (see pages 326–7). Many of the 'services' provided by the environment do not have a price, so there is no economic incentive to economise on their use. Yet most environmental resources are *scarce*: there is 'rivalry' in their use. At a zero price, these resources will be overused.

Externalities. One of the major problems of the environment being a public good is that of externalities. When people pollute the environment, the costs are borne mainly by others. The greater these external costs, the lower will be the socially efficient level of output (Q_3 in Figure 12.2). Because no one owns the environment, there is no one to enforce property rights over it. If a company pollutes the air that I breathe, I cannot stop it, because the air does not belong to me.

Ignorance. There have been many cases of people causing environmental damage without realising it, especially when the effects build up over a long time. Take the case of aerosols. It was not until the 1980s that scientists connected their use to ozone depletion. Even when the problems are known to scientists, consumers may not appreciate the full environmental costs of their actions. So even if people would like to be more 'environmentally friendly' in their activities, they might not have the knowledge to be so.

Intergenerational problems. The environmentally harmful effects of many activities are long term, whereas the benefits are immediate. Thus consumers and firms are frequently prepared to continue with various practices and leave future generations to worry about their environmental consequences. The problem, then, is a reflection of the importance that people attach to the present relative to the future.

economists adopt an approach that is consistent with the social efficiency view, and which can be easily modified to fit the conservationist view. The main area for disagreement within this approach is over the *value* to be put on specific environmental costs and benefits.

Let us take the case of the production of a good that yields benefits to consumers, but which involves pollution to the environment. What is the optimum level of output of the good? The choices are illustrated in Figure 12.2.

The line $MC_{pollution}$ shows the amount of pollution from each additional unit of the good. Up to level of activity Q_1 there is no pollution: the environment can cope with the waste generated. The curve gets steeper as output increases because the environment is increasingly unable to cope with the waste. The costs of pollution therefore accelerate.

The line $MB - MC$ shows the net marginal private benefit from the good (i.e. its private profitability). The curve slopes downwards for two reasons: marginal benefit falls as more of the good is consumed (the principle of diminishing marginal utility); marginal cost rises (diminishing marginal returns). It is privately profitable to produce extra units of the good up to Q_4. Total private gain is maximised at this output.

An otherwise perfect free market will produce Q_4 units of output, with a pollution cost of P_4. The *socially* efficient level of output, however, is Q_3, with the lower pollution cost, P_3. (We are assuming that there are no other externalities.) Here the marginal net private benefit is equal to the marginal external cost of the pollution (i.e. where there is a zero net *social* benefit: where $MSB = MSC$). Identifying this socially efficient level of output is not easy in practice, since it requires us to *measure* pollution costs, and that is fraught with problems. These problems were considered in section 11.4.

A more conservationist approach could be to set a maximum pollution cost of, say, P_2. This would reduce the

 Look through the categories of possible market failings in section 11.2 (pages 323–31). Are there any others, in addition to the four we have just identified, that will result in a socially inefficient use of the environment?

Section summary

1. The environment benefits humans in three ways: as an amenity, as a source of primary products and as a dump for waste.

2. Given the increasing population pressures and the demands for economic growth, the pressures on the environment are likely to grow. These pressures can be lessened, however, with the use of cleaner technology, a more efficient use of natural resources and 'greener' behaviour of consumers, firms and governments.

3. The concept of an 'optimum' use of the environment depends on people's attitudes towards sustainability. These attitudes vary from regarding the environment simply as a resource for human use at the one extreme

to seeing the environment as having moral rights at the other.

4. Under the social efficiency approach to sustainability, the optimum output of a good is where the marginal external environmental cost is equal to the marginal net benefit to users (assuming no other externalities).

5. The market fails to achieve a socially efficient use of the environment because large parts of the environment are a common resource, because production or consumption often generates environmental externalities, because of ignorance of the environmental effects of our actions, and because of a lack of concern for future generations.

12.2 POLICIES TO TACKLE POLLUTION AND ITS EFFECTS

Policies to tackle pollution fall into three broad categories: (a) those that attempt to work through the market by changing property rights or by changing market signals (e.g. through the use of taxes or subsidies); (b) those that involve the use of laws, regulations and other forms of non-market-based intervention; (c) those that attempt to combine the two approaches, the main example being that of 'cap and trade' – this is where the government gives firms permits to emit up to a certain limit (regulation) but then lets them trade these permits with each other (market-based).

Market-based policies

The policies that a government adopts to reduce pollution will depend on its attitudes towards sustainability: on how 'green' it is.

If governments adopt a social efficiency approach to sustainability, environmental problems are seen to be the result of prices not reflecting marginal social costs and benefits. In this section, we look at ways in which markets can be adjusted so that they do achieve social efficiency.

Extending private property rights

If those suffering from pollution are granted property rights, they can charge the polluters for the right to pollute. According to the Coase theorem (see page 336), this would result in the socially efficient level of output being achieved.

We can use Figure 12.2 to illustrate the Coase theorem. If output is initially less than Q_3, the marginal profit to the polluter will exceed the marginal pollution cost to the sufferer. In this case, if the sufferers impose a charge on the polluter that is greater than the sufferers' marginal

pollution cost but less than the polluter's marginal profit, both sides will benefit from more of the good being produced. Such a situation can continue up to Q_3. Beyond Q_3, the marginal pollution cost exceeds the marginal profit. There is no charge that would compensate for the victim's suffering and leave enough over for the polluter to make a profit. Equilibrium output is therefore at Q_3, the socially efficient output.

Similarly, if the polluting *firm* is given the right to pollute, victims could offer a payment to persuade it not to pollute. The victims would be prepared to pay only up to the cost to them of the pollution. The firm would cut back production only provided the payment was at least as great as the loss in profit. This would be the case at levels of output above Q_3. Once output falls below Q_3, the maximum that the victim would be prepared to pay would be less than the minimum that the firm would be prepared to accept. Again, equilibrium would be at Q_3.

Extending private property rights in this way is normally impractical whenever there are many polluters and many victims. But the principle of the victims paying polluters to reduce pollution is sometimes followed by governments. Thus, under Article 11 of the 1997 Kyoto Protocol, the developed countries agreed to provide financial assistance to the developing countries to help them reduce greenhouse gas emissions.

In addition, there are sometimes direct environmental gains to be made from extending private property rights to individuals. In many developing countries, tenant farmers or squatters in urban slums have no incentive to invest in the land where they work or live. Give such people secure property rights, however, and they are more likely to take care of the property. For example, farmers are much more likely to plant trees if they know they have the right to the wood or fruit several years later.

TC 2
p25

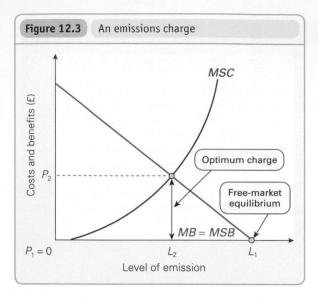

Figure 12.3 An emissions charge

Without a charge, the firm will emit L_1, since this is where its private marginal cost (= 0) equals its private marginal benefit. The socially efficient level of emission is L_2 and the socially efficient level of emissions charge, therefore, is P_2.

If these charges are to achieve a reduction in pollution, they must be a charge *per unit* of emissions or resource use (as in Figure 12.3). *Fixed total* charges, by contrast, such as water rates or council tax, will *not* encourage households to cut back on water use or reduce domestic refuse, since this will not save them any money: such charges have a *marginal* rate of zero. If the firm in Figure 12.3 were charged a fixed total pollution fee, it would still choose to emit L_1 waste.

Environmental ('green') taxes and subsidies

Rather than charging for environmental use, a tax could be imposed on the output (or consumption) of a *good*, wherever external environmental costs are generated. Such taxes are known as **green taxes**. In this case, the good already has a price: the tax has the effect of increasing the price. To achieve a socially efficient output, the rate of tax should be equal to the marginal external cost. The alternative is to subsidise activities that reduce pollution (such as the installation of loft insulation). Here the rate of subsidy should be equal to the marginal external benefit.

Figure 11.9 (on page 333) showed the optimum rate of pollution tax in an otherwise perfect market. In terms of Figure 12.2, this rate of tax would be P_3: i.e. equal to the marginal pollution cost at the socially optimum output Q_3. The tax, by adding to private costs, shifts the $MB - MC$ line downwards so that it crosses the horizontal axis at Q_3. Profit is maximised where $MB - MC = 0$: at Q_3.

Although green taxes and subsidies are theoretically a means of achieving social efficiency, they do have serious limitations (see Box 12.2).

Charging for use of the environment (as a resource or a dump)

One way of 'pricing the environment' is for the government to impose **environmental charges** on consumers or firms. Thus *emissions charges* could be levied on firms discharging waste. Another example is *user charges* to households for rubbish collection. If a social efficiency approach to sustainability is taken, the optimum level of environmental use would be where the marginal social benefits and costs of that use were equal. This is illustrated in Figure 12.3, which shows the emission of toxic waste into a river by a chemical plant.

It is assumed that all the benefits from emitting the waste into the river accrue to the firm (i.e. there is no external benefit). Marginal private and marginal social benefits are thus the same ($MB = MSB$). The curve slopes downwards because, with a downward-sloping demand curve for the good, higher output will have a lower marginal benefit, and so too will the waste associated with it.

But what about the marginal costs? Without charges, the marginal private cost of using the river for emitting the waste is zero. The pollution of the river, however, imposes an external cost on those using it for fishing or water supply. The marginal external cost rises as the river becomes less and less able to cope with increased levels of emission. As there is no private cost, the marginal social cost is the same as the marginal external cost.

 Draw a diagram like Figure 12.2, only this time assume that the activity has the effect of reducing pollution, with the result that the $MC_{pollution}$ curve lies below the horizontal axis, sloping downwards. Identify the socially optimal level of the activity. What would be the level of subsidy required to achieve this level of activity?

Non-market-based policies

Command-and-control systems (laws and regulations)

One way of tackling pollution has been to set maximum permitted levels of emission or resource use, or minimum acceptable levels of environmental quality, and then to fine firms contravening these limits. Measures of this type are known as ***command-and-control (CAC) systems***. Clearly, there have to be inspectors to monitor the amount of pollution, and the fines have to be large enough to deter firms from exceeding the limit.

Virtually all countries have environmental regulations of one sort or another. For example, the EU has over 230 items of legislation covering areas such as air and water pollution, noise, the marketing and use of dangerous chemicals, waste management, the environmental impacts of new projects (such as power stations, roads and quarries), recycling, depletion of the ozone layer and global warming.

Typically, there are three approaches to devising CAC systems:[1]

- ***Technology-based standards***. The focus could be on the amount of pollution generated, irrespective of its environmental impact. As technology for reducing pollutants improves, so tougher standards could be imposed, based on the 'best available technology' (as long as the costs were not excessive). Thus car manufacturers could be required to ensure that new car engines meet lower CO_2 emission levels as the technology enabled them to do so.
- ***Ambient-based standards***. Here the focus is on the environmental impact. For example, standards could be set for air or water purity. Depending on the location and the number of polluters in that area, a given standard would be achieved with different levels of discharge. If the object is a cleaner environment, this approach is more efficient than technology-based standards.
- ***Social-impact standards***. Here the focus is on the effect on people. Thus tougher standards would be imposed in densely populated areas. Whether this approach is more efficient than that of ambient-based standards depends on the approach to sustainability. If the objective is to achieve social efficiency, human-impact standards are preferable. If the objective is to protect the environment for its own sake (a deeper green approach), ambient standards would be preferable.

Assessing CAC systems. Given the uncertainty over the environmental impacts of pollutants, especially over the longer term, it is often better to play safe and set tough emissions or ambient standards. These could always be relaxed at a later stage if the effects turn out not to be so damaging, but it might be too late to reverse damage if the effects turn out to be more serious. Taxes may be a more sophisticated means of reaching a socially efficient output, but CAC methods are usually more straightforward to devise, easier to understand by firms and easier to implement.

Voluntary agreements

Rather than imposing laws and regulations, the government can seek to enter into voluntary agreements (VAs) with firms for them to cut pollution. Such agreements may involve a formal contract, and hence be legally binding, or they may be looser commitments by firms. VAs will be helped if (a) companies believe that this will improve their image with customers and hence improve sales; (b) there is an underlying threat by the government of introducing laws and regulations should VAs fail.

Firms often prefer VAs to regulations, because they can negotiate such agreements to suit their own particular circumstances and build them into their planning. The result is that the firms may be able to meet environmental objectives at lower cost. This clearly helps their competitive position.

The effectiveness of VAs depends on how tightly specified the agreements are and how easy they are for government inspectors to monitor. It also depends on there being genuine goodwill of firms. Without it, they may try to draw up agreements in a way that allows them to get around having to cut emissions as much as was intended by the government.

Education

People's attitudes are very important in determining the environmental consequences of their actions. Fortunately for the environment, people are not always out simply to maximise their own self-interest. If they were, then why would they buy more expensive 'green' products, such as environmentally friendly detergents? The answer is that many people like to do their bit, however small, towards protecting the environment. There is evidence that attitudes have changed markedly over the past few years. See Box 12.3 for more detail on this.

This is where education can come in. If children, and adults for that matter, were made more aware of environmental issues and the consequences of their actions, then people's consumption habits could change and more pressure would be put on firms to improve their 'green credentials'.

> ### Definitions
>
> **Command-and-control (CAC) systems** The use of laws or regulations backed up by inspections and penalties (such as fines) for non-compliance.
>
> **Technology-based standards** Pollution control that requires firms' emissions to reflect the levels that could be achieved from using the best available pollution control technology.
>
> **Ambient-based standards** Pollution control that requires firms to meet minimum standards for the environment (e.g. air or water quality).
>
> **Social-impact standards** Pollution control that focuses on the effects on people (e.g. on health or happiness).

[1] See R. K. Turner, D. Pearce and I. Bateman, *Environmental Economics* (Harvester Wheatsheaf, 1994), p. 198.

BOX 12.2 GREEN TAXES

Are they the perfect answer to the problem of pollution?

Increasingly countries are introducing 'green' taxes in order to discourage pollution as goods are produced, consumed or disposed of. The table shows the range of green taxes used around the world and the chart shows green tax revenues as a percentage of GDP in various countries.

As can be seen, they are higher than average in Scandinavian countries, reflecting the strength of their environmental concerns. They are lowest in the USA. By far the largest green tax revenues come from fuel taxes. Fuel taxes are relatively high in the UK and so, therefore, are green tax revenues.

There are various problems, however, with using taxes to tackle pollution.

Identifying the socially efficient tax rate. It will be difficult to identify the $MC_{pollution}$ curve for each firm (see Figure 12.2), given that each one is likely to produce different amounts of pollutants for any given level of output. Even if two firms produce identical amounts of pollutants, the environmental damage might be quite different, because the ability of the environment to cope with it will differ between the two locations. Also, the human impact will vary. We can add to these issues the fact that harmful effects are likely to build up over time, and predicting this is fraught with difficulty.

Problems of demand inelasticity. The less elastic the demand for the product, the less effective will a tax be in cutting production and hence in cutting pollution. Thus taxes on petrol (where we know demand is inelastic) would have to be very high to make significant reductions in the exhaust gases that contribute towards global warming and acid rain.

Problems with international trade. If a country imposes pollution taxes on its industries, its products will become less competitive in world trade. To compensate for this, it may be necessary to give the industries tax rebates for exports. Also, taxes would have to be imposed on imports of competitors' products from countries where there is no equivalent green tax.

Effects on employment. Reduced output in the industries affected by green taxes will lead to a reduction in employment. If, however, the effect was to encourage investment in new cleaner technology, employment might not fall. Furthermore, employment opportunities could be generated elsewhere, if the extra revenues from the green taxes were spent on alternative products (e.g. buses and trains rather than cars).

Types of environmental taxes and charges

Motor fuels	Other goods	Air transport
Leaded/unleaded	Batteries	Noise charges
Diesel (quality differential)	Plastic carrier bags	Aviation fuels
Carbon/energy taxation	Glass containers	*Water*
Sulphur tax	Drink cans	Water charges
Other energy products	Tyres	Sewage charges
Carbon/energy tax	CFCs/halons	Water effluent charges
Sulphur tax or charge	Disposable razors/cameras	Manure charges
NO_2 charge	Lubricant oil charge	*Direct tax provisions*
Methane charge	Oil pollutant charge	Tax relief on green investment
Agricultural inputs	Solvents	Taxation on free company cars
Fertilisers	*Waste disposal*	Employer-paid commuting expenses taxable
Pesticides	Municipal waste charges	Employer-paid parking expenses taxable
Manure	Waste-disposal charges	Commuter use of public transport tax deductible
Vehicle-related taxation	Hazardous waste charges	
Sales tax depends on car size	Landfill tax or charges	
Road tax depends on car size	Duties on waste water	

KI 15
p121

KI 9
p71

Tradable permits

A policy measure that has grown in popularity in recent years is that of **tradable permits**, also known as a 'cap-and-trade' system. This is a combination of command-and-control and market-based systems.

A maximum permitted level of emission is set for a given pollutant for a given factory, and the firm is given a permit to emit up to this amount. If it emits less than this amount, it is given a credit for the difference, which it can then use in

Definition

Tradable permits Each firm is given a permit to produce a given level of pollution. If less than the permitted amount is produced, the firm is given a credit. This can then be sold to another firm, allowing it to exceed its original limit.

Redistributive effects. Many green taxes are regressive. The poor spend a higher proportion of their income on domestic fuel than the rich. A 'carbon tax' on such fuel therefore has the effect of redistributing incomes away from the poor. The poor also spend a larger proportion of their income on food than the rich do. Taxes on agriculture, designed to reduce the intensive use of fertilisers and pesticides, also tend to hit the poor proportionately more than the rich.

Not all green taxes, however, are regressive. The rich spend a higher proportion of their income on motoring than the poor (see Figure 12.4 on page 370). Thus petrol and other motoring taxes could have a progressive effect.

Despite these problems, such taxes can still move output closer to the socially efficient level. What is more, they do have the major advantage of providing a continuing incentive to firms to find cleaner methods of production and thereby save more on their tax bills.

1. *Is it a good idea to use the revenues from green taxes to subsidise green alternatives (e.g. using petrol taxes for subsidising rail transport)? Consider the implications for wider tax policy in your answer.*
2. *If a green tax is highly regressive, does this mean that a government concerned with inequality should avoid implementing it? Consider the long-term impact of climate change on welfare in your answer.*

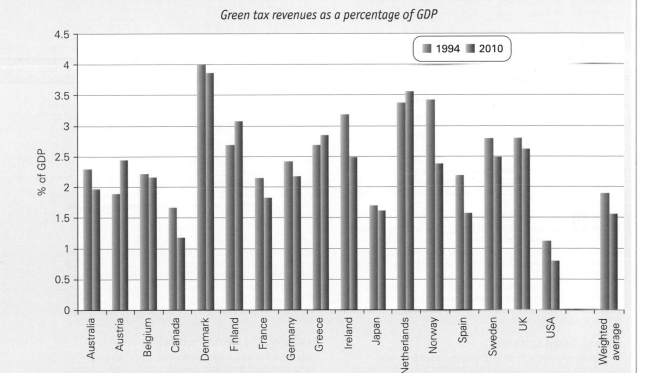

Green tax revenues as a percentage of GDP

Source: Based on data in *Environmentally related taxes database* (OECD).

another of its factories, or sell to other firms. These other firms are then permitted to go that amount *over* their permitted level. Thus the overall level of emissions is set by CAC methods, whereas their distribution is determined by the market.

Take the example of firms A and B, which are currently producing 12 units of a pollutant each. Now assume that a standard is set permitting them to produce only 10 units each. If firm A managed to reduce the pollutant to 8 units, it would be given a credit for 2 units. It could then sell this to firm B, enabling B to continue emitting 12 units. The effect

would still be a total reduction of 4 units between the two firms. However, the trade in pollution permits allows pollution reduction to be concentrated where it can be achieved at lowest cost. In our example, if it cost firm B more to reduce its pollution than firm A, the permits could be sold from A to B at a price that was profitable to both (i.e. at a price above the cost of emission reduction to A, but below the cost of emission reduction to B).

The principle of tradable permits can be used as the basis of international agreements on pollution reduction. Each

TC 2
p25

BOX 12.3 ARE WE ALL GREEN NOW?

Changing attitudes to the environmental agenda

It wasn't very long ago that concern about the environment and a willingness to take sustainability seriously were seen as eccentric. For every scientist predicting the potentially serious results of climate change, another suggested that humanity's impact on the planet was of little consequence. However, while it would be complacent to suggest that all individuals and businesses are fully signed up to the green agenda, there are signs that over the past few years there has been a fundamental change in attitudes.

Individuals' attitudes and behaviour

In 2009, the Department for Environment, Food and Rural Affairs (Defra) and the Energy Saving Trust conducted a survey[1] into attitudes and behaviours towards the environment. This was the latest in a series of similar surveys undertaken for Defra or its predecessors since 1986. They demonstrated that in recent years the public have put an increasing emphasis on green issues.

The 2009 results continue this trend, despite the financial crisis and subsequent recession. Three-quarters of those surveyed said they felt that if most people in the UK recycled more, cut down on car use

or flew less, it would have a medium or major impact on the UK's contribution to climate change. In the survey the environment was rated the third most important issue for government to address. Surveys undertaken in the late 1990s and early 2000s suggested that individuals were previously less convinced about the impact that their own behaviour could have on climate change.

If we look further at the statistics, it seems that that these changing attitudes are feeding through to many areas of household behaviour. By 2009/10, 91 per cent of respondents reported that they were recycling at least some items, rather than throwing them away. In total, households were recycling 40 per cent of rubbish compared with 33 per cent in 2007/8 and only 23 per cent in 2004/5. (Local authorities have been set a recycling target of 50 per cent by 2020.) The 2009/10 survey also reported that 84 per cent of people were taking their own bags when shopping, a big increase from the 51 per cent in 2007. There were also continued increases in the use of public transport, particularly in the South-East.

Of course some of these behavioural changes will reflect new policies; for example, many local authorities have adopted rubbish

BOX 12.4 INTERNATIONAL CO-ORDINATION ON CLIMATE CHANGE

The market-led solution of the Kyoto Protocol

In 1997, a draft accord to reduce greenhouse gas emissions was agreed by most nations of the world at the UN international climate change conference in Kyoto, Japan. It was based on principles established in a framework convention signed in 1992. The 'Kyoto Protocol' was designed to reduce greenhouse gas emissions by an average of 5.2 per cent (based on 1990 levels) by the year 2012. A second set of emission targets was later put in place for the period 2012–20.

To become a legally binding treaty, it had to be signed and ratified by nations accounting for at least 55 per cent of greenhouse gas emissions from industrialised countries. Because the Bush administration decided not to ratify the agreement, the 55 per cent target could be met only if Russia signed, which it eventually did in November 2004.

The treaty came into force on 16 February 2005, having been ratified by 141 parties. This has since increased to a total of 192 parties and, of these, 39 Annex 1 countries (those that are developed or 'in transition') agreed to emissions reductions.

Market-based systems

The agreement, although not originally envisaged in this way, involves the climate being turned into a market, where the right to pollute can be bought and sold through a system of emissions credits. These credits can be earned by reducing emission levels below those agreed or by creating conditions that help to minimise the impact of greenhouse gases on global warming: for example, by planting a forest (which absorbs carbon).

Within the Kyoto Protocol there are three distinct market-based mechanisms:

- Emissions trading.
- Joint Implementation (JI).
- Clean Development Mechanism (CDM).

Emissions trading. The countries that have ratified the Kyoto Protocol are allowed to trade amongst themselves rights to emit six greenhouse gases. If a country reduces emissions below its agreed limit, it will be able to sell the additional reduction as a credit. So if a country is finding it difficult to cut emissions, it will be able to buy these credits within some kind of marketplace. (As you will

see in Box 12.5, CO_2 emissions trading began within the EU in January 2005.)

Joint implementation. Under Article 6 of the protocol, an industrialised country can earn credits by investing in projects that reduce emissions in other industrialised countries (primarily former Soviet countries). These credits, in this case called 'emission reduction units' (ERUs), then reduce its own requirement to cut emissions.

Clean Development Mechanism. This is similar to the joint implementation process above, but involves a country or company from the industrialised world earning credits, in this case called 'certified emissions reductions' (CERs), by investing in emissions reduction schemes in *developing* countries. For example, a typical CDM or JI project might involve installing solar panels, planting forests, or investing in a factory producing energy-efficient light bulbs.

Assessing the Kyoto Protocol

While the use of such market mechanisms may make it easier to meet the Kyoto targets, many have claimed that the targets are too low. The Intergovernmental Panel on Climate Change estimates that a 60 to 80 per cent cut in greenhouse gas emissions from 1990 levels will ultimately be needed to avert serious climate disruption. In the light of this, a 5.2 per cent reduction, which will probably not be met anyway, seems irrelevant.

There is also the danger that reductions achieved would have taken place anyway. For example, Russia has CO_2 emissions considerably below its 1990 level and so has a massive emissions credit for sale. However, this is not the result of Russian environmental policy, but rather the consequence of the collapse of much of Russian industry in the early 1990s and the replacing of dirty inefficient factories with more profitable cleaner ones. The EU has consistently argued that, to ensure that some real gains are made, no more than 50 per cent of the emissions reduction should be achieved through these market-based mechanisms.

One of the biggest problems with the Kyoto treaty is that developing countries are not required to cut their emissions, although they do have to monitor and report the levels. Instead,

collection systems that encourage recycling, while a number of stores have started charging for plastic carrier bags. However, we might argue that changing attitudes have enabled those policies to be put in place.

The 2009 survey was the last to be conducted in the previous formats. Since then the government's focus has moved towards a broader 'well-being' agenda.

Businesses

Past attitudes of business towards the environment have been summarised as falling into two camps: a few firms were interested in 'saving the planet', while the majority felt that this conflicted with profit maximisation. Two things have challenged the approach of the majority.

First, in an era of real increases in commodity prices, and particularly of higher energy costs, a responsible attitude towards the environment and profit maximisation both suggest similar strategies; firms are investing in new technologies that will reduce long-term energy consumption, and sustainability has become a crucial plank of corporate social responsibility.

Second, changes in public attitudes have opened up a new approach for astute businesses: if consumers are themselves becoming environmentally aware, this presents business with opportunities for new approaches to marketing and innovation.

1. *New car registrations rose 10.8 per cent between 2012 and 2013. Does this suggest that, despite the reported change in attitudes, households are failing to cut back on motoring?*
2. *An experiment was conducted looking at the amount of waste recycled in an office. In some rooms, the bins for rubbish that cannot be recycled were labelled 'General Rubbish'. In others, they were labelled 'Land-fill'. What would you predict was the outcome? In your answer refer back to section 4.4 on pages 125–8.*

¹ Alex Thornton, *Public Attitudes and Behaviours towards the Environment – Tracker Survey: A Report to the Department for Environment, Food and Rural Affairs*, TNS (Defra, London, 2009).

recognising that developed nations have benefited from 150 years of industrial activity, the Protocol places a greater onus on those nations under the principle of 'common but differentiated responsibilities'. Most of these 'non-obligated' countries remain very poor; however, this group also includes fast-growing economies such as China, India and Brazil.

China's increasing emissions, in particular, have been the subject of much criticism. They more than doubled between 1990 and 2007; at one point it was building an average of two coal-fired power stations every week. In 2007 it responded to concerns by unveiling a climate change plan and promising to put the issue at the heart of its energy policies. This does seem to have had an impact and within two years China was being described as the world's leading builder of low-pollution, clean-technology power stations. Despite this, as countries such as China and India continue with their rapid industrialisation, emissions are likely to increase rapidly. Finally, the USA, under the Bush administration, having opted out of the Kyoto Protocol, clearly weakened the effectiveness of the treaty.

The USA and the Kyoto Protocol

So did the Bush administration take any measures to cut greenhouse gases? In its 'clear skies and global climate change initiative', launched in February 2002, the USA stated that its aim was to cut the growth in greenhouse gas emissions relative to the growth in the economy. There would be tax incentives to encourage renewable energy schemes and fuel efficiency schemes, but corporations would not be obliged to meet any CO_2 targets. The effect would still be one of a *growth* in greenhouse gases.

Despite this lack of political willpower in the Bush administration, elsewhere in the USA action was being taken. From January 2007 eight north-eastern states became involved in a regional cap-and-trade programme, while California has committed to reducing emissions by 25 per cent by 2020.

Following the election of Barack Obama in late 2008, there was renewed optimism about the US approach to climate change. He was elected on a campaign that included a pledge to reduce emissions by 28 per cent by 2020 and by 80 per cent by 2050. He also committed to invest $150 billion in new, energy-saving technologies. By 2010 his administration had undertaken a number of initiatives on

clean energy, eliminating fossil fuel subsidies and monitoring of greenhouse gas emissions. Yet despite this progress, the President remained under pressure from business and the Republican Party to soften his approach.

Beyond Kyoto

In December 2007, a UN climate change convention took place in Bali. Recognising that the Kyoto agreement lasted only to 2012, delegates agreed on a roadmap to making much deeper cuts in emissions. The intention was that a final agreement would be reached at a UN summit in December 2009 in Copenhagen. After a fortnight of wrangling between leaders, however, all that resulted was a non-binding 'accord'. This merely recognised the need for keeping global temperature rises to a maximum of 2°C without any specific commitments to achieving that goal.

In December 2010 a modest agreement was reached, following a two-week summit held in Cancún in Mexico. The agreement included a 'Green Climate Fund', set up by rich nations to help poor countries defend themselves against climate change.

In 2011 Canada became the first country to announce its withdrawal from the Kyoto Accord. It argued that Kyoto was not effective as neither China nor the USA were part of the Accord and several countries outside the EU were falling well short of their Kyoto targets. Japan and Russia announced that they would take on no further Kyoto targets in the post-2012 period.

An extension to the Kyoto Protocol to run from 2012 to 2020 was agreed in Doha, Qatar, in December 2012, but there are only 37 parties with binding targets, all, with the exception of Australia, in Europe. Australia agreed to a 5 per cent cut in emissions by 2020. Most of the rest agreed to a 20 per cent cut.

Most commentators are resigned to the fact that the Kyoto initiative may have run its course. National agreements are now seen as key to reductions in emissions, rather than the global approach taken at successive Kyoto summits. The overview of the OECD and the IPCC (see Box 12.1) may prove more effective.

Explain who are likely to be the 'winners' and 'losers' as a result of talks on carbon dioxide emissions. Use the concepts of game theory to illustrate your argument.

country could be required to achieve a certain percentage reduction in a pollutant (e.g. CO_2 or SO_2), but any country exceeding its reduction could sell its right to these emissions to other (presumably richer) countries.

A similar principle can be adopted for using natural resources. Thus fish quotas could be assigned to fishing boats or fleets or countries. Any parts of these quotas not used could then be sold.

How are the permitted pollution levels (or fish quotas) to be decided? The way that seems to be the most acceptable is to base them on firms' *current* levels, with any subsequent reduction in total permitted pollution being achieved by requiring firms to reduce their emissions by the *same* percentage. This approach is known as ***grandfathering***. The main problem with this approach is that it could be seen as unfair by those firms that are already using cleaner technology. Why should they be required to make the same reductions as firms using dirty technology?

In the EU, a carbon Emissions Trading Scheme (ETS) has been in place since January 2005. This scheme is examined in Box 12.5.

Assessing the system of tradable permits

The main advantage of tradable permits is that they combine the simplicity of CAC methods with the benefits of achieving pollution reduction in the most efficient way. There is also the advantage that firms have a financial incentive to cut pollution. This might then make it easier

> ## Definition
>
> **Grandfathering** Where each firm's emission permit is based on its current levels of emissions (e.g. permitted levels for all firms could be 80 per cent of their current levels).

| **BOX 12.5** | **TRADING OUR WAY OUT OF CLIMATE CHANGE** |

The EU carbon trading system

In the EU, a carbon Emissions Trading Scheme (ETS) started in January 2005. It created a market in carbon with the intention of providing incentives to companies to reduce their emissions of CO_2 and thus to contribute to the EU's approach to meeting its targets under the Kyoto Treaty (see Box 12.4).

Trading Periods 1 and 2

The first phase of the scheme ran from January 2005 until December 2007. Around 12 000 industrial plants were allocated CO_2 emissions allowances, or credits, by their respective governments. These installations were collectively responsible for around 40 per cent of the EU's CO_2 emissions each year.

Companies that exceeded their limits could purchase credits to cover the difference, while those that reduced their emissions were able to sell their surplus credits for a profit. Companies were able to trade directly with each other or via brokers operating throughout Europe.

At the end of December 2007 all existing allowances became invalid and the second Trading Period began, to last until the end of 2012. Although this was run under the same general principles as Trading Period 1, it also allowed companies to use JI and CDM credits earned under the Kyoto Protocol's project-based mechanisms (see Box 12.4). In other words, companies could offset emissions in the EU against emission reductions they achieve in countries outside the EU.

Phase III

In January 2008 the European Commission published draft proposals for ETS Phase III, to run from 2013 to 2020. The long lead-in time ensured that all involved would be aware of proposed changes to the system and thus could adapt

strategies and processes in anticipation. These changes included centralised allocation of allowances rather than allocation by national governments, progressively replacing the free allocation of allowances by the auctioning of them, with at least 20 per cent of the revenues earmarked for measures to combat climate change (reaching full auctioning by 2020) and the inclusion of other greenhouse gases.

In December 2009, the EU agreed to a '20/20/20' package to tackle climate change. This would involve cutting greenhouse gases by 20 per cent by 2020 compared with 1990 levels, raising the use of renewable energy sources to 20 per cent of total energy usage and cutting energy consumption by 20 per cent. Much of the emission reductions would be achieved by tighter caps under the ETS, with binding national targets for non-ETS sectors, such as agriculture, transport, buildings and services. However, over half of the reductions could be achieved by international carbon trading, where permits could be bought from abroad: e.g. under the Clean Development Mechanism (see Box 12.4).

Assessing the ETS

The introduction of the world's largest market-based policy to address climate change was welcomed by many economists and policy makers. However, others have raised concerns about both the operation of the scheme and its likely impact on overall emissions.

Some of these concerns are valid. For example, there is evidence that not all countries across the EU have been operating the scheme in the same way. Some countries, including the UK, have set tough targets based on past emissions, while others have set more generous forward-looking limits, raising questions about the equity of the scheme. Furthermore, while the allocation of permits for

for governments to impose tougher standards (i.e. impose lower permitted levels of emission).

There are, however, various problems with tradable permits. One is the possibility that trade will lead to pollution being concentrated in certain geographical areas. Another is that it may reduce the pressure on dirtier factories (or countries) to cut their emissions. Additionally, the system will lead to significant cuts in pollution only if the permitted levels are low. Once the system is in place, the government might then feel that the pressure is off to *reduce* the permitted levels. In early 2011, a further problem came to light, when the EU ETS suspended trading in permits, following identification of a substantial fraud worth €7.5 million.

 What determines the size of the administrative costs of a system of tradable permits? For what reasons might green taxes be cheaper to administer than a system of tradable permits?

How much can we rely on governments?

If governments are to be relied upon to set the optimum green taxes or regulations, several conditions must be met.

First, they must have the will to protect the environment. But governments are accountable to their electorates and must often appease various pressure groups, such as representatives of big business. In the USA, for example, there has been great resistance to cuts in greenhouse gases from the automobile, power and various other industries, many of which have powerful representation in Congress. So there must be the political will in a country if significant environmental improvements are to be made. One of the problems here is that many of the environmental effects of our actions today will be on future generations; but governments are elected by today's generation, and today's generation may not be prepared to make the necessary sacrifices. This brings us back to the importance of education.

a whole Trading Period does provide certainty for firms, it also reduces the ability of the scheme to be responsive to changing conditions. This concern was addressed in Phase III, with the removal of National Allocation Plans; since 2013 there has been a single, EU-wide cap. This has been set at a level which is intended to result in a 21 per cent reduction in emissions from the traded sector, between 2005 and 2020.

What matters crucially for the reduction of pollution is the total number of credits permitted. And this is where the major criticism lies: that allocation has been far too generous. This was compounded by a lack of willingness to prosecute those infringing the rules. The result of all this was that in Trading Period 1 emissions across the EU actually rose, by 1.9 per cent, and carbon prices fell – from a peak of around €30 per tonne of carbon in 2006 to a minuscule €0.02 per tonne by the end of Trading Period 1.

But this is not a criticism of the system of trading, only of the limits set. As long as the demand for permits exceeds the supply at a zero price and as long as the scheme enables free trade in carbon across the EU, then firms will have an incentive to reduce their emissions and sell permits to others. However, the lower the price, the less the incentive.

In Trading Period 2 the cap on emissions was tightened by 7 per cent (although this percentage varies from country to country). As a result, the price rose again – to around €20 per tonne at the end of 2008. A problem, however, was that the credits earned through CDM and JI may have been from new investments that would have taken place anyway. These 'bogus' credits then permitted companies to carry on emitting in the EU. A further criticism arose as a consequence of the global economic slump from 2007. The inevitable outcome of the recession was lower emissions, with consequentially much less pressure on industry from 2010 to 2012 than there otherwise would have been. This led to debate about whether

the cap should be tightened within Trading Period 2 to take account of this, though this did not in fact happen.

From 2012 the ETS was extended to airline emissions, although the proposed cuts of 3 per cent from 2004–6 levels are less than in other industries. In fact, this is 90 per cent higher than 1990, the base year used for the 8 per cent cut in emissions from the other sectors. In March 2011, the China Air Transport Association made formal representations to the EU's proposals, urging the EU to undertake bilateral negotiations with the Chinese government.

Plans to bring shipping emissions within the scheme have been delayed. Shipping is a large and growing source of emissions. As a first step towards cutting these, the European Commission has proposed that owners of large ships using EU ports should report their verified emissions from 2018. Similarly, road transport, responsible for around 20 per cent of all emissions, remains outside the scheme.

Overall, it is difficult to assess the impact of the ETS, even as we are now well inside Trading Period 3. Disaggregating the effect of emissions credits from the effects of other economic factors and policy changes is enormously complicated. However, there is general agreement that the systems and processes set in place do have the potential to be effective. The question remains, however, whether there is the political will to tighten the cap in order to reduce emissions further.

 Consider a situation where all firms are of identical size and each is allocated credits that allow it to produce 10 per cent less than its current emissions. How would this compare with a situation where permits are allocated to 90 per cent of firms only? Consider both efficiency and equity in your answer.

Second, it must be possible to identify just what the optimum is. This requires a clear set of objectives concerning sustainability and any conflicts between human and ecological objectives. It also requires a knowledge of just what are the environmental effects of various activities, such as the emission of CO_2 into the atmosphere, and that is something on which scientists disagree.

Finally, there is the problem that many environmental issues are global and not just local or national. Many require concerted action by governments around the world. The history of international agreements on environmental issues, however, is one plagued with difficulties between countries, which seem more concerned with their own national interests. To understand the difficulties of reaching international agreements, we can draw on game theory (see section 7.3, pages 209–13).

Game theory and international agreements

Assume that the world would benefit from a reduction in greenhouse gases and that these benefits would exceed the costs of having to cut back on activities (such as motoring or the generation of electricity) that release such gases into the atmosphere. What would be in the interests of an *individual* country, such as the USA? Its optimum solution would be for *other* countries to cut their emissions, while maintaining its own levels. This approach would yield most of the benefits to the USA and none of the costs. However, when *all* countries refuse to cut emissions, no one gains! This is an example of the *prisoners' dilemma* (see Box 7.5, page 211), and is illustrated in Table 12.1.

Assume that there is an international agreement (as at the Kyoto summit in December 1997) to cut emissions. If all countries stick to the agreement, the outcome is Cell A: a moderate gain to all. What should Congress do? Whatever other countries do (all stick to the agreement, some stick to it, none stick to it), it will be in the USA's interests *not* to stick to it: this is the dominant strategy. Cell D is preferable to Cell A; E is preferable to B; F is preferable to C. But when *all* countries reason like this, the world ends up in Cell F, with no cut in pollution. Cell F is worse for all countries than Cell A.

KI 21
p198

Table 12.1	Outcomes for countries from strategies of pollution reduction

		Other countries' strategy		
		All cut pollution	Some cut pollution	None cut pollution
USA's strategy	Cut pollution	**A** Moderate net gain for all	**B** Small loss for USA; gain for countries not cutting pollution	**C** Large loss for USA; slight gain for other countries
	Don't cut pollution	**D** High gain for USA; small gain for other countries	**E** Fairly high gain for USA; loss for other countries	**F** No gain for any country

Only if countries believe that the other countries will (a) ratify the agreement and (b) stick to it once it is ratified will the agreement be likely to succeed. This requires trust on all sides as well as the ability to monitor the outcomes.

The other major problem area concerns equity. Most countries will feel that they are being asked to do too much and that others are being asked to do too little. Developed countries will want to adopt a grandfathering approach. The starting point with this approach would be current levels of pollution. Every country would then be required to make the same percentage cut. Developing countries, on the other hand, will want the bulk of the cuts, if not all of them, to be made by the developed countries. After all, the rich countries produce much higher levels of pollutants per capita than do the poor countries, and curbing growth in developing countries would have a far more serious impact on levels of absolute poverty.

KI 4
p13

How does an international negotiation 'game' differ from the prisoners' dilemma game?

Section summary

1. One approach to protecting the environment is to use the market. This can be done by extending private property rights. In many cases, however, this approach is impractical. Another approach is to impose charges for using the environment or taxes per unit of output. The problem with these methods is in identifying the appropriate charges or tax rates, since these will vary according to the environmental impact.

2. Another approach is to use command-and-control systems, such as making certain practices illegal or putting limits on discharges. This is a less sophisticated alternative to taxes or charges, but it is safer when the environmental costs of certain actions are unknown. Other alternatives to market-based approaches include voluntary agreements and education.

3. Tradable permits are a mix of command-and-control and market-based systems. Firms are given permits to emit a certain level of pollution and then these can be traded. A firm that can relatively cheaply reduce its pollution below its permitted level can sell this credit to another firm that

finds it more costly to do so. The system is an efficient and administratively cheap way of limiting pollution to a designated level. It can, however, lead to pollution being concentrated in certain areas and can reduce the pressure on firms to find cleaner methods of production.

4. Although governments can make a major contribution to reducing pollution, government action is unlikely to lead to the perfect outcome (however defined). Governments may be more concerned with short-run political considerations and will not have perfect information. What is more, given that many environmental effects spill over national borders, governments may 'play games' internationally to try to reduce the costs to their country of any international action to protect the environment.

12.3 THE ECONOMICS OF TRAFFIC CONGESTION

Traffic congestion is a problem that faces all countries, especially in the large cities and at certain peak times. This problem has grown at an alarming rate as our lives have become increasingly dominated by the motor car. Sitting in a traffic jam is both time-wasting and frustrating.

And it is not only the motorist that suffers. Congested streets make life less pleasant for the pedestrian, and increased traffic leads to increased accidents and significant problems of pollution.

Between 1980 and 2012, road traffic in Great Britain rose by 338 per cent, whereas the length of public roads rose by only 26 per cent (albeit some roads were widened). Most passenger and freight transport is by road. In 2012, just under 90 per cent of passenger kilometres and 68 per cent of freight tonnage kilometres in Great Britain were by road, whereas rail accounted for a mere 9 per cent of passenger traffic and 9 per cent of freight tonnage.

Motoring costs in 2012 amounted to some 11 per cent of household expenditure. Although there has been a focus on high fuel costs in the UK, it is worth noting that spend on motoring fell in the period 2008–12. Since petrol prices have risen, this implies that households have cut back on journeys taken, Table 12.2 shows the growth of passenger car transport relative to other modes, although the rail and air passenger transport proportions have increased in recent years.

But should the government do anything about the problem? Is traffic congestion a price worth paying for the benefits we gain from using cars? Or are there things that can be done to ease the problem?

We will look later in this section at various schemes and at their relative costs and benefits. But first it is necessary to examine the existing system of allocating road space to see the extent to which it meets or fails to meet society's transport objectives. This will enable us to identify the problems that the government must address. (Our discussion will focus on the motor car and passenger transport, but clearly lorries are another major source of congestion, and any comprehensive policy to deal with traffic congestion must also examine freight transport.)

The existing system of allocating road space

The allocation of road space depends on both demand and supply. Demand is by individuals who base their decisions on largely private considerations. Supply, by contrast, is usually by central government or local authorities. Let us examine each in turn.

Demand for road space (by car users)

The demand for road space can be seen largely as a *derived* demand. What people want is not the car journey for its own sake, but to get to their destination. The greater the benefit they gain at their destination, the greater the benefit they gain from using their car to get there.

The demand for road space, like the demand for other goods and services, has a number of determinants. If congestion is to be reduced, it is important to know how responsive demand is to a change in any of these: it is important to consider the various elasticities of demand.

Year	Cars, vans and taxis	Motor cycles	Buses and coaches	Bicycles	Rail	Air (UK)
1952	26.6	3.2	42.2	10.5	17.4	0.1
1962	56.5	3.3	24.5	3.1	13.2	0.4
1972	75.9	0.9	13.9	0.9	7.9	0.5
1982	80.5	2.0	9.5	1.3	6.1	0.6
1992	86.0	0.7	6.3	0.7	5.6	0.7
2002	85.5	0.7	6.0	0.6	6.2	1.1
2012	83.2	0.6	5.4	0.6	9.1	1.1

Table 12.2 Passenger transport in Great Britain: percentage of passenger kilometres

Source: Based on data from Table TSGB0101, *Transport Statistics of Great Britain Database 2013* (Department for Transport, December 2013).

Price. This is the *marginal cost* to the motorist of a journey. It includes petrol, oil, maintenance, depreciation and any toll charges.

 Are there any costs associated with motoring that would not be included as marginal costs? Explain why.

The price elasticity of demand for motoring tends to be relatively low. There can be a substantial rise in the price of petrol, for example, and there will be only a modest fall in traffic.

Recent estimates of the short-run price elasticity of demand for road fuel in industrialised countries typically range from –0.15 to –0.28. Long-run elasticities are somewhat higher, but are still generally inelastic.[1]

The low price elasticity of demand suggests that schemes to tackle traffic congestion that merely involve raising the costs of motoring will have only limited success.

In addition to monetary costs, there are also the time costs of travel. The opportunity cost of sitting in your car is the next best alternative activity you could have been pursuing – relaxing, working, sleeping or whatever. Congestion, by increasing the duration of the journey, increases the opportunity cost.

Income. As incomes rise, car ownership and usage increase substantially. Demand for road space is elastic with respect to income.

Figure 12.4 shows motoring costs as a percentage of UK household expenditure by quintile groups of household income. The higher the household income, the higher the percentage of income spent on motoring. Indeed, the richest quintile's expenditure on motoring is double that

[1] See *Environmentally Related Taxes in OECD Countries: Issues and Strategies* (OECD, 2001), pp. 99–103.

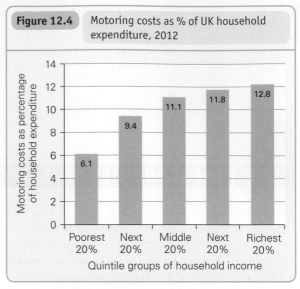

Figure 12.4 Motoring costs as % of UK household expenditure, 2012

Source: Based on data in Table 3.2 in *Family Spending 2012* (National Statistics, 2013)

of the poorest as a percentage of household expenditure. Clearly, the income elasticity of demand is significantly greater than 1.

This is also reflected in international statistics of car ownership. Figure 12.5 shows the growth of car ownership between 1980 and 2012 in selected European countries. As national incomes have risen, so has the proportion of car ownership. People see car transport as a 'luxury good' compared with alternatives such as public transport, walking or cycling. Also, the growth of suburbs has meant that many people travel longer distances to work.

The implication of this is that, if countries continue to experience economic growth, car ownership and usage are likely to increase substantially: a conclusion in line with most forecasts.

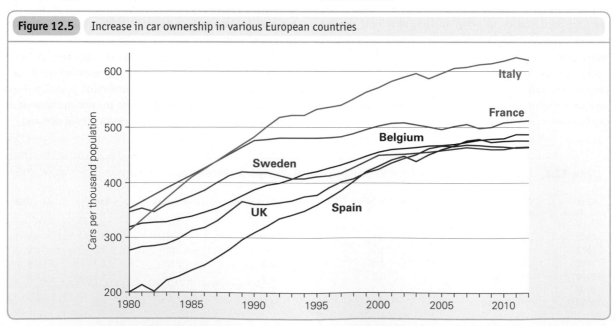

Figure 12.5 Increase in car ownership in various European countries

Source: Based on data in Table 2.6.2 ('Road: Motorisation') *Statistical Pocketbook 2014* (Mobility and Transport DG, European Commission).

Price of substitutes. If bus and train fares came down, people might switch from travelling by car. The cross-price elasticity, however, is likely to be relatively low, given that most people regard these alternatives as a poor substitute for travelling in their own car. Cars are seen as more comfortable and convenient.

The 'price' of substitutes also includes the time taken to travel by these alternatives. The quicker a train journey is compared with a car journey, the lower will be its time cost to the traveller and thus the more people will switch from car to rail.

Price of complements. Demand for road space will depend on the price of cars. The higher the price of cars, the fewer people will own cars and thus the fewer cars there will be on the road.

> *Is the cross-price elasticity of demand for road space with respect to the price of cars likely to be high or low?*

Demand will also depend on the price of complementary services, such as parking. A rise in car parking charges will reduce the demand for car journeys. But here again the cross elasticity is likely to be relatively low. In most cases, the motorist will either pay the higher charge or park elsewhere, such as in side streets.

> *Go through each of the determinants we have identified so far and show how the respective elasticity of demand makes the problem of traffic congestion difficult to tackle.*

Tastes/utility. Another factor explaining the preference of many people for travelling by car is the pleasure they gain from it compared with alternative modes of transport. Car ownership is regarded by many people as highly desirable, and once accustomed to travelling in their own car, most people are highly reluctant to give it up.

One important feature of the demand for road space is that it fluctuates. There will be periods of peak demand, such as during the rush hour or at holiday weekends. At such times, roads can get totally jammed. At other times, however, the same roads may be virtually empty.

Supply of road space

The supply of road space can be examined in two contexts: the short run and the long run.

The short run. In the short run, as we have seen, the supply of road space is constant. When there is no congestion, supply is more than enough to satisfy demand. There is spare road capacity. At times of congestion, there is pressure on this fixed supply. Maximum supply for any given road is reached at the point where there is the maximum flow of vehicles per minute along the road.

The long run. In the long run, the authorities can build new roads or improve existing ones. This will require an assessment of the costs and benefits of such schemes.

Identifying a socially efficient level of road usage (short run)

The existing system of *government* provision of roads and *private* ownership of cars is unlikely to lead to an optimum allocation of road space. So how do we set about identifying just what the social optimum is?

In the short run, the supply of road space is fixed. The question of the short-run optimum allocation of road space, therefore, is one of the optimum *usage* of existing road space. It is a question of *consumption* rather than supply. For this reason we must focus on the road user, rather than on road provision.

A socially efficient level of consumption occurs where the marginal social benefit of consumption equals its marginal social cost ($MSB = MSC$). So what are the marginal social benefits and costs of using a car?

Marginal social benefit of road usage

Marginal social benefit equals marginal private benefit plus externalities. Marginal private benefit is the direct benefit to the car user and is reflected in the demand for car journeys, the determinants of which we examined above. External benefits are few. The one major exception occurs when drivers give lifts to other people.

Marginal social cost of road usage

Marginal social cost equals marginal private cost plus externalities. Marginal private costs to the motorist include the costs of petrol, wear and tear, tolls, etc. They also include the time costs of travel. There may also be substantial external costs. These include the following.

Congestion costs: time. When a person uses a car on a congested road, it will add to the congestion. This will therefore slow down the traffic even more and increase the journey time of other car users.

This is illustrated in Table 12.3 (which uses imaginary figures).

Column (1) shows the number of cars travelling along a given road per minute. Column (2) shows the time taken for each car and thus can be seen as the marginal time cost to a motorist of making this journey. It is thus the *private* marginal time cost. With up to three cars per minute there is no congestion and therefore the traffic flows freely, each car taking 5 minutes to complete the journey. As traffic increases beyond this, however, the road becomes progressively more congested, and thus journey times increase. It is not just the additional cars that are forced to travel more slowly, but *all* the cars on the road. The extra cars thus impose a congestion cost on existing users of the road. By the time seven cars per minute are entering the road, journey time has increased to 16 minutes.

Column (3) shows the sum of the journey times of all the motorists on the road. For example, with six cars on the road, each taking 11 minutes, total journey time for all six is 66 minutes. Column (4) shows the increase in total journey

Table 12.3   Time taken to travel between two points along a given road

Traffic density (cars entering road per minute)	Journey time per car (marginal private time cost: in minutes)	Total journey time for all cars (total time cost: in minutes)	Extra total journey time as traffic increases by one more car (marginal social time cost: in minutes)	Additional time cost imposed on other road users by one more car (marginal external time cost: in minutes)
(1)	(2)	(3) = (1) × (2)	(4) = Δ(3)	(5) = (4) − (2)
1	5	5	5	0
2	5	10	5	0
3	5	15	5	0
4	6	24	9	3
5	8	40	16	8
6	11	66	26	15
7	16	112	46	30

time as one more car enters the road. Thus when the seventh car enters the road, total journey time increases from 66 to 112 minutes: an increase of 46 minutes. This is the additional cost to *all* road users: in other words, the marginal *social* cost. But of these 46 minutes, 16 are the private marginal costs incurred by the extra motorist. Only the remaining 30 minutes are *external* costs imposed on other road users. These external costs are shown in column (5).

 Complete Table 12.3 up to nine cars per minute, assuming that the journey time increases to 24 minutes for the eighth car and 35 minutes for the ninth car.

Time costs can be converted into money costs if we know the value of people's time. If time were valued at 10p per minute, the congestion costs (external costs) imposed by the seventh car would be £3 (i.e. 30 minutes × 10p per minute). Case Study 12.4 in MyEconLab examines the method used in the UK for estimating the value of time (in the context of evaluating new road schemes).

Congestion costs: monetary.   Congestion increases fuel consumption, and the stopping and starting increases the costs of wear and tear. When a motorist adds to congestion, therefore, there will be additional monetary costs imposed on other motorists. A table similar to Table 12.3 could be drawn to illustrate this.

Environmental costs.   When motorists use a road, they reduce the quality of the environment for others. Cars emit fumes and create noise. This is bad enough for pedestrians and other car users, but can be particularly distressing for people living along the road. Driving can cause accidents, a problem that increases as drivers become more impatient as a result of delays. Also, as we saw in section 12.1, exhaust gases contribute to global warming and acid rain.

The socially efficient level of road usage
The point where the marginal social benefit of car use is equal to the marginal social cost can be illustrated on a

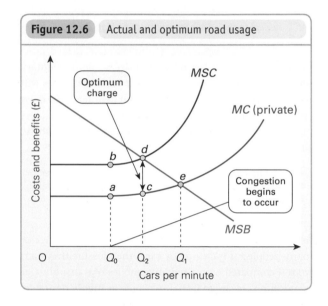

Figure 12.6   Actual and optimum road usage

diagram. In Figure 12.6, costs and benefits are shown on the vertical axis and are measured in money terms. Thus any non-monetary costs or benefits (such as time costs) must be given a monetary value. The horizontal axis measures road usage in terms of cars per minute passing a specified point on the road.

For simplicity it is assumed that there are no external benefits from car use and that therefore marginal private and marginal social benefits are the same. The *MSB* curve is shown as downward sloping. The reason for this is that different road users put a different value on this particular journey. If the marginal (private) cost of making the journey were high, only those for whom the journey had a high marginal benefit would travel along the road. If the marginal cost of making the journey fell, more people would make the journey: people choosing to make the journey at the point at which the marginal cost of using their car had fallen to the level of their marginal benefit. Thus the greater the number of cars in any given time period, the lower the marginal benefit.

KI 26
p315

The marginal (private) cost curve (MC) is likely to be constant up to the level of traffic flow at which congestion begins to occur. This is shown as point a in Figure 12.6. Beyond this point, marginal cost is likely to rise as time costs increase and as fuel consumption rises.

The marginal *social* cost curve (MSC) is drawn above the marginal private cost curve. The vertical difference between the two represents the external costs. Up to point b, external costs are simply the environmental costs. Beyond point b, there are also external congestion costs, since additional road users slow down the journey of *other* road users. These external costs get progressively greater as the volume of traffic increases (as column (5) of Table 12.3 illustrated).

The actual level of traffic flow will be at Q_1, where marginal private costs and benefits are equal (point e). The socially efficient level of traffic flow, however, will be at the lower level of Q_2, where marginal social costs and benefits are equal (point d). In other words, the existing system of allocating road space is likely to lead to an excessive level of road usage.

Identifying a socially optimum level of road space (long run)

In the long run, the supply of road space is not fixed. The authorities must therefore assess what new road schemes (if any) to adopt. This will involve the use of some form of *cost–benefit analysis* (see section 11.4).

The socially efficient level of construction will be where the marginal social benefit from construction is equal to the marginal social cost. This means that schemes should be adopted as long as their marginal social benefit exceeds their marginal social cost.

But how are these costs and benefits assessed in practice? Case Study 12.4 in MyEconLab examines the procedure used in the UK.

Section summary

1. Increased car ownership and car usage have led to a growing problem of traffic congestion.

2. The allocation of road space depends on demand and supply. Demand depends on the price to motorists of using their cars, incomes, the cost of alternative means of transport, the price of cars and complementary services (such as parking), and the comfort and convenience of car transport. The price and cross-price elasticities of demand for car usage tend to be low: many people are unwilling to switch to alternative modes of transport. The income elasticity, on the other hand, is high. The demand for cars and car usage grows rapidly as incomes grow.

3. The short-run supply of road space is fixed. The long-run supply depends on government road construction programmes.

4. The existing system of government provision of roads and private ownership of cars is unlikely to lead to the optimum allocation of road space.

5. In the short run, with road space fixed, allocation depends on the private decisions of motorists. The problem is that motorists create two types of external cost: pollution costs and congestion costs. Thus $MSC \times MC$. Because of these externalities, the actual use of road space (where $MB = MC$) is likely to be greater than the optimum (where $MSB = MSC$).

6. In the long run, the socially efficient amount of road space will be where $LRMSB = LRMSC$. New road schemes should be adopted as long as their $LRMSB > LRMSC$. Governments must therefore conduct some form of cost–benefit analysis in order to estimate these costs and benefits.

12.4   URBAN TRANSPORT POLICIES

We now turn to look at different solutions to traffic congestion. These can be grouped into three broad types: direct provision, regulation and legislation, and changing market signals.

Direct provision (supply-side solutions)

The road solution
One obvious solution to traffic congestion is to build more roads. There are serious problems, however, with this approach.

The objective of equity. The first problem concerns *equity*. After all, social efficiency is not the only possible economic objective. For example, when an urban motorway is built, those living beside it will suffer from noise and fumes. Motorway users gain, but the local residents lose. The question is whether this is fair.

The more the government tries to appeal to the car user by building more and better roads, the fewer will be the people who use public transport, and thus the more will public transport decline. Those without cars lose, and these tend to be from the most vulnerable groups – the poor, elderly and disabled people, and children.

Building more roads may lead to a *potential* Pareto improvement: in other words, if the gainers had fully to compensate the losers (e.g. through taxes or tolls), they would still have a net gain. The problem is that such compensation is rarely if ever paid. There is thus no actual Pareto improvement.

Congestion may not be solved. Increasing the amount of road space may encourage more people to use cars.

A good example is the London orbital motorway, the M25. In planning the motorway, not only did the government underestimate the general rate of traffic growth, but it also underestimated the direct effect it would have in encouraging people to use the motorway rather than using some alternative route, or some alternative means of transport, or even not making the journey at all. It also under-estimated the effect it would have in encouraging people to live further from their place of work and to commute along the motorway. The result is that there is now serious congestion on the motorway and many sections have been widened from the original dual three-lane model to dual four, five and, in some parts, six lanes.

Thus new roads may simply generate extra traffic, with little overall effect on congestion in the long term.

The environmental impact of new roads. New roads lead to the loss of agricultural land, the destruction of many natural habitats, noise, the splitting of communities and disruption to local residents. To the extent that they encourage a growth in traffic, they add to atmospheric pollution and a depletion of oil reserves. It is thus important to take account of these costs when assessing new road schemes. The problem, however, is that these environmental costs are frequently ignored, or only considered as an after-thought and not taken seriously. Part of the problem is that they are difficult to assess, and part is that there is often a strong road lobby which persuades politicians to ignore or play down environmental considerations.

Government or local authority provision of public transport

An alternative supply-side solution is to increase the provision of public transport. If, for example, a local authority ran a local bus service and decided to invest in additional buses, open up new routes and operate a low-fare policy, these services might encourage people to switch from using their cars.

To be effective, this would have to be an attractive alternative. Many people would switch only if the buses were frequent, cheap, comfortable and reliable, and if there were enough routes to take people close to where they wanted to go.

? *What other types of transport could be directly provided by the government or a local authority?*

A policy that has proved popular with many local authorities is to adopt park-and-ride schemes. Here the authority provides out-of-town parking and bus services from the car park to the town centre. Sometimes these are provided at low cost to the motorist. These schemes are likely to be most effective when used in combination with charges for private cars entering the inner city.

Regulation and legislation

An alternative strategy is to restrict car use by various forms of regulation and legislation.

Restricting car access

One approach involves reducing car access to areas that are subject to high levels of congestion. The following measures are widely used: bus and cycle lanes, 'high occupancy vehicle lanes' (confined to cars with two or more occupants), pedestrian-only areas and no entry to side streets from main roads.

There is, however, a serious problem with these measures. They tend not to solve the problem of congestion, but merely to divert it. Bus lanes tend to make the car lanes more congested; no entry to side streets tends to make the main roads more congested; and pedestrian-only areas often make the roads around these areas more congested, with drivers adopting side streets as 'rat-runs'.

Parking restrictions

An alternative to restricting road access is to restrict parking. If cars are not allowed to park along congested streets, this will improve the traffic flow. Also, if parking is difficult, this will discourage people from using their cars to come into city centres.

Apart from being unpopular with people who want to park, there are some serious drawbacks with parking restrictions:

- People may well 'park in orbit', driving round and round looking for a parking space, and in the meantime adding to congestion.
- People may park illegally. This may add to rather than reduce congestion, and may create a safety hazard.
- People may feel forced to park down side streets in residential areas, thereby causing a nuisance for residents.

Changing market signals

The solution favoured by many economists is to use the price mechanism. As we have seen, one of the causes of traffic congestion is that road users do not pay the full marginal social costs of using the roads. If they could be forced to do so, a social optimum usage of road space could be achieved.

In Figure 12.6 (page 372) this would involve imposing a charge on motorists of $d - c$. By 'internalising' the congestion and environmental externalities in this way, traffic flow will be reduced to the social optimum of Q_2.

So how can these external costs be charged to the motorist? There are several possible ways.

Extending existing taxes

Three major types of tax are levied on the motorist: fuel tax, taxes on new cars and car licences. Could increasing these taxes lead to the optimum level of road use being achieved?

Increasing the rates of new car tax and car licences may have *some* effect on reducing the total level of car ownership,

| BOX 12.6 | RESTRICTING CAR ACCESS TO ATHENS | CASE STUDIES AND APPLICATIONS |

A solution to local atmospheric pollution?

Athens lies in a bowl-shaped valley. When there are light winds, a humid atmosphere and sunshine, the levels of atmospheric pollution can soar to dangerous heights. The major cause of this chemical smog (the '*néfos*') is the emission of exhaust fumes.

The solution that the Greeks[1] have adopted is one of restricting the use of vehicles in the city. The restrictions are of two levels of severity. The more severe ones apply on Mondays to Fridays when there is a chemical smog emergency, typically two or three times a month; the less severe ones apply on all other Mondays to Fridays.

The city is divided into an inner zone and an outer zone. The levels of various pollutants (such as nitrogen dioxide and ozone) are constantly monitored by the city authorities, and when they reach certain critical levels a smog emergency is declared on radio, on television and in the press.

During an emergency, all cars and half the taxis are banned from use in the inner zone. On even-numbered dates, only taxis with an even-numbered registration can operate in the inner zone; on odd-numbered dates, only those with an odd-numbered registration can operate. In the outer zone, all taxis can operate, with the odd/even number plate system applying to cars. The police check on cars entering the zones and turn away those not allowed. The drivers of cars being used illegally in the zones are fined.

When an emergency is not in force, restrictions apply only to the inner zone. The even-numbered/odd-numbered registration restrictions apply to cars, but not to taxis or to cars with foreign number plates.

The measures are successful in one respect: very few cars are driven illegally in the zones (and it is not legal to have two number plates for the same car). But many commuters have resorted to owning two cars: one with an even-numbered plate and one with an odd-numbered one. The authorities even help in this by allowing people to request an even- or odd-numbered registration! Another problem with this is that people often buy an old, cheap second car, which is likely to have higher emissions. There is no incentive to buy cleaner cars with catalysts or particle filters.

A much more effective solution to traffic pollution is to have low-emission zones, where the most polluting vehicles are banned from entering or are charged to do so. According to Lucy Sadler, who runs the Low Emission Zones in Europe website:[2]

> Certainly, in terms of comparison between low emission zones and odd-and-even number plate schemes, it's a no-brainer. There is lots of good evidence saying low emission zones have a good impact on air quality and health. That's robust and well researched.[3]

In recent years, stimulated by hosting the Olympics in 2004, public transport has improved in Athens, with a large expansion of the metro system. Only with a more integrated transport system and tougher controls on emissions can Athens' serious pollution be significantly reduced.

Compare the relative advantages and disadvantages of the odd–even number plate system with those of charging people to come into the zones. Consider both the efficiency and equity aspects of the policy.

[1] Similar systems have been adopted in Beijing and Mexico City.
[2] www.lowemissionzones.eu/
[3] Karl Mathiesen, 'Why licence plate bans don't cut smog', *Guardian*, 20 March 2014.

---

but will probably have little effect on car use. The problem is that these taxes do not increase the *marginal* cost of car use and so do not discourage you from using your car.

Unlike the other two, fuel taxes are a marginal cost of car use. The more you use your car, the more fuel you use and the more fuel tax you pay. They are also mildly related to the level of congestion, since fuel consumption tends to increase as congestion increases. Nevertheless, they are not ideal. The problem is that *all* motorists would pay an increase in fuel tax, even those travelling on uncongested roads. To have a significant effect on congestion, there would have to be a very large increase in fuel taxes and this would be very unfair on those who are not causing congestion, especially those who have to travel long distances. Also, as the fuel protests in recent years have shown, increasing fuel taxes could make the government very unpopular.

Would a tax on car tyres be a good way of restricting car usage?

Introducing new taxes

An alternative to extending existing taxes is to introduce new ones. One that has received much attention in recent times has been the taxing of car parking spaces, particularly those provided by businesses for their employees. The problem with taxing car parking, however, is similar to that of restricting car parking places: people may simply try to park on neighbouring streets (a negative externality imposed on residents), and may spend longer driving around trying to find a space (thereby adding to congestion in the process).

Road pricing

Taxes are inevitably an indirect means of tackling congestion. Charging people for using roads, on the other hand, where the size of the charge reflects the marginal social cost, is a direct means of achieving an efficient use of road space. The higher the congestion, the higher should be the charge. This would encourage people not only to look for alternative means of transport, but also to travel, wherever possible, at off-peak times.

TC 11
p320

TC 2
p25

Variable tolls. Tolls are used in many countries, and could be adapted to reflect marginal social costs.

One obvious problem, however, is that, even with automatic tolls, there can be considerable tailbacks at peak times. Another problem is that they may simply encourage people to use minor roads into cities, thereby causing congestion on these roads. Cities have networks of streets and thus in most cases it is not difficult to avoid the tolls. Finally, if the tolls are charged to people *entering* the city, they will not affect *local* commuters. But it is these short-distance commuters *within* the city who are most likely to be able to find some alternative means of transport and who thus could make a substantial contribution to reducing congestion.

Area charges. One simple and practical means of charging people to use congested streets is the area charge. People would have to pay (normally by the day) for using their car in a city centre. Earlier versions of this scheme involved people having to purchase and display a ticket on their car, rather like a 'pay-and-display' parking system.

More recently, electronic versions have been developed. The London Congestion Charge is an example. Car drivers must pay a standard charge of £10 per day to enter the inner London area (or 'congestion zone') any time between 7.00 a.m. and 6.00 p.m., Monday to Friday. Payment can be made by various means, including post, online, telephone, mobile phone SMS text message and at various shops and petrol stations. Owners can pay in advance, within 24 hours for an extra £2, or can register for auto-pay. In this case they are billed for all charges and receive a £1 per day discount. Cars entering the congestion zone have their number plate recorded by camera and a computer check then leads to a penalty charge of £130 being sent to those who have not paid.

The London congestion charging system has reduced traffic in the zone by nearly 20 per cent and has significantly increased the rate of traffic flow. The charge is not a marginal one, however, in the sense that it does not vary with the degree of congestion or the amount of time spent or distance travelled by a motorist within the zone. This is an intrinsic problem of area charges. Nevertheless, their simplicity makes the system easy to understand and relatively cheap to operate. Nor is the charge designed to address pollution directly, although the original scheme did exempt electric and hybrid cars and those fuelled by natural gas or LPG.

In 2007 proposals were drawn up for a 'CO_2 charge' to be applied to vehicles in London. Those that emitted the highest levels of CO_2 would have faced a daily charge of £25. However, the plans were withdrawn by the incoming mayor, Boris Johnson, following his election in May 2008. Environmental campaigners were outspoken in their criticisms, suggesting that the mayor was putting business interests above the green agenda.

Despite this, there does seem to be an ongoing commitment to combining the congestion and emissions approaches within the charge. The alternative fuel discount has been replaced by a 'greener vehicle discount' exempting cars that emit 100 g/km of CO_2 or less. This approach recognises that new technologies are likely to result in continual improvements in emissions, even of cars fuelled by petrol. The scheme is also reviewed regularly, to ensure that both the congestion and environmental benefits are being maintained.

Variable electronic road pricing. The scheme most favoured by many economists and traffic planners is that of variable electronic road pricing. It is the approach that can most directly relate the price that the motorist is charged to the specific level of marginal social cost. The greater the congestion, the greater the charge imposed on the motorist. Ideally, the charge would be equal to the marginal congestion cost plus any marginal environmental costs additional to those created on non-charged roads.

Various systems have been adopted in various parts of the world, or are under consideration. One involves devices in the road which record the number plates of cars as they pass. Alternatively, cars may be required to be fitted with sensors. Charges are registered to cars on a central computer and owners are billed. Several cities around the world, including Barcelona, Dallas, Orlando, Lisbon, Oklahoma City and Oslo, are already operating such schemes.

Another system involves having a device installed in the car into which a 'smart card' is inserted. Beacons or overhead gantries automatically charge the cards at times of congestion. Such a system was introduced in 1997 on Stockholm's ring road, and in 1998 in Singapore (see Box 12.7).

With both these systems, the rate can easily be varied electronically according to the level of congestion (and pollution). The rates could be in bands and the current bands displayed by the roadside and/or broadcast on local radio so that motorists knew what they were being charged.

The most sophisticated scheme would involve equipping all vehicles with a receiver. Their position is located by satellites, which then send this information to a dashboard unit, which deducts charges according to location, distance travelled, time of day and type of vehicle. The charges can operate through either smart cards or central computerised billing. It is likely that such schemes would initially be confined to lorries.

Despite the enthusiasm for such schemes amongst economists, there are nevertheless various problems associated with them:

- Estimates of the level of external costs are difficult to make.
- Motorists have to be informed in advance what the charges will be, so that they can plan the timing of their journeys.
- There may be political resistance. Politicians may therefore be reluctant to introduce road pricing for fear of losing popular support.
- If demand is relatively inelastic, the charges might have to be very high to have a significant effect on congestion.

- The costs of installing road-pricing equipment could be very high.
- If road pricing were introduced only in certain areas, shoppers and businesses would tend to move to areas without the charge.
- A new industry in electronic evasion may spring up!

Subsidising alternative means of transport

An alternative to charging for the use of cars is to subsidise the price of alternatives, such as buses and trains. But cheaper fares alone may not be enough. The government may also have to invest directly in or subsidise an *improved* public transport service: more frequent services, more routes, more comfortable buses and trains.

Subsidising public transport need not be seen as an alternative to road pricing: it can be seen as complementary. If road pricing is to persuade people not to travel by car, the alternatives must be attractive. Unless public transport is seen by the traveller as a close substitute for cars, the elasticity of demand for car use is likely to remain low.

Part of an integrated transport policy

Singapore has some 230 vehicles per kilometre of road (this compares with 271 in Hong Kong, 222 in Japan, 77 in the UK, 75 in Germany and 37 in the USA). The average car in Singapore is driven some 19 000 kilometres per year, but with low car ownership (see below), this translates into a relatively low figure for kilometres travelled by car per person. Part of the reason is that Singapore has an integrated transport policy. This includes the following:

- A 153-kilometre-long mass rail transit (MRT) system with five main lines, 106 stations and subsidised fares. Trains are comfortable, clean and frequent. Stations are air-conditioned.
- A programme of building new estates near MRT stations.
- Cheap, frequent buses, serving all parts of the island.
- A modest expansion of expressways.

But it is in respect to road usage that the Singaporean authorities have been most innovative.

Area licences

The first innovation came in 1975. The city centre was made a restricted zone. Motorists who wished to enter this zone had to buy a ticket (an 'area licence') at any one of 33 entry points. Police were stationed at these entry points to check that cars had paid and displayed.

Then in 1990 a quota system for new cars was established. This makes cars in Singapore among the most expensive in the world. The government decides the total number of cars that the country should have in each of a number of categories, and issues just enough licences twice a month to maintain that total. These licences, or 'Certificates of Entitlement', are for 10 years and are offered at an online auction, with people being able to specify a maximum price (similar to the eBay system). Prices rise in the electronic bidding process until demand has been reduced to the number of certificates on offer. Their market price typically varies from around £30 000 to £40 000.

Partly as a result of the quota system, there are only 114 private cars per 1000 population. As you can see from Figure 12.5, this is only a small fraction of the figure for European countries.

A problem with the licences is that they are a once-and-for-all payment, which does not vary with the amount that people use their car. In other words, the marginal cost (for additional miles driven) is zero. There is therefore no disincentive for people to use their car as much as they want.

A similar problem occurs with import duties on cars, which are 150 per cent of the car's market value – much higher than in most other countries. Although these discourage the purchase of cars, they do not discourage their use once purchased.

Electronic road pricing

With traffic congestion steadily worsening, it was recognised that something more had to be done. The decision was taken to introduce electronic road pricing (ERP). This alternative would not only save on police labour costs, but enable charge rates to be varied according to levels of congestion, times of the day and locality.

Since 1998 all vehicles in Singapore have been fitted with an in-vehicle unit (IU). Every journey made requires the driver to insert a smart card containing pre-paid units into the IU. On specified roads, overhead gantries read the IU and deduct the appropriate charge from the card. If a car does not have sufficient funds on its smart card, the car's details are relayed to a control centre and a fine is imposed. The system has the benefit of operating on three-lane highways and does not require traffic to slow down.

The ERP system operates on roads subject to congestion and charges can vary every 5 or 20 minutes according to predicted traffic flows. Rates are published in advance but are reviewed every three months. The system is thus very flexible to allow traffic to be kept at the desired level.

The system was expensive to set up, however. Cheaper schemes have been adopted elsewhere, for example in Norway and parts of the USA. These operate by funnelling traffic into a single lane in order to register the car, but they have the disadvantage of slowing the traffic down.

One message is clear from the Singapore solution. Road pricing alone may not be enough. Unless there are fast, comfortable and affordable public transport alternatives, the demand for cars will be highly price inelastic.

 Explain how, by varying the charge debited from the smart card according to the time of day or level of congestion, a socially optimal level of road use can be achieved.

BOX 12.8   THE ECONOMY AND THE ENVIRONMENT

Green growth: a way forward

Recessions are generally bad news: output and jobs are lost, and both consumers and businesses face uncertainty. Yet, in the short run, a slump may have positive environmental effects. Between 2007 and 2008 road traffic fell by 0.8 per cent, with further falls of 0.9 and 1.6 per cent in 2009 and 2010 respectively. Probable causes were lower incomes, less freight being transported and fewer people driving to work. Non-renewable resources are depleted more slowly in a downturn, as households reduce consumption, increase recycling and reuse items that they might have discarded in a boom.

In other ways, however, a recession may lead to faster environmental degradation. Businesses are less likely to invest in clean technologies; consumers may put off replacing vehicles with more energy-efficient models; governments may choose to divert resources from environmental initiatives to job creation schemes.

Economic growth and the green agenda

Think back to the first chapter of this book, where we identified the fundamental economic problem of scarcity. We demonstrated how economic growth can provide a solution, allowing us to produce more and so satisfy more of our wants and needs. (We consider economic growth in more detail in Chapters 14 and 22.)

In general economists – and politicians – have presented economic growth as a 'good thing', resulting in higher levels of welfare and giving society the opportunity to redistribute further to reduce poverty. However, there has been less wholehearted support from the green lobby. Economic growth has been portrayed as fundamentally harmful with a widespread acceptance of the principle that there is a trade-off between growth and degradation of the environment.

The idea that growth may not be beneficial is not a new one. In 1848, John Stuart Mill wrote, 'Towards what ultimate point is society tending by its industrial progress? When the progress ceases, in what condition are we to expect that it will leave mankind?' In 1973 an influential collection of essays by E. F. Schumacher called 'Small is Beautiful' was published (see Case Study 1.1 in MyEconLab). This work led the debate on growth and its impact on well-being – a debate that continues today.

If you spend your time thinking that the most important objective of public policy is to get growth up from 1.9 per cent to 2 per cent and even better 2.1 per cent we're pursuing a sort of false god there. We're pursuing it first of all because, if we accept that, we will do things to the climate that will be harmful, but also because all the evidence shows that beyond the sort of standard of living which Britain has

---

This problem is recognised by the UK government, which encourages local authorities to use various forms of road pricing and charges on businesses for employee car parking spaces on condition that the revenues generated are ploughed back into improved public transport. All local authorities have to produce five-year Local Transport Plans covering all forms of transport. These include targets for traffic reduction and increases in the use of public transport.

Subsidising public transport can also be justified on grounds of equity, since it is used most by low-incomes groups.

 Which is preferable: general subsidies for public transport, or cheap fare policies for specific groups (such as children, students and pensioners)?

Conclusions

It is unlikely that any one policy can provide the complete solution. Certain policies or mixes of policies are better suited to some situations than others. It is important for governments to learn from experiences both within their own country and in others, in order to find the optimum solution to each specific problem.

Section summary

1. There are various types of solution to traffic congestion. These include direct provision by the government or local authorities (of additional road space or better public transport); regulation and legislation (such as restricting car access – by the use of bus and cycle lanes, or pedestrian-only areas – and various forms of parking restrictions); changing market signals (by the use of taxes, by road pricing and by subsidising alternative means of transport).

2. Problems associated with building additional roads include the decline of public transport, attracting additional traffic onto the roads, and environmental costs.

3. The main problem with restricting car access is that it tends merely to divert congestion elsewhere. The main problem with parking restrictions is that they may actually increase congestion.

4. Increasing taxes is effective in reducing congestion only if it increases the marginal cost of motoring. Even when it

does, as in the case of additional fuel tax, the additional cost is only indirectly related to congestion costs, since it applies to all motorists and not just those causing congestion.

5. Road pricing is the preferred solution of many economists. By the use of electronic devices, motorists can be charged whenever they add to congestion. This should encourage less essential road users to travel at off-peak times or to use alternative modes of transport, while those who gain a high utility from car transport can still use their cars, but at a price. Variable tolls and area charges are alternative forms of congestion pricing, but are generally less effective than the use of variable electronic road pricing.

6. If road pricing is to be effective, there must be attractive substitutes available. A comprehensive policy, therefore, should include subsidising efficient public transport. The revenues required for this could be obtained from road pricing.

now achieved, extra growth does not automatically translate into human welfare and happiness. (Lord Turner, Previously Chair of the UK Financial Services Authority)[2]

In 2010 the New Economics Foundation published a report entitled 'Growth isn't possible: why we need a new economic direction'. In this they argued that economic growth is constrained by the finite capacity of the Earth's resources.

However, given the levels of poverty seen across the world, a reduced commitment to growth must imply continuing inequality or an acceptance that industrialised countries will experience lower standards of living. This is unthinkable to many, who instead focus on achieving growth in a sustainable manner, one that allows for increased welfare while ensuring the long-term health of the planet. Much of the OECD's work in the environmental arena concentrates on this aspect – hardly surprising, given its remit to support global development. In 2012 it highlighted three issues which governments should consider in formulating growth policies:

- Putting a price on carbon emissions and other pollution.
- Supporting green innovation and ensuring that this spreads across national borders.
- Fostering private investment in capital that will support growth with cleaner technologies.

The OECD acknowledges that various governments across the world are making efforts to promote greener development. The European Union's Growth Strategy for 2020, Korea's National Strategy and five-year plan for Green Growth, the green development focus of China's 12th Five-year Plan and South Africa's New Growth Path and Green Economy Accord are just a few examples.

1. The UK government introduced a 'scrappage scheme' in 2009 to run for one year. Under this, motorists were given a £2000 grant towards the cost of a new car. To qualify they had to trade in a car that was more than 10 years old, which would then be scrapped. Explain how this scheme might be justified in the middle of a recession. Should there have been any restrictions on the new cars eligible for the grant?
2. Growth is largely seen as being associated with economic efficiency. Explain how it may also be an important issue when considering equity.
3. Under what circumstances will private investment be attracted to 'green' projects? Is there a role for government here?

[1] *Transport Statistics Great Britain* (Department for Transport, 2013).
[2] BBC Radio 4 interview, 1 January 2010.

END OF CHAPTER QUESTIONS

1. Assume that as traffic density increases along a given stretch of road, there comes a point when traffic begins to slow down. The following table gives the times taken for a car to travel the stretch of road (in minutes) according to the number of cars entering the road per minute.

Cars entering the road	5	6	7	8	9	10	11
Journey time	10	10	11	13	16	22	30

(a) Copy out the table and add the following rows: (i) total journey time for all cars; (ii) extra journey time as traffic increases by one more car (marginal social time cost); (iii) additional time cost imposed on other road users for each additional car entering the road (marginal external time cost). (See Table 12.3.)

(b) Assume that time is valued at 10p per minute. On a graph, plot the marginal private time cost (journey time) and the marginal social time cost.

(c) Assume that electronic road pricing is introduced. What charge should be levied when traffic density reaches (i) 6 cars per minute; (ii) 8 cars per minute; (iii) 11 cars per minute?

(d) What additional information would you need in order to work out the socially efficient traffic density on this particular stretch of road?

2. Assume that there are several chemical firms in an industry, each one producing different levels of an effluent, whose damage to the environment depends on the location of the firm. Compare the relative merits of using green taxes, tradable permits and controls as means of achieving the socially optimum levels of effluent from these firms.

3. Make out a case from a deep green perspective for rejecting the 'social efficiency' approach to the environment.

4. Why might efforts to address the issue of global warming be hampered by a lack of understanding of probability amongst the general public?

5. In 2007, China overtook the USA as the world's largest emitter of CO_2. Yet USA per capita emissions are three times that of China. What issues arise from this in the formulation of a global policy to reduce CO_2 emissions?

6. Make out a case for adopting a policy of individual tradable carbon permits, allocated to all citizens within a country. Could such a policy be extended globally?

7. Compare the relative merits of increased road fuel taxes, electronic road pricing and tolls as means of reducing urban traffic congestion. Why is the price inelasticity of demand for private car transport a problem here, whichever of the three policies is adopted? What could be done to increase the price elasticity of demand?

8. Why is the price inelasticity of demand for private car transport a problem when formulating a policy for the reduction of traffic congestion? What could be done to

change the price elasticity of demand in a desirable direction?

9. How would you set about measuring the external costs of road transport?

10. Many London Councils now have residents' street parking permits, with charges that vary according to the carbon emissions of the registered vehicle. Explain the thinking behind this policy.

11. Since 2008, the UK government has provided free off-peak bus travel for the over-60s in England and Wales. What do you think the impact of this policy has been on car usage? Is there a case for extending the policy to (a) bus travel for pensioners at all times of the day, as is the case in Scotland; (b) bus travel for all?

12. In 2010 the number of air passengers using UK airports fell by 3.4 per cent compared with 2009. In 2013, passengers were 3.5 per cent up compared with 2012. Can we deduce anything about people's attitude to the environment and their behaviour from this data?

Online resources

Additional case studies in MyEconLab

12.1 **Perverse subsidies.** An examination of the use of subsidies around the world that are harmful to the environment.

12.2 **Selling the environment.** This looks at the proposals made at international climate conferences to use market-based solutions to global warming.

12.3 **Environmental auditing.** Are businesses becoming greener? A growing number of firms are subjecting themselves to an 'environmental audit' to judge just how 'green' they are.

12.4 **Evaluating new road schemes.** The system used in the UK of assessing the costs and benefits of proposed new roads.

Websites relevant to this chapter

See sites listed at the end of Chapter 13 on page 398.

MyEconLab

This book can be supported by MyEconLab, which contains a range of additional resources, including an online homework and tutorial system designed to test and build your understanding.

You need both an access card and a course ID to access MyEconLab:

1. Is your lecturer using MyEconLab? Ask your lecturer for your course ID.

2. Has an access card been included with the book at a reduced cost? Check the inside back cover of the book.

3. If you have a course ID but no access card, go to: http://www.myeconlab.com/ to buy access to this interactive study programme.

Government Policy towards Business

CHAPTER MAP

13.1 Competition policy	**382**
Competition, monopoly and the public interest	382
The targets of competition policy	382
Competition policy in the European Union	383
UK competition policy	385
Assessment of competition policy	387
13.2 Privatisation and regulation	**389**
Nationalisation and privatisation	389
How desirable is privatisation?	389
Regulation: identifying the short-run optimum price and output	391
Regulation: identifying the long-run optimum price and output	392
Regulation in the UK	392
Increasing competition in the privatised industries	396

In this chapter we continue our examination of government policy to tackle market imperfections. The focus here is on the problem of market power. We examine various policies the government or its agencies can use to prevent firms abusing a monopolistic or oligopolistic position.

In section 13.1 we examine 'competition policy'. We will see that the targets of such policy include the abuse of monopoly power, the problem of oligopolistic collusion, and mergers that will result in the firm having a dominant position in the market.

Then, in section 13.2, we look at privatisation and the extent to which privatised industries should be regulated to prevent them abusing their market power. We also consider whether it is possible to introduce enough competition into these industries to make regulation unnecessary.

The relationship between government and business is always likely to be complex. Governments face the twin pressures of having to ensure consumer protection while needing a dynamic and profitable business environment that will ensure high levels of employment, output and growth. In this chapter we see the conflicts that can arise as a consequence.

13.1 COMPETITION POLICY

Competition, monopoly and the public interest

Most markets in the real world are imperfect, with firms having varying degrees of market power. But will this power be against the public interest? This question has been addressed by successive governments in framing legislation to deal with monopolies and oligopolies.

It might be thought that market power is always 'a bad thing', certainly as far as the consumer is concerned. After all, it enables firms to make supernormal profits, which implies they may be 'exploiting' the consumer. The greater the firm's power, the higher will prices be relative to the costs of production. Also, a lack of competition removes the incentive to become more efficient.

But market power is not necessarily a bad thing. Firms may choose not to fully exploit their position of power – perhaps thinking that very high profits would encourage other firms to overcome entry barriers, or perhaps because they are not aggressive profit maximisers. Even if they do make large supernormal profits, they may still charge a lower price than more competitive sectors of the industry because of their economies of scale. Finally, they may use profits for research and development and for capital investment. The consumer might then benefit from new or improved products at lower prices.

Competition policy could ban various structures. For example, there could be restrictions on mergers leading to market share of more than a certain amount. Most countries, however, focus on whether the practices of particular monopolists or oligopolists are anti-competitive. Some practices may be made illegal, such as price fixing by oligopolists; others may be assessed on a case-by-case basis. Such an approach does not presume that the existence of power is against the public interest, but rather that certain uses of that power may be.

 Try to formulate a definition of 'the public interest'.

The targets of competition policy

There are three possible targets of competition policy.

Abuse of the existing power of monopolies and oligopolies: monopoly policy

Monopoly policy seeks to prevent firms from abusing their economic power. Although it is referred to as 'monopoly' policy, it also applies to large oligopolists acting on their own. The most usual approach has been to weigh up the gains and losses to the public of individual firms' behaviour.

As we saw in Figure 6.10 (on page 184), faced with the same cost curves as an industry under perfect competition, a monopoly will charge a higher price, produce a lower output and make a larger profit. On the other hand, a monopolist may achieve substantial economies of scale, with lower costs and a price below the competitive price (see Figure 6.11 on page 186). It may retain profits for investment and research and development (R&D). This may result in better products and/or lower prices.

Thus the government (or regulatory authority, if separate from the government) has to work out whether a reduction in price would lower R&D and other investment, and whether the consumer would gain in the long run.

The growth of power through mergers and acquisitions: merger policy

The aim of merger policy is to have oversight of prospective mergers. The authorities will weigh up gains and losses to the public and the impact on the broader economy, and prevent or modify those that are considered to be against the public interest.

On the plus side, the merged firms may be able to rationalise and reduce costs. Horizontal mergers in particular may allow economies of scale to be gained, with production on fewer sites and more intensive utilisation of capital and labour. Also, a more efficient use may be made of warehousing and transport fleets, with distribution in greater bulk.

There may also be potential benefits with vertical mergers. It may be possible to concentrate various stages in the production process on one site, with consequent savings in transport and handling costs.

There are also cost savings that apply to all types of merger: horizontal, vertical and conglomerate. Central services such as finance and human resources (HR) can be merged and rationalised. Greater financial strength may allow the merged firm to drive down the prices charged by its suppliers and the combined profits may allow larger-scale investment and R&D.

However, mergers inevitably lead to a greater concentration of economic power, which could be used against the consumer's interests. This is particularly true of horizontal mergers, which will result in fewer firms and reduced consumer choice. But even conglomerate mergers can lead to anti-competitive activities. A conglomerate can use profits gained in one market where it already has monopoly power to *cross-subsidise* prices in a competitive market, thereby driving out competitors.

 What are the possible disadvantages of vertical mergers?

Definition

Cross-subsidise To use profits in one market to subsidise prices in another.

TC 5
p54

In deciding how tough to be with mergers, the government must consider how this will affect firms' behaviour. If the government adopts a liberal policy, this may actually encourage firms to be more efficient. If the managers of a firm are aware that it could be taken over, there is a greater incentive to ensure that the firm is strong and that it is perceived by shareholders to be more profitable than it would be under alternative ownership. This competition for corporate control (see page 186) may lower costs and benefit the consumer. It may, however, make firms keener to exploit any monopoly power, enabling the takeover of other firms, or persuading shareholders not to vote for being taken over.

Government policy towards corporate control will need to ensure that potential mergers encourage competition rather than reduce it.

Oligopolistic collusion: restrictive practice policy

In most countries, the approach towards oligopolistic collusion, known as **restrictive practices**, tends to be tougher. The firms are combining to exploit their joint power to make bigger profits. They could do this by working together to keep out new entrants; or they could agree to keep prices high and/or restrict output; or they could divide up the market between them, agreeing not to 'poach' on each other's territory. For example, two or more supermarket chains could agree to open only one supermarket in each district.

Banning formal cartels is easy. Preventing tacit collusion is another matter. It may be very difficult to prove that firms are making informal agreements behind closed doors.

Competition policy in the European Union

Relevant EU legislation is contained in Articles 101 and 102 of the 2009 Treaty of the Functioning of the European Union and in additional regulations covering mergers, which came into force in 1990 and were amended in 2004. Further minor amendments have been put in place since then, often focused on specific market regulation.

Article 101 is concerned with restrictive practices and Article 102 with the abuse of market power. The articles mainly concern firms trading between EU members and do not cover monopolies or oligopolies operating solely within a member country. The policy is implemented by the European Commission. If any firm appears to be breaking the provisions of either article, the Commission can refer it to the European Court of Justice.

EU restrictive practices policy

Article 101 covers agreements between firms, joint decisions, and concerted practices that prevent, restrict or distort competition. In other words, it covers all types of oligopolistic collusion that are against the interests of consumers.

Article 101 is designed to prevent collusive behaviour, not oligopolistic structures (i.e. the simple existence of

co-operation between firms). If the European Commission finds that firms are committing anti-competitive practices, they will be banned from doing so and possibly fined (up to 10 per cent of annual turnover), although firms do have the right of appeal to the European Court of Justice.

Practices considered anti-competitive include firms colluding to do any of the following:

- Fix prices (i.e. above competitive levels).
- Limit production, markets, technical development or investment.
- Share out markets or sources of supply.
- Charge discriminatory prices or operate discriminatory trading conditions, such as to benefit the colluding parties and disadvantage others.
- Make other firms that sign contracts with any of the colluding firms accept unfavourable obligations which have no connection with the subject of such contracts.

In recent years, the Commission has adopted a tough stance and has fined many firms. Case Study 6.4 in MyEconLab looks at the case of Microsoft, a firm whose abuse of its monopoly position has been the subject of ongoing investigations by both the US and EU authorities.

In 2008 the Commission announced new, streamlined procedures for dealing with cartel cases. The parties involved are shown the evidence against them and are given the opportunity to acknowledge their 'guilt'. In return any fines imposed are reduced by 10 per cent. The intention was to simplify the process and to reduce the number of cases going to the courts.

The first settlement under the new arrangements was made in 2008 and involved 10 companies making memory chips. Since then there have been a series of high-profile cases with huge fines being imposed. In 2012 Philips and five other electronics companies were fined a total of €1.47 billion, while in 2013 there were a number of cases focused on financial markets. (See Box 13.1 for a further example.)

EU monopoly policy

Article 102 relates to the abuse of market power and has also been extended to cover mergers. As with Article 101, it is the behaviour of firms that is the target of the legislation. The following are cited as examples of the abuse of market power. As you can see, they are very similar to those in Article 101.

- Charging unfairly high prices to consumers, or paying unfairly low prices to suppliers.

Definition

Restrictive practices Where two or more firms agree to adopt common practices to restrict competition.

BOX 13.1   SQUEAKY CLEAN COMPETITION?

The EU approach to cartels

As we have seen, EU competition policy applies to companies operating in two or more EU countries. The policy is implemented by the European Commission, which has the power to levy substantial fines on companies found to be in breach of the legislation.

In April 2011, the Commission announced fines of €315.2 million on two detergent manufacturers, Procter & Gamble and Unilever. They had been accused of operating a cartel with a third company, Henkel, in an EC investigation called 'Purity'. The three were the largest soap powder producers in Europe. Henkel was granted immunity from the fines, after revealing the existence of the cartel to the Commission in 2008. The company said that the cartel arrangements were detected by internal audit procedures and that it immediately informed the authorities.

The Commission announced that the three companies had operated a cartel for three years and across eight EU countries. The aim had been to stabilise their market positions and to coordinate prices. They found that the soap powder cartel started when the companies implemented a genuine and legal initiative, through their trade association, to improve the environmental performance of detergent products. But, in the course of this initiative, the companies strayed into illegal territory, agreeing measures to protect their market share, to maintain prices and, ultimately, to fix prices. Henkel, Procter & Gamble and Unilever did this on their own initiative and at their own risk.[1]

Joaquín Almunia, Vice-President of the Commission in charge of competition policy, said: 'By acknowledging their participation in the cartel, the companies enabled the Commission to swiftly conclude its investigation, and for this they got a reduction of the fine. But companies should be under no illusion that the Commission will pursue its relentless fight against cartels, which extract higher prices from consumers than if companies compete fairly and on the merits.'

This was the third cartel to be concluded under procedures introduced in 2008. From 2011 to 2013, 13 cartels were examined and led to fines totalling €4.83 billion. After a slow start it does appear that the Commission's stated aim of speeding up anti-competitive investigations is being achieved.

1. *What factors determine the likelihood that firms will collude to fix prices – despite the prospect of facing fines of up to 10 per cent of their annual global turnover?*
2. *The soap powder manufacturers were originally involved in a trade association environmental initiative to co-ordinate on packaging and presentation. Why is this legal under EU Competition law, while price fixing is not?*
3. *What possible advantages might there be to the consumer of the detergent cartel?*

[1] Europa Press Release IP 11/473, 13 April 2011 (http://europa.eu/rapid/pressReleasesAction.do?reference=IP/11/473).

- Limiting production, markets or technical developments to the detriment of consumers.
- Using price discrimination or other discriminatory practices to the detriment of certain parties.
- Making other firms that sign contracts accept unfavourable obligations which, by their nature, have no connection with the subject of such contracts.

Under Article 102, such practices can be banned and firms can be fined where they are found to have abused a dominant position. A firm need not have some specified minimum market share before Article 102 can be invoked. Instead, if firms are able to conduct anti-competitive practices, it is simply assumed that they must be in a position of market power. This approach is sensible, given the difficulties of identifying the boundaries of a market, in terms of either geography or type of product.

EU merger policy

Under current regulations (2004), mergers are prohibited which would significantly reduce competition in the EU.[1]

[1] See http://ec.europa.eu/competition/mergers/overview_en.html

Merging firms will automatically be referred to the European Commission if no more than two-thirds of each firm's EU-wide business is conducted in a single member state and if they exceed one or other of two turnover thresholds. These thresholds include combinations of worldwide annual sales and EU sales. For example, the first threshold is where worldwide sales exceed €5 billion and where EU sales of at least two of the companies exceed €250 million. Since 2008 the merger investigation process has been overseen by a Chief Competition Economist and a panel which scrutinises the investigating team's conclusions.

Relevant mergers must be notified to the Commission, which will then conduct preliminary investigations (Phase 1). A decision must then be made, normally within 25 working days, whether to conduct a formal investigation (Phase 2) or to let the merger proceed. A formal investigation must normally be completed within a further 90 working days (or 110 days in complex cases).

The process of EU merger control is thus both rapid and administratively inexpensive. The regulations are also potentially quite tough. Mergers are disallowed if they result in 'a concentration which would significantly impede effective competition, in particular by the creation or strengthening of a dominant position'.

But the regulations are also flexible, since they recognise that mergers may be in the interests of consumers if they result in cost reductions. In such cases they are permitted. This flexibility has led to criticism that the Commission has been too easily persuaded by firms, allowing mergers to go ahead with few, if any restrictions. Indeed, since the merger control measures were put in place, around 5500 mergers have been notified, with only around 4 per cent proceeding to Phase 2. By mid-2014 only 24 had been prohibited. When, in January 2011, the Commission prohibited a proposed merger between Greece's two largest airlines, Aegean Airline and Olympic Air, it was the 21st prohibition and the first since 2007.

This issue highlights a problem for EU policy makers: there is a trade-off between encouraging competition within the EU and supporting European companies to become world leaders. The ability to compete in world markets normally requires that companies are large, which may well imply having monopoly power within the EU.

 To what extent is Article 102 consistent with both these points of view?

UK competition policy

There have been substantial changes to UK competition policy since the first legislation was introduced in 1948. The current approach is based on the 1998 Competition Act and the 2002 Enterprise Act, together with Part 3 of the 2013 Enterprise and Regulatory Reform Act.

The Competition Act brought UK policy in line with EU policy, detailed above. The Act has two key sets (or 'chapters') of prohibitions. Chapter I prohibits various restrictive practices, and mirrors EU Article 101. Chapter II prohibits various abuses of monopoly power, and mirrors Article 102. The Enterprise Act strengthened the Competition Act and introduced new measures for the control of mergers.

Under the two Acts, the body charged with ensuring that the prohibitions were carried out was the Office of Fair Trading (OFT). The OFT could investigate any firms suspected of engaging in one or more of the prohibited practices. Where the OFT decided that an infringement of one of the prohibitions had occurred, it would be able to direct the offending firms to modify their behaviour or cease their practices altogether.

The Competition Act also set up a Competition Commission (CC) to which the OFT could refer cases for further investigation. The CC was charged with determining whether the structure of an industry or the practices of firms within it are detrimental to competition.

If a case was referred to the CC, it then carried out an investigation to establish whether competition had been adversely affected. If the CC found that it had, it decided on the appropriate remedies, such as prohibiting various practices.

In 2012 the government announced plans for the reform of the UK's competition regime. These followed the outcome of a consultation on the links between competition and economic growth and resulted in the 2013 Enterprise and Regulatory Reform Act. While retaining the principles and broad procedures of the 1998 and 2002 Acts, the 2013 Act resulted in the setting up of a new body – the Competition and Markets Authority (the CMA). Since April 2014 the CMA has undertaken most of the work previously carried out by the OFT and the CC. The intention was to reduce duplication of processes and costs and to increase business confidence in regulation. The government said that it hoped these proposals would make it easier to tackle anti-competitive mergers and to reform anti-trust rules.

UK restrictive practices policy

Under the 2002 Enterprise Act, it is a criminal offence to engage in cartel agreements (i.e. horizontal, rather than vertical, collusive agreements between firms), irrespective of whether there are appreciable effects on competition. Convicted offenders may receive a prison sentence of up to five years and/or an unlimited fine. Prosecutions could be brought by the Serious Fraud Office or the OFT. This role has now passed to the CMA, which has substantial powers: to enter premises, to seize documents and to require people to answer questions or provide information.

But what practices constitute 'cartel agreements'? These involve one or more of the following agreements by firms: price fixing; limiting supply, perhaps by each firm agreeing to an output quota; sharing out markets by geographical area, type or size of customer or nature of outlet (e.g. bus companies agreeing not to run services in each other's areas); *collusive tendering* for a contract, where two or more firms put in a tender at secretly agreed (high) prices; or agreements between purchasers (e.g. supermarkets) to keep down prices paid to suppliers (e.g. farmers).

 Are all such agreements necessarily against the interests of consumers?

In the case of other types of agreement, the CMA retains the discretion to decide, on a case-by-case basis, whether or not competition is appreciably restricted, and whether, therefore, they should be terminated or the firms should be exempted. Such cases included the following:

■ Vertical price-fixing agreements. These are price agreements between purchasing firms and their suppliers. An

Definition

Collusive tendering Where two or more firms secretly agree on the prices they will tender for a contract. These prices will be above those that would be put in under a genuinely competitive tendering process.

BOX 13.2   **MORE THAN A COINCIDENCE?**

School fees in the UK

In November 2005 the Office of Fair Trading announced that 50 independent schools had been found guilty of operating a fee-fixing cartel. The OFT found that schools had exchanged details of their planned fee increases between 2001 and 2004, in direct contravention of the 1998 Competition Act. Bursars of all the schools had participated in an annual round-robin message and the OFT found that 'this regular and systematic exchange of confidential information was anti-competitive and resulted in parents being charged higher fees than would otherwise have been the case'.

The investigation took nearly two years and uncovered evidence which showed that schools routinely exchanged both cost and pricing information when preparing fee recommendations to governors. One email, sent with details of over 20 competitor schools' proposed fee increases, contained the message 'Confidential please, so we aren't accused of being a cartel'.

Coincidence or cartel?

Having been found guilty, the schools could have faced large fines, totalling 10 per cent of their turnover. However, for the first time in a case of this nature the OFT negotiated a final settlement, allowing schools to pay a nominal penalty of £10 000 per school and to set up a charitable trust fund, to total £3 million, for the benefit of those who had been pupils at the relevant time.

The schools also had to admit that their participation in the exchange of information distorted competition. However, stepping back from their initial judgment, the OFT did not make any finding about the *effect* of the cartel. This final ruling acknowledged the schools' adamant defence that the sharing of information had not resulted in higher fees; indeed some of the schools involved maintained that the exchange of information resulted in *lower* rather than higher fees.

If this argument is plausible, then what could explain the fact that independent schools' fees rose by almost identical amounts each year? The answer lies in their cost structure;

the major input to schools is labour, and wage inflation for teachers will be determined by salaries offered in the (much larger) state sector. In addition, the top schools are likely to have very similar staff/student ratios. The result is that all the independent schools are likely to face very similar increases in wage costs; the schools claimed that this was the cause of the very similar increases in fees. In fact they went further and claimed that sharing good practice actually maximised operational efficiencies, something that is explicitly encouraged by the Charity Commission.

Charitable status

Government scrutiny of independent schools did not end with the OFT investigation. In 2006 the Charities Act was passed and under this Act various organisations, including independent schools and hospitals, lost their automatic right to charitable status. They now have to prove that 'people in poverty' benefit from their services even if they cannot afford their fees. The loss of charitable status would cost the schools £100 million a year in lost tax breaks.

In January 2008 the Charity Commission produced a landmark document which contained a series of recommendations for independent schools. Guidelines were designed to enable the schools to meet the 'public benefit' test to allow them to hold onto their charitable status. Amongst the proposals were suggestions that schools should offer bursaries to fund pupils from low-income households and that they should share facilities and staff with local state schools. In the guidance the Commission suggested that schools should still be able to charge 'reasonable and necessary' fees, but that those keeping fees to a minimum would be more likely to benefit the public.

 What costs, other than wages, would independent schools face? Would these costs support the schools' claim that identical fee increases are driven by identical costs, rather than by collusion?

---

example of this is ***resale price maintenance***. This is where a manufacturer or distributor sets the price for retailers to charge. It may well distribute a price list to retailers (e.g. a car manufacturer may distribute a price list to car showrooms). Resale price maintenance is a way of preventing competition between retailers driving down retail prices and ultimately the price they pay to the manufacturer. Both manufacturers and retailers, therefore, are likely to gain from resale price maintenance.

Definition

Resale (or retail) price maintenance Where the manufacturer of a product (legally) insists that the product should be sold at a specified retail price.

- Agreements to exchange information that could have the effect of reducing competition. For example, if producers exchange information on their price intentions, it is a way of allowing price leadership, a form of tacit collusion, to continue.

 What problems are likely to arise in identifying which firms' practices are anti-competitive? Should the CMA take firms' assurances into account when deciding whether to grant an exemption?

UK monopoly policy

Under the Chapter II prohibition of the 1998 Competition Act, it is illegal for a dominant firm to exercise its market power in such a way as to reduce competition. Any suspected case would be investigated by the CMA, which uses a two-stage process in deciding whether an abuse has taken place.

The first stage is to establish whether a firm has a position of dominance. The firm does not literally have to be a monopoly. 'Dominance' normally involves the firm having at least a 40 per cent share of the market (national or local, whichever is appropriate), although this figure will vary from industry to industry. Also, dominance depends on the barriers to entry to new competitors. The higher the barriers to the entry of new firms, the less contestable will be the market (see pages 181–2), and the more dominant a firm is likely to be for any given current market share.

If the firm is deemed to be dominant, the second stage involves the CMA deciding whether the firm's practices constituted an abuse of its position. As with restrictive practices, Chapter II follows EU legislation. It specifies the same four types of market abuse as does EU Article 102 (see above). Within these four categories, the CMA identifies the following practices as being overtly anti-competitive:

- Charging excessively high prices. These are prices above those that the firm would charge if it faced effective competition. One sign of excessively high prices is abnormally high rates of profit.
- Price discrimination, when it results in excessively higher prices or lower prices that are used to exclude competitors.
- Predatory pricing. This is where prices are set at loss-making levels, so as to drive competitors out of business (see page 217). The test is to look at the dominant firm's price in relation to its average costs. If its price is below average variable cost, predation would be assumed. If its price is above average variable cost, but below average total cost, then the CMA would need to establish whether the reason was to eliminate a competitor.
- *Vertical restraints*. This is where a supplying firm imposes conditions on a purchasing firm (or vice versa). For example, a manufacturer may impose rules on retailers about displaying the product or the provision of after-sales service, or it may refuse to supply certain outlets (as with perfume manufacturers refusing to supply discount chains such as Superdrug). Another example is *tie-in sales*. This is where a firm controlling the supply of a first product insists that its customers buy a second product from it rather than from its rivals.

The simple existence of any of these practices may not constitute an abuse. The CMA has to decide whether their effect is to restrict competition. This may require a detailed investigation to establish whether competition is restricted or distorted. If it were found to be so, the CMA would rule what actions must be taken to remedy the situation.

UK merger policy

Merger policy is covered by the 2002 Enterprise Act. It seeks to prevent mergers that are likely to result in a substantial lessening of competition.

A merger or takeover will be investigated by the CMA if the target company has a turnover of £70 million or more,

or if the merger will result in the new company having a market share of 25 per cent or more. The CMA will conduct a preliminary investigation to see whether competition is likely to be threatened. If it is, and if there are unlikely to be any substantial compensating benefit to consumers, there will be a further investigation.

If the merger is likely to lead to a significant reduction in competition, the CMA can prohibit the merger. Alternatively, it can require the merged firm to behave in certain ways in order to protect consumers' interests. In such cases, the CMA will then monitor the firm to ensure that it is meeting the required conditions.

The 2002 and 2013 Acts tightened up merger legislation. In the past, the vast majority of mergers were not referred to the CC (or its predecessor, the Monopolies and Mergers Commission). Yet studies had shown that mergers were generally not in the public interest. Mergers had contributed to a growing degree of market concentration in the UK and few benefits from cost reduction and research had occurred. The 2002 Act sought to rectify this problem.

Between 2005 and 2008 a number of mergers were referred to the CC; these included the merger of Heinz and HP Foods, the purchase of 115 Morrisons stores by Somerfield, and Sky's purchase of a 17.9 per cent stake in ITV.

However, in the autumn of 2008, following the announcement that a merger was proposed between Lloyds TSB and the troubled bank HBOS, the government said that it would overrule any objections raised by the competition authorities. This highlights the fact that governments may sometimes prefer to take a pragmatic view of competition policy, particularly in times of economic crisis.

 If anti-monopoly legislation is effective enough, is there ever any need to prevent mergers from going ahead?

Assessment of competition policy

With UK competition legislation in line with EU legislation, it is possible to consider the two together.

It is generally agreed by commentators that it is correct for the policy to concentrate on anti-competitive practices and their effects rather than simply on the existence of agreements or on the size of a firm's market share. After all, economic power is a problem only when it is abused. When, by contrast, it enables firms to achieve economies of scale,

---

> **Definitions**
>
> **Vertical restraints** Conditions imposed by one firm on another which is either its supplier or its customer.
>
> **Tie-in sales** Where a firm is only prepared to sell a first product on the condition that its customers buy a second product from it.

BOX 13.3 BUY NOW, PAY (A GREAT DEAL MORE) LATER

Is the consumer protected in the market for payday loans?

One of the biggest growth industries in the UK has been the market for payday loans. Borrowers, who are usually low-income and may be high-risk, are offered loans of a few hundred pounds. The terms range from 30 days to a few months and the rate of interest charged is extremely high, often in excess of 2000 per cent per annum. However, the actual cost may be perceived as affordable. For example, a £100 loan for 28 days might require total repayments of £127.

This is a highly profitable business, which has been imported from the USA over the last few years. Wonga, one of the market leaders, saw post-tax profits rise by 36 per cent in 2012 to £62.5 million. Four million loans, totalling £1.2 billion, were advanced to more than 1.2 million customers. The company is extremely efficient, knows its customers well and demonstrates an acute eye for humorous marketing.

However, the payday loan industry's critics highlight a number of practices which might be deemed unsavoury. Consumers may not fully understand the information they are given, or they may be so desperate to borrow money that they ignore the small print. If the loans are not repaid, they are often renewed at a higher rate of interest, while the option of extending the loan term is repeatedly offered. While the profit per loan is relatively small – Wonga's is quoted as averaging £15 – the overall profitability or return on capital is extremely high.

But does any of this imply that consumers are necessarily subject to unfair practice or uncompetitive behaviour? There are a large number of payday loan companies, offering varying terms and different, albeit high, rates of interest. Those borrowing are adults and may have good and rational reasons for needing a short-term loan; in the case of avoiding overdraft charges, they could even be saving money. Defenders of the industry point out that this is an efficient, fully functional market which has grown up in response to consumer demand.

Following debate and a number of high-profile campaigns, the OFT undertook a stage one investigation into the market, reporting in March 2013.[1] The conclusions were clear:

■ the payday loans market is not working well for many consumers;

■ there was evidence of irresponsible lending: people are given loans they can't afford and when they fail to repay are encouraged to extend them;

■ 28 per cent of loans are rolled over at least once, providing 50 per cent of lenders' revenues – in these instances the consumer has become 'captive' with no alternative supplier with which to engage;

■ 60 per cent of websites emphasise speed and simplicity over cost, implying that consumers are not receiving full and accurate information.

According to the OFT report, irresponsible lending was not confined to a few rogue traders, rather 'it has its roots in the way competition works in this market'. Firms which behaved in a proper manner, complying with national codes of lending conduct, would lose out to those which did not do so.

The OFT concluded that the problems identified were so extensive that the Competition Commission should undertake a market review. In the meantime it put in place a number of measures to address concerns relating to practice with respect to consumer credit, for which it was responsible at the time. These measures included:

■ starting formal investigations against a number of firms in the industry;

■ clarifying standards for all firms in the industry;

■ requiring that 50 firms (90 per cent of the industry) address areas of non-compliance within 12 weeks.

Since this report was published, the OFT's responsibility for consumer credit has passed to the Financial Conduct Authority. The Competition Commission instigated a full market investigation in 2013. This has now been taken over by the Competition and Markets Authority (CMA), which will report on its findings later in 2014.

1. What features of the market for payday loans distort competition?
2. Assess the arguments for and against the continued existence of payday loans companies.
3. How might the new body, the CMA, improve the UK's approach to competition and consumer protection?

[1] OFT Final Report Payday Lending, OFT 1481.

---

or more finance for investment, the result can be of benefit to consumers. In other words, the assumption that structure determines conduct and performance (see page 171) is not necessarily true, and certainly it is not necessarily true that market power is always bad and competitive industries are always good.

Also, most commentators favour the system of certain practices being prohibited, with fines applicable to the first offence. This acts as an important deterrent to anti-competitive behaviour.

A problem with any policy to deal with collusion is the difficulty in rooting it out. When firms do all their deals 'behind closed doors' and are careful not to keep records or give clues, then collusion can be very hard to spot. The cases that have come to light, such as that of collusive tendering between firms supplying ready-mixed concrete, may be just the tip of an iceberg.

If two or more firms were charging similar prices, what types of evidence would you look for to prove that this was collusion rather than coincidence?

13.2 PRIVATISATION AND REGULATION

Nationalisation and privatisation

One solution to market failure, advocated by some on the political left, is nationalisation. If industries are not being run in the public interest by the private sector, then bring them into public ownership. This way, so the argument goes, the market failures can be corrected. Problems of monopoly power, externalities, inequality, etc., can be dealt with directly if these industries are run with the public interest, rather than private gain, at heart.

Most nationalisation in the UK took place under the Labour government of 1945–51, when coal, railways, gas and steel were nationalised. The Labour Party at the time saw nationalisation not just as a means of correcting market failures, but as something that was morally desirable. It was seen to be much fairer and less divisive to have a society based on common ownership of the means of production than one where people were divided into separate classes: workers and capitalists.

By the mid-1970s, however, it became increasingly clear that the nationalised industries were inefficient and also a source of much industrial unrest. A change of policy was introduced from the early 1980s, when successive Conservative governments engaged in an extensive programme of 'privatisation', returning virtually all of the nationalised industries, including telecommunications, gas, water, steel, electricity and the railways, to the private sector. By 1997, the year the Conservatives left office, with the exception of the rail industry in Northern Ireland and

the water industry in Northern Ireland and Scotland, the only nationalised industry remaining in the UK was the Post Office (including post offices and mail). The Post Office and Royal Mail were split in 2012 and Royal Mail was privatised in October 2013. Post Office Ltd remains state owned but, under the 2011 Postal Services Act, there is the option for it to become a mutual organisation in the future.

Other countries have followed similar programmes of privatisation in what has become a worldwide phenomenon. Privatisation has been seen by many governments as a means of revitalising inefficient industries and as a golden opportunity to raise revenues to ease budgetary problems.

In 2008, however, many governments returned to the use of nationalisation, in order to 'rescue' banks which were at risk of going bankrupt. This was facilitated by the EU giving permission for member states to support financial institutions, subject to conditions under EU state aid rules. The use of nationalisation in this macroeconomic context of national or international economic crises is examined in section 23.4.

How desirable is privatisation?

Arguments for privatisation

Market forces. The first argument is that privatisation will expose these industries to market forces, from which will flow the benefits of greater efficiency, faster growth and greater responsiveness to the wishes of the consumer. There are three parts to this argument:

- Greater competition in the market. If privatisation involves splitting an industry into competing parts (e.g. separate power stations competing to sell electricity to different electricity distribution companies), the resulting competition may then drive costs and prices down.

- Greater competition for finance. After privatisation a company has to finance investment through the market: it must issue shares or borrow from financial institutions. In doing so, it will be competing for funds with other companies, and thus must be seen as capable of using these funds profitably.

- Accountability to shareholders. Shareholders want a good return on their shares and will thus put pressure on the privatised company to perform well. If the company does not make sufficient profits, shareholders will sell their shares. The share price will fall and the company will be in danger of being taken over. The market for corporate control thus provides incentives for private firms to be efficient. There has been considerable take-over activity in the water and electricity industries, with most of the 12 regional electricity companies and several of the water companies being taken over, often by non-UK companies.

Reduced government interference. In **nationalised industries**, managers may frequently be required to adjust their targets for political reasons. At one time they may have to keep prices low as part of a government drive against inflation. At another they may have to raise their prices substantially in order to raise extra revenue for the government and help finance tax cuts. At another they may find their investment programmes cut as part of a government economy drive.

Privatisation frees the company from these constraints and allows it to make more rational economic decisions and plan future investments with greater certainty.

Financing tax cuts. The privatisation issue of shares earns money directly for the government and thus reduces the amount it needs to borrow. Effectively, then, the government can use the proceeds of privatisation to finance tax cuts.

There is a danger here, however, that in order to raise the maximum revenue the government will want to make the industries as potentially profitable as possible. This may involve selling them as monopolies. But this, of course, would probably be against the interests of the consumer.

Potential problems with privatisation

The markets in which privatised industries operate are unlikely to be perfect. What is more, the process of privatisation itself can create problems.

Definition

Nationalised industries State-owned industries that produce goods or services that are sold in the market.

Natural monopolies. The market forces argument for privatisation largely breaks down if a public monopoly is simply replaced by a private monopoly, as in the case of the water companies. Critics of privatisation argue that at least a public-sector monopoly is not out to maximise profits and thereby exploit the consumer.

Some industries have such great economies of scale that there is only room for one firm in the industry. They are natural monopolies. The best examples of natural monopolies are the various grids that exist in the privatised utilities: the national electricity grid, the national gas pipe network, the network of railway lines. These grids account for a relatively high proportion of the total costs of these industries. The more intensively the electricity and gas grids are used, however, the lower their cost will become per unit of fuel supplied. Similarly with railways: the relatively high costs of providing track and signalling, etc., will become smaller per passenger, the more passengers use the railway.

In the short run, these costs are fixed. Average fixed costs must necessarily decline as more is produced: overheads are being spread over a greater output.

In the long run, when new (electricity, gas, railway) lines can be built, these costs become variable. It is still likely, however, that the costs per unit of output will decline, the higher the output becomes. A pylon carrying ten lines does not cost five times as much as one carrying two. This means that long-run average costs fall as more is produced.

In Figure 13.1, assume that the total industry output is Q_1. With just one company in the industry, long-run average cost is therefore $LRAC_1$. Now assume that the industry is split into two equal-sized companies, each with its own grid. If total output remains at Q_1, the two firms will produce Q_2 each at the higher long-run average cost of $LRAC_2$.

It is potentially more efficient, therefore, to have a single monopoly supplier whenever there is a natural monopoly. It avoids wasteful duplication.

The problem is that the monopoly producer in a free market could use its power to drive up prices. The long-run

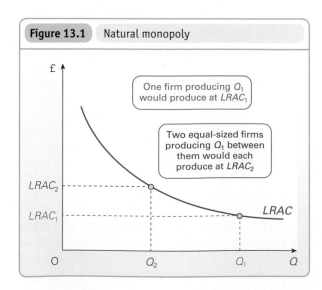

Figure 13.1 Natural monopoly

One firm producing Q_1 would produce at $LRAC_1$

Two equal-sized firms producing Q_1 between them would each produce at $LRAC_2$

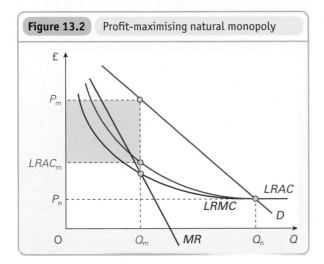

Figure 13.2 Profit-maximising natural monopoly

subsidised prices and that certain needy people (e.g. pensioners) should be charged lower prices.

Will such externalities and issues of equity be ignored under privatisation? The advocates of privatisation argue that externalities can be dealt with by appropriate taxes, subsidies and regulations even if the industry is privatised. Likewise questions of fairness and social justice can be dealt with by subsidies or regulations. A loss-making bus service can be subsidised so that it can be run profitably by a private bus company.

Critics argue that externalities are widespread and need to be taken into account by the industry itself and not just by an occasionally intervening government.

In assessing these arguments, a lot depends on the effectiveness of government legislation and regulation.

 To what extent can the problems with privatisation be seen as arguments in favour of nationalisation?

profit-maximising position is illustrated in Figure 13.2. The monopolist produces Q_m at a price P_m and at a cost of $LRAC_m$. There is a misallocation of resources.

If, however, the industry remained nationalised, or if it was privatised but regulated, it could be run as a monopoly and thus achieve the full economies of scale. And yet it could be directed to set a price that just covered costs (including normal profits), and thus make no more profit than a highly competitive industry. In Figure 13.2, it would produce Q_n at a price of P_n. We examine regulation later in this section.

Planning and the co-ordination of industry. Road use and road construction affect the demand for railways and vice versa. Decisions in the coal, electricity, gas and oil industries (and to a large extent in the steel industry) all affect each other. If these industries were nationalised, it should make their decisions easier to co-ordinate in the public interest and could help the sensible planning of the nation's infrastructure. If these industries were under private enterprise, however, either there would be little co-ordination, or alternatively co-ordination might degenerate into oligopolistic collusion, with the consumer losing out. In the extreme case, the same company may have a monopoly in more than one industry. For example, in some regions of the UK, one company runs both buses and trains.

KI 29
p323
Problems of externalities and inequality. Various industries may create substantial external benefits and yet may be privately unprofitable. A railway or an underground line, for example, may considerably ease congestion on the roads, thus benefiting road as well as rail users. Other industries may cause substantial external costs. Nuclear power stations may produce nuclear waste that is costly to dispose of safely, and/or provides hazards for future generations. Coal-fired power stations may pollute the atmosphere and cause acid rain.

For reasons of equity, it can be argued that various transport services should be subsidised in order to keep them **KI 4** **p13** going and/or to keep their prices down. For instance, it can be argued that rural bus services should be kept operating at

Regulation: identifying the short-run optimum price and output

Privatised industries, if left free to operate in the market, will have monopoly power; they will create externalities; and they will be unlikely to take into account questions of fairness. An answer to these problems is for the government or some independent agency to regulate their behaviour so that they produce at the socially optimum price and output.

Exactly what this optimum is depends on what problems need to be taken into account. Take three cases. In the first, the privatised industry is a monopoly (perhaps it is a natural monopoly), but there are no other problems. In the second case, there are also externalities to be considered, and in the third, questions of fairness too.

The privatised industry is a monopoly

The 'first-best' situation: P = MC. Assume that all other firms in the economy are operating under perfect competition, and thus producing where $P = MC$. This is the imaginary 'first-best' situation. If this were so, the privatised company should be required to follow the same pricing rule: $P = MC$. As we saw in section 11.1, this will give the Pareto optimal output, where total consumer plus producer surplus is maximised (see page 316).

KI 26
p315

The theory of the 'second best': P = MC + Z. Now let us drop the assumption that the rest of the economy operates under perfect competition. If other industries on average are charging a price, say, 10 per cent above MC, then the theory of the second best suggests that the privatised company should also charge a price 10 per cent above MC. At least that way it will not cause a diversion of consumption away from relatively low-cost industries (at the margin) to a relatively high-cost one. The second-best rule is therefore to set $P = MC + Z$, where Z in this case is 10 per cent.

The privatised industry produces externalities

In the first-best situation the privatised industry should produce where price equals marginal social (not private) cost: $P = MSC$. The second-best solution is to produce where $P = MSC + Z$ (where Z is the average of other industries' price above their MSC).

The difficulty for the regulator in applying these rules in practice is to identify and measure the externalities: not an easy task! (See section 11.4.)

The behaviour of the privatised industry involves questions of fairness

If the government wishes the regulator to insist on a price below MC because it wishes to help certain groups (e.g. pensioners, children, rural dwellers, those below certain incomes), what should this price be?

In practice, one of two simple rules could be followed. Either the industry could be required to charge uniform prices, despite higher costs for supplying certain categories of people (this could apply, for example, to rural customers of a privatised postal service); or a simple formula could be used (e.g. half price for pensioners and children). These are often the only practical solutions given the impossibility of identifying the specific needs of individual consumers.

Two further questions arise:

- Should the lower price be subsidised by central or local government, or by the privatised company and hence by other users of the service (i.e. by their paying higher prices)? Justice would suggest that support should come from the community as a whole – the taxpayer – and not just from other users of the service.
- If people require help, should they not be given general tax relief or benefits, rather than specifically subsidised services? For example, should pensioners not be paid better pensions, rather than be charged reduced fares on buses?

1. *In the case of buses, subsidies are often paid by local authorities to support various loss-making routes. Is this the best way of supporting these services?*
2. *In the case of postal services, profitable parts of the service cross-subsidise the unprofitable parts. Should this continue if the industry is privatised?*

Regulation: identifying the long-run optimum price and output

In the short run, certain factors of production are fixed in supply. For example, electricity output can be increased by using existing power stations more fully, but the number of power stations is fixed. There will thus be a limit to the amount of electricity that can be generated in the short run. As that limit is approached, the marginal cost of electricity is likely to rise rapidly. For example, oil-fired power stations, which are more costly to operate, will have to be brought on line.

In the long run, all factors are variable. New power stations can be built. The long-run marginal costs therefore will probably not rise as more is produced. In fact, they may even fall due to economies of scale.

Long-run marginal costs, however, unlike short-run marginal costs, will include the extra capital costs of increasing output. The long-run marginal cost of electricity will thus be all the extra costs of producing one more unit: namely, the extra operating costs (fuel, labour, etc.) plus the extra capital costs (power stations, pylons, etc.).

The rule for the optimum long-run price and output is simple. The regulator should require the industry to produce where price equals long-run marginal social cost ($LRMSC$). This is illustrated in Figure 13.3.

In the short run, optimum price and output are P_S and Q_S where $P = $ (short-run) MSC. This might mean that production is at quite a high cost: existing capital equipment is being stretched and diminishing returns have become serious.

In the long run, then, it will be desirable to increase capacity if $LRMSC < MSC$. Optimum long-run price and output are thus at P_L and Q_L where $P = LRMSC$.

This is the rule for the first-best situation. In the second-best situation, the industry should produce where $P = LRMSC + Z$ (where Z is the average of other industries' price above their $LRMSC$).

If the regulator imposed such rules, would they cause the firm to make a loss if it faced a downward-sloping LRMSC curve? (Clues: Where would the LRAC curve be relative to the LRMC curve? What would be the effect of externalities and the addition of the Z factor on the price?)

Regulation in the UK

To some extent the behaviour of privatised industries may be governed by general monopoly and restrictive practice legislation. For example, in the UK, privatised firms can be investigated by the CMA (Competition and Markets Authority).

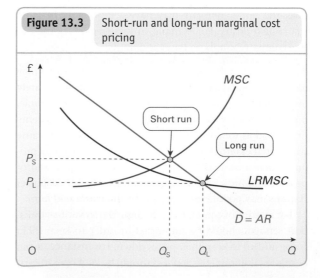

Figure 13.3 Short-run and long-run marginal cost pricing

In addition to this, there is a separate regulatory office to oversee the structure and behaviour of each of the privatised utilities. These regulators are as follows: the Office for Gas and Electricity Markets (Ofgem), the Office of Communications (Ofcom) (for telecommunications and broadcasting), the Office of Rail Regulation (ORR) and the Office of Water Services (Ofwat). The regulators set terms under which the industries have to operate. For example, ORR sets the terms under which rail companies have access to the track and stations. The terms set by the regulator can be reviewed by negotiation between the regulator and the industry. If agreement cannot be reached, the CMA acts as an appeal court and its decision is binding.

The regulator for each industry also sets limits to the prices that certain parts of the industry can charge (see Case Study 13.5 in MyEconLab). These parts are those where there is little or no competition – for example, the charges made to electricity and gas retailers by National Grid Transco, the owner of the electricity grid and major gas pipelines.

The price setting formulae have largely been of the 'RPI minus X' variety (although other factors, including competition and excessive profits, are also taken into account). What the RPI minus X formula means is that the industries can raise their prices by the rate of increase in the retail price index (RPI) (i.e. by the rate of inflation) minus a certain percentage (X) to take account of expected increases in efficiency. Thus if the rate of inflation were 3 per cent, and if the regulator considered that the industry (or firm) could be expected to reduce its costs by 2 per cent (X = 2 per cent), then price rises would be capped at 1 per cent. The RPI – X system is thus an example of ***price-cap regulation***. The idea of this system of regulation is that it will force the industry to pass on cost savings to the consumer.

Whether this will result in marginal cost pricing depends on what the price was in the first place. If the price was equal to marginal cost, and if the X factor is the amount by which the regulator expects the *MC* curve to shift downwards (after taking inflation into account), then the formula could result in marginal cost pricing.

 Why might it equally result in average cost pricing?

Assessing the system of regulation in the UK

The system that has evolved in the UK has various advantages over that employed in the USA and elsewhere, where regulation often focuses on the level of profits (see Case Study 13.5 in MyEconLab):

- It is a discretionary system, with the regulator able to judge individual examples of the behaviour of the industry on their own merits. The regulator has a detailed knowledge of the industry which would not be available to government ministers or other bodies such as the CMA. The regulator could thus be argued to be the best

person to decide on whether the industry is acting in the public interest.
- The system is flexible, since it allows for the licence and price formulae to be changed as circumstances change.
- The 'RPI minus X' formula provides an incentive for the privatised firms to be as efficient as possible. If they can lower their costs by more than X, they will, in theory, be able to make larger profits and keep them. There is thus a continuing pressure on them to cut costs. (In the US system, where profits rather than prices are regulated, there is little incentive to increase efficiency, since any cost reductions must be passed on to the consumer in lower prices, and do not, therefore, result in higher profits.)

TC 5
p 54

There are, however, some inherent problems with the regulation as it has been operated in the UK:

- The 'RPI minus X' formula was designed to provide an incentive for firms to cut costs. But if regulators underestimated the scope for cost reductions resulting from new technology and reorganisation, and set X too low, firms could make excessive profits. Where this has happened, regulators have changed the value of X after only one or two years. Alternatively, one-off price cuts have been ordered, as happened when the water companies were required by Ofwat to cut prices by an average of 10 per cent in 2000. In either case, this then removes the incentive for the industry to cut costs. What is the point of being more efficient if the regulator is merely going to take away the extra profits?
- With RPI minus X reducing firms' profits, the outcome may be reduced investment and innovation. Given the need for greater investment in power generation, in 2013 Ofgem introduced a new system for controlling prices in the distribution part of the energy sector. This is called RIIO (Revenue Incentives Innovation Outputs). This is a new performance-based model which aims to incentivise innovation and a reduction of future costs. It also allows the climate change agenda to be addressed as part of the price control process.
- Regulation has become increasingly complex. This makes it difficult for the industries to plan and may lead to a growth of 'short-termism' as firms are subjected to short-term changes in regulation or government intervention. It is likely to result in resources being wasted as the industry spends time and energy trying to outwit the regulator.
- Alternatively, there is the danger of ***regulatory capture***. As regulators become more and more involved in their

KI 23
p 225

KI 21
p 198

Definitions

Price-cap regulation Where the regulator puts a ceiling on the amount by which a firm can raise its price.

Regulatory capture Where the regulator is persuaded to operate in the industry's interests rather than those of the consumer.

BOX 13.4 SELLING POWER TO THE PEOPLE

The impact of privatisation and competition in the electricity industry

Competition is generally seen as better than regulation as a means of protecting consumers' interests, but there is evidence that this requires a strong regulatory framework to be retained. The electricity industry provides a good case study of the impact of the introduction of competition into a privatised industry.

The industry before privatisation

Under nationalisation, the industry in England and Wales was organised as a monopoly with the Central Electricity Generating Board (CEGB) supplying 99 per cent of all electricity. It operated the power stations and transmitted the electricity round the country via the national grid. However, the CEGB did not sell electricity directly to the consumer; rather it sold it to 12 regional boards, which in turn supplied it to the consumer.

Privatisation of the industry

Non-nuclear generation in England and Wales was privatised in 1990 as two companies: National Power (with just over 50 per cent of capacity) and PowerGen (with nearly 30 per cent). Nuclear power stations were privatised in 1996.

The 12 regional boards were privatised in 1991 as separate regional electricity companies (RECs), which were responsible for local distribution and supply to consumers. They would also be permitted to build their own power stations if they chose. The RECs jointly owned the national grid, but it was run independently. It was eventually sold as a separate company in 1996.

The electricity industry in England and Wales

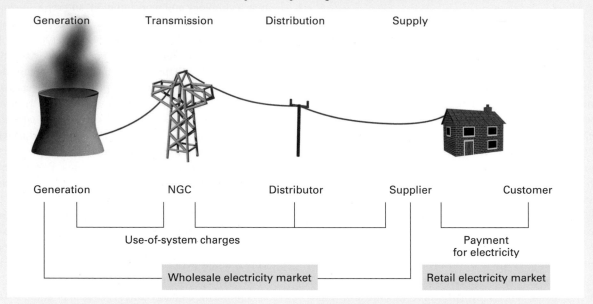

The diagram shows the structure of the industry. Electricity is produced by the *generators* (the power stations). The electricity is *transmitted* along the power lines of the national grid to different parts of the country. It is then transmitted locally by the *distributors*. There were originally 12 distribution companies, which were the *suppliers* of electricity to the customers. However, mergers have now resulted in nine distributors.

An Office of Electricity Regulation (OFFER) was set up to control prices in parts of the industry where there was no competition. The control was of the RPI – X variety (see page 393). For example, the charges paid by the generators and the suppliers to the transmission company are regulated. OFFER was later merged with the gas regulator to become the Office of Gas and Electricity Markets (Ofgem).

It was hoped that the new structure would allow a growth in competition, thereby making regulation increasingly unnecessary. So what was the nature of this competition? After all, National Power had over half of the generating capacity; NGET had a natural monopoly of electricity transmission; and the 12 RECs had a natural monopoly of distribution in each of their areas.

Competition was possible at two levels: at the *wholesale* level, with generators competing with each other to sell to suppliers; and at the *retail* level, with suppliers competing to sell to customers. Let us examine each of these markets in turn.

Competition in the wholesale market for electricity: NETA and BETTA

From 2001 in England and Wales electricity was traded in the wholesale market under the New Electricity Trading Arrangements (NETA). In April 2005, this system was extended to Scotland and renamed the British Electricity Trading and Transmission Arrangements (BETTA). Participants in the market include generators, suppliers, large commercial consumers of electricity and traders (i.e. dealers).

In this market, bulk electricity is traded 'forward' in bilateral contracts between individual buyers and sellers.

A forward contract means that a price is agreed today for an amount of electricity to be traded over a particular period in the future, which could be as soon as the next day or could be three or more years hence. The long forward contracts are to allow generators to plan to build extra capacity.

Of course, the future price will be based on anticipated demand, and demand in practice may not turn out as anticipated. To allow for this, BETTA operates a 'central balancing mechanism'. This is a system of buying and selling additional electricity where necessary to ensure that demand actually balances supply second by second. In practice, only about 2 per cent of electricity has to be traded under the balancing mechanisms; the remainder is traded in the forward contracts.

With more than 200 participants in BETTA, the system was initially seen as highly competitive, and in the first few months of NETA's operation wholesale prices fell by some 20–25 per cent. In December 2007 a report by Oxford Economic Research Associates found that the UK had the most competitive energy market both in the EU and in the G7.[1]

However, by 2008 there were increasing concerns about the UK wholesale electricity market. A number of mergers had taken place, resulting in greater concentration of market power. In February of the following year, the House of Commons Energy and Climate Change Committee criticised Ofgem for doing little to control the costs of managing electricity flows.

In response, Ofgem restated its commitment to enabling small/independent suppliers to enter the wholesale market. This would increase competitive pressure, particularly on the largest six suppliers, which account for over 99 per cent of the domestic retail customer market. However, it admitted that 'liquidity'[2] in the market had declined since 2001 and was low compared with that of many other countries and other commodity markets. A low level of liquidity makes it difficult for firms to enter the market and operate as a non-vertically integrated market participant.

In February 2010 Ofgem announced a consultation on proposed changes to the industry. This turned out to be a lengthy process with a final report on liquidity in wholesale markets published in 2013.

Competition in the retail market for electricity

The retail market is, by its nature, more competitive than the wholesale market. Since 1999 all customers, whether domestic or business, have been able to choose their supplier.

Over that period there have been several new entrants into the supplier market, including various gas companies diversifying into electricity supply.

By 2001, 38 per cent of customers had switched suppliers at least once and the former regional monopoly suppliers now had only 70 per cent of the market. In the light of this Ofgem announced that competition was sufficiently developed to allow all regulation of the retail market to be removed by April 2002. Indeed, by 2008, 80 per cent of customers had switched at least once and the former

suppliers' market share had been reduced below 50 per cent.

Failure to deliver on early promise

However, since 2008 concerns have been raised both about clarity of information on prices and about the increasing profits being made by suppliers. By 2011 the number of different tariffs on offer to domestic consumers had increased to more than 300. Yet this level of innovation appears not to have empowered consumers, but to have confused them.

Ofgem therefore revisited the regulation of retail suppliers and in 2013 after years of enquiry it published a full set of pricing rules. Energy companies are restricted to competing on a simple 'per-unit' price, allowing customers to compare tariffs at a glance.

Alongside the concerns about tariffs, there has been a focus on the increasing cost of power, with both electricity and gas companies coming under greater scrutiny. Ofgem has been subject to much criticism for its failure to secure competition and to protect the consumer interest. New suppliers have argued that their attempts to penetrate the market have been thwarted by the dominance of the big six suppliers, who control over 95 per cent of market share in both gas and electricity. Increasing vertical integration has resulted in rising prices and profits. It would be easy to conclude that the original state-owned monopoly has now become a very profitable, private oligopolistic industry.

In March 2014, following months of political pressure, Ofgem announced that it was referring the energy market to the Competition and Markets Authority (CMA).[3] Ofgem's initial report reinforced concerns about barriers to entry for independent suppliers and persistent high market shares of the largest energy companies. The retail profits of the energy suppliers had risen from £233 million in 2009 to £1.1 billion in 2012, with no clear evidence of equivalent cost reductions. At this point Ofgem concluded that its powers as a market regulator were not sufficient, and therefore asked the CMA to address any structural barriers that undermine competition.

1. *Does vertical integration matter if consumers still have a choice of suppliers and if generators are still competing with each other?*
2. *Wholesale and retail energy markets are expected to deliver on a number of targets including competitive pricing, environmental objectives and equity. Explain why this may present problems.*
3. *Does the 2014 referral by Ofgem to the CMA imply that the role of market regulators is no longer sufficient?*

[1] *Energy Market Competition in the EU and G7* (Oxera, 2007).
[2] Ofgem defines liquidity as the ability to quickly buy or sell a desired commodity or financial instrument without causing a significant change in its price and without incurring significant transaction costs. An important feature of a liquid market, it says, is that it has a large number of buyers and sellers willing to transact at all times. A high level of liquidity is seen as being good because it enables new players to enter the market and reduces the ability of incumbents to manipulate it (*Utility Week*, 3 September 2009).
[3] www.ofgem.gov.uk/press-releases-proposes-reference-cma-investigate-energy-market

industry and get to know the senior managers at a personal level, so they are increasingly likely to see the managers' point of view and will thus become less tough.

- The regulators could instead be 'captured' by the government. Rather than being totally independent, there to serve the interests of the consumer, they might bend to pressures from the government to do things that might help the government win the next election.

One way in which the dangers of ineffective or over-intrusive regulation can be avoided is to replace regulation with competition wherever this is possible. Indeed, one of the major concerns of the regulators has been to do just this. (See Box 13.4 for ways in which competition has been increased in the electricity industry.)

Increasing competition in the privatised industries

Where natural monopoly exists, competition is impossible in a free market. Of course, the industry could be broken up by the government, with firms prohibited from owning more than a certain percentage of the industry. But this would lead to higher costs of production. Firms would be operating further back up a downward-sloping long-run average cost curve.

But many parts of the privatised industries are not natural monopolies. Generally, it is only the grid that is a natural monopoly. In the case of gas and water, it is the pipelines. It would be wasteful to duplicate these. In the case of electricity, it is the power lines: the national grid and the local power lines. In the case of the railways, it is the track.

Other parts of these industries, however, have generally been opened up to competition (with the exception of water). Thus there are now many producers and sellers of electricity and gas. This is possible because they are given access, by law, to the national and local electricity grids and gas pipelines.

To help the opening up of competition, regulators have sometimes restricted the behaviour of the established firms

(like BT or British Gas), to prevent them using their dominance in the market as a barrier to entry of new firms.

As competition has been introduced into these industries, so price-cap regulation has been progressively abandoned. The intention is ultimately to confine price regulation to the operation of the grids: the parts that are natural monopolies.

Even for the parts where there is a natural monopoly, they could be made contestable monopolies. One way of doing this is by granting operators a licence for a specific period of time. This is known as *franchising*. This has been the approach used for the railways (see Case Study 13.5 in MyEconLab). Once a company has been granted a franchise, it has the monopoly of passenger rail services over specific routes. But the awarding of the franchise can be highly competitive, with rival companies putting in competitive bids, in terms of both price (or, in the case of many of the train operating companies, the level of government subsidy required) and the quality of service.

Another approach is to give all companies equal access to the relevant grid. For example, regional electricity companies have to charge the same price for using their local power lines to both rival companies and themselves.

But despite attempts to introduce competition into the privatised industries, they are still dominated by giant companies, which retain considerable market power. This is a long way from perfect competition and there is scope for price leadership or other forms of oligopolistic collusion. Although regulation through the price formula has been progressively abandoned as elements of competition have been introduced, the regulators have retained an important role in preventing collusion and the abuse of monopoly power.

> ### Definition
>
> **Franchising** Where a firm is granted the licence to operate a given part of an industry for a specified length of time.

Section summary

1. From around 1983 the Conservative government in the UK embarked on a large programme of privatisation. Many other countries have followed suit.

2. The economic arguments for privatisation include: greater competition, not only in the goods market but in the market for finance and for corporate control; reduced government interference; and raising revenue to finance tax cuts.

3. The economic arguments against privatisation of utilities include the following: the firms are likely to have monopoly power because their grids are natural monopolies; it makes overall planning and co-ordination of the transport and power sectors more difficult; and the industries produce substantial externalities and raise questions of fairness in distribution.

4. Regulators could require firms to charge the socially efficient price. In the first-best world, this will be where price equals marginal social cost. In the real world, this is not the case given that prices elsewhere are not equal to marginal social costs. Ideally, prices should still *reflect marginal social costs*, but there are difficulties in identifying and measuring social costs.

5. In the long run, the optimum price and output will be where price equals long-run marginal social cost. If $LRMSC < MSC$, it will be desirable to invest in additional capacity.

6. Regulation in the UK has involved setting up regulatory offices for the major privatised utilities. These use negotiation and bargaining to persuade the industries to behave in the public interest and set the terms under which firms can operate (e.g. access rights to the respective grid).

7. As far as prices are concerned, the industries have generally been required to abide by an 'RPI minus X' formula, or some variant of it, in all sectors where there is a lack of competition. This means that potential cost reductions are passed on to the consumer while allowing the industries to retain any additional profits gained from cost reductions greater than X. This has provided them with an incentive to achieve even greater increases in efficiency, but may not have incentivised innovation.

8. Many parts of the privatised industries are not natural monopolies. In these parts, competition has been seen as a more effective means of pursuing the public interest. Various attempts have been made to make the privatised industries more competitive, often at the instigation of the regulator. Nevertheless, considerable market power remains in the hands of many privatised firms, and thus regulators need to be able to retain the ability to prevent the abuse of monopoly power.

END OF CHAPTER QUESTIONS

1. Should governments or regulators always attempt to eliminate the supernormal profits of monopolists/oligopolists?

2. Compare the relative merits of banning certain types of market *structure* with banning certain types of market *behaviour*.

3. Consider the argument that whether an industry is in the public sector or private sector has far less bearing on its performance than the degree of competition it faces.

4. If two or more firms are charging similar prices, does this imply that collusion is taking place? What evidence would you need to determine the existence of collusion?

5. There exists a view that the UK is too small an economy to benefit from competition in many industries, with firms failing to reach minimum efficient scale. What does this imply for competition policy?

6. Should regulators of utilities that have been privatised into several separate companies allow (a) horizontal mergers (within the industry); (b) vertical mergers; (c) mergers with firms in other industries?

7. Summarise the relative benefits to consumers of (a) privatising a nationalised industry; (b) keeping it in the public sector but introducing competition.

8. If an industry regulator adopts an RPI – X formula for price regulation, is it desirable that the value of X should be adjusted as soon as cost conditions change?

9. Examine the case for public ownership of an industry where a natural monopoly exists.

10. If price regulation results in lower profits, will this always imply lower investment? How might a government incentivise innovation in a regulated industry?

11. Price-cap regulation was abandoned in the gas and electricity industries because the regulator (Ofgem) felt that there was sufficient competition. Consider whether this was a wise decision.

Online resources

Additional case studies in MyEconLab

13.1   **Cartels set in concrete, steel and cardboard.** This examines some of the best-known Europe-wide cartels of recent years.

13.2   **Taking your vitamins – at a price.** An examination of a global vitamins cartel and the action taken against it by the EU.

13.3   **A lift to profits?** The EC imposes a record fine on four companies operating a lift and escalator cartel.

13.4   **Misleading advertising.** Do firms intentionally mislead consumers and, if so, what can government do?

13.5   **Payday loans.** This case examines the rise of payday loans and looks at attempts to control their harsh terms and sky-high interest rates in order to protect the poor and vulnerable.

13.6   **Price-cap regulation in the UK.** How RPI – X regulation has been applied to the various privatised industries.

13.7   **Regulation US-style.** This examines rate-of-return regulation: an alternative to price-cap regulation.

13.8   **The right track to reform?** How successful has rail privatisation been in the UK?

13.9   **Privatisation in transition economies.** This extended case study examines state ownership under former communist countries of the USSR and how the transition of these countries to market economies involved a process of privatisation.

13.10 **Forms of privatisation in transition countries.** This focuses on how different types of privatisation are likely to affect the way industries are run.

Websites relevant to Chapters 11–13

Numbers and sections refer to websites listed in the Web Appendix and hotlinked from this book's website at **www.pearsoned.co.uk/sloman**.

- For news articles relevant to this and the previous chapter, see the *Economic News* section in MyEconLab.
- For general news on market failures and government intervention, see websites in section A, and particularly A1–5, 18, 19, 24, 31. See also links to newspapers worldwide in A38, 39, 43 and 44; and see A40 and 41 for links to economics news articles from newspapers worldwide.
- Site I11 has links to *Environmental Economics* and in the *Microeconomics* section to *Welfare Economics*.
- UK and EU departments relevant to competition policy can be found at sites E4, 10, 18; G7, 8.
- UK regulatory bodies can be found at sites E4, 11, 15, 16, 18, 19, 22, 29.
- For information on taxes and subsidies, see E25, 30, 36; G13. For use of green taxes (Box 12.2), see H5; G11; E2, 14, 30.
- For information on health and the economics of health care (Box 11.3), see E8; H8. See also links in I8 and 11.
- For sites favouring the free market, see C17; D34. See also C18 for the development of ideas on the market and government intervention.
- For the economics of the environment, see links in I7, 11, 14. For policy on the environment and transport, see E2, 7, 11, 14, 21, 29; G10, 11. See also H11.
- For student resources relevant to these three chapters, see sites C1–7, 9, 10, 19.
- For a simulation on tackling traffic congestion, see site D3.

MyEconLab

This book can be supported by MyEconLab, which contains a range of additional resources, including an online homework and tutorial system designed to test and build your understanding.

You need both an access card and a course ID to access MyEconLab:

1. Is your lecturer using MyEconLab? Ask your lecturer for your course ID.

2. Has an access card been included with the book at a reduced cost? Check the inside back cover of the book.

3. If you have a course ID but no access card, go to: http://www.myeconlab.com/ to buy access to this interactive study programme.

Foundations of Macroeconomics

14	The National Economy	400
15	Macroeconomic Issues and Analysis: An Overview	430
16	Macroeconomic Issues, Debates and Controversies	463

Why do economies sometimes grow rapidly, while at other times they suffer from recession? Why, if people want to work, do they sometimes find themselves unemployed? Why do economies experience inflation (rising prices), and does it matter if they do? Why do exchange rates change and what will be the impact of such changes on imports and exports? Why do individuals, firms and governments borrow and what are the implications of borrowing and debt for the economic health of countries? These macroeconomic issues affect all countries, and economists are called on to try to find explanations and solutions.

In the next three chapters we will be looking at these issues and giving you a preliminary insight into the causes of these problems and what governments can do to tackle them. In the third of these chapters (Chapter 16) we shall see how macroeconomics has developed over the years as economists have sought to explain the macroeconomic problems of the time – right up to the financial crisis and recession of recent years.

The National Economy

CHAPTER MAP

14.1 The scope of macroeconomics   401
Macroeconomic debates   401
The major macroeconomic issues   401
Government macroeconomic policy   404

14.2 The circular flow of income   405
The inner flow, withdrawals and injections   406
The relationship between withdrawals and injections   407
The circular flow of income and the four
    macroeconomic objectives   407
Equilibrium in the circular flow   408

14.3 Measuring national income and output   408
The three ways of measuring GDP   408
Taking account of inflation   409
Taking account of population: the use of
    per capita measures   409
Taking account of exchange rates: the use of
    PPP measures   410
Do GDP statistics give a good indication of a
    country's standard of living?   410

14.4 Short-term economic growth and the business cycle   414
The distinction between actual and potential growth   414
Economic growth and the business cycle   416
The business cycle in practice   416
Causes of fluctuations in actual growth   417

14.5 Long-term economic growth   419
Causes of long-term growth   419
Policies to achieve growth   424
Postscript: The role of investment   424

Appendix: Calculating GDP   425
The product method of measuring GDP   425
The income method of measuring GDP   426
The expenditure method of measuring GDP   427
From GDP to national income   427
Households' disposable income   428

We turn now to macroeconomics. This will be the subject of the second half of this book. As we have already seen, microeconomics focuses on individual markets. It studies the demand for and supply of, for example, oranges, music downloads, petrol and haircuts; bricklayers, doctors, office accommodation and computers. It examines the choices people make between goods, and what determines their relative prices and the relative quantities produced.

In macroeconomics we take a much broader view. We examine the economy as a whole. We still examine demand and supply, but now it is the total level of spending in the economy and the total level of production. In other words, we examine aggregate demand and aggregate supply.

We still examine output, employment and prices, but now it is national output and its rate of growth, national employment and unemployment, and the general level of prices and their rate of increase (i.e. the rate of inflation).

In this chapter, we identify the major macroeconomic objectives and have a preliminary look at the ways in which they may be related. Then we focus on national income and output. We look at how they are measured and what causes them to grow over time.

14.1 THE SCOPE OF MACROECONOMICS

Macroeconomic debates

Macroeconomics examines various issues affecting whole economies. Many of these are the big issues on which elections are won or lost. Is the economy growing and, if so, how rapidly? How can we avoid, or get out of, recessions? What causes unemployment and how can the rate be got down? Why is inflation a problem and what can be done to keep it at modest levels? What will happen to interest rates? How big a problem is government debt? Are banks lending too much or too little?

If there were agreement about the answers to these questions, macroeconomics would be simpler – but less interesting! As it is, macroeconomics is often characterised by lively debate. Economists can take different views on the importance of macroeconomic issues, their causes and the appropriate policy responses. They can also disagree about how to analyse macroeconomic phenomena and, therefore, the approach to take in modelling macroeconomic relationships.

We shall be looking at these different views throughout this second part of the book. This is not to suggest that economists always disagree; but they do sometimes.

Another factor is the difficulty of forecasting what will happen. It is relatively easy to explain things once they have happened. Predicting what is going to happen is another matter. Few economists – or anyone else – foresaw the global banking crisis, credit crunch and subsequent economic downturn of the late 2000s. Even those who thought banks had too little capacity to absorb losses and were making too many risky loans could not predict exactly when a crisis would occur.

A crucial element in macroeconomic activity is people's expectations. If people are optimistic about the future, consumers may be more inclined to spend and firms more inclined to invest. If they are pessimistic, spending may fall. But what drives these expectations? Again, this is a topic of lively debate.

Then there is the political context. Governments may be unwilling to take unpopular measures, especially when an election looms. So, should they give responsibility for decisions to other bodies? In many countries, interest rates are not set by the government but by the central bank. In the UK, for example, it is the Bank of England that sets interest rates at the monthly meetings of the Monetary Policy Committee.

So just what are the macroeconomic issues that we will be studying in the following chapters? We can group them under the following headings: economic growth, unemployment, inflation, the economic relationships with the rest of the world, the financial well-being of individuals, businesses and government and the relationship between the financial system and the economy. We will be studying other issues too, such as consumer behaviour and taxation, but these still link to these major macroeconomic issues and, more generally, to how economies function.

The major macroeconomic issues

Economic growth

Governments try to achieve high *rates of economic growth* over the long term – in other words, growth that is sustained over the years and is not just a temporary phenomenon. To this end, governments ordinarily try to achieve *stable* growth, avoiding both recessions and excessive short-term growth that cannot be sustained. As we shall see in later chapters, governments around the world were not very successful in preventing a recession in 2008–9.

KEY IDEA ?? *Economies suffer from inherent instability.* As a result, economic growth and other macroeconomic indicators tend to fluctuate.

Table 14.1 shows the average annual growth in output by decade since the 1960s for selected countries. As you can see, the differences between countries are quite substantial. 'Newly industrialised countries', such as Malaysia, Singapore and China, have experienced particularly rapid rates of economic growth.

There are also big differences between the growth rates of individual countries in different periods. Look, for example, at the figures for Japan. From being an 'economic miracle' in the 1960s, Japan by the 1990s had become a laggard, with a growth rate well below the OECD average.

Unemployment

Reducing unemployment is another major macroeconomic aim of governments, not only for the sake of the unemployed themselves, but also because it represents a waste of human resources and because unemployment benefits are a drain on government revenues.

Unemployment in the 1980s and early 1990s was significantly higher than in the 1960s and 1970s (see Table 14.1). Then, in the late 1990s and early 2000s, it fell in some countries, such as the UK and USA. In others, such as Germany and France, it remained stubbornly high. However, the

Definition

Rate of economic growth The percentage increase in national output, normally expressed over a 12-month period.

Table 14.1 Economic growth (average % per annum), unemployment (average %) and inflation (average % per annum)

	France	Germany	Japan	UK	USA	EU12[a]	OECD[b]	Brazil	Malaysia	Singapore	China
Growth											
1960	5.6	4.4	10.4	2.9	4.3	5.8	5.5	5.9	6.5	9.5	3.0
1970	3.7	3.1	5.2	2.4	3.2	3.8	3.7	7.9	7.8	9.6	7.1
1980	2.3	1.9	4.4	2.7	3.1	2.3	2.9	3.0	5.9	7.8	9.8
1990	1.9	2.2	1.5	2.8	3.2	2.2	2.5	1.7	7.2	7.3	10.0
2000	1.3	0.9	0.6	1.9	1.8	1.3	1.8	3.3	4.7	5.2	10.3
2010–15[c]	1.1	1.9	1.7	1.4	2.4	0.9	1.9	3.2	5.5	5.3	7.8
Unemployment											
1960	1.5	0.9	1.3	2.2	4.1	2.5	2.5	n.a.	n.a.	n.a.	n.a.
1970	3.7	2.3	1.7	4.5	6.1	4.0	4.3	n.a.	n.a.	3.6	n.a.
1980	8.2	6.9	2.5	9.9	7.3	9.3	7.2	5.5	7.2	4.4	2.7
1990	10.1	7.9	3.0	8.2	5.8	10.5	7.2	5.6	3.4	1.9	2.8
2000	8.8	9.0	4.7	5.4	5.5	8.5	6.5	9.9	3.5	2.9	4.0
2010–15[c]	10.4	5.8	4.5	7.7	8.1	11.3	8.1	6.1	3.1	2.2	4.1
Inflation											
1960	3.8	3.2	5.5	3.8	2.4	3.7	3.1	46.1	0.8	1.2	n.a.
1970	8.9	4.9	9.1	12.6	7.1	9.5	9.2	30.6	5.5	5.9	n.a.
1980	7.3	2.9	2.5	7.0	5.6	6.5	8.9	328.1	3.6	2.8	7.5
1990	1.9	2.4	1.2	3.3	3.0	2.9	4.4	854.8	3.7	1.9	7.8
2000	1.9	1.6	−0.3	1.8	2.6	2.1	2.7	6.9	2.2	1.5	1.9
2010–15[c]	1.7	1.8	0.6	2.9	1.9	1.3	2.0	5.8	2.3	3.4	3.2

[a] EU12 = the 12 original countries adopting the euro.
[b] The Organization for Economic Co-operation and Development (an organisation of 34 major industrialised countries).
[c] Figures from 2013 are based on forecasts.

global financial crisis and subsequent economic slowdown meant that unemployment rates were to rise generally in the late 2000s and into the early 2010s.

We take a preliminary look at the nature and causes of unemployment in Chapter 15.

Inflation

By inflation we mean a general rise in prices throughout the economy. Government policy here is to keep inflation both low and stable. One of the most important reasons for this is that it will aid the process of economic decision making. For example, businesses will be able to set prices and wage rates, and make investment decisions with far more confidence.

In recent years we have tended to become used to *inflation rates* of around 2 or 3 per cent, but it was not long ago that inflation in most developed countries was in double figures. Even though inflation rates rose in many countries in 2007–8 and again during 2010–11, figures remained much lower than in the past; in 1975, UK inflation reached 24 per cent. During the recession of 2008–9, inflation rates fell in most countries, becoming negative ('deflation') in some.

In most developed countries, governments have a particular target for the rate of inflation. In the UK the target is 2 per cent. The Bank of England then adjusts interest rates to try to keep inflation on target (we see how this works in Chapter 21).

The balance of payments and the exchange rate

We are concerned here with a country's foreign trade and its economic relationships with other countries.

A country's **balance of payments account** records all transactions between the residents of that country and the rest of the world. These transactions enter as either debit items or credit items. The debit items include all payments *to* other countries: these include the country's purchases of imports, the investments it makes abroad and the interest and dividends paid to people abroad who have invested in the country. The credit items include all receipts *from* other countries: these include the sales of exports, inflows of investment into the country and earnings of interest and dividends from abroad.

The sale of exports and any other receipts earn foreign currency. The purchase of imports or any other payments abroad requires foreign currency. If we start to spend more

Definitions

Rate of inflation The percentage increase in prices over a 12-month period.

Balance of payments account A record of the country's transactions with the rest of the world. It shows the country's payments to or deposits in other countries (debits) and its receipts or deposits from other countries (credits). It also shows the balance between these debits and credits under various headings.

foreign currency than we earn, then the balance of payments will go into deficit. If the government does nothing to correct the balance of payments deficit, the **exchange rate** must fall. (We will show just why this is so in section 15.4.) The exchange rate is the rate at which one currency exchanges for another. For example, the exchange rate of the pound into the dollar might be £1 = $1.60.

A falling exchange rate (e.g. from $1.60 to $1.50) is a problem because it pushes up the price of imports and may fuel inflation. Also, if the exchange rate fluctuates, this can cause great uncertainty for traders and can damage international trade and economic growth.

What are the underlying causes of balance of payments problems? How do the balance of payments and the exchange rate relate to the other macroeconomic issues? What are the best policies for governments to adopt? We take an initial look at these questions in Chapter 15 and then examine them in more detail in Chapters 25 and 26.

Sector accounts

There are two main types of accounts used to show the financial position of individuals, businesses and other organisations, governments and nations. The first type, known as an **income and expenditure account** or **profit and loss** account, shows *flows* of incomes and expenditure. The second type, known as a **balance sheet**, shows the *stock* of assets and liabilities. An **asset** is something owned by or owed to you. A **liability** is a debt: i.e. something you owe to someone else.

Note that it is also possible to make a separate record of the *changes* to a balance sheet over a given period of time, such as a month or a year. These changes are flows. Thus the acquisition of assets represents an inflow to the balance sheet and the disposal of assets represents an outflow.

> Is the balance of payments account an income and expenditure account or a balance sheet?

There are three key accounts which are compiled for the main sectors of the economy: the household, corporate and government sectors and the economy as whole.

- First, there is the *income account* which records the various flows of income alongside the amounts either spent or saved. Economic growth refers to the annual real growth in a country's income flows (i.e. after taking inflation into account).
- Second, there is the *financial account*. The financial *balance sheet* gives a complete record of the stocks of financial assets (arising from saving) and financial liabilities (arising from borrowing) of a sector, and include things such as currency, bank deposits, loans, bonds and shares. *Changes* in such balances over time (flows of new saving and borrowing) have been key in explaining the credit crunch and subsequent deep recession of the late 2000s/early 2010s.
- Third, there is the *capital account*, which records the stock of non-financial (physical) wealth, arising from acquiring

or disposing of physical assets, such as property and machinery. *Changes* over time (inflows and outflows) in the capital balance sheets of the different sectors give important insights into relationships between the sectors of the economy and to possible growing tensions.

The *national balance sheet* is a measure of the wealth of a country. It can be presented so as to show the contribution of each sector and/or the composition of wealth. The balance of a sector's or country's stock of both financial and non-financial wealth is referred to as its **net worth**.

Figure 14.1 presents the national balance sheet for the UK since 1987. In 2012, the net worth of the UK was £7.27 trillion, equivalent to 4.6 times the country's annual income or 'gross domestic product (GDP)' (see section 14.3 on the measurement of GDP). The stock of net worth fell for two consecutive years – 2008 and 2009 – at the height of the financial crisis and the economic slowdown.

These various accounts are part of an interconnected story detailing the financial well-being of a country's households, corporations and government. To illustrate how, consider what would happen if, over a period of time, you were to spend more than the income you receive. This would result in your income account deteriorating. To finance your excess spending you could perhaps draw on any financial wealth that you have accumulated through saving. Alternatively, you might fund some of your spending through a loan from a financial institution, such as a bank. Either way, your financial balance sheet will deteriorate. Or you may dispose of some physical assets, such as property. In this scenario your capital balance sheet will deteriorate. But however your excess spending is financed, your net worth declines.

The importance of balance sheet effects in influencing behaviour and, hence, economic activity has been increasingly recognised by both economists and policy makers, especially since the financial crisis of 2007–9. Yet there remains considerable work to be done in gaining a better understanding of the relationship and in devising the most appropriate policies.

Definitions

Exchange rate The rate at which one national currency exchanges for another. The rate is expressed as the amount of one currency that is necessary to purchase one unit of another currency (e.g. €1.20 = £1).

Income and expenditure account or **profit and loss account** A record of the flows of incomes, expenditure and saving of an individual or institution.

Balance sheet A record of the stock of assets and liabilities of an individual or institution.

Asset Possessions of an individual or institution or claims held on others.

Liability Claims by others on an individual or institution; debts of that individual or institution.

Net worth The market value of a sector's stock of financial and non-financial wealth.

KI 24
p 271

| Figure 14.1 | UK net worth |

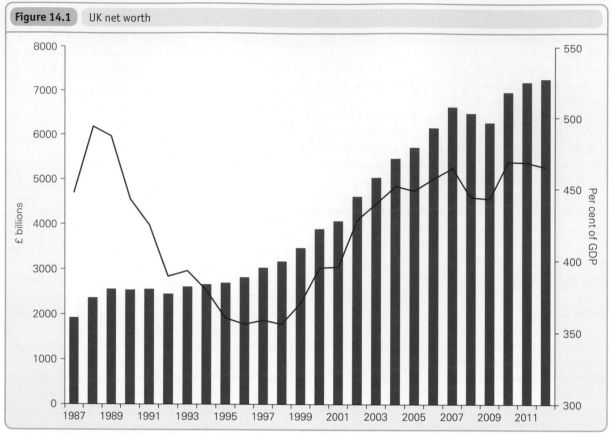

Source: Based on data from *National Balance Sheet* and Quarterly *National Accounts* (National Statistics).

KEY IDEA 33

Balance sheets affect people's behaviour. The size and structure of the liabilities and assets of governments, institutions and individuals affect economic well-being and can have significant effects on behaviour and economic activity.

Financial stability

A core aim of policy makers is to ensure the stability of the financial system. After all, financial markets and institutions are an integral part of economies. Their well-being is crucial to the well-being of an economy and, because of the global interconnectedness of financial institutions and markets, problems can spread globally like a contagion. The financial crisis of the late 2000s showed vividly how financially distressed financial institutions can cause serious economic upheaval on a global scale.

It perhaps seems self-evident, but a model of the macroeconomy is incomplete if it does not just incorporate financial markets and institutions but also capture the *interaction* between the financial system and the macroeconomy.

As we shall see in Chapter 18, a major part of the global response to the financial crisis has been to try to ensure that financial institutions are more financially resilient. In particular, financial institutions should have more loss-absorbing capacity and therefore be better able to withstand 'shocks' and deteriorating macroeconomic conditions.

Government macroeconomic policy

From the above issues we can identify a series of macroeconomic policy objectives that governments might typically pursue:

- High and stable economic growth.
- Low unemployment.
- Low inflation.
- The avoidance of balance of payments deficits and excessive exchange rate fluctuations.
- The avoidance of excessively financially distressed sectors of the economy, including government.
- A stable financial system.

Unfortunately, these policy objectives may conflict. For example, a policy designed to accelerate the rate of economic growth may result in a higher rate of inflation, a balance of payments deficit and excessive lending. Governments are thus often faced with awkward policy choices.

KEY IDEA 34

Societies face trade-offs between economic objectives. For example, the goal of faster growth may conflict with that of greater equality; the goal of lower unemployment may conflict with that of lower inflation (at least in the short run). This is an example of opportunity cost: the cost of achieving one objective may be achieving less of another. The existence of trade-offs means that policy makers must make choices.

14.2 THE CIRCULAR FLOW OF INCOME

One way in which the macroeconomic objectives are linked is through their relationship with **aggregate demand** (*AD*). This is the total spending on goods and services made within the country ('domestically produced goods and services'). This spending consists of four elements.

The first is **consumer spending on domestically produced goods and services** (C_d) (i.e. total consumer expenditure on all products (*C*) minus expenditure on imports (*M*)). The

other three elements are: investment expenditure by firms (*I*), government spending (*G*) and the expenditure by residents abroad on this country's exports (*X*). Thus,[1]

$$AD = C_d + I + G + X$$

or, put another way,

$$AD = C + I + G + X - M$$

To show how these objectives may be related to aggregate demand, we can use a simple model of the economy. This is the circular flow of income, and is shown in Figure 14.2. It is an extension of the model that we looked at back in Chapter 1 (page 17).

In the diagram, the economy is divided into two major groups: *firms* and *households*. Each group has two roles. Firms are producers of goods and services; they are also the

Definitions

Aggregate demand Total spending on goods and services produced in the economy. It consists of four elements: consumer expenditure (*C*), investment (*I*), government expenditure (*G*) and the expenditure on exports (*X*), less any expenditure on foreign goods and services (*M*). Thus $AD = C + I + G + X - M$, or $C_d + I + G + X$.

Consumption of domestically produced goods and services (C_d) The direct flow of money payments from households to firms.

[1] We assume, for simplicity, in this first equation that all investment, government expenditure and export expenditure is on domestic products. If, however, any part of these three went on imports, we would have to subtract this imported element (as we did with consumption). We would then have to write $AD = C_d + I_d + G_d + X_d$.

Figure 14.2 The circular flow of income

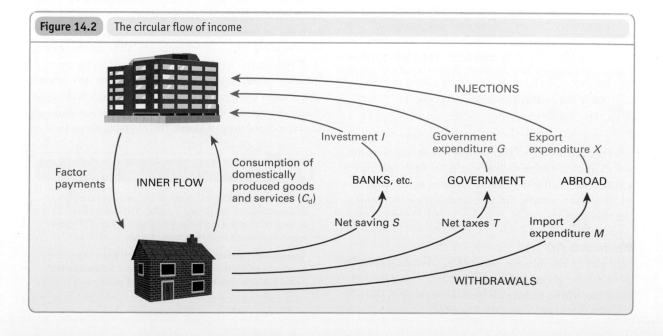

employers of labour and other factors of production. Households (which include all individuals) are the consumers of goods and services; they are also the suppliers of labour and various other factors of production. In the diagram there is an inner flow and various outer flows of incomes between these two groups.

Before we look at the various parts of the diagram, a word of warning. Do not confuse *money* and *income*. Money is a *stock* concept. At any given time, there is a certain quantity of money in the economy (e.g. £1 trillion). But that does not tell us the level of national *income*. Income is a *flow* concept (as is expenditure). It is measured as so much *per period of time*. The relationship between money and income depends on how rapidly the money *circulates*: its 'velocity of circulation'. (We will examine this concept in detail later on: see pages 470 and 561.) If there is £1 trillion of money in the economy and each £1 on average is paid out as income twice per year, then annual national income will be £2 trillion.

The inner flow, withdrawals and injections

The inner flow

Firms pay money to households in the form of wages and salaries, dividends on shares, interest and rent. These payments are in return for the services of the factors of production – labour, capital and land – that are supplied by households. Thus on the left-hand side of the diagram, money flows directly from firms to households as 'factor payments'.

Households, in turn, pay money to domestic firms when they consume domestically produced goods and services (C_d). This is shown on the right-hand side of the inner flow. There is thus a circular flow of payments from firms to households to firms and so on.

If households spend *all* their incomes on buying domestic goods and services, and if firms pay out *all* this income they receive as factor payments to domestic households, and if the velocity of circulation does not change, the flow will continue at the same level indefinitely. The money just goes round and round at the same speed and incomes remain unchanged.

Would this argument still hold if prices rose?

In the real world, of course, it is not as simple as this. Not all income gets passed on round the inner flow; some is *withdrawn*. At the same time, incomes are injected into the flow from outside. Let us examine these withdrawals and injections.

Withdrawals (W)

Only part of the incomes received by households will be spent on the goods and services of domestic firms. The remainder will be withdrawn from the inner flow. Likewise

only part of the incomes generated by firms will be paid to UK households. The remainder of this will also be withdrawn. There are three forms of **withdrawals** (or '**leakages**' as they are sometimes called).

Net saving (S).   Saving is income that households choose not to spend but to put aside for the future. Savings are normally deposited in financial institutions such as banks and building societies. This is shown in the bottom centre of the diagram. Money flows from households to 'banks, etc.'. What we are seeking to measure here, however, is the net flow from households to the banking sector. We therefore have to subtract from saving any borrowing or drawing on past savings by households to arrive at the *net* saving flow. Of course, if household borrowing exceeded saving, the net flow would be in the other direction: it would be negative.

Net taxes (T).   When people pay taxes (to either central or local government), this represents a withdrawal of money from the inner flow in much the same way as saving; only, in this case, people have no choice. Some taxes, such as income tax and employees' national insurance contributions, are paid out of household incomes. Others, such as VAT and excise duties, are paid out of consumer expenditure. Others, such as corporation tax, are paid out of firms' incomes before being received by households as dividends on shares. (For simplicity, however, taxes are shown in Figure 14.2 as leaving the circular flow at just one point.)

When, however, people receive *benefits* from the government, such as unemployment benefits, child benefit and pensions, the money flows the other way. Benefits are thus equivalent to a 'negative tax'. These benefits are known as **transfer payments**. They transfer money from one group of people (taxpayers) to others (the recipients).

In the model, 'net taxes' (T) represents the *net* flow to the government from households and firms. It consists of total taxes minus benefits.

Import expenditure (M).   Not all consumption is of totally home-produced goods. Households spend some of their incomes on imported goods and services, or on goods and services using imported components. Although the money that consumers spend on such goods initially flows to domestic retailers, it will eventually find its way abroad, either when the retailers or wholesalers themselves import them, or when domestic manufacturers purchase imported inputs to make their products. This expenditure on imports

---

Definitions

Withdrawals (*W*) (or leakages) Incomes of households or firms that are not passed on round the inner flow. Withdrawals equal net saving (*S*) plus net taxes (*T*) plus import expenditure (*M*): $W = S + T + M$.

Transfer payments Moneys transferred from one person or group to another (e.g. from the government to individuals) without production taking place.

constitutes the third withdrawal from the inner flow. This money flows abroad.

Total withdrawals are simply the sum of net saving, net taxes and the expenditure on imports:

$$W = S + T + M$$

Injections (J)

Only part of the demand for firms' output arises from consumers' expenditure. The remainder comes from other sources outside the inner flow. These additional components of aggregate demand are known as **injections** (J). There are three types of injection.

Investment (I). This is the money that firms spend after obtaining it from various financial institutions – either past savings or loans, or through a new issue of shares. They may invest in plant and equipment or may simply spend the money on building up stocks of inputs, semi-finished or finished goods.

Government expenditure (G). When the government spends money on goods and services produced by firms, this counts as an injection. Examples of such government expenditure include spending on roads, hospitals and schools. (Note that government expenditure in this model does not include state benefits. These transfer payments, as we saw above, are the equivalent of negative taxes and have the effect of reducing the T component of withdrawals.)

Export expenditure (X). Money flows into the circular flow from abroad when residents abroad buy our exports of goods and services.[1]

Total injections are thus the sum of investment, government expenditure and exports:

$$J = I + G + X$$

The relationship between withdrawals and injections

There are indirect links between saving and investment, taxation and government expenditure, and imports and exports, via financial institutions, the government (central and local) and foreign countries respectively. If more money

> ### Definition
>
> **Injections** (J) Expenditure on the production of domestic firms coming from outside the inner flow of the circular flow of income. Injections equal investment (I) plus government expenditure (G) plus expenditure on exports (X).

[1] Note that X would not include investment in the UK by foreign companies (i.e. credits on the financial account of the balance of payments). Foreign 'investment' involves the acquisition of assets in the UK and thus represents an income to the previous owners of these assets. It therefore represents an inflow from abroad to the household sector and thus has the effect of reducing M.

is saved, there will be more available for banks and other financial institutions to lend out. If tax receipts are higher, the government may be keener to increase its expenditure. Finally, if imports increase, incomes of people abroad will increase, which will enable them to purchase more of our exports.

These links, however, do not guarantee that $S = I$ or $G = T$ or $M = X$. Firms may wish to invest (I) more or less than people wish to save (S); governments can spend (G) more than they receive in taxes (T) or vice versa; and exports (X) can exceed imports (M) or vice versa.

A major point here is that the decisions to save and invest are made by different people, and thus they plan to save and invest different amounts. Likewise the demand for imports may not equal the demand for exports. As far as the government is concerned, it may choose not to make $T = G$. It may choose not to spend all its tax revenues to run a 'budget surplus' ($T > G$). Or it may choose to spend more than it receives in taxes – to run a budget deficit ($G > T$) – by borrowing or printing money to make up the difference.

Thus planned injections (J) may not equal planned withdrawals (W).

 Are the following net injections, net withdrawals or neither? If there is uncertainty, explain your assumptions.

(a) Firms are forced to take a cut in profits in order to give a pay-rise.

(b) Firms spend money on research.

(c) The government increases personal tax allowances.

(d) The general public invests more money in banks and building societies.

(e) UK investors earn higher dividends on overseas investments.

(f) The government purchases US military aircraft.

(g) People draw on their savings to finance holidays abroad.

(h) People draw on their savings to finance holidays in the UK.

(i) The government runs a budget deficit (spends more than it receives in tax revenues) and finances it by borrowing from the public.

(j) The government runs a budget deficit and finances it by printing more money.

The circular flow of income and the macroeconomic objectives

If planned injections are not equal to planned withdrawals, what will be the consequences? If, for example, injections exceed withdrawals, the level of expenditure will rise: there will be a rise in aggregate demand. This extra spending will increase firms' sales and thus encourage them to produce more. Total output in the economy will rise. Thus firms will pay out more in wages, salaries, profits, rent and interest. In other words, national income will rise.

The rise in aggregate demand will have the following effects upon the macroeconomic objectives:

- There will be economic growth. The greater the initial excess of injections over withdrawals, the bigger will be the rise in national income.

- Unemployment will fall as firms take on more workers to meet the extra demand for output.
- The rate of inflation will tend to rise. The greater the rise in aggregate demand relative to the capacity of firms to produce, the more will firms find it difficult to meet the extra demand, and the more likely they will be to raise prices.
- The exports and imports part of the balance of payments will tend to deteriorate. The higher demand sucks more imports into the country, and higher domestic inflation makes exports less competitive and imports relatively cheaper compared with home-produced goods. Thus imports will tend to rise and exports will tend to fall.
- The increase in aggregate demand and its impact on income, consumption and saving will be recorded on sector income accounts. These effects will impact on the financial and capital balance sheets of the various sectors and the economy as a whole. An increase in national income allows economic agents to accumulate financial and non-financial assets and/or to reduce holdings of financial liabilities. Exactly how the balance sheets are affected depends on the actual behaviour of economic agents.

 Now consider the situation where there is an initial excess of withdrawals over injections. What effect will there be on the macroeconomic objectives?

Equilibrium in the circular flow

When injections do not equal withdrawals, a state of disequilibrium will exist. This will set in train a process to bring the economy back to a state of equilibrium where injections are equal to withdrawals.

To illustrate this, let us again consider the situation where injections exceed withdrawals. Perhaps there has been a rise in business confidence so that investment has risen. Or perhaps there has been a tax cut so that withdrawals have fallen. As we have seen, the excess of injections over withdrawals will lead to a rise in national income.

But as national income rises, so households will not only spend more on domestic goods (C_d), but also save more (S), pay more taxes (T) and buy more imports (M). In other words, withdrawals will rise. This will continue until they have risen to equal injections. At that point, national income will stop rising, and so will withdrawals. Equilibrium has been reached.

Section summary

1. The circular flow of income model depicts the flows of money round the economy. The inner flow shows the direct flows between firms and households. Money flows from firms to households in the form of factor payments, and back again as consumer expenditure on domestically produced goods and services.

2. Not all income gets passed on directly round the inner flow. Some is withdrawn in the form of net saving, some is paid in net taxes, and some goes abroad as expenditure on imports.

3. Likewise, not all expenditure on domestic firms is by domestic consumers. Some is injected from outside the inner flow in the form of investment expenditure, government expenditure and expenditure on the country's exports.

4. Planned injections and withdrawals are unlikely to be the same.

5. If injections exceed withdrawals, national income will rise, unemployment will tend to fall, inflation will tend to rise, imports will tend to rise and exports fall. The reverse will happen if withdrawals exceed injections.

6. If injections exceed withdrawals, the rise in national income will lead to a rise in withdrawals. This will continue until $W = J$. At this point, the circular flow will be in equilibrium.

14.3 MEASURING NATIONAL INCOME AND OUTPUT

The circular flow of income is very useful as a model for understanding the working of an economy. It shows how national income can increase or decrease as a result of changes in the various flows. But just how do we measure national income or output? The measure we use is called *gross domestic product (GDP)*.

Definition

Gross domestic product (GDP) The value of output produced within the country over a 12-month period.

This section shows how GDP is calculated. It also looks at difficulties in interpreting GDP statistics. Can the figures be meaningfully used to compare one country's standard of living with another? The appendix to this chapter goes into more detail on the precise way in which the statistics for GDP are derived.

The three ways of measuring GDP

GDP can be calculated in three different ways, which should all result in the same figure. These three methods are illustrated in the simplified circular flow of income shown in Figure 14.3.

Figure 14.3	The circular flow of national income and expenditure

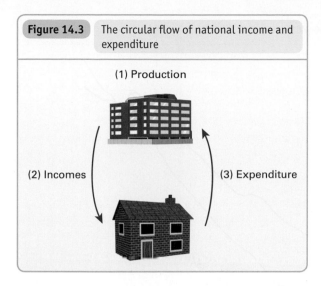

(1) Production

(2) Incomes   (3) Expenditure

The first method of measuring GDP is to add up the value of all the goods and services produced in the country, industry by industry. In other words, we focus on firms and add up all their production. This first method is known as the *product method*.

The production of goods and services generates incomes for households in the form of wages and salaries, profits, rent and interest. The second method of measuring GDP, therefore, is to add up all these incomes. This is known as the *income method*.

The third method focuses on the expenditures necessary to purchase the nation's production. In this simple model of the circular flow of income, with no injections or withdrawals, whatever is produced is sold. The value of what is sold must therefore be the value of what is produced. The *expenditure method* measures this sales value.

Because of the way the calculations are made, the three methods of calculating GDP *must* yield the same result. In other words,

national product = national income
= national expenditure

In the appendix to this chapter, we look at each of the three methods in turn, and examine the various factors that have to be taken into account to ensure that the figures are accurate.

Taking account of inflation

If we are to make a sensible comparison of one year's national income with another, we must take inflation into account. For example, if this year national income is 10 per cent higher than last year, but at the same time prices are also 10 per cent higher, then the average person will be no better off at all. There has been no *real* increase in income (see discussion in Appendix 1 at the end of the book on page A:6).

An important distinction here is between **nominal GDP** and **real GDP**. *Nominal* GDP, sometimes called 'money GDP', measures GDP in the prices ruling at the time and thus takes

no account of inflation. *Real* GDP, sometimes called 'GDP at constant prices', measures GDP in the prices that ruled in some particular year – the *base year*. Thus we could measure each year's GDP in, say, 2010 prices. This would enable us to see how much *real* GDP had changed from one year to another. In other words, it would eliminate increases in money GDP that were merely due to an increase in prices.

The official statistics give both nominal and real figures. (Case Study 14.1 in MyEconLab shows in more detail how real GDP figures are calculated.) Figure 14.4 shows nominal GDP and GDP at constant 2010 prices since 1950 in the UK. The real figures show the UK economy to be five times larger in 2015 than in 1950. If we had mistakenly used the nominal GDP figures to compare the size of output between these two dates we would have thought that the economy was over 120 times larger!

The real figures, as well as revealing the extent of long-term economic growth, also show the *variability* of economic growth from year to year. Indeed, we can see falls in output in the mid-1970s, early 1980s and early 1990s which are not directly observable from nominal GDP. Instead, nominal GDP continued to increase because of higher price levels. However, in 2009 output fell by over 5 per cent, which meant that even nominal GDP fell. In other words, price rises were not enough to offset a substantial decline in the volume of output.

Taking account of population: the use of per capita measures

The figures we have been looking at up to now are *total* GDP figures. Although they are useful for showing how big the total output or income of one country is compared with another, we are often more interested in output or income *per head*. Luxembourg obviously has a much lower total national income than the UK, but it has a higher GDP per head. In 2010 China overtook Japan to become the second-largest economy in the world, and some estimate that it will become the biggest economy by 2025. But these are total figures. In 2014, GDP per capita in China is estimated to be a mere 18 per cent of that of the USA (see Figure 27.2 on page 803), even after taking the different purchasing powers of the two currencies into account (see below, page 410). Even by 2025 it will still be only a small fraction.

Other per capita measures are sometimes useful. For example, measuring GDP per head of the *employed* population allows us to compare how much the average worker produces. A country may have a relatively high GDP per

Definitions

Nominal GDP GDP measured at current prices.

Real GDP GDP after allowing for inflation – GDP measured in constant prices: i.e. in terms of the prices ruling in some base year.

| Figure 14.4 | Nominal GDP and constant-price GDP, UK 1950–2015 |

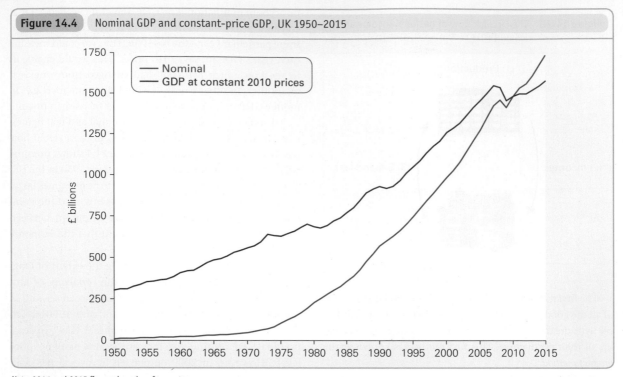

Note: 2014 and 2015 figures based on forecasts.
Source: Based on data from Quarterly National Accounts (ONS); forecasts based on data in Economic Outlook (IMF).

head of population, but also have a large proportion of people at work. Its output per worker will therefore not be so high.

 By what would we need to divide GDP in order to get a measure of labour productivity per hour?

Taking account of exchange rates: the use of PPP measures

There is a big problem with comparing GDP figures of different countries. They are measured in the local currency and thus have to be converted into a common currency (e.g. dollars or euros) at the current exchange rate. But the exchange rate may be a poor indicator of the purchasing power of the currency at home. For example, £1 may exchange for, say, ¥170. But will £1 in the UK buy the same amount of goods as ¥170 in Japan? The answer is almost certainly no.

To compensate for this, GDP can be converted into a common currency at a *purchasing-power parity rate*. This is a rate of exchange that would allow a given amount of money in one country to buy the same amount of goods in another country after exchanging it into the currency of the other country. For example, the OECD publishes PPP rates against the US dollar for all OECD currencies. Using such rates to measure GDP gives the *purchasing-power standard (PPS) GDP*.

Box 14.1 compares GDP with PPS GDP for various countries.

Do GDP statistics give a good indication of a country's standard of living?

If we take into account both inflation and the size of the population, and use figures for *real* per capita PPS GDP, will this give us a good indication of a country's standard of living? The figures *do* give quite a good indication of the level of production of goods and the incomes generated from it, provided we are clear about the distinctions between the different measures. But when we come to ask the more general question of whether the figures give a good indication of the welfare or happiness of the country's citizens, then there are serious problems in relying exclusively on GDP statistics.

Problems of measuring national output

The main problem here is that the output of some goods and services goes unrecorded and thus the GDP figures will understate the nation's output. There are two reasons why items are not recorded.

Definitions

Purchasing-power parity (PPP) exchange rate
An exchange rate corrected to take into account the purchasing power of a currency. $1 would buy the same in each country after conversion into its currency at the PPP rate.

Purchasing-power standard (PPS) GDP GDP measured at a country's PPP exchange rate.

| THRESHOLD CONCEPT 12 | THE DISTINCTION BETWEEN REAL AND NOMINAL VALUES | THINKING LIKE AN ECONOMIST |

Which would you rather have: (a) a pay rise of 5 per cent when inflation is 2 per cent, or (b) a pay rise of 10 per cent when inflation is 9 per cent? Which debt would you rather have: (a) one where the interest rate is 10 per cent and inflation is 8 per cent, or (b) one where the interest rate is 5 per cent and the inflation rate is 1 per cent?

To answer these questions, you need to distinguish between real and nominal values. *Nominal values* are measured in current prices and take no account of inflation. Thus in the questions above, the nominal pay rises are (a) 5 per cent and (b) 10 per cent; the nominal interest rates are (a) 10 per cent and (b) 5 per cent. In each case it might seem that you are better off with alternative (b).

But if you opted for answers (b), you would be wrong. Once you take inflation into account, you would be better off in each case with alternative (a). What we need to do is to use *real values*. Real values take account of inflation. Thus in the first question, although the nominal pay rise in alternative (a) is 5 per cent, the real pay rise is only 3 per cent, since 2 of the 5 per cent is absorbed by higher prices. You are only 3 per cent better off in terms of what you can buy. In alternative (b) the real pay rise is only 1 per cent, since 9 of the 10 per cent is absorbed by higher prices. Thus in real terms, alternative (a) is better.

In the second question, although in alternative (a) you are paying 10 per cent in nominal terms, your debt is being reduced in real terms by 8 per cent and thus you are paying a real rate of interest of only 2 per cent. In alternative (b), although the nominal rate of interest is only 5 per cent, your debt is being eroded by inflation by only 1 per cent. The real rate of interest is thus 4 per cent. Again, in real terms, you are better off with alternative (a).

The distinction between real and nominal values is a threshold concept, as understanding the distinction is fundamental to assessing statistics about the economy. Often politicians will switch between real and nominal values depending on which are most favourable to them. Thus a government wishing to show how strong economic growth has been will tend to use nominal growth figures. On the other hand, the opposition will tend to refer to real growth figures, as these will be lower (assuming a positive inflation rate).

It's easy to make the mistake of using nominal figures when we should really be using real ones. This is known as 'money illusion': the belief that a rise in money terms represents a real rise.

When comparing two countries' GDP growth rates, does it matter if we use nominal figures, provided we use them for both countries?

| BOX 14.1 | WHICH COUNTRY IS BETTER OFF? | CASE STUDIES AND APPLICATIONS |

Comparing national income statistics

Using PPS GDP figures can give a quite different picture of the relative incomes in different countries than using simple GDP figures. The table shows the GDP per head and PPS GDP per head in various countries. The figures are expressed as a percentage of the average of the EU-15 countries (i.e. those that were members prior to the entry of 10 new members in May 2004).

Thus in 2014, GDP per head in Australia was estimated to be 74 per cent higher than the EU-15 average. But, because of higher Australian prices, the average person in Denmark could buy only 16 per cent more goods and services. By contrast, GDP per head in Poland was only 31 per cent of the EU-15 average but, because of lower Polish prices, the average person there could buy 58 per cent as much as the average citizen of the EU-15 countries.

Referring to the figures in the table, which countries' actual exchange rates would seem to understate the purchasing power of their currency?

GDP per head as a percentage of the EU-15 average, 2014

	GDP per head	GDP (PPS) per head
Poland	30.5	57.9
Greece	46.4	60.8
Portugal	45.1	63.2
Czech Republic	41.5	68.3
Italy	74.4	81.6
Spain	66.4	82.2
France	90.9	91.6
UK	84.6	92.8
Japan	85.9	94.6
Germany	96.6	105.2
Denmark	130.5	107.6
Canada	118.9	108.1
Netherlands	104.4	109.0
Ireland	105.7	110.4
Sweden	134.6	110.9
Australia	173.7	116.0
USA	115.4	130.5
Luxembourg	248.4	224.0

Note: Figures based on forecasts.
Source: AMECO Database, European Commission, DGECFIN (Table 6.2).

Non-marketed items. If you employ a decorator to paint your living room, this will be recorded in the GDP statistics. If, however, you paint the room yourself, it will not. Similarly, if a nanny is employed by parents to look after their children, this childcare will form part of GDP. If, however, a parent stays at home to look after the children, it will not. The exclusion of these 'do-it-yourself' and other home-based activities means that the GDP statistics understate the true level of production in the economy. If over time there is an *increase* in the amount of do-it-yourself activities that people perform, the figures will also understate the *rate of growth* of national output. On the other hand, if in more and more families both partners go out to work and employ people to look after their children, this will overstate the rate of growth in output. The childcare that was previously unrecorded now enters into the GDP statistics.

 If we were trying to get a 'true' measure of national production, which of the following activities would you include: (a) washing up; (b) planting flowers in the garden; (c) playing an educational game with children in the family; (d) playing any game with children in the family; (e) cooking your own supper; (f) cooking supper for the whole family; (g) reading a novel for pleasure; (h) reading a textbook as part of studying; (i) studying holiday brochures? Is there a measurement problem if you get pleasure from the do-it-yourself activity itself as well as from its outcome?

The 'underground' economy. The underground economy consists of illegal and hence undeclared transactions. These could be transactions where the goods or services are themselves illegal, as with drugs, guns and prostitution. Alternatively, they could be transactions that are illegal only in that they are not declared for tax purposes. For example, to avoid paying VAT, a garage may be prepared to repair your car slightly more cheaply if you pay cash. Another example is that of 'moonlighting', where people do extra work outside their normal job and do not declare the income for tax purposes. For example, an electrician employed by a building contractor during the day may rewire people's houses in the evenings, again for cash. Unemployed people may do casual jobs that they do not declare, to avoid losing benefits.

Problems of using GDP statistics to measure welfare

GDP is essentially an indicator of a nation's *production*. But production may be a poor indicator of society's well-being for the following reasons.

Production does not equal consumption. Production is desirable only to the extent that it enables us to *consume* more. If GDP rises as a result of a rise in *investment*, this will not lead to an increase in *current* living standards. It will, of course, help to raise *future* consumption.

The same applies if GDP rises as a result of an increase in exports. Unless there is a resulting increase in imports,

it will be consumers abroad that benefit, not domestic consumers.

Production has human costs. If production increases, this may be due to technological advances. If, however, it increases as a result of people having to work harder or longer hours, its net benefit will be less. Leisure is a desirable good, and so too are pleasant working conditions, but these items are not included in the GDP figures.

GDP ignores externalities. The rapid growth in industrial society is recorded in GDP statistics. What the statistics do not record are the environmental side effects: the polluted air and rivers, the ozone depletion, the problem of global warming. If these external costs were taken into account, the *net* benefits of industrial production might be much less.

 Name some external benefits that are not included in GDP statistics.

The production of certain 'bads' leads to an increase in GDP. Some of the undesirable effects of growth may actually *increase* GDP! Take the examples of crime, stress-related illness and environmental damage. Faster growth may lead to more of all three. But increased crime leads to more expenditure on security; increased stress leads to more expenditure on health care; and increased environmental damage leads to more expenditure on environmental clean-up. These expenditures *add* to GDP. Thus, rather than reducing GDP, crime, stress and environmental damage actually increase it!

Total GDP figures ignore the distribution of income. If some people gain and others lose, we cannot say that there has been an unambiguous increase in welfare. A typical feature of many rapidly growing countries is that some people grow very rich while others are left behind. The result is a growing inequality. If this is seen as undesirable, then clearly total GDP statistics are an inadequate measure of welfare.

Conclusions

If a country's citizens put a high priority on a clean environment, a relaxed way of life, greater self-sufficiency, a less materialistic outlook, more giving rather than selling, and greater equality, then such a country will probably have a lower GDP than a similarly endowed country where the pursuit of wealth is given high priority. Clearly, we cannot conclude that the first country will have a lower level of well-being. However, this does not mean that we should reject GDP statistics as a means of judging economic performance. While GDP statistics are not a good measure of economic welfare, they are an effective measure of *output* or *income*, and should be seen in that context.

BOX 14.2 CAN GDP MEASURE NATIONAL HAPPINESS?

An alternative perspective on well-being

The domains of national well-being

GDP is not a complete measure of economic welfare; nor is it meant to be. Consequently, there is considerable interest in alternative methods of establishing the level of human well-being and happiness.

In 2010 the Office for National Statistics launched its *Measuring National Well-being (MNW) Programme*. The principal aim was to develop a set of national statistics which would both help people to gain a better understanding of well-being and allow well-being to be monitored. The data, for instance, would enable policy makers to make more informed policy decisions by better understanding the impact of their choices across society.

The MNW Programme has identified a series of 'domains' with associated measures. These domains include: the economy, the natural environment, personal finance, education and skills, health, where we live, governance, our relationships and individual well-being.

Individual well-being

Since 2011, adults in the UK over 16 have been asked the following four questions in an attempt to monitor individual well-being:

- Overall, how satisfied are you with your life nowadays?
- Overall, to what extent do you feel the things you do in your life are worthwhile?
- Overall, how happy did you feel yesterday?
- Overall, how anxious did you feel yesterday?

Respondents give their answers using a scale of 0 to 10 where 0 is 'not at all' and 10 is 'completely'.

In October 2013 the ONS published its first regional study of personal well-being.[1] Some of the findings help to demonstrate the complex relationship between economic variables and personal well-being. For example, within England the highest average personal well-being rating was in the South-West while the lowest was in the North-East. As contributory factors to high levels of personal well-being in the South-West, the study pointed to below-average unemployment rates, an above-average proportion of older people, high life expectancy rates and low population density. Meanwhile, among contributory factors to low levels of personal well-being in the North-East were above-average unemployment rates, the lowest gross value added per head of any English region and below-average life expectancy rates.

Interestingly, London had low personal well-being ratings despite having the highest income per head of any English region. Different factors were identified here, including the greatest range or degree of inequality of income per head of any region, the highest population density of any region and the lowest proportion of the population aged 65 or over of any region.

Our understanding of both national and individual well-being continues to evolve. However, it is, of course, debatable as to how close any measures of well-being can come to measuring such a thing. Further, how should the results of such investigations help governments devise policy? Will governments be any closer to measuring the costs and benefits of any policy decisions?

1. *Is well-being the same as happiness or utility?*
2. *For what reasons might a person have a high income but a poor level of well-being?*

[1] *Personal Well-being across the UK, 2012–13* (Office for National Statistics, October 2013).

Section summary

1. National income is usually expressed in terms of gross domestic product. This is simply the value of domestic production over the course of the year. It can be measured by the product, expenditure or income methods.

2. Real national income takes account of inflation by being expressed in the prices of some base year.

3. In order to compare living standards of different countries, national income has to be expressed per capita and at purchasing-power parity exchange rates.

4. Even if it is, there are still problems in using national income statistics for comparative purposes. Certain items will not be included: items such as non-marketed products, services in the family and activities in the underground economy. Moreover, the statistics include certain 'bads' and ignore externalities, and they also ignore questions of the distribution of income.

14.4 SHORT-TERM ECONOMIC GROWTH AND THE BUSINESS CYCLE

The distinction between actual and potential growth

Before examining the causes of economic growth, it is essential to distinguish between *actual* and *potential* economic growth. People frequently confuse the two.

Actual growth is the percentage annual increase in national output: the rate of growth in real GDP. When statistics on growth rates are published, it is actual growth they are referring to.

Potential growth is the speed at which the economy *could* grow. It is the percentage annual increase in the economy's *capacity* to produce: the rate of growth in *potential output*.

Potential output (i.e. potential GDP) is the level of output when the economy is operating at 'normal capacity utilisation'. This allows for firms having a planned degree of

Definitions

Actual growth The percentage annual increase in national output actually produced.

Potential growth The percentage annual increase in the capacity of the economy to produce.

Potential output The sustainable level of output that could be produced in the economy: i.e. one that involves a 'normal' level of capacity utilisation and does not result in rising inflation.

BOX 14.3 OUTPUT GAPS

A measure of excess or deficient demand

If the economy grows, how fast and for how long can it grow before it runs into inflationary problems? On the other hand, what minimum rate must be achieved to avoid rising unemployment?

To answer these questions, economists have developed the concept of 'output gaps'.[1] The output gap is the difference between actual output and potential output: i.e. normal-capacity output.

If actual output is below potential output (the gap is negative), there will be a higher than normal level of unemployment as firms are operating below their normal level of capacity utilisation. There will, however, be a downward pressure on inflation, resulting from a lower than normal level of demand for labour and other resources. If actual output is above potential output (the gap is positive), there will be excess demand and a rise in inflation.

Generally, the gap will be negative in a recession and positive in a boom. In other words, output gaps follow the course of the business cycle.

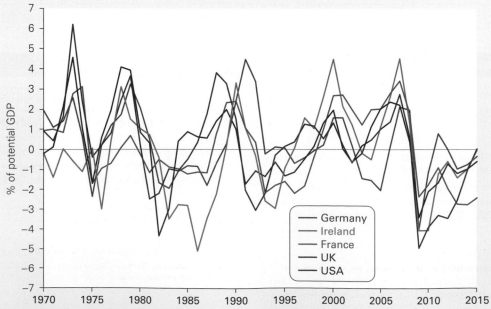

Output gaps, 1970–2015

Note: Figures for Germany based on West Germany only up to 1991; Figures from 2014 based on forecasts.
Source: Based on data from *AMECO Database* (European Commission, DGECFIN).

spare capacity to meet unexpected demand or for hold-ups in supply. It also allows for some unemployment as people move from job to job. Because potential output is normal-capacity output it is somewhat below full-capacity output, which is the absolute maximum that could be produced with firms working flat out.

The difference between actual and potential output is known as the *output gap*. Thus if actual output exceeds potential output, the output gap is positive: the economy is operating above normal capacity utilisation. If actual output is below potential output, the output gap is negative: the economy is operating below normal-capacity utilisation.

Definition

Output gap The difference between actual and potential output. When actual output exceeds potential output, the gap is positive. When actual output is less than potential output, the gap is negative.

Box 14.3 looks at the output gap since 1970 for five major industrial economies.

Two of the major factors contributing to potential economic growth are:

- An increase in resources – natural resources, labour or capital.
- An increase in the efficiency with which these resources are used, through advances in technology, improved labour skills or improved organisation.

If the actual growth rate is less than the potential growth rate, there will be an increase in spare capacity and probably an increase in unemployment: the output gap will become more negative (or less positive). To close a negative output gap, the actual growth rate would temporarily have to exceed the potential growth rate. In the long run, however, the actual growth rate will be limited to the potential growth rate.

There are thus two major policy issues concerned with economic growth: the short-run issue of ensuring that

Measuring the output gap

But how do we measure the output gap? There are two principal statistical techniques.

De-trending techniques. This approach is a purely mechanical exercise which involves smoothing the actual GDP figures. In doing this, it attempts to fit a trend growth path along the lines of the dashed line in Figure 14.5. The main disadvantage of this approach is that it is not grounded in economic theory and therefore does not account for those factors likely to determine normal-capacity output.

Production function approach. Many institutions, such as the European Union, use an approach which borrows ideas from economic theory. Specifically, it uses the idea of a production function which relates output to a set of inputs. Estimates of potential output are generated by using statistics on the size of a country's capital stock (see Box 22.1), the potential available labour input and, finally, the productivity or effectiveness of these inputs in producing output.

In addition to these statistical approaches use could be made of *business surveys*. In other words, we ask businesses directly. However, survey-based evidence can provide only a broad guide to rates of capacity utilisation and whether there is deficient or excess demand.

International evidence

The diagram shows output gaps for five countries from 1970 estimated using a production function approach. What is apparent from the chart is that all the countries have experienced significant output gaps, both positive and negative. This is consistent with a theme that we shall see throughout the second half of the book: economies are inherently volatile. In other words, countries experience business cycles.

The diagram does show that the characteristics of countries' business cycles can differ, particularly in terms of depth and duration. But we also see evidence of an international business cycle (see pages 781–3) where national cycles appear to share characteristics. This is true of the late 2000s and into the 2010s. Increasing global interconnectedness from financial and trading links meant that the financial crisis of the late 2000s spread like a contagion.

While output gaps vary from year to year, over the longer term the average output gap tends towards zero. As we can see from the table, this means that for our selection of countries from 1970 the actual rate of economic growth is approximately the same as the potential rate.

Average annual growth in actual and potential output, % (1970–2015)

	Average annual growth rates (%)	
	Actual output (real GDP)	**Potential output**
Germany	2.07	2.09
Ireland	4.23	4.20
France	2.34	2.28
UK	2.15	2.16
USA	2.81	2.85

Source: AMECO database (European Commission, DGECFIN).

 Under what circumstances would potential output (i.e. a zero output gap) move further away from the full-capacity output ceiling shown in Figure 14.5?

[1] See C. Giorno *et al.*, 'Potential output, output gaps and structural budget balances', *OECD Economic Studies*, no. 24 (1995), p. 1.

actual growth is such as to keep actual output as close as possible to potential output; and the long-run issue of what determines the rate of potential economic growth.

Economic growth and the business cycle

Although growth in potential output varies to some extent over the years – depending on the rate of advance of technology, the level of investment and the discovery of new raw materials – it nevertheless tends to be much steadier than the growth in actual output.

Actual growth tends to fluctuate. In some years, countries will experience high rates of economic growth: the country experiences a boom. In other years, economic growth is low or even negative: the country experiences a slowdown or recession.[1] This cycle of booms and recessions is known as the **business cycle** or **trade cycle**.

There are four 'phases' of the business cycle. They are illustrated in Figure 14.5.

1. *The upturn.* In this phase, a contracting or stagnant economy begins to recover, and growth in actual output resumes.
2. *The expansion.* During this phase, there is rapid economic growth: the economy is booming. A fuller use is made of resources, and the gap between actual and potential output narrows.
3. *The peaking out.* During this phase, growth slows down or even ceases.
4. *The slowdown, recession or slump.* During this phase, there is little or no growth or even a decline in output. Increasing slack develops in the economy.

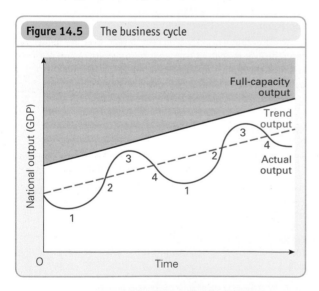

Figure 14.5 The business cycle

Definition

Business cycle or trade cycle The periodic fluctuations of national output around its long-term trend.

A word of caution: do not confuse a high *level* of output with a high rate of *growth* in output. The level of output is highest in phase 3. The rate of growth in output is highest in phase 2 (i.e. where the curve is steepest).

 Figure 14.5 shows a decline in actual output in recession. Redraw the diagram, only this time show a mere slowing down of growth in phase 4.

Long-term output trend

A line can be drawn showing the trend of national output over time (i.e. ignoring the cyclical fluctuations around the trend). This is shown as the dashed line in Figure 14.5. If, over time, firms on average operate with a 'normal' degree of capacity utilisation, the trend output line will be the same as the potential output line. Also, if the average level of capacity that is unutilised stays constant from one cycle to another, the trend line will have the same slope as the full-capacity output line. In other words, the trend (or potential) rate of growth will be the same as the rate of growth of capacity.

If, however, the level of unutilised capacity changes from one cycle to another, then the trend line will have a different slope from the full-capacity output line. For example, if unemployment and unused industrial capacity *rise* from one peak to another, or from one trough to another, the trend line will move further away from the full-capacity output line (i.e. it will be less steep).

 If the average percentage (as opposed to the average level) of capacity that was unutilised remained constant, would the trend line have the same slope as the potential output line?

The business cycle in practice

The business cycle illustrated in Figure 14.5 is a 'stylised' cycle. It is nice and smooth and regular. Drawing it this way allows us to make a clear distinction between each of the four phases. In practice, however, business cycles are highly irregular. They are irregular in two ways:

- *The length of the phases.* Some booms are short-lived, lasting only a few months or so. Others are much longer, lasting perhaps several years. Likewise some recessions are short while others are long.
- *The magnitude of the phases.* Sometimes in phase 2 there is a very high rate of economic growth, perhaps 4 per cent per annum or more. On other occasions in phase 2 growth is much gentler. Sometimes in phase 4 there is a

---

[1] In official statistics, a recession is defined as when an economy experiences falling national output (negative growth) for two or more quarters.

Figure 14.6	Growth rates in selected industrial economies

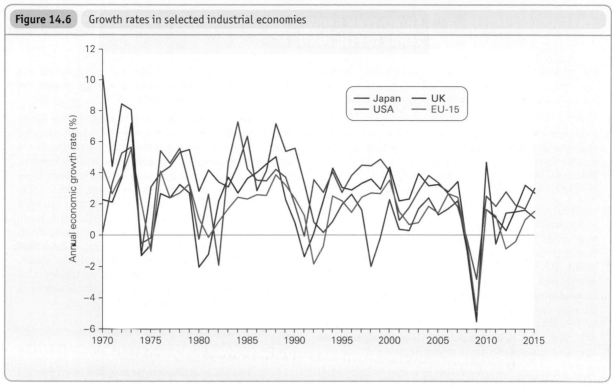

Note: Figures from 2014 based on forecasts; EU-15 = the member countries of the European Union prior to 1 May 2004.
Source: Based on data in *AMECO Database* (European Commission DGECFIN).

recession, with an actual decline in output, as occurred in 2008–9. On other occasions, phase 4 is merely a 'pause', with growth simply being low.

The essence of the business cycle is the variability of economic growth. This is more readily apparent when we look at the *rates of changes* in rather than the *levels* of real GDP. This is done in Figure 14.6, which shows the annual rate of growth in real GDP in selected industrial economies or groups of economies since 1970. As you can see, all of them suffered a slowdown in the mid 1970s, the early 1980s, the early 1990s and the early and late 2000s, and a boom in the early 1970s, the late 1970s, the late 1980s and, except in the case of Japan, the late 1990s.

But despite this broad similarity in their experience, there were nevertheless significant differences in the magnitude and timing of their individual cycles. For example, the economic downturn in the early 1980s was much more marked in the UK and the USA than in Japan. Also, the UK and the USA experienced negative growth in the early 1990s two years earlier than Japan or the EU-15.

Causes of fluctuations in actual growth

The major determinants of variations in the rate of actual growth in the *short run* are variations in the growth of aggregate demand. As we saw in section 14.2, aggregate demand is total spending on the goods and services produced in the economy:

$$AD = C + I + G + X - M$$

A rapid rise in aggregate demand will create shortages. This will tend to stimulate firms to increase output, thus reducing slack in the economy. Likewise, a reduction in aggregate demand will leave firms with increased stocks of unsold goods. They will therefore tend to reduce output.

Aggregate demand and actual output, therefore, fluctuate together in the short run. A boom is associated with a rapid rise in aggregate demand: the faster the rise in aggregate demand, the higher the short-run growth rate. A recession, by contrast, is associated with a reduction in aggregate demand.

A rapid rise in aggregate demand, however, is not enough to ensure a continuing high level of growth over a *number* of years. Without a corresponding expansion of potential output, rises in actual output must eventually come to an end as spare capacity is used up.

In the long run, therefore, there are two determinants of actual growth:

- The growth in aggregate demand. This determines whether potential output will be realised.
- The growth in potential output.

THRESHOLD CONCEPT 13 — SHORT-TERM GROWTH IN A COUNTRY'S OUTPUT TENDS TO FLUCTUATE

THINKING LIKE AN ECONOMIST

Countries rarely experience stable economic growth. Instead they experience business cycles. Periods of rapid economic growth are followed by periods of low growth or even a fall in output (negative growth).

Sometimes these cycles can be the result of government policy: raising taxes in a recession in order to compensate for falling tax revenues caused by lower incomes and lower expenditure. The higher taxation dampens consumer demand and causes firms to cut back on production to match the fall in sales.

Usually, however, economic fluctuations are simply the result of the workings of a market system. Some economists see the problem as rooted in fluctuations in aggregate demand. Consumer spending fluctuates; firms' investment fluctuates; export sales fluctuate. What is more, these various elements interact with each other. A rise in consumer expenditure can stimulate firms to invest in order to build up capacity to meet the extra demand. This, in turn, generates more employment in the capital goods industries and extra incomes for their employees. This further stimulates consumer demand. We examine these explanations in section 18.4.

Some economists see the problem as rooted in fluctuations in aggregate supply. These 'real-business-cycle' economists

argue that technological changes can boost output and employment and that these changes often come in waves. We look at these explanations in section 22.3.

But whatever the cause, it is vital to recognise the fundamental instability in market economies. This is what makes the business cycle a threshold concept. Analysing the causes and paths of business cycles occupies many macroeconomists. Their analysis leads to various policy conclusions. Some argue that it is best for the government or central bank to try to stabilise the cycle by active intervention: boosting aggregate demand (e.g. by cutting taxes, raising government expenditure or cutting interest rates) when the economy is experiencing low or negative growth, and dampening aggregate demand when the economy is experiencing unsustainably high growth. Others argue that it is best not to intervene, but to ride out the fluctuations, because attempting to manage aggregate demand often makes things worse.

1. *If people believe that the economy is about to go into recession (i.e. that real GDP will fall), how may their actions aggravate the problem?*
2. *Why will some people suffer more than others from a recession?*

BOX 14.4 — IS STABILITY ALWAYS DESIRABLE?

CASE STUDIES AND APPLICATIONS

Should firms sometimes be given a short, sharp shock?

Governments around the world aim for *stable* economic growth; they try to prevent the ups and downs of the business cycle. Gordon Brown, in his 10 years as Chancellor of the Exchequer, claimed to have 'put an end to boom and bust'. But why is stability desirable?

KI 11
p80

The first reason is that a stable economic environment allows firms to plan with more certainty and thus encourages investment. Instability, by contrast, makes firms cautious and unwilling to make long-term commitments, such as building a new factory; investment becomes more risky. Investment is thus lower and so too, as a result, is long-term economic growth.

The second reason is that some people suffer in times of recession. True, for most people recessions are relatively minor affairs, as long as they have a job and their pay is little affected. But some firms go out of business; some people lose their jobs. Personal lives are devastated, resulting in stress at the best and the break-up of relationships, depression, crime and suicide at worst. In other words, the effects of recessions are unequally spread.

KI 4
p13

The third reason concerns perception. Governments are often judged as successes or failures according to the state of the economy, and recessions are seen as a failure – whether or not the recession was caused by global factors largely beyond the scope of the government. Stable growth is thus a high policy priority for all governments.

When bad is good

But recessions can have benefits. If the economy is stable, firms may simply prefer to carry on doing what they have done before. If competition is strong, or where there is a risk of a takeover, this may not be possible. But when competition is weak, many firms can remain inefficient and still make reasonable profits.

When times are tough, however, firms may have to take a much closer look at how their business is operated and find new more efficient methods of production or new and better products. If they cannot, they may not survive. A recession, therefore, may be a useful means of getting rid of inefficient firms and releasing resources – labour, office space, raw materials, equipment, etc. – for the creation of new firms.

If the market is where the fittest survive, bad times are when you need to be fit – or rapidly become so.

KI 3
p13

1. *If, over a 10-year period, your income stayed constant at £20 000 per year, would you consider yourself to be better or worse off than if your income averaged £20 000 over the period but fluctuated from £5000 to £35 000 per year?*
2. *Explain whether a more risky business environment encourages higher or lower growth in potential output.*

Section summary

1. Actual growth must be distinguished from potential growth. The actual growth rate is the percentage annual increase in the output that is actually produced, whereas potential growth is the percentage annual increase in the capacity of the economy to produce (whether or not this capacity is utilised).

2. Actual growth will fluctuate with the course of the business cycle. The cycle can be broken down into four phases: the upturn, the expansion, the peaking out, and the slowdown or recession. In practice, the length and magnitude of these phases will vary: the cycle is thus irregular.

3. Actual growth is determined by potential growth and by the level of aggregate demand. If actual output is below potential output, actual growth can temporarily exceed potential growth, if aggregate demand is rising sufficiently. In the long term, however, actual output can grow only as fast as potential output will permit.

14.5 LONG-TERM ECONOMIC GROWTH

For growth to be sustained over the long term, there must be an increase in *potential* output. In other words, the country's capacity to produce must increase. In this section we see what determines this capacity and why some countries grow faster than others over the long term. What we are concerned with here, therefore, is the *supply* side of the economy, rather than the level of aggregate demand.

Causes of long-term growth

There are two main determinants of potential output: (a) the amount of resources available and (b) their productivity. If supply potential is to grow, then either (a) or (b) or both must grow.

Increases in the quantity of resources: capital, labour, land and raw materials

Capital. The nation's output depends on its stock of capital (*K*). An increase in this stock will increase output. If we ignore the problem of machines wearing out or becoming obsolete and needing replacing, then the stock of capital will increase by the amount of investment: $\Delta K = I$.

But by how much will this investment raise output? This depends on the productivity of this new capital: on the *marginal efficiency of capital* (see page 273). Let us define the nation's marginal efficiency of capital (*MEC*) as the annual extra income (ΔY) yielded by an increase in the capital stock, relative to the cost of that extra capital (ΔK):

$$MEC = \frac{\Delta Y}{\Delta K} = \frac{\Delta Y}{I}$$

Thus if £100 million of extra capital yielded an annual income of £25 million, the marginal efficiency of capital would be £25 million/£100 million = 1/4.

The rate of growth will depend on the fraction (*i*) of national income devoted to new investment (i.e. investment over and above what is necessary to replace worn-out equipment). The higher this rate of new investment, the higher will be the potential growth rate.

The relationship between the investment rate and the potential growth rate (g_p) is given by the simple formula

$$g_p = i \times MEC$$

Thus if 20 per cent of national income went in new investment (*i*), and if each £1 of new investment yielded 25p of extra income per year (*MEC* = 1/4), then the growth rate would be 5 per cent.

A simple example will demonstrate this. If national income is £2 trillion (i.e. £2000 billion), then £400 billion will be invested (*i* = 20 per cent). This will lead to extra annual output of £100 billion (*MEC* = 1/4). Thus national income grows to £2.1 trillion (i.e. £2100 billion): a growth of 5 per cent.

But what determines the rate of investment? There are a number of determinants. These include the confidence of businesspeople about the future demand for their products, the profitability of business, sources of finance for investment, the tax regime, the rate of growth in the economy and the rate of interest. We will examine these determinants in section 17.1.

Over the long term, if investment is to increase, then people must *save* more in order to finance that extra investment. Put another way, people must be prepared to consume less in order to allow more resources to be diverted into producing capital goods: factories, machines, etc.

Labour. If there is an increase in the working population, there will be an increase in potential output. This increase in working population may result from a higher 'participation rate': a larger proportion of the total population in work or seeking work. Examples include a greater proportion of women with children deciding to rejoin the labour market, people retiring later and people working part time deciding to work longer hours.

Alternatively, a rise in the working population may be the result of an increase in total population. There is a problem here, however. If a rise in total population does not result in a greater *proportion* of the population working,

THRESHOLD CONCEPT 14 — LONG-TERM GROWTH IN A COUNTRY'S OUTPUT DEPENDS ON A GROWTH IN THE QUANTITY AND/OR PRODUCTIVITY OF ITS RESOURCES

In the short term, economic growth is likely to be influenced by changes in aggregate demand. If the economy is in recession, an expansion in aggregate demand will help to bring the economy out of recession and move it closer to full employment.

Actual output, however, cannot continue growing faster than potential output over the longer term. Firms will start reaching capacity and actual growth will then have to slow. The rate of potential growth thus places a limit to the rate of actual growth over the longer term.

What then determines the rate of growth in potential output? The answer lies on the supply side. It depends on the rate of growth of factors of production. There are two key elements here. The first is growth in the *quantity* of factors: growth in the size of the workforce, of the available land and raw materials, and of the stock of capital. The second is productivity growth. This involves elements such as growth in the educational attainments and skills of the workforce, growth in technology, and growth in the efficiency with which resources are used.

To recognise the importance of resources and their productivity in determining long-term growth is a threshold concept. It helps in understanding the importance of designing appropriate supply-side policies: policies that focus on increasing aggregate supply rather than managing aggregate demand. It is easy to worry too much about the short term.

This is not to say that the short term should be neglected. The famous economist John Maynard Keynes argued that it was fundamentally important to focus on aggregate demand and the short term to avoid severe economic fluctuations, with the twin problems of high unemployment in recessions and high inflation in periods of unsustainably high growth. He used the famous phrase 'In the long term we're all dead.'

But although we all have to die sometime, we may have many years left to reap the benefits of appropriate supply-side policy. And even if we don't, our children will.

1. *Give some examples of supply-side policy (see Chapter 23 for some ideas if you are stuck).*
2. *If there is an increase in aggregate supply, will this result in an increase in potential growth?*

---

output *per head* of population may not rise at all. In practice, many developed countries are faced with a growing proportion of their population above retirement age, and thus a potential *fall* in output per head of population.

Land and raw materials. The scope for generating growth here is usually very limited. Land is virtually fixed in quantity. Land reclamation schemes and the opening up of marginal land can add only tiny amounts to national output. Even if new raw materials (e.g. oil) are discovered, this will result only in *short-term* growth, while the rate of extraction is building up. Once the rate of extraction is at a maximum, economic growth will cease. Output will simply remain at the new higher level, until eventually the raw materials begin to run out. Output will then fall back again.

The problem of diminishing returns. If a single factor of production increases in supply while others remain fixed, diminishing returns will set in. For example, if the quantity of capital increases with no increase in other factors of production, diminishing returns to capital will set in. The rate of return on capital will fall.

Unless *all* factors of production increase, therefore, the rate of growth is likely to slow down. It is not enough that labour and capital increase if there is a limited supply of land and raw materials. This was the worry of the classical economists of the nineteenth century, who were pessimistic about the future prospects for growth (see Box 14.5).

Then there is the problem of the environment. If a rise in labour and capital leads to a more *intensive* use of land and

KI 17
p135

natural resources, the resulting growth in output may be environmentally unsustainable.

The solution to the problem of diminishing returns is an increase in the *productivity* of resources.

Increases in the productivity of resources

Technological improvements can increase the marginal productivity of capital. Much of the investment in new machines is not just in extra machines, but in superior machines producing a higher rate of return. Modern computers can do the work of many people and have replaced many machines that were cumbersome and expensive to build. Improved methods of transport have reduced the costs of moving goods and materials. Improved communications (such as email and the Internet) have reduced the costs of transmitting information. The high-tech world of today would seem a wonderland to someone of 100 years ago.

As a result of technical progress, the productivity of capital has tended to increase, not decrease, over time. Similarly, as a result of new skills, improved education and training and better health the productivity of labour has also tended to increase over time.

But technical progress on its own is not enough. There must also be the institutions and attitudes that encourage *innovation*. In other words, the inventions must be exploited.

TC 14
p420

For what reasons might the productivity of land increase over time?

BOX 14.5 | **THEORIES OF GROWTH**

From dismal economics to the economics of optimism

The classical theory of growth

The classical economists of the nineteenth century were very pessimistic about the prospects for economic growth. They saw the rate of growth petering out as diminishing returns to both labour and capital led to low wages and a falling rate of profit. The only gainers would be landlords, who, given the fixed supply of land, would receive higher and higher rents as the demand for scarce land rose.

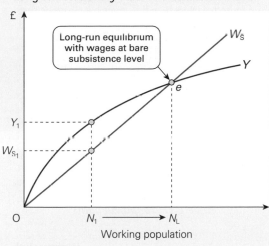

Long-run stationary state in the classical model

The classical position can be shown graphically. The size of the working population is plotted on the horizontal axis. If it is assumed that there is a basic minimum 'subsistence' wage that workers must earn in order to survive, then the line W_S traces out the total subsistence wage bill. It is a straight line because a doubling in the number of workers would lead to a doubling of the subsistence wage bill.

The line Y shows the total level of income that will be generated as more workers are employed, after subtracting rents to landlords. In other words, it is total wages plus profits. It gets less and less steep due to diminishing returns to labour and capital given the fixed supply of land.

As long as Y is above W_S (say, at a population of N_1), firms can make a profit. They will try to expand and will thus take on more labour.

Initially this will bid up the wage and will thus erode the level of profits. But the higher wages will encourage the population to expand. This increased supply of labour will compete wages back down to the subsistence level and will thus allow some recovery in profits. But profits will not be as high as they were before because, with an increase in workers, the gap between Y and W_S will have narrowed.

Firms will continue to expand and the population will continue to grow until point e is reached. At that point, even with wages at bare subsistence level, no profit can be made. Growth will cease. The economy will be in a long-run stationary state.

No wonder economics became dubbed 'the dismal science'.

New growth theory

Economists today are more optimistic about the prospects for economic growth. This is partly based on a simple appeal to the evidence. Despite a rapid growth in world population, most countries have experienced sustained economic growth. Over the past 100 years the industrialised countries have seen per capita growth rates averaging from just over 1 per cent to nearly 3 per cent per annum. This has resulted in per capita real incomes many times higher than in the nineteenth century.

This worldwide experience of economic growth has stimulated the development of new growth theories. These stress two features:

- The development and spread of new technology. The rapid advances in science and technology have massively increased the productivity of factors of production. What is more, new inventions and innovations stimulate other people, often in other countries, to copy, adapt and improve on them in order to stay competitive. Growth through technical progress stimulates more growth.
- The positive externalities of investment. If one firm invests in training in order to raise labour productivity, other firms will benefit from the improved stock of 'human capital'. There will be better-trained labour that can now be hired by other firms. Similarly, if one firm invests in research and development, the benefits can spill over to other firms. These spill-over benefits to other firms can be seen as the positive externalities of investment.

New growth theories seek to analyse the process of the spread of technology and how it can be influenced.

Given that technological progress allows the spectre of diminishing returns to be banished, or at least indefinitely postponed, it is no wonder that many economists are more optimistic about growth. Nevertheless, there are still serious grounds for concern:

- If the benefits of investment spill over to other firms (i.e. if there are positive externalities), the free market will lead to too little investment: firms considering investing will take into account only the benefits to themselves, not those to other firms. There is thus an important role for governments to encourage or provide training, research and capital investment. (We consider such policies in Chapter 23.)
- Potential growth may not translate into actual growth. A potentially growing economy may be languishing in a deep recession.
- There may be serious costs of economic growth (see Box 14.6).

KI 29
p323

Can growth go on for ever, given that certain resources are finite in supply?

BOX 14.6   THE COSTS OF ECONOMIC GROWTH

Is more necessarily better?

For many developing countries, economic growth is a necessity if they are to remove mass poverty. When the majority of their population is underfed and poorly housed, with inadequate health care and little access to education, few would quarrel with the need for an increase in productive potential. The main query is whether the benefits of economic growth will flow to the mass of the population, or whether they will be confined to the few who are already relatively well off.

For developed countries, the case for economic growth is less clear-cut. Economic growth is usually measured in terms of the growth in GDP. The problem is that there are many 'goods' and 'bads' that are not included in GDP (see Box 14.2). Economic growth, therefore, is not the same as growth in a nation's welfare.

So, what are the benefits and costs of economic growth?

The benefits of growth

It leads to increased levels of consumption.   Provided economic growth outstrips population growth, it will lead to higher real income per head. This can lead to higher levels of consumption of goods and services. If human welfare is related to the level of consumption, then growth provides an obvious gain to society.

It can help avoid other macroeconomic problems.   People aspire to higher living standards. Without a growth in productive potential, people's demands for rising incomes are likely to lead to higher inflation, balance of payments crises (as more imports are purchased), industrial disputes, etc. Growth in productive potential helps to meet these aspirations and avoid macroeconomic crises.

It can make it easier to redistribute incomes to the poor.   If incomes rise, the government can redistribute incomes from the rich to the poor without the rich losing. For example, as people's incomes rise, they automatically pay more taxes. These extra revenues for the government can be spent on programmes to alleviate poverty. Without a continuing rise in national income, the scope for helping the poor is much more limited.

Society may feel that it can afford to care more for the environment.   As people grow richer, they may become less preoccupied with their own private consumption and more concerned to live in a clean environment. The regulation of pollution tends to be tougher in developed countries than in the developing world.

The costs of growth

In practice, more consumption may not make people happier; economies may be no less crisis-riven; income may not be redistributed more equally; the environment may not be better protected. More than this, some people argue that growth may worsen these problems and create additional problems besides.

It has current opportunity costs.   To achieve faster growth, firms will probably need to invest more. This will require financing. The finance can come from more saving, higher retained profits or higher taxes. Either way, there must be a cut in consumption. In the short run, therefore, higher growth leads to less consumption, not more.

In the diagram, assume that consumption is currently at a level of C_1. Its growth over time is shown by the line out from C_1. Now assume that the government pursues a policy

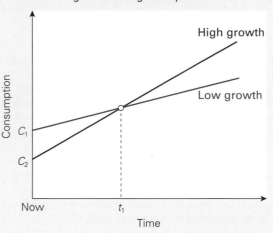

High- and low-growth paths

of higher growth. Consumption has to fall to finance the extra investment. Consumption falls to, say, C_2. The growth in consumption is now shown by the line out from C_2. Not until time t_1 is reached (which may be several years into the future) does consumption overtake the levels that it would have reached with the previous lower growth rate.

It may simply generate extra demands.   'The more people have, the more they want.' If this is so, more consumption may not increase people's utility at all. (Diagrammatically, indifference curves may move outwards as fast as, or even faster than, consumers' budget lines: see section 4.3.) It is often observed that happiness depends on relative rather than absolute incomes. Thus as developed countries get richer their citizens do not get happier.

It has social effects.   Many people claim that an excessive pursuit of material growth by a country can lead to a more greedy, more selfish and less caring society. As society becomes more industrialised, violence, crime, loneliness, stress-related diseases, suicides, divorce and other social problems are likely to rise.

By contrast, a life that is less materialistic may be more fulfilling. The term 'gross national happiness' was coined by King Jigme Singye of Bhutan. He argued that his people, although poor in materialistic terms, have a high quality of life living in harmony with their environment according to Buddhist philosophy.

It has environmental costs.   A richer society may be more concerned for the environment, but it is also likely to do more damage to it. The higher the level of consumption, the higher is likely to be the level of pollution and waste. What is more, many of the environmental costs are likely to be underestimated due to a lack of scientific knowledge. Acid rain and the depletion of the ozone layer have been two examples.

It uses non-renewable resources.   If growth involves using a greater amount of resources, rather than using the same amount of resources more efficiently, certain non-renewable resources will run out more rapidly. Unless viable alternatives can be found for various minerals and fossil fuels, present

growth may lead to shortages for future generations (see Box 9.11).

It has effects on the distribution of income.   While some people may gain from a higher standard of living, others are likely to lose. If the means to higher growth are greater incentives (such as cuts in higher rates of income tax), then the rich might get richer, with little or no benefit 'trickling down' to the poor.

Growth involves changes in production, both in terms of the goods produced and in terms of the techniques used and the skills required. The more rapid the rate of growth, the more rapid the rate of change. People may find that their skills are no longer relevant. Their jobs may be replaced by machines. People may thus find themselves unemployed and need to retrain, or they may be forced to take low-paid, unskilled work.

Conclusion

So should countries pursue growth? The answer depends on (a) just what costs and benefits are involved, (b) what weighting people attach to them and (c) how opposing views are to be reconciled.

A problem is that the question of the desirability of economic growth is a normative one. It involves a judgement about what a 'desirable' society should look like.

A simpler point, however, is that the electorate seems to want economic growth. As long as that is so, governments will tend to pursue policies to achieve growth. That is why we need to study the causes of growth and the policies that governments can pursue.

One thing the government can do is to view the problem as one of constrained optimisation. It sets constraints: levels of environmental protection, minimum wages, maximum rates of depletion of non-renewable resources, etc. It then seeks policies that will maximise growth, while keeping within these constraints.

1. *Is a constrained optimisation approach a practical solution to the possible costs of economic growth?*
2. *Are worries about the consequences of economic growth a 'luxury' that only rich countries can afford?*

KI 4
p13

KI 6
p29

*LOOKING AT THE MATHS

Assuming that the quantity of land is fixed, economic growth (g) results from three main sources: the rate of growth in the labour force ($\Delta L/L$), the rate of growth in the stock of capital ($\Delta K/K$) and the rate of growth in overall productivity in the economy or 'total factor productivity' ($\Delta TFP/TFP$). Thus

$$g = \frac{\Delta Y}{Y} = a\frac{\Delta L}{L} + b\frac{\Delta K}{K} + \frac{\Delta TFP}{TFP} \tag{1}$$

where a is the elasticity of national income (Y) with respect to labour. In other words, a is the percentage increase in national income that would result from a 1 per cent increase in the labour force. Similarly, b is the elasticity of national income with respect to capital: i.e. the percentage increase in national income from a 1 per cent increase in the capital stock.[1] If there are constant returns to scale, then

$a + b = 1$

In other words, an increase in both labour and capital of x per cent would lead to an x per cent increase in national income.

If the capital stock is held constant and the labour force increases, there will be diminishing returns to labour. This implies that

$a < 1$

and that the value of a gets less as the ratio of labour to capital increases. Similarly, if capital per head of the labour force increases, there will be diminishing returns to capital. This implies that

$b < 1$

and that the value of b gets less as the capital/labour ratio increases. In industrialised countries in the 2000s the value of

b is typically between 0.2 and 0.4, implying that a 10 per cent increase in the capital stock will increase national income by between 2 and 4 per cent. The value of a is typically between 0.6 and 0.8.

What about total factor productivity? Note that there is no 'c' term attached to $\Delta TFP/TFP$. What this means is that a total factor productivity increase of y per cent will lead to an increase in national income of y per cent for any given quantity of labour and capital. If we know the value of g, a, $\Delta L/L$, b and $\Delta K/K$, we can work out the rate of growth in total factor productivity. Rearranging equation (1) gives

$$\frac{\Delta TFP}{TFP} = g - \left(a\frac{\Delta L}{L} + b\frac{\Delta K}{K}\right) \tag{2}$$

Case study 14.4 in MyEconLab examines how equation (1) can be used for growth accounting: a system of measuring the contribution of increases in factor inputs to economic growth. It also looks at the evidence for the UK.

[1] The term b is the elasticity of Y with respect to changes in K: i.e.

$$b = \frac{\Delta Y}{\Delta K}\cdot\frac{K}{Y} = MEC \cdot \frac{K}{Y}$$

But, from equation (1), growth from a rise in capital alone is given by

$$g = b\frac{\Delta K}{K} = MEC \cdot \frac{K}{Y}\cdot\frac{\Delta K}{K}$$

Cancelling out the K terms gives

$$g = \frac{\Delta K}{Y}\times MEC = i\times MEC$$

which is the formula for the growth rate that we established on page 419.

The effects of actual growth on potential growth

Some economists argue that potential growth is not influenced by actual growth. It depends largely on growth in factor productivity, and that in turn depends on scientific and technical advance. Such advances, they argue, are independent of the state of the economy.

Other economists, however, argue that actual growth *stimulates* investment and the development of new technology. For these economists, therefore, it is vital for the achievement of high long-term growth rates that the economy experiences continuous and stable growth in actual output. Recessions breed pessimism and a lack of investment, a lack of research and a lack of innovation (see Box 14.4 on page 418).

Policies to achieve growth

How can governments increase a country's growth rate? Policies differ in two ways.

First, they may focus on the demand side or the supply side of the economy. In other words, they may attempt to create sufficient *aggregate demand* to ensure that firms wish to invest and that potential output is realised. Alternatively they may seek to increase *aggregate supply* by concentrating

on measures to increase potential output: measures to encourage research and development, innovation and training.

Second, they may be market-orientated or interventionist policies. Many economists and politicians, especially those on the political right, believe that the best environment for encouraging economic growth is one where private enterprise is allowed to flourish: where entrepreneurs are able to reap substantial rewards from investment in new techniques and new products. Such economists, therefore, advocate policies designed to free up the market. Others, however, argue that a free market will be subject to considerable cyclical fluctuations. The resulting uncertainty will discourage investment. These economists, therefore, tend to advocate active intervention by the government to reduce these fluctuations.

We focus on demand-side policies in Chapter 21 and on supply-side policies in Chapter 23. In each case we look at both interventionist and market-orientated policies.

Postscript: The role of investment

Investment plays a dual role in economic growth. It is a component of aggregate demand and thus helps determine the level of actual output. It is also probably the major determinant of potential output, since investment both increases the capital stock and leads to the development of new technology. It is important, therefore, that when investment rises, the resulting rise in aggregate demand matches the resulting rise in aggregate supply. There is a problem of timing here, however. Generally the effects on aggregate demand happen more quickly than those on aggregate supply.

Section summary

1. Growth in potential output is determined by the rate of increase in the quantity of resources: capital, labour, land and raw materials; and by the productivity of resources. The productivity of capital can be increased by technological improvements and a more efficient use of the capital stock; the productivity of labour can be increased by better education, training, motivation and organisation.

2. Whether governments can best achieve rapid growth through market-orientated or interventionist policies is highly controversial.

3. Investment plays a key role in determining growth, since it affects both aggregate demand and aggregate supply.

APPENDIX: CALCULATING GDP

As explained in section 14.3, there are three ways of estimating GDP. In this appendix, we discuss each method in more detail. We also look at some alternative measures of national income.

The product method of measuring GDP

This approach simply involves adding up the value of everything produced in the country during the year: the output of cars, timber, lollipops, shirts, etc.; and all the myriad of services such as football matches, haircuts, bus rides and insurance services. In the national accounts these figures are grouped together into broad categories such as manufacturing, construction and distribution. The figures for the UK economy for 2012 are shown in Figure 14.7.

When we add up the output of various firms, we must be careful to avoid *double counting*. For example, if a manufacturer sells a television to a retailer for £200 and the retailer sells it to the consumer for £300, how much has this television contributed to GDP? The answer is *not* £500. We do not add the £200 received by the manufacturer to the £300 received by the retailer: that would be double counting. Instead we either just count the final value (£300) or the *value added* at each stage (£200 by the manufacturer + £100 by the retailer).

The sum of all the values added at each of the stages of production by all the various industries in the economy is known as *gross value added at basic prices (GVA)*.

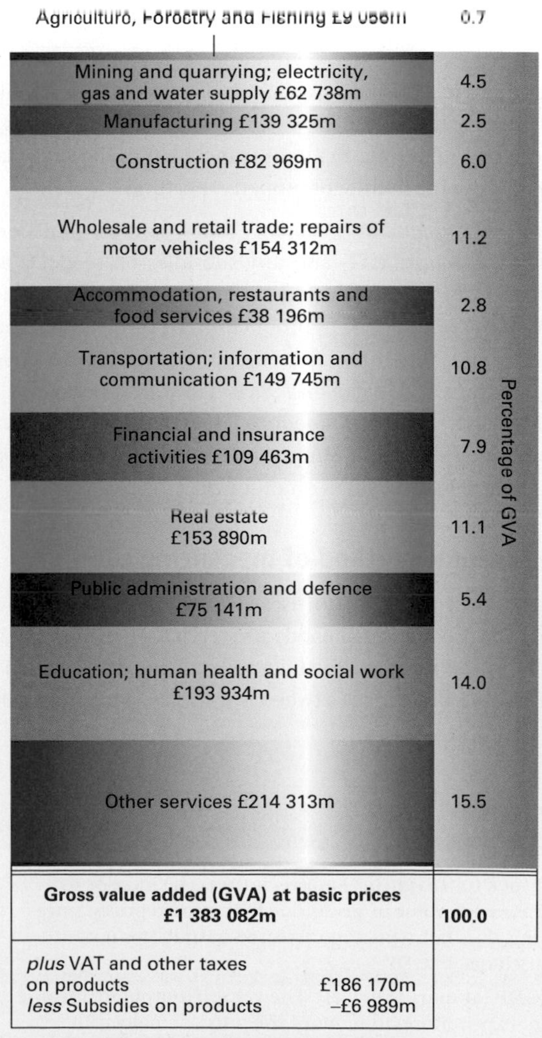

Definition

Gross value added at basic prices (GVA) The sum of all the values added by all industries in the economy over a year. The figures exclude taxes on products (such as VAT) and include subsidies on products.

Figure 14.7   UK GVA (product-based measure): 2012

	Percentage of GVA
Agriculture, Forestry and Fishing £9 056m	0.7
Mining and quarrying; electricity, gas and water supply £62 738m	4.5
Manufacturing £139 325m	2.5
Construction £82 969m	6.0
Wholesale and retail trade; repairs of motor vehicles £154 312m	11.2
Accommodation, restaurants and food services £38 196m	2.8
Transportation; information and communication £149 745m	10.8
Financial and insurance activities £109 463m	7.9
Real estate £153 890m	11.1
Public administration and defence £75 141m	5.4
Education; human health and social work £193 934m	14.0
Other services £214 313m	15.5
Gross value added (GVA) at basic prices £1 383 082m	**100.0**
plus VAT and other taxes on products £186 170m *less* Subsidies on products −£6 989m	
Total GDP (at market prices) £1 562 263m	

Some qualifications

Stocks (or inventories). We must be careful only to include the values added in the *particular year in question*. A problem here is that some goods start being produced *before* the year begins. Thus when we come to work out GDP, we must ignore the values that had previously been added to stocks of raw materials and goods. Similarly, other goods are only sold to the consumer *after* the end of the year. Nevertheless we must still count the values that have been added during *this* year to these stocks of partially finished goods.

A final problem concerned with stocks is that they may increase in value simply due to increased prices. This is known as **stock (or inventory) appreciation**. Since there has been no real increase in output, stock appreciation must be deducted from value added.

Government services. The output of private industry is sold on the market and can thus be easily valued. This is not the case with most of the services provided by the government. Such services (e.g. health and education) should be valued in terms of what they cost to provide.

Ownership of dwellings. When a landlord rents out a flat, this service is valued as the rent that the tenant pays. But owner-occupiers living in their own property do not pay rent and yet they are 'consuming' a similar 'service'. Here a rental value for owner-occupation is 'imputed'. In other words, a figure corresponding to a rent is included in the GDP statistics under the 'letting of property' heading.

Taxes and subsidies on products. Taxes paid on goods and services (such as VAT) and any subsidies on products are *excluded* from gross value added (GVA), since they are not part of the value added in production. Nevertheless the way GDP is measured throughout the EU and most other countries of the world is at *market prices*: i.e. at the prices actually paid at each stage of production. Thus **GDP at market prices** (sometimes referred to simply as GDP) is GVA *plus* taxes on products *minus* subsidies on products.

The income method of measuring GDP

The second approach focuses on the incomes generated from the production of goods and services. This must be the same as the sum of all values added, since value added is simply the difference between a firm's revenue from sales and the costs of its purchases from other firms. This difference is made up of wages and salaries, rent, interest and profit: the incomes earned by those involved in the production process.

Since GDP is the sum of all values added, it must also be the sum of all incomes generated: the sum of wages and salaries, rent, interest and profit.

 If a retailer buys a product from a wholesaler for £80 and sells it to a consumer for £100, then the £20 of value that has been added will go partly in wages, partly in rent and partly in profits. Thus £20 of income has been generated at the retail stage. But the good actually contributes a total of £100 to GDP. Where, then, is the remaining £80 worth of income recorded?

Figure 14.8 shows how these incomes are grouped together in the official statistics. By far the largest category is 'compensation of employees' – in other words, wages and salaries. As you can see, the total in Figure 14.8 is the same as in Figure 14.7, although the components are quite different. In other words, GDP is the same whether calculated by the product or the income method.

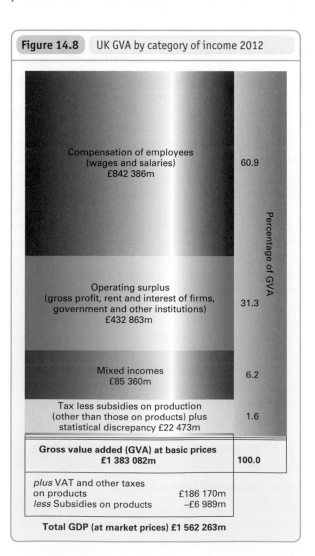

Figure 14.8 UK GVA by category of income 2012

Definitions

Stock (or inventory) appreciation The increase in monetary value of stocks due to increased prices. Since this does not represent increased output, it is not included in GDP.

GDP (at market prices) The value of output (or income or expenditure) in terms of the prices actually paid. GDP = GVA + Taxes on products − Subsidies on products.

Some qualifications

Stock (inventory) appreciation.   As in the case of the product approach, any gain in profits from inventory appreciation must be deducted, since they do not arise from a real increase in output.

Transfer payments.   GDP includes only those incomes that arise from the production of goods and services. We do not, therefore, include *transfer payments* such as social security benefits, pensions and gifts.

Direct taxes.   We count people's income *before* the payment of income and corporation taxes, since it is this *gross* (pre-tax) income that arises from the production of goods and services.

Taxes and subsidies on products.   As with the product approach, if we are working out GVA, we measure incomes before the payment of taxes on products or the receipt of subsidies on products, since it is these pre-tax-and-subsidy incomes that arise from the value added by production. When working out GDP, however, we add in these taxes and subtract these subsidies to arrive at a *market price* valuation.

The expenditure method of measuring GDP

The final approach to calculating GDP is to add up all expenditure on final output (which will be at market prices). This will include the following:

- Consumer expenditure (*C*). This includes all expenditure on goods and services by households and by non-profit institutions serving households (NPISH) (e.g. clubs and societies).
- Government expenditure (*G*). This includes central and local government expenditure on final goods and services. Note that it includes non-marketed services (such as health and education), but excludes transfer payments, such as pensions and social security payments.
- Investment expenditure (*I*). This includes investment in capital, such as buildings and machinery. It also includes the value of any increase (+) or decrease (–) in inventories, whether of raw materials, semi-finished goods or finished goods.
- Exports of goods and services (*X*).

We then have to *subtract* imports of goods and services (*M*) from the total in order to leave just the expenditure on *domestic* product. In other words, we subtract the part of consumer expenditure, government expenditure and investment that goes on imports. We also subtract the imported component (e.g. raw materials) from exports.

$$\text{GDP (at market prices)} = C + G + I + X - M$$

Table 14.2 shows the calculation of the 2012 UK GDP by the expenditure approach.

From GDP to national income

Gross national income

Some of the incomes earned in this country will go abroad. These include wages, interest, profit and rent earned in this country by foreign residents and remitted abroad, and taxes

Table 14.2	UK GDP at market prices by category of expenditure, 2012	
	£ million	**% of GDP**
Consumption expenditure of households and NPISH (*C*)	1 028 756	65.9
Government final consumption (*G*)	340 912	21.8
Gross capital formation (*I*)	231 033	14.8
Exports of goods and services (*X*)	492 810	31.5
Imports of goods and services (*M*)	–526 711	–33.7
Statistical discrepancy	–4 538	–0.3
GDP at market prices	**1 562 263**	**100.0**

Source: *Blue Book Tables* (National Statistics, 2013).

on production paid to foreign governments and institutions (e.g. the EU). On the other hand, some of the incomes earned by domestic residents will come from abroad. Again, these can be in the form of wages, interest, profit or rent, or in the form of subsidies received from governments or institutions abroad. Gross *domestic* product, however, is concerned only with incomes generated *within* the country, irrespective of ownership. If, then, we are to take 'net income from abroad' into account (i.e. these inflows minus outflows), we need a new measure. This is *gross national income (GNY)*.[1] It is defined as follows:

$$\text{GNY at market prices} = \text{GDP at market prices} \\ + \text{Net income from abroad}$$

Thus GDP focuses on the value of domestic production, whereas GNY focuses on the value of incomes earned by domestic residents.

Net national income

The measures we have used so far ignore the fact that each year some of the country's capital equipment wears out or becomes obsolete: in other words, they ignore capital depreciation. If we subtract from gross national income an allowance for *depreciation* (or 'capital consumption' as it is called in the official statistics), we get *net national income (NNY)*:

$$\text{NNY at market prices} = \text{GNY at market prices} \\ - \text{Depreciation}$$

Table 14.3 shows the 2012 GDP, GNY and NNY figures for the UK.

Although NNY gives a truer picture of a nation's income than GNY, economists tend to use the gross figures because depreciation is hard to estimate accurately.

Definitions

Gross national income (GNY) GDP plus net income from abroad.

Depreciation The decline in value of capital equipment due to age or wear and tear.

Net national income (NNY) GNY minus depreciation.

[1] In the official statistics, this is referred to as GNI . We use Y to stand for income, however, to avoid confusion with investment.

Table 14.3	UK GDP, GNY and NNY at market prices, 2012
	£ million
Gross domestic product (GDP)	**1 562 263**
Plus net income from abroad	−4 760
Gross national income (GNY)	**1 557 503**
Less capital consumption (depreciation)	176 050
Net national income (NNY)	**1 381 453**

Source: *Blue Book Tables* (National Statistics, 2013).

Households' disposable income

Finally, we come to a measure that is useful for analysing consumer behaviour. This is called *households' disposable income*. It measures the income that people have available for spending (or saving): i.e. after any deductions for income tax, national insurance, etc. have been made. It is the best measure to use if we want to see how changes in household income affect consumption.

Definition

Households' disposable income The income available for households to spend: i.e. personal incomes after deducting taxes on incomes and adding benefits.

How do we get from GNY at market prices to households' disposable income? As GNY measures the incomes that firms receive from production[1] (plus net income from abroad), we must deduct that part of their income that is *not* distributed to households. This means that we must deduct taxes that firms pay – taxes on goods and services (such as VAT), taxes on profits (such as corporation tax) and any other taxes – and add in any subsidies they receive. We must then subtract allowances for depreciation and any undistributed profits. This gives us the gross income that households receive from firms in the form of wages, salaries, rent, interest and distributed profits.

To get from this to what is available for households to spend, we must subtract the money that households pay in income taxes and national insurance contributions, but add all benefits to households, such as pensions and child benefit – in other words, we must *include* transfer payments:

> Households' disposable income = GNY at market prices
> – Taxes paid by firms + Subsidies received by firms
> – Depreciation – Undistributed profits – Personal taxes
> + Benefits

[1] We also include income from any public-sector production of goods or services (e.g. health and education) and production by non-profit institutions serving households.

Section summary

1. The product method measures the values added in all parts of the economy. Care must be taken in the evaluation of stocks, government services and the ownership of dwellings.

2. The income method measures all the incomes generated from domestic production: wages and salaries, rent, interest and profit. Transfer payments are not included; nor is stock appreciation.

3. The expenditure method adds up all the categories of expenditure: consumer expenditure, government expenditure, investment and exports. We then have to deduct the element of each that goes on imports in order to arrive at expenditure on domestic products. Thus $GDP = C + G + I + X − M$.

4. GDP at market prices measures what consumers pay for output (including taxes and subsidies on what they buy). Gross value added (GVA) measures what factors of production actually receive. GVA, therefore, is GDP at market prices minus taxes on products plus subsidies on products.

5. Gross national income (GNY) takes account of incomes earned from abroad (+) and incomes earned by people abroad from this country (−). Thus GNY = GDP plus net income from abroad.

6. Net national income (NNY) takes account of depreciation of capital. Thus NNY = GNY − Depreciation.

7. Personal disposable income is a measure of household income after the deduction of income taxes and the addition of benefits.

END OF CHAPTER QUESTIONS

1. The following table shows index numbers for real GDP (national output) for various countries (2008 = 100).

	2008	2009	2010	2011	2012	2013	2014	2015
Australia	100.00	102.09	104.57	108.09	111.85	114.71	117.90	121.25
Ireland	100.00	93.62	92.62	94.63	94.78	95.07	96.68	99.11
France	100.00	96.85	98.52	100.52	100.53	100.76	101.67	103.42
UK	100.00	94.83	96.40	97.48	97.60	98.91	101.14	103.52
USA	100.00	97.20	99.63	101.48	104.29	105.92	108.68	112.05
Japan	100.00	94.47	98.87	98.29	100.21	102.28	104.31	105.65
Canada	100.00	97.23	100.36	102.80	104.61	106.49	108.73	111.25
EU-15	100.00	95.07	96.65	97.80	96.96	96.55	97.49	98.98
Germany	100.00	94.85	98.66	101.95	102.65	103.13	104.88	106.92

Source: AMECO Database (European Commission, DGECFIN).

(a) Work out the growth rate for each country for each year from 2009 to 2015.

(b) Plot the figures on a graph. Describe the pattern that emerges.

2. In 1974 the UK economy shrank by 1.1 per cent before shrinking by a further 0.5 per cent in 1975. However, actual GDP rose by 13.4 per cent in 1974 and by 26.3 per cent in 1975. What explains these apparently contradictory results?

3. The following table shows the level of financial liabilities of UK households since 2003 along with the level of nominal GDP.

	2005	2006	2007	2008
Financial liabilities, £bn	1247.6	1399.5	1508.5	1536.2
GDP, £bn	1276.7	1349.5	1427.9	1462.1
Financial liabilities as % of GDP				

	2009	2010	2011	2012
Financial liabilities, £bn	1525.9	1529.2	1529.7	1546.7
GDP, £bn	1417.4	1485.6	1536.9	1564.6
Financial liabilities as % of GDP				

Source: National Balance Sheet and Quarterly National Accounts (National Statistics).

(a) Explain how the net worth of households is affected by their level of financial liabilities.

(b) Complete the final row of the table so as to present financial liabilities as a percentage of GDP.

4. Explain how equilibrium would be restored in the circular flow of income if there were a fall in investment.

5. Explain the circumstances under which an increase in pensions and child benefit would (a) increase national income; (b) leave national income unaffected; (c) decrease national income.

6. For what reasons might GDP be a poor indicator of (i) the level of development of a country; (ii) its rate of economic development?

7. Will the rate of actual growth have any effect on the rate of potential growth?

8. For what possible reasons may one country experience a persistently faster rate of economic growth than another?

9. Why will investment affect both actual (short-term) growth and the long-term growth in potential output? What will be the implications if these two effects differ in magnitude?

10. Explain how you would derive a figure for households' disposable income if you were starting from a figure for GDP.

Online resources

Additional case studies in MyEconLab

14.1 **The GDP deflator.** An examination of how GDP figures are corrected to take inflation into account.

14.2 **Taking into account the redistributive effects of growth.** This case study shows how figures for economic growth can be adjusted to allow for the fact that poor people's income growth would otherwise count for far less than rich people's.

14.3 **Simon Kuznets and the system of national income accounting.** This looks at the work of Simon Kuznets, who devised the system of national income accounting that is used around the world. It describes some of the patterns of economic growth that he identified.

14.4 **Growth accounting.** This case study identifies various factors that contribute to economic growth and shows how their contribution can be measured.

14.5 **How big is the underground economy?** This case study looks at the factors that determine the size of the underground economy.

14.6 **The use of ISEW.** This looks at an alternative measure of economic well-being popular among environment groups: the Index of Sustainable Economic Welfare.

Websites relevant to this chapter

See sites listed at the end of Chapter 15 on page 462.

MyEconLab

This book can be supported by MyEconLab, which contains a range of additional resources, including an online homework and tutorial system designed to test and build your understanding.

You need both an access card and a course ID to access MyEconLab:

1. Is your lecturer using MyEconLab? Ask your lecturer for your course ID.

2. Has an access card been included with the book at a reduced cost? Check the inside back cover of the book.

3. If you have a course ID but no access card, go to: http://www.myeconlab.com/ to buy access to this interactive study programme.

jobcentreplus

Part of the Department for Work and Pensions

Jobs

Macroeconomic Issues and Analysis: An Overview

CHAPTER MAP

15.1 The key issues: a recap	**431**
15.2 Unemployment	**431**
The meaning of 'unemployment'	432
Official measures of unemployment	432
The duration of unemployment	433
The composition of unemployment	435
Unemployment and the labour market	436
Disequilibrium unemployment	437
Equilibrium unemployment (or natural unemployment)	439
15.3 Aggregate demand and supply and the level of prices	**441**
The aggregate demand curve	441
The aggregate supply curve	442
Equilibrium	443
15.4 Inflation	**444**
The costs of inflation	446
Causes of inflation	446
Policies to tackle inflation	452
15.5 The balance of payments and exchange rates	**453**
The balance of payments account	453
Assessing the balance of payments figures	455
Exchange rates	456
The determination of the rate of exchange in a free market	457
Exchange rates and the balance of payments	458
Managing the exchange rate	459

In the previous chapter we examined the issue of economic growth. In this chapter we consider three further key macroeconomic issues: unemployment, inflation and the balance of payments. We give an overview of these problems: how they are measured and their effects on society. We also have a first look at the *causes* of these problems. This helps prepare the ground for the analyses in later chapters.

We saw in Chapter 14 that macroeconomics deals with economic problems in the aggregate (i.e. for the whole economy). An important tool for analysing these aggregate problems is aggregate demand and supply analysis. We look at this analysis in section 15.3. This is then the basis for our analysis of inflation in section 15.4.

15.1 THE KEY ISSUES: A RECAP

In Chapter 14 we identified a set of key macroeconomic issues: economic growth, unemployment, inflation, economic relationships with the rest of the world, the financial well-being of economic agents and the relationship between the financial system and the economy. We saw too how these issues can be related through their relationship with aggregate demand and, hence, the phase of the business cycle.

Thus, in a period of expansion economic growth is likely to be high, with unemployment falling; inflation is likely to rise, however, as will imports. In a recession, the reverse will be the case: economic growth will be negative and unemployment will probably rise; inflation, however, is likely to fall, as will imports.

One of the purposes of economic models, such as the circular flow model that we introduced in Chapter 14, is to help us get a better understanding of the ways in which macroeconomic issues are related. For instance, under what conditions might an economy be able to experience higher economic growth without there being significantly higher rates of inflation? Models can also show how these relationships evolve and how they differ between the short run and the long run.

By better understanding the key macroeconomic issues, their causes and the relationships between them, policy makers are in a position to make more informed policy decisions.

As the text progresses we will be looking further at the relationships between the key macroeconomic issues. Chapter 16 gives an overview of these debates. It helps to put in context the current state of macroeconomics: where economists have reached agreement and where they still disagree. But, in this chapter we take a deeper look at three key macroeconomic issues: unemployment, inflation and the balance payments and exchange rates. In doing so, we begin to think about their causes.

15.2 UNEMPLOYMENT

Unemployment fluctuates with the business cycle. In recessions, such as those experienced by most countries in the early 1980s, the early 1990s and the early and late 2000s, unemployment tends to rise. In boom years, such as the late 1980s, late 1990s and mid-2000s, it tends to fall. Figure 15.1 shows these cyclical movements in unemployment for selected countries.

As well as experiencing fluctuations in unemployment, most countries have experienced long-term changes in average unemployment rates. This is illustrated in Table 15.1, which shows average unemployment in a selection of industrialised countries. Average unemployment rates in the 1980s and 1990s were higher than in the 1970s, and average rates in the 1970s were, in turn, higher than in the 1950s and 1960s. In certain countries, such as the UK and the USA, the late 1990s and early 2000s saw a long-term fall in unemployment.

However, the global financial crisis of the late 2000s and subsequent economic downturn saw a marked upwards turn in unemployment rates. This was particularly so in

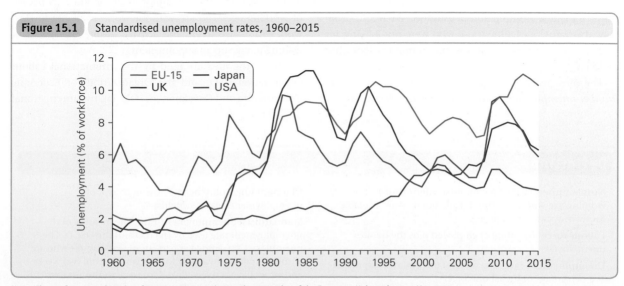

Figure 15.1 Standardised unemployment rates, 1960–2015

Notes: Figures from 2014 based on forecasts; EU-15 = the member countries of the European Union prior to 1 May 2004.
Source: Based on data in *AMECO Database* (European Commission, DGECFIN).

Table 15.1	Average unemployment rates (%)					
	1960s	1970s	1980s	1990s	2000s	2010–15
Australia	1.7	3.8	7.6	9.0	5.5	5.6
Canada	5.0	6.7	9.4	9.7	7.0	7.3
France	1.7	3.6	7.9	10.3	8.8	9.9
Germany	0.7	2.0	5.8	7.8	9.1	5.7
Greece	5.1	2.3	6.1	9.4	9.7	22.0
Ireland	5.3	7.5	14.2	11.9	5.4	13.0
Japan	1.3	1.7	2.5	3.2	4.7	4.3
Portugal	2.4	4.6	7.5	5.8	7.5	14.6
Spain	2.4	4.5	15.9	17.6	11.1	23.8
UK	1.6	3.5	9.5	8.1	5.4	7.4
USA	4.8	6.2	7.3	5.7	5.6	7.7
EU-15	2.2	3.6	8.3	9.3	7.9	10.3

Notes: (i) EU-15 = 15 members of the European Union prior to 1 May 2004; (ii) German figures relate to West Germany only up to 1991; (iii) figures from 2014 are forecasts.
Source: AMECO database (European Commission, DGECFIN).

countries where government finances were badly hit and where, as a result, governments looked to repair their balance sheets by restraining spending and/or raising taxes. In some countries, such as Ireland, Greece and Portugal, emergency loans had to be granted to help meet the rising costs of managing their rising stock of debt.

This section gives an overview of the problem of unemployment: how it is measured and what its costs are. Then we look at the range of possible causes of unemployment. We explore these causes and the policies for tackling unemployment in more detail as the text progresses.

The meaning of 'unemployment'

Unemployment can be expressed either as a number (e.g. 1.6 million) or as a percentage (e.g. 6 per cent). But just who should be included in the statistics? Should it be everyone without a job? The answer is clearly no, since we would not want to include children and pensioners. We would probably also want to exclude those who were not looking for work, such as parents choosing to stay at home to look after children.

The most usual definition that economists use for the **number unemployed** is: *those of working age who are without work, but who are available for work at current wage rates*. If the figure is to be expressed as a percentage, then it is a percentage of the total **labour force**. The labour force is defined as *those in employment plus those unemployed*. Thus if 30 million people were employed and 2.5 million people were unemployed, the **unemployment rate** would be

$$\frac{2.5}{30+2.5} \times 100 = 7.7\%$$

Official measures of unemployment

Claimant unemployment

Two common measures of unemployment are used in official statistics. The first is **claimant unemployment**. This is simply a measure of all those in receipt of unemployment-related benefits. In the UK claimants receive the 'jobseeker's allowance (JSA)'.

Claimant statistics have the advantage of being very easy to collect. However, they exclude all those of working age who are available for work at current wage rates, but who are *not* eligible for benefits. If the government changes the eligibility conditions so that fewer people are eligible, this will reduce the number of claimants and hence the official number unemployed, even if there has been no change in the numbers with or without work.

Several categories of people in the UK are ineligible for JSA and are thus not included in claimant unemployment. These include, among others, those aged 16 and 17, those over retirement age and those whose income or savings are too high. The net effect is that the claimant statistics understate the true level of unemployment.

Standardised unemployment rates

Recognising the weaknesses of the claimant statistics, the UK government since 1998 has used the **standardised unemployment rate** as the main measure of unemployment. In this measure, the unemployed are defined as people of working age who are without work, available to start work within two weeks and *actively seeking employment* or waiting to take up an appointment.

This is the measure used by the International Labour Organization (ILO) and the Organization for Economic Co-operation and Development (OECD), two international

Definitions

Number unemployed (economist's definition) Those of working age who are without work, but who are available for work at current wage rates.

Labour force The number employed plus the number unemployed.

Unemployment rate The number unemployed expressed as a percentage of the labour force.

Claimant unemployment Those in receipt of unemployment-related benefits.

Standardised unemployment rate The measure of the unemployment rate used by the ILO and the OECD. The unemployed are defined as persons of working age who are without work, are available to start work within two weeks and either have actively looked for work in the last four weeks or are waiting to take up an appointment.

Figure 15.2   UK unemployment by duration

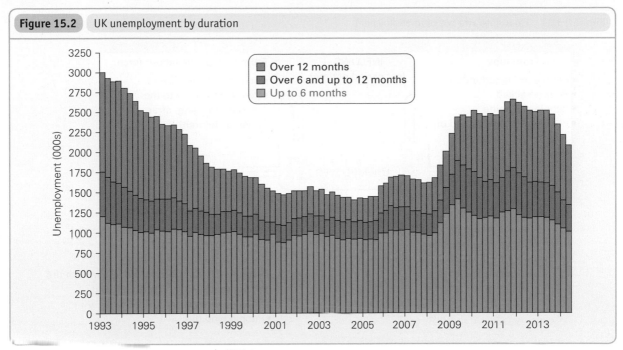

■ Over 12 months
■ Over 6 and up to 12 months
□ Up to 6 months

Source: Based on data from *Labour Market Statistics*, series YBWF, YBWG and TBWI (National Statistics)

---

organisations that publish unemployment statistics for many countries. The figures are compiled from the results of national labour force *surveys*. A representative cross-section of the population is asked whether they are employed, unemployed (using the above definition) or economically inactive. From their replies, national rates of unemployment can be extrapolated. In the UK, the Labour Force Survey is conducted quarterly.

As we have seen, the standardised rate is likely to be higher than the claimant rate to the extent that it includes people seeking work who are nevertheless not entitled to claim benefits. However, it will be lower to the extent that it excludes those who are claiming benefits and yet who are not actively seeking work. Over the period 2008 to 2013, the average claimant count rate in the UK was 4.3 per cent while the average standardised unemployment rate was 7.5 per cent.

 How does the ILO/OECD definition differ from the economist's definition? What is the significance of the phrase 'available for work at current wage rates' in the economist's definition?

The duration of unemployment

A few of the unemployed may never have had a job and maybe never will. For most, however, unemployment lasts only a certain period. For some it may be just a few days while they are between jobs. For others it may be a few months. For others – the long-term unemployed – it could be several years. Figure 15.2 shows the composition of standardised unemployment in the UK by duration.

What determines the average duration of unemployment? There are three important factors here.

The number unemployed (the size of the stock of unemployment). Unemployment is a 'stock' concept (see Box 9.9). It measures a *quantity* (i.e. the number unemployed) at a particular *point in time*. The higher the stock of unemployment, the longer will tend to be the duration of unemployment. There will be more people competing for vacant jobs.

The rate of inflow and outflow from the stock of unemployment. The people making up the unemployment total are constantly changing. Each week some people are made redundant or quit their jobs. They represent an inflow to the stock of unemployment. Other people find jobs and thus represent an outflow from the stock of unemployment. The various inflows and outflows are shown in Figure 15.3.

Unemployment is often referred to as 'the pool of unemployment'. This is quite a good analogy. If the water flowing into a pool exceeds the water flowing out, the level of water in the pool will rise. Similarly, if the inflow of people into unemployment exceeds the outflow, the level of unemployment will rise.

The duration of unemployment will depend on the *rate* of inflow and outflow. The rate is expressed as the number of people per period of time. Figure 15.4 shows the inflows and outflows in the UK since 1989.

Note the magnitude of the flows. In each of the years, the outflows (and inflows) exceed the total number unemployed. The bigger the flows are relative to the total number unemployed, the less will be the average duration of unemployment. This is because people move into and

Figure 15.3 Flows into and out of unemployment

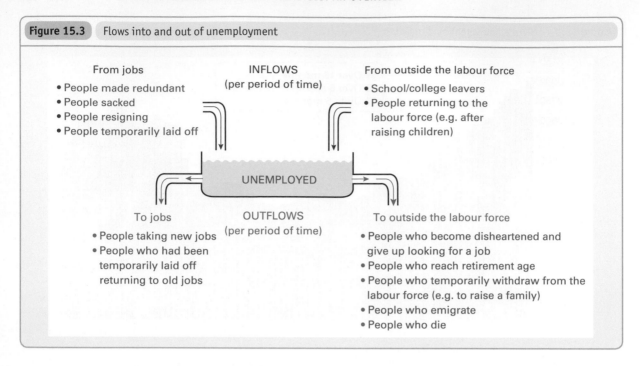

Figure 15.4 UK claimant unemployment: total stock and annual flows

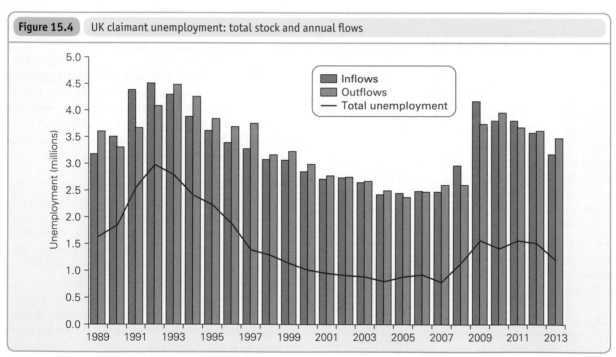

Source: Based on data from *Labour Market Statistics* (National Statistics).

out of the pool more quickly, and hence their average stay will be shorter.

1. *If the number unemployed exceeded the total annual outflow, what could we conclude about the average duration of unemployment?*
2. *Make a list of the various inflows to and outflows from employment from and to (a) unemployment; (b) outside the workforce.*

The phase of the business cycle. The duration of unemployment also depends on the phase of the business cycle. At the onset of a recession, unemployment will rise, but as yet the average length of unemployment is likely to have been relatively short. Once a recession has lasted for a period of time, however, people will on average have been out of work longer, and this long-term unemployment is likely to persist even when the economy is pulling out of recession.

The composition of unemployment

Unemployment rates vary enormously between countries and between different groups within countries.

Geographical differences. Table 15.2 illustrates the considerable differences in unemployment rates between countries. Countries have very different labour markets, very different policies on unemployment, training schemes, redundancy, etc., and very different attitudes of firms towards their workers. Also, countries may not be at precisely the same phase of their respective business cycles.

Unemployment also varies substantially within a country from one area to another. Most countries have some regions that are more prosperous than others. In the UK, unemployment across the north of England, Scotland and Northern Ireland is typically higher than in the south of England. For example, the average unemployment rate

over the period from 2008 to 2013 in South-East England (excluding London) was 5.9 per cent compared with 7.2 per cent in Scotland and 9.6 per cent in North-East England.

But geographical differences in unemployment are not just a regional problem. In many countries, inner city unemployment is very much higher than suburban or rural unemployment, and, as a result, most developed countries have schemes to attract employment to the inner cities. For example, the average standardised unemployment rate over the period 2008 to 2013 was 14 per cent in the City of Hull, 13.3 per cent in Birmingham City and 12.8 per cent in Newham in London. In contrast, the average rate was 3.9 per cent in both West Dorset and in West Oxfordshire and 3.2 per cent in the Shetland Islands.

Differences in unemployment rates between women and men. In many countries, female unemployment has traditionally been higher than male unemployment. Causes have included differences in education and training, discrimination by employers, more casual or seasonally related employment among women and other social factors. In many countries, however, the position has changed in recent years. In six of the countries in Table 15.2, including Ireland and the UK, male unemployment rates are higher than female rates. The main reason is the decline in many of the older industries, such as coal and steel, which employed mainly men.

Differences in unemployment rates between different age groups. Table 15.2 also shows that unemployment rates in the under-25 age group are higher than the average, and substantially so in many countries. In the EU as a whole the unemployment rate of the under-25s in the five-year period from September 2008 was more than double the average rate; in Italy it was more than triple. For some of the countries with the highest unemployment, this translates to a difference of over 20 percentage points – a considerable rise on the previous five years. These figures highlight that adverse economic conditions can disproportionally affect younger, inexperienced or less qualified members of the workforce. However, they also highlight other persistent underlying factors too.

Higher youth unemployment rates can be explained by the suitability (or unsuitability) of the qualifications of school leavers, the attitudes of employers to young people, and the greater willingness of young people to spend time unemployed looking for a better job or waiting to start a further or higher education course. The difference in rates is less in Germany, which has a well-established apprenticeship system.

Differences in unemployment rates between different ethnic groups. In many countries, members of ethnic minorities suffer from higher unemployment rates than the average. In the UK, the unemployment rate for Afro-Caribbeans was around 2.3 times higher than that for whites in 2013, while for those of Pakistani origin it was twice as high. Explanations are complex, but include differences in educational opportunities,

Table 15.2	Standardised unemployment rates by age and gender, average September 2008 to August 2013					
	All ages			Under 25		
	Total	Male	Female	Total	Male	Female
France	9.8	9.5	10.1	23.8	23.6	24.1
Germany	6.5	6.8	6.1	9.4	10.3	8.3
Greece	17.0	14.2	20.7	41.1	35.0	48.4
Ireland	13.4	16.3	9.9	27.1	32.8	21.1
Italy	9.1	8.3	10.4	30.2	28.3	32.3
Netherlands	4.7	4.7	4.6	8.6	8.5	8.6
Poland	9.4	8.8	10.0	24.0	22.3	26.4
Portugal	13.2	13.1	13.3	30.7	29.5	32.1
Spain	21.4	21.4	21.9	45.2	46.5	43.7
Sweden	8.0	8.2	7.9	23.7	24.8	22.7
UK	7.7	8.4	6.9	20.0	22.4	17.3
USA	8.6	9.2	8.0	17.0	18.9	15.0
EU-15	9.8	9.8	9.9	20.9	21.7	19.9
EU-28	9.7	9.7	9.8	21.4	22.1	20.6

Source: Based on data from Statistics Database (Eurostat, European Commission).

BOX 15.1 THE COSTS OF UNEMPLOYMENT

Who loses and by how much?

The most obvious cost of unemployment is to the unemployed themselves. There is the direct financial cost of the loss in their earnings. Then there are the personal costs of being unemployed. The longer people are unemployed, the more dispirited they may become. Their self-esteem is likely to fall, and they are more likely to succumb to stress-related illness.

Beyond the unemployed themselves, there are the costs to their families and friends. Personal relations can become strained, and there may be an increase in domestic violence and the number of families splitting up.

Then there are the broader costs to the economy. Unemployment represents a loss of output. In other words, actual output is below potential output. Apart from the loss of disposable income to the unemployed themselves, this underutilisation of resources leads to lower incomes for other people too:

- The government loses tax revenues, since the unemployed pay no income tax and national insurance, and, given that the unemployed spend less, they pay less VAT and excise duties. The government also incurs administrative costs associated with the running of benefit offices. It may also have to spend extra on health care, the social services and the police.
- Firms lose the profits that could have been made if there had been full employment.
- Other workers lose any additional wages they could have earned from higher national output.

What is more, the longer people remain unemployed, the more deskilled they tend to become. This scarring effect reduces potential as well as actual income.

 Why have the costs to the government of unemployment benefits not been included as a cost to the economy?

Finally, there is some evidence that higher unemployment leads to increased crime and vandalism. This obviously imposes a cost on the sufferers.

The costs of unemployment are to some extent offset by benefits. If workers voluntarily quit their jobs to look for better ones, then they must reckon that the benefits of a better job more than compensate for their temporary loss of income. From the nation's point of view, a workforce that is prepared to quit jobs and spend a short time unemployed will be a more adaptable, more mobile workforce – one that is responsive to changing economic circumstances. Such a workforce will lead to greater allocative efficiency in the short run and more rapid economic growth over the longer run.

Long-term involuntary unemployment is quite another matter. The costs clearly outweigh any benefits, both for the individuals involved and for the economy as a whole. A demotivated, deskilled pool of long-term unemployed is a serious economic and social problem.

 Which of the above costs would be recorded as a reduction in GDP?

---

a higher proportion of younger people, a greater sense of alienation among the unemployed, and the attitudes and prejudices of employers.

Unemployment and the labour market

We now turn to the causes of unemployment. These causes fall into two broad categories: *equilibrium* unemployment and *disequilibrium* unemployment. To make clear the distinction between the two, it is necessary to look at how the labour market works.

Figure 15.5 shows the **aggregate demand** for labour and **aggregate supply** of labour – that is, the total demand and supply of labour in the whole economy. The *real* average wage rate is plotted on the vertical axis. This is the average wage rate expressed in terms of its purchasing power: in other words, after taking prices into account.

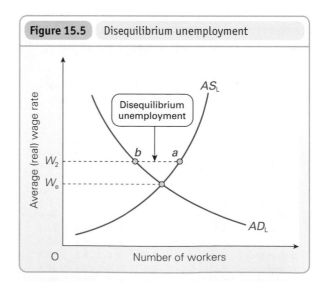

Figure 15.5   Disequilibrium unemployment

Definitions

Aggregate demand for labour curve A curve showing the total demand for labour in the economy at different average real wage rates.

Aggregate supply of labour curve A curve showing the total number of people willing and able to work at different average real wage rates.

The aggregate supply of labour curve (AS_L) shows the number of workers *willing to accept jobs* at each wage rate. This curve is relatively inelastic, since the size of the labour force at any one time cannot change significantly. Nevertheless it is not totally inelastic because (a) a higher wage rate will encourage some people to enter the labour market (e.g. parents raising children), and (b) the unemployed will be more willing to accept job offers rather than continuing to search for a better-paid job.

The aggregate demand for labour curve (AD_L) slopes downwards. The higher the wage rate, the more will firms attempt to economise on labour and to substitute other factors of production for labour.

The labour market is in equilibrium at a wage of W_e – where the demand for labour equals the supply.

If the wage rate were above W_e, the labour market would be in a state of disequilibrium. At a wage rate of W_1, there is an excess supply of labour of $a - b$. This is called ***disequilibrium unemployment***.

For disequilibrium unemployment to occur, two conditions must hold:

- The aggregate supply of labour must exceed the aggregate demand.
- There must be a 'stickiness' in wages. In other words, the wage rate must not immediately fall to W_e, the market-clearing wage.

Even when the labour market *is* in equilibrium, however, not everyone looking for work will be employed. Some people will hold out, hoping to find a better job. This is illustrated in Figure 15.6.

The curve N shows the total number in the labour force. The horizontal difference between it and the aggregate supply of labour curve (AS_L) represents the excess of people looking for work over those actually willing to accept jobs. Q_e represents the equilibrium level of employment and the distance $d - e$ represents the ***equilibrium level of***

Figure 15.7 Equilibrium and disequilibrium unemployment

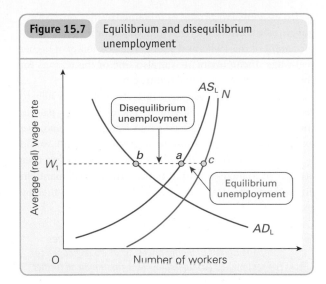

unemployment. This is sometimes known as the ***natural level of unemployment***.

Note that the AS_L curve gets closer to the N curve at higher wages. The reason for this is that the unemployed will be more willing to accept jobs, the higher the wages they are offered.

Figure 15.7 shows both equilibrium *and* disequilibrium unemployment. At a wage of W_1, disequilibrium unemployment is $a - b$; equilibrium unemployment is $c - a$; thus total unemployment is $c - b$.

But what are the causes of disequilibrium and equilibrium unemployment? We examine each in turn.

Disequilibrium unemployment

There are three possible causes of disequilibrium unemployment.

Real-wage unemployment

Real-wage unemployment occurs when trade unions use their monopoly power to drive wages above the market-clearing level. It could also be caused by the government setting the national minimum wage too high. In Figure 15.5, the wage rate is driven up above W_e.

Figure 15.6 Equilibrium unemployment

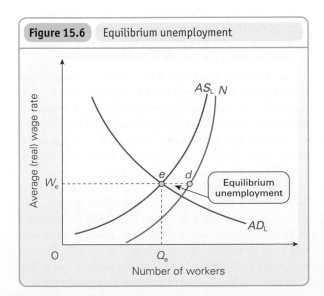

Excessive real wage rates were blamed by the Conservative governments under Thatcher and Major for the high unemployment of the 1980s and 1990s. The possibility of higher real-wage unemployment was also one of the reasons for their rejection of a national minimum wage.

One effect of high real wage rates, however, may help to reduce real-wage unemployment. The extra wages paid to those who are still employed could lead to extra *consumer* expenditure. This addition to aggregate demand would in turn lead to firms demanding more labour, as they attempted to increase output to meet the extra demand. In Figure 15.5, the AD_L curve will shift to the right, thereby reducing the gap $a - b$.

 If the higher consumer expenditure and higher wages subsequently led to higher prices, what would happen to (a) real wages; (b) unemployment (assuming no further response from unions)?

Demand-deficient or cyclical unemployment

Demand-deficient or **cyclical unemployment** is associated with economic recessions. As the economy moves into recession, consumer demand falls. Firms find that they are unable to sell their current level of output. For a time they may be prepared to build up stocks of unsold goods, but sooner or later they will start to cut back on production and reduce the amount of labour they employ. The deeper the recession becomes and the longer it lasts, the higher will demand-deficient unemployment become.

As the economy recovers and begins to grow again, so demand-deficient unemployment will start to fall again. Because demand-deficient unemployment fluctuates with the business cycle, it is sometimes referred to as 'cyclical unemployment'. Figure 15.1 (on page 431) showed the fluctuations in unemployment in various industrial countries. If you compare this figure with Figure 14.6 (on page 417), you can see how unemployment tends to rise in recessions and fall in booms.

Demand-deficient unemployment is also referred to as 'Keynesian unemployment', after John Maynard Keynes (see Case Study 16.6 in MyEconLab), who saw a deficiency of aggregate demand as the cause of the high unemployment between the two world wars. Today, many economists are known as 'Keynesian'. Although there are many strands of Keynesian thinking, these economists all see aggregate demand as important in determining a nation's output and employment.

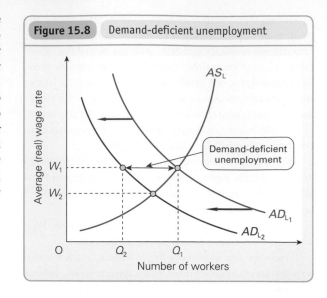

Figure 15.8   Demand-deficient unemployment

Demand-deficient unemployment is illustrated in Figure 15.8. Assume initially that the economy is at the peak of the business cycle. The aggregate demand for and supply of labour are equal at the current wage rate of W_1. There is no disequilibrium unemployment. Now assume that the economy moves into recession. Consumer demand falls and as a result firms demand less labour. The demand for labour shifts to AD_{L2}. If there is a resistance to wage cuts, such that the real wage rate remains fixed at W_1, there will now be disequilibrium unemployment of $Q_1 - Q_2$.

Some Keynesians specifically focus on the reluctance of real wage rates to fall from W_1 to W_2. This downward 'stickiness' in real wage rates may be the result of unions seeking to protect the living standards of their members (even though there are non-members out of work), or of firms worried about the demotivating effects of cutting the real wages of their workers. Sometimes it is simply that wage rates have been agreed through a process of collective bargaining for the following year or more, where the agreement includes an inflation-proofing element to ensure that they are *real* wage rates. For such economists, the problem of demand-deficient unemployment would be solved if there could somehow be a fall in real wage rates.

For other Keynesian economists, however, the problem is much more fundamental than a downward stickiness in real wages. For them the problem is that the low level of aggregate demand causes an *equilibrium* in the *goods* market at an output that is too low to generate full employment. Firms' supply is low (below the full-employment level of supply) because aggregate demand is low.

This low-level equilibrium in the goods market, and the corresponding disequilibrium in the labour market, may *persist*. This is the result of a lack of confidence on the part of firms. After all, why should firms produce more and take on more workers, if they believe that the recession will persist and that they will therefore not sell any more? The economy remains trapped in a low-output equilibrium.

TC 13
p418

Definition

Demand-deficient or cyclical unemployment
Disequilibrium unemployment caused by a fall in aggregate demand with no corresponding fall in the real wage rate.

In such cases, a fall in real wages would not cure the unemployment. In fact, it might even make the problem worse. In Figure 15.8, even if the average wage rate were to fall to W_2, demand-deficient unemployment would still persist. The reason is that this general cut in wages throughout the economy would reduce workers' incomes and hence reduce their *consumption of goods*. As the aggregate demand for goods fell, there would be a further reduction in demand for labour: the aggregate demand for labour curve would shift to the left again – to the left of AD_{L_2}. By the time the wage had fallen to W_2, W_2 would no longer be the equilibrium wage. There would still be demand-deficient unemployment.

 If this analysis is correct, that is if a reduction in wages will reduce the aggregate demand for goods, what assumption must we make about the relative proportions of wages and profits that are spent (given that a reduction in real wage rates will lead to a corresponding increase in rates of profit)?

Growth in the labour supply

If labour supply rises with no corresponding increase in the demand for labour, the equilibrium real wage rate will fall. If the real wage rate is 'sticky' downwards, disequilibrium unemployment will occur.

 On a diagram similar to Figure 15.8, illustrate how a growth in labour supply can cause disequilibrium unemployment.

This tends not to be such a serious cause of unemployment as demand deficiency, since the supply of labour changes relatively slowly. Nevertheless, there is a problem of providing jobs for school leavers each year with the sudden influx of new workers on to the labour market.

 From 2004, with the accession of eastern European countries to the EU, there were significant flows of migrants from eastern to western Europe. Does such immigration create disequilibrium unemployment?

Equilibrium unemployment (or natural unemployment)

Although there may be overall *macro*economic equilibrium, with the *aggregate* demand for labour equal to the *aggregate* supply, and thus no disequilibrium unemployment, at a *micro*economic level supply and demand may not match. There may be excess demand for labour (vacancies) in some markets and excess supply (unemployment) in others. There may be vacancies for computer technicians and unemployment in the steel industry, but unemployed steel workers cannot immediately become computer technicians. This is when equilibrium unemployment will occur.

There are various types of equilibrium unemployment.

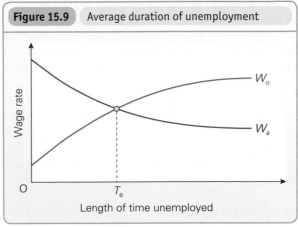

Figure 15.9 Average duration of unemployment

Frictional (search) unemployment

Frictional (search) unemployment occurs when people leave their jobs, either voluntarily or because they are sacked or made redundant, and are unemployed for a period of time while they are looking for a new job. They may not get the first job they apply for, despite a vacancy existing and despite their being suitably qualified.

The problem is that information is imperfect. Employers are not fully informed about what labour is available; workers are not fully informed about what jobs are available and what they entail. Both employers and workers, therefore, have to search: employers searching for the right labour and workers searching for the right jobs.

The longer people search for a job, the better the wage offers they are likely to be made. This is illustrated in Figure 15.9 by the curve W_o. It shows the highest wage offer that the typical worker will have received since being unemployed.

When they first start looking for a job, people may have high expectations of getting a good wage. The longer they are unemployed, however, the more anxious they are likely to be to get a job, and therefore the lower will be the wage they are prepared to accept. The curve W_a shows the wage that is acceptable to the typical worker.

KI 15
p121

TC 9
p121

 Why are W_o and W_a drawn as curves rather than straight lines?

The average duration of unemployment will be T_e. That is, workers will remain unemployed until they find a job at an acceptable wage.

Definition

Frictional (search) unemployment Unemployment that occurs as a result of imperfect information in the labour market. It often takes time for workers to find jobs (even though there are vacancies) and in the meantime they are unemployed.

One obvious remedy for frictional unemployment is to provide better job information through government job centres, private employment agencies or the media. This would have the effect of making the curve W_o reach its peak earlier, and thus of shifting the intersection of W_o and W_a to the left.

Another much more controversial remedy is for the government to reduce the level of unemployment benefit. This will make the unemployed more desperate to get a job and thus prepared to accept a lower wage. It will therefore have the effect of shifting the W_a curve downwards and again of shifting the intersection of W_o and W_a to the left.

Structural unemployment

Structural unemployment occurs where the structure of the economy changes. Employment in some industries may expand while in others it contracts. There are two main reasons for this.

A change in the pattern of demand. Some industries experience declining demand. This may be due to a change in consumer tastes as certain goods go out of fashion; or it may be due to competition from other industries. For example, consumer demand may shift away from coal and to other fuels. This will lead to structural unemployment in mining areas.

A change in the methods of production (technological unemployment). New techniques of production often allow the same level of output to be produced with fewer workers (see Case Study 15.2 in MyEconLab). This is known as 'labour-saving technical progress'. Unless output expands sufficiently to absorb the surplus labour, people will be made redundant. This creates **technological unemployment**. An example is the loss of jobs in the banking industry caused by the increase in the number of cash machines and by the development of telephone and Internet banking.

Structural unemployment often occurs in particular regions of the country. When it does, it is referred to as **regional unemployment**. Regional unemployment is due to the concentration of particular industries in particular areas. For example, the collapse in the South Wales coal-mining industry led to high unemployment in the Welsh valleys.

The level of structural unemployment will depend on three factors:

- The degree of regional concentration of industry. The more that industries are concentrated in particular regions, the greater will be the level of structural unemployment if particular industries decline.
- The speed of change of demand and supply in the economy. The more rapid the rate of technological change

or the shift in consumer tastes, the more rapid will be the rate of redundancies.

- The immobility of labour. The less able or willing workers are to move to a new job, the higher will be the level of structural unemployment. In Chapter 9 we made the distinction between geographical and occupational immobility. Geographical immobility is a particular problem with regional unemployment. Occupational immobility is a particular problem with technological unemployment where old skills are no longer required.

There are two broad approaches to tackling structural unemployment: *market-orientated* and *interventionist*.

A market-orientated approach involves encouraging people to look more actively for jobs, if necessary in other parts of the country. It involves encouraging people to adopt a more willing attitude towards retraining, and if necessary to accept some reduction in wages.

An interventionist approach involves direct government action to match jobs to the unemployed. Two examples are providing grants to firms to set up in areas of high unemployment (regional policy), and government-funded training schemes.

Policies to tackle structural unemployment are examined in detail in sections 23.2 and 23.3.

Seasonal unemployment

Seasonal unemployment occurs when the demand for certain types of labour fluctuates with the seasons of the year. This problem is particularly severe in holiday areas, such as Cornwall, where unemployment can reach very high levels in the winter months. Policies for tackling seasonal unemployment are similar to those for structural unemployment.

Definitions

Structural unemployment Unemployment that arises from changes in the pattern of demand or supply in the economy. People made redundant in one part of the economy cannot immediately take up jobs in other parts (even though there are vacancies).

Technological unemployment Structural unemployment that occurs as a result of the introduction of labour-saving technology.

Regional unemployment Structural unemployment occurring in specific regions of the country.

Seasonal unemployment Unemployment associated with industries or regions where the demand for labour is lower at certain times of the year.

Section summary

1. Who should be counted as 'unemployed' is a matter for some disagreement. The two most common measures of unemployment are claimant unemployment (those claiming unemployment-related benefits) and ILO/OECD standardised unemployment (those available for work and actively seeking work or waiting to take up an appointment).

2. The 'stock' of unemployment will grow if the inflow of people into unemployment exceeds the outflow (to jobs or out of the labour market altogether). The more rapid these flows, the shorter the average duration of unemployment.

3. In most countries, unemployment is unevenly distributed across geographical regions, between women and men, between age groups and between different ethnic groups.

4. The costs of unemployment include the financial and other personal costs to the unemployed person, the costs to relatives and friends, and the costs to society at large in terms of lost tax revenues, lost profits and lost wages to other workers, and in terms of social disruption.

5. Unemployment can be divided into disequilibrium and equilibrium unemployment.

6. Disequilibrium unemployment occurs when real wage rates are above the level that will equate the aggregate demand and supply of labour. It can be caused by unions or government pushing up wages (real-wage unemployment), by a fall in aggregate demand but a downward 'stickiness' in real wages (demand-deficient unemployment), or by an increase in the supply of labour with again a downward stickiness in wages.

7. In the case of demand-deficient unemployment, the disequilibrium in the labour market may correspond to a low-output equilibrium in the goods market. A fall in real wage rates may be insufficient to remove the deficiency of demand in the labour market.

8. Equilibrium unemployment occurs when there are people unable or unwilling to fill job vacancies. This may be due to poor information in the labour market and hence a time lag before people find suitable jobs (frictional unemployment), to a changing pattern of demand or supply in the economy and hence a mismatching of labour with jobs (structural unemployment – specific types being technological and regional unemployment), or to seasonal fluctuations in the demand for labour.

15.3 AGGREGATE DEMAND AND SUPPLY AND THE LEVEL OF PRICES

Before we examine the causes of inflation (the rate of increase in prices), we need to look at how the *level* of prices in the economy is determined. It is determined by the interaction of aggregate demand and aggregate supply. The analysis is similar to that of demand and supply in individual markets, although, as we shall see in later chapters, there are some crucial differences. Figure 15.10 shows an

aggregate demand and an aggregate supply curve. As with demand and supply curves for individual goods, we plot price on the vertical axis, except that now it is the *general* price level also referred to as to the **GDP deflator**; and we plot quantity on the horizontal axis, except that now it is the *total volume of national output* (GDP). Note that (as we saw in the Appendix to Chapter 14) national output and national income are just different ways of measuring GDP. It is conventional in macroeconomic diagrams, such as the *AD/AS* diagram of Figure 15.10. to use the term 'national income (Y)' rather than 'national output'.

Let us examine each curve in turn.

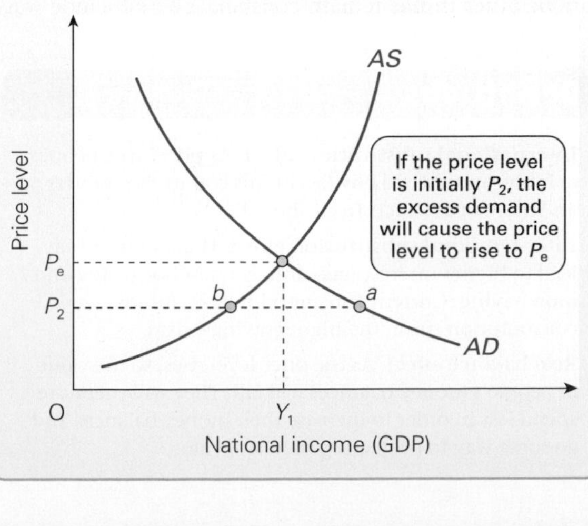

The aggregate demand curve

Remember what we said about aggregate demand in Chapter 14. It is the total level of spending in the economy and consists of four elements: consumer spending (C),

Figure 15.10   Aggregate demand and aggregate supply

If the price level is initially P_2, the excess demand will cause the price level to rise to P_e

Definition

GDP deflator The price index of all final domestically produced goods and services: i.e. all those items that contribute towards GDP.

private investment (*I*), government expenditure on goods and services (*G*) and expenditure on exports (*X*) less expenditure on imports (*M*). Thus

$$AD = C + I + G + X - M$$

The aggregate demand curve shows how much national output (GDP) will be demanded at each level of prices. But why does the *AD* curve slope downwards? Why will people demand less as prices rise? There are two effects that can cause this: income effects and substitution effects.

KI 7
p36

Income effects

For many people, when prices rise their wages will not rise in line, at least not in the short run. There will therefore tend to be a redistribution of income away from wage earners (and hence consumers) and to those charging the higher prices – namely, firms. Thus for consumers there has been an *income effect* of the higher prices. The rise in prices leads to a cut in real incomes and thus people will spend less. Aggregate demand will fall. The *AD* curve will be downward sloping, as in Figure 15.10.

To some extent this will be offset by a rise in profits, but it is unlikely that much of the additional profits will be spent by firms on investment, especially if they see consumer expenditure falling; and any increase in dividends to shareholders will take a time before it is paid, and then may simply be saved rather than spent. To summarise, if prices rise more than wages, the redistribution from wages to profits is likely to lead to a fall in aggregate demand.

Clearly, this income effect will not operate if wages rise in line with prices. Real incomes of wage earners will be unaffected. In practice, as we shall see at several places in this text, in the short run wages do lag behind prices.

An income effect is also likely to occur as a result of progressive taxes. As prices and incomes rise, so people will find that they are paying a larger proportion of their incomes in taxes. As a result, they cannot afford to buy so much.

Substitution effects

In the *micro*economic situation, if the price of one good rises, people will switch to alternative goods. This is the substitution effect of that price rise and helps to explain why the demand curve for a particular good will be downward sloping. At a *macro*economic level we can identify three main reasons why people will demand fewer products as prices:

■ An ***international substitution effect***. If prices rise, people will be encouraged to buy fewer of the country's products and more imports instead (which are now relatively cheaper); the country will also sell fewer exports (which are now less competitive). Thus imports (a withdrawal) will rise and exports (an injection) will fall. Aggregate demand, therefore, will be lower.

■ An ***inter-temporal substitution effect***. As prices rise, people will need more money to pay for their purchases. With a given supply of money in the economy, this will have the effect of driving up interest rates (we will explore this in Chapter 21). The effect of higher interest rates will be to discourage borrowing and encourage saving, with individuals postponing current consumption in favour of future consumption. The effect will be a reduction in spending and hence in aggregate demand.

■ A ***real balance effect***. If prices rise, the value of people's savings will be eroded. They may thus save more (and spend less) to compensate.

The shape of the aggregate demand curve

We have seen that both the income and substitution effects of a rise in the general price level will cause the aggregate demand for goods and services to fall. Thus the *AD* curve is downward sloping. The bigger the income and substitution effects, the more elastic will the curve be.

Shifts in the aggregate demand curve

The aggregate demand curve can shift inwards (to the right) or outwards (to the left), in exactly the same way as the demand curve for an individual good. A rightward shift represents an increase in aggregate demand, whatever the price level; a leftward shift represents a decrease in aggregate demand, whatever the price level.

A shift in the aggregate demand curve will occur if, for any given price level, there is a change in any of its components – consumption, investment, government expenditure or exports minus imports. Thus if the government decides to spend more, or if consumers spend more as a result of lower taxes, or if business confidence increases so that firms decide to invest more, the *AD* curve will shift to the right.

The aggregate supply curve

The aggregate supply (*AS*) curve shows the amount of goods and services that firms are willing to supply at each level of prices. To keep things simple, let us focus on the short-run *AS* curve. When constructing this curve, we assume that various other things remain constant. These include wage

Definitions

International substitution effect As prices rise, people at home and abroad buy less of this country's products and more of products from abroad.

Inter-temporal substitution effect Higher prices may lead to higher interest rates and thus less borrowing and more saving. Current consumption falls; future consumption (from the higher savings) rises.

Real balance effect As the price level rises, so the value of people's money balances will fall. They will therefore spend less in order to increase their money balances and go some way to protecting their real value.

rates and other input prices, technology and the total supply of factors of production (labour, land and capital).[1]

Why do we assume that wage rates and other input
prices are constant? Wage rates are frequently determined
by a process of collective bargaining and, once agreed, will
typically be set for a whole year, if not two. Even if they are
not determined by collective bargaining, wage rates often
change relatively infrequently. So too with the price of
other inputs: except in perfect, or near-perfect markets (such
as the market for various raw materials), firms supplying
capital equipment and other inputs tend to change their
prices relatively infrequently. They do not immediately
raise them when there is an increase in demand or lower
them when demand falls. Thus there is a 'stickiness' in both
wage rates and the price of many inputs.

The short-run aggregate supply curve slopes upwards, as
shown in Figure 15.10. In other words, the higher the level
of prices, the more will be produced. The reason is simple.
Because we are holding wages and other input prices constant, then as the prices of their products rise, firms' profitability at each level of output will be higher than before.
This will encourage them to produce more.

But what *limits* the increase in aggregate supply in response
to an increase in prices? In other words, why is the aggregate
supply curve not horizontal? There are two main reasons:

KI 17
p135

- Diminishing returns. With some factors of production
  fixed in supply, notably capital equipment, firms experience a diminishing marginal physical product from their
  other factors, and hence have an upward-sloping marginal cost curve. In microeconomic analysis the upward-
  sloping cost curves of firms explain why the supply
  curves of individual goods and services slope upwards.
  Here in macroeconomics we are adding the supply
  curves of all goods and services and thus the aggregate
  supply curve also slopes upwards.
- Growing shortages of certain variable factors. As firms
  collectively produce more, even inputs that can be
  varied may increasingly become in short supply. Skilled
  labour may be harder to find, and certain raw materials
  may be harder to obtain.

Thus rising costs explain the upward-sloping aggregate
supply curve. The more steeply costs rise as production
increases, the less elastic will the aggregate supply curve be.

---

[1] Long-run *AS* curves assume that these things *will* change – that they will be
affected by changes in aggregate demand and the price level. We will look at
long-run aggregate supply curves in later chapters.

It is likely that, as the level of national output (i.e. national
income) increases and firms reach full-capacity working, so
marginal costs will rise faster. The aggregate supply curve
will thus tend to get steeper (as shown in Figure 15.10).

Shifts in the aggregate supply curve

The aggregate supply curve will shift if there is a change in
any of the variables that are held constant when we plot the
curve. Several of these variables, notably technology, the
labour force and the stock of capital, change only slowly –
normally shifting the curve gradually to the right. This
represents an increase in potential output.

By contrast, wage rates and other input prices can change
significantly in the short run, and are thus the major causes
of shifts in the short-run supply curve. For example, a general
rise in wage rates throughout the economy reduces the amount
that firms wish to produce at any level of prices. The aggregate supply curve shifts to the left. A similar effect will occur
if other costs, such as oil prices or indirect taxes, increase.

Equilibrium

Equilibrium in the macroeconomy occurs when aggregate
demand and aggregate supply are equal. In Figure 15.10,
this is at the price level P_e and national income (GDP) of Y_e.
To demonstrate this, consider what would happen if aggregate demand exceeded aggregate supply, for example at P_2 in
Figure 15.10. The resulting shortages throughout the economy
would drive up prices. This would encourage firms to produce
more; there would be a movement up *along* the *AS* curve. At
the same time, the increase in prices would reduce the level
of aggregate demand – that is, there would also be a movement back up *along* the *AD* curve. The shortage would be
eliminated when price had risen to P_e.

TC 4
p47

Shifts in the AD or AS curves

If the *AD* or *AS* curve shifts, there will be a movement
along the other curve to the new point of equilibrium. For
example, if there is a cut in income taxes and a corresponding increase in consumer demand, the *AD* curve will shift
to the right. This will result in a movement up along the
AS curve to the new equilibrium point: in other words, to
a new higher level of national income and a higher price
level. The more elastic the *AS* curve, the more will output
rise relative to prices. We will consider the shape of the
AS curve in more detail in later chapters, and especially in
Chapters 16 and 20.

Section summary

1. An aggregate demand curve shows the relationship
   between aggregate demand ($C + I + G + X - M$) and the
   price level. The curve is downward sloping because of
   income and substitution effects.

2. If a rise in the price level causes wage rises to lag behind
   or causes a rise in the proportion of income paid in
   income tax, then consumers will respond to the resulting
   fall in their real incomes by cutting consumption. This is
   the income effect.

▶

3. If a rise in the price level causes (a) imports to rise and exports to fall, (b) people to spend less and save more because of a rise in interest rates and possibly (c) people to spend less in order to maintain the value of their bank balances. These effects too will result in a fall in the level of aggregate demand. These are all substitution effects.

4. If the determinant of any component of aggregate demand (other than the price level) changes, the aggregate demand will shift.

5. The (short-run) aggregate supply curve is upward sloping. This reflects the fact that at higher prices, firms will find it profitable to supply more. The curve will be more elastic, the less rapidly diminishing returns set in and the more elastic the supply of variable factors.

6. The aggregate supply curve will shift to the left (upwards) if wage rates or other costs rise independently of a rise in aggregate demand.

7. Equilibrium in the economy occurs when aggregate demand equals aggregate supply. A rise in the price level will occur if there is a rightward shift in the aggregate demand curve or a leftward shift in the aggregate supply curve.

15.4 INFLATION

The rate of inflation measures the annual percentage increase in prices. Typically inflation relates to *consumer* prices. The UK government publishes a consumer prices index (CPI) each month, and the rate of inflation is the percentage increase in that index over the previous 12 months. This index is used throughout the EU, where it generally goes under its full title of the Harmonised Index of Consumer Prices (HICP). The HICP covers virtually 100 per cent of consumer spending (including cross-border spending) and uses sophisticated weights for each item (see Appendix A, pages A:6–8 for an analysis of weighting in indices).

A broader measure of inflation relates to the rate at which the prices of all domestically produced goods and services are changing. The price index used in this case is the GDP deflator (see page 441 and Case Study 14.1 in MyEconLab). Figure 15.11 shows the annual rate of changes in the GDP deflator for the USA, Japan, the UK and the EU-15. As you can see, inflation was particularly severe in the mid-1970s, but rates have been relatively low in more recent years and indeed Japan has experienced falling prices.

Although inflation rates in most countries have followed a similar pattern over time, the average rates of inflation have differed substantially from one country to another (see Table 15.3). These differences, however, have tended to narrow in recent years as barriers to international trade and capital movements have been reduced and as increasing

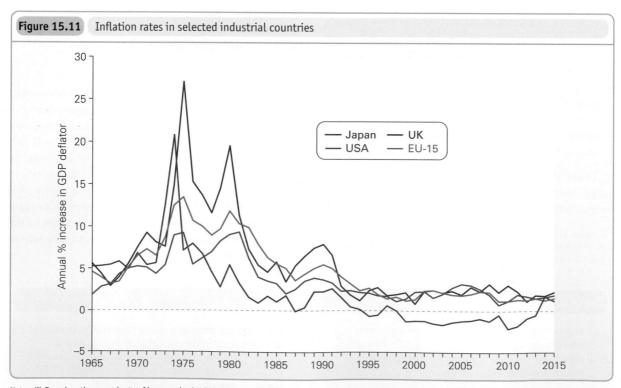

Figure 15.11 Inflation rates in selected industrial countries

Notes: (i) Based on the annual rate of increase in the GDP deflator; (ii) Figures from 2014 based on forecasts; (iii) EU-15 = the member countries of the European Union prior to 1 May 2004.

Source: Based on data in *AMECO Database* (European Commission, DGECFIN).

Table 15.3 Consumer price inflation rates for selected countries (average % per annum)

	1971–80	1981–90	1991–2000	2001–7	2008–12	1971–2012
Australia	10.5	8.1	2.2	3.0	2.8	5.8
Canada	8.1	6.0	2.0	2.3	1.8	4.4
France	9.7	6.4	1.7	1.8	1.7	4.7
Germany	5.1	2.6	2.4	1.6	1.6	2.9
Italy	13.9	9.8	3.8	2.3	2.3	7.2
Japan	9.1	2.1	0.9	−0.3	−0.2	2.8
Netherlands	7.3	2.5	2.4	2.2	2.0	3.5
New Zealand	12.6	10.8	1.8	2.6	2.7	6.7
Sweden	9.2	7.6	2.4	1.6	1.6	5.0
UK	13.8	6.0	2.7	1.7	3.3	6.0
USA	7.9	4.7	2.8	2.7	2.1	4.4
OECD	9.9	8.5	4.9	2.7	2.3	6.3

Source: Based on data in *Stat Extracts* (OECD).

numbers of countries have directed their macroeconomic policy towards achieving target rates of consumer price inflation of around 2 per cent.

*LOOKING AT THE MATHS

The inflation rate (π) is calculated from the following formula:

$$\pi_t = \frac{P_t - P_{t-1}}{P_{t-1}} \times 100$$

where P_t is the price index for year t and P_{t-1} is the price index for the previous year. Thus if the price index for year 1 is 140.0 and that for year 2 is 149.1, then inflation in year 2 is

$$\pi = \frac{149.1 - 140.0}{140.0} \times 100 = 6.5\%$$

It is also possible to give the rates of inflation for other prices. For example, indices are published for commodity prices, for food prices, for house prices, for import prices, for prices after taking taxes into account, and so on. Their respective rates of inflation are simply their annual percentage increases. Likewise it is possible to give the rate of inflation of wage rates ('wage inflation'). Figure 15.12 shows three inflation rate measures for the UK from 2001. The three annual inflation rates have differed considerably from each other over the period. Interestingly, from 2008 we see that the annual rate of CPI inflation – the Bank of England's target measure – consistently exceeded the annual growth of average weekly earnings. This meant that the purchasing power of weekly earnings was being eroded by higher consumer prices.

Figure 15.12 Selection of annual UK inflation rates

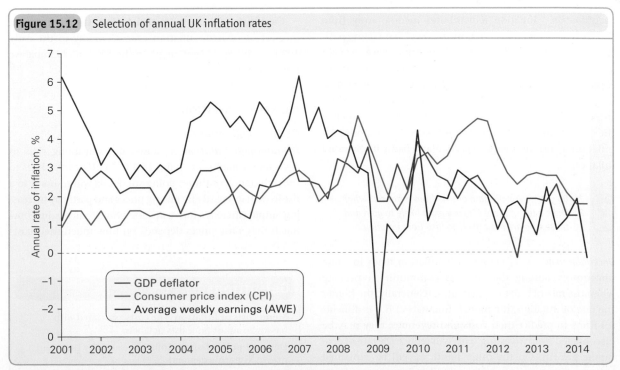

— GDP deflator
— Consumer price index (CPI)
— Average weekly earnings (AWE)

Notes: AWE is the average regular weekly pay (including bonuses) over the latest 3 months.
Source: Based on *Time Series Data*, series IHYU, D7G7 and KAC3 (National Statistics).

Before we proceed, a word of caution: be careful not to confuse a rise or fall in *inflation* with a rise or fall in *prices*. A rise in inflation means a *faster* increase in prices. A fall in inflation means a *slower* increase in prices (but still an increase as long as inflation is positive). (See Box A1.1 on page A:12.)

The costs of inflation

A lack of growth is obviously a problem if people want higher living standards. Unemployment is obviously a problem, both for the unemployed themselves and for society, which suffers a loss in output and has to support the unemployed. But why is inflation a problem? If prices go up by 10 per cent, does it really matter? Provided your wages kept up with prices, you would have no cut in your living standards.

If people could correctly anticipate the rate of inflation and fully adjust prices and incomes to take account of it, then the costs of inflation would indeed be relatively small. For us as consumers they would simply be the relatively minor inconvenience of having to adjust our notions of what a 'fair' price is for each item when we go shopping. For firms, they would again be the relatively minor costs of having to change price labels, or prices in catalogues or on menus, or adjust slot machines. These are known as **menu costs**.

In reality, people frequently make mistakes when predicting the rate of inflation and are not able to adapt fully to it. This leads to the following problems, which are likely to be more serious the higher the rate of inflation becomes and the more the rate fluctuates.

Redistribution. Inflation redistributes income away from those on fixed incomes and those in a weak bargaining position, to those who can use their economic power to gain large pay, rent or profit increases. It redistributes wealth to those with assets (e.g. property) that rise in value particularly rapidly during periods of inflation, and away from those with types of savings that pay rates of interest below the rate of inflation and hence whose value is eroded by inflation. Pensioners may be particularly badly hit by rapid inflation.

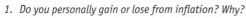

1. *Do you personally gain or lose from inflation? Why?*
2. *Make a list of those who are most likely to gain and those who are most likely to lose from inflation.*

Uncertainty and lack of investment. Inflation tends to cause uncertainty among the business community, especially when the rate of inflation fluctuates. (Generally, the higher the rate of inflation, the more it fluctuates.) If it is difficult for firms to predict their costs and revenues; they may be discouraged from investing. This will reduce the rate of economic growth. On the other hand, as will be explained below, policies to reduce the rate of inflation may them-

selves reduce the rate of economic growth, especially in the short run. This may then provide the government with a policy dilemma.

Balance of payments. Inflation is likely to worsen the balance of trade. If a country suffers from relatively high inflation, its exports will become less competitive in world markets. At the same time, imports will become relatively cheaper than home-produced goods. Thus exports will fall and imports will rise. This is an international substitution effect, an effect we identified earlier as contributing to the downward sloping aggregate demand curve (see page 442). As a result, the balance of trade will deteriorate and/or the exchange rate will fall. Both of these effects can cause problems. This is examined in more detail in section 15.4.

Resources. Extra resources are likely to be used to cope with the effects of inflation. Accountants and other financial experts may have to be employed by companies to help them cope with the uncertainties caused by inflation.

The costs of inflation may be relatively mild if inflation is kept to single figures. They can be very serious, however, if inflation gets out of hand. If inflation develops into 'hyperinflation', with prices rising perhaps by several hundred per cent or even thousands per cent per year, the whole basis of the market economy will be undermined. Firms constantly raise prices in an attempt to cover their soaring costs. Workers demand huge pay increases in an attempt to stay ahead of the rocketing cost of living. Thus prices and wages chase each other in an ever-rising inflationary spiral. People will no longer want to save money. Instead they will spend it as quickly as possible before its value falls any further. People may even resort to barter in an attempt to avoid using money altogether.

Case Study 15.5 in MyEconLab looks at three of the most severe case of hyperinflation ever: Germany in the early 1920s, Serbia and Montenegro in the 1990s and Zimbabwe more recently.

Causes of inflation

Demand-pull inflation

Demand-pull inflation is caused by continuing rises in aggregate demand. In Figure 15.13, the *AD* curve shifts to the right (and continues doing so). Firms will respond to a rise in demand partly by raising prices and partly by increasing output (there is a move up along the *AS* curve). Just how much they raise prices depends on how much their costs

---

Definitions

Menu costs of inflation The costs associated with having to adjust price lists or labels.

Demand-pull inflation Inflation caused by persistent rises in aggregate demand.

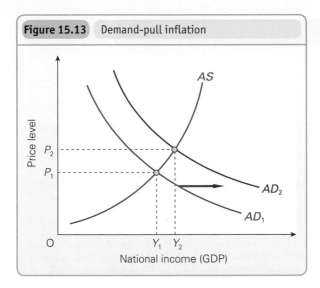

Figure 15.13   Demand-pull inflation

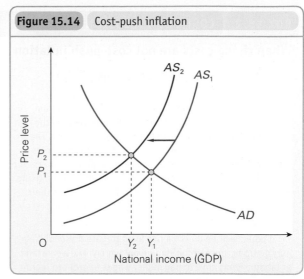

Figure 15.14   Cost-push inflation

rise as a result of increasing output. In other words, it will depend on the shape of the *AS* curve.

The aggregate supply curve will tend to become steeper as the economy approaches the peak of the business cycle. In other words, the closer actual output gets to potential output, and the less slack there is in the economy, the more will firms respond to a rise in demand by raising their prices.

Sometimes there may be a *single* increase in demand (or a 'demand shock'). This could be due, for example, to an increased level of government expenditure. The effect is to give a *single* rise in the price level. Although this causes inflation in the short run, once the effect has taken place inflation will fall back to zero. For inflation to persist, however, there must be *continuing* rightward shifts in the *AD* curve, and thus continuing rises in the price level. If inflation is to rise, these rightward shifts must get *faster*.

Demand-pull inflation is typically associated with a booming economy. Many economists therefore argue that it is the counterpart of demand-deficient unemployment. When the economy is in recession, demand-deficient unemployment is high, but demand-pull inflation is low. When, on the other hand, the economy is near the peak of the business cycle, demand-pull inflation is high, but demand-deficient unemployment is low.

Cost-push inflation

Cost-push inflation is associated with continuing rises in costs and hence continuing leftward (upward) shifts in the *AS* curve. Such shifts occur when costs of production rise *independently* of aggregate demand.

Definition

Cost-push inflation Inflation caused by persistent rises in costs of production (independently of demand).

If firms face a rise in costs, they will respond partly by raising prices and passing on the costs to the consumer, and partly by cutting back on production. This is illustrated in Figure 15.14. There is a leftward shift in the aggregate supply curve: from AS_1 to AS_2. This causes the price level to rise to P_2 and the level of national income to *fall* to Y_2.

Just how much firms raise prices and cut back on production depends on the shape of the aggregate demand curve. The less elastic the *AD* curve, the less will sales fall as a result of any price rise, and hence the more will firms be able to pass on the rise in their costs to consumers as higher prices.

Note that the effect on output and employment is the opposite of demand-pull inflation. With demand-pull inflation, output and hence employment tend to rise. With cost-push inflation, however, output and employment tend to fall.

As with demand-pull inflation, we must distinguish between *single* shifts in the aggregate supply curve (known as 'supply shocks') and *continuing* shifts. If there is a single leftward shift in aggregate supply, there will be a single rise in the price level. For example, if the government raises the excise duty on oil, there will be a single rise in oil prices and hence in firms' fuel costs. This will cause *temporary* inflation while the price rise is passed on through the economy. Once this has occurred, prices will stabilise at the new level and the rate of inflation will fall back to zero again. If cost-push inflation is to continue over a number of years, therefore, the aggregate supply curve must *continually* shift to the left. If cost-push inflation is to *rise*, these shifts must get *faster*.

Rises in costs may originate from a number of different sources, such as trade unions pushing up wages, firms with monopoly power raising prices in order to increase their profits, or increases in international commodity prices. With the process of globalisation and increased international competition, cost-push pressures have tended to decrease in recent years. One major exception has been the

BOX 15.2   COST-PUSH ILLUSION

When rising costs are not cost-push inflation

It is easy to get confused between demand-pull and cost-push inflation.

Frequently, inflationary pressures *seem* to come from the cost side. Shopkeepers blame their price rises on the rise in their costs – the wholesale prices they have to pay. The wholesalers blame their price rises on a rise in *their* costs – the prices they are charged by the various manufacturers. The manufacturers in turn blame rising raw material costs, rising wage rates, rising rents, and so on. Everyone blames their price rises on the rise in their costs.

But why have these costs risen?

It could well be due to a rise in aggregate *demand*! Wages may go up because of falling unemployment and a shortage of labour. Firms *have* to pay higher wages in order to recruit or maintain enough labour. Rents may rise because of the upsurge in demand. So too with raw materials: higher demand may pull up their prices too.

What we have then is a 'cost-push illusion'. Costs rise, it is true, but they rise because of an increase in demand.

So when does genuine cost-push inflation occur? This occurs when costs of production rise independently of demand. This will normally involve an increased use of monopoly power: unions becoming more powerful or militant and thus driving up wages; firms using their monopoly/oligopoly power to push up prices; commodity producers such as the OPEC countries forming cartels to push up their prices; the government using its power to raise indirect taxes (such as the increase in the UK in the standard rate of VAT from 17.5 to 20 per cent in January 2011).

In many cases, these cost-push or 'supply-side' shocks are one-off events and, after an initial rise in prices, prices settle at the new higher level. There is thus only a temporary inflationary effect while these cost rises work through the economy.

 If consumer demand rises and firms respond by raising prices, is this necessarily an example of demand-pull inflation? Could there be such a thing as demand-pull illusion? (Clue: why might consumer demand have risen?)

---

oil shocks that have occurred from time to time. For example, the near tripling of oil prices from $51 per barrel in January 2007 to $147 per barrel in July 2008, and again from $41 a barrel in January 2009 to $126 a barrel in April 2011, put upward pressure on costs and prices around the world.

Temporary supply shocks can come from bad harvests. Longer-term supply-side problems can come from the depletion of natural resources, such as the gradual running down of North Sea oil, pollution of the seas and hence a decline in incomes for nations with large fishing industries, and, perhaps the most devastating of all, the problem of 'desertification' in sub-Saharan Africa.

The interaction of demand-pull and cost-push inflation

Demand-pull and cost-push inflation can occur together, since wage and price rises can be caused both by increases in aggregate demand and by independent causes pushing up costs. Even when an inflationary process *starts* as either demand-pull or cost-push, it is often difficult to separate the two. An initial cost-push inflation may encourage the government to expand aggregate demand to offset rises in unemployment. Alternatively, an initial demand-pull inflation may strengthen the power of certain groups, which then use this power to drive up costs.

Either way, the result is likely to be continuing rightward shifts in the *AD* curve and leftward shifts in the *AS* curve. Prices will carry on rising. This is illustrated in Figure 15.15.

Structural (demand-shift) inflation

When the *pattern* of demand (or supply) changes in the economy, certain industries will experience increased demand and others decreased demand. If prices and wage

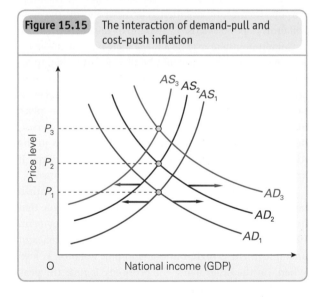

Figure 15.15   The interaction of demand-pull and cost-push inflation

rates are inflexible downwards in the contracting industries, and prices and wage rates rise in the expanding industries, the overall price and wage level will rise. The less elastic is supply to these shifts, the worse the problem will be.

Thus a more rapid structural change in the economy can lead to both increased structural unemployment and increased structural inflation. An example of this problem was the so-called north–south divide in the UK during the boom of the second half of the 1980s. The north experienced high structural unemployment as old industries declined, while the south experienced excess demand. This excess demand in the south, among other things, led to rapid house price inflation, and rapid increases in incomes

BOX 15.3   INFLATION OR DEFLATION?

Where's the danger?

During the first half of the 2000s it appeared that inflation was no longer a serious worry in many developed economies. Instead, 'deflation' (i.e. falling prices) had become a source of concern. The Japanese economy had experienced deflation for a decade or so and central banks, including the US Federal Reserve and the European Central Bank, were sounding warnings that deflation was a real and present danger to us all.

One of the main causes of declining prices was the process of globalisation. Imports from low-cost countries, such as China and India, drove prices down. What is more, outsourcing call-centre, back-office and IT work to developing countries put downward pressure on wages. This downward effect on prices and wages in the USA and other developed economies was dubbed the 'China price' effect.

A return of inflation?

The global economy grew strongly after 2003. Between 2004 and 2007 global growth averaged 3.9 per cent each year. The UK and USA saw average annual economic growth rates of 3.1 and 2.9 per cent respectively. These, however, were dwarfed by China and India, which experienced growth rates of 12.1 per cent and 9.1 per cent respectively.

The rapid growth in aggregate demand in many OECD countries, such as the UK and USA, put upward pressure on prices and wages but, unlike previously, the 'China price' effect was beginning to reinforce this upward pressure.

By 2007–8, the growth in China, India and other rapidly developing countries was causing significant inflation in commodity prices: i.e. in the prices of raw materials and primary agricultural products. This emergence of rapid commodity price inflation can be seen in the chart.

However, with the onset of recession in mid-2008, inflation started to fall. Once more there seemed to be a spectre of deflation. By 2009, many people were asking themselves why they should buy now when, by delaying, they might be able to get an item more cheaply later on. The effect of this would be a leftward shift in the *AD* curve, which forces prices down even further.

But the worry about deflation was short-lived. In 2010, the global economy expanded by 4.1 per cent and by a further 2.9 per cent in 2011. This was mirrored by the likes of China and India, which saw their respective economies expand by 10.4 per cent and 10.5 per cent in 2010 and by 9.3 per cent and 6.3 per cent in 2011. In the UK, the annual rate of CPI inflation peaked at 5.2 per cent in the 12 months to September 2011, significantly above the Bank of England's central inflation target of 2 per cent.

The years of 2012 and 2013 saw a slight easing of global growth, with the world economy expanding by 2.6 per cent and 2.3 per cent respectively. This was reflected in a cooling of the rate of commodity price inflation which, in turn, helped to moderate consumer price inflation rates. By October 2013, the rate of CPI inflation in the UK had fallen back to 2.2 per cent.

1. *What long-term economic benefits might deflation generate for business and the economy in general?*
2. *Would an inflationary China price effect be an example of demand-pull or cost-push inflation?*

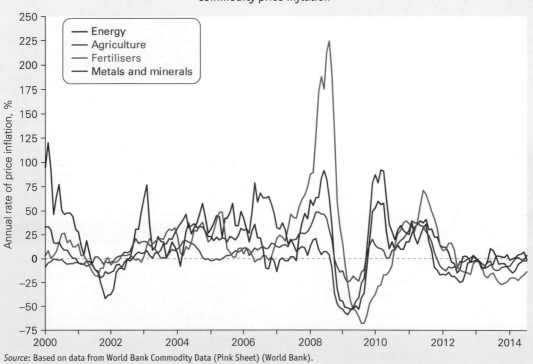

Commodity price inflation

Source: Based on data from World Bank Commodity Data (Pink Sheet) (World Bank).

for various groups of workers and firms. With many prices and wages being set *nationally*, the inflation in the south then 'spilt over' into the north.

 With the eurozone classed as a single economy with a single inflation rate, explain whether the above problems apply between the different countries using the euro.

Expectations and inflation

Workers and firms take account of the *expected* rate of inflation when making decisions.

Imagine that a union and an employer are negotiating a wage increase. Let us assume that both sides expect a rate of inflation of 5 per cent. The union will be happy to receive a

TC 9 p121

BOX 15.4 THE PHILLIPS CURVE

Is higher inflation the price for lower unemployment?

If inflation tends to be higher when the economy is booming and if unemployment tends to be higher in recessions, does this mean that there is a 'trade-off' between inflation and unemployment: that lower unemployment tends to be associated with higher inflation, and lower inflation with higher unemployment? Such a trade-off was observed by the New Zealand economist Bill Phillips (see Person Profile in MyEconLab), and was illustrated by the famous *Phillips curve*.

The original Phillips curve

In 1958, Phillips showed the statistical relationship between wage inflation and unemployment in the UK from 1861 to 1957. With the percentage annual wage inflation on the vertical axis and the percentage unemployment rate on the horizontal axis, a scatter of points was obtained. Each point represented the observation for a particular year. The curve that best fitted the scatter has become known as the 'Phillips curve'. It is illustrated in Figure (a) and shows an inverse relationship between inflation and unemployment.[1]

Given that wage increases over the period were approximately 2 per cent above price increases (made possible because of increases in labour productivity), a similar-shaped, but lower curve could be plotted showing the relationship between *price* inflation and unemployment.

The curve has often been used to illustrate the effects of changes in aggregate demand. When aggregate demand rose (relative to potential output), inflation rose and unemployment fell: there was an upward movement along the curve. When aggregate demand fell, there was a downward movement along the curve.

There was also a second reason given for the inverse relationship. If wages rose, the unemployed might have believed that the higher wages they were offered represented a *real* wage increase. That is, they might not have realised that the higher wages would be 'eaten up' by price increases: they might have suffered from **money illusion**. They would thus have accepted jobs more readily. The average duration of unemployment therefore fell. This is a reduction in *frictional* unemployment and is illustrated by an upward shift in the W_o curve in Figure 15.9 (on page 439).

The Phillips curve was bowed in to the origin. The usual explanation for this is that, as aggregate demand expanded, at first there would be plenty of surplus labour, which could meet the extra demand without the need to raise wages very much. But as labour became increasingly scarce, firms would find they had to offer increasingly higher wages to obtain the labour they required, and the position of trade unions would be increasingly strengthened.

The *position* of the Phillips curve depended on *non*-demand factors causing inflation and unemployment: frictional and structural unemployment; and cost-push, structural and expectations-generated inflation. If any of these non-demand factors changed so as to raise inflation or unemployment, the curve would shift outwards to the right. The relative stability of the curve over the 100 years or so observed by Phillips suggested that these non-demand factors had changed little.

The Phillips curve seemed to present governments with a simple policy choice. They could trade off inflation against unemployment. Lower unemployment could be bought at the cost of higher inflation, and vice versa. Unfortunately, the experience since the late 1960s has suggested that no such simple relationship exists beyond the short run.

TC 12 p411

KI 35 p475

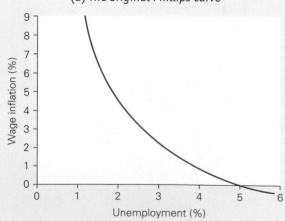

(a) *The original Phillips curve*

Definitions

Phillips curve A curve showing the relationship between (price) inflation and unemployment. The original Phillips curve plotted wage inflation against unemployment for the years 1861–1957.

Money illusion When people believe that a money wage or price increase represents a real increase: in other words, they ignore or underestimate inflation.

wage rise somewhat above 5 per cent. That way the members would be getting a *real* rise in incomes. The employers will be happy to pay a wage rise somewhat below 5 per cent. After all, they can put their prices up by 5 per cent, knowing that their rivals will do approximately the same. The actual wage rise that the two sides agree on will thus be somewhere around 5 per cent.

Now let us assume that the expected rate of inflation is 10 per cent. Both sides will now negotiate around this benchmark, with the outcome being somewhere around about 10 per cent. Thus the higher the expected rate of inflation, the higher will be the level of pay settlements and price rises, and hence the higher will be the resulting actual rate of inflation.

The breakdown of the Phillips curve

From about 1967 the Phillips curve relationship seemed to break down. The UK, and many other countries in the western world too, began to experience growing unemployment *and* higher rates of inflation.

Figure (b) shows price inflation (π) and (standardised) unemployment in the UK from 1960. From 1960 to 1967 a curve similar to the Phillips curve can be fitted through the data (the red line). From 1968 to the early 1990s, however, no simple picture emerges. Certainly the original Phillips curve could no longer fit the data; but whether the curve shifted to the right and then back again somewhat (the dashed lines), or whether the relationship broke down completely, or whether there was some quite different relationship between inflation and unemployment, is not clear by simply looking at the data.

Since 1997, the Bank of England has been targeting inflation (see section 21.5). For much of this period the 'curve' would seem to have become a virtually horizontal straight line. However, from the late 2000s, against a backdrop of significant economic volatility and uncertainty, the range of inflation rates increased despite inflation rate targeting. The hope was that as economic conditions normalised in the 2010s the variability in the rate of inflation would once again decline.

Over the years, there has been much debate among economists about the relationship between inflation and unemployment. The controversy will be examined in later chapters and particularly in Chapter 20. One thing does seem clear, however: the relationship is different in the short run and the long run.

Assume that there is a trade-off between unemployment and inflation, traced out by a 'Phillips curve'. What could cause a leftward shift in this curve?

[1] Phillips' estimated equation was $\omega = -0.9 + 9.638U^{-1.394}$.

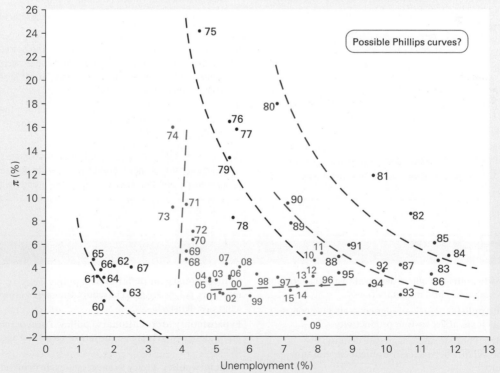

(b) The breakdown of the Phillips curve

Possible Phillips curves?

Source: Based on *Time Series Data* (National Statistics); forecasts based on data in Economic Outlook (IMF).

Just how expectations impact on inflation depends on how they are formed. We examine this in Chapter 20.

Policies to tackle inflation

We will be examining a number of different anti-inflationary policies in later chapters. These policies can be directed towards the control of either aggregate demand or aggregate supply, and hence are referred to as **demand-side** and **supply-side policies** respectively.

Demand-side policies

There are two types of demand-side policy.

Fiscal policy. **Fiscal policy** involves altering the level of government expenditure and/or rates of tax. Changes in fiscal policy can affect the level of aggregate demand. Cutting government expenditure or raising taxes will reduce aggregate demand. These are both examples of **contractionary** (or **deflationary**) fiscal policy.

Fiscal policy can also be used to *boost* aggregate demand, for example if there is a problem of demand-deficient unemployment. In this case, the government would raise government expenditure and/or cut taxes. This is called **expansionary** (or **reflationary**) fiscal policy.

Monetary policy. **Monetary policy** involves the central bank (the Bank of England in the UK) altering the supply of money in the economy or manipulating the rate of interest. For example, it can attempt to boost aggregate demand (a *contractionary* monetary policy) by cutting interest rates and thus making borrowing cheaper, or by acting to increase the supply of money available through the banking system, known as 'quantitative easing'. Conversely, by raising interest rates and/or cutting the money supply, the central bank can attempt to reduce aggregate demand.

Supply-side policies

The aim here is to reduce the rate of increase in costs. This will help reduce leftward (upward) shifts in the aggregate supply curve. This can be done either (1) by restraining monopoly influences on prices and incomes (e.g. by policies to restrict the activities of trade unions, or policies to restrict mergers and takeovers), or (2) by designing policies to increase productivity (e.g. giving various tax incentives, encouraging various types of research and development, giving grants to firms to invest in up-to-date equipment or in the training of labour).

We will examine all these various policies as the text progresses. As we shall see, just as economists sometimes disagree on the precise causes of inflation, so too they sometimes disagree on the most appropriate cure.

Section summary

1. Inflation redistributes incomes from the economically weak to the economically powerful; it causes uncertainty in the business community and as a result reduces investment; it tends to lead to balance of payments problems and/or a fall in the exchange rate; it leads to resources being used to offset its effects. The costs of inflation can be very great indeed in the case of hyperinflation.

2. Demand-pull inflation occurs as a result of increases in aggregate demand. This can be due to monetary or non-monetary causes.

3. Cost-push inflation occurs when there are increases in the costs of production independent of rises in aggregate demand. If there is a single supply-side shock, the inflation will peter out. For cost-push inflation to persist, there must be continuous increases in costs.

4. Cost-push and demand-pull inflation can interact to form spiralling inflation.

5. Inflation can also be caused by shifts in the pattern of demand in the economy, with prices rising in sectors of increasing demand but being reluctant to fall in sectors of declining demand.

6. Expectations play a crucial role in determining the level of inflation. The higher people expect inflation to be, the higher it will be.

7. Policies to tackle inflation can be either demand-side policies (fiscal or monetary) or supply-side policies (to reduce monopoly power or increase productivity).

Definitions

Demand-side policies Policies designed to affect aggregate demand: fiscal policy and monetary policy.

Supply-side policies Policies designed to affect aggregate supply: policies to affect costs or productivity.

Fiscal policy Policy to affect aggregate demand by altering the balance between government expenditure and taxation.

Contractionary (or deflationary) policy Fiscal or monetary policy designed to reduce the rate of growth of aggregate demand.

Expansionary (or reflationary) policy Fiscal or monetary policy designed to increase the rate of growth of aggregate demand.

Monetary policy Policy to affect aggregate demand by altering the supply or cost of money (rate of interest).

15.5   THE BALANCE OF PAYMENTS AND EXCHANGE RATES

The balance of payments account

All countries trade with and have financial dealings with the rest of the world. In other words, all countries are **open economies**. The flows of money between residents of a country and the rest of the world are recorded in the country's balance of payments account.

Receipts of money from abroad are regarded as *credits* and are entered in the accounts with a positive sign. *Outflows* of money from the country are regarded as *debits* and are entered with a negative sign.

There are three main parts of the balance of payments account: the *current account*, the *capital account* and the *financial account*. Each part is then subdivided. We shall look at each part in turn, and take the UK as an example. Table 15.4 gives a summary of the UK balance of payments for 2013.

The current account

The **current account** records payments for imports and exports of goods and services, plus incomes flowing into and out of the country, plus net transfers of money into and out of the country. It is normally split into four subdivisions.

The trade in goods account. This records imports and exports of physical goods (previously known as 'visibles'). Exports result in an inflow of money and are therefore a credit item. Imports result in an outflow of money and are therefore a debit item. The balance of these is called the **balance on**

trade in goods or **balance of visible trade** or **merchandise balance**. A *surplus* is when exports exceed imports. A *deficit* is when imports exceed exports.

The trade in services account. This records imports and exports of services (such as transport, tourism and insurance). Thus the purchase of a foreign holiday would be a debit, since it represents an outflow of money, whereas the purchase by an overseas resident of a UK insurance policy would be a credit to the UK services account. The balance of these is called the *services balance*.

The balance of both the goods and services accounts together is known as the **balance on trade in goods and services** or simply the **balance of trade**.

Definitions

Open economy One that trades with and has financial dealings with other countries.

Current account of the balance of payments The record of a country's imports and exports of goods and services, plus incomes and transfers of money to and from abroad.

Balance on trade in goods or balance of visible trade or merchandise balance Exports of goods minus imports of goods.

Balance on trade in goods and services or balance of trade Exports of goods and services minus imports of goods and services.

Table 15.4   UK balance of payments

	2013		Average 1990–2013 as % of GDP
	£m	% of GDP	
CURRENT ACCOUNT			
Balance on trade in goods	−107 797	−6.7	−4.1
Balance on trade in services	81 201	5.0	2.7
Balance of trade	**−26 596**	**−1.6**	**−1.4**
Income balance	−17 368	−1.1	0.4
Net current transfers	−27 114	−1.7	−0.9
Current account balance	**−71 078**	**−4.4**	**−1.9**
CAPITAL ACCOUNT			
Capital account balance	5 332	0.3	0.1
FINANCIAL ACCOUNT			
Net direct investment	11 297	0.7	−1.3
Portfolio investment balance	30 851	1.9	1.7
Other investment balance	29 036	1.8	1.7
Balance of financial derivatives	334	0.0	0.0
Reserve assets	−4 961	−0.3	−0.1
Financial account balance	**66 557**	**4.1**	**1.9**
Net errors and omissions	**−811**	**−0.1**	**−0.2**
Balance	**0**	**0.0**	**0.0**

Source: Balance of Payments (ONS).

Figure 15.16 Current account balance in selected industrial countries

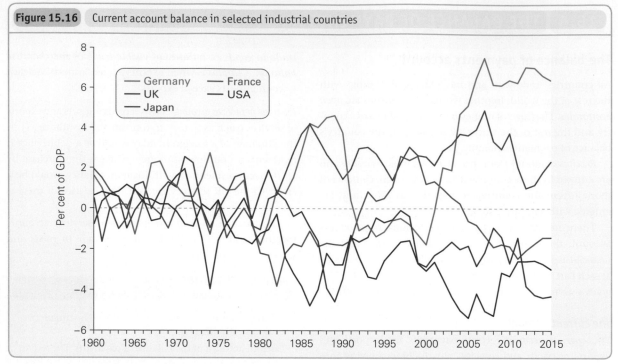

Notes: Figures from 2014 based on forecasts; German figures are West Germany up to 1991.
Source: Based on data in AMECO Database (European Commission, DGECFIN).

Income flows. These consist of wages, interest and profits flowing into and out of the country. For example, dividends earned by a foreign resident from shares in a UK company would be an outflow of money (a debit item).

Current transfers of money. These include government contributions to and receipts from the EU and international organisations, and international transfers of money by private individuals and firms for the purpose of *consumption*. Transfers out of the country are debits. Transfers into the country (e.g. money sent from Greece to a Greek student studying in the UK) would be a credit item.

The ***current account balance*** is the overall balance of all the above four subdivisions. A *current account surplus* is where credits exceed debits. A *current account deficit* is where debits exceed credits. Figure 15.16 shows the current account balances of a selection of countries as a proportion of their GDP since 1960. The chart shows how global imbalances on the current account have tended to increase over time, particularly since the 1980s. This is a theme that we return to in Chapter 26.

 Why are the US and UK current balances approximately a 'mirror image' of the Japanese and German current balances?

The capital account

The ***capital account*** records the flows of funds, into the country (credits) and out of the country (debits), associated with the acquisition or disposal of fixed assets (e.g. land or intangibles, such as patents and trademarks), the transfer of funds by migrants, the payment of grants by the government for overseas projects, debt forgiveness by the government

and the receipt of money for capital projects (e.g. from the EU's Agricultural Guidance Fund).

As Table 15.4 shows, the balance on the capital account is small in comparison to that on the current and financial accounts.

The financial account

The ***financial account*** of the balance of payments records cross-border changes in the holding of shares, property, bank deposits and loans, government securities, etc. In other words, unlike the current account, which is concerned with money incomes, the financial account is concerned with the purchase and sale of assets. Case Study 15.6 in MyEconLab considers some of the statistics behind the UK's financial account.

Investment (direct and portfolio). This account covers primarily long-term investment:

■ Direct investment. This involves a significant and lasting interest in a business in another country. If a foreign

Definitions

Balance of payments on current account The balance on trade in goods and services plus net investment incomes and current transfers.

Capital account of the balance of payments The record of the transfers of capital to and from abroad.

Financial account of the balance of payments The record of the flows of money into and out of the country for the purposes of investment or as deposits in banks and other financial institutions.

company invests money from abroad in one of its branches or associated companies in the UK, this represents an inflow of money when the investment is made and is thus a credit item. (Any subsequent profit from this investment that flows abroad will be recorded as an *investment income outflow* on the current account.) Investment abroad by UK companies represents an outflow of money when the investment is made. It is thus a debit item.

Note that what we are talking about here is the acquisition or sale of assets: e.g. a factory or farm, or the takeover of a whole firm, not the imports or exports of equipment.

- Portfolio investment. This relates to transactions in debt and equity securities which do not result in the investor having any significant influence on the operations of a particular business. If a UK resident buys shares (equity securities) in an overseas company, this is an outflow of funds and is hence a debit item.

Other financial flows. These consist primarily of various types of short-term monetary movement between the UK and the rest of the world. Deposits by overseas residents in banks in the UK and loans to the UK from abroad are credit items, since they represent an inflow of money. Deposits by UK residents in overseas banks and loans by UK banks to overseas residents are debit items. They represent an outflow of money.

Short-term monetary flows are common between international financial centres to take advantage of differences in countries' interest rates and changes in exchange rates.

1. Why may inflows of short-term deposits create a problem?
2. Where would interest payments on short-term foreign deposits in UK banks be entered on the balance of payments account?

Note that in the financial account, credits and debits are recorded *net*. For example, UK investment abroad consists of the net acquisition of assets abroad (i.e. the purchase less the sale of assets abroad). Similarly, foreign investment in the UK consists of the purchase less the sale of UK assets by foreign residents. Note that in either case the flow could be in the opposite direction. For example, if UK residents purchased fewer assets abroad than they sold, this item would be a net credit, not a debit (there would be a net return of money to the UK).

By recording financial account items net, the flows seem misleadingly modest. For example, if UK residents deposited an extra £100 billion in banks abroad but drew out £99 billion, this would be recorded as a mere £1 billion net outflow on the other financial flows account. In fact, *total* financial account flows vastly exceed current plus capital account flows.

Flows to and from the reserves. The UK, like all other countries, holds reserves of gold and foreign currencies. From time to time the Bank of England (acting as the government's agent) will sell some of these reserves to purchase sterling on the foreign exchange market. It does this normally as a

means of supporting the rate of exchange (see below). Drawing on reserves represents a *credit* item in the balance of payments accounts: money drawn from the reserves represents an *inflow* to the balance of payments (albeit an outflow from the reserves account). The reserves can thus be used to support a deficit elsewhere in the balance of payments.

Conversely, if there is a surplus elsewhere in the balance of payments, the Bank of England can use it to build up the reserves. Building up the reserves counts as a debit item in the balance of payments, since it represents an outflow from it (to the reserves).

When all the components of the balance of payments account are taken together, the balance of payments should exactly balance: credits should equal debits. As we shall see below, if they were not equal, the rate of exchange would have to adjust until they were, or the government would have to intervene to make them equal.

When the statistics are compiled, however, a number of errors are likely to occur. As a result, there will not be a balance. To 'correct' for this, a *net errors and omissions* item is included in the accounts. This ensures that there will be an exact balance. The main reason for the errors is that the statistics are obtained from a number of sources, and there are often delays before items are recorded and sometimes omissions too.

Assessing the balance of payments figures

It is often regarded as being undesirable for the combined current, capital and investment accounts to be in deficit. If they were in deficit, this would have to be covered by borrowing from abroad or attracting deposits from abroad. This might necessitate paying high rates of interest. It also leads to the danger that people abroad might at some time in the future suddenly withdraw their money from the country and cause a 'run on the currency'. An alternative would be to draw on reserves. But this too causes problems. If the reserves are run down too rapidly, it may cause a crisis of confidence, and again a run on the currency. Also, of course, reserves are limited and hence there is a limit to the extent to which they can be used to pay for a balance of payments deficit.

It is also often regarded as undesirable for a country to have a *current account* deficit, even if it is matched by a surplus on the other two accounts. Although this will bring the short-term benefit of a greater level of consumption through imports, and hence a temporarily higher living standard, the excess of imports over exports is being financed by foreign investment in the country. This will lead to greater outflows of interest and dividends in the future. On the other hand, inward investment may lead to increased production and hence possibly increased incomes for domestic residents.

With reference to the above, provide an assessment of the UK balance of payments in the years illustrated in Table 15.4.

Table 15.5	Sterling exchange rates: 1980–2013					
	Australian dollar	Canadian dollar	Euro[a]	Japanese yen	US dollar	Sterling exchange rate index (2005 = 100)
1980–3	1.80	2.29	1.72	441.37	1.91	95.88
1984–7	1.98	1.93	1.57	276.87	1.43	85.96
1988–91	2.23	2.06	1.44	237.20	1.74	88.03
1992–5	2.21	2.08	1.26	173.83	1.59	80.06
1996–9	2.34	2.31	1.42	192.21	1.62	90.93
2000–3	2.67	2.28	1.57	178.83	1.52	98.63
2004–7	2.43	2.21	1.47	212.08	1.87	101.56
2008–13	1.76	1.69	1.19	146.22	1.62	82.15

[a] The euro was introduced in 1999, with euro notes and coins circulating from January 2002. The exchange rates of the former eurozone currencies with the euro were fixed between 1999 and their disappearance in 2002. Their exchange rates with sterling during this period are the rates implied by the euro exchange rate with sterling. The euro figures prior to 1999 are projections backwards in time using synthetic data values (i.e. based on the weighted average exchange rates of the currencies that made up the euro).

Source: Based on data in the *Bank of England Statistical Interactive Database* (Bank of England).

What causes deficits to occur on the various parts of the balance of payments? The answer has to do with the demand for and supply of sterling on the foreign exchange market. Thus before we can answer the question, we must examine this market and in particular the role of the rate of exchange.

Exchange rates

An exchange rate is the rate at which one currency trades for another on the foreign exchange market.

If you live in the UK and go abroad, you will need to exchange your pounds into euros, dollars, Swiss francs or whatever. You will get the money at the exchange rate in operation at the time that you draw it from a cash machine abroad or from a bank – for example, €1.15 to the pound, or $1.60 to the pound. It is similar for firms. If an importer wants to buy, say, some machinery from Japan, it will require yen to pay the Japanese supplier. It will thus ask the foreign exchange section of a bank to quote it a rate of exchange of the pound into yen. Similarly, if you want to buy some foreign stocks and shares, or if companies based in the UK want to invest abroad, sterling will have to be exchanged into the appropriate foreign currency.

Likewise, if Americans want to come on holiday to the UK or to buy UK assets, or American firms want to import UK goods or to invest in the UK, they will require sterling. They will get it at an exchange rate such as £1 = $1.60. This means that they will have to pay $1.60 to obtain £1 worth of UK goods or assets.

Exchange rates are quoted between each of the major currencies of the world. These exchange rates are constantly changing. Minute by minute, dealers in the foreign exchange dealing rooms of the banks are adjusting the rates of exchange. They charge commission when they exchange currencies. It is important for them, therefore, to ensure that they are not left with a large amount of any currency unsold. What they need to do is to balance the supply and demand of each currency: to balance the amount they purchase to the amount they sell. To do this, they will need to

adjust the price of each currency, namely the exchange rate, in line with changes in supply and demand.

Not only are there day-to-day fluctuations in exchange rates, but also there are long-term changes in them. Table 15.5 shows the average exchange rate between the pound and various currencies for selected periods since 1980.

One of the problems in assessing what is happening to a particular currency is that its rate of exchange may rise against some currencies (weak currencies) and fall against others (strong currencies). In order to gain an overall picture of its fluctuations, therefore, it is best to look at a weighted average exchange rate against all other currencies. This is known as the ***exchange rate index***. The last column in Table 15.5 shows the sterling exchange rate index based on 2005 = 100.

The weight given to each currency in the index depends on the percentage of UK trade in goods and services done with that country. The weights are revised annually. Table 15.6 gives the 2014 weights of the various currencies that make up the sterling index. These are based on data from 2012.

Note that all the exchange rates must be consistent with each other. For example, if £1 exchanged for $1.50 or ¥150, then $1.50 would have to exchange for ¥150 directly (i.e. $1 = ¥100), otherwise people could make money by moving around in a circle between the three currencies in a process known as ***arbitrage***.

 How has the pound 'fared' compared with the US dollar and the yen from 1980? What conclusions can be drawn about the relative movements between these currencies?

Definitions

Exchange rate index A weighted average exchange rate expressed as an index, where the value of the index is 100 in a given base year. The weights of the different currencies in the index add up to 1.

Arbitrage Buying an asset in a market where it has a lower price and selling it again in another market where it has a higher price and thereby making a profit.

Table 15.6	The weights of foreign currencies in the sterling exchange rate index, 2014 weights (based on 2012 data)

Country	Weight (%)
Eurozone	46.2
USA	17.5
Germany	(12.0)
China	8.9
France	(6.9)
Netherlands	(6.2)
Belgium/Luxembourg	(4.7)
Ireland	(4.4)
Spain	(4.1)
Italy	(4.0)
Japan	3.7
Switzerland	3.3
India	2.1
Sweden	1.9
Australia	1.8
Poland	1.7
Canada	1.6
Singapore	1.6
Turkey	1.6
Russia	1.4
Denmark	1.2
Czech Republic	1.1
Hong Kong	1.1
Norway	1.1
Saudi Arabia	1.1
South Africa	1.0
Austria	(0.7)
Portugal	(0.7)
Finland	(0.6)
Greece	(0.6)
Slovakia	(0.5)
Cyprus	(0.3)
Slovenia	(0.2)
Estonia	(0.1)
Malta	(0.1)
Total	**100.0**

Note: The countries in brackets use the euro and hence are included in the eurozone weight.
Source: Bank of England.

The determination of the rate of exchange in a free market

In a free foreign exchange market, the rate of exchange is determined by demand and supply. This is known as a *floating exchange rate*, and is illustrated in Figure 15.17.

For the sake of simplicity, assume that there are just two countries: the UK and the USA. When UK importers wish to

Definition

Floating exchange rate When the government does not intervene in the foreign exchange markets, but simply allows the exchange rate to be freely determined by demand and supply.

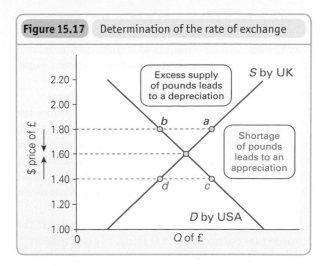

Figure 15.17 Determination of the rate of exchange

buy goods from the USA, or when UK residents wish to invest in the USA, they will *supply* pounds on the foreign exchange market in order to obtain dollars. The higher the exchange rate, the more dollars they will obtain for their pounds. This will effectively make American goods cheaper to buy, and investment more profitable. Thus the *higher* the exchange rate, the *more* pounds will be supplied. The supply curve of pounds, therefore, typically slopes upwards.

When US residents wish to purchase UK goods or to invest in the UK, they will require pounds. They *demand* pounds by selling dollars on the foreign exchange market. The lower the dollar price of the pound (the exchange rate), the cheaper it will be for them to obtain UK goods and assets, and hence the more pounds they are likely to demand. The demand curve for pounds, therefore, typically slopes downwards.

The equilibrium exchange rate is where the demand for pounds equals the supply. In Figure 15.17 this is at an exchange rate of £1 = $1.60. But what is the mechanism that equates demand and supply?

If the current exchange rate were above the equilibrium, the supply of pounds being offered to the banks would exceed the demand. For example, in Figure 15.17 if the exchange rate were $1.80, there would be an excess supply of pounds of *a* – *b*. The banks, wishing to make money by *exchanging* currency, would have to lower the exchange rate in order to encourage a greater demand for pounds and reduce the excessive supply. They would continue lowering the rate until demand equalled supply.

Similarly, if the rate were below the equilibrium, say at $1.40, there would be a shortage of pounds of *c* – *d*. The banks would find themselves with too few pounds to meet all the demand. At the same time, they would have an excess supply of dollars. The banks would thus raise the exchange rate until demand equalled supply.

In practice, the process of reaching equilibrium is extremely rapid. The foreign exchange dealers in the banks are continually adjusting the rate as new customers make new demands for currencies. What is more, the banks have to watch each other closely since they are constantly in competition with each other and thus have to keep their rates in line. The dealers receive minute-by-minute updates on their computer screens of the rates being offered round the world.

Shifts in the currency demand and supply curves

Any shift in the demand or supply curves will cause the exchange rate to change. This is illustrated in Figure 15.18, which shows the euro/sterling exchange rate. If the demand and supply curves shift from D_1 and S_1 to D_2 and S_2 respectively, the exchange rate will fall from €1.40 to €1.20. A fall in the exchange rate is called a *depreciation*. A rise in the exchange rate is called an *appreciation*.

But why should the demand and supply curves shift? The following are the major possible causes of a depreciation:

- *A fall in domestic interest rates*. UK rates would now be less competitive for savers and other depositors. More UK residents would be likely to deposit their money abroad (the supply of sterling would rise), and fewer people abroad would deposit their money in the UK (the demand for sterling would fall).
- *Higher inflation in the domestic economy than abroad*. UK exports will become less competitive. The demand for sterling will fall. At the same time, imports will become relatively cheaper for UK consumers. The supply of sterling will rise.
- *A rise in domestic incomes relative to incomes abroad*. If UK incomes rise, the demand for imports, and hence the supply of sterling, will rise. If incomes in other countries fall, the demand for UK exports, and hence the demand for sterling, will fall.
- *Relative investment prospects improving abroad*. If investment prospects become brighter abroad than in the UK, perhaps because of better incentives abroad, or because of worries about an impending recession in the UK, again the demand for sterling will fall and the supply of sterling will rise.
- *Speculation that the exchange rate will fall*. If businesses involved in importing and exporting, and also banks and other foreign exchange dealers, think that the exchange rate is about to fall, they will sell pounds *now* before the rate does fall. The supply of sterling will thus rise. People thinking of buying pounds will wait until the rate does fall and hence, in the meantime, the demand for sterling will fall. Speculation thus helps to bring about the very effect people had anticipated (see pages 75–7).
- *Longer-term changes in international trading patterns*. Over time the pattern of imports and exports is likely to change as (a) consumer tastes change, (b) the nature and

quality of goods change and (c) the costs of production change. If, as a result, UK goods become less competitive than, say, German or Japanese goods, the demand for sterling will fall and the supply will rise. These shifts, of course, are gradual, taking place over many years.

 Go through each of the above reasons for shifts in the demand for and supply of sterling and consider what would cause an appreciation of the pound.

Exchange rates and the balance of payments

In a free foreign exchange market, the balance of payments will *automatically* balance. But why?

The credit side of the balance of payments constitutes the demand for sterling. For example, when people abroad buy UK exports or assets, they will demand sterling in order to pay for them. The debit side constitutes the supply of sterling. For example, when UK residents buy foreign goods or assets, the importers of them will require foreign currency to pay for them. They will thus supply pounds. A floating exchange rate ensures that the demand for pounds always equals the supply. It thus also ensures that the credits on the balance of payments are equal to the debits: that the balance of payments balances.

This does not mean that each part of the balance of payments account will separately balance, but simply that any current account deficit must be matched by a capital plus financial account surplus and vice versa.

For example, suppose initially that each part of the balance of payments *did* separately balance. Then let us assume that interest rates rise. This will encourage larger short-term financial inflows as people abroad are attracted to deposit money in the UK: the demand for sterling would shift to the right (e.g. from D_2 to D_1 in Figure 15.18). It will also cause smaller short-term financial outflows as UK residents keep more of their money in the country: the supply of sterling shifts to the left (e.g. from S_2 to S_1 in Figure 15.18). The financial account will go into surplus. The exchange rate will appreciate.

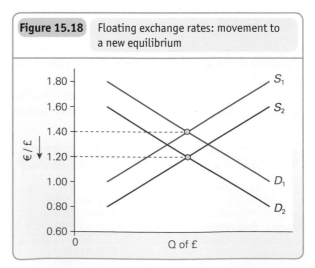

Figure 15.18 Floating exchange rates: movement to a new equilibrium

Definitions

Depreciation A fall in the free-market exchange rate of the domestic currency with foreign currencies.

Appreciation A rise in the free-market exchange rate of the domestic currency with foreign currencies.

| BOX 15.5 | DEALING IN FOREIGN EXCHANGE | CASE STUDIES AND APPLICATIONS |

A daily juggling act

Imagine that a large car importer in the UK wants to import 5000 cars from Japan costing ¥15 billion. What does it do?

It will probably contact a number of banks' foreign exchange dealing rooms in London and ask them for exchange rate quotes. It thus puts all the banks in competition with each other. Each bank will want to get the business and thereby obtain the commission on the deal. To do this it must offer a higher rate than the other banks, since the higher the ¥/£ exchange rate, the more yen the firm will get for its money. (For an importer a rate of, say, ¥140 to £1 is better than a rate of, say, ¥120.)

Now it is highly unlikely that any of the banks will have a spare ¥15 billion. But a bank cannot say to the importer 'Sorry, you will have to wait before we can agree to sell them to you.' Instead the bank will offer a deal and then, if the firm agrees, the bank will have to set about obtaining the ¥15 billion. To do this, it must offer to obtain pounds for Japanese who are *supplying* yen at a sufficiently *low* ¥/£

exchange rate. (The lower the ¥/£ exchange rate, the fewer yen the Japanese will have to pay to obtain pounds.)

The banks' dealers thus find themselves in the delicate position of wanting to offer a *high* enough exchange rate to the car importer in order to gain its business, but a *low* enough exchange rate in order to obtain the required amount of yen. The dealers are thus constantly having to adjust the rates of exchange in order to balance the demand and supply of each currency.

In general, the more of any foreign currency that dealers are asked to supply (by being offered sterling), the lower will be the exchange rate they will offer. In other words, a higher supply of sterling pushes down the foreign currency price of sterling (see Figure 15.18).

 Assume that an American firm wants to import Scotch whisky from the UK. Describe how foreign exchange dealers will respond.

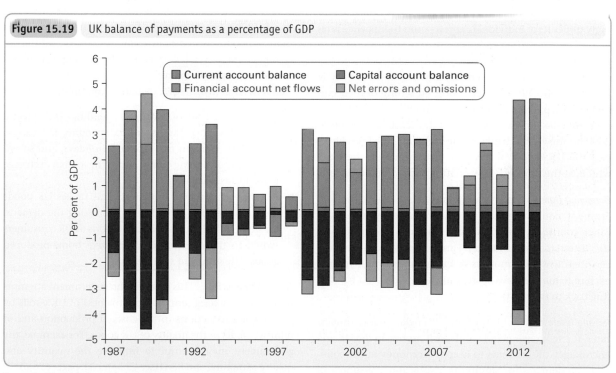

| Figure 15.19 | UK balance of payments as a percentage of GDP |

Source: Based on data from *Balance of Payments* (National Statistics).

As the exchange rate rises, this will cause imports to be cheaper and exports to be more expensive. The current account will move into deficit. There is a movement up along the new demand and supply curves until a new equilibrium is reached. At this point, any financial account surplus is matched by an equal current (plus capital) account deficit.

Figure 15.19 summarises the main accounts of the UK's balance of payments: financial, current and capital accounts. It presents each as a percentage of national income along with the net error and omissions item, which as we saw in

Table 15.4 averages close to zero over the long term. For much of the period, current account deficits have been offset by surpluses on the financial account.

Managing the exchange rate

The government may be unwilling to let the country's currency float freely. Frequent shifts in the demand and supply curves would cause frequent changes in the exchange rate. This, in turn, might cause uncertainty for businesses, which might curtail their trade and investment.

The government may thus ask the central bank (the Bank of England in the case of the UK) to intervene in the foreign exchange market. But what can it do? The answer to this will depend on the government's objectives. It may simply want to reduce short-term movements in the exchange rate that take it away from its longer-term equilibrium rate, or it may want to prevent longer-term, more fundamental shifts in the rate.

Reducing short-term fluctuations

Assume, for example, that the government believes that an exchange rate of €1.40 to the pound is approximately the long-term equilibrium rate. Short-term leftward shifts in the demand for sterling and rightward shifts in the supply, however, are causing the exchange rate to fall below this level (see Figure 15.18). What can be done? There are three possibilities.

Using reserves. The Bank of England can sell gold and foreign currencies from the reserves to buy pounds. This will shift the demand for sterling back to the right.

With the growth in short-term international financial flows over the past 30 years, however, it has become increasingly difficult for individual central banks to influence rates by buying and selling currencies. Today some $4 trillion a day is traded in foreign exchange markets compared with just over $1 trillion in 2001. Central bank reserves are nowhere near large enough to offset concerted selling of their currency. The combined actions of several central banks, however, may be sufficient. For example, combined action in 2000 by the central banks of the eurozone, the USA, Japan and the UK helped to prevent further falls in the euro, which, at the time, was depreciating against the US dollar.

Borrowing from abroad. In extreme circumstances, the government could negotiate a foreign currency loan from other countries or from an international agency such as the International Monetary Fund. The Bank of England can then use these moneys to buy pounds on the foreign exchange market, thus again shifting the demand for sterling back to the right.

Raising interest rates. If the Bank of England raises interest rates, it encourages people to deposit money in the UK and encourages UK residents to keep their money in the country. The demand for sterling increases and the supply of sterling decreases. Changing interest rates for the purpose of influencing exchange rates may not be possible, however, if interest rate changes in the opposite direction are required to keep inflation on target. We examine such policy conflicts in Chapters 21 and 25.

Maintaining a fixed rate of exchange over the longer term

Governments may choose to maintain a fixed rate over a number of months or even years. Indeed, from 1945 to 1972 the whole world operated under such a system. Countries used to 'peg' (i.e. fix) their currencies against the US dollar. This meant, therefore, that every currency was fixed with respect to every other currency (see pages 765–7).

But how can a government maintain an exchange rate that is persistently above the equilibrium? How can it resist the downward pressure on the exchange rate? After all, it cannot *order* dealers to keep the rate up: the dealers would run out of foreign currency. It cannot go on and on using its reserves to support the rate: the reserves would begin to run out. It will probably not want to go on borrowing from abroad and building up large international debts.

So what can it do? It must attempt to shift the demand and supply curves back again, so that they once more intersect at the fixed exchange rate. The following are possible methods it can use.

Deflation. This is where the government deliberately curtails aggregate demand by either fiscal policy or monetary policy or both.

Deflationary fiscal policy involves raising taxes and/or reducing government expenditure. Deflationary monetary policy involves reducing the supply of money and raising interest rates. Note that in this case we are not just talking about the temporary raising of interest rates to prevent a short-term outflow of money from the country, but the use of higher interest rates to reduce borrowing and hence dampen aggregate demand.

A reduction in aggregate demand works in two ways:

- It reduces the level of consumer spending. This directly cuts imports, since there is reduced spending on Japanese electronics, German cars, Spanish holidays, and so on. The supply of sterling coming onto the foreign exchange market thus decreases.
- It reduces the rate of inflation. This makes UK goods more competitive abroad, thus increasing the demand for sterling. It also cuts back on imports as UK consumers switch to the now more competitive home-produced goods. The supply of sterling falls.

Supply-side policies. This is where the government attempts to increase the long-term competitiveness of UK goods by encouraging reductions in the costs of production and/or improvements in the quality of UK goods. For example, the government may attempt to improve the quantity and quality of training and R&D (see Chapter 23, pages 698–702).

Controls on imports and/or foreign exchange dealing. This is where the government restricts the outflow of money, either by restricting people's access to foreign exchange, or by the use of tariffs and quotas. Tariffs are another word for customs duties. As taxes on imports, they raise their price and hence reduce their consumption. Quotas are quantitative restrictions on various imports.

What problems might arise if the government were to adopt this third method of maintaining a fixed exchange rate?

Section summary

1. The balance of payments account records all payments to and receipts from foreign countries. The current account records payments for imports and exports, plus incomes and transfers of money to and from abroad. The capital account records all transfers of capital to and from abroad. The financial account records inflows and outflows of money for investment and as deposits in banks and other financial institutions; it also includes dealings in the country's foreign exchange reserves.

2. The whole account must balance, but surpluses or deficits can be recorded on any specific part of the account.

3. It is generally regarded as undesirable to have persistent current account deficits.

4. The rate of exchange is the rate at which one currency exchanges for another. Rates of exchange are determined by demand and supply in the foreign exchange market. Demand for the domestic currency consists of all the credit items in the balance of payments account. Supply consists of all the debit items.

5. The exchange rate will depreciate (fall) if the demand for the domestic currency falls and/or the supply increases. These shifts can be caused by increases in domestic prices or incomes relative to foreign ones, reductions in domestic interest rates relative to foreign ones, worsening investment prospects at home compared with abroad, or the belief by speculators that the exchange rate will fall. The opposite in each case would cause an appreciation (rise).

6. The government can attempt to prevent the rate of exchange from falling by central bank purchases of the domestic currency in the foreign exchange market, either by selling foreign currency reserves or by using foreign loans. Alternatively, the central bank can raise interest rates. The reverse actions can be taken to prevent the rate from rising.

7. In the longer term, the government can prevent the rate from falling by pursuing deflationary policies or supply-side policies to increase the competitiveness of the country's exports, or by imposing import controls.

END OF CHAPTER QUESTIONS

1. The following table shows the GDP deflator for the years 1971–7 and 2006–12, based on 2010 = 100.

Year	1971	1972	1973	1974	1975	1976	1977
GDP deflator	10.0	10.8	11.6	13.3	16.9	19.5	22.2

Year	2006	2007	2008	2009	2010	2011	2012
GDP deflator	89.9	91.9	94.9	97.0	100.0	102.3	104.0

   (a) What is measured by the GDP deflator and how does it differ from the consumer prices index (CPI)?

   (b) What role does the GDP deflator play in the *AD/AS* framework?

   (c) Using the GDP deflator figures, work out the rate of inflation for each year from 1972 to 1977 and from 2007 to 2012. How do the rates of inflation in these two periods compare?

2. At what phase of the business cycle is the average *duration* of unemployment likely to be the highest? Explain.

3. Explain whether it would be desirable to have zero unemployment.

4. Consider the most appropriate policy for tackling each of the different types of unemployment.

5. Do any groups of people gain from inflation?

6. If everyone's incomes rose in line with inflation, would it matter if inflation were 100 per cent or even 1000 per cent per annum?

7. Imagine that you had to determine whether a particular period of inflation was demand-pull, or cost-push, or a combination of the two. What information would you require in order to conduct your analysis?

8. The following are the items in the UK's 1992 balance of payments.

	£ millions
Current account:	
Balance on trade in goods	−13 050
Balance on trade in services	9 706
Balance of trade	
Income balance	−1 835
Net current transfers	−5 228
Current account balance	
Capital account:	
Capital account balance	421
Financial account:	
Net direct investment	−1 837
Portfolio investment balance	−19 058
Other investment balance	34 546
Balance of financial derivatives	1 253
Reserve assets	1 407
Financial account net flows	
Net errors and omissions	

   (a) Complete the table by calculating the following: (i) the balance of trade; (ii) the current account balance; (iii) the financial account balance; (iv) net errors and omissions.

   (b) The UK's GDP in 1992 was estimated at £630 328 million. Calculate (i) the balance of trade, (ii) the current account balance and (iii) the financial account balance, each as a percentage of GDP.

   (c) Compare the value of each of the three items in (b) in both £millions and as a percentage of GDP with those 21 years later in 2013 (see Table 15.4 on page 453.)

▶

9. Explain how the current account of the balance of payments is likely to vary with the course of the business cycle.

10. The overall balance of payments must always balance. If this is the case, why might a deficit on one part of the balance of payments be seen as a problem?

11. List some factors that could cause an increase in the credit items of the balance of payments and a decrease in the debit items. What would be the effect on the exchange rate (assuming that it is freely floating)? What effect would these exchange rate movements have on the balance of payments?

12. What policy measures could the government adopt to prevent the exchange rate movements in question 11?

Online resources

Additional case studies in MyEconLab

15.1 **Do people volunteer to be unemployed?** Is it useful to make the distinction, often made, between voluntary and involuntary unemployment?

15.2 **Technology and employment.** Does technological progress create or destroy jobs?

15.3 **A high exchange rate.** This case looks at whether a high exchange rate is necessarily bad news for exporters.

15.4 **Disinflation.** The experience of Europe and Japan.

15.5 **Hyperinflation.** This looks at the extraordinarily high rates of inflation experienced in Germany in the early 1920s, Serbia and Montenegro in the 1990s and more recently in Zimbabwe.

15.6 **A W Phillips (1914–75).** A portrait of the discoverer of the Phillips curve, the New Zealand Economist, Bill Phillips.

15.7 **Making sense of the financial balances on the balance of payments.** An examination of the three main components of the financial account.

Websites relevant to Chapters 14 and 15

Numbers and sections refer to websites listed in the Web Appendix and hotlinked from this book's website at **www.pearsoned.co.uk/sloman**.

- For news articles relevant to this and the previous chapter, see the *Economics News Articles* link from the book's website.
- For general news on macroeconomic issues, both national and international, see websites in section A, and particularly A1–5, 7–9, 20–25, 31. See also links to newspapers worldwide in A38, 39, 43 and 44, and the news search feature in Google at A41. See also A42 for links to economics news articles from newspapers worldwide.
- For macroeconomic data, see links in B1 or 2; also see B4 and 12. For UK data, see B3 and 34. For EU data, see G1 > *The Statistical Annex*. For US data, see *Current economic indicators* in B5 and the *Data* section of B17. For international data, see B15, 21, 24, 31, 33, 35 and especially 36. For links to datasets, see B28, 33 and 36; I14.
- For national income statistics for the UK (Appendix), see B1, 1. *National Statistics* > the fourth link > *Economy* > *United Kingdom Economic Accounts* and *United Kingdom National Accounts – the Blue Book*.
- For data on UK unemployment, see B1, 1. *National Statistics* > the fourth link > *Labour Market* > *Labour Market Trends*. For international data on unemployment, see G1; H3 and 5.
- For international data on balance of payments and exchange rates, see *World Economic Outlook* in H4 and *OECD Economic Outlook* in B21 (also in section 6 of B1). See also the trade topic in I14.
- For details of individual countries' balance of payments, see B32.
- For UK data on balance of payments, see B1, 1. *National Statistics* > the fourth link > *Economy* > *United Kingdom Balance of Payments – the Pink Book*. See also B3, 34; F2. For EU data, see G1 > *The Statistical Annex* > *Foreign trade and current balance*.
- For exchange rates, see A3; B34; F2, 6, 8.
- For student resources relevant to Chapters 14 and 15, see sites C1–7, 9, 10, 19. See also the simulation *The trade balance and the exchange rate* in site D3.

MyEconLab

This book can be supported by MyEconLab, which contains a range of additional resources, including an online homework and tutorial system designed to test and build your understanding.

You need both an access card and a course ID to access MyEconLab:

1. Is your lecturer using MyEconLab? Ask your lecturer for your course ID.

2. Has an access card been included with the book at a reduced cost? Check the inside back cover of the book.

3. If you have a course ID but no access card, go to: http://www.myeconlab.com/ to buy access to this interactive study programme.

Macroeconomic Issues, Debates and Controversies

CHAPTER MAP

16.1 The macroeconomic environment and debates 464

16.2 Setting the scene: four key controversies 465
Controversy 1: the flexibility of prices and wages 465
Controversy 2: the flexibility of aggregate supply 466
Controversy 3: the role of expectations in the working of the market 467
Controversy 4: the significance of government budget deficits 467
Policy implications 467

16.3 Classical macroeconomics 468
The classical analysis of output and employment 468
The classical analysis of prices and inflation 469
The classical response to the Great Depression 470

16.4 The Keynesian revolution 473
Keynes' rejection of classical macroeconomics 473
Keynes' analysis of employment and inflation 474
The Keynesian policies of the 1950s and 1960s 476

16.5 The rise of the monetarist and new classical schools 477
Sowing the seeds of a new orthodoxy 477
The monetarist counter-revolution 477
The new classical school 479
Government policies 480

16.6 The Keynesian response 481
Market imperfections 481
Hysteresis 483
Government intervention 483

16.7 An emerging consensus up to the crisis of 2008 484
A new mainstream consensus 484
DSGE models – the new consensus macro model 484
Constrained policy discretion 485

16.8 The financial crisis and the search for a new consensus 486
The financial crisis and its aftermath 486
Fiscal expansion to fiscal austerity 486
Debates about the state of macroeconomics 487
Emergence of a new consensus? 488
Areas of general agreement? 488

In this final chapter of Part E we look at how macroeconomics has developed over the past 100 years. In doing so, we consider the debates surrounding our key macroeconomic issues: economic growth, unemployment, inflation, economic relationships with the rest of the world, the financial well-being of economic agents and the relationship between the financial system and the economy.

In reading this chapter you will see how macroeconomic debates have been shaped by events, such as the Great Depression of the 1930s, the rapid inflation of the 1970s or the global economic and financial crisis of the late 2000s. This should not surprise you since it is to help understand real problems, and to provide practical solutions to them, that many of the theories we shall be examining later in the book developed. But, you will also see how the development of economic ideas has affected actual policy, such as the granting of independence to central banks.

The unfolding of the 'macroeconomic story' allows us to see how different theories and approaches have developed. It also helps us to understand where there is greatest agreement among economists and where controversies remain.

16.1 THE MACROECONOMIC ENVIRONMENT AND DEBATES

In the previous two chapters, we began examining some key macroeconomic issues: growth, unemployment, inflation, our interconnectedness with foreign economies, the financial well-being of economic agents and the stability of the financial system. The focus of debates within macroeconomics tends to reflect the key macroeconomic issues of the time. It is not surprising that many of the debates and advancement of ideas have arisen because existing theories appeared unable to explain the prevailing macroeconomic conditions. Sometimes this has resulted in relatively small incremental changes to theory and to policy, but on other occasions very different views of how economies work have come to the fore and consequently policy has been radically reshaped.

Figure 16.1 plots the path of a selection of macroeconomic indicators since 1900. It helps to set the scene for some of the key macroeconomic debates over the past 100 years or so. Macroeconomics as a separate branch of economics had its birth with the mass unemployment experienced in the 1920s and 1930s. The old 'classical theories' of the time, which essentially said that free markets would

provide a healthy economy with full employment, could not provide solutions to the problem. Their analysis seemed totally at odds with the facts.

A new analysis of the economy – one that *did* offer solutions to mass unemployment – was put forward by the economist John Maynard Keynes. His book *The General Theory of Employment, Interest and Money*, published in 1936, saw the dawn of 'Keynesian economics'. Keynes advocated active intervention by governments, in particular using fiscal policy. By carefully managing aggregate demand, the government could prevent mass unemployment on the one hand, or an 'overheated' economy with unsustainable growth and high inflation on the other.

After the Second World War, governments around the world adopted Keynesian demand-management policies; and they seemed to be successful. The 1950s and 1960s were a period of low inflation, low unemployment and relatively high economic growth. Macroeconomists were largely concerned with refining Keynesian economics.

In the 1970s, however, the macroeconomic consensus broke down. As we can see from Figure 16.1, both inflation

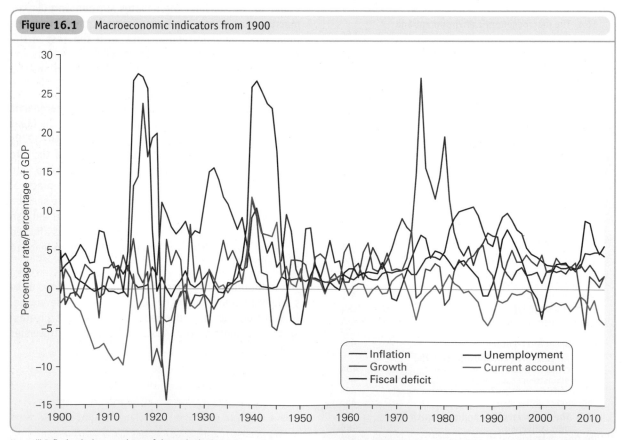

Figure 16.1 Macroeconomic indicators from 1900

Legend: Inflation, Growth, Fiscal deficit, Unemployment, Current account

Notes: (i) Inflation is the annual rate of change in the GDP deflator; (ii) Unemployment rate is based on administrative/claimant count rates; (iii) Growth is the annual growth in constant-price GDP; (iv) Current account as % of GDP; and (v) Fiscal deficit is public-sector net borrowing as a % of GDP.
Source: Based on data from Bank of England available at www.bankofengland.co.uk/publications/quarterlybulletin/threecenturiesofdata.xls and National Statistics (Various).

and unemployment rose and growth slowed. Macroeconomics became highly controversial. Different 'schools of thought' had their own explanations of what was going wrong, and each had its own solutions to the problems.

Then, as the macroeconomic environment generally improved in the 1990s, increasingly common ground was found and a new consensus emerged. This consensus was based around three general principles. First, economic agents are rational and forward-looking optimisers. Second, while markets adjust to equilibrium relatively quickly there exist frictions and imperfections that can affect both the speed of adjustment and the characteristics of the macroeconomic equilibrium. Third, random shocks frequently hit the economy.

While some economists were highly sceptical of the new consensus, it was the financial crisis of the late 2000s and the subsequent global economic downturn that re-energised long-standing debates and differences amongst macroeconomists. These differences were mirrored by the debates amongst politicians and policy makers and were significantly greater than they had been for many years.

In some ways, the debates of the late 2000s and early 2010s were a microcosm of much of the preceding 100 years

Many familiar questions were again being asked, not least concerning the role that governments should play in modern, developed economies. However, other questions emerged concerning the way that macroeconomic analysis and macroeconomic models had developed during the new orthodoxy.

The new consensus had largely sought to explain macroeconomic variables, such as the growth of real GDP or the rate of inflation, by building models that draw predictions based on aggregating the behaviour of representative rational forward-looking economic agents. Elaborately technical models began to characterise macroeconomics. But, in light of the general failure of macroeconomists to foresee the financial crisis, economists began to ask whether the models of the new orthodoxy had taken a wrong turn. New models began to be developed which put more emphasis on the role of the financial sector, debts and speculative behaviour.

While some disagreement amongst economists is inevitable, there exist some areas of broad agreement between many macroeconomists over the causes of macroeconomic problems and the appropriate policies to deal with them. Therefore, in this chapter we will be identifying areas not only where disagreement remains, but also where there is more agreement.

16.2 SETTING THE SCENE: FOUR KEY CONTROVERSIES

Most of the debate in macroeconomics has centred on the working of the market mechanism: just how well or how badly it achieves the various macroeconomic objectives. There have been four major areas of disagreement: (a) how flexible are wages and prices; (b) how flexible is aggregate supply; (c) what is the role of expectations; and (d) what is the impact of government budget deficits on markets? We examine each in turn.

Controversy 1: the flexibility of prices and wages

Generally, the political right has tended to ally with those economists who argue that prices and wages are relatively flexible. Markets tend to clear, they say, and clear fairly quickly.

Disequilibrium unemployment is likely to be fairly small, according to their view, and normally only a temporary, short-run phenomenon. Any long-term unemployment, therefore, will be equilibrium (or 'natural') unemployment. To cure this, they argue, encouragement must be given to the free play of market forces: to a rapid response of both firms and labour to changes in market demand and supply, to a more rapid dissemination of information on job vacancies, and generally to greater labour mobility, both geographical and occupational.

There are some on the political right, however, who argue that in the short run wages may not be perfectly flexible.

This occurs when unions attempt to keep wages above the equilibrium. In this case, disequilibrium unemployment may continue for a while. The solution here, they argue, is to curb the power of unions so that wage flexibility can be restored and disequilibrium unemployment cured.

The political centre and left have tended to ally with economists who reject the assumption of highly flexible wages and prices. There exist, they argue, frictions and market imperfections. If there is a deficiency of demand for labour in the economy, for example during a recession, there will be a resistance from unions to cuts in real wages and certainly to cuts in money wages. Any cuts that do occur will be insufficient to eliminate the disequilibrium, and will anyway serve only to reduce aggregate demand further, so that workers have less money to spend. The demand curve in Figure 15.8 (see page 438) would shift further to the left.

The prices of goods may also be inflexible in response to changes in demand. As industry became more concentrated and more monopolistic over the years, firms, it is argued, became less likely to respond to a general fall in demand by cutting prices. Instead, they were likely to build up stocks if they thought the recession was temporary, or cut production and hence employment if they thought the recession would persist. It is also argued that many firms use cost-plus methods of pricing. If wages are inflexible downwards, and if they form a major element of costs, prices will also be inflexible downwards.

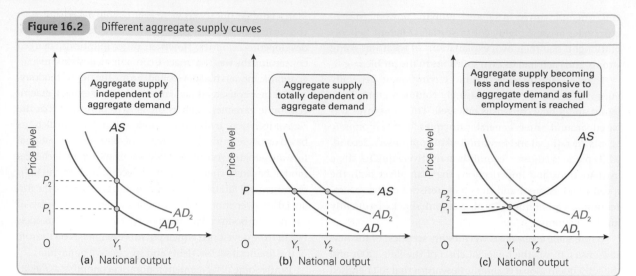

Figure 16.2 Different aggregate supply curves

(a) National output

(b) National output

(c) National output

Thus according to those who criticise the right, markets cannot be relied upon automatically to correct disequilibria and hence cure disequilibrium unemployment.

 Why are real wages likely to be more flexible downwards than money wages?

The process of globalisation has helped to offset the growth in market power in many industries in recent years. Competition from China and India, for example, has made prices in many markets more flexible. In other markets, however, particularly in the service sector, international competition is less relevant and, in others, global giants such as Apple, Monsanto, Boeing and GlaxoSmithKline have considerable price-setting power.

Controversy 2: the flexibility of aggregate supply

The question here is how responsive is national output (i.e. aggregate supply), and hence also employment, to a change in aggregate demand?

The arguments centre on the nature of the aggregate supply curve (*AS*). Three different *AS* curves are shown in Figure 16.2. In each of the three cases, it is assumed that the government raises aggregate demand through the use of fiscal and/or monetary policy. Aggregate demand shifts from AD_1 to AD_2. The effect on prices and output will depend on the shape of the *AS* curve.

TC 7
p72

Some economists, generally supported by the political right, argue that output is not determined by aggregate demand (except perhaps in the very short run). Instead, the rise in aggregate demand will simply lead to a rise in prices. They therefore envisage an *AS* curve like that in Figure 16.2(a). If the government wants to expand aggregate supply and get more rapid economic growth, it is no good, they argue, concentrating on demand. Instead, governments should

concentrate directly on supply by encouraging enterprise and competition, and generally by encouraging markets to operate more freely. For this reason, this approach is often labelled *supply-side economics*.

Their critics, however, argue that a rise in aggregate demand will lead to a rise in output. In the extreme case where actual output is well below potential output, prices will not rise at all. In this case, the *AS* curve is like that in Figure 16.2(b). Output will rise to Y_2 with the price level remaining at *P*.

Others argue that both prices and output will rise. In this case, the short-term curve will be like that in Figure 16.2(c). If there is plenty of slack in the economy – idle machines, unemployed labour, etc. – output will rise a lot and prices only a little. But as slack is taken up, the *AS* curve becomes steeper. Firms, finding it increasingly difficult to raise output in the short run, simply respond to a rise in demand by raising prices.

In recent years, some consensus has emerged. Most economists now maintain that the short-run *AS* curve is similar to that in Figure 16.2(c), but that in the long run, given time for prices and wages to adjust, the curve is much steeper, if not vertical. Any increase in aggregate demand will simply result in higher prices.

There is not total agreement, however. Some Keynesian economists argue that the long-run effects of an increase in aggregate demand could be a higher level of investment and hence higher capacity and thus a higher aggregate supply. In such a case, the long-run *AS* curve would be much flatter. Keynesian economists argued this in the recession

Definition

Supply-side economics An approach that focuses directly on aggregate supply and how to shift the aggregate supply curve outwards.

following the banking crisis of 2008. An expansion in aggregate demand, through fiscal and monetary policies, could result in higher investment and hence an increase in capacity of the economy, which would allow economic recovery to be sustained.

Would it be possible for a short-run AS curve to be horizontal (as in Figure 16.2(b)) at all levels of output?

Controversy 3: the role of expectations in the working of the market

How quickly and how fully will individuals and firms anticipate changes in prices and changes in output? How are their expectations formed, and how accurate are they? What effect do these expectations have? This has been the third major controversial topic.

The political right tended to ally with those economists who argue that people's expectations adjust rapidly and fully to changing economic circumstances. They emphasise the role of expectations of *price* changes.

If aggregate demand expands, they argue, people will expect higher prices. Workers will realise that the apparently higher wages they are offered are an illusion. The higher wages are 'eaten up' by higher prices. Thus workers are not encouraged to work longer hours, and unemployed workers are not encouraged to take on employment more readily. Likewise the higher prices that firms can charge are necessary to cover higher wages and other costs, and are not a reflection of higher real demand. Firms thus soon realise that any apparent increased demand for their products is an illusion. Their price rises will fully absorb the extra spending in money terms. There will be no increase in sales, and hence no increase in output and employment.

Thus, they argue, increased aggregate demand merely fuels inflation and can do no more than give a very temporary boost to output and employment. If anything, the higher inflation could damage business confidence and thus worsen long-term output and employment growth by discouraging investment.

Those who criticise this view argue that the formation of expectations is more complex than this. Whether people expect an increase in demand to be fully matched by inflation depends on the current state of the economy and how any increase in demand is introduced.

If there is a lot of slack in the economy (if unemployment is very high and there are many idle resources) and if an increase in demand is in the form, say, of direct government spending on production (on roads, hospitals, sewers and other infrastructure) then output and employment may quickly rise. Here the effect of expectations may be beneficial. Rather than expecting inflation from the increased demand, firms may expect faster growth and an expansion of markets. As a result, they may choose to invest, and this in turn will produce further growth in output and employment.

Views on expectations, therefore, tend to parallel views on aggregate supply. The right argues that a boost to demand will not produce extra output and employment: aggregate supply is inelastic (as in Figure 16.2(a)) and therefore the higher demand will merely fuel expectations of inflation. Critics argue that a boost to demand can increase aggregate supply and employment. If firms expect this, they will produce more.

If firms believe the aggregate supply curve to be moderately elastic, what effect will this belief have on the outcome of an increase in aggregate demand?

Controversy 4: the significance of government budget deficits

In a recession, the government's budget deficit tends automatically to rise as lower real incomes and spending lead to a fall in tax revenues, and as higher unemployment and lower real incomes lead to a rise in people claiming unemployment and other benefits.

The right tends to align with those economists who argue that it is important to reduce the deficit in order to restore confidence to financial markets and keep interest rates down. Cuts in public-sector expenditure and employment, it is argued, will be more than compensated by a rise in private-sector expenditure and employment. If the government tries to 'spend its way out of recession', any boost to the economy will be short-lived. The resulting increased public-sector borrowing will erode confidence and push up interest rates, thereby dampening private-sector expenditure.

The left tends to align with Keynesian economists, who argue that expansionary fiscal and monetary policies will stimulate economic growth and that this will increase the demand for the private sector, resulting in higher private-sector production and investment. The resulting economic growth will reduce the deficit as tax revenues increase and the number claiming benefits falls.

Policy implications

Generally, then, the economists supported by the political right tend to favour a policy of laissez-faire. Any intervention by government to boost demand will merely be inflationary and will thus damage long-term growth and employment. At most, governments should intervene to remove hindrances to the free and efficient operation of markets.

Economists supported by the political centre and left have tended to argue that disequilibrium unemployment may persist for several years and may be very high. The answer is to boost demand, thereby increasing aggregate supply and employment. They also argue that infrastructure investment by the government can make a significant difference in directly boosting aggregate supply.

Section summary

1. Macroeconomic debates tend to be shaped by the macroeconomic conditions of the time and this had led to developments in both macroeconomic theory and policy. Over the years there has been considerable debate among economists and politicians about how the market mechanism works at a macroeconomic level.

2. The right has tended to argue (a) that prices and wages are relatively flexible, (b) that aggregate supply is determined independently of aggregate demand and (c) that people's price and wage expectations adjust rapidly to shifts in aggregate demand so as to wipe out any output effect.

3. The centre and left to varying degrees have argued (a) that prices and wages are inflexible downwards, (b) that aggregate supply is relatively elastic when there is slack in the economy and (c) that positive expectations of output and employment can make investment and aggregate supply responsive to changes in aggregate demand.

4. The right generally supports policies to reduce government budget deficits even in a recession. The left generally supports expansionary fiscal policies in times of recession even though the size of the budget deficit is likely to increase temporarily. The deficit, it is argued, will fall again as the economy expands.

16.3 CLASSICAL MACROECONOMICS

The classical economists of the early nineteenth century held a pessimistic view of the long-term prospects for economic growth (see Boxes 5.1 and 14.5). Population growth combined with the law of diminishing returns would undermine any benefits from improved technology or the discovery of new sources of raw materials. What is more, there was little the government could do to improve these prospects. In fact governments, they argued, by interfering with competition and the functioning of the market would be likely to make things worse. They therefore advocated a policy of laissez-faire and free trade.

The classical school continued into the twentieth century. By then, its predictions about economic growth had become less pessimistic. After all, the Victorian years had been ones of rapid industrialisation and growth, with a massive expansion of the UK's overseas trade. This growing optimism had, if anything, strengthened the advocacy of laissez-faire. In the early years of the twentieth century, then, most economists, most politicians and virtually all bankers and businesspeople were relatively confident in the power of the free market to provide growing output and low unemployment.

The main role for the government was to provide 'sound finance' (i.e. not to print too much money), so as to maintain stable prices.

The classical analysis of output and employment

The classical theory predicted that, in the long run, equilibrium in the economy would be at virtually full employment. In the long run, any unemployment would be merely *frictional* unemployment: namely, people in the process of changing jobs.

There were two important elements in the classical theory.

The free-market economy works to equate demand and supply in all markets

This element of classical theory assumes flexible prices: of goods and services, of labour (i.e. wage rates) and of money (i.e. the rate of interest).

The classical economists argued that flexible prices would ensure that saving equalled investment ($S = I$) and that imports equalled exports ($M = X$). From this it follows that, if the government were to 'balance its budget' and make taxation equal to government expenditure ($T = G$), then total withdrawals would equal total injections ($W = J$):[1]

$$\left.\begin{array}{l} S = I \\ M = X \\ T = G \end{array}\right\} \rightarrow W = J$$

But why should flexible prices ensure that $S = I$ and $M = X$? The reasoning of the classical economists was as follows.

$S = I$. This would be brought about by flexible rates of interest (r) in the **market for loanable funds**. When firms want to invest in new plant and equipment, they will require finance. Investment demand, therefore, represents a demand for loanable funds from financial institutions (an outflow). The higher the rate of interest, the more expensive will borrowing be, and hence the less will be the demand for investment. The investment schedule will therefore be

Definition

Market for loanable funds The market for loans from and deposits into the banking system.

---

[1] The classical economists did not use the terms 'withdrawals' and 'injections': these are modern terms. Nevertheless, their analysis implied an automatic equation of W and J if markets cleared and the government balanced its budget.

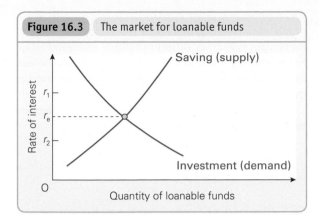

Figure 16.3 The market for loanable funds

downward sloping with respect to *r*. This is illustrated in Figure 16.3.

Saving represents a supply of loanable funds (an inflow). The saving schedule will be upward sloping. The higher the rate of interest, the more people will be attracted to save: that is, the more they will deposit in financial institutions.

Equilibrium will be at r_e, where $S = I$. If the rate of interest were above r_e, say at r_1, financial institutions would be accumulating funds. They would have to lower the rate of interest to attract sufficient borrowers. If the rate of interest were below r_e, say at r_2, financial institutions would find their funds were reducing. They would raise the rate of interest.

> *Assuming that rates of interest are initially above the equilibrium and that one particular financial institution chooses not to reduce its rate of interest, what will happen? What will be the elasticity of supply of loanable funds to an individual institution?*

$M = X$. This would be brought about by flexible UK prices and wages. Before 1914, and from 1925 to 1931, the UK was on the **gold standard**. This was a *fixed* exchange rate system in which each participating country's currency was valued at a certain fixed amount of gold.

If a country had a balance of payments deficit ($M > X$), this had to be paid for in gold from its reserves. A country was then supposed to respond to this outflow of gold by reducing the amount of money in the economy and hence reducing total expenditure. This would create surpluses in the goods and labour markets, which would, in turn, lead to a fall in prices and wages. This fall in the prices of UK goods would increase the sale of exports and reduce the consumption of the now relatively expensive imports. This whole process would continue until the balance of payments deficit was eliminated: until $M = X$.

> *What would have happened if countries in deficit had not responded to an outflow of gold by reducing total expenditure?*

(Note that, under a system of freely floating exchange rates, it is the flexibility in exchange rates, rather than the prices of goods and factors, that will ensure $M = X$.)

Provided the government balanced its budget ($T = G$), therefore, flexibility in the various markets would ensure that withdrawals equalled injections.

Say's law

J.-B. Say was a French economist of the early nineteenth century. **Say's law** states that *supply creates its own demand*. What this means is that the production of goods and services will generate expenditures sufficient to ensure that they are sold. There will be no deficiency of demand and no need to lay off workers. There will be full employment. The justification for the law is as follows.

When firms produce goods, they pay out money either directly to other firms, or as factor payments to households. The income that households receive is then partly paid back to firms in the form of consumption expenditure (C_d): the inner flow of the circular flow of income.

But any withdrawals by firms or households are also fully paid back to firms in the form of injections, since $S = I$, $M = X$ and $T = G$. Thus all the incomes generated by firms' supply will be transformed into demand for their products, either directly in the form of consumption, or indirectly via withdrawals and then injections. There will thus be no deficiency of demand.

Of course, although aggregate demand might equal aggregate supply, consumers may shift their demand away from some industries in favour of others. Structural unemployment (a form of equilibrium unemployment) may then occur. But then wages would fall in the declining industries and rise in the expanding industries. This would help to eliminate the structural unemployment.

The reduction in structural unemployment will be quicker (a) the more flexible are wages and (b) the more willing and able are workers to move to industries and towns where jobs are available (labour mobility). In other words, the better markets work, the lower will be the level of equilibrium unemployment.

The classical analysis of prices and inflation

The classical economists based their analysis of inflation on the **quantity theory of money**. In its simplest form, it states

Definitions

Gold standard The system whereby countries' exchange rates were fixed in terms of a certain amount of gold and whereby balance of payments deficits were paid in gold.

Say's law Supply creates its own demand. In other words, the production of goods will generate sufficient demand to ensure that they are sold.

Quantity theory of money The price level (P) is directly related to the quantity of money in the economy (M).

that the general level of prices (P) in the economy depends on the supply of money (M):[1]

$$P = f(M)$$

The greater the quantity of money, the higher the level of prices. Under this theory, inflation is simply caused by a rise in money supply.

To understand the reasoning behind the quantity theory of money, we need to examine the *equation of exchange*. This comes in various versions (see Case Study 16.1 in MyEconLab), but the one most useful for our purposes is the simple identity between national expenditure and national income. This identity may be expressed as follows:

$$MV = PY$$

M, as we have already seen, is the supply of money in the economy. V is the *velocity of circulation*. This is the number of times per year a unit of currency (e.g. £1) is spent on buying goods and services that make up GDP. Suppose that each pound's worth of money is typically spent six times per year on such goods and services, and that money supply is £300 billion. This would mean that total expenditure on GDP ($M \times V$) is £1.8 trillion (£1800 billion).

P, again as we have already seen, is the general level of prices. Let us define it more precisely as the price index based on some specific year (e.g. 2010), where the index in the base year is assumed to be 1.00 (not 100) (see pages A:6–8). Y is the real value of national income (i.e. GDP expressed in the prices of the base year). $P \times Y$, therefore, is simply the 'nominal' value of GDP (i.e. GDP expressed in *current* prices, rather than those of the base year). Thus if GDP in real terms (Y) (i.e. measured in base-year prices) were £1.5 trillion and if the current price index (P) were 1.2, then nominal GDP ($P \times Y$) would be £1.8 trillion.

Thus both MV and PY are equal to GDP and must, therefore, by definition be equal to each other.

The classical economists argued that both V and Y were determined independently of the money supply: i.e. a change in the money supply would *not* be expected to lead to a change in V or Y. The velocity of circulation (V),

they claimed, was determined by the frequency with which people were paid (e.g. weekly or monthly), the nature of the banking system and other institutional arrangements for holding money. As far as Y was concerned, Say's law would ensure that the real value of output (Y) was maintained at the full-employment level.

With V and Y as 'constants' with respect to M, therefore, the quantity theory must hold:

$$P = f(M)$$

Increases in money supply simply lead to inflation.

 Assuming that Y rises each year as a result of increases in productivity, can money supply rise without causing inflation? Would this destroy the validity of the quantity theory?

The classical response to the Great Depression

The classical economists had predicted that there would be virtually full employment. Any unemployment would simply be the frictional unemployment of people being 'between jobs'. Before the First World War their predictions were not far from the truth. Between the wars, however, the UK experienced a prolonged recession of unparalleled severity. Throughout this 'Great Depression' unemployment was very much higher than before the war, reaching over 22 per cent in the winter of 1932–3 with 3 million people unemployed. However, the depression eliminated inflation. In every year from 1921 to 1934 prices either were constant or fell. During this period the annual rate of inflation averaged –3 per cent while the unemployment rate averaged 10 per cent (see Figure 16.1).

Part of the cause of the depression was the decision in 1925 by Winston Churchill, the Chancellor of the Exchequer, to return to the gold standard at the pre-war rate of £1 = \$4.86. But with many export markets lost in the war and a rapid rise in imports for rebuilding the economy, the balance of payments was in severe deficit. To correct this deficit required severely deflationary policies. The aim was to drive wage rates down, reduce costs and restore the competitiveness of exports. The result, however, was a severe recession.

But while in the UK output slumped and unemployment soared, most of the rest of the industrialised world initially experienced a boom. But in 1929, after a decade of rapid growth and a huge rise in share values, Wall Street crashed. This sent the US economy plunging into deep recession, with the rest of the world following suit. As the world economy slumped, so did international trade. With a collapse of its exports, the UK dived even deeper into depression. Eventually, in 1932, it was forced to leave the gold standard and allow the pound to depreciate. (Case Study 16.3 in MyEconLab looks at the bitter experience of the return to the gold standard in 1925 and its aftermath.)

[1] In the quantity theory of money the letter M is used to refer to money supply, whereas in the circular flow of income it is used to refer to the expenditure on imports. Naturally this is potentially confusing, but unfortunately it is normal practice to use the letter M in both ways. To avoid any such confusion we will always specify which is being referred to. Elsewhere, however, you will just have to judge from the context! (There is the same problem with the letter P, which can refer either to price or to product.)

Definitions

Equation of exchange $MV = PY$. The total level of spending on GDP (MV) equals the total value of goods and services produced (PY) that go to make up GDP.

Velocity of circulation The average number of times annually that money is spent on goods and services that make up GDP.

Fiscal policy in the early 1930s

The budget must be balanced. All government expenditure should be financed from taxation. This was orthodox opinion in the 1920s.

But as unemployment increased during the Great Depression, spending on unemployment benefits (the most rapidly growing item of government expenditure) threatened the balanced budget principle. Other spending had to be cut to restore balance. The result was more unemployment, and hence the payment of more unemployment benefits.

Treasury officials and classical economists called for cuts in unemployment benefits. The May Committee, set up to investigate the budgetary problem, recommended a 20 per

cent reduction. Even the Labour government, elected on a mandate to tackle the unemployment problem, proposed a 10 per cent reduction in 1931. This contributed to its subsequent collapse.

Philip Snowdon, Labour's Chancellor of the Exchequer, remarked in 1931 how pensioners had returned their pension books and children sent in their savings to help the nation balance its budget. And yet, as Keynes argued, it was not saving that was necessary to cure the unemployment, but spending. Government deficits were *desirable*. Attempts to balance the budget merely deflated the economy further and deepened the problem of unemployment.

The deflationary policies of the 1920s seemed to be directly responsible for increasing unemployment. Many critics argued that the government ought deliberately to *expand* aggregate demand. However, the Treasury and other classical economists rejected the analysis that unemployment was caused by a lack of demand; they also rejected policies of reflation (e.g. increased government expenditure).

The classical Treasury view on unemployment

Would deflation of demand not lead to unemployment? According to the Treasury view, unemployment would occur only if labour markets *failed to clear*: if real wage costs did not fall sufficiently.

The Treasury concluded that people should be encouraged to take wage cuts. This would also help to reduce prices and restore export demand, thus correcting the balance of payments. People should also be encouraged to save. This would, via flexible interest rates, lead to more investment and hence a growth in output and demand for labour.

The classical Treasury view on public works

In the 1920s and 1930s, some politicians and economists argued that unemployment could be reduced if the government pursued a programme of public works: building roads, hospitals, houses, etc. The Treasury view was that this would not work and could have costly side effects.

A programme of public works could be funded in three ways: from extra taxation, from extra government borrowing or by printing extra money. *None* of these three ways would, according to the classical Treasury view, solve the unemployment problem.

- *Extra taxation* would merely have the effect of reducing the money that consumers would spend on private industry. Extra public-sector demand would thus be offset by a fall in private-sector demand.
- If the government *borrowed more*, it would have to offer higher interest rates in order to persuade people to buy the additional government securities. The private sector

would then have to offer higher interest rates, to compete for funds. As interest rates went up, private borrowing would go down. Thus public investment would **crowd out** private investment (see Box 16.2). This debate was to be revisited many years later when, following the financial crisis and subsequent economic downturn of the late 2000s, government borrowing rose sharply (see Figure 16.1).

- According to the quantity theory of money, printing extra money would simply lead to inflation. The assumption here is that the aggregate supply 'curve' is vertical. In Figure 16.4 a rise in aggregate demand from AD_1 to AD_2 (as a result of the extra money supply) would simply lead to

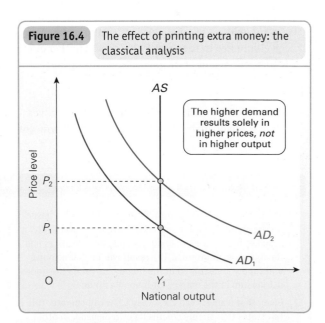

Figure 16.4 The effect of printing extra money: the classical analysis

The higher demand results solely in higher prices, *not* in higher output

Definition

Crowding out Where increased public expenditure diverts money or resources away from the private sector.

BOX 16.2 THE CROWDING-OUT EFFECT

When public expenditure replaces private

Critics of the use of government expenditure to stimulate output and employment often refer to the problem of *crowding out*. In its starkest form, the argument goes like this.

There is no point in the government embarking on a programme of public works to bring the economy out of recession. If it attempts to spend more, it can do so only by reducing private expenditure. The effect on total spending will be zero. This crowding out can take two main forms.

Resource crowding out

This is when the government uses resources such as labour and raw materials that would otherwise be used by the private sector. If the economy is operating near full capacity, then if resources are used by the government, they cannot at the same time be used by private companies.

The argument is far less convincing, however, if there is slack in the economy. If the government merely mobilises otherwise idle resources, there need be no reduction in private-sector output. In fact, if private-sector firms have spare capacity, they will respond to the higher demand by producing more themselves: aggregate demand will stimulate extra production.

Financial crowding out

This occurs when extra government spending diverts *funds* from private-sector firms and thus deprives them of the finance necessary for investment.

If the government spends more (without raising taxes or printing more money), it will have to borrow more and will therefore have to offer higher rates of interest. Private companies will then have to offer higher rates of interest themselves in order to attract funds. Alternatively, if they borrow from banks, and banks have less funds, the banks will charge them higher interest rates. Higher interest rates will discourage firms from borrowing and hence discourage investment.

The weakness with this argument is that it assumes that the supply of money is fixed. If the government spends more but increases the amount of money in the economy, it need not deprive the private sector of finance. Interest rates will not be bid up.

But would that not be inflationary? Not if there are idle resources and hence the extra money can be spent on extra output. Only if resource crowding out takes place would it be inflationary.

 Could resource crowding out take place at less than full employment?

---

a rise in the price level from P_1 to P_2. National output (and hence employment) would not increase. It would remain constant at Y_1. A re-emergence of inflation, which had been eliminated in the early 1920s, would further erode the competitiveness of UK goods, jeopardising the return to the gold standard at the pre-war exchange rate.

Treasury orthodoxy insisted, therefore, that the government should attempt to balance its budget, even if this meant cutting welfare benefits to the rising numbers of unemployed (see Box 16.1). The governments of the 1920s and early 1930s followed these classical recommendations. They attempted to balance their budgets and rejected policies of reflation. Yet mass unemployment persisted.

It is interesting to note that the policy of reducing deficits through cuts in government expenditure, even at a time of recession, has been a central part of Coalition policy in the early 2010s.

Section summary

1. The classical analysis of output and employment is based on the assumption that markets clear. More specifically, it assumes that there are flexible wages, flexible prices and flexible rates of interest. The result will be that demand and supply are equated in the labour market, in the goods market and in the market for loanable funds.

2. Given that markets will clear, Say's law will operate. This law states that supply creates its own demand. In other words, the production of goods and services will generate incomes for households, which in turn will generate consumption expenditure, ensuring that the goods are sold. If any incomes are not directly spent on domestic goods, flexible prices will help to ensure that any money withdrawn is re-injected. Flexible interest rates will ensure that investment equals saving, and flexible prices and wages will ensure that exports equal imports. Provided the government balances its budget, withdrawals will equal injections and Say's law will hold.

3. The classical economists based their analysis of prices on the quantity theory of money. This states that the level of prices is directly related to the quantity of money (M) in the economy. Their position can be demonstrated using the equation of exchange

    $$MV = PY$$

    where V is the velocity of circulation, P is the price index and Y is real national income expressed in the prices of the base year. The classical economists assumed that V

and Y were not affected by changes in the money supply and could thus be regarded as 'constants'. From this it follows that

$$P = f(M)$$

Increases in the money supply simply lead to inflation.

4. In 1925 the UK returned to the gold standard system of fixed exchange rates at the pre-war rate. But given the massive balance of payments deficit at this rate, it had to pursue tough deflationary policies. The result was mass unemployment.

5. The classical economists saw the remedy to the problem as lying in reductions in wages and prices. According to the classical theory, this would allow Say's law to operate and full employment to be restored. They rejected public works as the solution, arguing that it would lead to crowding out if financed by borrowing, and to inflation if financed by printing money.

16.4 THE KEYNESIAN REVOLUTION

Keynes' rejection of classical macroeconomics

The main critic of classical macroeconomics was John Maynard Keynes (see Case Study 16.6 in MyEconLab for a profile of Keynes). In his major work, *The General Theory of Employment, Interest and Money* (1936), he rejected the classical assumption that markets would clear. Disequilibrium could persist and mass unemployment could continue. There are two crucial markets in which disequilibrium could persist.

The labour market

Workers would resist wage cuts. Wages were thus 'sticky' downwards. In a recession, when the demand for labour is low, wages might not fall far or fast enough to clear the labour market.

In Figure 16.5 the recession has caused the aggregate demand for labour to shift to AD_{L2}. If the real wage rate were to remain at W_1, the supply and demand for labour would no longer be in equilibrium. There would exist disequilib-

rium (demand-deficient) unemployment. But even if wage cuts could be introduced, as advocated by classical economists, Keynes rejected that as the solution to demand deficiency. Workers are also consumers. A cut in workers' wages would mean less consumer spending. Firms would respond to this by reducing their demand for labour. Thus a lowering of wage rates below W_1 would lead to a leftward shift in the AD_L curve, and this would more than offset the reduction in wages. Wage rates would not fall fast enough to clear the market. Disequilibrium would worsen. The recession would deepen.

Employers might well find that labour was cheaper to employ, but if demand for their product were falling, they would hardly be likely to take on more labour.

The market for loanable funds

Keynes also rejected the classical solution of increased saving as a means of stimulating investment and growth. Again the problem was one of market disequilibrium.

An increase in saving will cause a disequilibrium in the market for loanable funds. The rate of interest will fall from

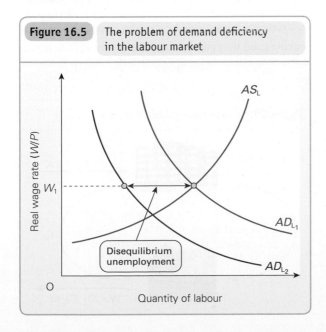

Figure 16.5 The problem of demand deficiency in the labour market

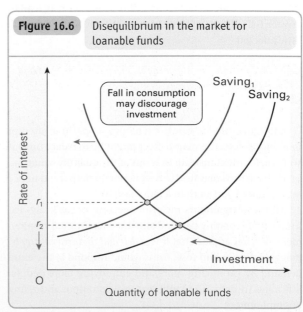

Figure 16.6 Disequilibrium in the market for loanable funds

BOX 16.3 **WILL WAGE CUTS CURE UNEMPLOYMENT?**

Keynes' dismissal of the classical remedy

In *The General Theory of Employment, Interest and Money*, Keynes rejects the classical argument that unemployment is due to excessive wages. In Chapter 2 he argues:

> [T]he contention that the unemployment which characterises a depression is due to a refusal by labour to accept a reduction of money wages is not clearly supported by the facts. It is not very plausible to assert that unemployment in the United States in 1932 was due either to labour obstinately refusing to accept a reduction of money wages or to its obstinately demanding a real wage beyond what

the productivity of the economic machine was capable of furnishing. Wide variations are experienced in the volume of employment without any apparent change either in the minimum real demands of labour or in its productivity. Labour is not more truculent in the depression than in the boom – far from it. Nor is its physical productivity less. These facts from experience are a prima facie ground for questioning the classical analysis.[1]

[1] J. M. Keynes, *The General Theory of Employment, Interest and Money* (Macmillan, 1967), p. 9.

---

r_1 to r_2 in Figure 16.6. But an increase in saving means a fall in consumption. As a result, firms will sell less and will thus be discouraged from investing. The investment demand curve will shift to the left. The rate of interest will have to fall *below* r_2 to clear the market.

The demand for investment, according to Keynes, depends very much on business confidence in the future. A slide into recession could shatter such confidence. The resulting fall in investment would deepen the recession.

The problem of disequilibrium in the market for loanable funds is made worse, according to Keynes, because neither saving nor investment is very responsive to changes in interest rates, and thus very large changes in interest rates would be necessary if equilibrium were ever to be restored after any shift in the saving or investment curves.

Keynes also rejected the simple quantity theory of money. Increases in money supply will not necessarily lead merely to rises in prices. If there is a lot of slack in the economy, with high unemployment, idle machines and idle resources, an increased spending of money may lead to substantial increases in real income (Y) and leave prices (P) little affected.

 Demonstrate this argument on an aggregate demand and supply diagram.

If the government were to cut money supply in an attempt to reduce prices, the major effect might be to reduce output and employment instead. In terms of the quantity equation, a reduction in M may lead to a reduction in output and hence real income Y rather than a reduction in P.

All these arguments meant a rejection of Say's law. Far from supply creating demand and thus ensuring full employment, Keynes argued that it was *demand that created supply*. If aggregate demand rose, firms would respond to the extra demand by producing more and employing more people. But a fall in demand would lead to less output and rising unemployment.

Keynes' central point was that an unregulated market economy *could not ensure sufficient demand*. Governments should therefore abandon laissez-faire, and should intervene to *control* aggregate demand.

Keynes' analysis of employment and inflation

Keynes' analysis of unemployment can be explained most simply in terms of the circular flow of income (see Figure 16.7). Keynes himself did not use this exact model, but it clearly explains the essence of his argument.

If injections (J) do not equal withdrawals (W), a state of disequilibrium exists. What will bring them back into equilibrium, however, is not a change in prices (of labour or of loanable funds), but rather a change in *national income* and *employment*.

Start with a state of equilibrium, where injections equal withdrawals, but with substantial unemployed resources (as was the case in the Great Depression). If there is now a rise in injections – for example, a rise in government expenditure – aggregate demand ($C_d + J$) will be higher. Firms will respond to this increased demand by using more labour and other resources and thus paying out more incomes (Y) to households. Household consumption will rise and so firms will sell more.

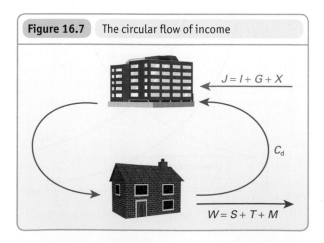

Figure 16.7 The circular flow of income

$$J = I + G + X$$

$$C_d$$

$$W = S + T + M$$

Firms will respond by producing more, and thus using more labour and other resources. Household incomes will rise again. Consumption and hence production will rise again, and so on. There will thus be a multiplied rise in incomes and employment. This is known as the *multiplier effect* and is an example of the 'principle of cumulative causation'.

 KEY IDEA 35 *The principle of cumulative causation.* An initial event can cause an ultimate effect that is much larger.

The process, however, does not go on for ever. Each time household incomes rise, households save more, pay more taxes and buy more imports. In other words, withdrawals rise. When withdrawals have risen to match the increased injections, equilibrium will be restored and national income and employment will stop rising. The process can be summarised as follows:

$$J > W \rightarrow Y\uparrow \rightarrow W\uparrow \text{ until } J = W$$

Similarly, an initial fall in injections (or rise in withdrawals) will lead to a multiplied fall in national income and employment:

$$J < W \rightarrow Y\downarrow \rightarrow W\downarrow \text{ until } J = W$$

Thus equilibrium in the circular flow of income can be at *any* level of output and employment.

If aggregate demand is too low, there will be a recession and high unemployment. In Figure 16.8 it is assumed that there is some level of national income and output (Y_F) at which there would be full employment of resources. This represents a limit to output. If aggregate demand were initially at AD_1, equilibrium would be at Y_1, considerably below the full-employment potential.

In this case, argued Keynes, governments should intervene to boost aggregate demand. There are two policy instruments that they can use.

Fiscal policy

Remember how we defined fiscal policy in Chapter 15 (page 452). It is where the government alters the balance between government expenditure (G) and taxation (T), and thereby alters the balance between injections and withdrawals. In this way, it controls aggregate demand. Faced with a recession, it should raise G and/or lower T. In other words, the government should run a budget deficit rather than a balanced budget. There will then be a multiplier effect:

$$G\uparrow \text{ or } T\downarrow \rightarrow J > W \rightarrow Y\uparrow \rightarrow W\uparrow \text{ until } J = W$$

Definition

Multiplier effect An initial increase in aggregate demand of £xm leads to an eventual rise in national income that is greater than £xm.

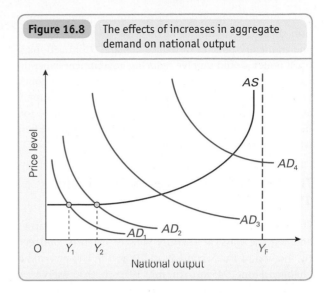

Figure 16.8 The effects of increases in aggregate demand on national output

If the eventual rise in aggregate demand were to, say, AD_2 in Figure 16.8, output would rise to Y_2.

Monetary policy

This is where the central bank alters the supply of money in the economy and/or manipulates interest rates. If it were to raise money supply, there would be more available in the economy for spending, interest rates would fall and aggregate demand would rise. Keynes argued that this was a less reliable policy than fiscal policy, since some of the extra money could be used for speculating in paper assets rather than spending on real goods and services. The details of how the central bank controls money supply and interest rates and the effects of such actions on the economy are examined in later chapters.

It is most effective if both fiscal and monetary policies are used simultaneously. For example, if the government undertook a programme of public works (fiscal policy) and financed it through increases in money supply (monetary policy), there would be no crowding out. There would be a significant rise in output and employment.

 What would be the classical economists' criticisms of this argument?

If aggregate demand rises too much, however, inflation becomes a problem. (This was the case during the Second World War, with the high expenditure on the war effort.) As Y_F is approached, with more and more firms reaching full capacity and with fewer and fewer idle resources, so additional increases in aggregate demand lead more and more to higher prices rather than higher output. This can be seen in Figure 16.8 as aggregate demand rises from AD_2 to AD_3 to AD_4.

 Might the AS curve shift to the right in the meantime? If it did, how would this influence the effects of the rises in aggregate demand?

Governments faced with the resulting demand-pull inflation should, according to Keynes, use *contractionary* fiscal and monetary policies to reduce demand. Contractionary fiscal policy would involve reducing government expenditure and/or raising taxes. Contractionary monetary policy would involve reducing the rate of growth of money supply and/or raising interest rates. Keynes argued that here too fiscal policy was the more reliable, but again that the best solution was to combine both policies.

The Keynesian policies of the 1950s and 1960s

During the 1920s and 1930s, UK governments of all parties adopted the classical Treasury view of balanced budgets. By the end of the Second World War, the consensus had changed. From 1945 up to the mid-1970s, both Conservative and Labour governments pursued Keynesian *demand-management policies* in an attempt to stabilise the economy and avoid excess or deficient demand.

When the economy began to grow too fast, with rising inflation and balance of payments deficits, the government adopted *deflationary* (contractionary) fiscal and monetary policies. When inflation and the balance of payments were sufficiently improved, but probably with recession looming, threatening rising unemployment and little or no growth, governments adopted *reflationary* (expansionary) fiscal and monetary policies (see Case Study 16.5 in MyEconLab). This succession of deflationary and reflationary policies to counteract the effect of the business cycle became known as *stop–go policies*.

During the 1950s and 1960s, inflation in the UK averaged just 3.9 per cent and unemployment a mere 1.4 per cent (see Case Study 16.6 in MyEconLab). Similarly low rates of inflation and unemployment were experienced in other industrialised countries. Nevertheless, from the mid-1960s onwards there was increasing criticism of short-term demand-management policies. Criticisms included the following:

- The policies were not very successful in stabilising the economy. Fluctuations still existed. Some economists even claimed that demand-management policies made fluctuations worse. The main reason given was the time it took for policies to be adopted and to work. If time lags are long enough, a deflationary policy may begin to work only when the economy has already turned down into recession. Likewise a reflationary policy may begin to work only when the economy is already booming, thus further fuelling inflation.

- The UK's post-war growth rate of around 2.75 per cent per annum was appreciably lower than that of other industrialised countries. Some of the blame for this was attributed to an overconcentration on short-term policies of stabilisation, and a neglect of underlying structural problems in the economy.

- Persistent balance of payments problems meant that governments often had to pursue deflationary policies even when the economy was running below capacity and unemployment was rising. At the time, there was a virtually fixed rate of exchange and thus *depreciation* of the exchange rate was not a means of correcting balance of payments deficits. Only in extreme circumstances could the exchange rate be 'devalued', i.e. fixed at a new lower rate. (This is explained in Chapter 25, page 765–7.)

- The simple Phillips curve relationship between inflation and unemployment was breaking down (see Box 15.4). If reflationary policies were the cure for unemployment and deflationary policies were the cure for inflation, what policies should be pursued when both inflation *and* unemployment were rising?

- The most fundamental criticism of all came from a group of economists called 'monetarists'. They rejected Keynesianism as a whole, with its concentration on demand. They returned to the earlier classical analysis, with its concentration on supply, and extended it to take account of the increasingly important role of price expectations in explaining 'stagflation' – the problem of slow growth and rising unemployment (i.e. stagnation) combined with rising inflation (see the next section).

From the mid-1970s onwards, the Keynesian/monetarist split between economists was reflected in the political parties. The Conservative leadership in the UK embraced monetarism, whereas the other political parties continued to embrace variants of Keynesianism.

Definitions

Demand-management policies Demand-side policies (fiscal and/or monetary) designed to smooth out the fluctuations in the business cycle.

Stop–go policies Alternate deflationary and reflationary policies to tackle the currently most pressing of the four problems that fluctuate with the business cycle.

Section summary

1. Keynes rejected the classical assumption that all markets would clear. Disequilibrium could persist in the labour market. A fall in aggregate demand would not simply lead to a fall in wages and prices and a restoration of the full-employment equilibrium. Instead there would be demand-deficient unemployment: as demand fell, there would be less demand for labour.

2. Disequilibrium could also persist in the market for loanable funds. As aggregate demand fell, and with it business confidence, so the demand for loanable funds for investment would shrink. Reductions in interest rates would be insufficient to clear the market for loanable funds.

3. Keynes also rejected the simple quantity theory. If there is slack in the economy, an expansion of the money supply can lead to an increase in *output* rather than an increase in prices.

4. Keynes argued that there would be a multiplier effect from changes in injections or withdrawals. A rise in investment, for example, would cause a multiplied rise in national income, as additional expenditures flowed round and round the circular flow, stimulating more and more production and thus generating more and more real income.

5. If the economy is operating below full employment, the government can use fiscal and/or monetary policies to boost aggregate demand and thereby take up the slack in the economy. Excessive aggregate demand, however, causes inflation. Deflationary fiscal and monetary policies can be used to remove this excess demand.

6. Keynesianism became the orthodoxy of the 1950s and 1960s. Governments used fiscal (and to a lesser extent monetary) policies to manage the level of aggregate demand.

7. After the mid-1960s, however, there was growing criticism of Keynesian demand management. The economy still fluctuated and the various macroeconomic problems seemed to be getting worse.

16.5 THE RISE OF THE MONETARIST AND NEW CLASSICAL SCHOOLS

Sowing the seeds of a new orthodoxy

As we saw in section 16.4, the Keynesian orthodoxy began to break down during the 1960s. This breakdown can be seen in the context of a more volatile macroeconomic environment (see Figure 16.1). The high inflation and low growth of the 1970s further helped to stimulate macroeconomic debates and, as we shall see, some of the resulting developments were to have a highly significant impact on macroeconomics, helping to shape a new orthodoxy.

In charting the path to a new orthodoxy, we begin by considering the rise of the monetarist and new classical schools. A distinguishing feature of both schools from the Keynesian orthodoxy is the belief that the market economy can deliver macroeconomic stability. Government intervention, they argue, can be a contributory factor to macroeconomic *instability*.

The monetarist counter-revolution

The chief advocate of monetarism was Milton Friedman, Professor of Economics at Chicago University and recipient of the Nobel Memorial Prize in Economics in 1976. Monetarists returned to the old classical theory as the basis for their analysis, and extended it to take account of the growing problem of *stagflation* – low growth accompanied by high inflation.

At the heart of monetarism is the quantity theory of money. Friedman examined the historical relationship between money supply and prices, and concluded that inflation was 'always and everywhere a monetary phenomenon'. If money supply over the long run rises faster than the potential output of the economy, inflation will be the inevitable result.

Monetarists argued that over the long run, in the equation $MV = PY$, *both* V and Y are independently determined and are not, therefore, affected by changes in M. Any change in money supply (M), therefore, will only affect prices (P). Whether or not monetarists were correct in arguing that V and Y are not affected by changes in M will be examined in later chapters.

Monetarists drew two important conclusions from their analysis:

■ The rising inflation from the mid-1960s onwards was entirely due to the growth in money supply increasingly outstripping the growth in output. If money supply rises,

Definition

Stagflation A term used to refer to the combination of stagnation (low growth and high unemployment) and high inflation.

they argued, then the resulting rise in aggregate demand will lead to higher output and employment at best for a few months. But soon people's expectations will adjust. Workers and firms come to expect higher wages and prices. Their actions then ensure that wages and prices *are* higher. Thus after one to two years the extra demand is fully taken up in inflation, and so output and employment fall back again. Then governments are tempted to raise money supply and aggregate demand again in a further attempt to get unemployment down. The effect of this over several years is for the inflation rate to get higher and higher.

- Reducing the rate of growth of money supply will reduce inflation without leading to long-run increases in unemployment. It *will* lead to temporary increases in unemployment, they argued, as the demand for goods and labour fall. But once price and wage inflation have adjusted down to this new level of demand, disequilibrium unemployment will be eliminated. This process will be hindered and high unemployment is likely to persist if workers persist in demanding excessive wage increases, or if firms and workers continue to expect high inflation rates.

Monetarists argued that inflation is damaging to the economy because it creates uncertainty for businesspeople and therefore reduces investment, and also because it reduces the country's competitiveness in international trade. They saw it as essential, therefore, for governments to keep a tight control over money supply and advocated the setting of money supply *targets*. Modest and well-publicised targets should help to reduce the *expected* rate of inflation. The UK government from the late 1970s to the mid-1980s set targets for the growth of money supply, and such targets were central to the Thatcher government's 'medium-term financial strategy'.

A vertical long-run Phillips curve

Monetarist analysis implied that the long-run Phillips curve (see Figure 16.9 and Box 15.4) is vertical at the equilibrium rate of unemployment (called the 'natural rate' by monetarists). In the *short run*, higher aggregate demand will reduce unemployment below the natural level. This is because there is a *real* increase in aggregate demand. But in the long run an increase in aggregate demand is fully absorbed by higher inflation. Therefore, a monetary expansion will increase output in the short run, but not so in the long run. The key to understanding why is the role of expectations.

Friedman argued that, in forming expectations of inflation, people learn from experience. If, for example, in the previous period, they underpredicted the rate of inflation, then this period they will adapt: they will revise their expectations of inflation upwards. This type of behaviour is thus known as **adaptive expectations**.

Assume that the economy is in equilibrium with unemployment at its natural rate (U_n) and that the authorities

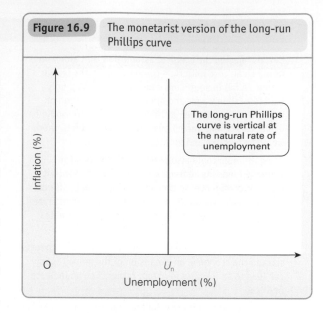

Figure 16.9 The monetarist version of the long-run Phillips curve

The long-run Phillips curve is vertical at the natural rate of unemployment

engage in a monetary expansion. This increases aggregate demand, resulting in an excess demand for goods and labour. The effect of this is to cause prices and nominal wages to rise. Even though *real* wages have not risen, workers could be 'fooled' into supplying more labour, believing that the rise in nominal wages represented a real rise. In fact, prices typically rise more quickly than nominal wages, resulting in a *fall* in real wages. Consequently, firms increase their demand for labour; output expands and unemployment falls below its natural level.

Gradually workers recognise that their real wages have fallen following the monetary expansion. This puts further upward pressure on money wages. In the long run, as expectations of inflation converge on actual inflation, all the extra demand is absorbed in higher inflation. Output falls to its potential level and unemployment rises back to the natural rate.

If unemployment is to be reduced in the long run, therefore, this vertical Phillips curve must be shifted to the left. This will be achieved by a reduction in the natural (equilibrium) rate of unemployment (U_n), *not* by an increase in demand. To reduce the natural rate, argued the monetarists, supply-side policies would be needed.

 Give some examples of supply-side policies that would help to reduce the natural rate of unemployment.

Definition

Adaptive expectations hypothesis The theory that people base their expectations of inflation on past inflation rates.

The new classical school

The **new classical school** took on increasing significance during the 1970s and 1980s. The monetarist view was that markets adjust relatively quickly, but that there may be disequilibrium in the short run.

In contrast, new classical economists believed that markets clear continuously. Market outcomes are the result of optimal responses of economic agents. The implication of **continuous market clearing** for the labour market is that all unemployment is equilibrium unemployment. The assumption of continuous market clearing has another important implication: the distinction between the short run and long run breaks down.

Another key assumption of the new classical school is **rational expectations**. This means that economic agents use all available information and predict inflation, or any other macroeconomic variable, as well as they can. The important point here is that, unlike with adaptive expectations, economic agents avoid making the same error repeatedly. Therefore, errors are random, which means that, on average, economic agents' expectations of inflation are correct.

The implication of these two assumptions, continuous market clearing and rational expectations, is that a change in aggregate demand will simply cause a change in prices, not a change in output and employment, even in the short run. This applies equally to both a rise and a fall in aggregate demand.

But, with market clearing and rational expectations, how did new classical models explain the business cycle?

Monetary surprises

The first strand of new classical models focused on how imperfect information could generate unexpected inflation. The work was led by Professor Robert Lucas, who, like Friedman, spent much of his career at the University of Chicago. Lucas was a recipient of the Nobel Memorial Prize in Economics in 1995 (see Box 20.5).

The monetary surprise model captured how *unexpected* changes in monetary policy could result in both firms and workers changing their supply decisions such that the economy temporarily deviated from equilibrium. Consider an unexpected monetary expansion that, because it causes aggregate demand to grow more than expected, results in the inflation rate being higher than expected. If, as general prices rise, workers and firms wrongly believe that the *real* price of their labour and output has increased, they will supply more. Conversely, an unexpected monetary contraction would see labour supply and output fall. This time, workers and firms would wrongly infer that a general fall in wages and prices represents a real fall in the price of labour and output.

Why are monetary surprises less likely with independent central banks pursuing an inflation target? Would monetary surprises still be possible in such circumstances?

The key to economic fluctuations in the monetary surprise model is errors in expectations of inflation that arise from imperfect information. Once economic agents recognise these errors, output and employment return to their equilibrium levels. In the presence of rational expectations and continuous market clearing, anticipated changes in economic policy have no effect on output and employment, which remain at their equilibrium levels. This prediction is known as the **policy ineffectiveness proposition**.

The monetary surprise models and the policy ineffectiveness proposition were highly contentious. Two principal concerns arose.

The first concern was the assumption of *continuous market clearing*. A key Keynesian response, as we shall see in the next section, was to explore why instead prices might adjust only *slowly* in clearing product and labour markets. If prices do adjust slowly then economic policy can have real effects on output and employment, even in the presence of rational expectations.

The second concern was the conclusion of *money neutrality*, whereby expected changes in monetary policy do not affect output. Could the business cycle be explained only by *monetary surprises?* It was this second concern that new classical economists attempted to address with the development of real business cycle models.

Real business cycles

Like the monetary surprise models, **real business cycle theories** also assume continuous market clearing and rational expectations. However, real business cycle theories challenge the traditional understanding of the business cycle as fluctuations in real GDP around potential (natural) output.

Definitions

New classical school A body of economists who believe that markets are highly competitive and clear very rapidly; any expansion of demand will feed through virtually instantaneously into higher prices, giving a vertical short-run as well as a vertical long-run Phillips curve.

Continuous market clearing The assumption that all markets in the economy continuously clear so that the economy is permanently in equilibrium.

Rational expectations Expectations based on the current situation. These expectations are based on the information people have to hand. While this information may be imperfect and therefore people will make errors, these errors will be random.

Policy ineffectiveness proposition The conclusion drawn from new classical models that when economic agents anticipate changes in economic policy, output and employment remain at their equilibrium (or natural) levels.

Real business cycle theories The new classical theory which explains fluctuations in real GDP in terms of economic shocks, especially technology shocks, and which have persistent effects on potential output.

Instead, it is argued, the business cycle is principally movements in potential output itself: in other words, shifts in aggregate supply, not aggregate demand. These movements come from frequent 'shocks' that hit the economy, which permanently affect the economy's growth path.

Real business cycle theories typically focus on supply-side shocks and, in particular, technology shocks. These shocks are also known as 'impulses'. For example, a technological breakthrough in telecommunications could shift aggregate supply to the right and generate economic growth.

By arguing that frequent technology shocks are an important explanation of business cycles, real business cycle theory challenges the traditional view that technology is important largely when explaining the *long-term* rate of economic growth and development. Instead, real business cycle theories dispense with the distinction between the business cycle and long-term economic growth; supply-side shocks are important both in the short run and in the long run.

The observed economic outcomes of economic shocks, such as those from technological change, are assumed to represent the optimal decisions of economic agents (firms, households, government, etc.). In making consumption and production choices, economic agents take into account the impact of their choices not only in the current period, but in all future periods too.

This implies that expansion in the economy's output (e.g. from a technological breakthrough) represents purposeful decisions by firms to increase output and workers to increase their labour supply.

Conversely, decreases in real GDP result from firms deciding to reduce output and workers to reduce labour supply. In such cases, the initial leftward shift in aggregate supply could come from a structural change: say, a decline in older manufacturing industries. Because of the immobility of labour, not all those laid off will find work elsewhere. Structural unemployment (part of equilibrium unemployment) rises and output falls. But there is no disequilibrium unemployment. All unemployment is still equilibrium unemployment.

The role of representative agents.   Real business cycle models frequently use a representative agent (i.e. a typical person or firm) in order to analyse and illustrate the impact of economic shocks (impulses). Agents are assumed to allocate their time between work and leisure in order to maximise lifetime utility.

Consider the effect of a positive supply-side shock, such as an improvement in the quality of capital. This enables the representative agents to produce and earn more now. If they believe that the benefits of this positive shock will be relatively short-lived, the incentive to work and earn more now is especially strong. Therefore, following positive economic shocks, economic agents actively choose to work more. In doing so, output rises. Some of the increased income from production is invested, raising the flow of investment and increasing the capital stock by more than would otherwise have been the case. The fact that the economy's capital stock rises increases possible future output levels.

Where economic shocks are negative, such as from declines in energy sources, economic agents choose to work less. This reduces current output and reduces the flow of investment. In this case, the capital stock will be lower than it would otherwise have been. This then reduces possible future output levels.

 Assume that there is a positive economic shock and the economy expands. Why may it continue to expand for some time? Why may the expansion eventually cease and be followed by a recession?

Government policies

Governments up to the late 1970s responded to rising unemployment by boosting aggregate demand (the balance of payments permitting). This, however, as monetarists and new classical economists predicted, led only to more inflation, fuelled by rising expectations of inflation.

When governments eventually did curb the growth in aggregate demand, as the Thatcher government did after 1979, it took time for expectations to adjust downwards. As we saw earlier, to help bring inflationary expectations down, the UK government from the late 1970s to the mid-1980s set targets for the growth of money supply – largely consistent with monetarist principles. In the meantime, there was a further temporary rise in unemployment due to wage rises being slow to moderate.

Nevertheless the pursuit of these policies did, according to monetarists, lead to a dramatic fall in the rate of inflation, and eventually the rise in unemployment was reversed.

The rise of monetarist and new classical macroeconomics was reflected in economic policy during the 1980s, in both the UK and the USA, and increasingly in other countries, by an increased reliance on the market. Policies of privatisation and deregulation were pursued; union power was curbed; and tax rates were cut. Controls over the financial system were reduced, as we shall see in Chapter 18, with banks given much more freedom to expand their activities. This 'supply-side' revolution was designed to increase incentives to work, to invest and to innovate. We explore these market-orientated supply-side policies in Chapter 23.

Section summary

1. Monetarists argued that there is a close correlation between the rate of growth of the money supply and the rate of inflation. Increases in money supply cause increases in aggregate demand, which in turn cause inflation. Along with the classical economists, they argued that output and employment are determined independently of money supply (at least in the long run). This means that a deflationary policy to cure inflation will *not* in the long run cause a fall in output or a rise in unemployment.

2. Monetarists thus argued that the long-run Phillips curve is vertical. Its position along the horizontal axis will depend on the level of equilibrium or 'natural' unemployment.

3. Building on monetarist ideas, early new classical macroeconomic models focused on how monetary surprises induce short-term deviations in unemployment from its natural rate. However, under the assumptions of rational expectations and continuous market clearing, unemployment does not deviate from its natural rate if monetary policy is anticipated.

4. Real business cycle theorists argued that the business cycle is caused by economic shocks, such as technology shocks, which affect the path of potential output. Observed economic outcomes, including the path of real GDP, are the result of optimal choices made by rational economic agents under continuous market clearing.

16.6 THE KEYNESIAN RESPONSE

Market imperfections

Monetarist and new classical ideas began radically to reshape macroeconomics through the 1970s and 1980s. Importantly, these ideas were affecting policy making too. In particular, there was a growing recognition of the significance of the supply side of the economy with less emphasis on government using its discretion over monetary and fiscal policy to fine-tune the economy.

Many Keynesians could agree with monetarists and new classical economists on one point. If demand is expanded too fast and for too long, inflation will result – and there will be a certain amount of unemployment of labour (and other resources too) that cannot be eliminated simply by expanding aggregate demand. However, their views on the behaviour of markets and, hence, the extent to which governments should 'sit back' differed markedly.

The task that a large number of academic Keynesians began addressing was to gain a better understanding of *aggregate supply*. The motivation was to develop stronger theoretical explanations of why markets may be slow to adjust. Consequently, a large amount of work was undertaken into market imperfections and the frictions which cause prices to be 'sticky'. Much of the focus was to establish stronger *microeconomic* foundations. The group of Keynesians who have taken this approach have been subsequently labelled *new Keynesians*.

Menu costs and nominal price rigidity

The assumption of continuous market clearing is seen by many Keynesians as the most controversial of the new classical assumptions. New Keynesians have focused on the *frictions* that may cause prices to adjust only slowly following economic shocks, especially to aggregate demand.

New Keynesians argue that firms are often operating in imperfectly competitive markets (see Chapter 7). Therefore, firms are price makers rather than price takers as portrayed in the perfectly competitive model (see Chapter 6). In other words, firms set not just quantity but also price, according to their estimated demand functions.

However, a firm's product price may exhibit *stickiness* in the presence of demand shocks because of the *menu costs* of price changes (see Chapter 15, page 481). Menu costs include both the physical costs to firms in updating price lists and the costs incurred in determining and negotiating prices with customers and suppliers.

If the menu costs to an individual firm are larger than the forsaken profit from not adjusting prices, then the rational firm will not change its prices. When price rigidity is commonplace throughout the economy, any change in aggregate demand can have a significant effect on national output.

To illustrate the effect of price rigidity, consider Figure 16.10, which shows the situation of a monopolistically competitive firm facing a *decrease* in demand for its produce as a result of a decrease in aggregate demand in the economy. The firm's demand curve (D_1) is downward sloping, the elasticity depending on how close its competitors' products are as substitutes to its own. The marginal revenue (MR_1) curve lies below the demand curve (average revenue curve), because in reducing price to sell more units all units attract the lower price (see Chapter 5 pages 160–1). For simplicity we assume that marginal cost (MC) is constant across all output levels.

Definition

New Keynesians Economists who seek to explain how market imperfections and frictions can result in fluctuations in real GDP and the persistence of unemployment.

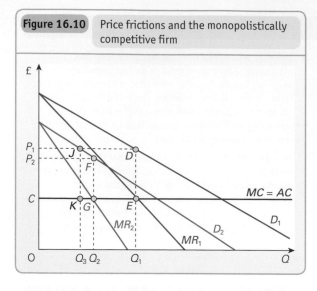

Figure 16.10 Price frictions and the monopolistically competitive firm

Before the decrease in aggregate demand, the firm is producing at output level Q_1, where marginal cost (MC) equals marginal revenue (MR_1), and selling its output at price P_1. Its profit is represented by the area CP_1DE.

The decrease in demand results in a leftward movement in both the demand curve (D_1 to D_2) and the marginal revenue curve (MR_1 to MR_2). In the absence of frictions, our price-setting firm will reduce price from P_1 to P_2 and output from Q_1 to Q_2. Profit falls to CP_2FG.

However, if frictions, such as those arising from menu costs, result in price stickiness, then output will fall further. If price remains at P_1 then output falls to Q_3. Profits fall to CP_1JK. Firms would be willing to incur this forsaken profit, $CP_2FG - CP_1JK$, if the menu costs incurred in reducing prices are greater.

The significance of menu costs in causing product prices to be sticky is that changes in aggregate demand can have significant effects on real GDP. Consequently, changes in the money supply affect the economy's output, meaning that money is not neutral as predicted by real business cycle theory. Furthermore, in the presence of frictions to market adjustment, government may need to intervene so as to affect the level of aggregate demand.

 What technological developments are likely to have reduced menu costs in recent years?

Sources of other frictions and imperfections

The extensive new Keynesian literature that has developed since the 1980s has identified a series of other market imperfections. These imperfections can help to reinforce the nominal rigidity in product prices arising from menu costs and so increase fluctuations in real GDP. Imperfections include the following:

- *Price inelasticity of demand*. Where competition is limited, demand will be less elastic. Under such circumstances a firm will be under less pressure to reduce prices if demand falls. In an economic downturn, therefore, firms may prefer to reduce output rather than cut prices. **KI 20 p171**

- *Anticipating other firms' pricing strategy*. If firms' products are close substitutes for one another, they are likely to be very wary of cutting prices for fear of retaliation from their rivals. They may prefer to reduce output during a downturn rather than risk a price war.

- *Sticky nominal wages*. Wage rates are largely determined through negotiation between workers and employers. The presence of contracts allows both sides to avoid the costs incurred in frequent wage negotiations and provide both with a degree of certainty. Even in the absence of contracts, workers are likely to be resistant to cuts in their money wages. They may prefer a reduction in hours, or the non-replacement of workers who leave, rather than take a cut in wages. Indeed, the flexibility of hours, often with 'zero-hours contracts', where workers have no guaranteed hours but are simply allocated hours on a weekly or monthly basis, means that employers are more likely to adjust hours than wage rates.

- *Real wage rigidity*. New Keynesians argue that equilibrium real wage rates may be above market-clearing levels. The result can be involuntary unemployment. As we saw in section 9.2 (pages 259–62), the **efficiency wage hypothesis** maintains that firms may pay wage rates *above* market levels in order to provide an incentive for workers. The implication that new Keynesians draw is that, in a downturn, a firm may be reluctant to cut real wages for fear of lowering morale and thereby reducing productivity. **TC 5 p54**

Insider–outsider theories emphasise the power of employees in resisting real wage cuts. Those currently employed (the **insiders**, see page 259) may, through their unions or close relationships with their employers, or because of the possession of specific skills, be able to prevent the unemployed (the **outsiders**) from competing wages down.

Definitions

Efficiency wage hypothesis The hypothesis that the productivity of workers is affected by the wage rate that they receive.

Insiders Those in employment who can use their privileged position (either as members of unions or because of specific skills) to secure pay rises, or resist wage cuts, despite an excess supply of labour (unemployment).

Outsiders Those out of work or employed on a casual, part-time or short-term basis, who have little or no power to influence wages or employment.

■ *Sources of finance.* During a downturn, both internal and external sources of finance for investment may diminish. The decline in demand will reduce profit and hence internal sources. What is more, banks may be less willing to lend, seeing risks rising in a downturn. The result is a decline in investment. During a boom, by contrast, sources of funds for investment are likely to increase. These 'pro-cyclical' changes in the availability of finance are thus likely to exacerbate existing fluctuations in real GDP.

■ *Attitudes towards debt.* In a boom, consumer and business confidence is likely to encourage borrowing. Debts are likely to rise. In a recession, however, with people more anxious about the future, consumers and firms may seek to reduce their debts by curbing spending. These effects could be reinforced by risk-averse financial institutions which reduce lending, seeing it as riskier when firms are more likely to go out of business or individuals more likely to lose their jobs. Again, this means that bank lending tends to be pro-cyclical and exacerbates existing fluctuations in real GDP.

Hysteresis

In the early 1980s there was a recession, or slowdown, throughout the industrialised world. Unemployment rose to unprecedented levels. But as the world began to recover, unemployment remained stubbornly high. This focused minds on the extent to which current rates of unemployment affect the future path of unemployment. Could there be a persistence or inertia in unemployment rates? And, if so, why?

Keynesians argued that the rise in unemployment, though largely caused by a lack of demand, could not simply be reversed by a *rise* in demand. The recession had itself *caused* higher rates of unemployment to become embedded in the economy. The reason is that during a recession many people become deskilled and/or demoralised and firms become more cautious about taking on workers, preferring to manage with a smaller, more efficient workforce. What is more, as we saw above, people who remain employed (the *insiders*) are often able to secure wage increases for themselves, and prevent the unemployed (the *outsiders*) from competing wages down. Many of the unemployed thus remain unemployed.

This persistence of high unemployment that characterised many developed economies through the 1980s and into the 1990s and once more in the late 2000s and into the 2010s is known as *hysteresis*. This term, used in physics, refers to the lagging or persistence of an effect, even when the initial cause has been removed. In our context, it refers to the persistence of unemployment even when the initial demand deficiency no longer exists.

Past levels of aggregate demand and unemployment were thus affecting what new classical and macroeconomists refer

to as the ***natural rate of unemployment*** or what some Keynesians prefer to call the ***non-accelerating-inflation rate of unemployment (NAIRU)***.

The natural rate of unemployment is the unemployment rate consistent with market clearing in the labour market. It is the equilibrium unemployment rate. On the other hand, the NAIRU is the rate of unemployment in a world characterised by market imperfections and frictions where there is no pressures for a change in the inflation rate. While strictly speaking the natural rate and the NAIRU are theoretically different, the concepts are often used interchangeably.

 Why has UK unemployment been less persistent following the recession of 2008–10 than following that in the early 1980s? In other words, why has hysteresis been less of a problem in the UK in recent times?

Government intervention

Targeted government intervention may be needed to help smooth the path of aggregate demand. A substantial increase in demand may be necessary if the economy is in danger of falling into deep recession, as was the case in 2008–9. The debate then concerns the form that this intervention should take.

One approach is for the government to increase its expenditure on public works such as roads, school building and housing. The advantages of such infrastructural projects is that they can directly impact on the economy's potential output and, because they have a relatively low import content, increased expenditure on such projects does not lead to balance of payments problems.

Thereafter the government should maintain a high and stable demand, by appropriate demand-management policies. This should keep unemployment down and set the environment for long-term investment and growth.

Definitions

Hysteresis The persistence of an effect even when the initial cause has ceased to operate. In economics, it refers to the persistence of unemployment even when the demand deficiency that caused it no longer exists.

Natural rate of unemployment or non-accelerating-inflation rate of unemployment (NAIRU) The rate of unemployment consistent with a constant rate of inflation: the rate of unemployment at which the vertical long-run Phillips curve cuts the horizontal axis.

bias is commonly identified as a key economic benefit of central bank independence.

By contrast, the central bank sticking to an inflation target creates the stable environment necessary for the market to flourish: expectations will adjust to the target rate of inflation (assuming central banks are successful in achieving the target) and firms will be able to plan with more confidence. Investment is thereby encouraged and this, in turn, encourages a growth in potential output. In other words, sticking to the targets creates the best environment for the expansion of aggregate *supply*.

From the mid-1990s to 2007–8, these policies seemed to be successful. The period was dubbed 'the great moderation', with low and stable inflation and continuous economic growth. But then things went horribly wrong!

Section summary

1. During the 1990s a new mainstream consensus began to develop. It drew ideas principally from the new classical and new Keynesian schools. Central to most new consensus models are representative forward-looking economic agents who form rational expectations.

2. Dynamic stochastic general equilibrium (DSGE) models became the standard model of the economy. These allowed economists to model the impact of frequent economic shocks under certain assumptions about competition in product and labour markets and the speed with which these markets adjust to equilibrium.

3. Government policy moved to one of constrained discretion, with fiscal and monetary targets. This, it was argued, would provide the stable environment for the mixed market system to flourish and for firms and consumers to take a longer-term perspective.

16.8 THE FINANCIAL CRISIS AND THE SEARCH FOR A NEW CONSENSUS

The financial crisis and its aftermath

Throughout the late 1990s/early 2000s, many banks had massively increased their lending. In 2007, several smaller banks were in difficulties and some had to be bailed out. Then, in 2008, Lehman Brothers in the USA collapsed and was liquidated. With many of the world's major banks being seen as having too little capital, there was a real danger that many more would collapse. Lending between banks dried up and several banks had to be bailed out by their governments. There was a sharp reduction in banks' lending to customers. This 'credit crunch' led to a deep recession in many developed countries.

The impact of the banking crisis on the economy was on such a scale that inevitably important debates followed. These debates challenged the new macroeconomic consensus; after all, why had so few economists predicted the global financial crisis? Indeed, Queen Elizabeth II, on a visit to the London School of Economics in November 2008, asked why economists had got it so wrong. But economists were not slow in providing explanations.

Economists on the right tended to argue that the banking crisis was the result of too much government intervention. Such intervention, it was argued, had distorted incentives such that banks believed that they would not be allowed to fail (a moral hazard: see page 124). Consequently, financial institutions took excessive risks, expanding their balance sheets aggressively with too little loss-absorbing capital.

Economists on the left tended to argue that the banking crisis was the result of too *little* intervention. Financial institutions had been too lightly regulated and it was this that had resulted in excessive risk taking. Some on the left argue that the banking sector is prone to excessive lending during times of prosperity, which ultimately sows the seeds for financial crises (see Box 8.2 on page 226). In other words, the financial system is an important contributory factor to the business cycle. There are some who argue that tighter regulation should not simply involve increasing the loss-absorbing capital that banks are required to hold, which has been the mainstream response since the crisis. Rather, they would advocate a return to controls on the flows of credit, a policy which many countries began abandoning from the late 1970s.

Fiscal expansion to fiscal austerity

Despite disagreement about the causes of the financial crisis, the immediate priorities of policy makers were to ensure the stability of the financial system and to mitigate the effects on aggregate demand of the limited levels of credit now available for households and firms. There was initially a general consensus on the medicine to be applied.

The initial expansionary policies. First, vast amounts of liquidity were supplied to the banking sector. Second, fiscal stimulus packages were used to boost aggregate demand. In other words, the consensus was that central banks and governments needed to act.

This was not a time for passive economic policy. Rules and frameworks were loosened or applied more flexibly and in some cases even abandoned completely. We discuss this in more detail in Chapter 21.

Followed by austerity policies.   This consensus was to be relatively short-lived, however, as many countries saw a marked deterioration in the state of their public finances. Governments began running relatively large fiscal deficits which needed financing. These deficits were worsened by governments having to bale out banks and by the recession which saw tax revenues fall and the number claiming benefits rising.

Cutting the deficit became the new priority of many governments, including the Coalition government in the UK formed in 2010. Consequently, in a short space of time the UK witnessed a fiscal policy yo-yo with fiscal austerity (spending cuts and tax rises) replacing fiscal loosening.

This was not confined to the UK. In the eurozone the **sovereign debt crisis** became so serious that Greece, Portugal, Ireland and later Cyprus had to receive bailouts from European funds and the IMF. In return they were obliged to agree to severe fiscal austerity measures.

Debates over policy.   In the light of this turmoil, debates re-emerged amongst academics and policy makers over the economic costs of fiscal deficits and of public expenditure crowding out private expenditure. In effect, we were witnessing a rerun of some the debates of the 1920s and 1930s between classical and Keynesian economists (see pages 470–6).

Those on the political left took a more Keynesian line, believing that cutting the deficit too quickly would endanger the economic recovery, with private-sector demand unable to offset the cuts to public expenditure.

Those on the political right argued in favour of rapid deficit reduction. Without this, they argued, there would be upward pressure on interest rates as the confidence in the government's finances was undermined and as the public sector competed with the private sector for scarce resources. This was the line taken in the UK by the Coalition government's Chancellor of the Exchequer, George Osborne.

Debates about the state of macroeconomics

While the financial crisis raised debates amongst academics and policy makers about its causes and its remedies, it also fuelled a debate about the state of macroeconomics. The new mainstream consensus came under scrutiny. We have seen how this consensus brought together ideas from different schools of thought and, in particular, from monetarist, new classical and new Keynesian economists.

However, it is important to recognise that the views of macroeconomists in relation to key issues, particularly the flexibility of prices, the flexibility of aggregate supply, the role of expectations and the role of government policy (see section 16.2 on pages 465–7), tend to fall along a spectrum, rather than being in some very specific camp. The term 'schools of thought', while useful for providing a

flavour of alternative views on some of the really key issues, can be rather rigid and pigeonhole economists.

At the one end of the *spectrum of views* are those who see the free market as working well and who generally blame macroeconomic problems on excessive government intervention. At the other are those who see the free market as fundamentally flawed.

Then there are economists who were never party to the consensus. In particular, objections were raised by a group of Keynesians who have become known as **post-Keynesians**. They highlight some of the key features of Keynes' *General Theory* to explain why economies are not self-correcting. In particular, they stress the importance of what Keynes called 'animal spirits', or what is today known as sentiment or confidence. Changes in confidence can have fundamental effects on the behaviour of economic agents. For instance, the mood of the country's business community can be crucial in determining firms' investment and output decisions. Without appropriate demand-management policy, this mood can remain depressed into the long term.

Post-Keynesians and other **heterodox economists** also challenge most of the microeconomic assumptions on which other more 'mainstream' macroeconomic theories are based. Firms, for example, are not cold, rational profit maximisers, making calm calculations based on marginal analysis. Instead, firms make output decisions largely in response to anticipated demand, again based on their *confidence* in their market. The result is that anticipated demand changes are likely to lead to *output* and *employment* changes, not price changes.

Post-Keynesians tend to focus on a country's *institutions* and *culture* to explain how firms and consumers respond to economic stimuli. In other words, they try to base their explanations and policies on real-world institutional and behavioural information rather than on abstract models.

 Two economists disagree over the best way of tackling the problem of unemployment arising from the credit crunch and recession. For what reasons might they disagree? Are these reasons positive or normative?

Definitions

Sovereign debt crisis The financial and economic problems caused by excessive public-sector debt and by the fear that governments will be unable to raise sufficient finance to repay maturing debt.

Post-Keynesians Economists who stress the importance of institutional and behavioural factors, and the role of confidence in explaining the state of the economy. They argue that firms are more likely to respond to changes in demand by changing output rather than prices.

Heterodox economists Economists who reject the assumptions of neoclassical economics, in particular the assumptions of rational optimising behaviour. They highlight the importance of institutional behaviour and factors influencing human behaviour.

Emergence of a new consensus?

While some groups, including post-Keynesians, have consistently voiced their concerns about the new consensus, a more broad-based debate began to develop in the aftermath of the financial crisis. The debate extended to the macroeconomics curriculum being taught in universities. Conferences and working parties have considered both what should be taught and how it should be taught.

Problems with relying on micro foundations

One concern was the extent to which the new consensus had focused too heavily on developing microeconomic foundations and thereby applying a 'bottom-up' approach to analysing macroeconomic aggregates. In the process, often very technical and mathematical models emerged based around representative agents with rational expectations. Some economists pointed to the acronym spelt out by 'representative agents with rational expectations' – RARE. This is a reminder of the importance of the behavioural assumptions we attach to economic agents in our economic models.

Another issue with a purely 'bottom-up' approach to macroeconomic analysis is the fallacy of composition. We first came across this in Chapter 3 (see page 88) in the context of poor harvests. When one farmer alone has a poor harvest his or her revenue falls, but if all farmers have poor harvests total revenue may well rise. More generally, what applies in one case does not necessarily apply when repeated in all cases. This is important in macroeconomics because we are analysing aggregates. For this reason the fallacy of composition is also known as the *paradox of aggregates*.

The paradox of thrift.   The most commonly cited paradox of aggregates is the paradox of thrift (see Box 16.4). If one individual increases his or her propensity to save, the individual's saving increases and the individual can consume more in the future. However, if this is repeated by all individuals, it can lead to a fall in aggregate saving because the fall in consumption causes firms to produce less, which reduces national income.

The example of the paradox of thrift nicely illustrates the importance, when building macroeconomic models, of taking into account not only how individuals behave but how they *interact*. Consequently, it also illustrates how aggregate or group behaviour impacts on individual behaviour and well-being.

A contemporary example of the paradox of thrift is the attempt by economic agents, following the financial crisis, to improve their financial well-being by cutting back on spending to reduce their debts. The effect of their actions is an example of *downward causation*: the general effect of a cutback in spending was a decline in sales and production. For this reason it is known as the *paradox of debt*. If people sell assets, for instance a household sells property or shares, they receive funds which can be used to reduce their liabilities. However, if *all* economic agents do this, the value of particular types of assets, like housing or shares, falls. The result is that the aggregate net worth of economic agents may fall.

The importance of the financial sector

Unsurprisingly, given the financial crisis, there has been a keen debate around the assumptions made about the financial system in economic models. Financial frictions and imperfections had been incorporated in new consensus models. However, the financial crisis illustrated the importance of the *behavioural assumptions* we make about financial institutions and the way in which we model their *interaction* with other economic agents. Financial institutions need to be fully and appropriately incorporated in macroeconomic models. As the financial crisis showed, financial institutions can be acutely destabilising.

Areas of general agreement?

As we have seen, the financial crisis and its aftermath have re-energised long-standing macroeconomic debates, while also fuelling important debates about the state of macroeconomics in the 2010s. Nonetheless, we can attempt to identify some general points of agreement that have emerged in recent years, at least among the majority of economists:

- In the short run, changes in aggregate demand can have a major effect on output and employment. If there is a collapse in demand, as in 2008, governments and/or central banks should intervene through expansionary fiscal and/or monetary policies. Only a few extreme new classical economists would disagree with this proposition.
- In the long run, changes in aggregate demand will have much less effect on output and employment and much more effect on prices. In fact, many economists say that there will be *no* effect at all on output and employment, and that the whole effect will be on prices. There is still a substantial body of Keynesians, however, especially post-Keynesians, who argue that changes in aggregate demand *will* have substantial effects on long-term output and employment via changes in investment and hence in potential output.

> ### Definitions
>
> **Downward causation** The name given to the impact on individual behaviour or well-being of aggregate or group effects. This is an example of cumulative causation (Key Idea 35).
>
> **Paradox of debt (or paradox of deleveraging)** The paradox that one individual can increase his or her net worth by selling assets, but if this is undertaken by a large number of people aggregate net worth declines because asset prices fall.

| BOX 16.4 | THE PARADOX OF THRIFT | EXPLORING ECONOMICS |

When prudence is folly

The classical economists argued that saving was a national virtue. More saving would lead via lower interest rates to more investment and faster growth. Keynes was at pains to show the opposite. Saving, far from being a national virtue, could be a national vice.

Remember the fallacy of composition (see Box 3.7 on page 88). Just because something is good for an individual, it does not follow that it is good for society as a whole. This fallacy applies to saving. If individuals save more, they will increase their consumption possibilities in the future. If society saves more, however, this may reduce its future income and consumption. As people save more, they will spend less. Firms will thus produce less. There will thus be a multiplied fall in income. The phenomenon of higher saving leading to lower national income is known as 'the paradox of thrift'.

But this is not all. Far from the extra saving encouraging more investment, the lower consumption will discourage firms from investing. There will then be a further multiplied fall in national income.

The paradox of thrift had in fact been recognised before Keynes, and Keynes himself referred to various complaints about 'underconsumption' that had been made back in the sixteenth and seventeenth centuries:

In 1598 Laffemas . . . denounced the objectors to the use of French silks on the grounds that all purchasers of French luxury goods created a livelihood for the poor, whereas the miser caused them to die in distress. In 1662 Petty justified 'entertainments, magnificent shews, triumphal arches, etc.', on the ground that their costs flowed back into the pockets of brewers, bakers, tailors, shoemakers and so forth . . . In 1695 Cary argued that if everybody spent more, all would obtain larger incomes 'and might then live more plentifully'.[1]

But despite these early recognitions of the danger of underconsumption, the belief that saving would increase the prosperity of the nation was central to classical economic thought.

? *Is an increase in saving ever desirable?*

[1] J. M. Keynes, *The General Theory of Employment, Interest and Money* (Macmillan, 1967), pp. 358–9.

- There is no simple long-run trade-off between inflation and unemployment. There is still disagreement, however, as to whether there is no relationship between them at all (i.e. the long-run Phillips curve is vertical), or whether they are connected indirectly via the long-term effects of changes in aggregate demand on investment etc.

- Expectations have an important effect on the economy. There is still disagreement, however, as to whether it is people's expectations of price changes or of output changes that are more important. Also it is difficult to model people's expectations when these can so easily be affected by random shocks; and also where optimism can sometimes build in a burst of 'irrational exuberance' or pessimism descend in a cloud of despondency, while at other times optimism or pessimism can quickly fade.

- Excessive growth in the money supply will lead to inflation. Some economists argue that the quantity theory of money holds in the long run (i.e. that inflation is *entirely* due to increases in the money supply). Others argue that the relationship is more general. Nevertheless, the consensus is that governments should avoid allowing the money supply to grow too rapidly.

- Controlling inflation through control of the money supply, however, is difficult, since money supply itself is not easy to control. Even if it were possible to control money supply accurately, there is a time lag between changes in money supply and the resulting changes in

inflation. This makes a precise control of inflation by this means very difficult. Most economists, therefore, argue that it is easier to control inflation by controlling interest rates, since this directly affects aggregate demand. Most central banks around the world today therefore use interest rate changes to achieve a target rate of inflation.

- If the economy is in deep recession, most economists agree that it may be necessary to expand the money supply, rather than relying on cuts in interest rates. However, monetary expansion (known as 'quantitative easing') does not directly affect spending. Banks have to be willing to lend the extra money and individuals and firms have to be willing to borrow and spend it.

- Macroeconomic policy should not focus exclusively on the demand side. Long-term growth depends primarily on changes in supply (i.e. in potential output). It is important, therefore, for governments to develop an effective supply-side policy if they want to achieve faster economic growth. There is still disagreement, however, over the forms that supply-side policy should take: should it focus on freeing up the market, or should it focus on various forms of government intervention to compensate for market deficiencies?

- Governments' ability to control their country's macroeconomic destiny is being increasingly eroded by the process of globalisation. As countries become more and more interdependent, and as capital moves more and more freely around the globe, so there is a growing need for co-ordinated policies between governments to tackle problems of global recessions or excessive exchange rate fluctuations. This lesson was brought home in 2008, when it became obvious that most countries were experiencing a collapse in aggregate demand following the banking crisis and the credit crunch. Leaders discussed common policy approaches at several international summits, including both bank rescue packages and expansionary fiscal and monetary policies.

It is perhaps too soon to say, particularly in the aftermath of the recent economic and financial crisis, what the future holds for the mainstream macroeconomic consensus. Nevertheless, economists are actively debating what the subject should like and what should be in the university macroeconomic curriculum.

As the book progresses, we will be looking at the various areas of agreement and disagreement in more detail. One thing is certain: these are incredibly fascinating times to be studying macroeconomics.

Section summary

1. During the 1990s a new mainstream consensus began to develop. It drew ideas principally from the new classical and new Keynesian schools. Central to most new consensus models are representative forward-looking economic agents who form rational expectations.

2. Dynamic stochastic general equilibrium (DSGE) models became the standard models of the economy. These allowed economists to examine the impact of frequent economic shocks under certain assumptions about competition in product and labour markets and the speed with which these markets adjust to equilibrium.

3. There are many shades of opinion among economists, from extreme new classical economists who advocate almost complete laissez-faire to post-Keynesian and heterodox economists who focus much more on individual and institutional behaviour and who see markets as having many failings. In between comes a whole spectrum of opinions and theories about the relative effectiveness of markets and the government in achieving the various macroeconomic goals.

4. The financial crisis and its aftermath reignited long-standing debates about policy, while also fuelling debates about the state of macroeconomics. Key concerns included the importance that had been placed on developing models with microeconomic foundations, the appropriateness of the behavioural assumptions of economic agents and assumptions made around the role of the financial system.

5. Despite these disagreements, most economists would agree on the following points: changes in aggregate demand have a direct effect on output and employment in the short run, but either no effect or a far less certain effect in the long run; there is no simple long-run trade-off between inflation and unemployment; expectations have an important effect on the economy, but can be affected in ways that are not easy to predict; excessive growth in the money supply causes inflation; it is easier to achieve inflation targets by controlling interest rates than by controlling money supply; monetary expansion is an important policy tool in tackling recession; changes on the supply side of the economy are the major determinant of long-term growth; globalisation reduces individual countries' ability to control their economies.

END OF CHAPTER QUESTIONS

1. In a given economy, the supply of money is £10 billion; the velocity of circulation of money (spent on final goods and services) is 3; and the price index is 2.00.
   (a) What is the level of real national income?
   (b) How much have prices risen (in percentage terms) since the base year?
   (c) Assume that money supply increases by 10 per cent and that the velocity of circulation remains constant. By what percentage will prices rise if
      (i) there is no increase in real national income;
      (ii) real national income increases by 10 per cent;
      (iii) real national income increases by 5 per cent?

2. In what way will the nature of aggregate supply influence the effect of a change in aggregate demand on prices and real national income?

3. Criticise the classical theory that higher government spending will necessarily crowd out private spending.

4. Criticise the use of increasing government expenditure as a means of reducing unemployment.

5. In what way may short-term demand-management policies help to stabilise the economy? What problems occur in the use of such policies?

6. What explanations can you give for the increase in *both* unemployment and inflation in the 1970s?

7. What do you understand by the policy invariance proposition? On what assumptions is the proposition based?

8. Identify a series of possible frictions which could affect the speed with which markets adjust or which affect the nature of market equilibria.

9. What is meant by hysteresis when applied to unemployment? How do you account for this phenomenon in the 1980s?

10. What will cause people to expect higher rates of inflation? How will expectations of inflation affect the actual rate of inflation?

11. Explain how pro-cyclical lending criteria applied by financial institutions could amplify fluctuations in real GDP.

12. What is meant by the paradox of aggregates? Of what importance might they be for how we analyse macroeconomic problems?

Online resources

Additional case studies in MyEconLab

16.1 **The equation of exchange.** This examines two more versions that are commonly used: the Fisher version and the Cambridge version.

16.2 **Money and inflation in ancient Rome.** A very early case study of the quantity theory of money: how the minting of extra coins by the Romans caused prices to rise.

16.3 **Thomas Malthus, David Ricardo and Jean-Baptiste Say.** A look at the work of three of the most famous classical economists and their degree of optimism or pessimism about the working of the free market.

16.4 **The Great Depression and the return to the gold standard.** A time of great hardship and sacrifice.

16.5 **Classical 'remedies' for unemployment.** How the policies advocated by the classical economists to cure unemployment would, according to Keynes, make the problem worse.

16.6 **John Maynard Keynes (1883–1946).** A profile of the great economist.

16.7 **A little bit less of this and a little bit more of that.** Fine-tuning in 1959 and 1960.

16.8 **'You've never had it so good.'** The claim in 1957 by Harold Macmillan, the UK Conservative Prime Minister, that governments were now able to manage the economy so as to give growing prosperity.

16.9 **Milton Friedman (1912–2006).** A profile of the most influential of the monetarist economists.

16.10 **A spectrum of views.** An overview of the different schools of macroeconomic thought.

Websites relevant to this chapter

See sites listed at the end of Chapter 17 on page 522.

MyEconLab

This book can be supported by MyEconLab, which contains a range of additional resources, including an online homework and tutorial system designed to test and build your understanding.

You need both an access card and a course ID to access MyEconLab:

1. Is your lecturer using MyEconLab? Ask your lecturer for your course ID.

2. Has an access card been included with the book at a reduced cost? Check the inside back cover of the book.

3. If you have a course ID but no access card, go to: http://www.myeconlab.com/ to buy access to this interactive study programme.

Macroeconomic Models, Theories and Policy

17	Short-run Macroeconomic Equilibrium	494
18	Banking, Money and Interest Rates	523
19	The Relationship between the Money and Goods Markets	560
20	Aggregate Supply, Unemployment and Inflation	593
21	Fiscal and Monetary Policy	625
22	Long-term Economic Growth	669
23	Supply-side Policies	684

We now build on the foundations of Part E. We will see why economies grow over the longer term but fluctuate in the short term and what governments can do to prevent these fluctuations.

In the following three chapters, we look at what determines the level of national income and the role that money plays in the process. Then, in Chapter 20 we look at the relationship between inflation and unemployment. In Chapter 21, we look at government policy to stabilise the economy. Finally, in Chapters 22 and 23, we turn to the long run and ask how economies can sustain faster growth.

Short-run Macroeconomic Equilibrium

CHAPTER MAP

17.1 Background to the theory	**495**
The relationship between aggregate demand and national income	495
Introducing the Keynesian 45° line diagram	495
Consumption	496
Withdrawals	499
Injections	501
17.2 The determination of national income	**507**
Equilibrium national income	507
The multiplier: the withdrawals and injections approach	507
The multiplier: the income and expenditure approach	510
*The multiplier: some qualifications	511
The relationship between the 45° line diagram and the aggregate demand and supply diagram	512
17.3 The simple Keynesian analysis of unemployment and inflation	**513**
'Full-employment' national income	513
The deflationary gap	513
The inflationary gap	513
Unemployment and inflation at the same time	514
The relationship between the *AD/AS* diagram and the 45° line diagram	515
17.4 The Keynesian analysis of the business cycle	**516**
Instability of investment: the accelerator	516
The multiplier/accelerator interaction	518
Fluctuations in stocks	518
Fluctuations in borrowing and debt	519
Determinants of the course of the business cycle	520

In this chapter we look at the determination of national income, employment and inflation in the short run: i.e. over a period of up to around two years. The analysis is based on a model developed by Keynesians. Although many economists argue that this is not appropriate for analysing the performance of the macroeconomy over the longer term, most agree that the analysis is essentially true over the short term.

The model assumes that aggregate demand determines the level of economic activity in the economy. In other words, the nation's production and employment depend on the amount of spending. Too little spending will lead to unemployment. More spending will stimulate firms to produce more and employ more people. Too much spending, however, will cause inflation. This chapter examines this relationship between aggregate demand and national income (GDP), employment and inflation.

One important simplifying assumption is made: the rate of interest is fixed. This allows us for the time being to ignore what is happening to the amount of money in the economy. A fixed interest rate effectively means that the supply of money will passively rise or fall as aggregate demand rises or falls. In other words, if spending rises and hence the demand for money from the banking system also rises, there will be a corresponding increase in the amount of money made available and hence no need for interest rates to rise. In subsequent chapters, we will drop this assumption and take specific account of the role of money in the economy.

17.1 BACKGROUND TO THE THEORY

The relationship between aggregate demand and national income

This chapter explains what determines the level of national income (GDP) in the short run. It is based on the model developed by John Maynard Keynes, back in the 1930s.

The basic explanation is quite simple: the level of production in the economy depends on the level of aggregate demand. If people buy more, firms will produce more in response to this, providing they have spare capacity. If people buy less, firms will cut down their production and lay off workers. But just *how much* will national income rise or fall as aggregate demand changes? We will answer this as the chapter progresses.

First, let us return to the circular flow of income that we looked at in Chapter 14. This is illustrated in Figure 17.1. Looking at the bottom of the diagram, the consumption of domestically produced goods (C_d) and the three withdrawals (W) – net saving (S), net taxes (T) and spending on imports (M) – all depend on the level of national income (Y). In fact, in the model, national income must always equal consumption of domestic goods plus withdrawals: there is nothing else people can do with their incomes!

$$Y \equiv C_d + W$$

Moving now to the top part of Figure 17.1, total spending in the economy on the goods and services of domestic firms is what we have already defined as aggregate demand (AD). In the Keynesian model that we are examining in this chapter, it is normally referred to as **aggregate expenditure (E)**. (This is useful to distinguish it from the AD and AS model that we looked at in Chapter 15.) Aggregate expenditure consists of C_d plus the three injections (J): investment in the domestic economy (I), government expenditure in the domestic economy (G) and expenditure from abroad on the country's exports (X):

$$AD \equiv E \equiv C_d + J$$

In equilibrium, withdrawals equal injections. (We demonstrated this in Chapter 14.) Since national income (Y) is simply withdrawals plus C_d, and aggregate expenditure (E) is simply injections plus C_d, it follows that in equilibrium national income must equal aggregate expenditure. To summarise:

$$W = J$$
$$\therefore \; C_d + W = C_d + J$$
$$\therefore \; Y = E (= AD)$$

Whenever aggregate expenditure ($C_d + J$) exceeds national income ($C_d + W$), injections will exceed withdrawals. Firms will respond to the extra demand by producing more and hence employing more factors of production. National income will thus rise. But as national income rises, so too will saving, imports and the amount paid in taxes: in other words, withdrawals will rise. Withdrawals will go on rising until they equal injections: until a new equilibrium has been reached. To summarise:

$$J > W \rightarrow Y \uparrow \rightarrow W \uparrow \text{ until } W = J$$

But *how much* will national income rise when aggregate demand (expenditure) rises? What will the new equilibrium level of national income be? To answer this question we must examine the relationship between national income and the component parts of the circular flow of income: consumption, withdrawals and injections. This relationship is shown in the Keynesian '45° line diagram'.

Introducing the Keynesian 45° line diagram

In this model, it is assumed that the levels of consumption and withdrawals are determined by the level of national income. Since national income is part of the model, we say that consumption and withdrawals are **endogenous**. This means that they vary with one of the other components of the model (i.e. income). Injections, however, are assumed to be **exogenous**: they are determined independently of what is going on in the model; they do *not* depend on the level of national income.

Figure 17.1   A simplified circular flow of income model

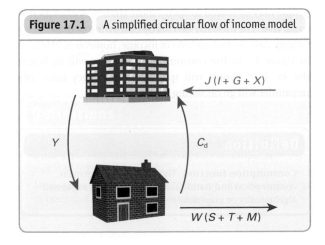

$J (I + G + X)$

Y

C_d

$W (S + T + M)$

Definitions

Aggregate expenditure (E) Aggregate demand in the Keynesian model: i.e. $C_d + J$.

Endogenous variable A variable whose value is determined by the model of which it is part.

Exogenous variable A variable whose value is determined independently of the model of which it is part.

balance sheets detail the sector's holding of financial assets and liabilities and of physical assets. The balance of financial assets over liabilities on the financial balance sheet is the household sector's net financial wealth. The household sector's net worth is the sum of its net financial wealth and its physical wealth.

Changes to the household balance sheets affect the sector's financial health – sometimes referred to as its level of financial distress. Such changes can have a significant impact on short-term prospects for household spending. For instance, a declining net worth to income ratio is an indicator of greater financial distress. This could be induced by falling house prices or falling share prices. In response to this we might see the sector engage in precautionary saving, whereby households attempt to build up a buffer stock of wealth. This buffer stock acts as a form of security blanket. Alternatively, households may look to repay some of their outstanding debt. Therefore, the impact of a worsening balance sheet may be to weaken spending, while improvements on the balance sheet may strengthen the growth of consumption. The household balance sheets are discussed in Box 17.2.

Consumer sentiment. If people are uncertain about their future income prospects, or fear unemployment, they are likely to be cautious in their spending. Surveys of consumer confidence are closely followed by policy makers (see Box 17.3) as an indicator of the level of future spending.

Expectations of future prices. If people expect prices to rise, they tend to buy durable goods such as furniture and cars before this happens.

The distribution of income. The poor have a higher *mpc* than the rich, with very little left over to save. A redistribution of national income from the poor to the rich will therefore tend to reduce the total level of consumption in the economy.

Tastes and attitudes. If people have a 'buy now, pay later' mentality, or a craving for consumer goods, they are likely to have a higher level of consumption than if their tastes are more frugal. The more 'consumerist' and materialistic a nation becomes, the higher will its consumption be for any given level of income.

The age of durables. If people's cars, carpets, clothes, etc., are getting old, they will tend to have a high level of 'replacement' consumption, particularly after a recession when they had cut back on their consumption of durables. Conversely, as the economy reaches the peak of the boom, people are likely to spend less on durables as they have probably already bought the items they want.

Movements along and shifts in the consumption function

The effect on consumption of a change in national income is shown by a movement *along* the consumption function.

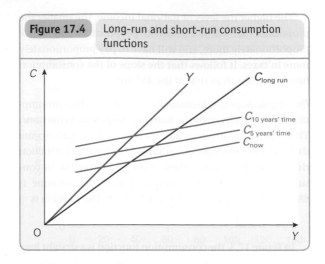

Figure 17.4 Long-run and short-run consumption functions

A change in any of the other determinants is shown by a *shift* in the consumption function.

 What effect will the following have on the mpc: (a) the rate of income tax rises; (b) the economy begins to recover from recession; (c) people anticipate that the rate of inflation is about to rise; (d) the government redistributes income from the rich to the poor? In each case sketch what would happen to the consumption function.

Long-run and short-run consumption functions

The long-run consumption function is likely to be steeper than the short-run one (see Figure 17.4).

In the short run, people may be slow to respond to a rise in income. Perhaps they are cautious about whether their higher income will last, or are slow to change their consumption habits. In the short run, then, people may have a relatively low *mpc*. In the long run, however, people have time to adjust their consumption patterns.

Assuming that national income rises over time, the long-run consumption function will be intersected by a series of short-run ones. Each year's short-run function will be above the previous year's.

 Which is likely to show the greater variation from one person to another at any given level of income: the short-run mpc or the long-run mpc?

Consumption of domestically produced goods (C_d)

The parts of consumption that go on imports and indirect taxes constitute withdrawals from the circular flow of income and thus do not contribute to aggregate demand. We shall concentrate on the part of consumption that *does*: namely, the consumption of domestic product (C_d). The C_d function lies below the C function, as in Figure 17.5. The gap between them constitutes imports of consumer goods and indirect taxes.

Figure 17.5 The consumption of domestic product

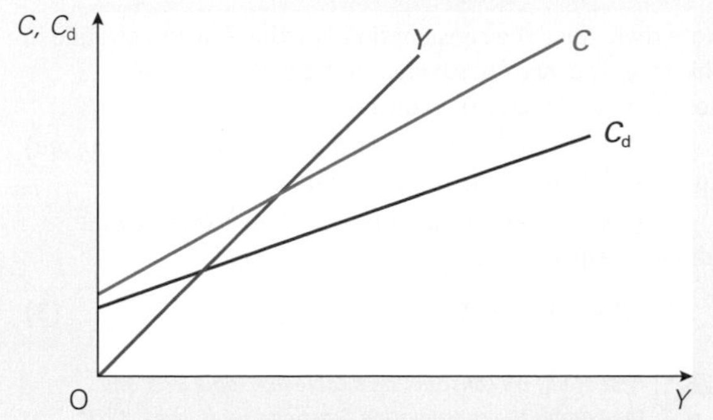

*LOOKING AT THE MATHS

Let us examine the relationship between C and C_d a bit more closely. When people make consumption decisions, this is largely based on their *disposable* income (Y_{dis}), where disposable income is income after the payment of income taxes and the receipt of benefits. We use the term 'net income taxes (T_i)' to refer to income taxes minus benefits. Thus

$$Y_{dis} = Y - T_Y$$

Also, people tend not to distinguish between domestic goods and imports when they make consumption decisions. Let us then focus on total consumption (C), not just the consumption of domestic products (C_d).

To get a better understanding of people's consumption behaviour, we could express the marginal propensity to consume all products (domestic and imported) relative to disposable income. Let us call this term mpc' (rather than mpc or $mpcd$) where

$$mpc' = \frac{\Delta C}{\Delta Y_{dis}} = \frac{\Delta C}{\Delta Y - \Delta T_Y} \qquad (1)$$

Note that the consumption term C refers to consumers' total consumption expenditure, not the net amount received by domestic firms (C_d). To get from C to C_d, we would have to subtract the amount spent on imports (M) and the amount paid in indirect taxes, such as VAT and excise duties, (T_E). Thus

$$C_d = C - M - T_E \text{ or } C = C_d + M + T_E$$

Thus

$$\Delta C = \Delta C_d + \Delta M + \Delta T_E \qquad (2)$$

Substituting equation (2) in equation (1) gives

$$mpc' = \frac{\Delta C_d + \Delta T_E + \Delta M}{\Delta Y - \Delta T_Y} \qquad (3)$$

Contrast this with the mpc_d, where

$$mpc_d = \frac{\Delta C_d}{\Delta Y} \qquad (4)$$

Withdrawals

All three withdrawals – net saving, net taxes and import expenditure – depend on the level of national income. They are thus all *endogenously* determined within the model.

Net saving

As with consumption, the major determinant of net saving (i.e. saving minus consumer borrowing and drawing on past savings) is income. As income increases, and a decreasing fraction of it goes on consumption, so an increasing fraction of it will be saved. The rich can afford to save a larger proportion of their income than the poor.

The proportion of an increase in national income that is saved is given by the **marginal propensity to save** (*mps*):

$$mps = \Delta S/\Delta Y$$

Other determinants of saving. To a large extent these are the same as the other determinants of consumption, since most things that encourage people to spend more will thereby encourage them to save less.

It might be easy to get the impression that saving is merely what is left over after consumption has taken place. In fact, for many people the decision to save is a very positive one. They might be saving up for something they are eager to buy but cannot afford at the moment, or saving for retirement. Indeed, people may be encouraged to save *more* by various factors, such as changes in pension provisions or new government-sponsored saving schemes.

> *Go through each of the determinants of consumption that were listed in the previous section and consider how they will affect saving. Are there any determinants of consumption that will not cause saving to rise if consumption is caused to fall?*

Net taxes

As national income increases, so the amount paid in tax will also increase. The **marginal tax propensity** (*mpt*) is the proportion of an increase in national income paid in taxes:[1]

$$mpt = \Delta T/\Delta Y$$

The *mpt* depends on tax rates. In a simple world where there was only one type of tax, which was charged at a

---

[1] We have defined net taxes as taxes minus benefits (i.e. the net flow from the household sector to the government). For our purposes, then, the *mpt* is the proportion of any rise in income going in taxes and reduced benefits.

Definitions

Marginal propensity to save The proportion of an increase in national income saved: $= \Delta S/\Delta Y$.

Marginal tax propensity The proportion of an increase in national income paid in tax: $= \Delta T/\Delta Y$.

*BOX 17.1 USING CALCULUS TO DERIVE THE *MPC*

The consumption function can be expressed as an equation. For example, the consumption function of Table 17.1 and Figure 17.3 is given by the equation

$$C = 10 + 0.8Y \qquad (1)$$

 Try using this equation to derive the figures in Table 17.1.

From this equation we can derive an equation for *mpc*. It is found by differentiating the consumption function. Remember from previous calculus boxes what it is we are doing when we differentiate an equation. We are finding its rate of change. Thus by differentiating the consumption function, we are finding the rate of change of consumption with respect to income. But this is what we mean by the *mpc*.

The difference between using differentiation and the formula $\Delta C/\Delta Y$ is that with the former we are looking at the *mpc* at a single point on the consumption function. With the $\Delta C/\Delta Y$ formula we were looking at the *mpc* between two points.

Differentiating equation (1) gives

$$mpc = dC/dY = 0.8 \qquad (2)$$

Note that, since the consumption function is a straight line in this case, the *mpc* (which measures the slope of the consumption function) is constant.

What would we do to find the *mpc* of a non-linear (curved) consumption function? The procedure is the same.

Assume that the consumption function is given by the following equation:

$$C = 20 + 0.9Y - 0.001Y^2 \qquad (3)$$

 First of all, try constructing a table like Table 17.1 and then graph the consumption function that it gives. What is it about equation (3) that gives the graph its particular shape?

The *mpc* is given by dC/dY:

$$mpc = 0.9 - 0.002Y$$

1. *What are the values of mpc at incomes of (a) 20; (b) 100?*
2. *What happens to the value of mpc as national income increases? Is this what you would expect by examining the shape of the consumption function?*

---

constant rate – for example, an income tax of 20 per cent – the *mpt* would be given directly by the tax rate. In this example, for each extra pound earned, 20p would be paid in income tax. The *mpt* = $\Delta T/\Delta Y = 20/100 = 0.20$. In practice, of course, there are many types of tax charged at many different rates, and thus working out the *mpt* is more complicated.

In most countries, the *mpt* rises as national income rises. This is because income tax is progressive. At higher incomes, people pay a higher marginal rate of income tax. In the UK and many other countries, however, income tax became much less progressive in the 1980s and 1990s, but the *mpt* remained roughly the same because of rises in indirect taxes.

Imports

The higher the level of national income, the higher will be the amount spent on imports. The **marginal propensity to import** (*mpm*) is the proportion of a rise in national income that goes on imports:

$$mpm = \Delta M/\Delta Y$$

Definition

Marginal propensity to import The proportion of an increase in national income that is spent on imports: $mpm = \Delta M/\Delta Y$.

Note that we only count that part of the expenditure on imports that actually goes abroad. Amounts retained by the retailer, the wholesaler and the importer, and amounts paid in indirect taxes, are excluded.

Whether the *mpm* rises or falls as national income rises depends on the nature of a country's imports. If a country imports predominantly basic goods, which have a relatively low income elasticity of demand, the rate of increase in their consumption would tail off rapidly as incomes increase. The *mpm* for such a country would thus also rapidly decrease.

If, however, a country's imports were mainly of luxury goods, they would account for an increasing proportion of any rise in national income: the *mpm* would rise.

 If a country imports a whole range of goods whose average income elasticity of demand is the same as for home-produced goods, will the mpm rise or fall as national income rises?

The determinants of the level of imports. Apart from national income, there are a number of other determinants of the level of imports:

■ *Relative prices.* If the prices of home-produced goods go up relative to the prices of imports, the level of imports will rise. The rate of exchange is a major influence here. The higher the rate of exchange, the cheaper will imports be and hence the more will be spent on them.

- *Tastes*. If consumer tastes shift towards foreign goods and services, imports will rise. For example, it might become more popular to go abroad for your holidays.
- *Relative quality*. If the quality of foreign goods and services increases relative to that of domestic goods and services, imports will rise.
- *The determinants of consumption*. Since imports of goods and services are part of *total* consumption (as opposed to C_d), the various determinants of consumption that we looked at on pages 496–8 will also be determinants of imports.

The total withdrawals function

Remember that withdrawals consist of the three elements net saving, net taxes and imports, all of which rise as national income rises. A withdrawals function along with the corresponding consumption of domestic goods function is shown in Figure 17.6.

Note the relationship between the C_d and W curves. The steeper the slope of the one, the flatter the slope of the other. The reason for this is that C_d and W add up to total national income (Y):

$$Y = C_d + W$$

Since the 45° line measures $C_d + W$, the distance between the C_d function and the 45° line must equal withdrawals. Thus at point x, where national income is £100 billion and C_d is £70 billion, W must be £30 billion – the gap between C_d and the 45° line.

The marginal propensity to withdraw

The formula for the **marginal propensity to withdraw** (*mpw*) is as we would expect:

$$mpw = \Delta W / \Delta Y$$

The *mpw* is the slope of the withdrawals function. Note that, since $W = S + T + M$, *mpw* must equal *mps* + *mpt* + *mpm*. For example, if for any rise in national income, 1/10 were saved, 2/10 paid in net taxes, and 2/10 spent on imports, then 5/10 must be withdrawn.

Note also that, since $C_d + W = Y$, $mpc_d + mpw$ must add up to 1. For example, if the country spends, say, 3/5 of any rise in income on domestically produced goods, the remaining 2/5 must go on withdrawals.

 If the slope of the C_d function is 3/4, what is the slope of the W function?

Injections

In simple Keynesian theory, injections are assumed not to depend on the level of national income: they are *exogenously* determined. This means that the injections function is drawn as a horizontal straight line. Injections will be at a given level irrespective of the level of national income. The injections function is the vertical addition of the investment, government expenditure and export functions, each of which is a horizontal straight line.

The assumption that injections are independent of national income makes the theory simpler. (It is possible to drop this assumption, however, without destroying the theory.) But is the assumption sufficiently realistic? Let us examine each of the injections in turn.

Investment

There are five major determinants of investment.

Increased consumer demand. Investment is to provide extra capacity. This will only be necessary, therefore, if consumer demand increases. The bigger the increase in consumer demand, the more investment will be needed.

You might think that, since consumer demand depends on the level of national income, investment must too, and that therefore our assumption that investment is independent of national income is wrong. But we are not saying that investment depends on the *level* of consumer demand; rather it depends on *how much it has risen*. If income and consumer demand are high but *constant*, there will be no point in firms expanding their capacity: no point in investing.

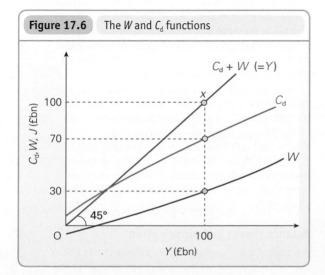

Figure 17.6 The W and C_d functions

Definition

Marginal propensity to withdraw The proportion of an increase in national income that is withdrawn from the circular flow: $mpw = \Delta W / \Delta Y$, where $mpw = mps + mpt + mpm$

BOX 17.2 THE HOUSEHOLD SECTOR BALANCE SHEETS

Net worth and consumption

Net worth

The national balance sheet details a country's net worth (i.e. wealth). This aggregates the net worth of the household sector, the corporate sector and the public sector.

We consider here the net worth of the household sector and the extent to which this may influence consumption (C).[1] The sector's net worth is the sum of its *net financial wealth* and *non-financial assets*:

- The household sector's net *financial* wealth is the stock of financial assets minus the stock of financial liabilities. Financial assets include money in savings accounts, shares and pension funds. Financial liabilities include debts secured against property, largely residential mortgages, and unsecured debts,

such as overdrafts and unpaid balances on credit cards.
- The stock of *non-financial* assets largely comprises the sector's residential housing wealth. Therefore, this is affected by changes in house prices.

The table summarises the net worth of the UK household sector. By the end of 2012 the sector had a stock of net worth estimated at over £7.61 trillion compared with £1.46 trillion at the end of 1987 – an increase of 420 per cent. This, of course, is a nominal increase, not a real increase, as part of it merely reflects the rise in asset prices.

Over the period net worth grew every year with the exceptions of 1994 (−2.1 per cent), 2001 (−2.0 per cent) and in 2008 (−11.7 per cent). The most rapid increase was observed in 1988 when net worth rose by 24 per cent.

Net worth of the household sector, 31 December 1987 and 2012

	1987			2012		
	£ billion	% of disposable income	% of GDP	£ billion	% of disposable income	% of GDP
Financial assets	840.0	319.0	195.5	4546.3	421.9	290.1
Financial liabilities	270.1	102.6	62.9	1546.7	143.5	98.7
Net financial wealth	**569.9**	**216.4**	**132.6**	**2999.6**	**278.3**	**191.4**
Non-financial assets	892.3	338.9	207.7	4611.0	427.9	294.2
Net worth	**1462.2**	**555.3**	**340.4**	**7610.7**	**706.2**	**485.6**

Source: Based on data from *National Balance Sheet, 2013 Estimates* and *Quarterly National Accounts, Q3 2013* (National Statistics).

To put the size of net worth and its components into context we can express them relative to annual disposable income or GDP. This shows that the household sector's net worth in 2012 was equivalent to 7.1 times the flow of household disposable income in that year, or 4.9 times GDP. In 1987 it was 5.6 times and 3.4 times respectively.

Chart (a) plots the components of the household sector's net worth (the figures are percentages of disposable income). The ratio of the sector's net worth to disposable income peaked in 2007 at 773 per cent, 256 percentage points higher than at the trough in 1994.

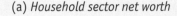

(a) *Household sector net worth*

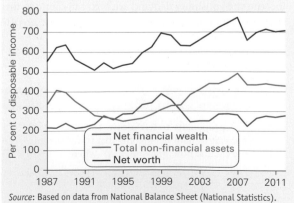

Source: Based on data from National Balance Sheet (National Statistics).

The chart shows the importance of non-financial wealth in the rise of net worth over this period. Non-financial wealth rose from £1.24 trillion (260 per cent of disposable income) in 1994 to £4.37 trillion (491 per cent of disposable income) in 2007. By contrast, the ratio of net *financial* wealth to disposable income peaked in 1999 at 388 per cent, and had fallen to 282 per cent in 2007.

The year 2008 saw an 11.7 per cent decline in net worth. The decline in net financial wealth was driven by a 33 per cent fall in the worth of holdings of shares and other equity as stock markets plummeted in the wake of the financial crisis. The decline in non-financial assets was driven by a 10 per cent fall in the value of dwellings.

The household sector's net worth then rose each year from 2009 to 2012, though not sufficiently to raise the ratio of net worth to disposable income above its 2007 peak.

Net financial wealth was 20 per cent higher in 2012 than in 2007, while the value of non-financial assets was 5.5 per cent higher. The rise in the value of net financial wealth was largely attributable to the rise in the value of currency and deposits held by households, which rose by 19 per cent.

Balance sheets and consumption

The state of the household sector's balance sheets affects the level of consumer spending (C) – something that was dramatically demonstrated in the credit crunch of 2008–9

(b) *Household sector financial balance sheet*

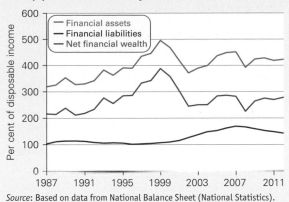

Source: Based on data from National Balance Sheet (National Statistics).

and the subsequent recession and slow recovery. Here we examine the various types of effect.

Financial wealth

The household sector has experienced significant growth in the size of its financial balance sheet. This is captured by Chart (b), which shows the components of net financial wealth: financial assets and liabilities. The ratio of financial liabilities to disposable income rose from 103 per cent in 1987 to 169 per cent in 2007; people were taking on more and more debt relative to their incomes, fuelled by the ease of accessing credit – both consumer credit (loans and credit-card debt) and mortgages. Then, in the aftermath of the credit crunch, the ratio fell each year up to 2012, when the ratio was 144 per cent.

The longer-term increase in the sector's debt-to-income ratio up to 2007 meant that interest payments involved increasingly significant demands on household budgets and hence on the discretionary income households had for spending. This made the sector's spending more sensitive to changes in interest rates. This became a worry as recovery gathered pace from 2014. A rise in interest rates could place a substantial burden on households, thereby curbing consumer expenditure and causing the recovery to stall.

Higher debt-to-income levels can fuel people's concerns about the potential risks arising from debt. If the prospects for income growth are revised down or become more uncertain, people may decide to cut their spending in order to pay off some of their debts.

Non-financial assets

The accumulation of household debt has gone hand-in-hand with the growth of non-financial assets, mainly housing. This is not a coincidence, since an important reason for the growth in household debt has been the sector's acquisition of property. *Secured debt* is debt where property acts as collateral. It accounts for nearly 90 per cent of household debt. Between 1988 and 2012 it grew on average by around 9 per cent per year. Over the same period, the stock of dwellings increased in value by around 7 per cent per year.

House prices display two characteristics: they are notoriously volatile in the short term but rise relative to general prices over the long term. House price volatility makes the net worth of the household sector volatile too. This impact of house price volatility on net worth had grown over the years as house prices had risen and hence the stocks of both housing assets and secured debt had risen. In 2012, 55 per cent of the household sector's net worth came from the value of dwellings. It had been as high as 61 per cent in 2007.

The precautionary effect.   The volatility in net worth from volatile house prices (and potentially the prices of other assets, such as shares) can induce volatility in consumption. If asset prices are falling, households may respond by cutting their spending and increasing saving. This is a *precautionary effect*. Conversely, higher asset prices enable households to reduce saving and spend more.

The collateral effect.   The trend for house prices to rise introduces another means by which the balance sheets affect spending: *a collateral effect*. As house prices rise, people's housing equity will tend to rise too. Housing equity is the difference between the value of a property and the value of any outstanding loan secured against it. House price movements affect the collateral that households have to secure *additional* lending.

When house prices are rising, households may look to borrowing additional sums from mortgage lenders for purposes other than either transactions involving property or spending on major home improvements. This is known as *housing equity withdrawal* (HEW). These funds can then be used to fund consumption, purchasing other assets (e.g. shares) or repaying other debts.

When house prices fall, households have less collateral to secure additional lending to fund spending. In these circumstances people may wish to restore, at least partially, their housing equity by increasing mortgage repayments (negative HEW), thereby further reducing consumption.

The period from 2002 to 2007 was one of high levels of HEW, averaging over £9.0 billion per quarter or 4.4 per cent of disposable income. From 2008 to 2013, however, HEW averaged *minus* £9.3 billion per quarter. This meant that households were *increasing* housing equity by the equivalent of 3.5 per cent of income per quarter – money that could have been spent on consumption. Case Study 17.4 in MyEconLab details the patterns in HEW and consumer spending.

 Draw up a list of the various factors that could affect the household sector's net worth and then consider how these could impact on consumer spending.

[1] The household sector in the official statistics also includes 'non-profit institutions serving households (NPISH)' such as charities, clubs and societies, trade unions, political parties and universities.

KI 10
p75

BOX 17.3 | **SENTIMENT AND SPENDING**

Does sentiment help forecast spending?

Each month, consumers and firms across the European Union are asked a series of questions, the answers to which are used to compile indicators of consumer and business confidence. For instance, consumers are asked about how they expect their financial position to change. They are offered various options such as 'get a lot better, 'get a lot worse' and balances are then calculated on the basis of positive and negative replies.[1]

Chart (a) plots economic sentiment in the EU across consumers and different sectors of business since 1985. It nicely captures the volatility of economic sentiment. This volatility is more marked amongst businesses than consumers and, in particular, in the construction sector.

Now compare the volatility of economic sentiment in Chart (a) with the annual rates of growth in household consumption and gross capital formation (investment), shown in Chart (b). The economy's capital spending is significantly more volatile than household spending. Therefore, the extent of the volatility in economic sentiment is reflected in patterns of expenditure.

What is less clear is the extent to which changes in sentiment *lead* to changes in spending. In fact, a likely scenario is that spending and sentiment interact. High rates

TC 9
p 121

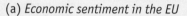

(a) *Economic sentiment in the EU*

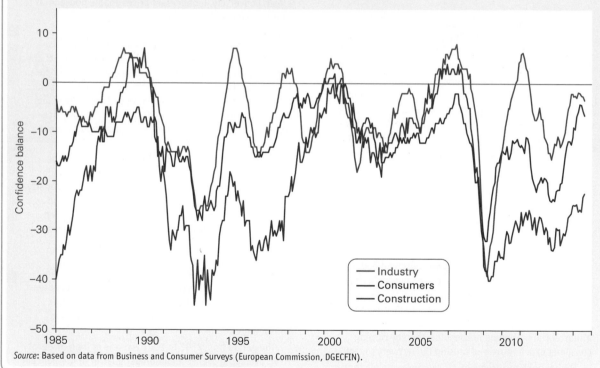

Source: Based on data from Business and Consumer Surveys (European Commission, DGECFIN).

The relationship between investment and *increased* consumer demand is examined by the 'accelerator theory'. We will look at this theory in section 17.4.

Expectations. Since investment is made in order to produce output for the future, investment must depend on firms' expectations about future market conditions.

The cost and efficiency of capital equipment. If the cost of capital equipment goes down or machines become more efficient,

the return on investment will increase. Firms will invest more. Technological progress is an important determinant here.

The rate of interest. The higher the rate of interest, the more expensive it will be for firms to finance investment, and hence the less profitable will the investment be. Just how responsive total investment in the economy is to changes in interest rates is a highly controversial issue and we will return to it later.

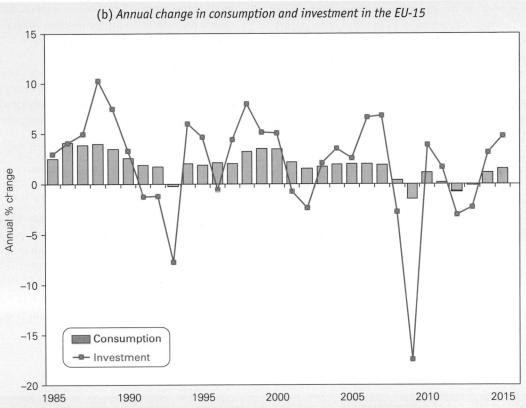

(b) *Annual change in consumption and investment in the EU-15*

Notes: Figures from 2014 based on forecasts; EU-15 = the member countries of the European Union prior to 1 May 2004.
Source: Based on data in *AMECO Database* (European Commission, DGECFIN).

of spending growth may result in high confidence through economic growth, which in turn leads to more spending. The reverse is the case when economic growth is subdued: low spending growth leads to a lack of confidence, which results in low spending growth and so low rates of economic growth.

What makes measures of confidence particularly useful is that they are published monthly. By contrast, measures of GDP and spending are published annually or quarterly and with a considerable time delay. Therefore, measures of confidence are extremely timely for policy makers and provide them with very useful information about the likely path of spending and output growth.

What factors are likely to influence the economic sentiment of (i) consumers; and (ii) businesses? Could the trends in the economic sentiment indicators for consumers and businesses diverge?

[1] More information on the EU programme of business and consumer surveys can be found at http://ec.europa.eu/economy_finance/db_indicators/surveys/index_en.htm

Availability of finance. Investment requires financing. Retained earnings provide one possible source. Alternatively, they could seek finance from banks, or perhaps issue debt instruments, such as bonds, or issue new shares. Therefore, difficulties in raising finance, such as seen in the late 2000s and early 2010s, can limit investment.

So if these are the main determinants of investment, does it mean that investment is totally independent of the level of national income? Not quite. Replacement of worn-out or outdated equipment *will* depend on the level of national income. The higher the current level of national income, the greater will be the stock of capital and therefore the more will need replacing each year. It is also possible that, if the level of national income is high and firms' profits are high, they will be able to *afford* more investment. However, it is not a gross distortion of reality to assume that investment and the level of national income are independent, at least in the short run.

Government expenditure

Government expenditure in any year is independent of the level of national income. In the months preceding the Budget each year, spending departments make submissions about their needs in the coming year. These are discussed with the Treasury and a sum is allocated to each department. That then (excepting any unforeseen events) fixes government expenditure on goods and services for the following financial year.

Thus, again, for our purposes we can take government expenditure as independent of national income in the short term. Even if tax revenues turn out to be more or less than expected, this will not influence that year's government spending. The government can end up running either a budget surplus ($T = G$) or a budget deficit ($G = T$).

Over the longer term, however, government expenditure *will* depend on national income. The higher the level of national income, the higher the amount of tax revenue that the government receives, and hence the more it can afford to spend. The governments of richer nations clearly spend much more than those of developing countries.

Exports

Exports are sold to people abroad, and thus depend largely on *their* incomes, not on incomes at home. Nevertheless, there are two indirect links between a country's national income and its exports:

- Via other countries' circular flows of income. If domestic incomes rise, more will be spent on imports. But this will cause a rise in other countries' incomes and lead them to buy more imports, part of which will be this country's exports.
- Via the exchange rate. A rise in domestic incomes will lead to a rise in imports. Other things being equal, this will lead to a depreciation in the exchange rate. This will make it cheaper for people in other countries to buy this country's exports. Export sales will rise.

However, it is useful in simple Keynesian models to assume that exports are determined independently of domestic national income.

Note that, although the injections function is assumed to be constant with respect to income and is drawn as a horizontal straight line, this does not mean that it will be constant *over time*. Investment can suddenly rise or virtually collapse as the confidence of businesspeople changes. Exports can change too, with shifts in the exchange rate or with speculation. The injections line, then, is constantly shifting up and down.

Section summary

1. In the simple Keynesian model, equilibrium national income is where withdrawals equal injections, and where national income equals the total expenditure on domestic products: where $W = J$ and where $Y = E$.

2. The relationships between national income and the various components of the circular flow of income can be shown on a 45° line diagram. In the diagram, C, C_d and W are endogenous variables. Each one rises as income rises. The relationships can also be expressed in terms of marginal propensities. The marginal propensity is given by $\Delta V/\Delta Y$ (where V is the variable in question).

3. Apart from being determined by national income, consumption is determined by wealth, taxation, the availability and cost of credit, expectations about future prices and incomes, the distribution of income, tastes and attitudes, and the average age of durables. Consumption of domestic product (C_d) is total consumption minus imports of goods and services and minus indirect taxes and plus subsidies on goods and services.

4. Like consumption, withdrawals (S, T and M) vary with national income. Net saving is also determined by the various factors that determine consumption: if these factors cause consumption to rise, then, except in the case of a cut in income taxes, they will cause saving to fall and vice versa. Net tax revenues, apart from being dependent on incomes, depend on the rates of tax and benefits that the government sets and how progressive or regressive they are. Imports depend on the relative prices and quality of domestic and foreign goods, total consumption and tastes.

5. In the simple Keynesian model, injections are assumed to be exogenous variables. They are therefore drawn as a horizontal straight line in the 45° line diagram. In practice, there will be *some* relationship between injections and national income. Replacement investment depends to some extent on the level of output; government expenditure depends to some extent on the level of tax revenues; and exports depend on exchange rates and foreign incomes, both of which will depend on the level of imports. Nevertheless, in the short run it is reasonable to assume that injections are independent of national income.

6. The determinants of investment include the rate of interest, the size of increases in consumer demand, the cost and efficiency of capital equipment, and expectations about prices, consumer demand, interest rates and other costs.

17.2 THE DETERMINATION OF NATIONAL INCOME

Equilibrium national income

We can now put the various functions together on one diagram. This is done in Figure 17.7. Note that there is a new line on the diagram that we have not looked at so far. This is the aggregate expenditure (i.e. the aggregate demand) function. We defined aggregate expenditure as $C_d + J$. Graphically, then, the E function is simply the C_d function shifted upwards by the amount of J.

Equilibrium national income can be found in either of two ways.

$W = J$

Withdrawals equal injections at point x in Figure 17.7. Equilibrium national income is thus Y_e. If national income were below this level, say at Y_1, injections would exceed withdrawals (by an amount $a - b$). This additional net expenditure injected into the economy would encourage firms to produce more and hence cause national income to rise. But as people's incomes rose, so they would save more, pay more taxes and buy more imports. In other words, withdrawals would rise. There would be a movement up along the W function. This process would continue until $W = J$ at point x.

If, on the other hand, national income were at Y_2, withdrawals would exceed injections (by an amount $c - d$). This deficiency of demand would cause production and hence national income to fall. As it did so, there would be a movement down along the W function until again point x was reached.

$Y = E$

If $W = J$, then $C_d + W = C_d + J$. In other words, another way of describing equilibrium is where national income ($Y \equiv C_d + W$) equals aggregate expenditure ($E \equiv C_d + J$). This is

shown at point z in Figure 17.7. This is where the expenditure function ($C_d + J$) crosses the 45° line ($C_d + W$).

If aggregate expenditure exceeded national income, say at Y_1, there would be excess demand in the economy (of $e - f$). In other words, people would be buying more than was currently being produced. Firms would find their stocks dwindling and would therefore increase their level of production. In doing so, they would employ more factors of production. National income would thus rise. As it did so, consumption and hence aggregate expenditure would rise. There would be a movement up along the expenditure function. But because not all the extra income would be consumed (i.e. some would be withdrawn), expenditure would rise less quickly than income (the E line is flatter than the Y line). As income rises towards Y_e, the gap between Y and E gets smaller. Once point z is reached, $Y = E$. There is then no further tendency for income to rise.

If national income exceeded national expenditure, at say Y_2, there would be insufficient demand for the goods and services currently being produced. Firms would find their stocks of unsold goods building up. They would thus respond by producing less and employing fewer factors of production. National income would thus fall and go on falling until Y_e was reached.

 Why is it the case that $a - b = e - f$, and $c - d = g - h$?

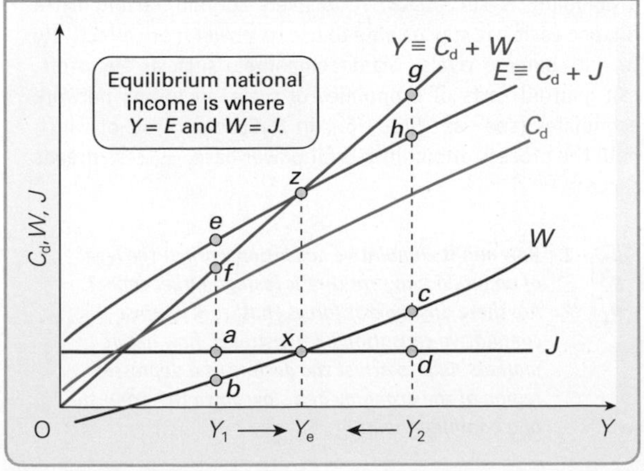

The multiplier: the withdrawals and injections approach

When injections rise (and continue at the higher level), this will cause national income to rise. But by how much?

In fact, national income will rise by *more* than injections: Y rises by a *multiple* of the rise in J.

$$\Delta Y > \Delta J$$

The number of times that the increase in income (ΔY) is greater than the increase in injections (ΔJ) is known as the *multiplier* (k):

$$k = \Delta Y / \Delta J$$

Thus if a £10 billion rise in injections caused a £30 billion rise in national income, the multiplier would be 3.

What causes the multiplier effect? The answer is that, when extra spending is injected into the economy, it will

---

Figure 17.7 Equilibrium national income

Equilibrium national income is where $Y = E$ and $W = J$.

$Y \equiv C_d + W$
$E \equiv C_d + J$
C_d
W
J

$Y_1 \longrightarrow Y_e \longleftarrow Y_2$

Definition

(Injections) multiplier The number of times by which a rise in income exceeds the rise in injections that caused it: $K = \Delta Y / \Delta J$.

KI 35
p475

then stimulate further spending, which in turn will stimulate yet more spending, and so on. For example, if firms decide to invest more, this will lead to more people being employed and hence more incomes being paid to households. Households will then spend part of this increased income on domestically produced goods (the remainder will be withdrawn). This increased consumption will encourage firms to produce more goods to meet the demand. Firms will thus employ more people and other factors of production. This leads to even more incomes being paid out to households. Consumption will thus increase yet again. And so the process continues.

TC 15
p508

The multiplier is an example of an important principle in economics: that of *cumulative causation* (see below). This is the last of our 15 threshold concepts.

Note that in this simple Keynesian theory we are assuming that prices are constant (i.e. that there is no inflation) and hence that any increase in income is a *real*

TC 12
p411

increase in income matched by extra production. So when we talk about extra injections into the economy causing

extra spending, it is the extra *output* that this spending generates that we are concerned with. If the multiplier were 3, for example, this would mean that an injection of £1 of expenditure into the economy would lead to an increase in *output* of £3.

But even if there were limitless resources, an increase in injections would not cause national income to go on rising for ever: the multiplier is not infinite. Each time people receive extra income, they will save some of it, pay some of it in taxes and spend some of it on imports: in other words, withdrawals will rise. Eventually, as income goes on rising, all the extra injections will have leaked away into the three withdrawals. At that point, the multiplier process will have ceased; a new equilibrium will have been reached.

What determines the size of the multiplier? This can be shown graphically using either withdrawals and injections or income and expenditure. The income/expenditure approach will be examined shortly. For now we will use the withdrawals/injections approach. This is illustrated in Figure 17.8.

Assume that injections rise from J_1 to J_2. Equilibrium will move from point a to point b. Income will thus rise from Y_{e_1} to Y_{e_2}. The multiplier is therefore

$$\frac{Y_{e_2} - Y_{e_1}}{J_2 - J_1}\left(\text{i.e. } \frac{\Delta Y}{\Delta J}\right)$$

It can be seen that the size of the multiplier depends on the slope of the W function. Remember that the slope of the

> ### Definition
>
> **Principle of cumulative causation** An initial event can cause an ultimate effect that is much larger.

THRESHOLD CONCEPT 15 | **CUMULATIVE CAUSATION**   THINKING LIKE AN ECONOMIST

Economic effects can snowball

Once an economy starts to expand, growth is likely to gather pace. Once it starts slowing down, this can gather pace too and end up in a recession. There are many other examples in economics of things getting 'onto a roll'. A rising stock market is likely to breed confidence in investors and encourage them to buy. This 'destabilising speculation' (see pages 76–7) will then lead to further rises in share prices. A fall in stock market prices can lead to panic selling of shares. The booming stock market of the late 1990s and 2003–8, and the falls in the early 2000s and 2008–9, are good examples of this (see chart in Box 2.3 on page 52).

This phenomenon of things building on themselves is known as 'cumulative causation' and occurs throughout market economies. It is a *threshold concept* because it helps us to understand the built-in instability in many parts of the economy and in many economic situations.

Central to explaining cumulative causation is people's psychology. Good news creates confidence and this optimism causes people to behave in ways that build on the good news. Bad news creates pessimism and this leads to people behaving cautiously, which tends to reinforce the bad news.

Take two regions of an economy: an expanding region and a declining region. The expansion of the first region encourages

workers to move there in search of jobs. The optimism in the area causes long-term investment as firms have confidence in an expanding market. This encourages house building and other forms of investment in infrastructure and services. And so the region thrives. Meanwhile the declining region suffers from deprivation as unemployment rises. This encourages people to move away and businesses to close. There is a further decline in jobs and further migration from the region.

Cumulative causation does not just occur at a macro level. If a company is successful, it is likely to find raising extra finance easier; it may be able to use its power more effectively to out-compete rivals. Giant companies, such as Microsoft, can gain all sorts of economies of scale, including network economies (see Case Study 6.4 in MyEconLab), all of which help the process of building their power base. Success breeds success.

1. *How might cumulative causation work at the level of an individual firm that is losing market share?*
2. *Are there any market forces that work against cumulative causation? For instance, how might markets help to arrest the decline of a depressed region of the economy and slow down the expansion of a booming region?*

Figure 17.8 The multiplier: a shift in injections

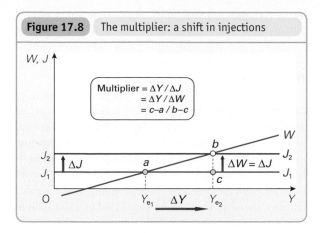

The multiplier can be expressed as the first derivative of national income with respect to injections:

$$k = \frac{dY}{dJ}$$

Since in equilibrium $J = W$, it is also the first derivative of income with respect to withdrawals. Thus

$$k = \frac{dY}{dW}$$

The marginal propensity to withdraw (i.e. the slope of the withdrawals curve) is found by differentiating the withdrawals function:

$$mpw - \frac{dW}{dY} = \frac{1}{k}$$

Thus

$$k = \frac{1}{mpw}$$

The algebra of the multiplier is explored in MyEconLab in Maths Case 17.1, which does not use calculus, and Maths Case 17.2, which does.

W function is given by the marginal propensity to withdraw ($\Delta W/\Delta Y$). The less steep the line (and hence the lower the mpw), the bigger will be the rise in national income: the bigger will be the multiplier.

 Try this simple test of the above argument. Draw a series of W lines of different slopes, all crossing the J line at the same point. Now draw a second J line above the first. Mark the original equilibrium and all the new ones corresponding to each of the W lines. It should be quite obvious that the flatter the W line is, the more Y will have increased.

The point here is that the less is withdrawn each time extra income is generated, the more will be recirculated and hence the bigger will be the rise in national income. The size of the multiplier thus varies inversely with the size of the mpw. The bigger the mpw, the smaller the multiplier; the smaller the mpw, the bigger the multiplier. In fact, the **multiplier formula** simply gives the multiplier as the inverse of the mpw:

$k = 1/mpw$

or alternatively, since $mpw + mpc_d = 1$ and thus $mpw = 1 - mpc_d$,

$k = 1/(1 - mpc_d)$

Thus if the mpw were $^1/_4$ (and hence the mpc_d were $^3/_4$), the multiplier would be 4. So if J increased by £10 billion, Y would increase by £40 billion.

But why is the multiplier given by the formula $1/mpw$? This can be illustrated by referring to Figure 17.8. The mpw is the slope of the W line. In the diagram, this is given by the amount $(b-c)/(c-a)$. The multiplier is defined as $\Delta Y/\Delta J$. In the diagram, this is the amount $(c-a)/(b-c)$. But this is merely the inverse of the mpw. Thus the multiplier equals $1/mpw$.[1]

A shift in withdrawals

A multiplied rise in income can also be caused by a fall in withdrawals. This is illustrated in Figure 17.9.

The withdrawals function shifts from W_1 to W_2. This means that, at the old equilibrium of Y_{e_1}, injections now exceed withdrawals by an amount $a - b$. This will cause national income to rise until a new equilibrium is reached at Y_{e_2} where $J = W_2$. Thus a downward shift of the withdrawals function of $a - b$ (ΔW) causes a rise in national income of

Figure 17.9 The multiplier: a shift in withdrawals

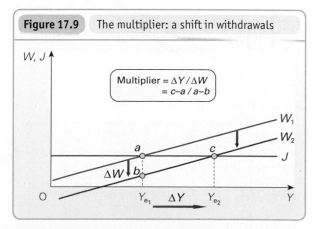

---

[1] In some elementary textbooks, the formula for the multiplier is given as $1/mps$. The reason for this is that it is assumed (for simplicity's sake) that there is only one withdrawal, namely saving, and only one injection, namely investment. As soon as this assumption is dropped, $1/mps$ becomes the wrong formula.

Definition

(Injections) multiplier formula The formula for the multiplier: $K = 1/mpw$ or $1/(1 - mpc_a)$.

$c - a$ (ΔY). The multiplier in this case is given by $\Delta Y/\Delta W$: in other words, $(c - a)/(a - b)$. Note that the multiplier is based on the *initial* fall in withdrawals. Once the multiplier effect has worked through, withdrawals will have risen back to equal injections at point c.

 Why is the 'withdrawals multiplier' strictly speaking a negative figure?

The multiplier: the income and expenditure approach

TC 15 p508 The multiplier can also be demonstrated using the income/expenditure approach. Assume in Figure 17.10 that the aggregate expenditure function shifts to E_2. This could be due either to a rise in one or more of the three injections, or to a rise in the consumption of domestically produced goods (and hence a fall in withdrawals). Equilibrium national income will rise from Y_{e_1} to Y_{e_2}.

What is the size of the multiplier? The initial rise in expenditure was $b - a$. The resulting rise in income is $c - a$. The multiplier is thus $(c - a)/(b - a)$.

The effect is illustrated in Table 17.2. Consumption of domestic product (C_d) is shown in the second column for various levels of national income (Y). For every £100 billion

rise in Y, C_d rises by £80 billion. Thus the $mpc_d = 0.8$. Assume initially that injections equal £100 billion at all levels of national income. Aggregate expenditure (the fourth column) equals $C_d + J$. Equilibrium national income is £700 billion. This is where $Y = E$.

Now assume that injections rise by £20 billion to £120 billion. Aggregate expenditure is now shown in the final column and is £20 billion higher than before at each level of national income (Y). At the original equilibrium national income (£700 billion), aggregate expenditure is now £720 billion. This excess of E over Y of £20 billion will generate extra incomes and continue doing so as long as E remains above Y. Equilibrium is reached at £800 billion, where once more $Y = E$. The initial rise in aggregate expenditure of £20 billion (from £700bn to £720bn) has led to an eventual rise in both national income and aggregate expenditure of £100 billion. The multiplier is thus 5 (i.e. £100bn/£20bn). But this is equal to $1/(1 - 0.8)$ or $1/(1 - mpc_d)$.

 1. *What determines the slope of the E function?*
2. *How does the slope of the E function affect the size of the multiplier? (Try drawing diagrams with E functions of different slopes and see what happens when they shift.)*

The multiplier: a numerical illustration

The multiplier effect does not work instantaneously. When there is an increase in injections, whether investment, government expenditure or exports, it takes time before this brings about the full multiplied rise in national income.

Consider the following example. Let us assume for simplicity that the mpw is $1/2$. This will give an mpc_d of $1/2$ also. Let us also assume that investment (an injection) rises by £160 million and stays at the new higher level. Table 17.3 shows what will happen.

As firms purchase more machines and construct more factories, the incomes of those who produce machines and those who work in the construction industry will increase by £160 million. When this extra income is received by households, whether as wages or profits, half will be withdrawn ($mpw = 1/2$) and half will be spent on the goods and services of domestic firms. This increase in consumption thus generates additional incomes for firms of £80 million

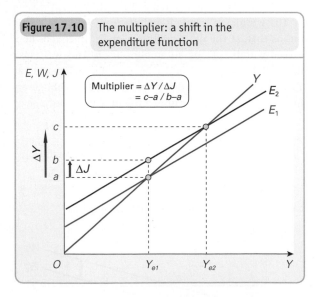

Figure 17.10 The multiplier: a shift in the expenditure function

Table 17.2 The effect of an increase in aggregate expenditure (£ billion)

Y	C_d	J (old)	E (old)	J (new)	E (new)
500	440	100	540	120	560
600	520	100	620	120	640
700	600	100	700	120	720
800	680	100	780	120	800
900	760	100	860	120	880

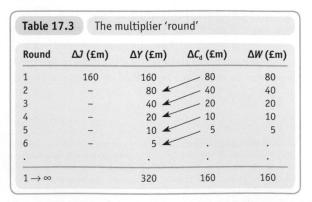

Table 17.3 The multiplier 'round'

Round	ΔJ (£m)	ΔY (£m)	ΔC_d (£m)	ΔW (£m)
1	160	160	80	80
2	–	80	40	40
3	–	40	20	20
4	–	20	10	10
5	–	10	5	5
6	–	5	.	.
.		.	.	.
$1 \to \infty$		320	160	160

BOX 17.4   **DERIVING THE MULTIPLIER FORMULA**   EXPLORING ECONOMICS

An algebraic proof

The formula for the multiplier can be derived using simple algebra. First of all, remember how we defined the multiplier:

$$k \equiv \Delta Y/\Delta J \qquad (1)$$

and the marginal propensity to withdraw:

$$mpw = \Delta W/\Delta Y \qquad (2)$$

If we now take the inverse of equation (2), we get

$$1/mpw \equiv \Delta Y/\Delta W \qquad (3)$$

But in equilibrium we know that $W = J$. Hence any change in injections must be matched by a change in withdrawals and vice versa, to ensure that withdrawals and injections remain equal. Thus

$$\Delta W/\Delta J \qquad (4)$$

Substituting equation (4) in equation (3) gives

$$1/mpw = \Delta Y/\Delta J \ (=k)$$

i.e. the multiplier equals $1/mpw$.

---

over and above the initial £160 million (which is still being generated in each time period). When this additional £80 million of incomes is received by households (round 2), again half will be withdrawn and half will go on consumption of domestic product. This increases national income by a further £40 million (round 3). And so each time we go around the circular flow of income, national income increases, but by only half as much as the previous time ($mpc_d = {}^1/_2$).

If we add up the additional income generated in each round (assuming the process goes on indefinitely), the total will be £320 million: twice the rise in injections. The multiplier is 2.

The bigger the mpc_d (and hence the smaller the mpw), the more will expenditure rise each time national income rises, and hence the bigger will be the multiplier.

*The multiplier: some qualifications

(This section examines the multiplier formula in more detail. You may omit it without affecting the flow of the argument.)

TC 15 p508

Some possible errors can easily be made in calculating the value of the multiplier. These often arise from a confusion over the meaning of terms.

The marginal propensity to consume domestic product

Remember the formula for the multiplier:

$$k = 1/(1 - mpc_d)$$

It is important to realise just what is meant by the mpc_d. It is the proportion of a rise in households' gross (i.e. pre-tax-and-benefit) income that actually accrues to domestic firms. It thus excludes that part of consumption that is spent on imports and that part which is paid to the government in VAT and other indirect taxes.

Up to now we have also been basing the mpc on gross income. As Case Study 17.1 in MyEconLab shows, however, the mpc is often based on *disposable* (i.e. post-tax-and-benefit)

income. After all, when consumers decide how much to spend, it is their disposable income rather than their gross income that they will consider. So how do we derive the mpc_d (based on gross income) from the mpc based on disposable income (mpc')? To do this, we must use the following formula:

$$mpc_d = mpc'(1 - t_E)(1 - t_Y) - mpm$$

where t_Y is the marginal rate of income tax, and t_E is the marginal rate of expenditure tax.

To illustrate this formula consider the following effects of an increase in national income of £100 million. It is assumed that $t_Y - 20$ per cent, $t_E - 10$ per cent and $mpc - 7/8$. It is also assumed that the mps (from gross income) = 1/10 and the mpm (from gross income) = 13/100. Table 17.4 sets out the figures.

Gross income rises by £100 million. Of this, £20 million is taken in income tax ($t_Y = 20$ per cent). This leaves a rise in disposable income of £80 million. Of this, £10 million is saved ($mps = 1/10$) and £70 million is spent. Of this, £7 million goes in expenditure taxes ($t_E = 10$ per cent) and £13 million leaks abroad ($mpm = 13/100$). This leaves £50 million that goes on the consumption of domestic product ($mpc_d = 50/100 = {}^1/_2$). Substituting these figures in the above formula gives

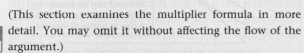

$$mpc_d = mpc(1 - t_E)(1 - t_Y) - mpm$$
$$= \tfrac{7}{8}(1 - \tfrac{1}{10})(1 - \tfrac{2}{10}) - \tfrac{13}{100}$$
$$= (\tfrac{7}{8} \times \tfrac{9}{10} \times \tfrac{8}{10}) - \tfrac{13}{100}$$
$$= \tfrac{63}{100} - \tfrac{13}{100} = \tfrac{50}{100} = \tfrac{1}{2}$$

Table 17.4   Calculating the mpc_d

	ΔY	–	ΔT_Y	=	ΔY_{dis}	
(£m)	100		20		80	
	ΔY_{dis}	–	ΔS	=	ΔC	
(£m)	80		10		70	
	ΔC	–	ΔT_E	–	ΔM	=	ΔC_d
(£m)	70		7		13		50

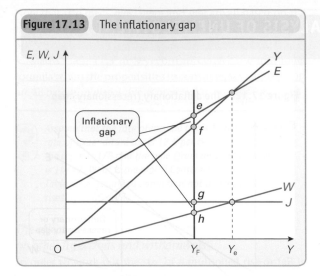

Figure 17.13 The inflationary gap

precise effect will depend on what happens to exchange rates – a subject we explore in Chapter 25.

Finally, as money incomes go up, people will tend to find themselves paying higher rates of tax (unless the government increases tax bands and allowances in line with inflation). This will shift the *W* line up and the *E* line down.

> *The present level of a country's exports is £12 billion; investment is £2 billion; government expenditure is £4 billion; total consumer spending (not C_d) is £36 billion; imports are £12 billion; and expenditure taxes are £2 billion. The economy is currently in equilibrium. It is estimated that an income of £50 billion is necessary to generate full employment. The mps is 0.1, the mpt is 0.05 and the mpm is 0.1.*
>
> *(a) Is there an inflationary or deflationary gap in this situation?*
>
> *(b) What is the size of the gap? (Don't confuse this with the difference between Y_e and Y_F.)*
>
> *(c) What would be the appropriate government policies to close this gap?*

This situation involves an ***inflationary gap***. This is the amount by which aggregate expenditure exceeds national income or injections exceed withdrawals at the full-employment level of national income. This is illustrated by the gaps $e - f$ and $g - h$ in Figure 17.13.

To eliminate this inflation, the inflationary gap must be closed by either raising withdrawals or lowering injections, or some combination of the two, until Y_e equals Y_F. This can be done by a deliberate government policy of deflation. This could be either a contractionary *fiscal* policy of lowering government expenditure and/or raising taxes, or a contractionary *monetary* policy of raising interest rates and reducing the amount of money in the economy.

Even if the government does not actively pursue a deflationary policy, the inflationary gap may still close automatically. If the rich are better able than the poor to defend themselves against inflation, there will be a redistribution from the poor to the rich. But the rich tend to have a higher marginal propensity to save than the poor. Thus saving will rise and consumption will fall. This will swing the *W* line up and the *E* line down, thus narrowing the inflationary gap.

Inflation will also tend to worsen the balance of payments. Higher money incomes at home will lead to more imports being purchased. Higher domestic prices will lead to fewer exports being sold and more imports being bought in preference to the now dearer home-produced goods. The effect of this will be to shift the *W* line up and the *J* and *E* lines down, thus helping to close the inflationary gap. The

Unemployment and inflation at the same time

The simple analysis of the preceding pages implies that the aggregate supply curve looks like AS_1 in Figure 17.14. Up to Y_F, output and employment can rise with no rise in prices at all. The deflationary gap is being closed. At Y_F no further rises in output are possible. Any further rise in aggregate demand is entirely reflected in higher prices. An inflationary gap opens. In other words, this implies that either inflation *or* unemployment can occur, but not both simultaneously.

Two important qualifications need to be made to this analysis to explain the occurrence of both unemployment *and* inflation at the same time.

First, there are *other* types of inflation and unemployment not caused by an excess or deficiency of aggregate

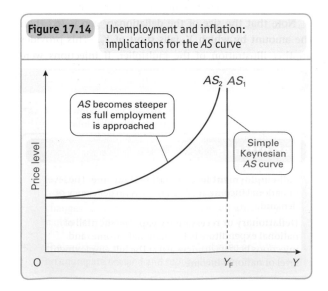

Figure 17.14 Unemployment and inflation: implications for the *AS* curve

AS becomes steeper as full employment is approached

Simple Keynesian *AS* curve

Definition

Inflationary gap The excess of national expenditure over income (and injections over withdrawals) at the full-employment level of national income.

demand: for example, cost-push and expectations-generated inflation; frictional and structural unemployment.

Thus, even if a government could manipulate national income so as to get Y_e and Y_F to coincide, this would not eliminate all inflation and unemployment – only demand-pull inflation and demand-deficient unemployment. Keynesians argue, therefore, that governments should use a whole package of policies, each tailored to the specific type of problem. But certainly one of the most important of these policies will be the management of aggregate demand.

Second, not all firms operate with the same degree of slack. Thus a rise in aggregate demand can lead to *both* a reduction in unemployment *and* a rise in prices: some firms responding to the rise in demand by taking up slack and hence increasing output; other firms, having little or no slack, responding by raising prices; others doing both. Similarly, labour markets have different degrees of slack and therefore the rise in demand will lead to various mixes of higher wages and lower unemployment. Thus the AS curve will look like AS_2 in Figure 17.14.

 How does the above argument about firms' responses to a rise in demand relate to the shape of their marginal cost curves?

These types of argument were used to justify a belief in a downward-sloping Phillips curve (see Box 15.4) by the majority of economists and politicians in the 1960s and into the 1970s. A modified version of these arguments is still used today by Keynesian economists. This is examined in more detail in Chapter 20.

The problem is that if there is a trade-off between unemployment and inflation, demand-management policies used to make one of the objectives better will succeed only in making the other one worse. It then becomes a matter of political judgement which of the objectives is the right one to direct demand-management policies towards. Is *inflation* public enemy number one, or is it *unemployment*?

The relationship between the *AD/AS* diagram and the 45° line diagram

Now that we have introduced the argument that inflation can begin to occur *before* the full-employment level of income is reached, how does this affect the relationship between our two models: the *AD/AS* model and the 45° line model? This is examined in Figure 17.15. Initial equilibrium is at Y_{e_1} in both parts of the diagram, where $AD_1 = AS$ and where E_1 crosses the 45° line.

Now let us assume that there is a rise in aggregate demand. The E line shifts initially to E_2 in diagram (b). If this rise in demand were to lead to a full multiplied rise in real income, equilibrium income would rise to Y_{e_2}. But we are now assuming that inflation can occur *before* the full-employment level of income is reached. In other words, we are assuming that the AS curve is upward sloping (not horizontal as it was in Figure 17.11).

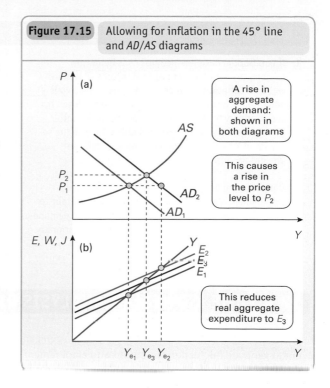

Figure 17.15 Allowing for inflation in the 45° line and *AD/AS* diagrams

In diagram (a), the rise in aggregate demand has shifted the AD curve from AD_1 to AD_2. Part of this increase in demand is reflected in higher prices – the price level rises to P_2 – and only *part* is reflected in higher output. Equilibrium real income therefore rises only to Y_{e_3} and not Y_{e_2}. In other words, it does not rise by the full extent of the multiplier.

In diagram (b), the effect of the higher prices is to reduce the real value of expenditure (E). In other words, a given amount of money buys fewer goods. If there is no compensating increase in money supply (which would shift the AD curve further to the right in diagram (a)), the E line must fall to the point where it intersects the 45° line at a real income of Y_{e_3}: the E line must fall to E_3.

What is the mechanism that drives down the expenditure function from E_2 to E_3?

- The shortage of money drives up interest rates. This reduces investment and encourages saving.
- Higher prices reduce the real value of people's savings. They may therefore save more to compensate for this.
- Higher prices of domestic goods reduce exports and increase imports.
- Given the progressive nature of the tax system, higher money incomes lead to increased taxes.
- Inflation is likely to redistribute income from the poor to the rich, who have a higher *mps*.

 If money supply did increase sufficiently for the E line to remain at E_2, what would be the position of the new AD curve?

Section summary

1. If equilibrium national income (Y_e) is below the full-employment level of national income (Y_F), there will be a deflationary (recessionary) gap. This gap is equal to $Y - E$ or $W - J$ at Y_F. This gap can be closed by expansionary fiscal or monetary policy, which will then cause a multiplied rise in national income (up to a level of Y_F) and will eliminate demand-deficient unemployment.

2. If equilibrium national income exceeds the full-employment level of income, the inability of output to expand to meet this excess demand will lead to demand-pull inflation. This excess demand gives an inflationary

gap, which is equal to $E - Y$ or $J - W$ at Y_F. This gap can be closed by deflationary policies.

3. This simple analysis tends to imply that the AS curve is horizontal up to Y_F and then vertical. In practice, the AS curve is likely to be upward sloping but getting steeper as full employment is approached and as bottlenecks increasingly occur.

4. An initial rise in aggregate demand (and an upward shift in the E curve) will be eroded to the extent that inflation reduces the real value of this demand: the E curve will shift back downwards again somewhat, unless there is a further boost to demand.

17.4   THE KEYNESIAN ANALYSIS OF THE BUSINESS CYCLE

Keynesian analysis focuses on how fluctuations in aggregate demand generate fluctuations in output and employment. Keynesians argue that private-sector spending is volatile. Therefore, understanding the causes of this volatility is crucial to understanding economic instability. As we saw in Chapter 16, new Keynesians argue that the impact of this instability on the economy can be magnified by market imperfections. For instance, the reluctance of firms to change prices because of menu costs (the costs incurred in adjusting prices) could see them change output levels substantially in response to fluctuations in demand.

The instability of aggregate demand, Keynesians argue, is central to explaining the business cycle. In the upturn (phase 1), aggregate demand starts to rise. It rises rapidly in the expansionary phase (phase 2). It then slows down and may start to fall in the peaking-out phase (phase 3). It then falls or remains relatively stagnant in the recession (phase 4) (see Figure 14.5 on page 416).

Keynesians argue that fluctuations in aggregate demand will often require the authorities to devise appropriate stabilisation policies to iron out these fluctuations. A more stable economy, they argue, provides a better climate for investment. With more investment, *potential* output grows more rapidly. This, given appropriate demand-management policy, then allows a faster growth in actual output to be maintained.

Instability of investment: the accelerator

The volatility of aggregate demand reflects the volatility of the expenditure components: C, I, G, X and M. Of these, the most volatile is investment (I).

When an economy begins to recover from a recession, investment can rise very rapidly. When the growth of the economy slows down, however, investment can fall dramatically, and during a recession it can all but disappear.

Since investment is an injection into the circular flow of income, these changes in investment will cause multiplied changes in income and thus heighten a boom or deepen a recession.

The theory that relates investment to *changes* in national income is called the **accelerator theory**. The term 'accelerator' is used because a relatively modest rise in national income can cause a much larger percentage rise in investment.

When there is no change in income and hence no change in consumption, the only investment needed is a relatively small amount of replacement investment for machines that are wearing out or have become obsolete. When income and consumption increase, however, there will have to be *new* investment in order to increase production capacity. This is called **induced investment** (I_i). Once this has taken place, investment will fall back to mere replacement investment (I_r) unless there is a further rise in income and consumption.

Thus induced investment depends on *changes* in national income (ΔY):

$$I_i = \alpha \Delta Y$$

where α is the amount by which induced investment depends on changes in national income, and is known as the **accelerator coefficient**. Thus if a £1 million *rise* in

Definitions

Accelerator theory The level of investment depends on the rate of change of national income, and as a result tends to be subject to substantial fluctuations.

Induced investment Investment that firms make to enable them to meet extra consumer demand.

Accelerator coefficient The level of induced investment as a proportion of a rise in national income: $\alpha = I_i/\Delta Y$.

Table 17.5	The accelerator effect						
	Year						
	0	1	2	3	4	5	6
Quantity demanded by consumers (sales)	1000	1000	2000	3000	3500	3500	3400
Number of machines required	10	10	20	30	35	35	34
Induced investment (I_i) (extra machines)		0	10	10	5	0	0
Replacement investment (I_r)		1	1	1	1	1	0
Total investment ($I_i + I_r$)		1	11	11	6	1	0

national income caused the *level* of induced investment to be £2 million, the accelerator coefficient would be 2.

The size of α depends on the economy's **marginal capital/output ratio** ($\Delta K/\Delta Y$). If an increase in the country's capital stock of £2 million (i.e. an investment of £2 million) is required to produce £1 million extra national output, the marginal capital/output ratio would be 2. Other things being equal, the accelerator coefficient and the marginal capital/output ratio will therefore be the same.

 How is it that the cost of an investment to a firm will exceed the value of the output that the investment will yield? Surely that would make the investment unprofitable? (Clue: the increase in output refers to output over a specific time period, usually a year.)

The following example (see Table 17.5) illustrates some important features of the accelerator. It looks at the investment decisions made by a firm in response to changes in the demand for its product. The firm is taken as representative of firms throughout the economy. The example is based on various assumptions:

- The firm's machines last exactly 10 years and then need replacing.
- At the start of the example, the firm has 10 machines in place, one 10 years old, one 9 years old, one 8 years old, one 7, one 6, and so on. Thus one machine needs replacing each year.
- Machines produce exactly 100 units of output per year. This figure cannot be varied.
- The firm always adjusts its output and its stock of machinery to match consumer demand.

The example shows what happens to the firm's investment over a six-year period when there is first a substantial rise in

consumer demand, then a levelling off and then a slight fall. It illustrates the following features of the accelerator:

- *Investment will rise when the growth of national income (and hence consumer demand) is rising* ($\Delta Y_{t+1} > \Delta Y_t$). Years 1 to 2 illustrate this (see Table 17.5). The rise in consumer demand is zero in year 1 and 1000 units in year 2. Investment rises from 1 to 11 machines. The growth in investment may be considerably greater than the growth in consumer demand, giving a large accelerator effect. Between years 1 and 2, consumer demand doubles but investment goes up by a massive *11* times!
- *Investment will be constant even when national income is growing, if the increase in income this year is the same as last year* ($\Delta Y_{t+1} = \Delta Y_t$). In years 2 to 3, consumer demand continues to rise by 1000 units, but investment is constant at 11 machines.
- *Investment will fall even if national income is still growing, if the rate of growth is slowing down* ($\Delta Y_{t+1} < \Delta Y_t$). In years 3 to 4, consumer demand rises by 500 units (rather than 1000 units as in the previous year). Investment falls from 11 to 6 machines.
- *If national income is constant, investment will be confined to replacement investment only.* In years 4 to 5, investment falls to the one machine requiring replacement.
- *If national income falls, even if only slightly, investment can be wiped out altogether.* In years 5 to 6, even though demand has fallen by only 1/35, investment will fall to zero. Not even the machine that is wearing out will be replaced.

In practice, the accelerator will not be as dramatic and clear-cut as this. The effect will be extremely difficult to predict for the following reasons:

- Many firms may have spare capacity and/or carry stocks. This will enable them to meet extra demand without having to invest.
- The willingness of firms to invest will depend on their confidence in *future* demand (see Box 17.3). Firms are not going to rush out and spend large amounts of money on machines that will last many years if it is quite likely that demand will fall back again the following year.
- Firms may make their investment plans a long time in advance and may be unable to change them quickly.

TC 9
p 121

KI 31
p 330

Definition

Marginal capital/output ratio The amount of extra capital (in money terms) required to produce a £1 increase in national output. Since $I_i = \Delta K$, the marginal capital/output ratio $\Delta K/\Delta Y$ equals the accelerator coefficient (α).

- Even if firms do decide to invest more, the producer goods industries may not have the capacity to meet a sudden surge in demand for machines.
- Machines do not as a rule suddenly wear out. A firm could thus delay replacing machines and keep the old ones for a bit longer if it was uncertain about its future level of demand.

All these points tend to reduce the magnitude of the accelerator and to make it very difficult to predict. Nevertheless the effect still exists. Firms still take note of changes in consumer demand when deciding how much to invest.

Box 17.5 looks at how fluctuations in investment in the UK have typically been far more severe than fluctuations in national income. This tends to suggest that there was a substantial accelerator effect operating during the period.

The multiplier/accelerator interaction

If there is an initial change in injections or withdrawals, then theoretically this will set off a chain reaction between the multiplier and the accelerator. For example, if there is a rise in government expenditure, this will lead to a multiplied rise in national income. But this *rise* in national income will set off an accelerator effect: firms will respond to the rise in income and the resulting rise in consumer demand by investing more. But this rise in investment constitutes a further rise in injections and thus will lead to a second multiplied rise in income. If this rise in income is larger than the first, there will then be a second rise in investment (the accelerator), which in turn will cause a third rise in income (the multiplier). And so the process continues indefinitely.

But does this lead to an exploding rise in national income? Will a single rise in injections cause national income to go on rising for ever? The answer is no, for two reasons. The first is that national income, in real terms, cannot go on rising faster than the growth in potential output. It will bump up against the ceiling of full employment, whether of labour or of other resources.

A second reason is that, if investment is to go on rising, it is not enough that national income should merely go on *rising*: instead, national income must *rise faster and faster*. Once the growth in national income slows down, investment will begin to fall, and then the whole process will be reversed. A fall in investment will lead to a fall in national income, which will lead to a massive fall in investment. The multiplier/accelerator interaction is shown more formally in Table 17.6. A numerical example is given in Case Study 17.7 in MyEconLab.

Fluctuations in stocks

Firms hold stocks (inventories) of finished goods. These stocks tend to fluctuate with the course of the business cycle, and these fluctuations in stocks themselves contribute to fluctuations in output.

Imagine an economy that is recovering from a recession. At first, firms may be cautious about increasing production. Doing so may involve taking on more labour or making additional investment. Firms may not want to make these commitments if the recovery could soon peter out. They may, therefore, run down their stocks rather than increase output. Initially the recovery from recession will be slow.

If the recovery does continue, however, firms will start to gain more confidence and will increase production. Also, they will find that their stocks have got rather low and will need building up. This gives a further boost to production, and for a time the growth in output will exceed the growth in demand. This extra growth in output will then, via the multiplier, lead to a further increase in demand.

Once stocks have been built up again, the growth in output will slow down to match the growth in demand. This slowing down in output will, via the accelerator and multiplier, contribute to the ending of the expansionary phase of the business cycle.

As the economy slows down, firms will find their stocks building up. Unless they cut back on production immediately, this increase in stocks cushions the effect of falling demand on output and employment.

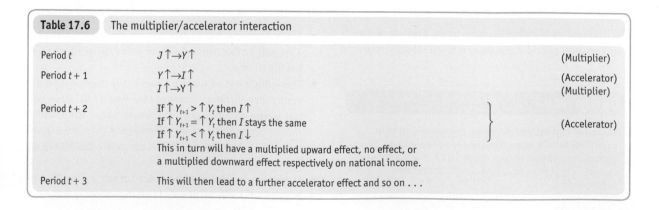

Table 17.6	The multiplier/accelerator interaction	
Period t	$J\uparrow\rightarrow Y\uparrow$	(Multiplier)
Period $t + 1$	$Y\uparrow\rightarrow I\uparrow$	(Accelerator)
	$I\uparrow\rightarrow Y\uparrow$	(Multiplier)
Period $t + 2$	If $\uparrow Y_{t+1} > \uparrow Y_t$ then $I\uparrow$	
	If $\uparrow Y_{t+1} = \uparrow Y_t$ then I stays the same	(Accelerator)
	If $\uparrow Y_{t+1} < \uparrow Y_t$ then $I\downarrow$	
	This in turn will have a multiplied upward effect, no effect, or a multiplied downward effect respectively on national income.	
Period $t + 3$	This will then lead to a further accelerator effect and so on . . .	

| BOX 17.5 | HAS THERE BEEN AN ACCELERATOR EFFECT IN THE UK? | CASE STUDIES AND APPLICATIONS |

The volatility of investment

If we look at the period from 1960 to 2014, the average annual rate of increase in GDP was 2.6 per cent while for investment it was 3.7 per cent. As the chart shows, investment is highly volatile. Economic growth has fluctuated with the business cycle; but investment has been subject to far more violent swings. The fastest annual rate of increase in GDP was 10.2 per cent (Q1 1973), while the sharpest rate of decline was 6.8 per cent (Q2 2009). By contrast, the fastest annual rate of increase in investment was 26.1 per cent (Q1 1964), while the sharpest rate of decline was 20.6 per cent (Q2 2000).

These figures are consistent with the accelerator theory, which argues that the level of investment depends on the rate of change of national income. A relatively small percentage change in national income can give a much bigger percentage change in investment.

The ups and downs in GDP and investment do not completely match because there are additional factors that determine investment other than simply changes in national income. These factors include interest rates, the availability of finance, exchange rates and businesses' expectations of future demand.

1. *Can you identify any time lags in the graph? Why might there be time lags?*
2. *Why does investment in construction and producer goods industries tend to fluctuate more than investment in retailing and the service industries?*

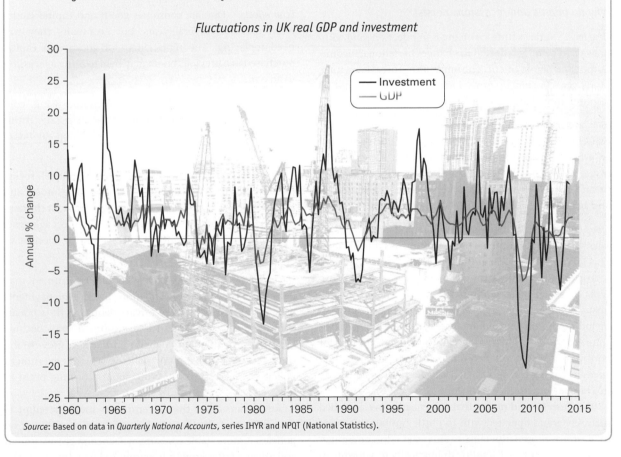

Fluctuations in UK real GDP and investment

Source: Based on data in *Quarterly National Accounts*, series IHYR and NPQT (National Statistics).

If the recession continues, however, firms will be unwilling to go on building up stocks. But as firms attempt to reduce their stocks back to the desired level, production will fall *below* the level of sales, despite the fact that sales themselves are lower. This could lead to a dramatic fall in output and, via the multiplier, to an even bigger fall in sales.

Eventually, once stocks have been run down to the minimum, production will have to rise again to match the level of sales. This will contribute to a recovery and the whole cycle will start again.

Fluctuations in borrowing and debt

During an upswing, when confidence is high, businesses will be more willing to borrow to invest and consumers will be more willing to borrow to spend. At the same time, banks will be more willing to lend, being confident in people's ability to repay. The extra borrowing and lending fuel the expansion. Private debt as a percentage of GDP thus tends to rise.

During a recession, banks are less willing to lend and both firms and consumers are less willing to borrow, fearing their ability to repay. Indeed, many people will seek to reduce their debts by increasing repayments. The reduction in borrowing and debt will push the economy deeper into recession.

We explored these balance sheet effects in Box 17.2 (page 502).

Determinants of the course of the business cycle

We are now in a position to paint a more complete Keynesian picture of the business cycle. We need to answer two key questions: (a) why do booms and recessions last for several months or even years, and (b) why do they eventually come to an end – what determines their turning points? Let us examine each in turn.

Why do booms and recessions persist?

Time lags.   It takes time for changes in injections and withdrawals to be fully reflected in changes in national income, output and employment. The multiplier process takes time. Moreover, consumers, firms and government may not all respond immediately to new situations.

'Bandwagon' effects.   Once the economy starts expanding, expectations become buoyant. People think ahead and adjust their expenditure behaviour: they consume and invest more *now*. Likewise in a recession, a mood of pessi-mism may set in. The effect is cumulative. The multiplier and accelerator interact: they feed on each other.

Group behaviour.   Individual consumers and businesses may take their lead from others and so mimic their behaviour. This helps to reinforce bandwagon effects.

For example, during the 2000s many financial institutions loosened their lending criteria. This helped to fuel unsustainable property booms in several countries, including the UK, Ireland and the USA. They engaged in a competitive race, offering evermore favourable terms for borrowers. Often the borrowers could only repay if their assets (e.g. property) appreciated in value, as they tend to do in a boom – but not in a recession.

This rush to lend meant that many banks overextended themselves and operated with too little capital. This made them much more vulnerable to financial crises and much more likely to cut back lending dramatically in a downturn – as indeed they did from 2008.

Group behaviour can therefore help to amplify economic upturns and downturns. By modelling representative agents with rational expectations, it is argued, we may fail to understand how the interaction between economic agents can affect macroeconomic aggregates (see Chapter 16 page 488).

Why do booms and recessions come to an end?

Ceilings and floors.   Actual output can go on growing more rapidly than potential output only as long as there is slack in the economy. As full employment is approached and as more and more firms reach full capacity, so a ceiling to output will be reached.

At the other extreme, there is a basic minimum level of consumption that people tend to maintain. During a recession, people may not buy many luxury and durable goods, but they will continue to buy food and other basic goods. There is thus a floor to consumption.

The industries supplying these basic goods will need to maintain their level of replacement investment. Also, there will always be some minimum investment demand as firms feel the need to install the latest equipment. There is thus a floor to investment too.

Echo effects.   Durable consumer goods and capital equipment may last several years, but eventually they will need replacing. The replacement of goods and capital purchased in a previous boom may help to bring a recession to an end.

The accelerator.   For investment to continue rising, consumer demand must rise at a *faster and faster* rate. If this does not happen, investment will fall back and the boom will break.

Random shocks.   National or international political, social, institutional or natural events can affect the mood and attitudes of firms, governments and consumers, or the conditions under which they operate, and thus affect aggregate demand. Changes in world oil prices, a war, an election or a banking crisis are all examples.

Changes in government policy.   In a boom, a government may become most worried by inflation, balance of payments deficits and rising levels of private debt, and thus pursue contractionary policies. In a recession, it may become most worried by unemployment and lack of growth and thus pursue expansionary policies. These government policies, if successful, will bring about a turning point in the cycle.

Keynesians argue that governments should attempt to reduce cyclical fluctuations by using active stabilisation policies. A more stable economy will encourage investment and allow a faster growth in output to be maintained. The policy traditionally favoured by Keynesians is *fiscal policy*. This is the subject of Chapter 21.

An analysis of the factors contributing to each of the four phases of the business cycle is given in Case Study 17.9 in MyEconLab.

Section summary

1. Keynesians explain cyclical fluctuations in the economy by examining the causes of fluctuations in the level of *aggregate demand*.

2. A major part of the Keynesian explanation of the business cycle is the instability of private-sector expenditure. Investment is the most volatile component of aggregate demand. The accelerator theory explains this volatility. It relates the level of investment to *changes* in national income and consumer demand. An initial increase in consumer demand can result in a very large percentage increase in investment; but as soon as the rise in consumer demand begins to level off, investment will fall; and even a slight fall in consumer demand can reduce investment to virtually zero.

3. The accelerator effect will be dampened by the carrying of stocks, the cautiousness of firms, forward planning by firms and the inability of producer goods industries to supply the capital equipment.

4. The interaction of the multiplier and accelerator will cause cycles.

5. Fluctuations in stocks and in levels of borrowing and debt are also major contributors to the business cycle.

6. Keynesians identify other causes of cyclical fluctuations, such as time lags, 'bandwagon' effects, ceilings and floors to output, echo effects, swings in government policy and random shocks.

END OF CHAPTER QUESTIONS

1. An economy is currently in equilibrium. The following figures refer to elements in its national income accounts.

	£ billion
Consumption (total)	60
Investment	5
Government expenditure	8
Imports	10
Exports	7

(a) What is the current equilibrium level of national income?

(b) What is the level of injections?

(c) What is the level of withdrawals?

(d) Assuming that tax revenues are £7 billion, how much is the level of saving?

(e) If national income now rose to £80 billion and, as a result, the consumption of domestically produced goods rose to £58 billion, what is the mpc_d?

(f) What is the value of the multiplier?

(g) Given an initial level of national income of £80 billion, now assume that spending on exports rises by £4 billion, spending on investment rises by £1 billion, while government expenditure falls by £2 billion. By how much will national income change?

(h) Given this new level of national income, assume that full employment is achieved at a national income of £100 billion. Is there an inflationary or a deflationary gap?

(i) What is the size of this gap?

2. What is the relationship between the *mpc*, the mpc_d and the *mpw*?

3. Why will the short-run consumption function be different from the long-run consumption function?

4. Construct a table similar to Table 17.3 (on page 510), only this time assume that the mpc_d is 3/4. Show that national income will increase by £640 million.

5. Assume that the multiplier has a value of 3. Now assume that the government decides to increase aggregate demand in an attempt to reduce unemployment. It raises government expenditure by £100 million with no increase in taxes. Firms, anticipating a rise in their sales, increase investment by £200 million, of which £50 million consists of purchases of foreign machinery. How much will national income rise? (Assume *ceteris paribus*.)

6. What factors could explain why some countries have a higher multiplier than others?

7. How can the interaction of the multiplier and the accelerator explain cyclical fluctuations in national income?

8. Why is it difficult to predict the size of the accelerator?

Online resources

Additional case studies in MyEconLab

17.1 **Keynes' views on the consumption function.** An analysis of how the assumptions made by Keynes affect the shape of the consumption function.

17.2 **Consumption and saving in practice.** An international comparison of consumption and saving rates over time.

17.3 **The relationship between income and consumption.** This examines three different theories of the consumption function – the absolute income hypothesis, the relative income hypothesis and the permanent income hypothesis. Each one is based on different assumptions about consumer behaviour.

17.4 **Trends in housing equity withdrawal (HEW).** An analysis of the patterns in HEW and consumer spending.

17.5 **An international comparison of household wealth and indebtedness.** An examination of households' financial assets and liabilities relative to disposable income in seven developed countries (the G7).

17.6 **Business expectations and their effects on investment.** An examination of business surveys in Europe and the effects of business sentiment on investment.

17.7 **The multiplier/accelerator interaction.** A numerical example showing how the interaction of the multiplier and accelerator can cause cycles in economic activity.

17.8 **Heavenly cycles.** An examination of the claim by Jevons in the late nineteenth century that the business cycle depends on the sunspot cycle!

17.9 **The phases of the business cycle.** A demand-side analysis of the factors contributing to each of the four phases.

Maths Case 17.1 Calculating the value of the multiplier. Examining the algebra.

Maths Case 17.2 Calculating the value of the multiplier. Using calculus.

Maths Case 17.3 Calculating the value of the multiplier with marginal propensities based on disposable income. Examining the algebra.

Websites relevant to Chapters 16 and 17

Numbers and sections refer to websites listed in the Web Appendix and hotlinked from this book's website at **www.pearsoned.co.uk/sloman**.

- For news articles relevant to this and the previous chapter, see the *Economic News* section in MyEconLab.

- For general news on national economies and the international economy, see websites in section A, and particularly A1–5, 7–9, 13, 20–26, 31, 33, 35, 36. See also links to newspapers worldwide in A38, 39, 42, 43 and 44, and the news search feature in Google at A41.

- For information on the development of ideas, see C12, 18; also see links under *Methodology* and *History of Economic Thought* in C14; links to economists in I4 and 17. See also sites I7 and 11 > *Economic Systems and Theories* > *History of Economic Thought*.

- For data on economic growth, employment and the business cycle, see links in B1; also see B4 and 12. For UK data, see B3, 5 and 34. For EU data, see B38 > *Statistical Annex*. For US data, see B15 and the *Data* section of B17. For international data, see B15, 21, 24, 31, 33, 35, 37, 40, 43, 48 and 49. For links to datasets, see B28; I14.

- For a model of the economy (based on the Treasury model), see *The Virtual Economy* (site D1). In addition to the model, where you can devise your own Budget, there are worksheets and outlines of theories and the work of famous economists.

- For student resources relevant to this chapter, see sites C1–7, 9, 10, 19.

MyEconLab

This book can be supported by MyEconLab, which contains a range of additional resources, including an online homework and tutorial system designed to test and build your understanding.

You need both an access card and a course ID to access MyEconLab:

1. Is your lecturer using MyEconLab? Ask your lecturer for your course ID.

2. Has an access card been included with the book at a reduced cost? Check the inside back cover of the book.

3. If you have a course ID but no access card, go to: http://www.myeconlab.com/ to buy access to this interactive study programme.

Banking, Money and Interest Rates

CHAPTER MAP

18.1 The meaning and functions of money — 524
The functions of money — 524
What should count as money? — 525

18.2 The financial system — 525
The role of the financial sector — 525
The banking system — 526
Deposit taking and lending — 527
Liquidity, profitability and capital adequacy — 532
The central bank — 537
The money markets — 541

18.3 The supply of money — 543
Definitions of the money supply — 543
The creation of credit: the simplest case — 545
The creation of credit: the real world — 546
What causes money supply to rise? — 548
The flow-of-funds equation — 549
The relationship between money supply and
   the rate of interest — 551

18.4 The demand for money — 553
The motives for holding money — 553
The transactions plus precautionary demand
   for money: L_1 — 553
The speculative (or assets) demand for
   money: L_2 — 554
The total demand for money: $L_1 + L_2$ — 555

18.5 Equilibrium — 557
Equilibrium in the money market — 557
Equilibrium in the foreign exchange market — 558

In this chapter and the next, we are going to look at the role that money and financial institutions play in an economy. The financial crisis that developed during the late 2000s vividly demonstrated the significance of the financial system to modern-day economies. It is generally recognised that changes in the amount of money can have a powerful effect on all the major macroeconomic indicators, such as inflation, unemployment, economic growth, interest rates, exchange rates and the balance of payments. But, the financial crisis did more than this: it demonstrated the systemic importance of financial institutions.

Inevitably, there will continue to be a vibrant debate about how, if at all, we can avoid a repeat of the recent financial crisis. Governments and regulators worldwide are grappling with many very important questions. For instance, are some financial institutions simply *too big to fail*? How can we ensure that banks operate with adequate loss-absorbing capacity? Can we prevent financial institutions from contributing to excessive cycles in the credit extended to households and firms? Can we better align the incentives of banks with those of the wider community? These and other questions about financial institutions are considered here.

The chapter begins by defining what is meant by money and examining its functions. Then in sections 18.2 and 18.3 we look at the operation of the financial sector of the economy and its role in determining the supply of money. It is here we consider the possible causes of the financial crisis, its impact on financial institutions themselves and some of the responses by central banks to the problems faced by financial institutions and, as a result, the economy.

In section 18.4 we turn to look at the demand for money. What we are asking is: how much of people's assets do they want to hold in the form of money? Finally, in section 18.5 we put supply and demand together to see how free-market interest rates – which have a crucial impact on aggregate demand – are determined.

Table 18.1 Balance sheet of UK banks and building societies: January 2014

Sterling liabilities	£bn	%	Sterling assets	£bn	%
Sight deposits		(39.6)	Notes and coin	9.3	(0.3)
UK banks, etc.	136.4		Balances with Bank of England		(8.5)
UK public sector	15.5		Reserve balances	297.5	
UK private sector	1058.5		Cash ratio deposits	4.1	
Non-residents	138.1		Market loans		(11.3)
Time deposits		(34.3)	UK banks, etc.	291.3	
UK banks, etc.	153.6		UK banks' CDs, etc.	5.4	
UK public sector	17.0		Non-residents	103.7	
UK private sector	814.1		Bills of exchange	10.6	(0.3)
Non-residents	214.8		Reverse repos	261.3	(7.4)
Certificates of deposit (CDs)	148.8	(4.3)	Investments	502.8	(14.2)
Repos	293.6	(8.4)	Advances	1953.0	(55.2)
Sterling capital & other funds	425.7	(12.2)	Other	96.9	(2.7)
Other	41.5	(1.2)			
Total sterling liabilities	**3493.9**	**(100.0)**	**Total sterling assets**	**3535.9**	**(100.0)**
Liabilities in other currencies	3930.1		Assets in other currencies	3888.1	
Total liabilities	**7424.0**		**Total assets**	**7424.0**	

Source: Based on data in *Bankstats* (Bank of England), Table B1.4, Data published March 2014.

Liabilities

Customers' deposits in banks (and other deposit-taking institutions such as building societies) are *liabilities* to these institutions. This means simply that the customers have the claim on these deposits and thus the institutions are liable to meet the claims.

There are five major types of liability: sight deposits, time deposits, certificates of deposit (CDs), 'repos' and capital.

Sight deposits. **Sight deposits** are any deposits that can be withdrawn on demand by the depositor without penalty. In the past, sight accounts did not pay interest. Today, however, there are many sight accounts that do. In fact, there is quite aggressive competition nowadays between banks to offer apparently very attractive interest rates on such accounts, although these are often on balances up to a relatively small amount.

The most familiar form of sight deposits are current accounts at banks. Depositors are issued with chequebooks and/or debit cards (e.g. Visa debit or MasterCard's Maestro) that enable them to spend the money directly without first having to go to the bank and draw the money out in cash. In the case of debit cards, the person's account is electronically debited when the purchase is made and the card is 'swiped' across the machine and the pin entered. This process is known as EFTPOS (electronic funds transfer at point of sale). Money can also be transferred between individuals and businesses through direct debits, standing orders and Internet banking transfers.

An important feature of current accounts is that banks often allow customers to be overdrawn. That is, they can draw on their account and make payments to other people in excess of the amount of money they have deposited.

Time deposits. **Time deposits** require notice of withdrawal. However, they normally pay a higher rate of interest than sight accounts. With some types of account, a depositor can withdraw a certain amount of money on demand, but there will be a penalty of so many days' lost interest. They are not chequebook or debit-card accounts, although some allow customers to use cash cards. The most familiar form of time deposits are the deposit and savings accounts in banks and the various savings accounts in building societies. No overdraft facilities exist with time deposits.

A substantial proportion of time deposits are from the banking sector. Interbank lending grew over the years as money markets were deregulated and as deposits were moved from one currency to another to take advantage of different rates of interest between different countries. A large proportion of overseas deposits are from foreign banks.

Certificates of deposit. **Certificates of deposit** are certificates issued by banks to customers (usually firms) for large deposits of a fixed term (e.g. £100 000 for 18 months). They can be sold by one customer to another, and thus provide a means whereby the holders can get money quickly if they need it

Definitions

Sight deposits Deposits that can be withdrawn on demand without penalty.

Time deposits Deposits that require notice of withdrawal or where a penalty is charged for withdrawals on demand.

Certificates of deposit (CDs) Certificates issued by banks for fixed-term interest-bearing deposits. They can be resold by the owner to another party.

without the banks that have issued the CDs having to supply the money. (This makes them relatively 'liquid' to the depositor but 'illiquid' to the bank: we examine this below.) The use of CDs has grown rapidly in recent years. Their use by firms has meant that, at a wholesale level, sight accounts have become less popular.

Sale and repurchase agreements (repos). If banks have a temporary shortage of funds, they can sell some of their financial assets to other banks or to the central bank – the Bank of England in the UK and the European Central Bank in the eurozone (see below) – and later repurchase them on some agreed date, typically a fortnight later. These **sale and repurchase agreements (repos)** are in effect a form of loan – the bank borrowing for a period of time using some of its financial assets as the security for the loan. One of the major assets to use in this way are government bonds (issued when the government borrows), normally called 'gilt-edged securities' or simply 'gilts' (see below). Sale and repurchase agreements involving gilts are known as gilt repos. Gilt repos play a vital role in the operation of monetary policy (see section 21.2).

Capital and other funds. This consists largely of the share capital in banks. Since shareholders cannot take their money out of banks (although they can sell their shares to other investors on the stock market), share capital provides a source of funding to meet sudden increases in withdrawals from depositors and to cover bad debts.

It is vital that banks have sufficient capital. As we shall see, an important part of the response to the financial crisis has been to require banks to hold relatively larger amounts of capital. At the beginning of 2014, the aggregate amount of sterling capital held by banks based in the UK was equivalent to 12 per cent of their sterling liabilities.

Assets

A bank's financial *assets* are its claims on others. There are three main categories of assets.

Cash and reserve balances in the central bank (Bank of England in the UK, ECB in the eurozone). Banks need to hold a certain amount of their assets as cash. This is largely used to meet the day-to-day demands of customers. They also keep 'reserve balances' in the central bank. In the UK these earn interest at the Bank of England's repo rate (or 'Bank Rate' as it is called), if, in normal times, they are kept within an agreed target range. These are like the banks' own current accounts and are used for clearing purposes (i.e. for settling the day-to-day payments between banks). They can be withdrawn in cash on demand. With interbank lending being seen as too risky during the crisis of the late 2000s, many banks resorted to depositing surplus cash in the Bank of England, even though Bank Rate was lower than the interbank lending rate or LIBOR ('London interbank offered rate') (see Box 18.3).

In the UK, banks and building societies are also required to deposit a small fraction of their assets as 'cash ratio deposits' with the Bank of England. These cannot be drawn on demand and earn no interest.

As you can see from Table 18.1, cash and balances in the Bank of England account for a very small proportion of banks' assets. The vast majority of banks' assets are in the form of various types of loan – to individuals and firms, to other financial institutions and to the government. These are 'assets' because they represent claims that the banks have on other people. Loans can be grouped into two types: short and long term.

Short-term loans. These are in the form of market loans, bills of exchange or reverse repos. The market for these various types of loan is the money market.

- **Market loans** are made primarily to other financial institutions. This interbank lending consists of (a) money lent 'at call' (i.e. reclaimable on demand or at 24 hours' notice); (b) money lent for periods up to one year, but typically a few weeks; (c) CDs (i.e. certificates of deposits made in other banks or building societies).
- **Bills of exchange** are loans either to companies (*commercial bills*) or to the government (*Treasury bills*). These are, in effect, an IOU, with the company issuing them (in the case of commercial bills), or the government (in the case of Treasury bills), promising to pay the holder a specified sum on a particular date (the 'maturity date'), typically three months later. Since bills do not pay interest, they are sold below their face value (i.e. at a 'discount'), but redeemed on maturity at the face value. This enables the purchaser, in this case the bank, to earn a return. The market for new or existing bills is therefore known as the **discount market**.

KI 25
p272

Definitions

Sale and repurchase agreements (repos) An agreement between two financial institutions whereby one in effect borrows from another by selling its assets, agreeing to buy them back (repurchase them) at a fixed price and on a fixed date.

Assets Possessions, or claims held on others.

Market loans Short-term loans (e.g. money at call and short notice).

Bills of exchange Certificates promising to repay a stated amount on a certain date, typically three months from the issue of the bill. Bills pay no interest as such, but are sold at a discount and redeemed at face value, thereby earning a rate of discount for the purchaser.

Commercial bills Bills of exchange issued by firms.

Treasury bills Bills of exchange issued by the Bank of England on behalf of the government. They are a means whereby the government raises short-term finance.

Discount market An example of a money market in which new or existing bills, such as Treasury bills or commercial bills, are bought and sold at a discount below their face value: i.e. the value at which they will be redeemed on maturity.

| BOX 18.2 | THE GROWTH OF BANKS' BALANCE SHEETS |

The rise of wholesale funding

Banks' traditional funding model relied heavily on deposits as the source of funds for loans. However, new ways for financial institutions to access funds to generate new loans have evolved. These reflect the deregulation of financial markets and the rapid pace of financial innovation.

Increasingly, financial institutions have made greater use of *wholesale funds*: i.e. funds from other financial institutions.

In addition, we have seen a growth in the 'securitisation' of non-marketable banks' assets, such as residential mortgages, which have regular income streams (e.g. from payments of interest and capital). Securitisation involves the conversion of such assets into tradable financial instruments, namely securities, which can be bought and sold on financial markets. These provide lenders who originate the loans with a source of funds for further loans. The growth of securitisation is discussed in more detail in Box 18.3.

With an increasing use of money markets by financial institutions, vast sums of funds became available for lending. One consequence of this, as illustrated in the chart, was an expansion of the aggregate balance sheets of financial institutions from £2.5 trillion (3 times GDP) at the start of 1998 to £8.5 trillion (6 times GDP) at the start of 2010.

The growth in banks' balance sheets was accompanied by a change in their composition. First, the profile of banks' assets became less liquid as they extended more long-term credit to households and firms. Second, there was a general increase in the use of fixed-interest bonds as opposed to ordinary shares (equities) for raising capital. The ratio of bonds to shares is known as the *gearing* (or *leverage*) ratio. The increase in leverage meant that, prior to the financial crisis, banks were operating with lower and lower levels of loss-absorbing capital, such as ordinary shares. If banks run at a loss, dividends on shares can be suspended; payments to

bond holders cannot. This meant that as the crisis unfolded, policy makers were facing a liquidity problem, not among one or two financial institutions, but across the financial system generally.

The market failure we are describing is a form of *co-ordination failure* and is an example of the *fallacy of composition*. When one bank pursues increased earnings by borrowing from and lending to other financial institutions, this is not necessarily a problem. But if many institutions build their balance sheets by borrowing from and lending to *each other*, then it becomes a problem for the whole financial system. The apparent increase in liquidity for individual banks, on which they base credit, is not an overall increase in liquidity for the financial system as a whole. The effect is to create a credit bubble.

The dangers of the bubble for the financial system and beyond were magnified by the increasingly tangled web of interdependencies between financial institutions, both nationally and globally. There was a danger that this complexity was masking fundamental weaknesses of many financial institutions and too little overall liquidity.

Things came to a head in 2007 and 2008. Once one or two financial institutions failed, such as Northern Rock in the UK in August 2007 and Lehman Brothers in the USA in September 2008, the worry was that failures would spread like a contagion. Banks could no longer rely on each other as their main source of liquidity.

The problems arising from the balance sheet expansion, increased leverage and enhanced maturity mismatch, meant that central banks around the world, including the Bank of England, were faced with addressing a liquidity problem of huge proportions. They had to step in to supply central bank money to prevent a collapse of the banking system.

KI 12 **p88**

The price paid for bills will depend on demand and supply. For example, the more Treasury bills that are offered for sale (i.e. the higher the supply), the lower will be their equilibrium price, and hence the higher will be their rate of return (i.e. their rate of interest, or 'rate of discount').

Normally, a bank will buy commercial bills only if they have been first 'accepted' by another financial institution (typically an investment bank). This means that the investment bank will redeem the bill (i.e. pay up) on the maturity date, if the firm issuing the bill defaults

on payment. Of course the investment bank charges for this insurance (or 'underwriting'). Bills that have been accepted in this way are known as **bank bills**.

■ *Reverse repos*. When a sale and repurchase agreement is made, the financial institution purchasing the assets (e.g. gilts) is, in effect, giving a short-term loan. The other party agrees to buy back the assets (i.e. pay back the loan) on a set date. The assets temporarily held by the bank making the loan are known as 'reverse repos'. Reverse repos are typically for one week, but can be for as little as overnight or as long as one year.

Definitions

Gearing or leverage (US term) The ratio of debt capital to equity capital: in other words, the ratio of borrowed capital (e.g. bonds) to shares.

Co-ordination failure When a group of firms (e.g. banks) acting independently could have achieved a more desirable outcome if they had co-ordinated their decision making.

Bank bills Bills that have been accepted by another financial institution and hence insured against default.

Reverse repos Gilts or other assets that are purchased under a sale and repurchase agreement. They become an asset to the purchaser.

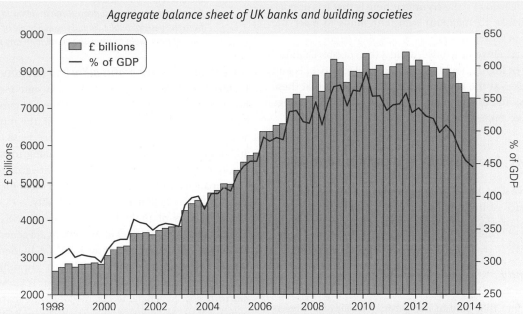

Aggregate balance sheet of UK banks and building societies

Sources: (i) Data showing liabilities of banks and building societies based on series LPMALOA and RPMTBJF (up to the end of 2009) and RPMB3UQ (from 2010) from *Statistical Interactive Database*, (Bank of England) (data published 1 July 2014, not seasonally adjusted). (ii) GDP data from *Quarterly National Accounts*, (Office for National Statistics) (GDP figures are the sum of the latest four quarters).

Subsequently, the Basel Committee on Banking Supervision (see pages 536–7) agreed a set of measures, to be applied globally, designed to ensure the greater financial resilience of banks and banking systems. It is notable from the chart how the early 2010s saw a consolidation of the aggregate balance sheet of UK banks. By the middle of 2014 the aggregate balance sheet had fallen to around £7 trillion.

This was equivalent to 4.5 times GDP as compared to almost 6 times GDP at the start of the decade.

What are the potential costs and benefits for financial institutions, lenders and borrowers and for the wider economy arising from maturity transformation? Are these dangers an inherent and unavoidable consequence of maturity transformation?

Longer-term loans. These consist primarily of loans to customers, both personal customers and businesses. These loans, also known as advances, are of four main types: fixed-term (repayable in instalments over a set number of years – typically, six months to five years), overdrafts (often for an unspecified term), outstanding balances on credit-card accounts, and mortgages (typically for 25 years).

Banks also make investments. These are partly in government bonds (gilts), which are effectively loans to the government. The government sells bonds, which then pay a fixed sum each year as interest. Once issued, they can then be bought and sold on the stock exchange. Banks are normally only prepared to buy bonds that have less than five years to maturity (the date when the government redeems the bonds). Banks also invest in various subsidiary financial institutions and in building societies.

Taxing the balance sheets

In January 2011, the UK introduced the bank levy: a tax on the liabilities of banks and building societies operating in

the UK. The design of the levy built on proposals presented by the International Monetary Fund in June 2010. There were two key principles. First, the revenues raised should be able to meet the full fiscal costs of any future support for financial institutions. Second, it should provide banks with incentives to reduce risk-taking behaviour and so reduce the likelihood of future financial crises.

The UK bank levy has two rates: a full rate on taxable liabilities with a maturity of less than one year and a half rate on taxable liabilities with a maturity of more than one year. The intention is to discourage excessive short-term borrowing by the banks in their use of wholesale funding. The levy rates are designed to raise at least £2.5 billion each year. The full rate was initially set at 0.075 and the half rate at 0.0375. By January 2014 the full rate had risen to 0.142 and the half rate to 0.071.

Not all liabilities are subject to the levy. First, it is not imposed on the first £20 billion of liabilities. This is to encourage small banks (note that the largest UK banks, such as HSBC, Barclays and RBS, each have liabilities of over £2 trillion). Second, various liabilities are excluded.

These are: (a) gilt repos; (b) retail deposits insured by public schemes such as the UK's Financial Services Compensation Scheme, which guarantees customers' deposits of up to £85 000; (c) a large part of a bank's capital known as Tier 1 capital (see below) – the argument here is that it is important for banks to maintain sufficient funds to meet the demands of its depositors.

Banks are also able to offset against their taxable liabilities holdings of highly liquid assets, such as Treasury bills and cash reserves at the Bank of England. It is hoped that these exclusions and deductions will encourage banks to engage in less risky lending.

Liquidity, profitability and capital adequacy

As we have seen, banks keep a range of liabilities and assets. The balance of items in this range is influenced by three important considerations: profitability, liquidity and capital adequacy.

Profitability

Profits are made by lending money out at a higher rate of interest than that paid to depositors. The average interest rate received by banks on their assets is greater than that paid by them on their liabilities.

Liquidity

The *liquidity* of an asset is the ease with which it can be converted into cash without loss. Cash itself, by definition, is perfectly liquid.

Some assets, such as money lent at call to other financial institutions, are highly liquid. Although not actually cash, these assets can be converted into cash virtually on demand with no financial penalty. Other short-term interbank lending is also very liquid (at least to individual banks: see Box 18.2). The only issue here is one of confidence that the money will actually be repaid. This was a worry in the financial crisis of 2008–9 when many banks stopped lending to each other on the interbank market for fear that the borrowing bank might become insolvent.

Other assets, such as gilts, can be converted into cash straight away by selling them on the Stock Exchange, but with the possibility of some financial loss, given that their market price fluctuates. Such assets, therefore, are not as liquid as money at call.

Other assets are much less liquid. Personal loans to the general public or mortgages for house purchase can be redeemed by the bank only as each instalment is paid. Other advances for fixed periods are repaid only at the end of that period.

Banks must always be able to meet the demands of their customers for withdrawals of money. To do this, they must hold sufficient cash or other assets that can be readily turned into cash. In other words, banks must maintain sufficient liquidity.

1. If a bank buys a £500 000 Treasury bill at the start of its 91-day life for £480 000, at roughly what price could it sell it to another financial institution after 45 days? Why is it not possible to predict the precise price when the bill is first purchased?

2. Suppose there were a sudden surge in demand for cash from the general public. Would the existence of interbank market loans help to meet the demand in any way?

The balance between profitability and liquidity

Profitability is the major aim of banks and most other financial institutions. However, the aims of profitability and liquidity tend to conflict. In general, the more liquid an asset, the less profitable it is, and vice versa. Personal and business loans to customers are profitable to banks, but highly illiquid. Cash is totally liquid, but earns no profit. Thus financial institutions like to hold a range of assets with varying degrees of liquidity and profitability.

For reasons of profitability, the banks will want to 'borrow short' (at low rates of interest, as are generally paid on current accounts) and 'lend long' (at higher rates of interest, as are normal on personal loans). The difference in the average maturity of loans and deposits is known as the *maturity gap*. In general terms, the larger the maturity gap between loans and deposits, the greater the profitability. For reasons of liquidity, however, banks will want a relatively small gap: if there is a sudden withdrawal of deposits, banks will need to be able to call in enough loans.

The ratio of an institution's liquid assets to total assets is known as its *liquidity ratio*. For example, if a bank had £100 million of assets, of which £10 million were liquid and £90 million were illiquid, the bank would have a 10 per cent liquidity ratio. If a financial institution's liquidity ratio is too high, it will make too little profit. If the ratio is too low, there will be the risk that customers' demands may not be able to be met: this would cause a crisis of confidence and possible closure. Institutions thus have to make a judgement as to what liquidity ratio is best – one that is neither too high nor too low.

Balances in the central bank, short-term loans (i.e. those listed above) and government bonds with less than 12 months to maturity would normally be regarded as liquid assets.

Why are government bonds that still have 11 months to run regarded as liquid, whereas overdrafts granted for a few weeks are not?

Definitions

Liquidity The ease with which an asset can be converted into cash without loss.

Maturity gap The difference in the average maturity of loans and deposits.

Liquidity ratio The proportion of a bank's total assets held in liquid form.

Over the years, banks had reduced their liquidity ratios (i.e. the ratio of liquid assets to total assets). This was not a problem as long as banks could always finance lending to customers by borrowing on the interbank market. In the late 2000s, however, banks became increasingly worried about bad debt. They thus felt the need to increase their liquidity ratios and hence cut back on lending and chose to keep a higher proportion of deposits in liquid form. In the UK, for example, banks substantially increased their reserve accounts at the Bank of England.

Capital adequacy

In addition to sufficient liquidity, banks must have sufficient capital (i.e. funds) to allow them to meet all demands from depositors and to cover losses if borrowers default on payment. Capital adequacy is a measure of a bank's capital relative to its assets, where the assets are weighted according to the degree of risk. The more risky the assets, the greater the amount of capital that will be required.

A measure of capital adequacy is given by the *capital adequacy ratio (CAR)*. This is given by the following formula:

$$CAR = \frac{\begin{array}{c}\text{Common equity Tier 1 capital} + \\ \text{Additional Tier 1 capital} + \text{Tier 2 capital}\end{array}}{\text{Risk-weighted assets}}$$

Common equity Tier 1 capital includes bank reserves (from retained profits) and ordinary share capital (equities), where dividends to shareholders vary with the amount of profit the bank makes. Such capital thus places no burden on banks in times of losses as no dividend need be paid. What is more, unlike depositors, shareholders cannot ask for their money back.

Additional Tier 1 (AT1) capital consists largely of preference shares. These pay a fixed dividend. But although preference shareholders have a prior claim over ordinary shareholders on company profits, dividends need not be paid in times of loss.

Tier 2 capital is subordinated debt with a maturity greater than five years. Subordinated debt holders only have a claim on a company after the claims of all other bond holders have been met.

Risk-weighted assets are the value of assets, where each type of asset is multiplied by a risk factor. Under the internationally agreed Basel II accord, cash and government bonds have a risk factor of zero and are thus not included. Interbank lending between the major banks has a risk factor of 0.2 and is thus included at only 20 per cent of its value; residential mortgages have a risk factor of 0.35; personal loans, credit-card debt and overdrafts have a risk factor of 1; loans to companies carry a risk factor of 0.2, 0.5, 1 or 1.5, depending on the credit rating of the company. Thus the greater the average risk factor of a bank's assets, the greater will be the value of its risk-weighted assets, and the lower will be its CAR.

The greater the CAR, the greater the capital adequacy of a bank. Under Basel II, banks were required to have a CAR of at least 8 per cent (i.e. 0.08). They were also required to meet two supplementary CARs. First, banks needed to hold a ratio of Tier 1 capital to risk-weighted assets of at least 4 per cent and, second, a ratio of ordinary share capital to risk-weighted assets of at least 2 per cent. It was felt that these three ratios would provide banks with sufficient capital to meet the demands from depositors and to cover losses if borrowers defaulted. The financial crisis, however, meant a rethink.

Secondary marketing and securitisation

As we have seen, one way of reconciling the two conflicting aims of liquidity and profitability is for financial institutions to hold a mixture of liquid and illiquid assets. Another way is through the *secondary marketing* of assets. This is where holders of assets sell them to someone else before the maturity date. This allows banks to close the maturity gap for liquidity purposes, but maintain the gap for profitability purposes.

Certificates of deposit (CDs) are a good example of secondary marketing. CDs are issued for fixed-period deposits in a bank (e.g. one year) at an agreed interest rate. The bank does not have to repay the deposit until the year is up. CDs are thus illiquid liabilities for the bank, and they allow it to increase the proportion of illiquid assets without having a dangerously high maturity gap. But the holder of the CD in the meantime can sell it to someone else (through a broker). It is thus liquid to the holder. Because CDs are liquid to the holder, they can be issued at a relatively low rate of interest and thus allow the bank to increase its profitability.

Another example of secondary marketing is when a financial institution sells some of its assets to another financial institution. The advantage to the first institution is that it gains liquidity. The advantage to the second one is that it gains profitable assets. The most common method for the sale of assets has been through a process known as *securitisation*.

Definitions

Capital adequacy ratio (CAR) The ratio of a bank's capital (reserves and shares) to its risk-weighted assets.

Secondary marketing Where assets are sold before maturity to another institution or individual. The possibility of secondary marketing encourages people or institutions to buy assets/grant loans in the primary market, knowing that they can sell them if necessary in the secondary market. The sale of existing shares and bonds on the stock market is an example of secondary marketing.

Securitisation Where future cash flows (e.g. from interest rate or mortgage payments) are turned into marketable securities, such as bonds. The sellers (e.g. banks) get cash immediately rather than having to wait and can use it to fund loans to customers. The buyers make a profit by buying below the discounted value of the future income. Such bonds can be very risky, however, as the future cash flows may be less than anticipated.

BOX 18.3   THE RISE OF SECURITISATION

Spreading the risk or securing a crisis?

The conflict between profitability and liquidity may have sown the seeds for the credit crunch that affected economies across the globe in the second half of the 2000s.

To understand this, consider the size of the 'advances' item in the banking sector's balance sheet – nearly 55 per cent of the value of sterling assets (see Table 18.1). The vast majority of these are to households. Advances secured against property have, in recent times, accounted for around 80 per cent by value of all household advances. *Residential mortgages* involve institutions lending long.

The number of UK residential mortgages has grown over time because of increases in the size of the housing stock and the proportion of households who are owner-occupiers. The number of households in the UK has increased from 19 million in 1971 to 27 million in 2014. Over the same period the owner-occupation rate has risen from 50 per cent to 64 per cent, though this is down from its peak of 70 per cent in 2002. The growth in the *value* of residential mortgages has been further fuelled by the long-term increase in house prices, including a period of strong and protracted growth between 1996 and 2008.

Securitisation of debt

One way in which individual institutions can achieve the necessary liquidity to expand the size of their mortgage lending (illiquid assets) is through *securitisation*. Securitisation grew especially rapidly in the UK and USA. In the UK this was particularly true amongst banks; building societies have historically made greater use of retail deposits to fund advances.

Figures from the Bank of England show that the value of lending to individuals which was securitised increased from just over £0.8 billion in 1998 to £103.6 billion in 2008 (see chart). As we can see from the chart, the majority of debt that has been securitised is secured debt: i.e. residential mortgages.

Securitisation is a form of financial engineering. It provides banks (originator-lenders) with liquidity and enables them to engage in further lending opportunities. It provides the special purpose vehicles with the opportunity to issue profitable securities.

The increase in securitisation up to 2008 highlights the strong demand amongst investors for these securities. The attraction of these fixed-income products for the noteholders was the potential for higher returns than on (what were) similarly rated products. However, investors have no recourse should people with mortgages fall into arrears or, worse still, default on their mortgages.

Risk and the sub-prime market

The securitisation of assets is not without risks for all those in the securitisation chain and consequently for the financial system as a whole.

The pooling of advances in itself *reduces* the cash-flow risk facing investors. However, there is a **moral hazard** problem here (see page 124). The pooling of the risks may encourage originator-lenders to lower their credit criteria by offering higher income multiples (advances relative to annual household incomes) or higher loan-to-value ratios (advances relative to the price of housing).

Towards the end of 2006 the USA witnessed an increase in the number of defaults by households on residential mortgages. This was a particular problem in the sub-prime market – higher-risk households with poor credit ratings. Similarly, the number falling behind with their payments rose. This was on the back of rising interest rates.

These problems in the US sub-prime market were the catalyst for the liquidity problem that beset financial systems in 2007 and 2008. Where these assets were securitised, investors, largely other financial institutions, suffered from the contagion arising from arrears and defaults.

Securitisation occurs when a financial institution pools some of its assets, such as residential mortgages, and sells them to an intermediary known as a *special purpose vehicle (SPV)*. SPVs are legal entities created by the financial institution. In turn, the SPV funds its purchase of the assets by issuing bonds to investors (noteholders). These bonds are known as *collateralised debt obligations (CDOs)*. Through this process, the financial institution removes the assets from its own balance sheets and so frees up capital for further advances. However, it continues to generate a return

---

Definitions

Moral hazard The temptation to take more risks when you know that someone else will cover the risks if you get into difficulties. In the case of banks taking risks, the 'someone else' may be another bank, the central bank or the government.

Special purpose vehicle (SPV) Legal entity created by financial institutions for conducting specific financial functions, such as bundling assets together into fixed-interest bonds and selling them.

Collateralised debt obligations (CDOs) These are a type of security consisting of a bundle of fixed-income assets, such as corporate bonds, mortgage debt and credit-card debt.

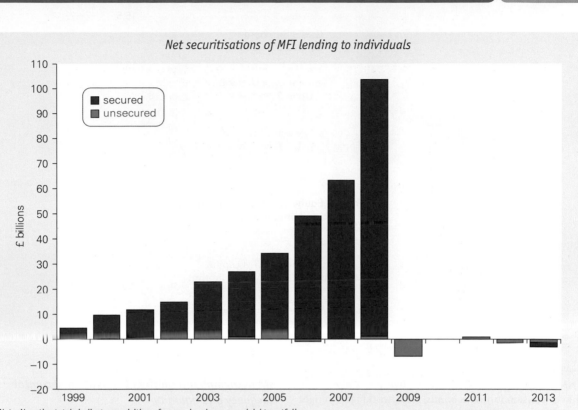

Net securitisations of MFI lending to individuals

Note: Negative totals indicate acquisition of secured and unsecured debt portfolios.
Source: Based on data from *Statistical interactive Database*, series LPQB3XE and LPQB3HK (Bank of England) (data published 29 January 2014).

Securitisation also internationalised the contagion. Investors are global so that advances, such as a US family's residential mortgage, can cross national borders. This resulted in institutions writing off debts, a deterioration of their balance sheets, the collapse in the demand for securitised assets and the drying up of liquidity.

The chart shows the collapse of the market for securitised assets. In 2009, 2012 and 2013 banks were acquiring debt portfolios. This occurs when banks buy debt portfolios from SPVs, including unsold portfolios.

 Does securitisation necessarily involve a moral hazard problem?

on its former assets by receiving a fee from the SPV for the servicing. In this way, it retains its relationships with its customers despite ceasing to own the assets. Indeed customers are very unlikely to be aware that their advance has been securitised.

The securitisation chain is illustrated in Figure 18.1. The financial institution looking to sell its assets is referred to as the 'originator' or the 'originator-lender'. Working from left to right, we see that the originator-lender sells its assets to another financial institution, the SPV, which then bundles

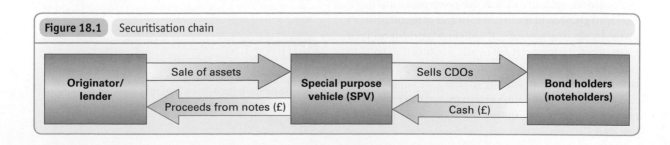

Figure 18.1 Securitisation chain

Figure 18.2   Basel III minimum capital requirements, by 1 January 2019

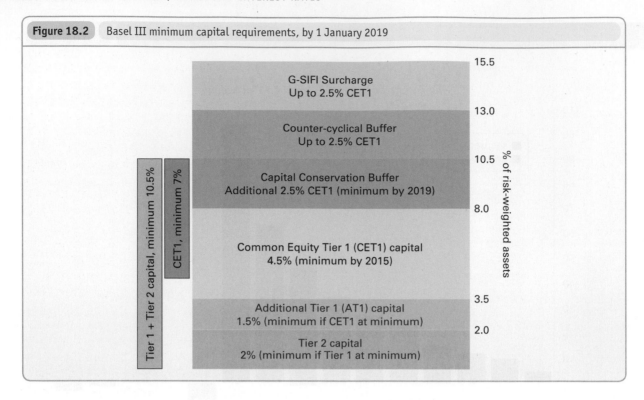

assets together into CDOs and sells them to investors (e.g. banks or pension funds) as bonds. Now, working from right to left, we see that by purchasing the bonds issued by the SPV, the investors provide the funds for the SPV's purchase of the lender's assets. The SPV is then able to use the proceeds from the bond sales (CDOs' proceeds) to provide the originator-lender with liquidity.

The effect of secondary marketing is to reduce the liquidity ratio that banks feel they need to keep. It has the effect of increasing their maturity gap.

Dangers of secondary marketing.   There are dangers to the banking system, however, from secondary marketing. To the extent that banks individually feel that they can operate with a lower liquidity ratio, so this will lead to a lower national liquidity ratio. This may lead to an excessive expansion of credit (illiquid assets) in times of economic boom.

Also, there is an increased danger of banking collapse. If one bank fails, this will have a knock-on effect on those banks which have purchased its assets. In the specific case of securitisation, the strength of the chain is potentially weakened if individual financial institutions move into riskier market segments, such as **sub-prime** residential mortgage markets. Should the income streams of the originator's assets dry up – for instance, if individuals default on their loans – then the impact is felt by the whole of the chain. In other words, institutions and investors are exposed to the risks of the originator's lending strategy.

The issue of securitisation and its impact on the liquidity of the financial system during the 2000s is considered in Box 18.3.

Strengthening international regulation of capital adequacy and liquidity

Capital adequacy.   In the light of the financial crisis of 2008–9, international capital adequacy requirements were strengthened by the *Basel Committee on Banking Supervision* in 2010–11. The new 'Basel III' capital requirements, as they are called, will be phased in by 2019. They are summarised in Figure 18.2. The revisions are to be phased in to prevent any harm to the economic recovery as banks begin adopting the new tighter regulatory requirements.

From 2013, banks continued to need a CAR of at least 8 per cent (i.e. 0.08). But by 2015 they were required to operate with a ratio of CET1 to risk-weighted assets of at least 4.5 per cent. The phased introduction of a *capital conservation buffer* from 2016 raises the CET1 ratio to no less than 7 per cent by 2019. This will take the overall CAR to at least 10.5 per cent.

On top of this, national regulators will be required to assess the financial resilience across all financial institutions under their jurisdiction, particularly in light of economic

Definition

Sub-prime debt   Debt where there is a high risk of default by the borrower (e.g. mortgage holders who are on low incomes facing higher interest rates and falling house prices).

conditions. This is *macro-prudential regulation*. If necessary, regulators will then apply a *counter-cyclical buffer* to all banks so increasing the CET1 ratio by up to a further 2.5 per cent. This will allow financial institutions to build up a capital buffer in boom times to allow it to be drawn on in times of recession or financial difficulty. It should also help to reduce the likelihood of financial institutions destabilising the economy by amplifying the business cycle.

Large global banks, known as *global systemically important banks* (G-SIBs), will be required to operate with a CET1 ratio of up to 3.5 per cent higher than other banks. The global and systemic importance of these institutions is scored against a series of indicators which determine the magnitude of their additional capital requirements. These indicators include their size and the extent of cross-border activity. The reason for this extra capital requirement is that the failure of such an institution could trigger a global financial crisis. This would potentially take the overall CAR for very large financial institutions in 2019 to 15.5 per cent (see Figure 18.2).

To supplement the risk-based capital requirements, the Basel III framework introduced a *non-risk-based leverage ratio*. Described by regulators as complementary to the risk-based framework, this requires financial institutions to operate with a Tier 1 capital-to-asset ratio of 3 per cent. In contrast to the risk-based ratios, the assets in the denominator in this ratio are *not* weighted by risk factors.

Liquidity. The financial crisis drew attention for the need of banks not only to hold adequate levels of capital but also to manage their liquidity better. The Basel III framework includes a *liquidity coverage ratio* (LCR). This requires that financial institutions have high-quality liquid assets (HQLAs) to cover the expected net cash flow over the next 30 days. Beginning in 2015, the minimum LCR ratio (HQLAs relative to the expected 30-day net cash flow) will rise from 60 per cent to 100 per cent by 2019.

Net stable funding ratio (NSFR). As part of Basel III, it is intended to introduce a *net stable funding ratio* (NSFR) by 2018. This takes a longer-term view of the funding profile of banks relative to their assets. Stable funding is defined as the amount of liabilities expected to be reliable sources of funds in circumstances of extreme stress. The NSFR is the ratio of stable liabilities to assets likely to require funding (i.e. assets where there is a likelihood of default).

On the liabilities side, these are to be weighted by their expected reliability – in other words, by the stability of these funds. This weighting will reflect the maturity of the liabilities and the propensity of lenders to withdraw their funds. For example, Tier 1 and 2 capital will have a weighting of 100 per cent; term deposits with less than one year to maturity will have a weighting of 50 per cent; and unsecured wholesale funding will have a weighting of 0 per cent. The result of these weightings is a measure of stable funding.

The *required* NSFR will be determined by the profile of assets. The various assets on banks' balance sheets are to be weighted by the likelihood that they will have to be funded over the course of one year. This means that they will be weighted by their liquidity, with more liquid assets requiring less funding. Thus cash will have a zero weighting, while more risky assets will have weightings up to 100 per cent. The result is a measure of required funding. Banks will need to hold a stable-liabilities-to-required-funding ratio (NSFR) of 100 per cent or more.

The central bank

The Bank of England is the UK's central bank. The European Central Bank (ECB) is the central bank for the countries using the euro. The Federal Reserve Bank of America (the Fed) is the USA's central bank. All countries with their own currency have a central bank. It fulfils two vital roles in the economy.

The first is to oversee the whole monetary system and ensure that banks and other financial institutions operate as stably and as efficiently as possible.

The second is to act as the government's agent, both as its banker and in carrying out monetary policy. The Bank of England traditionally worked in very close liaison with the Treasury, and there used to be regular meetings between the Governor of the Bank of England and the Chancellor of the Exchequer. Although the Bank may have disagreed with Treasury policy, it always carried it out. With the election of the Labour government in 1997, however, the Bank of England was given independence to decide the course of monetary policy. In particular, this meant that the Bank of England and not the government would now decide interest rates.

Another example of an independent central bank is the European Central Bank, which operates the monetary policy for the eurozone countries. Similarly, the Fed is independent of both the President and Congress, and its chair is generally regarded as having great power in determining the country's economic policy. Although the degree of independence of central banks from government varies considerably around the world, there has been a general move in recent years to make central banks more independent.

If the UK were ever to adopt the euro, there would be a much reduced role for the Bank of England. At present, however, within its two broad roles, it has a number of different functions. Although we will consider the case of the

KI 22
p 223

Definitions

Macro-prudential regulation Regulation which focuses not on a single financial institution but on the financial system as a whole and which monitors its resilience to shocks and its impact on the wider economy.

Global systemically important banks (G-SIBs) Banks identified by a series of indicators as being significant players in the global financial system.

| Table 18.2 | Balance sheet of the Bank of England: start of January 2008 and 2014 |

Liabilities, £ billion			Assets, £ billion		
	Jan 08	**Jan 14**		**Jan 08**	**Jan 14**
Issue Department			**Issue Department**		
Notes in circulation	34.5	62.5	Short-term open-market operations	2.4	0.0
			Long-term reverse repos	13.5	0.1
			Ways and Means advances to HM government	13.4	0.4
			Bonds and other securities acquired	0.0	4.2
			Deposits with banking department	5.2	57.8
Issue Department liabilities	34.5	62.5	**Issue Department assets**	34.5	62.5
Banking Department			**Banking Department**		
Reserve balances	23.6	297.0	Short-term open-market operations	0.0	0.0
Short-term open-market operations	0.0	0.0	Long-term reverse repos	10.0	0.1
Foreign currency public securities issued	4.9	3.6	Bonds and other securities acquired	7.6	12.2
Cash ratio deposits	2.9	4.1	Other assets	44.1	384.4
Other liabilities	30.3	91.8	*Of which:*		
			APF loan investment in corporate bonds and commercial papers		*0.0*
			APF loan investment in gilts		*375.0*
Banking Department liabilities	61.7	396.6	**Banking Department assets**	61.7	396.6

Source: Based on data in *Bankstats* (Bank of England), Tables B1.1.1 and D2.3.1, Data published January 2014.

Bank of England, the same principles apply to other central banks.

It issues notes

The Bank of England is the sole issuer of banknotes in England and Wales. (In Scotland and Northern Ireland, retail banks issue notes.) The issue of notes is done through the Issue Department, which organises their printing. This is one of two departments of the Bank of England. The other is the Banking Department, through which it deals with banks. Table 18.2 shows the balance sheets of these two departments at the start of 2008 and 2014. A significant expansion of the Bank's aggregate balance sheet occurred over this period.

The balance sheet of the Issue Department shows the outstanding value of the banknote issue and the assets that back this issue. The Ways and Means advances on the balance sheet of the Issue Department represent the UK central government's overdraft facility at the Bank.

As you can see from the balance sheet for the Issue Department, the note issue is largely backed by a mixture of short-term and long-term repos and more recently by deposits with the Banking Department.

The amount of banknotes issued by the Bank of England depends largely on the demand for notes from the general public. If people draw more cash from their bank accounts, the banks will have to draw more cash from their balances in the Bank of England. These balances are held in the Banking Department. The Banking Department will thus have to acquire more notes from the Issue Department, which will simply print more in exchange for extra government or other securities supplied by the Banking Department, which

are entered as 'deposits with Banking Department' in the assets of the Issue Department.

It acts as a bank

To the government. It keeps the two major government accounts: the 'Exchequer' and the 'National Loans Fund'. Taxation and government spending pass through the Exchequer. Government borrowing and lending pass through the National Loans Fund. The government tends to keep its deposits in the Bank of England (the public deposits item in the balance sheet) to a minimum. If the deposits begin to build up (from taxation), the government will probably spend them on paying back government debt. If, on the other hand, it runs short of money, it will simply borrow more.

To banks. Banks' deposits in the Bank of England consist of reserve balances and cash ratio deposits (see Table 18.1). The reserve balances are used for clearing purposes between the banks but are also a means by which banks can manage their liquidity risk. Therefore, the reserve balances provide banks with an important buffer stock of liquid assets.

To overseas central banks. These are deposits of sterling (or euros in the case of the ECB) made by overseas authorities as part of their official reserves and/or for purposes of intervening in the foreign exchange market in order to influence the exchange rate of their currency.

It operates the government's monetary policy

The Bank of England's Monetary Policy Committee (MPC) sets Bank Rate at its monthly meetings. This nine-member committee consists of four experts appointed by the Chancellor of the Exchequer and four senior members of the Bank of England, plus the Governor in the chair.

By careful management of the liquidity of the financial system the Bank of England aims to keep interest rates in line with the level decided by the MPC. It is able to do this through operations in the money markets. These are known as *open-market operations (OMOs)*. If shortages of liquidity are driving up short-term interest rates above the desired level, the Bank of England purchases securities (gilts and/or Treasury bills) on the open market: e.g. through reverse repos (a repo to the banks). This releases liquidity into the financial system and puts downward pressure on interest rates. Conversely, if excess liquidity is driving down interest rates, the Bank of England will sell more securities. When these are purchased, this will reduce banks' reserves and thereby put upward pressure on interest rates.

In normal times the Bank of England manages the aggregate amount of reserves through weekly auctions of 1-week repos. It also agrees with commercial banks an *average* amount of overnight reserve balances they would hold over the period between MPC meetings. Individual banks are then able to deposit or borrow reserves using the Bank of England's *operational standing facilities*. Banks deposit reserves at the deposit facility rate if they have an excess of reserves or borrow reserves from the Bank of England if they are short of reserves through overnight repo operations priced at the lending facility rate. The deposit rate is set below the Bank Rate, while the borrowing rate is set above the Bank Rate. This process is known as *reserve averaging*.

The operational standing facilities are designed to provide banks with excess or surplus reserves as an incentive to trade them with other banks. Banks would prefer to borrow reserves at a lower interest rate or deposit reserves at a higher interest rate than they can through the operational standing facilities. By managing the aggregate amount of reserves, agreeing an average overnight holding of reserves and providing operational standing facilities, the Bank of England aims to establish a 'corridor' for interbank rates between its lending and deposit rates.

From its inception in March 2006 up until the middle of 2007 the corridor system kept short-term money market rates close to Bank Rate. But then, with growing concerns about the solvency of banks, the interbank market ceased to operate effectively and banks were forced to make greater use of the more costly operational standing facilities and draw reserves from the Bank. In other words, banks could no longer trade reserves with each other (in order to meet their average reserve target) at a lower cost than by using the Bank's standing facilities.

As the financial crisis unfolded it became increasingly difficult for the Bank to meet its monetary policy objectives while maintaining financial stability. New policies were thus adopted. October 2008 also saw the Bank of England stop short-term open-market operations. The key priority was now ensuring sufficient liquidity and so the focus switched to longer-term OMOs.

March 2009 saw the Bank begin its programme of quantitative easing (see Box 21.9). This involved the Bank purchasing assets, mainly government bonds, predominantly from non-deposit-taking financial institutions (sometimes known as 'Other Financial Institutions' or simply OFCs), such as unit trusts, insurance companies and pension funds. In doing so, the Bank supplied them with reserves.

Given this large quantity of 'new money' being supplied to the banking system it was decided to end the practice of banks voluntarily setting their own reserve targets between meetings of the MPC. Instead, all reserves were now to be remunerated at the official bank rate. The effect of remunerating all reserves was to replace the 'corridor system' with a 'floor system' since no commercial bank would be willing to lend surplus reserves at any rate lower than the Bank Rate. Therefore, the interbank rate would not fall below the Bank Rate.

The Bank of England's programme of asset purchases can be observed on the balance sheet of the Banking Department in Table 18.2 (these are shown under 'Other assets'). The purchases were conducted by a subsidiary of the Bank of England known as the Asset Purchase Facility (APF).

Although the financial crisis saw changes to the Bank's monetary framework, the Bank argued that, in normal times, the reserve averaging framework remained an effective framework for implementing monetary policy. The case for resuming the framework was thus to be kept under review.

It provides liquidity, as necessary, to banks

Financial institutions engage in maturity transformation. While most customer deposits can be withdrawn instantly, financial institutions will have a variety of lending commitments, some of which span many years. Hence, the Bank of England acts as a 'liquidity backstop' for the banking system. It attempts to ensure that there is always an adequate supply of liquidity to meet the legitimate demands of depositors in banks.

Definitions

Open-market operations (OMOs) The sale (or purchase) by the authorities of government securities in the open market in order to reduce (or increase) money supply and thereby affect interest rates.

Operational standing facilities Central bank facilities by which individual banks can deposit reserves or borrow reserves.

Reserve averaging The process whereby individual banks manage their average level of overnight reserves between MPC meetings using the Bank of England's operational standing facilities and/or the interbank market.

Banks' reserve balances provide them with some liquidity insurance. However, the Bank of England needs other means by which to provide both individual banks and the banking system with sufficient liquidity. The financial crisis, for instance, saw incredible pressure on the aggregate liquidity of financial system. The result is that the UK has three principal liquidity insurance facilities:

- *Index long-term repos (ILTRS)*. Each month the Bank of England provides MFIs with reserves for a six-month period secured against collateral and indexed against the Bank Rate. Financial institutions can borrow reserves against different levels of collateral. These levels reflect the quality and liquidity of the collateral. The reserves are distributed through an auction where financial institutions indicate, for their particular level of collateral, the number of basis points over the Bank Rate (the 'spread') they are prepared to pay. Successful bidders pay a uniform price: this is the clearing price at which the Bank of England's preparedness to lend reserves has been met. The Bank of England will provide a greater quantity of reserves if, from the bids, it observes a greater demand for it to provide liquidity insurance.

- *Discount window facility (DWF)*. This on-demand facility allows financial institutions to borrow government bonds (gilts) for 30 days against different classes of collateral. They pay a fee to do so. The size of the fee is determined by both the level of collateral and the size of the collateral being traded. Gilts are long-term government debt instruments used by government as a means of financing its borrowing. Gilts can be used in repo operations as a means of securing liquidity. In this way, financial institutions are performing a liquidity upgrade of their collateral. However, the Bank may agree to lend cash rather than gilts if gilt repo markets cease to provide the necessary amount of liquidity, perhaps because the cost of doing so becomes prohibitively high. Financial institutions can look to roll over the funds obtained from the DWF beyond the normal 30 days.

- *Contingent term repo facility (CTRP)*. This is a facility which the Bank of England can activate in exceptional circumstances. As with the ILTRS, financial institutions can obtain liquidity secured against different levels of collateral through an auction. However, the terms, including the maturity of the funds, are intended to be more flexible.

It oversees the activities of banks and other financial institutions

The Bank of England requires all recognised banks to maintain adequate liquidity: this is called **prudential control**.

In May 1997, the Bank of England ceased to be responsible for the detailed supervision of banks' activities. This responsibility passed to the Financial Services Authority (FSA). But the financial crisis of the late 2000s raised concerns about whether the FSA, the Bank of England and HM Treasury were sufficiently watchful of banks' liquidity and the risks of liquidity shortage. Some commentators argued that a much tighter form of prudential control needed to be imposed.

The early 2010s saw the implementation of a new regulatory framework with an enhanced role for the Bank of England.

First, the Bank's *Financial Policy Committee* became responsible for macro-prudential regulation. This type of regulation takes a broader view of the financial system. It considers, for instance, its health or resilience to possible shocks and its propensity to create macroeconomic instability through credit creation.

Second, the prudential regulation of individual firms was transferred from the FSA to the *Prudential Regulation Authority*, a subsidiary of the Bank of England. Meanwhile, the *Financial Conduct Authority (FCA)* took responsibility for consumer protection and the regulation of markets for financial services. The FCA is an independent body accountable to HM Treasury. The FSA was wound up.

1. *Would it be possible for an economy to function without a central bank?*
2. *What effect would a substantial increase in the sale of government bonds and Treasury bills have on interest rates?*

It operates the government's exchange rate policy

The Bank of England manages the country's gold and foreign currency reserves on behalf of the Treasury. This is done through the **exchange equalisation account**. The Treasury sets the Bank an annual remit for the management of the account (e.g. setting a limit on changes in the level of reserves).

By buying and selling foreign currencies on the foreign exchange market, the Bank of England can affect the exchange rate. For example, if there were a sudden selling of sterling (due, say, to bad trade figures and a resulting fear that the pound would depreciate), the Bank of England could help to prevent the pound from falling by using reserves to buy up pounds on the foreign exchange market. Intervention in the foreign exchange market is examined in detail in Chapter 25.

Definitions

Prudential control The insistence by the Bank of England that recognised banks maintain adequate liquidity.

Exchange equalisation account The gold and foreign exchange reserves account in the Bank of England.

The money markets

We now turn to the money markets, where participants, including financial institutions, are able to lend and borrow to and from each other. In these markets debts typically have maturities of less than one year.

It has been traditional to distinguish money markets from another set of financial markets known as *capital markets*. In capital markets borrowing typically takes place over a longer duration. Capital markets include the market for ordinary shares and longer-term government debt instruments, known in the UK as gilts, which pay periodic fixed payments (known as 'coupons'). However, as we shall see, the boundaries in practice between these markets are rather difficult to pinpoint.

Central banks are also important participants in money markets. It is through the money markets that a central bank exercises control over interest rates. As we have seen throughout this chapter, the financial system has evolved rapidly and the money markets are no exception. This has widened the lending and borrowing opportunities for financial institutions.

We take the case of the London money market, which is normally divided into the 'discount' and 'repo' markets and the 'parallel' or 'complementary' markets.

 What how might the development of new financial instruments affect a central bank's conduct of monetary policy?

The discount and repo markets

The discount market is the market for commercial or government bills. In the UK government bills are known as Treasury bills and operations are conducted by the Debt Management Office, usually on a weekly basis. Treasury Bills involve short-term lending, say for one or three months, which, in conjunction with their low default risk, make them highly liquid assets. These markets are examples of *discount markets* because the instruments being traded are issued at a discount. In other words, the redemption price of the bills is greater than the issue price. The redemption price is fixed, but the issue price depends on demand and supply in the discount market. The rate of discount on bills can be calculated by the size of the discount relative to the redemption value and is usually expressed as an annual rate.

The discount market is also known as the 'traditional market' because it was the market in which many central banks traditionally used to supply central bank money to financial institutions. For instance, if the Bank of England wanted to increase liquidity in the banking system it could purchase from the banks Treasury bills which had yet to reach maturity. This process is known as *rediscounting*. The Bank of England would pay a price below the face value, thus effectively charging interest to the banks. The price could be set so that the 'rediscount rate' reflected the Bank Rate.

The emergence of the repo market is a more recent development dating back in the UK to the 1990s. As we saw earlier, repos have become an important source of wholesale funding for financial institutions. But they have also become an important means by which central banks can affect the liquidity of the financial system both to implement monetary policy and to ensure financial stability.

By entering into a repo agreement the Bank of England can buy securities, such as gilts, from the banks (thereby supplying them with money) on the condition that the banks buy them back at a fixed price and on a fixed date. The repurchase price will be above the sale price. The difference is the equivalent of the interest that the banks are being charged for having what amounts to a loan from the Bank of England. The repurchase price (and hence the 'repo rate') is set by the Bank of England to reflect the Bank Rate chosen by the MPC.

The Bank of England first began using repo operations to manage the liquidity of the financial system in 1997 when it undertook daily operations, with the repurchases of securities usually occurring two weeks after the initial sale. This system was refined so that in 2006 operations became weekly and the repurchase period typically shortened to one week.

However, the financial crisis caused the Bank to modify its repo operations to manage liquidity for both purposes of monetary policy, but increasingly to ensure financial stability. These changes included a widening of the securities eligible as collateral for loans, a move to longer-term repo operations and a consequent suspension of short-term repo operations. Whilst the financial crisis may have enduring effects on the nature of repo operations, they remain an important monetary instrument.

So central banks, like the Bank of England, are prepared to provide central bank money through the creation of bank reserves. Central banks are thus the ultimate guarantor of sufficient liquidity in the monetary system and, for this reason, are known as the *lender of last resort*.

Definitions

Capital market A financial market where longer-term debt instruments, like government bonds (gilts), can be bought and sold.

Discount market The market for corporate bills and Treasury bills whose initial price is below the redemption value.

Rediscounting bills of exchange Buying bills before they reach maturity.

Lender of last resort The role of the Bank of England as the guarantor of sufficient liquidity in the monetary system.

Figure 18.3 One-month LIBOR and Bank Rate

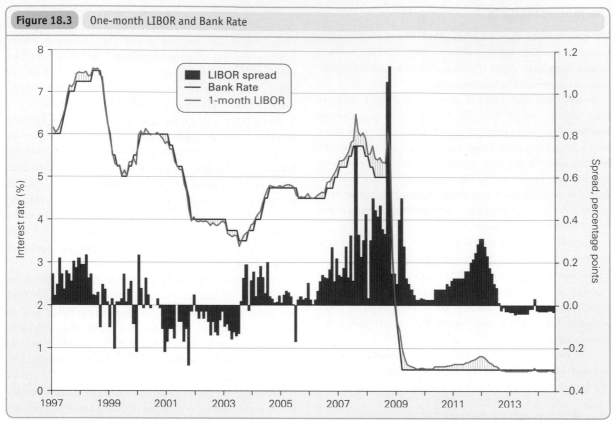

Source: Based on data from *Statistical Interactive Database*, Bank of England, series IUMMAM IH and IUMVNEA (data published 1 August 2014).

The parallel money markets

Like repo markets, complementary or parallel money markets have grown rapidly in recent years. In part, this reflects the opening up of markets to international dealing, the deregulation of banking and money market dealing and the desire of banks to keep funds in a form that can be readily switched from one form of deposit to another, or from one currency to another.

Examples of parallel markets include the markets for *certificates of deposit* (CDs), *foreign currencies markets* (dealings in foreign currencies deposited short term in the country) and *the interbank market*. We focus here on the important interbank market (details on other parallel markets can be found in Case Study 18.11 in MyEconLab).

The interbank market involves wholesale loans from one bank to another over periods from one day to up to several months. Banks with surplus liquidity lend to other banks, which then use this as the basis for loans to individuals and companies.

The rate at which banks lend to each other is known as the IBOR (interbank offered rate). The IBOR has a major influence on the other rates that banks charge. In the eurozone, the IBOR is known as Euribor. In the UK, it is known as the LIBOR (where 'L' stands for 'London'). As interbank loans can be anything from overnight to 12 months, the IBOR will vary from one length of loan to another.

Interbank interest rates tend to be higher than those in the discount and repo markets and sensitive to the aggregate level of liquidity in the financial system. As Figure 18.3 shows, during the financial crisis of 2008 interbank lending rates rose significantly above the Bank Rate. At the same time lending virtually ceased as banks became worried that the bank they were lending to might default.

 Why should Bank of England determination of the rate of interest in the discount and repo markets also influence rates of interest in the parallel markets?

Section summary

1. Central to the financial system are the retail and wholesale arms of banks. Between them they provide the following important functions: giving expert advice, channelling capital to areas of highest return, maturity transformation, risk transformation and the transmission of payments. During the financial crisis the systemic importance of some of these banks meant they had to be rescued by governments. They were seen as too important or too big to fail (TBF).

2. Banks' liabilities include both sight and time deposits. They also include certificates of deposit and repos. Their assets include: notes and coin, balances with the Bank of England, market loans, bills of exchange (Treasury bills and commercial bills), reverse repos, advances to customers (the biggest item – including overdrafts, personal loans, credit-card debt and mortgages) and investments (government bonds and interbank investments). In recent years they have increasingly included securitised assets.

3. Banks aim to make profits, but they must also have a sufficient capital base and maintain sufficient liquidity. Liquid assets, however, tend to be relatively unprofitable and profitable assets tend to be relatively illiquid. Banks therefore need to keep a balance of profitability and liquidity in their range of assets.

4. The Bank of England is the UK's central bank. It issues notes; it acts as banker to the government, to banks and to various overseas central banks; it ensures sufficient liquidity for the financial sector; it operates the country's monetary and exchange rate policy.

5. The money market is the market in short-term deposits and loans. It consists of the discount and repo markets and the parallel money markets.

6. Through repos the Bank of England can provide liquidity to the banks at the rate of interest chosen by the Monetary Policy Committee (Bank Rate). It is always prepared to lend in this way in order to ensure adequate liquidity in the economy. The financial crisis saw the Bank adapt its operations in the money market and introduce new mechanisms for providing liquidity insurance, including the Discount Window Facility which facilitates asset-swaps with commercial banks.

7. The parallel money markets consist of various markets in short-term finance between various financial institutions.

18.3 THE SUPPLY OF MONEY

Definitions of the money supply

If money supply is to be monitored and possibly controlled, it is obviously necessary to measure it. But what should be included in the measure? Here we need to distinguish between the monetary base and broad money.

The *monetary base* (or 'high-powered money') consists of cash (notes and coin) in circulation outside the central bank. Thus, in the eurozone, the monetary base is given by cash (euros) in circulation outside the ECB.[1] In 1970, the stock of notes and coins in circulation in the UK was around £4 billion, equivalent to 8 per cent of annual GDP. By 2014 this had grown to over £70 billion, but equivalent to only about 4 per cent of annual GDP.

But the monetary base gives us a very poor indication of the effective money supply, since it excludes the most important source of liquidity for spending: namely, bank deposits. The problem is which deposits to include. We need to answer three questions:

- Should we include just sight deposits, or time deposits as well?
- Should we include just retail deposits, or wholesale deposits as well?
- Should we include just bank deposits, or building society (savings institution) deposits as well?

In the past there has been a whole range of measures, each including different combinations of these accounts. However, financial deregulation, the abolition of foreign exchange controls and the development of computer technology have led to huge changes in the financial sector throughout the world. This has led to a blurring of the distinctions between different types of account. It has also made it very easy to switch deposits from one type of account to another. For these reasons, the most usual measure that countries use for money supply is *broad money*, which in most cases includes both time and sight deposits, retail and wholesale deposits, and bank and building society (savings institution) deposits.

[1] Before 2006, there used to be a measure of narrow money called 'M0' in the UK. This included cash in circulation outside the Bank of England and banks' non-interest-bearing 'operational balances' in the Bank of England, with these balances accounting for a tiny proportion of the whole. Since 2006, the Bank of England has allowed banks to hold interest-bearing reserve accounts, which are much larger than the former operational balances. The Bank of England thus decided to discontinue M0 as a measure and focus on cash in circulation as its measure of the monetary base.

Definitions

Monetary base Notes and coin outside the central bank.

Broad money Cash in circulation plus retail and wholesale bank and building society deposits.

BOX 18.4   UK AND EUROZONE MONETARY AGGREGATES

How long is a piece of string?

UK measures

There are two main measures of the money supply in the UK: cash in circulation (i.e. outside the Bank of England) and M4. Cash in circulation is referred to as the 'monetary base' or 'narrow money' and M4 is referred to as 'broad money' or simply as 'the money supply'. In addition, there is a measure called 'Retail deposits and cash in M4' (previously known as M2). This measure excludes wholesale deposits.

The definitions are as follows:

Cash in circulation.   This is all cash held outside the Bank of England: in other words, by individuals, firms, banks and the public sector.

Retail deposits and cash in M4.   Cash in circulation with the public (but not cash in banks and building societies) + private-sector *retail* sterling deposits in banks and building societies.

M4.   Retail deposits and cash in M4 + private-sector wholesale sterling deposits (including repos) in banks and building societies + private-sector holdings of sterling certificates of deposit, commercial paper and other short-term paper issued by MFIs.

Table (a) gives the figures for these aggregates for the end of December 2013.

(a) *UK monetary aggregates, end December 2013 (not seasonally adjusted)*

		£ billion
	Cash in circulation (i.e. outside the Bank of England)[a]	68.57
−	Cash in banks and cash held outside the UK[b]	−8.53
+	Private-sector retail bank and building society deposits	1352.82
=	**Retail deposits and cash in M4**	**1412.86**
+	Private-sector wholesale bank and building society deposits + CDs	691.48
=	**M4**	**2104.35**

[a] Cash in circulation is calculated mid-month and thus the figure slightly understates the end-month value.
[b] Row 4 minus rows 3 and 1.
Source: Based on data in *Bankstats* (Bank of England), Tables A1.1.1 and A2.2.1, Data published January 2014.

 Why is cash in banks and building societies not included in M4?

Eurozone measures

Although the ECB uses three measures of the money supply, they are different from those used by the Bank of England. The narrowest definition (M1) includes overnight deposits (i.e. call money) as well as cash, and is thus much broader than the UK's narrow money measure. The broadest eurozone measure (M3) is again broader than the UK's broadest measure (M4), since the eurozone measure includes various other moderately liquid assets. The definitions of the three eurozone aggregates are:

M1.   Cash in circulation with the public + overnight deposits.

M2.   M1 + deposits with agreed maturity up to two years + deposits redeemable up to three months' notice.

M3.   M2 + repos + money market funds and paper + debt securities with residual maturity up to two years.

Table (b) gives the figures for UK money supply for each of these three ECB measures – again, for the end of December 2013.

(b) *UK money supply using ECB measures: end December 2013 (not seasonally adjusted)*

		£ billion
	Currency in circulation	60.68
+	Overnight deposits	1218.67
=	**M1**	**1279.35**
+	Deposits with agreed maturity up to 2 years	213.65
+	Deposits redeemable up to 3 months' notice	590.55
=	**M2**	**2083.55**
+	Repos	222.01
+	Money market funds and paper	51.35
=	**M3**	**2356.91**

Note: M1, M2 and M3 estimates relate to non-MFI residents, excluding central government and contain deposits in all currencies.
Source: Bankstats (Bank of England), Table A2.3, Data published January 2014.

 What are the benefits of including these additional items in the broad measure of money supply?

In the UK this measure of broad money is known as M4. In most other European countries and the USA it is known as M3. There are, however, minor differences between countries in what is included. (Official UK and eurozone measures of money supply are given in Box 18.4.)

In 1970, the stock of M4 in the UK was around £25 billion, equivalent to 50 per cent of annual GDP. By 2014 this had grown to £2.1 trillion, equivalent to about 130 per cent of annual GDP.

As we have seen, bank deposits of one form or another constitute by far the largest component of (broad) money supply. To understand how money supply expands and contracts, and how it can be controlled, it is thus necessary to understand what determines the size of bank deposits.

Table 18.3	Banks' original balance sheet		
Liabilities	**£bn**	**Assets**	**£bn**
Deposits	100	Balances with the central bank	10
		Advances	90
Total	100	Total	100

Banks can themselves expand the amount of bank deposits, and hence the money supply, by a process known as 'credit creation'.

The creation of credit: the simplest case

To illustrate this process in its simplest form, assume that banks have just one type of liability – deposits – and two types of asset – balances with the central bank (to achieve liquidity) and advances to customers (to earn profit).

Banks want to achieve profitability while maintaining sufficient liquidity. Assume that they believe that sufficient liquidity will be achieved if 10 per cent of their assets are held as balances with the central bank. The remaining 90 per cent will then be in advances to customers. In other words, the banks operate a 10 per cent liquidity ratio.

Assume initially that the combined balance sheet of the banks is as shown in Table 18.3. Total deposits are £100 billion, of which £10 billion (10 per cent) are kept in balances with the central bank. The remaining £90 billion (90 per cent) are lent to customers.

Now assume that the government spends more money – £10 billion, say, on roads or hospitals. It pays for this with cheques drawn on its account with the central bank. The people receiving the cheques deposit them in their banks. Banks return these cheques to the central bank and their balances correspondingly increase by £10 billion. The combined banks' balance sheet now is shown in Table 18.4.

But this is not the end of the story. Banks now have surplus liquidity. With their balances in the central bank having increased to £20 billion, they now have a liquidity ratio of 20/110, or 18.2 per cent. If they are to return to a 10 per cent

Table 18.4	The initial effect of an additional deposit of £10 billion		
Liabilities	**£bn**	**Assets**	**£bn**
Deposits (old)	100	Balances with the central bank (old)	10
Deposits (new)	10	Balances with the central bank (new)	10
		Advances	90
Total	110	Total	110

Table 18.5	The full effect of an additional deposit of £10 billion		
Liabilities	**£bn**	**Assets**	**£bn**
Deposits (old)	100	Balances with the central bank (old)	10
Deposits (new: initial)	10	Balances with the central bank (new)	10
(new: subsequent)	90	Advances (old)	90
		Advances (new)	90
Total	200	Total	200

liquidity ratio, they need only retain £11 billion as balances at the central bank (£11 billion/£110 billion = 10 per cent). The remaining £9 billion they can lend to customers.

Assume now that customers spend this £9 billion in shops and the shopkeepers deposit the cheques in their bank accounts. When the cheques are cleared, the balances in the central bank of the *customers'* banks will duly be debited by £9 billion, but the balances in the central bank of the shopkeepers' banks will be credited by £9 billion, leaving overall balances in the central bank unaltered. There is still a surplus of £9 billion over what is required to maintain the 10 per cent liquidity ratio. The new deposits of £9 billion in the shopkeepers' banks, backed by balances in the central bank, can thus be used as the basis for further loans. Ten per cent (i.e. £0.9 billion) must be kept back in the central bank, but the remaining 90 per cent (i.e. £8.1 billion) can be lent out again.

When the money is spent and the cheques are cleared, this £8.1 billion will still remain as surplus balances in the central bank and can therefore be used as the basis for yet more loans. Again, 10 per cent must be retained and the remaining 90 per cent can be lent out. This process goes on and on until eventually the position is as shown in Table 18.5.

The initial increase in balances with the central bank of £10 billion has allowed banks to create new advances (and hence deposits) of £90 billion, making a total increase in money supply of £100 billion.

This effect is known as the **bank deposits multiplier**. In this simple example with a liquidity ratio of 1/10 (i.e. 10 per cent), the bank deposits multiplier is 10. An initial increase in deposits of £10 billion allowed total deposits to rise by £100 billion. In this simple world, therefore, the bank deposits multiplier is the inverse of the liquidity ratio (l): i.e. $1/l$.

Definition

Bank deposits multiplier The number of times greater the expansion of bank deposits is than the additional liquidity in banks that causes it: $1/l$ (the inverse of the liquidity ratio).

If banks choose to operate a 20 per cent liquidity ratio and receive extra cash deposits of £10 million:
(a) How much credit will ultimately be created?
(b) By how much will total deposits have expanded?
(c) What is the size of the bank deposits multiplier?

*LOOKING AT THE MATHS

The process of credit creation can be expressed mathematically as the sum of an infinite series. If a is the proportion of any deposit that is lent by banks, where $a = 1 - l$, then total deposits will expand by

$$D_r = D_0(1 + a + a^2 + a^3 + \ldots)$$
$$= D_0(1/1 - a)$$
$$= D_0(1/l) \qquad \textbf{(1)}$$

Thus if there were an initial additional deposit (D_0) of £100 and if $a = 0.8$, giving a liquidity ratio (l) of 0.2, total deposits would expand by £100 × 1/0.2 = £500. The bank deposits multiplier is 5.

Proof of equation (1) is given in Maths Case 18.1 in MyEconLab.

Note that the maths of the bank deposits multiplier is very similar to that of the Keynesian expenditure multiplier of section 17.2 (see Maths Case 17.1 in MyEconLab). The economics, however, is quite different. The Keynesian multiplier is concerned with the effects of increased demand on real national output. The bank deposits multiplier is simply concerned with money creation.

TC 12
p411

The creation of credit: the real world

In practice, the creation of credit is not as simple as this. There are three major complications.

Banks' liquidity ratio may vary

Banks may choose a different liquidity ratio. At certain times, banks may decide that it is prudent to hold a bigger proportion of liquid assets. For example, if banks are worried about increased risks of default on loans, they may choose to hold a higher liquidity ratio to ensure that they have enough to meet customers' needs. This was the case in the late 2000s when many banks became less willing to lend to other banks for fear of the other banks' assets containing sub-prime debt. Banks, as a result, hoarded cash and became more cautious about granting loans.

On the other hand, there may be an upsurge in consumer demand for credit. Banks may be very keen to grant additional loans and thus make more profits, even though they have acquired no additional assets. They may simply go ahead and expand credit, and accept a lower liquidity ratio.

Customers may not want to take up the credit on offer. Banks may wish to make additional loans, but customers may not want to borrow. There may be insufficient demand. But will the banks not then lower their interest rates, thus encouraging people to borrow? Possibly; but if they lower the rate they charge to borrowers, they must also lower the rate they pay to depositors. But then depositors may switch to other institutions such as building societies.

How will an increased mobility of savings and other capital between institutions affect this argument?

Banks may not operate a simple liquidity ratio

The fact that banks hold a number of fairly liquid assets, such as short-term loans to other banks on the interbank market, bills of exchange and certificates of deposit, makes it difficult to identify a simple liquidity ratio. For example, if banks use £1 million in cash to purchase £1 million of bills, can we assume that the liquidity ratio has remained exactly the same? In other words, can we assume that *near money* assets, such as bills, are just as liquid as cash? If we assume that they are not, then has the liquidity ratio fallen? If so, by how much?

Banks do not see a clear-cut dividing line between liquid and non-liquid assets. They try to maintain a rough balance across the liquidity range, but the precise composition of assets will vary as interest rates on the various assets vary, and as the demands for liquidity vary.

In practice, therefore, the size of the bank deposits multiplier will vary and is thus difficult to predict in advance.

Is the following statement true: 'The greater the number of types of asset that are counted as being liquid, the smaller will be the bank deposits multiplier'?

Some of the extra cash may be withdrawn by the public

If extra cash comes into the banking system, and as a result extra deposits are created, part of them may be held by households and non-bank firms (known in this context as the *non-bank private sector*) as cash outside the banks. In other words, some of the extra cash leaks out of the banking system. This will result in an overall multiplier effect that is smaller than the full bank deposits multiplier. This overall multiplier is known as the *money multiplier*. It is defined as the rise in total money supply expressed as a proportion of the rise in the monetary base that caused it: $\Delta M_s / \Delta M_b$ (where M_s is total broad money supply and M_b is the monetary base). Box 18.5 shows how the money multiplier is calculated.

The broad money multiplier in the UK

In the UK, the principal money multiplier measure is the broad money multiplier. This is given by $\Delta M4/\Delta cash$ in circulation with the public and in banks' interest-bearing deposits (reserve accounts) at the Bank of England.

Definitions

Near money Highly liquid assets (other than cash).

Non-bank private sector Households and non-bank firms. In other words, everyone in the country other than banks and the government (central and local).

Money multiplier The number of times greater the expansion of money supply is than the expansion of the monetary base that caused it: $\Delta M_s / \Delta M_b$.

Figure 18.4   UK broad money multiplier

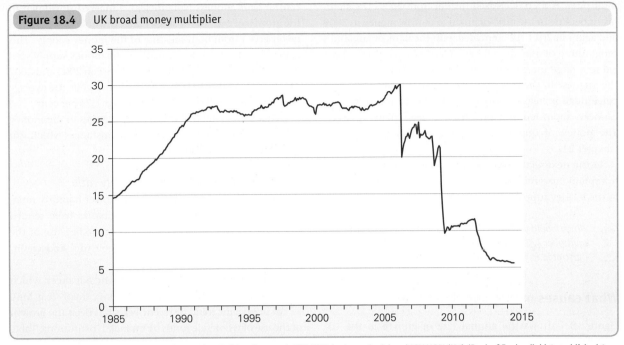

Source: Based on *Statistical Interactive Database*, series LPMBL22 (reserves), LPMAVAB (notes and coin) and LPMAUYN (M4) (Bank of England) (data published 6 August 2014, seasonally adjusted except for reserves).

Another indicator of the broad money multiplier is simply the ratio of the *level* of M4 relative to the cash in circulation with the public and banks' reserve accounts at the central bank. It is shown in Figure 18.4 and helps in analysing the longer-term relationship between the stocks of broad money and the monetary base. From it we can see how broad money grew rapidly relative to the monetary base during the late 1980s and into the early 1990s. From the early 1990s to the mid-2000s, the level of M4 relative to the monetary base fluctuated in a narrow range.

From May 2006 the Bank of England began remunerating banks' reserve accounts at the official bank rate. This encouraged banks to increase their reserve accounts at the Bank of England and led to a sharp fall in the broad money

---

*BOX 18.5   CALCULATING THE MONEY MULTIPLIER

The money multiplier (m) is the rise in total money supply (ΔM_s) divided by the rise in the monetary base (ΔM_b):

$$m = \Delta M_s / \Delta M_b \tag{1}$$

The total money supply (M_s) consists of deposits in banks and building societies (D) plus cash held by the public (C). Thus a rise in money supply would be given by

$$\Delta M_s = \Delta D + \Delta C \tag{2}$$

The monetary base (M_b) consists of bank and building society reserves (R) plus cash held by the public (C). Thus a rise in the monetary base would be given by

$$\Delta M_b = \Delta R + \Delta C \tag{3}$$

Thus, by substituting equations (2) and (3) into equation (1), the money multiplier is given by

$$m = \frac{\Delta D + \Delta C}{\Delta R + \Delta C} \tag{4}$$

Assume now that banks wish to hold a given fraction (r) of any rise in deposits in the form of reserves: i.e.

$$r = \Delta R / \Delta D \tag{5}$$

and that the public wishes to hold a given fraction (c) of any rise in its deposits as cash: i.e.

$$c = \Delta C / \Delta D \tag{6}$$

If we now divide the top and bottom of equation (4) by ΔD, we get

$$m = \frac{\Delta D/\Delta D + \Delta C/\Delta D}{\Delta R/\Delta D + \Delta C/\Delta D} = \frac{1+c}{r+c} \tag{7}$$

Thus if c were 0.2 and r were 0.1, the money multiplier would be

$$(1 + 0.2)/(0.1 + 0.2) = 1.2/0.3 = 4$$

or

$$\Delta M_s = 4 \times \Delta M_b$$

1. *If c were 0.1 and r were 0.01, by how much would money supply expand if the monetary base rose by £1 million?*
2. *Money supply (M4) includes wholesale as well as retail deposits. Given that firms will wish to keep only a very small fraction of a rise in wholesale deposits in cash (if any at all), how will a change in the balance of wholesale and retail deposits affect the value of c and hence of the money multiplier?*

multiplier. It then decreased further from 2009. The significant decline in the ratio of broad to narrow money in 2009 and again in 2011–12 coincided with the Bank of England's programme of asset purchases (quantitative easing) which led to a large increase in banks' reserves. The point is that the increase in the monetary base did not lead to the same percentage increase in broad money, as banks were more cautious about lending and chose to keep higher reserves. The policy of quantitative easing is discussed more in Chapter 21.

In the next section we focus on those factors which help to explain movements in the money multiplier and changes in the money supply.

 Which would you expect to fluctuate more, the money multiplier (ΔM4/Δcash), or the simple ratio, M4/cash, illustrated in Figure 18.4?

What causes money supply to rise?

Figure 18.5 shows the annual rate of growth in the UK money supply. It plots the nominal growth of M4 with and without other financial corporations (OFCs). As we saw earlier, OFCs include unit trusts, insurance companies and pension funds as well as special purpose vehicles (SPVs) which are used in the process of securitisation (see pages 534–5 and Box 18.3). By excluding OFCs we capture the money holdings of households and non-financial corporations.

While the general patterns in both measures of the growth in the money supply are similar, the effect of quantitative easing on money holdings of OFCs from 2009 is especially marked. OFCs were a major seller of assets to the Bank of England in exchange for which they received

central bank money. Nonetheless, a marked slowdown in the growth of the money supply after the financial crisis can be observed from both measure of the money supply. This contrasts with the robust growth in the money supply seen during the earlier part of the 2000s. Between 2002 and 2007 M4 grew at an annual rate of 10 per cent, while the average rate of consumer price inflation was just 1.75 per cent.

What factors might explain such changes in the money supply? We consider four sets of circumstances which can cause the money supply to *rise*.

Banks choose to hold a lower liquidity ratio

If banks collectively choose to hold a lower liquidity ratio, they will have surplus liquidity. The banks have tended to choose a lower liquidity ratio over time because of the increasing use of direct debits and debit-card and credit-card transactions.

Surplus liquidity can be used to expand advances, which will lead to a multiplied rise in broad money supply (e.g. M4).

An important trend in recent years has been the growth of the use of wholesale funds by financial institutions. Table 18.1 showed that short-term loans to other banks (including overseas banks) are now the largest element in banks' liquid assets. These assets may be used by a bank as the basis for expanding loans and thereby starting a chain of credit creation. But although these assets are liquid to an individual bank, they do not add to the liquidity of the banking system as a whole. By using them for credit creation, the banking system is operating with a lower overall liquidity ratio.

This was a major element in the banking crisis of the late 2000s. By operating with a collectively low liquidity ratio, banks were vulnerable to people defaulting on debt, such as mortgages. The problem was compounded by the holding

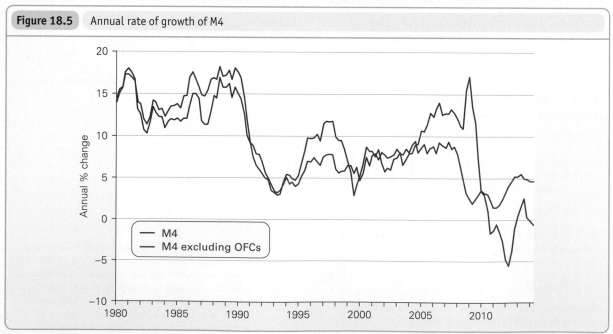

Figure 18.5 Annual rate of growth of M4

Note: OFC are other financial corporations.

Source: M4 growth rate from *Statistical Interactive Database*, series LPQVQJW and LPQBE24 (Bank of England) (data published 29 July 14, seasonally adjusted).

of sub-prime debt in the form of securitised assets. Realising the vulnerability of other banks, banks became increasingly unwilling to lend to each other. The resulting decline in interbank lending reduced the amount of credit created, thereby depressing the money supply (see Figure 18.4). In Box 18.6 we discuss in more detail the effect of credit cycles on the UK money supply.

 What effects do debit cards and cash machines (ATMs) have on (a) banks' prudent liquidity ratios; (b) the size of the bank deposits multiplier?

The non-bank private sector chooses to hold less cash

Households and firms may choose to hold less cash. Again, the reason may be a greater use of cards, direct debits, etc. This means that a greater proportion of the cash base will be held as deposits in banks rather than in people's wallets, purses or safes outside banks. The extra cash deposits allow banks to create more credit.

The above two reasons for an expansion of broad money supply (M4) are because more credit is being created for a given monetary base. The other two reasons for an expansion of money supply are reasons why the monetary base itself might expand.

An inflow of funds from abroad

When sterling to is used to pay for UK exports and is deposited in UK banks by the exporters, credit can be created on the basis of it. This leads to a multiplied increase in the domestic money supply.

The money supply will also expand if depositors of sterling in banks overseas then switch these deposits to banks in the UK. This is a direct increase in the money supply. In an open economy like the UK's movements of sterling and other currencies into and out of the country can be very large, leading to large fluctuations in the money supply.

A public-sector deficit

The public-sector net cash requirement (PSNCR) is the difference between public-sector expenditure and public-sector receipts. To meet this deficit, the government has to borrow money by selling interest-bearing securities (Treasury bills and gilts). In general, the bigger the PSNCR, the greater will be the growth in the money supply. Just how the money supply will be affected, however, depends on who buys the securities.

Consider first the case where government securities are purchased by the non-bank private sector. When people or firms buy the bonds or bills, they will draw money from their banks. When the government spends the money, it will be re-deposited in banks. There is no increase in money supply. It is just a case of existing money changing hands.

This is not the case when the securities are purchased by monetary financial institutions, including the central bank. Consider the purchase of Treasury bills by commercial banks: there will be a multiplied expansion of the money supply.

The reason is that, although banks' balances at the central bank will go down when the banks purchase the bills, they will go up again when the government spends the money. In addition, the banks will now have additional liquid assets (bills), which can be used as the basis for credit creation. This effect could be partly mitigated if the government is able to issue debt instruments of longer maturity (gilts) since these are less liquid.

If there is a public-sector *surplus* (a negative PSNCR), this will either reduce the money supply or have no effect, depending on what the government does with the surplus. The fact that there is a surplus means that the public sector is spending less than it receives in taxes etc. The initial effect, therefore, is to reduce the money in the economy: it is being 'retired' in the central bank.

If, however, the government then uses this money to buy back securities from the non-bank private sector, the money will merely return to the economy, and there will be no net effect on money supply.

 If the government borrows but does not spend the proceeds, what effect will this have on the money supply if it borrows from
(a) the banking sector;
(b) the non-bank private sector?

The flow-of-funds equation

All these effects on money supply can be summarised using a *flow-of-funds equation*. This shows the components of a change in money supply (ΔM_s). The following flow-of-funds equation is the one most commonly used in the UK, that for M4. It consists of four items (or 'counterparts' as they are known):

$\Delta M4$	*equals*	PSNCR	(Item 1)
	minus	Sales of public-sector debt to (or plus purchases of public-sector debt from) the non-bank private sector	(Item 2)
	plus	Banks' and building societies' sterling net lending to the UK private sector	(Item 3)
	plus	External effect	(Item 4)

Public-sector borrowing (item 1) will lead to a direct increase in the money supply, but not if it is funded by selling bonds and bills to the non-bank private sector. Such sales (item 2) have therefore to be subtracted from the PSNCR. But conversely, if the government buys back old bonds from the non-bank private sector, this will further increase the money supply.

Definition

Flow-of-funds equation The various items making up an increase (or decrease) in money supply.

BOX 18.6 CREDIT, THE MONEY SUPPLY AND MINSKY'S FINANCIAL INSTABILITY HYPOTHESIS

Are credit cycles inevitable?

Patterns in lending and the money supply

M4 is the UK's main broad aggregate measure of the money supply. It is defined as the UK non-bank private sector's holdings of notes and coin, sterling deposits and other short-term financial instruments issued by banks and building societies (up to five years).

As we can see from Figure 18.5 (see page 548) its growth is highly variable. Nonetheless, the weakness in the growth of M4 from the late 2000s was especially marked. An important reason for this was the collapse in the flows of credit from MFIs to the rest of the private sector.

As we saw on pages 545–8, when financial institutions grant credit, further deposits are created when the non-bank private sector looks to spend this credit. This, in turn, can lead to further credit being given and so further deposits created.

The chart considers the quarterly *flows* of net lending to the non-bank private sector: the household sector, non-financial corporations and other financial corporations (OFCs). Net lending is *additional* credit and is calculated by subtracting repayments from the total amount of gross lending by MFIs.

The chart shows the marked growth in credit during the late 1980s, particularly to households, which contributed to the

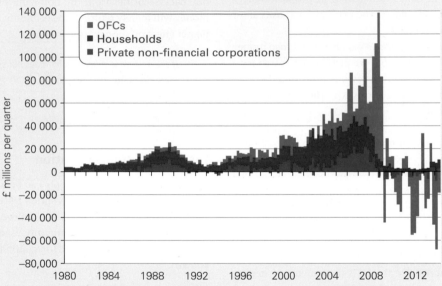

Quarterly flows of net lending to non-bank private sector

Source: *Statistical Interactive Database*, series LPQVWNL, LPQVWNQ and LPQVWNV (Bank of England) (data published 1 September 2014, seasonally adjusted).

The initial increase in liquidity from the sale of government securities to the banking sector is given by item 1. This increase in their liquidity will enable banks to create credit. To the extent that this extra lending is to the UK private sector (item 3), money supply will increase, and by a multiple of the initial increase in liquidity (item 1). Bank lending may also increase (item 3) even if there is no increase in liquidity or even a reduction in liquidity (item 1 is zero or negative), if banks respond to increases in the demand for loans by accepting a lower liquidity ratio, or if, through securitisation and other forms of secondary marketing, individual banks gain extra liquidity from each other, even though there is no total increase in liquidity in the banking system. Item 3 will be reduced if banks choose to hold more capital.

Finally, if there is a net inflow of funds from abroad (item 4), this too will increase the money supply.

The flow-of-funds equation that we have just described is a simplified version of the one actually used in official

statistics to analyse the components of changes in M4. The equation can easily be modified to show changes in retail deposits in M4 or the eurozone measure of M3.

Table 18.6 shows the components of changes in M4 since 2005. As Figure 14.4 showed, the period from 2010 to 2012 was characterised by a contraction in total M4, with then only a small increase in 2013. The period was also characterised by large public-sector deficits. Consider 2010, when the public-sector net cash requirement (item 1) was around £156 billion. Deficits tend to increase the money supply. However, this effect was counteracted by sales of government debt to the non-bank private sector (item 2), by an outflow of funds abroad (item 4), but, more especially, by a very large decrease in the flow of bank lending (item 3). Indeed, the negative figure for net lending indicates that the private non-bank sector was repaying existing debts more than it was acquiring new debt. We can see that this phenomenon was observed throughout the early 2010s.

stock of M4 increasing at an average rate of 16 per cent per year over the second half of the 1980s. A marked slowdown in the growth of credit followed with the recession of the early 1990s. Unsurprisingly M4 growth slowed too, with the annual growth rate falling to only a little over 2 per cent during 1993.

From the mid-1990s up to the late 2000s we observe a period of prolonged and robust credit growth. During 2006 and 2007 net lending to the non-bank private sector averaged around £72 billion per quarter with net lending to households of £25 billion per quarter. Again this helped to fuel the growth in M4. The average annual rate of growth in M4 over 2006 and 2007 was 13 per cent.

But the story was to change dramatically from 2008 onwards as the 'credit crunch' began to bite. We began to see extraordinarily low levels of net lending. Net lending to households slumped to levels not seen since the late 1970s. Meanwhile non-financial corporations and OFCs began reducing their existing bank debts by more than they were acquiring in new debts.

While the repayment of debt by OFCs was aided by the Bank of England's programme of asset purchases (quantitative easing), the late 2000s marked a new phase in the credit cycle. But how inevitable was this slump and the exuberance in lending that preceded it? How inevitable are credit cycles?

Minsky's credit cycles

Hyman Minsky (1919–96) was a Belarus-born American economist. He is known for his work on understanding the relationship between the financial system and the macroeconomy. His *financial instability hypothesis* proposes that financial cycles are an inherent part of the economic cycle and, indeed, are a key cause of the fluctuations in real GDP.

The key to the financial instability hypothesis is that the accumulation of credit by the non-bank private sector is pro-cyclical and destabilising. The extension of credit by MFIs can be seen to go through different phases. During these phases credit criteria and the ability of borrowers to afford their debts vary. Credit flows are therefore endogenous to the state of the economy.

Minsky argued that credit flows will tend to increase after a period of sustained growth. This causes banks and investors to develop a heightened euphoria and confidence in the economy and in the returns of assets. As a result, economic agents begin to take on bigger debts to acquire assets. These debts increasingly stretch their financial well-being. A point is reached, perhaps triggered by an economic shock or a tightening of economic policy, when the euphoria stops and confidence is replaced with pessimism. This is sometimes referred to as a *Minsky moment*.

The result of a Minsky moment is that lenders reduce their lending, and economic agents look to increase their net worth (i.e. reduce debts or increase savings) to ensure their financial well-being. However, the result of these individual actions causes a decline in spending and in national income. In other words, we observe a balance sheet recession or economic downturn. Furthermore, by selling assets to improve financial well-being, the value of assets falls. This paradoxical reduction of net worth is known as the paradox of debt (see Chapter 16, page 488).

Minsky believed that credit cycles are inevitable in a free-market economy. Hence, the authorities will need to take action to moderate credit cycles. The significance given to macro-prudential regulation by policy makers in the response to the financial crisis is recognition of the dangers posed to the economy by credit cycles.

 What demand-side and supply-side factors can influence the flows of net lending by financial institutions to households and non-financial corporations?

This is a balance sheet effect (see pages 548–9) which helped to reduce the growth of the money supply.

The relationship between money supply and the rate of interest

Simple monetary theory often assumes that the supply of money is totally independent of interest rates. This is illustrated in Figure 18.6. The money supply is *exogenous*. It is assumed to be determined by the government or central bank ('the authorities'): what the authorities choose it to be, or what they allow it to be by their choice of the level and method of financing the PSNCR.

In practice, however, even if narrow money were to be tightly controlled by the central bank (which it is not), it would be very hard to have a precise control of broad money. More complex models, therefore, and especially Keynesian models, assume that money supply is *endogenous*: that it

Definitions

Financial instability hypothesis During periods of economic growth, economic agents (firms and individuals) tend to borrow more and MFIs are more willing to lend. This fuels the boom. In a period of recession, economic agents tend to cut spending in order to reduce debts and MFIs are less willing to lend. This deepens the recession. Behaviour in financial markets thus tends to amplify the business cycle.

Exogenous money supply Money supply that does not depend on the demand for money but is set by the authorities.

Endogenous money supply Money supply that is determined (at least in part) by the demand for money.

Table 18.6 Counterparts to changes in M4 (£m)

	PSNCR (+) (Public-Sector Net Cash Requirement) (1)	Sales (−)/ Purchases (+) to/ from non-bank private sector(2)	Banks' and building societies net lending to UK private sector (less increase in bank's capital) (3)	External effect: inflows (+)/ outflows (−)(4)	Total change in M4
2005	41 386	−11 527	118 071	2 941	150 871
2006	33 771	−20 943	188 113	−33 915	167 026
2007	32 770	−999	234 042	−77 260	188 553
2008	107 061	−55 795	99 064	108 542	258 872
2009	197 080	29 057	88 295	−184 962	129 470
2010	156 449	−36 030	−123 988	−28 910	−32 479
2011	119 308	−19 906	−118 728	−32 320	−51 646
2012	106 591	17 365	−19 870	−127 455	−23 369
2013	75 922	−4 753	−29 447	−40 193	1 529

Source: Based on data in *Bankstats* (Bank of England), Table A3.2, data published January 2014.

Figure 18.6 The supply of money curve: exogenous money supply

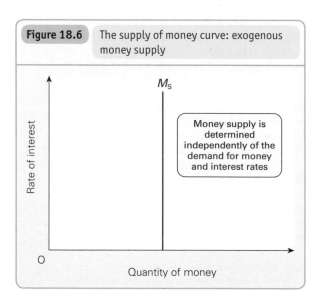

Figure 18.7 The supply of money curve: endogenous money supply

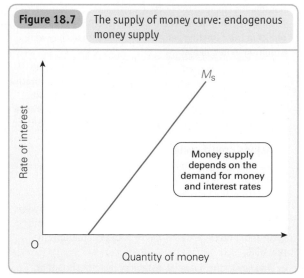

depends on the demand for money. The argument is that higher money demand will result in higher interest rates and in higher levels of money supplied. The result is an upward-sloping money supply curve, as in Figure 18.7. The reasons for this are as follows:

■ Increases in money supply may occur as a result of banks expanding credit in response to the demand for credit. This assumes that banks have surplus liquidity in the first place, or are happy to operate with lower liquidity, or can increase liquidity through secondary marketing of otherwise illiquid assets, or can obtain liquidity from the central bank through repos. Higher demand for credit will drive up interest rates, making it more profitable for banks to supply more credit.

■ Higher interest rates may encourage depositors to switch their deposits from sight accounts (earning little or no interest) to time accounts. Since money is less likely to be withdrawn quickly from time accounts, banks may feel the need to hold less liquidity, and

therefore may decide to increase credit, thus expanding the money supply.

■ Higher interest rates attract deposits from overseas. This increases the money supply to the extent that the Bank of England does not allow the exchange rate to appreciate in response.

To summarise, an increase in demand for money raises interest rates, which in turn increases the quantity of money supplied (see sections 18.4 and 18.5): a movement along an upward-sloping money supply curve.

Some economists go further still. They argue that not only is money supply endogenous, but the 'curve' is effectively horizontal; money supply expands passively to match the demand for money. In practice, the shape varies with the confidence of MFIs. In periods of optimism, banks may be willing to expand credit to meet the demand from customers. In periods of pessimism, such as that following the financial crisis, banks may be very unwilling to grant credit when customers seek it.

Section summary

1. Money supply can be defined in a number of different ways, depending on what items are included. A useful distinction is between narrow money and broad money. Narrow money includes just cash, and possibly banks' balances at the central bank. Broad money also includes deposits in banks and possibly various other short-term deposits in the money market. In the UK, M4 is the preferred measure of broad money. In the eurozone it is M3.

2. Bank deposits are a major proportion of broad money supply. The expansion of bank deposits is the major element in the expansion of the money supply.

3. Bank deposits expand through a process of credit creation. If banks' liquid assets increase, they can be used as a base for increasing loans. When the loans are redeposited in banks, they form the base for yet more loans, and thus a process of multiple credit expansion takes place. The ratio of the increase of deposits to an expansion of banks' liquidity base is called the 'bank deposits multiplier'. It is the inverse of the liquidity ratio.

4. In practice, it is difficult to predict the precise amount by which money supply will expand if there is an increase in cash. The reasons are that banks may choose to hold a different liquidity ratio; customers may not take up all the credit on offer; there may be no simple liquidity ratio given the range of near money assets; and some of the extra cash may leak away into extra cash holdings by the public.

5. Money supply will rise if (a) banks choose to hold a lower liquidity ratio and thus create more credit for an existing amount of liquidity; (b) people choose to hold less cash outside the banks; (c) there is a net inflow of funds from abroad; (d) the government runs a PSNCR and finances it by borrowing from the banking sector or from abroad.

6. The flow-of-funds equation shows the components of any change in money supply. A rise in money supply equals the PSNCR *minus* sales of public-sector debt to the non-bank private sector, *plus* banks' lending to the private sector (less increases in banks' capital), *plus* inflows of money from abroad.

7. Simple monetary theory assumes that the supply of money is independent of interest rates. In practice, a rise in interest rates (in response to a higher demand for money) will often lead to an increase in money supply.

18.4 THE DEMAND FOR MONEY

The motives for holding money

The demand for money refers to the desire to hold money: to keep your wealth in the form of money, rather than spending it on goods and services or using it to purchase financial assets such as bonds or shares. It is usual to distinguish three reasons why people want to hold their assets in the form of money. Note that we are talking here about broad money: M4 in the UK.

The transactions motive

Since money is a medium of exchange, it is required for conducting transactions. But since people receive money only at intervals (e.g. weekly or monthly) and not continuously, they require to hold balances of money in cash or in current accounts.

The precautionary motive

Unforeseen circumstances can arise, such as a car breakdown. Thus individuals often hold some additional money as a precaution. Firms too keep precautionary balances because of uncertainties about the timing of their receipts and payments. If a large customer is late in making payment, a firm may be unable to pay its suppliers unless it has spare liquidity.

The speculative or assets motive

Certain firms and individuals who wish to purchase financial assets, such as bonds, shares or other securities, may prefer to wait if they feel that their price is likely to fall. In the meantime, they will hold money balances instead. This speculative demand can be quite high when the price of securities is considered certain to fall. Money when used for this purpose is a means of temporarily storing wealth.

Similarly, people who will require foreign currency at some time in the future (people such as importers, holiday-makers, or those thinking of investing abroad or in foreign securities) may prefer to wait before exchanging pounds into the relevant foreign currencies if they believe that the sterling price of these currencies is likely to fall (the pound is likely to appreciate).

The transactions plus precautionary demand for money: L_1

The transactions plus precautionary demand for money is termed L_1. 'L' stands for **liquidity preference**: that is, the desire to hold assets in liquid form. Money balances held for these two purposes are called *active balances*: money to be

Definitions

Liquidity preference The demand for holding assets in the form of money.

Active balances Money held for transactions and precautionary purposes.

used as a medium of exchange. What determines the size of L_1?

The major determinant of L_1 is nominal national income (i.e. national income at current prices). The higher people's money income, the greater their expenditure and the bigger their demand for active balances. The frequency with which people are paid also affects L_1. The less frequently they are paid, the greater the level of money balances they will require to tide them over until the next payment.

 Will students in receipt of a grant or an allowance who are paid once per term have a high or a low transactions demand for money relative to their income?

The rate of interest has some effect on L_1, albeit rather small (see Figure 18.8). At high rates of interest, people may choose to spend less and save more of their income: e.g. by buying shares. The effect is likely to be bigger on the precautionary demand: a higher interest rate may encourage people to risk tying up their money. Firms' active balances are more likely to be sensitive to changes in r than those of individuals.

Other determinants of L_1 include the season of the year: people require more money balances at Christmas, for example. Also, any other factors that affect consumption will affect L_1.

The increased use of credit cards in recent years has reduced both the transactions and precautionary demands. Paying once a month for goods requires less money on average than paying separately for each item purchased. Moreover, the possession of a credit card reduces or even eliminates the need to hold precautionary balances for many people. On the other hand, the increased availability of cash machines, the convenience of debit cards and the ability to earn interest on current accounts have all encouraged people to hold more money in bank accounts. The net effect has been an increase in the demand for (broad) money.

The speculative (or assets) demand for money: L_2

The speculative demand for money balances is termed L_2. Money balances held for this purpose are called **idle balances**.

People who possess wealth, whether they are wealthy or simply small savers, have to decide the best form in which to hold that wealth. Do they keep it in cash in a piggy bank, or in a current account in a real bank; or do they put it in some interest-bearing time account; or do they buy stocks and shares or government bonds; or do they buy some physical asset such as a car or property?

In making these decisions, people will have to weigh up the relative advantages and disadvantages of the various alternative assets. Assets can be compared according to two criteria: liquidity and the possibility of earning income.

Just as we saw in the case of a bank's assets, these two criteria tend to conflict. The more liquid an asset is, the lower is likely to be the income earned from holding it. Thus cash is totally liquid to the holder: it can be used to buy other assets (or spent on goods) instantly, but it earns no interest. Shares, on the other hand, are not very liquid since they cannot be sold instantly at a guaranteed price. (They can be sold pretty well instantly, but if share prices are depressed, a considerable loss may be incurred in so doing. In other words, they are a risky means of holding wealth.) But shares have the potential of earning quite a high income for the holder, not only in terms of the dividends paid out of the firms' profits, but also in terms of the capital gain from any increase in the shares' prices.

 Buying something like a car is at the other end of the spectrum from holding cash. A car is highly illiquid, but yields a high return to the owner. In what form is this 'return'?

There are three major determinants of the speculative demand for money. Let us examine each in turn.

The rate of interest (or rate of return) on assets

The higher the rate of return on assets, such as shares and bonds, the greater the opportunity cost of holding money and therefore the lower the speculative demand for money.

The rate of return on assets varies inversely with their price. Take the case of a government bond (which pays a fixed sum of money throughout its life). Assume that the government issued a £100 bond at a time when interest rates were 10 per cent. Thus the bond must pay £10 per year. Although the government will not redeem bonds until their maturity date, which could well be 20 years from when they

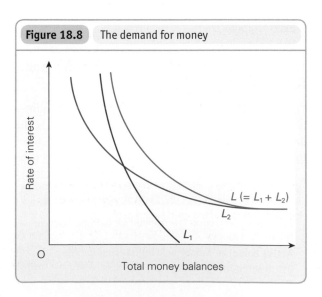

Figure 18.8　The demand for money

Rate of interest (vertical axis)
Total money balances (horizontal axis)

$L (= L_1 + L_2)$
L_2
L_1

Definition

Idle balances Money held for speculative purposes: money held in anticipation of a fall in asset prices.

were issued, holders can sell bonds at any time on the stock market. Their market price will reflect market rates of interest. Assume, for example, that interest rates fall to 5 per cent. What will happen to the market price of the bond paying £10 per year? It will be driven up to £200. At that price, the £10 per year is worth the current market rate of 5 per cent. Thus the market price of bonds varies inversely with the rate of interest.

Expectations of changes in the prices of securities and other assets

If people believe that share prices are about to rise rapidly on the stock market, they will buy shares and hold smaller speculative balances of money. If they think that share prices will fall, they will sell them and hold money instead. Some clever (or lucky) individuals anticipated the 2000–3 stock market decline (see figure in Box 2.3 on page 52). They sold shares and 'went liquid'. Some people made a similar move in the stock market decline of 2007–8.

If the market price of securities is high, the rate of interest (i.e. the rate of return) on these securities will be low. Potential purchasers of these securities will probably wait until their prices fall and the rate of interest rises. Similarly, existing holders of securities will probably sell them while the price is high, hoping to buy them back again when the price falls, thus making a capital gain. In the meantime, therefore, large speculative balances of money will be held. L_2 is high.

If, on the other hand, the rate of interest is high, then L_2 is likely to be low. To take advantage of the high rate of return on securities, people buy them now instead of holding onto their money.

Would the demand for securities be low if their price was high, but was expected to go on rising?

The relationship between L_2 and the rate of interest (r) is again shown in Figure 18.8. The inverse relationship between r and L_2 gives a downward-sloping curve.

Speculative demand and the exchange rate

In an open economy like the UK where large-scale movements of currencies across the foreign exchanges take place, expectations about changes in the exchange rate are a major determinant of the speculative demand for money.

If people believe that the pound is likely to appreciate, they will want to hold sterling until it does appreciate. For example, if the current exchange rate is £1 = $1.50 and speculators believe that it will shortly rise to £1 = $1.75, then if they are correct they will make a 25¢ per £1 profit by holding sterling. The more quickly the exchange rate is expected to rise, the more people will want to hold sterling (as money). If, however, they believe that it will be a slow rise over time, they will want to buy sterling assets (such as UK government bonds) rather than money, since such assets will also earn the holder a rate of interest.

Conversely, if people believe that the exchange rate is likely to fall in the near future, they will economise on their holdings of sterling, preferring to hold their liquid assets in some other currency – the one most likely to appreciate against other currencies.

Graphically, changes in expectations about the exchange rate will have the effect of shifting the L_2 curve in Figure 18.8.

There is a further complication here. Expectations about changes in the exchange rate will themselves be influenced by the interest rate (relative to overseas interest rates). If the UK rate of interest goes up, people will want to deposit their money in the UK. This will increase the demand for sterling on the foreign exchange market: there will be a short-term financial inflow into the UK (the financial account of the balance of payments will go into surplus). The effect will be to drive up the exchange rate. Thus if people believe that the UK rate of interest will rise, they will also believe that the rate of exchange will appreciate, and they will want to hold larger speculative balances of sterling.

The introduction of the 'foreign exchange dimension' into our analysis will have two effects on the L_2 curve. First, the curve will become more volatile. If the rate of interest is low and is thought likely to rise, the speculative demand is likely to be very high. Not only will people hold money in anticipation of a fall in security prices, but they will also hold money (sterling) in anticipation of an appreciation of the exchange rate.

Second, the curve will become more unstable. Expectations of changes in the exchange rate do not just depend on current domestic interest rates. They depend on the current and anticipated future state of the balance of trade, the rate of inflation, the current and anticipated levels of interest rates in other major trading countries, the price of oil, and so on. If any of these cause people to expect a lower exchange rate, the speculative demand for money will fall: L_2 will shift to the left.

Which way is the L_2 curve likely to shift in the following cases?
(a) The balance of trade moves into deficit.
(b) People anticipate that foreign interest rates are likely to rise substantially relative to domestic ones.
(c) The domestic rate of inflation falls below that of other major trading countries.
(d) People believe that the pound is about to depreciate.

The total demand for money: $L_1 + L_2$

Figure 18.8 also shows the total demand for money balances (L). This is found by the horizontal addition of curves L_1 and L_2. This curve is known as the 'liquidity preference curve' or simply the demand for money curve.

Any factor, other than a change in interest rates, that causes the demand for money to rise will shift the L curve to the right. For example, a rise in national income will cause L_1 to increase, and thus L will shift to the right.

Additional effects of expectations

We have talked about expectations and their importance in determining the speculative demand for money. In particular, we have looked at (a) the effect of interest rates on people's anticipations of future security prices and (b) the effect of expectations about exchange rate movements. There are two other ways in which expectations can influence the demand for money, and make it more unstable.

Expectations about prices. If people expect prices to rise, they may reduce their money balances and purchase goods and assets now, before prices do rise. This will tend to shift L to the left. (Note, though, that once prices have risen, people will need more money to conduct the same amount of transactions.)

Expectations of interest rate levels over the longer term. If people come to expect that interest rates will normally be higher than they used to be, then any given interest rate will seem lower relative to the 'normal' rate than it used to be. People will be more inclined to hold speculative balances of money in anticipation of a rise in interest rates. This will tend to shift L upwards.

---

*LOOKING AT THE MATHS

The demand for money (L) can be expressed by the following function:

$$L = L_1 + L_2$$
$$= l_1(PY, f, i) + l_2(i, er^e)$$
$$= l_1(PY, f, (r + \pi^e)) + l_2((r + \pi^e), er^e) \tag{1}$$

This states that L_1 is a function l_1 of nominal national income (i.e. real national income (Y) multiplied by the price index (P)), the frequency with which people are paid (f) and the (nominal) rate of interest (i), which equals the real rate of interest (r) on alternative assets to money plus the expected rate of inflation (π^e). L_2 is a function of the nominal rate of interest (i) and the expected value of the exchange rate er^e.

The advantage of specifying a relationship in this way is that it gives a simple way of representing a situation where something depends on a number of determinants. It is a convenient shorthand. Indeed, a more complex function could easily be specified where the demand for money depends on a longer list of variables. The one above, however, identifies the main determinants. By putting plus and minus signs under each of the terms, we could also identify whether the relationship with each of the determinants is a positive or negative one (i.e. whether the respective partial derivative is positive or negative). Equation (1) could thus be written

$$\begin{array}{c} L = l_1(PY, f, i) + l_2(i, er^e) \\ {}_{+\ \ -\ \ -} \quad {}_{-\ \ +} \end{array} \tag{2}$$

This merely states that the demand for money will rise as PY and er^e rise and f and i fall.

In an era of uncertainty about inflation, interest rates and exchange rates, people's expectations will be hard to predict. They will be volatile and susceptible to rumours and political events. In such circumstances, the L curve itself will be hard to predict and will be subject to considerable shifts. Generally, it is likely that the greater the uncertainty, the greater will be the preference for liquidity, and the greater the risk of tying wealth up in illiquid assets.

Section summary

1. The three motives for holding money are the transactions, precautionary and speculative (or assets) motives.

2. The transactions-plus-precautionary demand for money (L_1) depends primarily on the level of nominal national income, the frequency with which people are paid and institutional arrangements (such as the use of credit or debit cards). It also depends to some degree on the rate of interest.

3. The speculative demand for money (L_2) depends on the rate of return on assets and on anticipations about future movements in security prices (and hence their rate of return) and future movements in exchange rates. If security prices are anticipated to fall or the exchange rate to rise, people will hold more money balances.

4. The demand for money is also influenced by expectations of price changes and the levels of interest rates over the longer term.

18.5 EQUILIBRIUM

Equilibrium in the money market

Equilibrium in the money market is where the demand for money (L) is equal to the supply of money (M_s). This equilibrium is achieved through changes in the rate of interest.

In Figure 18.9, equilibrium is achieved with a rate of interest r_e and a quantity of money M_e. If the rate of interest were above r_e, people would have money balances surplus to their needs. They would use these to buy shares, bonds and other assets. This would drive up the price of these assets and drive down the rate of interest.

As the rate of interest fell, so there would be a contraction of the money supply (a movement down along the M_s curve) and an increase in the demand for money balances, especially speculative balances (a movement down along the liquidity preference curve). The interest rate would go on falling until it reached r_e. Equilibrium would then be achieved.

Similarly, if the rate of interest were below r_e, people would have insufficient money balances. They would sell securities, thus lowering their prices and raising the rate of interest until it reached r_e.

A shift in either the M_s or the L curve will lead to a new equilibrium quantity of money and rate of interest at the new intersection of the curves. For example, a rise in the supply of money will cause the rate of interest to fall.

In practice, there is no one single rate of interest. Different assets have different rates of interest. Table 18.7 gives examples of the rates of interest on various financial instruments.

 What patterns in interest rates emerged between 2008 and 2013?

Equilibrium in the money markets, therefore, will be where demand and supply of each type of financial asset separately balance. If, for example, there were excess demand for short-term loans (such as one-month intebank lending) and excess supply of money to invest in long-term assets (such as bonds), short-term rates of interest would rise relative to long-term rates. Generally, however, different interest rates tend to move roughly together as the overall demand for money and other liquid assets (or their supply) changes. Thus interest rates may generally rise or generally fall.

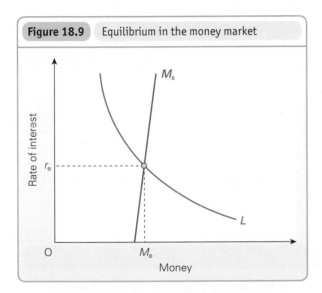

Figure 18.9 Equilibrium in the money market

Table 18.7	Selected rates of interest: January 1997 to December 2013 (monthly averages)					
		Rate of interest, per cent per annum			
Financial instrument	**Period of loan**	**Average Jan 1997–Dec 2007**	**Average Jan 2008–Dec 2013**	**Jan 1997**	**Dec 2013**
Call money	Overnight	5.16	1.17	5.90	0.42
Gilt repos	1 week	5.09	1.19	5.91	0.40
Interbank loans	1 month	5.23	1.38	6.14	0.49
Treasury bills	3 months	5.04	1.07	6.01	0.26
British government securities[1]	20 years	4.82	4.02	7.74	3.71
Bank and building society mortgages[2]	Variable (25 years typical)	6.86	4.60	7.18	4.39
Credit card	–	17.86	16.70	22.14	18.15
(Banks' base rate = Bank Rate)	–	5.19	1.22	5.94	0.50

[1] Zero coupon, nominal yields (series IUMALNZC).
[2] Standard variable rate for UK MFIs (series IUMTLMV).
Source: Statistical Interactive Database (Bank of England). Data published January 2014.

Equilibrium in the foreign exchange market

Changes in the money supply also affect the foreign exchange market. In a free foreign exchange market, equilibrium will be achieved by changes in the exchange rate. Assume that the money supply increases. This has three direct effects:

- Part of the excess money balances will be used to purchase foreign assets. This will therefore lead to an increase in the supply of domestic currency coming onto the foreign exchange markets.
- The excess supply of money in the domestic money market will push down the rate of interest. This will reduce the return on domestic assets below that on foreign assets. This, like the first effect, will lead to an increased demand for foreign assets and thus an increased supply of the domestic currency on the foreign exchange market. It will also reduce the demand for domestic assets by those outside the country, and thus reduce the demand for the domestic currency.
- Speculators will anticipate that the higher supply of the domestic currency will cause the exchange rate to depreciate. They will therefore sell domestic currency and buy foreign currencies before the expected depreciation takes place.

The effect of all three is to cause the exchange rate to depreciate.

 Trace through the effects on the foreign exchange market of a fall in the money supply.

Section summary

1. Equilibrium in the money market is where the supply of money is equal to the demand. Equilibrium will be achieved through changes in the rate of interest.

2. A rise in money supply causes money supply to exceed money demand. This causes interest rates to fall and a movement down along both the supply of money curve and the demand for money curve until money supply is equal to money demand.

3. Equilibrium in the foreign exchange market is where the demand and supply of a currency are equal. A rise in money supply causes interest rates to fall. The rise in money supply plus the fall in interest rates cause an increased supply of domestic currency to come onto the foreign exchange market and a reduced demand for the domestic currency. This causes the exchange rate to depreciate.

END OF CHAPTER QUESTIONS

1. Imagine that the banking system receives additional deposits of £100 million and that all the individual banks wish to retain their current liquidity ratio of 20 per cent.

   (a) How much will banks choose to lend out initially?

   (b) What will happen to banks' liabilities when the money that is lent out is spent and the recipients of it deposit it in their bank accounts?

   (c) How much of these latest deposits will be lent out by the banks?

   (d) By how much will *total* deposits (liabilities) eventually have risen, assuming that none of the additional liquidity is held outside the banking sector?

   (e) How much of these are matched by (i) liquid assets; (ii) illiquid assets?

   (f) What is the size of the bank deposits multiplier?

   (g) If one-half of any additional liquidity is held *outside* the banking sector, by how much less will deposits have risen compared with (d) above?

2. What is meant by the terms *narrow money* and *broad money*? Does broad money fulfil all the functions of money?

3. How does money aid the specialisation and division of labour?

4. What enables banks safely to engage in both maturity transformation and risk transformation?

5. Why do banks hold a range of assets of varying degrees of liquidity and profitability?

6. What is meant by the securitisation of assets? How might this be (a) beneficial and (b) harmful to banks and the economy?

7. What were the causes of the credit crunch and the banking crisis of the late 2000s?

8. If the government reduces the size of its public-sector net cash requirement, why might the money supply nevertheless increase more rapidly?

9. Why might the relationship between the demand for money and the rate of interest be an unstable one?

10. What effects will the following have on the equilibrium rate of interest? (You should consider which way the demand and/or supply curves of money shift.)

   (a) Banks find that they have a higher liquidity ratio than they need.

   (b) A rise in incomes.

   (c) A growing belief that interest rates will rise from their current level.

Online resources

Additional case studies in MyEconLab

18.1 Barter: its use in Russia in the 1990s. When barter was used as an alternative to money.

18.2 The attributes of money. What distinguishes it from other assets?

18.3 From coins to bank deposit money. This case traces the evolution of modern money.

18.4 Changes in the banking industry. Is bigger better?

18.5 Gresham's law. This examines the famous law that 'bad money drives good money out of circulation'.

18.6 German banking. This case compares the tradition of German banks with that of UK retail banks. Although the banks have become more similar in recent years, German banks have a much closer relationship with industry.

18.7 Residential mortgages and securitisation. Was the bundling of residential mortgage debt into securitised assets the cause of the 2008 credit crunch?

18.8 Bailing out the banks. An overview of the concerted efforts made to rescue the banking system in the crisis of 2007–9.

18.9 Making money grow. A light-hearted illustration of the process of credit creation.

18.10 Consolidate MFI balance sheet. A look at the *consolidated* balance sheet of UK monetary and financial institutions, including the Bank of England

18.11 Parallel money markets. A description of the variety of short-term financial instruments available in the parallel money markets.

18.12 Are the days of cash numbered? Are credit and debit cards and direct money transfers replacing cash transactions?

Maths Case 18.1 Calculating the value of the bank multiplier. Looking at the algebra.

Websites relevant to this chapter

See sites listed at the end of Chapter 19 on page 592.

MyEconLab

This book can be supported by MyEconLab, which contains a range of additional resources, including an online homework and tutorial system designed to test and build your understanding.

You need both an access card and a course ID to access MyEconLab:

1. Is your lecturer using MyEconLab? Ask your lecturer for your course ID.

2. Has an access card been included with the book at a reduced cost? Check the inside back cover of the book.

3. If you have a course ID but no access card, go to: http://www.myeconlab.com/ to buy access to this interactive study programme.

The Relationship between the Money and Goods Markets

CHAPTER MAP

19.1 The effects of monetary changes on national income — 561
The quantity theory of money — 561
The interest rate transmission mechanism — 561
The exchange rate transmission mechanism — 565
The portfolio balance effect — 567
How stable is the velocity of circulation? — 567

19.2 The monetary effects of changes in the goods market — 572
The monetary effects of an increase in injections — 572
Crowding out — 573
Is money supply exogenous or endogenous? — 575

19.3 The interaction of monetary policy and the goods market — 575
The goods and money markets — 575
The *IS* curve — 576
The *MP* curve — 577
Equilibrium — 578
Full effect of changes in the goods and money markets — 579

19.4 *ADI/ASI* model — 582
IS/MP and the *ADI/ASI* model — 582
Aggregate demand and supply plotted against inflation — 582
Response to changes in aggregate demand and supply — 584

*Appendix: The *IS/LM* model — 585
The *IS* curve — 586
The *LM* curve — 586
Equilibrium — 587
Full effects of changes in the goods and money markets — 589
Deriving an *AD* curve from the *IS/LM* model — 590

In Chapter 17 we saw how equilibrium national output was determined. In other words, we looked at macro-economic equilibrium in goods markets. In Chapter 18 we saw how equilibrium was determined in the money market. In this chapter we combine the analysis of the two chapters.

In section 19.1 we examine how changes in money supply affect real national income. In other words, we see how changes in money markets are transmitted through to goods markets: how monetary changes affect real output. Then, in section 19.2, we look at things the other way round. We examine the effects on money markets and interest rates of changes in the goods market. For example, if aggregate demand increases and firms start to produce extra goods, to what extent will money markets act as a constraint on this process?

In the remaining sections we look at the interplay of goods and money markets. In doing so, we introduce models which allow us to study how these markets interact. In sections 19.3 and 19.4 the interaction is analysed in the contemporary context of central banks setting interest rates to target the rate of inflation. In doing so, we introduce two complementary frameworks: the *IS/MP* model and the *ADI/ASI* models. In the appendix to the chapter we introduce the *IS/LM* model. This helps us to see how the two markets interact when interest rates adjust to bring about equilibrium in the money market.

19.1 THE EFFECTS OF MONETARY CHANGES ON NATIONAL INCOME

In this section we examine the impact on the economy of changes in money supply and interest rates: how they affect aggregate demand and how this, in turn, affects national income. A simple way of understanding the issues is in terms of the *quantity theory of money*.

The quantity theory of money

In section 16.2 (pages 469–70), we looked at the following version of the quantity equation:

$$MV = PY$$

In case you did not study Chapter 16, let us state the theory again. First a definition of the terms: M is the supply of money; V is the income velocity of circulation (the number of times money is spent per year on national output (GDP)); P is the price index (where the index = 1 in the base year); and Y is the real value of national income (= national output) for the year in question (i.e. GDP measured in base-year prices).

MV is the total spending on national output. For example, if total money supply (M) was £1 trillion and each pound was spent on average twice per year (V) on national output, then total spending on national output (MV) would equal £2 trillion for that year. MV is thus simply (nominal) aggregate demand, since total spending on national output consists of the four elements of aggregate demand: consumer spending (C), investment expenditure (I), government spending (G), and expenditure on exports less expenditure on imports ($X - M$), all measured in current prices.

TC 12
p411

PY is the money value of national output: in other words, GDP measured at *current* prices. For example, if real national income (Y) (i.e. in base-year prices) were £1 trillion, and the price index (P) were 2 (in other words, prices were twice as high as in the base year), then the value of national output in current prices would be £2 trillion.

Because of the way we have defined the terms, MV must equal PY. A simple way of looking at this is that MV and PY are both ways of measuring GDP. MV measures it in terms of national expenditure. PY measures it in terms of the value of what is produced.

The effect of a change in money supply

If money supply (M) changes, how will it affect the other three elements of the quantity equation? Will a rise in money supply simply lead to a rise in prices (P), or will there be a rise in real national income (Y): i.e. a rise in real GDP? What will happen to the velocity of circulation (V)? Can we assume that it will remain constant, or will it change?

Clearly the relationship between money supply and prices depends on what happens to V and Y. What happens to them has been the subject of considerable debate between economists over the years. Keynesians have generally had different views from monetarists and new classical economists.

Essentially there are two issues. In this chapter we look at the first one: the variability of V. If V is constant, a change in money supply (M) will directly affect nominal aggregate demand (MV) and hence nominal national income (PY). If, however, V varies, a change in M may have a much less predictable effect on PY.

The second issue is examined in Chapter 20. This concerns the variability of Y. Will a rise in aggregate demand lead to increased employment and output (Y), or will it simply lead to higher prices (P), or some combination of the two?

TC 12
p411

1. If V is constant, will (a) a £10 million rise in M give a £10 million rise in MV; (b) a 10 per cent rise in M give a 10 per cent rise in MV?
2. If both V and Y are constant, will (a) a £10 million rise in M lead to a £10 million rise in P; (b) a 10 per cent rise in M lead to a 10 per cent rise in P?

The interest rate transmission mechanism

Two principal means by which a rise in money supply can cause a rise in aggregate demand are the ***interest rate transmission mechanism*** and the ***exchange rate transmission mechanism***. These are illustrated in Figure 19.1.

The interest rate transmission mechanism is illustrated in the top part of Figure 19.1. This is graphed in Figure 19.2. It is a three-stage process:

KI 5
p22

1. Figure 19.2(a) shows the money market. A rise in money supply from M to M' leads to a surplus of money at i_1, and hence a fall in the rate of interest from i_1 to i_2.
2. Figure 19.2(b) shows the relationship between investment (I) and the rate of interest. A fall in the rate of interest from i_1 to i_2 leads to a rise in investment (and any other interest-sensitive expenditures) from I_1 to I_2. Note that it also encourages consumers to spend, since borrowing through credit cards and personal loans is now cheaper. At the same time, it discourages saving.
3. Figure 19.2(c) is the Keynesian withdrawals and injections diagram. A rise in investment leads to a multiplied rise in national income (from Y_1 to Y_2). If saving fell, there would also be a downward shift in the W line.

However, the increase in income to Y_2 shown in Figure 19.2(c) does not take into account the likelihood that any

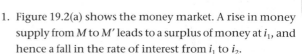

Definitions

Interest rate transmission mechanism How a change in money supply affects aggregate demand via a change in interest rates.

Exchange rate transmission mechanism How a change in money supply affects aggregate demand via a change in exchange rates.

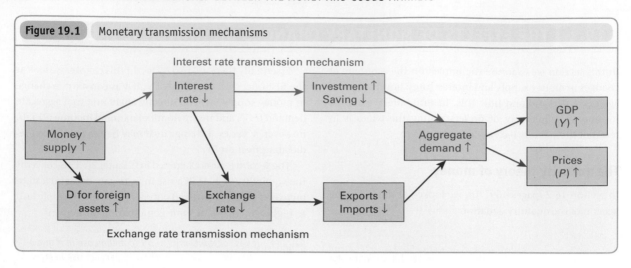

Figure 19.1 Monetary transmission mechanisms

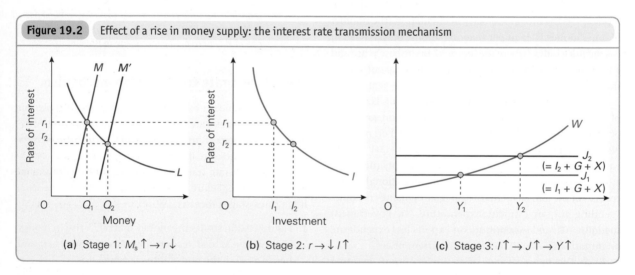

Figure 19.2 Effect of a rise in money supply: the interest rate transmission mechanism

(a) Stage 1: $M_s \uparrow \rightarrow r \downarrow$

(b) Stage 2: $r \rightarrow \downarrow I \uparrow$

(c) Stage 3: $I \uparrow \rightarrow J \uparrow \rightarrow Y \uparrow$

rise in income will lead to a rise in the transactions demand for money, L_1. In other words, L will shift to the right in Figure 19.2(a), and thus r will not fall as much as illustrated. Thus investment (Figure 19.2(b)) and national income (Figure 19.2(c)) will not rise as much as illustrated either.

The overall effect of a change in money supply on national income will depend on the size of the effect in each of the three stages. This will depend on the shapes of the curves in each of the three diagrams and whether they are likely to shift. The effect will be bigger:

■ the less elastic the liquidity preference curve (L): this will cause a bigger change in the rate of interest;

■ the more interest-elastic the investment curve (I): this will cause a bigger change in investment;

■ the lower the marginal propensity to withdraw (mpw), and hence the flatter the withdrawals function: this will cause a bigger multiplied change in national income and aggregate demand.

The problem is that stages 1 and 2 may be both weak and unreliable, especially in the short run. This problem is stressed by Keynesians.

Problems with stage 1: the money–interest link

An interest-elastic demand for money. According to Keynesians, the speculative demand for money is highly responsive to changes in interest rates. If people believe that the rate of interest will rise, and thus the price of bonds and other securities will fall, few people will want to buy them now. Instead there will be a very high demand for money and near money as people prefer to hold their assets in liquid form. The demand for money will therefore be very elastic in response to changes in interest rates. In such circumstances, the demand-for-money curve (the liquidity preference curve, L) will be relatively flat and may even be infinitely elastic at some minimum interest rate. This is the point where everyone believes interest rates will rise, and therefore no one wants to buy bonds.

With a very gently sloping L curve (as in Figure 19.3), a rise in money supply from M to M' will lead to only a small fall in the rate of interest from i_1 to i_2. Once people believe that the rate of interest will not go any lower, any further rise in money supply will have no effect on i. The additional money will be lost in what Keynes called the

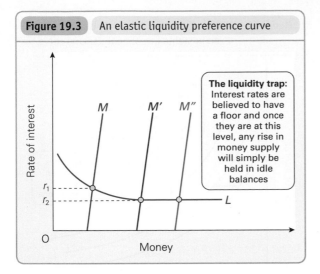

Figure 19.3   An elastic liquidity preference curve

The liquidity trap: Interest rates are believed to have a floor and once they are at this level, any rise in money supply will simply be held in idle balances

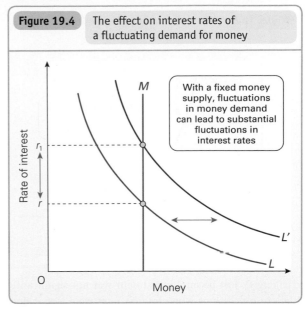

Figure 19.4   The effect on interest rates of a fluctuating demand for money

With a fixed money supply, fluctuations in money demand can lead to substantial fluctuations in interest rates

liquidity trap. People simply hold the additional money as idle balances.

Keynes himself saw the liquidity trap as merely a special case: the case where the economy is in deep recession. In normal times, an expansion of money supply would be likely to have some effect on interest rates. But in a deep recession an expansion of money supply may have no effect on the economy.

The possibility that additional money might simply find itself lost in a liquidity trap, with individuals and firms unwilling to spend it, was of concern to policy makers who responded to the financial crisis of the late 2000s by increasing the money supply.

In the UK, with the Bank of England's base rate at 0.5 per cent, the money supply was increased by the Bank purchasing gilts in exchange for central bank money (see Box 21.9 on quantitative easing). The hope was that this would increase bond prices as well as other asset prices, so reducing interest rates throughout the economy and hence the cost of borrowing. In turn, it was hoped that this would generate higher rates of spending growth than would otherwise have been the case.

In practice, the effectiveness of such policies is constrained by a liquidity trap. Extra money may be held as additional liquidity rather than boosting spending.

 How might we go about assessing whether quantitative easing actually worked?

An unstable demand for money. Another problem is that the liquidity preference curve (*L*) is *unstable*. People hold

KI 32
p401

Definition

Liquidity trap The absorption of any additional money supply into idle balances at very low rates of interest, leaving aggregate demand unchanged.

speculative balances when they anticipate that interest rates will rise (security prices will fall). But it is not just the current interest rate that affects people's expectations of the future direction of interest rates. Many factors could affect such expectations. These could include, for instance, economic policy announcements from government or newly released inflation figures indicating the possibility of imminent changes to monetary policy.

Thus the *L* curve can be highly volatile. With an unstable demand for money, it is difficult to predict the effect on various interest rates of a change in money supply.

A policy of *targeting* money supply can be criticised for similar reasons. A volatile demand for money can cause severe fluctuations in interest rates if the supply of money is kept constant (see Figure 19.4). These fluctuations will cause further uncertainty and further shifts in the speculative demand for money. Targeting the money supply can therefore add to the volatility of the velocity of circulation (*V*).

Problems with stage 2: the interest rate–investment link

An interest-inelastic investment demand. In the 1950s and 1960s, many Keynesians argued that investment was unresponsive to interest rate changes: that the *I* curve in Figure 19.2(b) was steep. In these circumstances, a very large change in interest rates would be necessary to have any significant effect on investment and aggregate demand.

KI 9
p71

Investment, it was argued, depends on confidence in future markets. If confidence is high, firms will continue to invest even if interest rates are high. They can always pass on the higher costs to the consumer. If confidence is low, firms will not invest even if interest rates are low and borrowing is cheap. Evidence seemed to confirm the interest inelasticity of investment demand.

Few Keynesians hold this extreme position today. The evidence for an inelastic investment demand has been

TC 9
p121

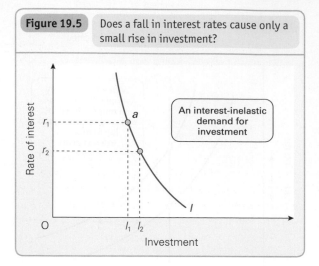

Figure 19.5 Does a fall in interest rates cause only a small rise in investment?

An interest-inelastic demand for investment

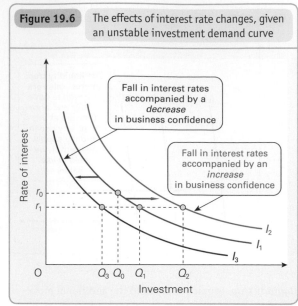

Figure 19.6 The effects of interest rate changes, given an unstable investment demand curve

Fall in interest rates accompanied by a *decrease* in business confidence

Fall in interest rates accompanied by an *increase* in business confidence

challenged. Just because investment was not significantly higher on occasions when interest rates were low, it does not follow that investment is unresponsive to interest rate changes. There may have been changes in *other* factors that helped to *curb* investment: in other words, the *I* curve shifted to the left. For example, a fall in consumer demand would both cause the low interest rate *and* discourage investment.

Figure 19.5 shows a steep investment demand curve. If the rate of interest falls from r_1 to r_2, there is only a small rise in investment from I_1 to I_2. Now draw a much more elastic I curve passing through point a. Assume that this is the true I curve. Show how the rate of interest could still fall to r_2 and investment still only rise to I_2 if this curve were to shift.

Even if fixed investment in plant and machinery is not very interest sensitive, other components of aggregate demand may well be: for example, investment in stocks, consumer demand financed through credit cards, bank loans or hire purchase, and the demand for houses financed through mortgages.

An unstable investment demand. Today the major worry about the interest–investment link is not that the investment curve is inelastic, but rather that it shifts erratically, driven by changes in the confidence of investors, the availability of finance and the financial well-being of economic agents.

KI 32
p401

The erratic nature of investment means that the investment curve in Figure 19.5 is frequently shifting. This affects the level of investment at a given rate of interest. An increase in confidence, more abundant finance and higher net worth of economic agents will tend to move the curve rightwards. This happened in the mid-2000s. In contrast, as in the late 2000s, falling confidence, more limited access to finance and a decline in economic agents' net worth move the investment curve leftwards.

Now consider the effect of interest rate changes given an unstable investment curve.

Assume in Figure 19.6 that the initial investment demand curve is given by I_1. Now assume that the central bank reduces interest rates from r_0 to r_1. Other things being equal, the level of investment will rise from Q_0 to Q_1. However, the fall in interest rates might be accompanied by other changes that affect investment too. For example, if firms believe that the economy will now pull out of recession, their confidence will increase. Firms may also believe that this growth will help to improve their balance sheets and hence their financial well-being, while financial institutions might be more confident to provide finance. The investment curve will shift to I_2 and investment will increase quite markedly to Q_2.

KI 10
p75

If, on the other hand, firms believe that inflation will now rise, which in turn will later force the central bank to raise interest rates again, their confidence may well decrease. The investment curve will shift to I_3 and the level of investment will actually fall to Q_3.

What we have seen here is that the effectiveness of monetary (and fiscal policy) is dependent on how people respond. Its effectiveness is therefore dependent on a range of factors, many of which are peculiar to that moment in time. Nonetheless, monetary policy is likely to be more effective if people have confidence in its effectiveness. This *psychological* effect can be quite powerful. This helps to explain the co-ordinated responses of central bankers to the financial crisis of 2007–9 and the concerted attempts to inject extra liquidity into the banking system. By doing so they were trying to reassure individuals and firms that the measures would work. Further expansions of liquidity by the Federal Reserve and other central banks in the early 2010s were again, in part, an attempt to reassure investors that the world would not be allowed to slip back into a double-dip recession, despite the tightening of fiscal policy as governments grappled with mounting public-sector debt.

Another example of attempting to reassure investors occurred in July 2012, when Mario Draghi, President of the European Central Bank, promised to 'do whatever it takes' to preserve the euro and support recovery in the eurozone. This was taken to mean that the ECB would buy bonds of weaker member countries, thereby pushing down their interest rates and increasing the money supply.

Balance sheets. Increasingly economists have become interested in how the balance sheets of economic agents affect the impact of changes from monetary (and fiscal) policy on economic activity.

The financial well-being of households, businesses and government has significance for their spending and saving decisions. Consider first the *precautionary effect* arising from the balance sheets. Assume that economic agents are looking to increase their net worth, perhaps concerned about their size of their financial liabilities. In such a scenario, a fall in interest rates may have little impact in boosting spending. Rather, economic agents would be making attempts to repay debt early and/or to increase their savings.

Consider now the *cash-flow effects* arising from the assets and liabilities comprising the balance sheets. Assume that interest rates are falling. This reduces the interest payments on those debts which are subject to variable interest rates, giving people more money to spend. However, it also reduces the interest receipts on financial assets: i.e. savings income. The net effect on aggregate demand will depend on which of these two counteracting effects is stronger. Nonetheless, for many economic agents, including many highly indebted households with mortgages, the effect of a fall in interest rates would be to generate a positive cash flow. This helps to boost spending and so reinforces the interest rate mechanism.

In the late 2000s and early 2010s, the precautionary behaviour of economic agents was a constraint on attempts to boost spending by increasing the money supply. This occurred because many sectors were simultaneously looking to repair their financial and capital balance sheets (see page 403). Consequently, spending levels were lower than they would otherwise have been. During this period the precautionary effect was particularly strong, thereby weakening the monetary transmission mechanism.

The exchange rate transmission mechanism

A second transmission mechanism is the exchange rate transmission mechanism. This is illustrated in the bottom half of Figure 19.1 (on page 562) and graphed in Figure 19.7. This mechanism backs up the interest rate mechanism. It includes the exchange rate as an intermediate variable between changes in the money supply and changes in aggregate demand. There are four stages in this exchange rate transmission mechanism (see Figure 19.7):

1. In Figure 19.7(a), a rise in money supply causes a fall in domestic interest rates from r_1 to r_2.

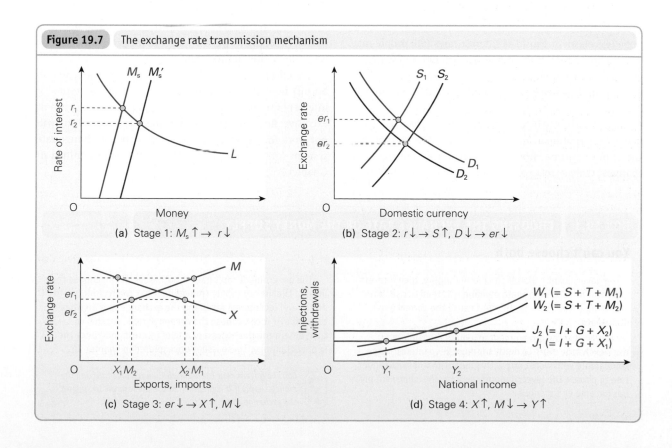

Figure 19.7 The exchange rate transmission mechanism

(a) Stage 1: $M_s \uparrow \rightarrow r \downarrow$

(b) Stage 2: $r \downarrow \rightarrow S \uparrow, D \downarrow \rightarrow er \downarrow$

(c) Stage 3: $er \downarrow \rightarrow X \uparrow, M \downarrow$

(d) Stage 4: $X \uparrow, M \downarrow \rightarrow Y \uparrow$

2. In Figure 19.7(b), the fall in domestic interest rates leads to an increased outflow of short-term finance from the country as people demand more foreign assets instead. There will also be a reduced inflow, as depositors seek to take advantage of relatively higher interest rates abroad. The supply of the domestic currency on the foreign exchange market rises from S_1 to S_2 and the demand falls from D_1 to D_2. This causes a depreciation of the exchange rate from er_1 to er_2 (assuming the authorities allow it). In addition, part of the increased money supply will be used to buy foreign assets directly, further contributing to the rightward shift in the supply curve. What is more, the depreciation in the exchange rate may be speeded up or amplified by speculation.

3. In Figure 19.7(c), the depreciation of the exchange rate causes a rise in demand for exports (X), since they are now cheaper for people abroad to buy (there is a movement down along the X curve). It also causes a fall in demand for imports (M), since they are now more expensive (there is a movement up along the M curve). Note that the rise in exports and fall in imports gives a current account balance of payments surplus (assuming a previous balance). This is matched by the financial account deficit resulting from the lower interest rate encouraging people to buy foreign assets and people abroad buying fewer of this country's assets.

4. In Figure 19.7(d), the rise in exports (an injection) and a fall in imports (a withdrawal) will cause a multiplied rise in national income.

Stage 1 will tend to be more powerful in a more open economy. The liquidity preference curve will tend to be less elastic because, as interest rates fall, people may fear a depreciation of the domestic currency and switch to holding other currencies. Just how strong stage 1 will be depends on *how much* people think the exchange rate will depreciate.

Stage 2 is likely to be very strong indeed. Given the openness of international financial markets, international financial flows can be enormous in response to interest rate changes. Only a relatively small change in interest rates is necessary to cause a relatively large financial flow. Monetarists and new classical economists stress the importance of this effect. Any fall in interest rates, they argue, will have such a strong effect on international financial flows and the exchange rate that the rise in money supply will be relatively quickly and fully transmitted through to aggregate demand.

Stage 3 may be quite strong in the long run. Given time, both the demand by consumers abroad for this country's exports and the domestic demand for imports may be quite elastic. In the short run, the effect may be rather limited. However, the size of the effect depends on people's expectations of exchange rate movements. If people think that the exchange rate will fall further, importers will buy *now* before the rate does fall. Exporters, on the other hand, will hold back as long as possible before shipping their exports. These actions will tend to push the exchange rate down. But such speculation is very difficult to predict as it depends on often highly volatile expectations.

 If importers and exporters believe that the exchange rate has 'bottomed out', what will they do?

Stage 4 is the familiar multiplier, only this time triggered by a change in imports and exports.

Again, as with the interest rate transmission mechanism, the full effect is unlikely to be as large as that illustrated. This is because the increased national income will cause an increased *transactions* demand for money. This will shift the L curve to the right in Figure 19.7(a), and thus lead to a smaller fall in the rate of interest than that illustrated. The overall effect can be quite strong, but the precise magnitude is usually highly unpredictable.

The effects of changes in money supply will depend also on just how free the exchange rate is. If the government intervenes to 'peg' (i.e. fix) the exchange rate or to prevent excessive fluctuations, the transmission mechanism will not work in the way described. Alternative exchange rate systems (or 'regimes', as they are called) are examined in Chapter 25.

You can't choose both

If the government expands the money supply, then interest rates will fall and aggregate demand will tend to rise. With a floating exchange rate, this will cause the currency to depreciate.

But what if the government attempts to maintain a fixed exchange rate? To do this it must keep interest rates comparable with world rates. This means that it is no longer free to choose the level of money supply. The money supply has become endogenous.

The government can't have it both ways. It can choose the level of the money supply (providing it has the techniques to do so) and let interest rates and the exchange rate be what they will. Or it can choose the exchange rate, but this will then determine the necessary rate of interest and hence the supply of money. These issues are explored in Chapter 25.

 Can the government choose both the exchange rate and the money supply if it is prepared to use the reserves to support the exchange rate?

The portfolio balance effect

Money can also impact on the economy through a process of 'portfolio adjustment': a mechanism that was stressed by monetarists. If money supply increases, people will have more money than they require to hold. They will spend this surplus. Much of this spending will go on goods and services, thereby directly increasing aggregate demand:

$$M_s \uparrow \rightarrow M_s > M_d \rightarrow AD \uparrow$$

The theoretical underpinning for this is given by the *theory of* **portfolio balance**. People have a number of ways of holding their wealth: as money, or as financial assets such as bills, bonds and shares, or as physical assets such as houses, cars and televisions. In other words, they hold a whole portfolio of assets of varying degrees of liquidity – from cash to property.

If money supply expands, people may find themselves holding more money than they require: their portfolios are unnecessarily liquid. Some of this money will be used to purchase financial assets, and some to purchase *goods and services*. As more assets are purchased, this will drive up their price. This will effectively reduce their 'yield'. For bonds and other financial assets, this means a reduction in their rate of interest. For goods and services, this means a reduction in their marginal utility/price ratio: a higher level of consumption will reduce their marginal utility and drive up their price. The process will stop when a balance has been restored in people's portfolios. In the meantime, there will have been extra consumption and hence a rise in aggregate demand.

 Do you think that this is an accurate description of how people behave when they acquire extra money?

Many Keynesian economists, however, argue that this mechanism may be weak and unreliable. What is more, a rise in money supply may itself come about as a result of a direct change in one of the components of aggregate demand, making it difficult to identify how much of any effect is due solely to the change in money supply.

Consider an increase in government expenditure financed by purchases of Treasury bills by the banking system. Will any impact on output and prices come primarily from the extra liquidity in the balance sheets of households and firms, or will it come directly from the higher government expenditure?

Even if there is a direct increase in liquidity (e.g. through quantitative easing) without any accompanying change in

Definition

Portfolio balance The balance of assets, according to their liquidity, that people choose to hold in their portfolios.

government expenditure or taxation, the effect of this additional liquidity will depend on the extent to which banks use it to extend new credit. This, in turn, will depend on the *demand* for credit, which in a recession may fall as people try to rein in their spending.

The question then is the extent to which any extra money will be passed on around the economy. Box 19.2 looks at this process.

Portfolio balance and the interest rate mechanism

The holding of a range of assets in people's portfolios can strengthen the interest rate transmission mechanism by making the liquidity preference curve less elastic (curve *L* in Figure 19.2(a) is relatively steep). The reason is that speculative balances of money may now have a much smaller role. But why?

A reduction in the rate of interest (*r*) following an increase in the money supply may well make bond holding less attractive, but this does not mean that the extra money will be mainly held in idle balances. Again, it can be used to purchase other assets such as property. Idle balances may expand only slightly.

 Redraw the three diagrams of Figure 19.2 with a steeper L curve. Show how an increase in money supply will have a larger effect on national income.

How stable is the velocity of circulation?

Short-run variability of V

Most economists agree that there is some variability of the velocity of circulation (*V*) in the short run if the money supply is changed. To the extent that interest rates and yields do fall with an expansion of the money supply, people may well hold somewhat larger money balances: after all, the interest sacrificed by not holding bonds etc. has been reduced. If people hold relatively more money, the velocity of circulation is thereby reduced, thus reducing the effect on aggregate demand. Furthermore, the direct mechanism may take time to operate. In the meantime, *V* will fall.

Also, the demand for money can shift unpredictably in the short run with changing expectations of prices, interest rates and exchange rates. Thus *V* is unpredictable in the short run, and so is the effect of monetary policy on aggregate demand. For these reasons, changing the money supply may not be an effective means of short-run demand management.

Long-run stability of V

The main claim of monetarists is that the velocity of circulation (*V*) is relatively stable over the longer run, and any changes that do occur are the predictable outcome of institutional changes, such as the increased use of credit cards (see Box 19.3).

One explanation of why *V* remains relatively stable in the long run, despite an increase in money supply, is that

BOX 19.2   PARTY GAMES AND THE VELOCITY OF MONEY

Are you ready for a game of pass-the-parcel?

What will be the effect of an increase in money supply on prices and output? To answer this we need to understand how money supply interacts with money demand. This requires an analysis of the velocity of circulation of money (V).

An interesting way of thinking about V and what it might mean for the economy is to consider changes in money in the context of a game of pass-the-parcel! Assume there has been an increase in money supply and that this causes individuals and firms to have excess money balances. In response, they may look to pass on the excess to somebody else and, of course, if that individual or firm also has excess money balances they too will look to pass it on. The consequence is a game of pass-the-parcel, where the parcel is money and the passing occurs through spending. The quicker the 'parcel' is passed, the more V will rise. If the extra spending is not matched by extra output (Y), then we would expect prices (P) to rise too.

But what if the increase in money occurred at a time when people are looking to increase their money holdings? This time there will be little impact on activity and prices as people hold on tightly to the parcel and refuse to play the game. In this case the velocity of circulation would fall.

The growth in money and spending

One way of assessing the extent to which the non-bank private sector might be holding excess money balances is to compare the annual growth in broad money with the annual growth in nominal spending (nominal GDP). Chart (a) is an indicator of the *excess nominal money balances* of the UK's non-bank private sector.

Positive values show excess money holdings: the velocity of circulation has slowed. To restore the balance of their portfolios, individuals and firms would be expected to pass the parcel more quickly, so causing the velocity of circulation to increase again. In turn, this would be expected to result in increasing economic activity, but in inflationary pressures too.

On the other hand, negative values indicate a deficit of liquid funds: the velocity of circulation has increased. To restore balance in this case, individuals and firms would look to increase money balances and so pass the parcel more slowly. This would act to constrain economic activity.

Money balances in different sectors

Our excess money balance indicator is an imperfect indicator of short-term activity and price movements, however, not

(a) *Annual money growth minus annual spending growth*

Sources: (i) *Statistical Interactive Database*, series LPQVQJW (Bank of England) (data published 29 July 2014) and (ii) *Quarterly National Accounts*, series YBHA (National Statistics).

least because the non-bank private sector comprises three groups: households, non-financial corporations (firms) and other financial corporations (e.g. insurance companies, pension funds and unit trusts). The key point is that the implications for economic activity and prices may depend on which of these three groups is experiencing excess or deficit money balances. Moreover, the ways in which these groups adjust their portfolios can have quite different economic effects.

Chart (b) shows, alongside the annual rate of growth of M4, the growth in the stock of M4 held by each of the groups comprising the non-bank private sector since 2000. From the second half of the 2000s we observe markedly contrasting rates of growth in their money holdings. The particular concern of the Bank of England was the dramatic slowdown from 2008 in the growth of broad money holdings of households and firms. This was not entirely surprising given the substantial retrenchment of lending and so of credit creation by financial institutions.

As if the negative impact of this on spending growth was not enough, households and firms were also looking to rebuild their balance sheets and reduce their debt exposure. An important element of this was their increased demand for money balances. In what were incredibly uncertain times, and with the markets for shares and housing depressed, households and firms looked to increase the liquidity of their portfolios. It was almost as if the music for our game of pass-the-parcel had stopped. Inevitably, the growth in nominal spending fell sharply, economic activity floundered and the economy entered into recession.

By contrast, broad money holdings of other financial corporations (OFCs) grew rapidly in the late 2000s before declining in the early 2010s.

Some of the initial rise in money holdings by OFCs related to unsold liquid securities issued by special purpose vehicles (SPVs) to fund the purchase of securitised assets, such as residential mortgages, from banks (see section 18.2). However, some of the increased money holdings were the result of quantitative easing, with OFCs exchanging gilts for money from the Bank of England. This increased the liquidity of OFCs' balance sheets. If money holdings are excessive, they can be passed on by purchasing other assets. In doing so, asset prices tend to rise and their yields fall. Therefore, it was hoped that amongst the positive effects of passing-the-parcel would be lower borrowing costs, a boost to the wealth of asset holders and increased economic activity.

 What can we infer from Charts (a) and (b) about the stability of the velocity of circulation in the short run? What can we learn from Chart (b) about the association between the growth of money holdings and that in nominal GDP?

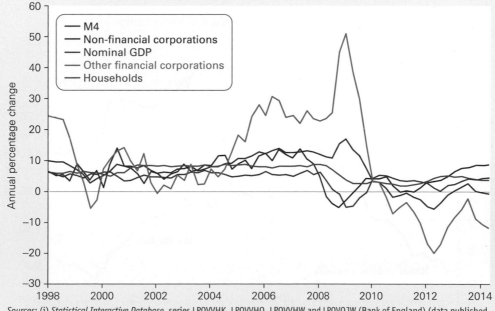

(b) *Annual growth rates of broad money and nominal GDP*

Sources: (i) *Statistical Interactive Database*, series LPQVVHK, LPQVVHQ, LPQVVHW and LPQVQJW (Bank of England) (data published 29 July 2014) and (ii) *Quarterly National Accounts*, series YBHA (National Statistics).

sufficient time has elapsed for the direct mechanism to have worked fully through.

Another explanation is the effect on inflation and consequently on interest rates. This works as follows.

Assume an initial increase in money supply. Interest rates fall. *V* falls. But if money supply goes on rising and hence expenditure goes on rising, inflation will rise. This will drive up *nominal* interest rates (even though *real* interest rates will stay low). But in choosing whether to hold money or to buy assets, it is the nominal rate of interest that people look at, since that is the opportunity cost of holding money. Thus people economise on money balances and *V* rises back again.

In extreme cases, *V* will even rise to levels higher than before. This is likely if people start speculating that prices will rise further. People will rush to buy goods and assets before their prices rise further. This action will help to push the prices up even more. This form of destabilising speculation took place in the hyperinflation of Germany in the 1920s and in Zimbabwe in the years up to 2008, as people spent their money as quickly as possible (see Case Study 15.5 in MyEconLab).

| BOX 19.3 | THE STABILITY OF THE VELOCITY OF CIRCULATION |

What is the evidence?

How stable is the velocity of circulation (*V*) in practice? Does the evidence support the monetarist case that it is relatively stable or the Keynesian case that it fluctuates unpredictably, at least in the short run? Unfortunately, the facts do not unequivocally support either side.

The evidence

How has *V* behaved over time? To answer this we need to measure *V*. A simple way of doing this is to use the formula $V = PY/M$ (rearranging the terms in the quantity equation $MV = PY$). Thus we need to measure *PY* and *M*. *PY* is simply the money value of national output: in other words, GDP at current prices. The value of *M* (and hence *V*) will depend on which measure of the money supply we use.

The diagram shows how the velocities of circulation in the UK of both broad money (M4) and narrow money (notes and coin) have changed over the years.

The long run

Broad money.   Long-term increases in the velocity of broad money from 1973 to 1979 are explained by the increase in money substitutes and credit cards, and thus smaller holdings of money balances. The decrease after 1980 reflects falling inflation and nominal interest rates,

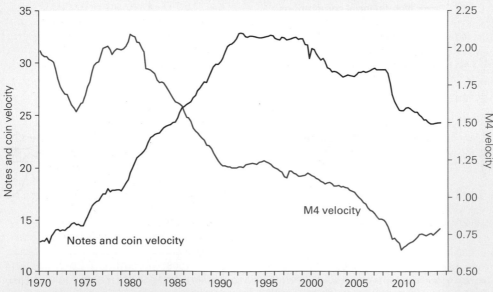

Velocity of circulation for narrow and broad money

Sources: (i) *Statistical Interactive Database*, series LPMAVAB and LPQAUYN (Bank of England) (data published 6 August 2014) and (ii) *Quarterly National Accounts*, series YBHA (National Statistics).

With a predictable *V* in the longer run, monetarists have claimed that monetary policy is the essential means of controlling long-term aggregate demand. For this reason, they have favoured a longer-term approach to monetary policy, including targets for the growth of the money supply (see page 478).

In the 1990s and 2000s, most governments adopted a policy of setting a target for the rate of inflation. This involves the central bank controlling aggregate demand by choosing an appropriate rate of interest. In these circumstances, the money supply must be *passively* adjusted to ensure that the chosen rate of interest is the equilibrium rate. This means expanding the money supply in line with the increase in real national income (*Y*) and the targeted increase in the price level (*P*). These rules were somewhat relaxed, however, following the recession of 2008–9 and subsequent rises in inflation. Preventing a double-dip recession became more important than strictly adhering to a (short-run) inflation target.

We explore inflation targeting and its effects in section 19.4. We explore the operation of monetary policy in section 21.2.

CASE STUDIES AND APPLICATIONS

with people being increasingly prepared to hold money in sight accounts; the growth in wholesale deposits (which earn interest); and people putting a larger proportion of their savings into bank and building society accounts, attracted by higher real interest rates and new types of high interest instant access account. As the pace of these changes slowed, so the fall in velocity became gentler after 1990.

However, in the second half of 2000s the velocity of broad money once again fell sharply. The financial and economic upheaval of this period is likely to have increased the demand for liquid assets.

Narrow money. The velocity of narrow money more than doubled between 1974 and 1993. One reason for this was the increased use of credit and debit cards, which reduce the amount of cash people need to hold. The growth of cash machines also reduced the need to hold so much cash, given that many people could easily obtain more at any time. The relatively smaller amount of cash thus circulated faster. But, as with broad money, these changes in the velocity of narrow money ceased in the early 1990s.

During the 2000s, the velocity of narrow money actually fell back to levels seen in the late 1980s. Low inflation rates, by reducing the opportunity cost of holding cash, contributed to the fall during the first half of 2000s. As with broad money, the impact of the economic and financial crisis contributed to a further fall in the velocity of narrow money during the second half of the 2000s.

The point made by monetarists is that these changes are predictable and gradual and do not, therefore, undermine the close relationship between *M* and *PY*.

The short run

Evidence shows periods when the velocity of circulation has been relatively stable in the short run, especially during the 1990s. However, this is largely because changes in money supply were not used to manipulate aggregate demand and hence national income. However, in response to the financial crisis of the late 2000s, the Bank of England embarked on a policy known as quantitative easing to increase the money supply. As we discussed in Box 19.2, the success of this was to depend on the responses of individuals and firms and so the extent to which *V* would fluctuate.

The direction of causality

Monetary and real changes often work together – especially in the long run. An expansionary fiscal policy over a number of years will increase the public-sector deficit, which in turn will lead to an increase in money supply (*M*). If the fiscal policy increases nominal national income (*PY*), *V* may well as a result remain constant. But it does not follow from this that it was the growth in *M* that caused the growth in *PY*. On the few occasions when fiscal and monetary policy work in opposite directions, the evidence is unclear as to which has the bigger effect – especially as the time period is rarely long enough for the full effects to be identified.

What we are concerned about here is the direction of causality. Changes in aggregate demand may go together with changes in money supply. But is it higher money supply causing higher aggregate demand, or the other way round, or the two simply occurring simultaneously?

Monetarists argue that increases in money supply cause (nominal) aggregate demand to expand (with a lag of perhaps a few months). For them money supply is exogenous: determined independently by the central bank. Keynesians, by contrast, argue that higher aggregate demand causes an increased demand for bank loans, and banks are only too happy to create the necessary credit, thus expanding the money supply. For them, money supply is endogenous.

 Why might it be difficult to establish the direction of causality from the evidence?

Section summary

1. The quantity equation $MV = PY$ can be used to analyse the possible relationship between money and prices. Whether and how much increases in money supply (M) affect the price level (P) depends on whether the velocity of circulation (V) and the level of real national income (Y) are independent of money supply (M).

2. The interest rate transmission mechanism works as follows: (a) a rise in money supply causes money supply to exceed money demand; interest rates fall; (b) this causes investment to rise; (c) this causes a multiplied rise in national income; but (d) as national income rises, so the transactions demand for money rises, thus preventing quite such a large fall in interest rates.

3. The effect will be weak if the demand for money curve (L) is elastic and the investment demand curve is inelastic. The effects may also be unreliable because of an unstable and possibly inelastic investment demand.

4. The exchange rate transmission mechanism works as follows: (a) a rise in money supply causes interest rates to fall; (b) the rise in money supply plus the fall in interest rates cause an increased supply of domestic currency to come onto the foreign exchange market; this causes the exchange rate to fall; (c) this causes increased exports and reduced imports, and hence a multiplied rise in national income.

5. According to the theory of portfolio balance, if people have an increase in money in their portfolios, they will attempt to restore portfolio balance by purchasing assets, including goods. Thus an increase in money supply is transmitted directly into an increase in aggregate demand.

6. The demand for money is more stable in the long run than in the short run. This leads to a greater long-run stability in V (unless it changes as a result of other factors, such as institutional arrangements for the handling of money).

19.2 THE MONETARY EFFECTS OF CHANGES IN THE GOODS MARKET

If there is an expansion in one of the components of aggregate demand (C, I, G or $X - M$), what will be the monetary effects? Will the current level of money supply act as a constraint on the growth in national income? In other words, will an expansion of one component of aggregate demand, such as government expenditure, be at the expense of another component, such as investment?

The monetary effects of an increase in injections

Let us assume that business confidence grows and that, as a result, the level of investment increases. Let us also assume that there is a given quantity of money in the economy. Will the rise in investment lead to a full multiplier effect on national income?

The effect of the rise in investment is illustrated in Figure 19.8. In Figure 19.8(a), the rise in investment leads to a rise in injections to J_2. Other things being equal, national income would rise to Y_2. But this increase in national income also leads to a rise in the transactions demand for money. In Figure 19.8(b), the demand-for-money curve shifts from L to L'.

If the central bank does not wish to allow money supply to rise, the higher demand for money will force it to raise interest rates to r_2. The effect of the higher interest rates is to reduce the level of investment. The overall rise in injections will be smaller than the rise from J_1 to J_2. Also net saving (i.e. saving minus borrowing) will rise as the higher interest rate acts as both an incentive for households to save and a disincentive for them to borrow. This causes an upward shift in the W curve. The result is that national income will not rise

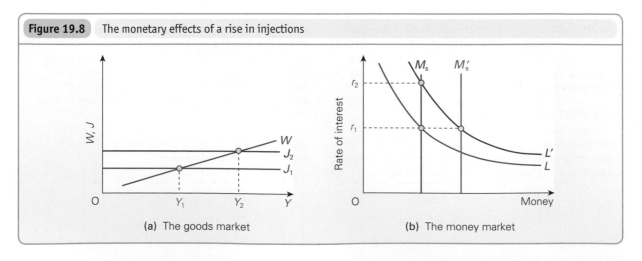

Figure 19.8 The monetary effects of a rise in injections

(a) The goods market

(b) The money market

as far as Y_2. In the extreme case, there would be no rise in national income at all.

If, however, the central bank responded to the increase in investment by expanding the money supply to M_s', there would be no change in the rate of interest and hence no dampening effect on either investment or consumption.

Assume that the government cuts its expenditure and thereby runs a public-sector surplus.
(a) What will this do initially to equilibrium national income?
(b) What will it do to the demand for money and initially to interest rates?
(c) Under what circumstances will it lead to
  (i) a decrease in money supply;
  (ii) no change in money supply?
(d) What effect will (i) and (ii) have on the rate of interest compared with its original level?

Crowding out

Another example of the monetary constraints on expansion in the goods market is the phenomenon known as **financial crowding out**. This is where an increase in public-sector spending reduces private-sector spending (see Box 16.2 on page 472).

To illustrate the effects, assume that previously the government has had a balanced budget, but that now it chooses to expand the level of government expenditure without raising additional taxes. As a result, it runs a budget deficit ($G > T$). But this deficit will have to be financed by borrowing. The resulting public-sector net cash requirement will lead to an increase in the money supply if it is financed by sales of government debt to financial institutions,

especially debt with shorter maturity. Alternatively, if it is financed by selling bills or bonds outside the banking sector, there will be no increase in the money supply.

The effect can once more be shown in Figure 19.8. The rise in government expenditure will cause injections to rise to J_2 and, other things being equal, national income will rise to Y_2. But, as with the case of increased investment, this increase in national income will lead to a rise in the demand for money. In Figure 19.8(b), the demand-for-money curve shifts from L to L'. If the PSNCR is financed in such a way as to allow money supply to expand to M_s', there will be no change in the interest rate and no crowding-out effect. If, however, the money supply is not allowed to expand, interest rates will rise to r_2. This in turn will reduce investment: crowding out will occur. Injections will fall back again below J_2. In the extreme case, injections could even fall back to I_1 and thus national income return to Y_1. Here crowding out is total.

The extent of crowding out

Just how much crowding out will occur when there is an expansionary fiscal policy, but when money supply is *not* allowed to expand, depends on two things.

The responsiveness (elasticity) of the demand for money to a change in interest rates. If the demand is relatively *elastic* (as in Figure 19.9(a)), the increase in demand, represented by a *horizontal* shift in the liquidity preference curve from L to L', will lead to only a small rise in interest rates. If, however, the demand is relatively inelastic (as in Figure 19.9(b)), the same horizontal shift will lead to a bigger rise in interest rates.

As we saw in section 19.1, Keynesians generally see the liquidity preference curve as being more elastic than do monetarists and new classical economists. They therefore argue that a rise in money demand normally leads to only a relatively modest rise in interest rates.

The responsiveness (elasticity) of investment to a change in interest rates. As we saw on pages 563–4, Keynesians argue that investment is relatively *unresponsive* to changes in interest rates. Businesspeople are much more likely to be affected by the state of the market for their product than by interest

KI 9
p71

Definition

Financial crowding out Where an increase in government borrowing diverts money away from the private sector.

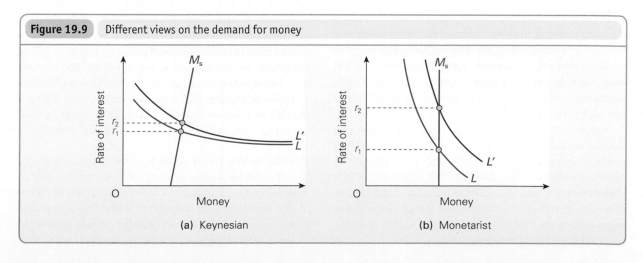

Figure 19.9 Different views on the demand for money

(a) Keynesian

(b) Monetarist

BOX 19.4   CROWDING OUT IN AN OPEN ECONOMY

Taking exchange rate effects into account

Will fiscal policy be crowded out in an open economy with floating exchange rates? Assume that the government increases its expenditure but does not allow the money supply to expand: a case of pure fiscal policy. What will happen?

- The increased government expenditure will increase the demand for money (see Figure 19.8(b)).
- This will drive up interest rates – the amount depending on the elasticity of the liquidity preference curve.
- This will lead to an inflow of finance from abroad, which in turn will lead to an appreciation of the exchange rate.

- The higher exchange rate will reduce the level of exports (an injection) and increase the level of imports (a withdrawal). This will add to the degree of crowding out.

Thus, in an open economy with floating exchange rates, an expansionary fiscal policy will be crowded out not only by higher interest rates, but also by a higher exchange rate.

 We have argued that the short-term inflow of finance following a rise in the rate of interest will drive up the exchange rate. Are there any effects of expansionary fiscal policy on the demand for imports (and hence on the current account) that will go some way to offsetting this?

Figure 19.10   Different views on the demand for investment

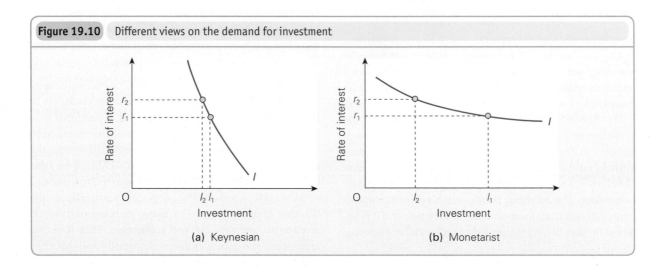

(a) Keynesian   (b) Monetarist

---

rates. Thus in Figure 19.10(a), there is only a small fall in investment. Monetarists and new classical economists, however, argue that investment is relatively *responsive* to changes in interest rates. Thus in Figure 19.10(b), there is a bigger fall in investment.

In the Keynesian case, therefore, the increase in demand for money arising from an expansionary fiscal policy will have only a small effect on interest rates and an even smaller effect on investment. Little or no crowding out takes place. In fact, the expansion of demand might cause an increase in investment through the accelerator effect (see pages 516–8).

Monetarists and new classical economists argue that interest rates will rise significantly and that there will be a severe effect on investment. Crowding out is substantial. For this reason they argue that, if money supply is to be kept under control to prevent inflation rising, it is vital for governments to reduce the size of their budget deficit. They argue that, in the long run, crowding out is total, given the long-run stability of the velocity of circulation.

The debate about crowding out in the early 2010s

There was a general tightening of fiscal policy around the world in the early 2010s, as governments sought to tackle the huge rises in public-sector debt that had resulted from bank bailouts and the fiscal stimulus packages that had been used to tackle the recession. Many governments, including the UK Coalition government, were unwilling to adopt a more expansionary fiscal policy for fear of crowding out private-sector investment and 'spooking' the markets that they were not serious about deficit reductions.

However, bankers and many economists were urging a relaxing of fiscal restraint. For example, a report by economists at Bank of America/Merrill Lynch stated that:

while fiscal austerity could help the long-run outlook, near-term fiscal consolidation threatens the recovery in developed economies . . . Interest rates are already quite low, signalling limited market pressure to reduce deficits. As a result, near-term fiscal austerity would do little to lower rates. Moreover, companies are flush with cash.

TC 15
p 508

Investment is low because of a lack of confidence in the recovery – not because government borrowing is crowding them out.[1]

Is money supply exogenous or endogenous?

Money supply is *exogenous* (independently determined) if it can be fixed by the authorities and if it does not vary with aggregate demand and interest rates. The money supply 'curve' would be vertical, as in Figure 19.9(b). It would shift only if the government or central bank *chose* to alter the money supply.

Money supply is *endogenous* (determined within the model) if it is determined by aggregate demand and hence the demand for money: banks expanding or contracting credit in response to customer demand. In such a case, the money supply curve would be upward sloping or even horizontal. The more that money supply expands in response to an increase in aggregate demand, the more gently upward sloping the money supply curve would be.

The more elastic the money supply curve, the less will money act as a constraint on expansion in the goods market,

and the less will a rise in government expenditure crowd out private expenditure. In other words, the less will interest rates rise in response to a rise in the demand for money.

The extreme monetarist position is that money supply is wholly exogenous. The extreme Keynesian position is that money supply is wholly endogenous: money simply passively expands to meet the demand for money.

In reality, money supply is partly exogenous and partly endogenous. The authorities are able to influence money supply, but banks and other financial institutions have considerable scope for creating credit in response to demand. If control of the money supply is adopted as the basis for policy, the authorities must reduce the endogenous element to a minimum.

The authorities in many countries recognise the difficulties in controlling the money supply directly. They therefore influence the supply of money indirectly by controlling interest rates and hence the demand for money.

Sometimes, however, in extreme circumstances, the authorities may attempt to control money supply directly. As we saw in Chapter 18, central banks in several countries, including the USA, the UK and Japan, injected large amounts of liquidity into the financial system during and after the financial crisis in an attempt to stabilise their financial systems and to stimulate bank lending. This use of 'quantitative easing' is examined in section 21.2.

---

[1] Quoted in Stephanie Flanders, 'Restraint or stimulus. Markets and governments swap roles', BBC News, 7 September 2011, www.bbc.co.uk/news/business-14823501

Section summary

1. Changes in injections or withdrawals will have monetary implications. If there is a rise in investment with no change in the money supply, the increased demand for money will drive up interest rates and reduce both investment and consumption. The resulting rise in income will be smaller.

2. Similarly, if there is a fiscal expansion and *no* change in the money supply, the increased demand for money will again drive up the interest rate. This will to some extent crowd out private expenditure and thus reduce the effectiveness of the fiscal policy.

3. The extent of crowding out will depend on the shape of the liquidity preference curve and the investment demand

curve. The less elastic the demand for money, and the more elastic the investment demand, the more crowding out will take place, and the less effective will fiscal policy be.

4. If there is a rise in aggregate demand, money supply may rise in response to this. The more elastic the supply of money curve, the less crowding out will take place.

5. Money supply is not totally exogenous. This makes it hard for the authorities to control it precisely. Generally, therefore, central banks try to control *interest rates* and attempt to alter liquidity to back this up. Sometimes, however, they may take more deliberate steps to inject extra liquidity into the financial system.

19.3 MODELLING THE INTERACTION OF MONETARY POLICY AND THE GOODS MARKET

The goods and money markets

In this chapter, we have shown that there are two key markets in the economy at macroeconomic level, and that these two markets interact. The first is the goods market; the second is the money market. Each of these two markets has been analysed by using a model.

In the case of the goods market, the model is the Keynesian injections/withdrawals model. Any change in injections or withdrawals will cause national income to change. For example, a rise in government expenditure shifts the *J* line upwards and causes a rise in equilibrium real national income. In other words, an increase in the demand for goods and services causes a (multiplied) rise in the output of goods and services (assuming that there are sufficient idle resources).

In the case of the money market, the model is the one showing the demand for money (L) and the supply of money (M) and their effect on the rate of interest. A change in the supply or demand for money will cause the equilibrium rate of interest to change. Monetary policy operates directly in this market, either by affecting the supply of money or by operating on interest rates.

What we have shown in this chapter is that the two markets *interact*: that changes in one market cause changes in the other. Therefore, we need a model which allows us to *combine* the goods and money markets. The traditional approach has been through a model known as the *IS/LM* model. The *IS* curve is based on equilibrium in the goods market; the *LM* curve is based on equilibrium in the money market. By examining the interaction of both markets we can see the implication for interest rates *and* output.

In many countries today interest rates have become the key tool of monetary policy. Money supply is therefore controlled only indirectly. In the UK, the Bank of England supplies an aggregate level of reserves (central bank money) so that, given the demand for money, it is able to influence the structure of interest rates. It does this to affect the growth of aggregate demand and inflationary expectations. In both the UK and the eurozone, the target inflation rate is 2 per cent.

Under inflation targeting the authorities use monetary policy to affect equilibrium in the goods market. Therefore, the modern approach to modelling the interaction between the goods and money markets retains the *IS* curve. The *IS* curve relates to equilibrium in the goods market. However, the *LM* curve is replaced with a monetary policy curve – the *MP* curve.

We now develop the *IS/MP* model. The traditional *IS/LM* model can be found in the appendix to this chapter.

The *IS* curve

Deriving the IS curve

To explain how the *IS* curve is derived, let us examine Figure 19.11, which, as you can see, is in two parts. The top part shows the familiar Keynesian injections and withdrawals diagram, only in this case, for simplicity, we are assuming that saving is the only withdrawal from the circular flow of income, and investment the only injection. Thus in equilibrium $I = S$ (i.e. $J = W$). The bottom part of Figure 19.11 shows the *IS* curve. This shows all the various combinations of real interest rates (i) and national income (Y) at which $I = S$. The interest rate is the *real* interest rate. This is the nominal (actual) interest rate (r) *less* the rate of inflation (π). We shall assume that actual inflation is constant at a particular moment of time.

Let us assume that initially the real interest rate is i_1. Both investment and saving are affected by interest rates, and thus, other things being equal, an interest rate of i_1 will give particular investment and saving schedules. Let us say that, in the top part of Figure 19.11, these are shown by the

TC 12 p411

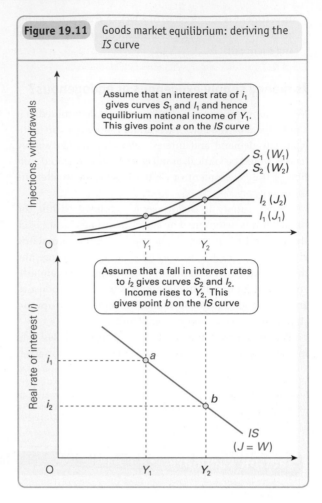

Figure 19.11 Goods market equilibrium: deriving the *IS* curve

Assume that an interest rate of i_1 gives curves S_1 and I_1 and hence equilibrium national income of Y_1. This gives point a on the *IS* curve

Assume that a fall in interest rates to i_2 gives curves S_2 and I_2. Income rises to Y_2. This gives point b on the *IS* curve

curves I_1 and S_1. Equilibrium national income will be where $I = S$: i.e. at Y_1. Thus in the lower part of Figure 19.11, an interest rate of i_1 will give a level of output Y_1. Thus point a is one point on the *IS* curve. At an interest rate of i_1 the goods market will be in equilibrium at output Y_1.

Now what will happen if the real rate of interest changes? Let us assume that it falls to i_2. This will cause a rise in investment and a fall in saving. A rise in investment is shown in the top part of Figure 19.11 by a shift in the investment line to I_2. Likewise a fall in saving is shown by a shift in the saving curve to S_2. This will lead to a multiplied rise in income to Y_2 (where $I_2 = S_2$). This corresponds to point b in the lower diagram, which therefore gives a second point on the *IS* curve.

Thus *lower* interest rates are associated with *higher* national income, if equilibrium is to be maintained in the goods market ($I = S$).

The elasticity of the IS curve

The elasticity of the IS curve (i.e. the responsiveness of national income to changes in interest rates) depends on two factors.[1]

KI 9 p71

---

[1] Note that, as with demand and supply curves, the elasticity of the *IS* curve will vary along its length. Therefore we should really talk about the elasticity at a particular point on the curve, or between two points.

The responsiveness of investment and saving to interest rate changes. The more investment and saving respond to a change in the rate of interest, the bigger will be the vertical shift in the *I* and *S* curves in the top part of Figure 19.11, and thus the bigger will be the effect on national income. The bigger the effect on national income, the more elastic will be the *IS* curve.

The size of the multiplier. This is given by $1/mps$ (i.e. $1/mpw$ in the full model). The *mps* is given by the slope of the *S* curve. The flatter the curve, the bigger the multiplier. The larger the value of the multiplier, the bigger will be the effect on national income of any rise in investment and fall in saving, and the more elastic therefore will be the *IS* curve. Thus the flatter the *S* curve in the top part of Figure 19.11, the flatter the *IS* curve in the bottom part.

 In a complete model where there were three injections (I, G and X) and three withdrawals (S, T and M), what else would determine the shape of the 'JW' curve?

Keynesians argue that the *IS* curve is likely to be fairly inelastic. The reason they give is that investment is not very responsive to changes in interest rates: the demand for investment curve in Figure 19.2(b) on page 562 is relatively inelastic. Saving also, claim Keynesians, is unresponsive to interest rate changes. The effect of this is that there will only be a relatively small shift in the *I* and *S* curves in response to a change in interest rates, and thus only a relatively small change in national income.

Monetarists, by contrast, argue that investment and saving are relatively responsive to changes in interest rates and that therefore the *IS* curve is relatively elastic.

Shifts in the IS curve

A change in interest rates will cause a movement *along* the *IS* curve. As we saw in Figure 19.11, a reduction in interest rates from i_1 to i_2 causes a movement *along* the *IS* curve from point *a* to point *b*.

A change in any *other* determinant of investment or saving, however, will *shift* the whole curve. The reason is that it will change the equilibrium level of national income at any given rate of interest.

An increase in investment, other than as a result of a fall in interest rates, will shift the *IS* curve to the *right*. This could happen, for example, if there were an increase in business confidence. A rise in business confidence *at the current interest rate* will cause an upward shift of the *I* curve in the top part of Figure 19.11, which will cause a multiplied rise in income. Thus in the lower part of Figure 19.11 a higher equilibrium income is now associated with each level of the interest rate: the *IS* curve has shifted to the right. Likewise, for any given interest rate, a fall in saving, and hence a rise in consumption, would also shift the *IS* curve to the right.

In a complete model (with three injections and three withdrawals), where the *IS* curve was a '*J* = *W*' curve rather than a simple '*I* = *S*' curve, similar shifts would result from changes in other injections or withdrawals. Thus an expansionary fiscal policy that increased government expenditure (*G*) or cut taxes (*T*) would shift the '*IS*' curve (i.e. the *JW* curve) to the right.

 In a complete JW model, what else would cause the JW curve (a) to shift to the right; (b) to shift to the left?

The MP curve

Deriving the MP curve

To help analyse the monetary policy (*MP*) curve consider Figure 19.12. Unlike the *IS* curve, which was developed as part of the *IS/LM* model (see the appendix to this chapter) in the 1930s, the *MP* curve is a relatively new model, developed in the context of inflation targeting by central banks.[1] The central bank is assumed to raise interest rates when inflation rises above the target (π^*) and to lower them when inflation falls below the target.

The *MP* curve is drawn as upward sloping. Potential national income is assumed to be constant. Assume too that inflation is currently at the target level. If aggregate demand now rises and hence real national income (*Y*) rises, thereby pushing firms closer to full capacity, this will raise inflation (π) above the target (π^*). The central bank will respond by raising the rate of interest. This gives an upward-sloping *MP* curve. A rise in national income will cause the central bank to raise the rate of interest; a fall in national income will cause the central bank to lower the rate of interest.

The relationship can be summarised as follows:

$$Y\uparrow \rightarrow \pi > \pi^* \rightarrow i\uparrow$$

$$Y\downarrow \rightarrow \pi < \pi^* \rightarrow i\downarrow$$

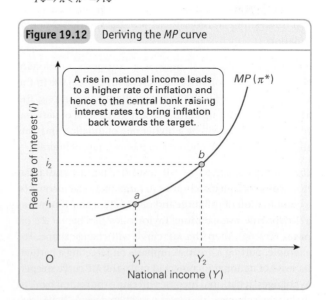

Figure 19.12 Deriving the *MP* curve

A rise in national income leads to a higher rate of inflation and hence to the central bank raising interest rates to bring inflation back towards the target.

[1] In fact, there are different versions of the *MP* curve. One version focuses on an interest rate target, rather than an inflation target. Another focuses on a complex target that is a combination of both inflation and national income or inflation and unemployment. The version we develop here is the most useful in the context of a specific inflation target and where the interest rate set by the central bank is only an intermediate variable determined by the actual rate of inflation relative to the target rate.

The elasticity of the MP curve

KI 9
p71 The elasticity of the *MP* curve (i.e. the responsiveness of interest rates to changes in national income) depends on the degree of slack in the economy.

If the economy is operating well below potential national income – a large negative output gap – a rise in national income (Y) will have little effect on inflation and hence little effect on central bank interest rates (r) and the real rate of interest (i). The *MP* curve will be relatively flat (elastic). If, however, there is a positive output gap, with firms operating close to full capacity, a rise in income will be reflected largely in a rise in inflation, causing the central bank to make a relatively large change to interest rates. The *MP* curve will be relatively steep (inelastic).

This means that the curve is likely to get steeper as national income rises, as in Figure 19.12. The closer the economy gets to full employment (i.e. the smaller the negative output gap or the bigger the positive output gap), the less slack there is in the economy. The less the slack, the more firms are likely to respond to a rise in demand by raising real prices (i.e. raising their prices above the rate of inflation) and the greater the resulting rise in inflation and the rise in central bank interest rates.

Shifts in the MP curve

A particular *MP* curve assumes a particular central bank target and a particular level of potential income. If either of these changes, a new *MP* curve will have to be drawn.

Change in the target rate of inflation. If the central bank chooses to lower the target rate of inflation, the *MP* curve will shift upwards. Any given level of national income and hence inflation will now result in the central bank setting a higher real interest rate in order to achieve the new lower rate of inflation.

An inflationary shock. If there is a cost-push inflationary shock, such as an oil price increase, a substantial rise in the minimum wage or a rise in inflationary expectations, the **KI 10**
p75 *MP* curve will shift upwards. For any given level of national income (Y), there will be a higher rate of inflation and thus the central bank will choose a higher real rate of interest.

Change in central bank policy. If, instead of targeting just inflation, the central bank chooses to target national income or a combination of inflation and national income (known as a Taylor rule: we examine Taylor rules in Chapter 21 on pages 659–64), then the *MP* curve will change shape. For example, putting a greater emphasis on targeting a particular level of national income will make the *MP* curve steeper, as changes in national income will cause the central bank to make larger changes in interest rates than it would have done if it targeted inflation alone. In the extreme case of targeting just national income and not inflation at all, the curve would be vertical at the targeted level of national income.

Alternatively, the central bank may target unemployment alongside inflation. Again this will tend to make the curve steeper, the more closely unemployment is aligned to national income. Indeed, in recent years central banks have taken more explicit account of unemployment. Under their policy of 'forward guidance', both the Fed (in 2012) and the Bank of England (in 2013) announced that they would not raise interest rates until unemployment had fallen to a particular level.

Change in potential national income. Potential national income is likely to rise over time. This rise in aggregate supply is the result of increased investment, new technology, greater labour efficiency, etc. A rise in potential national income will shift the *MP* curve to the right, as a given rate of inflation will be associated with a higher and higher level of national income.

 If the central bank targets real national income rather than inflation, what will be the shape of the MP curve?

Equilibrium

Equilibrium national income and the rate of interest are given by the intersection of the *IS* and *MP* curves. This is shown as **TC 10**
p317 point *a* in Figure 19.13, giving equilibrium national income of Y_e and an interest rate of i_e.

To demonstrate why this is an equilibrium, consider what would happen if national income were not at Y_e but at Y_1. According to the *MP* curve (point *b*), the higher inflation associated with this higher level of national income would lead the central bank to set an interest rate of i_1. But this higher interest rate of i_1 will dampen aggregate demand. According to point *c* on the *IS* curve, the goods market will be in equilibrium at a level of national income of Y_2. This will cause inflation to fall and hence the central bank to lower the real rate of interest. As it does so, there will be a **KI 8**
p46 movement down along the *IS* curve and a rise in national income until equilibrium is reached at Y_e.

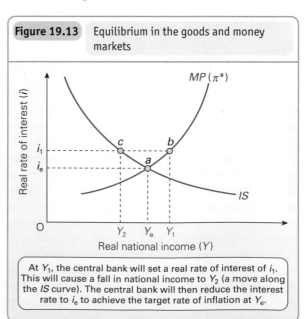

Figure 19.13 Equilibrium in the goods and money markets

At Y_1, the central bank will set a real rate of interest of i_1. This will cause a fall in national income to Y_2 (a move along the *IS* curve). The central bank will then reduce the interest rate to i_e to achieve the target rate of inflation at Y_e.

In practice, if the two markets are not in equilibrium, the central bank will attempt to move straight to i_e and Y_e by forecasting the likely movements in the economy and the results of its actions. The Bank of England, for example, at the monthly meetings of the Monetary Policy Committee, examines forecasts of inflation and output contained in its quarterly *Inflation Report* and other models of the economy.

The next step in the analysis is to consider how shifts in either curve affect national income, inflation and interest rates.

---

*LOOKING AT THE MATHS

Equilibrium in the *IS/MP* model is where the two functions, *IS* and *MP*, are equal. The simplest mathematical representation of this is where both *IS* and *MP* are simple linear (i.e. straight-line) functions. The *IS* function could be expressed as

$$i = a - bY \tag{1}$$

In other words, the higher the real rate of interest (i), the lower will be the level of aggregate demand and hence national income (Y).[1] This is consistent with a downward-sloping *IS* curve.

The *MP* function can be written as

$$i = c + dY \tag{2}$$

In other words, the higher the level of real national income (and hence the higher the rate of inflation), the higher will be the real rate of interest set by the central bank. This is consistent with an upward-sloping *MP* curve.

Equation (?) can be derived from the relationships between inflation (π) and national income and between inflation and the rate of interest. The relationship between inflation and national income is given by

$$\pi = e + f(Y - Y_p) \tag{3}$$

where Y_p is potential national income. The greater the excess of actual (short-run) income over potential income (i.e. the bigger the positive output gap), the higher will be the rate of inflation.

The relationship between inflation and the rate of interest is given by the central bank response function, which, in its simplest form, is given by

$$i = g + h(\pi - \pi^*) \tag{4}$$

where π^* is the target rate of inflation. The higher the actual inflation rate is relative to the target rate, the higher will the rate of interest set by the central bank. Substituting equation (4) in equation (3) gives

$$i = g + h(e + f(Y - Y_p) - \pi^*) \tag{5}$$

Assuming that Y_p and π^* are constant, equation (5) can be simplified as equation (2):

$$i = c + dY \tag{2}$$

We can then solve for Y from equations (1) and (2) by setting the two equations equal. Thus

$$a - bY = c + dY$$

that is,

$$bY + dY = a - c$$

giving

$$Y = \frac{a - c}{b + d}$$

Note that a change in any of the factors affecting Y, other than i, will shift the *IS* curve. Such factors include taxes, government expenditure, the exchange rate, expectations about income and prices, and so on.

Similarly, a change in any of the factors affecting i, other than Y, will shift the *MP* curve. Such factors include potential national income (Y_p), cost pressures, inflationary expectations and the inflation target (π^*).

The IS function can be written as

$$Y = IS(i, G, t, X, M, er, Y^e \ldots)$$

where G is government expenditure, t is the tax rate, X and M are the levels of exports and imports, er is the exchange rate, Y^e is the expected level of real national income and '...' represents other unspecified determinants.

Write an MP function in the form $i = MP(-----)$ identifying each of the determinants.

[1] Note that although equation (1) shows i as a function of Y, the model in fact has Y as the dependent variable. In other words, i determines Y. We express equation (1) this way to make it consistent with equation (2), where i is the dependent variable.

Full effect of changes in the goods and money markets

Changes in goods market equilibrium resulting from changes to aggregate demand are illustrated by a shift in the *IS* curve. Changes to monetary policy or potential national income are illustrated by a shift in the *MP* curve.

Shifts in the IS curve

Assume in Figure 19.14(a) that equilibrium is at point *a*, at a level of national income of Y_1. Now assume that a positive demand shock occurs resulting in a rightward shift in the *IS* curve from IS_1 to IS_2. This could arise, for example, because confidence rises and economic agents decide to increase spending or because of a loosening of fiscal policy (e.g. an increase in government purchases). This causes national income and inflation to rise. The central bank responds to the higher inflation by raising the rate of interest. There is a movement up along the *MP* curve. Equilibrium is reached at point *b* at a level of national income of Y_2 and a rate of interest of i_2.

Shifts in the MP curve

As we noted earlier, many countries have adopted some form of inflation targeting. However, inflation targeting can take many different forms and the policy rule can be changed or adapted. For example, the Federal Reserve from 2008 and the Bank of England from 2013 supplemented

Figure 19.14   *IS/MP* analysis of changes in the goods and money markets

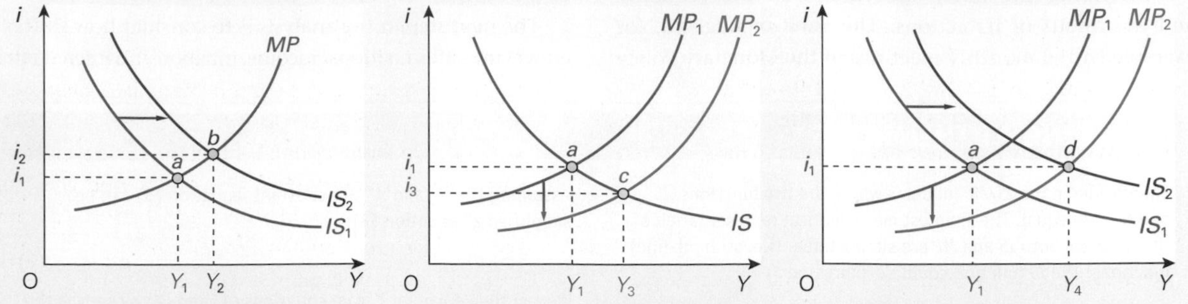

(a) A rise in injections

(b) A loosening of monetary policy or a rise in potential national income

(c) A shift in both curves

their existing policy frameworks with forward guidance: statements about the likely path of future interest rates. The intention was to signal that interest rates were likely to remain low for some time given the fragile economic conditions following the financial crisis. The hope was that this would give economic agents confidence to bring forward spending.

To illustrate a change to the monetary policy rule using the *IS/MP* framework, consider the case where the central bank now sets a lower interest rate for any given level of output and rate of inflation. The effect of this looser monetary policy rule is to move the *MP* curve vertically downwards. This is illustrated by a move from MP_1 to MP_2 in Figure 19.14(b).

BOX 19.5   THE FINANCIAL ACCELERATOR

Interest rate differentials and models of the goods market

The interest rate differential

The financial system is characterised by a range of interest rates rather than a single interest rate. For example, real borrowing rates (i_b) are higher than those on saving (i_s). This differential reflects the risks attached to lending to economic agents and the costs incurred by financial institutions in screening clients and then in arranging and managing loans. The bigger the risk, the bigger the differential.

However, this differential can exacerbate or amplify the magnitude of the business cycle. This is because the interest rate differential ($i_b - i_s$) tends to vary across the course of business cycle: falling in a boom and rising in a slowdown or recession.

But why does it fall in a boom? As far as lending is concerned, financial institutions may see rising output levels as a signal that lending is becoming less risky (see Chapter 16 page 403). After all, the financial well-being of economic agents typically improves as national income rises. Consequently, banks tend to reduce the differential of borrowing rates over saving rates in periods of rapid economic growth. At the same time, with economic agents gaining more confidence, they may decide to spend more and reduce their level of savings. Banks may thus offer higher interest rates on savings, further reducing the differential between borrowing and saving rates.

Conversely, the financial crisis and subsequent recession of the late 2000s saw interest rates fall dramatically. But saving rates fell more than borrowing rates, thereby widening the differential. Also the differential between interbank rates (at which banks borrow from each other) and the central bank rate (which more closely mirrors the saving rate) increased significantly (see Figure 18.2).

Effects on the goods market

The fact that the size of the interest rate differential is negatively related to changes in national income introduces another means by which the goods market is affected by national income. As national income rises, not only are there the normal multiplier and accelerator effects, but a reduction in the interest rate differential increases investment and consumption relative to saving.

An important effect of interest rate differentials is that injections cease to be determined independently of national income. More specifically, injections are now positively related to national income. Consider the top half of Figure 19.11: the injections–withdrawal model. The injections function will now be *positively sloped*: as national income rises, investment rises because the interest rate on borrowing falls relative to the saving rate.

Similarly, in the presence of an interest rate differential, the aggregate expenditure line in the Keynesian cross diagram of Figure 17.2 is now *steeper*. A rise in national income results in a larger increase in aggregate expenditure, while a fall in national income results in a larger decrease in aggregate expenditure. Therefore, the effect is to amplify the business cycle. The process is known as the *financial accelerator*.

Modelling the effect of the financial accelerator

Interest rate differentials and the IS curve.   When applying the *IS/MP* framework we need to identify which interest rate is on the vertical axis. Since rates on saving typically track the central

---

Definition

Financial accelerator When a change in national income is amplified by changes in the money market, such as changes in interest rate differentials or changes in the willingness of banks to lend.

TC 15
p 508

TC 15
p 508

The central bank reduces the nominal rate of interest so as to give a real rate of interest of i_3. As a result there is a movement along the IS curve to point c and national income rises to Y_3.

A similar effect would be caused by a rise in potential income. This again can be illustrated by a shift in the MP curve from MP_1 to MP_2 in Figure 19.14(b). With a rise in potential income, a higher level of actual income is now associated with any given rate of inflation and hence central bank interest rate.

Shifts in the both curves

If potential national income increases and also aggregate demand, actual income can rise without imposing extra inflationary pressures. This is illustrated in Figure 19.14(c). National income rises to Y_3. The central bank does not need to raise interest rates as there is no upward movement in inflation.

Size of the effect on national income of shifts in either or both curves

The magnitude of a change in income resulting from a shift in one or both curves depends not only on the size of the shift, but on the shape of the curves:

- The flatter the MP curve and the steeper the IS curve, the bigger will be the effect of a shift in the IS curve. When MP is relatively flat (e.g. when there is plenty of slack in the economy), a rightward shift in IS will lead to only a small rise in the real rate of interest (i) by the central bank. If IS is steep (i.e. aggregate demand being relatively unresponsive to changes in interest rates), this rise in i will lead to only a small curtailing of investment. In these two circumstances, the dampening effect on investment and consumption is limited. There will be a large increase in national income (Y).

- The effect of a shift in the MP curve will be bigger when the MP curve is steep (e.g. when the economy is near full employment) and the IS curve is relatively flat. When the MP curve is steep, there will be a relatively large downward shift in the MP curve for any fall in the inflation target and hence a relatively large fall in i. When IS is relatively flat, this fall in i will lead to a relatively large increase in investment and hence Y.

- The effect of a shift in either curve will be bigger if matched by a similar shift in the other curve.

EXPLORING ECONOMICS

bank rate most closely, we will label the vertical axis the real interest rate on saving (i_s).

The variation of the interest rate differential with national income affects the slope of the IS curve. This is illustrated in the diagram. IS_1 shows the IS curve when there is no differential between the saving and borrowing rate. IS_2 shows the IS curve in the presence of an interest rate differential. This curve is flatter, as a given fall in saving rates will produce a bigger rise in national income as borrowing rates will have fallen more as the differential narrows.

This flatter curve, IS_2, converges on IS_1 as output rises because the differential declines. Conversely, at lower levels of output the borrowing rate becomes relatively higher, causing investment, and hence aggregate expenditure, to be increasingly lower than it otherwise would be.

IS curve with interest rate differential

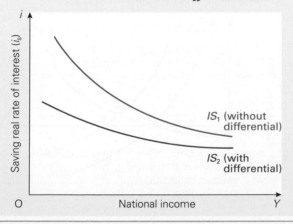

Other causes of the financial accelerator.   The amplification of the business cycle through the financial accelerator is caused not just by changes in interest rate differentials, but also by changes in the willingness of financial institutions to lend. They are likely to be more willing to lend in a period when the economy is operating near full employment and less willing to lend in a recession.

Modelling the effects of the financial crisis and recession of 2008–9.   We can see how the financial accelerator amplified the recession that followed the financial crisis.

The effect can be seen in three models. First, in terms of the top half of Figure 19.11 (injections–withdrawal diagram), our now positively sloped injections function moved vertically downwards. Second, the now steeper aggregate expenditure line in Figure 17.2 (Keynesian cross diagram) also moved vertically downward. Finally, there was a leftward shift of the now flatter IS curve. Each of these shifts had a bigger effect on output than in the simple models with no interest rate differential.

The size of the shifts was amplified by a reduction in the willingness of banks to lend and a desire of households and firms to reduce debt levels and increase saving. The size of the leftward movement of the IS curve was so significant that it meant that many countries saw a marked reduction in output.

With nominal interest rates having fallen to near zero, the ability of central bankers to respond by making further reductions in interest rates was effectively eliminated. Without unconventional monetary policy measures or a significant fiscal expansion, the fear was that the economy might have to endure a period of exceptionally low output. We examine these policy responses in Chapter 21.

 Using the IS/MP model, trace through the possible effects of an increase in the interest rate differential on real interest rates, output and inflation.

Section summary

1. The *IS/MP* model allows us to model the interaction between the goods and the money market. The model shows the relationship between national income and interest rates where central bankers set interest rates.

2. Equilibrium in the goods market is shown by the *IS* curve. This shows all the combinations of the real rate of interest and national income where investment (*I*) equals saving (*S*) (or, in a complete Keynesian model, where injections equal withdrawals). As the rate of interest rises, so investment will fall and saving will rise: thus equilibrium national income will fall. The *IS* curve is thus downward sloping.

3. The *MP* curve shows the real rate of interest that the central bank would choose at any particular level of national income. We assume that the rate of inflation

rises with the level of national income. The central bank will thus raise the real rate of interest (i.e. the nominal rate plus the rate of inflation) as national income rises. This gives an upward-sloping *MP* curve. A higher potential national income, by putting downward pressure on inflation at any given level of actual national income, will shift the *MP* curve to the right. A lower inflation target will shift the curve upwards.

4. Equilibrium occurs where *IS = MP*. At this point the goods market is in equilibrium at the real interest rate chosen by the central bank.

5. A shift in either curve will lead to a new equilibrium. The resulting size of the change in real national income and real interest rates will depend on the size of the shift and the shape of the other curve.

19.4 THE *ADI/ASI* MODEL

IS/MP and the *ADI/ASI* model

The *IS/MP* model allows us to analyse the interaction between monetary policy and the goods market and to show the impact of various shocks. The model has been developed to incorporate an important feature of contemporary monetary policy: central banks setting interest rates to meet an inflation target (or a more complex target). We will explore in more detail developments in monetary policy and the objectives of central bankers in Chapter 21.

Another complementary framework is the *ADI/ASI* model. This plots aggregate demand and supply against inflation (as opposed to the *level* of prices in the conventional *AD/AS* model). It shows graphically the relationship between national income and inflation. As with the *IS/MP* model, it allows us to incorporate inflation targeting, or other monetary policy frameworks.

Together, we can use both models to analyse the interaction of the goods and money markets for national income, real interest rates and inflation.

Aggregate demand and supply plotted against inflation

The *ADI/ASI* model is illustrated in Figures 19.15 and 19.16.

In this version, the horizontal axis, as before, measures real national income (*Y*). The vertical axis, however, measures the *rate of inflation*, not the *level* of prices. The aggregate demand and supply curves are labelled *ADI* and *ASI* to distinguish them from the curves in the normal aggregate demand and supply diagram. We also add a line showing the target rate of inflation.

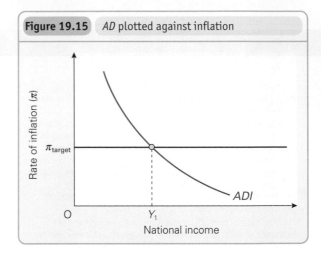

Figure 19.15   *AD* plotted against inflation

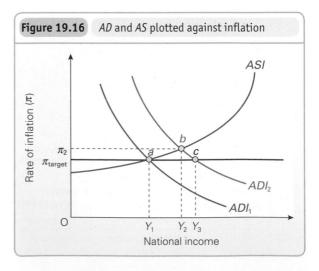

Figure 19.16   *AD* and *AS* plotted against inflation

Before we look at the properties of the model, let us examine each of the three lines in turn. The first two are illustrated in Figure 19.15.

The inflation target line

This is simply a horizontal line at the target rate of inflation (π_{target}). If inflation is above target, real interest rates will be raised by the central bank. If it is below target, real interest rates will be cut.

If the government or central bank changes the target, the line will shift to the new target rate.

The aggregate demand/inflation curve

As with the normal *AD* curve, the *ADI* curve is downward sloping. In other words, a higher rate of inflation leads to a lower level of (real) aggregate demand. But why?

The reason is simple. It consists of a two-stage process:

1. If the rate of inflation (π) goes above the target level, the central bank will raise the *real* rate of interest (i). In other words, it will raise the nominal rate *more* than the rise in the inflation rate. Thus if the rate of inflation goes up from a targeted 2 per cent to 3 per cent, the nominal interest rate (r) must rise by more than 1 percentage point in order to achieve a rise in the real interest rate.

2. The higher real rate of interest will then reduce (real) aggregate demand (*AD*), through both the interest rate and exchange rate mechanisms (see pages 561–6). In terms of the *IS/MP* framework, there is a movement leftwards along the *IS* curve.

To summarise:

$$\pi\!\uparrow \rightarrow i\!\uparrow \rightarrow AD\!\downarrow$$

Similarly, a fall in the rate of inflation will cause the central bank to lower the real rate of interest. This will then lead to an increase in aggregate demand.

The slope of the ADI curve.   The slope of the *ADI* curve depends on the strength of the two stages. The curve will be relatively flat:

- the more the central bank adjusts real interest rates in response to a change in inflation. The faster the central bank wants to get inflation back to its target level and the less concerned it is about cutting back on aggregate demand and hence output and employment, the larger interest rate changes will be.
- the more responsive investment, consumption and exports (i.e. the components of aggregate demand) are to a change in interest rates.

A movement along the ADI curve.   This will be caused by a change in the rate of inflation. If inflation rises, there will be a movement up the curve as the central bank raises the real rate of interest and this causes real income to fall. When *inflation* begins to fall in response to the higher rate of interest, there will be a movement back down the curve again.

The position of the ADI curve.   A given *ADI* curve represents a given monetary policy (the vertical position of the *MP* curve for a given inflation target). The particular *ADI* curve in Figure 19.15 intersects the inflation target line at a real income of Y_1. This means that if inflation is on target, real national income will be Y_1. The central bank will need to consider whether this is consistent with long-term equilibrium in the economy: in other words, whether Y_1 is the *potential* level of national output: i.e. the level of income with a zero output gap (see Box 14.3 on pages 414–5). If it is, then the monetary policy it has chosen is appropriate.

A shift in the ADI curve.   Any factor that causes aggregate demand to change, other than the central bank responding to inflation being off target, will cause the *ADI* curve to shift. A rightward shift represents an increase in aggregate demand. A leftward shift represents a decrease.

Examples of a rightward shift include cuts in tax rates, an increase in government expenditure and a rise in consumer or business confidence. These also cause the *IS* curve to shift rightwards. The *ADI* curve will also shift to the right if the government or central bank sets a higher target rate of inflation. The reason is that this will lead to lower interest rates at every level of inflation. This causes the *MP* curve to move vertically downwards.

The curve will also shift if the central bank changes its monetary policy, such that it no longer wants Y_1 to be the equilibrium level of national income. For example, if Y_1 in Figure 19.15 were below the potential level, and there was therefore demand-deficient unemployment, the central bank would want to reduce real interest rates in order to achieve a higher level of aggregate demand at the target rate of inflation. This will shift the *ADI* curve to the right. In other words, each level of inflation along this new *ADI* curve would correspond to a lower real rate of interest (i) and hence a higher level of aggregate demand.

But what determines the level of Y? This is determined by the interaction of aggregate demand and aggregate supply. To show this we introduce a third line: the *ASI* curve.

The aggregate supply/inflation curve

The *ASI* curve, like the normal *AS* curve, is upward sloping. In the short run it will be relatively flat. In the long run it will be relatively steep, if not vertical at the potential level of national income. The curve illustrated in Figure 19.16 is the short-run *ASI* curve. But why is it shaped this way? Why will a higher rate of inflation lead to higher real national income?

Assume that the economy is currently generating a real national income of Y_1 and that inflation is on target (π_{target}). Equilibrium is at point a. Assume also that Y_1 represents the long-run potential level of output.

Now assume that consumer confidence rises, and that, as a result, the *ADI* curve shifts to ADI_2. Firms will respond to the higher aggregate demand partly by raising prices more than the current (i.e. target) rate of inflation and partly by

TC 9 p121

increasing output: there is a movement along the *ASI* curve. Equilibrium moves to point *b*, where *ADI* = *ASI*.

But why will firms raise output as well as prices? The reason is that wage rises lag behind price rises. This is because of the time it takes to negotiate new wage rates and the fact that people were probably anticipating that inflation would stay at its target level. The higher prices now charged by firms will generate bigger profit margins for them, and thus they will be willing to supply more.

Over time, however, if the higher demand persists, wage rises would get higher. This would be the result of firms trying to obtain more labour to meet the higher demand and of unions seeking wage increases to compensate for the higher rate of inflation. Thus, assuming no increase in productivity, the *ASI* curve would shift upwards and continue doing so until real national income returned to the potential level Y_1. The long-run *ASI* curve would be vertical through point *a*.

Response to changes in aggregate demand and supply

A rise in aggregate demand

Assume, in Figure 19.16, that there has been a rise in real aggregate demand and that the *ADI* curve has shifted to ADI_2. Assume also that Y_1 is the potential level of national output. If inflation remained at its target level, the economy would move to point *c*, with national income increasing to Y_3. But as firms respond partly by increasing prices more rapidly, equilibrium is reached at point *b*. In other words, there has been a movement up along the *ASI* curve from point *a* to point *b* and back up along the new *ADI* curve from point *c* to point *b*. This movement along curve ADI_2 is the result of the higher interest rates imposed by the central bank in response to inflation rising to π_2.

But equilibrium at point *b* is above the target rate. This is unsustainable, even in the short run. One of two things must happen. The first option is for the central bank (or government) to accept a higher target rate of inflation: i.e. π_2. But if it does this, real income can only remain above its potential level in the short run. Soon, higher prices will feed through into higher wages and back into higher prices, and so on. The *ASI* curve will shift upwards.

The second option – the only effective option in the long run – is for the central bank to reduce aggregate demand back to ADI_1. This will mean changing monetary policy, such that a higher real rate of interest is chosen for each rate of inflation. This tighter monetary policy shifts the *ADI* curve to the left.

In other words, if the central bank is adhering strictly to an inflation target, any rise in real aggregate demand can have only a temporary effect, since the higher inflation that results will force the central bank to bring aggregate demand back down again.

The one exception to this would be if the higher aggregate demand encouraged firms to invest more. When the effects of this on aggregate supply began to be felt in terms of higher output, the short-term *ASI* curve itself would shift

to the right, leading to a new equilibrium to the right of point *a*. In such a case, there would have been a long-term increase in output, even though the central bank was sticking to an inflation target.

 Using a graph similar to Figure 19.16, trace through the effect of a reduction in aggregate demand.

A rise in aggregate supply

Assume now that aggregate supply rises. This could be a temporary 'supply shock', such as a cut in oil prices or a good harvest, or it could be a permanent increase caused, say, by technical progress. Let us take each in turn.

A temporary supply shock. In Figure 19.17, initial equilibrium is at point *a*, with curves ADI_1 and ASI_1 intersecting at the target rate of inflation. The rise in aggregate supply causes the *ASI* curve temporarily to shift from ASI_1 to ASI_2. Inflation thus falls below the target rate. As a result, the central bank reduces the real rate of interest (*i*). The effect is to increase aggregate demand. This is shown by a movement *along* curve ADI_1 from point *a* to point *d*. Inflation has fallen to π_3 and real national income has risen to Y_4. Since this is only a temporary increase in aggregate supply, the central bank will not change its monetary policy. The *ADI* curve, therefore, will not shift.

As the supply shock subsides, aggregate supply will fall again. The *ASI* curve will shift back from ASI_2 to ASI_1, causing inflation to rise again. The result is a move back up the ADI_1 curve from point *d* to point *a*.

 1. *Trace through the effect of an adverse supply shock, such as a rise in oil prices.*
2. *What determines the amount that national income fluctuates when there is a temporary shift in the ASI curve?*

A permanent increase in aggregate supply. Now assume that ASI_2 represents a permanent shift. As before, the reduction in inflation causes the central bank to reduce interest rates. If there is no change in monetary policy, there would simply

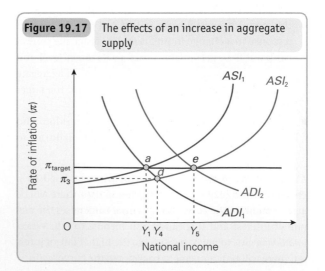

Figure 19.17 The effects of an increase in aggregate supply

be, once more, a movement from point *a* to point *d* with inflation now at π_3.

Once the central bank realises that the rise in aggregate supply is permanent, it will want to move to equilibrium at point *e*. To do this it will have to *change* its monetary policy and adopt a lower real interest rate at each rate of inflation (a move downwards of the *MP* curve). This will shift the *ADI* curve to ADI_2. If it does this, equilibrium will be restored at the target rate of inflation. Y_5 will be the new sustainable level of real national income.

In other words, the central bank, by maintaining an inflation target, will allow aggregate demand to expand sufficiently to accommodate the full rise in aggregate supply.

In Chapter 21 we explore policies to control aggregate demand. In the final section of that chapter (section 21.3), we look at whether it is best for a central bank to target inflation or whether it should adopt an alternative target. We also look at the more general issue of whether governments ought to set targets and stick to them, or whether they should allow themselves more discretion in managing the economy.

In the next chapter we expand our analysis of aggregate demand and supply to take account of unemployment and also the role of expectations. We look at how the various schools of thought model the macroeconomy in this more complete framework.

Section summary

1. The effects of adhering to an inflation target can be illustrated in a modified version of the aggregate demand and supply diagram. Inflation, rather than the price level, is plotted on the vertical axis. The aggregate demand curve in this diagram (labelled *ADI*) is downward sloping. This is because higher inflation encourages the central bank to raise interest rates and this leads to a fall in real national income.

2. The aggregate supply (*ASI*) curve in the short run is upward sloping. This is because wage rises lag behind price rises and thus firms are encouraged to supply more in response to a rise in demand knowing that their profits will increase.

3. If aggregate demand rises, the *ADI* curve will shift to the right. Inflation will rise above its target level. This is shown by a movement up the *ASI* curve and back up the new *ADI* curve to the new intersection point (as in Figure 19.16). The movement up the new *ADI* curve is in response to the higher interest rate now set by the central bank as it attempts to bring inflation back down to its target level.

4. Since the new equilibrium is above the target rate of inflation, the central bank must change to a tighter monetary policy and raise the real rate of interest. This shifts the *ADI* curve back to the left, and equilibrium is restored back at its original level. The rise in aggregate demand (unless accompanied by a rightward shift in aggregate supply) has had only a temporary effect on real national income.

5. A rise in aggregate supply (unless merely a temporary supply shock) will have a permanent effect on real national income. A rightward shift in aggregate supply will lead to an initial equilibrium at a rate of inflation below target and some rise in real national income as the rate of interest is reduced (as in Figure 19.17). The equilibrium is now below the target rate of inflation. The central bank must therefore change to a looser monetary policy and reduce the real rate of interest. This will shift the *ADI* curve to the right, causing a further rise in real national income that now fully reflects the rise in aggregate supply.

*APPENDIX: THE *IS/LM* MODEL

In section 19.3 we applied a framework known as the *IS/MP* model to analyse the interaction between monetary policy and the goods market. This framework recognises that many central bankers today attempt to achieve a target rate of inflation. They do this by seeking to influence the structure of interest rates in the economy and thereby to affect aggregate demand. We look at central bank objectives and their evolution in greater detail in Chapter 21.

The predecessor to the *IS/MP* model was the **IS/LM model**. As with the *IS/MP* model, the *IS/LM* model allows us to examine the effects of changes originating in the money or goods markets on *both* national income *and* interest rates: it shows what the equilibrium will be in both the goods and the money markets simultaneously. The

difference with the *IS/MP* model is that there is no inflation target. Instead, interest rates are purely market determined. The central bank is assumed to conduct monetary policy through changes in money supply.

As we saw earlier, the *IS* curve is based on equilibrium in the goods market. The *LM* curve is concerned with equilibrium

Definition

IS/LM model A model showing simultaneous equilibrium in the goods market ($I = S$) and the money market ($L = M$).

in the money market. It shows all the various combinations of interest rates and national income at which the demand for money (L) equals the supply (M). The LM curve is different from the MP curve in that it analyses how the interest rate adjusts to help bring money demand into equilibrium with money supply. In other words, the interest rate equilibrates the money market at any given level of national income.

In constructing the IS/LM model we assume, for simplicity, that prices are constant: i.e. there is an absence of inflation. Therefore, there is no difference between the nominal and real interest rate.

The *IS* curve

We analysed the *IS* curve in depth in section 19.3, so only a brief overview is provided here. The curve shows combinations of national income and interest rates at which planned expenditure equals national income. This occurs when the flow of injections (J) is matched by the flow of withdrawals (W). Hence, when we consider all injections (I, G and X) and withdrawals (S, T and M), rather than just investment and saving, we may think of the curve as the JW curve.

When the real rate of interest (i) rises, there is a fall in investment and a fall in saving. This will lead to a multiplied fall in income. Thus *higher* interest rates are associated with *lower* national income, if equilibrium is to be maintained in the goods market ($J = W$). The IS curve is therefore drawn as downward sloping, as illustrated in Figure 19.11 (on page 576).

A change in *interest rates* causes movements *along* the IS curve. Changes in any *other* determinant of injections and withdrawals *shift* the whole curve. The reason is that changes in other determinants will change the equilibrium level of national income at any given rate of interest. For example, if, in response to a decline in their net worth, firms reduce their investment at *the current interest rate* (resulting in a downward shift of the *I* curve in the top part of Figure 19.11), there is a multiplied fall in national income. Thus a lower equilibrium income is now associated with each level of the interest rate. The *IS* curve has shifted to the left.

The *LM* curve

Deriving the LM curve

To explain how the LM curve is derived consider Figure 19.18. The left-hand part of the diagram is the familiar money market diagram, showing a liquidity preference (demand for money) curve (L) and a supply of money curve (M).

At any given level of national income, there will be a particular level of transactions-plus-precautionary demand for money, and hence a given overall demand for money curve (L). Let us assume that, when national income is at a level of Y_1 in the right-hand part of Figure 19.18, the demand-for-money curve is L'. With the given money supply curve M_s, the equilibrium real rate of interest will be i_1. Thus point c is one point on the LM curve. At a level of national income Y_1, the money market will be in equilibrium at a real rate of interest of i_1. (Note that we are assuming that the money supply curve is not totally exogenous; in other words, the

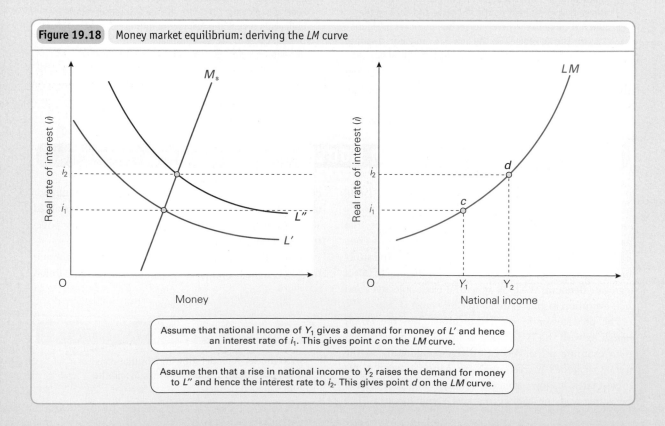

Figure 19.18   Money market equilibrium: deriving the *LM* curve

Assume that national income of Y_1 gives a demand for money of L' and hence an interest rate of i_1. This gives point c on the *LM* curve.

Assume then that a rise in national income to Y_2 raises the demand for money to L'' and hence the interest rate to i_2. This gives point d on the *LM* curve.

curve is upward sloping. In simple *IS/LM* models, the money supply curve is (unrealistically) assumed to be vertical.)

Now what will happen if the level of national income changes? Let us assume that national income rises to Y_2. The effect is to increase the transactions-plus-precautionary demand for money. The *L* curve shifts to the right: to, say, L''. This will cause the real rate of interest to rise to the new equilibrium level of i_2. This therefore gives us a second point on the *LM* curve (point *d*).

Thus *higher* national income leads to a greater demand for money and hence *higher* interest rates if equilibrium is to be maintained in the money market. The *LM* curve is therefore upward sloping.

The elasticity of the LM curve

The elasticity of the *LM* curve (i.e. the responsiveness of interest rate changes to a change in national income) depends on two factors.[1]

The responsiveness of the demand for money to changes in national income. The greater the marginal propensity to consume, the more will the transactions demand for money rise as national income rises, and thus the more the *L* curve will shift to the right. Hence the more the equilibrium interest rate will rise, and the steeper will be the *LM* curve.

The endogeneity of money will lessen this effect. In the case of an upward-sloping money supply curve (as in Figure 19.18), the less steep it is, the more will money supply expand in response to a rise in the demand for money and the less will interest rates rise. Hence the flatter will be the *LM* curve. Where money supply simply expands passively to meet any rise in demand, the *LM* curve will be horizontal.

The responsiveness of the demand for money to changes in interest rates. The more the demand for money responds to a change in interest rates, the flatter will be the liquidity preference curve in the left-hand part of Figure 19.18. The flatter the *L* curve, the less will the equilibrium interest rate change for any given horizontal shift in the *L* curve (arising from a change in *Y*). The less the equilibrium interest rate changes, the flatter will be the *LM* curve.

The Keynesian and monetarist views on the shape of the *LM* curve reflect their respective views on the elasticity of the *L* curve. Keynesians argue that the *L* curve is likely to be relatively flat given the responsiveness of the speculative demand for money to changes in interest rates and the endogeneity of money. They thus argue that the *LM* curve is correspondingly relatively flat (depending, of course, on the scales of the axes). Monetarists, on the other hand, argue that the *LM* curve is relatively steep. This is because they see the demand for money as insensitive to changes in interest rates and the supply of money as being exogenous.

[1] Note that the rate of interest is the dependent variable and the level of national income is the independent variable. Thus the more elastic is the *LM* curve (i.e. the more responsive interest rates are to changes in national income), the *steeper* it will be.

Shifts in the LM curve

A change in *national income* will cause a movement *along* the *LM* curve to a new equilibrating interest rate. Thus in Figure 19.18 a rise in national income from Y_1 to Y_2 leads to a movement along the *L* curve from point *c* to point *d* and hence a rise in the rate of interest from i_1 to i_2.

A change in any *other* determinant of the demand and supply of money will *shift* the whole curve. The reason is that it will change the equilibrium level of interest associated with any given level of national income.

An increase in the demand for money, other than as a result of a rise in income, will shift the *L* curve to the *right*. This could be due to people being paid less frequently, or a greater use of cash, or increased speculation that the price of securities will fall. This increased demand for money will raise the equilibrium rate of interest at the current level of national income. The *LM* curve will shift upwards.

An increased supply of money by the authorities will shift the M_s curve to the right. This will lower the rate of interest (in the left-hand part of Figure 19.18). This will shift the *LM* curve downwards: a lower rate of interest will be associated with any given level of national income.

Draw a diagram like Figure 19.18, only with just one L curve. Assume that the current level of national income is Y_1. Now assume that the supply of money decreases. Show the effect on:
(a) the rate of interest;
(b) the position of the LM curve.

Equilibrium

The *IS* curve shows all the combinations of the rate of interest (*i*) and national income (*Y*) at which the *goods* market is in equilibrium. The *LM* curve shows all the combinations of *i* and *Y* at which the *money* market is in equilibrium. *Both* markets will be in equilibrium where the curves intersect. This is at i_e and Y_e in Figure 19.19.

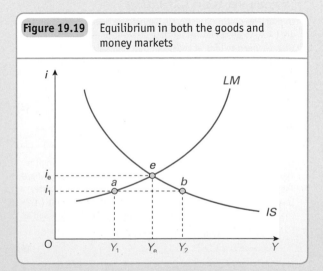

Figure 19.19 Equilibrium in both the goods and money markets

KI 5
p 22

But what would happen if both markets were not simultaneously in equilibrium? How would equilibrium be achieved?

Let us suppose that the current level of national income is Y_1. This will create a demand for money that will lead to an equilibrium interest rate of i_1 (point *a* on the *LM* curve). But at this low interest rate, the desired level of investment and saving would generate an income of Y_2 (point *b* on the *IS* curve). Thus national income will rise. But as national income rises, there will be a movement up along the *LM* curve from point *a*, since the higher income will generate a higher demand for money and hence push up interest rates.

And as interest rates rise, so the desired level of investment will fall and the desired level of saving will rise so as to reduce the equilibrium level of national income below Y_2. There will be a movement back up along the *IS* curve from point *b*. Once the interest rate has risen to i_e, the actual level of income will be at the equilibrium level (i.e. *on* the *IS* curve). Both markets will now be in equilibrium.

Assume that national income is initially at Y_2 in Figure 19.19. Describe the process whereby equilibrium in both markets will be achieved.

*LOOKING AT THE MATHS

Equilibrium in the *IS/LM* model is where the two functions, *IS* and *LM*, are equal. The simplest mathematical representation of this is where both *IS* and *LM* are simple linear (i.e. straight-line) functions. The *IS* function could be expressed as

$$i = a - bY \tag{1}$$

In other words, the higher the real rate of interest (i), the lower will be the level of aggregate demand and hence national income (Y).[1] This is consistent with a downward-sloping *IS* curve.

The *LM* function can be written as

$$i = g + hY \tag{2}$$

In other words, the higher the level of real national income (and hence the higher the demand for money), the higher will be the real rate of interest. This is consistent with an upward-sloping *LM* curve.

We can then solve for Y by setting the two equations equal. Thus

$$a - bY = g + hY$$

that is,

$$bY + hY = a - g$$

giving

$$Y = \frac{a - g}{h + b}$$

More complex IS and LM functions

In practice, neither function is likely to be linear. Both *IS* and *LM* are likely to be curves rather than straight lines. To understand why, we need to look at the other determinants of Y in the case of the *IS* curve and of i in the case of the *LM* curve. Let us first examine the *IS* function.

Real national income consists of five elements:

$$Y = C + I + G + X - M \tag{3}$$

or

$$Y = C(Y, T, i, \pi^e) + I(i, \pi^e, \Delta Y) + G + X(er) - M(Y, T, i, \pi^e, er) \tag{3a}$$

Equation (3a) is simply an expansion of equation (3) listing the key determinants of each of the variables in equation (3), where *T* is taxes, π^e is expected inflation and *er* is the exchange rate. Investment being a function of changes in national income (ΔY) is the accelerator effect. Thus an *IS* function could be expressed as

$$Y = IS(i, T, \pi^e, \Delta Y, G, er) \tag{4}$$
$$\quad\quad - - + \quad + + -$$

All the variables in this function are contained in equation (3a). It is highly likely that the relationship between Y and most, if not all, of these variables is non-linear (i.e. contains squared or higher-power terms).

The sign under each of the variables indicates the direction in which Y changes when the variable changes. For example, the negative sign under the *T* term means that a rise in taxes would lead to a *fall* in Y. Put another way, the sign indicates the sign of the partial derivative of Y with respect to each variable. For example, the positive sign under the expected inflation term (π^e) means that when you differentiate Y with respect to π^e, you end up with a positive number. This simply means that a rise in π^e leads to a *rise* in Y.

Note that a change in i would lead to a movement along the *IS* curve. A change in any of the other determinants in equation (4) would shift the curve. A rise in any of the determinants with a positive sign would result in a rightward shift in the curve; a rise in any of the determinants with a negative sign would result in a leftward shift.

Turning to the *LM* function, this can be expressed as

$$i = LM\left[Y, \frac{M_s}{P}, \pi^e, er^e, f\right] \tag{5}$$
$$\quad\quad + \;-\; + + \;-$$

where M_s/P is the real money supply, π^e is the expected rate of inflation, er^e is the expected exchange rate and f is the frequency with which people are paid. The *LM* curve assumes equilibrium in the money market. It therefore represents all the combinations of i and Y where the real demand for money is equal to the real supply. The real supply of money is given by the term M_s/P and the real demand for money depends on the other terms in equation (5) (see page 558).

A rise in Y would cause a movement up along the *LM* curve. A rise in any of the other determinants would shift the curve: upwards in the case of the determinants with a positive sign; downwards in the case of those with a negative sign.

As with the *IS* function, it is highly likely that the relationship between i and most, if not all, of the variables in the *LM* function is likely to be non-linear.

Maths Case 19.1 in MyEconLab shows how equilibrium in the *IS/LM* model can be derived from specific *IS* and *LM* functions.

TC 12
p411

---

[1] Note that although equation (1) shows i as a function of Y, the model in fact has Y as the dependent variable. In other words, i determines Y. We express equation (1) this way to make it consistent with equation (2), where i is the dependent variable.

| **Figure 19.20** | *IS/LM* analysis of changes in the goods and money markets |

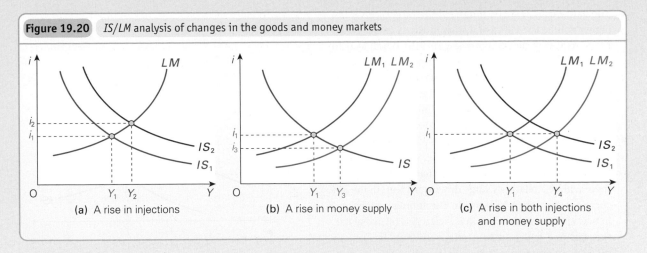

(a) A rise in injections (b) A rise in money supply (c) A rise in both injections and money supply

Full effects of changes in the goods and money markets

IS/LM analysis can be used to examine the full effects of changes in the goods market. Such changes are illustrated by a shift in the *IS* curve. Likewise, the full effects of changes in the money market can be illustrated by a shift in the *LM* curve.

Changes in the goods market

Consider a positive demand-side shock where the confidence of economic agents begins to rise. Assume that this leads firms to increase their investment and consumers to reduce their precautionary saving. The resulting increase in aggregate expenditure leads to a rightward shift in the *IS* curve. This is illustrated in Figure 19.20(a). It is assumed that there is no exogenous increase in the money supply and that, therefore, the *LM* curve does not shift. Income rises to Y_2, but interest rates also rise (to i_2).

The rise in the rate of interest to i_2 restricts the rise in national income, since the higher interest rate dampens both investment and consumption. The net rise in aggregate expenditure is less than the original increase. The steeper the *LM* curve, the less national income rises. The equilibrating effect of interest rates in the money market therefore 'chokes off' some of the increase in national income originating from the positive demand-side shock.

The *IS/LM* framework allows us to see how monetary policy could accommodate the positive demand-side shock. If money supply is expanded to meet the extra demand for money, then interest rates will not have to rise. This is illustrated in Figure 19.20(c). The rightward shift in the *IS* curve is matched by a downward shift in the *LM* curve. The rate of interest remains at i_1 and there is a full multiplied rise in national income to Y_4.

In the context of the early 2010s, central banks like the Federal Reserve and the Bank of England were keen that monetary policy helped to accommodate economic recovery. While remaining watchful of inflation, monetary policy was predominantly geared to supporting the still fragile economic recovery. This saw the authorities boost the money supply through asset purchases (see Boxes 21.4 and 21.9). One effect of this was to put downward pressure on the general structure of interest rates. As we saw in section 18.5, there is not a single interest rate. Rather, there is a myriad of interest rates on a range of financial instruments.

The *IS/LM* framework demonstrates nicely the policy dilemma facing the authorities in the early 2010s as aggregate demand recovered: how quickly to put the brakes on quantitative easing. To do so too quickly ran the risk of stalling the recovery as general interest rates rose, even if the authorities maintained a low policy rate. As argued in Box 19.5, interest rate differentials tend to be greatest when output levels are relatively low. The authorities therefore looked to apply the monetary policy handbrake gently.

Changes in the money market

Now consider an increase in money supply. The *LM* curve shifts downwards. This is illustrated in Figure 19.20(b). Interest rates fall and this encourages an increase in borrowing and hence an increase in investment and consumption. This is shown by a movement down along the *IS* curve. National income rises. Equilibrium is reached at a rate of interest of i_3 and a national income of Y_3.

The fall in the rate of interest means that some of the extra money is absorbed in idle balances and is not all used to finance additional expenditure, and this reduces the resulting increased national income. The effect on national income also depends on the elasticity of the *IS* curve. The steeper the *IS* curve, the less will national income rise. This will be the case when investment is relatively insensitive to cuts in interest rates.

If, however, the rise in money supply is accompanied by an autonomous rise in injections (e.g. a rise in government expenditure), then the effect can be much bigger. If the downward shift in the *LM* curve is matched by a rightward shift in the *IS* curve, then the effect is once more illustrated in Figure 19.20(c).

To summarise: the effect on national income of a change in either market depends on the slope of the *IS* and *LM* curves:

- The flatter the *LM* curve and the steeper the *IS* curve, the bigger will be the effect of a shift in the *IS* curve. When *LM* is relatively flat, a rightward shift in *IS* will lead to only a small rise in the rate of interest (i). If *IS* is steep, this rise in i will lead to only a small curtailing of investment. In these two circumstances, the dampening effect on investment and consumption is limited. There will be a large increase in national income (Y).
- The effect of a shift in the *LM* curve will be bigger when the liquidity preference curve (*L*) (e.g. in Figure 19.18(a)) is steep and the *IS* curve is relatively flat. When *L* is steep, there will be a relatively large downward shift in the *LM* curve for any given increase in the money supply and hence a relatively large fall in i. When *IS* is relatively flat, this fall in i will lead to a relatively large increase in investment and hence *Y*.
- The effect of a shift in either curve will be bigger if matched by a similar shift in the other curve.

 On a diagram similar to Figure 19.19, trace through the effects of (a) a fall in investment and (b) a fall in the money supply. On what does the size of the fall in national income depend?

Deriving an *AD* curve from the *IS*/*LM* model

In section 15.2, we saw why the aggregate demand curve is downward sloping. Now we have looked at the *IS*/*LM* model, we can give a more formal explanation of the shape of the *AD* curve.

Figure 19.21 shows both an *IS*/*LM* diagram and an *AD* curve. In the top part of the figure, both goods and money markets are in equilibrium at point *a* (the point where the *IS* and *LM* curves cross). National income is Y_1 and the rate of interest is i_1. Turning to the bottom part, let us assume that with national income at Y_1, the price level happens to be P_1. The aggregate demand curve thus passes through point a'.

TC 12
p411 Now let us assume that the price level rises to P_2. The effect of the higher price is to raise the demand for (nominal) money balances: after all, people will need bigger money balances if they are to pay higher prices for goods. The higher demand for money balances will raise the equilibrium rate of interest at the current level of national income. In the top diagram, the *LM* curve will shift upwards.

Figure 19.21   Deriving the *AD* curve from an *IS*/*LM* diagram

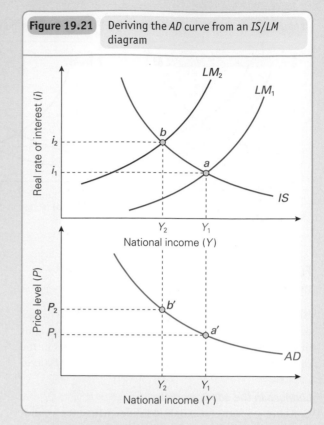

Assuming that the *LM* curve shifts to LM_2, equilibrium will now be at point *b*. National income will fall to Y_2. Thus a rise in the price level to P_2 has caused national income to fall to Y_2. In the bottom diagram, the *AD* curve must now pass through point b'.

If the *IS* curve shifts, or if the *LM* curve shifts other than as a result of a change in the price level, the *AD* curve must shift. For example, if investment rises, the *IS* curve will shift to the right. National income will rise for any given price level, and hence the *AD* curve must shift to the right. To summarise: rightward shifts in the *IS* or *LM* curve will lead to rightward shifts in the *AD* curve.

1. Trace through the effects of a fall in the price level to show how a further point on the AD curve can be derived.
2. Explain what could cause a downward shift in the LM curve and how this would affect the AD curve.

Section summary

1. The *IS/LM* model allows equilibrium to be shown in both goods and money markets simultaneously. The model shows the relationship between national income and interest rates.

2. Equilibrium in the goods market is shown by the *IS* curve. As the rate of interest rises, so investment will fall and saving will rise: thus equilibrium national income will fall. The *IS* curve is thus downward sloping.

3. A change in interest rates will cause a movement along the *IS* curve. A change in anything else that affects national income causes a shift in the *IS* curve.

4. Equilibrium in the money market is shown by the *LM* curve. This shows all the combinations of national income and the rate of interest where the demand for money (*L*) equals the supply (*M*). As national income rises, so the demand for money will rise: thus the equilibrium rate of interest in the money market will rise. The *LM* curve is thus upward sloping.

5. A change in national income will cause a movement along the *LM* curve. A change in anything else that affects interest rates (i.e. a change in the demand or supply of money other than as a result of a change in national income) will shift the *LM* curve.

6. Simultaneous equilibrium in both goods and money markets (i.e. the equilibrium national income *and* the equilibrium rate of interest) is where *IS = LM*.

7. A change in injections or withdrawals will shift the *IS* curve. A rise in injections will shift it to the right. This will cause a rise in both national income and the rate of interest. The rise in income will be bigger and the rise in the rate of interest smaller, the steeper is the *IS* curve and the flatter is the *LM* curve.

8. A rise in money supply will shift the *LM* curve downwards. This will cause a fall in interest rates and a rise in national income. The rise in national income will be larger, the flatter is the *IS* curve and the steeper is the liquidity preference curve (*L*) and hence the bigger the downward shift in the *LM* curve for any given increase in the money supply.

9. An *AD* curve can be derived from an *IS/LM* diagram. A higher price level will shift the *LM* curve upwards. This will lead to a lower level of national income. The higher price level and lower national income gives a new point on the *AD* curve.

END OF CHAPTER QUESTIONS

1. Using one or more diagrams like Figures 19.2, 19.7, 19.8, 19.9 and 19.10, illustrate the following:

   (a) The effect of a contraction in the money supply on national income. Refer to both the interest rate and exchange rate transmission mechanisms and show how the shapes of the curves affect the outcome.

   (b) The effect of a fall in investment on national income. Again show how the shapes of the curves affect the outcome. Specify your assumptions about the effects on the *supply* of money.

2. Controlling the money supply is sometimes advocated as an appropriate policy for controlling inflation. What implications do different assumptions about the relationships between *M* and *V*, and *M* and *Y*, in the equation $MV = PY$ have for the effectiveness of this policy?

3. Why may an expansion of the money supply have a relatively small effect on national income? Why may any effect be hard to predict?

4. What impact might the balance sheets of economic agents have on the influence of interest rates in affecting aggregate expenditure?

5. Why does the exchange rate transmission mechanism strengthen the interest rate transmission mechanism?

6. Explain how the holding of a range of assets in people's portfolios may help to create a more direct link between changes in money supply and changes in aggregate demand.

7. Explain how financial crowding out can reduce the effectiveness of fiscal policy. What determines the magnitude of crowding out?

8. What determines the shape and position of the *IS* curve?

9. What determines the shape and position of the *MP* curve?

10. Using the *IS/MP* model analyse the possible effect of an increase in aggregate expenditure on output, the real interest rate and inflation.

11. Using the *IS/MP* model analyse how a lower bound on real interest rates might cause the economy to enter a deflationary spiral following a significant decrease in aggregate expenditure.

12. What would cause (a) a steep *ADI* curve; (b) a gently sloping *ADI* curve? Compare the short-run and long-run effects of (i) a temporary adverse supply shock and (ii) a permanent supply reduction under each of (a) and (b).

13. Under what circumstances would a rightward shift in the *ADI* curve lead to a permanent increase in real national income?

*14. Using the *IS/LM* model, under what circumstances will (a) a rise in investment and (b) a rise in money supply cause a large rise in national income?

*15. Using the *IS/LM* model explain what would cause the aggregate demand curve to be steep.

Online resources

Additional case studies in MyEconLab

19.1 Crowding out. This case looks at a different version of crowding out from that analysed in section 19.2.

Maths Case 19.1 Using *IS* and *LM* equations to find the equilibrium national income and interest rate. Using the algebra in a worked example.

Websites relevant to Chapters 18 and 19

Numbers and sections refer to websites listed in the Web Appendix and hotlinked from this book's website at **www.pearsoned.co.uk/sloman**.

- For news articles relevant to this and the previous chapter, see the *Economic News* section in MyEconLab.
- For general news on money and banking, see websites in section A, and particularly A1–5, 7–9, 20–22, 25, 26, 31, 36.
- For monetary and financial data (including data for money supply and interest rates), see section F and particularly F2. Note that you can link to central banks worldwide from site F17. See also the links in B1 or 2.
- For monetary targeting in the UK, see F1 and E30. For monetary targeting in the eurozone, see F6 and 5.
- For links to sites on money and monetary policy, see the *Financial Economics* sections in I7, 11, 17.
- For student resources relevant to Chapters 18 and 19, see sites C1–7, 9, 10, 12, 19. See also '2nd floor – economic policy' in site D1.

MyEconLab

This book can be supported by MyEconLab, which contains a range of additional resources, including an online homework and tutorial system designed to test and build your understanding.

You need both an access card and a course ID to access MyEconLab:

1. Is your lecturer using MyEconLab? Ask your lecturer for your course ID.
2. Has an access card been included with the book at a reduced cost? Check the inside back cover of the book.
3. If you have a course ID but no access card, go to: http://www.myeconlab.com/ to buy access to this interactive study programme.

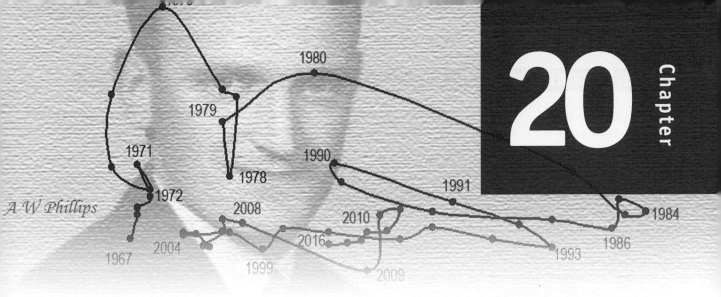

Aggregate Supply, Unemployment and Inflation

CHAPTER MAP

20.1 Aggregate supply	**594**
Short-run aggregate supply	594
Long-run aggregate supply	595
Long-run aggregate supply: the classical model of labour markets	596
Long-run aggregate supply: Keynesian models of labour markets	597
Aggregate demand and supply, and inflation	598
20.2 The expectations-augmented Phillips curve	**602**
Adaptive expectations	602
The accelerationist theory	602
The long-run Phillips curve and the natural rate of unemployment	604
The effects of contractionary policy	604
Explanations of stagflation	605
Evidence	605
Policy implications	608
Limitations of the adaptive expectations hypothesis	608
20.3 Inflation and unemployment: the new classical position	**609**
Aggregate supply and the Phillips curve when expectations are correct	610
Aggregate supply and the Phillips curve when expectations are incorrect	611
Policy implications	613
Real business cycles	613
20.4 Inflation and unemployment: the modern Keynesian position	**615**
Modern developments of the Keynesian model	615
Changes in equilibrium unemployment	615
The persistence of demand-deficient unemployment	616
The incorporation of expectations	616
The Keynesian criticism of non-intervention	617
*20.5 Output, inflation and expectations: an integrated model	**618**
An integrated model	618
Analysis of the 2008–9 banking crisis and the subsequence recession and slow recovery	621
20.6 Postscript: The state of macroeconomic thinking post-crisis	**622**
Areas of general agreement	622
The causes of longer-term growth	623
Soul-searching by economists	623

The focus so far of Part F has been to develop a better understanding of aggregate demand. We have looked at a variety of influences on aggregate demand and its components, including the effects of financial institutions and money markets. Now we consider in more detail the interaction of aggregate demand and aggregate supply. We will see that the effects of changes in aggregate demand on output, employment and prices depend crucially on the responsiveness of aggregate supply.

We begin this chapter by examining what determines this responsiveness: in other words, we examine what determines the shape of the aggregate supply curve. As we shall see, there are different views on this. Also, the effect will be different in the long run from the short run.

Then we turn to the relationship between inflation and unemployment, examining a range of alternative perspectives. Again, what is crucial here is the response of aggregate supply to a change in aggregate demand, in this case reflected in the shape of the Phillips curve. If aggregate supply responds to changes in aggregate demand, then a rise in aggregate demand should lead to a fall in unemployment, but will probably lead to a rise in inflation.

Finally, we integrate the *IS/MP* and *ADI/ASI* models. This allows us simultaneously to analyse the relationship between output and inflation when central banks set interest rates in order to achieve specific macroeconomic objectives, such as an inflation rate target.

20.1 AGGREGATE SUPPLY

The effect of an increase in aggregate demand on output, employment and prices is crucial for macroeconomic policy and is at the heart of macroeconomic debate. The debate hinges on the shape of the aggregate supply curve and how it varies with time.

The extreme Keynesian and new classical positions are shown in Figure 20.1. The extreme Keynesian position is that up to full employment (Y_F) the aggregate supply (AS) curve is *horizontal*, at least in the short run. A rise in aggregate demand from AD_1 to AD_2 will raise output from Y_1 to Y_2, but there will be *no effect on prices* until full employment is reached. In this model, aggregate supply up to the full-employment level is determined entirely by the level of aggregate demand. But there is no guarantee that aggregate demand will intersect aggregate supply at full employment. Therefore governments should manage aggregate demand by appropriate fiscal and monetary policies to ensure production at Y_F.

Many economists argue that the aggregate supply curve is *vertical* in the long run. New classicists argue that it is vertical in the short run too. Any rise in aggregate demand will have *no effect on output and employment*. It will merely lead to higher prices. Thus it is essential to keep (nominal) demand under control if *prices* are to be kept under control. To raise output and employment, however, will require supply-side policies: to shift the AS curve to the right.

If AS is somewhere between these two extremes, an increase in AD will have some effect on prices and some effect on output and employment (see Figure 20.1(c)).

In this chapter we analyse the shape of the AS curve in practice, and the implications that follow for policies to cure inflation and unemployment. First we must distinguish between short-run and long-run aggregate supply curves.

1. *In the extreme Keynesian model, is there any point in supply-side policies?*
2. *In the new classical model, is there any point in using supply-side policies to tackle inflation?*

Short-run aggregate supply

To understand the shape of the short-run AS curve, it is necessary to look at its microeconomic foundations. How will *individual* firms and industries respond to a rise in demand? What shape will their individual supply curves be?

In the short run, we assume that firms respond to the rise in demand for their product without considering the effects of a general rise in demand on their suppliers or on the economy as a whole. We also assume that the prices of inputs, including wage rates, are constant.

In the case of a profit-maximising firm under monopoly or monopolistic competition, there will be a rise in price and a rise in output. In Figure 20.2, profit-maximising output rises from where $MC = MR_1$ to where $MC = MR_2$. Just how much price changes compared with output depends on the slope of the marginal cost (MC) curve.

The nearer the firm is to full capacity, the steeper the MC curve is likely to be. Here the firm is likely to find diminishing returns setting in rapidly, and it is also likely to have to use more overtime with correspondingly higher unit labour costs. If, however, the firm is operating well below capacity, it can probably supply more with little or no increase in price. Its MC curve may thus be horizontal at lower levels of output.

Under oligopoly, where there is a tendency for prices to be more stable, firms may respond to an increase in demand without raising prices, even if their costs rise somewhat.

When there is a general rise in demand in the economy, the *aggregate* supply response in the short run can be seen as

KI 9
p71

KI 19
p154

KI 17
p135

Figure 20.1   Contrasting views on the aggregate supply curve

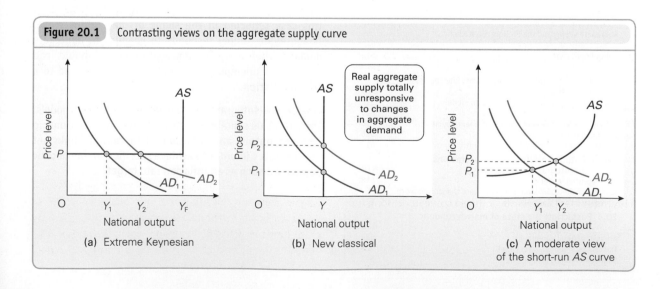

(a) Extreme Keynesian

(b) New classical

(c) A moderate view of the short-run AS curve

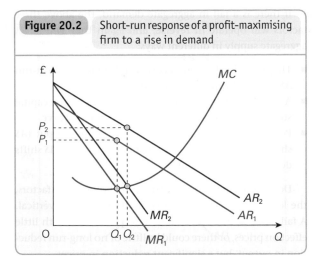

Figure 20.2 Short-run response of a profit-maximising firm to a rise in demand

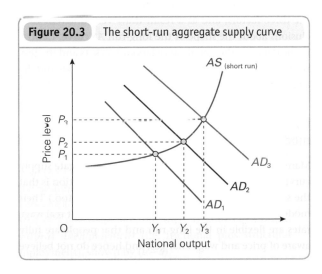

Figure 20.3 The short-run aggregate supply curve

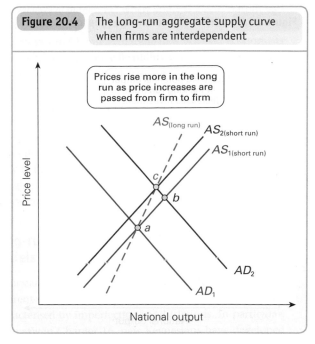

Figure 20.4 The long-run aggregate supply curve when firms are interdependent

Prices rise more in the long run as price increases are passed from firm to firm

simply the sum of the responses of all the individual firms. The short-run *AS* curve will look something like that in Figure 20.3. If there is generally plenty of spare capacity, a rise in aggregate demand (e.g. from AD_1 to AD_2) will have a big effect on output and only a small effect on prices. However, as more and more firms find their costs rising as they get nearer to full capacity, so the *AS* curve becomes steeper. Further increases in aggregate demand (e.g. from AD_2 to AD_3) will have bigger effects on prices and smaller effects on output.

A general rise in prices, of course, means that individual firms were mistaken in assuming that a rise in price from P_1 TC 12 to P_2 in Figure 20.2 was a *real* price rise (i.e. relative to prices p411 elsewhere).

Long-run aggregate supply

Three important factors affect the *AS* curve in the long run.

The interdependence of firms

A rise in aggregate demand will lead firms throughout the economy to raise their prices (in accordance with the

short-run *AS* curve). But as raw material and intermediate good producers raise their prices, this will raise the costs of production further up the line. A rise in the price of steel will raise the costs of producing cars and washing machines. At the same time, workers, experiencing a rise in demand for labour, and seeing the prices of goods rising, will demand higher wages. Firms will be relatively willing to grant these wage demands, since they are experiencing buoyant demand.

The effect of all this is to raise firms' costs, and hence their prices. As prices rise for any given level of output, the short-run *AS* curve shifts upwards.

These long-run effects of a rise in aggregate demand are TC 10 shown in Figure 20.4. Aggregate demand shifts to AD_1. The p317 economy moves from point *a* to point *b* along the short-run *AS* curve (AS_1). As rising costs are passed on throughout the economy, the short-run *AS* curve shifts to AS_2, and the economy moves to point *c*. Thus the long-run *AS* curve passing through points *a* and *c* is steeper than the short-run *AS* curve. A rise in aggregate demand will therefore have a smaller effect on output and a bigger effect on prices in the long run than in the short run.

 Under what circumstances would this interdependence of firms give a vertical long-run AS curve?

Investment

With a rise in demand, firms may be encouraged to invest in new plant and machinery (the accelerator effect). In so doing, they may well be able to increase output significantly in the long run with little or no increase in their prices. This would make their long-run *MC* curves much flatter than their short-run *MC* curves.

Figure 20.7 Short-run response to a fall in the aggregate demand for labour: sticky wages

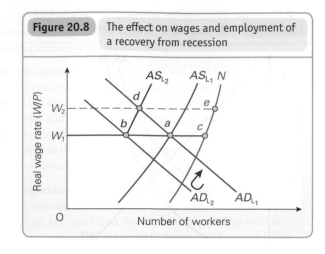

Figure 20.8 The effect on wages and employment of a recovery from recession

This gives a short-run aggregate supply (of goods) curve that is highly elastic below the current wage. A fall in aggregate demand will lead to a large fall in output and only a small fall in prices. The flatter are firms' marginal cost curves, the smaller will be the fall in prices.

But what about the *long* run? Clearly it depends on how long the long run is. Many Keynesians argue that prices and especially wages exhibit a degree of inflexibility over quite a long period of time, and over this period of time, therefore, the aggregate supply curve would not be vertical. What is more, Keynesians argue that the long-run *AS* curve is unlikely to be vertical for a number of other reasons.

Hysteresis. As you may have seen on page 483, *hysteresis* refers to the lagging or persistence of an effect, even when the initial cause has been removed. In other words, an equilibrium position depends on the path taken to arrive there. In this context, hysteresis would be where long-run aggregate supply depends on what has been happening to aggregate demand and supply in the short run. Assume that the economy goes into recession, with a corresponding rise in demand-deficient unemployment and a fall in output. In Figure 20.8, aggregate demand has fallen from AD_{L_1} to AD_{L_2}. Demand-deficient unemployment is $a - b$ (the short-run effect).

As the recession persists, those previously laid off may not be readily re-employable, especially if they have been out of work for some time and have become deskilled and demoralised. The aggregate supply of labour curve has shifted to the left, perhaps as far as AS_{L_2}. In such a case, there would now no longer be an excess supply of labour that firms regard as 'employable' ($AD_{L_2} = AS_{L_2}$). There is no downward pressure on real wages: a long-run equilibrium has been reached. The implication of this is that the long-run aggregate supply (of goods) curve is *not* vertical. A leftward shift in aggregate demand has led to a long-run fall in output.

Assume now that the government pursues a reflationary policy, and that the aggregate demand for labour shifts back to AD_{L_1}. There will be a move up along AS_{L_2} to point *d*. Unemployment is now $e - d$, higher than the original level of $c - a$.

Expectations of output. If aggregate demand falls and the economy moves into recession, business confidence may fall and businesses' financial well-being may deteriorate too. This could lead to reduced investment and the capital stock falling. This reduces aggregate supply. Unless confidence quickly returns, and there is no guarantee that it will, the recession may be long-lived. The reduction in aggregate supply will be *long*-term.

The reduction in the capital stock will magnify the leftward shift in the aggregate demand for labour and increase the level of unemployment.

Long-run money illusion. The problem of demand deficiency will be compounded if there is long-run money illusion. Assume again that there is a fall in aggregate demand. Workers may be reluctant to accept a reduction in money wages, not appreciating that there has been a corresponding fall in prices. Thus real wages may be forced up, compounding the problem of disequilibrium unemployment.

Aggregate demand and supply, and inflation

Aggregate demand and supply analysis can be used to distinguish between demand-pull and cost-push inflation.

Demand-pull inflation

Assume that aggregate demand rises. In Figure 20.9(a), there is some increase in output, and the price level rises from P_0 to P_1. If demand goes on rising, so that the *AD* curve goes on shifting to the right, the price level will go on rising and there will be demand-pull inflation. There will be a movement from point *a* to *b* to *c* in Figure 20.9(b).

But sooner or later the short-run aggregate *supply* curve will start shifting. If the effects of rising costs and rising price expectations offset any stimulus to investment, the

Figure 20.9 Demand-pull inflation

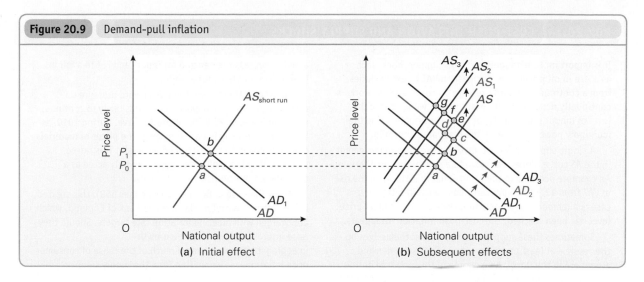

(a) Initial effect

(b) Subsequent effects

short-run *AS* curve will shift upwards. This will lead to a falling back of output but a further rise in prices as the economy moves to point *d*. If the government responds by giving a further boost to demand in order to keep expansion going, there will be a movement outward again to point *e*, but a further rise in prices. Then the *AS* curve will probably continue shifting upwards and the economy will move to point *f*.

If the government now makes the control of inflation its main policy objective, it may stop any further increases in aggregate demand. Aggregate supply may continue shifting upwards for a while as cost increases and expectations feed through. The economy moves to point *g*. In the extreme case, point *g* may be vertically above point *a*. The only effect of the shift in *AD* to *AD*₃ has been inflation.

Note that, although costs in Figure 20.9(b) have increased and hence the *AS* curves have shifted upwards, this is not *cost-push* inflation because the rise in costs is the result of the rise in *demand*.

If point g is vertically above point a, does this mean that the long-run AS curve is vertical? Are there any circumstances where point g might be to the left of point a?

Cost-push inflation

Assume that there is some exogenous increase in costs: a sharp increase in world oil prices, or an increase in wages due to increased trade union activity, or firms raising prices to cover the costs of a rise in interest rates. In Figure 20.10(a), the short-run *AS* curve shifts to *AS*₁. Prices rise to P_1 and there is a fall in national output.

If these increases in costs continue for some time, the *AS* curve will go on shifting upwards. Price rises will continue and there is cost-push inflation. The economy will move from point *a* to *b* to *c* in Figure 20.10(b). Continuous upward shifts in the *AS* curve are particularly likely if there is a continuing struggle between different groups (e.g. unions and employers' organisations) for a larger share of national income.

Figure 20.10 Cost-push inflation

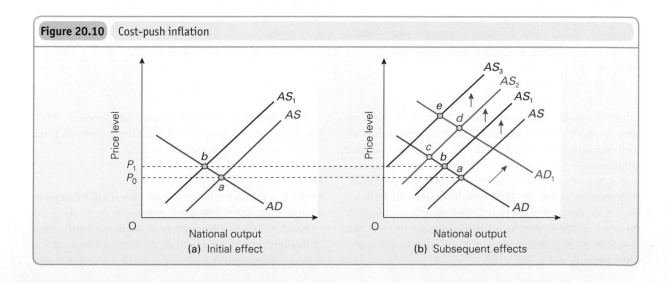

(a) Initial effect

(b) Subsequent effects

BOX 20.1 **COST-PUSH INFLATION AND SUPPLY SHOCKS**

It is important to distinguish a *single* supply shock, such as a rise in oil prices or an increase in VAT or excise duties, from a continuing upward pressure on costs, such as workers continually demanding increases in real wages above the level of labour productivity, or firms continually using their monopoly power to increase the real value of profits.

A single supply shock will give a *single* upward movement in the *AS* curve. Prices will move to a new higher equilibrium. An example occurred in the UK in January 2011, with the rise in VAT from 17.5 to 20 per cent. Cost-push inflation in this case is a *temporary* phenomenon. Once the new higher price level has been reached, the cost-push inflation disappears.

Sometimes these supply-side shocks can themselves be the result – at least partially – of an increase in demand elsewhere in the world. An example of this occurred during 2008 when the prices of materials and fuels used by industry began rising sharply, partly in response to the rapid growth in developing countries, such as China and India. As we can see from the chart, this caused the rate of input price inflation amongst manufacturers to rise to 35 per cent. But this spike in prices was temporary as the global downturn

acted to depress the demand for inputs and led to a fall in their prices – at least for a while.

But what if there is continuous upward pressure on costs? In this case, cost-push inflation is likely to continue, resulting in repeated shifts of the *AS* curve. During 2010, as the global economy began to recover, the prices of materials and fuels began to rise sharply once again. This raised concerns that the global slowdown had only acted as a temporary brake on rising input prices.

As we shall see in Box 21.10 (on pages 658), this created a dilemma for central banks, like the Bank of England, which are charged with meeting inflation rate targets. Should they raise interest rates to slow the growth in aggregate demand, even if much of the cause of consumer price inflation was emanating from the supply side?

 Give some examples of single shocks and continuing changes on the demand side. Does the existence of multiplier and accelerator effects make the distinction between single shocks and continuing effects more difficult to make on the demand side than on the supply side?

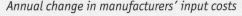

Annual change in manufacturers' input costs

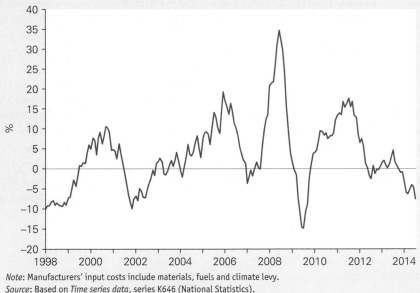

Note: Manufacturers' input costs include materials, fuels and climate levy.
Source: Based on *Time series data*, series K646 (National Statistics).

After a time, aggregate demand is likely to rise. This may be due to the government using expansionary fiscal and monetary policies to halt the falling output and employment. Or it may be due to money supply expanding endogenously as workers and firms need larger money balances to allow for increasingly costly transactions. Aggregate demand shifts to AD_1 and there is a movement to point *d*. There may be a further increase in costs and a movement to point *e*, and then a further increase in aggregate demand, and so on.

Note again that, although demand has increased, this is not *demand-pull* inflation because the rise in demand is the result of the upward pressure on *costs*.

What causes inflation in practice?

Inflation targeting, with the use of interest rate changes to achieve the target, implies that inflation is generally of the demand-pull variety. Forecasts of inflation (e.g. by the Bank of England) tend to concentrate on various factors affecting aggregate demand, such as the size of the government's

BOX 20.2 **ANALYSING DEMAND-PULL AND COST-PUSH INFLATION USING THE ADI/ASI MODEL**

Types of inflation under a policy of inflation targeting

We can use the *ADI/ASI* model to analyse the implications of demand-pull and cost-push pressures under a policy of inflation targeting. The diagram below is similar to Figure 19.17 (on page 584). Assume that the central bank operates with an inflation target of π_{target} and that the economy is currently in equilibrium at point *a* with aggregate demand and supply given by ADI_1 and ASI_1 respectively. Real national income is at the potential (or 'natural') level of Y_1.

Demand-pull inflation

If there is a rise in aggregate demand to ADI_2, this will result in demand-pull pressures on inflation. The government or central bank could respond in either of two ways:

- Fiscal or monetary policy could be tightened to shift the *ADI* curve back to ADI_1, thereby maintaining inflation at the target level.

- A new higher inflation target could be adopted (e.g. π_2), allowing an equilibrium at point *b*. Note, however, that if the potential level of income remains at Y_1, Y_2 will not be sustainable. In the long run, the *ASI* curve will drift upwards, pushing inflation above the new higher target level. A tighter monetary policy (ADI_3) would then be needed to bring national income back down to the potential level, Y_1.

Cost-push inflation

If costs now rise faster than the rate of inflation (a *real* rise in costs), the *ASI* line will shift upwards (e.g. to ASI_2). Again, the government or central bank could respond in either of two ways:

- The central bank could stick to its target and adopt a tighter monetary policy. In this case the *ADI* curve will shift to the left to give an equilibrium at point *c* at the target rate of inflation. The potential level of output is now at the lower level of Y_3.

- The central bank could be given a higher target rate of inflation (π_2) to prevent real income falling. It will thus expand aggregate demand and the *ADI* line will shift to ADI_3. Equilibrium would now be at point *d*. The problem with this second approach is that if there has been a long-term reduction in potential output to Y_3, there will be further upward pressure on inflation: the *ASI* curve will continue shifting upwards as long as real national income remains above Y_3. It will only be possible to keep to the target rate of inflation, at any level, if *ADI* is allowed to fall so that it intersects with *ASI* at Y_3.

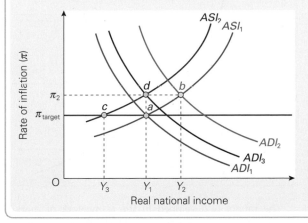

Demand-pull and cost-push inflation

If cost-push pressures reduce the potential level of real national income (e.g. from Y_1 to Y_3 in the diagram), why do demand-pull pressures not increase the potential level of real national income (e.g. from Y_1 to Y_2 in the diagram)?

---

deficit and business and consumer confidence. In most cases, changes in inflation are indeed caused by changes in the rate of growth of aggregate demand.

There are, however, occasions when there are exogenous changes in costs. In the short run, these can be shocks such as a rise in oil or other commodity prices (see Box 20.1) or a period of industrial unrest.

In the longer term, technological changes can affect the rate of growth of aggregate supply. If this slows down, then for any given rate of growth in aggregate demand, there will be a higher rate of inflation. This rise in inflation could be described as 'cost push'. Under a policy of inflation targeting, however, the response to this problem would be one

of slowing down the rate of growth in aggregate demand to match the slower growth in aggregate supply. In other words, a higher interest rate would be needed to achieve the target rate of inflation (a vertical upward move of the *MP* (monetary policy) curve – see pages 577–8).

One of the key determinants of inflation is people's *expectations*. The higher inflation is expected to be, the higher it will be. In the remainder of the chapter we look at just how expectations affect inflation and how they affect the relationship between inflation and unemployment. In doing so we will look at theories that develop the old Phillips curve (see Box 15.4).

Section summary

1. The short-run aggregate supply curve depends on firms' short-run marginal cost curves. The more rapidly costs rise as output increases, the less elastic will the *AS* curve be.

2. The long-run *AS* curve will be less elastic (a) the more that cost increases are passed on from one part of the economy to another, (b) the less that increases in aggregate demand stimulate cost-reducing investment and (c) the more that people expect prices to rise as a result of the increase in demand.

3. Classical assumptions imply that the long-run aggregate supply curve is vertical. The key assumptions here are flexible prices and wages, and an absence of money illusion.

4. Keynesians argue that the long-run supply curve will not be vertical. It will be more elastic the greater the problem of hysteresis, the more that firms react to changes in aggregate demand by changing the level of investment and hence the size of the capital stock, and the greater the degree of long-run money illusion.

5. Demand-pull inflation occurs where there are continuous rightward shifts in the *AD* curve. Cost-push inflation occurs where there are continuous upward shifts in the *AS* curve. In practice, it is difficult to separate demand-pull and cost-push inflation as there are often exogenous and endogenous factors affecting both demand and costs simultaneously.

20.2 THE EXPECTATIONS-AUGMENTED PHILLIPS CURVE

A major contribution to the theory of unemployment and inflation was made by Milton Friedman (see Person Profile in MyEconLab) and others in the late 1960s. They incorporated people's expectations about the future level of prices into the Phillips curve. In its simplest form, this *expectations-augmented Phillips curve* may be expressed as

$$\pi = f(1/U) + \pi^e + k \qquad (1)$$

This states that the rate of price inflation (π) depends on three things:

- First, it is a function (f) of the inverse of unemployment ($1/U$). This is simply the normal Phillips curve relationship. A rise in aggregate demand will lead to a fall in unemployment (a rise in $1/U$) and a rise in inflation: e.g. a movement from point *a* to point *b* in Figure 20.11.

- Second, the expected rate of inflation π^e must be added to the inflation that would result simply from the level of excess demand represented by ($1/U$).

- Third, if there are any exogenous cost pressures on inflation (k) (such as increases in international commodity prices), this must be added too.

Thus if people expected a 3 per cent inflation rate ($\pi^e = 3$ per cent) and if excess demand were causing demand-pull inflation of 2 per cent ($f(1/U) = 2$ per cent) and exogenous increases in costs were adding another 1 per cent to inflation ($k = 1$ per cent), actual inflation would be $3 + 2 + 1 = 6$ per cent.

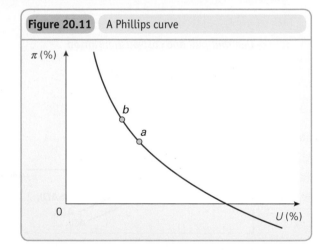

Figure 20.11 A Phillips curve

The model is developed in the framework of market clearing. Wages are not sticky downwards, at least not in the long run. There can be no long-run disequilibrium unemployment: no long-run deficiency of demand.

Adaptive expectations

What determines the expected rate of inflation (π^e)? In the model we are developing it depends on inflation rates *in the past*. This is the *adaptive expectations hypothesis* that we introduced in section 16.5. To keep the analysis straightforward, we will assume that the expected rate of inflation this year (π^e_t) is last year's actual inflation rate year (π_{t-1}):

$$\pi^e_t = \pi_{t-1} \qquad (2)$$

The accelerationist theory

Let us trace the course of inflation and expectations over a number of years in an imaginary economy. To keep the

Definition

Expectations-augmented Phillips curve A (short-run) Phillips curve whose position depends on the expected rate of inflation.

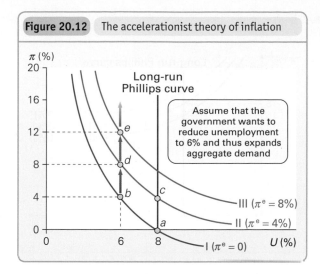

Figure 20.12 The accelerationist theory of inflation

Table 20.1 The accelerationist theory of inflation and inflationary expectations

Year	Point on graph	π	=	$f(1/U)$	+	π^e
1	a	0	=	0	+	0
2	b	4	=	4	+	0
3	c	4	=	0	+	4
4	d	8	=	4	+	4
5	e	12	=	4	+	8

analysis simple, assume there is no growth in the economy and no exogenous cost pressures on inflation ($k = 0$ in equation (1)).

Year 1. Assume that at the outset, in year 1, there is no inflation of any sort; that none is expected; that $AD = AS$; and that equilibrium unemployment is 8 per cent. The economy will be at point *a* in Figure 20.12 and Table 20.1.

Year 2. Now assume that the government expands aggregate demand in order to reduce unemployment. Unemployment falls to 6 per cent. The economy moves to point *b* along curve I. Inflation has risen to 4 per cent, but people, basing their expectations of inflation on year 1, still expect zero inflation. There is therefore no shift as yet in the Phillips curve. Curve I corresponds to an expected rate of inflation of zero. (See Case Study 20.1 in MyEconLab for an explanation of why the short-run Phillips curve slopes downwards.)

Year 3. People now revise their expectations of inflation to the level of year 2. The Phillips curve shifts up by 4 percentage points to position II. If *nominal* aggregate demand (i.e. demand purely in monetary terms, irrespective of the level of prices) continues to rise at the same rate, the whole of the increase will now be absorbed in higher prices. *Real* aggregate demand will fall back to its previous level and the economy will move to point *c*. Unemployment will return to 8 per cent. There is no *demand-pull* inflation now ($f(1/U) = 0$), but inflation is still 4 per cent due to expectations ($\pi^e = 4$ per cent).

TC 12
p411

Year 4. Assume now that the government expands *real* aggregate demand again so as to reduce unemployment once more to 6 per cent. This time it must expand *nominal* aggregate demand by *more* than it did in year 2, because this time, as well as reducing unemployment, it also has to validate the 4 per cent expected inflation. The economy moves to point *d* along curve II. Inflation is now 8 per cent.

Year 5. *Expected* inflation is now 8 per cent (the level of actual inflation in year 4). The Phillips curve shifts up to position III. If at the same time the government tries to keep unemployment at 6 per cent, it must expand nominal aggregate demand 4 per cent faster in order to validate the 8 per cent expected inflation. The economy moves to point *e* along curve III. Inflation is now 12 per cent.

Year 6 onwards. To keep unemployment at 6 per cent, the government must continue to increase nominal aggregate demand by 4 per cent more than the previous year. As the expected inflation rate goes on rising, the Phillips curve will go on shifting up each year.

Thus in order to keep unemployment below the initial equilibrium rate, price rises must go on *accelerating* each year. For this reason, the adaptive expectations theory of the Phillips curve is sometimes known as the ***accelerationist theory***.

The more the government reduces unemployment, the greater the rise in inflation that year, and the more the rise in expectations the following year and each subsequent year; and hence the more rapidly will price rises accelerate. Thus the true longer-term trade-off is between unemployment and the rate of *increase* in inflation:

$$\Delta\pi = f(1/U) \tag{3}$$

(Note that $\Delta\pi$ may be written $\dot{\pi}$.)

Note that the upward shift in the Phillips curve will be less rapid if expectations do not fully adjust to the previous year's inflation rate. The upward shift will be more rapid if expectations adjust to the rate of *increase* in inflation last year ($\Delta\pi_{t-1}$).

 Construct a table like Table 20.1, only this time assume that the government wishes to reduce unemployment to 5 per cent. Assume that every year from year 1 onwards the government is prepared to expand aggregate demand by whatever it takes to do this. If this expansion of demand gives $f(1/U) = 7$ per cent, fill in the table for the first six years. Do you think that after a couple of years people might begin to base their expectations differently?

Definition

Accelerationist theory The theory that unemployment can be reduced below the natural rate only at the cost of accelerating inflation.

The long-run Phillips curve and the natural rate of unemployment

As long as there are demand-pull pressures ($f(1/U) > 0$), inflation will rise as the expected rate of inflation (π^e) rises. In the long run, therefore, the Phillips curve will be *vertical* at the rate of unemployment where real aggregate demand equals *real* aggregate supply. This is the *equilibrium* rate of unemployment which monetarists refer to as the **natural rate** (U_n), but which, because of market imperfections and frictions, Keynesians often prefer to call the **non-accelerating-inflation rate of unemployment (NAIRU)** (see pages 615–17). In Figure 20.12, $U_n = 8$ per cent.

The implication for government policy is that expansionary monetary and fiscal policy can reduce unemployment below U_n only in the *short* run. In the long run, the effect will be purely inflationary.

 What will determine the speed at which inflation accelerates?

The effects of contractionary policy

Let us now move on a few years from Table 20.1. Assume that the economy has returned to the natural rate of unemployment: $f(1/U) = 0$. The economy is therefore on the long-run Phillips curve. But, due to past excess demand, the expected rate of inflation is 20 per cent. The economy is thus at point *j* on short-run Phillips curve X in Figure 20.13.

The government now decides to make the control of inflation its main priority. It therefore reduces the growth of nominal aggregate demand *below* the rate of inflation.

Definition

Natural rate of unemployment or **non-accelerating-inflation rate of unemployment (NAIRU)** The rate of unemployment consistent with a constant rate of inflation: the rate of unemployment at which the vertical long-run Phillips curve cuts the horizontal axis.

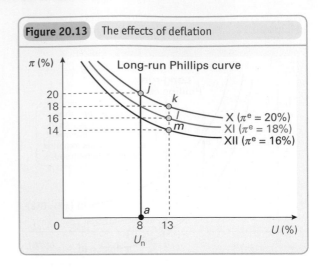

Figure 20.13 The effects of deflation

Real aggregate demand falls. Let us assume that there is a 2 per cent downward pressure on inflation: $f(1/U) = -2$. Inflation thus falls to 18 per cent. But unemployment rises, let us assume, from 8 per cent to 13 per cent. The economy moves along curve X to point *k*.

The following year the expected rate of inflation will fall to 18 per cent to match, and if real demand is still being deflated by the same amount ($f(1/U) = -2$), actual inflation will fall to 16 per cent. The economy moves to point *l* on curve XI.

If the government maintains unemployment at 13 per cent, inflation will continue to fall by 2 per cent a year. After 10 years of unemployment at 13 per cent, the economy could return to point *a*, with unemployment falling back to U_n.

 Construct a table like Table 20.1, only this time assume that in year 1 the economy is in recession with high unemployment, but also high inflation due to high inflationary expectations as a result of past excess demand. Assume that in year 1, $\pi = 30$ per cent, $f(1/U) = -6$ per cent and $\pi^e = 36$ per cent. Continue the table for as many years as it takes for inflation to be 'squeezed out' of the economy (assuming that the government keeps aggregate demand at a low enough level to maintain $f(1/U) = -6$ per cent throughout).

More sophisticated adaptive expectations models

More complex adaptive expectations models assume that π^e is a weighted average of past rates of inflation:

$$\pi^e_t = a\pi_{t-1} + b\pi_{t-2} + c\pi_{t-3} + \ldots + m\pi_{t-n} \quad (1)$$

where $a + b + c + \ldots + m = 1$, and where $a > b > c$, etc.

In other words, people will base their expectations of inflation on the actual inflation rates over the last few years, but with last year's inflation having a bigger influence on people's expectations than the previous year's, and so on.

In times of rapidly accelerating inflation, people may adjust their expectations of inflation upwards by the amount that inflation rose last year ($\Delta\pi_{t-1}$). This gives

$$\Delta\pi^e_t = \Delta\pi_{t-1} \quad (2)$$

Under what circumstances will term a in equation (1) be large relative to terms b, c, etc.?

How quickly can inflation be eliminated?

The short-run Phillips curve may be relatively shallow to the right of U_n. The more sticky downwards wages and prices are in the short run, the shallower the curve will be. Thus to get a relatively rapid fall in inflation, unemployment may have to be very high indeed.

According to the adaptive expectations model, there are two alternative routes to eliminating inflation.

The quick route. This involves a *severe* contraction. Unemployment rises to very high rates and the economy is plunged into a deep recession. However, the short-run Phillips curve shifts down fairly rapidly as the expected rate of inflation (π^e) falls quite quickly. Inflation may be squeezed out of the economy within two or three years. This approach could be called the 'short, sharp shock'.

The slow route. This involves a *mild* contraction. Unemployment rises perhaps one or two percentage points above the natural rate. Inflation falls only slightly in the first year, and thus π^e falls only slowly the next year and each subsequent year. Although less painful, this approach may take many years to eliminate inflation.

Explanations of stagflation

In the 1970s, many countries experienced 'stagflation' – a simultaneous rise in unemployment and inflation. Monetarists used the adaptive expectations model to explain why this occurred. The explanation involved clockwise loops and rightward shifts in the long-run Phillips curve.

Clockwise Phillips loops

Consider a 10-year cycle. This is illustrated in Figure 20.14. The economy starts at position *a* in year 0. There is no inflation and the economy is at the natural rate of unemployment. The government pursues an expansionary policy over the next three years in order to reduce unemployment. The economy moves up through points *b*, *c* and *d*.

The government then starts worrying about inflation. It allows unemployment to rise somewhat, but as it is still below U_n there is still demand-pull inflation. The economy moves to point *e*. The government now allows unemployment to rise to U_n, but the Phillips curve still shifts up as expectations catch up with last year's inflation. The economy moves from point *e* to point *f*.

Thereafter the government allows unemployment to rise further, and the economy eventually returns to point *a*, via points *g*, *h*, *i* and *j*. The economy has thus moved through a clockwise loop.

Stagflation is easy to see. From points *d* to *f*, both unemployment *and* inflation are rising. What is more, several points are to the 'north-east' of other earlier points. For example, point *g* is north-east of point *c*. In other words, inflation *and* unemployment in year 6 (point *g*) are higher than in year 2 (point *c*).

 Under what circumstances would a Phillips loop be (a) tall and thin; (b) short and wide?

Rightward shifts in the long-run Phillips curve

If frictional or structural unemployment rises (due, say, to increased unemployment benefits), U_n will increase. The long-run Phillips curve will shift to the right.

Assume that the economy was initially on the long-run Phillips curve with $U_n = 8$ per cent and a stable inflation rate of 5 per cent. U_n now rises to 12 per cent. The government uses demand-management policy to keep the rise in unemployment to only 10 per cent. But this is now *below* U_n and thus inflation will increase. Thus both inflation *and* unemployment have risen.

Evidence

The evidence for the UK since 1967 is consistent with the adaptive expectations model. (But note that it is consistent with other explanations too!) In Figure 20.15 loops can clearly be seen up to around 1993, when inflation targeting began (see section 21.5). At the same time, U_n would seem to have increased from about 4.5 per cent in the mid-1970s to around 11 per cent in the mid-1980s, and to have fallen to about 8 per cent in the late 1980s/early 1990s and to about 5 per cent in the mid-2000s.

Since the mid-1990s, hitting the inflation target has been the central aim of monetary policy and people had grown to believe that the target would be achieved. Figure 20.16 shows forecast and actual RPI inflation from 1998 to 2015. The forecasts are the average of at least 20 independent forecasts and thus can be taken as an indicator of expectations. As you can see, until the credit crunch of 2008, inflation forecasts were pretty accurate and reflected belief that the Bank of England would be successful in meeting its inflation target (2.5 per cent RPI inflation up to December 2003 and 2 per cent CPI inflation thereafter – CPI inflation is typically about 0.5 to 0.8 percentage points below RPI inflation).

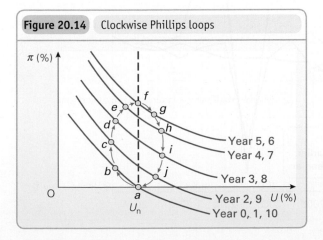

Figure 20.14 Clockwise Phillips loops

Figure 20.15 Phillips loops in the UK

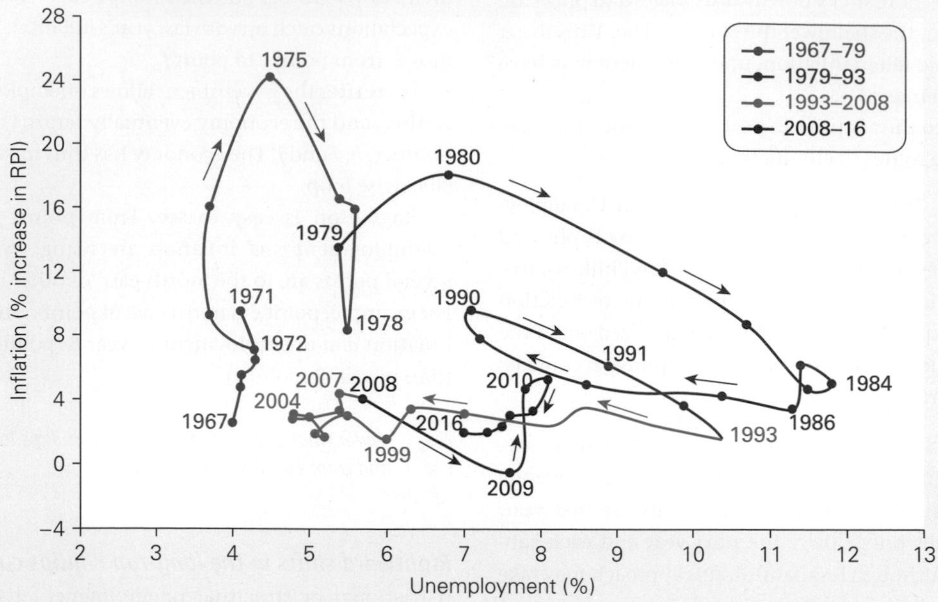

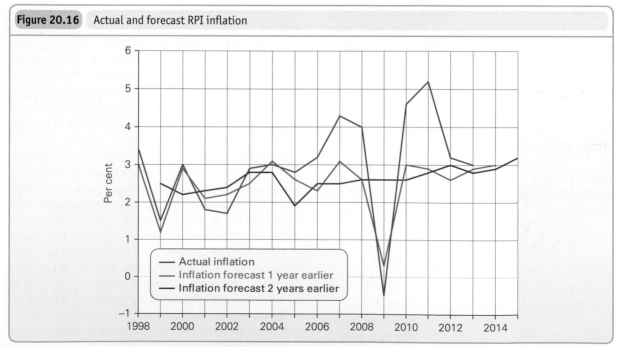

Note: 2015 and 2016 figures based on forecasts.
Source: Based on *Time Series Data* (National Statistics).

The credit crunch and the onset of recession, however, initially affected the accuracy of 24-month forecasts. Subsequently, the 12-month forecasts became less accurate too as inflation rose as a result of rapid rises in food, oil and other commodity prices.

So, does this mean that the Phillips curve has now become horizontal? The answer is that it depends on policy and, hence, on the central bank's remit. If inflation remains central to this remit, is successfully kept on target and people believe that it will remain so, the path of inflation and unemployment will be a horizontal straight line. Movements left and right along the line will depend on what happens to unemployment.

Even if the central bank remains committed to inflation targeting and does succeed in achieving the target rate of inflation, in the short term, unemployment will fluctuate

Figure 20.16 Actual and forecast RPI inflation

Note: Based on average of between 20 and 30 independent forecasts.
Source: *Forecasts for the UK Economy* (HM Treasury, various years).

Figure 20.17   Economic growth and inflation

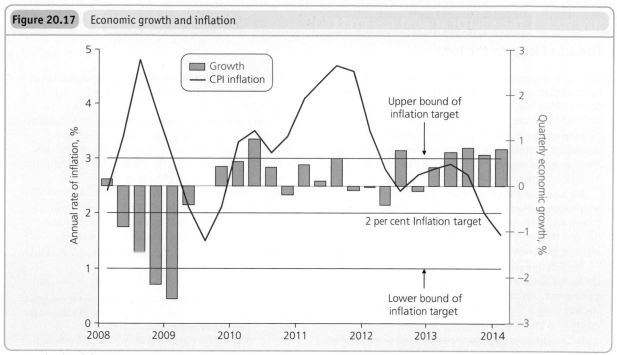

Source: National Statistics.

with the business cycle. Thus there may be movements left or right from one year to the next depending on the level of economic activity. Such fluctuations in unemployment are consistent with a stable inflation rate, provided that the fluctuations are mild and are not enough to alter people's expectations of inflation.

Over the medium term (3–6 years), there may be a leftward movement along the horizontal 'curve' if the economy starts in recession and then the output gap is gradually closed through a process of steady economic growth (growth that avoids 'boom and bust'). Demand-deficient unemployment will be gradually eliminated. Thus between 1992 (the trough of the recession) and 1996, the output gap was closed from 3 per cent below potential output to zero (see the diagram in Box 14.3 on page 414). Provided the process is gradual, inflation can stay on target.

Over the longer term, movements left (or right) will depend on what happens to equilibrium unemployment. A reduction in equilibrium unemployment will result in a leftward movement. Evidence suggests that between the mid-1980s and the financial crisis of the late 2000s, the equilibrium unemployment rate halved from around 10 per cent to around 5 per cent. The precise amount, however, is not certain as it is subject to measurement errors.

What if the central bank's remit changed?

Changes to a central bank's remit affect the objectives or priorities of monetary policy. Consequently, they affect the monetary policy (*MP*) curve introduced in Chapter 19, which captures the responsiveness of interest rates to changes in national income. The less strictly the central bank targets inflation and instead targets growth in national income (or reductions in unemployment), the smaller will be changes

in interest rates in response to rises in national income.

If inflation targeting were relaxed, perhaps as part of a shift to a broader remit, or even abandoned and then aggregate demand expanded rapidly, the short-run Phillips curve could re-emerge. A rapid expansion of aggregate demand would both reduce unemployment below the equilibrium rate and raise inflation. There would be a positive output gap. This position could not be sustained, however, as inflationary expectations would rise and the short-run Phillips curve would begin shifting upwards (as in Figure 20.12 on page 603).

Rising food and commodity prices both before and after the global economic slowdown of the late 2000s (see Box 20.1) provided the Bank of England (and other central banks too) with a dilemma. As we can see from Figure 20.17 it contributed to significant spikes in the annual rate of CPI inflation in the UK. Should the Bank continue rigidly targeting inflation, which would mean raising interest rates, or should it help to boost aggregate demand by cutting or keeping interest rates low? As it turned out, it was able to start cutting interest rates in late 2008 to boost aggregate demand without compromising its inflation target. This is because inflation fell in late 2008 and the output gap rose substantially; inflation was forecast to fall well below the target rate at the 24-month horizon.

The policy dilemma facing the Bank of England was in some ways trickier during 2010 and 2011 as inflation picked up because economic growth remained fragile and unemployment was rising. The increase in the standard rate of VAT from 17.5 per cent to 20 per cent at the start of 2011 further helped to raise the inflation rate. Despite inflation consistently exceeding the upper bound of the Bank of England's target the judgement of the MPC was to keep Bank Rate at 0.5 per cent throughout 2010 and into 2011

The art of looping the loop

Imagine that a politically naive government has been fulfilling election promises to reduce unemployment, cut taxes and increase welfare spending. In Figure 20.14 this is shown by a move from points *a* to *b* to *c*.

To its dismay, by the time the next election comes, inflation is accelerating and unemployment is rising again. The economy is moving from point *d* to *e* to *f*. You would hardly be surprised to learn that it loses the election!

But now suppose a much more politically skilful government is elected. What does it do? The answer is that it does politically unpopular things at first, so that before the next election it can do nice things and curry favour with the electorate.

The first thing it does is to have a tough Budget. 'We are having to clear up the economic mess left by the last government.' It thus engineers a recession and begins to squeeze down inflationary expectations. The economy moves from point *f* to *g* to *h*.

But people have very short memories (despite opposition attempts to remind them). After a couple of years of misery, the government announces that the economy has 'begun to turn the corner'. Things are looking up. Inflation has fallen and unemployment has stopped rising. The economy has moved from point *h* to *i* to *j*.

'Thanks to prudent management of the economy', claims the Chancellor, 'I am now in a position to reduce taxes and to allow modest increases in government expenditure.' Unemployment falls rapidly; the economy grows rapidly; the economy moves from point *j* to *a* to *b*.

The government's popularity soars; the pre-election 'give-away' Budget is swallowed by the electorate who trustingly believe that similar ones will follow if the government is returned to office. The government wins the election.

Then comes the nasty medicine again. But who will be blamed this time?

1. *Why might a government sometimes 'get it wrong' and find itself at the wrong part of the Phillips loop at the time of an election?*
2. *How will the move in the UK to fixed parliamentary election periods of five years affect the likelihood of political business cycles?*

---

believing that inflation would return to its central target within the 24-month horizon.

Critics argued that the Bank's response during 2010 and 2011 compromised the inflation target and meant higher inflationary expectations. These concerns were further heightened when in 2013 the Bank of England began a policy of *forward guidance*. This is intended to give economic agents an indication of the likely direction and level of interest rates.

In August 2013 the Bank announced that it was not minded to raise the policy rate of interest from its historic low of 0.5 per cent at least until the unemployment rate had fallen to 7 per cent or less.

However, by February 2014 it had further revised its forward guidance as the rate of unemployment, which had fallen during the latter half of 2013 and into 2014, stood at close to 7 per cent. Yet, the Bank judged that real national income was still well below its potential level. The Bank thus changed its forward guidance to say that, in setting interest rates, it would be guided not only by the rate of unemployment but by the amount of slack in the economy. It advised that when it did begin to raise rates the process would be a gradual one and that rates would remain 'materially below' the 5 per cent level prior the financial crisis.

The hope was that, by providing households and businesses with greater certainty about the path of interest rates, forward guidance would give them the confidence to bring forward expenditure and so boost aggregate demand. Critics argued that the benefits from a straightforward inflation target in securing consistently low expectations of inflation could be lost. We examine these policy issues more closely in the next chapter.

How would you explain the apparent re-emergence of a Phillips loop after 2004?

Policy implications

The implications of the expectations-augmented Phillips curve are that monetary and fiscal policies can have no *long-run* effect on unemployment. They can only be used to influence the inflation rate. Ultimately, monetary and fiscal policies merely move the economy up or down the vertical long-run Phillips curve. An expansionary policy, for example, could only ever bring a *temporary* reduction in unemployment below U_n.

To reduce unemployment permanently, *supply-side* policies should be used. These could either be market-orientated policies of removing impediments to the working of the market (see section 23.3) or interventionist policies, such as improving education and training or the country's transport and communications infrastructure (see section 23.4). By reducing frictional and/or structural unemployment, such policies will shift the long-run Phillips curve back to the left.

Limitations of the adaptive expectations hypothesis

The adaptive expectations hypothesis suffers from a serious flaw: it assumes that people base their expectations on the past. So if inflation is on an upward trend, the future of inflation will always be underestimated. Similarly, inflation will always be overestimated if it is on a downward trend. Thus people will normally be wrong.

But people will soon realise that it is not rational to base their expectations blindly on the past. They will look at the *current* situation and what is likely to affect inflation. Thus, it is argued, adaptive expectations cannot be a rational basis of behaviour. An alternative view of price expectations was subsequently developed. We look at it in the next section.

Section summary

1. A refinement of the simple Phillips curve involves the incorporation of people's expectations about the rate of inflation. This gives an expectations-augmented Phillips curve. One explanation of how people form these expectations is given by the adaptive expectations hypothesis. In its simplest form, the hypothesis states that the expected rate of inflation this year is what it actually was last year: $\pi_t^e = \pi_{t-1}$.

2. If there is excess demand in the economy, producing upward pressure on wages and prices, initially unemployment will fall. The reason is that workers and firms will believe that wage and price increases represent *real* wage and price increases respectively. Thus workers are prepared to take jobs more readily and firms choose to produce more. But as people's expectations adapt upwards to these higher wages and prices, so ever-increasing rises in nominal aggregate demand will be necessary to maintain unemployment below the natural rate. Price and wage rises will accelerate: i.e. inflation will rise.

3. The Phillips curve, according to this analysis, is thus vertical at the natural rate of unemployment.

4. If an economy suffering from high inflation is deflated, initially unemployment will rise above the natural rate.

   But as expectations adapt downwards, so the short-run Phillips curve will shift downwards and inflation will fall. Eventually the economy will return to zero inflation at the natural rate of unemployment.

5. This position can be reached more quickly if the government deflates sharply, but then in the short run the rate of unemployment may rise substantially above the natural rate.

6. Stagflation can be explained in this model either by a movement from 9 o'clock to 12 o'clock round a clockwise Phillips loop, or by a rightward shift in the vertical Phillips curve combined with a mild expansionary policy.

7. Evidence shows that the effects of inflation targeting on expectations has tended to make the time path of the Phillips curve horizontal at the target rate of inflation. This does not mean, however, that a vertical long-run Phillips curve would not soon become apparent if inflation targeting were abandoned or the central bank's remit revised.

8. The weakness of the adaptive expectations hypothesis is that people do not just base expectations of inflation on the past. They are also likely to base them on *current* events and conditions.

20.3 INFLATION AND UNEMPLOYMENT: THE NEW CLASSICAL POSITION

Economists of the *new classical school* (see section 16.5) go further than the monetarist theory described above. They argue that even the short-run Phillips curve is vertical: that there is *no* trade-off between unemployment and inflation, even in the short run. They base their arguments on two key assumptions:

- Prices and wages are flexible, and thus markets clear very rapidly.
- Expectations are 'rational', but are based on imperfect information.

Flexible wages and prices

New classical economists assume that there is a process of continuous market clearing. This is likely, they argue, in modern economies with flexible labour markets (see Box 9.8 on pages 264–5) and facing global competition. There is

thus no disequilibrium unemployment, even in the short run. All unemployment, therefore, is *equilibrium* unemployment, or 'voluntary unemployment' as new classical economists tend to call it. Increases in unemployment are therefore due to an increase in the natural level of unemployment, as people choose not to take jobs because of a lack of incentives to do so.

Rational expectations

The analysis of the previous section was based on *adaptive* expectations. Expectations of inflation are based on *past* information and therefore take a time to catch up with changes in aggregate demand. Thus, for a short time, a rise in aggregate demand will raise output and employment above the natural level, while prices and wages are still relatively low.

BOX 20.5   **THE RATIONAL EXPECTATIONS REVOLUTION**

Trying to 'unfool' the economics profession

The rational expectations revolution swept through the economics profession in the 1970s in a way that no other set of ideas had done since Keynes. Although largely associated with the free-market, non-interventionist wing of economics, the rational expectations revolution has been far more wide-reaching. Even economists implacably opposed to the free market nevertheless incorporated rational expectations into their models. Hence, rational expectations became part of the mainstream consensus that emerged up to the financial crisis of the late 2000s (see section 16.7).

The rational expectations revolution is founded on a very simple idea. People base their expectations of the future on the information they have available. They don't just look at the past; they also look at current information, including what the government is saying and doing and what various commentators have to say.

The new classical economists use rational expectations in the following context. If the *long-run* Phillips curve is vertical, so that an expansionary policy will in the end merely lead to inflation, it will be difficult for the government to fool people that this will not happen. If employers, unions, city financiers, economic advisers, journalists, etc., all expect this to happen, then it will; and it will happen in the *short run*. Why should firms produce more in response to a rise in demand if their costs are going to rise by just as much? Why should higher wages attract workers to move jobs, if wages everywhere are going up? Why should firms and unions not seek price and wage rises fully in line with the expected inflation?

But can the government not surprise people? The point here is that 'surprising' people really only means 'fooling' them – making them believe that an expansionary policy really *will* reduce unemployment. But why should the public be fooled? Why should people believe smooth-talking government ministers rather than the whole host of critics of the government, from the opposition, to economic commentators, to the next-door neighbour?

The rational expectations school revised the old saying 'You can't fool all the people all the time' to 'You can hardly fool the people at all'. And if that is so, argue the new classical economists, unemployment can only momentarily be brought below its natural level.

Two of the most famous rational expectations economists are Robert Lucas and Thomas Sargent. Robert Lucas, like Milton Friedman and many other famous conservative economists, has his academic base in the University of Chicago, where he has been a Professor since 1974. In 1995, like Milton Friedman in 1976, Lucas was awarded the Nobel Prize in Economics. Tom Sargent is Professor of Economics at New York University and Senior Fellow at the Hoover Institution of Stanford University. He was Professor of Economics at Chicago in the 1990s.

In recent years, rational expectations have been incorporated into models characterised by market imperfections and frictions, such as those developed by new Keynesians (see section 16.6). In this context, government policy *can* be effective. For example, supply-side policies can be directed to removing market distortions.

As we saw in Chapter 16, the new classical analysis is based on *rational expectations*. Rational expectations are not based on past rates of inflation. Instead they are based on the current state of the economy and the current policies being pursued by the government. Workers and firms look at the information available to them – at the various forecasts that are published, at various economic indicators and the assessments of them by various commentators, at government pronouncements, and so on. From this information they predict the rate of inflation as well as they can. It is in this sense that the expectations are 'rational': people use their reason to assess the future on the basis of current information.

But forecasters frequently get it wrong, and so do economic commentators! And the government does not always do what it says it will. Thus workers and firms base their expectations on *imperfect information*. Other versions assume that they may make very poor use of information. But either way, people frequently forecast incorrectly. The crucial point about the rational expectations theory, however, is that these errors in prediction are *random*. People's predictions of inflation are just as likely to be too high as too low.[1]

Aggregate supply and the Phillips curve when expectations are correct

If people are correct in their expectations, and if the long-run aggregate supply and Phillips curves are vertical, so too will be the short-run curves. In the new classical (rational expectations) model, unlike the adaptive expectations model, there is *no* lag in expectations. If their information is correct, people will rationally predict that output and employment will stay at the natural level. They predict that any change in *nominal* aggregate demand will be reflected purely in terms of changes in prices, and that real aggregate demand will remain the same. If real aggregate demand remains the same, so will the demand for and supply of

---

[1] The rational expectations hypothesis can be stated as

$$\pi_t = \pi_{t-1} + \left(\sum_{t=1}^{t=\infty} \varepsilon_t \right) (\varepsilon = 0)$$

In other words, the rate of inflation for any time period (π_t) will be the rate that people expected in that time period (π_t^e) plus an error term (ε_t). This error term may be quite large but is equally likely to be positive or negative. Thus when you sum (Σ) the error terms over the years (strictly speaking, to infinity), the positive and negative values will cancel each other out and the sum will therefore be zero.

Figure 20.18   The effects of an increase in aggregate demand

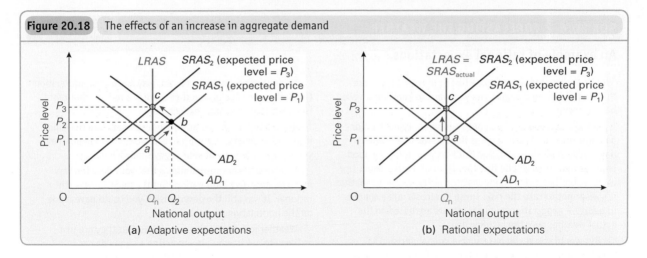

(a) Adaptive expectations

(b) Rational expectations

labour and the demand for and supply of goods. Thus, even in the *short* run, output and employment will stay at the natural level.

Let us see how the adaptive expectations and the rational expectations models analyse the effects of an increase in aggregate demand. Figure 20.18 uses simple aggregate demand and supply curves. Figure 20.18(a) gives the adaptive expectations analysis. Figure 20.18(b) gives the rational expectations analysis.

In both diagrams, there is an initial equilibrium at point *a*. This is a long-run equilibrium, where aggregate demand (AD_1) equals long-run aggregate supply ($LRAS$). Price is stable and is at the level of P_1. The short-run supply curve with P_1 as the *expected* price level is given by $SRAS_1$. Note that this is upward sloping in *both* diagrams because it shows how much will be supplied *if* (and only if) people expect price to remain at P_1.

Now assume that the government raises aggregate demand to AD_2. What will happen to prices and output?

In Figure 20.18(a), people base their expectations of prices on the past. In other words, at first they expect the price level to stay at P_1. The economy thus moves to point *b*, where $AD_2 = SRAS_1$. Output rises to Q_2 and the price level rises to P_2. Then, over time, as price expectations rise, the short-run aggregate supply curve shifts upwards, eventually reaching $SRAS_2$. Long-run equilibrium is thus at point *c*, where $AD_2 = LRAS$. In the short run, therefore, if the government expands aggregate demand, there will be a rise in output and employment. It is only in the long run that the effect is confined to higher prices. The actual length of time it takes to reach point *c* will depend on how quickly expectations adjust upwards.

In Figure 20.18(b), people correctly anticipate the full price effects of any increase in aggregate demand. The short-run aggregate supply curve based on a particular price (e.g. $SRAS_1$ based on a price level P_1) cannot be moved along. The moment aggregate demand shifts to the right, people will correctly anticipate a rise in the price level. Thus the moment the economy begins to move up along $SRAS_1$

from point *a*, the whole $SRAS$ curve will shift upwards. As a result, the economy moves *directly* to point *c*. Thus the *actual* short-run supply curve is vertical and, assuming expectations are correct, will be identical to the long-run 'curve'.

 Show these effects of an increase in aggregate demand from both the adaptive expectations and rational expectations points of view, only this time show the effects on Phillips curves.

Aggregate supply and the Phillips curve when expectations are incorrect

Although over the years people's expectations are assumed to be correct on average, it is more than likely that in any one year they will be wrong. Economic shocks, which for instance lead to unexpected changes in aggregate demand, mean that households and businesses are subject to 'surprises' (see section 16.5). The following analysis looks at the implication of this for output and employment.

The goods market

Assume that aggregate demand increases but that firms *under*predict the resulting rate of inflation: $\pi^e < \pi$. Firms do not realise that the increased expenditure on their product will be offset by an increase in costs. As a result, as profit maximisers, they decide to produce more. Thus if the government catches people unawares and unexpectedly boosts demand, then output will rise as firms, underpredicting the rate of inflation, believe that *real* demand has risen.

But in a rational expectations framework, this is just luck on the government's side. Firms might just as well have thought the government would give an even bigger boost to aggregate demand than it actually did. In this case, firms would have *over*predicted the rate of inflation, and as a result would have cut their output, believing that real demand had fallen. (A graphical analysis of these arguments is given in Case Study 20.3 in MyEconLab.)

TC 9
p121

BOX 20.6   FORECASTING THE WEATHER

An example of rational expectations

'What's the weather going to be like tomorrow?' If you are thinking of having a picnic, you will want to know the answer before deciding.

So what do you do? You could base your assessment on past information. Yesterday was fine; so was the previous day. Today is glorious. So, you think to yourself, it's a good bet that tomorrow will be fine too. If, on the other hand, the weather has been very changeable recently, you may feel that it's wiser not to take the risk. These 'forecasts' are examples of *adaptive* expectations: your forecasts are based on the actual weather over the last few days.

But would you really base such a crucial decision as whether or not to have a picnic on something so unreliable? Wouldn't you rather take on board more information to help you make up your mind?

The first thing that might come to mind is the old saying that a British summer is three fine days and a thunderstorm. We've just had the three fine days, you think to yourself, so perhaps we'd better stay at home tomorrow.

Or, being a bit more scientific about it, you turn on the weather forecast. Seeing loads of sunshine symbols all over the map, you decide to take a chance.

Basing your expectations in this way on current information (including even seeing whether there is a red sky that night) is an example of *rational* expectations.

So you go on your picnic and, guess what, it rains! 'I bet if we had decided to stay at home, it would have been fine', you grumble, as you eat your soggy sandwiches.

What you are acknowledging is that your decision was made on *imperfect* information. But the decision was still rational. It was still the best decision you could have made on the information available to you.

Weather forecasters make mistakes. But they are just as likely to get it wrong in predicting a sunny day as in predicting a wet day. It is still rational to base your decisions on their forecasts provided they are reasonably accurate.

Under what circumstances might weather forecasters have a tendency to err on the side of pessimism or optimism? If you knew this tendency, how would this affect your decisions about picnics, hanging out the washing or watering the garden?

The labour market

Let us assume that the government raises aggregate demand more than people expect, so that people underpredict the rate of inflation: $\pi^e < \pi$.

This means that workers will believe that they are getting a higher real wage (W/P) than they really are: $(W/P)^e > W/P$. They will supply more labour. In Figure 20.19, the labour supply curve shifts from AS_{L_1} to AS_{L_2}. Employment rises above the natural level Q_1 (where expectations are correct), to Q_2. If only labour (and not firms) underpredict the rate of inflation, this rise in employment to Q_2 is the only short-run effect.

If, however, firms underpredict the rate of inflation too, the effect on employment will be more complicated. On the one level, as explained above, firms will want to produce more, and thus the demand for labour will tend to increase. For example, it might shift to AD_{L_2} in Figure 20.19, and thus employment would rise to Q_3. On the other hand, given that they are underpredicting the rate of inflation, they will believe that any given level of money wages (W) represents a higher level of *real* wages $(W/P)^e$ than it really does (W/P). They will tend, therefore, to employ fewer people at each wage rate, and the demand curve will shift to the left. Thus, depending on which way the demand curve shifts, firms could employ more or less labour than Q_2.

If people *over*predict the rate of inflation, employment will fall as workers believe that their real wage is lower than it really is and therefore work less; and output may well fall as firms believe their product's relative price has fallen.

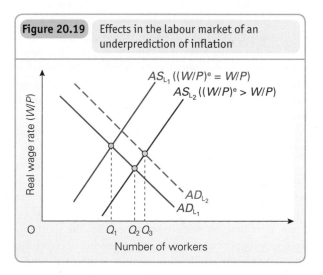

Figure 20.19   Effects in the labour market of an underprediction of inflation

Thus output and employment can vary from their natural level when people make errors in their predictions of inflation. But the short-run *AS* and Phillips curves will still be vertical because these errors are random. Errors in prediction simply shift the curves. This is shown in Figure 20.20. Underprediction of inflation shifts the short-run Phillips curve to the left (and the *AS* curve to the right) as unemployment temporarily falls below the natural rate (and output rises above its natural level). Overprediction of inflation shifts the Phillips curve to the right (and the *AS* curve to the left). The average position for the short-run Phillips curve will be at U_n.

Figure 20.20 Short-run Phillips curves

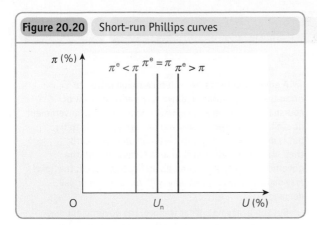

Should the government therefore simply give up as far as curing unemployment is concerned? (For the answer, see below.)

Policy implications

If the new classical 'surprise model' is correct, anticipated changes in aggregate demand will have no effect on output and employment. *Un*anticipated changes in aggregate demand will have some effect, but only for as long as it takes people to realise their mistake and for their wages and prices to be corrected. Given rational expectations, people can be fooled in this way only by luck. There is no way that a government can *systematically* use demand-management policy to keep output and employment above the natural level.

The new classical economists therefore totally reject Keynesian demand-management policy, even in the short run. Monetary policy should be used to control inflation, but neither fiscal nor monetary policy can be used systematically to increase output and employment. Similarly, there is no fear of a deflationary monetary policy reducing output and employment and leading to a recession. The reduction in aggregate demand will simply lead to lower inflation. Output and unemployment will remain at the natural level.

Thus, for new classicists, the problems of inflation and unemployment are totally separate. Inflation is caused by excessive growth in the money supply and should be controlled by monetary policy. Unemployment will be at the natural rate and should be reduced by supply-side policies designed to increase the incentives to work.

To prevent unanticipated changes in aggregate demand and thus to prevent unemployment deviating from its natural level, new classical economists advocate the announcement of clear monetary rules and then sticking to them. The delegation of monetary policy to independent central banks with clear remits, such as inflation rate targets, can form part of this approach.

1. *If the government announced that it would, come what may, reduce the growth of money supply to zero next year, what (according to new classical economists) would happen? How might their answer be criticised?*

2. *For what reasons would a new classical economist support the policy of the Bank of England publishing its inflation forecasts and the minutes of the deliberations of the Monetary Policy Committee?*

Real business cycles

As we saw in section 16.5 (page 479), a problem for new classical 'surprise models' is explaining the extent of economic volatility. If unemployment and output fluctuate only *randomly* from the natural level, and then only in the short run, how can we explain the frequency and magnitude of booms and recessions?

Unlike traditional Keynesian analysis, the focus of new classical *real business cycle theory* lies not in fluctuations in aggregate demand, but rather in shifts in aggregate *supply*. In a recession, the vertical short- and long-run aggregate supply curves will shift to the left (output falls) and the vertical short- and long-run Phillips curves will shift to the right (unemployment rises). The reverse happens in a boom.

The initial shifts in aggregate supply are caused by 'impulses'. An impulse could come from a structural change: say, a shift in demand from older manufacturing industries to new service industries. Because of the immobility of labour, not all those laid off in the older industries will find work in the new industries. Structural unemployment (part of equilibrium unemployment) rises and output falls.

Alternatively, the impulse could be a change in technology. For example, a technological breakthrough in telecommunications could shift aggregate supply to the right. Or it could come from an oil price increase, shifting aggregate supply to the left.

The persistence of supply-side effects

Real business cycle theory stresses that the effects of impulses on the economy persist. There are two main reasons. The first is that several changes may take months to complete. For example, a decline in demand for certain older industries, perhaps caused by growing competition from abroad, does not take place overnight. Likewise, a technological breakthrough does not affect all industries simultaneously.

The second reason is that these changes affect the profitability of investment. If investment rises, this will increase firms' capacity and aggregate supply will shift to the right. If investment falls, aggregate supply will shift to the left. In other words, investment is causing changes in output not through its effect on aggregate *demand* (through the multiplier), but rather through its effect on aggregate *supply*.

Turning points

So far we have seen how the theory of real business cycles explains persistent rises or falls in aggregate supply. But how does it explain *turning points*? Why do recessions and booms come to an end? The most likely explanation is that once a shock has worked its way through, aggregate supply will stop shifting. If there is then any shock in the other

---

BOX 20.7 | **THE BOY WHO CRIED 'WOLF'**

A government had better mean what it says

Do you remember the parable of the boy who cried 'Wolf!'?

There was once this little village on the edge of the forest. The villagers used to keep chickens, but, when no one was around, wolves would come out of the forest and carry off the chickens. So one of the boys in the village was given the job of keeping a lookout for wolves.

One day for a joke the boy called out 'Wolf, wolf! I see a wolf!' even though there was none. All the villagers came rushing out of their houses or back from the fields to catch the wolf. As you might expect, they were very angry to find that it was a false alarm.

The next day, thinking that this was great fun, the boy played the same trick again. Everyone came rushing out, and they were even more angry to find that they had been fooled again. But the boy just grinned.

The next day, when everyone was away in the fields, a wolf stalked into the village. The boy, spotting the animal, cried out 'Wolf, wolf! I see a wolf!' But the people in the fields said to each other 'We're not going to be fooled this time. We've had enough of his practical jokes.' And so they carried on working. Meanwhile, back in the village, the wolf was killing all the chickens.

You can probably guess what the villagers said when they returned in the evening to find just a large pile of feathers.

A government says 'We will take tough action to bring the rate of inflation down to 2 per cent.' Now of course this might be a 'joke' in the sense that the government doesn't really expect to succeed or even seriously to try, but is merely attempting to persuade unions to curb their wage demands. But if unions *believe* in both the government's intentions and its ability to succeed, the 'joke' may pay off. Some unions may well moderate their pay demands.

But some may not. What is more, the government may decide to give tax cuts to boost its popularity and stimulate growth, knowing that union pay demands are generally quite moderate. As a result, inflation soars.

But can the government get away with it a second or third time? It's like the boy who cried 'Wolf!' After a time, people will simply not believe the government. If they see the government boosting aggregate demand, they will say to themselves, 'Here comes inflation. We'd better demand higher wages to compensate.'

Does this parable support the adaptive or the rational expectations hypothesis?

---

direction, aggregate supply will start moving back again. For example, after a period of recession, an eventual rise in business confidence will cause investment to rise and hence aggregate supply to shift back to the right. Since these 'reverse shocks' are likely to occur at irregular intervals, they can help to explain why real-world business cycles are themselves irregular.

Assume that there are two shocks. The first causes aggregate supply to shift to the left. The second, occurring several months later, has the opposite effect on aggregate supply. Show that if both these effects persist for some time, but gradually fade away, the economy will experience a recession that will bottom out and be followed in smooth succession by a recovery.

Section summary

1. New classical theories assume continuous market clearing with flexible prices and wages in the short run as well as in the long run. It also assumes that people base their expectations of inflation on a rational assessment of the *current* situation.

2. People may predict wrongly, but they are equally likely to underpredict as to overpredict. On average, over the years, they will predict correctly.

3. The assumptions of continuous market clearing and rational expectations imply that not only the long-run but also the short-run *AS* and Phillips curves will be vertical. If people correctly predict the rate of inflation, they will correctly predict that any increase in nominal aggregate demand will simply be reflected in higher prices. Total output and employment will remain the same: at the natural level.

4. If people underpredict the rate of inflation, they will believe that there has been a *real* increase in aggregate demand, and thus output and employment will increase. But they are just as likely to overpredict the rate of inflation, in which case they will believe that real aggregate demand has fallen. The result is that output and employment will fall.

5. When the government adopts fiscal and monetary policies, people will rationally predict their effects. Given that people's predictions are equally likely to err on either side, fiscal and monetary policies are useless as means of controlling output and employment.

6. With a vertical aggregate supply curve, cyclical fluctuations must arise from shifts in aggregate supply, not shifts in aggregate demand. Real business cycle theory thus focuses on aggregate supply shocks, which then persist for a period of time. Eventually their effect will peter out, and supply shocks in the other direction can lead to turning points in the cycle.

20.4 INFLATION AND UNEMPLOYMENT: THE MODERN KEYNESIAN POSITION

Keynesians in the 1950s and early 1960s looked to aggregate demand to explain inflation and unemployment. Their approach was typically that of the inflationary/deflationary gap model (see pages 513–14). Although they recognised the existence of some cost-push inflation and some equilibrium unemployment, these factors were seen as relatively constant. As a result, there was thought to be a relatively stable inverse relationship between inflation and unemployment, as depicted by the Phillips curve. Governments could trade off inflation against unemployment by manipulating aggregate demand.

Modern developments of the Keynesian model

Keynesians still see aggregate demand as playing the crucial role in determining the level of inflation, output and employment. They still argue that the free market works inefficiently: it frequently fails to clear; price signals are distorted by economic power; most wages and many prices are 'sticky'; and, most important, the free market is unlikely to settle at full employment.

They still argue, therefore, that it is vital for governments to intervene actively to prevent either a slump in demand or an overexpansion of demand.

Nevertheless the Keynesian position has undergone some major modifications in recent years (see section 16.6). This has been in response to apparent shifts in the Phillips curve and the inability of the traditional Keynesian model to explain it.

The breakdown of the Phillips curve in the 1970s and the growing problem of 'stagflation' (see page 605) led many Keynesians to focus on cost-push causes of inflation. These causes included increased power and militancy of trade unions, a growing concentration of monopoly power in industry, and rising oil and other commodity prices. The effect was to push the short-run Phillips curve outwards.

Later, with a decline in industrial unrest in the 1990s and a growth of international competition keeping prices down, the Phillips curve apparently shifted inwards again. Keynesians attributed this partly to a *decline* in cost-push inflation. (These cost-push explanations are examined in Case Study 20.4 in MyEconLab.)

More recently, Keynesian analysis has incorporated three major modifications:

- An increased importance attached to equilibrium unemployment.
- A rationale for the persistence of demand-deficient unemployment.
- The incorporation of the theory of expectations: either adaptive or rational.

Changes in equilibrium unemployment

Changes in structural unemployment

Most Keynesians include growth in equilibrium unemployment (NAIRU) as part of the explanation of the apparent rightward shift in the Phillips curve in the 1970s and 1980s. In particular, Keynesians highlight the considerable structural rigidities that existed in the economy in a period of rapid industrial change. The changes include the following:

- Dramatic changes in technology. The microchip revolution, for example, made many traditional jobs obsolete.
- Competition from abroad. The introduction of new products from abroad, often of superior quality to domestic goods, or produced at lower costs, had led to the decline of many older industries (e.g. the textile industry).
- Shifts in demand away from the products of older labour-intensive industries to new 'high-tech' capital-intensive products.

Keynesians argue that the free market simply could not cope with these changes without a large rise in structural/technological unemployment. Labour was not sufficiently mobile – either geographically or occupationally – to move to areas where there were labour shortages or into jobs where there were skill shortages. A particular problem here was the lack of investment in education and training, with the result that the labour force was not sufficiently flexible to respond to changes in demand for labour.

1. *What effect did these developments have on (a) the Phillips curve; (b) the aggregate supply curve?*
2. *What policy implications follow from these arguments?*

From the mid-1980s up to the financial crisis of the late 2000s, structural unemployment was thought to have fallen as labour markets become more flexible and as various government supply-side policies took effect (see Chapter 23).

Hysteresis

If a recession causes a rise in unemployment which is not then fully reversed when the economy recovers, there is a problem of hysteresis (see page 483). Recessions can lead to a growing number of people becoming both deskilled and demotivated. What is more, many firms, in an attempt to cut costs, cut down on training programmes. In these circumstances, a rise in aggregate demand would not simply enable the long-term unemployed to be employed again. The effect is a rightward shift in the Phillips curve: a rise in the NAIRU. To reverse this, argue Keynesians, the government should embark on a radical programme of retraining.

Recessions also cause a lack of investment. The reduction in their capital stock means that many firms cannot respond to a recovery in demand by making significant increases in output and taking on many more workers. Instead they are more likely to raise prices. Unemployment may thus fall only modestly and yet inflation may rise substantially. The NAIRU increases: the Phillips curve shifts to the right.

These arguments hold in reverse. A period of sustained growth can reduce the NAIRU: the Phillips curve shifts to the left.

The persistence of demand-deficient unemployment

If there is demand-deficient unemployment, why may there not be a long-run fall in real wage rates so as to eliminate the surplus labour? Keynesians give two major explanations for the persistence of real wage rates above equilibrium:

- *Efficiency wages*. Wage rates work not only to balance the demand and supply of labour but also to motivate workers. If real wage rates are reduced when there is a surplus of labour (demand-deficient unemployment), then those workers already in employment may become dispirited and work less hard. If, on the other hand, firms keep wage rates up, then by maintaining a well-motivated workforce, by cutting down on labour turnover and by finding it easier to attract well-qualified labour, firms may find that their costs are reduced: a higher real wage rate is thus more profitable for them. The maximum-profit real wage rate (the *efficiency wage rate*: see pages 259–62) is likely to be above the market-clearing real wage rate. Demand-deficient unemployment is likely to persist.

- *Insider power*. If those still in employment (the insiders) are members of unions while those out of work (the outsiders) are not, or if the insiders have special skills or knowledge that give them bargaining power with employers while the outsiders have no influence, then there is no mechanism whereby the surplus labour – the outsiders – can drive down the real wage rate and eliminate the demand-deficient unemployment.

These two features help to explain why real wage rates did not fall during the recessions of the early 1980s and early 1990s. With the more flexible labour markets of more recent years, however, real wages did fall consistently in the period following the financial crisis (see Figure 15.12). Over the period 2009–12, the annual rate of consumer price inflation typically exceeded annual earnings growth by 1.6 percentage points.

The incorporation of expectations

Some Keynesians incorporate adaptive expectations into their models. Others incorporate rational expectations. Either way, their models differ from new classical models in two important respects:

- Prices and wages are not perfectly flexible. Markets are characterised by various frictions and imperfections.

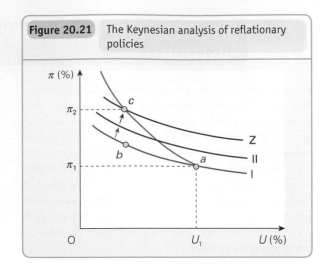

Figure 20.21 The Keynesian analysis of reflationary policies

- Expectations influence *output* and *employment* decisions, not just pricing decisions.

Price and wage rigidities are likely to be greater *downwards* than upwards. It is thus necessary to separate the analysis of a decrease in aggregate demand from that of an increase.

Expansion of aggregate demand

Unless the economy is at full employment or very close to it, Keynesians argue that an expansion of demand *will* lead to an increase in output and employment, even in the long run after expectations have fully adjusted.

In Figure 20.21, assume that the economy has a fairly high level of unemployment (U_1) but at the same time some cost inflation. Inflation is constant at π_1, with expectations of inflation at π_1 also. The economy is at point *a*.

Now assume that the economy begins to recover. Aggregate demand rises. As there is plenty of slack in the economy, output can rise and unemployment fall. The economy moves to point *b* on short-run Phillips curve I. The rise in inflation will feed through into expectations. The short-run Phillips curve will shift upwards. With adaptive expectations, it will initially shift up, say, to curve II.

But will the short-run Phillips curve not go on shifting upwards as long as there is any upward pressure on inflation? Keynesians reject this argument for two reasons:

- If there is a gradual but sustained expansion of aggregate demand, firms, seeing the economy expanding and seeing their orders growing, will start to invest more and make longer-term plans for expanding their labour force. People will generally *expect* a higher level of output, and this optimism will cause that higher level of output to be produced. In other words, expectations will affect output and employment as well as prices. The Phillips curve will shift downwards to the left, offsetting (partially, wholly or more than wholly) the upward shift from higher inflationary expectations. The NAIRU has fallen.

■ If U_1 includes a considerable number of long-term unemployed, then the expansion of demand may be *initially* inflationary, since many of the newly employed will require some retraining (a costly exercise). But as these newly employed workers become more productive, their lower labour costs may offset any further upward pressure on wages from the expansion of demand. At the same time, the higher investment may embody new, more productive, techniques that will also help to prevent further acceleration in costs. These factors occurred in the 1990s as the economy recovered from recession.

It is quite likely that these effects can prevent any further rises in inflation. Inflation can become stable at, say, π_2, with the economy operating at point *c*. The short-run Phillips curve settles at position Z. There is thus a long-run downward-sloping Phillips curve passing through points *a* and *c*. What this analysis is assuming is that, in the medium to long run, the NAIRU itself is responsive to changes in real aggregate demand.

 Would it in theory be possible for this long-run Phillips curve to be horizontal or even upward sloping over part of its length?

If expectations are formed rationally rather than adaptively, there will merely be a quicker movement to this long-run equilibrium. If people rationally predict that the effect of government policy will be to move the economy to point *c*, then their predictions will bring this about. All rational expectations do is to bring the long run about much sooner! The theory of rational expectations on its own does not provide support specifically for either the new classical or the Keynesian position.

The lesson here for governments, however expectations are formed, is that a sustained, but moderate, increase in aggregate demand can lead to a sustained growth in aggregate supply. What should be avoided is an excessive and unsustainable expansion of aggregate demand, as occurred in the late 1980s in the UK and in the late 1990s in the USA. This will lead to a boom, only to be followed by a 'bust' and a consequent recession.

Contraction of aggregate demand

Many Keynesians argue that the short-run Phillips curve is kinked at the current level of real aggregate demand. A reduction in real aggregate demand will have only a slight effect on inflation, since real wages are sticky downwards. Unions may well prefer to negotiate a reduction in employment levels, preferably by natural wastage (i.e. not replacing people when they leave), rather than accept a reduction in real wages. Thus in Figure 20.22, to the right of point *a*, the short-run Phillips curve is very shallow.

As long as this curve is not totally horizontal to the right of *a*, the introduction of expectations into the analysis will cause the short-run curve to shift downwards over time (if unemployment is kept above U_1) as people come to expect a lower rate of inflation.

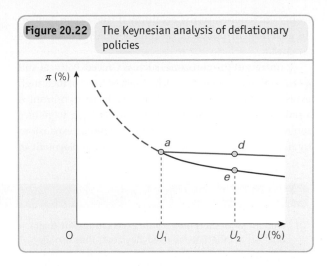

Figure 20.22   The Keynesian analysis of deflationary policies

With *adaptive* expectations, however, the curve could shift downwards very slowly indeed. If a movement from point *a* to point *d* represents only a 1 per cent reduction in inflation, and if it takes, say, two years for this to be fully reflected in expectations, then if unemployment is kept at U_2, inflation will reduce (i.e. the curve shifts downwards) by only 0.5 per cent a year. This may be totally unacceptable politically if inflation is already at very high levels, and if U_2 is also very high.

Even with *rational* expectations the response may be too slow. If there is a resistance from unions to receiving increases in wages below the current rate of inflation, or if they are attempting to 'catch up' with other workers, then even if they rationally predict the correct amount by which inflation will fall, inflation will fall only slowly. People will rationally predict the *resistance* to wage restraint, and sure enough, therefore, inflation will fall only slowly.

The worst scenario is when the government, in its attempt to eliminate inflation, keeps unemployment high for a number of years. As the core of long-term unemployed workers grows, an increasing number of workers become deskilled and therefore effectively unemployable. The effective labour supply is reduced, and firms find there is no longer a surplus of employable labour *despite* high unemployment. The NAIRU increases. A long-term equilibrium is reached at, say, point *e* with still substantial inflation. The *long*-run Phillips curve too may thus be relatively shallow to the right of point *a*.

As we saw earlier, the downward stickiness of wages was significantly less in the recession of 2008–9. This gave a steeper Phillips curve to the right of point *a* than in previous recessions.

The Keynesian criticism of non-intervention

Keynesians are therefore highly critical of the new classical conclusion that governments should not intervene other than to restrain the growth of money supply. High unemployment may persist for many years and become deeply entrenched in the economy if there is no deliberate government policy of creating a steady expansion of demand.

Countries in the eurozone, such as Greece, Portugal and Spain, which have had to seek bailouts because of their high levels of debt, have found themselves in this position. A condition of being granted bailouts has been to reduce public-sector debt. This has ruled out Keynesian expansionary fiscal policy. The very high levels of unemployment in these countries, especially amongst the young (rates of over 50 per cent in Greece and Spain in the 15–24 age group), have resulted in a problem of entrenchment and hysteresis that will make reductions in unemployment slow and difficult to achieve.

 Why is it important in the Keynesian analysis for there to be a steady expansion of demand?

Section summary

1. Modern Keynesians incorporate expectations into their analysis of inflation and unemployment. They also see an important role for cost-push factors and changes in equilibrium unemployment in explaining the position of the Phillips curve.

2. A growth in equilibrium unemployment in the 1970s and 1980s was caused by rapid changes in technology, greater competition from abroad and more rapid changes in demand patterns. It was also due to the persistence of unemployment beyond the recessions of the early 1980s and early 1990s and, to a lesser extent, the early 2010s, because of a deskilling of labour during the recessions (an example of hysteresis). The effect of increased equilibrium unemployment was to shift the Phillips curve to the right.

3. Demand-deficient unemployment may persist because real wage rates may be sticky downwards, even into the longer term. This stickiness may be the result of efficiency real wage rates being above market-clearing real wage rates and/or outsiders not being able to influence wage bargains struck between employers and insiders.

4. If expectations are incorporated into Keynesian analysis, the Phillips curve will become steeper in the long run (and steeper in the short run too in the case of rational expectations). It will not become vertical, however, since people will expect changes in aggregate demand to affect output and employment as well as prices.

5. If people expect a more rapid rise in aggregate demand to be sustained, firms will invest more, thereby reducing unemployment in the long run and not just increasing the rate of inflation. The NAIRU will fall. The long-run Phillips curve will be downward sloping.

6. The short- and long-run Phillips curves may be kinked. Reductions in real aggregate demand may have only a slight effect on inflation if real wage rates are sticky downwards.

*20.5 OUTPUT, INFLATION AND EXPECTATIONS: AN INTEGRATED MODEL

This chapter has examined alternative views on the relationships between output, unemployment and inflation. In many countries, it is important to understand these relationships in the context of central bankers with pre-defined macroeconomic objectives. Many central banks around the world target the inflation rate. This objective is often supplemented with a requirement that the central bank be mindful of the implications of its monetary policy for other macroeconomic variables, such as growth or employment.

We will look at variations in actual mandates set for central banks in Chapter 21, including the Federal Reserve, the European Central Bank and the Bank of England.

An integrated model

Here we are going to integrate the two models of the goods and money markets from sections 19.3 and 19.4, namely the *IS/MP* model and the *ADI/ASI* model.[1] We shall also introduce the role of expectations.

We will assume, as in Chapter 19, that the central bank sets interest rates to meet its macroeconomic objectives, which have been set for it by government. In the simplest version of the model, the central bank is required to meet an

---

[1] In some articles, economists refer to either the *ADI* curve or the *MP* curve as a monetary rule (*MR*) curve, as each is constructed on the basis that the central bank follows some particular monetary rule. It avoids confusion if the separate labels *ADI* and *MP* are used to distinguish the two curves. Also some economists refer to the *ASI* curve as a Phillips curve. This too is confusing, as although, as we shall see below, the *ASI* curve is based on the same analysis as the Phillips curve (*PC*), the Phillips curve normally refers to the relationship between *unemployment* and inflation, not *real national income* and inflation. It makes more sense, therefore, to refer to the *ASI* curve when looking at the relationship between real national income and inflation. When, therefore, some economists refer to an *IS–PC–MR* model, this is the integrated model we are developing here.

inflation rate target for the next period. It is not difficult, however, to introduce a more complex target which includes national income or unemployment.

We will make the new Keynesian assumption that there are market imperfections and frictions, such as contracts for prices and wages. As a result, wages and prices exhibit a degree of stickiness. This will be reinforced by the extent to which expectations of inflation are determined by past inflation rates.

Combining the IS/MP and ADI/ASI models

The short-run *ASI* curve, which we examined in section 19.4, is very similar to the Phillips curve, only instead of plotting unemployment on the horizontal axis, which gives a downward-sloping short-run curve, we plot real national income, which gives an upward-sloping curve. The short-run *ASI* curve, as is the short-run Phillips curve, is based on the assumption of constant inflationary expectations. The short-run *ASI* curve is shown in the bottom part of Figure 20.23. It is assumed to get steeper, the further national income is above potential national income, as firms find it increasingly difficult to respond to an increase in demand by raising output and, instead, raise prices.

Assume initially that the economy is in long-run equilibrium, with real national income at the potential level (Y_p) and inflation at the target rate (π^*). This is shown as point *a* in the lower diagram. In the upper diagram, the economy is at point *a'*: the central bank sets a real rate of interest of i_1.

Now assume that there is a rise in aggregate demand – from, say, a rise in real government expenditure. The *ADI* and *IS* curves shift to the right, to ADI_2 and IS_2 respectively. The rise in aggregate demand causes a rise in real national income, but also a rise in inflation. This is shown by a movement upwards along the short-run *ASI* curve (which corresponds to movement upwards along the traditional short-run Phillips curve). The new short-run equilibrium is at point *b*.

In response to the higher rate of inflation of π_2, the central bank raises the nominal rate of interest more than the rise in inflation, thereby raising the *real* rate of interest (*i*). There is a movement upwards along the short-run *MP* curve in the top part of the diagram. The new short-run equilibrium is reached at point *b'* with real interest rate of i_2.

But, as we saw on pages 582–4 and in Figure 19.16, equilibrium at point *b* gives an inflation rate (π_2) which is above the target rate of inflation (π^*). If the central bank is to return the economy to point *a*, with inflation on target and real national income at the potential level, it must shift the *ADI* curve back again. It does this by adopting a tighter monetary policy (i.e. a higher real interest rate for each rate of inflation). It thus raises the real interest rate above i_2, initially to i_3 as shown in the top part of Figure 20.24. In other words, the *MP* curve will shift upwards to MP_2.

The effect of the tighter monetary policy will be to shift the ADI_2 curve back towards ADI_1 and equilibrium will be restored at point *a*. In other words, the expansionary fiscal policy is being offset by a tighter monetary policy, the net effect being neutral on both real national income and inflation. In the top diagram, the tighter monetary policy is represented by a movement up *along* curve IS_2 to point *c'* (as the higher interest rate is shown on the vertical axis).

But once we introduce expectations, the effect is slightly different.

 How will the composition of aggregate demand at points a' and c' in the top half of Figure 20.24 differ?

Figure 20.23 Combining the *IS/MP* and *ADI/ASI* models

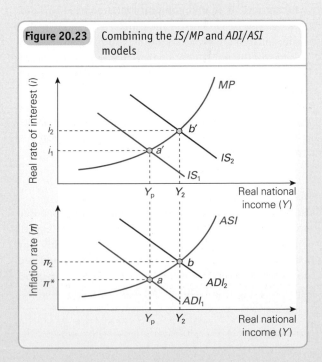

Figure 20.24 Effect of an increase in real aggregate demand in the *IS/MP* and *ADI/ASI* models

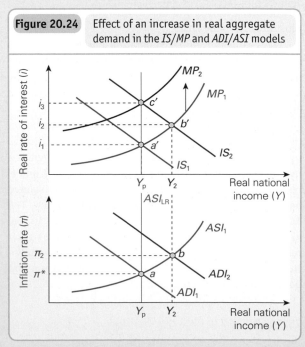

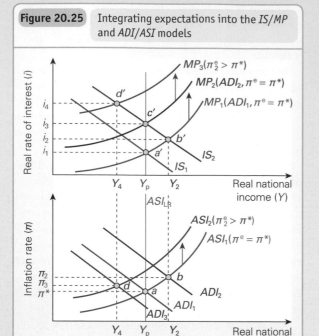

Figure 20.25   Integrating expectations into the *IS/MP* and *ADI/ASI* models

But, as we have seen, the *ASI* and *MP* curves are based on a particular expected rate of inflation (π^e). In the case of ASI_1 and MP_1 and now MP_2, the expected rate is the target rate ($\pi^e = \pi^*$). But with inflation having risen, people in the next time period adjust their expectations upwards, which, in turn, drives up the actual rate of inflation. This causes an upward shift in the *ASI* and *MP* curves, say to ASI_2 and MP_3.

Assume, as before, that the tighter monetary policy (as in MP_2) has moved the *ADI* curve back to ADI_1. However, with the new higher *ASI* curve (ASI_2), the effect of the even tighter monetary policy (as shown in curve MP_3) will bring a short-run equilibrium at point d' in the upper diagram. This even tighter monetary policy will shift the *ADI* curve further to the left, say to ADI_3, giving equilibrium at point d.

Real national income is now below Y_p. Inflation will fall (in this case to π_3), and expected inflation will then fall too. The *ASI* and *MP* curves will shift downwards again; monetary policy will be eased and the *ADI* curve will shift back to the right. Equilibrium will be restored at points a and a' with real national income at the potential level.

If the government through its fiscal policy now attempts to achieve real national income above Y_p (a positive output gap) for a longer period of time, then, assuming no change in Y_p, the *ASI* and *MP* curves will continue shifting upwards and inflation will accelerate. If, eventually, the government uses fiscal policy to reverse this process, there may have to be a substantial period of time where real national income is kept below Y_p in order to bring inflationary expectations back down. What we would be tracing out here is an anti-clockwise loop, mirroring the clockwise Phillips loops that we examined on page 605.

The quicker expectations adjust, the quicker the economy will return to its equilibrium position at point a. This process can also be hastened if the central bank, anticipating rising inflationary expectations, acts to dampen these by raising real interest rates more than that implied by the *MP* curve. This could be represented by a steeper *MP* curve and hence *ASI* curve.

Incorporating expectations

Each short-run *ASI* curve and each short-run *MP* curve are based on a given expected rate of inflation, which will directly impact on the actual rate of inflation. Because it is assumed that there is a lag in the adjustment of expectations, whether because of adaptive expectations or market imperfections, there can be a movement along a given *ASI* or *MP* curve in the short run. But what happens in the next time period when expectations adjust? The answer is that both short-run curves shift upwards if the expected rate of inflation rises, and shift downwards if it falls. This is illustrated in Figure 20.25.

Again we assume initial equilibrium at the potential level of real national income (Y_p), with inflation on target and no upward pressure on inflation. Thus expected inflation is the actual (targeted) inflation ($\pi^e = \pi^*$). Equilibrium is at points a and a' in the lower and upper diagrams respectively.

Now, as before, assume a rise in real government expenditure. This rise in aggregate demand shifts the *ADI* curve to ADI_2 and the *IS* curve to IS_2. In the short run there is a movement along the ASI_1 and MP_1 curves to point b and b' respectively. But, with Y_2 above Y_p, this cannot be sustained and the central bank tightens its monetary policy. The *MP* curve shifts to MP_2 and the central bank raises its real interest rate to i_3. With no effect on expectations, the tighter monetary policy will shift the *ADI* back again and equilibrium will be restored at point a in the lower diagram and point c' in the upper one.

 If expectations were formed rationally with no time lags, what would be the implications for short-run ASI curves and for the response to a rise in aggregate demand?

Assumptions about potential national income

Keynesians argue that potential national income depends to some extent on aggregate demand. If the economy experiences high aggregate demand and high output, this may encourage investment, both domestic and inward, and lead to an expansion of capacity and hence in potential national income. A rightward shift in the *ADI* curve may thus also result in a rightward shift in both the short-run and vertical long-run *ASI* curves.

If the increase in potential national income also corresponds to a lower natural rate of unemployment or lower NAIRU, the vertical long-run Phillips curve will also shift to the left.

Under what circumstances would a rise in potential real income not result in a fall in the NAIRU?

Alternative central bank remits

Instead of targeting just the rate of inflation, the central bank may also target a level of real national income, a rate of economic growth or a rate of unemployment.

Assume, for example, that the central bank targets the rate of economic *growth* as well as inflation. If real income and inflation rise (a movement along the *ASI* curve), the central bank will raise interest rates less than with a pure inflation target in order not to dampen growth too much. In other words, it will tolerate higher inflation in return for higher real income. This will make the *MP* curve flatter. The greater the weighting attached to economic growth, the flatter the *MP* curve will be.

If, however, the central bank gave a greater weighting to targeting the *level* of income *at* the potential level, this would make the *MP* curve *steeper*. Any movement away from Y_p would lead to a bigger adjustment in the real rate of interest (*i*) in the attempt not to allow national income to deviate from Y_p.

Analysis of the 2008–9 banking crisis and the subsequent recession and slow recovery

The *ADI/ASI* and *IS/MP* models can be used to show what happened in the period following the banking crisis. For simplicity, we focus on just the *IS/MP* model. Conventional monetary policy seemed powerless to bring economies out of recession. Nominal interest rates (*r*) were cut to virtually zero in most countries. But this was not enough to provide a sufficient boost to demand and central banks were unwilling to cut nominal rates below zero. Since real interest rates (*i*) equal the nominal rate minus inflation ($i = r - \pi$), this meant that real central bank interest rates were negative. This is illustrated in Figure 20.26.

Assume, before the financial crisis, that the economy was in equilibrium at point *a*, with national income at its potential level of Y_p and a real rate of interest of i_1. Then, with the financial crisis that led to a massive reduction in credit and a collapse in consumer and business confidence and a desire to cut spending in order to rebuild economic worth, aggregate demand fell massively (a 'Minsky moment'

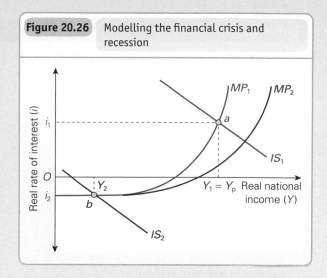

Figure 20.26 Modelling the financial crisis and recession

– see Box 18.6 on page 550). This is illustrated by the shift in the *IS* curve to IS_2. Central banks cut nominal interest rates to near zero, giving negative real interest rates (*i*). Equilibrium national income fell to Y_2.

But what could central banks do next? A relaxing of conventional monetary policy would shift the *MP* curve to the right. This is illustrated as the move to MP_2. But this would have no effect on real national income as nominal rates could fall no further.

In fact, as inflation gradually fell, the problem got worse. The fall in inflation gradually closed the gap between real and nominal interest rates, causing the *MP* curve to shift upwards, thereby leading to an intersection with the *IS* curve even further to the left.

At the same time as central banks and savings accounts were paying interest rates close to zero, borrowing rates, although lower than before, did not fall so much. The gap between borrowing and saving rates had widened, thereby further dampening demand (see Box 19.5 on page 580) and causing the *IS* curve to be further to the left than it would otherwise have been.

In terms of interest rates, all central banks could do was to attempt to reduce the risks of banks by acting as lender of last resort (see page 541) and providing as much liquidity as necessary to get interbank markets moving again. One hope of this was that this would narrow the gap between borrowing and lending rates: in other words, it would reduce borrowing rates at i_2 in Figure 20.26 and thereby stimulate aggregate demand.

To supplement such policies, central banks engaged in policies of massively expanding money supply through a process known as quantitative easing. We examine this in section 21.2.

Section summary

1. Many central banks today are tasked with using monetary policy to help deliver pre-defined macroeconomic objectives. This frequently involves targeting inflation. Therefore, by combining the *ADI/ASI* and *IS/MP* models it is possible to analyse the relationships between output, unemployment and inflation in a contemporary monetary policy-making context. The combined frameworks can be used to plot both the path of the economy and the monetary policy responses resulting from changes in the macroeconomic environment.

2. If aggregate demand rises, both the *ADI* and *IS* curves shift to the right. This is mirrored by movements up the *ASI* and *MP* curves respectively (as in Figure 20.23). In response to higher inflation the central bank raises the nominal interest rate by more than inflation, causing the real interest rate to rise. Assuming that output is now above its potential level and that the rate of inflation has risen above its target level, the central bank will need to respond further by adopting a tighter monetary policy.

3. If inflationary expectations remain unchanged, the path of the economy is represented by a leftward shift of the *ADI* curve along the *ASI* curve so that output is again at its potential level. The tighter monetary policy is captured by a vertical upward shift of the *MP* curve (a higher real interest rate at each level of national income) along the new *IS* curve. It acts to offset the initial increase in real aggregate demand.

4. When we incorporate inflationary expectations into the analysis, the response of the monetary authorities and the path of the economy to its long-run equilibrium are affected. If an increase in inflation leads people to raise their expectations of inflation, there will be an upward shift of the *ASI* curve and a larger upward shift of the *MP* curve than if expectations remain unchanged. This could mean output falling below its potential level and inflation falling below its target, until monetary policy is subsequently relaxed.

5. The combined framework can be used to illustrate the banking crisis of the late 2000s. The extent of the contraction in aggregate demand (leftward shifts of *ADI* and *IS* curves) meant that central banks cut interest rates close to zero. The leftward shift of the *IS* curve was amplified by savings rates falling more than borrowing rates. Consequently, in the *IS/MP* framework, equilibrium output lay in the flat region of the *MP* curve. Central banks responded by providing substantial amounts of liquidity and, in some cases, by engaging in quantitative easing.

20.6 POSTSCRIPT: THE STATE OF MACROECONOMIC THINKING POST-CRISIS

Areas of general agreement

Whilst there is some disagreement among economists over the nature of the aggregate supply and Phillips curves, and hence over the effects of changes in aggregate demand, it is important not to get the impression that economists disagree over everything. There is, in fact, quite a lot of common ground among the majority of economists over the issues that we have examined in this chapter.

If you look back to pages 488–90, we identified several areas where there is a high measure of agreement among economists. Let us restate three of these areas in the light of the theories we have covered in this chapter.

In the short run, changes in aggregate demand will have a major effect on output and employment

With the exception of extreme new classical economists, who argue that markets clear instantly and that expectations are formed rationally, all other economists would accept that the short-run *AS* and *ASI* curves are upward sloping, albeit getting steeper as full-capacity output is approached. Similarly, they would argue that the short-run Phillips curve is downward sloping. There are two major implications of this analysis:

TC 13
p418

- Reductions in aggregate demand can cause reductions in output and increases in unemployment. In other words, too little spending will cause a recession. This was the case in 2008–9.

- An expansion of aggregate demand by the government (whether achieved by fiscal or monetary policy, or both) will help to pull an economy out of a recession. There was consensus among most economists and politicians in 2008–9 that this approach was necessary. There may be considerable time lags, however, before the economy responds fully to such expansionary policies. Also if the central bank nominal rate is near zero, there may be little or no scope for further interest rate reductions.

In the long run, changes in aggregate demand will have much less effect on output and employment and much more effect on prices

As we have seen, new classical economists and others argue that both the long-run *AS* and *ASI* curves and the long-run Phillips curve are vertical. Many Keynesian economists, while arguing that these curves are not vertical, would still see them as less elastic than the short-run curves.

One of the problems is in financing any fiscal expansion. Indeed, the rapid rise in government deficits and debt

KI 9
p71

around the world in 2009–10 caused many governments to rein in spending for fear of 'spooking' the markets and increasing the cost of financing the debts. Further expansion of public-sector demand would have crowded out private demand.

Nevertheless, many Keynesians argue that changes in aggregate demand, if steady, will have substantial effects on long-term output and employment via changes in investment and hence in potential output (see Figure 20.5 on page 596).

Expectations have important effects on the economy

In fact, they are crucial in determining the success of government policy on unemployment and inflation. Whatever people expect to happen, their actions will tend to make it happen.

KI 9
p71

If people believe that an expansion of money supply will lead merely to inflation (the monetarist and new classical position), then it will. Firms and workers will adjust their prices and wage rates upwards. Firms will make no plans to expand output and will not take on any more labour. If, however, people believe that an expansion of demand will lead to higher output and employment (the Keynesian position), then, via the accelerator mechanism, it will.

Similarly, just how successful a deflationary policy is in curing inflation depends in large measure on people's expectations (but, as explained above, it also depends on the downward stickiness of real wages). If people believe that a deflationary policy will cause a recession, firms will stop investing and will cut their workforce. If they believe that it will cure inflation and restore firms' competitiveness abroad, firms may increase investment.

To manage the economy successfully, therefore, the government must convince people that its policies will work. This is as much a job of public relations as of pulling the right economic levers.

TC 9
p121

1. *If constant criticism of governments in the media makes people highly cynical about any government's ability to manage the economy, what effect will this have on the performance of the economy?*

2. *Suppose that, as part of the national curriculum, everyone in the country had to study economics up to the age of 16. Suppose also that the reporting of economic events by the media became more thorough (and interesting!). What effects would these developments have on the government's ability to manage the economy? How would your answer differ if you were a Keynesian from if you were a new classicist?*

The causes of longer-term growth

One other area where there is considerable agreement among economists concerns the causes of longer-term growth. Although demand-side policy may be important for ensuring that economies achieve their potential output, only by increasing that potential itself can growth be sustained. To achieve higher rates of economic growth over the long term, therefore, the government should focus on means of getting potential output to grow more rapidly, and this requires an appropriate supply-side policy.

Chapter 22 examines long-term growth and Chapter 23 discusses various types of supply-side policy open to governments.

Soul-searching by economists

Despite these areas of agreement, the financial crisis of 2007–8, and the subsequent recession and painfully slow recovery, took many economists by surprise. There has been considerable debate about economic models and how fit for purpose they are.

Although much of the analytical framework could cope with what had happened, it is now generally agreed that there was too little attention paid to balance sheets, deficits and debt, the drivers of expectations and risk attitudes. We hope that we have sufficiently accounted for them in this edition! We examine these issues further in the next chapter.

We turn now to demand-side policy. As we shall see, there have been considerable changes to the approaches to both fiscal and monetary policies post-crisis.

END OF CHAPTER QUESTIONS

1. Assume that inflation depends on two things: the level of aggregate demand, indicated by the inverse of unemployment ($1/U$), and the expected rate of inflation (π_t^e). Assume that the rate of inflation (π_t) is given by the equation

$$\pi_t = (48/U - 6) + \pi_t^e$$

Assume initially (year 0) that the actual and expected rate of inflation is zero.

(a) What is the current (natural) rate of unemployment?

(b) Now assume in year 1 that the government wishes to reduce unemployment to 4 per cent and continues to expand aggregate demand by as much as is necessary to achieve this. Fill in the rows for years 0 to 4 in the following table. It is assumed for simplicity that the expected rate of inflation in a given year (π_t^e) is equal

▶

to the actual rate of inflation in the previous year (π_{t-1}).

Year	U	48/U – 6	+	π^e	=	π
0	. . .	. . .	+	. . .	=	. . .
1	. . .	. . .	+	. . .	=	. . .
2	. . .	. . .	+	. . .	=	. . .
3	. . .	. . .	+	. . .	=	. . .
4	. . .	. . .	+	. . .	=	. . .
5	. . .	. . .	+	. . .	=	. . .
6	. . .	. . .	+	. . .	=	. . .
7	. . .	. . .	+	. . .	=	. . .

(c) Now assume in year 5 that the government, worried about rising inflation, reduces aggregate demand sufficiently to reduce inflation by 3 per cent in that year. What must the rate of unemployment be raised to in that year?

(d) Assuming that unemployment stays at this high level, continue the table for years 5 to 7.

2. For what reasons might the long-run aggregate supply curve be (a) vertical; (b) upward sloping; (c) downward sloping?

3. How would you attempt to assess whether a particular period of inflation was the result of cost-push or demand-pull pressures?

4. What is the difference between adaptive expectations and rational expectations?

5. How can adaptive expectations of inflation result in clockwise Phillips loops? Why would these loops not be completely regular?

6. What implications would a vertical short-run aggregate supply curve have for the effects of demand-management policy?

7. For what reasons may the NAIRU increase?

8. Given the Keynesian explanation for the persistence of high levels of unemployment after the recessions of the early 1980s and early 1990s, what policies would you advocate to reduce unemployment in the years following a recession?

9. Using the integrated *ADI/ASI* and *IS/MP* framework, analyse the possible impact of a relaxation by banks of their lending criteria when the central bank strictly adheres to an inflation target.

10. Repeat question 9, but now assume that there is a significant contraction of lending by banks.

Online resources

Additional case studies in MyEconLab

20.1 **Explaining the shape of the short-run Phillips curve.** This shows how money illusion on the part of workers can explain why the Phillips curve is downward sloping.

20.2 **The quantity theory of money restated.** An examination of how the vertical long-run *AS* curve in the adaptive expectations model can be used to justify the quantity theory of money.

20.3 **Getting predictions wrong.** How incorrect predictions can lead to a rise or fall in output in the new classical model.

20.4 **Cost-push factors in Keynesian analysis.** How Keynesians incorporated cost-push inflation into their analysis of shifts in the Phillips curve.

Websites relevant to this chapter

See sites listed at the end of Chapter 23 on page 704.

MyEconLab

This book can be supported by MyEconLab, which contains a range of additional resources, including an online homework and tutorial system designed to test and build your understanding.

You need both an access card and a course ID to access MyEconLab:

1. Is your lecturer using MyEconLab? Ask your lecturer for your course ID.

2. Has an access card been included with the book at a reduced cost? Check the inside back cover of the book.

3. If you have a course ID but no access card, go to: http://www.myeconlab.com/ to buy access to this interactive study programme.

Fiscal and Monetary Policy

CHAPTER MAP

21.1 Fiscal policy	**626**
Government finances: some terminology	626
Public-sector deficits and surpluses and the government's 'fiscal stance'	628
Automatic fiscal stabilisers	630
The effectiveness of automatic stabilisers	630
Discretionary fiscal policy	631
The effectiveness of discretionary fiscal policy	632
Problems of magnitude	632
Problems of timing	635
Fiscal rules	636
21.2 Monetary policy	**640**
The policy setting	640
Control of the money supply over the medium and long term	640
The operation of monetary policy in the short term	642
Techniques to control the money supply	642
Changing the method of funding the national debt	645
Difficulties in controlling money supply	645
Techniques to control interest rates	648
Problems with controlling interest rates	652
Using monetary policy	654
21.3 The policy-making environment	**656**
The case for rules	657
The case for discretion	657
Conclusions	664
*Appendix *IS/LM* analysis of fiscal and monetary policy	**665**
The Keynesian position	665
The monetarist/new classical position	666

Both fiscal and monetary policy can be used to control aggregate demand. Excessive growth in aggregate demand can cause unsustainable short-term growth and higher rates of inflation. Too little aggregate demand can result in a recession, with negative growth and rising unemployment.

Fiscal policy seeks to control aggregate demand by altering the balance between government expenditure (an injection into the circular flow of income) and taxation (a withdrawal). Monetary policy seeks to control aggregate demand by directly controlling the money supply or by altering the rate of interest and then backing this up by any necessary change in money supply. A reduction in interest rates will encourage more borrowing and hence raise aggregate demand. A rise in interest rates will dampen aggregate demand.

The first two sections of this chapter examine fiscal and monetary policy in turn: how they work and how effective they are.

We then turn to consider the arguments as to how much discretion or control policy makers should have over fiscal and monetary policy. Should governments adopt fixed targets for policy (e.g. inflation targets) or should they adjust policies according to circumstances? This is a debate reinvigorated by the global financial and economic crisis of the late 2000s.

In the appendix to the chapter we show how *IS/LM* analysis can be used to compare the relative effectiveness of the two policies.

21.1 FISCAL POLICY

Fiscal policy has two possible roles as far as controlling aggregate demand is concerned. The first is to remove any severe deflationary or inflationary gaps. In other words, expansionary fiscal policy could be used to prevent an economy experiencing a severe or prolonged recession, such as that experienced in the Great Depression of the 1930s or in east and south-east Asia, Russia and Brazil in the late 1990s. It has also been used for this purpose in Japan in recent years (see Case Study 21.6 in MyEconLab), and around the world in 2008 when substantial tax cuts and increased government expenditure were used by many countries, including the UK and the USA (see Box 21.1), to combat the onset of recession. Likewise, deflationary fiscal policy could be used to prevent rampant inflation, such as that experienced in the 1970s. To summarise, this first role is to prevent the occurrence of *fundamental* disequilibrium in the economy.

The second role is to smooth out the fluctuations in the economy associated with the business cycle. This involves reducing government expenditure or raising taxes when the economy begins to boom. This will dampen down the expansion and prevent 'overheating' of the economy, with its attendant problems of rising inflation and a deteriorating current account balance of payments. Conversely if a recession looms, the government should cut taxes or raise government expenditure in order to boost the economy. If these stabilisation policies are successful, they will amount merely to 'fine-tuning'. Problems of excess or deficient demand will never be allowed to get severe. Any movement of aggregate demand away from a steady growth path would be quickly 'nipped in the bud'.

Fiscal policy can also be used to influence aggregate *supply*. For example, government can increase its expenditure on infrastructure, or give tax incentives for investment. These supply-side policies are considered in Chapter 23.

Before we look at just how fiscal policy can be used, it is important to understand some of the terminology of government spending and taxation.

Government finances: some terminology

Central government

Central government deficits and surpluses. Since an expansionary fiscal policy involves raising government expenditure and/or lowering taxes, this has the effect of either increasing the **budget deficit** or reducing the **budget surplus**. A budget deficit in any one year is where central government's expenditure (including benefits) exceeds its revenue from taxation. A budget surplus is where tax revenues exceed central government expenditure.

For most of the past 50 years, governments around the world have run budget deficits. In the 1990s and early 2000s, however, many countries, the UK included, made substantial efforts to reduce their budget deficits, and some achieved budget surpluses for periods of time. The position changed dramatically in 2008–9, however, as governments around the world increased their expenditure and cut taxes in an attempt to stave off recession. Government deficits, and hence stocks of government debt, in many countries soared.

To finance a deficit, the government will have to borrow (e.g. through the issue of bonds (gilts) or Treasury bills). As we saw in section 18.3, this will lead to an increase in the money supply to the extent that the borrowing is from the banking sector. The purchase of bonds or Treasury bills by the (non-bank) private sector, however, will not lead to an increase in the money supply.

The national debt. The budget deficit refers to the debt that the government incurs in one year. If the government runs persistent deficits over many years, these debts will accumulate. The accumulated debt is known as the **national debt**. Note that the national debt is *not* the same thing as the country's overseas debt. In the case of the UK, only around 32 per cent of national debt is owed overseas. The remainder is owed to UK residents. In other words, the government finances its budget deficits largely by borrowing at home and not from abroad.

General government

'General government' includes central and local government. Thus we can refer to **general government deficits and surpluses** and **general government debt**. Table 21.1 shows government deficits/surpluses and debt for selected countries. They are expressed as a proportion of GDP.

As you can see, in the period from 1997 to 2007, all countries, with the exception of Ireland and Sweden, averaged a deficit. In the period from 2008 to 2015 the average deficits increased for most countries. And the bigger the deficit relative to GDP, the faster debt increased.

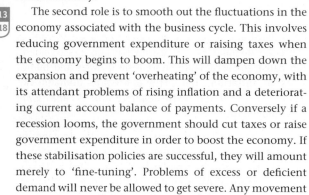

Definitions

Budget deficit The excess of central government's spending over its tax receipts.

Budget surplus The excess of central government's tax receipts over its spending.

National debt The accumulated budget deficits (less surpluses) over the years: the total amount of government borrowing.

General government deficit (or surplus) The combined deficit (or surplus) of central and local government.

General government debt The combined accumulated debt of central and local government.

Table 21.1	General government deficits/surpluses and debt as percentage of GDP			
	General government deficits (−) or surpluses (+)		General government debt	
	Average 1995–2007	Average 2008–15	Average 1995–2007	Average 2008–15
Belgium	−1.2	−3.3	106.5	97.3
France	−3.0	−5.3	60.7	86.6
Germany	−2.9	−1.0	62.2	77.0
Greece	−5.6	−9.0	100.9	155.5
Ireland	1.2	−11.1	42.8	97.9
Italy	−3.5	−3.3	110.1	123.5
Japan	−5.8	−7.4	115.3	227.7
Netherlands	−1.4	−3.5	57.6	68.1
Portugal	−4.2	−6.7	58.8	107.9
Spain	−1.4	−8.8	54.3	76.1
Sweden	0.0	−0.1	57.7	39.9
UK	−2.0	−7.7	43.1	81.2
USA	−2.8	−9.6	61.7	96.3
EU-15	−2.4	−4.6	65.2	84.8

Note: Data for 2014 and 2015 are forecasts.
Source: Based on data from *AMECO database*, Tables 16.3 and 18.1 (European Commission, DG ECFIN).

The whole public sector

To get a more complete view of public finances, we would need to look at the deficit or surplus of the entire public sector: namely, central government, local government and public corporations.

There is one important caveat to this: we have to be aware that corporations can transfer between the public and private sectors (a result of privatisation or nationalisation). Consequently, public finance statistics can be distorted by such movements. As we shall see in Chapter 23, privatisation is an example of a supply-side initiative: i.e. a policy to affect the economy's aggregate supply. In recent times, many countries have privatised major industries, such as transport, energy and telecommunications.

The financial crisis of the late 2000s saw various banking corporations transferred wholly or partly to the public sector (nationalisation) in order to ensure their survival and the stability of the financial system. In the UK, this included banking groups such as Lloyds, Northern Rock and the Royal Bank of Scotland. The hope was to return these institutions to the private sector in due course. Case 21.1 in MyEconLab discusses the government's financial interventions during the financial crisis and their cost to the public purse.

Total public expenditure.   In presenting the public finances it has become custom to distinguish between *current* and *capital expenditures*. Current expenditures include items such as wages and salaries of public-sector staff, administration and the payments of welfare benefits. Capital expenditures give rise to a stream of benefits *over time*. Examples include expenditure on roads, hospitals and schools. Of course, this distinction is not without

issues. Teachers and doctors, for instance, whose wages form part of public-sector current expenditure, would reasonably argue that their work generates benefits for future generations.

We can also distinguish between *final expenditure* on goods and services, and *transfers*. This distinction recognises that the public sector directly adds to the economy's aggregate demand through its spending on goods and services, including the wages of public-sector workers, but also that it redistributes incomes between individuals and firms. Transfers include subsidies and benefit payments, such as payments to the unemployed.

Since 1990 the UK's public expenditure has typically been split 93 to 7 per cent between current and capital expenditure, and 62 to 38 per cent between final expenditure and transfers (including interest payments). These figures contrast with those over the 1960s and 1970s. Then,

Definitions

Current expenditure Recurrent spending on goods and factor payments.

Capital expenditure Investment expenditure; expenditure on assets.

Final expenditure Expenditure on goods and services. This is included in GDP and is part of aggregate demand.

Transfers Transfers of money from taxpayers to recipients of benefits and subsidies. They are not an injection into the circular flow but are the equivalent of a negative tax (i.e. a negative withdrawal).

Table 21.2	Key UK fiscal indicators			
	£ billion	Percentage of GDP		
	2013	2013	1995–2007	2008–13
Deficit on current budget	67.4	4.2	0.6	5.4
Net investment	23.5	1.4	0.9	2.1
Net borrowing	90.9	5.6	1.7	7.5
Net debt	1254.5	75.7	36.7	63.2

Notes: The data exclude financial sector interventions; net debt is gross debt *less* liquid financial assets (deposits and official reserves).
Source: Based on data from *Public Sector Finances* (National Statistics).

the current–capital split was 80 to 20 per cent while the final expenditure–transfer split was 70 to 30 per cent.

The current budget. If the sum of the public sector's current expenditure is less than it earns (through taxes and the revenues of public corporations, etc.), then it runs a **surplus on the current budget**. In other words, the cost of public-sector current expenditure is being fully met out of the public-sector receipts and the sector can meet some of the cost of its net investment (i.e. gross capital expenditure less depreciation).

On the other hand, if it is running a deficit on the current budget, the public sector is not generating sufficient receipts to afford its current expenditures, let alone to contribute to its net investment expenditure. Table 21.2 shows that while the UK public sector has typically run a small deficit on the current budget, it significantly increased following the global financial crisis of the late 2000s.

 What could have driven the changes in the composition of UK public expenditure? Do such changes matter?

Public-sector deficits. If the public sector spends more than it earns, it will have to finance the deficit through borrowing, known as **public-sector net borrowing (PSNB)**. The principal form of borrowing is through the sale of gilts (bonds). Since 1965, the UK's public-sector net borrowing has averaged nearly 3.25 per cent of GDP. The precise amount of money the public sector requires to borrow in any one year is known as the **public-sector net cash requirement (PSNCR)**. It differs slightly from the PSNB because of time lags in the flows of public-sector incomes and expenditure.

Figure 21.1 shows both the PSNB and PSNCR since the 1960s. As you can see, in most years the UK's public expenditures have exceeded what it earns and, after accounting for financial transactions, it has needed to generate further cash to fund its spending. We can also see the dramatic impact of the economic downturn at the end of the 2000s as tax revenues fell and the government spent more on various projects to help stimulate the economy. A similar pattern was repeated in many countries as the global recession took hold.

The persistent deficits run by the public sector over the years have meant that the sector's financial liabilities have increased. However, in assessing the sustainability of the accumulated stock of debt and, hence, in assessing the sector's financial well-being it is usual to focus on **public-sector net debt**. This is the sector's gross debt less its liquid assets, which comprise official reserves and deposits held with financial institutions. The ratio of public-sector net debt to GDP increased significantly in many countries at the end of the 2000s. In the UK the ratio more than doubled from 37 per cent in 2007 to 76 per cent in 2013 (see Table 21.2 and Chart (b) in Box 21.3).

Public-sector deficits and surpluses and the government's 'fiscal stance'

The government's *fiscal stance* refers to whether it is pursuing an expansionary or contractionary fiscal policy. Does the fact that there was a public-sector deficit in the UK from 1971 to 1986 mean that the government's fiscal stance was expansionary throughout this period? Would the mere existence of a surplus mean that the stance was contractionary? The answer is no. Whether the economy expands or contracts depends on the balance of *total* injections and *total* withdrawals.

What we need to focus on is *changes* in the size of the deficit or surplus. If the deficit this year is lower than last year, then (*ceteris paribus*) aggregate demand will be lower this year than last. The reason is that either government expenditure (an injection) must have fallen, or tax revenues (a withdrawal) must have increased, or a combination of the two.

The fiscal stance and the state of the economy

Another problem is that the size of the deficit or surplus is not entirely due to deliberate government policy. It may

---

Definitions

Surplus on the current budget The amount by which public-sector receipts exceed those expenditures classified as current expenditures.

Public-sector net borrowing (PSNB) The difference between the expenditures of the public sector and its receipts from taxation and the revenues from public corporations.

Public-sector net cash requirement (PSNCR) The (annual) deficit of the public sector, and thus the amount that the public sector must borrow. In the UK the principal measure, which takes into account financial transactions by the public sector, is known as the public-sector net cash requirement.

Public-sector net debt Gross public-sector debt minus liquid financial assets.

Fiscal stance How expansionary or contractionary the Budget is.

Figure 21.1	UK public-sector deficit measures, % of GDP

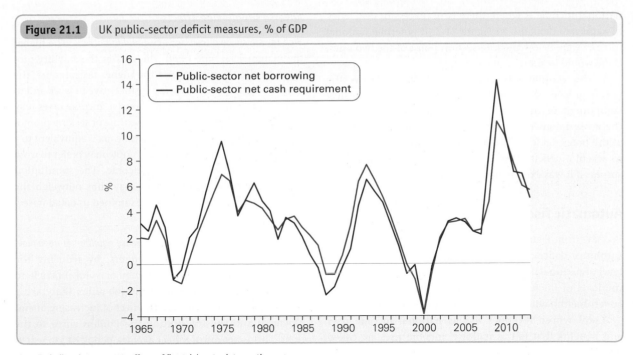

Note: Excluding the temporary effects of financial sector interventions.
Source: Based on data from *Public Sector Finances Supplementary Tables*, series J5II and JW38 (National Statistics); *Quarterly National Accounts*, series YRHA (National Statistics)

not give a very good guide, therefore, to government intentions. The size of the deficit or surplus is influenced by the state of the economy. If the economy is booming with people earning high incomes, the amount paid in taxes will be high. In a booming economy the level of unemployment will be low. Thus the amount paid out in unemployment benefits will also be low. The combined effect of increased tax revenues and reduced benefits is to give a public-sector surplus (or a reduced deficit). By contrast, if the economy were depressed, tax revenues would be low and the amount paid in benefits would be high. The public-sector deficit would thus be high.

This relationship between the budget deficit or surplus and the state of the economy is illustrated in Figure 21.2. The tax revenue function is upward sloping. Its slope depends on tax rates. The government expenditure function (which in this diagram includes transfer payments on

benefits) is drawn as downward sloping, showing that at higher levels of income and employment less is paid out in benefits. As can be clearly seen, there is only one level of income (Y_1) where there is a public-sector financial balance. Below this level of income there will be a public-sector deficit. Above this level there will be a surplus. The further income is from Y_1, the bigger will be the deficit or surplus. This is illustrated in Table 21.2.

During the boom that was experienced in Europe and North America between 1996 and 2000, deficits fell. Japan, by contrast, was experiencing a prolonged recession. Its deficit rose, partly as a result of falling tax revenues and partly from a deliberately expansionary fiscal policy (see Case Study 21.6 in MyEconLab).

To conclude, the size of the deficit or surplus is a poor guide to the stance of fiscal policy. A large deficit *may* be due to a deliberate policy of increasing aggregate demand, but it may be due simply to the fact that the economy is depressed.

The structural balance

The public-sector deficit or surplus that would arise if the economy were producing at the potential level of national income (see Box 14.3 on page 414) is termed the *structural deficit or surplus*. Remember that the potential level of

Figure 21.2	National income and the size of the public-sector deficit or surplus

Definition

Structural deficit (or surplus) The public-sector deficit (or surplus) that would occur if the economy were operating at the potential level of national income: i.e. one where there is a zero output gap.

national income is where there is no excess or deficiency of aggregate demand. In Figure 21.2, if potential national income were below the intersection point of the two lines, there would be a structural deficit.

If the economy is producing above or below the potential level of national income, there will be a cyclical component of the public-sector deficit or surplus. Thus the government could aim for a *structural* balance (*G = T* at the potential level of national income), but be prepared to accept a deficit if the economy was in a recession, or a surplus if it was experiencing a boom.

Automatic fiscal stabilisers

We saw from Figure 21.2 that the size of the public-sector surplus or deficit will automatically vary according to the level of national income. The effect of this will be to reduce the level of fluctuations in national income without the government having to take any deliberate action.

Taxes whose revenues rise as national income rises and benefits that fall as national income rises are called **automatic stabilisers**. They have the effect of reducing the size of the multiplier, reducing both upward and downward movements of national income. Thus, in theory, the business cycle should be dampened by such built-in stabilisers. The more taxes rise or benefits fall, the bigger will be the *mpt* (the net marginal tax propensity). Remember that we defined this as the proportion of any rise in income going in taxes and reduced benefits. The bigger the *mpt*, the smaller will be the multiplier and the greater will be the stabilising effect.

 Draw an injections and withdrawals diagram, with a fairly flat W curve. Mark the equilibrium level of national income. Now draw a second steeper W curve passing through the same point. This second W curve would correspond to the case where tax rates were higher. Assuming now that there has been an increase in injections, draw a second J line above the first. Mark the new equilibrium level of national income with each of the two W curves. You can see that national income rises less with the steeper W curve. The higher tax rates are having a dampening effect on the multiplier.

The effectiveness of automatic stabilisers

Automatic stabilisers have the obvious advantage that they act instantly as soon as aggregate demand fluctuates. By contrast, it may take some time before the government can institute discretionary changes in taxes or government expenditure, especially if forecasting is unreliable.

Nevertheless automatic stabilisers can never be the complete answer to the problem of fluctuations. Their effect is merely to reduce the multiplier – to reduce the severity of fluctuations, not to eliminate them altogether.

In addition, they tend to suffer two specific drawbacks: adverse effects on aggregate supply and the problem of 'fiscal drag'. Let us examine each in turn.

Adverse supply-side effects

High tax rates may discourage effort and initiative. The higher the marginal tax rate (*mpt*), the greater the stability provided by the tax system. But the higher tax rates are, the more likely they are to create a disincentive to work and to invest. For example, steeply progressive income taxes may discourage workers from doing overtime or seeking promotion. A higher marginal rate of income tax is equivalent to a higher marginal cost of working. People may prefer to work less and substitute leisure for income. The substitution effect of more progressive taxes may thus outweigh the income effect. These issues were examined in detail in section 10.2 (see pages 303–6).

High unemployment benefits may increase equilibrium unemployment. High unemployment benefits, by reducing the hardship of being unemployed, may encourage people to spend longer looking for the 'right' job rather than taking the first job offered. This has the effect of increasing unemployment and thus of shifting the Phillips curve to the right. This is because a longer average period of job search represents a higher level of *friction* in the economy and thus a higher *natural* (or *equilibrium*) level of unemployment.

High income-related benefits may create a poverty trap. The higher the level of income-related benefits and the more steeply they taper off, the greater will be the problem of the 'poverty trap'. What is the point in unemployed people seeking jobs, or people in very low-paid jobs seeking better ones, if as a result they lose their benefits and end up being little or no better off than before? The more that people are discouraged in this way, the lower will be the level of aggregate supply. The question of the poverty trap was also examined in Chapter 10 (see page 308).

The problem of fiscal drag

Automatic stabilisers help to reduce upward and downward movements in national income. This is fine if the current level of income is the *desirable* level. But suppose that there is currently a deep recession in the economy, with mass unemployment. Who would want to stabilise the economy at this level?

In these circumstances, if the economy began to recover, the automatic stabilisers would act as a drag on the expansion. This is known as **fiscal drag**. By reducing the size of the multiplier, the automatic stabilisers reduce the magnitude

> ## Definitions
>
> **Automatic fiscal stabilisers** Tax revenues that rise and government expenditure that falls as national income rises. The more they change with income, the bigger the stabilising effect on national income.
>
> **Fiscal drag** The tendency of automatic fiscal stabilisers to reduce the recovery of an economy from recession.

of the recovery. Similarly, they act as a drag on discretionary policy: the more powerful the automatic stabilisers are, the bigger the change in G or T that would be necessary to achieve a given change in national income.

Discretionary fiscal policy

Automatic stabilisers cannot prevent fluctuations. They merely reduce their magnitude. If there is a fundamental disequilibrium in the economy or substantial fluctuations in other injections and withdrawals, the government may choose to *alter* the level of government expenditure or the rates of taxation. This is known as *discretionary fiscal policy*. It involves *shifting* the J and W lines.

In the UK, changes in taxation and some changes in government expenditure are announced by the Chancellor of the Exchequer in the Budget (which usually takes place in March). Some of these changes apply to the coming financial year (beginning 6 April); some apply to the next financial year or even the one after that.

Since Budgets are normally held only once per year, 'fine-tuning' aggregate demand on a week-by-week or month-by-month basis is left to monetary policy – to changes in interest rates (see section 21.2). Very occasionally, however, changes are made between Budgets. Thus in September 2008 the government raised the threshold above which stamp duty must be paid on house purchase in an attempt to help first-time buyers. Then, in the Pre-Budget Report of November 2008, as recession deepened, VAT was cut and planned public-sector projects were brought forward (see Box 21.3).

Note that discretionary changes in taxation or government expenditure, as well as being used to alter the level of aggregate demand (fiscal policy), are also used for other purposes, including the following:

- Altering aggregate supply. Examples include tax incentives to encourage people to work more, or increased government expenditure on training or on transport infrastructure (e.g. roads and railways). We look at such 'supply-side policies' in Chapter 23.
- Altering the distribution of income. As Chapter 10 explained, taxation and benefits are the government's major means of redistributing incomes from the rich to the poor.

Let us now compare the relative effects of changing government expenditure and changing taxes. Will a £100 million increase in government expenditure have the same effect as a £100 million cut in taxes? Will the multiplier be the same in each case?

Definition

Discretionary fiscal policy Deliberate changes in tax rates or the level of government expenditure in order to influence the level of aggregate demand.

Discretionary fiscal policy: changing G

If government expenditure on goods and services (roads, health care, education, etc.) is raised, this will create a full multiplied rise in national income. The reason is that all the money gets spent and thus all of it goes to boosting aggregate demand.

 Show the effect of an increase in government expenditure by using (a) the injections and withdrawals diagram; (b) the income/expenditure diagram (see Figures 17.8 and 17.10 on pages 509 and 510).

Discretionary fiscal policy: changing T

Cutting taxes by £1 million will have a smaller effect on national income than raising government expenditure on goods and services by £1 million. The reason is that cutting taxes increases people's *disposable* incomes, of which only *part* will be spent. Part will be withdrawn into extra savings, imports and other taxes. In other words, not all the tax cuts will be passed on round the circular flow of income as extra expenditure.

The proportion of the cut in taxes that will be withdrawn is given by the mpw, and the proportion that will circulate round the flow is given by the mpc_d. Thus if the mpc_d were 4/5, the tax multiplier would only be 4/5 of the normal multiplier.[1] If the mpc_d were 2/3, the tax multiplier would only be 2/3 of the normal multiplier, and so on. The formula for the tax multiplier (k_t) becomes

$$k_t = mpc_d \times k$$

Thus if the normal multiplier were 5 (given an mpc_d of 4/5), the tax multiplier would be $4/5 \times 5 = 4$. If the normal multiplier were 4 (given an mpc_d of 3/4), the tax multiplier would be $3/4 \times 4 = 3$, and so on. It should be obvious from this that the tax multiplier is always 1 less than the normal multiplier:

$$k_t = k - 1$$

Since the tax multiplier is smaller than the government expenditure multiplier, to achieve a given rise in income through tax cuts would therefore require a bigger budget deficit than if it were achieved through increased government expenditure. In other words, the required tax cut would be bigger than the required government expenditure increase.

 Why will the multiplier effect of government transfer payments such as child benefit, pensions and social security be less than the full multiplier effect given by government expenditure on goods and services? Will this 'transfer payments multiplier' be the same as the tax multiplier? (Clue: will the recipients of such benefits have the same mpc_d as the average person?)

---

[1] Strictly speaking, the tax multiplier is negative, since a *rise* in taxes causes a *fall* in national income.

BOX 21.1   UK AND US FISCAL POLICY DURING AND AFTER THE FINANCIAL CRISIS

From fiscal expansion to fiscal consolidation

The impact of the financial crisis on economic growth in both the UK and USA was marked. In 2006 the UK and US economies had expanded by 2.8 per cent and 2.7 per cent respectively, but by 2009 they were contracting by 4.9 per cent and 2.6 per cent respectively. This box describes the active fiscal policies pursued in both the UK and the USA in the late 2000s in response to the economic slowdown. It then looks at how, in response to burgeoning budget deficits, the UK and then the USA turned rapidly towards fiscal consolidation.

US fiscal measures

During the first quarter of 2008 the US economy contracted by 0.2 per cent. In January 2008, President Bush announced an emergency $154 billion stimulus package of tax rebates, worth 1.1 per cent of GDP. The intention was to boost consumer spending. Growth returned in the second quarter of 2008, but this was short-lived as the financial crisis took hold. By the third quarter GDP was declining and the country was heading into recession.

Shortly after coming into office in 2009, President Obama signed into law a major fiscal stimulus package, worth $787 billion – the American Recovery and Investment Act. This was in addition to monetary policies designed to increase the flow of credit. The aim of the fiscal stimulus was to create 3.6 million jobs and reverse the collapse in aggregate demand that had followed the credit crunch.

The package included $212 billion in tax cuts for individuals and business, but the main feature was targeted increases in government expenditure to improve infrastructure: doubling the production of renewable energy, modernising some 75 per cent of government buildings to save energy, and large-scale investment in schools, colleges and public universities, in nationwide broadband, in science, research and technology.

In the third quarter of 2009 the US economy came out of recession after four consecutive quarters of declining output. During 2010 the economy grew by 2.9 per cent. However, despite the return of economic growth, unemployment rates took time to respond. The standardised unemployment rate peaked in October 2009 at 10.0 per cent, before then beginning to fall. In the meantime, the US general government deficit grew rapidly. In 2007, before the economic downturn, the deficit was just $385 billion or 2.75 per cent of GDP. By 2009 it had risen to $1818 billion

(or 13.0 per cent of GDP), but fell back somewhat to $1443 billion (9.6 per cent of GDP) by 2011. With high deficits, the stock of debt grew rapidly: general government gross debt rose from $9.4 trillion (67 per cent of GDP) in 2007, to $15.5 trillion (103 per cent of GDP) in 2011.

In response to the deteriorating public finances, President Obama outlined proposals to reduce the budget deficit to $627 billion (3 per cent of GDP) by 2017 with two-thirds of the reduction to come from spending cuts. However, a Republican-led House of Representatives rejected these proposals, arguing for deeper cuts. The political debate intensified as the national debt continued to rise towards the latest self-imposed ceiling agreed in February 2010 of $14.294 trillion. On 31 July 2011, Congress agreed to raise the debt limit by $900 billion in return for $917 billion of spending cuts over 10 years.

In September 2011, with growth remaining fragile and unemployment stubbornly high, President Obama outlined a new $447 billion plan to boost jobs. The proposal included a halving of the 6.2 per cent payroll tax on most businesses, providing money to states to protect the employment of public-sector workers and increased expenditure on infrastructure programmes. The money would be recouped later in the 10-year spending reduction plan – a plan made that much harder by these new proposals.

Political wrangling continued. This culminated in October 2013 with a partial shutdown of government when agreement over the budget for the fiscal year starting 1 October could not be reached. A deal was finally agreed by both Houses of Congress, less than 12 hours before the deadline of 17 October, when the USA would have once again bumped up against the debt ceiling of $16.699 trillion.

Debates over the budget remain highly polarised. However, as the economy expanded (real GDP grew by 2.8 per cent in 2012 and 1.9 per cent in 2013) and unemployment fell (the unemployment rate had fallen to 6.6 per cent by January 2014) the general government deficit-to-GDP ratio began falling (the ratio fell from 12 per cent in 2010 to 5 per cent in 2014). The growth in debt consequently slowed (see chart).

UK fiscal measures

The UK economy entered recession in the second quarter of 2008, one quarter earlier than in the USA. In the Pre-Budget Report of November 2008, among other

The effectiveness of discretionary fiscal policy

How successful will discretionary fiscal policy be? Can it 'fine-tune' demand? Can it achieve the level of national income that the government would like it to achieve?

There are two main problem areas with discretionary fiscal policy. The first concerns the *magnitude* of the effects. If *G* or *T* is changed, how much will *total* injections and withdrawals change? What will be the size of the multiplier? How much will a change in aggregate demand affect output and employment, and how much will it affect prices?

The second concerns the *timing* of the effects. How quickly can policy be changed and how quickly will the changes affect the economy?

Problems of magnitude

Before changing government expenditure or taxation, the government will need to calculate the effect of any such change on national income, employment and inflation. Predicting these effects, however, is often very unreliable for a number of reasons.

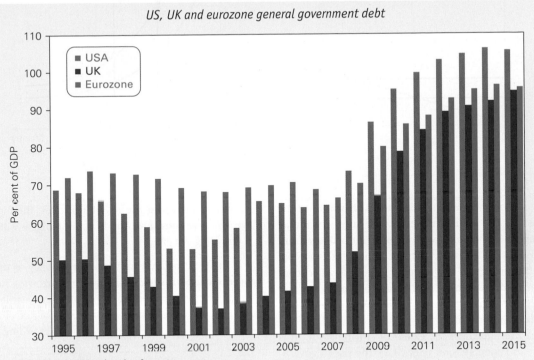

US, UK and eurozone general government debt

Note: 2014 and 2015 are based on forecasts.
Source: *AMECO* database (European Commission, DGECFIN).

measures, the government introduced a 13-month cut in VAT from 17.5 per cent to 15 per cent. It also brought forward from 2010/11 £3 billion of capital spending on projects such as motorways, new social housing, schools and energy efficiency.

The UK came out of recession in the fourth quarter of 2009 after six consecutive quarters of declining output. From 5.2 per cent at the start of 2008, the rate of unemployment peaked at 8 per cent in early 2010 and stood at 7.8 per cent in May when 13 years of Labour government came to an end. Not only did this mark a change of government as a Conservative–Liberal coalition took charge, but also a marked change in fiscal policy.

In 2010/11, public-sector net borrowing was running at 9.3 per cent of GDP, up from 2.6 per cent in 2007/8. Meanwhile, public-sector net debt had grown from £538 billion (37 per cent of GDP) in 2007/8 to £1.0 trillion (66 per cent of GDP) in 2010/11.

The response was the *fiscal mandate*: a balanced current budget (after adjusting for the position in the economic cycle) five years ahead. Therefore, at the end of a rolling five-year forecast period public-sector receipts should at least equal public-sector current expenditures, after adjusting for the economy's output gap.

To achieve this, the new government embarked on a series of spending cuts and tax rises. This started with a 'discretionary consolidation' of £8.9 billion in 2010/11 comprising spending cuts of £5.3 billion and tax increases worth £3.6 billion. It was announced that the consolidation would continue up to 2015/16, but with spending cuts accounting for over three-quarters of the consolidation. The Coalition government's fiscal mandate is discussed further in Box 21.3.

 Which is likely to have the largest impact on aggregate demand: tax rises of a given amount targeted on (a) the rich, or (b) the poor?

Predicting the effect of changes in government expenditure

A rise in government expenditure of £x may lead to a rise in total injections (relative to withdrawals) that is smaller than £x. This will occur if the rise in government expenditure *replaces* a certain amount of private expenditure. For example, a rise in expenditure on state education may dissuade some parents from sending their children to private schools. Similarly an improvement in the National Health Service may lead to fewer people paying for private treatment.

Crowding out. If the government relies on **pure fiscal policy** – that is, if it does not finance an increase in the budget deficit by increasing the money supply – it will have to borrow the money from the non-bank private sector. It will thus be competing with the private sector for finance and

Definition

Pure fiscal policy Fiscal policy that does not involve any change in money supply.

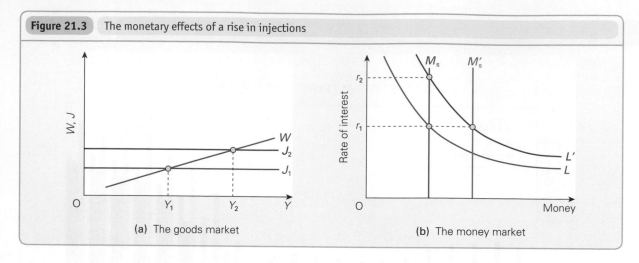

Figure 21.3 The monetary effects of a rise in injections

(a) The goods market

(b) The money market

will have to offer higher interest rates. This will force the private sector also to offer higher interest rates, which may discourage firms from investing and individuals from buying on credit. Thus government borrowing *crowds out* private borrowing. In the extreme case, the fall in consumption and investment may completely offset the rise in government expenditure, with the result that aggregate demand does not rise at all.

Figure 21.3 illustrates the extent of crowding out. (It is the same as Figure 19.8 on page 572.) The rise in government expenditure shifts the injections line from J_1 to J_2 in Figure 21.3(a). The full multiplier effect of this would be a rise in national income to Y_2. However, the increased government expenditure leads to an increased demand for money. In Figure 21.3(b), the liquidity preference curve shifts to L'. This raises the interest rate to r_2. Note that we are assuming that the money supply is purely *exogenous* (i.e. does not vary with the demand for money) and that, therefore, the money supply 'curve' is a vertical straight line (M_s).

The higher rate of interest reduces investment. The injections line falls below J_2, and, as a result, national income does not rise as far as Y_2. The amount by which actual income falls short of Y_2 measures the extent of crowding out.

The amount of crowding out from pure fiscal policy depends on three things:

- The shape of the L curve. The flatter the curve, the less will interest rates rise. A greater amount of liquidity will be released from idle balances and there will be a bigger increase in the velocity of circulation.
- Whether money supply is exogenous. If the extra demand for money leads to banks creating extra credit, the money supply curve will be upward sloping, not vertical. The more money is created, the flatter will be the M_s curve, the less interest rates will rise and the less will be the crowding out.
- The responsiveness of investment (and consumption) to a change in interest rates. The more responsive

investment is to a rise in interest rates, the more will the J curve shift downwards and the bigger will be the crowding-out effect.

If the fiscal policy is not *pure* fiscal policy, if the extra government borrowing is financed by borrowing from the banking sector, then the supply of money curve will shift to the right. If it were to shift as far as M'_s, the rate of interest would remain at r_1 and there would be no crowding out.

 How do people's expectations influence the extent of crowding out?

Predicting the effect of changes in taxes

A cut in taxes, by raising people's real disposable income, increases not only the amount they spend but also the amount they save. The problem is that it is not easy to predict the relative size of these two increases. In part it depends on whether people feel that the cut in tax is only temporary, in which case they may simply save the extra disposable income, or permanent, in which case they may adjust their consumption upwards.

 Do theories of the long-run and short-run consumption function help us to understand consumer reactions to a change in taxes? (See section 17.1 and Case Studies 17.1, 17.2 and 17.3 in MyEconLab.)

Predicting the resulting multiplied effect on national income

Even if the government *could* predict the net initial effect on injections and withdrawals, the extent to which national income will change is still hard to predict for the following reasons:

- The size of the *multiplier* may be difficult to predict. This is because the mpc_d and mpw may fluctuate. For example, the amount of a rise in income that households save or consume will depend on their expectations about future price and income changes.

- Induced investment through the *accelerator* (see pages 516–18) is also extremely difficult to predict. It may be that a relatively small fiscal stimulus will be all that is necessary to restore business confidence, and that induced investment will rise substantially. In such a case, fiscal policy can be seen as a 'pump primer'. It is used to start the process of recovery, and then the continuation of the recovery is left to the market. But for pump priming to work, businesspeople must believe that it will work. Business confidence can change very rapidly and in ways that could not have been foreseen a few months earlier.

- Multiplier/accelerator interactions. If the initial multiplier and accelerator effects are difficult to estimate, their interaction will be virtually impossible to estimate. Small divergences in investment from what was initially predicted will become magnified as time progresses

Random shocks

Forecasts cannot take into account the unpredictable, such as the attack on the World Trade Center in New York in September 2001. Even events that, with hindsight, should have been predicted, such as the banking crisis of 2007–9, often are not. Unfortunately, unpredictable or unpredicted events do occur and may seriously undermine the government's fiscal policy.

 Give some examples of these random shocks.

Problems of timing

 Fiscal policy can involve considerable time lags. If these are long enough, fiscal policy could even be *de*stabilising. Expansionary policies taken to cure a recession may not come into effect until the economy has *already* recovered and is experiencing a boom. Under these circumstances, expansionary policies are quite inappropriate: they simply worsen the problems of overheating. Similarly, contractionary policies taken to prevent excessive expansion may not take effect until the economy has already peaked and is plunging into recession. The contractionary policies only deepen the recession.

This problem is illustrated in Figure 21.4. Path (a) shows the course of the business cycle without government intervention. Ideally, with no time lags, the economy should be dampened in stage 2 and stimulated in stage 4. This would make the resulting course of the business cycle more like path (b), or even, if the policy were perfectly stabilising, a straight line.

With time lags, however, contractionary policies taken in stage 2 may not come into effect until stage 4, and expansionary policies taken in stage 4 may not come into effect until stage 2. In this case, the resulting course of the business cycle will be more like path (c). Quite obviously, in these circumstances 'stabilising' fiscal policy actually makes the economy less stable.

There are five possible lags associated with fiscal policy.

Time lag to recognition. Since the business cycle can be irregular and forecasting unreliable, governments may be unwilling to take action until they are convinced that the problem is serious.

Time lag between recognition and action. Most significant changes in government expenditure have to be planned well in advance. The government cannot increase spending on motorways overnight or suddenly start building new hospitals. As far as taxes are concerned, these can normally be changed only at the time of the Budget, and will not be instituted until the new financial year or at some other point in the future. As Budgets normally occur annually, there could be a considerable time lag if the problems are recognised a long time before the Budget.

Time lag between action and changes taking effect. A change in tax rates may not immediately affect tax payments, as some taxes are paid in arrears and new rates may take a time to apply.

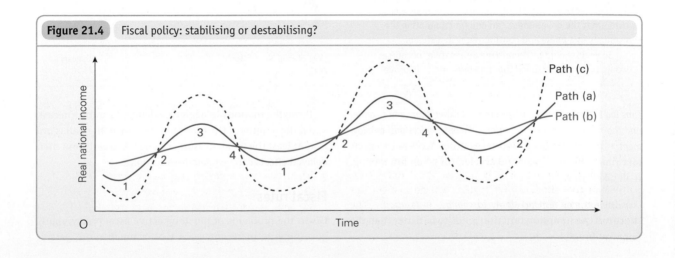

Figure 21.4 Fiscal policy: stabilising or destabilising?

BOX 21.2 **RIDING A SWITCHBACK**

A parable for Chancellors

Imagine that you are driving a car along a straight but undulating road. These undulations are not regular: some of the hills are steep, some are gentle; some are long, some are short.

You are given the instruction that you must keep the car going at a constant speed. To do this, you will need to accelerate going up the hills and brake going down them.

There is a serious problem, however. The car is no ordinary car. It has the following distinctly unusual features:

- The front windscreen and side windows are blacked out, so you cannot see where you are going! All you can see is where you have been by looking in your rear-view mirror.
- The brake and accelerator pedals both work with a considerable and unpredictable delay.
- The car's suspension is so good that you cannot feel whether you are going up or downhill. You can only judge this by looking in your mirror.
- Finally (you are relieved to know), the car has a special sensor and automatic steering that keep it in the correct lane.

As you are going along, you see that the road behind you is higher, and you realise that you are going downhill. The car gets faster and faster. You brake – but nothing happens. In your zeal to slow the car down, you put your foot down on the brake as hard as you can.

When the brake eventually does come on, it comes on very strongly. By this time, the car has already reached the bottom of the hill. As yet, however, you do not realise this and are still braking. But now the car is going up the next hill with the brakes still on. Looking in your mirror, you eventually realise this. You take your foot off the brake and start accelerating. But the pedals do not respond. The car is still slowing down rapidly, and you only just manage to reach the top of the hill.

Then, as you start going down the other side, the brakes eventually come off and the accelerator comes on . . .

This famous parable – first told by Frank Paish, Professor of Economics at the LSE, some 40 years ago – demonstrates how 'stabilising' activity can in fact be destabilising. When applied to fiscal policy, long and uncertain time lags can mean that the government can end up stimulating the economy in a boom and contracting it in a slump.

So what should be done? One alternative, of course, would be to try to reduce the time lags and to improve

forecasting. But failing this, the best policy may be to do nothing: to take a 'steady as you go' or 'fixed throttle' approach to running the economy. Going back to the car analogy, a fixed throttle will not prevent the car from going faster downhill and slower uphill, but at least it will not make the speed even more irregular.

A recent version of the parable

In an article in the *New Statesman*[1] on what Keynes' response would have been to the recovery and getting the public-sector deficit down, Vince Cable, the UK Business Secretary, wrote:

> As in many economic policy disputes, much of the ideological rhetoric conceals different forecasting assumptions – in respect of the cyclical, as opposed to structural, deficit; the influence of asset prices on consumer behaviour; the impact of the unorthodox monetary policy of quantitative easing (QE) and its interaction with the velocity of circulation of money; and the weight to be attached to business confidence and sentiment in financial markets. Amidst such uncertainty, economic policymaking is like driving a car with an opaque windscreen, a large rear-view mirror and poor brakes.

So what are the policy implications of this uncertainty and the time lags in response to government policy initiatives? The Coalition government saw the answer in a fiscal rule of getting the deficit down and thereby restoring long-term confidence in financial markets and encouraging private investment.

Critics of the government argued that policy needed to be flexible and responsive to current circumstances. Even with the time lags associated with fiscal policy, it was probably better to ease back on cutting the deficit so quickly if demand appeared to falter rather than just sticking with the planned government expenditure cuts.

But at least there were the automatic fiscal stabilisers – the car's accelerator would automatically come on and the brake would be eased if the economy slowed down.

 What would a fixed throttle approach to fiscal policy involve?

[1] Vince Cable, 'Keynes would be on our side', *New Statesman*, 12 January 2011.

KI 31 p330

Time lag between changes in government expenditure and taxation and the resulting change in national income, prices and employment. The multiplier round takes time. Accelerator effects take time. The multiplier and accelerator go on interacting. It all takes time.

Consumption may respond slowly to changes in taxation. The short-run consumption function tends to be flatter than the long-run function.

If the fluctuations in aggregate demand can be forecast, and if the lengths of the time lags are known, then all is not lost. At least the fiscal measures can be taken early and their delayed effects can be taken into account.

Fiscal rules

Given the problems of pursuing active fiscal policy, many governments in recent years took a much more passive approach. Instead of the policy being changed as the economy changes, countries applied a set of fiscal rules. These rules typically relate to measures of government deficits and to the stock of accumulated debt. Taxes and government expenditure can then be planned to meet these rules.

But rules cannot cope with severe disruption to the global economy, such as occurred in the credit crunch of 2008. Countries around the world resorted to discretionary fiscal policy to boost aggregate demand. They abandoned fiscal rules – at least temporarily. Rules were generally reinstated around the world, however, as the global economy pulled out of recession. In Box 21.3 we detail how the fiscal rules applied in the UK and the eurozone countries evolved following the events of the late 2000s.

Section summary

1. The government's fiscal policy influences the size of the budget deficit or surplus. Its size alone, however, is a poor guide to the government's fiscal stance. A large deficit, for example, may simply be due to the fact that the economy is in recession and therefore tax receipts are low. A better guide is whether the change in the deficit or surplus will be expansionary or contractionary.

2. Automatic fiscal stabilisers are tax revenues that rise, and benefits that fall, as national income rises. They have the effect of reducing the size of the multiplier and thus reducing cyclical upswings and downswings.

3. Automatic stabilisers take effect as soon as aggregate demand fluctuates, but they can never remove fluctuations completely. They also create disincentives and act as a drag on recovery from recession.

4. Discretionary fiscal policy is where the government deliberately changes taxes or government expenditure in order to alter the level of aggregate demand. Changes in government expenditure on goods and services have a full multiplier effect. Changes in taxes and benefits, however, have a smaller multiplier effect. The tax multiplier has a value 1 less than the full multiplier.

5. There are problems in predicting the magnitude of the effects of discretionary fiscal policy. Expansionary fiscal policy can act as a pump primer and stimulate increased private expenditure, or it can crowd out private expenditure. The extent to which it acts as a pump primer depends crucially on business confidence – something that is very difficult to predict beyond a few weeks or months. The extent of crowding out depends on monetary conditions and the government's monetary policy.

6. There are five possible time lags involved with fiscal policy: the time lag before the problem is diagnosed, the lag between diagnosis and new measures being announced, the lag between announcement and implementation, the lag while the multiplier and accelerator work themselves out, and the lag before consumption fully responds to new economic circumstances.

7. In recent years, many governments preferred a more passive approach towards fiscal policy. Targets were set for one or more measures of the public-sector finances, and then taxes and government expenditure were adjusted so as to keep to the target.

8. Nevertheless, in extreme circumstances, as occurred in 2008–9, governments were prepared to abandon rules and give a fiscal stimulus to their economies.

| BOX 21.3 | THE EVOLVING FISCAL FRAMEWORKS IN THE UK AND EUROZONE | CASE STUDIES AND APPLICATIONS |

Constraining government discretion over fiscal policy

If the government persistently runs a budget deficit, the national debt will rise. If it rises faster than GDP, it will account for a growing proportion of GDP. There is then likely to be an increasing problem of 'servicing' this debt: i.e. paying the interest on it. The government could find itself having to borrow more and more to meet the interest payments, and so the national debt could rise faster still. As a government borrows more and more, it has to pay higher interest rates to attract finances. If it is successful in this, borrowing and hence investment by the private sector could be crowded out (see page 573).

The possibility of financial crowding out contributed to governments, including the UK Coalition government, embarking on a strategy of fiscal consolidation during the 2010s. But the recognition of this problem and the need for a fiscal framework has in fact shaped fiscal policy across Europe for some time. However, the financial crisis called into question how rigid any framework should be and hence how much discretion over fiscal policy national governments should have. In this box, we consider the recent turbulent evolution of fiscal frameworks adopted across Europe and how they have been affected by recent economic turmoil.

Preparing for the euro

In signing the Maastricht Treaty in 1992, the EU countries agreed that to be eligible to join the single currency (i.e. the euro), they should have sustainable deficits and debts. This was interpreted as follows: the general government deficit should be no more than 3 per cent of GDP and general government debt should be no more than 60 per cent of GDP, or should at least be falling towards that level at a satisfactory pace.

But in the mid-1990s, several of the countries that were subsequently to join the euro had deficits and debts substantially above these levels (see Table 21.1 on page 627). Getting them down proved a painful business. Government expenditure had to be cut and taxes increased. These fiscal measures, unfortunately, proved to be powerful! Unemployment rose and growth remained low.

The EU Stability and Growth Pact (SGP)

In June 1997, at the European Council meeting in Amsterdam, the EU countries agreed that governments adopting the euro should seek to balance their budgets (or even aim for a surplus) averaged over the course of the business cycle, and that deficits should not exceed 3 per cent of GDP in any one year. A country's deficit was permitted to exceed 3 per cent only if its GDP has declined by at least 2 per cent (or 0.75 per cent with special permission from the Council of Ministers). Otherwise, countries with deficits exceeding 3 per cent were required to make deposits of money with the European Central Bank. These would then become fines if the excessive budget deficit were not eliminated within two years.

There were two main aims of targeting a zero budget deficit over the business cycle. The first was to allow automatic stabilisers to work without 'bumping into' the 3 per cent deficit ceiling in years when economies were slowing. The second was to allow a reduction in government debts as a proportion of GDP (assuming that GDP grows on average at around 2–3 per cent per year).

From 2002, with slowing growth, Germany, France and Italy breached the 3 per cent ceiling (see Chart (a)). By 2007, however, after two years of relatively strong growth, deficits had been reduced well below the ceiling.

But then the credit crunch hit. As the EU economies slowed, so deficits rose. To combat the recession, in November 2008 the European Commission announced a €200 billion fiscal stimulus plan, mainly in the form of increased public expenditure. €170 billion of the money would come from member governments and €30 billion from the EU, amounting to a total of 1.2 per cent of EU GDP. The money would be for a range of projects, such as job training, help to small businesses, developing green energy technologies and energy efficiency. Most member governments quickly followed in announcing how their specific plans would accord with the overall plan.

The combination of the recession and the fiscal measures pushed most eurozone countries' budget deficits well above the 3 per cent ceiling. The recession in EU countries deepened markedly in 2009, with GDP declining by 4.3 per cent in the eurozone as a whole, and by 5.1 per cent in Germany and Italy, 3.7 per cent in Spain and 2.7 per cent in France. Consequently, the deficits were not seen to breach SGP rules.

The Fiscal Compact

As the European economy began to recover in 2010, there was tremendous pressure on member countries to begin reining in their deficits. The average eurozone deficit had risen to 6.2 per cent of GDP, and some countries' deficits were very much higher. Indeed, with the Spanish, Greek and Irish deficits being 9.6, 10.8 and 31.3 per cent respectively, reigning in deficits would prove to be especially painful for these and several other eurozone countries.

The SGP was no longer seen as a credible vehicle for constraining deficits: it needed reform. The result was an intense period of negotiation that culminated in early 2012 with a new intergovernmental treaty on limiting spending and borrowing. The treaty, known as the Fiscal Compact, requires that from January 2013 national governments not only abide by the excessive deficit procedure of the SGP but also keep structural deficits no higher than 0.5 per cent of GDP.

(a) *General government deficits in the eurozone*

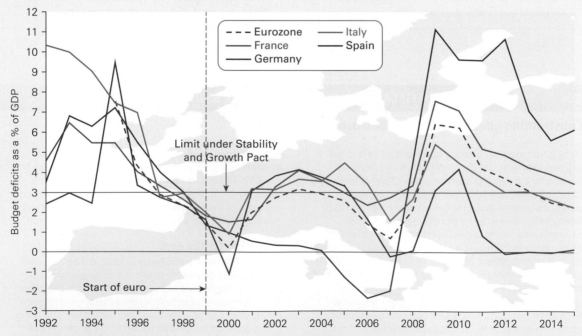

Note: 2014 and 2015 based on forecasts.
Source: Based on data in *European Economy* (European Commission).

Structural deficits are that part of a deficit not directly related to the economic cycle and so would exist even if the economy were operating at its potential output. In the cases of countries with a debt-to-GDP ratio significantly below 60 per cent, the structural deficit is permitted to reach 1 per cent of GDP. Finally, where the debt-to-GDP ratio exceeds 60 per cent, countries should, on average, reduce it by one-twentieth per year.

Where a national government is found by the European Court of Justice not to comply with the Fiscal Compact, it has the power to fine that country up to 0.1 per cent of GDP payable to the European Stability Mechanism (ESM). The ESM is a fund from which loans are provided to support a eurozone government in severe financing difficulty; alternatively it can be used to purchase that country's bonds in the primary market.

The UK Labour government's golden rule

On being elected in 1997, the Labour government in the UK adopted a similar approach to that of the SGP. It introduced two fiscal rules.

First, under its 'golden rule', the government pledged that over the economic cycle, it would borrow only to invest (e.g. in roads, hospitals and schools) and not to fund current spending (e.g. on wages, administration and benefits). Investment was exempted from the zero borrowing rule because it contributes towards the growth of GDP.

Second, under its 'sustainable investment rule', the government also set itself the target of maintaining a stable public-sector debt/GDP ratio at no more than 40 per cent over the economic cycle.

As with the SGP, the argument for the golden rule was that by using an averaging rule over the cycle, automatic stabilisers would be allowed to work. Deficits of receipts over current spending could occur when the economy is in recession or when growth is sluggish (as in 2001–3), helping to stimulate the economy.

The global financial crisis saw the UK fiscal framework suspended. The priority was to proactively support the economy through discretionary fiscal policy. Measures

included a 13-month cut in VAT from 17.5 per cent to 15 per cent and bringing forward from 2010/11 £3 billion of capital spending (see Box 21.1).

The fiscal approach of the Coalition government

May 2010 saw a Coalition government formed. Its fiscal priority was to get the deficit down. In 2010 public-sector net borrowing (see Figure 21.1) was around 10 per cent of GDP, one of the highest percentages in the developed world. The new government set itself a 'fiscal mandate': to achieve a cyclically adjusted current balance at the end of the five-year forecast period. Hence, it is similar to the golden rule. The initial hope was for the structural current deficit, which was running in excess of 5 per cent in 2009/10, to be zero by 2015/16.

The fiscal mandate was subsequently supplemented by a target for public-sector net debt as a percentage of GDP to be falling by 2015/16. This is designed to ensure that the public finances are on a sustainable path.

To achieve its fiscal mandate meant sharp government expenditure cuts and tax rises. In 2010/11 the government announced a total consolidation of £128 billion per year by 2015/16. Around 77 per cent (£99 billion per year) was to come from spending cuts and the remaining 23 per cent (£29 billion per year) from tax increases.

On its own, the much tighter fiscal policy would substantially dampen aggregate demand. The question was whether the recovery in private-sector expenditure would be sufficient to offset this. This, in turn, depended on the confidence of economic agents and on monetary policy (see section 21.2). Although economic activity picked up during 2013/14, the structural current budget deficit persisted and so the initial deadlines for meeting the fiscal mandate and the supplementary target for public-sector debt were missed (see Chart (b)).

1. *What effects will an increase in government investment expenditure have on general government deficits (a) in the short run; (b) in the long run?*
2. *If there is a danger of recession, should governments loosen the strait-jacket of fiscal policy targets?*

(b) *Public-sector net debt and cyclically adjusted current budget surplus (% of GDP)*

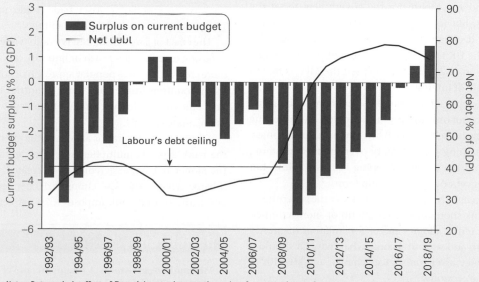

Notes: Data exclude effect of financial sector interventions; data from 2013/14 are forecasts.
Source: *Public Finances Databank* (Office for Budget Responsibility).

21.2 MONETARY POLICY

Each month the Bank of England's Monetary Policy Committee (MPC) meets to set the Bank Rate and possibly consider whether or not to alter the money supply directly through quantitative easing. The event often gets considerable media coverage, especially when a change is expected.

The fact is that changes in interest rates have gained a central significance in macroeconomic policy. And it is not just in the UK. Whether it is the European Central Bank setting interest rates for the eurozone countries, or the Federal Reserve Bank setting US interest rates, or any other central bank around the world choosing what the level of interest rates should be, monetary policy is seen as having a major influence on a whole range of macroeconomic indicators.

But is setting interest rates simply a question of making an announcement? In reality, it involves the central bank intervening in the money market to ensure that the interest rate announced is also the *equilibrium* interest rate.

The policy setting

In framing its monetary policy, the government must decide on what the goals of the policy are. Is the aim simply to control inflation, or does the government wish also to affect output and employment, or does it want to control the exchange rate?

The government also has to decide the role of the central bank in carrying out monetary policy. There are three possible approaches.

In the first, the government both sets the policy and decides the measures necessary to achieve it. Here the government would set the interest rate, with the central bank simply influencing money markets to achieve this rate. This first approach was used in the UK before 1997.

The second approach is for the government to set the policy *targets*, but for the central bank to be given independence in deciding interest rates. This is the approach adopted in the UK today. The government has set a target rate of inflation of 2 per cent, but then the MPC is free to choose the rate of interest.

The third approach is for the central bank to be given independence not only in carrying out policy, but in setting the policy targets itself. The ECB, within the statutory objective of maintaining price stability over the medium term, has decided on the target of keeping inflation below, but close to, 2 per cent over the medium term.

Finally, there is the question of whether the government or central bank should take a long-term or short-term perspective. Should it adopt a target for inflation or money supply growth and stick to it come what may? Or should it adjust its policy as circumstances change and attempt to 'fine-tune' the economy?

We will be looking primarily at *short-term* monetary policy – that is, policy used to keep to a set target for inflation or

money supply growth, or policy used to smooth out fluctuations in the business cycle.

It is important first, however, to take a longer-term perspective. Governments generally want to prevent an excessive growth in the money supply over the longer term. Likewise they want to ensure that money supply grows enough and that there is not a shortage of credit, such as that during the credit crunch. If money supply grows too rapidly, then inflation is likely to be high; if money supply grows too slowly, or even falls, then recession is likely to result.

Control of the money supply over the medium and long term

There are two major sources of monetary growth: (a) banks choosing to hold a lower liquidity ratio (probably in response to an increase in the demand for loans); (b) public-sector borrowing financed by borrowing from the banking sector. If the government wishes to restrict monetary growth over the longer term, it could attempt to control either or both of these.

Banks' liquidity ratio

The central bank could impose a statutory **minimum reserve ratio** on the banks, *above* the level that banks would otherwise choose to hold. Such ratios come in various forms. The simplest is where the banks are required to hold a given minimum percentage of deposits in the form of cash or deposits with the central bank. Other versions are where they are required to hold a given minimum percentage of certain specified types of deposit in the form of various liquid assets. This was the system used in the UK up to 1981. Various types of liquid asset had to add up to at least 12.5 per cent of certain 'eligible liabilities'.

The effect of a minimum reserve ratio is to prevent banks choosing to reduce their cash or liquidity ratio and creating more credit. This was a popular approach of governments in many countries in the past. Some countries imposed very high ratios indeed in their attempt to slow down the growth in the money supply.

Minimum reserve ratios also have the effect of reducing the bank deposits multiplier, since, for any expansion of the monetary base, *less* credit can be created. For example, if banks would otherwise choose a 10 per cent cash ratio, and if the central bank imposes a 20 per cent cash ratio,

---

Definition

Minimum reserve ratio A minimum ratio of cash (or other specified liquid assets) to deposits (either total or selected) that the central bank requires banks to hold.

the bank deposits multiplier is reduced from 10 (= $1/^1/_{10}$) to 5 (= $1/^1/_5$).

A major problem with imposing restrictions of this kind is that banks may find ways of getting round them. After all, normally banks would like to lend and customers would like to borrow. It is very difficult to regulate and police every single part of countries' complex financial systems.

Nevertheless, attitudes changed substantially after the excessive lending of the mid-2000s. The expansion of credit had been based on 'liquidity' achieved through secondary marketing between financial institutions and the growth of securitised assets containing sub-prime debt (see pages 533–6 and Box 18.3). After the credit crunch and the need for central banks or governments to rescue ailing banks, such as Northern Rock and later the Royal Bank of Scotland in the UK and many other banks around the world, there were calls for greater regulation of banks to ensure that they had sufficient capital and operated with sufficient liquidity and that they were not exposed to excessive risk of default. As we saw in section 18.2, a number of measures were taken.

Public-sector deficits

In section 18.3, we showed how government borrowing tends to lead to an increase in money supply. To prevent this, deficits must be financed by selling *bonds* (as opposed to bills, which could well be taken up by the banking sector, thereby increasing money supply). However, to sell extra bonds the government will have to offer higher interest rates. This will have a knock-on effect on private-sector interest rates. The government borrowing will thus crowd out private-sector borrowing and investment.

If governments wish to reduce monetary growth and yet avoid financial crowding out, they must therefore reduce deficits. Monetarism, which reached its high point in the 1980s, advocated governments making reductions in their deficits (as a proportion of national income) the central part of their medium- and longer-term monetary strategy. Not only would this help to restrict monetary growth, but, if it involved cutting government expenditure (as opposed to increasing taxes), it would also increase the size of the private sector relative to the public sector – and it was the private sector that monetarists saw as the main source of long-term growth in output and employment.

In the UK, the Conservative government's medium-term financial strategy, introduced in 1980, attempted to do just this. As well as setting targets for the growth of money supply, it also set targets for the PSNCR as a percentage of GDP.

 How could long-term monetary growth come about if the government persistently ran a public-sector surplus?

Once inflation is at or near its target rate, longer-term control of the monetary base is largely a matter of ensuring that government borrowing is kept in check (see Box 21.3). Keeping bank lending under control is achieved by *short-term* measures to keep inflation at its target rate (see below).

However, achieving longer-term control of the money supply when the authorities are embarking on a policy of bringing inflation down can be more problematic. The higher the initial rate of inflation, and the more rapidly the government wishes to reduce it, the bigger the problems can be. The government must reduce deficits, but this will be a contractionary *fiscal* policy. This could lead to a recession, given that inflation may be slow to fall.

Adverse effects of automatic stabilisers. In a recession, automatic fiscal stabilisers come into force that will tend to push deficits back up again. Lower incomes and lower expenditure will mean that less taxes are paid. At the same time, higher unemployment will involve increased government expenditure on unemployment benefits. The early 1990s recession in the UK turned a public-sector surplus of £14.5 billion (2.9 per cent of GDP) in 1988/89 into a massive deficit, as measured by the PSNCR, of £46 billion (6.8 per cent of GDP) by 1993/94 while the recession of the late 2000s saw a deficit of £23 billion (1.9 per cent of GDP) in 2007/8 balloon to £202 billion (14.1 per cent of GDP) in 2009/10. Some argued that in both cases attempts to cut the size of the PSNCR by fiscal tightening only helped to prolong the weakness of economic growth.

It is for this reason that the fiscal frameworks operating in eurozone countries and in the UK (see Box 21.3) have rules relating to cyclically adjusted deficits. Such rules take into account the effect of the business cycle on the financial position of governments.

Long-term monetary control and inflation

Although there are issues with achieving long-term control of the money supply, there is widespread agreement that it is important to do so. The argument is that *increasing* the money supply cannot increase output in the long run; all that will happen is an increase in prices.

It is widely agreed that in the long run – after all adjustments in the economy have worked through – a change in the quantity of money in the economy will be reflected in a change in the general level of prices. But it will not induce permanent changes in real variables such as real output or unemployment.

This general principle, referred to as the **long-run neutrality of money**, underlies all standard macroeconomic thinking. Real income or the level of employment are, in the long term, essentially determined by real factors, such as technology, population growth or the preferences of economic agents.[1]

[1] European Central Bank, www.ecb.int/mopo/intro/role/html/index.en.html

If inflation is to be kept under control, therefore, it is important to control the supply of money. And if long-term control is to be achieved, it is also important not to allow excessive expansion (or contraction) of the money supply in the short term too. But what instruments does a central bank have at its disposal? We examine these next.

The operation of monetary policy in the short term

Inflation may be off target. Alternatively, the government (or central bank) may wish to alter its monetary policy. Assume, for example, that it wishes to operate a tighter monetary policy in order to reduce aggregate demand and inflation. What can it do?

For any given supply of money (M_s) there will be a particular equilibrium rate of interest at any one time: where the supply of money (M_s) equals the demand for money (L). This is shown as r_1 in Figure 21.5.

Thus to operate a tighter monetary policy, the authorities can do the following:

■ Reduce money supply and accept whatever equilibrium interest rate results. Thus if money supply is reduced to Q_2 in Figure 21.5, a new higher rate of interest, r_2, will result.

■ First raise interest rates to r_2 and then manipulate the money supply to reduce it to Q_2. The more endogenous the money supply is, the more this will occur automatically through banks adjusting credit to match the lower demand at the higher rate of interest and the less the central bank will have to take deliberate action to reduce liquidity.

There is another possibility. This is to keep interest rates low (at r_1), but also reduce money supply to a level of Q_2. The trouble here is that the authorities cannot both control the money supply *and* keep interest rates down without running into the problem of disequilibrium. Since the demand for money now exceeds the supply by $Q_1 - Q_2$, some form of credit rationing would have to be applied.

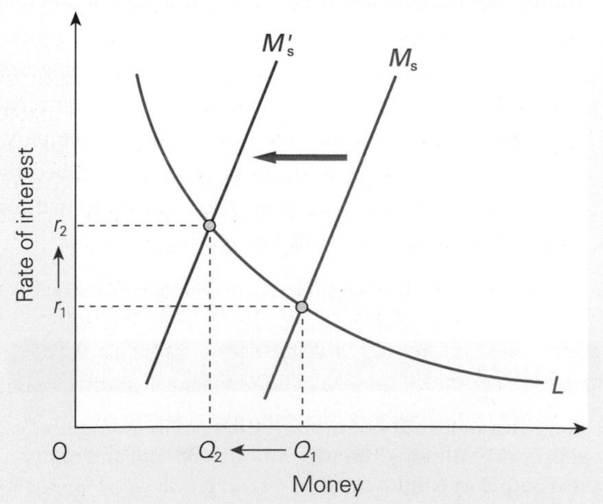

Credit rationing was widely used in the past, especially during the 1960s. The aim was to keep interest rates low, so as not to discourage investment, but to restrict credit to more risky business customers and/or to consumers. In the UK the Bank of England could order banks to abide by such a policy, although in practice it always relied on persuasion. The government also, from time to time, imposed restrictions on hire-purchase credit, by specifying minimum deposits or maximum repayment periods.

Such policies were progressively abandoned around the world from the early 1980s. They were seen to stifle competition and prevent efficient banks from expanding. Hire-purchase controls could badly hit certain industries (e.g. cars and other consumer durables), whose products are bought largely on hire-purchase credit. What is more, with the deregulation and globalisation of financial markets up to 2007, it had become very difficult to ration credit. If one financial institution was controlled, borrowers could simply go elsewhere.

With the excessive lending in sub-prime markets that had triggered the credit crunch of 2007–9, however, there were calls around the world for tighter controls over bank lending. But this was different from credit rationing as we have defined it. In other words, tighter controls, such as applying counter-cyclical buffers of capital to all banks, would be used to prevent reckless behaviour by banks, rather than to achieve a particular level of money at a lower rate of interest.

We thus focus on the two major approaches to monetary policy: (a) controlling the money supply and (b) controlling interest rates.

Techniques to control the money supply

There are two broad approaches to controlling the money supply.

The first is to alter the level of liquidity in the banking system, on which credit is created. Suppose, for example, that banks operate a rigid 10 per cent cash ratio and have just two types of asset: cash and advances. Suppose also that the authorities are able to reduce cash in banks by £1 million. With a bank multiplier of 10 (= 1/cash ratio), advances must be reduced by £9 million, and hence (broad) money supply by £10 million (see Table 21.3).

Figure 21.5 The demand for and supply of money

(Graph: vertical axis "Rate of interest" with r_2 and r_1 marked; horizontal axis "Money" from O, with $Q_2 \leftarrow Q_1$ marked. Curves M'_s and M_s (upward sloping) and L (downward sloping). An arrow points left showing the shift from M_s to M'_s.)

Table 21.3 Reducing the money supply

Liabilities		Assets	
Deposits	£10m ↓	Cash	£1m ↓
		Advances	£9m ↓

If banks operated a rigid 5 per cent cash ratio and the government reduced cash in banks by £1 million, how much must credit contract? What is the bank deposits multiplier?

The second approach is to alter the size of the bank deposits multiplier, by altering the ratio of reserves to deposits. Thus if the bank deposits multiplier can be reduced, credit will have to be reduced for any given reserve base.

Before they can actually apply techniques of monetary control, the authorities must make two preliminary decisions:

- Should a statutory minimum reserve or a minimum liquidity ratio be imposed on the banks, or should the banks be allowed to choose whatever ratios they consider to be prudent?
- Should the authorities attempt to control a range of liquid assets, or should they focus on controlling just the monetary base?

There are four techniques that a central bank could use to control the money supply. Assume in each case that the central bank wishes to *reduce* money supply.

Open-market operations

Open-market operations (OMOs) are the most widely used of the four techniques around the world. They alter the monetary base (cash in circulation outside the central bank). This then affects the amount of credit that banks can create and hence the level of broad money (M4 in the UK).

Open-market operations involve the sale or purchase by the central bank of government securities (bonds or bills) in the open market. These sales or purchases are *not* in response to changes in the level of government deficits/surpluses. Rather, they are being conducted to implement monetary policy. Hence, they are best understood in the context of an unchanged PSNCR.

Now assume that the central bank wishes to *reduce* the money supply. It will conduct OMOs so as to reduce financial institutions' reserves. It can do this by borrowing from financial institutions against government securities (reverse repos on banks' balance sheets). These securities include government bonds or short-term Treasury or central bank bills. Alternatively the central bank can sell securities outright.

The borrowing or sale of securities reduces the reserve balances of financial institutions at the central bank. If the reduction in banks' balances brings bank reserves below their prudent ratio (or statutory ratio, if one is in force), banks will reduce advances. There will be a multiple

KI 5
p22

Definition

Open-market operations The sale (or purchase) by the authorities of government securities in the open market in order to reduce (or increase) money supply.

contraction of credit and hence of (broad) money supply. (Details of how OMOs work in the UK are given below in Box 21.4.)

The effect will be limited if the extra securities are bills (as opposed to bonds) and if some are purchased by banks. The reduction in one liquid asset (balances with the central bank) will be offset to some extent by an increase in another liquid asset (bills). OMOs are more likely to be effective in reducing the money supply, therefore, when conducted in the bond market.

1. *Explain how open-market operations could be used to increase the money supply.*
2. *Why would it be difficult for a central bank to predict the precise effect on money supply of open-market operations?*

Adjusting central bank lending to the banks

The central bank in most countries is prepared to provide extra money to banks (through rediscounting bills, gilt repos or straight loans). If banks obtain less money in this way, they will have to cut back on lending. Less credit will be created and broad money supply will thereby be reduced.

Whether or not banks choose to obtain extra money from the central bank depends on (a) the rate of interest charged by the central bank (i.e. its discount rate, repo rate or lending rate); and (b) its willingness to lend (or repurchase securities).

In some countries, it is the policy of the central bank to keep its interest rate to banks *below* market rates, thereby encouraging banks to borrow (or sell back securities) whenever such facilities are available. By controlling the amount of money it is willing to provide at these low rates, the central bank can control the monetary base and hence the amount of credit that banks can create.

In other countries, such as the UK and the eurozone countries, it is not so much the amount of money made available that is controlled, but rather the rate of interest (or discount). The higher this rate is relative to other market rates, and hence the lower the monetary base, the less willing banks will be to borrow. Raising this rate, therefore, has the effect of reducing the money supply.

In some countries, central banks operate two rates: a main repo rate (or 'refinancing rate') on a set amount of money that the central bank wants to be made available, and a higher rate (a penal rate) used for 'last-resort' lending to banks short of liquidity. The European Central Bank operates such a system (see Box 21.6). Its higher rate is known as the 'marginal lending facility rate'.

In response to the credit crunch of the late 2000s, central banks in several countries extended their willingness to lend to banks. The pressure on central banks to act as the 'liquidity backstop' grew as the interbank market ceased to function effectively in distributing reserves and, hence, liquidity between financial institutions. As a result, interbank rates rose sharply relative to the policy rate (see Figure 21.8 on page 652). Increasingly, the focus of central banks was

BOX 21.4   THE OPERATION OF MONETARY POLICY IN THE UK

What goes on at Threadneedle Street?

The Bank of England (the 'Bank') does not normally attempt to control money supply directly. Instead it seeks to control interest rates. There are two principal elements to the framework in which it conducts monetary policy. First, it conducts *open-market operations* (OMOs) to adjust the aggregate amount of banks' reserves. Second, *standing facilities* allow individual banks to borrow reserves overnight directly from the Bank or to deposit reserves overnight at the Bank.

The framework is designed to determine short-term interest rates, which then have a knock-on effect on longer-term rates, as returns on different forms of assets must remain competitive with each other.

Normal operation of the monetary framework

Each month the Monetary Policy Committee (MPC) of the Bank of England meets to decide on Bank Rate. Changes in the Bank Rate are intended to affect the whole structure of interest rates in the economy, from interbank rates to bank deposit rates and rates on mortgages and business loans. The monetary framework works to affect the general structure of interest rates, principally by affecting short-term *interbank rates*.

Central to the process are the reserve accounts of financial institutions at the Bank of England (see section 18.2, pages 538–9). From the inception of the current system in May 2006, commercial banks have agreed with the Bank of England the average amount of reserve balances they would hold between MPC meetings. So long as the average over the month is within a small range, the reserves are remunerated at Bank Rate.

In order for individual banks to meet their reserve targets, the Bank of England needs to provide sufficient reserves. To do so, it uses OMOs. In normal circumstances, the Bank of England conducts short-term OMOs every week (on a Thursday) at Bank Rate. The size of the weekly OMO is adjusted to help banks maintain reserves at the target level and to reflect variations in the amount of cash withdrawn or deposited in banks.

To supply reserves the Bank of England will either enter into short-term repo operations lending against collateral ('high-quality' government securities), or buy securities outright. Although there is usually a shortage of liquidity in the banking system, in some weeks there may be a surplus. This would ordinarily drive market interest rates down. Depending on the Bank Rate, the Bank may look to reduce banks' reserves. To do this it can sell government securities on a repo basis, invite bids for Bank of England one-week sterling bills or sell outright some of its portfolio of securities.

At the end of the monthly period between MPC interest rate decisions, the Bank of England conducts a 'fine-tuning' OMO. This is conducted on a Wednesday – the day before the MPC decision on interest rates. The idea is to ensure that banks meet their reserve targets as closely as possible. This OMO could expand or contract liquidity as appropriate.

Longer-term finance is available through longer-term OMOs. Prior to the financial crisis of the late 2000s, longer-term OMOs would normally be conducted once per month. As well as the outright purchase of gilts, the Bank of England would conduct repo lending with 3-, 6-, 9- or 12-month maturities.

The rate of interest on the repos is market determined. Banks bid for the money and the funds are offered to the successful bidders. The bigger the demand for these funds by banks and the lower the supply by the Bank of England, the higher will be the interest rate that banks must pay. By adjusting the supply, therefore, the Bank of England can look to influence longer-term interest rates too.

With the aggregate amount of banks' reserves determined by the Bank of England's OMOs, the task now is for individual banks to meet their agreed reserve targets. This requires that they manage their balance sheets and, in particular, their level of liquidity. In doing so, commercial banks can make use either of the *interbank* market or the 'standing facilities' at the Bank of England. These standing facilities allow individual banks to borrow overnight (secured against high-quality collateral) at a rate *above* Bank Rate or to deposit reserves with the Bank at a rate *below* Bank Rate. Consequently, banks will trade reserves with each other if interbank rates fall within the corridor created by the interest rates of the standing facilities.

The financial crisis and the monetary framework

The financial crisis meant that normal OMOs were no longer sufficient to maintain liquidity for purposes of monetary policy. There was a severe liquidity crisis – one which posed grave risks for financial stability. In response, from January 2009 the Bank of England deliberately injected narrow money in a process known as 'quantitative easing' (see Box 21.9). This involved the Bank of England purchasing assets, largely gilts, from banks. The Bank argued that its asset purchase programme was an important monetary policy tool in meeting its inflation rate target. Between January 2009 and July 2012 the Bank of England injected £375 billion by such means. Quantitative easing thus massively extended the scope of OMOs.

As a result of this significant increase in aggregate reserves, banks were no longer required to set reserve targets. The supply of reserves was now being determined by MPC policy decisions. All reserves were to be remunerated at the Bank Rate.

Furthermore, short-term OMOs were temporarily suspended. Long-term repo operations continued but these were modified to allow financial institutions to sell a wider range of securities. The Bank also adapted its means of providing liquidity insurance (see section 18.2, pages 539–40). This includes the introduction of the Discount Window Facility (DWF), which enables banks to borrow government bonds (gilts) against a wide range of collateral which can then be used in repo operations to secure liquidity.

 Assume that the Bank of England wants to raise interest rates. Trace through the process by which it achieves this.

Table 21.4	Effect of raising the minimum reserve ratio from 10 to 20 per cent						
Initial position: 10% reserve ratio				**New position: 20% reserve ratio**			
Liabilities		**Assets**		**Liabilities**		**Assets**	
Deposits	£100bn	Reserve assets	£10bn	Deposits	£50bn	Reserve assets	£10bn
		Advances, etc.	£90bn			Advances, etc.	£40bn
Total	£100bn	Total	£100bn	Total	£50bn	Total	£50bn

on providing the necessary liquidity to ensure the stability of the financial system. Yet, at the same time, by providing more liquidity, central banks were ensuring monetary policy was not being compromised. The additional liquidity was needed to alleviate the upward pressure on market interest rates.

Changing the method of funding the national debt

Rather than focusing on controlling the monetary base (as in the case of the above two techniques), an alternative is for the authorities to attempt to alter the overall liquidity position of the banks. An example of this approach is a change, by the authorities – the Debt Management Office in the UK – in the balance of *funding* the national debt. To reduce money supply the authorities issue more bonds and fewer bills. Banks' balances with the central bank will be little affected, but to the extent that banks hold fewer bills, there will be a reduction in their liquidity and hence a reduction in the amount of credit created. Funding is thus the conversion of one type of government debt (liquid) into another (illiquid).

One problem with this approach is that bonds are likely to command a higher interest rate than bills. By switching from bills to bonds, the government will be committing itself to these interest rates for the life of the bond.

 If the Bank of England issues £1 million of extra bonds and buys back £1 million of Treasury bills, will there automatically be a reduction in credit by a set multiple of £1 million?

Variable minimum reserve ratios

If banks are required to maintain a statutory minimum reserve ratio and if the central bank is free to alter this ratio, it can use it as a means of controlling the money supply. It does this by affecting not the monetary base, but the size of the bank multiplier.

Assume that there are just two types of asset – cash and advances – and that banks are required to maintain a minimum 10 per cent cash ratio (a ratio above that which the banks would have chosen for reasons of prudence). The bank multiplier is thus 10 (= $1/^1/_{10}$). Assume that banks' total assets are £100 billion, of which £10 billion are cash reserves and £90 billion are advances. This is illustrated in the first part of Table 21.4.

Now assume that the central bank raises the minimum reserve ratio to 20 per cent. Banks still have £10 billion cash reserves, and so they have to reduce their advances to £40 billion (giving total assets of £50 billion, of which the £10 million cash is the required 20 per cent). This is shown in the second part of Table 21.4. The bank multiplier has been reduced to 5 (= $1/^1/_5$).

In the past, central banks that imposed minimum reserve ratios on the banks tended to vary them in this way as a means of altering the money supply for any given monetary base. For example, several of the EU countries used this technique before joining the euro. Increasingly, countries that still have minimum reserve ratios are relying on OMOs or direct lending to banks, rather than on varying the ratio. This is the case with the ECB, which has a fixed reserve ratio of 2 per cent. The USA, however, still uses variable minimum reserve ratios in this way (see Box 21.5).[1]

Difficulties in controlling money supply

The authorities may experience considerable difficulties in controlling broad money supply. Difficulties occur whether they focus on doing this via control of narrow money – the 'monetary base' – or whether they attempt to control a wider range of liquid assets.

Problems with monetary base control

Assume that the authorities seek to control narrow money: i.e. notes and coin. This could be done by imposing a statutory cash ratio on banks. Assume that a statutory ratio of 10 per cent is imposed. Then provided the authorities control the

---

Definition

Funding (in monetary policy) Where the authorities alter the balance of bills and bonds for any given level of government borrowing.

---

[1] In one sense, it could be argued that the imposition of a minimum reserve ratio is a *form* of credit rationing. It restricts the ability of banks to expand credit as much as they would like for the amount of reserves they hold. In Figure 21.5, however, higher minimum reserves would still shift the *supply* curve, given that this curve measures broad money and not the monetary base. It is for this reason that we considered minimum reserve ratios under the heading of 'techniques to control the money supply'.

How the 'Fed' works

The central bank in the USA is called the Federal Reserve System (or 'Fed'). It was set up in 1913 and consists of 12 regional Federal Reserve Banks, each of which is responsible for distributing currency and regulating banks in its region. But despite its apparent regional nature, it is still a national system. The Federal Reserve Board, based in Washington, decides on monetary policy and then the Federal Open Market Committee (FOMC) decides how to carry it out. The FOMC meets eight times a year. The Fed is independent of both the President and the Congress, and its chairman is generally regarded as having great power in determining the country's economic policy.

Its macroeconomic objectives include low inflation, sustainable economic growth, low unemployment and moderate long-term interest rates. Of course, these objectives may well conflict from time to time. In such a case, an assessment has to be made of which is the most pressing problem.

When there is no threat of rising inflation, the Fed may use monetary policy aggressively to pursue these other goals. Thus, from January to December 2001, with the US economy moving into recession, the FOMC cut interest rates 10 times. In January the rate was 6 per cent; by December it was down to 1.75 per cent.

Even when inflation is rising, the Fed may still cut interest rates if the economy is slowing. With the onset of the credit crunch of 2007–8, the Fed cut rates several times. In August 2007, the rate was 5.25 per cent. By August 2008 it had been cut to 2 per cent, even though inflation was rising (see Chart (a) in Box 21.11). Then as inflation fell and recession deepened, rates were cut again to stand at between 0 and 0.25 per cent by December 2008.

To carry out its objectives, the FOMC has traditionally had three policy instruments. The most important one is *open-market operations*. These are conducted through the Federal Reserve Bank of New York, which buys and sells Treasury bills and government bonds. For example, if the FOMC wishes to increase money supply, the New York Fed will buy more of these securities. The purchasers, whether they be banks, corporations or individuals, will have their bank accounts duly credited. In other words, the Fed credits

the accounts of sellers with a deposit and this enables a multiple increase in credit.

The second policy instrument is the *discount rate*. Known as the 'federal funds rate', this is the rate of interest at which the Fed is willing to lend to banks, thereby providing them with liquidity on which they can create credit. This is known as 'lending through the discount window'. If this rate is raised, banks are discouraged from borrowing, and credit is thereby squeezed. Since 1995, the FOMC has published its target federal funds rate. Sometimes this rate merely mirrors other market rates and is not, therefore, an active instrument of policy. On other occasions, however, the Fed changes it ahead of other market rates in order to signal its intention to tighten (or loosen) monetary policy.[1]

The final instrument is *reserve requirements*. Banks are legally required to hold a certain minimum percentage of eligible deposit liabilities as reserves. Interest is paid on these reserves. The reserve requirement is dependent on the size of a bank's eligible deposit liabilities. Banks with an amount of liabilities falling within an adjustable exemption range have no reserve requirement. Above this is the 'low-reserve tranche' range. As of January 2014, banks with eligible deposit liabilities within this range must hold 3 per cent of deposits in reserves. Banks with an eligible deposit total in excess of this must hold 10 per cent in reserves.

Currently the only deposit accounts subject to reserve requirements are transaction accounts, which include sight accounts ('checking accounts') and time deposits. The Fed can vary the types of deposits subject to the reserve requirement as well as the size and number of bands and the reserve ratios. Given that any change in the reserve ratio causes a multiplied effect on advances, changes are made only occasionally and by a small amount.

Response to the credit crunch

With the credit crunch of 2007–8 and the difficulties of banks in obtaining finance from the interbank market, the Fed extended its activities. It made considerable liquidity available to banks by swapping Treasury bills for hard-to-trade securities, such as mortgage-backed bonds and other securitised assets, including those backed by student loans.

---

supply of cash by, say, OMOs, it would seem that they can thereby control the creation of credit and hence deposits. There would be a bank multiplier of 10. For every £1 million decrease in cash held by the banks, money supply would fall by £10 million. There are serious problems, however, with this form of *monetary base control*:

Monetary base control Monetary policy that focuses on controlling the monetary base (as opposed to broad liquidity).

- Banks could hold cash in excess of the statutory minimum. For a time, therefore, they could respond to any restriction of cash by the authorities by simply reducing their cash ratio towards the minimum, rather than having to reduce credit.
- Unless cash ratios were imposed on every single financial institution, the control of certain institutions' lending would merely shift business to other uncontrolled institutions, including overseas ones. Banks operate in a global market. Thus UK banks can do business with UK borrowers using money markets abroad, thereby diverting potentially profitable business away from London. This is an example of Goodhart's law (see Box 21.7 on page 653).

KI 36
p653

It also extended the period of its short-term loans through the discount window and was now willing to lend not only to retail banks but to investment banks and mortgage lenders too.

Then in October 2008, the US government adopted a $700 billion rescue package for the ailing US financial system. This was known as the Troubled Asset Relief Program (TARP). The plan was to purchase 'distressed assets' including collateralised debt obligations (see section 18.2). The purchases were designed to provide liquidity for the holders of these CDOs, to stabilise the financial system and, in turn, encourage bank lending. In return for participating in TARP, financial institutions effectively gave the US Treasury part-ownership. Revisions to the TARP saw the first $250 billion allocated for the programme used to purchase preference shares from nine of the largest US banks. Subsequently, purchases of toxic assets took place, including mortgage-backed securities.

The US government's measures were backed up by the Fed, which embarked on an aggressive policy of increasing the money supply through the purchase of long-term securities. It announced in November 2008 that it planned to purchase $100 billion of corporate debt issued by government-sponsored financial enterprises and $500 billion of mortgage-backed securities (MBS), including MBS guaranteed by mortgage lenders Fannie Mae and Freddie Mac, which had recently been nationalised to save them from collapse.

In March 2009, the Fed announced that it would increase its purchases of debt issued by government-sponsored financial enterprises by a further $100 billion and its purchases of MBS by a further $750 billion. The hope was to stimulate bank lending and revive the collapsed housing market. It also announced that it would purchase $300 billion of longer-term Treasury securities.

In total, $1.25 trillion of MBS were purchased between January 2009 and March 2010. But still the economy remained fragile. In November 2010 a second round of quantitative easing was announced. This was to be dubbed QE2. Between November 2010 and June 2011 the Fed expanded its holding of longer-term Treasury securities by $600 billion. The aim was 'to promote a stronger pace of economic recovery'.

In September 2011 the Fed announced that in the period up to June 2012 it would buy up to $400 billion of long-term government bonds in the market and sell an equal amount of shorter-dated ones (of less than three years). The plan became known as 'Operation Twist'. It is a way of altering the *funding* of national debt, rather than directly altering the monetary base. The idea was to drive up the price of long-term bonds and hence drive down their yield and thereby drive down long-term interest rates. The hope was to stimulate investment and longer-term borrowing. The plan was expanded in June 2012 with the sale of a further $267 billion in Treasury securities by the end of the year.

In September 2012 the Fed launched a third round of quantitative easing, dubbed QE3. The hope was that the resulting growth in money supply would stimulate spending and thereby increase growth and employment. Under QE3, the Fed would purchase $40 billion of MBS per month, extended to $85 billion per month in December 2012. And this would go on for as long as it took for the employment market to show significant improvements. It was this open-ended commitment which made QE3 different from QE1 and QE2. Under QE1 and QE2, the Fed purchased a fixed amount of assets, namely $2.3 trillion of bonds.

In December 2013, the Fed announced the start of a tapering off of its quantitative easing programme. In other words, monthly purchases of MBS and longer-term Treasury securities were reduced. The expectation was that the programme would continue to wind down over 2014, contingent on labour market conditions and the expected longer-term path of inflation.

1. In what ways is the Fed's operation of monetary policy (a) similar to and (b) different from the Bank of England's?
2. Could there be a potential moral hazard problem arising out of the actions taken by the Fed and the US government in response to the financial crisis?

[1] For details of the Fed's interest rate policy, see www.federalreserve.gov/fomc/fundsrate.htm

■ Alternatively, if those banks subject to statutory cash requirements were short of cash, they could attract cash away from the uncontrolled institutions.

The switching of business away from controlled banks is known as **disintermediation**. To avoid this problem and to allow the greatest freedom of competition between financial institutions, the alternative is to use monetary base control with no *statutory* cash ratio.

But two major problems with monetary base control, with or without a statutory cash ratio, are the most serious of all. The first is that central banks *are always prepared to increase the monetary base, through repos or rediscounting, if it is demanded.* This makes it virtually impossible to have a precise control of the monetary base.

The second is the size and variability of the money multiplier. As we saw in section 18.3 (page 546), the money multiplier is the number of times greater the rise in (broad) money supply is than the rise in the monetary base. As Figure 18.4 (see page 547) demonstrates, the broad money

Definition

Disintermediation The diversion of business away from financial institutions that are subject to controls.

TC 15
p 508

multiplier can be highly variable. In other words, controlling the monetary base would have a highly unpredictable effect on the money supply.

For these reasons, the support for monetary base control has waned in recent years.

1. *Trace through the effects of a squeeze on the monetary base from an initial reduction in cash to banks' liquidity being restored through gilt repos. Will this restoration of liquidity by the central bank totally nullify the initial effect of reducing the supply of cash? (Clue: what is likely to happen to the rate of interest?)*
2. *Given the difficulties of monetary base control, would you expect cash in circulation and broader measures of the money supply, such as M4, to rise and fall by the same percentage as each other?*

Problems with controlling broad money supply

One solution to the problems of monetary base control would be for the authorities to attempt to control broader money supply directly. In the UK, targets for the growth in broad money were an important part of monetary policy from 1976 to 1985. The UK has not targeted money supply growth since the 1980s, however. The European Central Bank has a 'reference value' of 4.5 per cent for M3 growth of the euro (see Box 18.4 on page 544 for a definition of M3). This, however, is only a guideline and not a strict target.

How would such a policy work? Assume that the authorities want to operate a tight monetary policy. They sell bonds on the open market. Banks, now short of cash, obtain money from the central bank through rediscounting bills or through repos. Thus although the central bank has been obliged to restore the amount of cash it had withdrawn from the system, there has been a decrease in bills and short-term bonds held by the banks. Banks' *overall* liquidity has thus been reduced. Such measures could be backed up by changing the funding methods.

But, as with monetary base control, there are problems with attempting to control broad money supply. Banks may be prepared to reduce their liquidity ratio. This is likely if they already have surplus liquidity, or if their customers are prepared to switch from sight to time accounts (for which banks require fewer cash reserves). This will involve offering higher interest rates on time accounts, and hence charging higher interest rates on bank loans. But if the demand for loans is relatively insensitive to interest rate changes, this will have little effect on credit or on overall deposits.

The use of open-market operations or funding to reduce money supply involves selling more bonds. But if potential purchasers believe interest rates will rise in the future (highly likely when the government is attempting to operate a tighter monetary policy), they will hold off buying bonds now and may even attempt to sell bonds before bond prices fall. Thus the authorities may be forced into a large immediate increase in bond interest rates.

In circumstances where the central bank wants to *increase* broad money, the problem can be even more

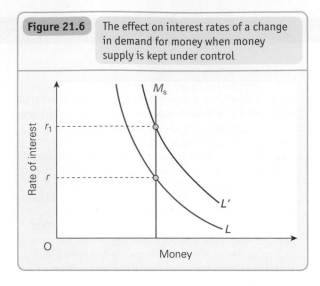

Figure 21.6 The effect on interest rates of a change in demand for money when money supply is kept under control

serious. Purchasing bonds may increase liquidity in the banking sector, but (a) people may not want to borrow if the economy is going into recession and people are trying to cut back on spending; (b) banks may be reluctant to lend, preferring to keep the extra liquidity in reserve as a precaution against people defaulting on debts. These were problems facing the Bank of England as it started on its programme of large-scale asset purchases (quantitative easing) in March 2009 (see Box 21.9).

Perhaps the biggest problem is the effect on interest rates.

The effect on interest rates

A policy of controlling money supply can lead to severe fluctuations in interest rates. This can cause great uncertainty for business and can be very damaging to long-term investment and growth.

The problem is more acute if the overall demand for money is inelastic and is subject to fluctuations. In Figure 21.6, with money supply controlled at M_s, even a fairly moderate increase in demand from L to L' leads to a large rise in interest rates from r to r_1.

And yet, if the authorities are committed to controlling money supply, they will have to accept that equilibrium interest rates may well fluctuate in this way.

Because of the above difficulties in controlling the money supply directly, countries have become increasingly reliant on controlling interest rates (backed up, normally, by open-market operations).

Techniques to control interest rates

The approach to monetary control today in many countries is to focus directly on interest rates. Normally an interest rate change will be announced, and then open-market operations will be conducted by the central bank to ensure that the money supply is adjusted so as to make the announced interest rate the *equilibrium* one. Thus, in Figure 21.5, the central bank might announce a rise in interest rates from r_1 to r_2 and then conduct open-market operations to ensure that the money supply is reduced from Q_1 to Q_2.

In the UK, since the Bank of England was made independent in 1997, interest rate changes have been made by the Bank's Monetary Policy Committee (MPC) at its monthly meetings. These are then backed up through the Bank's operations in the gilt repo and discount markets (see Box 21.4). Similarly, in the eurozone, the ECB's Governing Council sets interest rates at its fortnightly meetings (see Box 21.6).

Let us assume that the central bank decides to raise interest rates. What does it do? In general, it will seek to keep banks short of liquidity. This will happen automatically on any day when tax payments by banks' customers exceed the money they receive from government expenditure. This excess is effectively withdrawn from banks and ends up in the government's account at the central bank. Even when this does not occur, sales of bills by the central bank will effectively keep the banking system short of liquidity.

This 'shortage' can then be used as a way of forcing through interest rate changes. Banks will obtain the necessary liquidity from the central bank through gilt repos or by selling it back bills. The central bank can *choose the rate of interest to charge* (i.e. the gilt repo rate or the bill rediscount rate). This will then have a knock-on effect on other interest rates throughout the banking system.

The effects can be illustrated as in Figure 21.7, both parts of which assume that the central bank wishes to raise the interest rate (the repo or discount rate) from r_1 to r_2.

In Figure 21.7(a), it is assumed that banks are short of liquidity and are seeking to sell gilts to the central bank on a repo basis. It is assumed that the central bank will supply as much cash (i.e. demand as many gilts through repos) as banks choose, but only at the central bank's chosen repo rate. The demand for gilts is thus perfectly elastic at the central bank's repo rate. The supply curve of gilts by the banks represents their demand for cash from the central

bank, and hence is *downward* sloping: the lower the repo rate, the cheaper it is for the banks to obtain cash. If the central bank raises the repo rate to r_2, banks will supply fewer gilts (i.e. demand less cash from the central bank). If there is less liquidity in the banking system, the money supply will fall.

In the event of banks having a surplus of liquidity, Figure 21.7(b) applies. Here banks are seeking to use their surplus liquidity to *buy* bills from the central bank. Their demand curve is *upward* sloping: the higher the rate of discount (i.e. the lower the price that banks have to pay for bills), the more the banks will demand. In this case, the central bank can raise the rate of discount by offering more bills for sale. By increasing the supply of bills from S_1 to S_2, it can increase the equilibrium rate from r_1 to r_2.

In both cases, the central bank will first decide on the repo rate (or discount rate) and then adjust the supply or demand of gilts or bills to ensure that the chosen rate is the equilibrium rate (see Boxes 21.4, 21.5 and 21.6 for details of how the Bank of England, the Fed and the ECB do this in practice).

A change in the repo rate will then have a knock-on effect on other interest rates. For example, in the UK, banks normally automatically adjust their base rates (to which they gear their other rates) when the Bank of England announces a change in Bank Rate (i.e. the repo rate). Thus a 0.25 percentage point rise in Bank Rate will normally mean a 0.25 percentage point rise in banks' deposit rates, overdraft rates, etc.

Changes in Bank Rate, however, will not necessarily have an *identical* effect on other interest rates. This is illustrated in Figure 21.8, which shows the UK's Bank Rate alongside the average mortgage rate and 1-month LIBOR (*interbank* lending rate). Banks are often slow to adjust mortgage rates. As you can see, the average mortgage rate did not fall nearly as much as Bank Rate in 2008/9 and remained some 3.5 percentage points above Bank Rate, compared with around 2 percentage points previously.

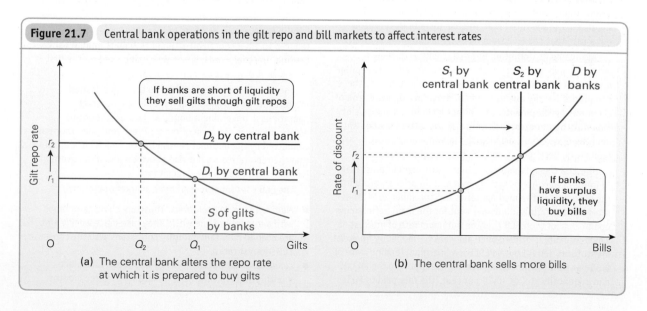

Figure 21.7 Central bank operations in the gilt repo and bill markets to affect interest rates

(a) The central bank alters the repo rate at which it is prepared to buy gilts

(b) The central bank sells more bills

BOX 21.6   **MONETARY POLICY IN THE EUROZONE**

The role of the ECB

The European Central Bank (ECB) is based in Frankfurt and is charged with operating the monetary policy of those EU countries that have adopted the euro. Although the ECB has the overall responsibility for the eurozone's monetary policy, the central banks of the individual countries, such as the Bank of France and Germany's Bundesbank, were abolished. They are responsible for distributing euros and for carrying out the ECB's policy with respect to institutions in their own countries. The whole system of the ECB and the national central banks is known as the European System of Central Banks (ESCB).

In operating the monetary policy of a 'euro economy' roughly the size of the USA, and in being independent from national governments, the ECB's power is enormous and is equivalent to that of the Fed (see Box 21.5). So what is the structure of this giant on the European stage, and how does it operate?

The structure of the ECB

The ECB has two major decision-making bodies: the Governing Council and the Executive Board:[1]

- The Governing Council consists of the members of the Executive Board and the governors of the central banks of each of the eurozone countries. The Council's role is to set the main targets of monetary policy and to take an oversight of the success (or otherwise) of that policy.
- The Executive Board consists of a president, a vice-president and four other members. Each serves for an eight-year, non-renewable term. The Executive Board is responsible for implementing the decisions of the Governing Council and for preparing policies for the Council's consideration. Each member of the Executive Board has a responsibility for some particular aspect of monetary policy.

The targets of monetary policy

The overall responsibility of the ECB is to achieve price stability in the eurozone. The target is a rate of inflation below, but close to, 2 per cent over the medium term. It is a weighted average rate for all the members of the eurozone, not a rate that has to be met by every member individually.

Alongside its definition of price stability, the ECB's monetary policy strategy comprises what it calls 'a two-pillar approach to the analysis of the risks to price stability'. These two pillars are any analysis of monetary developments and of economic developments. The former includes an analysis of monetary aggregates, including M3. The latter includes an analysis of economic activity, the labour market, cost indicators, fiscal policy and the balance of payments.

The ECB then attempts to 'steer' short-term interest rates to influence economic activity to maintain price stability in the euro area in the medium term. In September 2014, the rates were as follows: 0.05 per cent for the main 'refinancing operations' of the ESCB (i.e. the minimum rate of interest at which liquidity is offered once per week to 'monetary financial institutions' (MFIs) by the ESCB); a 'marginal lending' rate of 0.30 per cent (for providing overnight support to the MFIs); and a 'deposit rate' of −0.20 per cent (the rate paid to MFIs

for depositing overnight surplus liquidity with the ESCB). The negative deposit rate meant that banks were being charged for 'parking' money with the ECB rather than lending it. The hope was that this would encourage banks to lend to each other or to households and businesses and, consequently, help stimulate the eurozone economy.

Interest rates are set by the Governing Council by simple majority. In the event of a tie, the president has the casting vote.

The operation of monetary policy

The ECB sets a minimum reserve ratio. It argues that this gives greater stability to the system and reduces the need for day-to-day intervention by the ECB. The ECB argues that, if there were no minimum reserves, with banks free to use as much of their reserves with the ESCB as they chose, then they would do so if there were an upsurge in demand from customers. After all, the banks know that they can always borrow from the ESCB to meet any liquidity requirements. In such a situation, the ECB would be forced to rely much more on open-market operations to prevent excessive lending by banks to their customers, and hence excessive borrowing from the ESCB, and this would mean much greater fluctuations in interest rates.

Without the use of a minimum reserve system, the ESCB would be faced with a relatively high volatility of money market rates, which would require the frequent use of open-market operations for fine-tuning purposes. Such a situation would have clear disadvantages in practical terms and could undermine the operational efficiency of monetary policy, as central bank signals may become blurred if markets have difficulty distinguishing policy signals from technical adjustments.[2]

The minimum reserve ratio was not designed, however, to be used to make changes in monetary policy. In other words, it was not used as a variable minimum reserves ratio, and for this reason it was set at a low level. From 1 January 1999 to 17 January 2012 the ratio (all known as the reserve coefficient) was 2 per cent of key liquid and relatively liquid liabilities. However, as of 18 January 2012 the ratio was reduced to 1 per cent in an attempt to help stimulate bank lending. In other words, it was now being used for the first time as part of an active monetary policy.

The main instrument for keeping the ECB's desired interest rate as the equilibrium rate is open-market operations in government bonds and other recognised assets, mainly in the form of repos. These repo operations are conducted by the national central banks, which must ensure that the repo rate does not rise above the marginal overnight lending rate or below the deposit rate.

The ECB uses four types of open-market operations:

- *Main refinancing operations*. These are short-term repos with a maturity of one week. They take place weekly and are used to maintain liquidity consistent with the chosen ECB interest rate.
- *Longer-term refinancing operations*. These take place monthly and typically have a maturity of three months.

Longer maturities are available, but such operations are conducted more irregularly. They are to provide additional longer-term liquidity to banks as required at rates determined by the market, not the ECB.

- *Fine-tuning operations*. These can be short-term sales or purchases of short-term assets. They are designed to combat unexpected changes in liquidity and hence to keep money market rates at the ECB's chosen rate.
- *Structural operations*. These are used as necessary to adjust the amount of liquidity in the eurozone. They can involve either the purchase or sale of various assets.

ECB independence

The ECB is one of the most independent central banks in the world. It has very little formal accountability to elected politicians. Although its president can be called before the European Parliament, the Parliament has virtually no powers to influence the ECB's actions. Also, its deliberations are secret. Unlike those of the Bank of England's Monetary Policy Committee, the minutes of the Council meetings are not published.

There is one area, however, where the ECB's power is limited by politicians and this concerns the exchange rate of the euro. Under the Maastricht Treaty, EU finance ministers have the responsibility for deciding on exchange rate policy (even though the ECB is charged with carrying it out). If the finance ministers want to stop the exchange rate of the euro rising, in order to prevent putting EU exporters at a competitive disadvantage, this will put pressure on the ECB to lower interest rates, which might run directly counter to its desire to meet its inflation and money supply targets. This is an example of the principle of 'targets and instruments'. If you have only one instrument (the rate of interest), it cannot be used to achieve two targets (the exchange rate and inflation) if these two targets are in conflict (see Box 21.8).

Financial crisis

The financial crisis put incredible strains on commercial banks in the eurozone and, hence, on the ECB's monetary framework. Consequently, monetary operations were gradually modified.

A Securities Market Programme (SMP) began in May 2010 designed to supply liquidity to the ailing banking system. It allowed for ECB purchases of central government debt in the secondary market (i.e. not directly from governments) as well as purchases in both primary and secondary markets of private-sector debt instruments. By June 2012, €214 billion of purchases had been made, largely of government bonds issued by countries experiencing financing difficulties, including Portugal, Ireland, Greece and Spain.

As we saw earlier, the reserve ratio was reduced in January 2012 from 2 per cent to 1 per cent, so helping to alleviate some of the constraints on the volume of bank lending by banks. This move was preceded in December 2011 by three-year refinancing operations (LTROs) worth €529.5 billion and involving some 800 banks. By the end of February 2012, a further €489.2 billion of three-year loans

to 523 banks took place, taking the ECB's repo operations to over €1 trillion. The hope was that the funds would help financially distressed banks pay off maturing debt and again increase their lending.

Then in September 2012, with worries about the continuing difficulties of some eurozone countries, such as Greece, Spain and Italy, to borrow at affordable rates and possibly, as a result, their being driven from the euro, the ECB announced a replacement for the SMP. This would involve a more extensive programme of purchasing existing government bonds with up to three years of maturity in the secondary market. The aim would be to drive down these countries' interest rates and thereby make it cheaper to issue new bonds when old ones matured. These Outright Monetary Transactions (OMTs) were in principle unlimited, with the ECB President, Mario Draghi, saying that the ECB would do 'whatever it takes' to hold the single currency together.

Critics argued that this would still not be enough to stimulate the eurozone economy and help to bring countries out of recession. They gave two reasons.

The first is that the programme of OMTs typically differed from the quantitative easing programmes used in the UK and the USA. ECB purchases of these bonds generally did not increase the eurozone money supply as the ECB would sell off other assets to compensate. This process is known as *sterilisation*.

The second reason is the OMTs were *only* conducted if countries stuck to previously agreed austerity measures. Despite the eurozone economy contracting by 0.6 per cent in 2012 and by a further 0.4 per cent in 2013, OMTs had still not been used.

Subsequent measures followed. In June 2014, the ECB announced that it was adopting a negative deposit rate (see above), that it was embarking on a further series of targeted long-term refinancing operations so as provide long-term loans to commercial banks at cheap rates until September 2018, and that it would stop sterilising its SMP programme. Then in September 2014, it announced that it would be commencing the purchase of asset-backed securities, such as securitised mortgages and commercial loans (see section 18.2). Nonetheless, some feared that the announcements still did not go far enough given the problems facing the eurozone economy.

 What are the arguments for and against publishing the minutes of the meetings of the ECB's Governing Council and Executive Board?

---

[1] See www.ecb.int/ecb/orga/decisions/govc/html/index.en.html
[2] 'The use of a minimum reserve system by the European System of Central Banks in Stage Three', www.ecb.int/press/pr/date/1998/html/pr981013r3.en.html

Definition

Sterilisation Actions taken by a central bank to offset the effects of foreign exchange flows or its own bond transactions so as to leave money supply unchanged.

Figure 21.8 Average monthly interest rates

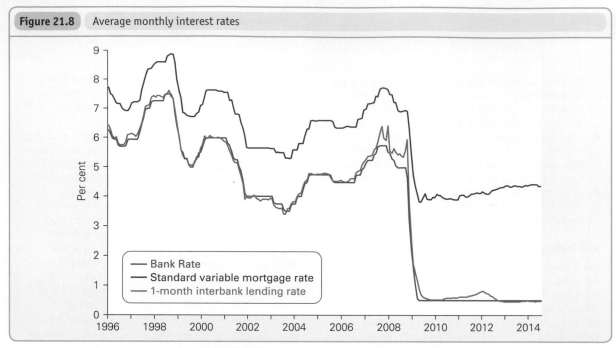

Source: Based on *Statistical Interactive Database*, series IUMABEDR (Bank Rate), IUMTLMV (mortgage rate) and IUMAVNEA (interbank rate) (Bank of England) (data published 3 August 2014, seasonally adjusted except for reserves).

Interbank rates also may not follow Bank Rate changes precisely. During the height of the credit crunch in 2008, the LIBOR diverged considerably from Bank Rate as banks became reluctant to lend to each other for fear that banks would default on their loans.

Problems with controlling interest rates

Even though central bank adjustment of the repo rate is the current preferred method of monetary control in most countries, it is not without its difficulties. The problems centre on the nature of the demand for loans. If this demand is (a) unresponsive to interest rate changes or (b) unstable because it can be significantly affected by other determinants (e.g. anticipated income or foreign interest rates), it will be very difficult to control by controlling the rate of interest.

Problem of an inelastic demand for loans

If the demand for loans is inelastic, as in Figure 21.9, any attempt to reduce demand (e.g. from Q_1 to Q_2) will involve large rises in interest rates (r_1 to r_2). The problem will be compounded if the demand curve shifts to the right, due, say, to a consumer spending boom. High interest rates lead to the following problems:

- They may discourage long-term investment (as opposed to current consumption) and hence long-term growth.
- They add to the costs of production, to the costs of house purchase and generally to the cost of living. They are thus cost inflationary.
- They are politically unpopular, since the general public do not like paying higher interest rates on overdrafts, credit cards and mortgages.

Figure 21.9 An inelastic demand for loans

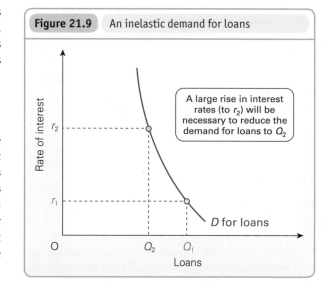

A large rise in interest rates (to r_2) will be necessary to reduce the demand for loans to Q_2

- The authorities may need to ensure a sufficient supply of longer-term securities so that liquidity can be constrained. This could commit the government to paying high rates on these bonds for some time.
- High interest rates encourage inflows of money from abroad. This makes it even more difficult to restrain bank lending.
- Inflows of money from abroad drive up the exchange rate. This can be very damaging for export industries and industries competing with imports. Many firms in the UK suffered badly between 1998 and 2007 from a high exchange rate (see Table 15.5 on page 456) induced partly by higher interest rates than those in the eurozone.

Evidence suggests that the demand for loans may indeed be quite inelastic, especially in the short run. Although

| BOX 21.7 | GOODHART'S LAW | EXPLORING ECONOMICS |

'To control is to distort'

'If you want to tackle a problem, it's best to get to the root of it.'

This is a message that economists are constantly preaching. If you merely treat the symptoms of a problem rather than its underlying causes, the problem may simply manifest itself in some other form. What is more, the symptoms (or lack of them, if the treatment makes them go away) will now be a poor indicator of the problem. Let's illustrate this with a medical example.

Assume that you suffer from deteriorating eyesight. As a result, you get increasingly bad headaches. The worse the headaches become, the worse it suggests your eyesight is getting. The headaches are thus a symptom of the problem and an indicator of the problem's magnitude. So what do you do? One approach is to treat the symptoms. You regularly take painkillers and the headaches go away. But you haven't treated the underlying problem – by getting stronger glasses, or perhaps even having eye surgery – all you have done is to treat the symptoms. As a result, headaches (or rather the lack of them) are now a poor indicator of your eyesight.

If you control the indicator rather than the underlying problem, the indicator ceases to be a good indicator. 'To control [the indicator] is to distort [its use as an indicator].' This is *Goodhart's law* and it has many applications in economics, especially when targets are set by the government. Let us take the example of a money supply target.

> *Goodhart's law:* Controlling a symptom (i.e. an indicator) of a problem will not cure the problem. Instead, the indicator will merely cease to be a good indicator of the problem.

Money as an indicator of aggregate demand

Monetarists argue that the level of money supply determines the level of nominal aggregate demand and prices. They therefore argue in favour of setting targets for the growth of money supply. Critics, however, argue that the level of money supply is only an indicator of the level of nominal aggregate demand (and a poor one at that). As soon as you start to control money supply, they say, the relationship between them breaks down. If, for example, you restrict the amount of money and yet people still want to borrow, money will simply circulate faster (the velocity of circulation (V) will rise), and hence aggregate demand may not decline.

The choice of money supply target

If targets for the growth of money supply are to be set, which measure of money supply should be chosen? Goodhart's law suggests that whichever measure is chosen it will, by virtue of its choice, become a poor indicator. If the government targets cash in circulation and directs its policy to reducing the amount of notes and coin in the economy, banks may try to reduce their customers' demand for cash by, say, increasing the charges for cash advances on credit cards. As a result, cash may well be constrained, but M4 may well go on rising.

The choice of institutions

If bank advances are a good indicator of aggregate demand, the government may choose to control bank lending. But as soon as it does so, bank lending will become a poor indicator. If people's demand for loans is still high and bank loans are becoming difficult to obtain, people will simply go elsewhere to borrow money. If you regulate part of the financial system, you are likely to end up merely diverting business to other parts which are unregulated.

1. *Give some everyday examples of Goodhart's law.*
2. *How may the use of targets in the health service (such as getting waiting lists down) provide an example of Goodhart's law?*

---

investment plans may be curtailed by high interest rates, borrowing to finance current expenditure by many firms cannot easily be curtailed. Similarly, while householders may be discouraged from taking on new mortgages, they may find it difficult to reduce current expenditure as a means of reducing their credit-card debt. What is more, although high interest rates may discourage many firms from taking out long-term fixed-interest loans, some firms may merely switch to shorter-term variable-interest loans.

Problem of an unstable demand

Accurate monetary control requires the authorities to be able to predict the demand curve for money. Only then can they set the appropriate level of interest rates. Unfortunately, the demand curve may shift unpredictably, making control very difficult. The major reason is *speculation*:

- If people think interest rates will rise and bond prices fall, in the meantime they will want to hold their assets in liquid form. The demand for money will rise.
- If people think exchange rates will rise, they will want sterling while it is still relatively cheap. The demand for money will rise.
- If people think inflation will rise, the transactions demand for money may rise. People spend now while prices are still relatively low.
- If people think the economy is going to grow faster, the demand for loans will increase as firms seek to increase their investment.

Definition

Goodhart's law Controlling a symptom of a problem or only one part of the problem will not cure the problem: it will simply mean that the part that is being controlled now becomes a poor indicator of the problem.

It is very difficult for the authorities to predict what people's speculation will be. Speculation depends largely on world political events, rumour and 'random shocks'.

If the demand curve shifts very much, and if it is inelastic, monetary control will be very difficult. Furthermore, the authorities will have to make frequent and sizeable adjustments to interest rates. These fluctuations can be very damaging to business confidence and may discourage long-term investment.

> *Why does an unstable demand for money make it difficult to control the supply of money?*

The net result of an inelastic and unstable demand for money is that substantial interest rate changes may be necessary to bring about the required change in aggregate demand. An example occurred in 2001, when the US Federal Reserve, seeing the economy moving rapidly into recession, had to cut interest rates several times. At the beginning of 2001, the US 'federal funds rate' was 6 per cent. By the end of the year it had been reduced to 1.75 per cent.

Similar moves were made to prevent recession arising from the credit crunch. In August 2007, the rate was 5.25 per cent. By December 2008, the Fed had cut it to between 0 and 0.25 per cent. But even this was not enough to give a sufficient boost to lending and borrowing. The Fed had to resort to a large expansion of money supply by extraordinary means: the policy of quantitative easing (see Box 21.9).

Using monetary policy

It is impossible to use monetary policy as a precise means of controlling aggregate demand. It is especially weak when it is pulling against the expectations of firms and consumers, and when it is implemented too late. However, if the authorities operate a tight monetary policy firmly enough and long enough, they should eventually be able to reduce lending and aggregate demand. But there will inevitably be time lags and imprecision in the process.

An expansionary monetary policy is even less reliable. If the economy is in recession, no matter how low interest rates are driven, people cannot be forced to borrow if they do not wish to. Firms will not borrow to invest if they predict a continuing recession.

A particular difficulty in using interest rate reductions to expand the economy arises if the repo rate is nearly zero but this is still not enough to stimulate the economy. The problem is that (nominal) interest rates cannot be negative, for clearly nobody would be willing to lend in these circumstances. While this situation was experienced by many countries as a result of the financial crisis of the late 2000s, Japan had faced a similar situation back in the early 2000s. It found itself caught in the 'liquidity trap' (see pages 562–3).

One way in which central banks, like the Federal Reserve, the Bank of England and the ECB, attempted to encourage spending following the financial crisis of the late 2000s was

---

| BOX 21.8 | USING INTEREST RATES TO CONTROL *BOTH* AGGREGATE DEMAND *AND* THE EXCHANGE RATE | EXPLORING ECONOMICS |

A problem of one instrument and two targets

Assume that the central bank is worried about excessive growth in the money supply and rising inflation. It thus decides to raise interest rates. One effect of these higher interest rates is to attract deposits into the country (causing a financial account surplus) and thus drive up the exchange rate. This makes imports cheaper and exports less competitive. This will result in a current account deficit, which will match the financial (plus capital) account surplus.

Now let us assume that the central bank becomes worried about the damaging effect on exports and wants to reduce the exchange rate. If it uses interest rates as the means of achieving this, it will have to lower them: lower interest rates will cause deposits to flow out of the country, and this will cause the rate of exchange to depreciate.

But there is a dilemma here. The central bank wants high interest rates to contain inflation, but low interest rates to help exporters. If interest rates are the only policy instrument, one objective will have to be sacrificed for the other.

Another example, but this time the reverse case, was when the UK was forced out of the 'exchange rate mechanism' (ERM) in September 1992. As we shall see in section 26.2, the ERM was a system of semi-fixed exchange rates between

European currencies. The UK joined the ERM in 1990 at a relatively high rate of exchange. In its attempt to stay in the ERM and prevent speculation driving down the exchange rate, it had to keep interest rates at very high levels. But the economy was deep in recession and a lower interest rate would have helped to stimulate investment and aggregate demand generally. On this occasion the government wanted high interest rates to support the exchange rate, but low interest rates to revive the economy. Once the country had left the ERM and the pound was allowed to float, interest rates were reduced. There was no longer any conflict.

These examples illustrate a rule in economic policy: you must have at least as many instruments as targets. If you have two targets (e.g. low inflation and a low exchange rate), you must have at least two policy instruments (e.g. interest rates and one other).

1. *Give some other examples of the impossibility of using one policy instrument to achieve two policy objectives simultaneously.*
2. *If the central bank wanted to achieve a lower rate of inflation and also a higher exchange rate, could it under these circumstances rely simply on the one policy instrument of interest rates?*

BOX 21.9 **QUANTITATIVE EASING**

Rethinking monetary policy in hard times

As the economies of the world slid into recession in 2008, central banks became more and more worried that the traditional instrument of monetary policy – controlling interest rates – was insufficient to ward off a slump in demand.

Running out of options?

Interest rates had been cut at an unprecedented rate. Central banks were reaching the end of the road for interest rate cuts. The Fed was the first to be in this position. It had made several cuts in the target federal funds rate – the overnight rate at which the Fed lends to banks. By December 2008 it had been cut to a range between 0 and 0.25 per cent. Meanwhile, in the UK, Bank Rate had fallen to 0.5 per cent by March 2009. But you cannot cut nominal rates below zero – otherwise you would be paying people to borrow money, which would be like giving people free money!

The problem was that there was an acute lack of willingness of banks to lend and firms and consumers to borrow as people saw the oncoming recession. So the cuts in interest rates were not having enough effect on aggregate demand.

Increasing the money supply

So what were central banks to do? The answer was to increase money supply directly, in a process known as *quantitative easing*. This involves an aggressive version of open-market operations, where the central bank buys up a range of assets, such as securitised mortgage debt and long-term government bonds. The effect is to pump large amounts of additional cash into the economy in the hope of stimulating demand and, through the process of credit creation, to boost broad money too.

In the USA, in December 2008, at the same time as the federal funds rate was cut to a range of 0 to 0.25 per cent, the Fed was already embarking on large-scale quantitative easing. As we saw in Box 21.5, the Fed began buying hundreds of billions of dollars' worth of mortgage-backed securities on the open market and planned also to buy large quantities of long-term government debt. The Federal Open Market Committee (the interest-rate-setting body in the USA) said: 'The focus of the committee's policy going forward will be to support the functioning of financial markets and stimulate the economy through open-market operations and other measures that sustain the size of the Federal Reserve's balance sheet at a high level.' The result was that considerable quantities of new money were injected into the system.

A similar approach was adopted in the UK. In January 2009, the Bank of England was given powers by the Treasury to buy on the open market up to £50 billion of existing government bonds (gilts) and high-quality private-sector assets, such as corporate bonds and commercial paper. The purchases, largely from private investors, such as insurance companies and pension funds, were with newly created electronic money. When the money found its way back into the banking system, it resulted in an increase in banks' reserve balances in the Bank of England. But this was only the start.

In March 2009, as the recession deepened, the Chancellor agreed to increase the scale and range of assets to be purchased. This effectively marked the beginning of the second and substantive phase of quantitative easing. This saw the Monetary Policy Committee vote not only on the level of Bank Rate, but also on the size of asset purchases. These purchases, mainly government bonds (gilts), resulted in a substantial increase in banks' reserves at the Bank of England and hence in the Bank's balance sheet (see Table 18.2 on 528). By November 2009 the MPC had sanctioned asset purchases of £200 billion.

With recovery still weak, the MPC sanctioned further asset purchases in October 2011 (£75bn), February 2012 (£50bn) and July 2012 (£50bn), bringing the total to £375 billion.

The transmission mechanism of asset purchases

By financing asset purchases through the creation of central bank reserves, quantitative easing involves increasing the amount of narrow money. It can also, indirectly, increase broad money. There are two principal ways in which this can happen.

The first is through the effects on asset prices and yields. When non-bank financial intermediaries, including insurance companies and pension funds, sell assets to the central bank they can use the money to purchase other assets. In doing so, this will drive up their prices. This, in turn, reduces the yields on these assets (at a higher price there is less dividend or interest per pound spent on them), which should help to reduce interest rates and make the cost of borrowing cheaper for households and firms, so boosting aggregate demand.

Also, for those holding these now more expensive assets there is a positive wealth effect. For instance, households with longer-term saving plans involving securities will now have greater financial wealth. Again, this will boost spending.

The second mechanism is through bank lending. Banks will find their reserve balances increase as those selling assets deposit the proceeds in their bank accounts. This will increase the liquidity ratio of banks, which could encourage them to grant more credit.

However, it is all very well increasing the monetary base, but a central bank cannot force banks to lend or people to borrow. That requires confidence. We observed in Box 18.6 the continued weakness of bank lending to the non-bank private sector through the late 2000s and into the early 2010s.

This is not to say that quantitative easing failed in the UK: growth in credit and broad money could have been weaker still. However, it does illustrate the potential danger of this approach if in the short run little credit creation takes place. In the equation $MV = PY$, the rise in (narrow) money supply (M) may be largely offset by a fall in the velocity of circulation (V) (see Box 19.2 on page 568).

On the other hand, there is also the danger that if this policy is conducted for too long, the growth in money supply could prove to be excessive, resulting in inflation rising above the target level. It is therefore important for central banks to foresee this and turn the monetary 'tap' off in time.

Definition

Quantitative easing A deliberate attempt by the central bank to increase the money supply by buying large quantities of securities through open-market operations. These securities could be securitised mortgage and other private-sector debt or government bonds.

 Would it be appropriate to define the policy of quantitative easing as 'monetarist'?

by publicly indicating the expected path of future interest rates. By stating that interest rates were likely to remain low for some time, central banks hoped that *forward guidance* would give economic agents confidence to bring forward their spending.

Despite these problems, changing interest rates can be quite effective in the medium term. After all, they can be changed very rapidly. There are not the time lags of implementation that there are with various forms of fiscal policy. Indeed, since the early 1990s, most governments or central banks have used interest rate changes as the major means of keeping inflation and/or aggregate demand under control.

In the UK, the eurozone and many other countries, the government or central bank sets a target for the rate of infla-tion for the medium term. In the UK, the target is 2 per cent CPI inflation in two years' time plus or minus 1 per cent. In the eurozone, the target is a rate of CPI inflation[1] below, but close to, 2 per cent over the medium term (where the precise period is unspecified). If forecasts suggest that inflation is going to be off target, interest rate changes are announced, and then appropriate open-market operations are con-ducted to support the new interest rate. The use of such targets is examined in section 21.3.

One important effect of changing interest rates in this very public way is that it sends a clear message to people that inflation *will* be kept under control. People will there-fore be more likely to adjust their expectations accordingly and keep their borrowing in check.

KI 10 p75

Section summary

1. Control of the growth in the money supply over the longer term will normally involve governments attempting to restrict the size of their deficits. While this is relatively easy once inflation has been brought under control, it can lead to serious problems if inflation is initially high. Increases in taxes and cuts in government expenditure are not only politically unpopular, but could also result in a recession.

2. In the short term, the authorities can use monetary policy to restrict the growth in aggregate demand in one of two major ways: (a) reducing money supply directly; (b) reducing the demand for money by raising interest rates.

3. The money supply can be reduced directly by using open-market operations. This involves the central bank selling more government securities and thereby reducing banks' reserves when their customers pay for them from their bank accounts. Alternatively, the central bank can reduce the amount of lending or rediscounting it is prepared to do (other than as a last-resort measure). Rather than controlling the monetary base in either of these two ways, the central bank could adjust its funding of the national debt. This would involve increasing the sale of bonds relative to bills, thereby reducing banks' liquid assets. Finally, it could operate a system of variable minimum reserve ratios. Increasing these would force banks to cut back the amount of credit they create.

4. Controlling either the monetary base or broad liquidity in the short term, however, is difficult given that central banks are always prepared to provide liquidity to the banks on demand. Even if the authorities are successful in controlling the money supply, there then arises the problem of severe fluctuations in interest rates if the demand for money fluctuates and is relatively inelastic.

5. The current method of control in the UK and many other countries involves the central bank influencing interest rates by its operations in the gilt repo and discount markets. The central bank keeps banks short of liquidity and then supplies them with liquidity, largely through gilt repos, at its chosen interest rate (gilt repo rate). This then has a knock-on effect on interest rates throughout the economy.

6. With an inelastic demand for loans, however, changes in interest rates may have to be very large to bring the required changes in monetary growth. High interest rates are politically unpopular and discriminate against those with high borrowing commitments. They also drive up the exchange rate, which can damage exports. Controlling aggregate demand through interest rates is made even more difficult by fluctuations in the demand for money. These fluctuations are made more severe by speculation against changes in interest rates, exchange rates, the rate of inflation, etc.

7. It is impossible to use monetary policy as a precise means of controlling aggregate demand in the short term. Nevertheless, controlling interest rates is a rapid way of responding to changing forecasts, and can be an important signal to markets that inflation will be kept under control, especially when, as in the UK and the eurozone, there is a firm target for the rate of inflation.

21.3 THE POLICY-MAKING ENVIRONMENT

Debates over the control of demand have shifted ground somewhat in recent years. There is now less debate over the relative effectiveness of fiscal and monetary policy in influ-encing aggregate demand. There is general agreement that a *combination* of fiscal and monetary policies will have a more powerful effect on demand than either used separately.

Economists have become increasingly interested in the environment within which policy is made. In this section we analyse debates around the extent to which governments

---

[1] In the eurozone the CPI is known as the 'harmonised index of consumer prices (HICP)'.

ought to pursue active demand-management policies or adhere to a set of policy rules.

Those in the Keynesian tradition prefer discretionary policy – changing policy as circumstances change. Those in the monetarist and new classical tradition prefer to set firm rules (e.g. targets for inflation, public deficits or growth in the money supply) and then stick to them.

The case for rules

There are two important arguments against discretionary policy.

Political behaviour. The first concerns the motivation of government. Politicians may attempt to manipulate the economy for their own political purposes – such as the desire to be re-elected. As we saw in Box 20.4 on the political business cycle (see page 608), the government, if not constrained by rules, may overstimulate the economy some time before an election so that growth is strong at election time. After the election, the government strongly dampens the economy to deal with the higher inflation which is now beginning to accelerate, and to create enough slack for another boost in time for the next election.

A less extreme version is where governments from time to time use monetary and fiscal policy to try to boost their popularity. The manipulation of policy instruments is not necessarily systematic or regular in the way that the political business cycle model implies. Nonetheless, the manipulation is intended to court short-term favour with the public and may store up problems for the economy and, in the case of fiscal policy, for the public finances.

When politicians behave in this way, they may lose credibility concerning sound economic management. This can lead to higher inflationary expectations, uncertainty and lower long-term investment. Trade unions are likely to bargain for increases in wages that protect their purchasing power should government loosen its policy stance to try and boost its popularity. The result could be an inflation bias (see section 16.7, page 485), with inflation typically higher than it would otherwise be, but with unemployment no lower.

Time lags with discretionary policy. Both fiscal and monetary policies can involve long and variable time lags, which can make the policy at best ineffective and at worst destabilising. Taking the measures *before* the problem arises, and thus lessening the problem of lags, is usually not an option since forecasting tends to be unreliable.

By contrast, by setting and sticking to rules, and then not interfering further, the government can provide a sound monetary framework in which there is maximum freedom for individual initiative and enterprise, and in which firms are not cushioned from market forces and are therefore encouraged to be efficient. By the government setting a target for a steady reduction in the growth of money supply,

or a target for the rate of inflation, and then resolutely sticking to it, people's expectations of inflation will be reduced, thereby making the target easier to achieve.

This sound and stable monetary environment, with no likelihood of sudden contractionary or expansionary fiscal or monetary policy, will encourage firms to take a longer-term perspective and to plan ahead. This could then lead to increased capital investment and long-term growth.

The optimum situation is for all the major countries to adhere to mutually consistent rules, so that their economies do not get out of line. This will create more stable exchange rates and provide the climate for world growth (we explore this issue in section 26.1).

Advocates of this point of view in the 1970s and 1980s were the monetarists, but in recent years support for the setting of targets has become widespread. As we have seen, in both the UK and the eurozone countries, targets are set for both inflation and public-sector deficits.

 Would it be desirable for all countries to stick to the same targets?

The case for discretion

Keynesians reject the argument that rules provide the environment for high and stable growth. Demand, argue Keynesians, is subject to many and sometimes violent exogenous shocks: e.g. changes in expectations, domestic political events (such as an impending election), financial market effects (such as the credit crunch), world economic factors (such as the world economic recession of 2008–9) or world political events (such as a war). The resulting shifts in injections or withdrawals cause the economy to deviate from a stable full-employment growth path.

Any change in injections or withdrawals will lead to a cumulative effect on national income via the multiplier and accelerator and via changing expectations. These endogenous effects take time and interact with each other, and so a process of expansion or contraction can last many months before a turning point is eventually reached.

Since the exogenous changes in demand occur at irregular intervals and are of different magnitudes, the economy is likely to experience cycles of irregular duration and of varying intensity.

Given that the economy is inherently unstable and is buffeted around by various exogenous shocks, Keynesians argue that the government needs actively to intervene to stabilise the economy. Otherwise, the uncertainty caused by unpredictable fluctuations will be very damaging to investment and hence to long-term growth in potential output (quite apart from the short-term effects of recessions on actual output and employment).

If demand fluctuates in the way Keynesians claim, and if the policy of having a money supply or inflation rule is adhered to, interest rates must fluctuate. But excessive fluctuations in interest rates will discourage long-term business

| BOX 21.10 | INFLATION TARGETING | EXPLORING ECONOMICS |

The fashion of the age

Many countries have turned to inflation targeting as their main macroeconomic policy. The table gives the targets for a selection of countries (as of 2014).

Part of the reason is the apparent failure of discretionary macroeconomic policies. Discretionary fiscal and monetary policies suffer from time lags, from being used for short-term political purposes and from failing to straighten out the business cycle. But if discretionary policies have seemed not to work, why choose an inflation target rather than a target for the money supply or the exchange rate?

Money supply targets were adopted by many countries in the 1980s, including the UK, and this policy too was largely a failure. Money supply targets proved very difficult to achieve. As we have seen, money supply depends on the amount of credit banks create, and this is not easy for the authorities to control. Then, even if money supply is controlled, this does not necessarily mean that aggregate demand will be controlled: the velocity of circulation may change. Nevertheless, many countries do still target the money supply, although in most cases it is not the main target.

Exchange rate targets, as we shall see in Chapter 25, may have serious disadvantages if the equilibrium exchange rate is not the one that is being targeted. The main instrument for keeping the exchange rate on target is the rate of interest. But, as we saw in Box 21.8 (on page 654), if the rate of interest is being used to achieve an exchange rate target, it cannot be used for other purposes, such as controlling aggregate demand or inflation. Raising interest rates to achieve an exchange rate target may lead to a recession.

Inflation targets have proved relatively easy to achieve. There may be problems at first, if the actual rate of inflation is way above the target level. The high rates of interest necessary to bring inflation down may cause a recession. But once inflation has been brought down and the objective is then simply to maintain it at the target level, most countries have been relatively successful. And the more successful they are, the more people will expect this success to be maintained, which in turn will help to ensure this success.

So, have there been any problems with inflation targeting? Ironically, one of the main problems lay in its success. With worldwide inflation having fallen, and with global trade and competition helping to keep prices down, there was now less of a link between inflation and the business cycle. Booms no longer seemed to generate the inflation they once did. Gearing interest rate policy to maintaining low inflation could still see economies experiencing unsustainable booms, followed by recessions. Inflation may be controlled, but the business cycle may not be.

Then there is the periodic problem of rising world inflation resulting from rapidly developing economies, such as China, India and Brazil (see Box 27.5). The resulting rise in food and commodity prices pushes up inflation rates around the world. Too strict an adherence to an inflation target could see higher interest rates and slow economic growth.

This was a problem in many countries during 2011 (see Box 20.1 on page 600). Take the case of the UK. Despite having only just emerged from recession and the government embarking on a significant fiscal consolidation, inflationary pressures meant that the rate of inflation again began rising. Yet, with the economy expected to continue operating significantly below potential output for some time, the Monetary Policy Committee maintained Bank Rate at its low of 0.5 per cent. It subsequently confirmed its intention for interest rates to remain low when in August 2013 the Bank began a policy of forward guidance: statements about the future path of interest rates. In its first statement, it indicated that interest rates were likely to remain at 0.5 at least until the unemployment rate had fallen to 7 per cent or less. In February 2014, it further advised that when it did begin to raise rates the process would be a gradual one and that rates would remain 'materially below' the 5 per cent level prior the financial crisis.

 Why may there be problems in targeting (a) both inflation and money supply; (b) both inflation and the exchange rate?

Country	Inflation target (%)	Details
Australia	2–3	Average over the medium term
Brazil	4.5	Tolerance band of ±2 percentage points
Canada	2	Tolerance band of ±2 percentage points
Chile	3	Tolerance band of ±1 percentage point
Czech Republic	2	Tolerance band of ±1 percentage point
Eurozone	<2 but close to it	Average for eurozone as a whole; over medium term
Hungary	3	Tolerance band of ±1 percentage point
Iceland	2.5	Tolerance band of ±1.5 percentage points
Israel	1–3	
Japan	2	
Mexico	3	Tolerance band of ±1 percentage point
New Zealand	1–3	On average over the medium term
Norway	2.5	Close to 2.5 per cent over time
Peru	2	Tolerance band of ±1 percentage point
Poland	2.5	Tolerance band of ±1 percentage point
South Africa	3–6	
South Korea	2.5–3.5	
Sweden	2	1–2 year horizon; tolerance band of ±1 percentage point
Switzerland	<2 but close to it	
Thailand	0–3.5	Core inflation – CPI inflation excluding fresh food and energy prices
UK	2	Forward-looking inflation target; tolerance band of ±1 percentage point

Source: Various bank websites. See www.bis.org/cbanks.htm

planning and investment. What is more, the government may find it difficult to keep to its targets. This too may cause uncertainty and instability.

Difficulties with the choice of target

If the government is to adopt a target, which one should it choose? If a money supply measure is to be chosen, which one? They frequently do not grow at the same rate. What is more, the adoption of one measure as the target may lead to distortions as people switch the form of their holdings of liquidity and wealth (Goodhart's law).

KI 36
p 653

If an inflation target is chosen, then again Goodhart's law is likely to apply. Inflation may become a poor indicator of the state of the economy. If people believe that the central bank will be successful in achieving its inflation target, then those expectations will feed into their inflationary expectations, and not surprisingly the target will be met.

But that target rate of inflation may now be consistent with both a buoyant and a depressed economy. In other words, the Phillips curve may become *horizontal*. Similarly, in terms of Figure 19.16 (on page 582), the *ASI* curve will be horizontal (at least up to near full capacity in the economy). Shifts in the *ADI* curve will simply lead to changes in real national income. Thus achieving an inflation target may not tackle the much more serious problem of creating stable economic growth and an environment which will therefore encourage long-term investment.

In extreme cases, as occurred in 2008, the economy may slow down rapidly and yet cost-push factors cause inflation to rise. Strictly adhering to an inflation rate target in these circumstances would demand *higher* interest rates, which could further restrict growth.

Use of a Taylor rule

For this reason, many economists have advocated the use of a ***Taylor rule***,[1] rather than a simple inflation target. A Taylor rule takes *two* objectives into account – (1) inflation and (2) either real national income or unemployment – and seeks to get the optimum degree of stability of the two. The degree of importance attached to each of the two objectives can be decided by the government or central bank. The central bank adjusts interest rates when either the rate of inflation diverges from its target or the level of real national income (or unemployment) diverges from its potential (or natural) level.

Take the case where inflation is above its target level. The central bank following a Taylor rule will raise the rate of interest. It knows, however, that this will reduce real

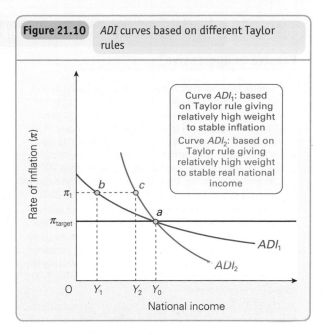

Figure 21.10 *ADI* curves based on different Taylor rules

> Curve ADI_1: based on Taylor rule giving relatively high weight to stable inflation
>
> Curve ADI_2: based on Taylor rule giving relatively high weight to stable real national income

national income. This, therefore, limits the amount that the central bank is prepared to raise the rate of interest. The more weight it attaches to stabilising inflation, the more it will raise the rate of interest. The more weight it attaches to stabilising real national income relative to its potential level, the less it will raise the rate of interest.

We can illustrate the economic significance of the relative weights given by the central bank to inflation and real national income using the *ADI/ASI* framework introduced in Section 19.4. Consider Figure 21.10. It shows two alternative *ADI* curves (aggregate demand curves plotted against inflation). Assume that the economy is currently at point *a*, with inflation on target and real national income at Y_0, which happens to be the potential level. Now assume that inflation rises to π_1. As this is above the target level, the central bank raises the rate of interest. This causes real national income to fall and is represented by a movement up along the *ADI* curve.

If the central bank puts a high weight on controlling inflation rather than on stabilising real national income around its potential level, the curve will be relatively flat, like ADI_1 in Figure 21.10. The bank will be prepared to raise interest rates a lot and, as a result, see real national income fall a lot in the short term.

Definition

Taylor rule A rule adopted by a central bank for setting the rate of interest. It will raise the interest rate if (a) inflation is above target or (b) real national income is above the potential level (or unemployment is below the natural rate). The rule states how much interest rates will be changed in each case.

---

[1] Named after John Taylor, from Stanford University, who proposed that for every 1 per cent that GDP rises above potential GDP, real interest rates should be raised by 0.5 percentage points, and that for every 1 per cent that inflation rises above its target level, real interest rates should be raised by 0.5 percentage points (i.e. nominal rates should be raised by 1.5 percentage points).

BOX 21.11 | **INTEREST RATE RESPONSES AND THE FINANCIAL CRISIS OF 2007–9**

Passive or aggressive?

The Federal Reserve, the European Central Bank (ECB) and the Bank of England are examples of independent central banks. In each case the responsibility for setting interest rates has been delegated to a decision-making board of the central bank. However, the policy remit of each of these banks is different. We consider here how this may have influenced interest rate decisions in the period from 2005 and, in particular, in the aftermath of the liquidity crisis that hit financial systems across the world from summer 2007.

In the USA the goals of monetary policy are set down in the Federal Reserve Act, originally proposed in 1913. The Federal Open Market Committee (FOMC) has eight regularly scheduled meetings each year. It is charged with ensuring that there is long-run economic growth so as to achieve the goals of maximum employment, stable prices and moderate long-term interest rates.

The ECB's independence is laid down in the institutional framework for the single monetary policy. Its aim is to promote price stability. For operational purposes the ECB has a target rate of inflation below, but close to, 2 per cent over the medium term. It is a weighted average across the eurozone. At the end of the first of two monthly meetings the Governing Council takes its interest rate decision.

The 1998 Bank of England Act gave the Bank independence in setting interest rates. The Bank's Monetary Policy Committee meets at the beginning of each month to decide on interest rates. Although elements of the remit have been adapted as a result of the financial crisis of the late 2000s (see below), the focus of the remit remains to deliver

price stability. Operationally, this is a symmetrical target around a 2 per cent inflation rate. The target applies at all times reflecting the 'primacy' of the inflation rate target for UK monetary policy. Furthermore, the inflation target is forward-looking so ensuring that inflationary expectations remain 'anchored' over the medium term.

In setting interest rates the view of the MPC is that 'official interest rate decisions have their fullest effect on output with a lag of around one year, and their fullest effect on inflation with a lag of around two years'.[1] Hence, the Bank of England effectively targets inflation 24 months hence. If current inflation exceeds or undershoots this target by more than one percentage point then the Governor is forced to write an open letter to the Chancellor of the Exchequer communicating the strategy for returning inflation to target.

Different policy responses?

The goals set for the Federal Reserve are broader than those of its two European counterparts. This would be expected to impact on the relationship between interest rates and inflation observed across the three central banks. For more detail on alternative policy rules see Box 21.12.

Chart (a) displays the annual rates of consumer price inflation for the USA, the eurozone and the UK from 2005. The US rate of inflation was consistently higher than those in the UK and the eurozone throughout 2005 and into the autumn of 2006. During much of this period the Federal Reserve was raising interest rates. This can be observed in Chart (b), which plots the interest rates set by the decision-making boards of

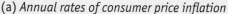

(a) *Annual rates of consumer price inflation*

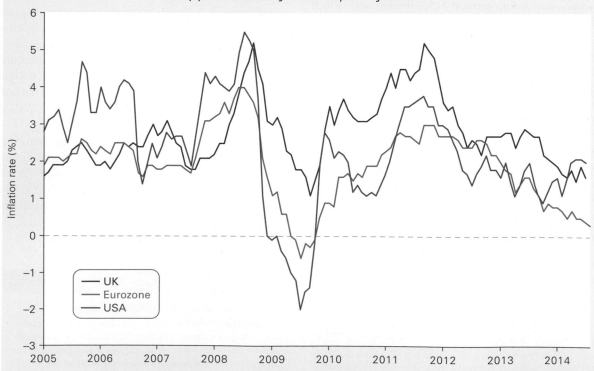

Sources: Bureau of Labor Statistics, Eurostat and Office for National Statistics.

(b) *Central bank interest rates*

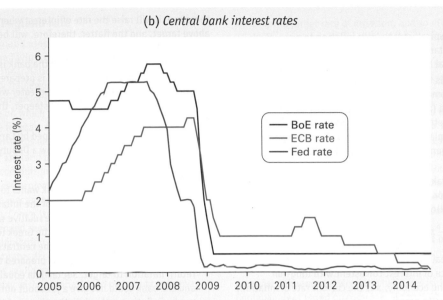

Note: Federal reserve rate is the federal funds effective rate.
Sources: Federal Reserve Bank, European Central Bank and Bank of England.

the three central banks. From 2.25 per cent at the start of 2005 the Fed increased rates to 5.25 per cent by June 2006.

The Fed kept interest rates at 5.25 per cent until the liquidity crisis hit global financial systems in late summer 2007. Interestingly, its broader policy remit appears to have enabled it to respond more aggressively to the impact of financial instability on the macroeconomy. The responses of the ECB and the Bank of England were constrained by their policy remits and, specifically, their inflation rate targets. This was because inflationary pressures were emerging at around the same time as the liquidity crisis with significant increases in food and commodity prices. Therefore, the ECB and the Bank of England felt unable to cut rates. They were concerned about easing the brake on aggregate demand and further fuelling inflation, both directly and through raising inflation expectations.

The ECB looks to have been especially concerned to suppress inflation. It raised interest rates from 3.75 to 4 per cent in June 2007 and maintained them at this level until July 2008, when it raised them again to 4.25 per cent. In sharp contrast, the Fed's rate fell from 5.25 per cent in August 2007 to 2 per cent by April 2008.

The Bank of England's interest rate policy from the time of the liquidity crisis was to tread carefully in the presence of inflation rate fears. It eased rates in December 2007 from 5.75 to 5.5 per cent and to 5.25 per cent in February and 5 per cent in April 2008.

Recession and falling inflation rates

From late 2008, inflation rates started to fall as recession around the world took hold and the USA experienced deflation in the early months of 2009. The different remits of the central banks now no longer mattered so much. Whether the remit was to keep inflation to target or to follow a Taylor rule (see Box 21.12), both required a cut in interest rates.

As you can see from Chart (b), all three banks cut interest rates. The Fed was the earliest and most aggressive cutter and the ECB the least. But by May 2009, all three had made substantial cuts, with the Bank of England's rate at 0.5 per cent, the Fed's rate between 0 and 0.25 per cent and the ECB's at 1.0 per cent. These low rates were to continue for some time.

The quite distinctive responses of three of the most important central banks in the world from late summer 2007 raise questions about the rights and wrongs of alternative policy rules. Is it better to stick to a firm inflation target, like the ECB? Or is it better to allow central banks to have more discretion to take a number of economic indicators into account, as is the case with the Fed?

In March 2013 the Bank of England's remit was amended. It continues to stress the primacy of the inflation target. However, it states that when inflation departs from target, policy decisions should take into account the possible volatility in output that may result in returning inflation to target. Consequently, the MPC may wish for inflation to deviate from its target 'temporarily' if, in bringing inflation back to target too quickly, the result is 'undesirable' volatility or, alternatively, posed a risk to financial stability. In other words, the remit allows for a longer adjustment period for inflation to return to target and places more significance of interest rate changes on the volatility of output.

 In which of the following circumstances are the three central banks more likely to respond in a similar way: (a) rising demand-pull inflation; (b) rising cost-push inflation? Explain.

[1] 'The transmission mechanism of monetary policy', *The Monetary Policy Committee, Bank of England*, www.bankofengland.co.uk/publications/Documents/other/monetary/montrans.pdf

If, however, it puts a relatively high weight on stabilising real national income around its potential level, the curve will be relatively steep, like ADI_2. The bank will not be prepared to see real national income fall very much and will thus only raise interest rates modestly.

Thus the central bank has to trade off inflation stability against real income stability. Its Taylor rule shows its optimum trade-off and is illustrated by the slope of the ADI curve.

KI 34
p404

The Taylor rule is explored in more detail in Box 21.12 and is compared with the rule followed by the Bank of England of having an inflation target based on forecast inflation (rather than current inflation).

Difficulties with the target level

KI 2
p11

When a target is first set, the short-term costs of achieving it may be too high. If expectations are slow to adjust downwards and inflation remains high, then adherence to a tight monetary or inflation rule may lead to a very deep and unacceptable recession. This was a criticism made by many economists of monetarist policies between 1979 and 1982.

When a target has been in force for some time, it may cease to be the appropriate one. Economic circumstances might change. For example, a faster growth in productivity or a large increase in oil revenues may increase potential growth and thus warrant a faster growth in money supply. Or an extended period of relatively low inflation may warrant a lower inflation target. The government must at least have the discretion to *change* the rules, even if only occasionally.

But if rules should not be stuck to religiously, does this mean that the government can engage in fine-tuning? Keynesians today recognise that fine-tuning may not be possible; nevertheless, significant and persistent excess or deficient demand *can* be corrected by demand-management policy. For example, the actions taken in the USA by the Federal Reserve Bank in 2001 and again in 2007–8 to cut interest rates substantially, and by the US government to increase its expenditure and to cut taxes, helped to stave off even deeper recessions in 2001–2 and 2008–9.

Improvements in forecasting, a willingness of governments to act quickly and the use of quick-acting policies can all help to increase the effectiveness of discretionary demand management.

Under what circumstances would adherence to money supply targets lead to (a) more stable interest rates and (b) less stable interest rates than pursuing discretionary demand-management policy?

Conclusions

The resolution of this debate will depend on the following factors:

- The confidence of people in the effectiveness of either discretionary policies or rules: the greater the confidence, the more successful is either policy likely to be.
- The degree of self-stabilisation of the economy (in the case of rules), or conversely the degree of inherent instability of the economy (in the case of discretion).
- The size and frequency of exogenous shocks to demand: the greater they are, the greater the case for discretionary policy.
- In the case of rules, the ability and determination of governments to stick to the rules and the belief by the public that they will be effective.
- In the case of discretionary policy, the ability of governments to adopt and execute policies of the correct magnitude, the speed with which such policies can be effected and the accuracy of forecasting.

Case Study 21.14 in MyEconLab looks at the history of fiscal and monetary policies in the UK from the 1950s to the current day. It illustrates the use of both rules and discretion and how the debates about policy shifted with historical events.

Section summary

1. The case against discretionary policy is that it involves unpredictable time lags that can make the policy destabilising. Also, the government may ignore the long-run adverse consequences of policies designed for short-run political gain.

2. The case in favour of rules is that they help to reduce inflationary expectations and thus create a stable environment for investment and growth.

3. The case against sticking to money supply or inflation rules is that they may cause severe fluctuations in interest rates and thus create a less stable economic environment for business planning. Given the changing economic environment in which we live, rules adopted in the past may no longer be suitable for the present.

4. Although perfect fine-tuning may not be possible, Keynesians argue that the government must have the discretion to change its policy as circumstances demand.

APPENDIX: IS/LM ANALYSIS OF FISCAL AND MONETARY POLICY

IS/LM analysis can be used to examine the effects of fiscal and monetary policy, taking both goods and money market effects into account simultaneously.

Assume that the economy is in recession and that the government wishes to raise the level of national income. Figure 21.11 illustrates the policy alternatives.

Figure 21.11(a) shows the effect of an increase in government expenditure (G) or a cut in taxes (T), but with no increase in money supply. The *IS* curve shifts to the right. Income rises to Y_2, but real interest rates also rise (to i_2). Thus some crowding out occurs.

Figure 21.11(b) shows the effect of an increase in money supply. The *LM* curve shifts downwards. Real interest rates fall to i_3 and this encourages an increase in investment. As a result of this, income rises to Y_3.

Figure 21.11(c) shows what happens when the government finances higher government expenditure or lower taxes by increasing the money supply. There is no rise in interest rates, and thus no crowding out. National income rises by a greater amount than in (a) or (b) to Y_4.

The effectiveness of fiscal and monetary policy

The effectiveness of fiscal and monetary policy depends on the slope of the two curves. Fiscal policy is more effective the flatter the *LM* curve and the steeper the *IS* curve. When *LM* is relatively flat, a rightward shift in *IS* will lead to only a small rise in the real rate of interest (i). If *IS* is relatively steep, this rise in i will lead to only a small curtailing of investment. In these two circumstances, crowding out is minimised. There will be a large increase in national income (Y).

Monetary policy, by contrast, is most effective when the *LM* curve is relatively steep and the *IS* curve is relatively flat. When *LM* is relatively steep, a rightward shift in *LM* will lead to a relatively large fall in i. When *IS* is relatively flat, a fall in i will lead to a relatively large increase in investment and hence Y.

Fiscal and monetary policies will be most effective when applied simultaneously, as in Figure 21.11(c).

The Keynesian position

Keynesian analysis has traditionally made the following assumptions:

- *The LM curve is relatively flat.* This is because the liquidity preference curve (*L*) is relatively flat, due to the important role of the speculative demand for money (see Figure 19.9(a) on page 573).
- *The IS curve is relatively steep.* This is because the investment demand curve is relatively inelastic, due to the unresponsiveness of investment to changes in interest rates (see Figure 19.10(a) on page 574). Also, saving is relatively unresponsive to interest rate changes.

Under these circumstances, fiscal policy is more effective than monetary policy in controlling aggregate demand. Figure 21.12(a) shows a bigger increase in national income with expansionary fiscal policy, than does Figure 21.12(b) with expansionary monetary policy. Monetary policy is weak because increases in money supply lead to substantially increased holdings of idle balances and hence only a small fall in interest rates and a small downward shift in the *LM* curve.

 According to Keynesians, which will have a bigger effect on national income and employment: (unforeseen) fluctuations in investment or (unforeseen) fluctuations in the money supply?

If money supply is endogenous, fiscal policy will be more effective still. A relatively elastic supply of money curve in the left-hand diagram of Figure 19.18 (on page 586) will give an even flatter *LM* curve.

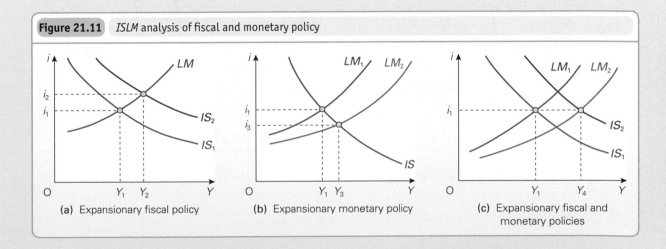

Figure 21.11 *ISLM* analysis of fiscal and monetary policy

(a) Expansionary fiscal policy

(b) Expansionary monetary policy

(c) Expansionary fiscal and monetary policies

Figure 21.12   Keynesian analysis of fiscal and monetary policy

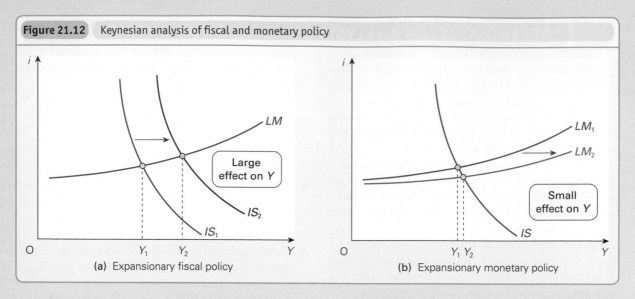

(a) Expansionary fiscal policy   (b) Expansionary monetary policy

Keynesians also stress that the *IS* curve tends to be *unstable* (e.g. as investment fluctuates with business confidence). Fluctuations in a steep *IS* curve will lead to substantial fluctuations in national income (Y). To avoid this, argue Keynesians, active demand-management (fiscal) policy will be required.

The monetarist/new classical position

Monetarist/new classical analysis has traditionally made the following assumptions:

■ *The LM curve is relatively steep.* This is because the *L* curve is relatively steep (see Figure 19.9(b)), due to the relatively small role of speculative balances of money, and the general interest inelasticity of the demand for money.

■ *The IS curve is relatively flat.* This is because the *I* curve is relatively flat (see Figure 19.10(b)), due to the wide range of interest-sensitive expenditures.

Under these circumstances, monetary policy is more effective than fiscal policy. Figure 21.13(b) shows a bigger increase in income with expansionary monetary policy than does Figure 21.13(a) with expansionary fiscal policy.

According to these assumptions, fiscal policy is weak because of crowding out. This is illustrated in Figure 21.13(a) by the steepness of the *LM* curve. The increased transactions demand resulting from a rise in income will lead to a large rise in interest rates. The reason is that there are few speculative holdings of money, and therefore a large rise in interest rates will be necessary to release sufficient money balances to meet the new higher transactions demand.

Figure 21.13   Monetarist analysis of fiscal and monetary policy

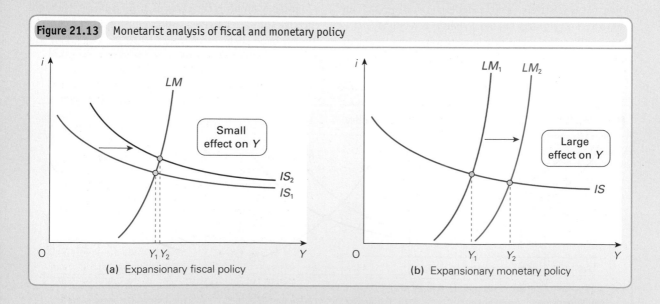

(a) Expansionary fiscal policy   (b) Expansionary monetary policy

Section summary

1. Fiscal policy shifts the *IS* curve. An expansionary fiscal policy shifts it to the right. This causes a rise in both national income and the rate of interest. The steeper the *IS* curve and the flatter the *LM* curve, the bigger will be rise in income and the smaller the rise in the rate of interest.

2. Keynesians argue that fiscal policy is relatively effective and that there will be relatively little crowding out because the *IS* curve is relatively steep (due to an inelastic investment demand schedule) and the *LM* curve is relatively flat (due to an elastic liquidity preference curve).

3. Monetarists argue the opposite: that fiscal policy is relatively ineffective and that there will be substantial crowding out because the *IS* curve is relatively flat (due to the wide range of interest-sensitive expenditures) and the *LM* curve is relatively steep (due to the small role of speculative balances).

4. Monetary policy shifts the *LM* curve. An expansionary monetary policy shifts it downwards. This causes a fall in interest rates and a rise in national income. The flatter the *IS* curve and the steeper the liquidity preference curve (*L*), and hence the bigger the downward shift in the *LM* curve for any given increase in the money supply, the larger will be the rise in national income. This means that monetarists argue that monetary policy is relatively effective, whereas Keynesians argue that it is relatively ineffective.

5. Fiscal and monetary policy operating together will have the most powerful effect. An expansionary fiscal policy accompanied by a rise in money supply can lead to an increase in national income with no rise in interest rates and thus no crowding out, irrespective of the shapes of the *IS* and *LM* curves.

END OF CHAPTER QUESTIONS

1. The following table shows part of a country's national expenditure schedule (in £ billion):

National income (*Y*)	100	120	140	160	180	200	220
National expenditure (*E*)	115	130	145	160	175	190	205

(a) What is the government expenditure multiplier?

(b) What is the tax multiplier?

Assume that full employment is achieved at a level of national income of £200 billion.

(c) Is there an inflationary or a deflationary gap, and what is its size?

(d) By how much would government expenditure have to be changed in order to close this gap (assuming no shift in other injections or withdrawals)?

(e) Alternatively, by how much would taxes have to be changed in order to close the gap (again assuming no shift in other injections or withdrawals)?

(f) Alternatively, assuming that there were initially a balanced budget, and that the government wanted to maintain a balanced budget, by how much would both government expenditure and taxes have to be changed in order to close the gap?

2. What are the problems of relying on automatic fiscal stabilisers to ensure a stable economy at full employment?

3. Does it matter if a country has a large national debt as a proportion of its national income?

4. If the government is running a budget deficit, does this mean that national income will increase?

5. What factors determine the effectiveness of discretionary fiscal policy?

6. Why is it difficult to use fiscal policy to 'fine-tune' the economy?

7. Assume that a bank has the following simplified balance sheet, and is operating at its desired liquidity ratio:

Liabilities	(£m)	Assets	(£m)
Deposits	100	Balances with central bank	10
		Advances	90
	100		100

Now assume that the central bank repurchases £5 million of government bonds on the open market. Assume that the people who sell the bonds all have their accounts with this bank and keep a constant amount of cash outside the bank.

(a) Draw up the new balance sheet directly after the purchase of the bonds.

(b) Now draw up the eventual balance sheet after all credit creation has taken place.

(c) Would there be a similar effect if the central bank rediscounted £5 billion of Treasury bills?

(d) How would such open-market operations affect the rate of interest?

8. Is it possible for the government to target the money supply over the longer term without targeting the level of public-sector net borrowing?

9. What are the mechanics whereby the central bank raises the rate of interest?

10. What is Goodhart's law? How is it relevant to (a) monetary policy; (b) using assignment grades to assess a student's ability; (c) paying workers according to the amount of output they produce; (d) awarding local authority contracts to cleaning or refuse disposal companies on the basis of tendered prices?

11. 'It is easier to control the monetary base than broader money, but it is less relevant to do so.' Do you agree with this statement?

12. Is there a compromise between purely discretionary policy and adhering to strict targets?

13. Assume that the economy is at potential output and inflation is at the target rate set for the central bank by the government. Assume now that aggregate demand falls. Using the *ADI/ASI* framework compare the path of the economy when the central bank strictly targets inflation to that when it also considers output volatility. Assume that inflation expectations remain anchored at the target rate and that potential output is unaffected.

14. Compare the relative merits of targeting (a) the money supply; (b) the exchange rate; (c) the rate of inflation.

*15. Using diagrams like Figures 21.12 and 21.13 compare Keynesian and monetarist analyses of contractionary fiscal and monetary policy.

Online resources

Additional case studies in MyEconLab

21.1 **Banks, taxes and the fiscal costs of the financial crisis.** A discussion of the government's financial interventions during the financial crisis and their impact on the public finances.

21.2 **The national debt.** This explores the question of whether it matters if a country has a high national debt.

21.3 **Trends in public expenditure.** This case examines attempts to control public expenditure in the UK and relates them to the crowding-out debate.

21.4 **Injections against the contagion.** The use of discretionary fiscal policy in the late 1990s.

21.5 **Any more G and T?** Does the Code for Fiscal Stability mean that the UK government balances its books? An examination of the evidence.

21.6 **Discretionary fiscal policy in Japan.** Attempts by successive Japanese governments since 1992 to bring the economy out of recession though expansionary fiscal policy.

21.7 **Monetary policy in the eurozone.** This is a more detailed examination of the role of monetary policy and the ECB than that contained in Box 21.6.

21.8 **The Bank of England's response to the financial crisis.** Focusing on the Bank of England, this case shows the timeline of the responses between 2007 and 2014.

21.9 **Credit and the business cycle.** This case traces cycles in the growth of credit and relates them to the business cycle. It also looks at some of the implications of the growth in credit.

21.10 **Effective monetary policy versus banking efficiency and stability.** This case examines potential conflicts between banking stability, efficiency and the effective operation of monetary policy.

21.11 **Should central banks be independent of government?** An examination of the arguments for and against independent central banks.

21.12 **Managing the macroeconomy.** This considers whether there have been conflicts of objectives in recent UK macroeconomic policy.

21.13 **Monetary targeting: its use around the world.** An expanded version of Box 21.6.

21.14 **Fiscal and monetary policy in the UK.** An historical overview of UK fiscal and monetary policy.

Websites relevant to this chapter

Nmbers and sections refer to websites listed in the Web Appendix and hotlinked from this book's website at **www.pearsoned.co.uk/sloman.**

- For news articles relevant to this chapter, see the *Economics News Articles* section in MyEconLab.
- For general news on fiscal and monetary policies, see websites in section A, and particularly A1–5. See also links to newspapers worldwide in A38, 39, 42, 43 and 44, and the news search feature in Google at A41.
- For information on UK fiscal policy and government borrowing, see sites E30, 36; F2. See also sites A1–8 at Budget time. For fiscal policy in the eurozone, see *Public Finances in EMU* in G1.
- For a model of the economy (based on the Treasury model), see *The Virtual Economy* (site D1). In addition to the model, where you can devise your own Budget, there are worksheets and outlines of theories and the work of famous economists.
- For monetary policy in the UK, see F1 and E30. For monetary policy in the eurozone, see F6 and 5. For monetary policy in the USA, see F8. For monetary policy in other countries, see the respective central bank site in section F.
- For links to sites on money and monetary policy, see the *Financial Economics* sections in I7, 11, 17.
- For demand-side policy in the UK, see the latest Budget Report (e.g. section on maintaining macroeconomic stability) at site E30.
- For inflation targeting in the UK and eurozone, see sites F1 and 6.
- For student resources relevant to this chapter, see sites C1–7, 9, 10, 12, 19. See also '2nd floor – economic policy' in site D1.

MyEconLab

This book can be supported by MyEconLab, which contains a range of additional resources, including an online homework and tutorial system designed to test and build your understanding.

You need both an access card and a course ID to access MyEconLab:

1. Is your lecturer using MyEconLab? Ask your lecturer for your course ID.

2. Has an access card been included with the book at a reduced cost? Check the inside back cover of the book.

3. If you have a course ID but no access card, go to: http://www.myeconlab.com/ to buy access to this interactive study programme.

Long-term Economic Growth

CHAPTER MAP

22.1 Long-run economic growth in industrialised countries 670
Twin characteristics of growth 670
Growth over the decades 670
Comparing the growth performance of different countries 671
The causes of economic growth 672

22.2 Economic growth without technological progress 673
Capital accumulation 673
A model of economic growth 673
An optimum rate of saving? 675
An increase in the workforce 675

22.3 Economic growth with technological progress 678
The effect of technological progress in output 678
Endogenous growth theory 679

In this chapter we turn our attention to the determinants of long-run economic growth. All developed countries have experienced economic growth over the past 60 years, but rates have differed significantly from one country to another. We look at some of these differences in section 22.1.

If an economy is to achieve sustained economic growth over the longer term, there must be a sustained increase in potential output. This means that there has to be a continuous rightward shift in aggregate supply.

The main ingredient in long-term economic growth is a growth in labour productivity. This, in turn, depends on two major factors: a growth in the amount of capital that workers use, and technological progress. We can see these two elements if we look around us. Take a modern car factory, with its high-tech robot-driven equipment: it is no surprise that workers' productivity is much higher than it was, say, 30 years ago. Take a modern office, with powerful computers: again it is no surprise that today's office staff are much more productive than their counterparts of years gone past.

In section 22.2 we look at the effects of an increase in the rate of capital investment when there is no change in technology. As we shall see, the effect will simply be growth to a new higher level of national income, not a permanently higher rate of economic growth.

If economic growth is to be higher over the long term, therefore, there must be an increase in the rate of technological progress. We look at how this affects economic growth in section 22.3. We also examine what determines the rate of invention, technological development and the use of new technology. It is important to understand this if the government is to develop appropriate supply-side policies – the subject of Chapter 23.

22.1 LONG-RUN ECONOMIC GROWTH IN INDUSTRIALISED COUNTRIES

Twin characteristics of growth

Economies are inherently volatile. Quite naturally, governments and individuals are concerned with the ups and downs of the business cycle. How does this year's economic performance compare with last year's? Are the various macroeconomic indicators such as growth, unemployment and inflation getting better or worse?

Yet when we step back and look at the longer span of history, these short-term fluctuations take on less significance. What we see is that economies tend to experience long-term economic growth. Therefore, long-run growth seems to go hand-in-hand with short-run economic instability.

These twin characteristics of growth are nicely captured in Figure 22.1, which plots for the UK both the *level* of real GDP and annual percentage *changes* in real GDP. It shows that while the rate of economic growth is volatile, the volume of output grows over time.

The rate of long-term economic growth in developed nations, such as the UK, has meant that average living standards have improved markedly. When measured in terms of real GDP per head, all developed nations are considerably richer today than they were 50 or 60 years ago.

The picture, however, is not one of universal improvement. People are not necessarily happier; there are many stresses in modern living; the environment is in many respects more polluted; inequality has increased in most countries, especially over the past 20 years; for many people work is more demanding and the working day is longer than in the past; there is more crime and more insecurity. If you look back to Boxes 14.4 and 14.6, you will see that 'more' is not always 'better'.

Nevertheless, most people *want* more consumer goods; they want higher incomes. In this chapter, we examine what causes long-term economic growth, and how it can be increased. We leave you to judge whether a materially richer society is a better society.

Growth over the decades

Despite economic volatility, most countries have experienced long-term economic growth. Figure 22.2 shows the path of real GDP (output) in six developed economies, including the UK, from 1960. As you can see, the fluctuations in output appear relatively minor compared with the long-term growth in output.

Figure 22.1   Output and economic growth in the UK

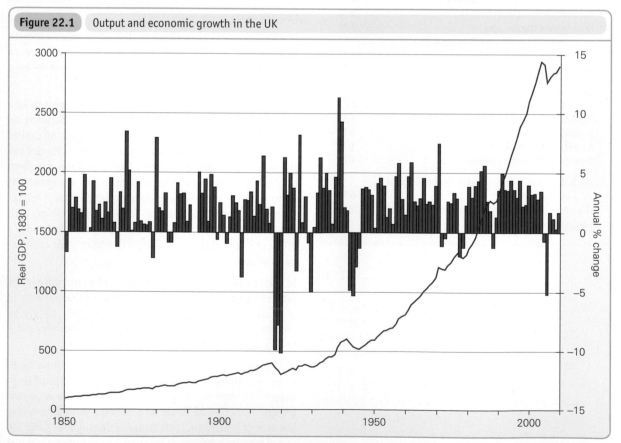

Note: Growth is the annual growth in constant-price GDP.

Sources: 1850–1948 based on data from Bank of England available at http://www.bankofengland.co.uk/publications/quarterlybulletin/threecenturiesofdata.xls; from 1949 based on data from *Quarterly National Accounts* (National Statistics).

Figure 22.2 Long-term output growth (real GDP, 1960 = 100)

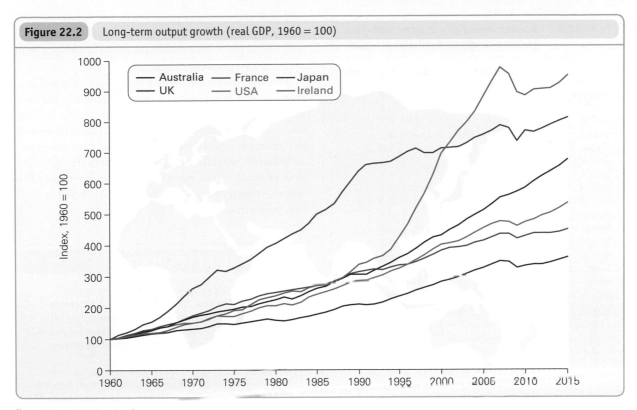

Note: 2014 and 2015 based on forecasts.
Source: Based on data in *AMECO database* (European Commission, DGECFIN).

Table 22.1 Average annual percentage growth rates, 1961–2015

	Real GDP	Real GDP per worker	Real GDP per capita
Canada	3.3	1.3	2.0
France	2.8	2.3	2.1
Germany	2.4	1.9	2.1
Ireland	4.2	3.1	3.3
Italy	2.5	2.3	2.2
Japan	4.0	3.4	3.4
Netherlands	2.7	1.9	2.0
Spain	3.4	2.9	2.7
UK	2.4	1.9	2.0
USA	3.1	1.7	2.1

Notes: (i) Figures for 2014 and 2015 are based on forecasts; (ii) German figures based on West Germany only up to 1991.
Source: Based on data from *AMECO database* (European Commission, DGECFIN).

Table 22.2 Output ratios, 2015 relative to 1960

	Real GDP	Real GDP per worker	Real GDP per capita
Canada	5.7	2.0	2.9
France	4.5	3.5	3.2
Germany	4.1	2.5	2.7
Ireland	9.5	5.4	5.8
Italy	3.8	3.4	3.2
Japan	8.1	6.0	6.0
Netherlands	4.3	2.9	3.0
Spain	6.2	4.6	4.1
UK	3.6	2.8	2.9
USA	5.4	2.5	3.0

Notes: (i) Figures for 2014 and 2015 are based on forecasts; (ii) German figures based on West Germany only in 1960.
Source: Based on data from *AMECO database* (European Commission DGECFIN).

Such growth cannot be explained by a closing of the gap between actual and potential output: by an expansion of aggregate demand leading to a fuller use of resources. Instead, the explanation lies on the supply side. Countries' economic *capacity* has increased. There has been a growth in the average output per worker and in the average output per head of the population (per capita). Table 22.1 shows the average *annual* growth in output per employed person and in output per capita for several developed countries since the 1960s, alongside that for output (real GDP). The effect of even very small differences can be significant when looked at over many years. Table 22.2 shows how many times greater output, output per person employed and output per capita in 2015 were compared with those in 1960.

Comparing the growth performance of different countries

As you can see from these two tables, there has been a considerable difference in the rates of growth experienced by the different countries. Such differences have implications

Table 22.3	Average annual growth rates 1995–2015 at constant prices: total and per capita	
	Real GDP	**Real GDP per capita**
Australia	3.3	1.9
Brazil	3.0	1.8
Canada	2.5	1.5
China	9.4	8.7
France	1.5	1.0
Germany	1.3	1.3
India	6.6	4.9
Ireland	4.5	3.2
Italy	0.7	0.3
Japan	0.9	0.9
Malaysia	5.1	2.9
Netherlands	1.8	1.3
Russia	3.3	3.6
Singapore	5.3	2.9
Spain	2.1	1.3
UK	2.2	1.6
USA	2.5	1.5

Note: 2014 and 2015 figures based on forecasts.
Source: Authors' calculations based on data from *World Economic Outlook Database, October 2013* (International Monetary Fund).

for the longer-term living standards of countries' populations. However, if economic growth is to give an indication of an increase in living standards, it has to be measured per head of the population.

Table 22.3 considers the average annual growth rates from 1995 to 2015, both overall and per capita, for a wider range of countries than we have so far considered. Canada and the USA had faster absolute growth rates than the UK, but after taking into account their more rapid increase in populations, they experienced a lower per capita growth rate. Russia, with a decline in its population, experienced higher growth per capita than absolute growth.

In general, the richer developed countries have grown at a slower rate than the less rich ones. The result has been a narrowing of the gap. For example, in 1950 GDP per head in the USA (in purchasing-power standard terms) was 2.5 times that in West Germany and 20 times that in Japan. By 2015, GDP per head in the USA was only 24 per cent higher than that in Germany and 47 per cent higher than that in Japan.

This ***convergence in GDP per head***, however, has not been universal across the world. Although countries like Brazil, China, India and many other Asian countries have grown very rapidly, some of the poorest developing

Definition

Convergence in GDP per head The tendency for less rich developed countries to catch up with richer ones. Convergence does not apply to many of the poorer developing countries, however; the gap between them and richer countries has tended to widen.

countries, and especially those in sub-Saharan Africa, have grown at pitifully slow rates, and in some cases GDP per head has declined. We examine the causes of low growth in developing countries in Chapter 27.

Although recent generations have come to expect economic growth, it is a relatively new phenomenon. For most of the last 2000 years, countries have experienced virtually static output per head over the long term. Economic growth has become significant only once countries have undergone an industrial revolution, and it is only with the technological advances of the twentieth and now the twenty-first centuries that long-term growth rates of 2 per cent or more have been achieved.

*LOOKING AT THE MATHS

Since 1961, the UK economy has grown on average by 2.4 per cent per annum. This means that it has doubled in size roughly every 29 years. Over the same period, the Irish economy has grown by an average of 4.2 per cent per annum. As a result, its economy has doubled in size roughly every 17 years. But how do we work out these numbers of years? To do this we use logarithms. To find the number of years, *n*, that it takes an economy to grow by a factor *x* (e.g. 2 in the case of a doubling), we divide the log of *x* by the log of the factor by which the economy is growing each year, *g* (so *g* = 1.024 for 2.4 per cent and *g* = 1.042 for 4.2 per cent):

$$n = \frac{\log x}{\log g}$$

We can use our calculators to find the logs. Thus, in the case of the UK:

$$n = \frac{\log x}{\log g} = \frac{\log 2}{\log 1.024} = 29.2$$

and in the case of Ireland:

$$n = \frac{\log x}{\log g} = \frac{\log 2}{\log 1.042} = 16.8$$

In practice, these figures are only approximate as the two countries' growth rates varied from year to year.

 How long would it take an economy, like China's, growing at an annual rate of close to 10 per cent to (a) double in size; (b) triple in size?

The causes of economic growth

The sources of economic growth can be grouped into two broad categories:

■ An increase in the *quantity* of factors. Here we would include an increase in the workforce or the average number of hours that people work, an increase in raw materials (e.g. discoveries of oil) and an increase in capital. Of these, for most countries, it is an increase in the capital stock, brought about by investment, that is the most important source of growth. The amount of capital per worker – the capital/labour ratio (K/L) – has increased over time and has resulted in a greater output per worker (Y/L).

- An increase in the *productivity* of factors. Here we would include an increase in the skills of workers, a more efficient organisation of inputs by management and more productive capital equipment. Most significant here is technological progress. Developments of computer technology, of new techniques in engineering, of lighter, stronger and cheaper materials, of digital technology

in communications and of more efficient motors have all contributed to a massive increase in the productivity of capital. Machines today can produce much more output than machines in the past that cost the same to manufacture.

In the next two sections, we will examine these two sources of growth and focus first on capital accumulation (an increase in the *quantity* of capital) and then on technological progress (an increase in the *productivity* of factors).

Section summary

1. The determinants of economic growth in the long run lie primarily on the supply side.

2. Most developed countries have experienced average annual rates of economic growth of 2 per cent or more over the last 50 years, but there have been considerable differences between countries.

3. The income gap between developed countries has tended to narrow as the less rich ones have grown faster than the

richer ones. Some of the poorest countries of the world, however, have experienced very low rates of growth, with the result that the gap between them and richer countries has widened.

4. Determinants of economic growth can be put into two broad categories: an increase in the quantity of factors and an increase in the productivity of factors.

22.2 ECONOMIC GROWTH WITHOUT TECHNOLOGICAL PROGRESS

Capital accumulation

An increase in capital per worker will generally increase output. In other words, the more equipment that is used by people at work, the more they are likely to produce. But to increase capital requires investment, and that investment requires resources – resources that could have been used for producing consumer goods. Thus more investment means diverting resources away from producing finished goods into producing machines, buildings and other capital equipment. This is the opportunity cost of investment.

TC 1 p11

If we take a simple circular flow of income model, with saving as the only withdrawal and investment as the only injection, then saving will be equal to investment ($S = I$). An increase in saving, therefore, will enable more investment and more output for the future. Thus sacrifices today, in terms of more saving and less consumption, will mean more output and hence possibly more consumption for the future.

A model of economic growth

In Chapter 14, we looked at a simple growth model (see pages 419–20). This stated that growth depends on the proportion of a rise in income that is saved and hence invested (i) and the marginal efficiency of capital (*MEC*):

$$g = i \times MEC$$

Thus if 15 per cent of national income is saved and invested (i = 15 per cent) and if a 1 per cent increase in the

capital stock ($\Delta K = I$) leads to a $^1/_3$ per cent increase in annual output ($MEC = {}^1/_3$), then the rate of growth will be 5 per cent. For example, if national income is £2 trillion, £300 billion will be invested (i = 15 per cent), and this will yield extra annual output of £100 billion ($MEC = {}^1/_3$). Thus national income has grown by 5 per cent (from £2 trillion to £2.1 trillion).

 What would be the rate of economic growth if 20 per cent of national income were saved and invested and the marginal efficiency of capital were $^2/_5$?

However, we need to make two qualifications to this simple model. The first is that the marginal efficiency of capital is likely to decline as the amount of capital per worker increases. This is because of diminishing returns to capital. The second is that a proportion of investment has to be used for replacing worn-out or obsolete equipment. The problem here is that, the larger the capital stock, the greater the proportion of investment that will be needed for replacement purposes, and the smaller the proportion that can be used for increasing the size of the capital stock.

KI 17 p135

Growth to a long-run equilibrium level of national income

Let us now incorporate these two qualifications into a model of growth. This is known as the neoclassical or 'Solow' growth model, after the MIT economics professor and Nobel Prize winner, Robert Solow. In this model, we are assuming for simplicity that the size of the workforce is

KI 8 p46

Figure 22.3 Steady-state output

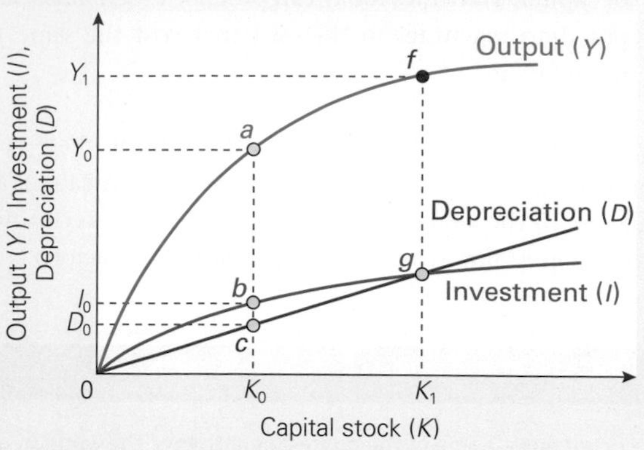

constant. Any increase in the capital stock, therefore, means an increase in the average amount of capital per worker.

The model is illustrated in Figure 22.3. The size of the capital stock (K) is measured on the horizontal axis; the level of national output (Y) is measured on the vertical axis.

We start by looking at the effects of a growth in the capital stock on national output (i.e. on real national income (Y)). This is shown by the green output curve. As the capital stock increases, so output increases, but at a diminishing rate (the curve gets less and less steep). The reason for this is the law of diminishing returns: in this case, diminishing returns to capital. For example, if, in an office, you start equipping workers with computers, at first output will increase very rapidly. But as more and more workers have their own computer rather than having to share, so the rate of increase in output slows down. When everyone has their own, output is likely to be at a maximum. Any additional computers (of the same specification) will remain unused.

Increased output will mean increased saving and hence increased investment (the amount depending on the level of i). This is shown by the blue investment (I) curve. In this simple model, the vertical distance between the Y and I curves represents consumption ($C = Y − I$).

The magenta (D) line shows the amount of depreciation of capital that takes place, and hence the amount of replacement investment required. The bigger the capital stock, the larger the amount of replacement investment required .

Assume initially that the size of the capital stock is K_0. This will generate an output of Y_0 (point a). This output, in turn, will generate saving and investment of I_0, but of this, D_0 will have to be used for replacement purposes. The difference ($b − c$) will be available to increase the size of the capital stock. The capital stock will thus increase up to K_1 (point g). At this point, all investment will be required for replacement purposes. Output will therefore cease growing. Y_1 represents the **steady-state level of national income**.

Effect of an increase in the saving rate

In the simple model, $g = i × MEC$, an increase in the saving rate will increase i and hence the growth rate (g). When we

take into account diminishing returns to capital and depreciation, however, an increase in the saving rate will lead to only a temporary increase in output, and to no long-term *growth* at all!

*LOOKING AT THE MATHS

Steady-state equilibrium in the Solow growth model is achieved where investment (I) equals depreciation (D).

Investment is assumed to be a given fraction (s) of the level of national income Y, where national income is a function of the total capital stock (K): $K = f(K)$. Thus

$$I = sY$$
$$= s × f(K) \tag{1}$$

Depreciation in the model is assumed to be a fixed proportion (d) of the capital stock (K). Thus

$$D = dK \tag{2}$$

In steady-state equilibrium, given that $I = D$, from equations (1) and (2) we can write

$$s × f(K) = dK$$

Thus

$$K = \frac{s × f(K)}{d}$$

Thus if we know the production function ($Y = f(K)$), the saving rate (s) and the depreciation rate (d), we can solve for the steady-state equilibrium value of K and hence also for Y. Maths Case 22.1 in MyEconLab gives a worked example of this.

This is illustrated in Figure 22.4. If the saving rate increases, the investment curve will shift upwards. This is shown by a shift from I_1 to I_2. Investment is now above that which is necessary to maintain the capital stock at K_1. The capital stock will grow, therefore, and so will national income. But this growth is only temporary. Once the capital stock has risen to K_2, all the new higher level of investment will be absorbed in replacing capital ($I = D$ at point n). National income stops rising. Y_2 represents the new steady-state national income.

Does this mean, therefore, that there is no long-term gain from an increase in the saving rate? There *is* a gain, to the extent that income per worker is now higher (remember that we are assuming a constant labour force), and this higher income will be received not just once, but every year from now on as long as the saving rate remains at the new higher level. There is no increase in the long-term *growth rate*, however. To achieve that, we would have to look to the other determinants of growth.

Definition

Steady-state level of national income The long-run equilibrium level of national income. The level at which all investment is used to maintain the existing capital stock at its current level.

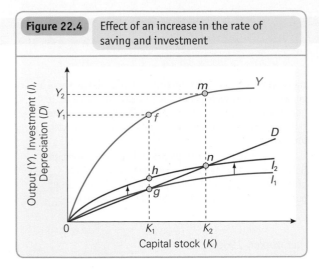

Figure 22.4   Effect of an increase in the rate of saving and investment

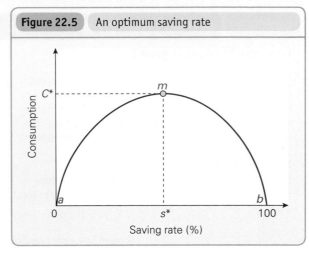

Figure 22.5   An optimum saving rate

Human capital and education

The analysis of Figures 22.3 and 22.4 need not be confined to the stock of *physical* capital: machines, buildings, tools, etc. It can also apply to *human capital*. Human capital, as we saw in Chapter 9, refers to the skills and expertise of workers that have been acquired through education and training. If part of saving is used for investment in education and training, then the productivity of workers will rise, and so will output. In Figures 22.3 and 22.4, therefore, the horizontal axis measures both physical and human capital. An increase in either has the effect of increasing the steady-state level of national income.

 If there were a gradual increase in the saving rate over time, would this lead to sustained economic growth?

An optimum rate of saving?

 If an increase in the saving rate does at least lead to a higher level of output, is there an *optimum* level of saving? Clearly we would need to define 'optimum'. One definition would be where *consumption* per head is maximised.

Assuming a fixed population and a fixed workforce, higher saving will do two things. First, it will directly decrease consumption, since what is saved is not directly spent. Second, as we have seen, it will lead to higher output and hence higher income. So, with a higher saving rate, consumption will be a smaller proportion, but of a higher income. This implies that there will be some optimum saving rate at which consumption is maximised. This is illustrated in Figure 22.5.

If the saving rate is zero, the capital stock will be zero. Output and consumption will thus be zero (point *a*). As saving rises above zero, so the capital stock will grow, as will output and consumption. At the other extreme, if the saving rate were 100 per cent, although the capital stock would be high, all of the nation's income would go on maintaining that capital stock: there would be no consumption (point *b*). A saving rate somewhere between 0 and

100 per cent, therefore, will give the maximum consumption. In Figure 22.5, this is a rate of *s**, giving a level of consumption of *C** (point *m*). This is sometimes known as the **golden-rule saving rate**.

Evidence suggests that all countries have saving rates below the golden-rule level. Thus increases in saving rates would result in increases in consumption.

 If this is true, why do people not increase their rate of saving?

An increase in the workforce

An increase in the workforce, or in the number of hours worked by the existing workforce, will have the effect of shifting both the *Y* and *I* lines upwards in Figures 22.3 and 22.4. In other words, if a given amount of capital is used by more workers or for longer periods, output and hence saving and investment will increase. As more labour hours are used with any given amount of capital, diminishing returns to labour will set in. Output will grow, but at a diminishing rate. The marginal and average product of labour will fall (see Figure 5.1 on page 136). Thus although national output has risen (the new steady-state income is higher), the output per labour hour is less.

The effect on GDP per head of the population

If the rise in total hours worked is the result of an increased **participation rate** (i.e. a greater proportion of the population wishing to work) or of people working longer hours, then GDP per capita will be higher, even though output per hour

Definitions

Golden-rule saving rate The rate of saving that maximises the level of long-run consumption.

Participation rate The percentage of the working-age population that is part of the workforce.

BOX 22.1   GETTING INTENSIVE WITH CAPITAL

How quickly does it grow?

In this box we take a look at two issues relating to capital. First, we consider what counts as capital in a country's national accounts. Second, we compare the growth of the capital stock in a sample of developed economies and then see how this compares with their rates of economic growth.

What is capital?

In a country's national accounts, capital consists of non-financial *fixed assets*. It does not include goods and services

transformed or used up in the course of production; these are known as *intermediate goods and services*. Furthermore, it does not relate directly to the stock of human capital: the skills and attributes embodied in individuals that affect production.

Estimates of human capital are still quite experimental. But, an estimate of the UK's *employed human capital* produced by the Office for National Statistics for 2012 puts it at £17.1 trillion. This is based on the expected

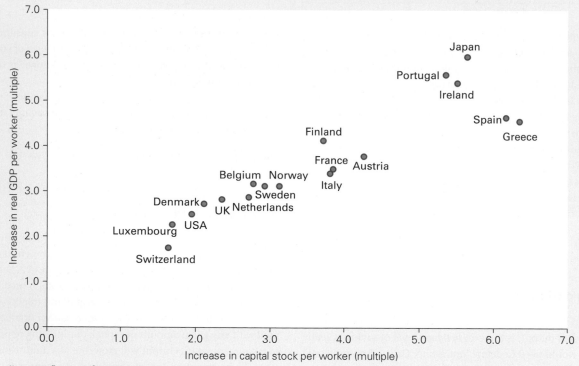

Growth in capital and output per worker, 1960–2015

Note: 2015 figures are forecasts.
Source: Based on data from AMECO database (European Commission).

worked will be lower. If, however, the increased hours worked are the result of an increased *population*, with no increase in the participation rate or number of hours worked per worker, then, because of diminishing returns to labour, output per head of the population will have gone down: GDP per capita will be lower.

1. *If there were a higher participation rate and GDP per capita rose, would output per worker also have risen?*
2. *If people worked longer hours and, as a result, GDP per capita rose, how would you assess whether the country was 'better off'?*

If, however, there is an increase in both labour *and* capital, GDP per capita need not fall, even with the same number of hours worked per head. There are likely to be constant returns to scale. For example, if country A has double the population and double the capital stock of country B, its GDP is likely to be approximately double, and its GDP per head approximately the same.

What should be clear from the above analysis is that, without technological progress or some other means of increasing output from a given quantity of inputs, long-term growth cannot be sustained.

lifetime earnings of those in employment. When those unemployed are included, the UK's *full human capital* rises to £17.5 trillion. Case study 22.3 in MyEconLab analyses the UK statistics on human capital in more detail.

A country's stock of fixed assets can be valued at its replacement cost, regardless of its age: this is its gross value. It can also be valued at its written-down value known as its net value. The net value takes into account the consumption of capital which occurs through wear and tear (depreciation) or when capital becomes naturally obsolescent.

The table shows that the estimated net capital stock of the UK in 2012 was £3.59 trillion. To put this into context, this is about 2.3 times the value of GDP.

UK net capital stock, 2012

Type	£ billion	% of fixed assets	% of GDP
Dwellings	1487.0	41.4	95.2
Other buildings and structures	1342.5	37.4	85.9
Other machinery, equipment and cultivated assets	552.3	15.4	35.4
Intangible assets	117.5	3.3	7.5
Transport equipment	91.0	2.5	5.8
All fixed assets	3590.3	100.0	229.8

Source: Based on data from National Statistics.

The table shows that there are five broad categories of fixed assets. The largest of these by value is *dwellings*, which includes houses, bungalows and flats. Residential housing yields rental incomes for landlords and, more generally, provides all of us with important consumption services, most notably shelter.

The second largest component by value is *other buildings and structures*. This includes buildings, other than residential dwellings, and most civil engineering and construction work. It also includes structures such as factories, schools and hospitals and the country's railway track.

The third largest component by value is *other machinery, equipment and cultivated assets*. It includes electricity and telephone lines as well as tractors and fork lift trucks, while cultivated assets include livestock and forests. Next by value is *intangible assets*. This includes computer software, original works of literature or art and mineral exploration. The smallest component by value is *transport equipment*. This includes lorries for haulage, buses and railway rolling stock for transportation and all civil aircraft.

How quickly does capital grow? An international comparison

In models of economic growth an important measure of how much capital is being used is the amount of capital per person employed (per worker). This is also known as *capital intensity*. In the chart we plot the ratio of capital per worker in 2015 to that in 1960 (*x* axis) against the ratio of real GDP per worker in 2015 to that in 1960 (*y* axis) in a selection of developed countries.

For each country we observe an increase in capital intensity, although the rates of capital accumulation differ quite significantly. For instance, in Japan capital per worker in 2015 is 5.6 times higher than in 1960; in the UK it is 2.4 times higher; while in the USA it is not quite twice as large.

We would expect that the higher the level of capital per worker, the greater will be the level of output (real GDP) per worker. This is largely borne out in the chart. However, while there is a strong statistical association between capital accumulation and economic growth, economic theory plays an important role in helping us to gain a better understanding of this apparent relationship. As you can see from this chapter, there is considerable debate about the determinants of capital accumulation and its significance for economic growth.

1. *How does human capital (the skills and expertise of the workforce) fit into a national account's definition of capital?*
2. *Does the composition of a country's capital affect its long-run economic growth?*

Section summary

1. An increased saving rate will lead to higher investment and hence to an increase in the capital stock. This, in turn, will lead to a higher level of national income.

2. A larger capital stock, however, will require a higher level of replacement investment. Once this has risen to absorb all the extra investment, national income will stop rising: growth will cease. A steady-state level of national income has been achieved. An increased saving rate will therefore lead only to a rise in output, not to a long-term rise in the rate of growth.

3. An optimum rate of saving could be defined as one where consumption per head is maximised. This is sometimes known as the 'golden-rule saving rate'.

4. An increase in the workforce will lead to higher total output, but unless accompanied by an increase in the capital stock, it will generally lead to a reduction in output per worker.

22.3 ECONOMIC GROWTH WITH TECHNOLOGICAL PROGRESS

The effect of technological progress on output

Technological progress has the effect of increasing the output from a given amount of investment. This is shown in Figure 22.6. Initial investment and income curves are I_1 and Y_1; steady-state income is at a level of Y_1 (point f). A technological advance has the effect of shifting the Y line upwards, say to Y_2. The higher income curve leads to a higher investment curve (for a given *rate* of saving). This is shown by curve I_2. The new long-term equilibrium capital stock is thus K_2, and the new steady-state level of income is Y_2 (point p).

If there is a 'one-off' technological advance, the effect is the one we have just illustrated. Income rises to a higher level, but does not go on rising once the new steady-state level has been reached. But technological progress marches on over time. New inventions are made; new processes are discovered; old ones are improved. In terms of Figure 22.6, the Y curve *goes on* shifting upwards over time.

The faster the rate of technological progress, the faster will the Y curve shift upwards and the higher will be the rate of economic growth. This is illustrated in Figure 22.7, which shows the increase in output over time. The faster the rate of technological progress, the higher the rate of growth of output.

Maths Case 22.2 in MyEconLab explores the algebra of technological progress.

The effect of an increase in the saving rate with a given rate of technological progress

Figure 22.8 shows the combined effects of an increased saving rate and continuing technological progress. The rate of technological progress gives the slope of the **steady-state growth path**. This is the growth path for any given saving rate. The saving rate determines the *position* (as opposed to slope) of the curve. Assume that the economy is on steady-state

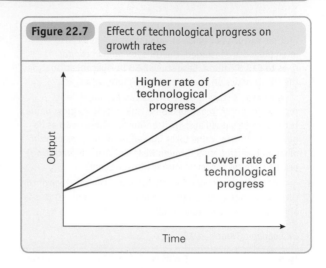

Figure 22.7 Effect of technological progress on growth rates

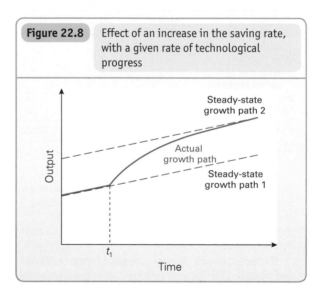

Figure 22.8 Effect of an increase in the saving rate, with a given rate of technological progress

growth path 1. Then, at time t_1, there is an increase in the saving rate. This has the effect of increasing output and the economy will move towards steady-state growth path 2. But the full effect does not take place immediately, since new capital equipment takes time to plan and install and then to generate additional income, part of which will be used for more investment. Thus the actual growth path will follow the green line, gradually converging on steady-state growth path 2.

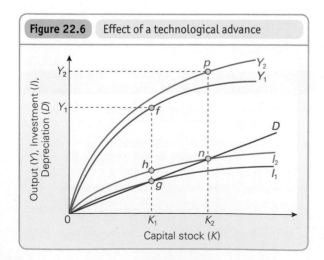

Figure 22.6 Effect of a technological advance

Definition

Steady-state growth path The growth path for a given saving rate (where growth results from technological progress).

Endogenous growth theory

It should be clear from our argument that an increase in technological progress is essential if a country wants to achieve faster rates of growth in the long term. But is this purely in the lap of the scientists and engineers? In the Solow growth model that we have been considering up to now, this is the type of assumption made. In other words, technological progress is simply a 'given': it is exogenously determined.

While the neoclassical model identifies the importance of technological progress for enduring growth, it does not offer governments actual policy prescriptions. What can be done to speed up the rate of innovation? Can governments adopt policies that encourage scientific breakthroughs and technological developments? An ***endogenous growth model*** attempts to answer such questions as this by incorporating technological advancement *within* the model.

 What is endogenous about endogenous growth theory?

Endogenous growth models stress the importance of research and development, education and training and fostering innovation. As you can imagine, there is considerable interest and debate surrounding endogenous growth models not just amongst academics but policy makers too. Policy makers are interested in appropriate policies that might make their country a world leader in innovation and technological advancement, especially if this helps to sustain higher long-run rates of economic growth, and so higher standards of living.

  In such models, a major determinant of technological progress is the size and composition of the capital stock. As economies accumulate capital, they are likely to devote more resources to the development and maintenance of capital goods industries. In other words, they are likely to have a larger sector devoted to producing and developing capital goods. This in turn may raise the rate of technological progress and enable further capital accumulation. A virtuous circle is created.

Investment in research and development can be encouraged through the use of patents and copyrights. These provide some protection to firms, enabling them to capture more of the benefits from their own ideas and thus providing them with an incentive to create and innovate. Furthermore, the striving for profit or the pursuit of competitive advantage over rivals are incentives that can drive this innovation and creativity.

But there are limits to the ability of firms to exclude other firms from prospering from their own ideas, such as the

development of products, processes and people. The virtuous circle is thus reinforced by externalities: the spill-over of ideas from one firm to another. New ideas cannot be put back into the metaphorical bottle once its lid is off.

A model of endogenous technological progress

Endogenous growth models argue two things. The first is that technological progress is *dependent* on various economic factors such as the rate of investment in research and development. This could be included as an element in the investment (I) term: i.e.

$$I = I_n + I_c$$

where I_n is investment in research and development of new technology (it could also include investment in training) and I_c is investment in capital that uses current technology. The greater the value of I_n/I_c, the faster will the Y curve shift upwards in Figure 22.3 and the steeper will be the steady-state growth path in Figure 22.8. Any policy, then, that increases the proportion of national income being devoted to R&D and training will increase the long-run rate of economic growth.

The second factor is the responsiveness of Y to I_n. This will depend in part on the extent to which innovations spill over to other firms, which duplicate or adapt them, thereby adding to the increase in national income (ΔY). The greater the value of $\Delta Y/I_n$, the greater will be the rate of economic growth: the steeper will be the steady-state growth path.

The values of I_n and $\Delta Y/I_n$ are thought to depend on structural and institutional factors within the economy and on the role of government. These include:

- attitudes of business, such as the inclination to take risk;
- willingness of financial institutions to lend in order to support investment opportunities;
- tax incentives and government grants, for instance support for R&D;
- a research infrastructure (laboratories, the number and skills of researchers, etc.);
- the degree of competition over the development of new products and processes;
- the magnitude of external spill-overs from the generation of new products, processes and techniques.

As we have seen, endogenous growth models try to explain how the economy's production function shifts upwards over time. In some cases the production function may also become steeper – in other words, a larger rise in national income for a given rise in the capital stock. The reason is that the output from investment is not just confined to the firms doing the investing. Rather, it spills over to other firms, which duplicate or develop the original firm's ideas. Consequently, these spill-overs may positively impact on the overall marginal product of capital.

 Do all investment projects generate significant spill-overs?

> ## Definition
>
> **Endogenous growth models** Models where the rate of growth depends on the rate of technological progress and diffusion, both of which depend on institutions, incentives and the role of government.

BOX 22.2   LABOUR PRODUCTIVITY

How effective is UK labour?

KI 16
p133

A country's potential output depends on the productivity of its factors of production. There are two common ways of measuring labour productivity. The first is output per worker. This is the most straightforward measure to calculate. All that is required is a measure of total output and employment.

The second measure is output per hour worked. This has the advantage that it is not influenced by the number of hours worked. So for an economy like the UK's, with a very high percentage of part-time workers on the one hand, and long average hours worked by full-time employees on the other, such a measure would be more accurate in gauging worker efficiency.

Both measures focus solely on the productivity of labour. In order to account directly for the productivity of capital we need to consider the growth in total factor productivity (TFP). This measure analyses output relative to the amount of factors used. Changes in total factor productivity over time provide a good indicator of technical progress.

International comparisons of labour productivity

Charts (a) and (b) show comparative productivity levels of various countries and the G7 using GDP per hour worked. Chart (a) shows countries' productivity relative to the UK. As you can see, GDP per hour worked is lower in the UK than the other countries with the exception of Japan. For example, in 2012, compared with the UK, output per hour was 35 per cent higher in the USA, 32 per cent higher in France and 31 per cent higher in Germany.

Compared with the rest of the G7 countries, UK output per worker was 21 per cent lower – the highest productivity gap since 1992. A major explanation of lower productivity in the UK is the fact that for decades it has invested a smaller proportion of its national income than most other industrialised nations. Nevertheless, until 2006 the gap had been narrowing with the rest of the G7. This was because UK productivity, although lower than in many other countries, was growing faster. This can be seen Chart (b). Part of the reason for this was the inflow of investment from abroad.

Chart (c) compares labour productivity across both measures. Workers in the USA and the UK work longer hours than those in France and Germany. Thus whereas output *per hour worked* in the USA is only about 3 per cent higher than in France and 4 per cent higher than in Germany, output per person employed in the USA is about 28 per cent higher than in France and 37 per cent higher than in Germany.

The chart shows that UK labour productivity is lower than that in the USA, France and Germany on both measures but higher than that in Japan.

 What could explain the differences in productivity between the five countries in Chart (c), and why do the differences vary according to which of the two measures is used?

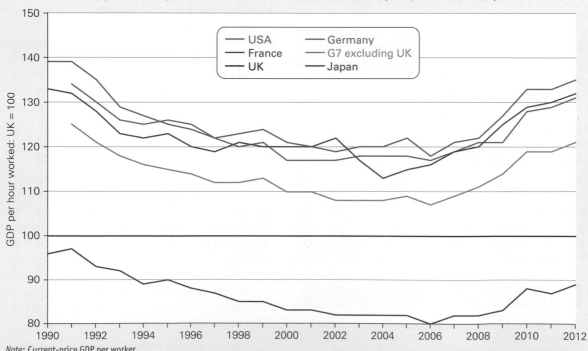

(a) *Productivity in selected economies relative to the UK (GDP per hour worked)*

Note: Current-price GDP per worker.

Source: Based on data in *International Comparisons of Productivity* (National Statistics, 2014).

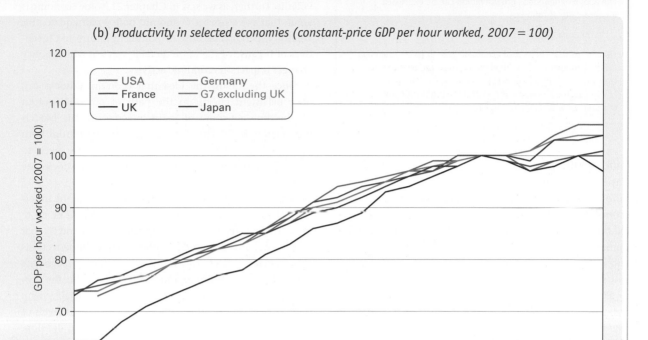

(b) *Productivity in selected economies (constant-price GDP per hour worked, 2007 = 100)*

Source: Based on data *in International Comparisons of Productivity* (National Statistics, 2014).

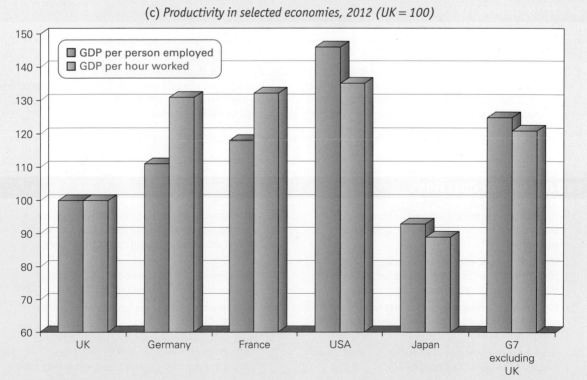

(c) *Productivity in selected economies, 2012 (UK = 100)*

Note: Current-price GDP per worker.
Source: Based on data in *International Comparisons of Productivity* (National Statistics, 2014).

The above endogenous growth model can be expressed algebraically as follows:

$$\Delta Y/Y = v(I_n/Y)$$

This states that the rate of economic growth ($\Delta Y/Y$) depends on the proportion of national income devoted to R&D and training (I_n/Y) by an amount v.

The higher the value of I_n/Y and the higher the value of v, the steeper will be the steady-state growth path.

Policy implications

If there is a virtuous circle arising from firms investing and innovating, how can governments encourage this? Many economists argue that this requires supply-side policies. Examples include policies to influence research and development, education and training, industrial organisation and work practices – in other words, policies to affect aggregate supply directly.

There is less agreement, however, as to whether these policies should focus on delivering market solutions or involve greater state intervention. We return to these themes in Chapter 23.

In fostering an environment conducive to innovation and progress many would agree that a stable macroeconomy

is desirable. It is not easy to plan ahead in times of great economic uncertainty. Of course, we have seen through the second half of the book that economies are inherently volatile. Further, as we saw in Chapter 21, some economists argue that government economic policy can add to this volatility, perhaps because of politically motivated incentives or because of the unpredictable ways in which policy changes impact on economic activity.

Since the 1990s, the idea that economic shocks can have persistent effects on the path of potential output has become a feature of many macroeconomic models (see section 16.7). These shocks can originate from both the demand and supply sides. Either way, we need to understand the mechanisms by which such shocks are propagated.

Some economists, however, argue that, given the inherent volatility of economies, governments *should* be more proactive. For instance, we saw in Chapters 16 and 20 that new Keynesians have identified how market imperfections and hysteresis effects can result in changes in aggregate demand having enduring and marked effects on the economy. For example, imperfections in the financial system, such as credit cycles, can have marked effects on levels of investment, including spending on research and development. They argue that governments have a role to play in helping to stabilise aggregate demand so as to support and encourage firms to invest and increase potential output.

Section summary

1. A higher long-term rate of growth will normally require a faster rate of technological progress.

2. The rate of technological progress determines the slope of the steady-state growth path (i.e. the rate of steady-state growth). If there is a rise in the saving rate, this will shift the steady-state growth path upwards (parallel) and the

actual growth path will gradually move from the lower to the higher path.

3. Endogenous growth theory argues that the rate of technological progress and its rate of diffusion depend on economic institutions and incentives. Supply-side policy could be used to alter these.

END OF CHAPTER QUESTIONS

1. For what reasons do countries experience very different long-run rates of economic growth from each other?

2. Why do developed countries experience a degree of convergence over time? Would you expect there to be total convergence of GDP per head?

3. If increased investment (using current technology) does not lead to increased long-run economic growth, does it bring any benefits?

4. What determines the rate of depreciation? What would happen if the rate of depreciation fell?

5. What is meant by the 'steady-state economic growth path'? What determines its slope?

6. What is the significance of the term 'endogenous' in endogenous growth theory? What, according to this theory, determines the long-run rate of economic growth?

7. Under what circumstances would a higher rate of investment lead to a higher rate of economic growth?

8. What determines the rate of growth in total factor productivity?

9. What policy prescriptions do the neoclassical and endogenous growth theories offer policy makers who are looking to raise their country's long-run growth rate?

10. For what possible reasons may a country experience a persistently faster rate of economic growth than another?

Online resources

Additional case studies in MyEconLab

22.1   **Productivity performance and the UK economy.** A detailed examination of how the UK's productivity compares with that in other countries.

22.2   **The USA: is it a 'new economy'?** An examination of whether US productivity increases are likely to be sustained.

22.3   **UK human capital.** An overview of official data estimating the UK's stock of human capital.

Maths Case 22.1 Finding the steady-state equilibrium in the Solow model. Using the algebra in a worked example.

Maths Case 22.2 The effect of technological progress in the Solow model. Using the algebra in a worked example.

Websites relevant to this chapter

See sites listed at the end of Chapter 23 on page 704.

MyEconLab

This book can be supported by MyEconLab, which contains a range of additional resources, including an online homework and tutorial system designed to test and build your understanding.

You need both an access card and a course ID to access MyEconLab:

1. Is your lecturer using MyEconLab? Ask your lecturer for your course ID.

2. Has an access card been included with the book at a reduced cost? Check the inside back cover of the book.

3. If you have a course ID but no access card, go to: http://www.myeconlab.com/ to buy access to this interactive study programme.

Supply-side Policies

CHAPTER MAP

23.1 Supply-side policies and the macroeconomy	**685**
Economic growth and supply-side policies	685
Supply-side policies and other macroeconomic objectives	685
23.2 Approaches to supply-side policy	**686**
The new classical approach	686
The Keynesian approach	686
'Third Way' supply-side policies	687
The link between demand-side and supply-side policies	687
23.3 Market-orientated supply-side policies	**687**
Supply-side policies in the 1980s	687
Reducing government expenditure	688
Tax cuts: the effects on labour supply and employment	688
Tax cuts for business and other incentives	690
Reducing the power of labour	690
Reducing welfare	691
Policies to encourage competition	694
Conclusions	695
23.4 Interventionist supply-side policy	**695**
The case against the market	696
The forms of intervention	698
Planning	698
Selective intervention	698
The case against intervention	702

As we saw in Chapter 22, long-run economic growth can only be achieved through an increase in aggregate supply. If growth is to continue and not peter out, this in turn requires an increase in productivity. But how can productivity be increased?

We begin this chapter by drawing out various policy conclusions from the growth models we examined in sections 22.2 and 22.3. They stress the importance of technological progress and innovation. We also examine how developments on the supply side can affect the other macroeconomic objectives of achieving low unemployment and low inflation.

We then focus on the various policy options to increase aggregate supply. In doing this we consider the different approaches to supply-side policy and how they relate to the analysis of the economy. For example, we contrast Keynesian and new classical approaches.

Supply-side policies can be put into two broad categories: market orientated and interventionist. Market-orientated policies focus on 'freeing up' markets and improving market incentives. They involve policies such as tax cuts, privatisation and deregulation. We look at such policies in section 23.3.

Interventionist policies, by contrast, focus on ways of countering the inadequacies of markets through direct government provision of transport infrastructure, training or R&D, or financial support for private provision. We look at this type of policy in section 23.4.

Not surprisingly, the political right argues in favour of 'freeing up' the market; the left argues in favour of intervention.

23.1 SUPPLY-SIDE POLICIES AND THE MACROECONOMY

Economic growth and supply-side policies

Governments across the world have increasingly focused on *supply-side policies*; these are policies designed to increase *potential* output and hence long-run aggregate supply. As we saw in the last chapter, an increase in aggregate supply can be achieved through an increase in the quantity and/or quality of factors of production. Supply-side policies, therefore, focus on stimulating investment to increase the capital stock and encouraging increases in productivity of both capital and labour.

An important element in the growth of productivity is technological progress. Supply-side policy thus seeks to encourage research and development. It also seeks to encourage firms to take advantage of new ideas and innovations by investing in new capital, new production processes and perhaps organisational structures. But they will also need workers and managers with the skills and flexibility to take full advantage of these innovations.

Thus supply-side policies to encourage economic growth should focus not just on research and development, but also on education and training, industrial organisation, work practices and the whole range of incentives that may be necessary to make the best use of new ideas and techniques.

TC 14 / p420

? *Why do Keynesians argue that, even in the long run, demand-side policies will still be required if faster growth in aggregate supply is to be achieved?*

Supply-side policies and other macroeconomic objectives

Unemployment

Supply-side policies can also be directed at other macroeconomic objectives. The cure for demand-deficient unemployment may lie on the demand side, but other types of unemployment require supply-side solutions.

Equilibrium unemployment – frictional, structural, etc. – is caused by rigidities or imperfections in the market. There is a mismatching of aggregate supply and demand, and vacancies are not filled despite the existence of unemployment. The problem is that labour is not sufficiently mobile, either occupationally or geographically, to respond to changes in the job market. Labour supply for particular jobs is too inelastic.

Supply-side policies aim to influence labour supply by making workers more responsive to changes in job opportunities. They may also aim to make employers more adaptable and willing to operate within existing labour constraints. Alternatively, they may seek to reduce the monopoly power of unions to drive real wages above the equilibrium.

Inflation and supply-side policies

If inflation is caused by cost-push pressures, supply-side policy can help to reduce it in three ways:

- By reducing the power of unions and/or firms (e.g. by the use of anti-monopoly legislation) and thereby encouraging more competition in the supply of labour and/or goods.
- By preventing people from exercising that power by some form of prices and incomes policy. (Such policies were used in the 1970s: see Case Study 23.3 in MyEconLab.)
- By encouraging increases in productivity through retraining, or by investment grants to firms, or by tax incentives, etc.

KI 20 / p171

> ### Definition
>
> **Supply-side policies** Government policies that attempt to influence aggregate supply directly, rather than through aggregate demand.

Section summary

1. Supply-side policies seek to increase productivity and, in particular, promote more rapid technological progress and its adoption by business.

2. Demand-side policies (fiscal and monetary) may be suitable for controlling demand-pull inflation or demand-deficient unemployment, but supply-side policies will be needed to control the other types of inflation and unemployment.

23.2 APPROACHES TO SUPPLY-SIDE POLICY

The new classical approach

New classical economists argue that demand-side policy (by which they mean monetary policy) can only control inflation; it cannot affect growth and employment. Supply-side policy is the appropriate policy to increase output and reduce the level of unemployment.

Supply-side policy can be used to shift the aggregate supply curve to the right: to increase the amount that firms wish to supply at any given price. In Figure 23.1, output rises to Y_2 and prices fall to P_2. In the labour market, it can also reduce the natural rate of unemployment, and thus shift the vertical long-run Phillips curve to the left.

New classical economists advocate policies to 'free up' the market: policies that encourage private enterprise, or provide incentives and reward initiative. Section 23.3 examines these ***market-orientated supply-side policies***.

TC 5
p54

This part of the new classical agenda has much in common with the ***neo-Austrian/libertarian school*** (see Box 11.8). The argument here is that a free market, with the absolute minimum of government interference, will provide the dynamic environment where entrepreneurs will be willing to take risks and develop new products and new techniques.

Unlike neoclassical economists, who concentrate on the desirability of achieving economic efficiency in competitive markets, the neo-Austrians take a longer-term perspective. They argue that the prospect of monopoly profits is often what provides a major motivation for firms to take risks. The search to achieve market advantages through new products and new techniques is just as important a part of competition, they argue, as competition in the market for existing goods. Thus private property rights are a key element in neo-Austrian thought: the right to keep the fruits of innovation and investment, with minimum taxation.

The Keynesian approach

Modern Keynesians do not just advocate the management of demand. They too advocate supply-side policies, but generally of a more ***interventionist*** nature (e.g. training schemes, or policies to encourage firms to set up in areas of high unemployment).

The appropriate balance between demand- and supply-side policies depends on the degree of slack in the economy. In Figure 23.2, if output is below Y_1 with aggregate demand below AD_1, the immediate policy requirement is to increase aggregate *demand* rather than aggregate supply. If, however, the economy is approaching full employment with aggregate demand at AD_2 and output at Y_2, the most appropriate policy to increase output is a supply-side policy. This will shift the AS curve to the right (e.g. to AS_2) and raise output (e.g. to Y_3).

 Does this mean that Keynesians would advocate using supply-side policies only at times of full employment?

Keynesians also advocate supply-side policies to shift the Phillips curve to the left. If successful, such policies could

Definitions

Market-orientated supply-side policies Policies to increase aggregate supply by freeing up the market.

Neo-Austrian/libertarian school A school of thought that advocates maximum liberty for economic agents to pursue their own interests and to own property.

Interventionist supply-side policies Policies to increase aggregate supply by government intervention to counteract the deficiencies of the market.

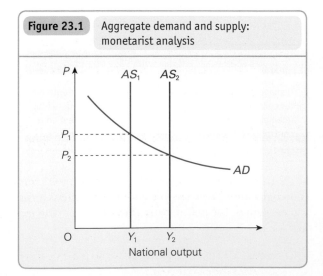

Figure 23.1 Aggregate demand and supply: monetarist analysis

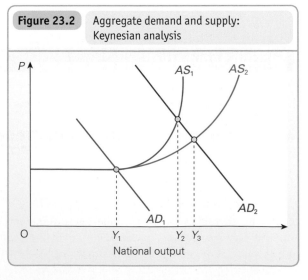

Figure 23.2 Aggregate demand and supply: Keynesian analysis

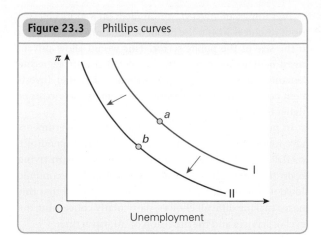

Figure 23.3   Phillips curves

lead simultaneously to lower unemployment and lower inflation. The economy could move from, say, point *a* to point *b* in Figure 23.3.

'Third Way' supply-side policies

During the early years of the Labour government in the UK from 1997 under Tony Blair, there was much discussion of a 'Third Way' between the unfettered market system advocated by many of those on the right and the interventionist approach advocated by those on the left. The Third Way borrows from the right in advocating incentives, low taxes and free movements of capital. It also borrows from the left in advocating means whereby governments can provide support for individuals in need while improving economic performance by investing in the country's infrastructure, such as its transport and telecommunication systems, and in its social capital, such as schools, libraries and hospitals.

Its main thrust is the concept of helping people to help themselves. Thus unemployment policies should be focused on helping the unemployed become employable, with unemployment benefits linked to the obligation actively to look for work. Growth policies should be a mixture of strengthening market incentives and keeping taxes low, regulation to encourage more competition and prevent monopoly abuse, and providing improved infrastructure and improved education and training.

To some extent, this approach was continued by the Coalition government, which came to office in 2010, albeit with somewhat more emphasis on freeing up the market.

The link between demand-side and supply-side policies

Policies can have both demand-side and supply-side effects. For example, many supply-side policies involve increased government expenditure, whether on retraining schemes, on research and development projects, or on industrial relocation. They will therefore cause a rise in aggregate demand (unless accompanied by a rise in taxes). Similarly, supply-side policies of tax cuts designed to increase incentives will increase aggregate demand (unless accompanied by a cut in government expenditure). It is thus important to consider the consequences for demand when planning various supply-side policies.

Likewise, demand-management policies often have supply-side effects. If a cut in interest rates boosts investment, there will be a multiplied rise in national income: a demand-side effect. But that rise in investment will also create increased productive capacity: a supply-side effect.

Section summary

1. Supply-side policies, if successful, will shift the aggregate supply curve to the right, and possibly shift the Phillips curve downwards/to the left.

2. New classical and neo-Austrian economists favour market-orientated supply-side policies. Keynesians tend to favour interventionist supply-side policies. The Third Way advocates carefully targeted government intervention, regulation, welfare and education programmes to encourage people better to help themselves and markets to work more effectively.

3. Supply-side policies often have demand-side effects, and demand-side policies often have supply-side effects. It is important for governments to take these secondary effects into account when working out their economic strategy.

23.3   MARKET-ORIENTATED SUPPLY-SIDE POLICIES

Supply-side policies in the 1980s

Radical market-orientated supply-side policies were first adopted in the early 1980s by the Thatcher government in the UK and the Reagan administration in the USA. The essence of these policies was to encourage and reward individual enterprise and initiative, and to reduce the role of government; to put more reliance on market forces and competition, and less on government intervention and regulation. The policies were thus associated with the following:

- Reducing government expenditure so as to release more resources for the private sector.

TC 5
p54

- Reducing taxes so as to increase incentives.
- Reducing the monopoly power of trade unions so as to encourage greater flexibility in both wages and working practices and to allow labour markets to clear.
- Reducing the automatic entitlement to certain welfare benefits so as to encourage greater self-reliance.
- Reducing red tape and other impediments to investment and risk taking.
- Encouraging competition through policies of deregulation and privatisation.
- Abolishing exchange controls and other impediments to the free movement of capital.

Such policies were increasingly copied by other governments around the world. Today most countries have adopted some or all of the above measures.

Reducing government expenditure

The desire by many governments to cut government expenditure is not just to reduce the size of deficits and hence reduce the growth of money supply; it is also an essential ingredient of their supply-side strategy.

In most countries the size of the public sector, relative to national income, had grown substantially by the 1980s (see Figure 23.4). A major aim of conservative governments throughout the world has been to reverse this trend. The public sector is portrayed as more bureaucratic and less efficient than the private sector. What is more, it is claimed that a growing proportion of public money has been spent on administration and other 'non-productive' activities, rather than on the direct provision of goods and services.

Two things are needed, it is argued: (a) a more efficient use of resources within the public sector and (b) a reduction in the size of the public sector. This would allow private investment to increase with no overall rise in aggregate demand. Thus the supply-side benefits of higher investment could be achieved without the demand-side costs of higher inflation.

In practice, as we can see in Figure 23.4, governments have found it very difficult to cut the share of expenditure in GDP. However, many countries were faced with trying to do this after the financial crisis and global economic slowdown of the late 2000s. Governments found that this meant making difficult choices, particularly concerning the level of services and the provision of infrastructure.

 Why might a recovering economy (and hence a fall in government expenditure on social security benefits) make the government feel even more concerned to make discretionary cuts in government expenditure?

Tax cuts: the effects on labour supply and employment

Cutting the marginal rate of income tax was a major objective of the Thatcher and Major governments (1979–97), as it was of the Reagan administration. In 1979, the standard rate of income tax was 33 per cent, with higher rates rising to 83 per cent. By 1997 the standard rate was only 23 per cent and the top rate was only 40 per cent. The Blair and Brown governments continued with this policy, so that by 2008 the standard rate was 20 per cent (but the lower rate had been abolished). From 2010, an additional 50 per cent

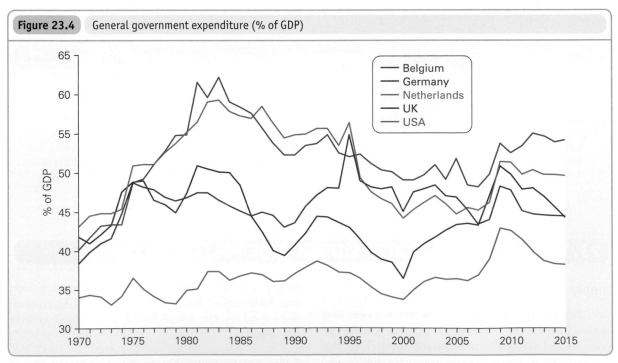

| Figure 23.4 | General government expenditure (% of GDP) |

Notes: Figures for Gemany based West Gemany only up to 1991; 2014 and 2015 based on forecasts.
Source: Based on data from *AMECO database* (European Commission, DGECFIN).

| BOX 23.1 | THE SUPPLY-SIDE REVOLUTION IN THE USA | CASE STUDIES AND APPLICATIONS |

'Reaganomics' and beyond

In both the UK and the USA, the 1980s proved to be years of radical political and economic change. Traditional economic and political practices were replaced by new and often controversial policies, although in theory many of the ideas advocated were based on old principles of laissez-faire capitalism.

In the USA, the era of 'Reaganomics' began in January 1981 when Ronald Reagan became president. With this new administration came a radical shift in policy aimed at directly tackling the supply side of the economy. This policy strategy involved four key strands:

- A reduction in the growth of Federal (central government) spending.
- A reduction in individual and corporate tax rates.
- A reduction in Federal regulations over private enterprise.
- A reduction in inflation through tight monetary policy.

On all four points, President Reagan was to achieve a degree of success. Federal spending growth was reduced even though military spending rocketed. Tax rates fell dramatically. Deregulation was speeded up. Inflation at first was stabilised and then fell sharply.

These supply-side measures were hailed as a great success by Republicans, and followers in both the UK and the USA were quick to advocate an even bigger reduction in the government's role.

Critics remained sceptical and pointed to the costs of Reaganomics. Huge budget deficits plagued the Reagan administration and the Bush Snr, Clinton and Bush Jnr

administrations that followed. The massive tax cuts were not matched by an equivalent cut in public expenditure; nor did they produce a sufficiently high rate of economic growth, through which additional tax revenues were to balance the budget. In the 1980s, 'civilian' or welfare spending was cut repeatedly in preference to the huge military budget. This led to increasing social hardship.

And such hardship still existed under George W. Bush. Indeed, with the onset of the credit crunch, things were to get worse as many poor people lost their houses. The emphasis had remained on cutting welfare and tightening requirements to receive state assistance. Critics claim that, even though the numbers on welfare might have fallen over the years, individuals and families remained in poverty, being forced to work for poverty wages as welfare support dwindled. The revolution was far from complete and its benefits to all social groups have been far from even.

The financial crisis of the late 2000s and the subsequent need for fiscal consolidation led to much debate, not only in the USA, about the form the fiscal consolidation should take and, more generally, about the role the state should play in modern economies. Whether, in such circumstances, current or future administrations will succeed in providing greater support for the poor without jeopardising the 'supply-side revolution' remains to be seen.

 Are market-orientated supply-side policies incompatible with policies to redistribute national income more equally?

---

tax rate was implemented for those earning in excess of £150 000, largely as a means of plugging the deficit in the public finances. This was subsequently reduced to 45 per cent from 2013.

Cuts in the marginal rate of income tax are claimed to have five beneficial effects: people work longer hours; more people wish to work; people work more enthusiastically; employment rises; unemployment falls. These are big claims. Are they true?

People work longer hours

A cut in the marginal rate of income tax has a *substitution effect* inducing people to work more and also an *income effect* causing people to work less. (At this point, you should review the arguments about the incentive effects of tax cuts: see pages 303–6.) Evidence suggests that the two effects will roughly cancel each other out. Anyway, for many people there is no such choice in the short run. There is no chance of doing overtime or working a shorter week. In the long run, there may be some flexibility in that people can change jobs.

More people wish to work

This applies largely to second income earners in a family, mainly women. A rise in after-tax wages may encourage

more women to look for jobs. It may now be worth the cost in terms of transport, childcare, family disruption, etc. The effects of a 1 or 2 per cent cut in income tax rates, however, are likely to be negligible. A more significant effect may be achieved by raising tax allowances. Part-time workers, especially, could end up paying no taxes. Of course, if unemployment is already high, the government will not want to increase the labour force.

People work more enthusiastically

There is little evidence to test this claim. The argument, however, is that people will be more conscientious and will work harder if they can keep more of their pay.

Employment rises

If wages are flexible, total employment will rise. This is illustrated in Figure 23.5. The N curve shows the total labour force. The AS_L curve shows the number of people who are actually qualified and willing to do the specific jobs they are offered at each (after-tax) wage rate. Equilibrium is where the aggregate demand for labour (AD_L) is equal to the labour cost to the employer (i.e. the pre-tax wage rate). Assume an initial income tax per worker of $a - b$. The equilibrium employment will be Q_1. Workers receive an after-tax wage

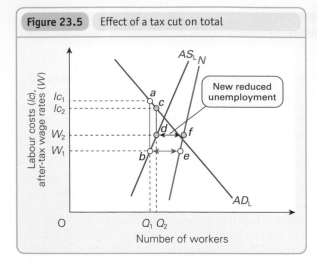

Figure 23.5   Effect of a tax cut on total

W_1 and thus supply Q_1 labour. Employers' labour cost is the pre-tax wage lc_1. At this wage, they demand Q_1 labour.

If the income tax per worker now falls to $c - d$, equilibrium employment will rise to Q_2. Firms will employ more workers because their labour costs have fallen to lc_2. More workers will take up jobs because their after-tax wages have risen to W_2.

Unemployment falls

One of the causes of natural (equilibrium) unemployment highlighted by new classical economists is the cushioning provided by unemployment benefit. If income tax rates are cut, there will be a bigger difference between after-tax wage rates and unemployment benefit. More people will be motivated to 'get on their bikes' and look for work.

In Figure 23.5, the horizontal gap between N and AS_L represents equilibrium unemployment. With a cut in income tax per worker from $a - b$ to $c - d$, equilibrium unemployment will fall from $e - b$ to $f - d$.

 What would happen to the AS_L curve and the level of unemployment if unemployment benefits were increased?

Despite the cuts in marginal rates of income tax in many countries, it has been commonplace for these to be offset by significant increases in other taxes. For example, in the UK, VAT was raised from 8 to 15 per cent per cent in 1979, to 17.5 per cent in 1992 and to 20 per cent in 2011.[1] The marginal rate of national insurance contributions was 6.5 per cent in 1979; in 2011 it was 12 per cent. The net effect was that government's receipts as a proportion of GDP were largely unchanged at close to 40 per cent.

 Does this mean that there were no positive incentive effects from the 1979–97 Conservative governments' tax measures?

[1] The rate was cut to 15 per cent in December 2008 for 13 months as part of the government's fiscal stimulus package.

To the extent that tax cuts do succeed in increasing take-home pay, there is a danger of 'sucking in' imports. In the UK, there is a high income elasticity of demand for imports. Extra consumer incomes may be spent on foreign-made electronic goods, foreign cars, holidays abroad, and so on. Tax cuts can therefore have a serious effect on the current account of the balance of payments.

Tax cuts for business and other investment incentives

A number of financial incentives can be given to encourage investment. Selective intervention in the form of grants for specific industries or firms is best classified as an interventionist policy and will be examined later in this chapter. Market-orientated policies seek to reduce the general level of taxation on profits, or to give greater tax relief to investment.

A cut in corporation tax (the tax on business profits) will increase after-tax profits. This will leave more funds for ploughing back into investment. Also, the higher after-tax return on investment will encourage more investment to take place. In 1983 the main rate of corporation tax in the UK stood at 52 per cent. A series of reductions have taken place since then. By 2011 the main rate had been halved to 26 per cent and by 2015 the rate was due to have fallen to 20 per cent

An alternative policy would be to increase investment allowances. These allow firms to offset the cost of investment against pre-tax profit, thereby reducing their tax liability. Successive governments have used a range of such allowances. For example, in the UK companies can offset a multiple of research and development costs against corporation tax. As of April 2012, the rate of relief for small and medium-sized enterprises (SMEs) was 225 per cent: taxable profits are reduced by £225 for every £100 of R&D expenditure. For larger companies the rate of relief was 130 per cent.

Since April 2013, firms have been subject to a lower rate of corporation tax on profits earned from patented inventions and certain other innovations. The idea is that firms will be provided with financial support to innovate where this results in their acquiring patents. Patents provide protection for intellectual property rights. From April 2013, firms are liable to corporation tax on the profits attributable to qualifying patents at a reduced rate of 10 per cent. The relief is being phased in, so that by 2017 all profits related to the patent will be subject to the reduced rate.

Reducing the power of labour

In Figure 23.6, if the power of unions to push wage rates up to W_1 were removed, then (assuming no change in the demand curve for labour) wage rates would fall to W_e. Disequilibrium unemployment ($Q_2 - Q_1$) would disappear. Employment would rise from Q_1 to Q_e.

Equilibrium unemployment, however, will rise somewhat as the gap between gross and effective labour supply

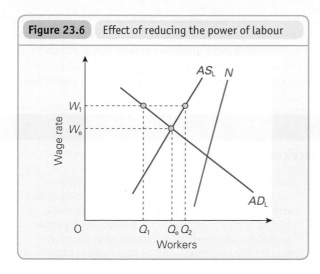

Figure 23.6 Effect of reducing the power of labour

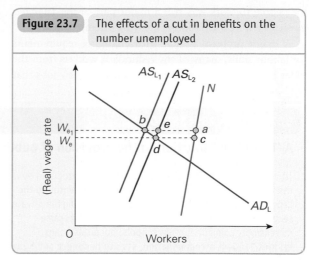

Figure 23.7 The effects of a cut in benefits on the number unemployed

widens. With the reduction in wage rates, some people may now prefer to remain on unemployment benefits.

If labour costs to employers are reduced, their profits will probably rise. This could encourage and enable more investment and hence economic growth. If the monopoly power of labour is reduced, then cost-push inflation will also be reduced.

The Thatcher government took a number of measures to weaken the power of labour. These included restrictions on union closed shops, restrictions on secondary picketing, financial assistance for union ballots, and enforced secret ballots on strike proposals (see Chapter 9). It also set a lead in resisting strikes in the public sector. Unlike previous Labour governments, it did not consult with union leaders over questions of economic policy. It was publicly very critical of trade union militancy and blamed the unions for many of the UK's economic ills. As a result, unions lost a lot of political standing and influence.

As labour markets have become more flexible, with increased part-time working and short-term contracts, and as the process of globalisation has exposed more companies to international competition, so the power of labour has been further eroded in many sectors of the economy.

 Is the number of working days lost through disputes a good indication of (a) union power; (b) union militancy?

Reducing welfare

New classical economists claim that a major cause of unemployment is the small difference between the welfare benefits of the unemployed and the take-home pay of the employed. This causes voluntary unemployment (i.e. frictional unemployment). People are caught in a 'poverty trap': if they take a job, they lose their benefits (see pages 308–9).

A dramatic solution to this problem would be to cut unemployment benefits. Unlike policies to encourage investment, this supply-side policy would have a very rapid

effect. It would shift the effective labour supply curve to the right. In Figure 23.7, equilibrium unemployment would fall from $a - b$ to $c - d$ if real wage rates were flexible downwards; or from $a - b$ to $a - e$ if they were not flexible. In the case of non-flexible real wage rates, the reduction in equilibrium unemployment would be offset by a rise in disequilibrium unemployment $(e - b)$.

Because workers would now be prepared to accept a lower wage, the average length of job search by the unemployed would be reduced. In Figure 23.8, the average duration of unemployment would fall from T_1 to T_2 (see pages 439–40).

 Would a cut in benefits affect the W_o curve? If so, with what effect?

In the early 1980s, the gap between take-home pay and welfare benefits to the unemployed did indeed widen. However, over the same period unemployment rose dramatically. Nevertheless, the claim that there was too little incentive

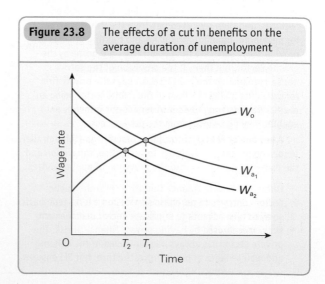

Figure 23.8 The effects of a cut in benefits on the average duration of unemployment

for people to work was still a major part of the Thatcher government's explanation of growing unemployment.

A major problem is that with changing requirements for labour skills, many of the redundant workers from the older industries are simply not qualified for new jobs that are created. What is more, the longer people are unemployed, the more demoralised they become. Employers would probably be prepared to pay only very low wage rates to such workers. To persuade these unemployed people to take these low-paid jobs, the welfare benefits would have

---

BOX 23.2 ASSESSING PFI

A 'Third Way' solution to the provision of public services

The Private Finance Initiative (PFI), although introduced by the Conservative government in 1992, became central to the Labour government's 'Third Way' approach of using the private sector to deliver public projects and services. It became increasingly common for new schools, hospitals, roads, bridges, student accommodation, etc., to be funded and built by private companies under PFI contracts (see table and figure). Well-known examples include the Channel Tunnel rail link and capital investment in the London Underground.

PFI Projects: total of current PFI projects across government as of March 2013

	Number of projects	Capital value (£m)
Health	121	11 804.5
Defence	44	9 076.7
Transport	61	7 278.0
Education	168	6 891.1
Scottish Government	83	5 690.0
Environment, Food and Rural Affairs	30	4 147.2
Communities and Local Government	68	2 366.3
Northern Ireland Executive	39	1 656.9
Work and Pensions	3	1 059.2
Home Office	28	1 047.9
HM Revenue & Customs	8	862.1
Justice	23	798.6
Welsh Government	24	568.6
Culture, Media and Sport	17	348.9
Other	8	615.2
Total	725	54 211.2

The government or local authority decides the service it requires, and then seeks tenders from the private sector for designing, building, financing and running projects to provide these services. The capital costs are borne by the private sector, but then, if the provision of the service is not self-financing, the public sector pays the private firm for providing it. Thus instead of the public sector being an owner of assets and provider of services, it is merely an enabler, buying services from the private sector.

A key aim of PFI is to introduce competition (through the tendering process), private-sector expertise, innovation and the management of risk into the provision of public services.

Under the Private Finance Initiative (PFI) the public sector contracts to purchase services on a long-term basis so as to take advantage of private-sector management skills incentivised by having private finance at risk. The private sector has always been involved in the building and maintenance of public infrastructure, but PFI ensures that contractors are bound into long-term maintenance contracts and shoulder responsibility for the quality of the work they do. With PFI, the public sector defines what is required to meet public needs and ensures delivery of the outputs through the contract. Consequently, the private sector can be harnessed to deliver investment in better quality public services while frontline services are retained within the public sector.[1]

Clearly, there are immediate benefits to the public finances from using private, rather than public, funds to finance a project. Later, however, there is potentially an extra burden of having to buy the services from the private provider at a price that includes an element for profit. What is hoped is that the costs to the taxpayer of these profits will be more than offset by gains in efficiency.

Critics, however, claim that PFI projects have resulted in low quality of provision and that cost control has often been poor, resulting in a higher burden for the taxpayer in the long term. What is more, many of the projects have turned out to be highly profitable, suggesting that the terms of the original contracts were too lax. Take the case of construction and maintenance company Carillion. By 2014 it had won 60 PFI projects in the UK and Canada, including hospitals, schools, university buildings, prisons, roads and railways. In 2005, it announced that the net present value of its then 18 UK PFI investments was £83 million. This compared with an investment cost of just £29 million.

There is also the question of what happens if the private company runs into financial difficulties. In 2005, the engineering company Jarvis only just managed to avoid bankruptcy by securing refinancing on all 14 of its PFI deals. This involved selling a large amount of assets and renegotiating loans.

It is estimated that PFI projects typically use around 90 per cent debt finance. With the credit crunch of 2008–9 many firms operating PFI projects found it difficult to raise finance. In March 2009, the government set up an Infrastructure Finance Unit to provide government loans, if necessary, on commercial terms. In April 2009 it provided a £120 million loan to help complete a waste treatment and power generation plant in Manchester. But this was an exception. Many projects either were held up or were faced with paying above-market interest rates.

Private Finance 2 (PF2)

Given the criticisms of PFI by both Conservatives and Liberal Democrats in opposition, in November 2011 the Coalition Chancellor, George Osborne, set up a review of PFI. The objective was to develop a new model for delivering public investment and services that takes advantage of private-sector expertise, but at lower cost to the taxpayer.

to be slashed. A 'market' solution to the problem, therefore, may be a very cruel solution. A fairer solution would be an interventionist policy: a policy of retraining labour.

Another alternative is to make the payment of unemployment benefits conditional on the recipient making a concerted effort to find a job. In the jobseeker's allowance scheme introduced in the UK in 1996, claimants must be available for, and actively seeking, work and must complete a Jobseeker's Agreement, which sets out the types of work the person is willing to do, and the plan to find work.

CASE STUDIES AND APPLICATIONS

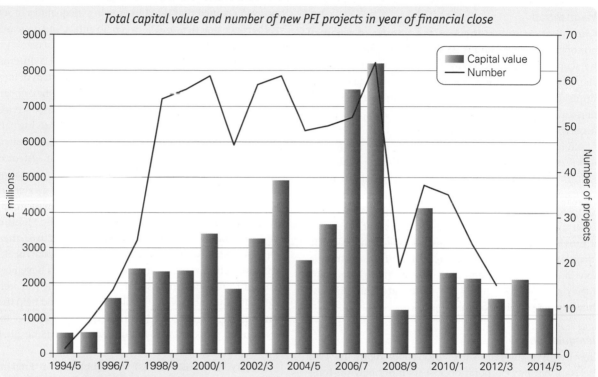

Total capital value and number of new PFI projects in year of financial close

Note: Capital values for 2013/14 and 2014/15 projected.
Source: PFI Projects Data (various years) (GOV.UK).

This review coincided with the introduction in 2010 of a National Investment Plan (NIP): a strategic plan to target public investment.

With some £270 billion in repayments on PFI contracts due to be made to private-sector companies over the next 50 years, and with the cost of capital for a typical PFI project at 8 per cent, double the long-term gilt rate of around 4 per cent, it was not surprising that government was looking to find cheaper ways of using private finance and expertise.

In December 2012 the Treasury published its New Approach to Public Private Partnerships. The publication set out the government's new approach: PF2. Changes include:

- government to act as a minority public equity co-investor in PF2 projects, with the public sector taking stakes of up to 49 per cent in individual private finance projects and appointing a director to the boards of each project;
- publication of an annual report detailing project and financial information on all projects where the government holds a public-sector equity stake;
- the competitive tendering phases for PF2 project to be no longer than 18 months unless agreed by the Chief Secretary to the Treasury;

- procurement processes to be centralised, with government departments taking charge of procurement;
- removing 'soft services', such as cleaning and catering from PF2 projects;
- the introduction of funding competitions for a portion of the private-sector equity to enable long-term equity providers to invest in projects before financial close;
- the tender process to require bidders to develop a long-term financing solution, where bank debt does not form the majority of the financing of the project.

In unveiling its guidelines for PF2, the government confirmed the new PF2 framework would be used for a £1.75 billion privately financed element of the Priority Schools Building Programme (PSBP). Hence, public–private partnerships were to remain an important means of delivering on the UK's National Infrastructure Plan (NIP).

 Do a news Web search for PFI projects and identify the issues currently surrounding the success or otherwise of PFI.

[1] Financial Statement and Budget Report, Chapter C (HM Treasury, 2005).

Payment can be refused if the claimant refuses to accept the offer of a job.

Policies to encourage competition

If the government can encourage more competition, this should have the effect of increasing national output and reducing inflation. Five major types of policy have been pursued under this heading.

Privatisation

If privatisation simply involves the transfer of a natural monopoly to private hands (as with the water companies), the scope for increased competition is limited. However, where there is genuine scope for competition (e.g. in the supply of gas and electricity), privatisation can lead to increased efficiency, more consumer choice and lower prices (but see Box 13.4 on page 394).

Alternatively, privatisation can involve the introduction of private services into the public sector (e.g. private contractors providing cleaning services in hospitals, or refuse collection for local authorities). Private contractors may compete against each other for the franchise. This may well lower the cost of provision of these services, but the quality of provision may also suffer unless closely monitored. The effects on unemployment are uncertain. Private contractors may offer lower wages and thus may use more labour. But if they are trying to supply the service at minimum cost, they may employ less labour.

Deregulation

This involves the removal of monopoly rights. In 1979 the National Bus Corporation lost its monopoly on long-distance coach haulage. Private operators were now allowed to compete. This substantially reduced coach fares on a number of routes. In 1986 competition was allowed in providing local bus services (see Case Study 23.1 in MyEconLab).

An example in the private sector was the so-called 'Big Bang' on the Stock Exchange in 1986. Under this, the monopoly power of jobbers to deal in stocks and shares on the Stock Exchange was abolished. In addition, stockbrokers now compete with each other in the commission rates that they charge, and online share dealing has become commonplace.

Introducing market relationships into the public sector

This is where the government tries to get different departments or elements within a particular part of the public sector to 'trade' with each other, so as to encourage competition and efficiency. The process often involves 'devolved budgeting'.

Devolved budgeting in the UK's National Health Service. One area of public policy in the UK which has been radically reshaped by devolved budgeting is health. The Thatcher government introduced an 'internal market' into the National Health Service (NHS). General practitioners were offered the opportunity to control their own budget. The size of the budget was determined by the number of patients and by their age and health profiles. GP fundholders purchased services directly from hospitals and had to cover their drugs bill. The suppliers of treatment, the hospitals, depended for much of their income on attracting the business of GP purchasers. They were thus put in competition with other hospitals.

Advocates of the internal market in the NHS argued that it created greater efficiency through competition. Critics, however, claimed that it led to growing inequalities of service between practices and between hospitals, and increased the administrative costs of the NHS.

The Labour government abolished the NHS internal market and replaced GP fundholding with a system of local primary care trusts (PCTs), which coordinated health-care provision in a particular locality. They also purchased services for patients from hospitals with the objective of giving patients, through their GPs, more choice of where to be treated.

In 2003, the government also introduced a system of 'foundation trusts'. Hospitals can apply for foundation trust status. If successful, they are given much greater financial autonomy in terms of purchasing, employment and investment decisions. Applications are judged by Monitor, the independent health regulator. By July 2013, there were 147 NHS foundation trusts and 41 mental health NHS foundation trusts. Critics argue that funds have been diverted to foundation hospitals away from the less well-performing hospitals where greater funding could help that performance. In the 2012 Health and Social Care Act the government proposed that in due course all NHS hospitals become foundation trusts.

Primary care trusts (PCTs) were abolished in England in April 2013. In their place were clinical commissioning groups (CCGs). These are formed of groups of GP practices. Clinical commissioning groups are responsible for arranging most of the NHS services within their boundaries. They oversee how NHS funds are spent. Therefore, as with GP fundholding, a key principle is to give GPs a choice of 'providers' with the hope of reducing costs and driving up standards.

The Private Finance Initiative (PFI)

This is where a private company, after a competitive tender, is contracted by a government department or local authority to finance and build a project, such as a new road or a prison. The government then pays the company to maintain and/or run it, or simply rents the assets from the company. The public sector thus becomes a purchaser of services rather than a direct provider itself. The benefits and costs of PFI are explored in Box 23.2.

Free trade and free capital movements

The opening up of international trade and investment is central to a market-orientated supply-side policy. One of the first measures of the Thatcher government (in October 1979) was to remove all exchange controls, thereby permitting the free inflow and outflow of capital, both long term and short term. Most other industrialised countries also removed or relaxed exchange controls during the 1980s and early 1990s.

The Single European Act of 1987, which came into force in 1993, was another example of international liberalisation. As we shall see in section 24.4, it was designed to create a 'single market' in the EU: a market without barriers to the movement of goods, services, capital and labour. This has been largely achieved, although some restrictions on trade between member states do still apply.

Conclusions

Although a number of supply-side measures have been taken in many countries during the past 35 years, many of the supply-side *effects* have been the result of changes in demand.

The recessions of the early 1980s and early 1990s caused many firms to fail. Those that survived were often able to do so only by increases in efficiency. Resistance from unions to the introduction of new labour-saving technology was weakened by high unemployment and the fear that, without the new technology, firms might be forced to close.

Similarly, demand had effects on the supply side during periods of expansion, such as the late 1980s and late 1990s.

Firms were encouraged to innovate and develop new products to take advantage of buoyant markets.

Even where supply-side changes cannot be traced directly to changes in aggregate demand, they often occur not as a result of government supply-side policy, but as a result of international competition and capital movements, new business practices, new inventions and new products.

Thus, although productivity in the UK and the USA grew more rapidly in the 1980s and 1990s than in the 1970s (see Box 22.2 on page 680), it is not clear to what extent this was the direct result of supply-side *policy*.

A similar debate can be had in explaining UK wage patterns during the period following the financial crisis of the late 2000s. As illustrated in Figure 15.12 (see page 445), many workers saw *real* wage rates fall as nominal wage rates failed to keep pace with the rate of inflation. This helped to limit the rise in the equilibrium level of unemployment. But to what extent was this driven by the fall in aggregate demand and economic uncertainty or by greater labour market flexibility brought about through supply-side reforms?

 If supply-side measures led to a 'shake out' of labour and a resulting reduction in overstaffing, but also to a rightward shift in the Phillips curve, would you judge the policy as a success?

Section summary

1. Market-orientated supply-side policies aim to increase the rate of growth of aggregate supply by encouraging private enterprise and the freer play of market forces.

2. Reducing government expenditure as a proportion of GDP is a major element of such policies.

3. Tax cuts can be used to encourage more people to take up jobs, and to encourage people to work longer hours and more enthusiastically. They can be used to reduce equilibrium unemployment and encourage employers to take on more workers. Likewise tax cuts for businesses or increased investment allowances may encourage higher investment. The effects of tax cuts depend on how people respond to incentives. For example, people will work longer hours only if the substitution effect outweighs the income effect.

4. Reducing the power of trade unions by legislation could reduce disequilibrium unemployment and cost-push inflation. It could also lead to a redistribution of income to profits, which could increase investment and growth (but possibly lead to greater inequality).

5. A reduction in welfare benefits, especially those related to unemployment, will encourage workers to accept jobs at lower wages and thus decrease equilibrium unemployment.

6. Various policies can be introduced to increase competition. These include privatisation, deregulation, introducing market relationships into the public sector, public–private partnerships and freer international trade and capital movements.

23.4 INTERVENTIONIST SUPPLY-SIDE POLICY

In this section, we look at the limitations of the market in stimulating supply-side improvements. We then look at ways in which the government can intervene to encourage more investment and a faster rate of economic growth. We will also assess the relative effectiveness of different types of interventionist policy.

 TC 6 p55

Many of these policies come under the general heading of *industrial policy*: the government taking an active role to

support investment in industry and to halt the decline of the manufacturing sector (see Box 23.3).

Definition

Industrial policies Policies to encourage industrial investment and greater industrial efficiency.

The case against the market

The basis of the case for government intervention is that the free market is likely to provide too little research and development, training and investment.

As we saw in Chapter 22, there are potentially large external benefits from research and development. Firms investing in developing and improving products, and especially firms engaged in more general scientific research, may produce results that provide benefits to many other firms and to the wider economy. Thus the social rate of return on investment may be much higher than the private rate of return. Investment that is privately unprofitable for a firm may therefore still be economically desirable for the nation.

Similarly, investment in training may continue yielding benefits to society that are lost to the firms providing the training when the workers leave.

Investment often involves risks. Firms may be unwilling to take those risks, since the costs of possible failure may be too high. When looked at nationally, however, the benefits of investment might well have substantially outweighed the costs, and thus it would have been socially desirable for firms to have taken the risk. Successes would have outweighed failures.

For decades, the UK has had a lower level of investment relative to GDP than other industrialised countries. This is illustrated in Table 23.1. It could be argued, therefore, that there is a particularly strong case in the UK for government intervention to encourage investment.

Imperfections in the capital market

Imperfections in the capital market may result in investment not being financed, even though it is privately profitable. Banks in the UK, unlike banks in France, Germany and Japan, have not traditionally been a source of finance for long-term investment by firms.

Similarly, if firms rely on raising finance by the issue of new shares, this makes them very dependent on the stock market performance of their shares, which depends on current profitability and expected profitability in the near future, not on long-term profitability. Shareholders, mainly financial institutions, tend to demand too high a dividend rate from the companies in which they invest. This, in part, is due to competition between financial institutions to attract savers to buy their savings packages. The result is that there is less profit left over for ploughing back into investment. The fear of takeovers (the competition for corporate control) again makes managers overconcerned to keep shareholders happy. Finally, floating successful companies on the Stock Exchange provides a large windfall gain to the original owners. This encourages entrepreneurs to *set up* companies, but discourages them from making *long-term* commitments to them. This has all led to the UK disease of 'short-termism': the obsession with short-term profits and the neglect of investment that yields profits only after a number of years.

Figure 23.9 shows the extent of net capital issues (capital issues less repayments) by, and net bank lending (gross lending less repayments) to, UK private non-financial corporations since 2003. Across the period the majority of the net capital issue involved the issue of fixed-interest bonds – over 90 per cent of the net issue. Until the financial crisis, net capital issues were low and firms relied much more heavily on bank loans. By contrast, the onset of the crisis saw bank lending drying up, with repayments exceeding loans. Many firms were forced to make increased use of capital issues.

Finally, in the case of ailing firms, if the government does not help finance a rescue investment programme, there may be substantial social costs from job losses. The avoidance of these social costs may make the investment socially, if not privately, profitable.

 How would the radical right reply to these arguments?

Table 23.1	Gross fixed capital formation as a percentage of GDP					
	1970–92		**1993–2015**		**1970–2015**	
	General government	**Private**	**General government**	**Private**	**General government**	**Private**
Belgium	3.5	18.1	1.7	18.7	2.6	18.4
Denmark	2.7	18.4	1.9	17.0	2.3	17.7
France	3.4	17.9	3.1	15.8	3.3	16.8
Germany	3.3	18.5	1.8	17.4	2.5	18.0
Ireland	3.9	17.8	3.1	15.8	3.5	16.8
Italy	3.0	20.9	2.2	17.4	2.6	19.1
Japan	5.2	26.1	4.4	19.5	4.8	22.8
Netherlands	3.9	18.7	3.3	16.4	3.6	17.6
Spain	3.1	20.4	3.2	20.4	3.2	20.4
UK	3.0	16.0	1.8	14.4	2.4	15.2
USA	2.4	19.9	2.3	18.6	2.3	19.2

Source: *AMECO database*, Tables 3.2 and 6.1 (European Commission, DGECFIN).

TC 3
p26

KI 29
p323

KI 11
p80

KI 23
p225

TC 1
p11

Figure 23.9   Net bank lending and net capital issue

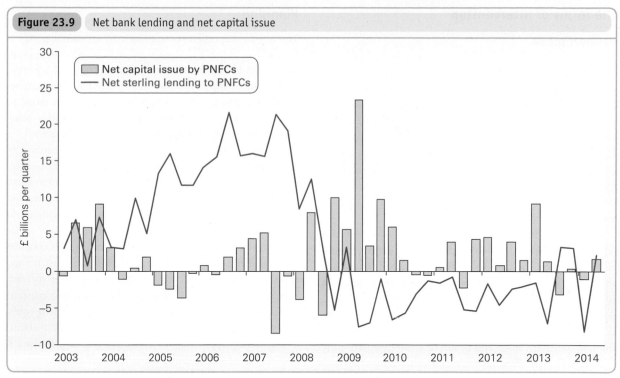

Source: Based on data from *Bankstats*, series LPQVWNQ and CPQB83I (Bank of England) (data published 1 September 2014).

BOX 23.3   **A NEW APPROACH TO INDUSTRIAL POLICY**   EXPLORING ECONOMICS

Industrial policy attempts to increase investment and halt or slow the shrinking of the industrial sector. As with many other areas of economic policy, industrial policy throughout most of the world has undergone a radical reorientation in recent years. The government's role has shifted from one of direct intervention in the form of subsidies and protecting industry from competition, to one of focusing upon the external business environment and the conditions that influence its competitiveness.

The reasons for such a change are both philosophical and structural:

■ The rise of the political right in the 1980s led to a shift away from interventionist and towards market-based supply-side policy.
■ Growing government debt, and a desire to curb public expenditure, acted as a key incentive to reduce the state's role in industrial affairs. This was argued to be one of the driving forces behind the European privatisation process since the 1980s.
■ Industry, during the 1980s, became progressively more global in its outlook. As such, its investment decisions were increasingly being determined by external environmental factors, especially the technology, productivity and labour costs of its international competitors.

The new approach to industrial policy, being widely adopted by many advanced countries, is to focus on improving those factors that shape a nation's competitiveness. This involves shifting away from particular sectors to targeting what are referred to as 'framework conditions for industry'. Policies include the following:

■ The promotion of investment in physical and human capital. Human capital in particular, and the existence of a sound skills base, are seen as crucial for attracting global business and ensuring long-run economic growth.
■ A reduction in non-wage employment costs, such as employers' social security and pension contributions. Many governments see these costs as too high and as a severe limitation on competitiveness and employment creation.
■ The promotion of innovation and the encouragement of greater levels of R&D.
■ Support for small and medium-sized enterprises. SMEs have received particular attention due to their crucial role in enhancing innovation, creating employment and contributing to skills development, especially in high-tech areas.
■ The improvement of infrastructure. This includes both physical transport, such as roads and railways, and information highways.
■ The protection of intellectual property by more effective use of patents and copyright. By reinforcing the law in these areas it is hoped to encourage firms to develop new products and commit themselves to research.

These policies, if they are to be truly effective, are likely to require co-ordination and integration, since they represent a radical departure from traditional industrial policy.

1. *In what senses could these new policies be described as (a) non-interventionist; (b) interventionist?*
2. *Does globalisation, and in particular the global perspective of multinational corporations, make industrial policy in the form of selective subsidies and tax relief more or less likely?*

KI 22
p 223

The forms of intervention

Nationalisation

This is the most extreme form of intervention, and one that most countries have in the past rejected, given the world-wide trend of privatisation. Nevertheless, many countries have stopped short of privatising certain key transport and power industries, such as the railways and electricity generation. Having these industries under public ownership may result in higher investment than if they were under private ownership. Thus French governments have invested heavily in the state-owned railway system. This has resulted in fast, efficient rail services, with obvious benefits to rail users and the economy generally.

Nationalisation may also be a suitable solution for rescuing vital industries suffering extreme market turbulence. This was the case in 2008 with many banks. With the credit crunch, overexposure to risky investments in securitised sub-prime debt, inadequate levels of capital, declining confidence and plummeting share prices, many banks were taken into full or partial public ownership. In the UK, Northern Rock and Bradford & Bingley were fully nationalised, while the government took a majority share-holding in the Royal Bank of Scotland and Lloyds Banking Group.

Direct provision

Improvements in infrastructure – such as a better motorway system – can be of direct benefit to industry. Alternatively, the government could provide factories or equipment to specific firms.

Grants

The government may sponsor research and development in certain industries (e.g. aerospace) or in specific fields (e.g. microprocessors). It may back investment programmes considered to benefit the economy as a whole.

Rationalisation

The government may encourage mergers or other forms of industrial reorganisation that will lead to greater efficiency and/or higher levels of investment. This could be done through government agencies or government departments.

Advice and persuasion

The government may engage in discussions with private firms in order to find ways to improve efficiency and innovation. It may bring firms together to exchange information and create a climate of greater certainty. It may bring firms and unions together to try to create greater industrial harmony.

Information

The government may provide various information services to firms: technical assistance, the results of public research, information on markets, etc.

Planning

The most comprehensive approach to industrial policy is for the government to engage in national economic planning. This is not the 'command planning' of the former Soviet Union, where factories were issued with instructions on what to produce, what inputs to use and how much to invest. Rather, it is 'indicative planning'. Indicative planning works alongside the market. It does not replace it.

In a free market, there are likely to be many uncertainties for firms. Industries are highly interconnected. For example, if the electricity industry plans to expand, it will want to know the likely availability of coal or other fuels. Unless firms can know the plans of other firms, they may be cautious about taking investment decisions.

Indicative planning is where the government consults with industry leaders to find out their intentions. It then seeks to co-ordinate the plans of firms, industries and sectors, and to recommend realistic and mutually consistent targets for output and investment. The government could also use persuasion or various financial incentives to obtain a consistent plan. The use of indicative planning in the UK is examined in Case Study 23.6 in MyEconLab.

Today in the UK and most other countries there is no comprehensive indicative planning at national level. Nevertheless, local authorities and government departments do consult with industry and with chambers of commerce to improve the flow of information. To this end, in 2011 the Coalition government established Local Enterprise Partnerships (LEPs) – partnerships between the private sector and local authorities – to promote local economic development.

What instruments might a government use to 'persuade' firms to abide by a national plan? What are their advantages and disadvantages?

Selective intervention

Conservative governments have never favoured a comprehensive industrial strategy. Nevertheless, governments of both parties have intervened selectively in areas where they have felt that the market has provided inadequate investment.

Research and development (R&D)

Around one-third of UK R&D is financed by the government, but around half of this has been concentrated in the defence, aerospace and nuclear power industries. As a result, there has been little government sponsorship of research in the majority of industry. Since the mid-1970s, however, there have been various government initiatives in the field of information technology. Even so, the amount of government support in this field has been very small compared with Japan, France and the USA. What is more, the amount of support declined between the mid-1980s and the late 1990s.

As we saw in section 23.3 (see page 690), the UK uses the tax system to encourage research and development (R&D). Despite this, UK gross expenditure on R&D as a percentage

KI 15 p121

TC 5 p54

Figure 23.10 Gross expenditure on R&D as a percentage of GDP

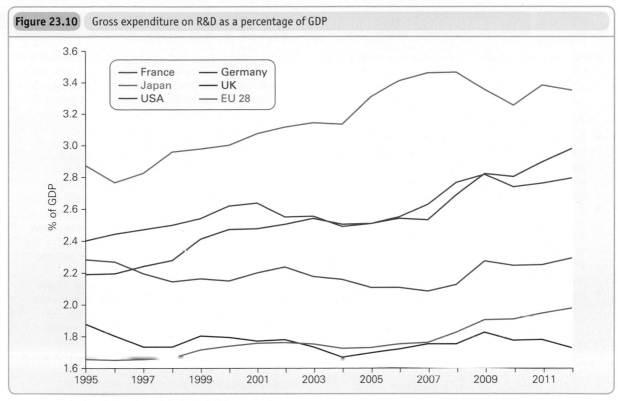

Note: EU 28 = the 28 member countries of the European Union since July 2013.
Source: Based on data in *Main Science and Technology Indicators* (OECD, 2014).

of GDP has been lower than that of its main economic rivals (see Figure 23.10). For instance, the UK's share of R&D expenditure in GDP has typically been only around 70 per cent of that in Germany and around 56 per cent of that in Japan.

Lower R&D has contributed to a productivity gap between the UK and other G7 countries (see Box 22.2). The UK's poor R&D record has occurred even though a sizeable number of UK-based companies regularly make a list of the world's largest R&D spending companies. In part, this reflects the limited R&D expenditure by government. But, it also reflects the low R&D intensity across the private sector. In other words, total R&D expenditure by UK firms has often been low *relative* to the income generated by sales.

Industrial reorganisation

UK Labour governments in the past were concerned with encouraging efficiency and investment via 'rationalisation'. For example, the Industrial Reorganisation Corporation (IRC) was set up in 1967 to provide loans to industry, and to arrange and finance mergers, where these were felt to lead to economies of scale and greater scope for investment. It was wound up in 1970 by the incoming Conservative government.

The main industrial reorganisation strategy pursued by the Conservative governments of the 1980s and 1990s was privatisation (see section 13.2 and page 694).

Training

The government may set up training schemes, or encourage educational institutions to make their courses more

vocationally relevant, or introduce new vocational qualifications (such as GNVQs, NVQs and foundation degrees in the UK). Alternatively, the government can provide grants or tax relief to firms which themselves provide training schemes. Alternative approaches to training in the UK, Germany, France and the USA are examined in Box 23.4.

Regional and urban policy

Certain parts of the country suffer from lower economic growth and higher unemployment than others. These can be broad regions, such as the north-east of England or Calabria in southern Italy, or much smaller areas, such as parts of inner cities. These regional and urban problems normally result from structural problems – the main one being the decline of certain industries, such as mining or heavy manufacturing industry, which had previously been concentrated in those areas.

When an area declines, there will be a downward *regional multiplier effect*. The decline in demand and loss of jobs lead to less money being spent in the local community; transport and other service industries lose custom. The whole region becomes more depressed.

Definition

Regional multiplier effects When a change in injections into or withdrawals from a particular region causes a multiplied change in income in that region. The regional multiplier (kr) is given by 1/$mpwr$, where the import component of *mpwr* consists of imports into that region either from abroad or from other regions of the economy.

BOX 23.4   ALTERNATIVE APPROACHES TO TRAINING AND EDUCATION

It is generally recognised by economists and politicians alike that improvements in training and education can yield significant supply-side gains.

Training and economic performance are linked in three main ways:

- *Labour productivity*. In various studies comparing the productivity of UK and German industry, education and training is seen as the principal reason for the productivity gap between the two countries (see Box 22.2).
- *Innovation and change*. A key factor in shaping a firm's willingness to introduce new products or processes will be the adaptability and skills of its workforce. If the firm has to spend a lot of money on retraining, or on attracting skilled workers away from other firms, the costs may prove prohibitive.
- *Costs of production*. A shortage of skilled workers will quickly create labour bottlenecks and cause production costs to increase. This will stifle economic growth.

If training is left to the employer, the benefits will become an externality if the workers leave to work elsewhere. Society has benefited from the training, but the firm has not. The free market, therefore, will provide a less than optimal amount of training. The more mobile the labour force, and the more 'transferable' the skills acquired from training, the more likely it is that workers will leave, and the less willing firms will be to invest in training.

In the UK, there is a high level of labour turnover. What is more, wage differentials between skilled and unskilled workers are narrower than in many other countries, and so there is less incentive for workers to train.

How can increased training be achieved? There are three broad approaches:

- Workers could be encouraged to stay with their employer so that employers would be more willing to invest in training. Externalities would be reduced.
- The government could provide subsidies for training. Alternatively, the government or some other agency could provide education and training directly.
- Firms could co-operate to prevent 'poaching' and set up industry-wide training programmes, perhaps in partnership with the government and unions.

Approaches to training in various countries

As far as the first approach is concerned, most countries have seen a movement *away* from workers staying with their employers and a movement towards greater labour mobility. The rise in the 'flexible firm' (see Box 9.8) has involved the employment of fewer permanent workers and more part-time and temporary workers.

Some countries, such as Japan and Germany, however, have a generally lower rate of labour turnover than most. In Japan, the relationship between employer and employee has traditionally extended well beyond a simple short-term economic arrangement. Workers give loyalty and commitment to their employers, who in return virtually guarantee long-term employment and provide various fringe benefits (such as housing, childcare, holiday schemes and health care). It is not surprising that Japanese firms invest highly in training.

In the USA, labour turnover is very high and yet there is little in the way of industry-wide training. Instead, the US government hopes, by having a high percentage of young people in further and higher education, that sufficient numbers and quality of workers are available for industry. As of 2011, 72 per cent of the US young adults entered higher education, compared with 64 per cent in the UK. However, the percentage taking vocational training courses is very low. Between 2005 and 2011, total public-sector expenditure on all types of training programmes averaged just 0.05 per cent of GDP.

In Germany, about 46 per cent of young adults entered higher education in 2011, considerably lower than the USA (and the UK) and below the OECD average of 60 per cent. However, public-sector expenditure on training accounts for 0.3 per cent of GDP, six times larger than the share in the USA. Three-quarters of this training is categorised as institutional training, whereby young people who do not enter higher education embark on some form of apprenticeship. They attend school for part of the week, and receive work-based training for the rest.

In the German model, the state, unions and employers' associations work closely in determining training provision, and they have developed a set of vocational qualifications based around the apprenticeship system. Given that virtually all firms are involved in training, the 'free-rider' problem of firms poaching labour without themselves paying for training is virtually eliminated. The result is that the German workforce is highly skilled. Many of the skills, however, are highly specific. This is a problem when the demand for particular skills declines and can result in high structural unemployment.

The UK approach

In the UK, the 1979–97 Conservative government's attitude towards training was initially influenced by its free-market approach to supply-side policy. Training was to be left largely to employers. However, with growing worries over the UK's 'productivity gap', the government set up Training and Enterprise Councils (TECs) in 1988. The TECs identified regional skills shortages, organised training and financed work-based training schemes.

In 2001, the Labour government (1997–2010) replaced the TECs by the Learning and Skills Council (LSC). This had a budget of over £10 billion and was responsible for planning and funding training in sixth forms and further education colleges, work-based training for young people aged 16 to 24 ('Apprenticeships' and 'Advanced Apprenticeships'), adult and community learning, the provision of information, advice and guidance for adults, and developing links between education and business.

KI 30
p326

In addition, a support service called 'Connexions' offered training and employment advice and support for young people between the ages of 13 and 19. In 2012, this was replaced by the National Careers Service. This is a single point of access for both young people and adults. Dedicated national Careers Direct advisers for young people are available online or by phone. Although careers advice is still provided by some local authorities, many of the Connexions centres have closed.

In March 2008 it was announced that the LSC was to be abolished. Funding responsibilities for 16- to 19-year-olds were transferred to local education authorities. A newly created Skills Funding Agency took responsibility for the funding and regulation of further education and training for adults in England.

Vocational qualifications.   Over the past 25 years there have been various new vocational qualifications introduced. In 1991, the National Vocational Qualification (NVQ) was launched. Students work for an employer, and receive on-the-job training. They also attend college on an occasional basis. The NVQ is awarded when they have achieved sufficient experience. In addition, the government launched General National Vocational Qualifications (GNVQs). These further-education qualifications were intended to bridge the gap between education and work, by ensuring that education was more relevant to work.

The GNVQ system was modelled on the system in France, where a clear vocational educational route is seen as the key to reducing skills shortages. At the age of 14, French students can choose to pursue academic or vocational education routes. The vocational route provides high-level, broad-based skills (unlike in Germany, where skills tend to be more job-specific).

However, GNVQs competed alongside other well-established vocational qualifications such as City and Guilds and BTEC certificates and diplomas. Such competition led to the withdrawal of the GNVQ by October 2007. The NVQ survives, largely because it complements other training: e.g. apprenticeship schemes.

In 2008, 14–19 Diplomas were launched. By 2011, these were offered in 14 vocational areas or 'lines of learning', such as engineering, IT, hair and beauty studies, retail business, construction and hospitality. They are studied in schools or colleges. All Diplomas are available at three levels: Foundation (level 1), Higher (level 2: equivalent to GCSE grades A* to C) and Advanced (level 3: equivalent to $3^1/_2$ A-levels). The diploma scheme was closed in 2013, however.

Another approach adopted by the Labour government was to encourage 'lifelong learning'. Measures included setting up the following:

■ A University for Industry, which through its 'Learndirect' brand offers online courses in a range of business, technical and IT subjects. Learndirect in England and Wales is now an independent training provider and since 2011 has been part of the Lloyds Banking Group. Learndirect Scotland was renamed My World of Work as part of Skills Development Scotland.

■ Some 700 UK Online centres. These offer access to the Internet, and helpers are on hand to provide basic IT, literacy and numeracy support. Today there are nearly 5000 such centres.

■ Two-year foundation degrees, offered by universities or higher education colleges. These are designed in conjunction with employers to meet various skill shortages. They are taken at the university or an associated college, normally on a part-time basis, and often include work-based study with local employers.

There has been considerable concern in the UK with respect to training and skilling the workforce to levels appropriate for future national prosperity. In 2004 the Labour government set up a committee under Lord Leitch to consider the most effective forms of training for increasing economic prosperity and productivity, and improving social justice. The assessment was rather gloomy; the Leitch Committee stated in its interim report that the UK had to 'raise its game' (see Case Study 22.1 in MyEconLab).

The final report of the Leitch Review released in December 2006 argued that all young people should continue in learning until they are 18. This has now been widely accepted across the political spectrum. The Coalition government formed in 2010 announced that it would be increasing the age to which all young people must continue in either education or training. The 'participation age' was increased to 17 in 2013 and 18 in 2015. Local authorities have a statutory duty to provide sufficient education and training provision for those young people aged 16 to 18.

In response to particular concerns about vocational education at the 16–19 level, the Coalition government set up an independent review under Professor Alison Wolf. Among the recommendations of the report, published in March 2011, were that vocational qualifications provide core skills, especially in maths and English, and that apprenticeships deliver the right skills for the workplace.

England has experienced a marked expansion in the number of apprenticeships in recent years. In 2012–13 there were 510 200 apprenticeship programme starts, of which 37 per cent were under 19s. This compares with 239 000 in 2008–9, of which 41 per cent were under 19s.

1. *Governments and educationalists generally regard it as desirable that trainees acquire transferable skills. Why may many employers disagree?*
2. *There are externalities (benefits) when employers provide training. What externalities are there from the undergoing of training by the individual? Do they imply that individuals will choose to receive more or less than the socially optimal amount of training?*

KI 29
p323

[1] Leitch Review of Skills, *Prosperity for All in the Global Economy – World Class Skills. Final Report* (HMSO, December 2006).

In addition, labour may be geographically immobile. The regional pattern of industrial location may change more rapidly than the labour market can adjust to it. Thus jobs may be lost in the depressed areas more rapidly than people can migrate from them. Unemployment rises. Even when people do leave the area, this can compound the downward multiplier effect as spending further declines.

If the capital market functioned well, this could help to arrest the decline. If wages were lower and land were cheaper in the depressed areas, capital would be attracted there. In practice, capital, like labour, is often relatively immobile. *Existing* capital stock is highly immobile. Buildings and most machinery cannot be moved to where the unemployed are! *New* capital is much more mobile. But there may be insufficient new investment, especially during a recession, to halt regional decline, and investors may be put off by the depressed and run down nature of the area, the lack of suitably qualified labour and lack of infrastructure.

A supply-side response to this problem is for governments or local authorities to provide support for such areas. This can come in various forms, such as giving grants or subsidies for the creation of jobs; expenditure on infrastructure, such as roads and communications, technical colleges, community facilities and housing; the siting of government offices in such areas; the setting up of government agencies to provide advice and support for incoming firms or local community action groups.

An example of such support was the setting up of Enterprise Zones by the Coalition government in 2011. As of April 2014, there were 24 Enterprise Zones across England. These zones are specific geographic locations where firms will benefit from reduced planning restrictions, tax breaks, and access to superfast broadband. Many of the Enterprise Zones encourage clustering: businesses in the same sector grouping together. The hope is that they can mutually benefit from cooperation and/or the sorts of technological spill-overs that we came across in the context of endogenous growth theory (see section 22.3).

To benefit from clustering effects, the zones typically focus on specific sectors, such as automotive and transport (e.g. the MIRA technology park near Hinckley, Leicestershire) or renewable energy (e.g. the Humber Renewable Energy Super Cluster, near Grimsby). The danger of such policies, particularly given the often small geographic area in question, is that they may merely divert investment away from other areas rather than resulting in *additional* investment.

Case Study 23.10 in MyEconLab is an extended case study of regional and urban policy in both the UK and the EU.

The case against intervention

New classical economists, monetarists, neo-Austrian economists and others advocating the free market argue the following:

- A poor investment record may be due to managerial inertia and union restrictive practices. Forcing firms and unions to face up to competition in the market may be a better way of encouraging willingness to accept change. Government subsidies may simply allow firms to continue producing inefficiently.
- The government may not make an efficient use of taxpayers' money by giving investment grants. The money may well go to extravagant and unprofitable projects, such as Concorde or the Millennium Dome.

- Private industry's low investment record may be due to a low potential return on investment. If market opportunities were good, firms would invest without the need of government support.
- UK investment has remained low in the past despite interventionist industrial policy.
- If the government is to help industry, it is best to reduce the tax burden generally, so as to increase the return on investment. The microeconomic allocation of investment resources will then still be provided by the market.

 Provide a critique of these arguments.

Moves towards more market-based policies in the UK

Welfare to work and the Work Programme. An example of a 'Third Way' approach to supply-side policy is the 'welfare to work' policy, set up by the UK Labour government elected in 1997 (see Case Study 23.9 in MyEconLab). This provided benefits and other support to unemployed people and people currently outside the workforce to seek employment. It was interventionist to the extent that it targeted support at particular people, but pro-market to the extent that it provided incentives for people to become more occupationally mobile.

In 2011, the previous system was replaced by the Work Programme. This consists of 18 providers, largely private companies, which seek to place the long-term unemployed in jobs. However, the House of Commons Public Accounts Committee found that the scheme had managed to get only 3.6 per cent of the people on the scheme off benefits and into secure employment in the first 14 months of its operation. This compares with a target of 11.9 per cent set by the Department for Work and Pensions.

Universal credit. An important aspect of a more market-based approach to welfare is the need to create the 'right incentives' to get people working. This is a central objective of Universal Credit, being rolled out in the UK between 2013 and 2017 to replace various income-related benefits, Housing Benefit and Tax Credits. The idea is to ensure that people do not lose all their benefit on taking up work and are thus encouraged to seek employment.

However, as we saw in section 10.2 (page 308), if benefits taper off too quickly, there may be too little incentive for people to take up work. If they taper off more slowly, however, this can make the scheme very expensive. The current withdrawal rate (tapering off rate) of 65 per cent for Universal Credit gives a marginal effective tax rate for a basic-rate income tax payer of 76.2 per cent (compared with 73 per cent for the former tax credits). This is argued by critics to be too high to create a sufficient incentive for many people to take up part-time work.

There is also the problem of a simplified scheme like this not being able to take sufficient account of people's individual circumstances.

Local Enterprise Partnerships and Enterprise Zones. The introduction by the Coalition government of Local Enterprise Partnerships (LEPs) and Enterprise Zones marked a shift towards a less interventionist industrial strategy. The nine regional development agencies (RDAs) were abolished. These had been important drivers in the English regions of the previous Labour government's regional economic strategy. Indeed, the scope and finances of the RDAs had tended to

TC 5
p54

increase over time. The Coalition government adopted an approach known as *localism*, arguing that the RDAs were unelected bodies detached from local people. More generally, it believed that government needed streamlining.

The LEPs are a natural outcome of localism involving local business and local authorities. However, they receive no direct funding from central government. This has led to concerns about their effectiveness at a time when local authority budgets are stretched.

A further issue is localism itself. LEPs are based on local authority boundaries, while Enterprise Zones typically cover very small geographic areas within the boundaries of an LEP. Some argue that the economic geography of the UK does not correspond straightforwardly to local authority boundaries. Consequently, it is argued by some that there should be mechanisms to ensure that the economic spillovers from one local economic area to another are sufficiently taken into account.

Section summary

1. Those in favour of interventionist industrial policy point to failings of the market, such as the externalities involved in investment and training, the imperfections in the capital market and the short-term perspective of decision makers.

2. Intervention can take the form of grants, the encouragement of mergers and other forms of rationalisation, advice and persuasion, the provision of information and the direct provision of infrastructure.

3. Selective intervention can take the form of grants for research and development, encouragement of reorganisation, assistance to small firms and help for training.

BOX 23.5   UNEMPLOYMENT AND SUPPLY-SIDE POLICIES

CASE STUDIES AND APPLICATIONS

Two approaches

Countries have had varying degrees of success in reducing unemployment through appropriate supply-side policies.

In 2006, the OECD put countries into four groups according to their policies towards labour markets. The first two groups have been successful in cutting unemployment. The other two have not.

The first group, labelled 'mainly English-speaking' by the OECD (Japan, South Korea and Switzerland are honorary Anglophones), tends to have weaker job protection, less generous unemployment benefits and thinner tax wedges than the average. Its employment rate is comfortably higher than the OECD average; its jobless rate [5.3 per cent] is comfortably lower [than the OECD average of 7.5 per cent]. In the second, 'northern European' group (Scandinavia, the Netherlands, Austria and Ireland), taxes and unemployment benefits are high and workers hard to fire. Yet the average employment rate is a little higher than the first group's and the unemployment rate a little lower [4.8 per cent].

There are two reasons why the second group can match the first. Their product markets are, like those of the first group, fairly loosely regulated, making the whole economy more dynamic. And they spend much more on schemes intended to ensure that the unemployed try hard to find work: in return for high benefits, they must accept that their search for a job will be closely watched and that some work-seeking programmes may be compulsory. That high unemployment benefits are a disincentive to seek work is not in doubt; but it seems that a sufficiently diligent and well-funded employment service can offset their effects . . .

Countries in the third group – mainly southern European ones, plus France and Germany – tend to pay high benefits too. But they have not offset these with labour-market programmes on the scale of the second group, and their product markets are more protected. [Unemployment in this group averages 9.0 per cent.]

In the last group, which includes the Czech Republic, Poland and Slovakia, benefits are low. But workers are not especially easy to fire; little is spent on pushing the jobless into work; and product markets are more regulated than in any other group. [Unemployment in this group averages 15.1 per cent.][1]

1. *How would you classify the approaches of the first two groups in terms of whether they are 'market-orientated' or 'interventionist'?*
2. *Is there an even more effective approach to reducing unemployment that uses elements of each?*

[1] 'Intricate workings', *The Economist*, 17 June 2006.

END OF CHAPTER QUESTIONS

1. Define *demand-side* and *supply-side* policies. Sometimes it is said that Keynesians advocate demand-side policies and monetarists advocate supply-side policies. Is there any accuracy in this statement?

2. What is the relationship between 'successful' supply-side policies and unemployment in (i) the short run and (ii) the long run, according to (a) Keynesian and (b) monetarist assumptions?

3. Why might market-orientated supply-side policies have undesirable side effects on aggregate demand?

4. What types of tax cuts are likely to create the greatest (a) incentives, (b) disincentives to effort?

5. Is deindustrialisation necessarily undesirable?

6. In what ways can interventionist industrial policy work with the market, rather than against it? What are the arguments for and against such policy?

7. Compare the relative merits of pro-market and interventionist solutions to regional decline.

8. What are the arguments for and against relying entirely on discretionary regional and urban policy?

9. Select a European country other than the UK and compare its regional and urban policy with that of the UK.

Online resources

Additional case studies in MyEconLab

23.1 **Deregulating the UK bus industry.** Has this led to greater competition and improved services?

23.2 **The R&D Scoreboard.** An international comparison of spending by companies on R&D.

23.3 **Controlling inflation in the past.** This case study looks at the history of prices and incomes policies in the UK.

23.4 **UK industrial performance.** This examines why the UK has had a poorer investment record than many other industrial countries and why it has suffered a process of 'deindustrialisation'.

23.5 **Technology and economic change.** How to get the benefits from technological advance.

23.6 **Indicative planning in the UK.** Experiments with planning in the 1960s and 1970s.

23.7 **Assistance to small firms in the UK.** An examination of current government measures to assist small firms.

23.8 **Small-firm policy in the EU.** This looks at the range of support available to small and medium-sized firms in the EU.

23.9 **Welfare to work.** An examination of the UK Labour government's policy of providing support to people looking for work.

23.10 **Regional and urban policy.** This extended case study looks at the causes of regional imbalance and urban decay, at various approaches to regional and urban policy and at how regional and urban policy are implemented in the UK and the EU.

Websites relevant to Chapters 20, 22 and 23

Numbers and sections refer to websites listed in the Web Appendix and hotlinked from this book's website at **www.pearsoned.co.uk/sloman**.

- For news articles relevant to these three chapters, see the *Economics News* section in MyEconLab.
- For general news on unemployment, inflation, economic growth and supply-side policy, see websites in section A, and particularly A1–5, 7–13, 37. See also links to newspapers worldwide in A38, 39, 42, 43 and 44, and the news search feature in Google at A41.
- For data on unemployment, inflation and growth, see links in B1; also see B4 and 12. For UK data, see B3 and 34. For EU data, see B38 > *European economic forecast* (click first on year) and B49. For US data, see the Data section of B17. For international data, see B15, 21, 24, 31, 33, 43 and 48. For links to datasets, see B28; I14.
- For specific data on UK unemployment, see B1, 1. *National Statistics* > Browse by theme > *Labour Market*. For international data on unemployment, see G1; H3 and 5.
- For information on the development of ideas, including information on classical, Keynesian, monetarist, new classical and new Keynesian thought, see C12, 18; also see links under *Methodology* and *History of Economic Thought* in C14. See also site I7 > *Economic Systems and Theories* > *History of Economic Thought*.
- For the current approach to UK supply-side policy, see the latest Budget Report (e.g. sections on productivity and training) at site E30. See also sites E5, 9 and 10.
- For support for a market-orientated approach to supply-side policy, see C17.
- For information on training in the UK and Europe, see sites E5; G5, 14.
- For information on the support for small business in the UK, see site E38.
- For information on regional policy in the UK, see site E2; and in the EU, see site G12.
- For student resources relevant to these three chapters, see sites C1–7, 9, 10, 19.

MyEconLab

This book can be supported by MyEconLab, which contains a range of additional resources, including an online homework and tutorial system designed to test and build your understanding.

You need both an access card and a course ID to access MyEconLab:

1. Is your lecturer using MyEconLab? Ask your lecturer for your course ID.

2. Has an access card been included with the book at a reduced cost? Check the inside back cover of the book.

3. If you have a course ID but no access card, go to: http://www.myeconlab.com/ to buy access to this interactive study programme.

G Part

The World Economy

24 International Trade 706

25 The Balance of Payments and Exchange Rates 741

26 Global and Regional Interdependence 778

27 Economics of Developing Countries 799

'Globalisation' is a word frequently used nowadays. But it neatly captures one of the key features of economics today: that it is global in nature. International trade has grown at a much faster rate than the levels of national output in any country. International financial flows have grown faster still. The result is that economies around the globe are intermeshed, and what happens in one country can have profound effects on others.

In Chapters 24 and 25 we look at the two key economic elements in this interdependence: international trade and international finance. Then in Chapter 26 we look at particular aspects of global interdependence. Finally we turn to the poorest countries of the world, whose development depends so much on the economic policies of the rich world.

International Trade

CHAPTER MAP

24.1 The advantages of trade   707
The growth of world trade   707
Specialisation as the basis for trade   707
The law of comparative advantage   708
The gains from trade based on comparative
   advantage   711
International trade and its effect on factor prices   713
Increasing opportunity costs and the limits to
   specialisation and trade   714
The terms of trade   714
*Intermediate analysis of gains from trade   716
Other reasons for gains from trade   717
The competitive advantage of nations   718

24.2 Arguments for restricting trade   719
Methods of restricting trade   720
Arguments in favour of restricting trade   720
Problems with protection   723
The World Trade Organization   727

24.3 Preferential trading   729
Types of preferential trading arrangement   729
The direct effects of a customs union: trade
   creation and trade diversion   730
Longer-term effects of a customs union   731
Preferential trading in practice   732

24.4 The European Union   733
Historical background   733
From customs union to common market   734
The benefits and costs of the single market   735
Completing the internal market   737

Without international trade we would all be much poorer. There would be some items like pineapples, coffee, cotton clothes, foreign holidays and uranium that we would simply have to go without. Then there would be other items like wine and spacecraft that we could produce only very inefficiently. International trade has the potential to benefit all participating countries. This chapter explains why.

Totally free trade, however, may bring problems to countries or to groups of people within those countries. Many people argue strongly for restrictions on trade. Textile workers see their jobs threatened by cheap imported cloth. Car manufacturers worry about falling sales as customers switch to Japanese or other east Asian models. But are people justified in fearing international competition, or are they merely trying to protect some vested interest at the expense of everyone else? Section 24.2 examines these arguments and also looks at world attitudes towards trade restrictions.

A step on the road to freer trade is for countries to enter free-trade agreements with just a limited number of other countries. Examples include the EU and more recently the North American Free Trade Agreement (NAFTA – the USA, Canada and Mexico). We consider such 'preferential trading systems' in section 24.3. Finally, we look in more detail at the EU and the development of the 'single European market'.

This chapter may be studied after Chapter 11 or Chapter 13 if you prefer.

24.1 THE ADVANTAGES OF TRADE

The growth of world trade

World trade has grown rapidly over the past 60 years and at consistently higher rates than world GDP. Table 24.1 shows exports as a percentage of various countries' GDP. As you can see, in all cases the proportion was higher in the 2010s than in 1960s, and in some cases considerably higher.

Developed economies have dominated world trade. In 2013, they accounted (by value) for 56.7 per cent of world exports and 60.4 per cent of world imports (see Figure 24.1). Their share of world trade, however, has declined over time because many of the countries with the most rapid *growth* in exports can be found in the developing world.

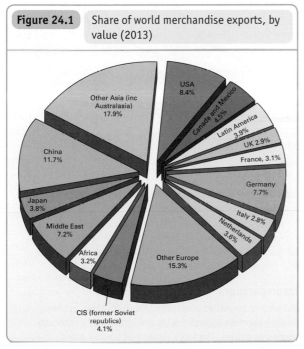

| Figure 24.1 | Share of world merchandise exports, by value (2013) |

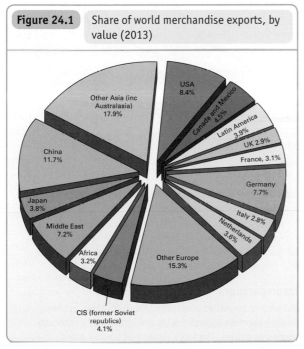

Source: Based on data in *International Trade and Tariff Data*, 2014 (WTO).

The growth in exports from the group of developing nations collectively known as the BRICS[1] (Brazil, Russia, India, China and South Africa) has been especially rapid. Between them they accounted for just 6.4 per cent of the value of world exports in 1994. By 2013 this had grown to 18.0 per cent (see Figure 24.2).

Specialisation as the basis for trade

Why do countries trade with each other, and what do they gain from it? The reasons for international trade are really only an extension of the reasons for trade *within* a nation. Rather than people trying to be self-sufficient and do everything for themselves, it makes sense to specialise.

Firms specialise in producing certain goods. This allows them to gain economies of scale and to exploit their entrepreneurial and management skills and the skills of their labour force. It also allows them to benefit from their particular location and from the ownership of any particular capital equipment or other assets they might possess. With the revenues firms earn, they buy in the inputs they need from other firms and the labour they require. Firms thus trade with each other.

Countries also specialise. They produce more than they need of certain goods. What is not consumed domestically is exported. The revenues earned from the exports are used to import goods that are not produced in sufficient amounts at home.

 Why does the USA not specialise as much as General Motors or Texaco? Why does the UK not specialise as much as Tesco? Is the answer to these questions similar to the answer to the questions 'Why does the USA not specialise as much as Luxembourg?' and 'Why does Tesco or Unilever not specialise as much as the local butcher?'?

[1] Sometimes the term is used to refer just to the first four countries. When South Africa is excluded, the term is written BRICs rather than BRICS.

| Table 24.1 | Exports of goods and services as percentage of GDP |

	1960s	1970s	1980s	1990s	2000s	2010–15
Australia	12.9	13.9	14.7	18.1	19.8	21.6
Canada	19.1	23.3	27.0	34.2	38.0	31.1
France	13.7	18.8	22.0	23.3	26.7	27.2
Germany	19.3	23.5	29.7	26.9	40.3	50.8
Ireland	32.0	38.7	50.9	71.5	87.2	106.0
Japan	9.7	11.7	12.6	9.8	13.6	15.7
Luxembourg	83.3	91.9	98.5	110.8	157.2	175.6
Netherlands	43.6	47.7	56.0	58.8	69.2	86.6
UK	19.4	25.6	26.2	26.2	27.1	31.0
USA	5.0	7.2	8.2	10.1	10.4	13.4
EU-15	19.1	24.4	28.3	28.9	36.4	42.9

Note: Figures for Germany based on West Germany only up to 1991.
Source: Based on data from *AMECO database* (European Commission, DGECFIN).

BOX 24.1 TRADING PLACES

Patterns and trends in world trade

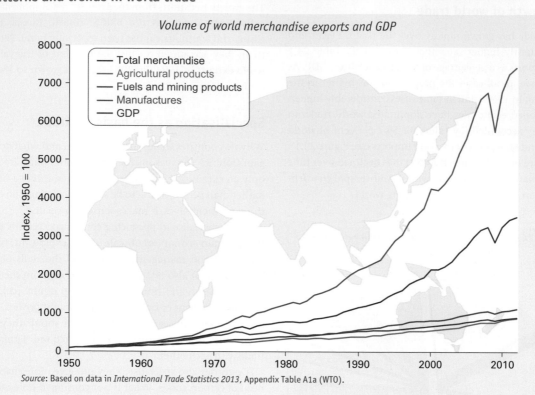

Volume of world merchandise exports and GDP

Legend:
— Total merchandise
— Agricultural products
— Fuels and mining products
— Manufactures
— GDP

Source: Based on data in *International Trade Statistics 2013*, Appendix Table A1a (WTO).

In 2012 the total *value* of the world's exports of goods and services was US$17.9 trillion compared with US$61.5 billion in 1950. Therefore, the value of trade in 2012 was over 290 times larger than in 1950. But given that prices had risen by more than 900 per cent over the period, a more useful figure is that for the volume of world trade (which is measured in constant prices). This grew by a factor of 35 over this period which is significantly more than world output which was 9 times larger in 2012 than in 1950.

The chart illustrates the growth in trade and world output from 1950 to 2012. It shows how the growth in the volume of world merchandise exports has been driven by *manufactures*, which have increased by a factor of 74, while the export of

fuels and mining products has increased by a factor of 11 and *agricultural* products by a factor of 9.

Table (a) shows the world's top five merchandise exporters and importers by value. It also shows trade figures for the UK. The four largest exporting nations are also the four largest importers of goods and services.

Trade partners

But who do countries trade with? Table (b) looks at the trading partners both of the UK and of the world's leading trading countries. The table shows that trading blocs (see section 24.3) and geography matter. For instance, in the cases of the UK and Germany over one-half of their trade is with other EU countries. Similarly, one-third of the value

---

But which goods should a country specialise in? What should it export and what should it import? The answer is that it should specialise in those goods in which it has a *comparative advantage*. Let us examine what this means.

The law of comparative advantage

Countries have different endowments of factors of production. They differ in population density, labour skills, climate, raw materials, capital equipment, etc. These differences tend to persist because factors are relatively immobile between countries. Obviously land and climate are totally immobile, but even with labour and capital there

are more restrictions on their international movement than on their movement within countries. Thus the ability to supply goods differs between countries.

What this means is that the relative cost of producing goods varies from country to country. For example, one country may be able to produce one fridge for the same cost as 6 tonnes of wheat or three compact disc players, whereas another country may be able to produce one fridge for the same cost as only 3 tonnes of wheat but four CD players. It is these differences in relative costs that form the basis of trade.

At this stage, we need to distinguish between *absolute advantage* and *comparative advantage*.

KI 2
p11

(a) *Top trading countries by value and world share, 2012*

Rank	Exporters	$ billion	Share	Rank	Importers	$ billion	Share
1	China	2049	11.1	1	USA	2336	12.6
2	USA	1546	8.4	2	China	1818	9.8
3	Germany	1407	7.6	3	Germany	1167	6.3
4	Japan	799	4.3	4	Japan	886	4.8
5	Netherlands	656	3.6	5	UK	690	3.7
11	UK	474	2.6	7	Netherlands	591	3.2

Source: International Trade Statistics, 2013 (WTO).

(b) *Merchandise trade by destination and origin, 2012*

(i) *Exports*

	UK		China		USA		Germany		Japan	
	Destination	%	Destination	%	Destination	%	Destination	%	Destination	%
1	EU-27	48.5	USA	17.2	Canada	18.8	EU-27	56.2	China	18.0
2	USA	13.3	EU-27	16.3	EU-27	17.1	USA	7.9	USA	17.8
3	Switzerland	3.4	Hong Kong	15.8	Mexico	13.9	China	6.1	EU-27	10.2
4	China	3.3	Japan	7.4	China	7.2	Switzerland	4.5	S Korea	7.7
5	Hong Kong	1.9	South Korea	4.3	Japan	4.5	Russia	3.5	Taiwan	5.8

(ii) *Imports*

	Origin	%	Origin	%	Origin	%	Origin	%	Origin	%
1	EU-27	47.4	EU-27	11.7	China	19.1	EU-27	56.0	China	21.2
2	USA	8.9	Japan	9.8	EU-27	16.7	China	8.6	EU-27	9.4
3	China	8.2	South Korea	9.3	Canada	14.0	USA	5.7	USA	8.8
4	Norway	4.8	Hong Kong	7.9	Mexico	12.0	Russia	4.7	Australia	6.4
5	Switzerland	4.0	USA	7.4	Japan	6.4	Switzerland	4.2	Saudi Arabia	6.2

Source: WTO Statistics Database.

of the USA's exports and one quarter of its imports can be attributed to Canada and Mexico, members of the North American Free Trade Agreement (NAFTA) (see page 732 and also Case Study 24.8 in MyEconLab).

 Does the fact that world trade has increased at a much faster rate than world GDP highlight the limitations of trade as a driver of economic growth?

Absolute advantage

When one country can produce a good with less resources than another country, it is said to have an ***absolute advantage*** in that good. If France can produce wine with less resources than the UK, and the UK can produce gin with less resources than France, then France has an absolute advantage in wine and the UK an absolute advantage in gin. Production of both wine and gin will be maximised by each country specialising and then trading with the other country. Both will gain.

Comparative advantage

The above seems obvious, but trade between two countries can still be beneficial even if one country could produce

all goods with less resources than the other, providing the *relative* efficiency with which goods can be produced differs between the two countries.

Take the case of a developed country that is absolutely more efficient than a less developed country at producing

> ### Definition
>
> **Absolute advantage** A country has an absolute advantage over another in the production of a good if it can produce it with less resources than the other country.

| **Figure 24.2** | Share of total world merchandise exports by the BRICS countries, by value (%) |

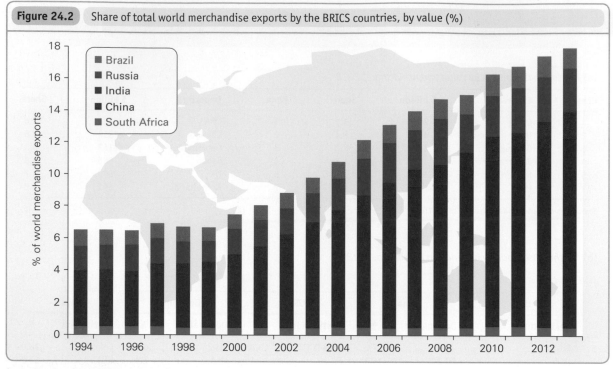

Source: Based on data in *WTO Statistics Database*.

both wheat and cloth. Assume that with a given amount of resources (labour, land and capital) the alternatives shown in Table 24.2 can be produced in each country.

Despite the developed country having an absolute advantage in both wheat and cloth, the less developed country (LDC) has a ***comparative advantage*** in wheat, and the developed country has a comparative advantage in cloth.

This is because wheat is relatively cheaper in the LDC: only 1 square metre of cloth has to be sacrificed to produce 2 kilos of wheat, whereas 8 square metres of cloth would have to be sacrificed in the developed country to produce 4 kilos of wheat (i.e. 2 square metres of cloth for every 1 kilo of wheat). In other words, the opportunity cost of wheat is four times higher in the developed country (8/4 compared with 1/2).

On the other hand, cloth is relatively cheaper in the developed country. Here the opportunity cost of producing 8 square metres of cloth is only 4 kilos of wheat, whereas in the LDC 1 square metre of cloth costs 2 kilos of wheat. Thus the opportunity cost of cloth is four times higher in the LDC (2/1 compared with 4/8).

Draw up a similar table to Table 24.2, only this time assume that the figures are: LDC 6 wheat or 2 cloth; DC 8 wheat or 20 cloth. What are the opportunity cost ratios now?

To summarise, countries have a comparative advantage in those goods that can be produced at a lower opportunity cost than in other countries.

If countries are to gain from trade, they should export those goods in which they have a comparative advantage and import those goods in which they have a comparative disadvantage. From this we can state a ***law of comparative advantage***.

KEY IDEA 37

The law of comparative advantage. Provided opportunity costs of various goods differ in two countries, both of them can gain from mutual trade if they specialise in producing (and exporting) those goods that have relatively low opportunity costs compared with the other country.

See Case Study 24.1 in MyEconLab for Ricardo's original statement of the law in 1817. **TC 1 p11**

But why do they gain if they specialise according to this law? And just what will that gain be? We will consider these questions next.

Definitions

Comparative advantage A country has a comparative advantage over another in the production of a good if it can produce it at a lower opportunity cost: i.e. if it has to forgo less of other goods in order to produce it.

Law of comparative advantage Trade can benefit all countries if they specialise in the goods in which they have a comparative advantage.

The gains from trade based on comparative advantage

Before trade, unless markets are very imperfect, the prices of the two goods are likely to reflect their opportunity costs. For example, in Table 24.2, since the less developed country can produce 2 kilos of wheat for 1 square metre of cloth, the *price* of 2 kilos of wheat will roughly equal the price of 1 square metre of cloth.

Assume, then, that the pre-trade exchange ratios of wheat for cloth are as follows:

LDC   : 2 wheat for 1 cloth
Developed country : 1 wheat for 2 cloth (i.e. 4 for 8)

Both countries will now gain from trade, provided the exchange ratio is somewhere between 2:1 and 1:2. Assume, for the sake of argument, that it is 1:1, that 1 wheat trades internationally for 1 cloth. How will each country gain?

The LDC gains by exporting wheat and importing cloth. At an exchange ratio of 1:1, it now only has to give up 1 kilo of wheat to obtain a square metre of cloth, whereas before trade it had to give up 2 kilos of wheat.

The developed country gains by exporting cloth and importing wheat. Again at an exchange ratio of 1:1, it now has to give up only 1 square metre of cloth to obtain 1 kilo of wheat, whereas before it had to give up 2 square metres of cloth.

Thus both countries have gained from trade.

The actual exchange ratios will depend on the relative prices of wheat and cloth after trade takes place. These prices will depend on total demand for and supply of the two goods. It may be that the trade exchange ratio is nearer to the pre-trade exchange ratio of one country than the other. Thus the gains to the two countries need not be equal. (We will examine these issues below.)

| Table 24.2 | Production possibilities for two countries |

		Kilos of wheat		Square metres of cloth
Less developed country	Either	2	or	1
Developed country	Either	4	or	8

1. Show how each country could gain from trade if the LDC could produce (before trade) 3 wheat for 1 cloth and the developed country could produce (before trade) 2 wheat for 5 cloth, and if the exchange ratio (with trade) was 1 wheat for 2 cloth. Would they both still gain if the exchange ratio was (a) 1 wheat for 1 cloth; (b) 1 wheat for 3 cloth?

2. In question 1, which country gained the most from a trade exchange ratio of 1 wheat for 2 cloth?

BOX 24.2   SHARING OUT THE JOBS

CASE STUDIES AND APPLICATIONS

A parable of comparative advantage

Imagine that you and a group of friends are fed up with the rat race and decide to set up a self-sufficient community. So you club together and use all your savings to buy an old run-down farmhouse with 30 acres of land and a few farm animals.

You decide to produce all your own food, make your own clothes, renovate the farmhouse, make all the furniture, provide all your own entertainment and set up a little shop to sell the things you make. This should bring in enough income to buy the few items you cannot make yourselves.

The day comes to move in, and that evening everyone gathers to decide how all the jobs are going to be allocated. You quickly decide that it would be foolish for all of you to try to do all the jobs. Obviously it will be more efficient to specialise. This does not necessarily mean that everyone is confined to doing only one job, but it does mean that each of you can concentrate on just a few tasks.

But who is to do which job? The answer would seem to be obvious: you pick the best person for the job. So you go down the list of tasks. Who is to take charge of the renovations? Pat has already renovated a cottage, and is brilliant at bricklaying, plastering, wiring and plumbing. So Pat would seem to be the ideal person. Who is to do the cooking? Everyone agrees on this. Pat makes the best cakes, the best quiches and the best Irish stew. So Pat is everyone's choice for cook. And what about milking the sheep? 'Pat used to keep sheep', says Tarquin, 'and made wonderful feta cheese.' 'Good old Pat!' exclaims everyone.

It doesn't take long before it becomes obvious that 'clever-clogs' Pat is simply brilliant at everything, from planting winter wheat, to unblocking drains, to doing the accounts, to tie-dyeing. But it is soon realised that, if Pat has to do everything, nothing will get done. Even Chris, who has never done anything except market research, would be better employed milking the sheep than doing nothing at all.

So what's the best way of allocating the jobs so that the work gets done in the most efficient way? Sharon comes up with the solution. 'Everyone should make a list of all the jobs they could possibly do, and then put them in order from the one they are best at to the one they are worst at.'

So this is what everyone does. And then people are allocated the jobs they are *relatively* best at doing. Chris escapes milking the sheep and keeps the accounts instead. And Pat escapes with an eight-hour day!

If Pat took two minutes to milk the sheep and Tarquin took six, how could it ever be more efficient for Tarquin to do it?

KI 37
p710

Figure 24.3 Effect of trade on consumption possibilities

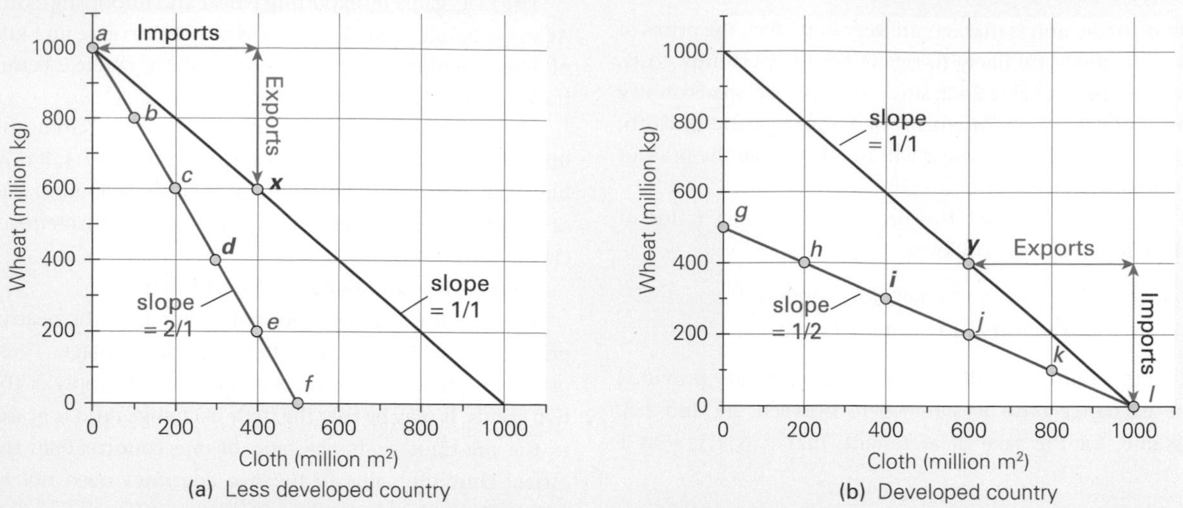

(a) Less developed country

(b) Developed country

Simple graphical analysis of comparative advantage and the gains from trade: constant opportunity cost

The gains from trade can be shown graphically using production possibility curves. Let us continue with the example of the developed and less developed countries that we looked at in Table 24.2, where both countries produce just two goods: wheat and cloth.

For simplicity, assume that the pre-trade opportunity costs of cloth in terms of wheat in the two countries do not vary with output: i.e. there are *constant opportunity costs* of cloth in terms of wheat of 2/1 in the LDC and 1/2 in the developed country. Let us assume that the pre-trade production possibilities are as shown in Table 24.3.[1]

For each 100 extra square metres of cloth that the LDC produces, it has to sacrifice 200 kilos of wheat. For each extra 100 kilos of wheat that the developed country produces, it has to sacrifice 200 square metres of cloth. Straight-

line pre-trade production possibility 'curves' can thus be drawn for the two countries with slopes of (minus) 2/1 and (minus) 1/2 respectively. These lines illustrate the various total combinations of the two goods that can be produced and hence consumed. They are shown as the blue lines in Figure 24.3.

Assume that before trade the LDC produces (and consumes) at point *d*: namely, 400 million kilos of wheat and 300 million square metres of cloth; and that the developed country produces at point *i*: namely, 300 million kilos of wheat and 400 million square metres of cloth.

If they now trade, the LDC, having a comparative advantage in wheat, will specialise in it and produce at point *a*. It will produce 1000 million kilos of wheat and no cloth. The developed country will specialise in cloth and produce at point *l*. It will produce 1000 million square metres of cloth and no wheat.

For simplicity, let us assume that trade between the two countries takes place at an exchange ratio of 1:1 (i.e. 1 kilo of wheat for 1 square metre of cloth). This means that the two countries can now *consume* along the red lines in Figure 24.3: at, say, points *x* and *y* respectively. At point *x* the LDC consumes 600 million kilos of wheat (a gain of 200 million kilos over the pre-trade position) and 400 million square metres of cloth (a gain of 100 million square metres over the pre-trade position). At point *y* the developed country consumes 400 million kilos of wheat (a gain of 100 million kilos over the pre-trade position) and 600 million square metres of cloth (a gain of 200 million square metres over the pre-trade position). Thus trade has allowed both countries to increase their consumption of both goods.

To summarise, before trade, the countries could only consume along their production possibility curves (the blue lines); after trade, they can consume along the higher red lines.

Table 24.3 Pre-trade production possibilities

Less developed country			Developed country	
Wheat (million kg)	Cloth (million m²)		Wheat (million kg)	Cloth (million m²)
A	1000	0	g	500	0
B	800	100	h	400	200
C	600	200	i	300	400
D	400	300	j	200	600
E	200	400	k	100	800
F	0	500	l	0	1000

[1] Note that, for simplicity, it is assumed that the size of the two economies is similar. The LDC can still have an *absolute* disadvantage in both goods, however, because it may take many more resources to produce these goods. For example, it may have a very much larger population than the developed country and hence a very much lower output per person.

KI 2
p11

TC 2
p25

KI 37
p710

Table 24.4 The production and consumption gains from trade

	Less developed country			Developed country			Total	
	Production	Consumption	Imports (−)/ Exports (+)	Production	Consumption	Imports (−)/ Exports (+)	Production	Consumption
No trade								
Wheat (million kg)	400	400	0	300	300	0	700	700
Cloth (million m²)	300	300	0	400	400	0	700	700
With trade								
Wheat (million kg)	1000	600	+400	0	400	−400	1000	1000
Cloth (million m²)	0	400	−400	1000	600	+400	1000	1000

Note that in this simple two-country model total production and consumption of the two countries for each of the two goods must be the same, since one country's exports are the other's imports. Thus if the LDC produces at point *a* and consumes at point *x*, the developed country, producing at point *l*, must consume at point *y*. The effects on trade of the two countries consuming at points *x* and *y* are shown in Table 24.4.

As complete specialisation has taken place in our example, the LDC now has to import all its cloth and the developed country has to import all its wheat. Thus, given the exchange ratio of 1:1, the LDC exports 400 million kilos of wheat in exchange for imports of 400 million square metres of cloth. (These imports and exports are also shown in Figure 24.3.)

The final two columns of Table 24.4 show that trade has increased the total production and consumption of the two countries.

1. *Draw a diagram with the same two countries and with the same production possibilities and exchange ratio as in Figure 24.3. But this time show how much would be imported and exported for each country if, after trade, the LDC consumes 500 million kilos of wheat. Fill the figures in on a table like Table 24.4.*

2. *If the opportunity cost ratio of wheat for cloth is 1/2 in the LDC, why is the slope of the production possibility curve 2/1? Is the slope of the production possibility curve always the reciprocal of the opportunity cost ratio?*

3. *Show (graphically) that, if the (pre-trade) opportunity cost ratios of the two countries were the same, there would be no gain from trade – assuming that the production possibility curves were straight lines and did not shift as a result of trade.*

International trade and its effect on factor prices

Countries tend to have a comparative advantage in goods that are *intensive in their abundant factor*. Canada has abundant land and hence it is cheap. Therefore Canada specialises in grain production since grains are land-intensive. South Asian countries have abundant supplies of labour with low wage rates, and hence specialise in clothing and other labour-intensive goods. Europe, Japan and the USA have relatively abundant and cheap capital, and hence specialise in capital-intensive manufactured goods.

Trade between such countries will tend to lead to greater equality in factor prices. For example, the demand for

---

BOX 24.3 TRADE AS EXPLOITATION?

EXPLORING ECONOMICS

Does free trade exploit cheap labour abroad?

People sometimes question the morality of buying imports from countries where workers are paid 'pittance' wages. 'Is it right', they ask, 'for us to support a system where workers are so exploited?' As is often the case with emotive issues, there is some truth and some misunderstanding in a point of view like this.

First the truth. If a country like the UK trades with a regime that denies human rights, and treats its workers very badly, we may thereby be helping to sustain a corrupt system. We might also be seen to be lending it moral support. In this sense, therefore, trade may not help the cause of the workers in these countries. It is arguments like these that were used to support the imposition of trade sanctions against South Africa in the days of apartheid.

Now the misunderstanding. If we buy goods from countries that pay low wages, we are *not* as a result contributing to their low-wage problem. Quite the reverse. If countries like India export textiles to the west, this will help to *increase* the wages of Indian workers. If India has a comparative advantage in labour-intensive goods, these goods will earn a better price by being exported than by being sold entirely in the domestic Indian market. Provided *some* of the extra revenues go to the workers, they will gain from trade.

Under what circumstances would a gain in revenues by exporting firms not lead to an increase in wage rates?

KI 4
p13

labour will rise in labour-abundant countries like India if they specialise in labour-intensive goods. This will push up wage rates in these low-wage countries, thereby helping to close the gap between their wage rates and those of the developed world. Without trade, wage rates would tend to be even lower.

Increasing opportunity costs and the limits to specialisation and trade

KI 2
p11 In practice, countries are likely to experience increasing opportunity costs (and hence have bowed-out production possibility curves). The reason for this is that, as a country increasingly specialises in one good, it has to use resources that are less and less suited to its production and which were more suited to other goods. Thus ever-increasing amounts of the other goods have to be sacrificed. For example, as a country specialises more and more in grain production, it has to use land that is less and less suited to growing grain.

These increasing costs as a country becomes more and more specialised lead to the disappearance of its comparative cost advantage. When this happens, there will be no point in further specialisation. Thus, whereas a country like Germany has a comparative advantage in capital-intensive manufactures, it does not produce only manufactures. It would make no sense not to use its fertile lands to produce food or its forests to produce timber. The opportunity costs of diverting all agricultural labour to industry would be very high.

Thus increasing opportunity costs limit the amount of a country's specialisation and hence the amount of its trade. There are also other limits to trade:

- Transport costs may outweigh any comparative advantage. A country may be able to produce bricks more cheaply than other countries, but their weight may make them too expensive to export.
- It may be the factors of production, rather than the goods, that move from country to country. Thus developed countries, rather than exporting finished goods to LDCs, may invest capital in LDCs to enable manufactures to be produced there. Also, labour may migrate from low-wage to high-wage countries.
- Governments may restrict trade (see section 24.2).

The terms of trade

What price will our exports fetch abroad? What will we have to pay for imports? The answer to these questions is given by the *terms of trade*.

To simplify matters, suppose there is only one exported good and only one imported good. In this case, the terms of trade are defined as P_x/P_m, where P_x is the price of the exported good and P_m is the price of the imported good. This is the reciprocal of the exchange ratio: for example, if 2x exchange for 1m (an exchange ratio of 2/1), the price of x will be half the price of m. The terms of trade will be 1/2.

1. *If 4x exchange for 3m, what are the terms of trade?*
2. *If the terms of trade are 3, how many units of the imported good could I buy for the money earned by the sale of 1 unit of the exported good? What is the exchange ratio?*

In the real world where countries have *many* exports and imports, the **terms of trade** are given by

$$\frac{\text{Average price of exports}}{\text{Average price of imports}}$$

expressed as an index, where price changes are measured against a base year in which the terms of trade are assumed to be 100. Thus if the average price of exports relative to the average price of imports has risen by 20 per cent since the base year, the terms of trade will now be 120. The terms of trade for selected countries are shown in Figure 24.4 (with 2005 as the base year).

If the terms of trade rise (export prices rising relative to import prices), they are said to have 'improved', since fewer exports now have to be sold to purchase any given quantity of imports. Changes in the terms of trade are caused by changes in the demand for and supply of imports and exports, and by changes in the exchange rate.

KI 5
p22

In Figure 24.4, which countries' terms of trade improved in the 2000s?

The terms of trade and comparative advantage

Assuming there are two goods, x and m, trade can be advantageous to a country as long as the terms of trade P_x/P_m are different from the opportunity cost ratios of the two goods, given by MC_x/MC_m. For example, if the terms of trade were greater than the opportunity cost ratio ($P_x/P_m > MC_x/MC_m$), it would benefit the country to produce more x for export in return for imports of m, since the relative value of producing x (P_x/P_m) is greater than the relative cost (MC_x/MC_m). KI 14
p107

With increasing opportunity costs, however, increasing specialisation in x will lead to MC_x rising (and MC_m falling), until $P_x/P_m = MC_x/MC_m$. At this point, there can be no more gain from further specialisation and trade: the maximum gain has been achieved and comparative cost advantages have been exhausted. TC 11
p320

The determination of the terms of trade

When countries import and export many goods, the terms of trade will depend on the prices of all the various exports and imports. These prices will depend on the demand and supply of each traded good and their elasticities in the respective countries. Take the case of good g in which

Definition

Terms of trade The price index of exports divided by the price index of imports and then expressed as a percentage. This means that the terms of trade will be 100 in the base year.

| Figure 24.4 | Terms of trade for selected countries (2000 = 100) |

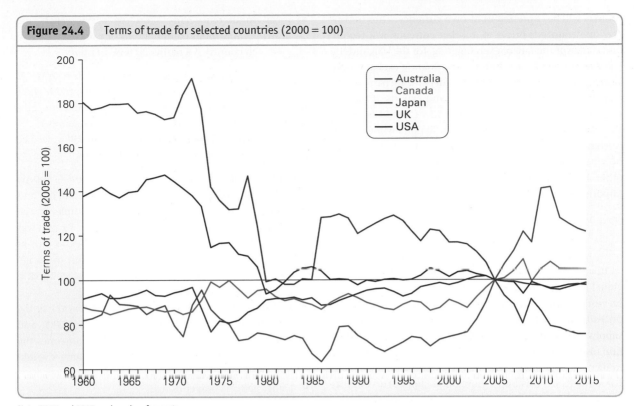

Note: 2014 and 2015 are based on forecasts.
Source: Based on data in *AMECO database* (European Commission, DGECFIN).

| Figure 24.5 | Determination of the price of an individual traded good |

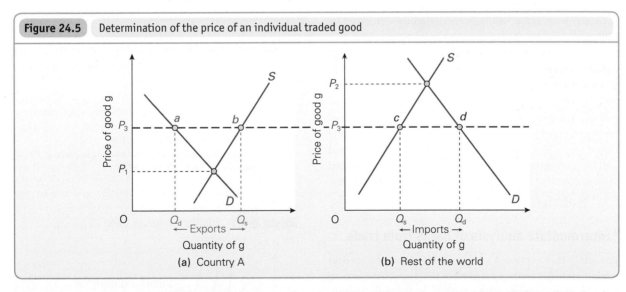

country A has a comparative advantage with respect to the rest of the world. This is illustrated in Figure 24.5.

Demand and supply curves of good g can be drawn for both country A and the rest of the world. (The upward-sloping supply curves imply increasing opportunity costs of production.) Before trade, country A has a low equilibrium price of P_1 and the rest of the world a high equilibrium price of P_2. After trade, price will settle at P_3 in both countries (assuming no transport costs), where total demand by both country A and the rest of the world together equals total supply, and thus where the imports of g into the rest of the world ($d - c$) equal the exports from country A ($b - a$). The

position of P_3 relative to P_1 and P_2 will depend on the elasticities of demand and supply.

A similar analysis can be conducted for all the other traded goods – both exports and imports of country A. The resulting prices will allow country A's terms of trade to be calculated.

Draw a similar diagram to Figure 24.5 showing how the price of an individual good imported into country A is determined.

The analysis is complicated somewhat if different national currencies are involved, since the prices in each

KI 8
p46

country will be expressed in its own currency. Thus to convert one country's prices to another currency will require knowledge of the rate of exchange: e.g. for the USA and the UK it might be $2 = £1. But under a floating exchange rate system, the rate of exchange will depend in part on the demand for and supply of imports and exports. If the rate of exchange depreciates – say, from $2 = £1 to $1.50 = £1 – the UK's terms of trade will worsen. Exports will earn less foreign currency per pound: e.g. £1 worth of exports will now be worth only $1.50 rather than $2. Imports, on the other hand, will be more expensive: e.g. $6 worth of imports previously cost £3; they now cost £4.

Why will exporters probably welcome a 'deterioration' in the terms of trade?

In a world of many countries and many goods, an individual country's imports and exports may have little effect on world prices. In the extreme case, the country may face prices totally dictated by the external world demand and supply. The country in this case is similar to an individual firm under perfect competition. The country is too small to influence world prices, and thus faces a horizontal demand curve for its exports and a horizontal supply curve for its imports. In foreign currency terms, therefore, the terms of trade are outside its control. Nevertheless, these terms of trade will probably be to its benefit, in the sense that the gains from trade will be virtually entirely received by this small country rather than the rest of the world. It is too small for its trade to depress the world price of its exports or drive up the price of its imports.

In general, a country's gains from trade will be greater the less elastic its own domestic demand and supply of tradable goods are, and the more elastic the demand and supply of other countries. You can see this by examining Figure 24.5. The less elastic the domestic demand and supply, the bigger will be the effect of trade on prices faced by that country. The more the trade price differs from the pre-trade price, the bigger the gain.

TC 7 p72

*Intermediate analysis of gains from trade

The analysis of section 11.1 (pages 320–2) can be used to demonstrate the welfare gains from trade and the limits to specialisation under conditions of increasing opportunity cost. A simple two-good model is used, and the pre-trade position is compared with the position with trade.

Pre-trade

Let us make the following simplifying assumptions:

- There are two goods, x and m.
- Country A has a comparative advantage in the production of good x.
- There are increasing opportunity costs in the production of both x and m. Thus the production possibility curve is bowed out.

- Social indifference curves can be drawn, each one showing the various combinations of x and m that give society in country A a particular level of utility.

Figure 24.6 shows the pre-trade position in country A. Production and consumption at P_1C_1 will give the highest possible utility. (All other points on the production possibility curve intersect with lower indifference curves.)

If there is perfect competition, production will indeed be at P_1C_1. There are four steps in establishing this:

- The slope of the production possibility curve ($-\Delta m/\Delta x$) is the marginal rate of transformation (*MRT*), and equals MC_x/MC_m (see page 321). For example, if the opportunity cost of producing 1 extra unit of x (Δx) was a sacrifice of 2 units of m ($-\Delta m$), then an extra unit of x would cost twice as much as an extra unit of m: i.e. $MC_x/MC_m = 2/1$, which is the slope of the production possibility curve, $-\Delta m/\Delta x$.
- The slope of each indifference curve ($-\Delta m/\Delta x$) is the marginal rate of substitution in consumption (*MRS*), and equals MU_x/MU_m. For example, if x had three times the marginal utility of m ($MU_x/MU_m = 3$), consumers would be willing to give up 3m for 1x ($-\Delta m/\Delta x = 3$).
- Under perfect competition,

$$\frac{MC_x}{MC_m} = \frac{P_x}{P_m} = \frac{MU_x}{MU_m}$$

- Thus the domestic pre-trade price ratio P_x/P_m under perfect competition must equal the slope of the production possibility curve (MC_x/MC_m) and the slope of the social indifference curve (MU_x/MU_m). This is the case at P_1C_1 in Figure 24.6.

KI 14 p107

1. If production were at point a in Figure 24.6, describe the process whereby equilibrium at point P_1C_1 would be restored under perfect competition.
2. Why would production be unlikely to take place at P_1C_1 if competition were not perfect?

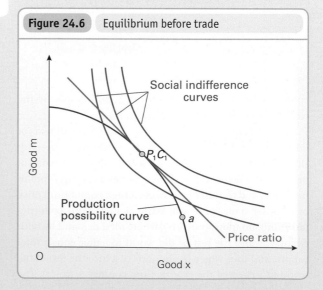

Figure 24.6 Equilibrium before trade

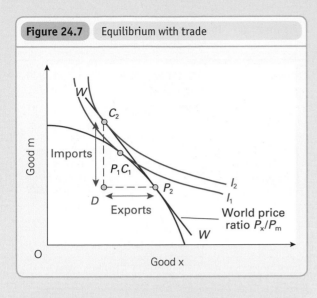

Figure 24.7 Equilibrium with trade

1. Draw a similar diagram to Figure 24.7, only this time assume that the two goods are good a measured on the vertical axis and good b measured on the horizontal axis. Assume that the country has a comparative advantage in good a. (Note that the world price ratio this time will be shallower than the domestic pre-trade price ratio.) Mark the level of exports of a and imports of b.
2. Is it possible to gain from trade if competition is not perfect?

With trade

If country A has a comparative advantage in good x, the price of x relative to m is likely to be higher in the rest of the world than in country A: i.e. world P_x/P_m > pre-trade domestic P_x/P_m. This is shown in Figure 24.7. The world price ratio is given by the slope of the line *WW*. With this new steeper world price ratio, the optimum production point will be P_2 where *MRT* (the slope of the production possibility curve) = world P_x/P_m (the slope of *WW*).

With production at P_2, the country can by trading consume *anywhere* along this line *WW*. The optimum consumption point will be C_2 where *MRS* (the slope of the indifference curve) = world P_x/P_m (the slope of *WW*). Thus trade has allowed consumption to move from point C_1 on the lower indifference curve I_1 to point C_2 on the higher indifference curve I_2. There has thus been a gain from trade. Perfect competition will ensure that this gain is realised, since production at P_2 and consumption at C_2 meet the equilibrium condition that

$$\frac{MC_x}{MC_m} = \frac{P_x}{P_m} = \frac{MU_x}{MU_m}$$

How much will be imported and how much will be exported? With production at P_2 and consumption at C_2, country A will import $C_2 - D$ of good m in exchange for exports of $P_2 - D$ of good x.

Similar diagrams to Figure 24.7 can be drawn for other countries. Since they show equilibrium for both imports and exports on the *one* diagram, economists refer to them as *general equilibrium diagrams* (see Figure 11.3 on page 322 for another example).

Definition

General equilibrium diagrams (in trade theory) Indifference curve/production possibility curve diagrams that show a country's production and consumption of both imports and exports.

Other reasons for gains from trade

Decreasing costs

Even if there are no initial comparative cost differences between two countries, it will still benefit both to specialise in industries where economies of scale (either internal or external) can be gained, and then to trade. Once the economies of scale begin to appear, comparative cost differences will also appear, and thus the countries will have gained a comparative advantage in these industries.

A similar argument applies to different models of the same product (e.g. different models of cars or electrical goods). Several countries, by specialising in just one or two models each, can gain the full economies of scale and hence a comparative advantage in their particular model(s). Then, through trade, consumers can gain from having a wider range from which to choose. Much of the specialisation that international trade permits is of this nature.

The decreasing cost reason for trade is particularly relevant for small countries where the domestic market is not large enough to support large-scale industries. Thus exports form a much higher percentage of GDP in small countries such as Singapore than in large countries such as the USA.

Would it be possible for a country with a comparative disadvantage in a given product at pre-trade levels of output to obtain a comparative advantage in it by specialising in its production and exporting it?

Differences in demand

Even with no comparative cost differences and no potential economies of scale, trade can benefit both countries if demand conditions differ.

If people in country A like beef more than lamb, and people in country B like lamb more than beef, then rather than A using resources better suited for lamb to produce beef and B using resources better suited for producing beef to produce lamb, it will benefit both to produce beef *and* lamb and to export the one they like less in return for the one they like more.

Increased competition

If a country trades, the competition from imports may stimulate greater efficiency at home. This extra competition may prevent domestic monopolies/oligopolies from charging high prices. It may stimulate greater research and development and the more rapid adoption of new technology. It may lead to a greater variety of products being made available to consumers.

Trade as an 'engine of growth'

In a growing world economy, the demand for a country's exports is likely to grow, especially when these exports have a high income elasticity of demand. This provides a stimulus to growth in the exporting country.

Non-economic advantages

There may be political, social and cultural advantages to be gained by fostering trading links between countries.

The competitive advantage of nations

The theory of comparative advantage shows how countries can gain from trade, but why do countries have a comparative advantage in some goods rather than others?

One explanation is that it depends on the resources that countries have. If a country has plenty of land, then it makes sense to specialise in products that make use of this abundant resource. Thus Canada produces and exports wheat. If a country has a highly skilled workforce and an established research base, then it makes sense to specialise in high-tech products and export these. Thus Germany exports many highly sophisticated manufactured products. By contrast, many developing countries with plentiful but relatively low-skilled workers specialise in primary products or simple manufactured products.

In other words, countries should specialise in goods which make intensive use of their abundant resources. But this still does not give enough detail as to why countries specialise in the precise range of products that they do. Also, why do countries both export and import the *same* products? Why do many countries produce and export cars, but also import many cars?

According to Porter,[1] there are four key determinants of why nations are highly competitive in certain products but less so in others. These are illustrated in a diagram which has become known as the 'Porter diamond' (see Figure 24.8).

Available resources. These include 'given' resources, such as raw materials, population and climate, but also specialised resources that have been developed by humans, such as the skills of the labour force, the amount and type of capital, the transport and communications infrastructure, and the science and technology base. These specialised resources vary in detail from one country to another and give them a competitive advantage in very specific products. Once an industry has started to develop, this may attract further research and development, capital investment and training, all of

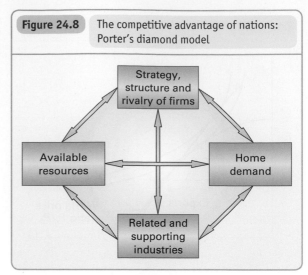

Figure 24.8 The competitive advantage of nations: Porter's diamond model

Source: M. E. Porter, *The Competitive Advantage of Nations* (The Free Press, 1998), p. 127.

which are very specific to that industry. This then further builds the country's competitive advantage in that industry. Thus the highly developed engineering skills and equipment in Germany give it a competitive advantage in producing well-engineered cars.

Demand conditions in the home market. The more discerning customers are within the country, the more this will drive the development of each firm's products and the more competitive the firm will then become in international markets. The demand for IT solutions within the USA drove the development of the software industry and gave companies such as Microsoft, Intel and Google an international advantage.

Strategy, structure and rivalry of firms. Competition between firms is not just in terms of price. Competitive rivalry extends to all aspects of business strategy, from product design, to marketing, to internal organisation, to production efficiency, to logistics. The very particular competitive conditions within each industry can have a profound effect on the development of firms within that industry and determine whether or not they gain an international competitive advantage. Strategic investments and rivalry gave Japanese electronics companies an international competitive advantage.

Related and supporting industries. Firms are more likely to be successful internationally if there are well-developed supporting industries within the home economy. These may be industries providing specialist equipment or specialist consultancy, or they may simply be other parts of the main value chain, from suppliers of inputs to distributors of the firms' output. The more efficient this value chain, the greater the competitive advantage of firms within the industry.

---

chael E. Porter, *The Competitive Advantage of Nations* (The Free Press, 1998).

KEY IDEA 38

The competitive advantage of nations is the ability of countries to compete in the market for exports and with potential importers to their country. The competitiveness of any one industry depends on the availability and quality of resources, demand conditions at home in that industry, the strategies and rivalry of firms within the industry and the quality of supporting industries and infrastructure. It also depends on government policies, and there is also an element of chance.

As the arrows in Figure 24.8 show, the four determinants of competitive advantage are interlinked and influence each other. For example, the nature of related and supporting industries can influence a firm's strategic decision about whether to embark on a process of vertical integration or de-integration. Similarly, the nature of related and supporting industries depends on demand conditions in these industries and the availability of resources.

With each of the four determinants in Figure 24.8, competitive advantage can be stimulated by appropriate government supply-side policies, such as a supportive tax regime, investment in transport and communications infrastructure, investment in education and training, competition policy and sound macroeconomic management of the economy. Also, chance often has a large part to play. Any pharmaceutical company which discovers a cure for AIDS or for various types of cancer will give a significant competitive advantage to the country in which it is based.

Section summary

1. Countries can gain from trade if they specialise in producing those goods in which they have a comparative advantage: i.e. those goods that can be produced at relatively low opportunity costs. This is merely an extension of the argument that gains can be made from the specialisation and division of labour.

2. If two countries trade, then, provided that the trade price ratio of exports and imports is between the pre-trade price ratios of these goods in the two countries, both countries can gain. They can both consume *beyond* their production possibility curves.

3. With increasing opportunity costs there will be a limit to specialisation and trade. As a country increasingly specialises, its (marginal) comparative advantage will eventually disappear. Trade can also be limited by transport costs, factor movements and government intervention.

4. The terms of trade give the price of exports relative to the price of imports. Additional trade can be beneficial if the terms of trade (P_x/P_m) are greater than the relative marginal costs of exports and imports (MC_x/MC_m).

5. A country's terms of trade are determined by the demand and supply of imports and exports and their respective elasticities. This will determine the prices at which goods are traded and affect the rate of exchange. A country's gains from trade will be greater the less elastic its own domestic demand and supply of tradable goods, and the more elastic the demand and supply of other countries.

*6. Trade allows countries to achieve a higher level of utility by consuming on a higher social indifference curve. The maximum gain from trade is achieved by consuming at the point where the world price ratio is tangential to both the production possibility curve and a social indifference curve. This would be achieved under perfect competition.

7. Gains from trade also arise from decreasing costs (economies of scale), differences in demand between countries, increased competition from trade and the transmission of growth from one country to another. There may also be non-economic advantages from trade.

8. Comparative advantage is related to competitive advantage. Countries tend to have a competitive advantage in those industries where specialist resources have been developed, where products have been developed in response to changing consumer demands, where business strategy is conducive and where there is a network of supporting industries and infrastructure.

24.2 ARGUMENTS FOR RESTRICTING TRADE

KI 2 p11

Most countries have not pursued a policy of totally free trade. Their politicians know that trade involves costs as well as benefits. In this section, we will attempt to identify what these costs are, and whether they are genuine reasons for restricting trade.

Although countries may sometimes contemplate having completely free trade, they usually limit their trade. However, they certainly do not ban it altogether. The sorts of questions that governments pose are (a) should they have freer or more restricted trade and (b) in which sectors should restrictions be tightened or relaxed? Ideally, countries should weigh up the marginal benefits against the marginal costs of altering restrictions, although just *what* benefits and costs should be taken into account, and what weighting should be attached to them, may be highly contentious. For example, should external costs and benefits be considered and should these include *global* externalities?

Methods of restricting trade

Tariffs (customs duties).   These are taxes on imports and are usually **ad valorem tariffs**: i.e. a percentage of the price of the import. Tariffs that are used to restrict imports are most effective if demand is elastic (e.g. when there are close domestically produced substitutes). Tariffs can also be used as a means of raising revenue, but in this case they are more effective if demand is inelastic. They can also be used to raise the price of imported goods to prevent 'unfair' competition for domestic producers.

Quotas.   These are limits imposed on the quantity of a good that can be imported. Quotas can be imposed by the government, or negotiated with other countries which agree 'voluntarily' to restrict the amount of exports to the first country.

Exchange controls.   These include limits on how much foreign exchange can be made available to importers (financial quotas), or to citizens travelling abroad, or for investment. Alternatively, they may take the form of charges for the purchase of foreign currencies.

Import licensing.   The imposition of exchange controls or quotas often involves requiring importers to obtain licences. This makes it easier for the government to enforce its restrictions.

Embargoes.   These are total government bans on certain imports (e.g. drugs) or exports to certain countries (e.g. to enemies during war).

Administrative barriers.   Regulations may be designed to exclude imports: examples include customs delays and excessive paperwork.

Procurement policies.   This is where governments favour domestic producers when purchasing equipment (e.g. defence equipment).

Dumping.   Alternatively, governments may favour domestic producers by subsidising their exports in a process known as **dumping**. The goods are 'dumped' at artificially low prices in the foreign market.

Arguments in favour of restricting trade

Economic arguments having some general validity

The infant industry argument.   Some industries in a country may be in their infancy, but have a potential comparative advantage. This is particularly likely in developing countries. Such industries are too small yet to have gained economies of scale; their workers are inexperienced; they lack back-up facilities, such as communications networks and specialist suppliers. They may have only limited access to finance for expansion. Without protection, these **infant industries** will not survive competition from abroad.

> ### Definitions
>
> **Ad valorem tariffs** Tariffs levied as a percentage of the price of the import.
>
> **Dumping** Where exports are sold at prices below marginal cost – often as a result of government subsidy.
>
> **Infant industry** An industry that has a potential comparative advantage, but which is as yet too underdeveloped to be able to realise this potential.

| BOX 24.4 | FREE TRADE AND THE ENVIRONMENT | CASE STUDIES AND APPLICATIONS |

Do whales, rainforests and the atmosphere gain from free trade?

International trade provides an outlet for hardwood from the rainforests, for tiger parts for medicines, for chemicals and other industrial products produced with little regard for safety or environmental standards, and for products produced using electricity generated from low-cost, high-sulphur, highly polluting coal.

The problem is that countries are likely to export goods that they can produce at a relatively low opportunity cost. But these opportunity costs are *private* costs. They do not take into account externalities. This is a powerful argument against free trade based on free-market prices.

Surely, though, the developed countries use taxes, legislation and other means to prevent the abuse of the environment? They may do, but this does not stop them importing products from countries that do not.

In reply, the advocates of free trade argue that it is up to each country to decide its own environmental standards. If a poor country produces a product in a cheap polluting way,

the gains from exporting it may more than offset the environmental damage done.

There is some strength in this argument provided (a) the government of that country has done a proper study of the costs and benefits involved, including the external costs; and (b) the externalities are confined to within the country's borders. Unfortunately, in many cases neither of these conditions holds. Much of the pollution generated from industrial production has global effects (e.g. global warming).

As countries such as China and India take an increasingly large share of world exports of industrial products (see Figure 24.2), so these problems are likely to grow. Both countries have much lower environmental protection standards than those in Europe and North America.

 Should the world community welcome the use of tariffs and other forms of protection by the rich countries against imports of goods from developing countries that have little regard for the environment?

Protection from foreign competition, however, will allow them to expand and become more efficient. Once they have achieved a comparative advantage, the protection can then be removed to enable them to compete internationally.

Similar to the infant industry argument is the *senile industry argument*. This is where industries with a potential comparative advantage have been allowed to run down and can no longer compete effectively. They may have considerable potential, but be simply unable to make enough profit to afford the necessary investment without some temporary protection. This is one of the most powerful arguments used to justify the use of special protection for the automobile and steel industries in the USA.

> *How would you set about judging whether an industry had a genuine case for infant/senile industry protection?*

To reduce reliance on goods with little dynamic potential. Many developing countries have traditionally exported primaries: foodstuffs and raw materials. The world demand for these, however, is fairly income inelastic, and thus grows relatively slowly. In such cases, free trade is not an engine of growth. Instead, if it encourages countries' economies to become locked into a pattern of primary production, it may prevent them from expanding in sectors like manufacturing that have a higher income elasticity of demand. There may thus be a valid argument for protecting or promoting manufacturing industry. (We explore these arguments in section 27.2.)

To prevent dumping and other unfair trade practices. A country may engage in dumping by subsidising its exports. The result is that prices may no longer reflect comparative costs. Thus the world would benefit from tariffs being imposed to counteract such practices.

> *Does the consumer in the importing country gain or lose from dumping?*

 It can also be argued that there is a case for retaliating against countries that impose restrictions on your exports. In the *short* run, both countries are likely to be made worse off by a contraction in trade. But if the retaliation persuades the other country to remove its restrictions, it may have a longer-term benefit. In some cases, the mere threat of retaliation may be enough to get another country to remove its protection.

 To prevent the establishment of a foreign-based monopoly. Competition from abroad, especially when it involves dumping or predatory pricing (see pages 217 and 387), could drive domestic producers out of business. The foreign company, now having a monopoly of the market, could charge high prices with a resulting misallocation of resources.

All of the above arguments suggest that governments should adopt a 'strategic' approach to trade. *Strategic trade theory* (see Box 24.5) argues that protecting certain industries

allows a net gain *in the long run* from increased competition in the market. This argument has been used to justify the huge financial support given to the aircraft manufacturer Airbus, a consortium based in four European countries. The subsidies have allowed it to compete with Boeing, which would otherwise have a monopoly in many types of passenger aircraft. Airlines and their passengers worldwide, it is argued, have benefited from the increased competition.

To spread the risks of fluctuating markets. A highly specialised economy – Zambia with copper, Cuba with sugar – is highly susceptible to world market fluctuations. Greater diversity and greater self-sufficiency can reduce these risks.

To reduce the influence of trade on consumer tastes. It is a mistake to assume that fixed consumer tastes dictate the pattern of production through trade. Multinational companies through their advertising and other forms of sales promotion may influence consumer tastes. Thus some restriction on trade may be justified in order to reduce this 'producer sovereignty'.

> *In what ways may free trade have harmful cultural effects on developing countries?*

To prevent the importation of harmful goods. A country may want to ban or severely curtail the importation of things such as drugs, pornographic literature and live animals.

To take account of externalities. Free trade will tend to reflect private costs. Both imports and exports, however, can involve externalities. The mining of many minerals for export may damage the health of miners; the production of chemicals for export may involve pollution; the importation of juggernaut lorries may lead to structural damage to houses; shipping involves large amounts of CO_2 emissions (estimates typically put this at between 3 and 5 per cent of total world emissions) (see Box 24.4).

In recent years some politicians and green groups have called for the imposition of 'carbon tariffs'. The rate of tariff would reflect the amount of carbon emitted in the production of the good being imported. Such tariffs would be hard to implement, however. Assessing and valuing the carbon emitted would be very difficult and could lead to arbitrary tariff rates. Also, domestic goods would have to be subject to similar taxes.

Definition

Strategic trade theory The theory that protecting/supporting certain industries can enable them to compete more effectively with large monopolistic rivals abroad. The effect of the protection is to increase long-run competition and may enable the protected firms to exploit a comparative advantage that they could not have done otherwise.

BOX 24.5 **STRATEGIC TRADE THEORY**

An argument for protection?

Lester Thurow is a professor of management and economics and former dean in the Sloan School of Management at the Massachusetts Institute of Technology (MIT). He is also an economics journalist and editor. He is also one of the USA's best-known and most articulate advocates of 'managed trade'.

Thurow (and others) have been worried by the growing penetration of US markets by imports from Japan and Europe and also from China and many other developing countries. Their response is to call for a carefully worked-out strategy of protection for US industries.

The *strategic trade theory* that they support argues that the real world is complex. It is wrong, they claim, to rely on free trade and existing comparative advantage. Particular industries will require particular policies of protection or promotion tailored to their particular needs:

- Some industries will require protection against unfair competition from abroad – not just to protect the industries themselves, but also to protect the consumer from the oligopolistic power that the foreign companies will gain if they succeed in driving the domestic producers out of business.
- Other industries will need special support in the form of subsidies to enable them to modernise and compete effectively with imports.
- New industries may require protection to enable them to get established – to achieve economies of scale and build a comparative advantage.
- If a particular foreign country protects or promotes its *own* industries, it may be desirable to retaliate in order to persuade the country to change its mind.

But, despite the enthusiasm of the strategic trade theorists, their views have come in for concerted criticism from

economic liberals. If the USA is protected from cheap imports from Asia, they claim, all that will be achieved is a huge increase in consumer prices. The car, steel, telecommunications and electrical goods industries might find their profits bolstered, but this is hardly likely to encourage them to be more efficient.

Another criticism of managed trade is the difficulty of identifying just which industries need protection, and how much and for how long. Governments do not have perfect knowledge. What is more, the political lobbyists from various interested groups are likely to use all sorts of tactics – legal or illegal – to persuade the government to look favourably on them. In the face of such pressure, will the government remain 'objective'? No, say the liberals.

So how do the strategic trade theorists reply? If it works for China and Japan, they say, it can work for the USA. What is needed is a change in attitudes. Rather than industry looking on the government as either an enemy to be outwitted or a potential benefactor to be wooed, and government looking on industry as a source of votes or tax revenues, both sides should try to develop a partnership – a partnership from which the whole country can gain.

But whether sensible, constructive managed trade is possible in the US democratic system, or the UK for that matter, is a highly debatable point. 'Sensible' managed trade, say the liberals, is just pie in the sky.

 Airbus, a consortium based in four European countries, has received massive support from the four governments, in order to enable it to compete with Boeing, which until the rise of Airbus had dominated the world market for aircraft. To what extent are (a) air travellers; (b) citizens of the four countries likely to have gained or lost from this protection? (See Case Study 24.9 in MyEconLab.)

Economic arguments having some validity for specific groups or countries

The arguments considered so far are of general validity: restricting trade for such reasons could be of net benefit to the world. There are other arguments, however, that are used by individual governments for restricting trade, where their country will gain, but at the *expense* of other countries, such that there will be a net loss to the world. Such arguments include the following.

The exploitation of market power. If a country, or a group of countries, has market power in the supply of exports (e.g. South Africa with diamonds, OPEC with oil) or market power in the demand for imports (e.g. the USA or other large wealthy countries), it can exploit this power by inter-vening in trade.

Let us first take the case of a country, or a group of coun-tries acting as a cartel, which has monopoly power in the sale of a particular export: for example, West African coun-

tries in the sale of cocoa. But let us assume that there are many individual producers that are therefore price takers and are thus not in a position to exploit the country's over-all market power. In Figure 24.9, these price-taking firms will collectively produce at point *a* where $P = MC$. Market equilibrium is at a trade price of P_1 and an output of Q_1.

The country's profit, however, would be maximised at point *b* where $MC = MR$, with output at the lower level of Q_2. By imposing an export tax of $P_2 - P_3$, therefore, the country can maximise its gain from this export. Producers will receive P_3 and will therefore supply Q_2. Market price will be P_2.

 1. How much would be the total tax revenue for the government?
2. Will the individual producers gain from the export tax?

Now let us take the case of a country that has *monopsony* power in the demand for an import. This is illustrated in

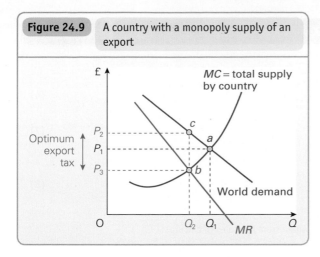

Figure 24.9 A country with a monopoly supply of an export

Figure 24.10 A country with a monopsony demand for an export

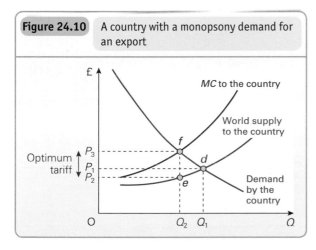

Figure 24.10. Without intervention, equilibrium will be at point *d* where demand equals supply. Q_1 would be purchased at a price of P_1.

But the marginal cost of imports curve will be *above* the supply curve because, given the country's size, the purchase of additional imports would drive up their price. This means that the cost of additional imports would be the new higher price (given by the supply curve) *plus* the rise in expenditure on the imports that would previously have been purchased at a lower price. The country will maximise its gain from trade at point *f* by importing Q_2, where demand equals marginal cost. Consumption can be reduced to Q_2 if the government imposes a tariff of $P_3 - P_2$. This is known as the ***optimum tariff***. The country now only pays P_2 to importers. Consumers have to pay P_3 (i.e. P_2 plus the tariff).

The country gains from such intervention, but only at the expense of the other countries with which it trades.

Definition

Optimum tariff A tariff that reduces the level of imports to the point where marginal social cost equals marginal social benefit.

To protect declining industries. The human costs of sudden industrial closures can be very high. In such circumstances, temporary protection may be warranted to allow industries that have lost comparative advantage to decline more slowly. Such policies will be at the expense of the consumer, who will be denied access to cheaper foreign imports.

To improve the balance of payments. Under certain special circumstances, when other methods of balance of payments correction are unsuitable, there may be a case for resorting to tariffs (see Chapter 25).

'Non-economic' arguments

A country may be prepared to forgo the direct economic advantages of free trade – consumption at a lower opportunity cost – in order to achieve objectives that are often described as 'non-economic':

- It may wish to maintain a degree of self-sufficiency in case trade is cut off in times of war. This may apply particularly to the production of food and armaments.
- It may decide not to trade with certain countries with which it disagrees politically.
- It may wish to preserve traditional ways of life. Rural communities or communities based on old traditional industries may be destroyed by foreign competition.
- It may prefer to retain as diverse a society as possible, rather than one too narrowly based on certain industries.

Pursuing such objectives, however, involves costs. Preserving a traditional way of life, for example, may mean that consumers are denied access to cheaper goods from abroad. Society must therefore weigh up the benefits against the costs of such policies.

 If economics is the study of choices of how to use scarce resources, can these other objectives be legitimately described as 'non-economic'?

Problems with protection

Tariffs and other forms of protection impose a cost on society. This is illustrated in Figure 24.11. It illustrates the case of a good that is partly home produced and partly imported. Domestic demand and supply are given by D_{dom} and S_{dom}. It is assumed that firms in the country produce under perfect competition and that therefore the supply curve is the sum of the firms' marginal cost curves.

Let us assume that the country is too small to affect world prices: it is a price taker. The world price is given, at P_w, and world supply to the country (S_{world}) is perfectly elastic. At P_w, Q_2 is demanded, Q_1 is supplied by domestic suppliers and hence $Q_2 - Q_1$ is imported.

Now a tariff is imposed. This shifts up the world supply curve to the country by the amount of the tariff. Price rises to $P_w + t$. Domestic production increases to Q_3, consumption falls to Q_4, and hence imports fall to $Q_4 - Q_3$.

What are the costs of this tariff to the country? Consumers are having to pay a higher price, and hence consumer

*BOX 24.6 THE OPTIMUM TARIFF OR EXPORT TAX

Using calculus

The size of the optimum export tax depends on the price elasticity of demand ($Pє_d$). You can see this if you imagine rotating the demand and MR curves in Figure 24.9. The less elastic the demand curve, the bigger will be the optimum export tax. The formula for the optimum export tax rate is

$$t = 1/Pє_d$$

The proof of this is as follows.

In Figure 24.9, the optimum tax rate is

$$(P_2 - P_3) \div P_2 \tag{1}$$

From the point of view of the country (as opposed to individual producers) this is simply

$$(P - MR) \div P \tag{2}$$

Remember from Box 3.3 (on page 69) that price elasticity of demand is given by

$$Pє_d = \frac{-dQ}{dP} \times \frac{P}{Q} \tag{3}$$

Remember also, from Box 5.9 (on page 165), that

$$MR = \frac{dTR}{dQ} = \frac{d(P \cdot Q)}{dQ} \tag{4}$$

From the rules of calculus:

$$\frac{d(P \cdot Q)}{dQ} = \frac{dP \cdot Q + dQ \cdot P}{dQ} \tag{5}$$

$$\therefore \quad P - MR = P - \frac{dP \cdot Q + dQ \cdot P}{dQ} \tag{6}$$

$$\frac{P}{P - MR} = \frac{P}{P - \dfrac{dP \cdot Q + dQ \cdot P}{dQ}} \tag{7}$$

$$= 1 - \frac{P}{P - \dfrac{dP \cdot Q + dQ \cdot P}{dQ}} \tag{8}$$

Again from the rules of calculus:

$$= 1 - \left(\frac{dQ \cdot P}{dP \cdot Q} + \frac{dQ \cdot P}{dQ \cdot P} \right) \tag{9}$$

$$= 1 - \frac{dQ \cdot P}{dP \cdot Q} - 1 \tag{10}$$

$$= \frac{-dQ \cdot P}{dP \cdot Q} = Pє_d \tag{11}$$

∴ from equations (2) and (11):

$$\frac{P - MR}{P} = \text{optimum tax rate} = \frac{1}{Pє_d}$$

See if you can devise a similar proof to show that the optimal import tariff, where a country has monopsony power, is $1/Pє_s$ (where $Pє_s$ is the price elasticity of supply of the import).

---

surplus falls from *ABC* to *ADE*. The cost to consumers in lost consumer surplus is thus *EDBC* (i.e. areas 1 + 2 + 3 + 4). *Part* of this cost, however, is redistributed as a *benefit* to other sections in society. *Firms* face a higher price, and thus gain extra profits (area 1): where profit is given by the area between the price and the *MC* curve. The *government* receives extra revenue from the tariff payments (area 3): i.e. $Q_4 - Q_3 \times$ tariff. These revenues can be used, for example, to reduce taxes.

But *part* of this cost is not recouped elsewhere. It is a net cost to society (areas 2 and 4).

Area 2 represents the extra costs of producing $Q_3 - Q_1$ at home, rather than importing it. If $Q_3 - Q_1$ were still imported, the country would only be paying S_{world}. By producing it at home, however, the costs are given by the domestic supply curve (= MC). The difference between MC and S_{world} (area 2) is thus the efficiency loss on the production side.

Area 4 represents the loss of consumer surplus by the reduction in consumption from Q_2 to Q_4. Consumers have saved area FBQ_2Q_4 of expenditure, but have sacrificed area DBQ_2Q_4 of utility in so doing – a net loss of area 4.

The government should ideally weigh up such costs against any benefits that are gained from protection.

In this model, where the country is a price taker and faces a horizontal supply curve (the small-country assumption), is any of the cost of the tariff borne by the overseas suppliers?

Apart from these direct costs to the consumer, there are several other problems with protection. Some are direct effects of the protection; others follow from the reactions of other nations.

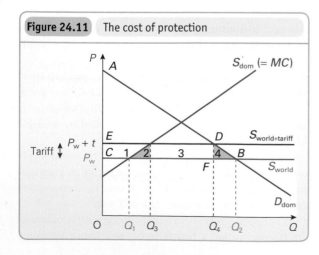

Figure 24.11 The cost of protection

BOX 24.7   GIVING TRADE A BAD NAME

Arguments that don't add up

'Why buy goods from abroad and deny jobs to workers in this country?' This is typical of the concerns that many people have about an open trade policy. However, these concerns are often based on arguments that do not stand up to close inspection. Here are four of them.

'Imports should be reduced since they lower the standard of living. The money goes abroad rather than into the domestic economy.' Imports are consumed and thus add directly to consumer welfare. Also, provided they are matched by exports, there is no net outflow of money. Trade, because of the law of comparative advantage, allows countries to increase their standard of living: to consume beyond their production possibility curve (see Figures 24.3 and 24.7).

'Protection is needed from cheap foreign labour.' Importing cheap goods from, say, Indonesia, allows more goods to be consumed. The UK uses less resources by buying these goods through the production and sale of exports than by producing them at home. However, there will be a cost to certain UK workers whose jobs are lost through foreign competition.

'Protection reduces unemployment.' At a microeconomic level, protecting industries from foreign competition may allow workers in those industries to retain their jobs. But if foreigners sell fewer goods to the UK, they will not be able to buy so many UK exports. Thus unemployment will rise in UK export industries. Overall unemployment, therefore, is little affected, and in the meantime the benefits from trade to consumers are reduced. Temporary protection given to declining industries, however, may help to reduce structural unemployment.

'Dumping is always a bad thing, and thus a country should restrict subsidised imports.' Dumping may well reduce world economic welfare: it goes against the law of comparative advantage. The importing country, however, may well gain from dumping. Provided the dumping is not used to drive domestic producers out of business and establish a foreign monopoly, the consumer gains from lower prices. The losers are the taxpayers in the foreign country and the workers in competing industries in the home country.

Go through each of these four arguments and provide a reply to the criticisms of them.

Protection as 'second best'.   Many of the arguments for protection amount merely to arguments for some type of government intervention in the economy. Protection, however, may not be the best way of dealing with the problem, since protection may have undesirable side effects. There may be a more direct form of intervention that has no side effects. In such a case, protection will be no more than a *second-best* solution.

For example, using tariffs to protect old inefficient industries from foreign competition may help prevent unemployment in those parts of the economy, but the consumer will suffer from higher prices. A better solution would be to subsidise retraining and investment in those areas of the country in *new efficient* industries – industries with a comparative advantage. In this way, unemployment is avoided, but the consumer does not suffer.

Even if the *existing* industries were to be supported, it would still be better to do this by paying them subsidies than by putting tariffs on imports. This argument can be expressed in terms of Figure 24.11. As we have seen, a tariff imposes costs on the consumer of areas 1 + 2 + 3 + 4. In the current example, area 2 may be a cost worth paying in order to increase domestic output to Q_3 (and hence reduce unemployment). Areas 1 and 3, as argued above, are merely *redistributed* elsewhere (to firms and the government respectively). But this still leaves area 4. This is a side-effect cost not recouped elsewhere.

A *subsidy*, on the other hand, would not have involved this side-effect cost. In order to raise output to Q_3, a rate of subsidy the same as the tariff rate would have to be given to producers. This would raise the amount they receive per unit to $P_w + t$. They would choose to supply Q_3. The price to the consumer, however, would *remain at the world price P_w*. There would thus be no cost to the consumer. The cost of the subsidy to the taxpayer would be areas 1 + 2. Area 1 would be redistributed to firms as extra profit. Area 2, as argued above, may be worth paying to achieve the desirable output and employment consequences.

If the aim is to increase output, a *production* subsidy is the best policy. If the aim is to increase employment, an *employment* subsidy is the best policy. In either case, to use *protection* instead would be no more than second best, since it would involve side effects.

To conclude: the best policy is to tackle the problem directly. Unless the aim is specifically to reduce imports (rather than help domestic industry), protection is an indirect policy, and hence never more than second best.

1. What would be the 'first-best' solution to the problem of an infant industry not being able to compete with imports?
2. Protection to allow the exploitation of monopoly/monopsony power can be seen as a 'first-best' policy for the country concerned. Similarly, the use of tariffs to counteract externalities directly involved in the trade process (e.g. the environmental costs of an oil tanker disaster) could be seen to be a first-best policy. Explain why.

World multiplier effects.   If the UK imposes tariffs or other restrictions, imports will be reduced. But these imports are

TC 15
p 508

other countries' exports. A reduction in their exports will reduce the level of injections into the 'rest-of-the-world' economy, and thus lead to a multiplied fall in rest-of-the-world income. This in turn will lead to a reduction in demand for UK exports. This, therefore, tends to undo the benefits of the tariffs.

 What determines the size of this world multiplier effect?

Retaliation. If the USA imposes restrictions on, say, imports from the EU, then the EU may impose restrictions on imports from the USA. Any gain to US firms competing with EU imports is offset by a loss to US exporters. What is more, US consumers suffer, since the benefits from comparative advantage have been lost.

The increased use of tariffs and other restrictions can lead to a trade war: each country cutting back on imports from other countries. In the end, everyone loses.

Protection may allow firms to remain inefficient. By removing or reducing foreign competition, protection may reduce firms' incentive to reduce costs. Thus, if protection is being given to an infant industry, the government must ensure that the lack of competition does not prevent it 'growing up'. Protection should not be excessive and should be removed as soon as possible.

TC 5
p54

Bureaucracy. If a government is to avoid giving excessive protection to firms, it should examine each case carefully. This can lead to large administrative costs.

Corruption. Some countries that have an extensive programme of protection suffer from corruption. Home

---

BOX 24.8 **THE DOHA DEVELOPMENT AGENDA**

A new direction for the WTO?

Globalisation, based on the free play of comparative advantage, economies of scale and innovation, has produced a genuinely radical force, in the true sense of the word. It essentially amplifies and reinforces the strengths, but also the weaknesses, of market capitalism: its efficiency, its instability, and its inequality. If we want globalisation not only to be efficiency-boosting but also fair, we need more international rules and stronger multilateral institutions.[1]

In November 1999, the members of the World Trade Organization met in Seattle in the USA. What ensued became known as the 'Battle of Seattle' (see Case Study 24.4 in MyEconLab). Anti-globalisation protesters fought with police; the world's developing economies fell out with the world's developed economies; and the very future of the WTO was called into question. The WTO was accused of being a free trader's charter, in which the objective of free trade was allowed to ride roughshod over anything that might stand in its way. Whatever the issue – the environment, the plight of developing countries, the dominance of trade by multinationals – free trade was king.

At Seattle, both the protesters and developing countries argued that things had gone far enough. The WTO must redefine its role, they argued, to respect *all* stakeholders. More radical voices called for the organisation to be scrapped. As Pascal Lamy, the EU Trade Commissioner, made clear in the speech quoted above, rules had to be strengthened, and the WTO had to ensure that the gains from trade were fairer and more sustainable.

The rebuilding process of the WTO began in Doha, Qatar, in November 2001. The meeting between the then 142 members of the WTO concluded with the decision to launch a new round of WTO trade talks, to be called the Doha Development Agenda (DDA). As with previous trade rounds, the talks were designed to increase the liberalisation of trade. However, this time such a goal was to be tempered by

a policy of strengthening assistance to developing economies.

At Doha it was agreed that the new trade talks would address questions such as:

- **Sustainable development and the environment.** In the past, international trade agreements always seemed to take precedence over international environmental agreements, even though they are legally equivalent. The hope this time was to achieve greater coherence between various areas of international policy making.
- **Trade and development.** The Doha round would attempt to address a number of issues of concern to developing countries as they become more integrated into the world's trading system. These included improving access to markets in developed countries and strengthening the special treatment that developing countries received, such as the ability to maintain higher rates of tariff protection.

Other areas identified for discussion include: greater liberalisation of agriculture; rules to govern foreign direct investment; the co-ordination of countries' competition policies; the use and abuse of patents on medicines; and the needs of developing countries.

The talks were originally scheduled for completion by January 2005, but this deadline was extended several times as new talks were arranged and failed to reach agreement. A particular sticking point was the unwillingness of rich countries, and the USA and the EU in particular, to make sufficient reductions in agricultural protection, given the pressure from their domestic farmers. The USA was unwilling to make substantial cuts in agricultural subsidies and the EU in agricultural tariffs.

There was also unwillingness on the part of large developing countries, such as India and Brazil, to reduce protection to their industrial and service sectors. What is more, there were large divergences in opinion between

producers want as much protection as possible. Importers want as much freedom as possible. It is very tempting for both groups to bribe officials to give them favourable treatment.

The World Trade Organization

After the Wall Street crash of 1929 (when prices on the US stock exchange plummeted), the world plunged into the Great Depression (see pages 470–6). Countries found their exports falling dramatically, and many suffered severe balance of payments difficulties. The response of many countries was to restrict imports by the use of tariffs and quotas. Of course, this reduced other countries' exports, which encouraged them to resort to even greater protectionism. The net effect of the Depression and the rise in

protectionism was a dramatic fall in world trade. The volume of world trade in manufactures fell by more than a third in the three years following the Wall Street crash. Clearly there was a net economic loss to the world from this decline in trade.

After the Second World War there was a general desire to reduce trade restrictions, so that all countries could gain the maximum benefits from trade. There was no desire to return to the beggar-my-neighbour policies of the 1930s.

In 1947, 23 countries got together and signed the General Agreement on Tariffs and Trade (GATT). By 2014, there were 159 members of its successor organisation, the World Trade Organization (WTO), which was formed in 1995. Between them, the members of the WTO account for around 98 per cent of world trade. The aims of GATT, and now the WTO, have been to liberalise trade.

CASE STUDIES AND APPLICATIONS

developing countries on how much they should reduce their own agricultural protection.

Breakdown of the talks

The talks seemed finally to have broken down at a meeting in Geneva in July 2008. Despite the willingness of developing countries to reduce industrial tariffs by more than 50 per cent, and of the USA and the EU to make deep cuts in agricultural subsidies and tariffs, the talks foundered over the question of agricultural protection for developing countries. This was item 18 on a 'to-do' list of 20 items; items 1 to 17 had already been agreed. China and India wanted to protect poor farmers by retaining the ability to impose temporary tariffs on food imports in the event of a drop in food prices or a surge in imports. The USA objected. When neither side would budge, the talks collapsed.

But even 'success' would not have addressed some thorny issues, such as achieving equal access to rich countries' markets by all banana-producing countries (see Case Study 24.5 in MyEconLab) and protecting cotton producers in developing countries from cheap subsidised cotton grown in the USA. And Africa's interests would not have been properly addressed. In fact, no African country was present in the inner circle of talks at the end.

Many commentators, however, argued that failure was no catastrophe. The gain from total liberalisation of trade would have boosted developing countries' GDP by no more than 1 per cent. And anyway, tariffs were generally falling and were already at an all-time low. But, with the global economic downturn of 2008–9, there were worries that protectionism would begin to rise again. This was a classic prisoner's dilemma (see pages 210–11 and 368). Policies that seemed to be in the interests of countries separately would be to the overall determinant of the world. The Nash equilibrium of such a 'game', therefore, is one where countries are generally worse off. As it turned out, the worries were largely unfounded.

The Bali Package and the push to agreement

At the WTO's Bali Ministerial Conference in December 2013, an agreement was reached on a package of issues. The result was a streamlining of trade, allowing developing countries more options for providing food security, boosting least developed countries' trade and, more generally, promoting development. The deal was the first substantial agreement since the WTO was formed in 1995.

At the heart of the agreement is the simplifying of customs procedures, making them more transparent, and ensuring that trade is made 'easier, faster and cheaper'. Meanwhile, the deal also permits developing countries to continue subsidising their agriculture in order to promote food security, provided the practice does not distort international trade.

According to the EU's Trade Commissioner, Karel De Gucht, about one quarter of the goals set for the Doha Round have been achieved in this agreement. This, of course, still leaves a long way to go if all the Doha objectives are to be met. World trade, although now likely to be somewhat freer, is still not free; developing countries will still find restricted access for their agricultural products, and manufactures too, to many markets in the rich world; rich countries will still find restricted access for their manufactured products and services to many markets in the developing world.

By the time you read this, completion of the Doha Development Agenda may have been reached – or probably not!

 Does the process of globalisation mean that the role of the WTO is becoming less and less important?

[1] 'Global policy without democracy' (speech by Pascal Lamy, EU Trade Commissioner, given in 2001).

WTO rules

The WTO requires its members to operate according to various rules. These include the following:

- Non-discrimination. Under the 'most favoured nations clause', any trade concession that a country makes to one member must be granted to *all* signatories. The only exception is with free-trade areas and customs unions (such as the EU). Here countries are permitted to abolish tariffs between themselves while still maintaining them with the rest of the world.
- Reciprocity. Any nation benefiting from a tariff reduction made by another country must reciprocate by making similar tariff reductions itself.
- The general prohibition of quotas.
- Fair competition. If unfair barriers are erected against a particular country, the WTO can sanction retaliatory action by that country. The country is not allowed, however, to take such action without permission.
- Binding tariffs. Countries cannot raise existing tariffs without negotiating with their trading partners.

Unlike the GATT, the WTO has the power to impose sanctions on countries breaking trade agreements. If there are disputes between member nations, these will be settled by the WTO, and if an offending country continues to impose trade restrictions, permission will be granted for other countries to retaliate.

For example, in March 2002 the Bush administration imposed tariffs on steel imports into the USA in order to protect the ailing US steel industry (see Case Study 24.7 in MyEconLab). The EU and other countries referred the case to the WTO, which in December 2003 ruled that they were illegal. This ruling made it legitimate for the EU and other countries to impose retaliatory tariffs on US products. President Bush consequently announced that the steel tariffs would be abolished.

 Could US action to protect its steel industry from foreign competition be justified in terms of the interests of the USA as a whole (as opposed to the steel industry in particular)?

The greater power of the WTO has persuaded many countries to bring their disputes to it. From January 1995 to April 2014 the WTO had considered, or was considering, 474 disputes (compared with 300 by GATT over the whole of its 48 years).

Trade rounds

Periodically, member countries have met to negotiate reductions in tariffs and other trade restrictions. There have been eight 'rounds' of such negotiations since the signing of GATT in 1947. The last major round to be completed was the Uruguay Round, which began in Uruguay in 1986, continued at meetings around the world and culminated in a deal being signed in April 1994. By that time, the average tariff on manufactured products was 4 per cent and falling. In 1947 the figure was nearly 40 per cent. The Uruguay Round agreement also involved a programme of phasing in substantial reductions in tariffs and other restrictions up to the year 2002 (see Case Study 24.2 in MyEconLab).

Despite the reduction in tariffs, many countries have still tried to restrict trade by various other means, such as quotas and administrative barriers. Also, barriers have been particularly high on certain non-manufactures. Agricultural protection in particular has come in for sustained criticism by developing countries. High fixed prices and subsidies given to farmers in the EU, the USA and other advanced countries mean that the industrialised world continues to export food to many developing countries that have a comparative advantage in food production! Farmers in developing countries often find it impossible to compete with subsidised food imports from the rich countries.

The most recent round of trade negotiations began in Doha, Qatar, in 2001 (see Box 24.8). The negotiations have focused on both trade liberalisation and measures to encourage development of poorer countries. In particular, the Doha Development Agenda, as it is called, is concerned with measures to make trade fairer so that its benefits are spread more evenly around the world. This would involve improved access for developing countries to markets in the rich world. The Agenda is also concerned with the environmental impacts of trade and development.

The negotiations were originally due to be completed in 2005, but, as Box 24.8 explains, deadlines continued to be missed. December 2013, however, saw a series of agreements at a WTO ministerial conference in Bali. The so-called Bali Package included commitments to streamline trade, boost trade among least developing countries and provide 'food security' for developing countries. The deal was proclaimed as the first substantial agreement since the WTO was formed in 1995. Nonetheless, considerable work remained in meeting the goals set in Doha.

Section summary

1. Countries use various methods to restrict trade, including tariffs, quotas, exchange controls, import licensing, export taxes, and legal and administrative barriers. Countries may also promote their own industries by subsidies.

2. Reasons for restricting trade that have some validity in a world context include the infant industry argument; the inflexibility of markets in responding to changing comparative advantage, dumping and other unfair

trade practices; the danger of the establishment of a foreign-based monopoly; the problems of relying on exporting goods whose market is growing slowly or even declining; the need to spread the risks of fluctuating export prices; and the problems that free trade may adversely affect consumer tastes, may allow the importation of harmful goods and may not take account of externalities.

3. Often, however, the arguments for restricting trade are in the context of one country benefiting even though other countries may lose more. Countries may intervene in trade in order to exploit their monopoly/monopsony power. In the case of imports, the optimum tariff would be that which would reduce consumption to the level where price was equal to the country's marginal cost. In the case of exports, the optimum export tax would be that which reduced production to the level where the country's marginal revenue was equal to marginal cost. Other 'beggar-my-neighbour' arguments include the protection of declining industries and improving the balance of payments.

4. Finally, a country may have other objectives in restricting trade, such as remaining self-sufficient in certain strategic products, not trading with certain countries of

which it disapproves, protecting traditional ways of life or simply retaining a non-specialised economy.

5. In general, trade brings benefits to countries, and protection to achieve one objective may be at a very high opportunity cost. Other things being equal, there will be a net loss in welfare from restricting trade, with any gain in government revenue or profits to firms being outweighed by a loss in consumer surplus. Even if government intervention to protect certain parts of the economy is desirable, restricting trade is unlikely to be a first-best solution to the problem, since it involves side-effect costs. What is more, restricting trade may have adverse world multiplier effects; it may encourage retaliation; it may allow inefficient firms to remain inefficient; it may involve considerable bureaucracy and possibly even corruption.

6. Most countries of the world are members of the WTO and in theory are in favour of moves towards freer trade. The Uruguay Round brought significant reductions in trade restrictions, both tariff and non-tariff. Nevertheless, countries have been very unwilling to abandon restrictions if they believe that they can gain from them, even though they might be at the expense of other countries.

24.3 PREFERENTIAL TRADING

The world economy seems to have been increasingly forming into a series of trade blocs, based upon regional groupings of countries: a European region centred on the European Union, an Asian region on Japan, a North American region on the USA and a Latin American region. Such trade blocs are examples of *preferential trading arrangements*. These arrangements involve trade restrictions with the rest of the world, and lower or zero restrictions between the members.

Although trade blocs clearly encourage trade between their members, many countries outside the blocs complain that they benefit the members at the expense of the rest of the world. For many developing economies, in need of access to the most prosperous nations in the world, this represents a significant check on their ability to grow and develop.

Types of preferential trading arrangement

There are three possible forms of such trading arrangements.

Free-trade areas
A *free-trade area* is where member countries remove tariffs and quotas between themselves, but retain whatever restrictions *each member chooses* with non-member countries. Some provision will have to be made to prevent imports from outside coming into the area via the country with the lowest external tariff.

Customs unions
A *customs union* is like a free-trade area, but in addition members must adopt *common* external tariffs and quotas with non-member countries.

Common markets
A *common market* is where member countries operate as a *single* market. As with a customs union, there are no tariffs and quotas between member countries and there are common external tariffs and quotas. But a common market goes further than this. A full common market includes the following features:

Definitions

Preferential trading arrangements A trade agreement whereby trade between the signatories is freer than trade with the rest of the world.

Free trade area A group of countries with no trade barriers between themselves.

Customs union A free-trade area with common external tariffs and quotas.

Common market A customs union where the member countries act as a single market with free movement of labour and capital, common taxes and common trade laws.

- *A common system of taxation.* In the case of a *perfect* common market, this will involve identical rates of tax in all member countries.
- *A common system of laws and regulations governing production, employment and trade.* For example, in a perfect common market, there would be a *single* set of laws governing issues such as product specification (e.g. permissible artificial additives to foods, or levels of exhaust emissions from cars), the employment and dismissal of labour, mergers and takeovers, and monopolies and restrictive practices.
- *Free movement of labour, capital and materials, and of goods and services.* In a perfect common market, this will involve a total absence of border controls between member states, the freedom of workers to work in any member country and the freedom of firms to expand into any member state.
- *The absence of special treatment by member governments of their own domestic industries.* Governments are large purchasers of goods and services. In a perfect common market, they should buy from whichever companies within the market offer the most competitive deal and not show favouritism towards domestic suppliers: they should operate a common procurement policy.

The definition of a common market is sometimes extended to include the following two features of *economic and monetary union*:

- *A fixed exchange rate between the member countries' currencies.* In the extreme case, this would involve a single currency for the whole market.
- *Common macroeconomic policies.* To some extent, this must follow from a fixed exchange rate, but in the extreme case it will involve a single macroeconomic management of the whole market, and hence the abolition of separate fiscal or monetary intervention by individual member states.

We will examine European economic and monetary union in section 26.2.

The direct effects of a customs union: trade creation and trade diversion

By joining a customs union (or free-trade area), a country will find that its trade patterns change. Two such changes can be distinguished: trade creation and trade diversion.

Trade creation
Trade creation is where consumption shifts from a high-cost producer to a low-cost producer. The removal of trade barriers allows greater specialisation according to comparative advantage. Instead of consumers having to pay high prices for domestically produced goods in which the country has a comparative disadvantage, the goods can now be obtained more cheaply from other members of the customs union. In return, the country can export to them goods in which it has a comparative advantage.

For example, suppose that the most efficient producer in the world of good x is France. Assume that, before it joined the EU in 2004, Poland had to pay tariffs on good x from France. After joining the EU, however, it was then able to import good x from France without paying tariffs. There was a gain to Polish consumers. This gain is illustrated in Figure 24.12. Curves S_{Pol} and D_{Pol} show the domestic supply and demand curves in Poland. The diagram assumes, for simplicity, that Poland is a price taker as an importer of good x from France: the EU price is given.

The diagram shows that, before joining the EU, Poland had to pay the EU price *plus* the tariff (i.e. P_1). At P_1 Poland produced Q_2, consumed Q_1 and thus imported $Q_1 - Q_2$. With the removal of tariffs, the price fell to P_2. Consumption increased to Q_3 and production fell to Q_4. Imports thus increased to $Q_3 - Q_4$. Trade had been created.

The gain in welfare from the removal of the tariff is also illustrated in Figure 24.12. A reduction in price from P_1 to P_2 leads to an increase in Polish consumer surplus of areas $1 + 2 + 3 + 4$. On the other hand, there is a loss in profits to domestic producers of good x of area 1 and a loss in tariff revenue to the government of area 3. There is still a net gain, however, of areas $2 + 4$.

The increased consumption of wine in the UK after joining the EU may be seen as trade creation.

Trade diversion
Trade diversion is where consumption shifts from a lower-cost producer outside the customs union to a higher-cost producer within the union.

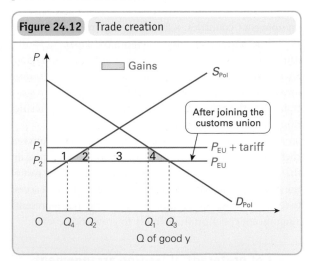

Figure 24.12 Trade creation

Definitions

Trade creation Where a customs union leads to greater specialisation according to comparative advantage and thus a shift in production from higher-cost to lower-cost sources.

Trade diversion Where a customs union diverts consumption from goods produced at a lower cost outside the union to goods produced at a higher cost (but tariff-free) within the union.

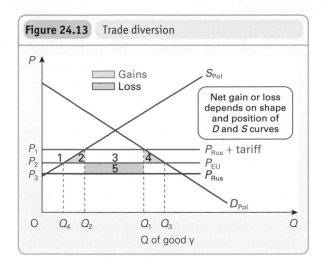

Figure 24.13 Trade diversion

Net gain or loss depends on shape and position of D and S curves

Under which of the following circumstances is there likely to be a net gain from trade diversion? (Refer to Figure 24.13.) (a) A small difference between the EU price and the Russian pre-tariff price, and a large difference between the EU price and the Russian price with the tariff, or vice versa. (b) Elastic or inelastic Polish demand and supply curves. (c) The Polish demand and supply curves close together or far apart.

A customs union is more likely to lead to trade diversion rather than trade creation:

- When the union's external tariff is very high. Under these circumstances, the abolition of the tariff within the union is likely to lead to a large reduction in the price of goods imported from other members of the union.
- When there is a relatively small cost difference between goods produced within and outside the union. Here the abolition of even relatively low tariffs within the union will lead to internally produced goods becoming cheaper than externally produced goods.

Longer-term effects of a customs union

The problem with the above analysis is that it assumes *static* demand and supply curves: in other words, supply and demand curves that are unaffected by changes in trading patterns. In reality, if a country joins a customs union, the curves are likely to shift. Membership itself affects demand and supply – perhaps beneficially, perhaps adversely.

Longer-term advantages (economic) include the following:

- Increased market size may allow a country's firms to exploit (*internal*) *economies of scale*. This argument is more important for small countries, which have therefore more to gain from an enlargement of their markets.
- *External economies of scale*. Increased trade may lead to improvements in the infrastructure of the members of the customs union (better roads, railways, financial services, etc.). This in turn could bring bigger long-term benefits from trade between members, and from external trade too, by making the transport and handling of imports and exports cheaper.
- The bargaining power of the whole customs union with the rest of the world may allow member countries to gain *better terms of trade*. This, of course, will necessarily involve a degree of political co-operation between the members.
- *Increased competition* between member countries may stimulate efficiency, encourage investment and reduce monopoly power. Of course, a similar advantage could be gained by the simple removal of tariffs with any competing country.
- Integration may encourage a *more rapid spread of technology*.

Assume that the most efficient producer of good y in the world was Russia – outside the EU. Assume that, before membership, Poland paid a similar tariff on good y from any country, and thus imported the product from Russia rather than the EU.

After joining the EU, however, the removal of the tariff made the EU product cheaper, since the tariff remained on the Russian product. Consumption thus switched to a higher-cost producer. There was thus a net loss in world efficiency. As far as Poland was concerned, consumers still gained, since they were paying a lower price than before, but this time the loss in profits to Polish producers plus the loss in tariff revenue to the Polish government might have outweighed these gains, giving a net loss.

These benefits and costs are shown in Figure 24.13. For simplicity it assumes a constant Russian and EU price (i.e. that their supply curves to Poland are infinitely elastic). The domestic supply curve (S_{Pol}) is upward sloping, and is assumed to be equal to marginal cost.

Before joining the EU, Poland was importing good y from Russia at a price P_1 (i.e. the Russian price plus the tariff). Poland thus consumed Q_1, produced Q_2 domestically and imported the remainder, $Q_1 - Q_2$. On joining the EU, it was now able to consume at the EU (tariff-free) price of P_2. (Note that this is above the tariff-free Russian price, P_3.) What are the gains and losses to Poland?

- Consumers' gain: Polish consumer surplus rises by areas $1 + 2 + 3 + 4$.
- Producers' loss: Polish producer surplus (profit) falls by area 1.
- Government's loss: previously tariffs of areas $3 + 5$ were paid. Now no tariffs are paid. The Polish government thus loses this revenue.

There is thus a net gain of areas $1 + 2 + 3 + 4$ minus areas $1 + 3 + 5$: i.e. areas $2 + 4$ minus area 5. If, however, area 5 is bigger than area $2 + 4$, there is a net loss.

TC 1
p11

When trade *diversion* takes place, therefore, there may still be a net gain, but there may be a net loss. It depends on circumstances.

Longer-term disadvantages (economic) include the following:

- *Resources may flow from a country* to more efficient members of the customs union, or to the geographical centre of the union (so as to minimise transport costs). This can be a major problem for a *common market* (where there is free movement of labour and capital). The country could become a depressed 'region' of the community, with adverse regional multiplier effects.

- If integration encourages greater co-operation between firms in member countries, it may also encourage *greater oligopolistic collusion*, thus keeping prices to the consumer higher. It may also encourage mergers and takeovers which would increase monopoly power.

- *Diseconomies of scale.* If the union leads to the development of very large companies, they may become bureaucratic and inefficient.

- The *costs of administering* the customs union may be high. The more the intervention in the affairs of individual members the worse this problem is likely to be.

It is extremely difficult to assess these arguments. To decide whether membership has been beneficial to a country requires a prediction of what things would have been like if it had not joined. No *accurate* predictions of this sort can be made, and they can never be tested. Also, many of the advantages and disadvantages are very long term, and depend on future attitudes, institutions, policies and world events, which again cannot be predicted.

In addition, some of the advantages and disadvantages are distinctly political, such as 'greater political power' or 'loss of sovereignty'.

How would you set about assessing whether or not a country had made a net long-term gain by joining a customs union? What sort of evidence would you look for?

Preferential trading in practice

Preferential trading has the greatest potential to benefit countries whose domestic market is too small, taken on its own, to enable them to benefit from economies of scale, and where they face substantial barriers to their exports. Most developing countries fall into this category, and as a result many have attempted to form preferential trading arrangements.

Examples in Latin America and the Caribbean include the Latin American Integration Association (LAIA), the Andean Community, the Central American Common Market (CACM) and the Caribbean Community (CARICOM). A Southern Common Market (MerCoSur) was formed in 1991, consisting of Argentina, Brazil, Paraguay and Uruguay. It has a common external tariff and most of its internal trade is free of tariffs.

In 1993, the six original ASEAN nations (Brunei, Indonesia, Malaysia, the Philippines, Singapore and Thailand) agreed to work towards an ASEAN Free Trade Area (AFTA). ASEAN (the Association of South-East Asian Nations) now has 10 members (the new ones being Laos, Myanmar, Vietnam and Cambodia) and is dedicated to increased economic co-operation within the region. What progress has been made in achieving AFTA? Virtually all tariffs between the six original members were eliminated by 2010 and there are plans to eliminate them for the remaining countries by 2015. ASEAN also plans to establish a common market, the ASEAN Economic Community (AEC), by 2020.

In Africa, the Economic Community of West African States (ECOWAS) has been attempting to create a common market between its 15 members. The West African franc is used in eight of the countries and another six plan to introduce a common currency, the eco, by 2015. The ultimate goal is to combine the two currency areas and adopt a single currency for all member states.

North American Free Trade Agreement (NAFTA)

Along with the EU, NAFTA is one of the two most powerful trading blocs in the world. It came into force in 1994 and consists of the USA, Canada and Mexico. These three countries agreed to abolish tariffs between themselves in the hope that increased trade and co-operation would follow. Tariffs between the USA and Canada were phased out by 1999, and tariffs between all three countries were eliminated as of 1 January 2008. New non-tariff restrictions will not be permitted either, but many existing ones can remain in force, thus preventing the development of true free trade between the members. Indeed, some industries, such as textiles and agriculture, will continue to have major non-tariff restrictions.

NAFTA members hope that, with a market similar in size to the EU, they will be able to rival the EU's economic power in world trade. Other countries may join in the future, so NAFTA may eventually develop into a Western Hemisphere free-trade association.

NAFTA is principally a free-trade area and not a common market. Unlike the EU, it does not seek to harmonise laws and regulations, except in very specific areas such as environmental management and labour standards. Member countries are permitted total legal independence, subject to the one proviso that they must treat firms of other member countries equally with their own firms – the principle of 'fair competition'. Nevertheless, NAFTA has encouraged a growth in trade between its members, most of which is trade creation rather than trade diversion.

Case Study 24.8 in MyEconLab looks at the costs and benefits of NAFTA membership to the three countries involved.

Asia-Pacific Economic Co-operation forum (APEC)

The most significant move towards establishing a more widespread regional economic organisation in east Asia appeared with the creation of the Asia-Pacific Economic

Association (APEC) in 1989. APEC links 21 economies of the Pacific Rim, including Asian, Australasian and North and South American countries (19 countries, plus Hong Kong and Taiwan). These countries account for around 55 per cent of world GDP and 45 per cent of world trade. At the 1994 meeting of APEC leaders, it was resolved to create a free-trade area across the Pacific by 2010 for the developed industrial countries, and by 2020 for the rest.

Unlike the EU and NAFTA, APEC is likely to remain solely a free-trade area and not to develop into a customs union, let alone a common market. Within the region there exists a wide disparity in GDP per capita, ranging in 2014 from $61 100 in Australia, $55 000 in the USA and $38 100 in Japan to a mere $2500 in Papua New Guinea and $2100 in Vietnam. Such disparities create a wide range of national

interests and goals. Countries are unlikely to share common economic problems or concerns. In addition, political differences and conflicts within the region are widespread, reducing the likelihood that any organisational agreement beyond a simple economic one would succeed.

The economic benefits from free trade, however, and the resulting closer regional ties, could be immense. If the whole of the US and Russian economies are included, then APEC accounts for nearly half of world trade – a truly massive trading zone.

The longest established and most comprehensive of preferential trading arrangements is the European Union. The remainder of this chapter is devoted to examining its evolution from a rather imperfect customs union to a common market (though still not perfect).

Section summary

1. Countries may make a partial movement towards free trade by the adoption of a preferential trading system. This involves free trade between the members, but restrictions on trade with the rest of the world. Such a system can be a simple free-trade area, or a customs union (where there are common restrictions with the rest of the world), or a common market (where in addition there is free movement of capital and labour, and common taxes and trade laws).

2. A preferential trading area can lead to trade creation where production shifts to low-cost producers within the area, or to trade diversion where trade shifts away from lower-cost producers outside the area to higher-cost producers within the area.

3. There is a net welfare gain from trade creation: the gain in consumer surplus outweighs the loss of tariff revenue and the loss of profit to domestic producers. With trade

diversion, however, these two losses may outweigh the gains to consumers; whether they do depends on the size of the tariffs and on the demand for and supply of the traded goods.

4. Preferential trading may bring dynamic advantages of increased external economies of scale, improved terms of trade from increased bargaining power with the rest of the world, increased efficiency from greater competition between member countries, and a more rapid spread of technology. On the other hand, it can lead to increased regional problems for members, greater oligopolistic collusion and various diseconomies of scale. There may also be large costs of administering the system.

5. There have been several attempts around the world to form preferential trading systems. The two most powerful are the European Union and the North American Free Trade Agreement (NAFTA).

24.4 THE EUROPEAN UNION

Historical background

The European Economic Community was formed by the signing of the Treaty of Rome in 1957 and came into operation on 1 January 1958.

The original six member countries of the EEC (Belgium, France, Italy, Luxembourg, the Netherlands and West Germany) had already made a move towards integration with the formation of the European Coal and Steel Community in 1952. This had removed all restrictions on trade in coal, steel and iron ore between the six countries. The aim had been to gain economies of scale and allow more effective competition with the USA and other foreign producers.

The EEC extended this principle and aimed eventually to be a full common market with completely free trade

between members in all products, and with completely free movement of labour, enterprise and capital.

All internal tariffs between the six members had been abolished and common external tariffs established by 1968. But this still only made the EEC a *customs union*, since a number of restrictions on internal trade remained (legal, administrative, fiscal, etc.). Nevertheless the aim was eventually to create a full common market.

In 1973 the UK, Denmark and Ireland became members. Greece joined in 1981, Spain and Portugal in 1986, and Sweden, Austria and Finland in 1995. In May 2004, a further 10 countries joined: Cyprus, the Czech Republic, Estonia, Hungary, Latvia, Lithuania, Malta, Poland, Slovakia and Slovenia. Bulgaria and Romania joined in 2007, before the European Union, as it is now called, reached 28 members in July 2013 with the accession of Croatia.

From customs union to common market

The EU is clearly a customs union. It has common external tariffs and no internal tariffs. But is it also a common market? For many years, there have been *certain* common economic policies.

The Common Agricultural Policy (CAP). The Union has traditionally set common high prices for farm products. This has involved charging variable import duties to bring foreign food imports up to EU prices and intervention to buy up surpluses of food produced within the EU at these above-equilibrium prices (see section 3.5). Although the main method of support has shifted to providing subsidies (or 'income support') unrelated to current output, this still represents a *common* economic policy.

Regional policy. EU regional policy provides grants to firms and local authorities in relatively deprived regions of the Union (see Case Study 23.10 in MyEconLab).

Competition policy. EU policy here has applied primarily to companies operating in more than one member state (see section 13.1). For example, Article 101 of the Treaty on the Functioning of the European Union (TFEU) prohibits agreements between firms operating in more than one EU country (e.g. over pricing or sharing out markets) which adversely affect competition in trade between member states (see pages 383–4).

Harmonisation of taxation. VAT is the standard form of indirect tax throughout the EU. However, there are substantial differences in VAT rates between member states, as there are with other tax rates.

 What would be the economic effects of (a) different rates of VAT, (b) different rates of personal income tax and (c) different rates of company taxation between member states if there were no other barriers to trade or factor movements?

Social policy. In 1989 the European Commission presented a *social charter* to the heads of state. This spelt out a series of worker and social rights that should apply in all member states (see Case Study 24.10 in MyEconLab). These rights were grouped under 12 headings covering areas such as the guarantee of decent levels of income for both the employed and the non-employed, freedom of movement of labour between member countries, freedom to belong to a trade union and equal treatment of men and women in the labour market. However, the charter was only a recommendation and each element had to be approved separately by the European Council of Ministers.

The social chapter of the Maastricht Treaty (1991) attempted to move the Community forward in implementing the details of the social charter in areas such as maximum hours, minimum working conditions, health and safety protection, information and consultation of workers, and equal opportunities.

The UK Conservative government refused to sign this part of the Maastricht Treaty. It maintained that such measures would increase costs of production and make EU goods less competitive in world trade. Critics of the UK position argued that the refusal to adopt minimum working conditions (and also a minimum wage) would make the UK the 'sweatshop' of Europe. One of the first acts of the incoming Labour government in 1997 was to sign up to the social chapter.

 Would the adoption of improved working conditions necessarily lead to higher labour costs per unit of output?

Despite these various common policies, in other respects the Community of the 1970s and 1980s was far from a true common market: there were all sorts of non-tariff barriers such as high taxes on wine by non-wine-producing countries, special regulations designed to favour domestic producers, governments giving contracts to domestic producers (e.g. for defence equipment), and so on.

The category often cited by businesses as being the most important single barrier was that of regulations and norms. In some cases, the regulations merely added to the costs of imports. But in the cases of many mechanical engineering and telecommunications products, technical and health and safety regulations sometimes ruled out foreign imports altogether.

Moves towards a single market

The Single European Act of 1986, which came into force in July 1987, sought to remove these barriers and to form a genuine common market by the end of 1992 (see Box 24.10).

One of the most crucial aspects of the Act was its acceptance of the principle of *mutual recognition*. This is the principle whereby if a firm or individual is permitted to do something under the rules and regulations of *one* EU country, it must also be permitted to do it in all other EU countries. This means that firms and individuals can choose the country's rules that are least constraining.

Mutual recognition also means that individual governments can no longer devise special rules and regulations that keep out competitors from other EU countries (see Box 24.9). Here was the answer to the dilemma of how to get all EU countries to agree to common sets of rules and regulations. All that was required was that they recognised the rules and regulations applying in each other's countries.

> ### Definition
>
> **Mutual recognition** The EU principle that one country's rules and regulations must apply throughout the EU. If they conflict with those of another country, individuals and firms should be able to choose which to obey.

| BOX 24.9 | MUTUAL RECOGNITION: THE CASSIS DE DIJON CASE | CASE STUDIES AND APPLICATIONS |

Or when is a liqueur not a liqueur?

Crème de Cassis is an alcoholic blackcurrant drink made by the French firm Cassis de Dijon. Added to white wine, it makes the drink kir. It is not just the French who like drinking kir; it is also drunk, among others, by the Germans. In this seemingly innocent fact lay the seeds for the dismantling of some of the most serious trade barriers in Europe!

The story starts back in 1978. The West German company Rewe Zentral AG wanted to import Cassis, but found that under West German law it could not. The problem was that Cassis does not contain enough alcohol to be classed as a liqueur, and it also fell outside any other category of alcoholic drink that was permitted by West German law.

But Rewe was not to be put off. It started legal proceedings in Europe to challenge the German law. The basis of Rewe's case was that this law discriminated against non-German companies. After much legal wrangling, the European Court of Justice in Luxembourg ruled that Germany had no right to prevent the importation of a product that was legitimately on sale in another member country (i.e. France). The only exceptions to this ruling would be if the product was barred for reasons of consumer protection, health or fair trade. None of these applied to Cassis, so the Germans can now drink kir to their hearts' content without having to become smugglers.

But what of the implications of the case? These are enormous and were spelt out in the Single European Act: 'the Council may decide that provisions in force in a member state must be recognised as being equivalent to those applied by another'. In other words, individuals and firms can choose which country's sets of regulations suit them the best and then insist that they be applied in all member states.

'Mutual recognition' of each other's laws tends to lead to deregulation, as people choose those countries' laws that give them the greatest freedom. This appeals to economic and political liberals. Equally, it worries those who argue that regulations and laws on industrial standards have been instituted for a purpose, and should not be undone just because some other member country has not been wise enough to institute them itself.

 How has the Cassis de Dijon ruling affected the balance of power in the EU between (a) individual states and the EU as a whole; (b) governments and the courts?

However, there was a danger that governments would end up competing against each other to provide the lightest set of regulations in order to attract firms to invest in their country. This could be to the detriment of consumers and workers.

Thus *some* common sets of rules and regulations were still required. One other feature of the Single European Act helped here. This was the institution of *majority* voting in questions of harmonisation of rules and regulations. Previously, unanimous approval had been necessary. This had meant that an individual country could veto the dismantling of barriers. This new system of majority voting, however, does not currently apply to the harmonisation of taxes, although the European Commission continues to propose that majority voting be extended to taxation while recognising that 'there is no need for across the board harmonisation' of taxes.

The benefits and costs of the single market

It is difficult to quantify the benefits and costs of the single market, given that many occur over a long period, and that it is hard to know to what extent the changes that are taking place are the direct result of the single market.

One study conducted in 1998 did, nevertheless, estimate the benefits in terms of increased consumption (see Table 24.5). This found that the benefits to the smaller, lower-income countries, such as Portugal and Greece, were the greatest. Such estimates, however, do depend crucially on the assumptions made and are thus open to substantial error.

Table 24.5	Gains from the single market

Countries	Extra consumption as % of GDP
France, Germany, UK, Italy	2–3
Denmark	2–5
Netherlands, Spain	3–4
Belgium, Luxembourg	4–5
Ireland	4–10
Greece	5–16
Portugal	19–20

Source: C. Allen, M. Gasiorek and A. Smith, 'The competition effects of the single market in Europe', *Economic Policy* (1998).

Then in 2012, the European Commission published *20 Years of the European Single Market*. This stated: 'EU27 GDP in 2008 was 2.13% or €233 billion higher than it would have been if the Single Market had not been launched in 1992. In 2008 alone, this amounted to an average of €500 extra in income per person in the EU27. The gains come from the Single Market programme, liberalisation in network industries such as energy and telecommunication, and the enlargement of the EU to 27 member countries.'

Even though the precise magnitude of the benefits is difficult to estimate, it is possible to identify the *types* of benefit that have resulted, many of which have been substantial.

Trade creation. Costs and prices have fallen as result of a greater exploitation of comparative advantage. Member countries can now specialise further in those goods and

 KI 37 p710

BOX 24.10 FEATURES OF THE SINGLE MARKET

Since 1 January 1993 trade within the EU has operated very much like trade within a country. In theory, it should be no more difficult for a firm in Birmingham to sell its goods in Paris than in London. At the same time, the single market allows free movement of labour and involves the use of common technical standards.

The features of the single market are summed up in two European Commission publications.[1] They are:

- Elimination of border controls on goods within the EU: no more long waits.
- Free movement of people across borders.
- Common security arrangements.
- No import taxes on goods bought in other member states for personal use.
- The right for everyone to live in another member state.
- Recognition of vocational qualifications in other member states: engineers, accountants, medical practitioners, teachers and other professionals able to practise throughout Europe.
- Technical standards brought into line, and product tests and certification agreed across the whole EU.
- Common commercial laws – making it attractive to form Europe-wide companies and to start joint ventures.
- Public contracts to supply equipment and services to state organisations now open to tenders across the EU.

So what does the single market mean for individuals and for businesses?

Individuals

Before 1993, if you were travelling in Europe, you had a 'duty-free allowance'. This meant that you could only take goods up to the value of €600 across borders within the EU without having to pay VAT in the country into which you were importing them. Now you can take as many goods as you like from one EU country to another, provided they are for your own consumption. But to prevent fraud, member states may ask for evidence that the goods have been purchased for the traveller's own consumption if they exceed specified amounts.

Individuals have the right to live and work in any other member state. Qualifications obtained in one member state must be recognised by other member states.

Firms

Before 1993 all goods traded in the EU were subject to VAT at every internal border. This involved some 60 million customs clearance documents at a cost of some €70 per consignment.[2]

This has all now disappeared. Goods can cross from one member state to another without any border controls; in fact, the concepts of 'importing' and 'exporting' within the EU no longer officially exist. All goods sent from one EU country to another will be charged VAT only in the country of destination. They are exempt from VAT in the country where they are produced.

One of the important requirements for fair competition in the single market is the convergence of tax rates. Although income tax rates, corporate tax rates and excise duties still differ between member states, there has been some narrowing in the range of VAT rates. Higher rates of VAT on luxury goods were abolished and countries are allowed to have no more than two lower rates of at least 5 per cent on 'socially necessary' goods, such as food and water supply.

There is now a lower limit of 15 per cent on the standard rate of VAT. Actual rates in January 2014 nonetheless varied from 15 per cent in Luxembourg to 27 per cent in Hungary. However, during the early 2010s several countries, including the UK, Ireland, Greece and Portugal, increased their standard rate of VAT as a means of reducing their budget deficits (see section 21.1). One effect of this is that the vast majority of EU countries now have a standard rate of VAT between 20 and 25 per cent.

 In what ways would competition be 'unfair' if VAT rates differed widely between member states?

---

[1] *A Single Market for Goods* (Commission of the European Communities, 1993); *10 Key Points about the Single European Market* (Commission of the European Communities, 1992).
[2] See *A Single Market for Goods* (Commission of the European Communities, 1993).

---

services that they can produce at a comparatively low opportunity cost.

Reduction in the direct costs of barriers. This category includes administrative costs, border delays and technical regulations. Their abolition or harmonisation has led in many cases to substantial cost savings.

Economies of scale. With industries based on a Europe-wide scale, many firms can now be large enough, and their plants large enough, to gain the full potential economies of scale (see Box 5.8 on pages 156–7). Yet the whole European market is large enough for there still to be adequate competition. Such gains have varied from industry to industry depending on the minimum efficient scale of a plant or firm. Economies of scale have also been gained from mergers and other forms of industrial restructuring.

Greater competition. Increased competition between firms has led to lower costs, lower prices and a wider range of products available to consumers. This has been particularly so in newly liberalised service sectors such as transport, financial services, telecommunications and broadcasting. In the long run, greater competition can stimulate greater innovation, a greater flow of technical information and the rationalisation of production.

Despite these gains, the single market has not received universal welcome within the EU. Its critics argue that, in a Europe of oligopolies, unequal ownership of resources, rapidly changing technologies and industrial practices, and factor immobility, the removal of internal barriers to trade has merely exaggerated the problems of inequality and economic power. More specifically, the following criticisms are made.

Radical economic change is costly. Substantial economic change is necessary to achieve the full economies of scale and efficiency gains from a single European market. These changes necessarily involve redundancies – from bankruptcies, takeovers, rationalisation and the introduction of new technology. The severity of this structural and technological unemployment depends on (a) the pace of economic change and (b) the mobility of labour – both occupational and geographical. Clearly, the more integrated markets become across the EU, the less the costs of *future* change.

Adverse regional multiplier effects. Firms are likely to locate as near as possible to the 'centre of gravity' of their markets and sources of supply. If, before barriers were removed, a firm's prime market was the UK, it might well have located in the Midlands or the north of England. If, however, with barriers now removed, its market has become Europe as a whole, so it may choose to locate in the south of England or in France, Germany or the Benelux countries instead. The creation of a single European market thus tends to attract capital and jobs away from the edges of the Union to its geographical centre.

In an ideal market situation, areas like Cornwall, the south of Italy or Portugal should attract resources from other parts of the Union. Since they are relatively depressed areas, wage rates and land prices are lower. The resulting lower industrial costs should encourage firms to move into the areas. In practice, regional multiplier effects may worsen the problem (see page 699). As capital and labour (and especially young and skilled workers) leave the extremities of the Union, so these regions are likely to become more depressed. If, as a result, their infrastructure is neglected, they then become even less attractive to new investment.

 Has the problem of adverse regional multiplier effects been made better or worse by the adoption of a single European currency? (This issue is explored in section 26.3.) (Clue: without a single currency, how would the devaluation of the drachma (the former Greek currency) have affected a depressed Greek economy?)

The development of monopoly/oligopoly power. The free movement of capital can encourage the development of giant 'Eurofirms' with substantial economic power. Indeed, recent years have seen some very large European mergers (see Box 8.5 on pages 236–7). This can lead to higher, not lower, prices and less choice for the consumer. It all depends on just how effective competition is, and how effective EU competition policy is in preventing monopolistic and collusive practices.

Trade diversion. Just as increased trade creation has been a potential advantage from completing the internal market, so trade diversion has been a possibility too. This is more likely if *external* barriers remain high (or are even increased) and internal barriers are *completely* abolished.

 Is trade diversion more likely or less likely in the following cases? (a) European producers gain monopoly power in world trade. (b) Modern developments in technology and communications reduce the differences in production costs associated with different locations. (c) The development of the internal market produces substantial economies of scale in many industries.

Perhaps the biggest objection raised against the single European market is a political one: the loss of national sovereignty. Governments find it much more difficult to intervene at a microeconomic level in their own economies.

 Why may the newer members of the Union have the most to gain from the single market, but also the most to lose?

Completing the internal market

Despite the reduction in barriers, the internal market is still not 'complete'. In other words, various barriers to trade between member states still remain. Thus, in June 1997, an Action Plan was adopted by the European Council. Its aim was to ensure that all barriers were dismantled by the launch of the euro in January 1999.

To monitor progress, an 'Internal Market Scoreboard' was established. This is published every six months and shows progress towards the total abandonment of any forms of internal trade restrictions (see Box 24.11). It shows the percentage of EU Single Market Directives still to be transposed into national law. In addition to giving each country's 'transposition deficit', the Scoreboard identifies the number of infringements of the internal market that have taken place. The hope is that the 'naming and shaming' of countries will encourage them to make more rapid progress towards totally free trade within the EU.

In 1997, the average transposition deficit of member countries was 6.3 per cent. By 1999, this had fallen to 3.5 per cent and by 2014 to 0.7 per cent. Despite this success, national governments have continued to introduce *new* technical standards, several of which have had the effect of erecting new barriers to trade. Also, infringements of single market rules by governments have not always been dealt with. The net result is that, although trade is much freer today than in the early 1990s, especially given the transparency of pricing with the euro, there still do exist various barriers, especially to the free movement of goods.

To counteract new barriers, the EU periodically issues new directives. If this process is more rapid than that of the transposition of existing directives into national law, the transposition deficit increases.

 If there have been clear benefits from the single market programme, why do individual member governments still try to erect barriers, such as new technical standards?

The effect of the new member states

Given the very different nature of the economies of many of the new entrants to the EU, and their lower levels of GDP per head, their potential gain from membership has been substantial. The gains come through trade creation, increased competition, technological transfer and inward investment, both from other EU countries and from outside the EU.

A study in 2004 concluded that Poland's GDP would rise by 3.4 per cent and Hungary's by almost 7 per cent.[1] Real wages would rise, with those of unskilled workers rising faster than those of skilled workers, in accordance with these countries' comparative advantage. There would also be benefits for the 15 pre-2004 members from increased

---

[1] M. Maliszewska, 'Benefits of the Single Market Expansion for current and new member states', *Centrum Analiz Społeczno-Ekonomicznych*, 2004.

BOX 24.11 THE INTERNAL MARKET SCOREBOARD

Keeping a tally on progress to a true single market

The success or otherwise of implementing EU internal market directives is measured by the Internal Market Scoreboard, which tracks the transposition (or 'implementation') deficit for each country. This is the percentage of directives that have failed to be implemented into national law by their agreed deadline.

The Scoreboard has been published every six months since 1997 and, in addition to tracking the deficit for each country, it also shows the average deficit across all EU countries. The chart shows that the average deficit was falling until May 2002, but then rose somewhat. Part of the problem is that new directives are being issued as existing ones are being implemented.

After 2004, the transposition deficit tended to fall, even with the accession of ten new members in 2004, two more in 2007 and one in 2013. An average deficit target of 1 per cent was set in 2007 and this was reached by 2008. The average deficit fell further in 2009 to 0.7 per cent but then rose to 0.9 per cent in 2010 and to 1.2 in 2011. It subsequently fell back in 2012 and 2013 to between 0.6 and 0.7 per cent.

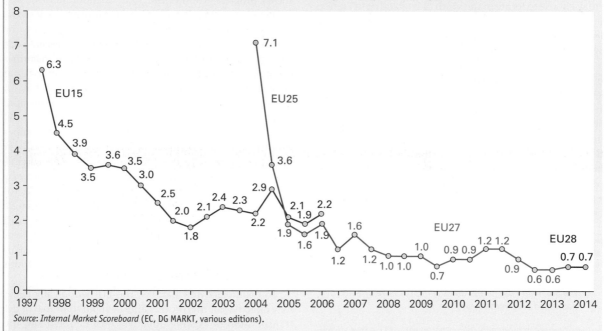

Internal Market Scoreboard: average transposition deficit

Source: *Internal Market Scoreboard* (EC, DG MARKT, various editions).

Behind the rise in the average deficit in 2010 and 2011 was a reduction in the speed with which directives were being enacted. To tackle delays, a target of 'zero tolerance' operates for delays of two years or more in transposing directives. Overly long delays are seen as impairing the functioning of the single market. In May 2011, member states took an extra 5.5 months on average to transpose EU directives after the transposition deadline has passed. By November 2011 this had risen to an extra 8 months. As of May 2014 member states were still taking an extra 7.5 months to transpose directives.

As well as the transposition deficit, the Scoreboard also measures the *compliance deficit*: the percentage of transposed directives where infringement proceedings for non-conformity have been initiated by the Commission. The target for the compliance deficit is 0.5 per cent. In November 2012 the compliance deficit was 0.6 per cent, the lowest level recorded. As of May 2014 the average compliance deficit had ticked up very slightly to 0.7 per cent. Nonetheless, this was still viewed as a 'good result'.

1. *What value are scoreboards for member states and the European Commission?*
2. *Why do you think that it is so important that legislation such as that governing the internal market is in place in all member states at the same time?*

Note: Further information and the latest statistics on the Single Market Scoreboard can be accessed at http://ec.europa.eu/internal_market/scoreboard/index_en.htm

trade and investment, but these would be relatively minor in comparison to the gains to the new members.

In future years, now that the euro is used by at least 18 of the member states, trade within the EU is likely to continue to grow as a proportion of GDP. We examine the benefits and costs of the single currency and the whole process of economic and monetary union in the EU in section 26.2.

To examine the arguments about full monetary union, we need first to look at the question of exchange rate determination and alternative exchange rate systems. This is the subject of the next chapter.

Section summary

1. The European Union is a customs union in that it has common external tariffs and no internal ones. But virtually from the outset it has also had elements of a common market, particularly in the areas of agricultural policy, regional policy, monopoly and restrictive practice policy, and to some extent in the areas of tax harmonisation and social policy.

2. Nevertheless, there have been substantial non-tariff barriers to trade within the EU, such as different tax rates, various regulations over product quality, licensing, state procurement policies, educational qualification requirements, financial barriers, various regulations and norms, and subsidies or tax relief to domestic producers.

3. The Single European Act of 1987 sought to sweep away these restrictions and to establish a genuine free market within the EU – to establish a full common market. Benefits from completing the internal market have included trade creation, cost savings from no longer having to administer barriers, economies of scale for firms now able to operate on a Europe-wide scale, and greater competition leading to reduced costs and prices, greater flows of technical information and more innovation.

4. Critics of the single market point to various changes in industrial structure that have resulted, bringing problems of redundancies and closures. They also point to adverse regional multiplier effects as resources are attracted to the geographical centre of the EU, to possible problems of market power with the development of giant 'Euro-firms', and to the possibilities of trade diversion.

5. The actual costs and benefits of EU membership to the various countries vary with their particular economic circumstances – for example, the extent to which they gain from trade creation, or lose from adverse regional multiplier effects and with their contributions to and receipts from the EU budget.

6. These cost and benefits in the future will depend on just how completely the barriers to trade are removed, on the extent of monetary union and on any further enlargements to the Union.

END OF CHAPTER QUESTIONS

1. Imagine that two countries, Richland and Poorland, can produce just two goods, computers and coal. Assume that for a given amount of land and capital, the output of these two products requires the following constant amounts of labour:

	Richland	Poorland
1 computer	2	4
100 tonnes of coal	4	5

Assume that each country has 20 million workers.

(a) Draw the production possibility curves for the two countries (on two separate diagrams).

(b) If there is no trade, and in each country 12 million workers produce computers and 8 million workers produce coal, how many computers and tonnes of coal will each country produce? What will be the total production of each product?

(c) What is the opportunity cost of a computer in (i) Richland; (ii) Poorland?

(d) What is the opportunity cost of 100 tonnes of coal in (i) Richland; (ii) Poorland?

(e) Which country has a comparative advantage in which product?

(f) Assuming that price equals marginal cost, which of the following would represent possible exchange ratios?
   (i) 1 computer for 40 tonnes of coal;
   (ii) 2 computers for 140 tonnes of coal;
   (iii) 1 computer for 100 tonnes of coal;
   (iv) 1 computer for 60 tonnes of coal;
   (v) 4 computers for 360 tonnes of coal.

(g) Assume that trade now takes place and that a computer exchanges for 65 tonnes of coal. Both countries specialise completely in the product in which they have a comparative advantage. How much does each country produce of its respective product?

(h) The country producing computers sells 6 million domestically. How many does it export to the other country?

(i) How much coal does the other country consume?

(j) Construct a table like Table 24.4 to show the no-trade and with-trade positions of each country.

2. If capital moves from developed to less developed countries, and labour moves from less developed to developed countries, what effects will these factor movements have on wage rates and the return on capital in the two types of country?

3. What factors determine a country's terms of trade?

4. Go through each of the arguments for restricting trade (both those of general validity and those having some validity for specific countries) and provide a counter-argument for not restricting trade.

5. If countries are so keen to reduce the barriers to trade, why do many countries frequently attempt to erect barriers?

6. What factors will determine whether a country's joining a customs union will lead to trade creation or trade diversion?

7. Why is it difficult to estimate the magnitude of the benefits of completing the internal market of the EU?

8. Look through the costs and benefits that we identified from the completion of the internal market. Do the same costs and benefits arise from the enlarged EU of 28 members?

Online resources

Additional case studies in MyEconLab

24.1 **David Ricardo and the law of comparative advantage.** The original statement of the law of comparative advantage by David Ricardo back in 1817.

24.2 **The Uruguay round.** An examination of the negotiations that led to substantial cuts in trade barriers.

24.3 **The World Trade Organization.** This looks at the various opportunities and threats posed by this major international organisation.

24.4 **The Battle of Seattle.** This looks at the protests against the WTO at Seattle in November 1999 and considers the arguments for and against the free-trade policies of the WTO.

24.5 **Banana, banana.** The dispute between the USA and the EU over banana imports.

24.6 **Beyond bananas.** Other US/EU trade disputes.

24.7 **Steel barriers.** This examines the use of tariffs by the George W. Bush administration in 2002 to protect the ailing US steel industry.

24.8 **Assessing NAFTA.** Who are the winners and losers from NAFTA?

24.9 **Strategic trade theory.** The case of Airbus.

24.10 **The social dimension of the EU.** The principles of the social charter.

24.11 **The benefits of the single market.** Evidence of achievements and the Single Market Action Plan of 1997.

Websites relevant to this chapter

Numbers and sections refer to websites listed in the Web Appendix and hotlinked from this book's website at **www.pearsoned.co.uk/sloman**.

- For news articles relevant to this chapter, see the *Economic News* section in MyEconLab.

- For general news on international trade, see websites in section A, and particularly A1–5, 7–9, 24, 25, 31. See also links to newspapers worldwide in A38, 39, 42, 43 and 44, and the news search feature in Google at A41.

- For international data on imports and exports, see site H16 > *Documents and Resources* > *Statistics*. See also *World Economic Outlook* in H4. See also the trade topic in I14. The ESDS International site (B35) has links to World Bank, IMF, OECD, UN and Eurostat datasets (but you will need to register, which is free to all UK higher education students).

- For UK data, see B1, 1. *National Statistics* > *Browse by theme* > *Economy*. See also B34. For EU data, see B38 > *Economic Forecasts (latest)*, Tables 45 to 60; see also B49 (*Ameco online*) sections 9 to 11.

- For discussion papers on trade, see H4 and 7.

- For trade disputes, see H16.

- For various pressure groups critical of the effects of free trade and globalisation, see H13, 14.

- For information on various preferential trading arrangements, see H20–23.

- For EU sites, see G1, 3, 7–14, 16–19.

- Site 17 contains links to various topics in *International economics* (*International trade*, *International agreements*, *Economic co-operation* and *EU Economics*). Site 12 gives links to various international organisations.

- For student resources relevant to this chapter, see sites C1–7, 9, 10, 19.

MyEconLab

This book can be supported by MyEconLab, which contains a range of additional resources, including an online homework and tutorial system designed to test and build your understanding.

You need both an access card and a course ID to access MyEconLab:

1. Is your lecturer using MyEconLab? Ask your lecturer for your course ID.

2. Has an access card been included with the book at a reduced cost? Check the inside back cover of the book.

3. If you have a course ID but no access card, go to: http://www.myeconlab.com/ to buy access to this interactive study programme.

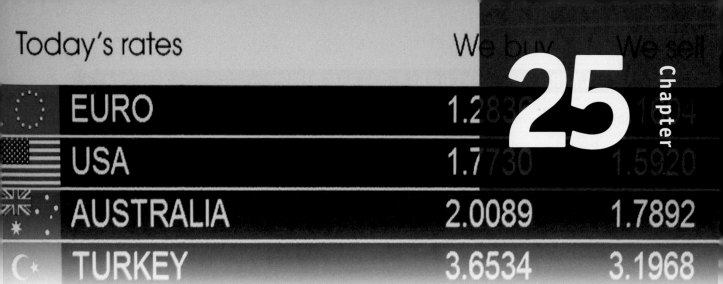

Today's rates

We buy   We sell

EURO	1.2830	1.0 4
USA	1.7730	1.5920
AUSTRALIA	2.0089	1.7892
TURKEY	3.6534	3.1968

25 Chapter

The Balance of Payments and Exchange Rates

CHAPTER MAP

25.1 Alternative exchange rate regimes	**742**
Policy objectives: internal and external	742
Nominal and real exchange rates	743
Alternative exchange rate regimes	745
Correction under fixed exchange rates	746
Correction under free-floating exchange rates	749
Intermediate exchange rate regimes	750
25.2 Fixed exchange rates	**752**
*Effects of shocks under fixed exchange rates	752
Causes of longer-term balance of payments problems under fixed exchange rates	753
Advantages of fixed exchange rates	754
Disadvantages of fixed exchange rates	754
25.3 Free-floating exchange rates	**757**
Floating exchange rates and the freeing of domestic policy	757
Response to shocks under a floating rate	757
Speculation	760
Advantages of a free-floating exchange rate	761
Disadvantages of a free-floating exchange rate	761
Conclusion	765
25.4 Exchange rate systems in practice	**765**
The adjustable peg system: 1945–73	765
Managed floating	767
Problems with managed floating since 1972	767
The volatility of exchange rates	769
*Appendix: The Open economy *IS/LM* analysis	**772**
Analysis under a fixed exchange rate	772
Fiscal policy under fixed exchange rates	773
Monetary policy under fixed exchange rates	774
Analysis under free-floating exchange rates	774
Fiscal policy under floating exchange rates	775
Monetary policy under floating exchange rates	775

We live in a world in which events in one country or group of countries can have profound effects on other countries. Look at what happened in 2007–8. Excessive sub-prime mortgage lending in the USA led to huge losses for many financial institutions. With such debt securitised into bonds held by financial institutions across the world, the credit crunch rapidly became global.

As globalisation has increased, with trade and international financial movements growing much more rapidly than countries' GDP, and becoming much freer at the same time, so countries' vulnerability to balance of payments problems and exchange rate fluctuations has increased.

This chapter explores the relationships between a country's balance of payments and its exchange rate. In particular, we ask whether a country should allow its exchange rate to be determined entirely by market forces, with the possible instability that this brings, or whether it should attempt to fix its exchange rate to another currency (such as the US dollar), or at the very least attempt to reduce exchange rate fluctuations through central bank intervention in the foreign exchange market. We also look at the experience of countries in operating different types of exchange rate system.

25.1 ALTERNATIVE EXCHANGE RATE REGIMES

Policy objectives: internal and external

A country is likely to have various *internal* and *external policy objectives*. *Internal* objectives include such things as economic growth, low unemployment and low inflation. *External* objectives include such things as avoiding current account balance of payments deficits, encouraging international trade and preventing excessive exchange rate fluctuations. Internal and external objectives may come into conflict, however.

KI 34
p404

A simple illustration of potential conflict is with the objectives of *internal balance* and *external balance*.

Internal balance. **Internal balance** is where the economy is at the potential level of national income: i.e. where the output gap is zero (see Box 14.3 on page 414). This can be expressed in various ways, depending on the model of the economy and the policy objectives being pursued.

Thus, in the simple Keynesian model, internal balance is where the economy is at the *full-employment* level of national income: i.e. where Y_e (equilibrium national income) = Y_f (full-employment national income) (see Chapter 17). In the monetarist and new classical models, it would be where the economy is on the vertical Phillips curve with stable inflation. In the context of inflation targeting, it would be where meeting the inflation target is consistent with achieving potential national income: i.e. where the *ADI* crosses the *ASI* curve at the targeted inflation rate (see Figure 19.17 on page 584).

If there is initially internal balance and then aggregate demand falls, in the short run output will fall below the potential level and disequilibrium unemployment will occur. Internal balance will be destroyed. The stickier wages and prices are, the longer it will take for internal balance to be restored.

External balance. **External balance** is the term for a *balance of payments* equilibrium. In the context of floating exchange rates, it is normally used in the narrow sense of a current account balance, and therefore also a capital plus financial account balance.

In the context of a fixed exchange rate, or an exchange rate target, it is often used more loosely to refer merely to a *total currency flow balance*. This is where the total demand and supply of the currency are equal at the targeted exchange rate with *no need for intervention from the reserves*: in other words, where any current account deficit is matched by a surplus on the other two accounts, and vice versa.

Conflicts between internal and external balance

It may, however, be difficult to achieve internal and external balance simultaneously. This is illustrated in Figure 25.1. Assume in Figure 25.1(b) that the exchange rate is er_1.

Currency demand and supply curves are given by D and S_1 and there is no central bank intervention. Thus er_1 is the *equilibrium* exchange rate and there is external balance in the loose sense. Assume also that there is external balance in the narrow sense: i.e. a current account balance.

Let us also assume, however, that there is a recession. This is illustrated in Figure 25.1(a). Equilibrium national income is Y_{e_1}, where W_1 equals J_1. There is a deflationary gap: Y_{e_1} is below the full-employment level, Y_F. There is no *internal* balance.

Now assume that the government expands aggregate demand through fiscal policy in order to close the deflationary gap and restore internal balance. It raises injections to J_2 and reduces withdrawals to W_2. National income rises to Y_{e_2}. But this higher national income leads to an increased demand for imports. The supply of sterling will shift to S_2 in Figure 25.1(b). There is now a current account deficit, which destroys external balance in the narrow sense. If the government maintains the exchange rate at er_1 (by buying sterling from the reserves), external balance will be destroyed in the loose sense too.

External balance in the loose sense could be restored by allowing the exchange rate to depreciate to er_2, so that the demand and supply of sterling are equated at the new lower exchange rate.

TC 4
p47

But will this also correct the current account deficit and restore external balance in the narrow sense? It will go *some* way to correcting the deficit, as the lower exchange rate will make imports relatively more expensive and exports relatively cheaper. The amount that imports fall and exports rise will depend on their price elasticity of demand.

TC 7
p72

But there may also be an effect on the financial account. The higher aggregate demand will lead to a higher demand for money. This will drive up interest rates unless money supply is allowed to expand to offset the higher demand for money. If interest rates rise, this will lead to an inflow of finance (a financial account surplus). In Figure 25.1(b), the

Definitions

Internal policy objectives Objectives relating solely to the domestic economy.

External policy objectives Objectives relating to the economy's international economic relationships.

Internal balance Where the equilibrium level of national income is at the desired level.

External balance Narrow definition: where the current account of the balance of payments is in balance (and thus also the capital plus financial accounts). Loose definition: where there is a total currency flow balance at a given exchange rate.

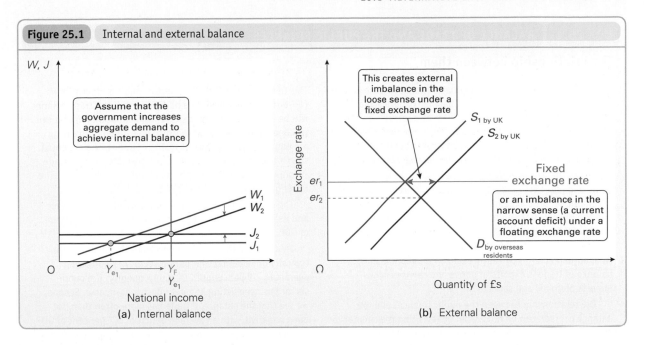

Figure 25.1 Internal and external balance

(a) Internal balance

(b) External balance

supply curve of sterling would shift to the left and the demand curve to the right. The exchange rate would not fall as far, therefore, as er_2. If the positive effect of higher interest rates on the financial account was bigger than the negative effect of higher imports on the current account, the exchange rate would actually *appreciate*.

Either way, there will be a current account deficit and an equal and opposite financial plus capital account surplus. Narrow external balance has not been restored in the short term. (We explore the long-term current account balance under floating exchange rates in section 25.3.)

Figure 25.2 shows the effect of various 'shocks' that can affect both internal and narrow external balance.

1. *Assume that there is both internal and narrow external balance. Now assume that as a result of inflation being below target, the central bank cuts interest rates. Into which of the four quadrants in Figure 25.2 will the economy move?*
2. *Imagine that there is an inflationary gap, but a current account equilibrium. Describe what will happen if the government raises interest rates in order to close the inflationary gap. Assume first that there is a fixed exchange rate; then assume that there is a floating exchange rate.*

The ability of the economy to correct these imbalances depends on the *exchange rate regime*. We examine alterna-

Figure 25.2 Effects on internal and (narrow) external balance

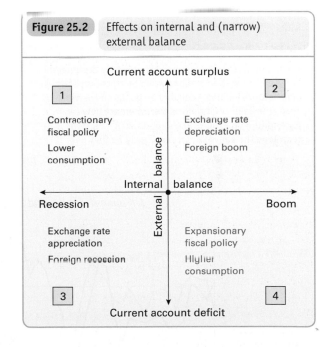

tive exchange rate regimes in the final part of this section, but first we must distinguish between nominal and real exchange rates.

Nominal and real exchange rates

A nominal exchange rate is simply the rate at which one currency exchanges for another. All exchange rates that you see quoted in the newspapers, on television or the Internet, or at travel agents, banks or airports, are nominal rates. Up to this point we have solely considered nominal rates.

Definition

Exchange rate regime The system under which the government allows the exchange rate to be determined.

BOX 25.1 BALANCE OF TRADE AND THE PUBLIC FINANCES

The relationship between them

We have seen that the external situation can affect the ability of an economy to achieve internal balance (where actual income is at the potential level). But it also impacts on the composition of aggregate demand. This is most readily demonstrated by observing the relationship between the *public sector's budget balance* and *the balance of trade*.

A measure of the budget balance is *public sector net borrowing* (see section 21.1). This is the difference between the public sector's expenditure and the receipts from taxation and the revenues of public corporations. The balance of trade is one of three principal items that comprise the balance of the current account; the other two are net investment income from abroad and net current transfers (see section 15.4). The balance of trade is exports of goods and services minus imports of goods and services ($X - M$).

The relationship between the public finances and the balance of trade can be illustrated by revisiting the circular flow of income that we introduced in Chapter 14. There we saw that actual (as opposed to planned) withdrawals from the circular flow (net saving (S) plus net taxes (T) plus imports (M)) must equal injections (investment (I) plus government expenditure (G) plus exports (X)):

$$S + T + M = I + G + X \qquad (1)$$

The public sector's budget balance is simply the difference between its taxation and operating receipts (net of transfer expenditures) and its spending on goods and services, or $T - G$. The balance of trade is the difference between expenditure on exports and imports, or $X - M$. If we rearrange the above condition slightly we find

$$(T - G) = (X - M) + (I - S) \qquad (2)$$

This tells us that if the public sector runs a budget surplus ($T - G$ is positive), there is a likelihood that the trade balance will be in surplus too. We can see from equation (2) that this will depend on the extent to which investment and saving are equal. In the case that investment and saving are equal then a budget surplus would be exactly matched by a trade surplus, or a budget deficit by an identical trade deficit. The latter gives rise to the term 'the twin deficits'.

The chart plots the UK's public sector's budget balance and its balance of trade. Each is presented as a percentage of GDP.

First, we see that from 1955 to 2013 the public sector typically ran a deficit with public-sector net borrowing averaging 2.9 per cent of GDP. Consequently, the public sector has been acting as a net injector of income. Second, we see that the balance of trade has more often than not been negative, with an average deficit of 0.7 per cent of GDP.

The size of the net withdrawal from the trade deficit does not quite match the net injection from the public sector. This means that private-sector investment expenditure has been less than private saving ($I < S$). It also reinforces the arguments that we examined in Chapters 16 and 21 that public-sector deficits can reduce private investment. This is known as crowding out. In the UK, public-sector borrowing has been financed partly through foreign borrowing from running a trade deficit and partly from the private saving that is not used for private investment.

 If the exchange rate depreciated, how would this affect the trade and budget balances?

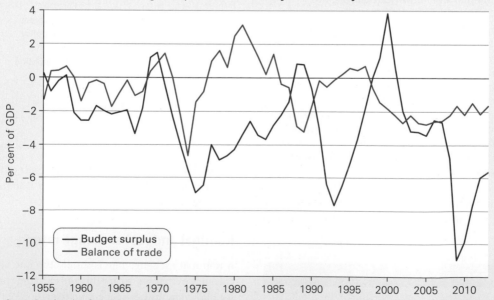

UK budget surplus and balance of trade as % of GDP

Source: Based on data from *Balance of Payments Quarterly First Release*, *Public Sector Finances First Release* and *Quarterly National Accounts* (National Statistics).

The *real exchange rate* is the exchange rate index adjusted for changes in the prices of imports (measured in foreign currencies) and exports (measured in domestic prices) – in other words, adjusted for the terms of trade. Thus if a country has a higher rate of inflation for its exports than the weighted average inflation of the imports it buys from other countries, its real exchange rate index (RERI) will rise relative to its nominal exchange rate index (NERI).

The real exchange rate index can be defined as

$$RERI = NERI \times P_X/P_M$$

where P_X is the domestic currency price index of exports and P_M is the foreign currencies weighted price index of imports. Thus if (a) a country's inflation is 5 per cent higher than the trade-weighted average of its trading partners (P_X/P_M rises by 5 per cent per year) and (b) its nominal exchange rate depreciates by 5 per cent per year (NERI falls by 5 per cent per year), its real exchange rate index will stay the same.

Take another example: if a country's export prices rise faster than the foreign currency prices of its imports (P_X/P_M rises), its real exchange rate will appreciate relative to its nominal exchange rate.

The real exchange rate thus gives us a better idea of the *quantity* of imports a country can obtain from selling a given quantity of exports. If the real exchange rate rises, the country can get more imports for a given volume of exports.

Figure 25.3 shows the nominal and real exchange rate indices of sterling. As you can see, the real exchange rate has tended to rise over time relative to the nominal exchange rate. This is because the UK has typically had a higher rate of inflation than the weighted average of its trading partners.

The real exchange rate also gives a better idea than the nominal exchange rate of how competitive a country is. The lower the real exchange rate, the more competitive will the country's exports be. Figure 25.3 shows that the UK became less competitive between 1996 and 2001, and remained at similarly uncompetitive levels until 2008, thanks not only to a rise in the nominal exchange rate index, but also to higher inflation than its trading partners.

Alternative exchange rate regimes

There are a number of possible exchange rate regimes. They all lie somewhere between two extremes. These two extreme regimes are a *totally fixed rate* and a *freely floating rate*.

In the case of a *fixed rate*, the government or central bank will almost certainly have to intervene in the foreign

---

Definitions

Exchange rate (real) A country's exchange rate adjusted for changes in the domestic currency prices of its exports relative to the foreign currency prices of its imports. If a country's prices rise (fall) relative to those of its trading partners, its real exchange rate will rise (fall) relative to the nominal exchange rate.

Fixed exchange rate (totally) Where the government takes whatever measures are necessary to maintain the exchange rate at some stated level.

Freely floating exchange rate Where the exchange rate is determined entirely by the forces of demand and supply in the foreign exchange market with no government intervention whatsoever.

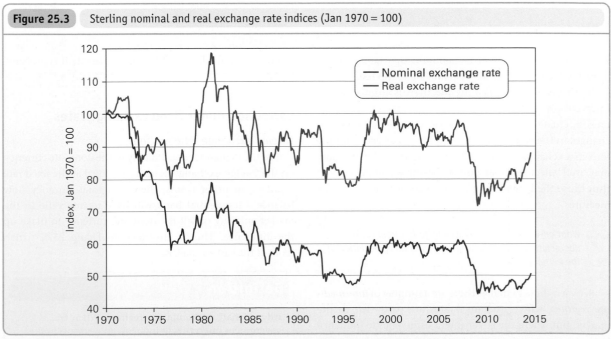

Figure 25.3 Sterling nominal and real exchange rate indices (Jan 1970 = 100)

Note: Exchange rate indices are BIS narrow indices comprising 27 countries, re-based by authors, Jan 1970 = 100.
Source: Based on data from Bank for International Settlements.

BOX 25.2   THE UK'S BALANCE OF PAYMENTS DEFICIT

A cyclical problem or a long-term trend?

In the late 1980s, the UK current account balance of payments moved sharply into deficit, as the chart shows. In 1989 the current account deficit was 4.6 per cent of GDP – the highest percentage ever recorded. Opinions differed dramatically, however, as to how seriously we should have taken these figures. Not surprisingly, the government claimed that the problem was merely temporary and was not something to cause serious concern. The opposition parties (also not surprisingly) saw the figures as disastrous and a sign that the economy was badly off-course.

So who was correct? In fact there was an element of truth in both these claims.

The government was correct to the extent that the severity of the deficit partly reflected the unprecedented boom of the late 1980s. An average growth rate of real GDP of 4 per cent between 1984 and 1988 had led to a huge increase in imports. Since the boom could not be sustained, the growth in imports was bound to slow down. Another factor contributing to the deficit was the fall in oil revenues caused by a fall in oil prices. Oil exports fell from £16.1 billion in 1985 to £5.9 billion in 1989. Again, this fall in oil revenues was unlikely to continue once oil prices began to rise again. The current account deficit was also a mirror image of the financial account surplus. This had been caused by a rise in interest rates, used to slow the economy down. As short-term finance flowed into the country to take advantage of the higher interest rate, so this drove the exchange rate up (see Table 15.5 on page 456). The higher exchange rate contributed to the fall in exports and the rise in imports.

But the opposition parties were also correct. The severity of the deficit reflected an underlying weakness of the UK's trading position. If the deficit had been merely a cyclical problem associated with the boom phase of the business cycle, the current account should have gone into *surplus* in the early 1990s as the economy moved into recession. But even in the depths of the recession in 1991, the current account deficit was still 1.4 per cent of GDP.

The government, however, sought to place a large portion of the blame on a falling demand for exports as the rest of the world began to move into recession.

Subsequent events appeared to support the Conservative government's interpretation. The world economy was recovering in 1994 and the current account deficit virtually disappeared. But then, with a large appreciation of sterling from 1996, and an even larger appreciation of the real exchange rate (see Figure 25.3), the current account started to deteriorate again, as the diagram shows. Optimists claimed that this was, once more, simply a temporary situation, caused by a high exchange rate and low growth in demand in the eurozone.

But, with a considerable worsening of the current account from 2008 to 2013, despite a large nominal and real depreciation of sterling (again see Figure 25.3), pessimists again pointed to a much deeper malaise in the UK exporting sector – that successive supply-side reforms had made too little difference.

Rebalancing the economy?

The Coalition government after 2010 stressed the need for a 'rebalancing' of the economy towards greater exports and investment. By 2013 Q3, however, the current account deficit had reached a record 5.6 per cent of GDP. The deficit on goods was also at a record 7.3 per cent of GDP, well above the average since 2000 of 5.5 per cent.

With the economy still recovering slowly, it would normally be expected that the trade deficit would be low. However, the exchange rate was now rising and this made it difficult for UK

---

exchange market in order to maintain that rate, and will probably have to take internal policy measures too.

In the case of a *freely floating rate*, there is no government intervention in the foreign exchange market. Exchange rates fluctuate according to market forces – according to changes in the demand for and supply of currencies on the foreign exchange market. Changes in the exchange rate may well affect internal policy objectives, however, and thus cause the government to take various internal policy measures.

> *What adverse internal effects may follow from (a) a depreciation of the exchange rate; (b) an appreciation of the exchange rate?*

Between these extremes there are a number of *intermediate regimes*, where exchange rates are partly left to the market, but where the government intervenes to influence the rate. These intermediate regimes differ according to how much the government intervenes, and thus according

to how much flexibility of the exchange rate it is prepared to allow.

Correction under fixed exchange rates

Foreign exchange intervention

Unless the demand for and supply of the domestic currency on the foreign exchange markets are equal at the fixed rate – unless, in other words, there is a total currency flow balance – the central bank will have to intervene in the market and buy or sell the domestic currency to make up the difference. This is illustrated in Figure 25.4, which looks at the case of the UK.

Definition

Intermediate exchange rate regimes Where the government intervenes to influence movements in the exchange rate.

exporters to compete. Also, with consumer confidence returning, imports were rising, again boosted by the appreciating exchange rate, which made imports cheaper.

The most dramatic change was in transfers and income flows (see chart) and particularly those from investment. Before the crash in late 2008, the returns to many of the risky investments abroad made by UK financial institutions were very high. From 2012 they then became negative

as UK institutions reduced their exposure to overseas investments and as earnings in the UK by overseas investors increased.

So should we worry about balance of payments deficits? What effect do they have on exchange rates, inflation, growth, unemployment, etc.? What should the government do? These are questions we shall look at in this chapter.

UK current account balance of payments as % of GDP, 1963–2013

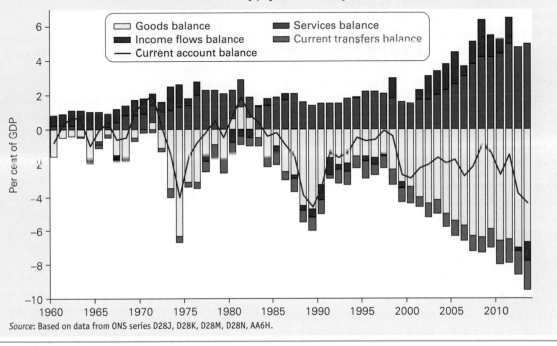

Source: Based on data from ONS series D28J, D28K, D28M, D28N, AA6H.

Figure 25.4(a) shows the case of a currency flow deficit (an excess of pounds) of an amount $a - b$. The Bank of England thus has to purchase these excess pounds by drawing on its foreign exchange reserves, or by borrowing foreign currency from foreign banks.

In Figure 25.4(b), there is a currency flow surplus of $c - d$. In this case, the Bank of England has to supply $c - d$ additional pounds to the market, and will acquire foreign currencies in exchange. It can use these to build up reserves or to pay back foreign loans.

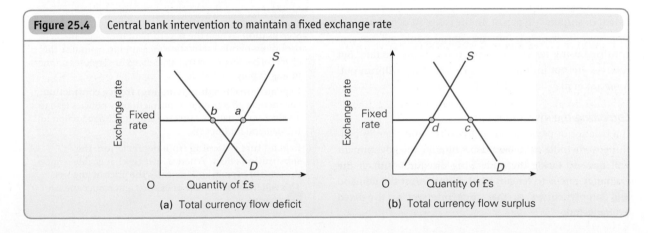

Figure 25.4 Central bank intervention to maintain a fixed exchange rate

(a) Total currency flow deficit

(b) Total currency flow surplus

Foreign exchange market intervention and the money supply. Maintaining a fixed exchange rate causes changes in the money supply. If the rate is maintained *above* the equilibrium (Figure 25.4(a)), there is a total currency flow deficit. The Bank of England buys pounds. It thereby withdraws them from circulation and reduces the money supply.

The effect of this reduction in money supply is to raise the equilibrium rate of interest. This attracts financial inflows and improves the financial account. It also dampens aggregate demand, and thus reduces imports and improves the current account. The net effect is to reduce the overall currency flow deficit and thus reduce the gap *a − b* in Figure 25.4(a). The problem here, of course, is that the lower aggregate demand may well result in a recession.

If the rate is maintained *below* equilibrium (Figure 25.4(b)), there is a total currency flow surplus. The Bank of England supplies additional pounds (which are spent by people abroad on UK exports etc. and are thus injected into the UK economy). It thereby increases the money supply.

The effect of the increased money supply is to reduce interest rates. This worsens the financial account and, by boosting aggregate demand, increases imports. The currency flow surplus is reduced. The gap *d − c* narrows.

Sterilisation. If the Bank of England did not want the money supply to alter, it would have to counter these effects with other monetary measures: e.g. open-market operations. Thus when there is a deficit and money supply falls, the Bank of England could buy back government bonds from the general public, thereby restoring the money supply to its previous level. This will prevent the economy moving into recession.

This process of countering the effects on money supply of a balance of payments deficit or surplus is known as **sterilisation**.

 Describe the open-market operations necessary to sterilise the monetary effects of a balance of payments surplus. Would this in turn have any effect on the current or financial accounts of the balance of payments?

There is a problem with sterilisation, however. If the money supply is not allowed to change, the currency flow deficit or surplus will persist. In the case of a deficit, a recession may be avoided, but the central bank will have to continue using reserves to support the exchange rate. But reserves are not infinite. Sooner or later they will run out! A recession may be inevitable.

Correcting the disequilibrium

If a balance of payments deficit persists, and reserves continue to dwindle or foreign debts mount, the government will have to tackle the underlying disequilibrium. If the exchange rate is to remain fixed, it must shift the demand and supply curves so that they intersect at the fixed exchange rate.

It can use contractionary fiscal and monetary policies for this purpose. Such policies have two main effects on the current account: an income effect (*expenditure reducing*) and a substitution effect between home and foreign goods (*expenditure switching*).

Expenditure reducing. Contractionary policy reduces national income. This in turn reduces expenditure, including expenditure on imports, shifting the supply of sterling curve to the left in Figure 25.4(a). The bigger the marginal propensity to import, the larger the shift.

There is a possible conflict here, however, between external and internal objectives. The balance of payments may improve, but unemployment is likely to rise and the rate of growth to fall.

 Under what circumstances would (a) contractionary and (b) expansionary policies cause no conflict between internal and external objectives?

Expenditure switching. If contractionary policies reduce the rate of inflation below that of foreign competitors, exports will become relatively cheaper compared with foreign competing goods and imports will become relatively more expensive compared with home-produced alternatives. Some foreign consumers will switch to UK exports. The more elastic the demand, the bigger the switch. Some UK consumers will switch from imports to home-produced goods. Again, the more elastic the demand, the bigger the switch. Demand in both cases will be more elastic the closer UK goods are as substitutes for foreign goods.

To the extent that contractionary policies result in expenditure switching rather than expenditure reducing, so this reduces the conflict between balance of payments and employment objectives.

Expenditure switching can also be achieved by placing restrictions on imports (tariffs and/or quotas) or the subsidising of exports. But this would conflict with the objective of free trade.

To the extent that fiscal and monetary policies affect interest rates, so this will affect the financial account of the

---

Definitions

Sterilisation Where the government uses open-market operations or other monetary measures to neutralise the effects of balance of payments deficits or surpluses on the money supply.

Expenditure changing (reducing) from a contraction: the income effect Where contractionary policies lead to a reduction in national income and hence a reduction in the demand for imports.

Expenditure switching from depreciation: the substitution effect Where a lower exchange rate reduces the price of exports and increases the price of imports. This will increase the sale of exports and reduce the sale of imports.

balance of payments. Higher interest rates will increase the demand for sterling and will thus lead to an improvement on the financial account. (The implications of this are explored in section 25.2.)

Correction under free-floating exchange rates

Freely floating exchange rates should automatically and immediately correct any balance of payments deficit or surplus: by depreciation and appreciation respectively. Foreign exchange dealers simply adjust the exchange rate so as to balance their books – in line with demand and supply.

KI 5
p 22

As with fixed rates, an income effect and a substitution effect of the correction process can be distinguished. But the nature of the income and substitution effects of depreciation/appreciation is quite different from that of deflation. It is only the substitution effect that corrects the disequilibrium. The income effect makes the problem *worse*! First the substitution effect: *expenditure switching*.

Expenditure switching (the substitution effect)

The process of adjustment. Assume a higher rate of inflation in the UK than abroad. As domestic prices rise relative to the price of imports, more imports will be purchased. The supply of pounds curve will shift to the right (to S_2 in Figure 25.5). UK exports will now be relatively more expensive for foreigners. Less will be sold. The demand for pounds curve will shift to the left (to D_2).

KI 7
p 36

Foreign exchange dealers will now find themselves with a glut of unsold pounds. They will therefore lower the exchange rate (to er_2 in Figure 25.5). The amount that the exchange rate has to change depends on:

■ The amount that the curves shift. Thus large differences in international inflation rates or large differences in international interest rates will cause large shifts in the demand for and supply of currencies, and hence large movements in exchange rates.

■ The elasticity of the curves. The less elastic the demand and supply curves of sterling, the greater the change in the exchange rate for any given shift in demand and supply.

But what determines the elasticity of the demand and supply curves? This is examined in Case Study 25.1 in MyEconLab.

KI 7
p 36

Expenditure changing (the income effect)

Depreciation, as well as affecting relative prices, will affect national income. This will cause *expenditure changing*.

We have already established that, as the exchange rate falls, so more exports will be sold and less imports purchased: this was the substitution effect. But this is only an initial effect.

Exports are an injection into, and imports a withdrawal from, the circular flow of income. There will thus be a multiplied rise in national income. This income effect (expenditure *increasing*) reduces the effectiveness of the depreciation. Two situations can be examined.

A rise in national income and employment, but no change in prices. Assume that there are substantial unemployed resources, so that an increase in aggregate demand will raise output and employment but not prices. As national income rises, so imports rise (thereby tending to offset the initial fall), but exports are unaffected.

This is illustrated by the line $(X - M)_1$ in Figure 25.6. At low levels of national income, spending on imports is low; thus exports (X) exceed imports (M). $X - M$ is positive. As national income and hence imports rise, $X - M$ falls, and after a point becomes negative. Thus the $X - M$ line is downward sloping.

Assume an initial equilibrium national income at Y_1, where national income (Y) equals national expenditure (E_1), but with imports exceeding exports by an amount $a - b$. The exchange rate thus depreciates.

This will cause a substitution effect: exports rise and imports fall. The $X - M$ line therefore shifts upwards. But this in turn causes an income effect. Aggregate demand rises, and the E line shifts upwards.

An eventual internal and external equilibrium is reached at Y_2, where $Y = E_2$ and $(X - M)_2 = 0$.

Figure 25.5 Adjustment of the exchange rate to a shift in demand and supply

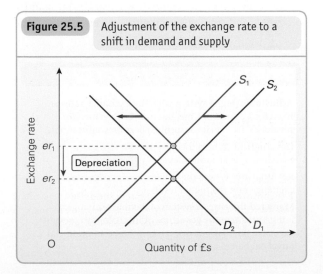

> ## Definitions
>
> **Expenditure switching from a contraction: the substitution effect** Where contractionary policies lead to a reduction in inflation and thus cause a switch in expenditure away from imports and towards exports.
>
> **Expenditure changing (increasing) from depreciation: the income effect** Where depreciation, via the substitution effect, will alter the demand for imports and exports, and this, via the multiplier, will affect the level of national income and hence the demand for imports.

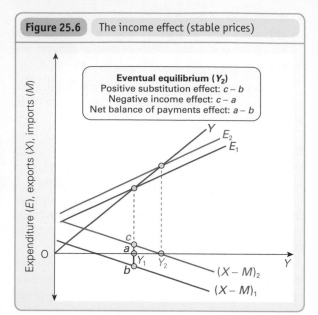

Figure 25.6 The income effect (stable prices)

The positive substitution effect of this depreciation is $c - b$. The negative income effect is $c - a$. The net effect is thus only $a - b$, which is the size of the initial deficit. Had it not been for this negative income effect, a smaller depreciation would have been needed.

At least in this case, the income effect is having a desirable *internal* consequence: reducing unemployment.

A rise in prices. If the economy is near full employment, the rise in aggregate demand from depreciation will make that depreciation even less effective. Not only will the higher demand lead directly to more imports, it will also lead to higher inflation. There will thus be an adverse substitution effect too. This will partially offset the beneficial substitution effect of the depreciation. The higher inflation will have the effect of shifting the $X - M$ line back down again somewhat.

In the extreme case, where money supply expands to accommodate the rise in aggregate demand, $X - M$ may simply return to its original position. The depreciation will fail to correct the balance of payments disequilibrium. In Figure 25.5, the fall in the exchange rate to er_2 will simply lead to a further rightward shift in supply and a leftward shift in demand, until the gap between them is the same as it was at er_1.

To offset the income effect, a government may feel it necessary to back up a currency depreciation with deflationary demand-management policies.

Intermediate exchange rate regimes

There are a number of possible intermediate systems between the two extremes of totally fixed and completely free-floating exchange rates.

Adjustable peg. The **adjustable peg** system is towards the fixed end of the spectrum. Exchange rates are fixed (or 'pegged') for a period of time – perhaps several years.

In the short and medium term, therefore, correction is the same as with a totally fixed system. Central banks have to intervene in the foreign exchange market to maintain the rate. If a deficit persists, then deflationary or other policies must be adopted to *shift* the currency demand and supply curves. This will be a problem, however, if there already exist substantial unemployed resources.

In the long term, if a fundamental disequilibrium occurs, the currency can be repegged at a lower or higher rate. Adjusting the peg downwards is known as **devaluation**. Adjusting it upwards is known as **revaluation**.

Alternatively, more frequent smaller adjustments could be made, thus moving the system away from the fixed end of the spectrum.

Managed floating. The **managed floating** system is towards the free-floating end of the spectrum. Exchange rates are not pegged: they are allowed to float. But the central bank intervenes from time to time to prevent excessive exchange rate fluctuations. It is thus a form of 'managed flexibility'.

Under such a system, the central bank does not seek to maintain a long-term or even medium-term disequilibrium rate. Rather it tries to allow an 'orderly' exchange rate adjustment to major changes in demand and supply, while preventing the violent short-term swings that can occur with a totally free float (swings arising from currency speculation).

To back up the central bank's use of reserves, it may also alter interest rates to prevent exchange rate fluctuations. If, for example, there were a large-scale selling of the domestic currency, the central bank could raise interest rates to counter this effect and prevent the exchange rate from falling.

 How would raising interest rates in this way affect the balance between the current and financial accounts of the balance of payments?

The degree of currency stability sought, and hence the degree of intervention required, will vary from country to country and from government to government. At one

Definitions

Adjustable peg A system whereby exchange rates are fixed for a period of time, but may be devalued (or revalued) if a deficit (or surplus) becomes substantial.

Devaluation Where the government repegs the exchange rate at a lower level.

Revaluation Where the government repegs the exchange rate at a higher level.

Managed floating A system of flexible exchange rates, but where the government intervenes to prevent excessive fluctuations or even to achieve an unofficial target exchange rate.

extreme, the government may intervene only if exchange rate fluctuations become very severe; at the other extreme, the government may try to maintain the exchange rate at some unofficial target level.

Crawling peg. The **crawling peg** system is midway between managed floating and the adjustable peg system. Instead of making large and infrequent devaluations (or revaluations), the government adjusts the peg by small amounts, but frequently – say, once a month, as the equilibrium exchange rate changes.

Joint float. Under a **joint float** a group of countries have a fixed or adjustable peg system between their *own* currencies, but *jointly float* against all other currencies.

Exchange rate band. With an **exchange rate band** the government sets a lower and an upper limit to the exchange rate: say, £1 = $1.60 and £1 = $1.80. It then allows the exchange rate to fluctuate freely within these limits. It will intervene, however, if the rate hits the floor or the ceiling. Exchange rate bands could be narrow (say ±1 per cent) or wide (say ±15 per cent).

Exchange rate bands can be incorporated in other systems – the band could be adjustable, crawling or fixed. For example, Figure 25.7 illustrates a crawling peg system with an exchange rate band.

The exchange rate mechanism (ERM) of the European Monetary System (EMS), which pre-dated the euro, was an example of a joint float against non-member currencies and an adjustably pegged exchange rate band with member currencies (see section 26.2). The ERM2 system for Denmark and Lithuania, and for new members of the EU prior to adopting the euro, is similar.

All these intermediate systems are attempts to achieve as many as possible of the advantages of both fixed and flexible exchange rates, with as few as possible of the attendant disadvantages. To assess any of these compromise systems, therefore, we must examine the advantages and disadvantages of fixed and flexible exchange rates. We do this in the next two sections.

Definitions

Crawling peg A system whereby the government allows a gradual adjustment of the exchange rate.

Joint float Where a group of currencies pegged to each other jointly float against other currencies.

Exchange rate band Where a currency is allowed to float between an upper and lower exchange rate, but is not allowed to move outside this band.

Figure 25.7 The crawling peg within exchange rate bands

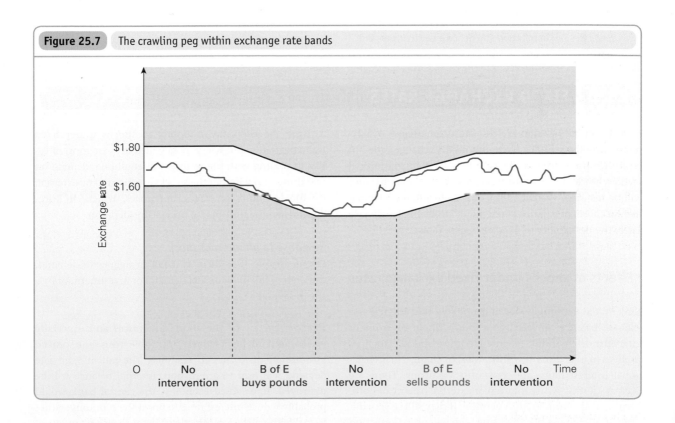

Section summary

1. There may be a conflict in achieving both internal and external balance simultaneously. The nature of the conflict depends on the exchange rate regime that the country adopts.

2. Nominal exchange rates are simply the rates at which one currency exchanges for another. Real exchange rates take account of differences in inflation rates between import and export prices and are a measure of the competitiveness of a country's exports.

3. Under a fixed exchange rate system, the government will have to intervene whenever the equilibrium exchange rate ceases to coincide with the fixed rate. If the equilibrium rate falls below the fixed rate, the government will have to buy in the domestic currency on the foreign exchange market. This will have the effect of reducing the money supply. Likewise, selling the domestic currency in order to prevent an appreciation will increase money supply. The government can prevent these changes in money supply by the use of appropriate open-market operations or other monetary measures. This is known as 'sterilisation'. Sterilisation, however, means that the disequilibrium is likely to go uncorrected.

4. If a deficit (or surplus) persists under a fixed rate, the government can attempt to shift the currency demand and supply curves. To cure a deficit, it can use contractionary fiscal or monetary policies. These have two effects. Deflation leads to a fall in national income (the income effect) and hence a fall in the demand for imports. It also leads to a fall in inflation and hence a switch in demand from foreign goods to home-produced goods (the substitution effect).

5. Correction under free-floating exchange rates also involves an income and a substitution effect. If there is a deficit, the exchange rate will depreciate. This will make imports more expensive and exports cheaper, and hence there will be a substitution effect as imports fall and exports rise.

6. The income effect of a depreciation, however, reduces its effectiveness. The rise in exports and fall in imports (i.e. the substitution effect of a depreciation) will lead to a multiplied rise in national income, which will cause imports to rise back again somewhat. The bigger this income effect, the bigger will be the depreciation necessary to achieve equilibrium in the foreign exchange market. Correction is made more difficult if any depreciation leads to increases in domestic prices and hence to a second substitution effect – only this time an adverse one.

7. There are intermediate exchange rate regimes between the extremes of fixed rates and free-floating rates. The exchange rate may be fixed for a period of time (the adjustable peg); or it may be allowed to change gradually (the crawling peg); or the government may merely intervene to dampen exchange rate fluctuations (managed floating); or the exchange rate may be allowed to fluctuate within a band, where the band in turn may be fixed, adjustable or crawling.

25.2 FIXED EXCHANGE RATES

In this section we examine the causes of balance of payments problems under fixed nominal exchange rates, in both the short run and the long run. First, in an optional section, we look at short-run causes and whether balance will be restored. We then look at longer-run, more fundamental causes of balance of payments problems. Finally, we assess the desirability of fixed exchange rates.

*Effects of shocks under fixed exchange rates

Under fixed exchange rates, it is unlikely that internal and external balance can persist for long without government intervention. Various macroeconomic 'shocks', such as changes in injections or withdrawals, or changes in international interest rates, are constantly occurring. These are likely to destroy either internal or external balance or both. Even with government intervention, it may still be very difficult, if not impossible, to restore both balances. Correction of balance of payments disequilibria will come into conflict with the other macroeconomic goals of growth, full employment and stable prices.

How the economy responds to shocks under fixed exchange rates, and which policy measures are most effective in dealing with the resultant disequilibria, depend on two things: (a) whether the shocks are internal or external; (b) the flexibility of wages and prices, which, in turn, depends on the time period under consideration.

Response to an internal shock

Let us assume that there is a fall in aggregate demand, caused by a fall in consumer demand or investment, or by a rise in saving.

Short-run effect. In the short run, prices and especially wages tend to be relatively inflexible (this is a central assumption of Keynesian analysis). The fall in aggregate demand will lead to a recession. Internal balance will be destroyed. In a closed economy, the central bank would probably reduce interest rates to boost the economy, either to tackle the recession directly or because *forecast* inflation had fallen below its target level.

In an open economy under fixed exchange rates, however, this is not possible. But why?

The lower aggregate demand will lead to a fall in imports, resulting in a *current account* surplus. There is an opposite effect on the *financial account*, however. The reduced aggregate demand will lead to a fall in the demand for money and hence downward pressure on interest rates. If interest rates were allowed to fall, there would be a resulting financial outflow and hence a financial account deficit.

But which would be the larger effect: the current account surplus or the financial account deficit? This depends on the marginal propensity to import (*mpm*) and the mobility of international finance. The higher the *mpm*, the bigger the current account surplus. The higher the international mobility of finance, the bigger the financial outflow and hence the bigger the financial account deficit. In today's world of massive financial flows across the foreign exchanges, international finance is highly, if not perfectly, mobile. If the central bank allows interest rates to fall, the financial account deficit will therefore exceed the current account surplus.

To prevent this happening, interest rates must not be allowed to fall or, at least, must fall only very slightly – just enough for the resulting financial account deficit to match the current account surplus. With hardly any fall in interest rates, money supply must thus be allowed to contract to match the fall in the demand for money.

Thus to maintain the fixed exchange rate (without massively draining reserves) interest rates will be determined by the balance of payments. They cannot be used for domestic purposes, such as targeting inflation, targeting real national income or some combination (e.g. a Taylor rule: see page 659). Internal imbalance will persist in the short run.

Long-run effect.   In the long run, there will be much greater, if not perfect, price and wage flexibility. Under new classical assumptions, such flexibility will exist in the short run too. This flexibility will ensure that internal balance is restored. The Phillips curve is vertical at the natural rate of unemployment.

But, with a fixed exchange rate, will it also ensure external balance? Again, let us assume that people decide to spend less and save more. As in the short run, this will lead to a *current account* surplus. This time, however, the effect is much bigger. In the short run, there was little or no price effect (i.e. no substitution effect) since there was little change in inflation. There was only an income effect from reduced imports caused by the recession. In the long run, however, the lower real aggregate demand reduces inflation. Assuming that inflation falls below that of trading partners, the *real* exchange rate falls. This makes exports relatively cheaper and imports relatively more expensive. This causes exports to rise and imports to fall.

The resulting rise in aggregate demand not only helps to eliminate the recession, but also helps to reduce the current account surplus.

 Thus, despite a fixed *nominal* exchange rate, wage and price flexibility cause the *real* exchange rate to be flexible.

This helps restore overall external balance. Nevertheless, a current account surplus may persist. Indeed, as the surplus is used to buy foreign assets, so, over time, these will yield an income, further crediting the current account.

But what is clear is that, although interest rates are determined by the need to maintain a fixed nominal exchange rate, wage and price flexibility in the long run will eventually restore internal balance. The question is, how long will the long run be? How long will the recession persist? If it is too long, and if interest rates cannot be cut, then can expansionary fiscal policy be used? We examine this in Box 25.3.

Response to an external shock

Assume now that there is a fall in demand for exports.

Short-run effect.   The fall in exports causes the *current account* to go into deficit. It also reduces aggregate demand, causing a multiplied fall in national income. This reduces the demand for imports: the larger the *mpm*, the bigger the reduction in imports. Aggregate demand will go on falling until the lower injections are matched by lower withdrawals. But the current account deficit will not be eliminated, since the fall in withdrawals to match the fall in exports consists only partly of lower imports; part will consist of lower saving and lower tax receipts.

The reduction in aggregate demand reduces the transactions demand for money, putting downward pressure on interest rates. This would result in a financial outflow and hence a *financial account* deficit, making the overall currency flow deficit worse. To prevent this happening, the central bank must prevent interest rates from falling by reducing the money supply (through open-market operations). Indeed, given the current account deficit, interest rates may have to be slightly higher than they were originally in order to create a financial account surplus sufficient to offset the current account deficit. This will make the recession worse.

Long-run effect.   The reduction in aggregate demand will put downward pressure on domestic inflation. This will help to reduce the *real* exchange rate and hence correct the current account deficit. It will also restore internal balance. Again, however, without fiscal policy, the long run may be some time in coming. The recession may persist.

Trace through the short-run and long-run internal and external effects (under a fixed exchange rate) of (a) a fall in domestic saving; (b) a rise in the demand for exports.

Causes of longer-term balance of payments problems under fixed exchange rates

With moderately flexible prices, current account balance may eventually be restored after 'one-off' shocks. However, long-term continuing shifts in the demand and supply of imports and exports can make balance of payments problems persist. We will examine four causes of these long-term shifts.

Different rates of inflation between countries. If a country has persistently higher rates of inflation than the countries with which it trades, it will have a growing current account deficit. Exports and import substitutes will become less and less competitive as its *real* exchange rate appreciates.

Different rates of growth between countries. If a country grows faster than the countries with which it trades, its imports will tend to grow faster than its exports.

Income elasticity of demand for imports higher than for exports. If the income elasticity of demand for imports is relatively high, and the income elasticity of demand for exports is relatively low, then as world incomes grow, the country's imports will grow faster than its exports. This has been a particular problem for many developing countries: they import manufactured goods and capital equipment, whose demand grows rapidly, and export primary products – food and raw materials – whose demand, until recent years, has grown relatively slowly (see section 27.2).

Long-term structural changes.

- Trading blocs may emerge, putting up tariff barriers to other countries. Australian and New Zealand exports were adversely affected when the UK joined the EEC.
- Countries may exercise monopoly power to a greater extent than previously. The OPEC oil price increases of 1973–4 and 1978–9 are examples.
- Countries may develop import substitutes. Thus plastics and other synthetics have in many cases substituted for rubber and metals, worsening the balance of payments of traditional primary exporters.
- The nature and quality of a country's products may change. Thus Japan has shifted from producing low-quality simple manufactured goods in the 1950s to producing high-quality sophisticated manufactured goods today. This has helped increase its exports.

To maintain a fixed exchange rate under such circumstances, governments have to take measures to correct the disequilibria. They can use demand-side policies (fiscal and monetary: see Box 25.3), supply-side policies or protectionist policies.

Advantages of fixed exchange rates

Many economists are opposed to fixed exchange rates, for reasons to be examined shortly. Nevertheless, many businesspeople are in favour of relatively rigid exchange rates. The following arguments are used.

 Certainty. With fixed exchange rates, international trade and investment become much less risky, since profits are not affected by movements in the exchange rate.

Little or no speculation. Provided the rate is *absolutely* fixed – and people believe that it will remain so – there is no point in speculating. For example, between 1999 and 2001, when the old currencies of the eurozone countries were still used,

but were totally fixed to the euro, there was no speculation that the German mark, say, would change in value against the French franc or the Dutch guilder.

 When the UK joined the ERM in 1990, it was hoped that this would make speculation pointless. As it turned out, speculation forced the UK to leave the ERM in 1992. Can you reconcile this with the argument that fixed rates discourage speculation?

Automatic correction of monetary errors. If the central bank allows the money supply to expand too fast, the resulting extra demand and lower interest rates will lead to a balance of payments deficit. This will force the central bank to intervene to support the exchange rate. Either it must buy the domestic currency on the foreign exchange market, thereby causing money supply to fall again (unless it sterilises the effect), or it must raise interest rates. Either way this will have the effect of correcting the error.

Preventing governments pursuing 'irresponsible' macroeconomic policies. If a government deliberately and excessively expands aggregate demand – perhaps in an attempt to gain short-term popularity with the electorate – the resulting balance of payments deficit will force it to constrain demand again (unless it resorts to import controls).

Disadvantages of fixed exchange rates

The new classical view

New classicists make two crucial criticisms of fixed rates.

Fixed exchange rates make monetary policy ineffective. Interest rates must be used to ensure that the overall balance of payments balances. As a result, money supply must be allowed to vary with the demand for money in order to keep interest rates at the necessary level. Thus monetary policy cannot be used for domestic purposes (see Box 25.3). Inflation depends on world rates, which may be high and domestically unacceptable. If the central bank tries to reduce inflation by attempting to reduce money supply and raise interest rates, the current and financial accounts will go into surplus. Money supply will thus increase until domestic inflation rises back to world levels.

Fixed rates contradict the objective of having free markets. Why fix the exchange rate, when a simple depreciation or appreciation can correct a disequilibrium? In the new classical world where markets clear, and supply and demand are relatively elastic, why not treat the foreign exchange market like any other, and simply leave it to supply and demand?

The Keynesian view

In the Keynesian world, wages and prices are relatively 'sticky', and demand-deficient unemployment and cost-push inflation may persist. As such, there is no guarantee of achieving both internal and external balance simultaneously when exchange rates are fixed. This leads to the following problems.

BOX 25.3 **THE EFFECTIVENESS OF FISCAL AND MONETARY POLICIES UNDER FIXED EXCHANGE RATES**

EXPLORING ECONOMICS

Monetary policy

Monetary policy is not very effective under fixed exchange rates.

Assume that the central bank, worried by rising inflation, wishes to reduce the growth in nominal aggregate demand. It thus reduces the rate of growth in money supply. This drives up interest rates and causes a fall in real national income.

What effect will this have on the balance of payments? The lower national income reduces expenditure on imports and hence leads to a surplus on the current account. Also, the higher interest rates encourage an inflow of finance and hence a surplus on the financial account too. This balance of payments surplus will *increase* money supply again and reduce interest rates back towards the original level. Aggregate demand will rise back towards its original level. Monetary policy has been ineffective.

But rather than changing the *supply* of money, can the government not directly alter interest rates? The problem here is that, in order to maintain the rate of exchange at the fixed level, the government's room for manoeuvre is very limited. For example, if it raises interest rates, the resulting inflow of finance will cause a balance of payments surplus. The government could, for a period of time, simply build up reserves, but it may not want to do this indefinitely.

The problem is more serious if the economy is in recession and the central bank wants to increase aggregate demand by *reducing* interest rates. The financial outflow will force the central bank to buy in the domestic currency by using its reserves. But it can do this for only so long. Eventually, it will be forced to raise interest rates again in order to stem the drain on the reserves. In today's world, with little in the way of exchange controls and with massive amounts of short-term international liquidity, such flows can be enormous. This gives the central bank virtually no discretion

over changing interest rates. Interest rates will have to be kept at a level so as to maintain the exchange rate. In the case of perfect mobility of international finance, interest rates must be kept at world rates. Monetary policy will be totally ineffective.

Fiscal policy

Fiscal policy is much more effective.

Assume that there is a recession and the government wishes to increase aggregate demand. It thus cuts taxes and/or raises government expenditure. This raises national income and increases expenditure on imports. Also, higher inflation raises the real exchange rate. This makes exports less competitive and imports relatively cheaper. The current account moves into deficit.

The increase in aggregate demand will raise the demand for money and hence put upward pressure on interest rates. This will lead to an inflow of finance and a financial account surplus. To prevent this swamping the current account deficit, the central bank must prevent interest rates from rising very much. In the case of an infinitely elastic supply of finance, interest rates must not be allowed to rise at all.

Thus money supply must be allowed to expand to keep interest rates down. This expansion of the money supply thus reinforces the expansionary fiscal policy and prevents crowding out.

Thus a high level of international financial mobility enhances the effectiveness of fiscal policy.

 Suppose that under a managed floating system the central bank is worried about high inflation and wants to keep the exchange rate up in order to prevent import prices rising. To tackle the problem of inflation, it raises interest rates. What will happen to the current and financial accounts of the balance of payments?

Balance of payments deficits can lead to a recession. A balance of payments deficit can occur even if there is no excess

KI 32 p401

demand. As we saw above, this could be caused by different rates of growth or different rates of inflation from trading partners, a higher income elasticity of demand for imports than for exports, and so on. If protectionism is to be avoided, and if supply-side policies work only over the long run, the government will be forced to reduce the rate of growth of aggregate demand. This will lead to higher unemployment and possibly a recession.

If wages and prices are sticky downwards, the contraction may have to be severe if a significant improvement in the *current* account is to be made. Here, reliance would have to be placed largely on lower *incomes* reducing the demand for imports. If the deflation is achieved through higher interest rates, however, an improvement on the *financial* account may remove the need for a severe deflation, especially given the high degree of financial mobility that exists

nowadays. Nevertheless, the rate of interest may still be higher than that desired for purely internal purposes.

If a country has a *persistent* current account deficit, it may need to have persistently higher interest rates than its competitors and suffer persistently lower growth rates as a result. It will also tend to build up short-term debts, as money is put on deposit in the country to take advantage of the higher interest rates. This can make the problem of speculation much more acute if people come to believe that the fixed rate cannot be maintained (see below).

Competitive deflations leading to world depression. If deficit countries deflated, but surplus countries *reflated*, there would be no overall world deflation or reflation. Countries may be quite happy, however, to run a balance of payments surplus and build up reserves. Countries may thus competitively deflate – all trying to achieve a balance of payments surplus. But this is beggar-my-neighbour policy. Not all

TC 15 p508

countries can have a surplus! Overall the world must be in balance. Such policies lead to general world deflation and a restriction in growth.

Problems of international liquidity. If trade is to expand, there must be an expansion in the supply of currencies acceptable for world trade (dollars, euros, gold, etc.): there must be adequate **international liquidity**. Countries' reserves of these currencies must grow if they are to be sufficient to maintain a fixed rate at times of balance of payments disequilibrium. Conversely, there must not be excessive international liquidity. Otherwise the extra demand that would result would lead to world inflation. It is important under fixed exchange rates, therefore, to avoid too much or too little international liquidity. The problem is how to maintain adequate control of international liquidity. The supply of dollars, for example, depends largely on US policy, which may be dominated by the US internal economic situation rather than by any concern for the well-being of the international community. Similarly, the supply of euros depends on the policy of the European Central Bank, which is governed by the internal situation in the eurozone countries.

 Why will excessive international liquidity lead to international inflation?

 KI 10 **p75** *Speculation.* If speculators believe that a fixed rate simply cannot be maintained, speculation is likely to be massive. If there is a huge deficit, there is no chance whatsoever of a *re*valuation. Either the rate will be devalued or it will remain the same. Speculators will thus sell the domestic currency. After all, it is a pretty good gamble: heads they win (devaluation); tails they don't lose (no devaluation). This speculative selling will worsen the deficit, and may itself force the devaluation. Speculation of this sort had disastrous effects on some south-east Asian currencies in 1997 (see Case Study 25.4 in MyEconLab) and on the Argentinean peso in 2002 (see Case Study 27.5).

 To what extent do Keynesians and new classicists agree about the role of fixed exchange rates?

Postscript

An argument used in favour of fixed rates is that they prevent governments from pursuing inflationary policies. But if getting inflation down is desirable, why do governments not pursue an anti-inflationary policy directly? Today, many governments (or central banks) make inflation targeting the goal of monetary policy. Most, however, have floating exchange rates.

> **Definition**
>
> **International liquidity** The supply of currencies in the world acceptable for financing international trade and investment.

Section summary

*1. Macroeconomic shocks are constantly occurring. Whether internal and external balance will be restored under a fixed exchange rate, following a shock, depends on price and wage flexibility and on the time period.

*2. In the short run there is a degree of wage and price inflexibility. If there is a fall in aggregate demand, the resulting fall in national income will reduce the demand for imports. This will cause a current account surplus. The fall in aggregate demand will also reduce the demand for money and put downward pressure on interest rates. This will cause a financial account deficit. This effect can be large, given the high mobility of international finance. Interest rates are thus constrained by the need for the financial account to balance the current account.

*3. In the long run, with wage and price flexibility, the real exchange rate can change. This will help to restore both internal and external balance.

4. Over the longer term, balance of payments disequilibria under fixed exchange rates can arise from different rates of inflation and growth between countries, different income elasticities of demand for imports and exports, and long-term structural changes.

5. Under fixed exchange rates, monetary policy will not be very effective, but fiscal policy will be much more effective.

6. Fixed exchange rates bring the advantage of certainty for the business community, which encourages trade and foreign investment. They also help to prevent governments from pursuing irresponsible macroeconomic policies.

7. Both new classical and Keynesian economists, however, see important disadvantages in fixed exchange rates. New classical economists argue that they make monetary policy totally ineffective, and that they run counter to the efficiency objective of having free markets. Keynesians argue that fixed rates can lead to serious internal imbalance with perhaps a persistent recession; that with competitive deflations a recession can be worldwide; that there may be problems of excessive or insufficient international liquidity; and that speculation could be very severe if people came to believe that a fixed rate was about to break down.

25.3 FREE-FLOATING EXCHANGE RATES

Floating exchange rates and the freeing of domestic policy

With a freely floating exchange rate there can be no overall balance of payments disequilibrium. Foreign exchange dealers will constantly adjust the exchange rate to balance their books, so that the demand for and supply of any currency are equal.

This, therefore, removes the balance of payments constraint on domestic policy that exists under a fixed exchange rate. No reserves are required, since there is no central bank intervention to support the exchange rate. The government would seem free to pursue whatever domestic policy it likes. Any resulting effects on the balance of payments are simply and automatically corrected by a depreciation or appreciation of the exchange rate.

In reality, however, things are not quite so simple. Even under a totally free-floating exchange rate, some constraints on domestic policy may be imposed by the effects of these exchange rate movements. For example, a depreciation of the exchange rate increases the price of imports. If the demand for imports is relatively inelastic, this may lead to a higher rate of inflation.

Response to shocks under a floating exchange rate

Internal shocks

Let us assume that there is a rise in aggregate demand that causes inflation. For the moment, however, let us also assume that monetary policy maintains real interest rates at international levels. For simplicity, let us assume that there is no inflation abroad. How will a floating exchange rate system cope with this internal shock of a rise in aggregate demand? The exchange rate will simply depreciate to maintain the competitiveness of exports and import substitutes.

For example, assume an initial exchange rate of £1 = $2. A UK product costing $2 in the USA will earn £1 for the UK exporter. If UK inflation now causes prices to double, the exchange rate will roughly halve. If it falls to £1 = $1, then the same product costing $2 in the USA will now earn £2 for the UK exporter, which in *real* terms is the same amount as before. This is the ***purchasing-power parity theory***. This states that domestic price changes will be offset by (nominal) exchange rate changes, thereby maintaining the same relative prices between countries as before.

 If this is the case, need firms worry about losing competitiveness in world markets if domestic inflation is higher than world inflation?

If we now drop the assumption that real interest rates are maintained at the same level as abroad, the purchasing-power parity theory will break down. Let us assume that the rise in aggregate demand causes a rise in UK real interest rates. This could be either the effect of the higher demand for money pushing up interest rates, or a deliberate act of the central bank to bring the inflation rate back down to the target level.

There are now two effects on the exchange rate. The higher aggregate demand and higher inflation will cause the current account to move into deficit, thereby putting downward pressure on the exchange rate. The higher real interest rates, however, will cause the financial account to move into surplus as depositors choose to hold their money in pounds. This will put upward pressure on the exchange rate. Whether the exchange rate actually falls or rises depends on which of the two effects is the bigger. In today's world of huge international financial flows, the effect on the financial account is likely to be the larger one: the exchange rate will thus *appreciate*. The greater the interest elasticity of supply of such flows, the greater the appreciation.

But either way, because of the financial account effect, the new equilibrium exchange rate will be above the purchasing-power parity rate. This will adversely affect export industries, since the exchange rate has not fallen sufficiently (if at all) to compensate for their higher sterling price. It will also adversely affect domestic industries that compete with imports, since again the exchange rate has not fallen sufficiently to retain their competitiveness with imports. The current account thus remains in deficit, matched by an equal and opposite financial plus capital account surplus.

This has been the position in the UK for several years. The rate of inflation has often been above that of major trading partners, while the current account has been persistently in deficit (see Box 25.2) and the capital plus financial account persistently in surplus (see Figure 15.19 on page 459). Furthermore, UK interest rates have been persistently above interest rates in the USA and, until the economic downturn of the late 2000s, above those in the eurozone. The result was an appreciating real exchange rate between 1996 and 2007 (see Figure 25.3).

The carry trade. The problem for current account deficit countries has often been made worse in recent years by the

TC 4 p47

TC 12 p411

TC 7 p72

Definition

Purchasing-power parity theory The theory that the exchange rate will adjust so as to offset differences in countries' inflation rates, with the result that the same quantity of internationally traded goods can be bought at home as abroad with a given amount of the domestic currency.

growth in the *carry trade*. This involves international investors taking advantage of nominal interest rate differences between countries.

Prior to the financial crisis of 2008, current account deficit countries, such as the UK, Australia and New Zealand, typically had relatively high interest rates, while current account surplus countries such as Japan and Switzerland had relatively low ones. It was thus profitable to borrow, say, yen at the low interest rate that obtains in Japan, exchange it

into sterling and deposit the money at the higher interest rate available in the UK. If there was no change in the exchange rate between the pound and the yen, the investor made a profit equal to the difference in the interest rates.

If, however, the higher interest rates in the UK and other deficit countries were simply to compensate investors for the risk of currency depreciation, then there would be no excessive inflow of finance. The benefit of the higher interest rate would be offset by a depreciating currency. But the carry trade had the effect of making deficit currencies *appreciate*, thereby further boosting the carry trade by speculation of further exchange rate rises.

Thus the currencies of deficit countries appreciated, making their goods less competitive and worsening their current account deficits. Between 1996 and 2006, the average current account deficits as a percentage of GDP for the USA, Australia and the UK were 3.3, 4.6 and 1.8 respectively. Between January 1996 and December 2006, the exchange

---

Definition

Carry trade Borrowing at low interest rates and then using it to buy assets that earn higher rates. In foreign exchange markets, the carry trade involves borrowing money in a currency of a country where interest rates are low and exchanging it for another currency where the country pays higher interest rates.

BOX 25.4	THE PRICE OF A BIG MAC

The Economist's guide to purchasing-power parity rates

At least once a year *The Economist* publishes its 'hamburger standard' exchange rates for currencies. It is a light-hearted attempt to see if currencies are exchanging at their purchasing-power parity rates. The test is the price at which a 'Big Mac' McDonald's hamburger sells in different countries! According to this simplified version of the purchasing-power parity theory, exchange rates should adjust so that a Big Mac costs the same in dollars everywhere.

If a Big Mac is taken as representative of all goods and services, then in January 2014, with a Big Mac selling for $4.62 in the USA, but only the equivalent of $2.74 in China, this implies that the Chinese yuan was undervalued by 41 per cent. As we can see from the table, it was not the only Asian currency to be undervalued in Big Mac PPP terms. The Malaysian ringgit and the Thai baht, for instance, were also substantially undervalued. In Malaysia it cost 7.40 ringgits, while in Thailand a Big Mac cost 96 bahts. With, at the time, exchange rates of 3.32 ringgits and 32.88 bahts to the dollar, this meant that in Malaysia a Big Mac cost $2.23, while in Thailand it cost $2.92. This implied that the Malaysian ringgit was undervalued in Big Mac PPP terms by 52 per cent while the Thai baht was undervalued by 37 per cent.

In India, the nearest product is a 'Maharajah Mac', which uses chicken rather than beef. Given that the meat accounts for less than 10 per cent of a burger's cost, it is a fair approximation to use this rather than a Big Mac. With a price of $1.54 at the exchange rate of the time, this implied that the rupee was undervalued by 67 per cent – the most undervalued currency in the sample.

While Asia was often found to be the cheapest place to eat a burger, Europe tended to be more expensive. For instance, the Norwegian kroner was estimated to be 69 per cent overvalued. At the prevailing exchange rate of 6.16 kroner to

The hamburger standard

Country	Big Mac price in dollars at current exchange rate	Under (−) or over (+) valuation against the dollar (%)
India	1.54	−67
South Africa	2.16	−53
Malaysia	2.23	−52
Indonesia	2.30	−50
Hong Kong	2.32	−50
Russia	2.62	−43
China	2.74	−41
Thailand	2.92	−37
Japan	2.97	−36
Poland	3.00	−35
Argentina	3.03	−34
Pakistan	3.04	−34
South Korea	3.47	−25
Singapore	3.60	−22
Turkey	3.76	−19
Australia	4.47	−3
USA[a]	4.62	0
UK	4.63	0
Uruguay	4.91	6
Eurozone[b]	4.96	7
Canada	5.01	8
Denmark	5.18	12
Brazil	5.25	13
Sweden	6.29	36
Switzerland	7.14	54
Venezuela	7.15	55
Norway	7.80	69

a Average of New York, Chicago, San Francisco and Atlanta.
b Weighted average of member countries.

rate index of the US dollar appreciated by 11.2 per cent, of the Australian dollar by 12.6 per cent and of sterling by some 38.5 per cent.

Currencies of surplus countries depreciated, making their goods more competitive and further boosting their current account surpluses. For example, between 2004 and 2006 the average current account surpluses as a percentage of GDP for Japan and Switzerland were 3.8 and 13.2 respectively. Their short-term interest rates averaged a mere 0.1 and 1.0 per cent respectively (compared with 3.4, 4.7 and 5.7 per cent for the USA, the UK and Australia). Yet, between January 2004 and December 2006, the exchange rate index of the yen depreciated by 14.3 per cent while that of the Swiss franc depreciated by 2.0 per cent.

With the credit crunch of 2007–8, however, short-term flows of finance declined significantly. This had the effect of reducing the carry trade and its effect on exchange rates. The current account became relatively more significant in determining exchange rates. The currencies of deficit countries, such as the UK and USA, began to depreciate and those of surplus countries, such as Japan and Switzerland, began to appreciate. Between September 2007 and September 2008, the US dollar and sterling depreciated by 2.5 and 13.7 per cent respectively; the yen and the Swiss franc appreciated by 5.8 and 4.3 per cent.

External shocks

Now let us assume that the rest of the world goes into recession (but with no change in international interest rates). The demand for UK exports will fall. This will lead to a depreciation of the exchange rate. This in turn will boost the demand for UK exports and domestic substitutes for imports. This boost to demand again will help to offset the dampening effect of the world recession.

Floating exchange rates thus help to insulate the domestic economy from world economic fluctuations.

CASE STUDIES AND APPLICATIONS

the dollar, a Big Mac in Norway cost the equivalent of $7.80. For a Big Mac to cost the same in Norway as in the USA, the exchange rate would have had to be 10.38 kroner to the dollar.

Across the eurozone a Big Mac in January 2014 cost on average €3.66. With an exchange rate of €1 = $1.36, the eurozone Big Mac cost $4.96, implying an overvaluation of the euro of 7 per cent.

So what of the UK? A Big Mac in January 2014 cost an average of £2.79. At the exchange rate at the time of £1 = $1.66, this meant a Big Mac cost $4.63 in the UK – almost exactly that in the USA. In June 2008, by contrast, the Big Mac report had estimated that the pound was overvalued by 28 per cent.

Generally, richer countries' currencies seem to be overvalued and poorer ones' undervalued (exceptions in the table being Uruguay and Venezuela). The explanation lies in differences in local costs, such as rents and wages. These are higher in rich countries. According to David Parsley, of Vanderbilt University, and Shang-Jin Wei, of the International Monetary Fund, non-traded inputs, such as labour, rent and electricity, account for between 55 and 64 per cent of the price of a Big Mac.[1]

With lower rents and wages,

. . . you would expect average prices to be cheaper in poor countries than in rich ones because labour costs are lower. This is the basis of the so-called 'Balassa-Samuelson effect'. Rich countries have much higher productivity and hence higher wages in the traded-goods sector than poor countries do. Because firms compete for workers, this also pushes up wages in non-tradable goods and services, where rich countries' productivity advantage is smaller.[2]

A Big Mac index is now produced adjusting for GDP per capita. In January 2014 it suggested that the Indian rupee was still significantly undervalued (39 per cent). On the other hand, the Chinese yuan was now very slightly overvalued (1 per cent). While this adjustment may capture some of the differences between countries, such as in labour costs, it cannot capture differences attributable to transportation costs, or to consumer tastes which affect the amount consumers are willing to pay.

Also, exchange rates can diverge from their PPP values because of factors influencing the *financial account* of the balance of payments: factors such as actual and expected interest rate differentials, investment prospects and speculation about exchange rate movements.

Nevertheless, despite the limitation of the original Big Mac index, it does give some indication of whether a currency is above or below its long-term equilibrium rate.

1. *If the Chinese yuan is undervalued by 41 per cent in PPP terms against the US dollar and the Norwegian kroner overvalued by 69 per cent, what implications does this have for the interpretation of Chinese, Norwegian and US GDP statistics?*
2. *Why do developing countries' currencies tend to be undervalued relative to those of developed countries (see table)?*
3. *At the time the table was compiled, the Big Mac PPP rate for the Swiss franc was $1 = SF1.41. What was the market exchange rate?*

[1] 'A prism into the PPP puzzles: the microfoundations of Big Mac real exchange rates', October 2004, www2.owen.vanderbilt.edu/david.parsley/research.htm
[2] *The Economist*, 30 July 2011.

Will there be any cost to the UK economy from a decline in the demand for exports resulting from a world recession?

The path to long-run equilibrium

If there is a single shock, and if there is initially both internal balance and also external balance in the narrow sense (i.e. a current account balance), eventually both internal balance and current account balance will be restored. Current account balance will be restored by a change in the exchange rate that restores purchasing-power parity. This is illustrated in Figure 25.8.

Assume that the country experiences the same long-term rate of inflation as its trading partners and that, therefore, the nominal exchange rate follows the same path as the real exchange rate. Assume also that there are no *long-term* changes to cause an appreciation or depreciation and that, therefore, the long-term equilibrium exchange rate is constant over time. This is shown by the horizontal line at er_L.

Now assume, as before, that there is a rise in aggregate demand and a resulting rise in interest rates. This occurs at time t_1. As the demand for imports rises, the current account goes into deficit. Higher interest rates, however, lead to a financial inflow and an immediate appreciation of the exchange rate to er_1. But then the exchange rate will gradually fall back to its long-run rate as the higher interest rates curb demand and interest rates can thus come back down.

What determines the level of er_1? This exchange rate must be high enough to balance the gain from the higher interest rate against the fact that the exchange rate will be expected to depreciate again back to its long-run equilibrium level er_L. For example, if the interest rate rises by 1 per cent, the exchange rate must rise to the level where people anticipate that it will fall by 1 per cent per year. Only that way will finance stop flowing into the country.

 Describe the exchange rate path if there were a single shock that caused interest rates to fall. What determines the magnitude and speed of changes in the exchange rate in such a scenario?

Speculation

In the real world, shocks are occurring all the time. Also there is considerable uncertainty over the future course of the exchange rate path. What is more, things are made more complicated by the activities of speculators. As soon as any exchange rate change is anticipated, speculators will buy or sell the currency.

Assume, for example, that there is a rise in UK inflation above international rates, but no change in interest rates. This causes a fall in the demand for exports and hence a fall in the demand for sterling (assuming a price elasticity of demand greater than 1), and a rise in imports and hence a rise in the supply of sterling. This is illustrated in Figures 25.9 and 25.10. The exchange rate depreciates from er_1 to er_2. Speculators seeing the exchange rate falling can react in one of two ways. The first is called *stabilising speculation*; the second is called *destabilising speculation* (see section 3.2).

Stabilising speculation

This occurs when speculators believe that any exchange rate change will soon be reversed.

In our example, speculators may anticipate that the central bank will raise interest rates or take some other measure to reduce inflation. They thus believe that the exchange rate will appreciate again. As a result, they buy more pounds and sell fewer. But this very act of speculation causes the appreciation they had anticipated.

This is illustrated in Figure 25.9. Inflation has caused the demand for and supply of pounds to shift from D_1 and S_1 to D_2 and S_2, and the exchange rate to fall from er_1 to er_2.

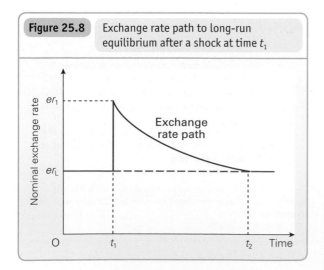

Figure 25.8 Exchange rate path to long-run equilibrium after a shock at time t_1

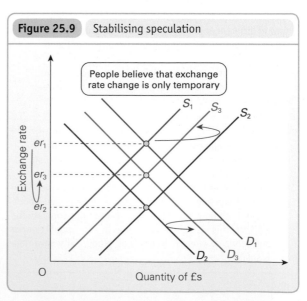

Figure 25.9 Stabilising speculation

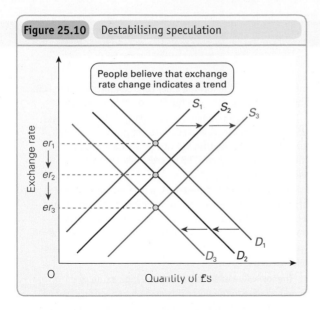

Figure 25.10 Destabilising speculation

People believe that exchange rate change indicates a trend

Stabilising speculation then shifts the curves back again, to D_3 and S_3, and the exchange rate rises again to er_3.

The action of speculators in this case, therefore, prevents excessively large exchange rate changes. In general, stabilising speculation occurs whenever speculators believe that the exchange rate has 'overreacted' to the current economic situation.

 Draw a similar diagram to Figure 25.9, showing how an initial appreciation of the exchange rate would similarly be reduced by stabilising speculation.

Destabilising speculation

This occurs when speculators believe that exchange rate movements will continue in the same direction.

KI 32 p401 In our example, speculators may believe that inflation will not be brought under control. They anticipate a continuing fall in the exchange rate and thus sell *now* before the exchange rate falls any further. In Figure 25.10, this speculation causes the demand and supply curves to shift further, to D_3 and S_3, and causes the exchange rate to fall further, to er_3.

Eventually, however, this destabilising speculation could cause **overshooting**, with the exchange rate falling well below the purchasing-power parity rate. At this point speculators, believing that the rate will rise again, will start buying pounds again. This causes the exchange rate to rise.

Definition

Exchange rate overshooting Where a fall (or rise) in the long-run equilibrium exchange rate causes the actual exchange rate to fall (or rise) by a greater amount before eventually moving back to the new long-run equilibrium level.

Obviously, governments prefer stabilising to destabilising speculation. Destabilising speculation can cause severe exchange rate fluctuations. The resulting uncertainty is very damaging to trade. It is very important, therefore, that governments create a climate of confidence. People must believe that the government can prevent economic crises from occurring.

Conclusion

Whatever speculators anticipate will happen to the exchange rate, their actions will help to bring it about. If they think the sterling exchange rate will fall, they will sell pounds, hence causing it to fall. Thus speculators as a whole will gain. This applies to both stabilising and destabilising speculation.

 If speculators on average gain from their speculation, who loses?

Advantages of a free-floating exchange rate

The advantages and disadvantages of free-floating rates are to a large extent the opposite of those of fixed rates.

Automatic correction. The government simply lets the exchange rate move freely to the equilibrium. In this way, balance of payments disequilibria are automatically and instantaneously corrected without the need for specific government policies – policies that under other systems can be mishandled. IL4 p47

No problem of international liquidity and reserves. Since there is no central bank intervention in the foreign exchange market, there is no need to hold reserves. A currency is automatically convertible at the current market exchange rate. International trade is thereby financed.

Insulation from external economic events. A country is not tied to a possibly unacceptably high world inflation rate, as it is under a fixed exchange rate. It can choose its own inflation target. It is also to some extent protected against world economic fluctuations and shocks (see pages 757–60).

Governments are free to choose their domestic policy. Under a fixed rate, a government may have to deflate the economy even when there is high unemployment. Under a floating rate, the government can choose whatever level of domestic demand it considers appropriate, and simply leave exchange rate movements to take care of any balance of payments effect. This is a major advantage, especially when the effectiveness of deflation is reduced by downward wage and price rigidity, and when competitive deflation between countries may end up causing a world recession.

Disadvantages of a free-floating exchange rate

Despite these advantages, there are still some serious problems with free-floating exchange rates.

BOX 25.5   THE EURO/DOLLAR SEESAW

Ups and downs in the currency market

For periods of time, world currency markets can be quite peaceful, with only modest changes in exchange rates. But with the ability to move vast sums of money very rapidly from one part of the world to another and from one currency to another, speculators can suddenly turn this relatively peaceful world into one of extreme turmoil – a turmoil that can be very damaging for business.

In this box we examine the huge swings of the euro against the dollar since the euro's launch in 1999.

First the down . . .

On 1 January 1999, the euro was launched and exchanged for $1.16. By October 2000 the euro had fallen to $0.85. What was the cause of this 27 per cent depreciation? The main cause was the growing fear that inflationary pressures were increasing in the USA and that, therefore, the Federal Reserve Bank would have to raise interest rates. At the same time, the eurozone economy was growing only slowly and

inflation was well below the 2 per cent ceiling set by the ECB. There was thus pressure on the ECB to cut interest rates.

The speculators were not wrong. As the diagram shows, US interest rates rose, and ECB interest rates initially fell, and when eventually they did rise (in October 1999), the gap between US and ECB interest rates soon widened again.

In addition to the differences in interest rates, a lack of confidence in the recovery of the eurozone economy and a continuing confidence in the US economy encouraged investment to flow to the USA. This inflow of finance (and lack of inflow to the eurozone) further pushed up the dollar relative to the euro.

The low value of the euro meant a high value of the pound relative to the euro. This made it very difficult for UK companies exporting to eurozone countries and also for those competing with imports from the eurozone (which had been made cheaper by the fall in the euro).

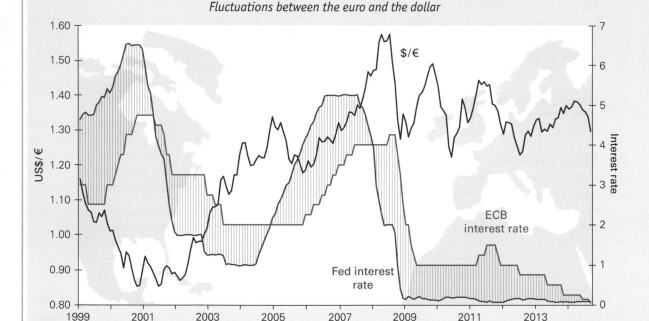

Fluctuations between the euro and the dollar

Note: Federal reserve rate is the federal funds effective rate.
Source: Federal Reserve Bank, European Central Bank and *Monthly Review of External Trade Statistics* (National Statistics).

Speculation.   Short-run instability can be lessened by stabilising speculation, thus making speculation advantageous. If, due to short-run inelasticity of demand, a deficit causes a very large depreciation, speculators will *buy* pounds, knowing that in the long run the exchange rate will appreciate again. Their action therefore helps to lessen the short-run fall in the exchange rate.

Nevertheless, in an uncertain world where there are few restrictions on currency speculation, where the fortunes and policies of governments can change rapidly, and where

large amounts of short-term deposits are internationally 'footloose', speculation can be highly destabilising in the short run. Considerable exchange rate overshooting can occur.

An example of such overshooting occurred between June 2008 and March 2009 when the pound depreciated 14 per cent against the euro, 28 per cent against the US dollar and 34 per cent against the yen (see Figure 25.11). The nominal sterling exchange rate index fell 16 per cent. Speculators were predicting that interest rates in the UK

In October 2000, with the euro trading at around 85¢, the ECB plus the US Federal Reserve Bank (the USA's central bank), the Bank of England and the Japanese central bank all intervened on the foreign exchange market to buy euros. This arrested the fall, and helped to restore confidence in the euro.

. . . Then the up

The position completely changed in 2001. With the US economy slowing rapidly and fears of an impending recession, the Federal Reserve Bank reduced interest rates 11 times during the year: from 6.5 per cent at the beginning of the year to 1.75 per cent at the end (see the chart). Although the ECB also cut interest rates, the cuts were relatively modest: from 4.75 at the beginning of the year to 3.25 at the end. With eurozone interest rates now considerably above US rates, the euro began to rise.

In addition, a massive deficit on the US balance of payments current account, and a budget deficit nearing 4 per cent of GDP, made foreign investors reluctant to invest in the US economy. In fact, investors were pulling out of the USA. One estimate suggests that European investors alone sold $70 billion of US assets during 2002. The result of all this was a massive depreciation of the dollar and appreciation of the euro, so that by December 2004 the exchange rate had risen to $1.36: a 60 per cent appreciation since June 2001!

In 2004–5, with the US economy growing strongly again, the Fed raised interest rates several times, from 1 per cent in early 2004 to 5.25 by June 2006. The ECB kept interest rates constant at 2 per cent until early 2006. The result was that the euro depreciated against the dollar in 2005. But then the rise of the euro began again as the US growth slowed and eurozone growth rose and people anticipated a narrowing of the gap between US and eurozone interest rates.

In 2007 and 2008, worries about the credit crunch in the USA led the Fed to cut interest rates to stave off recession. In August 2007 the US federal funds rate was 5.25 per cent. It was then reduced on several occasions to stand at between 0 and 0.25 per cent by December 2008. The ECB, in contrast, kept the eurozone rate at 4 per cent for the first part of this period and even raised it to 4.25 per cent temporarily in the face of rapidly rising commodity prices. As a result, short-term finance flooded into the eurozone and the euro

appreciated again, from $1.37 in mid-2007 to $1.58 in mid-2008.

Eventually, in September 2008, with the eurozone on the edge of recession and predictions that the ECB would cut interest rates, the euro at last began to fall. It continued to do so as the ECB cut rates. However, with monetary policy in the eurozone remaining tighter than in the USA, the euro began to rise again, only falling once more at the end of 2009 and into 2010 as US growth accelerated and speculators anticipated a tightening of US monetary policy.

. . . Then seesawing on the back of fiscal concerns

The early 2010s were characterised by concerns over levels of government borrowing and the growing stocks of national debt. These concerns contributed to the volatility of the euro. In particular, its value was to be affected by swings in investor confidence over countries' financial health and the adequacy of the mechanisms in place to deal with them (see Box 21.3).

Consequently, the euro would tend to weaken on fears of debt default as investors became increasingly reluctant to hold the currency. For instance, in early 2010, fear of a Greek default and growing worries about contagion to other highly indebted eurozone countries, such as Portugal, Ireland, Italy and Spain, led to speculation against the euro. In January 2010, the euro stood at $1.44; by early June, it had fallen to $1.19. This represented a 17 per cent depreciation.

But then the euro strengthened as discussions began over the design of funding mechanisms for eurozone countries in financial distress. By the end of October 2010 the euro was trading at $1.39.

The path of the euro shows that interest rate volatility and the relative level of interest rates in the USA and the eurozone have been a major contributory factor to exchange rate volatility between the euro and the dollar. However, more recently concerns over the fiscal health of national eurozone governments have played a particularly important role in explaining fluctuations in the euro.

 Find out what has happened to the euro/dollar exchange rate over the past 12 months (you can find the data from the Bank of England's Statistical Interactive Database at www.bankofengland.co.uk/statisticsindex.htm). Explain why the exchange rate has moved the way it has.

would fall further than in other countries and stay lower for longer. This was because recession was likely to be deeper in the UK, with inflation undershooting the Bank of England's 2 per cent target and perhaps even becoming negative. But the fall in the exchange rate represented considerable over-shooting and the exchange rate index rose by 9 per cent between March and May 2009.

This is just one example of the violent swings in exchange rates that have occurred in recent years. They even occur under managed floating exchange rate systems

where governments have attempted to dampen such fluctuations!

The continuance of exchange rate fluctuations over a number of years is likely to encourage the growth of speculative holdings of currency. This can then cause even larger and more rapid swings in exchange rates.

Uncertainty for traders and investors. The uncertainty caused by currency fluctuations can discourage international trade and investment. To some extent, the problem can be

Figure 25.11 Depreciating and then appreciating sterling from 2008

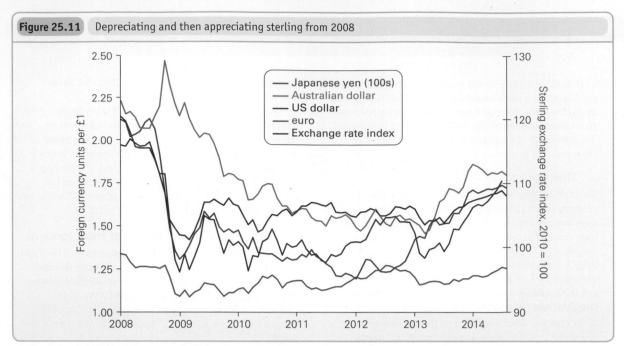

Note: Exchange rate index is BIS broad nominal index comprising 61 countries.
Source: Based on data in *Monthly Review of External Statistics* (National Statistics) and from Bank for International Settlements.

BOX 25.6 | **THE EFFECTIVENESS OF MONETARY AND FISCAL POLICIES UNDER FLOATING EXCHANGE RATES** | EXPLORING ECONOMICS

With a floating exchange rate, monetary policy is strong and fiscal policy is weak (the reverse of the case with fixed exchange rates).

Monetary policy

Assume that the economy is in recession and the central bank wishes to increase aggregate demand. It thus reduces interest rates. Three effects follow, each contributing to the effectiveness of the monetary policy.

1. *The expansionary monetary policy directly increases aggregate demand*. The size of the effect here depends on the amount that interest rates change and the elasticity of aggregate demand in response to the changes in interest rates.
2. *The exchange rate depreciates*. Higher aggregate demand increases imports and (via higher prices) reduces exports. This and the lower interest rates reduce the demand for and increase the supply of domestic currency on the foreign exchange market. The exchange rate thus depreciates.

    This reinforces the increase in domestic demand. A lower exchange rate makes exports less expensive again and therefore increases their demand (an injection). Imports become more expensive again and therefore their demand falls (a withdrawal). There is thus a further multiplied rise in income.
3. *Speculation may cause initial exchange rate overshooting*. Lower interest rates cause speculative financial outflows in anticipation of the depreciation. This causes the exchange rate to fall below its eventual rate – to overshoot, thus causing a further rise in aggregate demand.

This is only a short-term effect, however, since speculators will stop selling the domestic currency when the rate has gone so low that they feel it must rise again (back towards the purchasing-power parity level) sufficiently fast to offset the lower interest rates they are now getting. The greater the mobility of international finance and the better the information of the speculators, the shorter will the short run be.

Fiscal policy

Fiscal policy is relatively weak under a floating rate. Again let us assume that the objective is to raise aggregate demand to combat a recession. The government thus reduces taxes and/or increases its expenditure. The rise in aggregate demand raises imports and (via higher prices) reduces exports. This effect on the current account of the balance of payments puts downward pressure on the exchange rate.

The higher aggregate demand, however, increases the transactions demand for money and hence *raises* interest rates. These higher interest rates will lead to financial inflows. This will put upward pressure on the exchange rate, which is likely to swamp the downward pressure from the current account deficit. There will therefore be an *appreciation* of the exchange rate. This will increase imports and reduce exports, thus reducing aggregate demand again, and reducing the effectiveness of the fiscal expansion.

 Compare the relative effectiveness of fiscal and monetary policies as means of reducing aggregate demand under a system of floating exchange rates.

overcome by using the *forward exchange market*. Here traders agree with a bank *today* the rate of exchange for some point in the *future* (say, in six months' time). This allows traders to plan future purchases of imports or sales of exports at a known rate of exchange. Of course, banks charge for this service, since they are taking upon themselves the risks of adverse exchange rate fluctuations.

This will not help long-term investment, however, where decisions are made based on anticipated costs and revenue flows for many years to come. The possibility of exchange rate appreciation may well discourage firms from investing abroad.

 Why would banks not be prepared to offer a forward exchange rate to a firm for, say, five years from now?

Lack of discipline on the domestic economy. Governments may pursue irresponsibly inflationary policies. Also, unions and firms may well drive up wages and prices, without the same fear of losing overseas markets or of the government imposing deflationary policies. The depreciation resulting from this inflation will itself fuel the inflation by raising the price of imports.

Conclusion

Neither fixed nor free-floating exchange rates are free from problems. For this reason, governments have sought a compromise between the two, the hope being that some intermediate system will gain the benefits of both, while avoiding most of their disadvantages.

One compromise was tried after the Second World War. This was the *adjustable peg*. Another is the system that replaced the adjustable peg in the early 1970s and continues for much of the world today. This is the system of *managed floating*. We examine these systems in the next section.

Definition

Forward exchange market Where contracts are made today for the price at which a currency will be exchanged at some specified future date.

Section summary

1. Under a free-floating exchange rate, the balance of payments will automatically be kept in balance by movements in the exchange rate. This removes the *balance of payments* constraint on domestic policy. It does not, however, remove external constraints entirely.

2. According to the purchasing-power parity theory, any changes in domestic prices will simply lead to equivalent changes in the exchange rate, leaving the international competitiveness of home-produced goods unaffected. If, however, internal shocks cause changes in interest rates, there will be a change in the *financial* account balance. This will influence exchange rates and destroy the purchasing-power parity theory. The current account will go out of balance (in an equal and opposite way to the financial account).

3. This problem is made more acute by the carry trade, whereby people borrow money in low interest rate (current account surplus) countries and deposit them in high interest rate (current account deficit) countries. This causes deficit countries' exchange rates to appreciate, thereby worsening their current account deficit.

4. External shocks will be reflected in changes in exchange rates and will help to insulate the domestic economy from international economic fluctuations.

5. Exchange rate movements are highly influenced by speculation. If speculators believe that an appreciation or depreciation is merely temporary, their activities will help to stabilise the exchange rate. If, however, they believe that an exchange rate movement in either direction will continue, their activities will be destabilising and cause a bigger movement in the exchange rate.

6. The advantages of free-floating exchange rates are that they automatically correct balance of payments disequilibria; they eliminate the need for reserves; and they give governments a greater independence to pursue their chosen domestic policy.

7. On the other hand, a completely free exchange rate can be highly unstable, made worse by destabilising speculation. This may discourage firms from trading and investing abroad. What is more, a flexible exchange rate, by removing the balance of payments constraint on domestic policy, may encourage governments to pursue irresponsible domestic policies for short-term political gain.

25.4 EXCHANGE RATE SYSTEMS IN PRACTICE

The adjustable peg system: 1945–73

After the collapse in 1931 of the fixed exchange rate system of the gold standard (see section 16.2), the huge scale of the initial disequilibria caused wild swings in exchange rates. Many countries resorted to protectionism, given the great uncertainties associated with free trade under fluctuating exchange rates.

The Bretton Woods system

In 1944 the allied countries met at Bretton Woods in the USA to hammer out a new exchange rate system: one that would avoid the chaos of the 1930s and encourage free trade, but that would avoid the rigidity of the gold standard. The compromise they worked out was an adjustable peg system that lasted until 1971.

Under the **Bretton Woods system** there was a totally fixed dollar/gold exchange rate ($35 per ounce of gold). The USA guaranteed that it would freely convert dollars into gold. It was hoped that this would encourage countries to hold dollars as their major reserve currency. After all, if dollars were freely convertible into gold, they were as good as gold. All other countries pegged their exchange rate to the dollar.

To prevent temporary, short-term fluctuations in the exchange rate, central banks *intervened* on the foreign exchange markets using their foreign reserves. This enabled them to maintain the pegged rate within a 1 per cent band.

If the disequilibrium became more serious, governments were supposed to pursue policies of *deflation* or *reflation*. In the meantime, in the case of a deficit, the central bank might have insufficient reserves to maintain the exchange rate. The International Monetary Fund was set up to provide such liquidity. All countries were required to deposit a quota of funds with the IMF, depending on the size of their trade. The IMF would then lend to countries in balance of payments deficit to enable them to maintain their exchange rate. The more a country had to borrow from the IMF, the more the IMF would insist that it pursued appropriate deflationary policies to correct the disequilibrium.

If the deficit became severe, countries could *devalue*: the pegged rate could be adjusted (in consultation with the IMF).

 Under this system, how would you expect countries to respond to a balance of payments surplus? Would a revaluation benefit such countries?

Advocates of an adjustable peg system argue that the Bretton Woods arrangement made a significant contribution to the long boom of the 1950s and 1960s:

- Since rates were fixed for a long period of time – perhaps many years – uncertainty was reduced and trade was encouraged.
- Pegged rates, plus the overseeing role of the IMF, prevented governments from pursuing irresponsible policies, and helped to bring about an international harmonisation of policies. They kept world inflation in check.
- If a deficit became severe, countries could devalue. This prevented them being forced into a depression or into adopting protectionist policies. The IMF ensured an orderly process of devaluation.

However, there were two serious weaknesses with the system. These became more and more apparent during the 1960s, and eventually led to the system's downfall.

Problems of adjustment to balance of payments disequilibria

To avoid internal policy being governed by the balance of payments, and to avoid being forced into a depression, countries with a fundamental deficit were supposed to devalue. There were several difficulties here, however:

- Identifying whether a deficit was fundamental. Governments were frequently overoptimistic about the future balance of payments position.
- If devaluation did take place, it could be very disruptive to firms. A devaluation suddenly alters the costs and revenues of importers and exporters by a substantial amount. If a devaluation is felt to be imminent, it can cause great uncertainty and may make them reluctant to take on new trade commitments.

 Would this uncertainty have a similar or a different effect on exporting companies and companies using imported inputs?

- At first a devaluation might make a current account deficit *worse*: the **J-curve effect**. The price elasticities of demand for imports and exports may be low in the short run (see Case Study 25.1 in MyEconLab). Directly after devaluation, few extra exports may be sold, and more will have to be paid for imports that do not have immediate substitutes. There is thus an initial deterioration in the balance of trade before it eventually improves. In Figure 25.12, devaluation takes place at time t_1. As you can see, the diagram has a J shape.

Figure 25.12 The J-curve effect

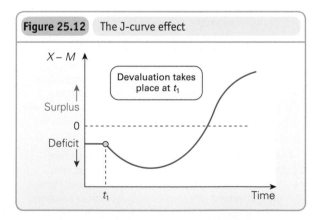

Definitions

Bretton Woods system An adjustable peg system whereby currencies were pegged to the US dollar. The USA maintained convertibility of the dollar into gold at the rate of $35 to an ounce.

J-curve effect Where a devaluation causes the balance of payments first to deteriorate and then to improve. The graph of the balance of payments over time thus looks like a letter J.

For these reasons, countries in deficit tended to put off devaluing until they were forced to by a crisis. The reluctance of countries to devalue caused other problems.

Stop–go policies.   Countries had to rely much more on *deflation* as a means of curing deficits. The UK in particular found that, whenever the economy started to grow, the balance of payments went into deficit. This forced the government to curb demand again through fiscal and/or monetary policies.

KI 32
p401

Speculation.   If countries delayed devaluing until a deficit became really severe, an eventual large devaluation became inevitable. This provided a field day for speculators: they could not lose, and there was a high probability of a substantial gain.

Large-scale disruption.   The delay in devaluing plus the build-up of speculative pressure could cause the devaluation to be very large when it eventually came. This could be highly disruptive.

Countries' balance of payments deficits could be reduced and adjustment made easier if surplus countries were willing to revalue. There was a reluctance to do this, however, by countries such as Japan. Revaluation was strongly opposed by exporters (and producers of import substitutes), who would find it suddenly more difficult to compete. What is more, there were not the same pressures for surplus countries to revalue as there were for deficit countries to devalue. A lack of reserves can force deficit countries to devalue. Surplus countries, however, may be quite happy to carry on building up reserves.

The USA was not allowed to devalue when in deficit. The onus was on other countries to revalue, which they were reluctant to do. Hence large US deficits persisted. The problem of these deficits was linked to the second major problem area: that of international liquidity.

Problems of international liquidity and the collapse of the system

With an adjustable peg system, there have to be sufficient stocks of internationally acceptable currencies or other liquid assets. This 'international liquidity' is necessary both to finance trade and to provide enough reserves for central banks to support their currencies whenever there is a currency flow deficit. Under the Bretton Woods system, there were three main sources of liquidity: gold, dollars and IMF quotas. But since IMF quotas were only in existing currencies, they were not a source of *additional* liquidity.

As world trade expanded, so deficits (and surpluses) were likely to be larger, and so more reserves were required. But the supply of gold was not expanding fast enough, so countries increasingly held dollars. After all, dollars earned interest. The willingness to hold dollars enabled the USA to run large balance of payments deficits. All the USA needed to do to pay for the deficits was to 'print' more dollars, which other countries were prepared to accept as reserves.

US balance of payments deficits in the 1960s got steadily worse. The financing of the Vietnam War, in particular,

deepened the deficit. Dollars flooded out of the USA. World liquidity thus expanded rapidly, fuelling world inflation. Furthermore, the rapid growth in overseas dollar holdings meant that US gold reserves were increasingly inadequate to guarantee convertibility. Some countries, fearful that the USA might eventually be forced to suspend convertibility, chose to exchange dollars for gold. US gold reserves fell, creating a further imbalance and a deepening of the crises.

Despite various attempts to rescue the system, with its overreliance on the dollar, it eventually collapsed. The dollar was devalued against gold by 8 per cent in December 1971. In June 1972 the pound was floated. Over the following year, other countries followed suit, and despite a further dollar devaluation the system was finally abandoned in 1973. By mid-1973 gold was trading at $120 per ounce.

Why would the adjustable peg system have been less suitable in the world of the mid-1970s than it was back in the 1950s?

Managed floating

The world has been on a floating exchange rate system since the breakdown of the Bretton Woods system in the early 1970s. This allows adjustment to be made to the inevitable shifts in demand and supply, shifts that got more extreme in the early 1970s with a quadrupling of oil prices in 1973–4 and rapid changes in world trading patterns. Domestic policy has been largely freed from balance of payments constraints. At the same time, *managed* floating was claimed to allow adjustment to be gentler, ideally avoiding wild swings in the exchange rate aggravated by speculation.

TC 6
p55

Some minor currencies remain pegged (but adjustable) to a major currency such as the dollar, but float along with it against other currencies. Other currencies are pegged to each other, but jointly float against the rest of the world. The most notable examples of this have been the currencies of the exchange rate mechanism (ERM) of the European Monetary System (see section 26.2) and now the members of ERM2 (see page 789).

Some countries allow their currencies to float freely. Most countries, however, from time to time have attempted to stabilise their exchange rate, and have thus been operating a system of 'managed flexibility'.

If the country decides to adopt a managed floating system, how could the central bank prevent the exchange rate from falling? There are two main methods:

- Using reserves or foreign loans to purchase domestic currency on the foreign exchange market.
- Raising interest rates to attract short-term financial inflows.

Problems with managed floating since 1972

Managing the exchange rate involved problems, however. Governments needed to know when to intervene, what exchange rate level they should aim to maintain, and how persistently they should try to maintain that rate in the face of speculative pressure.

Predicting the long-term equilibrium exchange rate

Differing inflation rates between countries will require exchange rate adjustments to maintain purchasing-power parity. It is not correct, however, for governments to assume that this will be the *only* cause of shifts in the long-term equilibrium exchange rate. For example, the 1973–4 and 1979–80 oil crises caused fundamental and unpredictable changes in currency demand and supply. So too did other factors, such as the dismantling of trade barriers within the EU, protectionist measures adopted in different parts of the world, changes in technology and changes in tastes.

It is therefore very difficult for the government to predict what the long-term equilibrium will be, and what propor-

tion of any exchange rate movement is therefore due to long-term and what proportion merely to short-term phenomena.

The growth in speculative financial flows

The OPEC oil price increase in 1973–4 caused huge balance of payments deficits for oil importers. The OPEC countries could not spend all of these surpluses on additional imports since (a) they did not have the capacity to consume such a huge increase in imports and (b) the oil-importing countries did not have the capacity to supply such a huge increase in exports. The surpluses were thus largely invested in short-term dollar (and, to a lesser extent, other major currency) assets. This created a large capacity for short-term loans by western banks. These moneys could be rapidly shifted from one world financial centre to

---

| BOX 25.7 | STERLING IN THE 1990S AND 2000S |

The sterling seesaw

Between October 1990 and September 1992, sterling was in the ERM, at a central rate of £1 = 2.95 German marks, with permitted fluctuations of ±6 per cent against any other ERM currency. However, this exchange rate proved unsustainably high and the UK was forced out of the ERM by a massive wave of speculation. Within two months of this, sterling had depreciated by some 15 per cent.

Since 1992, the UK has adopted a virtually free-floating exchange rate. Between 1992 and 1996, fluctuations in the exchange rate were relatively minor. The government was now targeting inflation, and with inflation coming down, it was at first able to reduce interest rates. But this mirrored reductions in inflation and interest rates in other countries, and thus there was little need for exchange rate changes.

Real exchange rate indices (2010 = 100)

Note: Exchange rate indices are BIS broad indices comprising 61 countries.
Source: Based on data from Bank for International Settlements.

another, depending on which country had the most favourable interest rates and exchange rates. This created a massive capacity for speculation, and thus made it difficult for countries to control exchange rates by currency sales alone.

Over the years, the scale of speculative flows has continued to increase. Some $4 trillion now passes across the international exchanges every day. Reserves and access to foreign loans are simply inadequate to prevent concerted speculative selling.

To manage the exchange rate, therefore, central banks would have to rely much more on using interest rates.

Conflicts with internal policy

Using interest rates to support the exchange rate has become more and more unpopular as countries have pre-ferred to use interest rates to keep inflation at or below a target level.

As a result of these problems, countries have increasingly opted for a system of freely floating exchange rates. The UK experience is considered in Case Study 25.6 in MyEconLab and in Box 25.7.

 Would any of these problems be lessened by the world returning to an adjustable peg system? If so, what sort of adjustable peg system would you recommend?

The volatility of exchange rates

Exchange rates have become extremely volatile. We continue to observe this volatility when we adjust for changes in the prices of exports (measured in domestic prices) relative

---

The rise in sterling

By the beginning of 1996, however, speculators began buying pounds, believing that the exchange rate would appreciate. They saw that the economy was now beginning to grow quite rapidly, and was likely to continue doing so, given that an election was coming up. Inflation was thus likely to rise and this would force the government to raise interest rates. Indeed, by mid-1996 interest rates bottomed out and began to rise.

When the new Labour government was elected in 1997, the Bank of England was made independent. Over the following months, the Bank raised interest rates several times in order to bring inflation down to the target level. The effect was a large-scale appreciation of sterling. Between January 1996 and April 1998, the real exchange rate index rose by 32 per cent (see chart). This made it more difficult for UK exporters and industries competing with imports.

From 1998 to 2007 the pound was well above its purchasing-power parity rate. This was largely the result of UK interest rates being higher than eurozone and Japanese rates, and frequently above US rates too.

With the growth of the carry trade (see pages 758–9), this had helped keep the exchange rate above the PPP rate. The overvaluation of the pound continued to put both the export and import-competing sectors in the UK under great competitive pressure. The current account remained in deficit and in most years deteriorated (see the chart in Box 25.2 on page 747).

The fall in sterling

In late 2007, at last the pound began depreciating. With the effects of speculation, this became rapid. Worries about recession suggested that the Bank of England would reduce interest rates – as indeed it did: Bank Rate fell from 5 per cent in October 2008 to 0.5 per cent in March 2009.

But other central banks were reducing their rates too (see the figure in Box 21.11), so why did the pound depreciate while other currencies, including the Japanese yen and Australian dollar, appreciated? There were various reasons for this:

- The cut in Bank Rate was greater than in the eurozone.
- There were worries that the recession would be deeper and more prolonged in the UK than elsewhere and that low interest rates would therefore persist for longer than in other countries.
- Investment in the UK was seen as more risky than in other countries, given the importance of the financial services sector in the UK (a sector badly hit by the credit crunch) and the more rapid rise in government borrowing than in many other countries.
- Commodity prices were rising, which pushed up the exchange rates for commodity-exporting countries, such as Australia.

Significantly, the carry trade began to unwind. With the onset of recession, the UK's high current account deficit was no longer seen as a reason to expect relatively high interest rates. Many who had borrowed in yen or other low-interest-rate currencies, to purchase sterling, now began selling sterling and returning to the original currencies, causing such currencies to appreciate substantially.

Between September 2008 and September 2010 the real sterling exchange rate depreciated by 8 per cent while the real exchange rate of the Japanese yen appreciated by 20 per cent. This appreciation of the yen prompted the Japanese central bank in September 2010 to begin intervening in the foreign exchange markets by selling yen and buying dollars.

Eventually, in mid-2013, sterling began to rise. With recovery gaining momentum more rapidly in the UK than in the eurozone, speculators were predicting that the Bank of England would raise rates before the ECB and that this would cause the pound to appreciate. The actions of speculators ensured that this occurred.

 What factors contributed to the appreciation of sterling from the mid 1990s?.

Figure 25.13   Real exchange rate indices (2010 = 100)

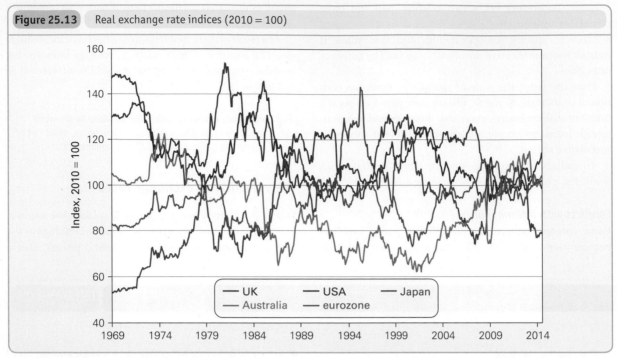

Note: Exchange rate indices are BIS narrow indices comprising 61 countries; prior to the introduction of the euro in 1999, eurozone figures are weighted average exchange rates of currencies that made up the euro.
Source: Based on data from Bank for International Settlements.

to the prices of imports (measured in foreign currencies). In other words, the real exchange rate is volatile too (see Figure 25.13). This means that nominal exchange rates have typically moved more than the relative prices of exported and imported goods and services.

As a result of exchange rate volatility, currencies can gain or lose several percentage points in the space of a few days. These changes can then make all the difference between profit and loss for trading companies. There are a number of reasons for this volatility:

- Inflation or money supply targets. Central banks may have to make considerable changes to interest rates in order to keep to their targets. These in turn cause exchange rate fluctuations.
- A huge growth in international financial markets. This has encouraged the international transfer of money and capital.
- The abolition of exchange controls in most industrialised countries.
- The growth in information technology. The simple use of a computer can transfer capital and finance internationally in a matter of seconds.
- The preference for liquidity. With the danger of currency fluctuations, companies prefer to keep their financial capital as liquid as possible. They do not want to be locked into assets denominated in a declining currency.
- The growing speculative activities of trading companies. Many large companies have a team of dealers to help manage their liquid assets: to switch them from

currency to currency in order to take advantage of market movements.
- The growing speculative activities of banks and other financial institutions.
- The growing belief that rumour and 'jumping on the bandwagon' are more important determinants of currency buying or selling than cool long-term appraisal. If people *believe* that speculation is likely to be destabilising, their actions will ensure that it is. Many companies involved in international trade and finance have developed a 'speculative mentality'.
- The growing belief that governments are powerless to prevent currency movements. As short-term capital (or 'hot money') grows relative to official reserves, it is increasingly difficult for central banks to stabilise currencies through exchange market intervention.

Although most governments and firms dislike highly volatile exchange rates, few today advocate a return to fixed exchange rates, or a system like the Bretton Woods one. In fact, apart from the Gulf states, very few countries still peg their currencies to the dollar. Even China, which from 1997 to 2005 was pegged to the dollar at $1 = 8.27 yuan, has moved to a managed float based round the weighted average of a basket of currencies. In September 2014, the yuan was trading at 6.14 to the dollar – an appreciation of almost 26 per cent since 2005.

Despite the preference of most countries for floating exchange rates, suggestions have been made for reducing volatility. We examine some of these in Chapter 26.

BOX 25.8 **DO INFLATION RATES EXPLAIN LONGER-TERM EXCHANGE RATE MOVEMENTS?**

Does PPP hold in the long run?

As we have seen in section 25.4, exchange rates have become extremely volatile. We can see from Figure 25.13 (page 770) that the trade-weighted *real* exchange rate of sterling exhibits considerable volatility. The real exchange rate adjusts for the terms of trade. The significance of movements in the real exchange rate is that it demonstrates that purchasing-power parity (PPP) fails to hold in the short run.

But does PPP hold in the long run? If so, differences in countries' inflation rates need to be reflected in changes in exchange rates. In this box, we consider whether long-term inflation rate differentials between the UK and 11 other countries have been reflected in long-term movements in the foreign currency price of sterling: i.e. in the number of foreign currency units per £.

Consider the chart. On the horizontal axis is plotted the average annual percentage change in the number of foreign currency units per £1 from 1981 to 2013. Positive values indicate that sterling appreciated against that currency; negative values that it depreciated. For instance, sterling appreciated by 7.8 per cent per annum against the South African rand, but depreciated by 2.7 per cent per annum against the Japanese yen.

On the vertical axis is plotted the inflation differential; this measures the difference between the average annual rate of inflation in the UK and that in each of the other 11 countries. For instance, the average annual UK inflation rate was 3.5 percentage points higher than in Japan, but 6.8 percentage points lower than in South Africa.

If inflation differentials are to be reflected in exchange rate changes we would expect to see the observations for the 11 countries lying along the downward-sloping blue line. This links positive values of the inflation differential with the equivalent percentage depreciation; this would be consistent with PPP holding in the long run.

Five of our observations lie *above* the blue line. This tells us that for the inflation rate differential with each country, sterling has appreciated more or depreciated less than we would have expected. This means that the *real* exchange rate of sterling has *appreciated* against each country's currency over the period of analysis.

Take Japan as an example. As we noted above, the inflation rate differential with the UK is 3.5 percentage points per annum. The higher rate of inflation in the UK means that the exchange rate would need to depreciate by 3.5 per cent per annum to compensate. Although sterling has indeed depreciated against the yen, it has done so by only 2.7 per cent per annum.

Six of our observations lie *below* the blue line. For these countries, sterling has appreciated less or depreciated more than we would have expected. Hence, the real exchange rate of sterling against each country's currency has *depreciated*.

Consider the case of New Zealand. Over the period from 1981 to 2013, the average UK annual rate of inflation has typically been 1.1 percentage points lower than in New Zealand. For PPP to hold, sterling would have needed to appreciate by 1.1 per cent per annum. In fact, it depreciated by 0.2 per cent per annum.

From observing the data, it would appear that long-term inflation differentials do affect movements in bilateral exchange rates. However, it also appears that we need to take into account more than just inflation differentials in understanding exchange rate movements. Other causes of exchange rate movements include changes in relative interest rates, various international shocks, longer-term shifts in demand and supply for imports and exports, and speculation.

Identify two factors in the UK economy which help to explain the appreciation of sterling against several currencies.

Inflation differentials and appreciation of sterling, 1981–2013

Source: Based on data in *Monthly Review of External Statistics* (National Statistics) and *World Economic Outlook* (IMF).

Section summary

1. Under the Bretton Woods system (1945–71), currencies were pegged to the US dollar. The rate was supported from countries' reserves and if necessary with loans from the IMF. If there was a moderate disequilibrium, countries were supposed to use deflationary/reflationary policies. If the disequilibrium became severe, they were supposed to devalue/revalue.

2. The system was claimed to bring certainty for business and a constraint on governments pursuing irresponsible fiscal and monetary policies, while avoiding the problem of a recession if a balance of payments deficit became severe.

3. However, it was sometimes difficult to identify whether a deficit was severe enough to warrant a devaluation; a devaluation itself could be very disruptive for firms; and devaluation at first could make the deficit worse (the J-curve effect). If a country was reluctant to devalue, it would have to rely on deflation and a possible recession to tackle a balance of payments deficit.

4. Problems for deficit countries were made worse by an unwillingness of surplus countries to revalue or reflate.

5. Dollars were the main source of international liquidity under the Bretton Woods system. The USA, by creating dollars to pay for balance of payments deficits, caused excessive liquidity. This caused worldwide inflation, a lack of confidence in the USA and an eventual collapse of the system.

6. Since the early 1970s the world has largely been on a managed floating exchange rate system. The degree of intervention varies from country to country and from time to time.

7. In theory, managed floating can give the necessary degree of exchange rate flexibility in a world where shifts in currency demand and supply have become much larger. It can also release domestic policy from being dominated by balance of payments considerations. At the same time, the intervention could (in theory) prevent violent exchange rate fluctuations and allow a more orderly adjustment to new equilibrium exchange rates.

8. Nevertheless, there are problems under managed floating of predicting long-term equilibrium exchange rates. What is more, with the massive growth in 'hot money' since the early 1970s, it has become increasingly difficult for countries on their own to counteract speculation. The main instrument of intervention has become the rate of interest. There may be a conflict, however, in using interest rates both to control exchange rates *and* to control the domestic economy.

9. Sterling exchange rates have shown considerable volatility over the years, with large divergences from the purchasing-power parity rate. For example, the rise in UK interest rates in 1997–8 caused a large appreciation of sterling, much to the consternation of exporters. The cut in interest rates in 2008 was accompanied by an equally large depreciation.

10. The volatility of exchange rates around the world has grown. Reasons include: a growth in international financial markets and a liberalisation of international financial movements combined with easier computer transfer of funds, a growth in speculative activities and a growing belief in the impotence of governments acting on their own to stabilise rates.

---

*APPENDIX: THE OPEN ECONOMY AND *IS/LM* ANALYSIS

In this appendix, we show how the *IS/LM* analysis that we examined in the appendix to Chapter 21 can be extended to incorporate the open economy. We will first assume a fixed rate of exchange and then later a free-floating rate.

Analysis under a fixed exchange rate

The BP curve

We start by introducing a third curve, the *BP* (balance of payments) curve. This curve, like the *IS* and *LM* curves, plots a relationship between the real rate of interest (*i*) and the level of national income (*Y*). All points along the *BP* curve represent a position of *balance of payments equilibrium*.

The curve slopes upwards from left to right (see Figure 25.14). Increases in the rate of interest (*i*) will cause the financial account to move into surplus as finance is attracted into the country. Increases in national income (*Y*), in contrast, will cause the current account to move into deficit as more imports are purchased. If the overall balance of payments

is to stay in equilibrium, current account deficits must be matched by financial (plus capital) account surpluses and vice versa. Thus a rise in *Y* must be accompanied by a rise in

Figure 25.14 The *BP* curve

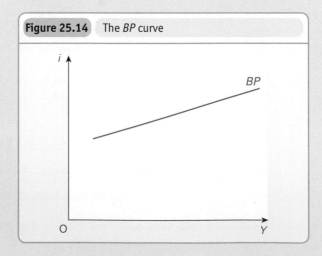

i, and reductions in *Y* must be accompanied by reductions in *i*. The *BP* curve therefore slopes upwards. Any point below the *BP* line represents a position of overall deficit; any point above the line, a position of surplus.

The slope of the *BP* curve depends on two factors.

The marginal propensity to import (mpm = ΔM/ΔY).   The higher the *mpm*, the steeper will be the *BP* curve. The reason is that with a high *mpm* there will be a correspondingly large rise in imports for any given rise in national income. This will cause a large current account deficit. To maintain an overall balance of payments equilibrium, this will require a correspondingly large financial account surplus. This in turn will require a large rise in interest rates. Thus the bigger the *mpm*, the larger the rise in interest rates that will be necessary to restore balance of payments equilibrium, and hence the steeper will be the *BP* curve.

KI 7
p36
The elasticity of supply of international finance.   The greater the elasticity of supply of international finance, the less will be the rise in interest rates necessary to attract an inflow of finance and thereby restore balance of payments equilibrium after a rise in national income, and hence the flatter will be the *BP* curve. In the case of a perfectly elastic supply of international finance, the *BP* curve will be horizontal at the world rate of interest.

Equilibrium in the model

If we now put the *BP* curve on an *IS/LM* diagram, we have the position shown in Figure 25.15. Point *a* represents full equilibrium. At i_1 and Y_1, investment equals saving (point *a* is on the *IS* curve), the demand for money equals the supply (point *a* is also on the *LM* curve), and finally the balance of **KI 8** payments is in balance (point *a* is also on the *BP* curve).
p46
But what is the mechanism that ensures that all three curves intersect at the same point? To answer this question, let us assume that the three curves just happen to intersect at the same point, and then let us examine the effects of changes in fiscal and monetary policies, which shift the *IS* and *LM* curves respectively. Will equilibrium be restored?

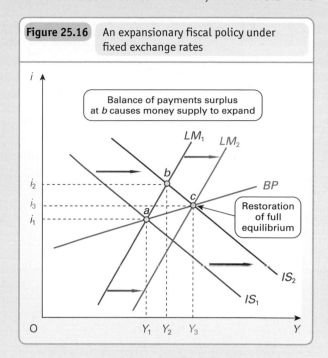

Figure 25.16 An expansionary fiscal policy under fixed exchange rates

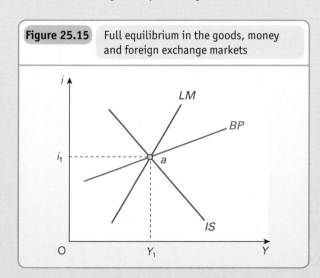

Figure 25.15 Full equilibrium in the goods, money and foreign exchange markets

The answer is yes, via a change in the money supply. Let us examine fiscal and monetary policy changes in turn.

Fiscal policy under fixed exchange rates

An expansionary fiscal policy (i.e. a rise in government spending and/or a reduction in tax) will have the effect of shifting the *IS* curve to the right (e.g. to IS_2 in Figure 25.16). The reason is that for any given rate of interest there will be a higher equilibrium level of national income than before.

This will increase national income, but the extra demand for money that results will drive up interest rates. In a *closed* economy, equilibrium would now be at point *b* (i_2, Y_2), where $IS_2 = LM_1$. But in our open economy model, this equilibrium is *above the BP curve*. There is a balance of payments surplus. The reason for this is that the higher interest rates have caused a financial account surplus that is bigger than the current account deficit that results from the higher national income.

Such a surplus will cause the money supply to rise as funds flow into the country. This will in turn cause the *LM* curve to shift to the right. Equilibrium will finally be achieved at point *c* (i_3, Y_3), where $IS_2 = LM_2 = BP$. Thus under these conditions, the monetary effect of the change in the balance of payments will *reinforce* the fiscal policy and lead to a bigger rise in national income.

 What will be the effect of an expansionary fiscal policy on interest rates and national income if there is a perfectly elastic supply of international finance?

If the *BP* curve were steeper than the *LM* curve, the effect would be somewhat different. (Remember the *BP* curve will

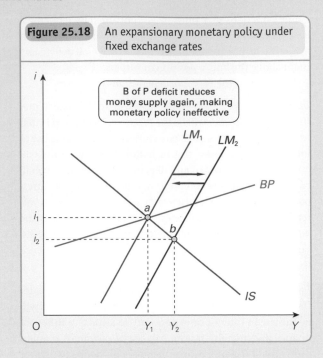

Figure 25.17 An expansionary fiscal policy under fixed exchange rates: a steep *BP* curve

Figure 25.18 An expansionary monetary policy under fixed exchange rates

be steep if there is a high *mpm* and an inelastic supply of international finance.) This is illustrated in Figure 25.17.

Under these circumstances, an initial rise in national income to Y_2 (where $IS_2 = LM_1$) will cause a balance of payments *deficit* (point *b* is *below the BP curve*). The reason is that this time the current account deficit is bigger than the financial account surplus (due to a large *mpm* and a small inflow of finance). This will reduce the money supply and cause the *LM* curve to shift to the left. Equilibrium will be achieved at point *c*, where $LM_2 = IS_2 = BP$.

When the *BP* curve is steeper than the *LM* curve, therefore, the monetary effect of the change in the balance of payments will *dampen* the effect of the fiscal policy and lead to a smaller rise in national income.

Monetary policy under fixed exchange rates

An expansionary monetary policy will cause the *LM* curve to shift to the right (e.g. to LM_2 in Figure 25.18). The increased supply of money will drive down the rate of interest and increase national income. In a closed economy, equilibrium would now be at point *b* (i_2, Y_2), where $LM_2 = IS$. But in an open economy, this extra demand will have sucked in extra imports, and the lower interest rate will have led to net financial outflows. There will be a balance of payments deficit: point *b* is below the *BP* curve.

The balance of payments deficit will cause the money stock to fall as money flows abroad. This will cause the *LM* curve to shift back again to its original position. The economy will return to its initial equilibrium at point *a*.

Thus, under a fixed exchange rate regime, monetary policy alone will have *no long-term effect* on national income and employment. Only when accompanied by an expansion in

aggregate demand (either through fiscal policy or through an autonomous rise in investment or a fall in saving) will an expansion of money supply lead to higher national income.

1. *Why does this conclusion remain the same if the BP curve is steeper than the LM curve?*
2. *Trace through the effects of a fall in exports (thereby shifting the BP curve).*
3. *Show what will happen if there is (a) a rise in business confidence and a resulting increase in investment; (b) a rise in the demand for money balance (say, for precautionary purposes).*

Analysis under free-floating exchange rates

As the exchange rate changes, the *BP* curve will shift (see Figure 25.19). If the *IS* and *LM* curves intersect *above* the *BP*

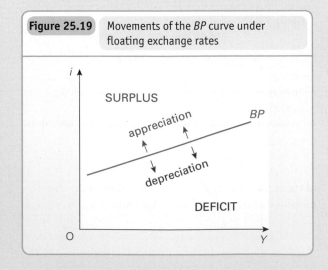

Figure 25.19 Movements of the *BP* curve under floating exchange rates

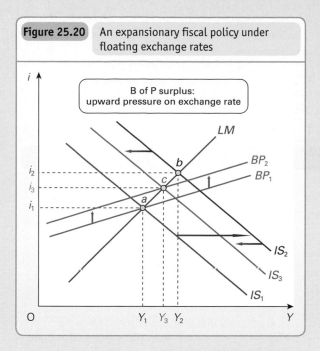

Figure 25.20 An expansionary fiscal policy under floating exchange rates

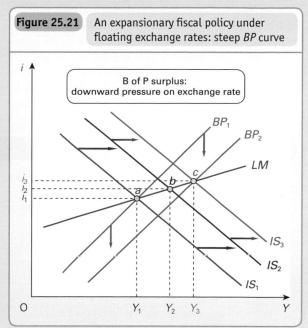

Figure 25.21 An expansionary fiscal policy under floating exchange rates: steep *BP* curve

curve, there will be a balance of payments surplus. This will cause the exchange rate to appreciate. The appreciation will cause the surplus to disappear. This in turn will cause the *BP* curve to shift upwards.

Similarly, if the *IS* and *LM* curves intersect *below* the *BP* curve, the resulting balance of payments deficit will cause a depreciation and a downward shift of the *BP* curve. Thus the *BP* curve will always shift so that it intersects where the *IS* and *LM* curves intersect.

Fiscal policy under floating exchange rates

Assume that the government pursues a reflationary fiscal policy. The *IS* curve shifts to IS_2 in Figure 25.20.

At point *b*, where the *LM* curve and the new *IS* curve intersect, there is a balance of payments surplus (due to higher financial inflows attracted by the higher rate of interest). This causes the exchange rate to appreciate and the *BP* curve to shift upwards.

But the higher exchange rate will cause a fall in exports and a rise in imports. This fall in aggregate demand will cause the *IS* curve to shift back towards the left. The new equilibrium will be at a point such as *c*. This represents only a modest change from point *a*. Thus under a floating exchange rate the effects of fiscal policy may be rather limited.

However, the steeper the *BP* curve, the stronger will be the effect. In Figure 25.21, the *BP* curve is steeper than the *LM* curve. This time a rise in the *IS* curve from IS_1 to IS_2 will lead to a balance of payments *deficit* and hence a *depreciation* of the exchange rate. The *BP* curve will shift *downwards*. The depreciation will cause a rise in exports and a fall in imports. This *rise* in aggregate demand will cause the *IS* curve to shift to the *right*. The new equilibrium will be at point *c*, which is at a higher level of national income, Y_3. Under

these circumstances, the balance of payments effect makes fiscal policy stronger.

 Under what circumstances would an expansionary fiscal policy have no effect at all on national income?

Monetary policy under floating exchange rates

An expansionary monetary policy will shift the *LM* curve to the right, to LM_2 in Figure 25.22. In a closed economy, equilibrium would now be at point *b*.

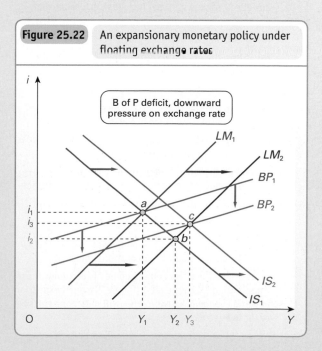

Figure 25.22 An expansionary monetary policy under floating exchange rates

In an open economy under a floating exchange rate, the fall in the rate of interest will cause the exchange rate to depreciate and the *BP* curve to shift downwards. The depreciation will cause exports to rise and imports to fall. This increase in aggregate demand will shift the *IS* curve to the right. The new equilibrium will thus be at point *c*, where $LM_2 = IS_2 = BP_2$. This represents a large change from the initial point *a*.

Thus monetary policy can have a substantial effect on the level of national income under a system of floating exchange rates.

 What will determine the size of the shift in the BP curve in each case?

Section summary

1. A BP curve can be added to an *IS/LM* diagram. It shows all the combinations of national income and real interest rates at which the balance of payments is in equilibrium. The curve is upward sloping, showing that a rise in national income (causing a current account deficit) will require a rise in interest rates to give a counterbalancing financial account surplus.

2. The lower the *mpm* and the more elastic the supply of international finance, the flatter will be the *BP* curve.

3. Under a fixed exchange rate, the flatter the *BP* curve, the larger will be the effect on national income of an expansionary fiscal policy. Provided the *BP* curve is flatter than the *LM* curve, an expansionary fiscal policy will cause a balance of payments surplus (via its effect of increasing interest rates). The resulting increase in money supply will strengthen the initial effect of the fiscal policy.

4. Monetary policy under fixed exchange rates will have no effect on national income. Any expansion of money supply will, by depressing interest rates, simply lead to a balance of payments deficit and thus a reduction in the money supply again.

5. Under a floating exchange rate an appreciation will shift the *BP* curve upwards and a depreciation will shift it downwards.

6. If the *BP* curve is flatter than the *LM* curve, fiscal policy under a floating exchange rate will be dampened by the resulting changes in the exchange rate. An expansionary fiscal policy will lead to an appreciation (due to the effects of higher interest rates), which in turn will dampen the rise in aggregate demand.

7. Monetary policy will have a relatively large effect on aggregate demand under floating rates. A rise in money supply will reduce interest rates and raise aggregate demand. This will cause a balance of payments deficit and thus a depreciation. This in turn will lead to a further expansion of aggregate demand.

END OF CHAPTER QUESTIONS

1. Assume a free-floating exchange rate. Draw a diagram like Figure 25.6 (on page 750), only this time show an initial equilibrium national income with a balance of payments surplus.

   (a) Mark the size of the surplus.

   (b) Show the resulting shifts in the (*X* − *M*) and the *E* curves.

   (c) Mark the eventual equilibrium.

   (d) Show the size of the income and substitution effects (of the change in the exchange rate).

   (e) Under what circumstances will the income effect be (i) 'desirable'; (ii) 'undesirable'?

   (f) Could the income effect of the change in the exchange rate ever be larger than the substitution effect?

2. Compare the relative effectiveness of fiscal and monetary policy under (a) fixed; (b) free-floating exchange rates. How is the effectiveness influenced by the elasticity of supply of international finance?

3. What will be the effects on the domestic economy under free-floating exchange rates if there is a rapid expansion in world economic activity? What will determine the size of these effects?

4. The following table shows a selection of nominal exchange rate indices (effective exchange rates) for the years 2007 to 2013, based on 2010 = 100.

	2007	2008	2009	2010	2011	2012	2013
Australian $	95.0	92.4	88.1	100.0	107.1	109.4	103.7
US $	129.6	97.9	103.5	100.0	95.4	98.2	99.5
Japanese yen	75.6	83.9	95.9	100.0	105.7	107.3	87.2
Sterling	129.6	113.2	100.5	100.0	99.3	103.3	101.2
Euro	102.0	105.6	107.5	100.0	100.5	95.8	100.2
Chinese yuan	90.4	96.4	102.0	100.0	100.1	105.7	111.9

Source: Based on data from Bank for International Settlements.

   (a) Explain what is meant by an exchange rate index/an effective exchange rate.

   (b) Calculate the annual rate of appreciation or depreciation for each currency for each year from 2008.

   (c) Calculate the percentage appreciation or depreciation of each currency when comparing 2013 with 2007.

5. For what reasons might the exchange rate diverge from the purchasing-power parity rate over the longer term?

6. Why does exchange rate overshooting occur? What determines its magnitude?

7. Consider the argument that in the modern world of large-scale, short-term international capital movements, the ability of individual countries to affect their exchange rate is very limited.

8. If speculators had better information about future exchange rates, would their actions be more or less stabilising than at present?

*9. Using *IS/LM/BP* analysis, trace through the effect of (a) a deflationary fiscal policy and (b) a deflationary monetary policy under (i) a fixed exchange rate; (ii) a free-floating exchange rate.

Online resources

Additional case studies in MyEconLab

25.1 **The Marshall–Lerner condition.** An analysis of the determinants of the elasticities of demand and supply of a currency.

25.2 **The gold standard.** A historical example of fixed exchange rates.

25.3 **The sterling crisis of early 1985.** When the pound fell almost to $1.00.

25.4 **Currency turmoil in the 1990s.** Two examples of speculative attacks on currencies: first on the Mexican peso in 1995; then on the Thai baht in 1997.

25.5 **The euro, the US dollar and world currency markets.** An analysis of the relationship between the euro and the dollar.

25.6 **UK experience of managed floating.** An historical account of the volatility in sterling since the early 1970s.

Websites relevant to this chapter

See sites listed at the end of Chapter 26 on page 798.

MyEconLab

This book can be supported by MyEconLab, which contains a range of additional resources, including an online homework and tutorial system designed to test and build your understanding.

You need both an access card and a course ID to access MyEconLab:

1. Is your lecturer using MyEconLab? Ask your lecturer for your course ID.

2. Has an access card been included with the book at a reduced cost? Check the inside back cover of the book.

3. If you have a course ID but no access card, go to: http://www.myeconlab.com/ to buy access to this interactive study programme.

Global and Regional Interdependence

CHAPTER MAP

26.1 Globalisation and the problem of instability   779
Interdependence through trade   779
Financial interdependence   780
International business cycles   781
The need for international policy co-ordination   784
International harmonisation of economic policies   784

26.2 European economic and monetary union (EMU)   788
The ERM (exchange rate mechanism)   788
The Maastricht Treaty and the road to the single currency   788
The birth of the euro   789
Advantages of the single currency   789
Opposition to EMU   790

26.3 Achieving greater currency stability   793
Controlling exchange transactions   793
Exchange rate target zones   794

One of the major causes of currency fluctuations is the very different conditions existing in different countries and the different policies they pursue. For example, an expansionary fiscal policy plus a tight monetary policy can lead to huge currency appreciation if other countries do not follow suit. This is what happened to the dollar in 1983 and 1984. Conversely, a persistent current account deficit, plus a policy of interest rate reductions in order to stimulate the economy, can lead to large-scale currency depreciation. This happened to sterling after it left the ERM in 1992 and to the dollar in 2007 and to sterling again in 2008.

Changes in exchange rates are then often amplified by speculation. And this problem is becoming worse. As we have seen, approximately $4 trillion per day passes across the foreign exchange markets. The scale of such movements makes any significant speculation simply too great for individual countries to resist. And on some occasions even the concerted action of groups of countries cannot maintain exchange rate stability.

In the first section, we explore the nature of the interdependence of economies and why countries are so vulnerable to international fluctuations. We then look at what can be done to create a greater co-ordination of international economic policies and consider the role of the G8 and G20 countries in this process.

The extreme solution to currency instability is for countries to adopt a common currency. In section 26.2, we look at the euro and how economic and monetary union (EMU) operates. The chapter finishes by looking at some alternative suggestions for reducing currency fluctuations.

26.1 GLOBALISATION AND THE PROBLEM OF INSTABILITY

We live in an interdependent world. Countries are affected by the economic health of other countries and by their governments' policies. Problems in one part of the world can spread like a contagion to other parts, with perhaps no country immune.

There are two major ways in which this process of 'globalisation' affects individual economies. The first is through trade. The second is through financial markets.

Interdependence through trade

So long as nations trade with one another, the domestic economic actions of one nation will have implications for those which trade with it. For example, if the US administration feels that the US economy is growing too fast, it might adopt various contractionary fiscal and monetary measures, such as higher tax rates or interest rates. US consumers will not only consume fewer domestically produced goods, but also reduce their consumption of imported products. But US imports are other countries' exports. A fall in these other countries' exports will lead to a multiplier effect in these countries. Output and employment will fall.

Changes in aggregate demand in one country thus send ripples throughout the global economy. The process whereby changes in imports into (or exports from) one country affect national income in other countries is known as the *international trade multiplier*.

 Assume that the US economy expands. What will determine the size of the multiplier effect on other countries?

The more open an economy, the more vulnerable it will be to changes in the level of economic activity in the rest of the world. This problem will be particularly acute if a nation is heavily dependent on trade with one other nation (e.g. Canada on the USA) or one other region (e.g. Switzerland on the EU).

International trade has been growing as a proportion of countries' national income for many years. This is illustrated in Figure 26.1, which shows the growth in world real exports and in real GDP. You can see that exports have been growing much more rapidly than GDP. From 1951 to 2015 the average annual growth in world output was 3.6 per cent, whereas the figure for world exports was 6.0 per cent.

With most nations committed to freer trade, and with the WTO overseeing the dismantling of trade barriers, international trade is likely to continue growing as a proportion of world GDP. This will increase countries' interdependence and their vulnerability to world trade fluctuations, such as the global recession of the late 2000s. World output fell by 2.4 per cent in 2009, while worldwide exports fell by 10.0 per cent. This was the biggest contraction in global trade since the Second World War.

 Are exports likely to continue growing faster than GDP indefinitely? What will determine the outcome?

Definition

International trade multiplier The effect on national income in country B of a change in exports (or imports) of country A.

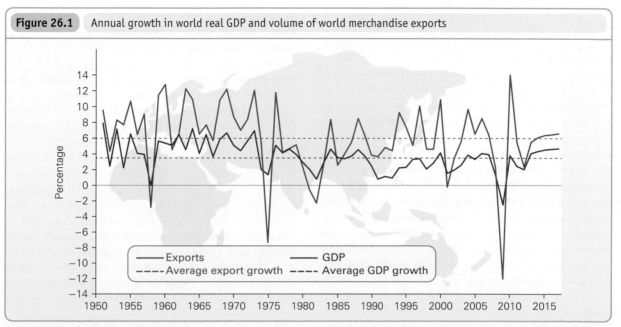

Figure 26.1 Annual growth in world real GDP and volume of world merchandise exports

Note: Data from 2013 based on forecasts.
Source: Based on data in International Trade Statistics, 2013 (WTO) and World Economic Outlook (IMF).

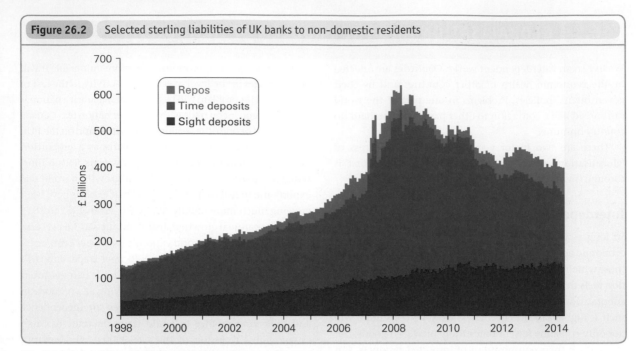

| **Figure 26.2** | Selected sterling liabilities of UK banks to non-domestic residents |

Note: Data include building societies from 2010; data are not seasonally adjusted.

Source: Based on series RPMTBFF, RPMTBFM, RPMTBFT (up to end of 2009) and RPMB3OM, RPMB3TM and RPMB3WM (from 2010) from Statistical Interactive Database, Bank of England (data published 2 June 2014).

Financial interdependence

International trade has grown rapidly over the past 30 years, but international financial flows have grown much more rapidly. Each day, some $4 trillion of assets are traded across the foreign exchanges. Many of the transactions are short-term financial flows, moving to where interest rates are most favourable or to currencies where the exchange rate is likely to appreciate. This has meant that non-deposit financial institutions like pension funds, insurance companies and investment trusts have become important players on foreign exchange markets.

In Chapter 18 we identified a variety of financial instruments. The global nature of financial systems means that these financial instruments readily cross national borders. It also means that financial institutions operating in one country will have liabilities to foreign residents (individuals and institutions). Figure 26.2 shows the growth in those claims of foreign residents on banks operating in the UK which take the form of sterling-denominated sight deposits, time deposits and repos. Holdings by foreign residents of these three financial instruments rose from £135 billion at the beginning of 1998 to nearly £630 billion in April 2008. By spring 2014, following the global banking crisis and subsequent consolidation by banks of their balance sheets, the value of these liabilities had fallen to close to £400 billion, but this was still well above the 1998 values, even after taking inflation into account.

Another demonstration of global financial interdependence is the foreign holdings of government securities. Figure 26.3 shows the importance of foreign demand for British gilts: i.e. for long-term UK government securities.

At the start of 1996 gilts worth about £50 billion were held overseas, the equivalent to 19 per cent of holdings of gilts. By the start of 2014 this had risen to over £400 billion or 30 per cent of holdings.[1] In Box 26.1 we consider the significance of foreign purchases of US government debt.

A stark example of global financial interdependence was the collapse of the sub-prime credit markets in the USA in the late 2000s, which spread like a contagion to cause a global recession. Household debt in many advanced economies, including the UK and USA, had grown markedly as a proportion of household disposable income. Between 2000 and 2008, the stock of debt held by UK households increased from around 116 per cent to 175 per cent of annual disposable income (see Box 17.2). In the USA over the same period, the stock of household debt increased from 104 to 135 per cent of annual disposable income.

As we discussed in section 18.2, the growth of domestic credit has been facilitated both by financial deregulation, including the removal of capital controls, and the greater use by financial institutions of wholesale funding. The process of securitisation (see pages 533–6), for instance, enabled financial institutions to raise capital from financial investors across the globe in order to provide domestic households with both mortgages and short-term credit. In other words, the aggressive expansion of domestic banks' balance sheets was funded by international financial flows.

Financial deregulation and innovation have therefore created a complex chain of interdependencies between

---

[1] Note that this still means that the bulk of national debt is held by residents in the UK. In other words, most of what the government owes is in the form of the savings by UK individuals and companies.

Figure 26.3 Overseas holdings of UK government gilts

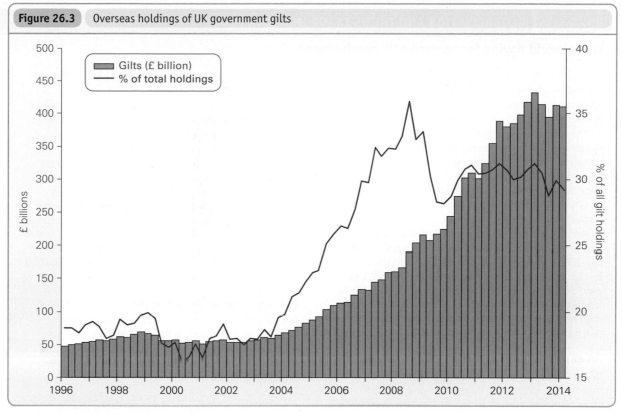

Source: Based on data from Debt Managemeent Office.

financial institutions, financial systems and economies. But this chain is only as strong as its weakest link. In the financial crisis of the late 2000s overly aggressive lending practices by banks in one part of the world impacted on financial investors worldwide. As US interest rates rose from 2004 to 2007 (see figure in Box 25.5), the income flows from US households to banks began to dry up; US households began to fall into arrears and, worse still, default on their loans. But these income flows were the source of the return for global financial investors who had purchased collateralised debt obligations (see page 534). Hence, the new financial order meant the contagion went international.

Global financial interdependence also means that changes in interest rates in one country can affect the economies of other countries. Assume that the Federal Reserve Bank in the USA, worried about rising inflation, decides to raise interest rates. What will be the effect on business in the USA's trading partners? There are three major effects:

- If aggregate demand in the USA falls, so will its expenditure on imports from firms abroad, thus directly affecting businesses exporting to the USA. With a decline in their exports, aggregate demand in these other countries falls.
- The higher interest rate in the USA will tend to drive up interest rates in other countries. This will depress investment. Again, aggregate demand will tend to fall in these countries.
- The higher interest rate will attract an inflow of funds to the USA from other countries. This will cause the dollar

to appreciate relative to other currencies. This will make these other countries' exports to the USA more competitive and imports from the USA relatively more expensive. This will result in an improvement in the current account of the USA's trading partners: their exports rise and imports fall. This represents a *rise* in aggregate demand in these countries – the opposite from the first two effects.

 What will be the effect on the UK economy if the European Central Bank cuts interest rates?

International business cycles

There is an old saying: 'If America sneezes, the rest of the world catches a cold.' Viruses of a similar nature regularly infect the world economy. The credit crunch of 2007–8 resulting from defaults on US sub-prime debt was a dramatic example of this. As a consequence of both trade and financial interdependence, the world economy, like the economy of any individual country, tends to experience periodic fluctuations in economic activity – an *international* business cycle. The implication of this is that countries will tend to share common problems and concerns at the same time. At one time, the most pressing problem may be world inflationary pressures; at another time, it may be a world recession.

In order to avoid 'beggar-my-neighbour' policies, it is better to seek *common* solutions to these common problems: i.e. solutions that are international in scope and design

BOX 26.1   GLOBALISATION AND THE US TRADE IMBALANCE

Is the world paying for excessive US expenditure?

In 2013 the USA had a current account deficit of $380 billion – the equivalent of 2.3 per cent of GDP (see chart). Since 2000, the US current account deficit has averaged 4 per cent of GDP, reaching as high as 5.8 per cent of GDP in 2006.

The current account deficit is offset by an equal and opposite capital-plus-financial account surplus, much of which consists of the purchase of US government bonds and Treasury bills. These massive inflows to the USA represent some 80 per cent of the savings which the rest of the world invests abroad. These financial inflows permitted the current account deficit to deepen.

And yet US interest rates for much of the 2000s have been at historically low levels. Nominal interest rates from mid-2003 to mid-2004 were a mere 1 per cent (see chart in Box 25.5 on page 762) and real rates were minus 1.3 per cent! Similarly, since the financial crisis of the late 2000s, interest rates have been very low in comparison with other countries. How is it, then, that with such low interest rates the USA has maintained such a large financial account surplus?

An answer in Asia

Several Asian currencies, including the Chinese yuan (or 'renminbi'), were pegged to the dollar and had been running large current account surpluses. For instance, the Chinese current account surplus since 2000 has averaged close to 4.5 per cent of GDP (see chart). Instead of letting their currencies appreciate against the dollar, Asian central banks were using their surpluses to buy dollars.

These countries saw a triple advantage in this. First, it allowed them to *build up reserves* and thereby bolster their ability to resist any future speculative attacks on their currencies. Since 2000 foreign exchange reserves across developing Asian economies are thought to have grown by more than 20 per cent per year. Chinese foreign exchange reserves rose from $172 billion in 2000 to approaching $4 trillion in early 2014 – a staggering 20-fold increase. The effect was a huge increase in global liquidity and hence money supply.

Second, and more important, it kept their exchange rates low and thereby helped to keep their exports competitive. This helped to sustain their rapid rates of economic growth. Third, it helped to keep US interest rates down and therefore boost US spending on Asian exports.

In 2005, the Chinese, after much international pressure, agreed to revalue the yuan and then peg it against a basket of currencies with subsequent further revaluations. Between July 2005 and July 2008 the yuan was allowed to appreciate by 17 per cent against the US dollar while the exchange rate index rose by 7 per cent (the exchange rate index of the US dollar fell by 15 per cent).

But, with the global economic downturn biting in 2008 and concerns about slowing Chinese export growth, the Chinese authorities effectively fixed the yuan once again.

This remained the case until June 2010 when again the yuan was revalued. Between June 2010 and January 2014 the yuan appreciated a further 10.5 per cent against the US dollar, though it depreciated by 12 per cent against a trade-weighted basket of currencies. Therefore, over the period from July 2005 to January 2014 the yuan appreciated by 26 per cent against the US dollar. But this rate of appreciation of the yuan has been considerably below the level necessary to achieve a PPP rate. It remains undervalued by some 40 per cent against the dollar in PPP terms.

Consequences of the imbalance

Can the USA simply continue with a massive current account deficit, financed by the acquisition of equally huge amounts of dollars by the rest of the world, and Asia in particular? Or must there be a correction of the current account imbalance?

A depreciation of the dollar.   From mid-2004, US interest rates began to rise – but not fast enough to prevent the dollar's slide on the foreign exchange market. From July 2004 to July 2008 the effective exchange rate of the dollar depreciated by 17 per cent. Initially, the current account worsened (see chart), consistent with a J-curve effect (see pages 766–7). It then modestly improved.

Many commentators, however, have argued that the rate would need to fall significantly more if the deficit was to be reduced to a sustainable size without injecting excessive liquidity into the world economy. This would mean an exchange rate perhaps as high as $1.80 to the euro and $2.30 to the pound, which would have devastating effects on European exports and make sustained European recovery much more difficult.

Chinese bubbles.   A real danger for the Chinese and other Asian economies is that real increases in output may not match the increase in money supply. The result would then be inflation, compounded by rising commodity prices. In 2008, inflation reached 8.7 per cent, the highest for 12 years, having averaged only 1.2 per cent from 2000 to 2006. The global economic recession helped to bring inflation down quickly with annual rates of deflation of 2 per cent during 2009. Interestingly, China's own rate of economic growth,

---

rather than narrowly based on national self-interest. For example, during a world recession, countries are likely to suffer from rising unemployment. Policies that lead to a depreciation of the exchange rate (such as cutting interest rates) will help to stimulate demand by making exports cheaper and imports more expensive. But this will then only worsen the trade balance of other countries, whose aggregate demand will thus fall. The first country is thus tackling its own unemployment at the expense of rising unemployment in other countries.

However, if other nations (which will also be experiencing higher unemployment) can be convinced to

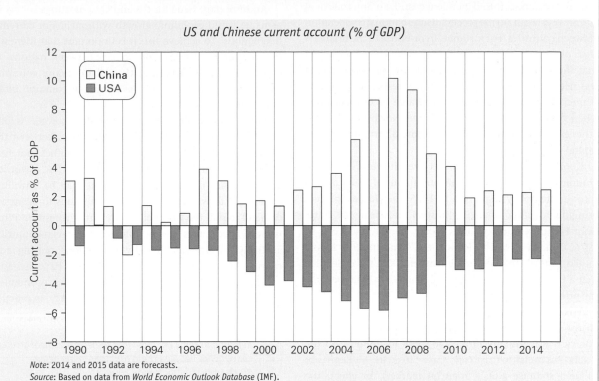

US and Chinese current account (% of GDP)

Note: 2014 and 2015 data are forecasts.
Source: Based on data from *World Economic Outlook Database* (IMF).

which peaked at 14 per cent in 2007, remained at between 9 and 10 per cent in the period from 2008 to 2011. When global growth returned in 2010–11, helping to refuel commodity price inflation, China's inflation rate was again to rise to 6.5 per cent.

A major concern for economic stability is the growth in domestic credit in China. The amount of domestic credit extended by the financial sector to all sectors of the economy, except central government, had risen from 88 per cent of GDP in 1995 to 155 per cent of in 2012. One manifestation of this credit growth was rising Chinese property prices. Annual rates of residential house price inflation topped 40 per cent in 2008.

China's concern about the inflationary impact of increased money supply resulted in its raising interest rates several times between 2004 and 2008, thereby helping to sterilise some of the currency flow surplus. Though rates fell at the end of 2008, they started rising again at the end of 2010 and continued doing so until the second half of 2012.

China was, however, concerned about raising rates too quickly, not only because of the potential impact on

economic growth, but also in case it attracted speculative capital resulting in a faster appreciation of the yuan. Another method used to constrain credit growth was to increase the deposit reserve ratio that the country's banks were required to meet. This ratio reached 21.5 per cent in June 2011 before being lowered slightly. In 2011 economic growth eased to 7.7 per cent, while annual house price inflation rates were close to zero by the end of the year.

Potential currency volatility. Perhaps the biggest long-term danger of the huge increase in international liquidity is the potential for large-scale selling of the dollar and consequent overshooting of the long-term equilibrium exchange rate. Between March 2009 and August 2011 the dollar exchange rate index fell by 16.7 per cent. Concerns about the size of the US fiscal deficit and the effects of quantitative easing only added to the danger of a significant overshoot.

 Examine the merits for the Chinese of (a) floating the yuan freely; (b) pegging it to a trade-weighted basket of currencies.

co-ordinate their policy actions, an expansionary *international* economic policy will benefit all. In addition to the resulting rise in their imports, all nations will also experience rising export sales.

Even if national policies are not in the strictest sense co-ordinated, discussions between nations regarding the

nature and magnitude of the problems they face may help to improve the policy-making process.

 Give some examples of beggar-my-neighbour policies.

The need for international policy co-ordination

Global economic interdependence and an international business cycle can aid the process of international co-operation between countries. For instance, in response to the financial crisis of the late 2000s world leaders were seriously worried that the whole world would plunge into recession. What was needed was a co-ordinated policy response from governments and central banks. This came in October 2008 when governments in the UK, Europe, North America and other parts of the world injected some $2 trillion of extra capital into banks.

Countries have frequently met over the years in various groupings to discuss economic and financial issues and to co-ordinate policy responses. In 1975, the G6 was formed, bringing together finance ministers and heads of states from France, Germany, Italy, Japan, the UK and USA. In 1976, Canada joined to form the G7 and in 1998 Russia joined to form the G8. In September 2009 it was decided that a broader grouping known as the G20 would become the principal economic forum.

The G20 represents 19 countries and the EU and includes all the G8 countries, but larger emerging economies too. The G20 was initially formed in 1999 in response to the Asian Financial Crisis (see Case 26.3 in MyEconLab) to help stabilise global financial markets. In effect, the emergence of the G20 as the premier forum recognises two important developments. First, there has been a remarkable growth seen in emerging economies like Brazil, India, China and South Africa which, along with Russia, are often collectively referred to as BRICS (see section 24.1 and Figure 24.2). Second, the increasing scale of interdependency through trade and finance typically requires a co-ordinated response from a larger representation of the international community.

Global interdependence also raises questions about the role that international organisations like the World Trade Organization (WTO) and the International Monetary Fund (IMF) should play. The WTO's role is to encourage freer trade. We considered its role in section 24.2. The IMF's remit is to promote global growth and stability, to help countries through economic difficulty and to help developing economies achieve macroeconomic stability and reduce poverty. In response to the global economic and financial crisis of the late 2000s, the IMF's budget was substantially increased and it became more actively involved with what were previously defined as 'strong performing economies' (see Box 26.2).

International harmonisation of economic policies

The five main underlying causes of exchange rate movements are divergences in *interest rates*, *growth rates*, *inflation rates*, *current account balance of payments* and *government*

deficits. Table 26.1 shows the variation in the levels of these indicators across a sample of eight countries. These divergences still remain considerable.

An important issue for G8 and G20 meetings is how to generate world economic growth without major currency fluctuations. To achieve this it is important that there is a *harmonisation* of economic policies between nations. In other words, it is important that all the major countries are pursuing consistent policies aiming at common international goals.

But how can policy harmonisation be achieved? As long as there are significant domestic differences between the major economies, there is likely to be conflict, not harmony. For example, if one country, say the USA, is worried about the size of its budget deficit, it may be unwilling to respond to world demands for a stimulus to aggregate demand to pull the world economy out of recession. What is more, speculators, seeing differences between countries, are likely to exaggerate them by their actions, causing large changes in exchange rates. The G8 countries have therefore sought to achieve greater *convergence* of their economies. But whilst convergence may be a goal of policy, in practice it has proved more elusive.

 Referring to Table 26.1, in what respects was there greater convergence between these countries in the period 2009–13 than in the period 2004–8?

Because of a lack of convergence, there are serious difficulties in achieving international policy harmonisation:

- Countries' budget deficits and national debt may differ substantially as a proportion of their national income. This puts very different pressures on the interest rates necessary to service these debts. In 2013, the UK had a general government net debt (debt less liquid assets) to GDP ratio of 72 per cent. This compared with 14 per cent for Australia, 39 per cent for Canada, 56 per cent for Germany, 88 per cent for France and 134 per cent for Japan.
- Harmonising rates of monetary growth or inflation targets would involve letting interest rates fluctuate with the demand for money. Without convergence in the demand for money, interest rate fluctuations could be severe.

> ### Definitions
>
> **International harmonisation of economic policies** Where countries attempt to co-ordinate their macroeconomic policies so as to achieve common goals.
>
> **Convergence of economies** When countries achieve similar levels of growth, inflation, budget deficits as a percentage of GDP, balance of payments, etc.

Table 26.1 International macroeconomic indicators

		Australia	Canada	China	France	Germany	Japan	UK	USA
Nominal exchange rate index (annual % change)	1989–1993	−2.8	−0.9	1.3	1.6	1.8	3.8	−3.2	−0.2
	1994–1998	0.3	−2.2	−2.8	0.4	−0.1	−1.2	3.7	2.7
	1999–2003	0.0	1.0	−1.4	−0.1	−0.1	2.4	−0.9	−0.9
	2004–2008	2.7	5.0	−0.6	1.0	1.3	0.2	−1.4	−3.9
	2009–2013	3.5	1.1	1.1	−0.6	−0.8	2.3	−2.0	0.5
Short-term (3-month) nominal interest rate (%)	1989–1993	10.8	9.2	8.0	9.7	8.3	5.6	11.1	6.0
	1994–1998	6.2	5.1	9.0	4.7	4.0	1.1	6.5	5.4
	1999–2003	5.1	4.0	2.7	3.5	3.5	0.2	4.8	3.7
	2004–2008	6.2	3.4	2.9	3.3	3.3	0.4	5.1	3.7
	2009–2013	3.9	1.0	3.7	0.8	0.8	0.2	0.8	0.4
Economic growth (% change in real GDP)	1989–1993	2.5	0.8	9.1	1.7	3.0	3.1	1.6	2.4
	1994–1998	4.2	3.5	10.2	2.2	1.7	1.0	4.0	3.9
	1999–2003	3.4	3.3	8.7	2.1	1.3	0.9	3.1	2.9
	2004–2008	3.4	2.4	11.6	1.8	1.9	1.3	2.4	2.3
	2009–2013	2.5	1.4	8.9	0.2	0.7	0.3	−0.1	1.2
Consumer price inflation (% change in CPI)	1989–1993	4.2	3.7	6.9	3.0	3.7	2.3	5.3	4.1
	1994–1998	2.1	1.3	10.3	1.5	1.6	0.6	2.1	2.4
	1999–2003	3.2	2.4	0.0	1.7	1.3	−0.6	1.2	2.5
	2004–2008	3.1	2.1	3.6	2.2	2.1	0.3	2.3	3.2
	2009–2013	2.4	1.5	2.7	1.5	1.5	−0.4	3.1	1.6
Current account balance (% of GDP)	1989–1993	−4.1	−3.6	0.9	−0.2	0.8	2.3	−2.5	−1.0
	1994–1998	−4.1	−1.1	1.9	1.5	−0.9	2.3	−0.4	−1.7
	1999–2003	−4.1	1.5	1.9	1.7	0.2	2.6	−2.3	−3.9
	2004–2008	−5.9	1.3	7.5	−0.7	5.9	3.9	−2.0	−5.2
	2009–2013	−3.6	−3.2	3.0	−1.6	6.8	2.1	−2.5	−2.7
General government surplus (% of GDP)	1989–1993	−1.8	−7.3	−2.1	−3.6	−2.8	0.5	−3.5	−5.3
	1994–1998	−1.1	−2.8	−2.1	−4.2	−4.1	−4.4	−3.7	−2.7
	1999–2003	0.8	1.1	−3.0	2.5	−2.3	−7.3	−0.1	−2.2
	2004–2008	1.0	1.1	−0.7	−3.0	−1.7	−4.1	−3.5	−5.1
	2009–2013	−4.3	−3.9	−2.0	−5.8	−1.6	−9.3	−8.6	−11.1

Note: Chinese short-term interest rate 1990–8 is the central bank discount rate (data commence 1990).
Sources: *Stat Extracts* (OECD), *Principal Economic Indicators* (IMF) and *AMECO database* (European Commission).

- Harmonising interest rates would involve abandoning monetary, inflation and exchange rate targets (unless interest rate 'harmonisation' meant adjusting interest rates so as to maintain monetary or inflation targets or a fixed exchange rate).
- Countries have different internal structural relationships. A lack of convergence here means that countries with higher endemic *cost* inflation would require higher interest rates and higher unemployment if international inflation rates were to be harmonised, or higher inflation if interest rates were to be harmonised.
- Countries have different rates of productivity increase, product development, investment and market penetration. A lack of convergence here means that the growth in exports (relative to imports) will differ for any given level of inflation or growth.
- Countries may be very unwilling to change their domestic policies to fall in line with other countries. They may prefer the other countries to fall in line with them!

If any one of the five – interest rates, growth rates, inflation rates, current account balance of payments or government deficits – could be harmonised across countries, it is likely that the other four would then not be harmonised.

Total convergence and thus total harmonisation may not be possible. Nevertheless most governments favour some movement in that direction: some is better than none. To achieve this, co-operation is necessary.

Although co-operation is the ideal, in practice discord often tends to dominate international economic relations. The reason is that governments are normally concerned with the economic interests of other countries only if they coincide with those of their own country. This, however, can create a prisoners' dilemma problem (see pages 210–11 and 368). With each country looking solely after its own interests, the world economy suffers and everyone is worse off.

 KI 22 p223

 If total convergence were achieved, would harmonisation of policies follow automatically?

BOX 26.2	DOCTOR, THE WORLD HAS CAUGHT A COLD

Global answers to global problems?

We don't have to look far to see how much economic and financial interdependence affects our daily lives. As you walk down the street to the supermarket, many of the passing cars originate overseas or perhaps were built here by foreign-owned companies. You look up and the airliner flying overhead is taking passengers to every corner of the world for both business and pleasure. As you enter the supermarket you see an array of goods from all over the world.

Clearly, interdependence through trade connects economies. The late 2000s have helped demonstrate just how interdependent financial systems and financial institutions have become. Financial products have a passport to travel, and travel they do!

Increasing economic and financial interdependence means that problems in one part of the world rapidly spread to other parts. Just look at what happened when the US sub-prime mortgage market collapsed. The USA's illness turned into the world's flu!

But who should dish out the medicine? How potent can the medicine of national governments be in isolation? What role is there for co-ordinated monetary and fiscal policies and does it require stronger international institutions to deal with world problems?

Iceland's cold

The decline in output in Iceland in 2009, at nearly 7 per cent, was especially stark. The country had been especially badly hit by the global financial crisis.

An aggressive strategy of credit expansion had seen the liabilities of the three largest Icelandic banks rise from 100 per cent of GDP in 2004 to 923 per cent in 2007. Some of the funds from this expansion came from the interbank market but also from deposits overseas in subsidiaries of these banks in the Nordic countries and the UK. When the credit crunch hit, they found it increasingly difficult to roll over loans on the interbank market. What is more, the sheer scale of the banks' expansion made it virtually impossible for Iceland's central bank to guarantee repayments of the loans.

The result was that four of its largest banks were nationalised and run by Iceland's Financial Supervisory Authority.

In November 2008, the International Monetary Fund's executive board approved a $2.1 billion loan to Iceland to support an economic recovery programme. An initial payment of $827 million was made with subsequent payments to be spread over time, subject to IMF quarterly reviews of the recovery programme.

A Greek Tragedy

Greece has been struggling with the burden of a huge budget deficit for some years, and following the credit crunch of 2008 its general government deficit soared. In 2008 it was 9.9 per cent of GDP; by 2009, it was 15.6 per cent – the highest in the EU at the time and over five times higher than EU rules allow. The annual cost to Greece of servicing the debt was running at about 12 per cent of GDP. In early 2010 the government estimated that it would need to borrow €53 billion to cover budget shortfalls. Greece, like many other countries, also experienced rising unemployment. By 2010 the unemployment rate was 12.5 per cent, up from 7.7 per cent in 2008.

Austerity measures, as part of an IMF and EU rescue package, aimed to reduce this deficit to less than 3 per cent of GDP by 2014. This was to be achieved through a variety of spending cuts and tax rises and was the price that Greece had to pay to receive a £95 billion bailout. However, the costs of the austerity measures in terms of disposable income and unemployment were high and there were widespread strikes by public-sector workers.

Subsequent events demonstrated that the debt crisis was not just confined to Greece. For instance, in November 2010 Ireland agreed a rescue package of up to €100 billion with the IMF and EU member states. The general government deficit in Ireland in 2010 was estimated at 31 per cent of GDP, up from 14.4 per cent in 2009. The aim was to reduce to this to 3 per cent of GDP by 2015.

IMF to the rescue?

We have seen how the IMF has been a major player in helping to finance rescue packages for countries like Iceland, Ireland and Greece. But what is the IMF? And what does it do?

The IMF is a 'specialised agency' of the United Nations and is financed by its 188 member countries (as of 2014). The role of the IMF is to ensure macroeconomic stability – as in the cases above – and to foster global growth. It also works with developing nations to alleviate poverty and to achieve economic stability. To do this it provides countries with loans.

The IMF has not been without controversy, however. Conditions attached to loans have often been very harsh, especially for some of the most indebted developing countries.

Section summary

1. Changes in aggregate demand in one country will affect the amount of imports purchased and thus the amount of exports sold by other countries and hence their national income. There is thus an international trade multiplier effect.

2. Changes in interest rates in one country will affect financial flows to and from other countries, and hence their exchange rates, interest rates and national income.

3. To prevent problems in one country spilling over to other countries and to stabilise the international business cycle will require co-ordinated policies between nations.

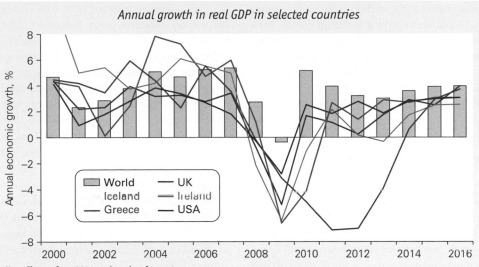

Annual growth in real GDP in selected countries

Note: Figures from 2014 are based on forecasts.
Source: Based on data in *World Economic Outlook*, April 2014 (International Monetary Fund).

The global economic and financial crisis provided the IMF with a challenge: which countries to support with a limited budget? Between 2007 and spring 2012, the IMF is estimated to have provided $300 billion of loans to member countries. During this period an increasing amount of assistance was being given to developed economies, especially within the EU.

Following crisis talks with finance ministers in Europe in May 2010, the IMF agreed to set aside €250 billion to support eurozone countries in financial difficulty. This would be in addition to €440 billion supplied by eurozone countries under the 'European Financial Stability Facility' and €60 billion from EU funds under the 'European Financial Stabilisation Mechanism'.

In October 2010 the EU agreed to establish a more permanent funding mechanism for eurozone countries in financial difficulties, known as the European Stability Mechanism (see Box 21.3). The Mechanism became operational in 2013. The IMF is a crucial stakeholder in the funding mechanism, both in committing funds but also in assessing, alongside the European Commission and the European Central Bank, the financial position of any country requesting help. This assessment includes possible 'macroeconomic adjustment programmes' for countries in receipt of funds.

Strengthening the IMF

World leaders meeting as part of the G20 in London in April 2009 announced the need to strengthen global financial institutions. They agreed that the resources available to the IMF should be trebled to $750 billion. They also agreed that the IMF would work with a new Financial Stability Board (FSB), made up, among others, of the G20 countries and the European Commission, so as to help in identifying potential economic and financial risks. Essentially, the G20 countries were looking for a better 'early warning system' to meet some of the challenges of an increasingly interdependent world.

However, the ongoing financial problems facing governments, particularly in the eurozone, led the international community in April 2012 to pledge an additional $430 billion in resources for the IMF. Further changes in members' subscriptions were expected from 2015 as part of the IMF's 15th periodic review of the 'quota system'. This is the system which helps determine members' subscriptions, their voting power and their access to financing. The intention was that the IMF has sufficient finances to create a credible 'firewall' to contain future financial crisis.

 Do you see any problems arising from a strengthening of global economic and financial institutions?

4. Currency fluctuations can be lessened if countries harmonise their economic policies. Ideally this will involve achieving compatible growth rates, inflation rates, balance of payments and government deficits (as percentages of GDP) and interest rates. The attempt to harmonise one of these goals, however, may bring conflicts with one of the other goals.

5. Leaders of the G8 and G20 countries meet at least annually to discuss ways of harmonising their policies. Usually, however, domestic issues are more important to the leaders than international ones, and frequently they pursue policies that are not in the interests of the other countries.

26.2 EUROPEAN ECONOMIC AND MONETARY UNION (EMU)

The ultimate way for a group of countries to achieve greater currency stability between themselves is to adopt a single currency and, therefore, to have a common central bank and a common monetary policy – to form an *economic and monetary union (EMU)*. This is what has happened in the EU, with countries coming together to adopt a single currency – the euro. The euro began in 1999, with notes and coins circulating from 2002. Initially 11 countries joined; by 2014 there were 18 members.

The ERM (exchange rate mechanism)

The forerunner to EMU was the *exchange rate mechanism (ERM)*. This was an adjustable peg system, where members pegged their exchange rates to each other while floating against the rest of the world. This encouraged trade between the members and enabled the combined reserves of all member countries to prevent excessive fluctuations of their currencies with the rest of the world.

Under the system, each currency was given a central exchange rate with each of the other ERM currencies in a grid. However, fluctuations were allowed from the central rate within specified bands, typically of up to 0.25 per cent. The central rates were adjusted from time to time by agreement. All the currencies floated jointly with currencies outside the ERM.

If a currency approached the upper or lower limit against *any* other ERM currency, intervention would take place to maintain the currencies within the band. This would take the form of central banks in the ERM selling the strong currency and buying the weak one. It could also involve the weak currency countries raising interest rates and the strong currency countries lowering them.

The ERM in practice

The ERM came into existence in March 1979 and the majority of the EU countries were members. The UK, however, initially chose not to join. Spain joined in 1989, the UK in 1990 and Portugal in April 1992.

Sterling entered the ERM at a central rate of £1 = 2.95 German marks with permitted fluctuations of ±6 per cent

against any other ERM currency. This rate proved unsustainable. German interest rates were rising to dampen inflationary pressures partly fuelled by substantial public expenditures following the reunification of Germany. US interest rates by contrast were falling to help stimulate economic growth in the face of recession. The result was a large outflow of capital from the USA, much of it going to Germany. The effect was to push up the value of the German mark. Consequently, currencies like sterling and the Italian lira were repeatedly at the bottom of their permitted exchange rate band with the mark. This was despite high and rising interest rates and, in the case of the UK, despite the economy sliding rapidly into recession.

In September 1992, things reached a crisis point. On 16 September – known thereafter as 'Black Wednesday' – the UK and Italy were forced to suspend their membership of the ERM. Both currencies were floated and depreciated substantially.

Turmoil returned in the summer of 1993, with pressure this time on the French franc. In response, EU finance ministers agreed to adopt very wide ±15 per cent bands, though with bands this wide it hardly seemed like a 'pegged' system at all. Within months, however, the crisis passed and exchange rate fluctuations began to fall within a very narrow range and for most of the time within ±2.25 per cent.

Italy rejoined the ERM in November 1996 as part of its bid to join the single European currency. Austria joined in 1995, Finland in 1996 and Greece in 1998. By the time the ERM was replaced by the single currency in 1999, only Sweden and the UK were outside the ERM. You can read more on how the ERM actually worked in practice in Case Study 26.5 in MyEconLab.

The Maastricht Treaty and the road to the single currency

The ERM was conceived as a stage on the road to complete economic and monetary union (EMU) of member states. Details of the path towards EMU were finalised in the Maastricht Treaty, which was signed in February 1992. The timetable for EMU involved the adoption of a single currency by 1999 at the latest.

One of the first moves was to establish a European Monetary Institute (EMI). Its role was to co-ordinate monetary policy and encourage greater co-operation between EU central banks. It also monitored the operation of the ERM and prepared the ground for the establishment of a European central bank in time for the launch of the single currency.

Before they could join the single currency, member states were obliged to achieve convergence of their economies. Each country had to meet five convergence criteria:

Definitions

Economic and monetary union (EMU) The adoption by a group of countries of a single currency with a single central bank and a single monetary policy. In the EU the term applies to the countries that have adopted the euro.

Exchange rate mechanism (ERM) A semi-fixed system whereby participating EU countries allow fluctuations against each other's currencies only within agreed bands. Collectively they float freely against all other currencies.

- Inflation: should be no more than 1.5 per cent above the average inflation rate of the three countries in the EU with the lowest inflation.
- Interest rates: the rate on long-term government bonds should be no more than 2 per cent above the average of the three countries with the lowest inflation rates.
- Budget deficit: should be no more than 3 per cent of GDP at market prices.
- National debt: should be no more than 60 per cent of GDP at market prices.
- Exchange rates: the currency should have been within the normal ERM bands for at least two years with no realignments or excessive intervention.

Before the launch of the single currency, the Council of Ministers had to decide which countries had met the convergence criteria and would thus be eligible to form a *currency union* by fixing their currencies permanently to the euro. Their national currencies would effectively disappear.

At the same time, a European System of Central Banks (ESCB) would be created, consisting of a European Central Bank (ECB) and the central banks of the member states. The ECB would be independent: independent from governments and also from EU political institutions. It would operate the monetary policy on behalf of the countries that had adopted the single currency.

The birth of the euro

In March 1998, the European Commission ruled that 11 of the 15 member states were eligible to proceed to EMU in January 1999. The UK and Denmark were to exercise their opt-out, and Sweden and Greece failed to meet one or more of the convergence criteria. (Greece joined the euro in 2001.)

All 11 countries unambiguously met the interest rate and inflation criteria, but doubts were expressed by many 'Eurosceptics' as to whether they all genuinely met the other three criteria:

- *Exchange rates*. Neither Finland nor Italy had been in the ERM for two years and the Irish punt was revalued by 3 per cent on 16 March 1998. However, the Commission regarded these three countries as being sufficiently close to the reference value.
- *Government deficits*. All 11 countries met this criterion, but some countries only managed to achieve a deficit of 3 per cent or below by taking one-off measures, such as a special tax in Italy and counting privatisation receipts in Germany. Yet, under the Stability and Growth Pact, eurozone countries would be required to keep their deficits

within the 3 per cent limit (see Box 20.4). The concern was that countries that only just met this criterion at time of entry would find it difficult to keep within the limit in times of recession or slow growth. This proved to be the case with France and Germany from 2002 to 2005.

- *Government debt*. Only four countries had debts that did not exceed 60 per cent (France, Finland, Luxembourg and the UK). However, the Maastricht Treaty allowed countries to exceed this value as long as the debt was 'sufficiently diminishing and approaching the reference value at a satisfactory pace'. Critics argued that this phrase was interpreted too loosely.

The euro came into being on 1 January 1999, but euro banknotes and coins were not introduced until 1 January 2002. In the meantime, national currencies continued to exist alongside the euro, but at irrevocably fixed rates. The old notes and coins were withdrawn a few weeks after the introduction of euro notes and coins.

Ten new members joined the EU in May 2004, and another two in January 2007. Under the Maastricht Treaty, they should all make preparations for joining the euro by meeting the convergence criteria. Estonia, Lithuania and Slovenia were the first to join ERM2 in June 2004 with Latvia, Cyprus, Malta and Slovakia following in 2005. They adopted the wide band of ±15 per cent against the euro. Slovenia adopted the euro in 2007, Malta and Cyprus in 2008, Slovakia in 2009, Estonia in 2011 and Latvia in 2014, making a total of 18 countries using the euro.

Advantages of the single currency

EMU has several major advantages.

Elimination of the costs of converting currencies.   With separate currencies in each of the EU countries, costs were incurred each time one currency was exchanged into another. The elimination of these costs, however, was probably the least important benefit from the single currency. The European Commission estimated that the effect was to increase the GDP of the countries concerned by an average of only 0.4 per cent. The gains to countries like the UK, which have well-developed financial markets, would be even smaller.

Increased competition and efficiency.   Despite the advent of the single market, large price differences remained between member states. Not only does the single currency eliminate the need to convert one currency into another (a barrier to competition), but it brings more transparency in pricing, and puts greater downward pressure on prices in high-cost firms and countries.

Elimination of exchange rate uncertainty (between the members).   Removal of exchange rate uncertainty has helped to encourage trade between the eurozone countries. Perhaps more importantly, it has encouraged investment by firms that trade between these countries, given the greater certainty in calculating costs and revenues from such trade.

Definition

Currency union A group of countries (or regions) using a common currency.

Figure 26.4 Inward investment to selected EU countries, % of total EU inward investment

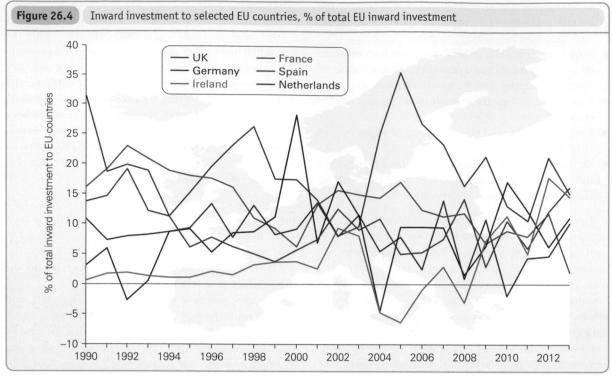

Source: Based on data in *UNCTADstat* (UNCTAD).

In times of economic uncertainty, such as the credit crunch of 2008, exchange rate volatility between countries can be high, as we saw with the experience of sterling. However, if the UK had adopted the euro, the uncertainty for the UK in its trade with the eurozone countries would have been eliminated.

Increased inward investment. Investment from the rest of the world is attracted to a eurozone of some 338 million inhabitants, where there is no fear of internal currency movements. By contrast, the UK, by not joining, has found that inward investment has been subject to more volatility and, periodically, flows appear to have been diverted away to countries within the eurozone.

From 1990 to 1998, the UK's share of inward investment to EU countries (including from other EU countries) averaged 20.4 per cent. From 1999 to 2003, it was 13.2 per cent (see Figure 26.4). From 2003 to 2005, as the UK economy grew more strongly than other major economies in the EU, its share increased to 35.3 per cent. This proved to be relatively short-lived, with the volatility of sterling acting as a deterrent to investment. By 2011, the UK's share of inward investment to EU countries had fallen to 10.4 per cent. This was to rise to 21.2 per cent in 2012, once more boosted by stronger growth in the UK than in the eurozone.

Lower inflation and interest rates. A single monetary policy forces convergence in inflation rates (just as inflation rates are very similar between the different regions within a country). With the ECB being independent from short-term political manipulation, this has resulted in a low average inflation rate in the eurozone countries. This, in turn, has

helped to convince markets that the euro will be strong relative to other currencies. The result is lower long-term rates of interest. This, in turn, further encourages investment in the eurozone countries, both by member states and by the rest of the world.

Opposition to EMU

European monetary union has, however, attracted considerable criticism. Many 'Eurosceptics' see within it a surrender of national political and economic sovereignty. Their arguments are essentially ones of principle.

Others, including those more sympathetic to monetary union in principle, raise concerns about the design of the monetary and fiscal systems within which monetary union operates – a design that, in principle, can be amended (see Boxes 21.3 and 21.6).

Arguments against EMU in principle

The lack of national currencies. This is a serious problem if an economy is at all out of harmony with the rest of the Union. For example, if countries such as Italy and Spain have higher rates of inflation (due, say, to greater cost-push pressures), then how are they to make their goods competitive with the rest of the Union? With separate currencies these countries could allow their currencies to depreciate. With a single currency, however, they could become depressed 'regions' of Europe, with rising unemployment and all the other problems of depressed regions *within* a country. This might then require significant regional policies – policies that might not be in place or, if they were, would be seen as too interventionist by the political right.

How might multiplier effects (the principle of cumulative causation) lead to prosperous regions becoming more prosperous and less prosperous regions falling even further behind?

TC 15 p508

Proponents of EMU argue that it is that it is better to tackle the problem of high inflation in such countries by the disciplines of competition from other EU countries, than merely to feed that inflation by keeping separate currencies and allowing repeated depreciation, with all the uncertainty that they bring. What is more, the high-inflation countries tend to be the poorer ones with lower wage levels (albeit faster wage *increases*). With the increased mobility of labour and capital as the single market deepens, resources are likely to be attracted to such countries. This could help to narrow the gap between the richer and poorer member states.

The critics of EMU counter this by arguing that labour is relatively immobile, given cultural and language barriers. Thus an unemployed worker in Dublin could not easily move to a job in Turin or Helsinki. What the critics are arguing here is that the EU is not an *optimal currency area* (see Box 26.3).

Loss of separate monetary policies. Perhaps the most serious criticism is that the same rate of interest must apply to all eurozone countries: the 'one-size-fits-all' problem. The trouble is that while one country might require a lower rate of interest in order to ward off recession (such as Portugal, Ireland and Greece in 2010–11), others might require a higher one to prevent inflation.

The greater the convergence between economies within the eurozone, the less serious this problem is. Consequently, it was hoped that, with common fiscal rules and free trade, these divergences would diminish over time. Eurosceptics, however, argue that there has been increasing *divergence* between members, especially in terms of the size of government deficits and debt and the confidence of the financial markets in countries' ability to tackle these deficits.

Asymmetric shocks. A third and related problem for members of a single currency occurs in adjusting to a shock when that shock affects members to different degrees. Such occurrences are known as *asymmetric shocks*. For example, the banking crisis affected the UK more severely than other countries,

given that London is a global financial centre. The less the factor mobility between member countries and the less the price flexibility within member countries, the more serious is this problem.

This problem, however, should not be overstated. Divergences between economies are often the result of a lack of harmony between countries in their demand-management policies, something that is impossible in the eurozone in the case of monetary policy, and more difficult in the case of fiscal policy, due in part, to the Fiscal Compact (see Box 21.3). Also, many of the shocks that face economies today are global and have similar (albeit not identical) effects on all countries. Adjustment to such shocks would often be better with a single co-ordinated policy, something that is much easier with a single currency and a single central bank.

Even when shocks are uniformly felt in the member states, however, there is still the problem that policies adopted centrally will have different impacts on each country.

This is because the transmission mechanisms of economic policy (i.e. the way in which policy changes impact on economic variables like growth and inflation) vary across countries.

Criticisms of the current design of EMU

Others, who are currently critical of the design of EMU, argue that with appropriate changes, the problems could be significantly reduced.

Monetary policy. In the case of monetary policy, it is argued that the ECB was not as proactive in tackling the recession that followed the aftermath of the financial crisis. Large-scale programmes of quantitative easing were adopted by the US Federal Reserve and the Bank of England (see Boxes 21.4, 21.5 and 21.9). The ECB, by contrast, was seen as more cautious.

The ECB's principal intervention took the form of large-scale, long-term repo operations. Over €1 trillion of long-term (three-year) repo loans were provided to banks between December 2011 and March 2012; €214 billion of purchases of assets, largely government bonds, took place between May 2010 and June 2012 under the Securities Market Programme (see Box 21.6). However, the effects on the money supply were sterilised by ECB sales of other assets. In other words, monetary operations were undertaken to offset the injected liquidity.

Critics point to the underlying weakness of a single currency operating alongside separate national government debt issues. The greater the divergence of the eurozone countries, in terms of growth, inflation, deficits, debt and the proportions of debt securities maturing in the short term, the greater this problem becomes.

KI 33 p404

Fiscal policy. Under the Stability and Growth Pact (SGP), countries were supposed to keep public-sector deficits below 3 per cent of GDP and their stocks of debt below 60 per cent of GDP (see Box 21.3 on pages 637–9). However, the Pact was not rigidly enforced. Furthermore, because the rules allowed for discretion in times of recession, deficits and debt rose sharply in the late 2000s (see Table 21.1 on page 627).

Definitions

Optimal currency area The optimal size of a currency area is the one that maximises the benefits from having a single currency relative to the costs. If the area were increased or decreased in size, the costs would rise relative to the benefits.

Asymmetric shocks Shocks (such as an oil price increase or a recession in another part of the world) that have different-sized effects on different industries, regions or countries.

BOX 26.3   OPTIMAL CURRENCY AREAS

When it pays to pay in the same currency

Imagine that each town and village used a different currency. Think how inconvenient it would be having to keep exchanging one currency into another, and how difficult it would be working out the relative value of items in different parts of the country.

Clearly, there are benefits of using a common currency, not only within a country but across different countries. The benefits include greater transparency in pricing, more open competition, greater certainty for investors and the avoidance of having to pay commission when you change one currency into another. There are also the benefits from having a single monetary policy if that is delivered in a more consistent and effective way than by individual countries.

So why not have a single currency for the whole world? The problem is that the bigger a single currency area gets, the more likely the conditions are to diverge in the different parts of the area. Some parts may have high unemployment and require expansionary policies. Others may have low unemployment and suffer from inflationary pressures. They may require *contractionary* policies.

What is more, different members of the currency area may experience quite different shocks to their economies, whether from outside the union (e.g. a fall in the price of one of their major exports) of from inside (e.g. a prolonged strike). These 'asymmetric shocks' would imply that different parts of the currency area should adopt different policies. But with a common monetary policy and hence common interest rates, and with no possibility of devaluation/revaluation of the currency of individual members, the scope for separate economic policies is reduced.

The costs of asymmetric shocks (and hence the costs of a single currency area) will be greater: (a) the less the mobility of labour and capital; (b) the less the flexibility of prices and wage rates; (c) the fewer the alternative policies there are that can be turned to (such as fiscal and regional policies).

So is the eurozone an optimal currency area? Certainly strong doubts have been raised by many economists:

- Labour is relatively immobile.
- There are structural differences between the member states.
- The transmission effects of interest rate changes are different between the member countries, given that countries have different proportions of borrowing at variable interest rates and different proportions of consumer debt to GDP.
- Exports to countries outside the eurozone account for different proportions of the members' GDP, and thus their economies are affected differently by a change in the rate of exchange of the euro against other currencies.
- Wage rates are relatively inflexible.
- Under the Stability and Growth Pact and the Fiscal Compact (see Box 21.3), the scope for using discretionary fiscal policy is curtailed except in times of severe economic difficulty (as in 2009).

This does not necessarily mean, however, that the costs of having a single European currency outweigh the benefits. Also, the problems outlined above should decline over time as the single market develops. Finally, the problem of asymmetric shocks can be exaggerated. European economies are highly diversified; there are often more differences within economies than between them. Thus shocks are more likely to affect different industries or localities, rather than whole countries. Changing the exchange rate, if that were still possible, would hardly be an appropriate policy in these circumstances.

 Why is a single currency area likely to move towards becoming an optimal currency area over time?

Subsequently, efforts have been made to change the framework within which national governments make their fiscal choices. The result is the Fiscal Compact, signed in March 2012 (see Box 21.3). This reaffirmed the Stability and Growth Pact rules, but added other requirements. For example, eurozone countries would now be required to keep structural deficits at or below 0.5 per cent of GDP and tougher penalties would be imposed on countries breaking the rules.

There are those who argue that, for eurozone members to benefit fully from monetary union, tighter fiscal rules alone are insufficient. Instead, they advocate greater fiscal harmonisation. In other words, the problem, they say, is one of incomplete integration.

The problem for economists is that the issue of monetary union is a very emotive one. 'Europhiles' often see monetary union as a vital element in their vision of a united Europe. Many Eurosceptics, however, see EMU as a surrender of sovereignty and a threat to nationhood. In such an environment, a calm assessment of the arguments and evidence is very difficult.

1. *By what means would a depressed country in an economic union with a single currency be able to recover? Would the market provide a satisfactory solution to its problems or would (union) government intervention be necessary, and if so, what form could that intervention take?*
2. *Is greater factor mobility likely to increase or decrease the problem of cumulative causation associated with regional multipliers? (See page 699.)*

The UK Labour government in the early 2000s specified five convergence criteria that would have to be met before it would put the question of UK adoption of the euro to the electorate in a referendum. These are examined in Case Study 26.7 in MyEconLab. However, with the forming of the Coalition government in the UK in 2010, there was now no possibility of the UK joining the euro.

Section summary

1. One means of achieving greater currency stability is for a group of countries to peg their exchange rates with each other and yet float jointly with the rest of the world. The exchange rate mechanism of the EU (ERM) was an example. Members' currencies were allowed to fluctuate against other member currencies within a band. The band was ±2.25 per cent for the majority of the ERM countries until 1993.

2. The need for realignments seemed to have diminished in the late 1980s as greater convergence was achieved between the members' economies. However, growing strains in the system in the early 1990s led to a crisis in September 1992. The UK and Italy left the ERM. The bands were widened in 1993 to ±15 per cent, although in practice fluctuations were kept within ±2.25 per cent for most of the time from 1993 to the start of the euro in 1999.

3. The ERM was seen as an important first stage on the road to complete economic and monetary union.

4. The euro was born on 1 January 1999. Twelve countries adopted it, having at least nominally met the Maastricht convergence criteria. Euro notes and coins were introduced on 1 January 2002, with the notes and coins of the old currencies withdrawn a few weeks later.

5. The advantages claimed for EMU are that it eliminates the costs of converting currencies and the uncertainties associated with possible changes in inter-EU exchange rates. This encourages more investment, both inward and by domestic firms. What is more, a common central bank, independent from domestic governments, provides the stable monetary environment necessary for a convergence of the EU economies and the encouragement of investment and inter-Union trade.

6. Critics claim, however, that it makes adjustment to domestic economic problems more difficult. The loss of independence in policy making is seen by such people to be a major issue, not only because of the loss of political sovereignty, but also because domestic economic concerns may be at variance with those of the Union as a whole. A single monetary policy is claimed to be inappropriate for dealing with asymmetric shocks. What is more, countries and regions at the periphery of the Union may become depressed unless there is an effective regional policy.

26.3 ACHIEVING GREATER CURRENCY STABILITY

One important lesson of recent years is that concerted speculation has become virtually unstoppable. This was made clear by the expulsion of the UK and Italy from the ERM in 1992, the collapse of various south-east Asian currencies and the Russian rouble in 1997–8, the collapse of the Argentinean peso in early 2002, the fall in the pound in 2008 and the fall in the euro in 2010. In comparison with the vast amounts of short-term finance flowing across the foreign exchanges each day, the reserves of central banks seem trivial.

If there is a consensus in the markets that a currency will depreciate, there is little that central banks can do. For example, if there were a 50 per cent chance of a 10 per cent depreciation in the next week, then selling that currency now would yield an 'expected' return of just over 5 per cent for the week (i.e. 50 per cent of 10 per cent): equivalent to just over 1200 per cent at an annual rate!

For this reason, many commentators have argued that there are only two types of exchange rate system that can work over the long term. The first is a completely free-floating exchange rate, with no attempt by the central bank to support the exchange rate. With no intervention, there is no problem of a shortage of reserves!

The second is to share a common currency with other countries: to join a common currency area, such as the eurozone, and let the common currency float freely. The country would give up independence in its monetary policy, but at least there would be no problem of exchange rate instability within the currency area. A similar alternative is to adopt a major currency of another country, such as the US dollar or the euro. Many smaller states have done this. For example, Kosovo and Montenegro adopted the German mark and then the euro; and Ecuador has adopted the US dollar.

An attempt by a country to peg its exchange rate is likely to have one of two unfortunate consequences. Either it will end in failure as the country succumbs to a speculative attack, or its monetary policy will have to be totally dedicated to maintaining the exchange rate.

So is there any way of 'beating the speculators' and pursuing a policy of greater exchange rate rigidity? Or must countries outside a currency union be forced to accept freely floating exchange rates, with all the uncertainty for traders that such a regime brings?

This section looks at two possible solutions. The first is to reduce international financial mobility, by putting various types of restriction on foreign exchange transactions. The second is to move to a new type of exchange rate regime that offers the benefits of a degree of rigidity without being susceptible to massive speculative attacks.

Controlling exchange transactions

Until the early 1990s, many countries retained restrictions of various kinds on financial flows. Such restrictions made it more expensive for speculators to gamble on possible exchange rate movements. It is not the case, as some commentators argue, that it is impossible to reimpose controls. Indeed, Malaysia did just that in 1998 when the ringgit was under speculative attack. Many countries in the developing world still retain controls, and the last ERM countries to give them up did so only in 1991. It is true that the complexity of modern financial markets provides the speculator with more opportunity to evade controls, but they will still have the effect of dampening speculation.

In September 1998, the IMF said that controls on inward movements of finance could be a useful tool, especially for countries that were more vulnerable to speculative attack. In its 1998 annual report, it argued that the Asian crisis of 1997–8 was the result not only of a weak banking system, but also of open financial accounts, allowing massive withdrawals of funds.

The aim of financial controls is not to prevent international flows of finance. After all, such flows are an important source of financing investment. Also, if finance moves from countries with a lower marginal productivity of capital to countries where it is higher, this will lead to an efficient allocation of world savings. The aim of financial controls must therefore be to prevent speculative flows that are based on rumour or herd instinct rather than on economic fundamentals.

Types of control

In what ways can movements of short-term finance be controlled? There are various alternatives, each one with strengths and drawbacks.

Quantitative controls.   Here the authorities would restrict the amount of foreign exchange dealing that could take place. Perhaps financial institutions would be allowed to exchange only a certain percentage of their assets. Developed countries and most developing countries have rejected this approach, however, since it is seen to be far too anti-market.

The exception is the use of special emergency measures to restrict capital movements in times of a currency crisis. According to Article 57 of the Treaty of Amsterdam, the EU Council of Ministers may 'adopt measures on the movement of capital to or from third countries'. Article 59 allows 'safeguard measures' to be taken if 'in exceptional circumstances, movements of capital to or from third countries cause . . . serious difficulties for the operation of economic and monetary union'. Article 60 allows member states to take 'unilateral measures against a third country with regard to capital movements and payments'.

A 'Tobin' tax.   This is named after James Tobin, who in 1972 advocated the imposition of a small tax of 0.1 to 0.5 per cent on all foreign exchange transactions, or just on financial account transactions.[1] This would discourage destabilising speculation (by making it more expensive) and would thus

impose some 'friction' in the foreign exchange markets, making them less volatile.

Calls for the use of Tobin taxes have become more frequent in recent years, particularly after the financial crisis of the late 2000s. Back in November 2001 the French National Assembly became the first national legislature to incorporate into law a Tobin tax of up to 0.1 per cent. Belgium followed in 2002. The EU finance ministers ordered the European Commission to undertake a feasibility study of such a tax. In late 2001, the charity War on Want declared that 13 March 2002 would be international 'Tobin tax day'. Ironically, Tobin died on 11 March 2002.

A problem with such a tax is that it would penalise transactions that were for normal trading or investment purposes as well as those for speculative purposes. Another problem is that the tax might have to be quite high to prevent speculation in times of uncertainty, and this would be very damaging to trade and investment. A possibility here would be to impose the tax only at times of exchange market turbulence, or to impose a higher tax at such times. At least a tax is far less distortionary than quantitative controls.

Box 26.4 considers the arguments for and against Tobin taxes in more detail and the growing momentum, particularly in Europe, for a financial transactions tax (FTT) on banks.

Non-interest-bearing deposits.   Here a certain percentage of inflows of finance would have to be deposited with the central bank in a non-interest-bearing account for a set period of time. Chile in the late 1990s used such a system. It required that 30 per cent of all inflows be deposited with Chile's central bank for a year. This clearly amounted to a considerable tax (i.e. in terms of interest sacrificed) and had the effect of discouraging short-term speculative flows. The problem was that it meant that interest rates in Chile had to be higher in order to attract finance.

One objection to all these measures is that they are likely only to dampen speculation, not eliminate it. If speculators believe that currencies are badly out of equilibrium and will be forced to realign, then no taxes on financial movements or artificial controls will be sufficient to stem the flood.

There are two replies to this objection. The first is that, if currencies are badly out of line, exchange rates *should* be adjusted. The second is that merely *dampening* speculation is probably the ideal. Speculation *can* play the valuable role of bringing exchange rates to their long-term equilibrium more quickly. Controls are unlikely to prevent this aspect of speculation: i.e. bringing about a more rapid adjustment to changes in economic fundamentals. If they help to lessen the wilder forms of destabilising speculation, so much the better.

Exchange rate target zones

One type of exchange rate regime that has been much discussed in recent years is that proposed by John Williamson,

[1] J. Tobin, 'A proposal for international monetary reform', *Eastern Economic Journal*, 4(3–4) (1978), pp. 153–9.

of Washington's Institute for International Economics.[1] Williamson advocated a form of crawling peg within broad exchange rate bands (see Figure 25.7 on page 751). This would have four major features:

- Wide bands. For example, currencies would be allowed to fluctuate by ±10 per cent of their central parity.
- Central parity set in *real* terms, at the 'fundamental equilibrium exchange rate' (FEER): i.e. a rate that is consistent with long-run balance of payments equilibrium.
- Frequent realignments. In order to stay at the FEER, the central parity would be adjusted frequently (say, monthly) to take account of the country's rate of inflation. If its rate of inflation were 2 per cent per annum above the trade-weighted average of other countries, the central parity would be devalued by 2 per cent per annum. Realignments would also reflect other changes in fundamentals, such as changes in the levels of protection, or major political events, such as German reunification.
- 'Soft buffers'. Governments would not be forced to intervene at the ±10 per cent mark or at some specified fraction of it. In fact, from time to time the rate might be allowed to move outside the bands. The point is that the closer the rate approached the band limits, the greater would be the scale of intervention.

[1] See, for example, J. Williamson and M. Miller, 'Targets and indicators: a blueprint for the international coordination of economic policy', *Policy Analyses in International Economics*, 22, IIE (1987).

There are two main advantages of this system. First, the exchange rate would stay at roughly the equilibrium level, and therefore the likelihood of large-scale devaluations or revaluations, and with them the opportunities for large-scale speculative gains, would be small. The reason why the narrow-banded ERM broke down in 1992 and 1993 was that the central parities were *not* equilibrium rates.

Second, the wider bands would leave countries freer to follow an independent monetary policy – one that could therefore respond to domestic needs.

The main problem with the system is that it may not allow an independent monetary policy. If the rate of exchange has to be maintained within the zone, monetary policy may sometimes have to be used for that purpose rather than controlling inflation.

Nevertheless, crawling bands have been used relatively successfully by various countries, such as Chile and Israel, over quite long periods of time. What is more, in 1999 Germany's former finance minister, Oskar Lafontaine, argued that they might be appropriate for the euro relative to the dollar and yen. A world with three major currencies, each changing gently against the other two in an orderly way, has a lot to commend it.

1. Would the Williamson system allow countries to follow a totally independent monetary policy?
2. If the euro were in a crawling peg against the dollar, what implications would this have for the ECB in sticking to its inflation target of no more than 2 per cent?

Section summary

1. Many economists argue that, with the huge flows of short-term finance across the foreign exchanges, governments are forced to adopt one of two extreme forms of exchange rate regime: free floating, or being a member of a currency union.

2. If financial flows could be constrained, however, exchange rates could be stabilised somewhat.

3. Forms of financial control include quantitative controls, a tax on exchange transactions, and non-interest-bearing deposits of a certain percentage of capital inflows with the central bank. Such controls can dampen speculation, but may discourage capital from flowing to where it has a higher marginal productivity.

4. An alternative means of stabilising exchange rates is to have exchange rate target zones. Here exchange rates are allowed to fluctuate within broad bands around a central parity, which is adjusted to the fundamental equilibrium rate in a gradual fashion.

5. The advantage of this system is that, by keeping the exchange rate at roughly its equilibrium level, destabilising speculation is avoided, and yet there is some freedom for governments to pursue an independent monetary policy. Monetary policy, however, may still from time to time have to be used to keep the exchange rate within the bands.

BOX 26.4 THE TOBIN TAX

A new panacea?

In the mid-1980s, the daily turnover in the world's foreign exchange markets was approximately $150 billion. By the early 2010s, it had risen to a truly massive $4 trillion. But only some 5 per cent of this was used for trade in goods and services.

With the massive growth in speculative flows, it is hardly surprising that this can cause great currency instability and financial crises at times of economic uncertainty. Global financial markets have often been decisive in both triggering and intensifying economic crises. The ERM crisis in 1992, the Mexican peso crisis in 1994, the south-east Asian crisis in 1997, the Russian rouble meltdown in 1998, the crisis in Argentina in 2001–2 and the currency instability of 2008–9 in the wake of the credit crunch are the most significant in a long list.

The main issue is one of volatility of exchange rates. If currency markets responded to shifts in economic fundamentals, then currency volatility would not be so bad. However, it is increasingly the case that vast quantities of money flow around the global economy on pure speculation, in which the herd instinct often drives speculative waves. Invariably, given the volume of speculative flows, exchange rates overshoot their natural equilibrium, intensifying the distortions created. Such currency movements are a huge destabilising force, not just for individual economies but for the global economy as a whole.

So is there anything countries can do to reduce destabilising speculation? One suggestion is the introduction of a Tobin tax.

The Tobin tax

Writing in 1972, James Tobin proposed a system for reducing exchange rate volatility without fundamentally impeding the operation of the market. This involved the imposition of an international tax of some 0.1 to 0.5 per cent payable on all spot or cash exchange rate transactions. He argued that this would make currency trading more costly and would therefore reduce the volume of destabilising short-term financial flows, which would invariably lead to greater exchange rate stability.

Tobin's original proposal suggested that the tax rate would need to be very low so as not to affect 'normal business'. Even if it was very low, speculators working on small margins would be dissuaded from regular movements of money, given that the tax would need to be paid per transaction. If a tax rate of 0.2 per cent was set, speculators who moved a sum of money once a day would face a yearly tax bill of approximately 50 per cent. An investor working on

a weekly movement of money would pay tax of 10 per cent per annum, and a monthly movement of currency would represent a tax of 2.4 per cent for the year. Given that 40 per cent of currency transactions have only a two-day time horizon, and 80 per cent have a time horizon of less than seven days, such a tax would clearly operate to dampen speculative currency movements.

In addition to moderating volatility and speculation, the Tobin tax might yield other benefits. It would, in the face of globalisation, restore to the nation state an element of control over monetary policy. In the face of declining governance over international forces, this might be seen as a positive advantage of the Tobin proposals.

The tax could also generate significant revenue. Estimates range from $150 to 300 billion annually. Many of the world's leading pressure groups, such as War on Want and Stamp out Poverty, have argued that the revenue from such an international tax could be used to tackle international problems, such as world poverty and environmental degradation. The World Bank estimates that some $225 billion is needed to eliminate the world's worst forms of poverty. The revenue from a Tobin tax would, in a relatively short period of time, easily exceed this amount. Even with a worldwide rate as low as 0.005 per cent (the rate recommended by Stamp out Poverty), the tax could still raise some $50 billion per year.

Problems with the Tobin tax

How far would a tax on currency transactions restrict speculative movements of money? The issue here concerns the rate of return investors might get from moving their money. If a currency were to devalue by as little as 3 to 4 per cent, a Tobin tax of 0.2 per cent would do little to deter a speculative transaction based upon such a potential return. Given devaluations of 50 per cent in Thailand and Indonesia following the 1997 crash, and an 82 per cent appreciation of the euro against the dollar from 2002 to 2008, along with severe short-term fluctuations, a 3 to 4 per cent movement in the currency appears rather modest. Raising the rate of the Tobin tax would be no solution, as it would begin to impinge upon 'normal business'.

One response to such a situation has been proposed by a German economist, Paul Bernd Spahn. He suggests that a two-tier system is used. On a day-to-day basis, a minimal tax rate, as originally envisaged by Tobin, is charged against each transaction conducted. However, during periods when exchange rates are highly unstable, a tax surcharge is levied. This would be at a far higher rate, and would only be triggered once a currency moved beyond some predetermined band of exchange rate variation.

A further problem identified with the Tobin tax concerns the costs of its administration. However, given interlinked computer systems and the progressive centralisation of foreign exchange markets – in terms of marketplaces, traders and currencies – effective administration is becoming easier. Most foreign exchange markets are well monitored already and extending such monitoring to include overseeing tax collection would not be overly problematic.

Another problem is tax avoidance. For example, the Tobin tax is a tax payable on spot exchange rate transactions. This could encourage people to deal more in futures. Foreign exchange futures are a type of 'derivative' that allow people to trade currencies in the future at a price agreed today (see Box 3.4). These would be far more difficult to monitor, since no currency is exchanged at the time of the agreement, and hence more difficult to tax. One solution would be to apply a tax on the notional value of a derivative contract. However, derivatives are an important way through which businesses hedge against future risk. Taxing them might seriously erode their use to a business and damage the derivatives market as a whole, making business more risky.

Even with avoidance, however, supporters of the Tobin tax argue that it is still likely to be successful. The main problem is the one of political will.

Although some countries, such as France, Canada, Belgium and Venezuela, have supported the introduction of a Tobin tax, most of the major economics are opposed to it. With reservations being expressed by the IMF, any concerted international action to control global financial movements will be difficult to put on the agenda, let alone put in place and administer.

A Tobin tax on financial transactions

In 2009, Adair Turner, Chairman of the Financial Services Authority (the UK's financial sector regulator until 2012), proposed the possible use of Tobin taxes to curb destabilising financial transactions. This was met with criticism from many bankers that the tax would be unworkable at a global level and if applied solely to the UK would divert financial business away from London.

Despite international opinion on the imposition of a FTT remaining divided, the European Commission favours a FTT. Eleven countries – France, Germany, Austria, Belgium, Estonia, Greece, Italy, Portugal, Slovakia, Slovenia and Spain – broadly favour the introduction of a FTT. In February 2013, the European Commission tabled a proposal for a Directive

which, once passed, will allow participating countries to transpose the directive into national law. They hope to raise billions of euros from the tax, which will apply whenever at least one of the parties to a trade is based in one of the 11 countries.

With a rate of 0.1 per cent on trading in bonds and shares and 0.01 per cent on trading in derivatives, the tax is designed to be too small to affect trading in shares or other financial products for purposes of long-term investment. It would, however, dampen speculative trades that take advantage of tiny potential gains from very short-term price movements.

Such trades account for huge financial flows between financial institutions around the world and tend to make markets more volatile. The short-term dealers are known as high-frequency traders (HFTs) and their activities now account for the majority of trading on exchanges. Most of these trades are by computers programmed to seek out minute gains and respond in milliseconds. And while they add to short-term liquidity for much of the time, this liquidity can suddenly dry up if HFTs become pessimistic.

Supporters of the tax claim that it will make a major contribution to tackling the deficit problems of many eurozone countries. The Commission estimates that revenues will be around €30 to €35 billion, or 0.4 to 0.5 per cent of the GDP of the participating member states.

The UK government remains opposed to such a tax, unless globally adopted, fearing that the UK's large financial services sector would suffer. Critics claim that it will dampen investment and growth and divert financial business away from the participating countries.

The implementation of the FTT was subsequently delayed, partly over concerns about the legality of the central plank of the tax: that it must be paid if one of the counterparties to the trade is based in one of the participating counties. Delays arose too as discussions continued among the 11 participating member states over the details of the tax, including its scope and the distribution of revenues. The tax was not expected to be implemented before 2015.

George Soros, multi-millionaire currency speculator, has referred to global capital markets as being like a wrecking ball rather than a pendulum, suggesting that such markets are becoming so volatile that they are damaging to all concerned, including speculators. What might lead Soros to such an observation?

END OF CHAPTER QUESTIONS

1. Under what circumstances does a growth in financial flows make exchange rates less stable?

2. Assume that countries in the eurozone decide to pursue a deflationary fiscal policy. What effect is this likely to have on the UK economy?

3. It is often argued that international convergence of economic indicators is a desirable objective. Does this mean that countries should all seek to achieve the same rate of economic growth, monetary growth, interest rates and budget deficits as a percentage of their GDP, etc.?

4. Did the exchange rate difficulties experienced by countries under the ERM strengthen or weaken the arguments for progressing to a single European currency?

5. Assume that just some of the members of a common market like the EU adopt full economic and monetary union, including a common currency. What are the advantages and disadvantages to those members joining the full EMU and to those not?

6. Is the eurozone an optimal currency area? Explain your answer.

7. How are asymmetric shocks dealt with within a country? To what extent can this process be mirrored within the eurozone?

8. Would the world benefit from the general imposition of controls on the movement of international finance?

Online resources

Additional case studies in MyEconLab

26.1 The new economy. Does globalisation bring economic success?

26.2 High oil prices. What is their effect on the world economy?

26.3 Crisis in south-east Asia. Causes of the severe recession in many south-east Asian countries in 1997–8.

26.4 The 1997–8 crisis in Asia: the role played by the IMF.

26.5 The ERM in practice. This looks at the ERM from its inception in 1979 to the birth of the euro in 1999.

26.6 Converging on the euro. Did the 11 countries that adopted the euro in 1999 genuinely meet the convergence criteria?

26.7 The UK Labour government's convergence criteria for euro membership. An examination of the five tests set by the UK government that would have to be passed before the question of euro membership would be put to the electorate in a referendum.

Websites relevant to Chapters 25 and 26

Numbers and sections refer to websites listed in the web appendix and hotlinked from this book's website at **www.pearsoned.co.uk/sloman**.

■ For news articles relevant to this and the previous chapter, see the *Economic News* section in MyEconLab.

■ For general news on countries' balance of payments and exchange rates, see websites in section A, and particularly A1–5, 7–9, 20–25, 31, 35, 36. For articles on various aspects of economic development, see A27, 28; I9. See also links to newspapers worldwide in A38, 39, 42, 43 and 44, and the news search feature in Google at A41.

■ For international data on balance of payments and exchange rates, see *World Economic Outlook* in H4 and *OECD Economic Outlook* in B21 (also in section 6 of B1). See also the trade topic in I14. The ESDS International site (B35) has links to World Bank, IMF, OECD, UN and Eurostat datasets (but you will need to register first, a service free to all UK higher education students).

■ For UK data on balance of payments, see B1, *1. National Statistics > Publications > United Kingdom Balance of Payments – the Pink Book*. See also B34. For EU data, see B38 > *Economic Forecasts* (click on latest year), tables 29, 30 and 45 to 60 in *Statistical Annex* at end; see also B49 (Ameco online) sections 10 and 11.

■ For exchange rates, see A3; B5, 34; F2, 6, 8. For real and nominal exchange rate indices, see B45.

■ For discussion papers on balance of payments and exchange rates, see H4 and 7.

■ For various pressure groups critical of the effects of free trade and globalisation, see H13 and 14.

■ For information on EMU, see sites G1, 2, 3 and 6; F3–6 and 9.

■ For student resources relevant to these two chapters, see sites C1–7, 9, 10, 19. See also *The trade balance and the exchange rate* in site D3.

MyEconLab

This book can be supported by MyEconLab, which contains a range of additional resources, including an online homework and tutorial system designed to test and build your understanding.

You need both an access card and a course ID to access MyEconLab:

1. Is your lecturer using MyEconLab? Ask your lecturer for your course ID.

2. Has an access card been included with the book at a reduced cost? Check the inside back cover of the book.

3. If you have a course ID but no access card, go to: http://www.myeconlab.com/ to buy access to this interactive study programme.

Economics of Developing Countries

CHAPTER MAP

27.1 The problem of underdevelopment	**800**
The gulf between rich and poor countries	800
The meaning of 'development'	800
27.2 International trade and development	**805**
The relationship between trade and development	805
Trade strategies	806
Approach 1: Exporting primaries – exploiting comparative advantage	806
Approach 2: Import-substituting industrialisation (ISI)	810
Approach 3: Exporting manufactures – a possible way forward?	813
27.3 Structural problems within developing countries	**817**
The neglect of agriculture	817
Inappropriate technology	818
Unemployment	819
27.4 The problem of debt	**823**
The oil shocks of the 1970s	823
Coping with debt: rescheduling	824
Dealing with debt: structural reform within the developing countries	825
Dealing with debt: debt forgiveness	826

In this final chapter, we turn to the economic problems of the poorer countries of the world. These include all the countries of Africa and Latin America and most of the countries of Asia. More than three-quarters of the world's population lives in these countries. As Theodore Schultz said when accepting the Nobel Prize in Economics in 1979:

> Most of the people of the world are poor, so if we knew the economics of being poor we would know much of the economics that really matters.

We start by looking at the nature and extent of their poverty and the means by which it can be measured. We then look at the trade relations between the poorer countries and the advanced industrialised world. As we shall see, most developing countries are highly dependent for their development, or lack of it, on their relationships with the rich world.

In section 27.3, the focus shifts to some of the internal problems faced by developing countries: problems such as the neglect of agriculture, the use of inappropriate technology and the rise in unemployment. The final section looks at one of the most serious problems facing poorer countries: the problem of huge international debts. We look at the growing calls for the debts of the poorest countries to be cancelled and at the response of the rich countries.

27.1   THE PROBLEM OF UNDERDEVELOPMENT

The gulf between rich and poor countries

The typical family in North America, western Europe, Japan and Australasia has many material comforts: plentiful food to eat; a house or apartment with electricity and running hot and cold water; an inside toilet connected to an underground sewerage system; access to free or affordable health care and education; numerous consumer durables; holidays away from home; visits to the cinema, concerts, sports events, etc. There are some people, it is true, who are very poor and, indeed, the problem of poverty in many developed countries has worsened in recent years. But it is only a small minority that cannot afford the basics of life, such as adequate food, shelter and clothing.

In most of Africa and large parts of Asia and Latin America, the picture is quite different. The majority of people live in poverty. For them life is a daily struggle for survival. Affluence does exist in these countries, but here it is the fortunate few who can afford good food, good housing and the various luxury items that typify life in the industrialised world.

A large proportion of the inhabitants live in the countryside. For many, this means living in a family with many children and working on a small amount of land with too little income to buy adequate agricultural machinery, fertilisers or pesticides. With a rapid growth in population there is less and less land to go round. As land is passed on from generation to generation, it is divided up between the offspring into smaller and smaller plots. Many who cannot make ends meet are forced to sell their land to the local landlords. Then as landless labourers they have to accept very low-paid jobs on the large farms or plantations. Others try to survive by borrowing, hoping to be able to pay off their debts with future crop sales. But often the only source of finance is again the local landlord who charges exorbitant rates of interest. As a result, they end up in a state of 'debt bondage' where they can never pay off their debts, but year in year out have to give part of their crops to the landlord as interest.

Others come to the rapidly growing cities. In the cities, at least there are some jobs. But typically more people migrate to the cities than there are jobs available. Thus the number of unemployed in the cities has grown inexorably. People are forced to do anything to earn a living: selling wares on street corners, or working as casual labourers, domestic servants or shoe shiners; some resort to prostitution and crime, others merely beg.

All round the outskirts of cities throughout the developing world, shanty towns mushroom as the poor flock in from the countryside. Families crowd into one- or two-roomed shacks, often with no electricity, no water and no sanitation. There are schools in these towns, but often parents cannot afford to allow their children to attend.

Instead they have to send them out to work to supplement the family's meagre income. In some emerging countries, programmes to provide work and education in the shanty towns have helped reduce the problem somewhat; in other countries, the problem continues to worsen.

Statistics cannot give the complete picture, but they can give us some indication of the gulf between rich and poor countries. Table 27.1 gives some details.

Some 82 per cent of the world's population lives in developing countries (low- and middle-income countries) but these people earn only 32 per cent of the world's income. However, as Figure 27.1 shows, this share has risen significantly since 2005. Between 1960 and 2004, the share of global GNY[1] attributable to developing economies averaged just 17.2 per cent and was as low as 13.5 per cent in the early 1990s.

In high-income countries, the average GNY per head in 2012 was just over $38 400. In low-income countries it was a mere $590. Even in purchasing-power parity terms, the figures were $38 500 and $1400 respectively. What is more, some of the poorest developing countries have the slowest rates of real per capita growth – just 0.8 per cent per annum from 1990 to 2012 for sub-Saharan African countries compared with the global average of 1.4 per cent. The gulf between rich and poor countries can also be seen in other basic indicators, including health, life expectancy and literacy (see Table 27.1).

Nevertheless, as the table shows, growth in GNY per capita over recent years has been faster in developing countries than in rich countries. The income gap between the developed and developing world has been narrowing.

The meaning of 'development'

Countries want to develop. But just what do we mean by 'development'? Clearly it is a normative concept. Its definition will depend on the goals that the economist assumes societies want to achieve. So how do economists define and measure development?

The basic needs approach
A starting point is to identify the basic needs that people have if they are to be able to realise their potential as human beings. Different economists have identified various lists of requirements, including the following items:

- Adequate food, shelter, warmth and clothing.
- Universal access to education.
- Availability of adequate health care.
- Availability of non-demeaning jobs.
- Sufficient free time to be able to enjoy social interaction.

[1] GNY (gross national income): see appendix to Chapter 14.

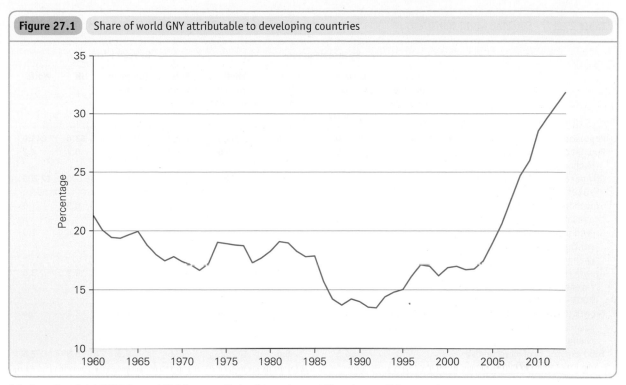

Figure 27.1 Share of world GNY attributable to developing countries

Note: Proportion of global GNY at current US dollars earned by low-income, lower-middle and upper-middle economies.
Source: Based on data from *World Development Indicators* (World Bank, 2014).

- Freedom to make one's own economic decisions.
- Freedom to participate in the decisions of government and other bodies that affect one's life.

 What other items might be included as basic needs?

There are four major problems with defining development in terms of a basic list of requirements.

The first is in deciding *what to include*. Any definition of *economic* development would clearly include people's *material* standard of living. But should development include social and political factors such as 'self-esteem', freedom from servitude and freedom of religion?

The second problem is in *measuring each of the items*. It is possible to measure such things as income per head, literacy rates and mortality rates. It is much more difficult, however, to measure the achievement of social and political objectives such as self-esteem.

The third problem is in arriving at a *single measure* of the level of development. You cannot add the average calorific intake to the number of doctors and nurses to the percentage of homes having various basic amenities such as running water. You can meaningfully add things up only if they are expressed in the same units, or if appropriate *weights* are attached to each of the items. Clearly, the assigning of any such weights would be highly controversial.

The fourth problem is in deciding the importance of the *distribution* of the various items. If, say, the average calorific intake increases, but the poorest sections of the population have less to eat, has the country really experienced an increase in the level of development?

However, many economists argue that the basic needs approach does provide a useful 'checklist' to see whether a country's development is broadly based or confined to just one or two indicators.

 Would it be possible with this basic needs approach to say (a) that one country was more developed than another; (b) that one country was developing faster than another?

Using GNY to measure development

The desire to have a single measure for development and thus to be able to make simple comparisons between countries has led to the universal use of real gross national income (GNY) per capita as the main indicator. It has some major advantages:

- It takes into account virtually all the goods and services produced in a country, and converts them into a single measure by the use of market prices.
- Although markets are by no means perfect, they do reflect the strength of demand and the opportunity costs of supply.
- The rules for the measurement of GNY are universally agreed.

Table 27.1 Selected world statistics

	By income groups				By region/country			
	Low-income economies	Lower-middle-income economies	Upper-middle-income economies	High-income economies	Sub-Saharan African	European Union	UK	World
Population (millions, 2012)	846.5	2 507.0	2 390.6	1 299.8	912.2	505.6	63.6	7 043.9
Population growth (average annual % change, 2003–12)	2.2	1.6	0.8	0.6	2.7	0.3	0.7	1.2
GNY per capita, PPP ($ per annum, 2012)	1 383	3 877	10 621	38 522	2 240	34 074	35 620	12 209
Growth in GNY per capita (average annual % change, 2003–12)	3.9	4.7	5.8	1.1	2.5	0.9	0.5	1.5
Growth in household consumption per capita (average annual % change, 2003–12)	2.5	4.4	4.7	1.2	1.6	0.7	0.4	1.3
Growth in gross capital formation (average annual % change, 2003–12)	9.2	10.0	10.2	1.3	8.2	0.6	0.9	3.6
Growth in exports in goods and services (average annual % change, 2003–12)	10.6	9.6	8.1	4.6	9.3	4.0	3.1	5.4
Food exports, % of merchandise exports (average 2003–12)	23.0	14.5	8.6	6.8	12.6	8.3	5.8	7.5
Domestic credit provided by financial sector as % of GDP (average 2003–12)	34.5	54.8	94.5	187.6	76.8	142.6	187.9	162.5
Health expenditure as % of GDP (average 2003–12)	5.3	4.4	5.8	11.6	6.6	9.8	8.8	10.1
Life expectancy at birth (years, 2012)	61.6	66.2	74.2	79.3	56.4	80.5	81.5	70.8
Under-5 mortality rate (per 1000 births, 2012)	81.8	61.2	20.2	6.2	97.5	4.8	4.8	47.8
Literacy rate (% of people aged 15 and over, 2011)	61.2	70.5	93.6	n.a.	59.8	99.1	n.a.	84.1
Public spending on education as % of GDP (average 2001–10)	3.6	4.0	4.5	5.2	3.8	5.3	5.3	4.5
Ratio of girls to boys in primary and secondary education (%, 2011)	93.1	94.8	101.7	99.3	90.2	99.1	100.4	97.2
Urban population (% of total, 2012)	28.2	38.9	60.7	80.2	36.8	41.3	79.8	52.5
Urban population growth (average annual % change, 2003–12)	3.6	2.7	2.6	1.0	3.9	0.6	0.8	2.2
Fixed broadband Internet subscribers (per 100 of population, 2012)	0.2	1.4	10.7	26.2	12.4	28.0	34.0	9.2
CO_2 emissions (average 2001–10, metric tonnes per capita)	0.3	1.4	4.3	12.0	0.8	7.9	8.7	4.5

Notes: (i) Low-income economies are those with GNY per capita of $1035 or less in 2012; lower middle income, $1036–$4085; upper middle income, $4086–$12 615; and high income, $12 616 or more; (ii) n/a = not available.
Source: *World DataBank, World Development Indicators* (World Bank).

- Virtually all countries compile GNY statistics.
- Although not every item that affects human welfare is included in GNY, a sustained rise in GNY is generally agreed to be a *necessary* condition for a sustained rise in welfare.
- There is a fairly close correlation between the level of per capita GNY and other indicators such as mortality rates, literacy rates, and calorific and protein intake.

However, there are four fundamental criticisms of relying on simple GNY per capita as an indicator of development.

Many items are excluded. Much of production that does not get bought and sold will escape being recorded. This is a particular problem with rural societies that are largely subsistence-based. People grow their own food, build their own houses, make their own clothes and provide their own entertainment. GNY statistics are therefore likely to *understate* the level of production in these societies.

On the other hand, as these societies 'develop', the size of the market sector is likely to grow. A larger proportion of people's consumption will be of items they have purchased and which therefore do enter into GNY statistics. Thus GNY

| Figure 27.2 | GNY per head as a percentage of US GNY per head, 2012 (using purchasing-power parity exchange rates) |

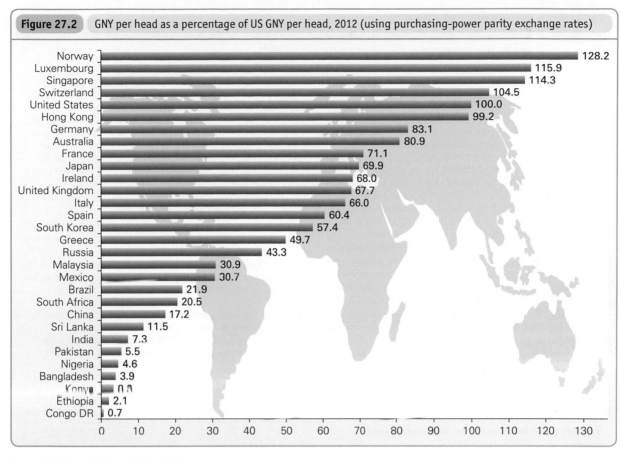

Norway 128.2
Luxembourg 115.9
Singapore 114.3
Switzerland 104.5
United States 100.0
Hong Kong 99.2
Germany 83.1
Australia 80.9
France 71.1
Japan 69.9
Ireland 68.0
United Kingdom 67.7
Italy 66.0
Spain 60.4
South Korea 57.4
Greece 49.7
Russia 43.3
Malaysia 30.9
Mexico 30.7
Brazil 21.9
South Africa 20.5
China 17.2
Sri Lanka 11.5
India 7.3
Pakistan 5.5
Nigeria 4.6
Bangladesh 3.9
Kenya 0.9
Ethiopia 2.1
Congo DR 0.7

0 10 20 30 40 50 60 70 80 90 100 110 120 130

Source: *World Economic Outlook* database (IMF).

figures will *overstate* the rate of growth of production and consumption.

As an economy becomes more urbanised, there is likely to be a growth in *external* costs of production and consumption, such as pollution and crime. Traditional ways of life will be destroyed; people may find themselves increasingly in a competitive, uncaring environment. Again the growth in GNY is likely to *overstate* the growth in human welfare.

Market prices may be highly distorted. GNY is based on market prices, but these prices may be distorted. Markets are often highly fragmented, and there is little competition to ensure that prices reflect undistorted marginal costs. Companies often have considerable monopoly power to push up prices of manufactured goods; landlords often have power to push up rents; governments may impose price controls on food; employers with monopsony power may be able to pay very low wages.

 How would a redistribution of income to the powerful be likely to affect GNY?

Exchange rates may not reflect local purchasing power. GNY statistics are initially compiled in terms of the domestic currency. For purposes of international comparison they

then have to be converted into a common currency – usually the US dollar – at the current exchange rate. But exchange rates reflect demand and supply of *traded* goods; they do not reflect the prices of *non-traded* goods. Generally, the price of non-traded goods and services in developing countries will be lower than the price of similar goods and services in advanced countries. The *level* of GNY is therefore likely to *understate* the level of production in poor countries. If, on the other hand, the proportion of traded goods increases over time, the *growth* of GNY will again *overstate* the growth in production.

It is much better, therefore, to estimate GNY using purchasing-power parity exchange rates. Even if this is done, however, massive differences remain in GNY per head between rich and poor countries. This is illustrated in Figure 27.2, which shows GNY per head at PPP exchange rates as a percentage of US GNY per head.

Simple GNY per head ignores the distribution of income. Since the early 1980s, many developing countries have achieved relatively rapid growth in per capita GNY as they have sought overseas investment, privatised their industries and cut the levels of public provision. But with a deepening of poverty, a growing inequality in the distribution of income and an increase in unemployment, few would argue that this constitutes genuine 'development'.

KI 29
p323

KI 4
p13

| BOX 27.1 | THE HUMAN DEVELOPMENT INDEX | EXPLORING ECONOMICS |

A measure of human welfare?

Since 1990, the United Nations Development Programme (UNDP) has published an annual Human Development Index (HDI). This is an attempt to provide a more broad-based measure of development than GDP or GNY. HDI is the average of three indices based on three sets of variables: (i) life expectancy at birth, (ii) education (a weighted average of (a) the mean years that a 25-year-old person or older has spent in school and (b) the number of years of schooling that a 5-year-old child is expected to have over their lifetime) and (iii) real GNY per capita, measured in US dollars at purchasing-power parity exchange rates. The 187 countries are then placed in one of four equal-sized groups according to their HDI: very high human development (top quartile), high human development (next quartile), medium human development (next quartile) and low human development (bottom quartile).

For each of the three indices making up the HDI, a sophisticated formula is used. Thus the index for GNY attempts to measure material well-being by building in the assumption of a rapidly diminishing marginal utility of income above average world levels.

The table, based on the 2013 Human Development Report, published in 2014, gives the 2012 HDIs for selected countries and their rankings. It also gives rankings for GNY per capita. The final column shows the divergence between the two rankings.

A positive number shows that a country has a higher ranking for HDI than GNY per capita. As can be seen, the rankings differ substantially in some cases between the two measures. For some countries, such as Australia, Ireland, South Korea and Cuba, GNY understates their relative level of human development, whereas for others, such as Singapore, Qatar, Kuwait, Turkey and South Africa, GNY per capita overstates their relative level of human development. Thus South Africa (PPP) GNY per capita is 75 per cent higher than that of Cuba and yet its HDI is lower.

The point is that countries with similar levels of national income may use that income quite differently.

Recently, work has been done to adjust HDI figures for various other factors, such as overall income distribution, gender inequalities and inequalities by region or ethnic group. Thus the overall HDI can be adjusted downwards to reflect greater degrees of inequality. Alternatively, separate HDIs can be produced for separate regions or ethnic groups, or for women and men within a country.

1. For what reasons are HDI and per capita GDP rankings likely to diverge?
2. Why do Kuwait and South Africa have such a large negative figure in the final column of the table?

Human Development Index for selected countries (2012)

Country	HDI rank	HDI value	GNY per head (PPP$)	GNY (PPP$) ranking	GNY (PPP$) rank minus HDI rank
Very high human development (top 47 countries by HDI)					
Norway	1	0.955	48 688	5	4
Australia	2	0.938	34 340	17	15
United States	3	0.937	43 480	9	6
Netherlands	4	0.921	37 282	12	8
Germany	5	0.920	35 431	15	10
Ireland	7	0.916	28 671	26	19
Japan	10	0.912	32 545	21	11
South Korea	12	0.909	28 231	27	15
Hong Kong	13	0.906	45 598	7	−6
Singapore	18	0.895	52 613	3	−15
France	20	0.893	30 277	24	4
Luxembourg	26	0.875	48 285	6	−20
United Kingdom	26	0.875	32 538	21	−5
Qatar	36	0.834	87 478	1	−35
United Arab Emirates	41	0.818	42 716	10	−31
High human development (next 47 countries by HDI)					
Bahamas	49	0.794	27 401	28	−21
Kuwait	54	0.790	52 793	3	−51
Russia	55	0.788	14 461	55	0
Saudi Arabia	57	0.782	22 616	36	−21
Cuba	59	0.780	5 539	103	44
Brazil	85	0.730	10 152	77	−8
Turkey	90	0.722	13 710	58	−32
Medium human development (next 47 countries by HDI)					
China	101	0.699	7 945	90	−11
Botswana	119	0.634	13 102	64	−55
South Africa	121	0.629	9 594	79	−42
India	136	0.554	3 285	133	−3
Kenya	145	0.519	1 541	160	15
Bangladesh	146	0.515	1 785	155	9
Pakistan	146	0.515	2 566	137	−9
Low human development (bottom 46 countries by HDI)					
Nigeria	153	0.471	2 102	147	−6
Uganda	161	0.456	1 168	166	5
Zimbabwe	172	0.397	424	186	14
Congo DR	186	0.304	319	186	0
Niger	186	0.304	701	182	−4

Source: *2013 Human Development Report* (United Nations Development Programme, 2014).

Many who have advocated the concentration on GNY and its rate of growth have argued that, while the rich may be the first to benefit from prosperity, gradually the benefits will 'trickle down' to the poor. In practice, the wealth has failed to trickle down in many countries. The rich have got richer while the poor have got poorer.

Given the weaknesses of GNY, but given the desirability of having a single measure of development, various composite indicators have been constructed. The most widely used is the ***Human Development Index (HDI)***, which is a combined measure of life expectancy, education and GDP per head at PPP exchange rates. This index is examined in Box 27.1.

Section summary

1. There are a number of ways of categorising countries according to their level of development.

2. The level of development of a country can be defined in terms of the extent to which it meets basic needs for human life. There is no universal agreement, however, about which items should be measured or about how to measure and weight them. Nevertheless, the approach provides a useful indicator of whether development is broadly based and how rapidly the most serious problems of poverty are being tackled.

3. The most widely used measure of development is GNY per head at PPP exchange rates. However, there are serious problems with using GNY: many items may be excluded, especially for a more subsistence-based society; prices may be highly distorted; and the statistics ignore the question of the distribution of income. Another widely used measure is the Human Development Index.

27.2 INTERNATIONAL TRADE AND DEVELOPMENT

International trade is one of the most contentious issues in development economics. Should countries adopt an open trading policy with few if any barriers to imports? Should governments actively promote trade by subsidising their export sector? Or should they restrict trade and pursue a policy of greater self-sufficiency? These are issues that we will be looking at in this section.

Whether it is desirable that developing countries should adopt policies of more trade or less, trade is still vital. Certain raw materials, capital equipment and intermediate products that are necessary for development can be obtained only from abroad. Others *could* be produced domestically, but only at much higher cost.

The relationship between trade and development

What makes the issue of trade so contentious is the absence of a simple relationship between trade and development. Instead the relationship is complex and determined by a series of interactions between variables affecting both trade and development. What is more apparent though is that while some countries have managed to use trade as an engine for economic growth and wider human development, others, despite trade liberalisation, have seen relatively little improvement either in their export performance or in human development.

In constructing a trade and development index, the UN[1] identified three broad groups of influences or dimensions which interact and affect a country's trade and development performance. Within these broad groups are various indicators which themselves interact. We consider briefly these three dimensions and some of the indicators within each dimension.

Structural and institutional dimension

Human capital. This relates to the skills and expertise of the workforce which affect a country's performance and its productivity. Education and health are key influences here. As well as affecting the economic growth of a country, higher educational attainment and better health conditions positively impact on social and human development.

Physical infrastructure. Infrastructure affects a country's productive capacity and so its potential output. Poor transport infrastructure, for example, is thought to be a major impediment to a country's export performance.

Financial environment. Credit is important to producers and consumers alike in helping to finance both short-term and longer-term commitments. For instance, it enables firms to finance day-to-day operational purchases but also longer-term investments in fixed assets such as buildings and machinery.

Definition

Human Development Index (HDI) A composite index made up of three elements: an index for life expectancy, an index for school enrolment and adult literacy, and an index for GDP per capita (in PPP$).

---

[1] Developing countries in international trade 2005: Trade and development index, United Nations, 2005.

Institutional quality. This relates to issues of governance not just of firms themselves, but also to institutions, largely governmental.

Environmental sustainability. The argument here is that excessive activity, particularly at the early stages of development, can result in environmental degradation. This can adversely affect human development and, in turn, economic development.

Trade policies and process dimension

Openness to trade. In the absence of market failures and externalities, trade liberalisation is argued to be a driver of development. However, as we shall see later, there can be significant human costs in the transition process.

Effective access to foreign markets. The success of a country's export performance is crucially dependent on its effective access to markets. Barriers to access include tariffs and non-tariff barriers, such as regulatory standards in the markets of recipient countries. A wider definition of 'effective' access recognises other factors too. These might include the size of foreign markets, transport links, the characteristics of the goods being exported – for example, how differentiated they are – as well as the cost of the exported goods.

Levels of development dimension

The third series of factors affecting both trade and human development relate to existing levels of development. In section 27.1 we discussed some of the issues in defining and measuring development. But, in general terms, we can think of the relevant development issues here as encompassing three components: economic development, social development and gender development.

Trade strategies

As we have seen, the relationship between trade and development is complex. Consequently, the impact of countries' approaches to trade on both trade performance and human development will depend on a series of factors.

Nonetheless, as they develop, countries' policies towards trade typically go through various stages. In the remainder of this section we consider these broad strategies before, in the next section, considering some of the particular issues that developing countries face in raising their trade performance and increasing levels of human development.

Primary outward-looking stage

Traditionally, developing countries have exported primaries – minerals such as copper, cash crops such as coffee, and non-foodstuffs such as cotton – in exchange for manufactured consumer goods. Having little in the way of an industrial base, if they want to consume manufactured goods, they have to import them.

Secondary inward-looking stage

In seeking rapid economic development, most developing countries drew lessons from the experience of the advanced countries. The main conclusion was that industrialisation was the key to economic success.

But industrialisation required foreign exchange to purchase capital equipment. This led to a policy of ***import-substituting industrialisation***, which involved cutting back on non-essential imports and thereby releasing foreign exchange. Tariffs and other restrictions were imposed on those imports for which a domestic substitute existed, or which were regarded as unimportant.

Secondary outward-looking stage

Once an industry had satisfied domestic demand, it had to seek markets abroad if expansion was to continue. What is more, as we shall see, import substitution brought a number of serious problems for developing countries. The answer seemed to be to look outward again, this time to the export of manufactured goods. Many of the most economically successful emerging countries (especially Hong Kong, Singapore, South Korea, Taiwan and, more recently, China and India) have owed their high growth rates to a rapid expansion of manufactured exports.

We will now examine the three stages in more detail.

Approach 1: Exporting primaries – exploiting comparative advantage

The importance of primary exports

Despite moves towards import substitution and secondary export promotion, many developing countries still rely heavily on primary exports. Consider the exports of foods and beverages. These constituted around 20 per cent of the value of total developing country exports during the 1980s. As we can see from Figure 27.3, by the 2000s this share has effectively halved. Nonetheless, developing countries typically remain more dependent on agricultural exports than do developed countries. A similar pattern is true for other primary products. Today, primary products in total account for around 40 per cent (by value) of developing countries' exports. This is double the share in advanced countries.

The justification for exporting primaries

Three major arguments have traditionally been used for pursuing a policy of exporting primaries. In each case, the arguments have also been used to justify a policy of free or virtually free trade.

> **Definition**
>
> **Import-substituting industrialisation** A strategy of restricting imports of manufactured goods and using the foreign exchange saved to build up domestic substitute industries.

Figure 27.3 Food exports as a percentage of total merchandise exports

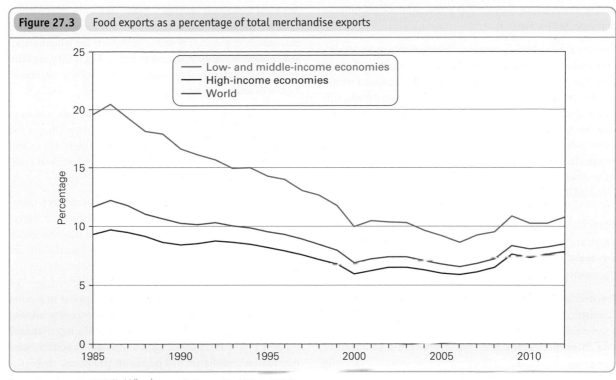

Source: Based on data from *World Development Indicators* (World Bank, 2014).

Exporting primaries exploits comparative advantage. Traditional trade theory implies that countries should specialise in producing those items in which they have a comparative advantage: i.e. those goods that can be produced at relatively low opportunity costs. For most developing countries, this means that a large proportion of their exports should be primaries.

 KI 37 p710

The reasons for differences in comparative costs were examined by two Swedish economists, Eli Heckscher and Bertil Ohlin. They believed that comparative cost differences arise from differences in factor endowments. The *Heckscher–Ohlin theory* states that *a country should specialise in those goods that are intensive in the country's abundant factor.* The more abundant a factor, the relatively cheaper it is likely to be, and thus the lower will be the opportunity cost of producing goods that are intensive in its use. Thus labour-abundant developing countries should specialise in labour-intensive products. By exporting these products, which will typically be primaries, they can earn the foreign exchange to import goods that use large amounts of capital and other resources that are in short supply.

According to this theory, international trade would lead not only to higher consumption, but also to *factor price equalisation*: i.e. the erosion of income inequalities between trading nations. For example, if wage rates are low in developing countries, trade will increase the demand for their labour-intensive products and thereby push up wage rates. International trade will also erode income differentials *within* countries. The demand for exports will increase the demand for the relatively cheap factors, and imports will

reduce the demand for the relatively expensive ones. Thus the cheap factors will go up in price and the expensive ones will come down.

1. *What effect will trade have on the price of capital in developing and developed countries?*
2. *It is sometimes claimed that trade with developing countries is unjust because it leads to the importation of goods produced at pitifully low wages. How can the Heckscher–Ohlin theory be used to refute this claim? Is there any validity in the claim? (See Box 24.3.)*

Exporting primaries provides a 'vent for surplus'. Trade offers a *vent for surplus*: i.e. a means of putting to use resources that would otherwise not be used. These surpluses will occur where the domestic market is simply not big enough to consume all the available output of a particular good. There is far too little demand within Zambia to consume its

---

Definitions

Heckscher–Ohlin version of comparative advantage A country has a comparative advantage in those goods that are intensive in the country's relatively abundant factor.

Factor price equalisation The tendency for international trade to reduce factor price inequalities both between and within countries.

Vent for surplus Where international trade enables a country to exploit resources that would otherwise be unused.

potential output of copper. The same applies to Namibian uranium or Peruvian tin.

Environmental primaries provides an 'engine for economic growth'. According to this argument, developing countries benefit from the growth of the economies of the developed world. As industrial expansion takes place in the rich North, this creates additional demand for primaries from the poor South. In more recent years, the rapid growth in China, India and other industrialising developing countries has seen a rapid growth in demand for commodities, many produced in the least developed countries. This has driven up commodity prices and benefited primary exporters (see Figure 27.4).

Traditional trade theory in the context of development
There are several reasons for questioning whether the above arguments justify a policy of relying on primary exports as the means to development.

Comparative costs change over time. Over time, with the acquisition of new skills and an increase in the capital stock, a developing country that once had a comparative advantage in primaries may find that it now has a comparative advantage in certain *manufactured* products, especially those that are more labour-intensive and use raw materials of which the country has a plentiful supply. The market, however, cannot necessarily be relied upon to bring about a smooth transition to producing such products.

KI 37
p710

KI 37
p710

Concentrating on primary production may hinder growth. The theory of comparative advantage shows how trade allows a country to consume beyond its production possibility curve (see pages 711–13 and 716–17). As its economy grows, however, this production possibility curve will *shift outwards*. By concentrating on primaries, the curve may shift outwards more slowly than if the country had pursued a policy of industrialisation. In other words, economic growth may be slower from a policy of exporting primaries than from a policy of industrialisation.

The benefits from trade may not accrue to the nationals of the country. If a mine or plantation is owned by a foreign company, it will be the foreign shareholders who get the profits from the sale of exports. In addition, these companies may bring in their own capital and skilled labour from abroad. The benefits gained by the local people will probably be confined to the additional wages they earn. With these companies being in a position of monopsony power, the wages are often very low.

In recent years the Fair Trade movement has focused attention on the low incomes received by many primary producers and their lack of market power. Only a tiny fraction of the price you pay for coffee, tea or bananas goes to local growers.

? *Why does this argument make GNY a better indicator of development than GDP? (See the appendix to Chapter 14.)*

Trade may lead to less equality. Trade shifts income distribution in favour of those factors of production employed intensively in the export sector. If exports are labour intensive, greater equality will tend to result. But if they are land or raw material intensive, trade will redistribute income in favour of large landowners or mine owners.

KI 4
p13

Exporting primary exports may involve external costs. Mining can lead to huge external costs, such as the despoiling of the countryside and damage to the health of miners. Mines and plantations can lead to the destruction of traditional communities and their values.

KI 29
p323

Trade may adversely influence tastes. The more freely a country trades, the more will people's aspirations for a 'better life' be fuelled. If people cannot afford to buy the goods imported from the affluent world, their frustrations are likely to increase.

These arguments cast doubt on whether a policy of relying on free trade in primary exports is the best way of achieving economic development. Various trends in the international economy have also worked against primary exporters, causing them serious balance of payments problems.

Balance of payments problems: long term
Long-term trends in international trade have caused problems for primary exporting countries in three ways: (a) exports have grown slowly; (b) imports have grown rapidly; (c) until recent years, the terms of trade have moved against them.

Low income elasticity of demand for primary products. As world incomes grow, so a smaller proportion of these incomes is spent on primaries. Since food is a necessity, consumers, especially in rich countries, already consume virtually all they require. A rise in incomes, therefore, tends to be spent more on luxury goods and services, and only slightly more on basic foodstuffs. The exceptions are certain 'luxury' imported foodstuffs such as exotic fruits. In the case of raw materials, as people's incomes grow, they tend to buy more and more expensive products. The extra value of these products, however, arises not from the extra raw materials they might contain, but from their greater sophistication.

KI 9
p71

This argument has not applied in recent years, however, as the rapid growth of countries such as China and India, where people spend a relatively large proportion of any increase in their income on food, has led to a rapid rise in world food prices (see Figure 27.4). This has been aggravated by poor harvests in many parts of the world and by switching land to growing crops for biofuels instead of food. There has also been a rapid growth in demand by such countries for raw materials as inputs into the construction industry and the expanding industrial sector.

Agricultural protection in advanced countries. Faced with the problem of a slowly growing demand for food produced by their own farmers, advanced countries increasingly imposed restrictions on imported food. Reducing these restrictions

| Figure 27.4 | World primary commodity prices (2000 = 100) |

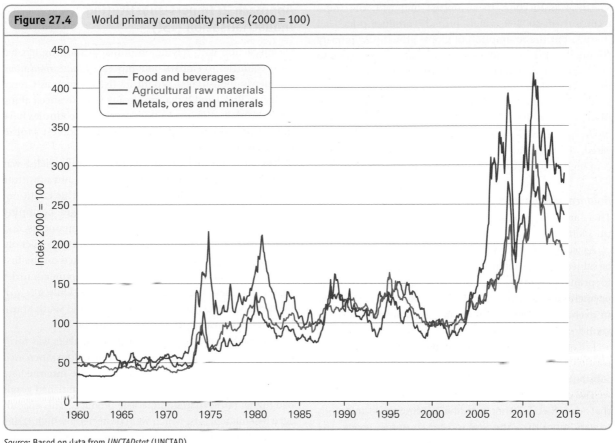

Source: Based on data from *UNCTADstat* (UNCTAD).

was one of the main aims of the Doha Development Agenda (the latest round of WTO trade negotiations: see Box 24.8 on pages 726–7).

Technological developments. Synthetic substitutes have in many cases replaced primaries in the making of consumer durables, industrial equipment and clothing. Also, the process of miniaturisation, as microchips have replaced machines, has meant that less and less raw materials have been required to produce any given amount of output.

Rapid growth in imports. There tends to be a high income elasticity of demand for imported manufactures. This is the result partly of better-off people in developing countries being able to afford luxury goods, and partly of the development of new tastes as people are exposed to the products of the developed world – products such as Coca-Cola, Levi jeans, mobile phones and iPods. In fact, the whole process has been dubbed 'Coca-Colanisation'. Because of a lack of domestic substitutes, the price elasticity of demand for manufactured imports is low. This gives market power to the overseas suppliers of these imports, which tends to raise their price relative to exports.

Deterioration in the terms of trade. The slow growth in demand for primary exports and the rapid growth in demand for manufactured imports led to chronic current account

balance of payments problems for primary exporters. This caused their exchange rates to depreciate and hence brought a decline in their terms of trade, where a country's terms of trade are defined as the average price of its exports divided by the average price of its imports (P_x/P_m).

This problem was compounded by adverse movements in international prices of primaries and manufactures. The overall demand for primaries tends to be relatively price inelastic. There is no substitute for food, and in the short run there is often no substitute for minerals. On the other hand, the demand for any *one* primary product, and especially the demand for any one *country's* primary exports, will be very price elastic: there are plenty of other countries producing substitutes. This will encourage countries to produce as much as possible (as long as price remains above marginal cost), but as all countries do the same, the low overall price elasticity will depress primary product prices. Between 1980 and 2000, the prices of many primary products declined. For instance, the nominal price index in 2000 for beverages (coffee and tea) was only one-third of its level in the late 1970s – and even less than that in real terms.

As Figure 27.4 shows, a quite different picture emerged in the 2000s. As the demand for food and raw materials grew rapidly, reflecting the rapid growth of China and various other emerging economies, so primary commodity prices rose sharply.

TC 7
p72

This was to come to an abrupt halt with the world recession of 2008–9, when primary product prices fell sharply. But the resumption of global growth saw primary commodity prices climb once more and in many cases to levels considerably higher than before the world recession. In the case of the minerals, ores and metals, for instance, average prices in April 2011 were some 47 per cent higher than in January 2007. Despite the subsequent easing of commodity prices, as the growth in demand for commodities again eased, the aggregate commodity price index was 159 per cent higher in July 2014 than 15 years earlier in July 1999.

Balance of payments problems: short term

There are also problems for primary exporting countries in the *short term*.

As we have just seen, the prices of primary products can be subject to large fluctuations. This causes great uncertainty for primary exporters. The current account of the balance of payments fluctuates wildly, which tends to cause large swings in exchange rates or requires massive government intervention to stabilise them.

Price fluctuations are caused partly by the low price elasticity of demand and supply of primaries, but also by substantial *shifts* in their demand and supply.

The demand for *food* tends to be relatively stable, but that for minerals varies with the business cycle and tends to vary more than the demand for consumer goods. The reason is the *accelerator principle* (see section 17.4). Since the *level* of investment demand depends on the size of *changes* in consumer demand, investment will fluctuate much more than consumer demand. But since many minerals are inputs into *capital* equipment, their demand is also likely to fluctuate more than consumer demand. For example, with the boom in construction in emerging economies in the mid-2000s and again in 2010–11, the prices of iron ore, copper, nickel and lead shot up.

The supply of minerals is relatively stable. The supply of cash crops, however, varies with the harvest. Many developing countries are subject to drought or flood, which can virtually wipe out their export earnings from the relevant crop.

 If a disastrous harvest of rice were confined to a particular country, would (a) the world price and (b) its own domestic price of rice fluctuate significantly? What would happen to the country's export earnings and the earnings of individual farmers?

With a price-inelastic world demand and supply for primaries, shifts in either curve will lead to substantial fluctuations in world prices. Figure 27.4 illustrates the extent of these fluctuations. The problem is most serious for countries that rely on just one or two primary products, such as Ghana, which relies on cocoa, and the Democratic Republic of Congo, which relies on copper. Diversification into other primaries would help to reduce their exposure.

Approach 2: Import-substituting industrialisation (ISI)

Dissatisfaction with relying on primary exporting has led most countries to embark on a process of *industrialisation*. The newly industrialised countries (NICs), such as China, Malaysia, Brazil and India, are already well advanced along the industrialisation road. Other developing countries have not yet progressed very far, especially the poorest African countries.

The most obvious way for countries to industrialise was to cut back on the imports of manufactures and substitute them with home-produced manufactures. This could not be done overnight: it had to be done in stages, beginning with assembly, then making some of the components, and finally making all, or nearly all, of the inputs into production. Most developing countries have at least started on the first stage. Several of the more advanced developing countries have component-manufacturing industries. Only a few of the larger NICs, such as China, India, Brazil and South Korea, have built extensive capital goods industries.

The method most favoured by policy makers was **tariff escalation**. Here tariff rates (or other restrictions) increased as one moved from the raw materials to the intermediate product to the finished product stage. Thus finished goods had higher tariffs than intermediate products. This encouraged assembly plants, which were protected by high tariffs from imported finished products, and were able to obtain components at a lower tariff rate.

One of the problems with ISI was that countries were desperately short of resources to invest in industry. As a result, a policy of ISI usually involved encouraging investment by multinational companies. But even without specific 'perks' (e.g. tax concessions, cheap sites, the cutting of red tape), multinationals would still probably be attracted by the protection afforded by the tariffs or quotas.

Adverse effects of import substitution

Some countries, such as South Korea and Taiwan, pursued an inward-looking ISI policy for only a few years. For them it was merely a stage in development, rapidly to be followed by a secondary outward-looking policy. Infant industries were initially given protection, but when they had achieved sufficient economies of scale, the barriers to imports were gradually removed.

The countries that continued to pursue protectionist ISI policies generally had a poorer growth record. They also tended to suffer from other problems, such as a deepening of inequality. The development of the modern industrial

---

Definition

Tariff escalation The system whereby tariff rates increase the closer a product is to the finished stage of production.

| BOX 27.2 | WHEN DRIVING AND ALCOHOL DO MIX | CASE STUDIES AND APPLICATIONS |

A case of import substitution in Brazil

Two major changes in world trade hit Brazil in the 1970s. The first was the fourfold increase in world oil prices. Brazil has very little oil of its own. The second was the slump in the world sugar cane market as a result of northern countries' protection of their sugar beet industries. Brazil was a major cane sugar exporter.

Faced with a resulting large increase in its import bill and a slump in its sugar exports, the Brazilian government came up with an ingenious solution. It could use surplus sugar cane to make alcohol, which could then be used instead of petrol for cars. Farmers were given subsidies to grown sugar cane.

Large distilleries were set up to convert the sugar cane into alcohol. At the same time, cars were produced (e.g. VW Beetles) that could run on alcohol (ethanol) rather than petrol.

Thus by one measure two problems were alleviated. By 1985, more than 90 per cent of cars produced in Brazil were designed to burn alcohol.

Then, with the decline in oil prices from the mid-1980s, the relative cost-efficiency of alcohol-powered cars declined: at times it was cheaper to import oil than to produce alcohol. The government cut subsidies and by 1997 less than 1 per cent of cars produced in Brazil were alcohol-powered.

The story illustrates the danger of basing major schemes on terms of trade existing at a particular time. If these terms of trade subsequently change, the schemes could prove to be uneconomical.

A new dawn for the biofuels industry

A more flexible solution was found in 2003 with the introduction of dual-fuel cars that could run on either alcohol or petrol or a mixture of the two. This gave consumers the chance of using whichever fuel was the cheapest at the time. The popularity of these 'flexi-fuel' cars has given a welcome boost to the sugar cane and ethanol industries. By 2006, 56 per cent of new Brazilian cars and vans were dual-fuel, and by 2013 the figure was over 84 per cent.

Although subsidies to the ethanol industry have been abolished, the industry is now well able to survive without. With oil prices over $50 per barrel, ethanol can be produced at half the cost of petrol.

The environmental benefits of renewable sources of fuel which do not displace food production or the rainforest are clear. However, the conditions for sugar cane workers are some of the toughest in the world.

Given the success of the alcohol programme and the huge savings in oil imports, Brazil has now embarked on another import-substituting drive: to displace diesel fuel with fuel produced from soybeans. Perhaps this 'biodiesel' will become the new dollar saver. But soya-based biodiesel can have very damaging effects on the environment. It is far less energy-efficient than sugar cane as a source of fuel and it absorbs less carbon per hectare as it grows. In fact, given that rainforest is being cleared to grow soya, the net effect is to reduce carbon capture substantially.

 Could a case be made out for a flexible tax on oil imports to ensure that it was always profitable to produce alcohol?

---

sector has often been to the detriment of the traditional sectors and also to the export sector.

The criticisms of ISI are numerous, and include the following.

It ran directly counter to the principle of comparative advantage. Rather than confining ISI to genuine infant industries and then gradually removing the protection, ISI was applied indiscriminately to a whole range of industries. Countries ended up producing goods in which they had a comparative *disadvantage*.

 If a country specialises in a good in which it has a comparative disadvantage, where will it be consuming with respect to its production possibility curve?

It cushioned inefficient practices and encouraged the establishment of monopolies. Without competition from imports, many of the industries were highly inefficient and wasteful of resources. What is more, in all but the largest or most developed of the developing countries the domestic market for many manufactures is small. If a newly established industry is to be large enough to gain the full potential economies of scale, it must be large relative to the market. This means that it will have considerable monopoly power.

It involved artificially low real interest rates. To encourage capital investment in the import-substituting industries, governments often intervened to keep interest rates low. This encouraged the use of capital-intensive technology with a consequent lack of jobs. It also starved other sectors (such as agriculture) of much needed finance, and it discouraged saving.

It led to urban wages above the market-clearing level. Wage rates in the industrial sector, although still low compared with advanced countries, are often considerably higher than in the traditional sectors:

- They are pushed up by firms seeking to retain labour in which they have invested training.
- Governments, seeking to appease the politically powerful urban industrial working class, have often passed minimum wage laws.
- Trade unions, although less widespread in developing than in advanced countries, are mainly confined to the new industries.

KI 20
p171

Higher industrial wages again encourage firms to use capital-intensive techniques.

It involved overvalued exchange rates. Restricting imports tends to lead to an appreciation of the exchange rate. This makes non-restricted imports cheaper. This then discourages the production of domestic goods, such as food and component parts, which compete with those imports. Also, a higher exchange rate discourages exports. Exports tend to be priced in dollars. If the exchange rate appreciates, domestic currency will buy more dollars; or put another way, a dollar will exchange for less domestic currency. Thus exporters will earn less domestic currency as the exchange rate appreciates.

Why is an overvalued exchange rate likely to encourage the use of capital-intensive technology?

It did not necessarily save on foreign exchange. Many of the new industries were highly dependent on the importation of raw materials, capital equipment and component parts. These imported inputs, unlike imports of finished goods, were often supplied by a single firm, which could thus charge monopoly prices. What is more, a large proportion of the extra incomes generated by these industries tended to be spent on imports by the new urban elites.

Protection was not applied evenly. Many different tariff rates were used in one country; in fact, a policy of tariff escalation demands this. In addition, governments often used a whole range of other protectionist instruments, such as the licensing of importers, physical and value quotas, and foreign exchange rationing. The result was that protection was highly uneven.

Economists have developed the concept of **effective protection** to measure the true degree of protection that an industry gets. Effective protection measures the extra domestic value added that protection gives an industry. By *domestic value added* we mean the difference between the world market price of the finished good and the cost of the imported inputs used to make the good.

The effective rate of protection is given by the formula

$$\frac{V^* - V}{V} \times 100$$

where V is the free-trade domestic value added, and V^* is the value added after the imposition of tariffs. There are three variables that determine the rate of effective protection:

- The tariff rate on the finished good (the nominal rate of protection). The higher this is, the higher will be the value of V^* relative to V, and hence the higher will be the effective rate of protection.
- The tariff rate (or rates) on the inputs. The higher these are, the lower will be the value of V^* relative to V, and hence the lower will be the effective rate of protection.
- The level of value added as a proportion of the price of the finished good. The higher this is, the lower will be the effective rate of protection (assuming tariff escalation).

To demonstrate this last point, work out the effective rate of protection in the following three cases:
(a) Free-trade finished good price = £100; free-trade cost of imported inputs = £40.
(b) Free-trade finished good price = £100; free-trade cost of imported inputs = £80.
(c) Free-trade finished good price = £100; free-trade cost of imported inputs = £100.
In each case, assume that a 50 per cent tariff is imposed on the finished good and a 10 per cent tariff on the imported inputs.

In many countries, effective protective rates varied massively from one industry to another. For example, according to World Bank estimates, in 1980 effective rates of protection in manufacturing ranged from −85 per cent to 219 per cent in Brazil and from −62 per cent to 1119 per cent in Nigeria! Clearly, such huge differences in effective protection imposed massive distortions on the market.

Under what circumstances could the effective rate of protection be negative?

Income distribution was made less equal. Additional incomes generated by the modern sector tended to be spent on modern-sector goods and imported goods. Thus there was a multiplier effect *within* the modern sector, but virtually none between the sectors. Also, as we saw above, an overvalued exchange rate leads to a bias against agriculture, and thus further deepens the divide between rich and poor. Finally, the relatively high wages of the modern sector encourage workers to migrate to the towns, where many, failing to get a job, live in dire poverty.

Social, cultural and environmental costs. A policy of ISI often involved imposing an alien set of values. Urban life can be harsh, competitive and materialistic. Moreover, a drive for industrialisation may involve major costs to the environment, as a result of waste products from new industries.

Finally, import substitution is necessarily limited by the size of the domestic market. Once that is saturated, ISI can come to an abrupt halt. At that stage, further expansion can come only from exporting; but if these industries have been overprotected, they will be unable to compete in world markets.

> ## Definition
>
> **Effective rate of protection** The percentage increase in an industry's domestic value added resulting from protection given to that industry.

Table 27.2	Growth rates and export performance of selected secondary outward-looking countries, 1985–2012			
	Average annual growth in real GDP (%)	Average annual growth in real GNY per capita (%)	Share of manufactures in merchandise exports (%)	Average annual growth rate of exports (%)
Brazil	3.0	1.7	50.3	5.4
China	10.0	8.9	80.6	13.3
Hong Kong	4.6	3.6	90.5	7.2
India	6.4	4.5	70.4	13.9
Malaysia	5.8	3.5	65.4	4.6
Singapore	6.4	3.9	76.4	8.5
South Korea	5.9	5.2	91.1	9.9
All developing countries	4.7	3.3	61.2	8.4
High-income economies	2.4	1.8	74.0	4.6
World	2.9	1.5	71.0	5.4

Source: Data drawn from *World Development Indicators* (World Bank, 2014).

This has been a long list of problems and different economists put different emphases on them. Neoclassical economists stress the problems of market distortions, arguing that ISI leads to great inefficiency. Neo-Marxist economists, on the other hand, stress the problems of *dependency*. Many of the new industries will be owned by multinational companies, which import unsuitable technologies. The countries will then become dependent on imported inputs and foreign sources of capital. (See Case Study 27.2 in MyEconLab.)

Approach 3: Exporting manufactures – a possible way forward?

The countries with the highest rates of economic growth are those that have successfully made the transition to being exporters of manufactures. Table 27.2 gives some examples.

The transition from inward-looking to outward-looking industrialisation

How is a country to move from import substituting to being outward-looking? One approach is to take it industry by industry. When an industry has saturated the home market and there is no further scope for import substitution, it should then be encouraged to seek markets overseas. The trouble with this approach is that, if the country is still protecting other industries, there will probably still be an overvalued exchange rate. Thus specific subsidies, tax concessions or other 'perks' would have to be given to this industry to enable it to compete. The country would still be highly interventionist, with all the distortions and misallocation of resources that this tends to bring.

The alternative is to wean the whole economy off protection. Three major things will need doing. There will need to be a devaluation of the currency in order to restore the potential profitability of the export sector. There will also need to be a dismantling of the various protective measures that had biased production towards the home market. Finally, there will probably need to be a removal or relaxing of price controls. But these are things that cannot be done 'at a stroke'. Firms may have to be introduced gradually to the greater forces of competition that an outward-looking trade policy brings. Otherwise there may be massive bankruptcies and a corresponding massive rise in unemployment.

The benefits from a secondary outward-looking policy

The advocates of outward-looking industrialisation make a number of points in its favour.

It conforms more closely to comparative advantage. Countries pursuing an open trade regime will be able to export only goods in which they have a comparative advantage. The resources used in earning a unit of foreign exchange from exports will be less than those used in saving a unit of foreign exchange by replacing imports with home-produced goods. In other words, resources will be used more efficiently.

Economies of scale. If the home market is too small to allow a firm to gain all the potential economies of scale, these can be gained by expanding into the export market.

Increased competition. By having to compete with foreign companies, exporters will be under a greater competitive pressure than industries shielded behind protective barriers. This will encourage (a) resource saving in the short run, both through their better *allocation* and through reductions in X inefficiency (see Box 6.5), and (b) innovation and investment, as firms attempt to adopt the latest technology, often obtained from developed countries.

> ## Definition
>
> **Dependency** Where the development of a developing country is hampered by its relationships with the industrialised world.

| BOX 27.3 | THE CHINESE ECONOMIC MIRACLE |

Riding the dragon

'China is amazing. It is capitalism, but at an unprecedented speed.' 'The talent of Chinese software engineers is unbelievable. I can't believe how effective they are.' (Bill Gates, Chairman, Microsoft)

'If your business isn't making money in China, it probably wouldn't make money anywhere else.' (Carlos Ghosn, President, Nissan Motor Company)[1]

On the basis of several indicators, China's economic performance is extraordinary. From 1990 to 2014 annual economic growth averaged 12 per cent. Its exports grew by an average of 14.6 per cent (see chart). In 2009 it overtook Germany to become the world's largest exporter (see Figure 24.1 on page 707). In PPP terms, China is the world's second-biggest economy after the USA, or third if the eurozone is taken as a single economy.

And as China's economy and exports have boomed, so foreign investment has flooded into the country. In 1990 foreign direct investment (FDI) into China was $3.5 billion. By 2012 the figure had risen to $121 billion.

Chinese export-orientated growth has been based on three key factors: specialising in goods in which it has

a comparative advantage; having an economy that is favourable to both domestic and inward investment; and having an exchange rate that is undervalued in PPP terms.

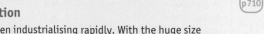

Specialisation

China has been industrialising rapidly. With the huge size of the domestic market and with an open policy towards exporting, China has specialised in goods that exploit its diverse but relatively well-trained labour force. Huge industrial complexes have sprung up along the coast from which it is easy to export.

Chinese firms have adapted to changing world markets and to their own changing comparative advantage. Twenty years ago, textiles and clothing were China's main export industry. These relatively labour-intensive industries were ideally suited to exploit the abilities of China's abundant labour. Today textiles and clothing account for a sixth of China's exports. Electronic goods, by contrast, account for more than a third and are growing at a rate three times as fast as textiles. Electronic goods exploit China's increasingly well-trained and well-educated workforce.

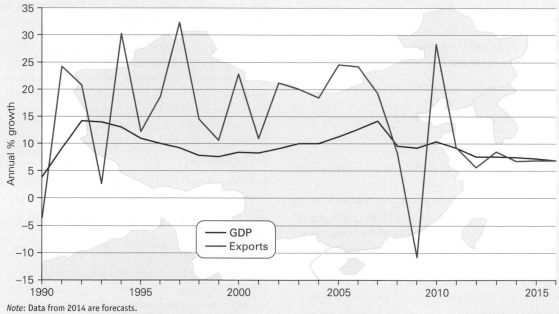

Growth in Chinese merchandise exports and GDP (%)

Note: Data from 2014 are forecasts.
Source: Based on data from *World Economic Outlook* database (IMF).

Increased investment. To the extent that outward-looking policies lead to a greater potential for economic growth, they may attract more foreign capital. To the extent that they lead to increased incomes, additional saving will be generated, especially given that the *marginal* propensity to save may be quite high. The extra savings can be used to finance extra investment.

It can lead to more employment and a more equal distribution of income. According to the Heckscher–Ohlin theory, the manufactured goods in which a country will have a comparative advantage are those produced by labour-intensive techniques. Export expansion will thus increase the demand for labour relative to capital, and create more employment. The increased demand for labour will tend to lead to a rise in wages relative to profits.

Investment

But why are foreign investors attracted to China? Is it simply that the economy is growing rapidly? Clearly that is part of the attraction, but it is more than that. For a start, the Chinese economy is huge. With a population of 1.4 billion and a GDP of close on $10 trillion in 2014 (which is expected to have risen to $15 trillion by the end of the 2010s), China represents a massive potential market. The government has also invested heavily in improving the country's transport, power and communications infrastructure.

What is more, much of the growth in income in the Chinese economy is concentrated in the hands of the middle class, which now constitutes over 20 per cent of the population and 50 per cent of the urban population. The demand for consumer goods by these middle-class Chinese is very income elastic. As a result, sales of electrical goods, furniture, cars and fashion clothing are growing rapidly. Not only foreign manufacturers, but foreign retailers too are taking advantage of this. For example, Wal-Mart entered China in 1996 and by 2014 had over 400 stores, largely sourcing its merchandise from local suppliers. Carrefour, the French supermarket chain, entered China in 1995 and by 2014 had more than 230 stores.

But foreign investors are not only attracted by the growing domestic Chinese market. They are also attracted by the opportunity to manufacture high-tech products with a highly skilled workforce.

More and more companies become cutting edge and leapfrog foreign rivals. Whether games consoles, DVD recorders or flat-screen monitors, Chinese factories are grabbing high-tech market share.

'Ten years ago, China was about low cost,' says Infineon's Ulrich Schumacher. 'Now it is at the forefront of technical development. Infineon can develop twice as fast in China as anywhere else.'

'Engineers are working in three shifts, seven days a week,' enthuses Mr Schumacher. 'In Germany that would not be possible: there, engineers don't work on weekends.'

Bill Gates is similarly impressed after his latest visit to Microsoft's research lab in Beijing, one of four in China and Hong Kong. 'The talent of the people there is unbelievable, I can't believe how effective they are,' he says.

All this is worrying news for high-tech workers in industrialised countries, who hoped their skills would give them a competitive advantage in the globalised economy.[2]

An undervalued exchange rate

Despite the booming economy and export sector, and a massive current account surplus against the USA ($162 billion in 2004), the Chinese yuan remained pegged to the US dollar at $1 = 8.28 yuan from 1995 to 2005. This undervaluation of the yuan against the dollar was a major contributing factor in the growth in Chinese exports.

The situation had become even more extreme with other countries. With the fall in the dollar in 2003–4 against the euro, yen and sterling, the dollar-pegged yuan thus also fell against these currencies. This made Chinese exports even cheaper in Europe and east Asia, further fuelling the trade imbalance.

The USA for some time had been pressing for a revaluation of the yuan or a floating of the yuan so that it could appreciate. Indeed, in 2005 the US Senate was pushing the Bush administration to adopt a 27.5 per cent tariff on all Chinese imports unless China revalued its currency.

In 2005 China eventually moved to a pegged exchange rate with a basket of 11 currencies, each currency being weighted in the basket by the amount of trade with China (see Box 26.1). It also revalued the yuan by 2.1 per cent.

By January 2014 the yuan–dollar exchange rate was $1 = 6.10 yuan, while the yuan's effective exchange rate was 19 per cent higher than in July 2005. Nonetheless, it was still considerably undervalued in PPP terms, giving China a strong competitive edge against other developing countries seeking export-led growth. The effect has been a huge current account surplus, which peaked at 10.1 per cent of GDP in 2007. Since then it has fallen and during the first half of the 2010s averaged close to 2.5 per cent of GDP.

The surplus has resulted in massive Chinese purchases of dollars and other currencies. By 2014 China had in excess of $4 trillion in foreign exchange reserves. The inflows have also allowed China to purchase stakes in many American and European companies and to make substantial investments in various developing countries.

1. *In what ways does a booming Chinese economy benefit the rest of the world?*
2. *Why may the Chinese be reluctant to adopt a freely floating exchange rate?*

[1] 'Is China a goldmine or minefield?', BBC News Online, 19 February 2004, http://news.bbc.co.uk/1/hi/business/3494069.stm
[2] Ibid.

 Will the adoption of labour-intensive techniques necessarily lead to a more equal distribution of income?

It removes many of the costs associated with ISI. Under a policy of ISI, managers may spend a lot of their time lobbying politicians and officials, seeking licences (and sometimes paying bribes to obtain them), adhering to norms and regulations or trying to find ways round them. If an outward-looking policy involves removing all this, managers can turn their attention to producing goods more efficiently.

TC 5 p22

Drawbacks of an export-orientated industrialisation strategy

The export of manufactures is seen by many developed countries as very threatening to their own industries. Their response has often been to erect trade barriers. These barriers have tended to be highest in the very industries (such as textiles, footwear and processed food) where developing countries have the greatest comparative advantage. Even if the barriers are *currently* low, developing countries may feel that it is too risky to expand their exports of these products for fear of a future rise in barriers. Recognising this problem, the World Trade Organization is very keen to ensure fair access for developing countries to the markets of the rich world. This has been a core focus of the Doha Round of trade negotiations (see Box 24.8 on pages 726–7).

 Consider the arguments from the perspective of an advanced country for and against protecting its industries from imports of manufactures from developing countries.

The successes of developing countries such as China, Malaysia and South Korea in exporting manufactures (see Table 27.2) do not imply that other developing countries will have similar success. As additional developing countries attempt to export their manufactures, they will be facing more and more competition from each other.

Another problem is that, if a more open trade policy involves removing or reducing exchange and capital controls, the country may become more vulnerable to speculative attack. This was one of the major contributing factors to the east Asian crisis of the late 1990s (see Case Study 27.3 in MyEconLab). Gripped by currency and stock market speculation, and by banking and company insolvency, many countries of the region found that economic growth had turned into a major recession. The 'miracle' seemed to be over. Nevertheless, the countries with the fewest distortions fared the best during the crisis. Thus Singapore and Taiwan, which are open and relatively flexible, experienced only a slowdown, rather than a recession.

Exporting manufactures may thus be a very risky strategy for the least developed countries, such as many in Africa. Perhaps the best hope for the future may be for a growth in manufacturing trade *between* such developing countries. That way they can gain the benefits of specialisation and economies of scale that trade brings, while at the same time producing for a growing market. The feasibility of this approach depends on whether developing countries can agree to free-trade areas or even customs unions between themselves (see section 24.3).

There does, however, seem to be a strong movement in this direction (see pages 732–3). The share of trade between developing countries (so-called South–South trade) in total world exports has doubled over the past 20 years, to over 25 per cent. Manufactured goods now account for nearly 60 per cent of South–South trade, respectively.

Section summary

1. Trade is of vital importance for the vast majority of developing countries, and yet most developing countries suffer from chronic balance of trade deficits.

2. Developing countries have traditionally been primary exporters. This has allowed them to exploit their comparative advantage in labour-intensive goods and has provided a market for certain goods that would otherwise have no market at home.

3. However, with a low income elasticity of demand for primary products in developed countries, with the development of synthetic substitutes and with the protection of agriculture in Europe and the USA, the demand for primary exports has, until recent years, grown only slowly. At the same time, the demand for manufactured imports into developing countries has grown rapidly. The result has been a worsening balance of trade problem; and with a price-inelastic demand for both imports and exports, the terms of trade worsened too. There is also the danger that comparative costs may change over time; that most of the benefits from primary exports may accrue to foreign owners of mines and plantations, or to wealthy elites in the domestic population; that mines and plantations can involve substantial environmental and other external costs; and that export earnings can fluctuate, given instabilities in supply and unstable world prices.

4. Import-substituting industrialisation was seen to be the answer to these problems. This was normally achieved in stages, beginning with the finished goods stage and then working back towards the capital goods stage. ISI, it was hoped, would allow countries to benefit from the various dynamic advantages associated with manufacturing.

5. For many countries, however, ISI brought as many, if not more, problems than it solved. It often led to the establishment of inefficient industries, protected from foreign competition and facing little or no competition at home either. It led to considerable market distortions, with tariffs and other forms of protection haphazardly applied and with resulting huge variations in effective rates of protection; to overvalued exchange rates with a resulting bias against exports and the agricultural sector generally; to a deepening of inequalities and to large-scale social and environmental problems as the cities expanded and as poverty and unemployment grew. Finally, the balance of payments was in many cases made worse as the new industries became increasingly dependent on imported inputs and as growing urbanisation caused a growing demand for imported consumer goods.

6. The most rapidly growing of the developing countries are those that have pursued a policy of export-orientated industrialisation. This has allowed them to achieve the benefits of economies of scale and foreign competition. It has allowed them to specialise in goods in which they have a comparative advantage (i.e. labour-intensive goods) and yet which have a relatively high income elasticity of demand. Whether countries that have pursued ISI can successfully turn to an open, export-orientated approach depends to a large extent on the degree of competition they face, not only from rich countries, but also from other developing countries.

27.3 STRUCTURAL PROBLEMS WITHIN DEVELOPING COUNTRIES

The neglect of agriculture

The drive to industrialise by many developing countries has often been highly damaging to agriculture, especially in the poorest countries such as those of sub-Saharan Africa. With a backward and run down agricultural sector, with little or no rural infrastructure, many countries today face a food crisis of immense proportions.

Over the years, opinions have gradually changed. It is now realised that the relief of poverty, unemployment and the maldistribution of income can best be achieved by improving productivity and incomes in the rural sector. No longer is agriculture seen as a sector to be 'squeezed' like an orange. Rather it is seen as a sector that must be developed in harmony with the urban sector. Agricultural output must be increased for the benefit of rural and urban dwellers alike. At the same time, industrial output can be given new markets in the rural sector if rural incomes expand. The following are some of the possible ways forward.

Price reform. The price of food needs to be raised relative to the price of industrial goods. This may be achieved simply through the reduction of protection of manufactured products. Higher relative food prices increase the profitability of agricultural production and enable farmers to afford to invest in irrigation, agricultural implements, land improvement, etc.

A particular problem has come from cheap subsidised food 'dumped' on the markets of developing countries by the EU and the USA. A substantial reduction in such subsidies has been one of the major demands by developing countries in the Doha round of trade negotiations (see Box 24.8 on pages 726–7).

Rising world food prices in recent years (see Figure 27.4) have provided much needed help for farmers who make a living selling food. But they have worsened the plight of city dwellers, who naturally demand lower prices. In most developing countries only a minority of households sell more food than they buy.

Devaluation. If the currency is devalued, or allowed to depreciate, this increases the price of food imports and thus makes it easier for domestic food producers to compete. It also increases the profitability of food exports (in domestic currency).

Government support for rural infrastructure projects. If food is to be marketed, there must be adequate rural infrastructure. Government road-building schemes and the setting up of marketing boards can make a dramatic difference to the viability of commercial food production.

The provision of finance. Farmers need access to cheap finance and not to be forced to borrow at sky-high interest rates from local moneylenders. This can be achieved by setting up rural banks specialising in the provision of finance to small farmers. These could be nationalised institutions, or the government could give incentives to private banks to expand into the rural sector.

The adoption of new technologies and practices. There have been rapid advances in agricultural technology in recent years. The development of new fertilisers, pesticides, simple but effective agricultural machinery, and most of all of new high-yielding strains of grain, especially wheat and rice, have helped to transform traditional agriculture in certain developing countries such as India. There has been a *Green Revolution*, hastened in recent years by the production of genetically modified strains of crops.

Other countries, however, and especially those of sub-Saharan Africa, have made slower progress in adopting these technologies. This is due partly to an inability to afford the new equipment, chemicals and seeds, partly to the lack of infrastructure to make them available, and partly to their unsuitability to the generally more arid African conditions. When the technologies are adopted, it is often only by large multinationals operating in plantations. For example, companies like Monsanto have been the main developers and users of genetically modified crops.

Governments can help by funding research into the best farming methods and inputs for local conditions. They can also help by providing finance for the adoption of the new methods.

Education and advice. Many farmers are simply unaware of new, more efficient farming methods. Training schemes or rural advisers can help here.

Land reform. As population grows, land holdings are divided and subdivided as they are passed from generation to generation. Thus many farmers operate on tiny plots of land that can never yield an adequate income. Increasingly, they get into debt and are forced to mortgage their land to large landowners at high interest rates, or to sell it to them at low prices. The number of landless labourers or farmers in 'debt bondage' therefore grows.

A solution to this problem is the redistribution of land. Clearly, this cannot be done unless there is a government sympathetic to the rural poor and willing to take on the inevitable opposition from the large farmers. Often these large farmers are politically powerful and have the police on their side.

The encouragement of rural co-operatives. If small farmers get together and form co-operatives, they may be able to afford to share agricultural equipment such as tractors and harvesters, and undertake irrigation schemes; they may be able to set up input-purchasing and crop-marketing and distribution organisations, and gain easier access to credit. In many countries, national or local governments have actively encouraged such co-operatives by providing subsidies, tax incentives and advice, and by passing favourable legislation.

Inappropriate technology

The technology employed in a country depends on the type of development strategy it is pursuing. Some strategies lead to the adoption of relatively labour-intensive technologies, others to relatively capital-intensive ones.

Neoclassical theory suggests that countries should use techniques that are intensive in their abundant factor. This is simply an extension of the Heckscher–Ohlin theory, only this time it is applied to the choice of techniques rather than to the choice of goods. The theory implies that (labour-abundant) developing countries should adopt labour-intensive techniques; techniques that use relatively more of the cheap factor (labour) and relatively less of the expensive factor (capital).

With the advent of policies of industrialisation, however, came strong arguments for adopting capital-intensive technology. Capital-intensive technologies were seen to be more advanced. These were the technologies that were developed in rich countries, countries with sophisticated research facilities. The argument here was that, despite having a higher capital/labour ratio, these techniques nevertheless had a low capital/output ratio. The equipment might be expensive, but it would yield a very high output and would thus cost less *per unit* of output.

 If a modern capital-intensive technique has a higher capital/labour ratio and a lower capital/output ratio than a traditional labour-intensive one, what can we say about its labour/output ratio relative to the traditional technique?

A second argument was that, if multinationals were to be encouraged to invest in developing countries, they had to be allowed to bring with them their own technology – technology that was almost invariably capital-intensive. In other words, the choice was not between more labour-intensive and more capital-intensive techniques, but rather between having *extra* capital (by allowing multinationals to invest) and not having it at all.

A final argument in favour of capital-intensive technology was that it provides a greater level of profit, and that this profit will then be reinvested, thereby causing a faster rate of economic growth.

Given these arguments, many governments of developing countries actively encouraged the use of capital-intensive techniques; some still do. But also there were other features of ISI that unintentionally led to biases in favour of capital-intensive technology. These included the following:

- Wage rates above the market-clearing level, driven up by minimum wage legislation, trade union activity, or firms trying to ensure that workers they had trained were not 'poached' by other firms.

- Low interest rates to encourage investment. The effect of this, plus relatively high wage rates in the expanding industries, is to encourage the substitution of capital for labour.
- An overvalued exchange rate. This lowers the relative price of imported inputs, which under a policy of tariff escalation have low tariffs. This encourages the use of import-intensive technology, which also tends to be capital-intensive.
- The ignorance of many multinational companies of alternative efficient labour-intensive technology.
- The bias of engineers. It is engineers rather than economists who are often instrumental in deciding which production techniques a firm will use. Engineers tend to be biased in favour of mechanically efficient techniques, which tend to be capital-intensive, rather than economically efficient techniques, which may well be labour-intensive.

? *What is the difference between mechanical efficiency and economic efficiency?*

In recent years, with the criticism of ISI has come the criticism of capital-intensive technologies:

- Capital-intensive equipment may require more maintenance.
- It may have to be imported, and may use a high proportion of imported inputs. This will put a strain on the country's balance of trade. If less domestic inputs are used, there will be less spread effect to other sectors of the economy: there will be a smaller multiplier effect.
- There may be problems of hold-ups, breakdowns and incorrect usage due to problems in obtaining parts and an absence of properly trained maintenance staff.
- Even if the technologies do generate higher profits, there is no guarantee that these will be reinvested. They may simply flow abroad to foreign shareholders, or be spent largely on luxury consumption if the profits initially stay within the country (and a high proportion of luxury goods are imported anyway).
- Capital-intensive techniques often involve large-scale production. There have been many examples of countries opening up plants that are simply too large relative to the market. As a result, they never operate at full capacity, and thus may operate inefficiently.

In addition, capital-intensive technologies have other detrimental effects. As we shall see shortly, they may worsen the unemployment problem. Also, as they are large-scale technologies, the firms using them usually locate in the cities. This tends to worsen the problem of ***dualism***. Inequality

> ### Definition
>
> **Dualism** The division of an economy into a modern (usually urban) sector and a poor traditional (usually rural) sector.

KI 37
p710

KI 4
p13

between urban and rural incomes tends to grow; and with relatively few workers being employed in these industries, at relatively high wages, the gap between their wages and those of the urban poor tends to grow also.

 The concentration of large-scale plants in cities can cause severe problems of pollution, especially if the government is not very strict in enforcing pollution control.

 Why may governments of developing countries be less strict than developed countries in controlling pollution?

So what can be done to encourage a more appropriate technology? Part of the solution lies in correcting market distortions: there will probably need to be a devaluation of the currency and a rise in interest rates. This would remove two of the key factors favouring capital-intensive industry.

 Then there will probably also need to be positive encouragement given to the invention or adoption of *efficient* labour-intensive technologies. This could involve government-sponsored research, information centres to provide details of the various techniques used around the world, education and training schemes for managers and workers, the provision of advice on production, marketing, distribution, etc., and incentives for inventions (such as subsidies or patent protection).

The government could help to encourage small businesses (which typically use more labour-intensive techniques) by, for example, setting up development banks that provide services specifically for small businesses (including farms and other rural businesses), and which grant loans at similar rates to those charged to large firms; encouraging the formation of co-operatives through tax concessions or subsidies, or by reducing the amount of red tape such organisations are likely to encounter; and providing small workshops at low or zero rent.

 What difficulties is a government likely to encounter in encouraging the use of labour-intensive technology?

Unemployment

Imagine the choice of living in a large family in the countryside with too little land to be able to feed you and the other family members, or of seeking your fortune in the city where there are nowhere near enough jobs to go round. It is not much of a choice. But it is the sort of choice that millions of people are forced to make. Open unemployment rates in developing countries are generally much higher than in developed countries: rates in excess of 15 per cent are not uncommon.

But even these high rates grossly understate the true extent of the problem. With the system of extended families, where the family farm or the family trade occupies all the family members, people may not be out looking for jobs and are thus not openly unemployed, but their output is nevertheless

very low. There is simply not enough work to occupy them fully. This is the problem of *disguised unemployment*. Then there are those who manage to do a few hours' work each week as casual labourers or as petty traders. These people are *underemployed*. When you add the problem of disguised unemployment and underemployment to the problem of open unemployment, the problem becomes overwhelming.

The causes of the unemployment problem are deep-seated and complex, but four stand out as being particularly important in most developing countries.

Rapid population growth

With reductions in mortality rates (due to improved health care) that have not been matched by equivalent reductions in birth rates, populations in most developing countries have grown rapidly for many years now. The labour force has thus grown rapidly too. The growth in production has simply not been fast enough to create enough jobs for these extra workers.

Capital-intensity bias

As we have seen, import-substituting industrialisation has involved a bias in favour of capital-intensive technology. This has led to the production of goods and to the use of processes that provide only limited employment opportunities. As long as the relative price of capital to labour is kept low, or as long as there is a lack of modern, efficient *labour-intensive* techniques available, or as long as multinational companies choose to bring in their own (capital-intensive) technology, there will continue to be a lack of demand for labour.

Rural–urban migration

Throughout the developing world, people flock from the countryside to the towns and thereby swell the numbers of urban unemployed. Migration accounts for some 55 per cent of urban population growth in developing countries. But if life in the shanty towns is wretched, what is the point? The point is that for most of the migrants there was no chance at all of getting another job in the countryside, whereas in the towns there is at least some chance. If one in five migrants gets a job, then you might be the lucky one.

The decision to migrate thus depends on four main factors:

■ The income differential between the countryside and the town. The more that jobs in the town pay relative to what the migrant could earn by staying behind, the more the person is likely to migrate. If their decision was to be totally rational, they would also take into account the differences in the cost of living between the two areas.

Definitions

Disguised unemployment Where the same work could be done by fewer people.

Underemployment Where people who want full-time work are only able to find part-time work.

*BOX 27.4   UNEMPLOYMENT IN DEVELOPING COUNTRIES

Three simple models

In this box we will look at three models that have been developed to explain Third World unemployment.

Limited choice of techniques

The simplest version of this model assumes that there is only one technique available to firms and that just two factors of production are involved – labour and capital. Firms will thus face a right-angled isoquant (see section 5.3). This is illustrated in Figure (a).

Each isoquant shows a particular level of output (Q). Given that there is only one choice of technique, involving a particular combination of labour and capital, then for each amount of capital used a particular amount of labour will be needed – no more and no less. Any extra labour will simply be idle.

For example, if each machine required one operative and if 10 machines were available, then 10 operatives would be required. An 11th would add nothing to output. Similarly, if there were 10 operatives available, an 11th machine would be idle.

If, in Figure (a), the total supply of capital were $\bar{K}$, then firms would require L_1 of labour. But if the total labour force were $\bar{L}$, then $\bar{L} - L_1$ workers would be unemployed.

Thus the lack of availability of labour-intensive techniques means that there is not enough capital to employ everyone.

Capital-intensity bias

This model assumes that there are labour-intensive techniques available, but that firms choose not to use them. Assuming

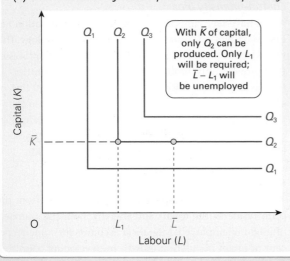

(a) *Limited choice of techniques: one technique only*

With $\bar{K}$ of capital, only Q_2 can be produced. Only L_1 will be required; $\bar{L} - L_1$ will be unemployed

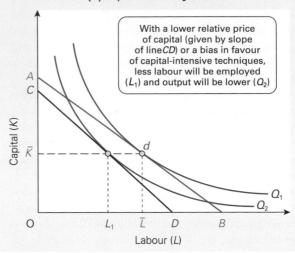

(b) *Capital intensity bias*

With a lower relative price of capital (given by slope of line CD) or a bias in favour of capital-intensive techniques, less labour will be employed (L_1) and output will be lower (Q_2)

- The chance of getting a job. The higher the rate of urban unemployment, the less the chance of getting a job and thus the less likely the person is to migrate.
- The 'risk attitude' of the person: in other words, how willing potential migrants are to take the gamble of whether or not they will get a job.
- The degree of misinformation. People may migrate to the towns, attracted by the 'bright lights' of the city and the belief (probably misplaced) that their prospects are much better there.

Box 27.4 presents three simple, but more formalised models examining the impact of technology and migration in unemployment in developing countries.

What would be the effect on the levels of migration and urban unemployment of the creation of jobs in the towns?

External influences

Most developing countries are highly dependent on international economic forces. If the world economy goes into recession, or world interest rates rise, or protectionist policies are pursued by developed countries, this will have a damaging effect on industry in developing countries. Their exports will fall and unemployment will rise.

There is no simple cure for unemployment in developing countries. Nevertheless, there are certain measures that governments can take which will help to reverse its growth:

again that there are just the two factors, labour and capital, this time firms will face curved isoquants. In other words, the firm can choose to combine labour and capital in any proportions it chooses. This is illustrated in Figure (b).

Assume that the total supplies of capital and labour are $\bar{K}$ and $\bar{L}$ respectively. With a price ratio given by the slope of the isocost AB, the factor market will clear. All capital and all labour will be employed at point d on isoquant Q_1.

Managers, however, may have a bias in favour of capital-intensive techniques. Alternatively, the price of labour may be above the market-clearing level, or the price of capital may be below the market-clearing level, so that the isocost is steeper than AB (e.g. CD). In either case, if $\bar{K}$ capital is used, less than $\bar{L}$ labour will be employed. With an isocost of CD, only L_1 will be employed. $\bar{L} - L_1$ will be unemployed. There will also be a lower level of output, since production is now on the lower isoquant Q_2.

If there were three techniques available, what would the isoquant look like? Would it make any difference to the conclusions of this model?

Rural–urban migration

This model assumes that migration depends first on the difference between urban wages (W_u) and rural wages (W_r). The bigger the differential, the more will people wish to migrate. Second, it depends on the likelihood of getting a job. The more likely people are to find a job, the more likely they are to migrate.

These two can be combined in the concept of an expected urban wage (W_u^e). This is the actual average urban wage multiplied by the probability of getting a job. Thus if the average wage were £40 per week, and if there were a 50 per cent chance of getting a job, the expected urban wage would be £20. If the chance were only 25 per cent, the expected

wage would be only £10, and so on. This can be expressed formally as

$$W_u^e = W_u L_m / L_u$$

where L_m is the total number of workers employed in the urban sector and L_u is the total labour supply (employed and unemployed). Thus L_m/L_u is the employment rate, which can be taken as an indication of the probability of getting a job.

So when will rural workers migrate to the towns? According to the model this will occur when

$$W_u^e > (W_r + \alpha)$$

where α is a term representing the costs of migration. In other words, people will migrate when, after taking the cost of migrating into account, they can expect to earn more in the towns than in the countryside.

But as people migrate, W_r will tend to rise as the supply of rural labour falls, and W_u^e will tend to fall as the new arrivals in the towns increase L_u and thus reduce the likelihood of others getting a job. An equilibrium urban unemployment will be reached when

$$W_u^e = W_r + \alpha$$

At that point, migration will stop.

Thus in this model, urban unemployment will be greater (a) the higher is the level of the actual urban wage (W_u), (b) the lower is the level of the rural wage (W_r) and (c) the lower are the costs of migrating (α).

If more jobs were created in the towns, how, in the rural–urban migration model, would this affect (a) the level of urban unemployment; (b) the rate of urban unemployment?

■ The government can encourage the use of more labour-intensive techniques by adopting the sorts of policy outlined earlier.
■ It can help to reverse rural–urban migration by reducing the rural 'push'. This will involve policies of encouraging rural development and thereby providing jobs away from the big towns.
■ It can provide jobs directly by embarking on labour-intensive infrastructure construction projects. For example, it can employ gangs of workers to build roads or dig irrigation ditches.
■ It can adopt policies that help to reduce the rate of population growth: policies such as educational and propaganda programmes to persuade people to have

smaller families, measures to raise the economic and social status of women so that they have a freer choice over family size, and policies directed at tackling extreme poverty so that the very poor do not feel the need to have a large family as an insurance that they will be supported in their old age.

1. *Is there any potential conflict between the goals of maximising economic growth and maximising either (a) the level of employment or (b) the rate of growth of employment?*
2. *What is the relationship between unemployment and (a) poverty; (b) inequality?*

BOX 27.5   THE BUILDING BRICS OF DEVELOPMENT

The importance of infrastructure development for emerging economies

A key supply-side constraint on development is poor-quality transport, communications and power infrastructure. Indeed, the World Bank constructs a Logistic Performance Index based on survey responses of organisations involved with international freight. One dimension of this index is the quality of trade- and transport-related infrastructure (e.g. ports, railroads, roads, information technology). This infrastructure is rated from 1 (very low) to 5 (very high).

The table shows the evolution of this index since its inception in a selection of countries. It identifies that the quality of infrastructure is a key concern in developing economies, though the general trajectory is upwards.

Logistics performance indicator: quality of trade and transport-related infrastructure

	2007	2010	2012
UK	4.05	3.95	3.95
Brazil	2.75	3.10	3.07
Russia	2.23	2.38	2.45
India	2.83	2.54	2.54
China	2.28	2.59	2.72
Developing countries	2.22	2.27	2.45
High-income economies	3.41	3.46	3.50
World	2.58	2.64	2.77

Source: *World Development Indicators* (World Bank, 2014).

Forecast infrastructure investment, 2008–17 ($ trillion)

Source: Forecast by Morgan Stanley in *The Economist*, 5 June 2008.

Some of the most rapidly growing emerging economies have invested heavily in construction, whether through state investment or by encouraging private construction projects.

Infrastructure investment now accounts for a higher proportion of world GDP than at any time in history and over half of such investment is taking place in emerging countries. Around three-quarters of this is in the four large emerging countries – Brazil, Russia, India and China, the so-called BRICs.[1] According to forecasts by Morgan Stanley, over the period from 2008 to 2017 total infrastructure investment in the BRICs will be some $15.4 trillion (see chart).

Infrastructure investment can yield big economic gains. Building roads or railways immediately boosts output and jobs, but it also helps to spur future growth – provided the money is spent wisely. Better transport helps farmers to get their produce to cities, and manufacturers to export their goods overseas. Countries with the lowest transport costs tend to be more open to foreign trade and so enjoy faster growth. Clean water and sanitation also raise the quality of human capital, thereby lifting labour productivity. The World Bank estimates that a 1% increase in a country's infrastructure stock is associated with a 1% increase in the level of GDP. Other studies have concluded that East Asia's much higher investment in infrastructure explains a large part of its faster growth than Latin America.[2]

What is more, there is a process of cumulative causation between consumption and infrastructure investment. Infrastructure construction boosts incomes and employment. But as people get richer and as more live in towns, so they demand better facilities, such as sealed roads, running water, sanitation, electricity, a good phone network and access to the Internet. All this stimulates the production of these facilities, whether through market forces or through political pressure for public provision.

 Why might an outward-looking economy experience higher infrastructure investment than an inward-looking one?

TC 15
p 508

[1] Sometimes South Africa is included, thus making the BRICs the BRICS.
[2] 'Economics focus', *The Economist, 5 June 2008.*

Section summary

1. The urban/industrial bias of many development programmes has led to the neglect of agriculture. The effect has been a deepening of rural poverty and a growing inability of the rural sector to feed the towns. Policies to reverse this trend include the raising of food prices, devaluation of the currency, government support for rural infrastructure projects, the provision of lower-interest finance to the rural sector, encouragement for the adoption of new labour-intensive techniques in farming and the use of new high-yielding seeds, land reform and the setting up of rural co-operatives.

2. Development programmes have often encouraged the use of capital-intensive technology through policies of low interest rates, relatively high urban wages, an overvalued exchange rate or encouraging investment by multinational companies. These capital-intensive technologies were often seen as advantageous in that they yielded higher profits and thus more surplus for reinvestment. Often they were more sophisticated than labour-intensive techniques, and sometimes they had a lower capital/output ratio despite having a higher capital/labour ratio. Nevertheless, labour-intensive techniques may involve less maintenance and less reliance on imported inputs and foreign skilled personnel; the profits generated from them are more likely to be retained within the country; they are likely to create more employment and a more equal spread of the benefits of economic growth; and they may be less polluting.

3. Unemployment is a major problem for most developing countries, both in the countryside and in the ever-growing shanty towns surrounding the cities. The causes are complex, but include rapid population growth, biases towards the use of capital-intensive technology, and a vulnerability to world economic changes. Urban unemployment has grown rapidly as people have migrated from the countryside, attracted by the relatively higher wages, the 'bright lights of the city' and at least the possibility (however remote) of getting a job.

27.4 THE PROBLEM OF DEBT

A serious consequence of the oil shocks of the 1970s and the reactions of the developed world to these shocks was a major debt crisis in developing countries. Attempts to service these debts – to pay interest and instalments on capital repayments – have placed severe strains on the economies of many developing countries. By the early 1980s, the problem had become so severe that many developing countries found it virtually impossible to continue servicing their debt. There was a growing fear that countries would default on payment, thereby precipitating an international banking crisis.

Although today, from the perspective of the rich world, the debt problem is no longer seen as a 'crisis', this is largely because the world financial system has found ways of coping with the debt, and threats of default have subsided.

From the perspective of the majority of poor countries, however, the problems are still acute. While, for most, their total debt is falling, it still remains at levels where the costs of servicing it put huge strains on their economies and represent a massive transfer of moneys to the rich world. Table 27.3 shows the growth of debt from the early 1970s.

In this final section, we look first at the origins of the debt crisis and then at schemes that have been adopted to cope with it. We then turn finally to look at ways in which the problem of debt can be tackled.

The oil shocks of the 1970s

In 1973–4, oil prices quadrupled and the world went into recession. Oil imports cost much more and export demand was sluggish. The current account deficit of oil-importing developing countries rose from 1.1 per cent of GNY in 1973 to 4.3 per cent in 1975.

It was not difficult to finance these deficits, however. The oil surpluses deposited in commercial banks in the industrialised world provided an important additional source of finance. The banks, flush with money and faced with slack demand in the industrialised world, were very willing to lend. Bank loans to developing countries rose from $3 billion in 1970 to $12 billion in 1975. These flows enabled developing countries to continue with policies of growth.

Table 27.3	Debt in developing countries as a percentage of GNY (average per period)							
	1973–7	1978–2	1983–7	1988–92	1993–7	1998–2002	2003–7	2008–12
Low-income economies	19.6	32.4	56.2	68.9	83.4	71.3	52.0	31.2
Lower-middle-income economies	20.1	26.8	42.5	53.8	53.6	50.9	33.1	26.4
Upper-middle-income economies	14.4	26.5	36.6	33.7	32.8	33.3	26.5	20.8

Source: *World Development Indicators* (World Bank, 2014).

Figure 27.5 Debt servicing costs as a percentage of gross national income (GNY)

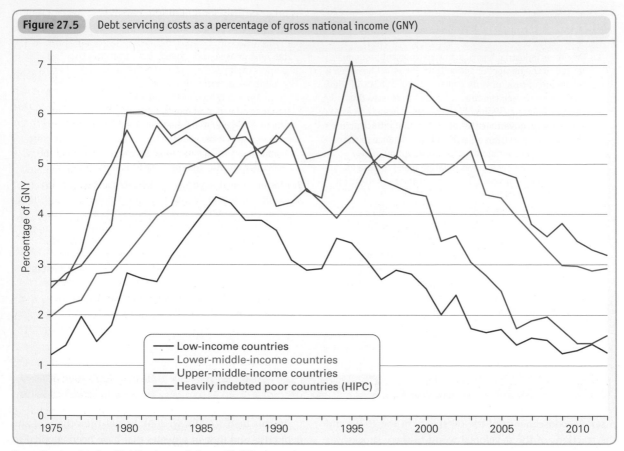

- Low-income countries
- Lower-middle-income countries
- Upper-middle-income countries
- Heavily indebted poor countries (HIPC)

Source: Based on data from *World Development Indicators* (World Bank, 2014).

The world recession was short-lived, and with a recovery in the demand for their exports and with their debts being eroded by high world inflation, developing countries found it relatively easy to service these increased debts (i.e. pay interest and make the necessary capital repayments).

In 1979–80 world oil prices rose again (from $15 to $38 per barrel). This second oil shock, like the first one, caused a large increase in the import bills of developing countries. But the full effects on their economies this time were very much worse, given the debts that had been accumulated in the 1970s and given the policies adopted by the industrialised world after 1979.

The debt position worsened after 1979, compared with that in 1974. Some countries fared very badly. For example, in 1985 the ratio of debt service (i.e. interest and capital repayments) to GNY was 15.9 per cent in Nigeria, 10.5 per cent for Kenya, 8.7 per cent for Mexico and 7.5 per cent for Bolivia.

But why were things so much worse this time?

- The world recession was deeper and lasted longer (1980–3), and when recovery came, it came very slowly. Developing countries' current account balance of payments deteriorated sharply. This was due to both a marked slowing down in the growth of their exports and a fall in their export prices.

- The tight monetary policies pursued by the industrialised countries led to a sharp increase in interest rates, and the resulting fall in inflation meant, therefore, that there was a very sharp increase in real interest rates. This greatly increased developing countries' costs of servicing their debts (see Figure 27.5).

- The problem was made worse by the growing proportion of debt that was at variable interest rates. This was largely due to the increasing proportion of debt that was in the form of loans from commercial banks.

After 1979, many developing countries found it increasingly difficult to service their debts. Then in 1982 Mexico, followed by several other countries such as Brazil, Bolivia, Zaire and Sudan, declared that it would have to suspend payments. There was now a debt crisis, which threatened not only the debtor countries, but also the world banking system.

Coping with debt: rescheduling

There have been two dimensions to tackling the debt problems of developing countries. The first is to cope with difficulties in servicing their debt. This usually involves some form of rescheduling of the repayments. The second dimension is to deal with the causes of the problem. Here we will focus on rescheduling.

Rescheduling official loans

Official loans are renegotiated through the Paris Club. Industrialised countries are members of the Club, which arranges terms for the rescheduling of their loans to developing countries. Agreements normally involve delaying the date for repayment of loans currently maturing, or spreading the repayments over a longer period of time. Paris Club agreements are often made in consultation with the IMF, which works out a programme with the debtor country for tackling its underlying economic problems.

The main recipients of official loans are low-income and lower-middle-income countries (the upper-middle-income countries relying largely on commercial bank loans). Between 1982 and 1987, demands by low-income countries for Paris Club renegotiations increased dramatically. By 1987 virtually all the sub-Saharan African countries had sought repeated Paris Club assistance. By 1987 it was becoming clear that the existing arrangements were inadequate for many countries.

Several attempts have been made since the mid-1980s to make rescheduling terms more generous, with longer periods before repayments start, longer to repay when they do start, and lower interest rates. In return, the developing countries have had to undertake various 'structural adjustment programmes' supervised by the IMF (see below).

But despite the apparent advances made by the Paris Club in making its terms more generous, the majority of low-income countries failed to meet the required IMF conditions, and thus failed to have their debts reduced. What is more, individual Paris Club members were often reluctant to reduce debts unless they were first convinced that other members were 'paying their share'. Nevertheless, some creditor countries unilaterally introduced more generous terms and even cancelled some debts.

The net effect of rescheduling, but only very modest debt forgiveness, can be seen in Figure 27.5. By the mid-1990s average debt service ratios had fallen from the levels of the mid 1980s and yet the ratio of total debt to GNY was higher. There were thus growing calls for the cancellation of debts (see below).

Rescheduling commercial bank loans

After the declarations by Mexico and other countries of their inability to service their debts, there was fear of an imminent collapse of the world banking system. Banks realised that disaster could be averted only by collective action of the banks to reschedule debts. This has normally involved the creditor banks forming a Bank Advisory Committee (BAC) – a small committee that liaises with the country and the banks concerned. Such arrangements have sometimes been referred to as the 'London Club'. The BAC negotiates a rescheduling agreement with the debtor country. When all creditor banks have approved the agreement, it is signed by each of them.

The approach of banks in the 1980s was to reschedule some of the debts – the minimum necessary to avoid default – and to provide some additional loans in return for debtor countries undertaking structural adjustment (as described below). Additional loans, however, fell well short of the amount that was needed. Banks were unwilling to supply extra money to deal with current debt servicing problems when they saw the problem as a long-term one of countries' inability to pay. Nevertheless, banks were increasingly setting aside funds to cover bad debt, and thus the crisis for the banks began to recede.

As banks felt less exposed to default, so they became less worried about it and less concerned to negotiate deals with debtor countries. Many of the more severely indebted countries, however, found their position still deteriorating rapidly. What is more, many of them were finding that the IMF adjustment programmes were too painful (often involving deep cuts in government expenditure) and were therefore abandoning them. Thus in 1989 US Treasury Secretary Nicholas Brady proposed measures to *reduce* debt.

The *Brady Plan* involved the IMF and the World Bank lending funds to debtor countries to enable them to repay debts to banks. In return for this instant source of liquidity, the banks would have to be prepared to accept repayment of less than the full sum (i.e. they would sell the debt back to the country at a discount). To benefit from such deals, the debtor countries would have to agree to structural adjustment programmes. Several such agreements were negotiated; much of the debt reduction has involved debt swaps of one sort or another (see Box 27.7).

 What are the relative advantages and disadvantages to a developing country of rescheduling its debts compared with simply defaulting on them (either temporarily or permanently)?

Dealing with debt: structural reform within the developing countries

The severe structural adjustment programmes frequently demanded by the IMF before it is prepared to sanction the rescheduling of debts include:

- Tight fiscal and monetary policies to reduce government deficits, reduce interest rates and reduce inflation.
- Supply-side reforms to encourage greater use of the market mechanism and greater incentives for investment.
- A more open trade policy and devaluation of the currency in order to encourage more exports and more competition.

These policies, however, often brought extreme hardship as countries were forced to deflate. Unemployment and poverty increased and growth slowed down or became negative. Even though in the long run some developing countries emerged as more efficient and better able to compete in international trade, in the short run the suffering for many was too great to bear. Popular unrest and resentment against the IMF and the country's government led to riots in many countries and a breakdown of law and order.

BOX 27.6   'ECOCIDE'

Debt and the environment

Faced with mounting debts and the need to service them, many developing countries have attempted to increase their export earnings. One way of achieving this is through the intensified extraction of minerals and ores or intensified farming, often by multinational corporations. But a consequence of this may be massive environmental damage. Some examples include:

- Long-term degradation of the soil from monoculture and from the increased use of chemical pesticides and fertilisers.
- Overfishing of rivers and seas.
- Chopping down forests for timber.
- Clearing forests for grazing cattle or for growing cash crops.
- 'Desertification', as a lack of forest cover leads to the encroachment of deserts in marginal areas.
- Open-cast mining, with little concern for the direct effect on the environment, or for poisonous waste products tipped into rivers.
- Burning highly polluting low-grade coal for electricity generation.
- Building dams for electricity generation and irrigation which flood large areas of land and destroy communities.

Brazil.   An example of a country forced into what has been called 'ecocide' in response to its huge debt burden is Brazil. One of the most environmentally damaging of all Brazilian projects has been the Grande Carajas iron ore project. Proposed in 1980, the Carajas scheme cost some $62 billion and has involved massive deforestation of an area larger than France and Great Britain together. The Brazilian government has been willing to allow this environmental damage because Carajas is seen as a 'national export project'.

Venezuela.   Another example of ecocide has occurred in Venezuela. The country has huge gold reserves – some

12 per cent of the world total. With the fall in oil prices in the 1990s, and hence a fall in revenues for Venezuela, one of the world's leading oil exporters, the Venezuelan authorities sought to exploit the country's gold reserves more aggressively. By 1994, the state had contracted out some 436 sites, covering 12 839 km^2. By 2000, this had risen to 30 000 km^2 (an area the size of Belgium), earning revenue of some $250 million per year.

The extraction of gold, however, has wrought great environmental damage. The richest gold reserves are in the region of Guayana, which makes up part of the Amazon river basin. It is an area rich, and in many respects unique, in its biodiversity. The environmental impact of open-cast mining within the region is already being felt. One of the most serious consequences has been the poisoning of rivers with mercury (used to separate gold from other minerals). In addition to the destruction of the forests and rivers, there are many cases where Indigenous peoples have had their human rights violated and have even been murdered to make way for the mines.

Indonesia.   The misuse and destruction of rainforests caused dramatic effects in 1997. In large parts of Indonesia (another highly indebted country), it is normal practice to burn land after forests have been felled, either to clear it for crops or for replanting. In 1997, the El Niño effect on ocean currents had caused a major drought and the forest fires got out of hand. As a result, air pollution on a massive scale affected many countries in south-east Asia. Most of Indonesia, Malaysia and Singapore became covered with a haze of dense smoke. The international air pollutant index has a scale on which readings above 500 are considered extremely hazardous. In parts of Malaysia readings of 1200 were recorded – equivalent to smoking a couple of packs of cigarettes a day. Schools and airports were closed, and income from tourism was lost throughout the region.

A more 'complete' structural adjustment would extend beyond simple market liberalisation and tough monetary policies to much more open access to the markets of the rich countries, to more aid and debt relief being channelled into health and education, and to greater research and development in areas that will benefit poor people (e.g. into efficient labour-intensive technology and into new strains of crops that are suitable for countries' specific climate and soil conditions, and which do not require large amounts of chemicals).

Dealing with debt: debt forgiveness

By the end of the 1990s, the debt burden of many of the poorest countries had become intolerable. Despite portions of their debt being written off under Paris Club terms, the

debts of many countries were still rising. Between 1980 and 2000, the debt of sub-Saharan Africa had increased some 3.5 times, from $61 billion to $212 billion. Some countries, such as Ethiopia and Mozambique, were spending nearly half their export earnings on merely servicing their debt.

Even with substantial debt rescheduling and some debt cancellation, highly indebted countries were being forced to make savage cuts in government expenditure, much of it on health, education and transport. The consequence was a growth in poverty, hunger, disease and illiteracy. African countries on average were paying four times more to rich countries in debt servicing than they were spending on health and education: it was like a patient giving a blood transfusion to a doctor! The majority of these countries had no chance of 'growing their way out of debt'. The only

Biodiesel.   A recent case of ecocide is the production of palm oil as a biofuel. The environmental justification was that the carbon dioxide given off by burning the fuel is offset by the carbon absorbed by growing the oil palm trees. But this has turned out to be only part of the story. The production of the additional palm oil has involved either cutting down rainforest, which, apart from being a much more efficient carbon absorber than oil palm trees, is habitat for many endangered species, or the draining and burning of peat lands, which sends huge amounts of carbon dioxide into the atmosphere.

Changing international attitudes

In recent years, there has been growing international awareness of the scale of the environmental destruction that is taking place. In particular, the rich countries have begun to realise that they too might suffer from this destruction, with its consequences for global warming and the loss of many unique species of plants and animals. Increasingly, international agencies such as the IMF and the World Bank are taking ecological issues into account when considering appropriate development and adjustment programmes.

Many in the developed world now realise that development must be sustainable. It is no good trying to secure 'development' for the current generation if, in the process, the environment is damaged and future generations suffer. This is a message that has been well understood by Indigenous peoples for countless generations, especially those living on marginal lands: from the Aborigines of the Australian outback to the tribes of the African bush. It is seen as a moral imperative that the land bequeathed by one's ancestors should be passed on in just as good a state to one's descendants (see pages 355–7).

In 1992 in Rio de Janeiro, the United Nations Conference on Environment and Development (UNCED) put forward a programme for environmentally responsible development.

In Agenda 21 it set out various policies that could be carried out by the international community. The policies, which were approved by 178 countries, included: targeting aid to projects that helped improve the environment (such as providing clean water); research into environmentally friendly farming methods; and programmes that help reduce population growth (such as family planning and education).

The test of such sentiments, however, is action. To monitor this, a Commission on Sustainable Development (CSD) was established in December 1992. In 2003 it set out a programme until 2015. Every two years from 2004 there would be a particular focus for action:

- 2004–5 water, sanitation and human settlements;
- 2006–7 energy for sustainable development, industrial development, air pollution and climate change;
- 2008–9 agriculture, rural development, land, drought, desertification and Africa;
- 2010–11 transport, chemicals, waste management, mining and long-term consumption and production patterns;
- 2012–13 forests, biodiversity, mountains and tourism;
- 2014–15 oceans and seas, marine resources, small island developing states and disaster management and vulnerability.

In 2016–17 there is due to be an overall appraisal of the CSD's multi-year programme of work since 2004.

1. *If reductions in developing countries' debt are in the environmental interests of the whole world, then why have developed countries not gone much further in reducing or cancelling the debts owed to them?*
2. *Would it be possible to devise a scheme of debt repayments that would both be acceptable to debtor and creditor countries and not damage the environment?*

solution for them was for a more substantial proportion of their debt to be written off.

The heavily indebted poor countries (HIPC) initiative

In 1996 the World Bank and the IMF launched the HIPC initiative. A total of 42 countries, mainly in Africa, were identified as being in need of substantial debt relief. This number was subsequently reduced to 39, of which 29 are in sub-Saharan Africa. The object of the initiative has been to reduce the debts of such countries to 'sustainable' levels by cancelling debts above 200–250 per cent of GDP (this was reduced to 150 per cent in 1999 and to a lower level still for five countries).

The HIPC process involves countries passing through two stages. In the first stage, eligible countries must demonstrate a track record of 'good performance'. This means that

they must satisfy the IMF, the World Bank and the Paris Club that they are undertaking adjustment measures, such as cutting government expenditure and liberalising their markets. It also involves the countries preparing a Poverty Reduction Strategy Paper (PRSP) to show how they will use debt relief to tackle poverty, and especially how they will improve health and education. Once the IMF and the World Bank are satisfied that the country is making sufficient progress, the 'decision point' is reached and the level of debt relief would be determined. The country would then enter the second stage.

During this second stage, some interim debt relief is provided. Meanwhile the country must establish a 'sound track record' by implementing policies established at the decision point and based on the PRSP. The length of this stage depends on how long it takes the country to implement the policies.

BOX 27.7 **SWAPPING DEBT**

A solution to developing countries' debt?

Faced with the inability of many developing countries to service, let alone repay, their debts, many banks have collaborated with debtor countries or companies in ingenious schemes to convert debt into some other form. There are a number of types of these 'debt swaps', as they are called.

Debt-for-equity swaps

Banks sell a certain amount of a country's debt at a discount in the secondary market. The purchaser (a firm or a bank) then swaps the debt with the central bank of the developing country for local currency, which is then used to buy shares in one or more of the country's companies. Sometimes debt–equity swaps are part of a privatisation programme, the debt being swapped for shares in a newly privatised company.

As far as the debtor country is concerned, this has the benefit of both reducing the debt and increasing the amount of investment in domestic companies. It has the drawback, however, of increasing foreign ownership and control in the country.

Debt-for-cash swaps

This is where the banks allow a debtor country to 'buy back' (i.e. repay) its debt at a discount. In order to do this, the developing country will probably have to secure a loan from another source. The developing country gains from achieving a net reduction in its debt. The bank gains by achieving an instant repayment of a percentage of the original debt.

Debt-for-bonds swaps

Here debt is converted into lower-interest-rate or lower-value bonds. The developing country gains by having to pay a lower rate of interest. The bank gains by having a greater certainty of payment. A version of this system was adopted by Argentina in 2005 (see Case Study 27.5 in MyEconLab) when it agreed to swap old bonds, on which it had defaulted, for new ones worth only 35 per cent of the old ones, but which would at least be honoured.

Debt-for-export swaps

Under these schemes, banks arrange for developing countries to sell exports that they would otherwise have difficulty in selling (perhaps because of industrial country protection), provided the revenues are used to pay off specific debt. Clearly, the developing country can gain from the development of new export markets, but there is a danger that, by being a form of 'export protection', it could encourage the production of goods in which the country has a comparative disadvantage, and encourage inefficiency in production.

Debt-to-local-debt swaps

This is where external debt is converted into debt in the local currency (usually indexed to the US dollar).

The original creditor sells the debt to a company that requires local currency to finance a subsidiary operating in the debtor country. The company benefits from a cheap source of local currency. The country benefits from a reduction in the need for scarce foreign currency.

Debt-for-nature or debt-for-development swaps

In recent years, the process of debt swapping has been applied directly to specific projects. A debt-for-nature swap is where debts are cancelled in return for investment in environmental projects. There are two types of scheme: bilateral and commercial.

In a bilateral swap, a creditor country agrees to cancel debt in return for the debtor country investing a proportion of the amount in environmental projects. In a commercial swap, the debt owed to banks is sold to an international environmental agency at a substantial discount (or sometimes even given away); the agency then agrees to cancel this debt in return for the country funding the agency to carry out various environmental projects. By 2007, the total debt cancelled through debt-for-nature swaps was just over $870 million.

Like debt-for-nature swaps, debt-for-development swaps involve the selling or donating of debt to an international development agency, which then cancels it in return for the country carrying out specific projects in the fields of education, transport infrastructure, health, agriculture, etc.

Most of these types of debt swaps have taken place with HIPC countries. By 2007, of the $15.0 billion of debt reduced by debt-for-development swaps, $11.4 billion involved HIPC countries. But these countries would probably have had such debts cancelled anyway. What is more, the size of such debt swaps has been tiny compared with the total stock of debt, which in 2007 was $3357 billion. But debt-for-development swaps can still make a useful contribution to debt relief.

> Despite their limitations, swaps can produce creative and participatory projects. Swaps can be beneficial in terms of local development and small-scale projects. As suggested by some civil society organisations such as Jubilee Peru, swaps that are well conceived and carried out 'can re-energise local development and strengthen poorest communities by promoting projects that respond to local needs. They can also strengthen participative democracy by offering local communities good opportunities.'[1]

Would the objections of developing countries to debt–equity swaps be largely overcome if foreign ownership were restricted to less than 50 per cent in any company? If such restrictions were imposed, would this be likely to affect the 'price' at which debt is swapped for equity?

[1] Marta Ruiz, *Debt Swaps for Development* (EURODAD, 2007), p. 26.

Table 27.4	Debt indicators of 36 post-decision-point HIPCs		
		1999 (%)	**2012 (%)**
Present value of debt-to-exports		457	75
Present value of debt-to-GDP		114	20
Debt service-to-exports		18	5
Present value of debt-to-revenue		552	104
Debt service-to-revenue		22	7

Source: *HIPC At-A-Glance Guide* (IMF, Autumn 2013).

At the end of the second stage, the country reaches the 'completion point' and debts are cancelled (as agreed at the decision point) by the various creditors, on a pro rata basis, to bring the debt to the sustainable threshold.

In 2006, debt relief for the HIPCs that reach the completion point was extended under the Multilateral Debt Relief Initiative (MDRI). This involves cancelling multilateral debt incurred before 2004.

By 2013, 35 of the HIPCs had reached the completion point and were receiving MDRI relief, one country was at the decision point and three were at the pre-decision point. By 2012, $74.3 billion had been cancelled under the HIPC programme and a further $39.7 billion under MDRI. The debt stocks of the 36 post-decision-point HIPCs had been reduced by over 90 per cent. The effect on various debt indicators is shown in Table 27.4. As you can see, the improvement has been dramatic.

Despite this substantial relief, the programme has been heavily criticised for taking too long and for imposing excessively harsh conditions on the HIPC countries. The required reductions in government expenditure have led to deep cuts in basic health and education, and deflationary policies have led to reductions in investment.

Then there are the non-HIPCs. Many of these countries are also suffering debts which divert a large percentage of their income from poverty relief. Just because non-HIPCs can manage to service their debts, it does not make it desirable that they should be forced to do so.

According to many charities, such as Oxfam, a much better approach would be to target debt relief directly at poverty reduction, with the resources released being used for investment in fields such as health, education, rural development and basic infrastructure. The focus, they argue, should be on what countries can afford to pay *after* essential spending on poverty relief and human development.

Imagine that you are an ambassador of a developing country at an international conference. What would you try to persuade the rich countries to do in order to help you and other poor countries overcome the debt problem? How would you set about persuading them that it was in their own interests to help you?

Should all debt be cancelled and aid increased?

In recent years there have been growing calls for the cancellation of debts and a significant increase in aid, especially for the poorest developing countries, many ravaged by war, drought or AIDS. The United Nations has for many years called on wealthy countries to give 0.7 per cent of their GDP in aid. In practice they give only a little over 0.2 per cent.

As we have seen, the HIPC and MDRI relief has reduced such countries' debt dramatically. However, as of 2012 low-income countries' debt still amounted to $134 billion and developing countries as a whole owed some $4.8 trillion. Then there is the plight of many non-HIPC countries, such as Kenya, which could be argued to be in greater need of debt relief than some HIPC countries.

In 2000, the net flow of official aid from the 22 countries which are members of the OECD's Development Assistance Committee (DAC) amounted to $54 billion, a mere 0.22 per cent of GNY – well short of the UN target of 0.7 per cent. By 2013, this had risen to $133.1 billion, but it still constituted only 0.30 per cent of GNY – still well below the 0.7 per cent target. The percentages for France, Germany and the USA were 0.41, 0.38 and 0.19 respectively. However, 2013 saw the UK hit the UN target, with the figure having risen to 0.72 – up from 0.56 in 2012.

The argument against debt cancellation and a substantial increase in aid is that this could represent a 'moral hazard' (see Box 4.6 on page 124). Once the burden of debt had been lifted and aid had been increased, countries might be tempted to squander the money. It might also encourage them to seek further loans, which might again be squandered.

For this reason, much of the disbursement of funds by donor countries, the IMF and other agencies has been conditional on countries pursuing policies of fiscal restraint and supply-side reform. But also, in recent years, conditionality has required recipient countries to pursue key poverty-reducing projects, such as health, education, clean water and other basic infrastructure projects. (Case Study 27.7 in MyEconLab examines some of the issues surrounding aid.)

Section summary

1. After the 1973 oil crisis, many developing countries borrowed heavily in order to finance their balance of trade deficits and to maintain a programme of investment. Despite this increase in debt, a combination of low real interest rates, a recovery in the world economy and high international rates of inflation allowed developing countries to sustain moderate rates of economic growth after 1975.

2. After the 1979 oil price rises, however, there was a much deeper world recession than in the mid-1970s, and real interest rates were much higher. Debt increased dramatically, and much of it was at variable interest rates.

3. Rescheduling can help developing countries to cope with increased debt in the short run. Official loans are renegotiated through the Paris Club. This will normally involve some combination of longer repayment periods, grace periods in which payments may be delayed and either lower interest rates or partial cancellation of debts. Commercial bank loans have also frequently been renegotiated through a Bank Advisory Committee of the banks concerned. This has normally involved delaying paying loans for a period of time and the extension of the repayment period.

4. If the problem is to be tackled, however, then either debts have to be written off – something that banks have been increasingly forced to do – or the developing countries themselves must take harsh corrective measures. The IMF has traditionally favoured 'structural adjustment' policies of deflation and market-orientated supply-side policies. An alternative is to use debt relief and aid to invest in health, education, roads and other infrastructure.

5. In 1996 the World Bank and the IMF launched the HIPC initiative to help reduce the debts of heavily indebted poor countries to sustainable levels. HIPC relief has been criticised, however, for being made conditional on the debtor countries pursuing excessively tough IMF adjustment programmes, for having an excessively long qualifying period and debt sustainability thresholds that are too high, and for delays in its implementation. A better approach might be to target debt relief directly at programmes to help the poor.

END OF CHAPTER QUESTIONS

1. Compare the relative merits of using GNY statistics with those of various basic needs indicators when assessing both the level and the rate of a country's economic development.

2. If a developing country has a comparative advantage in primary products, should the government allow market forces to dictate the pattern of trade?

3. What are the advantages and disadvantages for a developing country of pursuing a policy of ISI?

4. Should all developing countries aim over the long term to become exporters of manufactured products?

5. How would you attempt to assess whether the technology used by an industry in a developing country was 'inappropriate'?

6. What policies could be adopted to reduce urban unemployment in developing countries?

7. To what extent was the debt crisis of the early 1980s caused by inappropriate policies that had been pursued by the debtor countries?

8. What are the advantages and disadvantages of debt swapping as a means of reducing the debts of developing countries?

Online resources

Additional case studies in MyEconLab

27.1 **Theories of development.** This looks at different approaches to the analysis of poverty and development.

27.2 **Multinational corporations and developing countries.** This examines whether multinational investment is a net benefit to developing countries.

27.3 **A miracle gone wrong.** Lessons from east Asia.

27.4 **Ethical business.** An examination of the likelihood of success of companies which trade fairly with developing countries.

27.5 **Argentina in crisis.** An examination of the collapse of the Argentinean economy in 2001–2, the default on its debts and the subsequent recovery.

27.6 **The great escape.** This case examines the problem of capital flight from developing countries to rich countries.

27.7 **Economic aid.** Does aid provide a solution to the debt problem?

Websites relevant to this chapter

Numbers and sections refer to websites listed in the Web Appendix and hotlinked from this book's website at **www.pearsoned.co.uk/sloman**.

- For news articles relevant to this chapter, see the *Economic News* section in MyEconLab.
- For news on various aspects of economic development, see A27, 28; I9. See also links to newspapers worldwide in A38, 39, 42, 43 and 44, and the news search feature in Google at A41.
- For links to a range of development sites, see sites I9 and 10.
- For data on developing countries, see sites B1, 19, 23, 31, 33, 35, 43 and 47.
- For data on debt and development, see B24 and 35 (*Global Development Finance*) and B31. Also see the debt section in I14.
- For information on trade and developing countries, see H4, 7, 9, 10, 16, 17.
- For information on debt and developing countries, see H4, 7, 9, 10, 12–14, 17–19.
- Site I7 contains links to *Capital flows and aid* and *Trade and trade policy* in *Development Economics*. Site I11 has a link to *Development economics*.
- For student resources relevant to this chapter, see sites C1–7, 9, 10, 19. See also *Virtual Developing Country* in *Virtual Worlds* in site C2.

MyEconLab

This book can be supported by MyEconLab, which contains a range of additional resources, including an online homework and tutorial system designed to test and build your understanding.

You need both an access card and a course ID to access MyEconLab:

1. Is your lecturer using MyEconLab? Ask your lecturer for your course ID.

2. Has an access card been included with the book at a reduced cost? Check the inside back cover of the book.

3. If you have a course ID but no access card, go to: http://www.myeconlab.com/ to buy access to this interactive study programme.

Postscript: The Castaways or Vote for Caliban

The Pacific Ocean –
A blue demi-globe.
Islands like punctuation marks.

A cruising airliner,
Passengers unwrapping pats of butter.
A hurricane arises,
Tosses the plane into the sea.

Five of them flung onto an island beach,
Survived.

Tom the reporter.
Susan the botanist.
Jim the high-jump champion.
Bill the carpenter.
Mary the eccentric widow.

Tom the reporter sniffed out a stream of drinkable water.
Susan the botanist identified a banana tree.
Jim the high-jump champion jumped up and down and gave them each a bunch.
Bill the carpenter knocked up a table for their banana supper.
Mary the eccentric widow buried the banana skins,
But only after they had asked her twice.

They all gathered sticks and lit a fire.
There was an incredible sunset.

Next morning they held a committee meeting.
Tom, Susan, Jim and Bill
Voted to make the best of things.
Mary, the eccentric widow, abstained.

Tom the reporter killed several dozen wild pigs.
He tanned their skins into parchment
And printed the Island News with the ink of squids.

Susan the botanist developed new strains of banana
Which tasted of chocolate, beefsteak, peanut butter,
Chicken and bootpolish.

Jim the high-jump champion organised organised games
Which he always won easily.
Bill the carpenter constructed a wooden water wheel
And converted the water's energy into electricity.
Using iron ore from the hills, he constructed lampposts.

They all worried about Mary, the eccentric widow,
Her lack of confidence and her –
But there wasn't time to coddle her.

The volcano erupted, but they dug a trench
And diverted the lava into the sea
Where it formed a spectacular pier.
They were attacked by pirates but defeated them
With bamboo bazookas firing
Sea-urchins packed with home-made nitro-glycerine.
They gave the cannibals a dose of their own medicine
And survived an earthquake thanks to their skill in jumping.

Tom had been a court reporter
So he became a magistrate and solved disputes.
Susan the botanist established
A university which also served as a museum.
Jim the high-jump champion
Was put in charge of law enforcement –
Jumped on them when they were bad.
Bill the carpenter built himself a church,
Preached there every Sunday.

But Mary the eccentric widow . . .
Each evening she wandered down the island's main street,
Past the Stock Exchange, the Houses of Parliament,
The prison and the arsenal.
Past the Prospero Souvenir Shop,
Past the Robert Louis Stevenson Movie Studios,
Past the Daniel Defoe Motel
She nervously wandered and sat on the end of the pier of lava.

Breathing heavily,
As if at a loss,
As if at a lover,
She opened her eyes wide
To the usual incredible sunset.

Adrian Mitchell

1. Had the castaways reduced their problem of scarcity by the end of the poem?
2. Could the 'usual incredible sunset' be described as an economic good?

Appendix 1: Some Techniques of Economic Analysis

As you will see if you flick back through the pages, there are many diagrams and tables and several equations. But this does not mean that there are many mathematical techniques that you will have to master in order to study this book. In fact there are relatively few techniques, but they are ones which we use many times in many different contexts. You will find that if you are new to the subject, you will very quickly become familiar with these techniques. If you are not new to the subject, perhaps you could reassure your colleagues who are!

On some university courses, however, you will take mathematics to a higher level. To meet your needs there are a number of optional 'Looking at the Maths' sections scattered throughout the book. These use maths to express arguments that have just been covered in words or diagrams. Most of these 'Looking at the Maths' sections also refer to 'Maths Cases' in MyEconLab. These cases consist of worked examples and also have one or more questions at the end for you to test your understanding of the relevant technique. The answers to these questions are also given in MyEconLab.

But please note that the 'Looking at the Maths' sections are purely optional and will not be suitable for many courses. In such cases you can simply ignore them.

Diagrams as pictures

On many occasions, we use diagrams simply to provide a picture of a relationship. Just as a photograph in a newspaper can often depict an event much more vividly than any verbal account, so too a diagram in economics can often picture a relationship with a vividness and clarity that could never be achieved by words alone.

For example, we may observe that as people's incomes rise, they spend a lot more on entertainment and only a little more on food. We can picture this relationship very nicely by the use of a simple graph.

In Figure A1.1, an individual's income is measured along the horizontal axis and expenditure on food and entertainment is measured up the vertical axis. There are just two lines on this diagram: one showing how the expenditure on entertainment rises as income rises, the other how the expenditure on food rises as income rises. Now we could use a diagram like this to plot actual data. But we may simply be using it as a sketch – as a picture. In this case we do not necessarily need to put figures on the two axes. We are simply showing the relative *shapes* of the two curves. These shapes tell us that the person's expenditure on entertainment rises more quickly than that on food, and that above a certain level of income the expenditure on entertainment becomes greater than that on food.

 What else is the diagram telling us?

Figure A1.1   Effect of a rise in an individual's income on his or her expenditure on food and entertainment

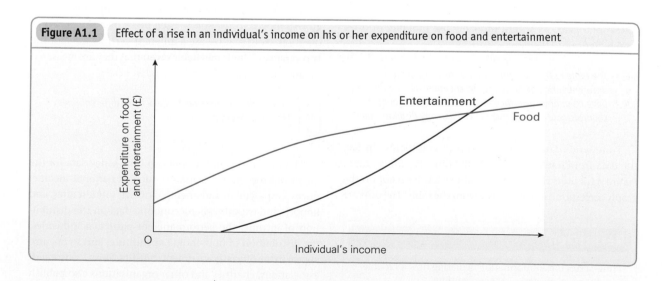

Table A1.1	UK unemployment, 2007 Q1–2014 Q2														
	2007				2008				2009				2010			
	Q1	Q2	Q3	Q4	Q1	Q2	Q3	Q4	Q1	Q2	Q3	Q4	Q1	Q2	Q3	Q4
Unemployment (millions)	1.70	1.66	1.65	1.61	1.62	1.67	1.84	2.00	2.23	2.44	2.46	2.44	2.51	2.47	2.44	2.48

	2011				2012				2013				2014			
	Q1	Q2	Q3	Q4	Q1	Q2	Q3	Q4	Q1	Q2	Q3	Q4	Q1	Q2		
Unemployment (millions)	2.46	2.51	2.62	2.66	2.61	2.56	2.51	2.50	2.52	2.51	2.47	2.34	2.21	2.08		

Source: Based on *Time Series Data*, series MGSC (National Statistics, 2014).

Representing real-life statistics

In many cases, we will want to depict real-world data. We may want to show, for example, how unemployment has changed over the years in a particular country, or how income is distributed between different groups in the population. In the first we will need to look at *time-series* data. In the second we will look at *cross-section* data.

Time-series data

Table A1.1 shows the level of UK unemployment between the first quarter of 2007 and the second quarter of 2014. A table like this is a common way of representing **time-series data**. It has the advantage of giving the precise figures, and is thus a useful reference if we want to test any theory and see if it predicts accurately.

Notice that in this particular table the figures are given quarterly. Depending on the period of time over which we want to see the movement of a variable, it may be more appropriate to use a different interval of time. For example, if we wanted to see how unemployment had changed over the past 50 years, we might use annual figures or even average figures for longer periods of time. If, however, we wanted to see how unemployment had changed over the course of a year, we would probably use monthly or even weekly figures.

 The table in Box 1.2 shows time-series data for four different variables for four different countries. Would there have been any advantage in giving the figures for each separate year? Would there have been any disadvantage?

Time-series data can also be shown graphically. In fact the data from a table can be plotted directly onto a graph. Figure A1.2 plots the data from Table A1.1. Each dot on the graph corresponds to one figure from the table. The dots are

Definition

Time-series data Information depicting how a variable (e.g. the price of eggs) changes over time.

then joined up to form a single line. Thus if you wanted to find the level of unemployment at any time between 2007 Q1 and 2011 Q3, you would simply find the appropriate date on the horizontal axis, read vertically upwards to the line you have drawn, then read across to find the level of unemployment.

Although a graph like this cannot give you quite such an accurate measurement of each point as a table does, it gives a much more obvious picture of how the figures have moved over time and whether the changes are getting bigger (the curve getting steeper) or smaller (the curve getting shallower). We can also read off what the likely figure would be for some point *between* two observations.

 What was the level of unemployment midway between quarter 3 and quarter 4 2008?

It is also possible to combine *two* sets of time-series data on one graph to show their relative movements over time. Table A1.2 shows the figures for UK economic growth for the same time period. Figure A1.3 plots these data along with those from Table A1.1. This enables us to get a clear picture of how unemployment and the rate of economic growth moved in relation to each other over the period in question. Note that we use a different vertical scale for the two variables. This is inevitable given that they are measured in different units.

 How would it be possible to show three different lines on the same diagram?

All developed countries publish time-series data for the major macroeconomic variables such as national income, prices, employment and unemployment, interest rates, and imports and exports. Microeconomic data on the distribution of income, the performance of particular industries, the distribution of household expenditure, and so on, also appear in the official government statistics. Firms, consumers' associations, charities and other organisations also publish microeconomic statistics.

Figure A1.2   UK unemployment: 2007 Q1–2014 Q2

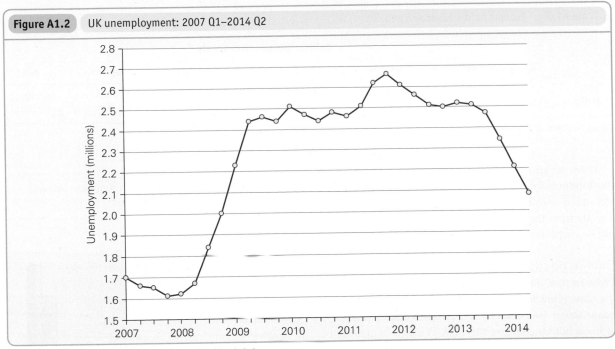

Source: Based on *Time Series Data*, series MGSC (National Statistics).

Table A1.2   UK economic growth, 2007 Q1–2014 Q2 (% increase over equivalent quarter in previous year)

	2007				2008				2009				2010			
	Q1	Q2	Q3	Q4	Q1	Q2	Q3	Q4	Q1	Q2	Q3	Q4	Q1	Q2	Q3	Q4
Economic growth (%)	2.4	3.3	4.3	3.7	2.8	0.6	−2.1	−4.3	−6.8	−6.3	−5.0	−2.5	0.5	2.0	2.4	1.8

	2011				2012				2013				2014	
	Q1	Q2	Q3	Q4	Q1	Q2	Q3	Q4	Q1	Q2	Q3	Q4	Q1	Q2
Economic growth (%)	1.7	0.8	1.0	1.1	0.6	0.1	0.3	0.2	0.5	1.7	1.8	2.7	3.1	3.2

Source: Based on *Time Series Data,* series IHYR (National Statistics, 2014).

Figure A1.3   UK unemployment and economic growth: 2007 Q1–2014 Q2

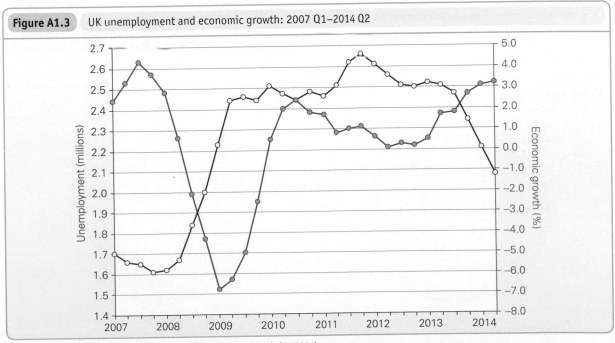

Source: Based on *Time Series Data*, series MGSC and IHYR (National Statistics, 2014).

Table A1.3	Income before taxes and benefits					
	Quintile groups of households					
	Bottom 20%	Next 20%	Middle 20%	Next 20%	Top 20%	Total
1977	4	10	18	26	42	100
2012/13	3	7	14	24	51	100

Source: *The Effects of Taxes and Benefits on Household Income, 2012/13* (National Statistics, 2014).

There are also several sources of data freely available on the Internet. Section B of Appendix 2 gives a number of websites containing datasets. These websites can be accessed directly from the hotlinks section of this book's own website (www.pearsoned.co.uk/sloman).

Cross-section data

Cross-section data show different observations made at the same point in time. For example, they could show the quantities of food and clothing purchased at various levels of household income, or the costs to a firm or industry of producing various quantities of a product.

Table A1.3 gives an example of cross-section data. It shows the distribution of household income in the UK before the deduction of taxes and the addition of benefits. It puts households into five equal-sized groups (or 'quintiles') according to their income. Thus the poorest 20 per cent of households are in one group, the next poorest 20 per cent are in the next and so on. Looking just at the 2012/13 figures, they show that the poorest 20 per cent earned just

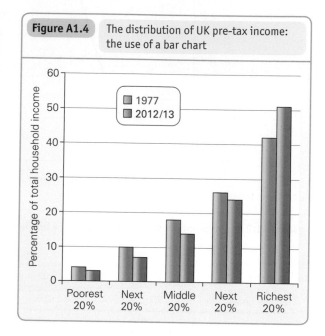

Figure A1.4   The distribution of UK pre-tax income: the use of a bar chart

3 per cent of total household incomes, whereas the richest 20 per cent earned 51 per cent.

Cross-section data like these are often represented in the form of a chart. Figure A1.4 shows the data as a *bar chart*, and Figure A1.5 as two *pie charts*.

It is possible to represent cross-section data at two or more different points in time, thereby presenting the figures

Definition

Cross-section data Information showing how a variable (e.g. the consumption of eggs) differs between different groups or different individuals at a given time.

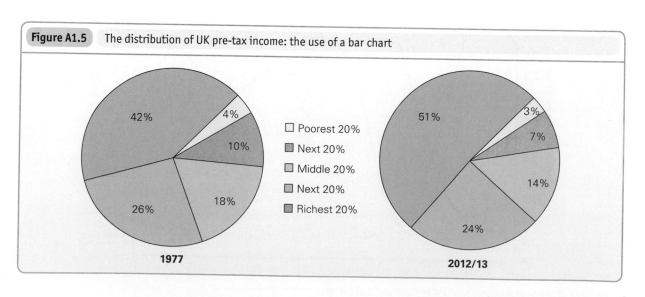

Figure A1.5   The distribution of UK pre-tax income: the use of a bar chart

as a time series. In Table A1.3, figures are given for just two time periods. With a more complete time series we could graph the movement of the shares of each of the five groups over time.

 Could bar charts or pie charts be used for representing time-series data?

Getting a true picture from the statistics

'There are lies, damned lies and statistics.' This well-known saying highlights the abuse of statistics – abuse, unfortunately, that is commonplace. Have you noticed how politicians always seem to be able to produce statistics to 'prove' that they are right and that their opponents are wrong? And it's not just politicians. Newspapers frequently present statistics in the most 'newsworthy' way; companies try to show their performance in the most flattering way; pressure groups fighting for a cause (such as the protection of the environment) again present statistics in the way that best supports their case.

It is not difficult to present data in such a way as to give a grossly distorted picture of a situation. Let us have a look at some of the most common examples.

Selective use of data

This is where people select only those statistics that support their case and ignore those that do not. For example, assume that unemployment has risen but inflation has fallen. The government highlights the inflation statistics to show how successful its policies have been. The opposition

parties do the opposite: they concentrate on the unemployment statistics to demonstrate the failure of government policy.

Graphical presentation of data

Two graphs may present exactly the same data and yet convey a quite different impression about them. Figure A1.6 shows how the amount that people buy of a particular foodstuff varies with their income. It is based on the information in Table A1.4.

Diagram (a) shows *exactly the same* information as diagram (b), and yet at a glance it would seem from diagram (a) that people buy a lot more as their incomes rise, whereas from diagram (b) it would seem that people only buy a little more.

Clearly the choice of *scales* for the two axes will determine the shape of the graph.

 1. *If the vertical scale for Figure A1.2 ran from 0 to 5 million, how would this alter your impression of the degree to which unemployment had changed?*
2. *What are the advantages and disadvantages of presenting data graphically with the axes starting from zero?*

Use of absolute or proportionate values

'People are paying more taxes now than they did when the government came to office', claims the opposition.

'Since coming into office we have cut taxes substantially', claims the government.

So who is right? Do we pay more or less tax? Quite possibly they are both right. If incomes have risen, we probably

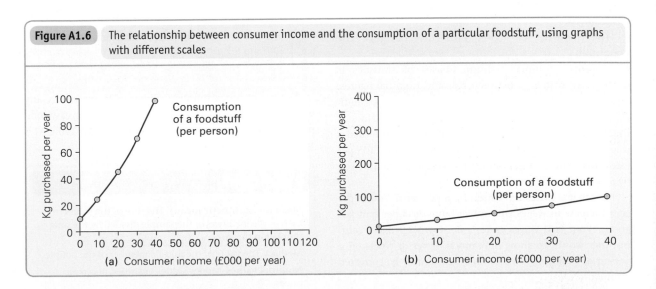

Figure A1.6 The relationship between consumer income and the consumption of a particular foodstuff, using graphs with different scales

(a) Consumer income (£000 per year)

(b) Consumer income (£000 per year)

Table A1.4	Annual purchases per person of a particular foodstuff				
Consumer income (£ per year)	0	10 000	20 000	30 000	40 000
Foodstuff purchased per person (kg per year)	10	25	45	70	100

do pay more tax in total. After all, the more we earn, the greater the sum of money we will be paying in income tax; and the more we spend, the more we will be paying out in VAT. Thus in *absolute* terms we probably are paying more in taxes.

On the other hand, if the government has cut the rates of tax, we may be paying a smaller *proportion* of our income. In other words, a smaller proportion of a larger total can still represent an absolute increase.

Ignoring questions of distribution

'The average person has become better off under this government', claims a minister.

'Poverty has increased steeply under this government', claims the opposition. 'More than half the population are worse off now than when the government came to office.'

Surely, this time one of the claims must be wrong? But again, both could be right. The term 'average' normally refers to the *mean*. The mean income is simply the total national income divided by the number in the population: i.e. income *per head*. If this is what is meant by the average, then the government may well be correct. Income per head may have risen.

If, however, a small number of people have got a lot richer and the rest have got a little poorer, the *median* income will have fallen. The median income is the income of the *middle* person. For example, if the population were 50 million, the median income would be the income of the 25 millionth richest person. This person's income may have fallen.

Real or nominal values

'Incomes have risen by 5 per cent this last year', claims the government.

'The standard of living has fallen', claims the opposition.

One of the most common abuses of statistics is deliberately switching between real and nominal figures, depending on what message you want to give your audience. *Nominal* figures are the simple monetary values at the prices ruling at the time. For example, if you earned a wage of £100 per week last year and are earning £105 per week this year, then in nominal terms your wage has risen by 5 per cent.

But what if prices have risen by 8 per cent? Your 5 per cent increase in wages will in fact buy you 3 per cent *less* goods. Your *real* wages have gone down by 3 per cent. In other words, to show how much better or worse off a person or nation is, the nominal figure must be corrected for inflation.

 KEY IDEA 39 *The distinction between nominal and real figures.* Nominal figures are those using current prices, interest rates, etc. Real figures are figures corrected for inflation.

Thus:

Real growth = Nominal growth – Inflation

1. *If a bank paid its depositors 3 per cent interest and inflation was 5 per cent, what would be the real rate of interest?*
2. *Has your real income gone up or down this last year?*

The time chosen for comparison

'Between 1982 and 1990, Britain's real growth rate averaged 3.5 per cent per year', boasted the Conservative government of the time.

'Between 1979 and 1993, Britain could only manage a real growth rate of 1.6 per cent per year', chided the opposition.

Again both were correct, but they had chosen either to include or to ignore the periods from 1979 to 1982 and from 1990 to 1993 when the real growth rate was negative.

Index numbers

Time-series data are often expressed in terms of *index numbers*. Consider the data in Table A1.5. It shows index numbers of manufacturing output in the UK from 1985 to 2013.

One year is selected as the *base year* and this is given the value of 100. In our example this is 2010. The output for other years is then shown by their percentage variation from 100. For 1985 the index number is 86.1. This means that manufacturing output was 13.9 per cent lower in 1985 than in 2010. The index number for 2007 is 109.9. This means that manufacturing output was 9.9 per cent higher in 2007 than in 2010.

 Does this mean that the value of manufacturing output in 2007 was 9.9 per cent higher than 2010 in money terms?

The use of index numbers allows us to see clearly any upward and downward movements and to make an easy comparison of one year with another. For example, Table A1.5

Definitions

Mean (or arithmetic mean) The sum of the values of each of the members of the sample divided by the total number in the sample.

Median The value of the middle member of the sample.

Nominal values Money values measured at *current* prices.

Real values Money values corrected for inflation.

Index number The value of a variable expressed as 100 plus or minus its percentage deviation from a base year.

Base year (for index numbers) The year whose index number is set at 100.

| Table A1.5 | UK manufacturing output (2010 = 100) |

1985	1986	1987	1988	1989	1990	1991	1992	1993	1994	1995	1996	1997	1998	1999
86.1	87.2	91.4	98.0	102.0	101.8	96.7	96.6	98.1	102.7	104.2	105.0	106.8	107.4	107.9

2000	2001	2002	2003	2004	2005	2006	2007	2008	2009	2010	2011	2012	2013
110.3	108.4	105.8	105.3	107.3	107.1	109.0	109.9	106.9	96.0	100.0	101.8	100.1	99.4

Source: Time Series Data, series K22A (National Statistics, various years).

shows quite clearly that manufacturing output fell from 1989 to 1992 and did not regain its 1989 level until 1994. It fell again from 2007 to 2009 and from 2011 to 2013.

Using index numbers to measure percentage changes

To find the annual percentage growth rate in any one year we simply look at the percentage change in the index from the previous year. To work this out we use the following formula:

$$\left(\frac{I_t - I_{t-1}}{I_{t-1}}\right) \times 100$$

where I_t is the index in the year in question and I_{t-1} is the index in the previous year.

Thus to find the growth rate in manufacturing output from 1987 to 1988 we first see how much the index has risen ($I_t - I_{t-1}$). The answer is 98.0 − 91.4 = 6.6. But this does *not* mean that the growth rate is 6.6 per cent. According to our formula, the growth rate is equal to

$$\frac{98.0 - 91.4}{91.4} \times 100$$
$$= 6.6/91.4 \times 100$$
$$= 7.22$$

 What was the growth rate in manufacturing output from (a) 1986 to 1987; (b) 2008 to 2009?

The price index

Perhaps the best known of all price indices is the **consumer prices index (CPI)**. It is an index of the prices of goods and services purchased by the average household. Movements in this index, therefore, show how the cost of living has changed. Annual percentage increases in the CPI are the commonest definition of the rate of inflation. Thus if the CPI went up from 100 to 110 over a 12-month period, we would say that the rate of inflation was 10 per cent.

 If the CPI went up from 150 to 162 over 12 months, what would be the rate of inflation?

The use of weighted averages

The CPI is a **weighted average** of the prices of many items. The index of manufacturing output that we looked at previously was also a weighted average, an average of the output of many individual products.

To illustrate how a weighted average works, consider the case of a weighted average of the output of just three industries, A, B and C. Let us assume that in the base year (year 1) the output of A was £7 million, of B £2 million and of C £1 million, giving a total output of the three industries of £10 million. We now attach weights to the output of each industry to reflect its proportion of total output. Industry A is given a weight of 0.7 because it produces seven-tenths of total output. Industry B is given a weight of 0.2 and industry C a weight of 0.1. We then simply multiply each industry's index by its weight and add up all these figures to give the overall industry index.

The index for each industry in year 1 (the base year) is 100. This means that the weighted average index is also 100. Table A1.6 shows what happens to output in year 2. Industry A's output falls by 10 per cent, giving it an index of 90 in year 2. Industry B's output rises by 10 per cent and industry C's output rises by 30 per cent, giving indices of 110 and 130, respectively. But as you can see from the table, despite the fact that two of the three industries have had a rise in output, the total industry index has *fallen* from 100 to 98. The reason is that industry A is so much larger than the other two that its decline in output outweighs their increase.

The consumer prices index is a little more complicated. This is because it is calculated in two stages. First, products are grouped into categories such as food, clothing and services. A weighted average index is worked out for each group. Thus the index for food would be the weighted average of

Table A1.6	Constructing a weighted average index				
		Year 1		**Year 2**	
Industry	Weight	Index	Index times weight	Index	Index times weight
A	0.7	100	70	90	63
B	0.2	100	20	110	22
C	0.1	100	10	130	13
Total	1.0			100	98

the indices for bread, potatoes, cooking oil, etc. Second, a weight is attached to each of the groups in order to work out an overall index.

Functional relationships

Throughout economics we examine how one economic variable affects another: how the purchases of cars are affected by their price; how consumer expenditure is affected by taxes, or by incomes; how the cost of producing washing machines is affected by the price of steel; how the rate of unemployment is affected by the level of government expenditure. These relationships are called *functional relationships*. We will need to express these relationships in a precise way, preferably in the form of a table or a graph or an equation.

Simple linear functions

These are relationships which produce a straight line when plotted on a graph. Let us take an imaginary example of the relationship between total value added tax receipts in an economy (V) and the level of consumer expenditure (C). This functional relationship can be written as

$$V = f(C)$$

This is simply shorthand for saying that VAT receipts are a function of (i.e. depend on) the level of consumer expenditure.

If we want to know just *how much* VAT revenue will be at any given level of consumer expenditure, we will need to spell out this functional relationship. Let us do this in each of the three ways.

As a table. Table A1.7 gives a selection of values of C and the corresponding level of V. It is easy to read off from the table the level of VAT receipts at one of the levels of consumer expenditure listed. It is clearly more difficult to

Table A1.7	A VAT function
Consumer expenditure (£bn per year)	VAT receipts (£bn per year)
0	0
10	2
20	4
30	6
40	8
50	10

work out the level of VAT receipts if consumer expenditure is £23.4 billion or £47.6 billion.

As a graph. Figure A1.7 plots the data from Table A1.7. Each of the dots corresponds to one of the points in the table. By joining the dots up into a single line we can easily read off the value for VAT receipts at some level of consumption other than those listed in the table. A graph also has the advantage of allowing us to see the relationship at a glance.

It is usual to plot the *independent variable* (i.e. the one that does not depend on the other) on the horizontal or x axis, and the *dependent variable* on the vertical or y axis. In our example, VAT receipts *depend* on consumer expenditure. Thus VAT receipts are the dependent variable and consumer expenditure is the independent variable.

As an equation. The data in the table can be expressed in the equation

$$V = 0.2C$$

This would be the equation if the VAT rate were 20 per cent on all goods and services.

Definition

Functional relationships The mathematical relationships showing how one variable is affected by one or more others.

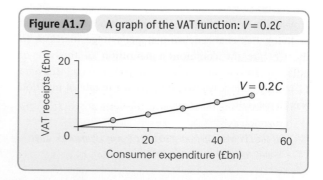

Figure A1.7	A graph of the VAT function: $V = 0.2C$

Table A1.8 $y = 4 + 2x$

x	y
0	4
1	6
2	8
3	10
4	12
5	14

Figure A1.8 $y = 4 + 2x$

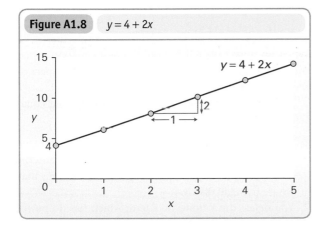

 On a diagram like Figure A1.8 draw the graphs for the following equations: $y = -3 + 4x$; $y = 15 - 3x$.

Note that in the second equation of the question, the x term is negative. This means that y and x are *inversely related*. As x increases, y decreases.

Non-linear functions

With these functions the equation involves a squared term (or other power terms). Such functions will give a curved line when plotted on a graph. As an example, consider the following equation:

$$y = 4 + 10x - x^2$$

Table A1.9 and Figure A1.9 are based on it.

As you can see, y rises at a decelerating rate and eventually begins to fall. This is because the negative x^2 term is becoming more and more influential as x rises and eventually begins to outweigh the $10x$ term.

 What shaped graph would you get from the equations

$$y = -6 + 3x + 2x^2 \text{ and } y = 10 - 4x + x^2?$$

(If you cannot work out the answer, construct a table like Table A1.9 and then plot the figures on a graph.)

An equation has the major advantage of being precise. We could work out *exactly* how much would be paid in VAT at any given level of consumption.

This particular function starts at the origin of the graph (i.e. the bottom left-hand corner). This means that when the value of the independent variable is zero, so too is the value of the dependent variable.

When a graph does not pass through the origin its equation will have the form

$$y = a + bx$$

where y stands for the dependent variable and x for the independent variable, and a and b will have numbers assigned in an actual equation. For example, the equation might be

$$y = 4 + 2x$$

This would give Table A1.8 and Figure A1.8.

Notice two things about the relationship between the equation and the graph:

- The point where the line crosses the vertical axis (at a value of 4) is given by the constant (a) term. If the a term is negative, the line will cross the vertical axis *below* the horizontal axis.
- The slope of the line is given by the b term. The slope is 2/1: for every 1 unit increase in x there is a 2 unit increase in y.

Table A1.9 $y = 4 + 10x - x^2$

x	y
0	4
1	13
2	20
3	25
4	28
5	29
6	28
7	25

Figure A1.9 $y = 4 + 10x - x^2$

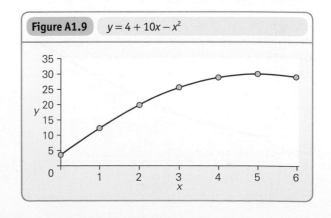

*Elementary differentiation

In several starred boxes and 'Looking at the Maths' sections we use some elementary calculus. The part of calculus we use is called *differentiation*. This is a technique to enable us to calculate the rate of change of a variable. The purpose of this section is not to explain why differentiation involves the procedures it does, but simply to state the rules that are necessary for our purposes. You will need to consult a maths book if you want to know how these rules are derived.

First, let us see when we would be interested in looking at the rate of change of a variable. Take the case of a firm thinking of expanding. It will want to know how much its costs will increase as its output increases. It will want to know the rate of change of costs with respect to changes in output.

Let us assume that it faces a cost function of the form

$$C = 20 + 5Q + Q^2 \qquad (1)$$

where C is the total cost of production and Q is the quantity produced. Table A1.10 and Figure A1.10 are derived from this equation.

The rate of increase in its costs with respect to increases in output is given by the *slope* of the cost curve in Figure A1.10. The steeper the slope, the more rapidly costs increase. At point a the slope of the curve is 11. This is found by drawing the tangent to the curve and measuring

the slope of the tangent. At this point on the curve, what we are saying is that for each one unit increase in output there is an £11 increase in costs. (Obviously as the graph is curved, this rate of increase will vary at different outputs.)

This rate of increase in costs is known as the *marginal cost*. It is the same with other variables that increase with quantity: their rate of increase is known as *marginal*. For example, *marginal revenue* is the rate of increase of sales revenue with respect to output.

We can use the technique of differentiation to derive a marginal from a total equation: in other words, to derive the slope of the total curve. Let us assume that we have an equation

$$y = 10 + 6x - 4x^2 + 2x^3 \qquad (2)$$

When we differentiate it, we call the new equation dy/dx: this stands for the rate of increase in y (dy) with respect to the increase in x (dx).

The rules for differentiating a simple equation like equation (2) are very straightforward:

1. You delete the constant term (10). The reason for this is that, being constant, by definition it will not cause an increase in y as x increases, and it is the *increase* in y that we are trying to discover.
2. You delete the x from the x term which has no power attached, and just leave the number. Thus the term $6x$ becomes simply 6.
3. For any term with a power in it (a square, a cube, etc.), its value should be *multiplied* by the power term and the power term reduced by one. Thus in the term $4x^2$, the 4 would be multiplied by 2 (the power term), and the power term would be reduced from 2 to 1 (but x to the power of 1 is simply x). After differentiation, therefore, the term becomes $8x$. In the term $2x^3$, the 2 would be multiplied by 3 (the power term), and the power term would be reduced from 3 to 2. After differentiation, therefore, the term becomes $6x^2$.

Applying these three rules to the equation

$$y = 10 + 6x - 4x^2 + 2x^3 \qquad (2)$$

gives

$$dy/dx = 6 - 8x + 6x^2 \qquad (3)$$

To find the rate of change of y with respect to x at any given value of x, therefore, you simply substitute that value of x into equation (3).

Table A1.10	$C = 20 + 5Q + Q^2$

x	y
0	20
1	26
2	34
3	44
4	56
5	70
6	86
7	104
8	124

Figure A1.10	A total cost function: $C = 20 + 5Q + Q^2$

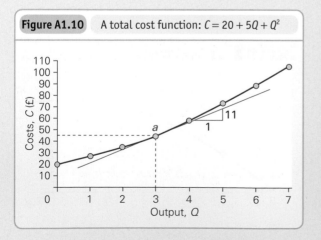

Definitions

Differentiation A mathematical technique to find the rate of change of one variable with respect to another.

Marginal cost The rate of increase in costs with respect to output.

Thus when $x = 4$, $dy/dx = 6 - (8 \times 4) + (6 \times 16) = 70$. In other words, when $x = 4$, for every 1 unit increase in x, y will increase by 70.

Returning to our cost function in equation (1), what is the marginal cost equation? Applying the three rules to the equation

$$C = 20 + 5Q + Q^2 \qquad (1)$$

gives

$$dC/dQ = 5 + 2Q \qquad (4)$$

Thus at an output of 3, the marginal cost (dC/dQ) is $5 + (2 \times 3) = 11$, which is the slope of the tangent to point a.

What would be the marginal cost equation if the total cost equation were

$$C = 15 + 20Q - 5Q^2 + Q^3?$$

What would be the marginal cost at an output of 8?

Finding the maximum or minimum point of a curve

The other important use we can make of calculus is to find the maximum or minimum point of a curve. This has a number of important applications. For example, a firm may want to know the minimum point on its average cost curve (a curve which shows how costs per unit of output vary as output increases). Also it is likely to want to know the output at which it will earn maximum profit. Let us examine this particular case.

Assume that the equation for total profit (Π) is

$$\Pi = -20 + 12Q - Q^2 \qquad (5)$$

This gives profit at various outputs as shown in Table A1.11. The corresponding graph is plotted in Figure A1.11.

What is the meaning of a negative profit?

Figure A1.11 A total profit function:
$\Pi = -20 + 12Q - Q^2$

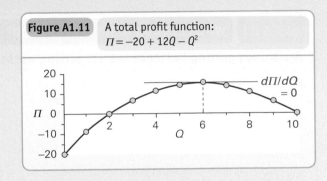

It can be seen at a glance that profits are maximised at an output of 6 units. But we could have worked this out directly from the profit equation without having to draw up a table or graph. How is this done?

Remember that when we differentiate a curve, the equation we get (known as 'the first derivative') gives us the slope of the curve. You can see that at the point of maximum profit (the top of the curve) its slope is zero: the tangent is horizontal. So all we have to do to find the top of the curve is to differentiate its equation and set it equal to zero.

Given that

$$\Pi = -20 + 12Q - Q^2 \qquad (5)$$

then:

$$d\Pi/dQ = 12 - 2Q \qquad (6)$$

Setting this equal to zero gives

$$12 - 2Q = 0$$
$$\therefore \quad 2Q = 12$$
$$\therefore \quad Q = 6$$

Thus profits are maximised at an output of 6 units – the result we obtained from the table and graph.

The second-derivative test

There is a problem with this technique, however. How can we tell from equation (6) that we have found the *maximum* rather than the *minimum*? The problem is that *both* the maximum *and* the minimum points of a curve have a zero slope.

The answer is to conduct a *second-derivative test*. This involves differentiating the equation a second time. This gives the rate of change of the *slope* of the original curve. If you look at Figure A1.11, as output increases, the tangent moves from being upward sloping, to horizontal, to downward sloping. In other words, the slope is getting less and

Q	Π
0	−20
1	−9
2	0
3	7
4	12
5	15
6	16
7	15
8	12
9	7
10	0

Table A1.11 $\Pi = -20 + 12Q - Q^2$

Definition

Second-derivative test If on differentiating an equation a second time the answer is negative (positive), the point is a maximum (minimum).

*BOX A1.1 | WHEN IS GOOD NEWS REALLY GOOD?

Are things getting better or merely getting worse more slowly?

From the second quarter of 2008 unemployment rose continuously for several months. By the third quarter of 2009 unemployment had increased by some 0.75 million. What good news could the government possibly draw from this?

Governments, always in search of any glimmer of good economic news, proclaimed that unemployment was rising more slowly (in other words, that the rate of increase in unemployment was *falling*). This was perfectly correct.

To show this, let us assume that N is the number of people out of work. The rate of change of unemployment is therefore given by dN/dt (where t is time). A positive figure for dN/dt represents a rise in unemployment, a negative figure a fall. Its value is given by the slope of the green line in the diagram. From the second quarter of 2008 this figure was positive. Bad news!

But the government sought a rosier interpretation. By using a second-order derivative, d^2N/dt^2, it could show that the rate of increase in unemployment from early 2009 had been falling. The value of this is given by the slope of the red line in the diagram and by the level of the green line. The government proclaimed that this was evidence that the economy was beginning to recover. Good news!

The use of calculus in this manner is a two-edged sword and such statistical sophistry is open to the political opposition, who could at a later date, if they so wished, claim that a fall in unemployment was bad economic news. Dare they?

 If the opposition were indeed to claim that a fall in unemployment was bad news, what would have to be the value of d^2N/dt^2: positive or negative?

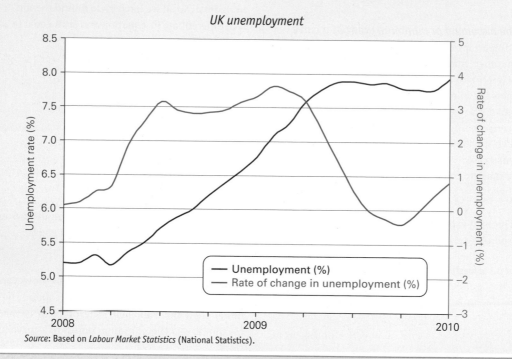

UK unemployment

Source: Based on *Labour Market Statistics* (National Statistics).

less. Its rate of change is *negative*. Thus if we differentiate the equation for the slope (i.e. the first derivative), we should get a negative figure.

When we differentiate a second time we get what is called the **second derivative**. It is written d^2y/dx^2.

If we differentiate equation (6)

$$d\Pi/dQ = 12 - 2Q \qquad (6)$$

we get

$$d^2\Pi/dQ^2 = -2 \qquad (7)$$

(Note that the rules for differentiating a second time are the same as for the first time.) Given that the second derivative in this case is negative, we have demonstrated that we have indeed found the maximum profit point (at $Q = 6$), and not the minimum.

Given the following equation for a firm's average cost (AC), that is the cost per unit of output (Q):

$$AC = 60 - 16Q + 2Q^2$$

(a) At what output is AC at a minimum?
(b) Use the second-derivative test to prove that this is a minimum and not a maximum.

Partial differentiation

Many relationships in economics involve more than two variables. For example, the demand for a product depends not just on its price, but also on income, the price of substitutes, the price of complements, etc. Similarly, a firm's cost of production depends not just on the quantity of output it produces, but also on wage rates, the prices of the various materials it uses, the productivity of its workers and machinery, and so on.

Such relationships can be expressed as a function as follows:

$$y = f(x_1, x_2, x_3, \ldots, x_n)$$

where x_1, x_2, etc., are the various determinants of y.

Let us take a simple example where a firm's total cost (TC) depends on just two things: the quantity produced (Q) and the wage rate (W). The cost function will be of the form

$$TC = f(Q, W)$$

Assume that in the case of a particular firm the function is

$$TC = 20 + 10Q - 4Q^2 + 2Q^3 + 6W \qquad (8)$$

What we are likely to want to know is how this firm's total cost changes as quantity changes, assuming the wage rate is held constant. Alternatively we may wish to know how its total cost changes as the wage rate changes, assuming that

output is held constant. To do this we use the technique of **partial differentiation**. This involves the same technique as simple differentiation but applied to just the one variable that is not held constant.

Thus to find the rate of change of costs with respect to quantity in equation (8), we differentiate the equation with respect to Q and ignore the W term. We ignore it as it is held constant and is thus treated like the constant (20) term in the equation. Using the rules of differentiation, the **partial derivative** is thus

$$\frac{\partial TC}{\partial Q} = 10 - 8Q + 6Q^2 \qquad (9)$$

Note that instead of using the symbol 'd' that we used in simple differentiation, we now use the symbol '∂'. Apart from that, the rules for partial differentiation are exactly the same as with simple differentiation.

If we now wanted to see how this firm's costs vary with the wage rate for any given output, then we would partially differentiate equation (8) with respect to W, giving

$$\frac{\partial TC}{\partial W} = 6$$

In other words, for each £1 rise in the wage rate, total cost would rise by £6.

Assume that the demand for a product is given by the following function:

$$Q_D = 1000 - 50P + 2P^2 + 10P_S + P_S^2$$

where Q_D is the quantity demanded, P is the price of the good and P_S is the price of a substitute good. What is the partial derivative of this demand function with respect to (a) the price of the good; (b) the price of the substitute good? Interpret the meaning of each partial derivative.

Definitions

Second derivative The rate of change of the first derivative, found by differentiating the first derivative.

Partial differentiation A mathematical technique used with functions containing two or more independent variables. The technique is used to find the rate of change of the dependent variable with respect to a single independent variable assuming that the other independent variables are held constant.

Partial derivative The partial derivative of a function of two or more independent variables is the derivative with respect to just one of those variables, while holding the others constant.

Appendix summary

1. Diagrams in economics can be used as pictures: to sketch a relationship so that its essentials can be perceived at a glance.

2. Tables, graphs and charts are also used to portray real-life data. These can be time-series data or cross-section data or both.

3. In order to get a true picture from economic data it is important to be aware of various ways that statistics can be abused: these include a selective use of data, a choice of axes on a graph to make trends seem more or less exaggerated or to make a curve more or less steep, confusing absolute and relative values, ignoring questions of distribution, confusing nominal and real values, and selecting the time period to make the statistics look the most favourable or unfavourable.

4. Presenting time-series data as index numbers gives a clear impression of trends and is a good way of comparing how two or more series (perhaps originally measured in different units) have changed over the same time period. A base year is chosen and the index for that year is set at 100. The percentage change in the value of a variable is given by the percentage change in the index (I). The formula is

$$\left(\frac{I_t - I_{t-1}}{I_{t-1}}\right) \times 100$$

Several items can be included in one index by using a weighted value for each of the items. The weights must add up to 1, and each weight will reflect the relative importance of that particular item in the index.

5. Functional relationships can be expressed as an equation, a table or a graph. In the linear (straight-line) equation $y = a + bx$, the a term gives the vertical intercept (the point where the graph crosses the vertical axis) and the b term gives the slope. When there is a power term (e.g. $y = a + bx + cx^2$), the graph will be a curve.

*6. Differentiation can be used to obtain the rate of change of one variable with respect to another. The rules of differentiation require that in an equation of the form

$$y = a + bx + cx^2 + dx^3$$

the a term disappears, the bx term simply becomes b, the cx^2 term becomes $2cx$, the dx^3 becomes $3dx^2$, and so on, with each extra term being multiplied by its power term and its power term being reduced by 1.

*7. To find the value of the x term at which the y term is at a maximum or minimum, the equation should be differentiated and set equal to zero. To check which it is – maximum or minimum – the second derivative should be calculated. If it is negative, then setting the first derivative equal to zero has yielded a maximum. If the second derivative is positive, then setting the first derivative to zero has yielded a minimum value.

Appendix 2: Websites

All the following websites can be accessed from this book's own website (www.pearsoned.co.uk/sloman). When you enter the site, click on **Hotlinks**. You will find all the following sites listed. Click on the one you want and the 'hot link' will take you straight to it.

The sections and numbers below refer to the ones used in the websites listed at the end of each chapter. Thus if the list contained the number A21, this would refer to the Moneyextra site.

(A) General news sources

As the title of this section implies, the websites here can be used for finding material on current news issues or tapping into news archives. Most archives are offered free of charge. However, some do require you to register. As well as key UK and US news sources, you will also notice some slightly different places from where you can get your news, such as the *St Petersburg Times* and *Kyodo News* (from Japan). Check out site numbers 38. *Refdesk*, 43. *Guardian World News Guide* and 44. *Online newspapers* for links to newspapers across the world. Try searching for an article on a particular topic by using site number 41. *Google News Search*.

1. BBC News
2. The Economist
3. The Financial Times
4. The Guardian
5. The Independent
6. ITN
7. The Observer
8. The Telegraph
9. Aljazeera
10. The New York Times
11. Fortune
12. Time Magazine
13. The Washington Post
14. Moscow Times (English)
15. St Petersburg Times (English)
16. Straits Times (Singapore)
17. New Straits Times (Malaysia)
18. The Scotsman
19. The Herald
20. Euromoney
21. Moneyextra
22. Market News International
23. Bloomberg Businessweek
24. International Business Times
25. CNN Money
26. Wall Street Journal
27. Asia News Network
28. allAfrica.com
29. Greek News Sources (English)
30. Kyodo News: Japan (English)
31. Euronews
32. The Australian
33. Sydney Morning Herald
34. Japan Times
35. Reuters
36. Bloomberg
37. David Smith's Economics UK.com
38. Refdesk (links to a whole range of news sources)
39. Newspapers and Magazines on World Wide Web
40. Yahoo News Search
41. Google News Search
42. ABYZ news links
43. Guardian World News Guide
44. Online newspapers

(B) Sources of economic and business data

Using websites to find up-to-date data is of immense value to the economist. The data sources below offer you a range of specialist and non-specialist data information. Universities have free access to the *MIMAS* and *UK Data Service* sites (sites 12 and 15 in this set), which are huge databases of statistics. Site 34, the *Treasury Pocket Data Bank*, is a very useful source of key UK and world statistics, and is updated monthly; it downloads as an Excel file. The Economics Network's *Economic data freely available online* (site 1) gives links to various sections in over 40 UK and international sites.

1. Economics Network gateway to economic data
2. Biz/ed Gateway to economic and company data
3. National Statistics
4. Data Archive (Essex)
5. Bank of England Statistical Database
6. Economic Resources (About)
7. Nationwide House Prices Site
8. House Web (data on housing market)
9. Economist global house price data
10. Halifax House Price Index
11. House prices indices from ONS

12. Manchester Information and Associated Services (MIMAS)
13. Economist economic and financial indicators
14. FT market data
15. Economagic
16. Groningen Growth and Development Centre
17. AEAweb: Resources for economists on the Internet (RFE): data
18. Joseph Rowntree Foundation
19. Intute: Social Sciences (Economics) (archive site)
20. Energy Information Administration
21. OECD Statistics
22. CIA world statistics site (World Factbook)
23. UN Millennium Country Profiles
24. World Bank statistics
25. Federal Reserve Bank of St Louis, US Economic Datasets (FRED)
26. Ministry of Economy, Trade and Industry (Japan)
27. Financial data from Yahoo
28. DataMarket
29. Index Mundi
30. Oanda Currency Converter
31. World Economic Outlook Database (IMF)
32. Telegraph shares and markets
33. OFFSTATS links to data sets
34. Treasury Pocket Data Bank (source of UK and world economic data)
35. UK Data Service (incorporating ESDS)
36. BBC News, market data
37. NationMaster
38. Statistical Annex of the European Economy
39. Business and Consumer Surveys (all EU countries)
40. Gapminder
41. WebEc Economics Data
42. WTO International Trade Statistics database
43. UNCTAD trade, investment and development statistics (UNCTADstat)
44. London Metal Exchange
45. Bank for International Settlements, global nominal and real effective exchange rate indices
46. EconStats from EconomyWatch
47. AMECO database

(C) Sites for students and teachers of economics

The following websites offer useful ideas and resources to those who are studying or teaching economics. It is worth browsing through some just to see what is on offer. Try out the first four sites, for starters. The *Internet for Economics* (site 8) is a very helpful tutorial for economics students on using the Internet.

1. The Economics Network
2. Biz/ed
3. Ecedweb
4. Studying Economics
5. Economics and Business Education Association
6. Tutor2U
7. Council for Economic Education
8. Internet for Economics (tutorial on using the Web)
9. Econoclass: Resources for economics teachers
10. Teaching resources for economists (RFE)
11. METAL – Mathematics for Economics: enhancing Teaching And Learning
12. Federal Reserve Bank of San Francisco: Economics Education
13. Excel in Economics Teaching (from the Economics Network)
14. WebEc resources
15. Dr. T's EconLinks: Teaching Resources
16. Online Opinion (Economics)
17. The Idea Channel
18. History of Economic Thought
19. Resources For Economists on the Internet (RFE)
20. Classroom Expernomics
21. Bank of England education resources
22. Why Study Economics?
23. Economic Classroom Experiments
24. Veconlab: Charles Holt's classroom experiments
25. Embedding Threshold Concepts
26. MIT Open Courseware in Economics

(D) Economic models, simulations and classroom experiments

Economic modelling is an important aspect of economic analysis. There are several sites that offer access to a model or simulation for you to use: e.g. *Virtual economy* (where you can play being Chancellor of the Exchequer). Using such models can be a useful way of finding out how economic theory works within an environment that claims to reflect reality.

1. Virtual Economy
2. Virtual Factory
3. Virtual Learning Arcade
4. About.com Economics
5. Classic Economic Models
6. Economics Network Handbook, Chapter on Simulations, Games and Role-play
7. Classroom Experiments, Internet Experiments, and Internet Simulations
8. Simulations
9. Experimental economics: Wikipedia
10. Software available on the Economics Network site
11. RFE Software
12. Virtual Worlds
13. Veconlab: Charles Holt's classroom experiments
14. EconPort
15. Denise Hazlett's Classroom Experiments in Macroeconomics
16. Games Economists Play

17. Finance and Economics Experimental Laboratory at Exeter (FEELE)
18. Classroom Expernomics
19. The Economics Network's Guide to Classroom Experiments and Games
20. Economic Classroom Experiments (Wikiversity)

(E) UK government and UK organisations' sites

If you want to see what a government department is up to, then look no further than the list below. Government departments' websites are an excellent source of information and data. They are particularly good at offering information on current legislation and policy initiatives.

1. Gateway site (GOV.UK)
2. Department for Communities and Local Government
3. Prime Minister's Office
4. Competition Commission
5. Department for Education
6. Department for International Development
7. Department for Transport
8. Department of Health
9. Department for Work and Pensions
10. Department for Business, Innovation and Skills
11. Environment Agency
12. Department of Energy and Climate Change
13. Low Pay Commission
14. Department for Environment, Food and Rural Affairs
15. Office of Communications (Ofcom)
16. Office of Gas and Electricity Markets (Ofgem)
17. Official Documents OnLine
18. Office of Fair trading (OFT)
19. Office of Rail Regulation (ORR)
20. The Takeover Panel
21. Sustainable Development Commission
22. OFWAT
23. National Statistics (ONS)
24. List of ONS releases from UK Data Explorer
25. HM Revenue and Customs
26. UK Intellectual Property Office
27. Parliament website
28. Scottish Government
29. Scottish Environment Protection Agency
30. Treasury
31. Equality and Human Rights Commission
32. Trades Union Congress (TUC)
33. Confederation of British Industry
34. Adam Smith Institute
35. Chatham House
36. Institute for Fiscal Studies
37. Advertising Standards Authority
38. Businesses and Self-employed
39. Campaign for Better Transport
40. New Economics Foundation

(F) Sources of monetary and financial data

As the title suggests, here are listed useful websites for finding information on financial matters. You will see that the list comprises mainly central banks, both within Europe and further afield. The links will take you to English language versions of non-English-speaking countries' sites.

1. Bank of England
2. Bank of England Monetary and Financial Statistics
3. Banque de France
4. Bundesbank (German central bank)
5. Central Bank of Ireland
6. European Central Bank
7. Eurostat
8. US Federal Reserve Bank
9. Netherlands Central Bank
10. Bank of Japan
11. Reserve Bank of Australia
12. Bank Negara Malaysia
13. Monetary Authority of Singapore
14. Bank of Canada
15. National Bank of Denmark
16. Reserve Bank of India
17. Links to central bank websites from the Bank for International Settlements
18. The London Stock Exchange

(G) European Union and related sources

For information on European issues, the following is a wide range of useful sites. The sites maintained by the European Union are an excellent source of information and are provided free of charge.

1. Economic and Financial Affairs: (EC DG)
2. European Central Bank
3. EU official Web site
4. Eurostat
5. Employment, Social Affairs and Inclusion: (EC DG)
6. Booklets on the EU
7. Enterprise and Industry: (EC DG)
8. Competition: (EC DG)
9. Agriculture and Rural Development: (EC DG)
10. Energy: (EC DG)
11. Environment: (EC DG)
12. Regional Policy: (EC DG)
13. Taxation and Customs Union: (EC DG)
14. Education and Culture: (EC DG)
15. European Patent Office
16. European Commission
17. European Parliament
18. European Council
19. Mobility and Transport: (EC DG)
20. Trade: (EC DG)
21. Internal Market and Services: (EC DG)

(H) International organisations

This section casts its net beyond Europe and lists the Web addresses of the main international organisations in the global economy. You will notice that some sites are run by charities, such as Oxfam, while others represent organisations set up to manage international affairs, such as the International Monetary Fund and the United Nations.

1. Food and Agriculture Organization (FAO)
2. United Nations Conference on Trade and Development (UNCTAD)
3. International Labour Organization (ILO)
4. International Monetary Fund (IMF)
5. Organization for Economic Co-operation and Development (OECD)
6. OPEC
7. World Bank
8. World Health Organization (WHO)
9. United Nations (UN)
10. United Nations Industrial Development Organization (UNIDO)
11. Friends of the Earth
12. Institute of International Finance
13. Oxfam
14. Christian Aid (reports on development issues)
15. European Bank for Reconstruction and Development (EBRD)
16. World Trade Organization (WTO)
17. United Nations Development Programme
18. UNICEF
19. EURODAD – European Network on Debt and Development
20. NAFTA
21. South American Free Trade Areas
22. ASEAN
23. APEC

(I) Economics search and link sites

If you are having difficulty finding what you want from the list of sites above, the following sites offer links to other sites and are a very useful resource when you are looking for something a little bit more specialist. Once again, it is worth having a look at what these sites have to offer in order to judge their usefulness.

1. Gateway for UK official sites
2. Alta Plana
3. Data Archive Search
4. Inomics (search engine for economics information)
5. RePEc bibliographic database
6. Estima: Links to economics resources sites
7. Intute: Social Sciences (Economics) (archive site)
8. WebEc
9. One World (link to economic development sites)
10. Economic development sites (list) from OneWorld.net
11. DMOZ Open Directory: Economics
12. Web links for economists from the Economics Network
13. Yahoo's links to economic data
14. OFFSTATS links to data sets
15. Excite Economics Links
16. Internet Resources for Economists
17. National Association for Business Economics links
18. Resources for Economists on the Internet
19. UK University Economics Departments
20. Economics education links
21. Development Gateway
22. Find the Best

(J) Internet search engines

The following search engines have been found to be useful.

1. Google
2. Bing
3. Whoosh UK
4. Excite
5. Go.com
6. Search.com
7. MSN
8. Economics search engine (from RFE)
9. Yahoo
10. Ask
11. Kartoo
12. Blinkx (for videos and audio podcasts)

Threshold Concepts and Key Ideas

THRESHOLD CONCEPTS

		Page
1.	Choice and opportunity cost	11
2.	People gain from voluntary economic interaction	25
3.	Markets may fail to meet social objectives	26
4.	Markets equate demand and supply	47
5.	People respond to incentives. So it's important to get them right	54
6.	Governments can sometimes improve market outcomes	55
7.	Elasticity: of a variable to a change in a determinant	72
8.	Rational decision making involves choices at the margin	105
9.	People's actions depend on their expectations	121
10.	General equilibrium: when all markets are in balance	317
11.	Allocative efficiency: private and social	320
12.	The distinction between real and nominal values	411
13.	Short-term growth in a country's output tends to fluctuate	418
14.	Long-term growth in a country's output depends on a growth in the quantity and/or productivity of its resources	420
15.	Cumulative causation: economic effects can snowball	508

KEY IDEAS

		Page
1.	**Scarcity** is the excess of human wants over what can actually be produced. Because of scarcity, various choices have to be made between alternatives.	7
2.	The **opportunity cost** of any activity is the sacrifice made to do it. It is the best thing that could have been done as an alternative.	11
3.	**Economic efficiency** is thus achieved when each good is produced at the minimum cost and where individual people and firms get the maximum benefit from their resources.	13
4.	**Equity** is where income is distributed in a way that is considered to be fair or just. Note that an equitable distribution is not the same as an equal distribution and that different people have different views on what is equitable.	13
5.	**Changes in demand or supply cause markets to adjust**. Whenever such changes occur, the resulting 'disequilibrium' will bring an automatic change in prices, thereby restoring equilibrium (i.e. a balance of demand and supply).	22
6.	**The importance of the positive/normative distinction**. Economics can only contribute to policy issues in a positive way. Economists, as scientists, should not make normative judgements. They can make them only as individual people, with no more moral right than any other individual.	29
7.	The **income and substitution effects** are useful concepts as they help to explain why people react to a price rise by buying less. The size of these effects depends on a range of factors. These factors determine the shape of the demand curve.	36
8.	**Equilibrium is the point where conflicting interests are balanced**. Only at this point is the amount that demanders are willing to purchase the same as the amount that suppliers are willing to supply. It is a point that will be automatically reached in a free market through the operation of the price mechanism.	46

9. **Elasticity**. The responsiveness of one variable (e.g. demand) to a change in another (e.g. price). This concept is fundamental to understanding how markets work. The more elastic variables are, the more responsive is the market to changing circumstances. 71

10. **People's actions are influenced by their expectations**. People respond not just to what is happening now (such as a change in price), but to what they anticipate will happen in the future. 75

11. **People's actions are influenced by their attitudes towards risk**. Many decisions are taken under conditions of risk or uncertainty. Generally, the lower the probability of (or the more uncertain) the desired outcome of an action, the less likely people will be to undertake the action. 80

12. **The fallacy of composition**. What applies in one case will not necessarily apply when repeated in all cases. 88

13. **The principle of diminishing marginal utility**. The more of a product a person consumes, the less will be the additional utility gained from one more unit. 101

14. **The equi-marginal principle**. The optimum amount of two alternatives consumed (or produced) will be where the marginal benefit ratios of the two alternatives are equal to their marginal cost ratios: 107

$$\frac{MU_A}{MU_B} = \frac{P_A}{P_B}$$

15. **Good decision making requires good information**. Where information is poor, decisions and their outcomes may be poor. 121

16. **Output depends on the amount of resources and how they are used**. Different amounts and combinations of inputs will lead to different amounts of output. If output is to be produced efficiently, then inputs should be combined in the optimum proportions. 133

17. **The law of diminishing marginal returns** states that when increasing amounts of a variable factor are used with a given amount of a fixed factor, there will come a point when each extra unit of the variable factor will produce less extra output than the previous unit. 135

18. The **'bygones' principle** states that sunk (fixed) costs should be ignored when deciding whether to produce or sell more or less of a product. Only variable costs should be taken into account. 139

19. **Fixed costs and the time period**. Fixed costs occur only in the short run, since in the long run all inputs can be varied. 154

20. **Market power**. When firms have market power over prices, they can use this to raise prices and profits above the perfectly competitive level. Other things being equal, the firm will gain at the expense of the consumer. Similarly, if consumers or workers have market power, they can use this to their own benefit. 171

21. **People often think and behave strategically**. How you think others will respond to your actions is likely to influence your own behaviour. Firms, for example, when considering a price or product change will often take into account the likely reactions of their rivals. 198

22. **The nature of institutions and organisations is likely to influence behaviour**. There are various forces influencing people's decisions in complex organisations. Assumptions that an organisation will follow one simple objective (e.g. short-run profit maximisation) is thus too simplistic in many cases. 223

23. **The principal–agent problem**. Where people (principals), as a result of a lack of knowledge, cannot ensure that their best interests are served by their agents. Agents may take advantage of this situation to the disadvantage of the principals. 225

24. **Stocks and flows**. A stock is a quantity of something at a given point in time. A flow is an increase or decrease in something over a specified period of time. This is an important distinction and a common cause of confusion. 271

25. **The principle of discounting**. People generally prefer to have benefits today rather than in the future. Thus future benefits have to be reduced (discounted) to give them a present value. 272

26. **Allocative efficiency (simple formulation) in any activity is achieved where marginal benefit equals marginal cost**. Private efficiency is achieved where marginal private benefit equals marginal private cost ($MB = MC$). Social efficiency is achieved where marginal social benefit equals marginal social cost ($MSB = MSC$). 315

27. **Social efficiency (equi-marginal formulation)** is achieved where the marginal social benefit ratios are equal to the marginal social cost ratios for any two alternatives. In the case of two alternatives X and Y, this will be where 320

$$\frac{MSB_x}{MSB_y} = \frac{MSC_x}{MSC_y}$$

28. **Markets generally fail to achieve social efficiency**. There are various types of market failure. Market failures provide one of the major justifications for government intervention in the economy. 323

29. **Externalities are spill-over costs or benefits**. Where these exist, even an otherwise perfect market will fail to achieve social efficiency.   323

30. **The free-rider problem**. People are often unwilling to pay for things if they can make use of things other people have bought. This problem can lead to people not purchasing things that would be to the benefit of them and other members of society to have.   326

31. **The problem of time lags**. Many economic actions can take a long time to take effect. This can cause problems of instability and an inability of the economy to achieve social efficiency.   330

32. **Economies suffer from inherent instability**. As a result, economic growth and other macroeconomic indicators tend to fluctuate.   401

33. **Balance sheets affect people's behaviour**. The size and structure of the liabilities and assets of governments, institutions and individuals affect economic well-being and can have significant effects on behaviour and economic activity.   404

34. **Societies face trade-offs between economic objectives**. For example, the goal of faster growth may conflict with that of greater equality; the goal of lower unemployment may conflict with that of lower inflation (at least in the short run). This is an example of opportunity cost: the cost of achieving one objective may be achieving less of another. The existence of trade-offs means that policy makers must make choices.   404

35. **The principle of cumulative causation**. An initial event can cause an ultimate effect that is much larger.   475

36. **Goodhart's law**: Controlling a symptom (i.e. an indicator) of a problem will not cure the problem. Instead, the indicator will merely cease to be a good indicator of the problem.   653

37. **The law of comparative advantage**. Provided opportunity costs of various goods differ in two countries, both of them can gain from mutual trade if they specialise in producing (and exporting) those goods that have relatively low opportunity costs compared with the other country.   710

38. **The competitive advantage of nations**. The ability of countries to compete in the market for exports and with potential importers to their country. The competitiveness of any one industry depends on the availability and quality of resources, demand conditions at home in that industry, the strategies and rivalry of firms within the industry and the quality of supporting industries and infrastructure. It also depends on government policies and there is also an element of chance.   719

39. **The distinction between nominal and real figures**. Nominal figures are those using current prices, interest rates, etc. Real figures are figures corrected for inflation.   A:6

Glossary

Abduction Using pieces of evidence to develop a plausible explanation. This can then be tested by gathering more evidence.

Absolute advantage A country has an absolute advantage over another in the production of a good if it can produce it with less resources than the other country can.

Accelerationist theory The theory that unemployment can only be reduced below the natural rate at the cost of accelerating inflation.

Accelerator coefficient The level of induced investment as a proportion of a rise in national income: $\alpha = I_i/\Delta Y$.

Accelerator theory The *level* of investment depends on the *rate of change* of national income, and as result tends to be subject to substantial fluctuations.

Active balances Money held for transactions and precautionary purposes.

Actual growth The percentage annual increase in national output actually produced.

Ad valorem **tariffs** Tariffs levied as a percentage of the price of the import.

Ad valorem **tax** A tax on a good levied as a percentage of its value. It can be a single-stage tax or a multi-stage tax (such as VAT).

Adaptive expectations hypothesis The theory that people base their expectations of inflation on past inflation rates.

Adjustable peg A system whereby exchange rates are fixed for a period of time, but may be devalued (or revalued) if a deficit (or surplus) becomes substantial.

Adverse selection The tendency of those who are at greatest risk to take out insurance.

Aggregate demand Total spending on goods and services made in the economy. It consists of four elements, consumer spending (C), investment (I), government spending (G) and the expenditure on exports (X), less any expenditure on imports of goods and services (M): $AD = C + I + G + X - M$.

Aggregate demand for labour curve A curve showing the total demand for labour in the economy at different levels of real wage rates.

Aggregate expenditure (E) Aggregate demand in the Keynesian model: i.e. $C_d + J$.

Aggregate supply The total amount of output in the economy.

Aggregate supply of labour curve A curve showing the total number of people willing and able to work at different average real wage rates.

Allocative efficiency A situation where the current combination of goods produced and sold gives the maximum satisfaction for each consumer at their current levels of income. Note that a redistribution of income would lead to a different combination of goods that was allocatively efficient.

Alternative theories of the firm Theories of the firm based on the assumption that firms have aims other than profit maximisation.

Ambient-based standards Pollution control that requires firms to meet minimum standards for the environment (e.g. air or water quality).

Appreciation A rise in the free-market exchange rate of the domestic currency with foreign currencies.

Arbitrage The practice of taking advantage of price differentials in markets by buying in the low-priced markets and selling in the high-priced ones. The practice of buying and selling will tend to eliminate the price differentials. Interest rate arbitrage involves borrowing at low interest rates and lending at high rates. This will tend to eliminate the interest rate differentials.

Arc elasticity The measurement of elasticity between two points on a curve.

Assets Possessions of an individual or institution, or claims held on others.

Assisted areas Areas of high unemployment qualifying for government regional selective assistance (RSA) and grants from the European regional development fund (ERDF).

Asymmetric information Where one party in an economic relationship (e.g. an agent) has more information than another (e.g. the principal).

Asymmetric shocks Shocks (such as an oil price increase or a recession in another part of the world) that have different-sized effects on different industries, regions or countries.

Authorised institutions The institutions comprising the monetary (or banking) sector.

Automatic fiscal stabilisers Tax revenues that rise and government expenditure that falls as national income rises. The more they change with income, the bigger the stabilising effect on national income.

Average cost pricing or mark-up pricing Where firms set the price by adding a profit mark-up to average cost.

Average fixed cost Total fixed cost per unit of output: $AFC = TFC/Q$.

Average (or 'midpoint') formula for price elasticity of demand ΔQ_D/average $Q_D \div \Delta P$/average P.

Average physical product Total output (TPP) per unit of the variable factor in question: $APP = TPP/Q_v$.

Average rate of income tax Income taxes as a proportion of a person's total (gross) income: T/Y.

Average revenue Total revenue per unit of output. When all output is sold at the same price average revenue will be the same as price: $AR = TR/Q = P$.

Average (total) cost Total cost (fixed plus variable) per unit of output: $AC = TC/Q = AFC + AVC$.

Average variable cost Total variable cost per unit of output: $AVC = TVC/Q$.

Balance of payments account A record of the country's transactions with the rest of the world. It shows the country's payments to or deposits in other countries (debits) and its receipts or deposits from other countries (credits). It also shows the balance between these debits and credits under various headings.

Balance of payments on current account The balance on trade in goods and services plus net investment income and current transfers.

Balance of trade Exports of goods and services minus imports of goods and services. If exports exceed imports, there is a 'balance of trade surplus' (a positive figure). If imports exceed exports, there is a 'balance of trade deficit' (a negative figure).

Balance on trade in goods Exports of goods minus imports of goods.

Balance on trade in goods and services (or balance of trade) Exports of goods and services minus imports of goods and services.

Balance on trade in services Exports of services minus imports of services.

Balance sheet A record of the stock of assets and liabilities of an individual or institution.

Balancing item (in the balance of payments) A statistical adjustment to ensure that the two sides of the balance of payments account balance. It is necessary because of errors in compiling the statistics.

Bank (or deposits) multiplier The number of times greater the expansion of bank deposits is than the additional liquidity in banks that causes it: $1/L$ (the inverse of the liquidity ratio).

Bank bills Bills that have been accepted by another institution and hence insured against default.

Barometric firm price leadership Where the price leader is the one whose prices are believed to reflect market conditions in the most satisfactory way.

Barriers to entry Anything that prevents or impedes the entry of firms into an industry and thereby limits the amount of competition faced by existing firms.

Barter economy An economy where people exchange goods and services directly with one another without any payment of money. Workers would be paid with bundles of goods.

Base year (for index numbers) The year whose index number is set at 100.

Basic needs approach The attempt to measure development in terms of a country's ability to meet the basic requirements for life.

Basic rate of tax The main marginal rate of tax, applying to most people's incomes.

Behavioural theories of the firm Theories that attempt to predict the actions of firms by studying the behaviour of various groups of people within the firm and their interactions under conditions of potentially conflicting interests.

Benefit principle of taxation The principle that people ought to pay taxes in proportion to the amount they use government services.

Benefits in kind Goods or services which the state provides directly to the recipient at no charge or at a subsidised price. Alternatively, the state can subsidise the private sector to provide them.

Bilateral monopoly Where a monopsony buyer faces a monopoly seller.

Bill of exchange A certificate promising to repay a stated amount on a certain date, typically three months from the issue of the bill. Bills pay no interest as such, but are sold at a discount and redeemed at face value, thereby earning a rate of discount for the purchaser.

Bounded rationality When the ability to make rational decisions is limited by lack of information or the time necessary to obtain such information or by a lack of understanding of complex situations.

Bretton Woods system An adjustable peg system whereby currencies were pegged to the US dollar. The USA maintained convertibility of the dollar into gold at the rate of $35 to an ounce.

Broad money in UK (M4) Cash in circulation plus retail and wholesale bank and building society deposits.

Budget deficit The excess of central government's spending over its tax receipts.

Budget line A graph showing all the possible combinations of two goods that can be purchased at given prices and for a given budget.

Budget surplus The excess of central government's tax receipts over its spending.

Buffer stocks Stocks of a product used to stabilise its price. In years of abundance, the stocks are built up. In years of low supply, stocks are released onto the market.

Buffer-stock saving Saving undertaken in order that the stock of wealth is kept at a desired level.

Business cycle or Trade cycle The periodic fluctuations of national output round its long-term trend.

Capital All inputs into production that have themselves been produced: e.g. factories, machines and tools.

Capital account of the balance of payments The record of the transfers of capital to and from abroad.

Capital adequacy ratio (CAR) The ratio of a bank's capital (reserves and shares) to its risk-weighted assets.

Capital expenditure Investment expenditure; expenditure on assets.

Capital market A financial market where longer-term debt instruments, like government bonds (gilts), can be bought and sold.

Carry trade Borrowing at low interest rates and then using it to buy assets that earn higher rates. In foreign exchange markets, the carry trade involves borrowing money in a currency of a country where interest rates are low and exchanging it for another currency where the country pays higher interest rates.

Cartel A formal collusive agreement.

Central bank Banker to the banks and the government.

Centrally planned or command economy An economy where all economic decisions are taken by the central authorities.

Certificates of deposit (CDs) Certificates issued by banks for fixed-term interest-bearing deposits. They can be resold by the owner to another party.

Ceteris paribus Latin for 'other things being equal'. This assumption has to be made when making deductions from theories.

Change in demand This is the term used for a shift in the demand curve. It occurs when a determinant of demand *other* than price changes.

Change in supply The term used for a shift in the supply curve. It occurs when a determinant *other* than price changes.

Change in the quantity demanded The term used for a movement along the demand curve to a new point. It occurs when there is a change in price.

Change in the quantity supplied The term used for a movement along the supply curve to a new point. It occurs when there is a change in price.

Claimant unemployment Those in receipt of unemployment-related benefits.

Classical model A macroeconomic model that assumes prices and wages are fully flexible.

Clearing system A system whereby interbank debts are settled.

Closed shop Where a firm agrees to employ only union members.

Coase theorem By sufferers from externalities doing deals with perpetrators (by levying charges or offering bribes), the externality will be 'internalised' and the socially efficient level of output will be achieved.

Cobb–Douglas production function Like other production functions, this shows how output (*TPP*) varies with inputs of various factors (F_1, F_2, F_3, etc.). In the simple two-factor case it takes the following form:

$$TPP = f(F_1, F_2) = AF_1^{\alpha}F_2^{\beta}$$

If $\alpha + \beta = 1$, there are constant returns to scale; if $\alpha + \beta > 1$, there are increasing returns to scale; if $\alpha + \beta < 1$, there are decreasing returns to scale.

Collateralised debt obligations (CDOs) These are a type of security consisting of a bundle of fixed-income assets, such as corporate bonds, mortgage debt and credit-card debt.

Collusive oligopoly Where oligopolists agree (formally or informally) to limit competition between themselves. They may set output quotas, fix prices, limit product promotion or development, or agree not to 'poach' each other's markets.

Collusive tendering Where two or more firms secretly agree on the prices they will tender for a contract. These prices will be above those which would be put in under a genuinely competitive tendering process.

Command-and-control (CAC) systems The use of laws or regulations backed up by inspections and penalties (such as fines) for non-compliance.

Command economy An economy where all economic decisions are made by a central planning process.

Commercial bills Bills of exchange issued by firms.

Common market A customs union where the member countries act as a single market with free movement of labour and capital, common taxes and common trade laws.

Comparative advantage A country has a comparative advantage over another in the production of a good if it can produce it at a lower opportunity cost: i.e. if it has to forgo less of other goods in order to produce it.

Competition for corporate control The competition for the control of companies through takeovers.

Complementary goods A pair of goods consumed together. As the price of one goes up, the demand for both goods will fall.

Compounding The process of adding interest each year to an initial capital sum.

Compromise strategy A strategy whose worst outcome is better than under a high-risk strategy and whose best outcome is better than under a low-risk strategy.

Conglomerate merger When two firms in different industries merge.

Consortium Where two or more firms work together on a specific project and create a separate company to run the project.

Constrained discretion A set of principles or rules within which economic policy operates. These can be informal or enshrined in law.

Consumer durable A consumer good that lasts a period of time, during which the consumer can continue gaining utility from it.

Consumer prices index (CPI) An index of the prices of goods bought by a typical household.

Consumer sovereignty A situation where firms respond to changes in consumer demand without being in a position in the long run to charge a price above average cost.

Consumer surplus The excess of what a person would have been prepared to pay for a good (i.e. the utility) over what that person actually pays.

Consumers' share of a tax on a good The proportion of the revenue from a tax on a good that arises from an increase in the price of the good.

Consumption The act of using goods and services to satisfy wants. This will normally involve purchasing the goods and services.

Consumption function The relationship between consumption and national income. It can be expressed algebraically or graphically.

Consumption of domestically produced goods and services (C_d) The direct flow of money payments from households to firms.

Consumption smoothing The act by households of smoothing their levels of consumption over time despite facing volatile incomes.

Contingent convertible debt instruments (Co-Cos) Debt instruments, like corporate bonds, which may be converted into equity capital when a trigger point, such as the level of financial distress of a corporation, is reached.

Continuous market clearing The assumption that all markets in the economy continuously clear so that the economy is permanently in equilibrium.

Contractionary (or deflationary) policy Fiscal or monetary policy designed to reduce the rate of growth of aggregate demand.

Convergence in GDP per head The tendency for less rich developed countries to catch up the richer ones. Convergence does not apply to many of the poorer developing countries, however, where the gap between them and richer countries has tended to widen.

Convergence of economies When countries achieve similar levels of growth, inflation, budget deficits as a percentage of GDP, balance of payments, etc.

Co-ordination failure When a group of firms (e.g. banks) acting independently could have achieved a more desirable outcome if they had coordinated their decision making.

Core workers Workers, normally with specific skills, who are employed on a permanent or long-term basis.

Cost–benefit analysis The identification, measurement and weighing up of the costs and benefits of a project in order to decide whether or not it should go ahead.

Cost-plus pricing (full-cost pricing) When firms price their product by adding a certain profit 'mark-up' to average cost.

Cost-push inflation Inflation caused by persistent rises in costs of production (independently of demand).

Countervailing power When the power of a monopolistic/oligopolistic seller is offset by powerful buyers who can prevent the price from being pushed up.

Cournot equilibrium Where the outputs chosen by each firm are consistent with each other: where the two firms' reaction curves cross.

Cournot model of duopoly A model where each firm makes its price and output decisions on the assumption that its rival will produce a particular quantity.

Crawling peg A system whereby the government allows a gradual adjustment of the exchange rate.

Credible threat (or promise) One that is believable to rivals because it is in the threatener's interests to carry it out.

Credit crunch A sudden reduction in the availability of loans or credit from banks and other financial institutions.

Cross-price elasticity of demand The percentage (or proportionate) change in quantity demanded of one good divided by the percentage (or proportionate) change in the price of another.

Cross-price elasticity of demand (formula) ($C\epsilon_{P_{AD}}$) The percentage (or proportionate) change in demand for good A divided by the percentage (or proportionate) change in price of good B: $\%\Delta Q_{DA} \div \%\Delta P_B$.

Cross-price elasticity of demand (arc formula) $\Delta Q_{DA}/$ average $Q_{DA} + \Delta P_B/$ average P_B.

Cross-section data Information showing how a variable (e.g. the consumption of eggs) differs between different groups or different individuals at a given time.

Cross-subsidise To use profits in one market to subsidise prices in another.

Crowding out Where increased public expenditure diverts money or resources away from the private sector.

Cumulative causation (principle of) When an initial change causes an eventual change that is larger.

Currency union A group of countries (or regions) using a common currency.

Current account balance of payments Exports of goods and services minus imports of goods and services plus net incomes and current transfers from abroad. If inflows of money (from the sale of exports etc.) exceed outflows of money (from the purchase of imports etc.) there is a 'current account surplus' (a positive figure). If outflows exceed inflows there is a 'current account deficit' (a negative figure).

Current expenditure (by the government) Recurrent spending on goods and factor payments.

Customs union A free-trade area with common external tariffs and quotas.

Deadweight loss of an indirect tax The loss of consumers' plus producers' surplus from the imposition of an indirect tax.

Deadweight welfare loss The loss of consumers' plus producers' surplus in imperfect markets (when compared with perfect competition).

Debentures (company bonds) Fixed-interest loans to firms. These assets can be traded on the stock market and their market price is determined by demand and supply.

Debt servicing Paying the interest and capital repayments on debt.

Debt-servicing costs The costs incurred when repaying debt, including debt interest payments.

Deciles Divisions of the population into 10 equal-sized groups (an example of a quantile).

Decision tree (or game tree) A diagram showing the sequence of possible decisions by competitor firms and the outcome of each combination of decisions.

Deduction Using a theory to draw conclusions about specific circumstances.

Deflationary (or recessionary) gap The shortfall of national expenditure below national income (and injections below withdrawals) at the full-employment level of national income.

Deflationary policy Fiscal or monetary policy designed to reduce the rate of growth of aggregate demand.

Demand curve A graph showing the relationship between the price of a good and the quantity of the good demanded over a given time period. Price is measured on the vertical axis; quantity demanded is measured on the horizontal axis. A demand curve can be for an individual consumer or group of consumers, or more usually for the whole market.

Demand function An equation which shows the mathematical relationship between the quantity demanded of a good and the values of the various determinants of demand.

Demand schedule (market) A table showing the different total quantities of a good that consumers are willing and able to buy at various prices over a given period of time.

Demand schedule for an individual A table showing the different quantities of a good that a person is willing and able to buy at various prices over a given period of time.

Demand-deficient or **cyclical unemployment** Disequilibrium unemployment caused by a fall in aggregate demand with no corresponding fall in the real wage rate.

Demand-management policies Demand-side policies (fiscal and/or monetary) designed to smooth out the fluctuations in the business cycle.

Demand-pull inflation Inflation caused by persistent rises in aggregate demand.

Demand-side policies Policies designed to affect aggregate demand: fiscal policy and monetary policy.

Demand-side policy Government policy designed to alter the level of aggregate demand, and thereby the level of output, employment and prices.

Dependency Where the development of a developing country is hampered by its relationships with the industrialised world.

Depreciation (of a currency) A fall in the free-market exchange rate of the domestic currency with foreign currencies.

Depreciation (of capital) The decline in value of capital equipment due to age, or wear and tear.

Deregulation Where the government removes official barriers to competition (e.g. licences and minimum quality standards).

Derived demand The demand for a factor of production depends on the demand for the good which uses it.

Destabilising speculation Where the actions of speculators tend to make price movements larger.

Devaluation Where the government re-pegs the exchange rate at a lower level.

Differentiation A mathematical technique to find the rate of change of one variable with respect to another.

Diminishing marginal rate of substitution The more a person consumes of good X and the less of good Y, the less additional Y will that person be prepared to give up in order to obtain an extra unit of X: i.e. $\Delta Y/\Delta X$ diminishes.

Diminishing marginal returns When one or more factors are held fixed, there will come a point beyond which the extra output from additional units of the variable factor will diminish.

Diminishing marginal utility As more units of a good are consumed, additional units will provide less additional satisfaction than previous units.

Diminishing marginal utility of income Where each additional pound earned yields less additional utility.

Direct income support or **direct aid** A fixed grant to farmers that does not vary with current output. It may be based on acreage, number of livestock or past output.

Direct monetary transmission mechanism A change in money supply having a direct effect on aggregate demand.

Direct taxes Taxes on income and wealth. Paid directly to the tax authorities on that income or wealth.

Dirty floating (managed flexibility) A system of flexible exchange rates but where the government intervenes to prevent excessive fluctuations or even to achieve an unofficial target exchange rate.

Discount market An example of a money market in which new or existing bills, such as Treasury bills or commercial bills, are bought and sold at a discount below their face value: i.e. the value at which they will be redeemed on maturity.

Discounting The process of reducing the value of future flows to give them a present valuation.

Discretionary fiscal policy Deliberate changes in tax rates or the level of government expenditure in order to influence the level of aggregate demand.

Diseconomies of scale Where costs per unit of output increase as the scale of production increases.

Disequilibrium unemployment Unemployment resulting from real wage rates in the economy being above the equilibrium level.

Disguised unemployment Where the same work could be done by fewer people.

Disintermediation The diversion of business away from financial institutions which are subject to controls.

Disposable income Household income after the deduction of taxes and the addition of benefits.

Distribution of income by class of recipient Measurement of the distribution of income between the classes of person who receive it (e.g. homeowners and non-homeowners or those in the North and those in the South).

Diversification This is where a firm expands into new types of business.

Dominant firm price leadership When firms (the followers) choose the same price as that set by a dominant firm in the industry (the leader).

Dominant strategy game Where different assumptions about rivals' behaviour lead to the adoption of the same strategy.

Downward causation The name given to the impact on individual behaviour or well-being of aggregate or group effects. This is an example of cumulative causation (Key Idea 35).

Dualism The division of an economy into a modern (usually urban) sector and a poor traditional (usually rural) sector.

Dumping When exports are sold at prices below marginal cost – often as a result of government subsidy.

Duopoly An oligopoly where there are just two firms in the market.

Dynamic stochastic general equilibrium (DSGE) models Models that seek to explain macroeconomic phenomena by examining the microeconomic behaviour of rational forward-looking individual economic agents acting in a variety of market conditions. The microeconomic equilibria are subject to random shocks, such as technological change, political events or changes in the supply of natural resources.

Econometrics The science of applying statistical techniques to economic data in order to identify and test economic relationships.

Economic and monetary union (EMU) The adoption by a group of countries of a single currency with a single central bank and a single monetary policy. In the EU the term applies to the countries that have adopted the euro.

Economic discrimination When workers of identical *ability* are paid different wages or are otherwise discriminated against because of race, age, sex, etc.

Economic efficiency A situation where each good is produced at the minimum cost and where individual people and firms get the maximum benefit from their resources.

Economic model A formal presentation of an economic theory.

Economic rent The excess that a factor is paid over the amount necessary to keep it in its current employment.

Economies of scale When increasing the scale of production leads to a lower long-run cost per unit of output.

Economies of scope When increasing the range of products produced by a firm reduces the cost of producing each one.

ECU (European Currency Unit) The predecessor to the euro: a weighted average of EU currencies. It was used as a reserve currency and for the operation of the exchange rate mechanism (ERM).

Effective rate of protection The percentage increase in an industry's domestic value added resulting from protection given to that industry.

Efficient (capital) market hypothesis The hypothesis that new information about a company's current or future performance will be quickly and accurately reflected in its share price.

Efficiency wage hypothesis The hypothesis that the productivity of workers is affected by the wage rate that they receive.

Efficiency wage rate The profit-maximising wage rate for the firm after taking into account the effects of wage rates on worker motivation, turnover and recruitment.

Elastic demand (with respect to price) Where quantity demanded changes by a larger percentage than price. Ignoring the negative sign, it will have a value greater than 1.

Elasticity A measure of the responsiveness of a variable (e.g. quantity demanded or quantity supplied) to a change in one of its determinants (e.g. price or income).

EMS (The European Monetary System, mark 1) A system whereby EC countries co-operated to achieve greater exchange rate stability. It involved use of the exchange rate mechanism (the ERM).

Endogenous growth models Models which demonstrate that the rate of economic growth depends on the rate of technological progress and diffusion, both of which depend on institutions, incentives and the role of government.

Endogenous money supply Money supply that is determined (at least in part) by the demand for money.

Endogenous variable A variable whose value is determined by the model of which it is part.

Engel curve A line showing how much of a good people will demand at different levels of income.

Entrepreneurship The initiating and organising of the production of new goods, or the introduction of new techniques, and the risk taking associated with it.

Envelope curve A long-run average cost curve drawn as the tangency points of a series of short-run average cost curves.

Environmental charges Charges for using natural resources (e.g. water or national parks), or for using the environment as a dump for waste (e.g. factory emissions or sewage).

Equation of exchange $MV = PY$. The total level of spending on GDP (MV) equals the total value of goods and services produced (PY) that go to make up GDP.

Equilibrium A position of balance. A position from which there is no inherent tendency to move away.

Equilibrium price The price where the quantity demanded equals the quantity supplied: the price where there is no shortage or surplus.

Equilibrium ('natural') unemployment The difference between those who would like employment at the current wage rate and those willing and able to take a job.

Equi-marginal principle Consumers will maximise total utility from their incomes by consuming that combination of goods where $MU_a/P_a = MU_b/P_b = MU_c/P_c = \ldots = MU_n/P_n$.

Equities Company shares. Holders of equities are owners of the company and share in its profits by receiving dividends.

Equity A distribution of income that is considered to be fair or just. Note that an equitable distribution is not the same as an equal distribution and that different people have different views on what is equitable.

ERM (the exchange rate mechanism) A system of semi-fixed exchange rates used by most of the EU countries prior to adoption of the euro. Members' currencies were allowed to fluctuate against each other only within agreed bands. Collectively they floated against all other currencies.

Excess burden (of a tax on a good) The amount by which the loss in consumer plus producer surplus exceeds the government surplus.

Excess capacity (under monopolistic competition) In the long run, firms under monopolistic competition will produce at an output below their minimum-cost point.

Exchange equalisation account The gold and foreign exchange reserves account in the Bank of England.

Exchange rate The rate at which one national currency exchanges for another. The rate is expressed as the amount of one currency that is necessary to purchase *one unit* of another currency (e.g. $1.60 = £1).

Exchange rate band Where a currency is allowed to float between an upper and lower exchange rate, but is not allowed to move outside this band.

Exchange rate index A weighted average exchange rate expressed as an index where the value of the index is 100 in a given base year. The weights of the different currencies in the index add up to 1.

Exchange rate mechanism See ERM.

Exchange rate overshooting Where a fall (or rise) in the long-run equilibrium exchange rate causes the actual exchange rate to fall (or rise) by a greater amount before eventually moving back to the new long-run equilibrium level.

Exchange rate: real A country's exchange rate adjusted for changes in the domestic currency prices of its exports relative to the foreign currency prices of its imports. If a country's prices rise (fall) relative to those of its trading partners, its real exchange rate will rise (fall) relative to the nominal exchange rate.

Exchange rate regime The system under which the government allows the exchange rate to be determined.

Exchange rate transmission mechanism How a change in money supply affects aggregate demand via a change in exchange rates.

Exogenous money supply Money supply that does not depend on the demand for money but is set by the authorities.

Exogenous variable A variable whose value is determined independently of the model of which it is part.

Expansion path The line on an isoquant map that traces the minimum-cost combinations of two factors as output increases. It is drawn on the assumption that both factors can be varied. It is thus a long-run path.

Expansionary (or reflationary) policy Fiscal or monetary policy designed to increase the rate of growth of aggregate demand.

Expectations-augmented Phillips curve A (short-run) Phillips curve whose position depends on the expected rate of inflation.

Expected value The value of a possible outcome multiplied by the probability of its occurrence.

Expenditure changing (increasing) from depreciation: the income effect Where depreciation, via the substitution effect, will alter the demand for imports and exports, and this will, via the multiplier, affect the level of national income and hence the demand for imports.

Expenditure changing (reducing) from a contraction: the income effect Where contractionary policies lead to a reduction in national income and hence a reduction in the demand for imports.

Expenditure changing (reducing) from deflation: the income effect Where deflationary policies lead to a reduction in national income and hence a reduction in the demand for imports.

Expenditure switching from a contraction: the substitution effect Where contractionary policies lead to a reduction in inflation and thus cause a switch in expenditure away from imports and towards exports.

Expenditure switching from deflation: the substitution effect Where deflationary policies lead to a reduction in inflation and thus cause a switch in expenditure away from imports and also towards exports.

Expenditure switching from depreciation: the substitution effect Where a lower exchange rate reduces the price of exports and increases the price of imports. This will increase the sale of exports and reduce the sale of imports.

Explicit costs The payments to outside suppliers of inputs.

External balance (in the economy) Narrow definition: where the current account of the balance of payments is in balance (and thus also the capital plus financial accounts). Loose definition: where there is a total currency flow balance at a given exchange rate.

External benefits Benefits from production (or consumption) experienced by people *other* than the producer (or consumer).

External costs Costs of production (or consumption) borne by people *other* than the producer (or consumer).

External diseconomies of scale Where a firm's costs per unit of output increase as the size of the whole *industry* increases.

External economies of scale Where a firm's costs per unit of output decrease as the size of the whole *industry* grows.

External policy objectives Objectives relating to the economy's international economic relationships.

Externalities Costs or benefits of production or consumption experienced by society but not by the producers or consumers themselves. Sometimes referred to as 'spill-over' or 'third-party' costs or benefits.

Factor price equalisation The tendency for international trade to reduce factor price inequalities both between and within countries.

Factors of production (or resources) The inputs into the production of goods and services: labour, land and raw materials, and capital.

Fallacy of composition What applies to the individual does not necessarily apply to the whole.

Final expenditure Expenditure on goods and services. This is included in GDP and is part of aggregate demand.

Financial accelerator When a change in national income is amplified by changes in the money market, such as a changes in interest rate differentials or changes in the willingness of banks to lend.

Financial account of the balance of payments The record of the flows of money into and out of the country for the purposes of investment or as deposits in banks and other financial institutions.

Financial crowding out When an increase in government borrowing diverts money away from the private sector.

Financial deregulation The removal of or reduction in legal rules and regulations governing the activities of financial institutions.

Financial flexibility Where employers can vary their wage costs by changing the composition of their workforce or the terms on which workers are employed.

Financial instability hypothesis During periods of economic growth, economic agents (firms and individuals) tend to borrow more and monetary financial institutions (MFIs) are more willing to lend. This fuels the boom. In a period of recession, economic agents tend to cut spending in order to reduce debts and MFIs are less willing to lend. This deepens the recession. Behaviour in financial markets thus tends to amplify the business cycle.

Financial instruments Financial products resulting in a financial claim by one party over another.

Financial intermediaries The general name for financial institutions (banks, building societies, etc.) which act as a means of channelling funds from depositors to borrowers.

Fine-tuning The use of demand-management policy (fiscal or monetary) to smooth out cyclical fluctuations in the economy.

First-best solution The solution of correcting a specific market distortion by ensuring that the whole economy operates under conditions of social efficiency (Pareto optimality).

First-degree price discrimination Where a firm charges each consumer for each unit the maximum price which that consumer is willing to pay for that unit.

First-mover advantage When a firm gains from being the first one to take action.

Fiscal drag The tendency of automatic fiscal stabilisers to reduce the recovery of an economy from recession.

Fiscal policy Policy to affect aggregate demand by altering the balance between government expenditure and taxation.

Fiscal stance How deflationary or reflationary the Budget is.

Fixed costs Total costs that do not vary with the amount of output produced.

Fixed exchange rate (totally) Where the government takes whatever measures are necessary to maintain the exchange rate at some stated level.

Fixed factor An input that cannot be increased in supply within a given time period.

Flat organisation Where the senior management communicate directly with those lower in the organisational structure, bypassing middle management.

Flexible firm A firm that has the flexibility to respond to changing market conditions by changing the composition of its workforce.

Floating exchange rate When the government does not intervene in the foreign exchange markets, but simply allows the exchange rate to be freely determined by demand and supply.

Flow An amount of something occurring over a *period of time*: e.g. production per week, income per year, demand per week. (Contrasts with *stock*.)

Flow-of-funds equation The various items making up an increase (or decrease) in money supply.

Forward exchange market Where contracts are made today for the price at which currency will be exchanged at some specified future date.

Franchise A formal agreement whereby a company uses another company to produce or sell some or all of its product.

Franchising Where a firm is given the licence to operate a given part of an industry for a specified length of time.

Freely floating exchange rate Where the exchange rate is determined entirely by the forces of demand and supply in the foreign exchange market with no government intervention whatsoever.

Free-market economy An economy where all economic decisions are taken by individual households and firms and with no government intervention.

Free-rider problem When it is not possible to exclude other people from consuming a good that someone has bought.

Free-trade area A group of countries with no trade barriers between themselves.

Frictional (search) unemployment Unemployment which occurs as a result of imperfect information in the labour market. It often takes time for workers to find jobs (even though there are vacancies) and in the meantime they are unemployed.

Full-employment level of national income The level of national income at which there is no deficiency of demand.

Functional distribution of income Measurement of the distribution of income according to the source of income (e.g. from employment, from profit, from rent, etc.).

Functional flexibility Where employers can switch workers from job to job as requirements change.

Functional relationships The mathematical relationship showing how one variable is affected by one or more others.

Funding (in monetary policy) Where the authorities alter the balance of bills and bonds for any given level of government borrowing.

Future price A price agreed today at which an item (e.g. commodities) will be exchanged at some set date in the future.

Futures or forward market A market in which contracts are made to buy or sell at some future date at a price agreed today.

Gaia philosophy The respect for the rights of the environment to remain unharmed by human activity. Humans should live in harmony with the planet and other species. We have a duty to be stewards of the natural environment, so that it can continue to be a self-maintaining and self-regulating system.

Game theory (or the theory of games) A mathematical method of decision making in which alternative strategies are analysed to determine the optimal course of action for the interested party, depending on assumptions about rivals' behaviour. Widely used in economics, game theory is also used as a tool in biology, psychology and politics.

GDP (gross domestic product at market prices) The value of output (or income or expenditure) in terms of the prices actually paid. GDP = GVA + taxes on products – subsidies on products.

GDP deflator The price index of all final domestically produced goods and services: i.e. all those items that contribute towards GDP.

Gearing or **Leverage (US term)** The ratio of debt capital to equity capital: in other words, the ratio of borrowed capital (e.g. bonds) to shares.

General equilibrium A situation where all the millions of markets throughout the economy are in a simultaneous state of equilibrium.

General equilibrium diagrams (in trade theory) Indifference curve/production possibility curve diagrams that show a country's production and consumption of both imports and exports.

General government debt The combined accumulated debt of central and local government.

General government deficit (or surplus) The combined deficit (or surplus) of central and local government.

Geographical immobility The lack of ability or willingness of people to move to jobs in other parts of the country.

Giffen good An inferior good whose demand increases as its price increases as a result of a positive income effect larger than the normal negative substitution effect.

Gini coefficient The area between the Lorenz curve and the 45° line divided by the total area under the 45° line.

Global systemically important banks (G-SIBs) Banks identified by a series of indicators as being significant players in the global financial system.

GNY (gross national income) GDP plus net income from abroad.

Gold standard The system whereby countries' exchange rates were fixed in terms of a certain amount of gold and whereby balance of payments deficits were paid in gold.

Golden-rule saving rate The rate of saving that maximises the level of long-run consumption.

Goodhart's law Controlling a symptom of a problem or only one part of the problem will not *cure* the problem: it will simply mean that the part that is being controlled now becomes a poor indicator of the problem.

Government bonds or 'gilt-edged securities' A government security paying a fixed sum of money each year. It is redeemed by the government on its maturity date at its face value.

Government surplus (from a tax on a good) The total tax revenue earned by the government from sales of a good.

Grandfathering Where each firm's emission permit is based on its *current* levels of emission (e.g. permitted levels for all firms could be 80 per cent of their current levels).

Green tax A tax on output designed to charge for the adverse effects of production on the environment. The socially efficient level of a green tax is equal to the marginal environmental cost of production.

Gross domestic product (GDP) The value of output produced within the country over a 12-month period.

Gross national income (GNY) GDP plus net income from abroad.

Gross value added at basic prices (GVA) The sum of all the values added by all industries in the economy over a year. The figures exclude taxes on products (such as VAT) and include subsidies on products.

Growth maximisation An alternative theory that assumes that managers seek to maximise the growth in sales revenue (or the capital value of the firm) over time.

Heckscher–Ohlin version of comparative advantage A country has a comparative advantage in those goods that are intensive in the country's relatively abundant factor.

Heterodox economists Economists who reject the assumptions of neoclassical economics, in particular the assumptions of rational optimising behaviour. They highlight the importance of institutional behaviour and factors influencing human behaviour.

Heuristics The use of strategies that draw on simple lessons from past experience when faced with similar, although not identical, choices.

H-form organisation (holding company) Where the parent company holds interests in a number of subsidiary companies.

Historic costs The original amount the firm paid for factors it now owns.

Hit-and-run competition When a firm enters an industry to take advantage of temporarily high profits and then leaves again as soon as the high profits have been exhausted.

Horizontal equity The equal treatment of people in the same situation.

Horizontal merger When two firms in the same industry at the same stage in the production process merge.

Households' disposable income The income available for households to spend: i.e. personal incomes after deducting taxes on incomes and adding benefits.

Human capital The qualifications, skills and expertise that contribute to a worker's productivity.

Human Development Index (HDI) A composite index made up of three elements: an index for life expectancy, an index for school enrolment and adult literacy, and an index for GDP per capita (in PPP$).

Hysteresis The persistence of an effect even when the initial cause has ceased to operate. In economics, it refers to the persistence of unemployment even when the demand deficiency that caused it no longer exists.

Identification problem The problem of identifying the relationship between two variables (e.g. price and quantity demanded) from the evidence when it is not known whether or how the variables have been affected by *other* determinants. For example, it is difficult to identify the shape of a demand curve simply by observing price and quantity when it is not known whether changes in other determinants have *shifted* the demand curve.

Idle balances Money held for speculative purposes: money held in anticipation of a fall in asset prices.

Imperfect competition The collective name for monopolistic competition and oligopoly.

Implicit costs Costs which do not involve a direct payment of money to a third party, but which nevertheless involve a sacrifice of some alternative.

Import-substituting industrialisation (ISI) A strategy of restricting imports of manufactured goods and using the foreign exchange saved to build up domestic substitute industries.

Incidence of tax The distribution of the burden of tax between sellers and buyers.

Income and expenditure account or profit and loss account A record of the flows of incomes, expenditure and saving of an individual or institution.

Income effect (of a price change) The effect of a change in price on quantity demanded arising from the consumer becoming better or worse off as a result of the price change.

Income effect of a rise in wage rates Workers get a higher income for a given number of hours worked and may thus feel they need to work *fewer* hours as wage rates rise.

Income effect of a tax rise Tax increases reduce people's incomes and thus encourage people to work more.

Income elasticity of demand The percentage (or proportionate) change in quantity demanded divided by the percentage (or proportionate) change in income.

Income elasticity of demand (arc formula) ΔQ_D/average $Q_D \div \Delta Y$/average Y.

Income–consumption curve A line showing how a person's optimum level of consumption of two goods changes as income changes (assuming the price of the goods remains constant).

Increasing opportunity costs of production When additional production of one good involves ever-increasing sacrifices of another.

Independence (of firms in a market) Where the decisions of one firm in a market will not have any significant effect on the demand curves of its rivals.

Independent risks Where two risky events are unconnected. The occurrence of one will not affect the likelihood of the occurrence of the other.

Index number The value of a variable expressed as 100 plus or minus its percentage deviation from a base year.

Indifference curve A line showing all those combintions of two goods between which a consumer is indifferent: i.e. those combinations that give the same level of utility.

Indifference map A graph showing a whole set of indifference curves. The further away a particular curve is from the origin, the higher the level of satisfaction it represents.

Indifference set A table showing the same information as an indifference curve.

Indirect monetary transmission mechanism A change in money supply affecting aggregate demand indirectly via some other variable.

Indirect taxes Taxes on expenditure (e.g. VAT). They are paid to the tax authorities, not by the consumer, but indirectly by the suppliers of the goods or services.

Indivisibilities The impossibility of dividing a factor into smaller units.

Induced investment Investment firms make to enable them to meet extra consumer demand.

Induction Constructing general theories on the basis of specific observations.

Industrial policies Policies to encourage industrial investment and greater industrial efficiency.

Industry's infrastructure The network of supply agents, communications, skills, training facilities, distribution channels, specialised financial services, etc., that supports a particular industry.

Inelastic demand (with respect to price) Where quantity demanded changes by a smaller percentage than price. Ignoring the negative sign, it will have a value less than 1.

Infant industry An industry that has a potential comparative advantage, but which is as yet too underdeveloped to be able to realise this potential.

Inferior goods Goods whose demand *decreases* as consumer incomes increase. Such goods have a negative income elasticity of demand.

Inflation bias Excessive inflation that results from people raising their expectations of the inflation rate following expansionary demand-management policy, encouraging government to loosen policy even further.

Inflation rate The percentage increase in prices over a 12-month period.

Inflationary gap The excess of national expenditure over income (and injections over withdrawals) at the full-employment level of national income.

Informal sector The parts of the economy that involve production and/or exchange, but where there are no money payments.

Infrastructure (industry's) The network of supply agents, communications, skills, training facilities, distribution channels, specialised financial services, etc., that supports a particular industry.

Injections (J) Expenditure on the production of domestic firms coming from outside the inner flow of the circular flow of income. Injections equal investment (I) plus government expenditure (G) plus expenditure on exports (X).

(Injections) multiplier The number of times by which a rise in income exceeds the rise in injections that caused it: $k = \Delta Y/\Delta J$.

(Injections) multiplier formula The formula for the multiplier: $k = 1/mpw$ or $1/(1 - mpc_d)$.

Input–output analysis This involves dividing the economy into sectors where each sector is a user of inputs from and a supplier of outputs to other sectors. The technique examines how these inputs and outputs can be matched to the total resources available in the economy.

Insiders Those in employment who can use their privileged position (either as members of unions or because of specific skills) to secure pay rises despite an excess supply of labour (unemployment).

Interdependence (under oligopoly) One of the two key features of oligopoly. Each firm will be affected by its rivals' decisions. Likewise its decisions will affect its rivals. Firms recognise this interdependence. This recognition will affect their decisions.

Interest rate transmission mechanism How a change in money supply affects aggregate demand via a change in interest rates.

Intermediate exchange rate regimes Where the government intervenes to influence movements in the exchange rate.

Internal balance (of an economy) Where the equilibrium level of national income is at the desired level.

Internal policy objectives (national) Objectives relating solely to the domestic economy.

Internal rate of return The rate of return of an investment: the discount rate that makes the net present value of an investment equal to zero.

International harmonisation of economic policies Where countries attempt to co-ordinate their macroeconomic policies so as to achieve common goals.

International liquidity The supply of currencies in the world acceptable for financing international trade and investment.

International substitution effect As prices rise, people at home and abroad buy less of this country's products and more of products from abroad.

International trade multiplier The effect on national income in country B of a change in exports (or imports) of country A.

Inter-temporal substitution effect Higher prices may lead to higher interest rates and thus less borrowing and more saving. Current consumption falls; future consumption (from the higher savings) rises.

Intervention price (in the CAP) The price at which the EU is prepared to buy a foodstuff if the market price were to be below it.

Interventionist supply-side policies Policies to increase aggregate supply by government intervention to counteract the deficiencies of the market.

Investment The production of items that are not for immediate consumption. This can include investment in plant and equipment: such investment builds the stock of firms' capital and yields a flow of future output. Investment also includes adding to stocks of goods or resources which are not sold or used in the current period, but will be in the future.

IS/LM model A model showing simultaneous equilibrium in the goods market ($I = S$) and the money market ($L = M$).

IS/MP model A model showing simultaneous equilibrium in the goods market ($I = S$) and the money market, where the central bank sets interest rates according to a monetary policy rule (MP).

Isocost A line showing all the combinations of two factors that cost the same to employ.

Isoquant A line showing all the alternative combinations of two factors that can produce a given level of output.

J-curve effect Where a devaluation causes the balance of trade first to deteriorate and then to improve. The graph of the balance of trade over time thus looks like a letter J.

Joint float Where a group of currencies pegged to each other jointly float against other currencies.

Joint supply Where the production of more of one good leads to the production of more of another.

Joint venture Where two or more firms set up and jointly own a new independent firm.

Just-in-time methods Where a firm purchases supplies and produces both components and finished products as they are required. This minimises stock holding and its associated costs. It does, however, put pressure on the supply chain and increases the probability that on occasion firms may not be able to meet demand – for example, in times of bad weather.

Kinked demand theory The theory that oligopolists face a demand curve that is kinked at the current price, demand being significantly more elastic above the current price than below. The effect of this is to create a situation of price stability.

Labour All forms of human input, both physical and mental, into current production.

Labour force The number employed plus the number unemployed.

Land (and raw materials) Inputs into production that are provided by nature: e.g. unimproved land and mineral deposits in the ground.

Law of comparative advantage Trade can benefit all countries if they specialise in the goods in which they have a comparative advantage.

Law of demand The quantity of a good demanded per period of time will fall as price rises and will rise as price falls, other things being equal (*ceteris paribus*).

Law of diminishing (marginal) returns When one or more factors are held fixed, there will come a point beyond which the extra output from additional units of the variable factor will diminish.

Law of large numbers The larger the number of events of a particular type, the more predictable will be their average outcome.

Lender of last resort The role of the Bank of England as the guarantor of sufficient liquidity in the monetary system.

Leverage (US term) or **Gearing** The ratio of debt capital to equity capital: in other words, the ratio of borrowed capital (e.g. bonds) to shares.

Liability Claim by others on an individual or institution; debt of that individual or institution.

Liabilities All legal claims for payment that outsiders have on an institution.

Libertarian school A school of thought that advocates maximum liberty for economic agents to pursue their own interests and to own property.

Limit pricing Where a monopolist (or oligopolist) charges a price below the short-run profit maximising level in order to deter new entrants.

Liquidity The ease with which an asset can be converted into cash without loss.

Liquidity preference The demand for holding assets in the form of money.

Liquidity ratio The proportion of a bank's total assets held in liquid form.

Liquidity trap The absorption of any additional money supply into idle balances at very low rates of interest, leaving aggregate demand unchanged.

Lock-outs Union members are temporarily laid off until they are prepared to agree to the firm's conditions.

Long run The period of time long enough for *all* factors to be varied.

Long run under perfect competition The period of time that is long enough for new firms to enter the industry.

Long-run average cost curve A curve that shows how average cost varies with output on the assumption that *all* factors are variable. (It is assumed that the least-cost method of production will be chosen for each output.)

Long-run marginal cost The extra cost of producing one more unit of output assuming that all factors are variable.

(It is assumed that the least-cost method of production will be chosen for this extra output.)

Long-run neutrality of money Changes in money supply over the long run will only affect prices and not real output or employment.

Long-run profit maximisation An alternative theory of the firm which assumes that managers aim to *shift* cost and revenue curves so as to maximise profits over some longer time period.

Long-run shut-down point This is where the *AR* curve is tangential to the *LRAC* curve. The firm can just make normal profits. Any fall in revenue below this level will cause a profit-maximising firm to shut down once all costs have become variable.

Lorenz curve A curve showing the proportion of national income earned by any given percentage of the population (measured from the poorest upwards).

Macro-prudential regulation Regulation which focuses not on a single financial institution but on the financial system as a whole and which monitors its overall stability, its resilience to shocks and its impact on the wider economy.

Macroeconomics The branch of economics that studies economic aggregates (grand totals): e.g. the overall level of prices, output and employment in the economy.

Managed floating (dirty floating) A system of flexible exchange rates but where the government intervenes to prevent excessive fluctuations or even to achieve an unofficial target exchange rate.

Marginal benefit The additional benefit of doing a little bit more (or 1 unit more if a unit can be measured) of an activity.

Marginal capital/output ratio The amount of extra capital (in money terms) required to produce a £1 increase in national output. Since $I_i = \Delta K$, the marginal capital/output ratio $\Delta K/\Delta Y$ equals the accelerator coefficient (α).

Marginal consumer surplus The excess of utility from the consumption of one more unit of a good (MU) over the price paid: $MCS = MU - P$.

Marginal cost (of an activity) The additional cost of doing a little bit more (or 1 unit more if a unit can be measured) of an activity.

Marginal cost (of production) The cost of producing one more unit of output: $MC = \Delta TC/\Delta Q$.

Marginal disutility of work The extra sacrifice/hardship to a worker of working an extra unit of time in any given time period (e.g. an extra hour per day).

Marginal efficiency of capital or **internal rate of return** The rate of return of an investment: the discount rate that makes the net present value of an investment equal to zero.

Marginal physical product The extra output gained by the employment of one more unit of the variable factor: $MPP = \Delta TPP/\Delta Q_v$.

Marginal productivity theory The theory that the demand for a factor depends on its marginal revenue product.

Marginal propensity to consume The proportion of a rise in national income that goes on consumption: $mpc = \Delta C/\Delta Y$.

Marginal propensity to import The proportion of an increase in national income that is spent on imports: $mpm = \Delta M/\Delta Y$.

Marginal propensity to save The proportion of an increase in national income saved: $mps = \Delta S/\Delta Y$.

Marginal propensity to withdraw The proportion of an increase in national income that is withdrawn from the circular flow: $mpw = \Delta W/\Delta Y$, where $mpw = mps + mpt + mpm$.

Marginal rate of factor substitution The rate at which one factor can be substituted by another while holding the level of output constant: $MRS = \Delta F_1/\Delta F_2 = MPP_{F_2}/MPP_{F_1}$.

Marginal rate of income tax The income tax rate. The rate paid on each *additional* pound earned: $\Delta T/\Delta Y$.

Marginal rate of substitution (between two goods in consumption) The amount of one good (Y) that a consumer is prepared to give up in order to obtain one extra unit of another good (X): i.e. $\Delta Y/\Delta X$.

Marginal revenue The extra revenue gained by selling one more unit per time period: $MR = \Delta TR/\Delta Q$.

Marginal revenue product (of a factor) The extra revenue a firm earns from employing one more unit of a variable factor: $MRP_{factor} = MPP_{factor} \times MR_{good}$.

Marginal tax propensity The proportion of an increase in national income paid in tax: $mpt = \Delta T/\Delta Y$.

Marginal utility The extra satisfaction gained from consuming one extra unit of a good within a given time period.

Market The interaction between buyers and sellers.

Market clearing A market clears when supply matches demand, leaving no shortage or surplus.

Market for loanable funds The market for loans from and deposits into the banking system.

Market loans Short-term loans (e.g. money at call and short notice).

Market-orientated supply-side policies Policies to increase aggregate supply by freeing up the market.

Mark-up A profit margin added to average cost to arrive at price.

Marshall–Lerner condition Depreciation will improve the balance of payments only if the sum of the price elasticities of demand for imports and exports is greater than 1.

Maturity gap The difference in the average maturity of loans and deposits.

Maturity transformation The transformation of deposits into loans of a longer maturity.

Maximum price A price ceiling set by the government or some other agency. The price is not allowed to rise above this level (although it is allowed to fall below it).

Mean (or arithmetic mean) The sum of the values of each of the members of the sample divided by the total number in the sample.

Means-tested benefits Benefits whose amount depends on the recipient's income or assets.

Median The value of the middle member of the sample.

Medium of exchange Something that is acceptable in exchange for goods and services.

Medium-term financial strategy (MTFS) The policy of the Conservative government in the UK during the 1980s of setting targets for the PSBR and the growth of money supply for the following four years.

Menu costs of inflation The costs associated with having to adjust price lists or labels.

Merit goods Goods which the government feels that people will underconsume and which therefore ought to be subsidised or provided free.

M-form (multi-divisional form) of corporate organisation Where the firm is split into a number of separate divisions (e.g. different products or countries), with each division then split into a number of departments.

Microeconomics The branch of economics that studies individual units: e.g. households, firms and industries. It studies the interrelationships between these units in determining the pattern of production and distribution of goods and services.

Minimum price A price floor set by the government or some other agency. The price is not allowed to fall below this level (although it is allowed to rise above it).

Minimum reserve ratio A minimum ratio of cash (or other specified liquid assets) to deposits (either total or selected) that the central bank requires banks to hold.

Mixed command economy A planned economy that nevertheless makes some use of markets.

Mixed economy An economy where economic decisions are made partly by the government and partly through the market. In practice all economies are mixed.

Mixed market economy A market economy where there is some government intervention.

Mobility of labour The willingness and ability of labour to move to another job.

Monetarists Those who attribute inflation solely to rises in money supply.

Monetary base Notes and coin outside the central bank.

Monetary base control Monetary policy that focuses on controlling the monetary base (as opposed to broad liquidity).

Monetary financial institutions (MFIs) Deposit-taking institutions including banks, building societies and the Bank of England.

Monetary policy Policy to affect aggregate demand by altering the supply or cost of money (rate of interest).

Money illusion When people believe that a money wage or price increase represents a *real* increase: in other words, they ignore or underestimate inflation.

Money market The market for short-term debt instruments, such as government bills (Treasury bills), in which financial institutions are active participants.

Money multiplier The number of times greater the expansion of money supply is than the expansion of the monetary base that caused it: $\Delta M_s/\Delta M_b$.

Monopolistic competition A market structure where, like perfect competition, there are many firms and freedom of entry into the industry, but where each firm produces a differentiated product and thus has some control over its price.

Monopoly A market structure where there is only one firm in the industry.

Monopsony A market with a single buyer or employer.

Moral hazard The temptation to take more risks when you know that someone else will cover the risks if you get into difficulties. In the case of banks taking risks, the 'someone else' may be another bank, the central bank or the government.

Multiplier (injections multiplier) The number of times a rise in income exceeds the rise in injections that caused it: $k = \Delta Y/\Delta J$.

Multiplier effect An initial increase in aggregate demand of £x million leads to an eventual rise in national income that is greater than £x million.

Multiplier formula (injections multiplier) The formula for the multiplier is $k = 1/mpw$ or $1/(1 - mpc_d)$.

Mutual recognition The EU principle that one country's rules and regulations must apply throughout the EU. If they conflict with those of another country, individuals and firms should be able to choose which to obey.

Nash equilibrium The position resulting from everyone making their optimal decision based on their assumptions about their rivals' decisions. Without collusion, there is no incentive for any firm to move from this position.

National debt The accumulated budget deficits (less surpluses) over the years: the total amount of government borrowing.

National expenditure on domestic product (E) Aggregate demand in the Keynesian model: i.e. $C_d + J$.

Nationalised industries State-owned industries that produce goods or services that are sold in the market.

Natural level of output The level of output in monetarist analysis where the vertical long-run aggregate supply curve cuts the horizontal axis.

Natural level of unemployment The level of equilibrium unemployment in monetarist and new classical analysis measured as the difference between the (vertical) long-run gross labour supply curve (N) and the (vertical) long-run effective labour supply curve (AS_L).

Natural monopoly A situation where long-run average costs would be lower if an industry were under monopoly than if it were shared between two or more competitors.

Natural rate of unemployment or non-accelerating-inflation rate of unemployment (NAIRU) The rate of unemployment at which there is no excess or deficiency of demand for labour. The rate of unemployment consistent, therefore, with a constant rate of inflation: the rate of unemployment at which the vertical long-run Phillips curve cuts the horizontal axis.

Natural wastage When a firm wishing to reduce its workforce does so by not replacing those who leave or retire.

Near money Highly liquid assets (other than cash).

Negative income tax A combined system of tax and benefits. As people earn more they gradually lose their benefits until beyond a certain level they begin paying taxes.

Neo-Austrian/libertarian school A school of thought that advocates maximum liberty for economic agents to pursue their own interests and to own property.

Net investment Total investment minus depreciation.

Net national income (NNY) GNY minus depreciation.

Net present value of an investment The discounted benefits of an investment minus the cost of the investment.

Net worth The market value of a sector's stock of financial and non-financial wealth.

Network (business) An informal arrangement between businesses to work together towards some common goal.

Network economies The benefits to consumers of having a network of other people using the same product or service.

Neutrality of money (long run) Changes in money supply over the long run will only affect prices and not real output or employment.

New classical school The school of economists which believes that markets clear virtually instantaneously and that expectations are formed 'rationally'. Any expansion of demand will feed through virtually instantaneously into higher prices, giving a vertical short-run as well as a vertical long-run Phillips curve.

New Keynesians Economists who seek to explain how market imperfections and frictions can result in fluctuations in real GDP and the persistence of unemployment. They argue that governments may have to expand aggregate demand when demand-deficient unemployment is persistent.

Nominal GDP GDP measured at current prices.

Nominal national income National income measured at current prices.

Nominal values Money values measured at *current* prices.

Non-accelerating-inflation rate of unemployment (NAIRU) The rate of unemployment consistent with a constant rate of inflation. (In monetarist analysis this is the same as the natural rate of unemployment: the rate of unemployment at which the vertical long-run Phillips curve cuts the horizontal axis.)

Non-bank private sector Households and non-bank firms: in other words, everyone in the country other than banks and the government (central and local).

Non-collusive oligopoly Where oligopolists have no agreement between themselves that is formal, informal or tacit.

Non-excludability Where it is not possible to provide a good or service to one person without it thereby being available for others to enjoy.

Non-price competition Competition in terms of product promotion (advertising, packaging, etc.) or product development.

Non-rivalry Where the consumption of a good or service by one person will not prevent others from enjoying it.

Normal goods Goods whose demand increases as consumer incomes increase. They have a positive income elasticity of demand. Luxury goods will have a higher income elasticity of demand than more basic goods.

Normal profit The opportunity cost of being in business: the profit that could have been earned in the next best alternative business. It is counted as a cost of production.

Normal rate of return The rate of return (after taking risks into account) that could be earned elsewhere.

Normative statement A value judgement.

Number unemployed (economist's definition) Those of working age who are without work, but who are available for work at current wage rates.

Numerical flexibility Where employers can change the size of their workforce as their labour requirements change.

Occupational immobility The lack of ability or willingness of people to move to other jobs irrespective of location.

Oligopoly A market structure where there are few enough firms to enable barriers to be erected against the entry of new firms.

Oligopsony A market with just a few buyers or employers.

Open economy One that trades with and has financial dealings with other countries.

Open-market operations The sale (or purchase) by the authorities of government securities in the open market in order to reduce (or increase) money supply or influence interest rates.

Operational standing facilities Central bank facilities by which individual banks can deposit reserves or borrow reserves.

Opportunity cost Cost measured in terms of the best alternative forgone.

Optimal currency area The optimal size of a currency area is the one that maximises the benefits from having a single currency relative to the costs. If the area were increased or decreased in size, the costs would rise relative to the benefits.

Optimum tariff A tariff that reduces the level of imports to the point where the country's marginal social cost equals marginal social benefit.

Organisational slack Where managers allow spare capacity to exist, thereby enabling them to respond more easily to changed circumstances.

Output gap The difference between actual and potential output. When actual output exceeds potential output, the gap is positive. When actual output is less than potential output, the gap is negative.

Outsiders Those out of work or employed on a casual, part-time or short-term basis, who have little or no power to influence wages or employment.

Overheads Costs arising from the general running of an organisation, and only indirectly related to the level of output.

Paradox of debt (or paradox of deleveraging) The paradox that one individual can increase his or her net worth by selling assets, but if this is undertaken by a large number of people aggregate net worth declines because asset prices fall.

Paradox of thrift If society saves more, this may *reduce* its future income and consumption. The reason is that as people save more, they will spend less. Firms will thus produce less. There will thus be a multiplied *fall* in income.

Pareto improvement Where changes in production or consumption can make at least one person better off without making anyone worse off.

Pareto optimality Where all possible Pareto improvements have been made: where, therefore, it is impossible to make anyone better off without making someone else worse off.

Partial derivative The partial derivative of a function of two or more independent variables is the derivative with respect to just one of those variables, while holding the others constant.

Partial differentiation A mathematical technique used with functions containing two or more independent variables. The technique is used to find the rate of change of the dependent variable with respect to a single independent variable assuming that the other independent variables are held constant.

Participation rate The percentage of the working-age population that is part of the workforce.

Partnership A firm owned by two or more people. They each have unlimited liability for the firm's debts.

Peak-load pricing Price discrimination (second or third degree) where a higher price is charged in peak periods and a lower price in off-peak periods.

Perfect competition A market structure where there are many firms, none of which is large; where there is freedom of entry into the industry; where all firms produce an identical product; and where all firms are price takers.

Perfectly contestable market A market where there is free and costless entry and exit.

Phillips curve A curve showing the relationship between (price) inflation and unemployment. The original Phillips curve plotted *wage* inflation against unemployment for the years 1861–1957.

Picketing When people on strike gather at the entrance to the firm and attempt to persuade workers or delivery vehicles from entering.

Plant economies of scale Economies of scale that arise because of the large size of the factory.

Point elasticity The measurement of elasticity at a point on a curve. The formula for price elasticity of demand using the point elasticity method is: $dQ/dP \times P/Q$, where dQ/dP is the inverse of the slope of the tangent to the demand curve at the point in question.

Policy ineffectiveness proposition The conclusion drawn from new classical models that when economic agents anticipate changes in economic policy, output and employment remain at their equilibrium (or natural) levels.

Poll tax A lump-sum tax per head of the population. Since it is a fixed *amount*, it has a marginal rate of zero with respect to both income and wealth.

Polluter pays principle The principle that polluters ought to be charged (e.g. through green taxes) for the external environmental costs that they generate.

Pooling risks (for an insurance company) The more policies an insurance company issues and the more independent the risks of claims from these policies are, the more predictable will be the number of claims.

Portfolio balance The balance of assets, according to their liquidity, that people choose to hold in their portfolios.

Positive statement A value-free statement which can be tested by an appeal to the facts.

Post-Keynesians Economists who stress the importance of institutional and behavioural factors, and the role of business confidence in explaining the state of the economy. They argue that firms are more likely to respond to changes in demand by changing output rather than prices.

Potential growth The percentage annual increase in the capacity of the economy to produce.

Potential output The sustainable level of output that could be produced in the economy: i.e. one that involves a 'normal' level of capacity utilisation and does not result in rising inflation.

Poverty trap (for developing countries) When countries are too poor to save and invest enough to achieve real per capita growth.

Poverty trap (for individuals) Where poor people are discouraged from working or getting a better job because any extra income they earn will be largely taken away in taxes and lost benefits.

Predatory pricing Where a firm sets its prices below average cost in order to drive competitors out of business.

Preferential trading arrangements A trade agreement whereby trade between the signatories is freer than trade with the rest of the world.

Present value approach to appraising investment This involves estimating the value *now* of a flow of future benefits (or costs).

Price benchmark A price which is typically used. Firms, when raising prices, will usually raise it from one benchmark to another.

Price-cap regulation Where the regulator puts a ceiling on the amount by which a firm can raise its price.

Price–consumption curve A line showing how a person's optimum level of consumption of two goods changes as the price of one of the two goods changes (assuming that income and the price of the other good remain constant).

Price discrimination Where a firm sells the same product at different prices.

Price elasticity of demand The responsiveness of quantity demanded to a change in price.

Price elasticity of demand (arc formula) ΔQ/average $Q \div \Delta P$/average P. The average in each case is the average between the two points being measured.

Price elasticity of demand (formula) ($P\epsilon_D$) The percentage (or proportionate) change in quantity demanded divided by the percentage (or proportionate) change in price: $\%\Delta Q_D \div \%\Delta P$.

Price elasticity of supply The responsiveness of quantity supplied to a change in price.

Price elasticity of supply ($P\epsilon_S$) The percentage (or proportionate) change in quantity supplied divided by the percentage (or proportionate) change in price: $\%\Delta Q_S \div \%\Delta P$.

Price elasticity of supply (arc formula) ΔQ_S/average $Q_S \div \Delta P$/average P.

Price mechanism The system in a market economy whereby changes in price in response to changes in demand and supply have the effect of making demand equal to supply.

Price taker A person or firm with no power to be able to influence the market price.

Prices and incomes policy When the government seeks to restrain price and wage increases. This may be in the form of a voluntary agreement with firms and/or unions, or there may be statutory limits imposed.

Primary labour market The market for permanent full-time core workers.

Primary market in capital Where shares are sold by the issuer of the shares (i.e. the firm) and where, therefore, finance is channelled directly from the purchasers (i.e. the shareholders) to the firm.

Principal–agent problem Where people (principals), as a result of lack of knowledge, cannot ensure that their best interests are served by their agents.

Principle of cumulative causation An initial event can cause an ultimate effect that is much larger.

Prisoners' dilemma Where two or more firms (or people), by attempting independently to choose the best strategy for whatever the other(s) are likely to do, end up in a worse position than if they had co-operated in the first place.

Private efficiency Where a person's marginal benefit from a given activity equals the marginal cost.

Private limited company A company owned by its shareholders. Shareholders' liability is limited to the value of their shares. Shares can only be bought and sold privately.

Problem of the second best The difficulty of working out the best way of correcting a specific market distortion if distortions in other parts of the market continue to exist.

Producers' share of a tax on a good The proportion of the revenue from a tax on a good that arises from a reduction in the price to the producer (after the payment of the tax).

Product differentiation   When one firm's product is sufficiently different from its rivals' to allow it to raise the price of the product without customers all switching to the rivals' products. A situation where a firm faces a downward-sloping demand curve.

Production   The transformation of inputs into outputs by firms in order to earn profit (or meet some other objective).

Production function   The mathematical relationship between the output of a good and the inputs used to produce it. It shows how output will be affected by changes in the quantity of one or more of the inputs.

Production possibility curve   A curve showing all the possible combinations of two goods that a country can produce within a specified time period with all its resources fully and efficiently employed.

Productive efficiency   A situation where firms are producing the maximum output for a given amount of inputs, or producing a given output at the least cost. The least-cost combination of factors for a given output.

Productivity deal   When, in return for a wage increase, a union agrees to changes in working practices that will increase output per worker.

Profit (rate of)   Total profit (Π) as a proportion of the total capital employed (K): $r = \Pi/K$.

Profit and loss account or income and expenditure account   A record of the flows of incomes, expenditure and saving of an individual or institution.

Profit satisficing   Where decision makers in a firm aim for a target level of profit rather than the absolute maximum level.

Profit-maximising rule   Profit is maximised where marginal revenue equals marginal cost.

Progressive tax   A tax whose average rate with respect to income rises as income rises.

Proportional tax   A tax whose average rate with respect to income stays the same as income rises.

Prudential control   The insistence by the Bank of England that recognised banks maintain adequate liquidity.

Public good   A good or service that has the features of non-rivalry and non-excludability and as a result would not be provided by the free market.

Public limited company   A company owned by its shareholders. Shareholders' liability is limited to the value of their shares. Shares may be bought and sold publicly – on the Stock Exchange.

Public-sector net borrowing (PSNB)   The difference between the expenditures of the public sector and its receipts from taxation and the revenues from public corporations.

Public-sector net cash requirement (PSNCR)   The (annual) deficit of the public sector, and thus the amount that the public sector must borrow. In the UK the principal measure, which takes into account financial transactions by the public sector, is known as the public-sector net cash requirement.

Public-sector net debt   Gross public-sector debt minus liquid financial assets.

Public-sector surplus or **Public-sector debt repayment (PSDR)**   The (annual) surplus of the public sector, and thus the amount of debt that can be repaid when public-sector income exceeds public-sector expenditures.

Purchasing-power parity (PPP) exchange rate   An exchange rate corrected to take into account the purchasing power of a currency. $1 would buy the same in each country after conversion into its currency at the PPP rate.

Purchasing-power parity theory   The theory that the exchange rate will adjust so as to offset differences in countries' inflation rates, with the result that the same quantity of internationally traded goods can be bought at home as abroad with a given amount of the domestic currency.

Purchasing-power standard (PPS) GDP   GDP measured as a country's PPP exchange rate.

Pure fiscal policy   Fiscal policy which does not involve any change in money supply.

Quantile   Divisions of the population into equal-sized groups.

Quantitative easing   Where the central bank increases the monetary base by a deliberate amount through the open-market purchase of government bonds or other securities from banks. When banks lend the money, broad money expands by a multiple of this through the process of credit creation.

Quantity demanded   The amount of a good a consumer is willing and able to buy at a given price over a given period of time.

Quantity theory of money   The price level (P) is directly related to the quantity of money in the economy (M).

Quasi-rent   Temporary economic rent arising from short-run supply inelasticity.

Quintiles   Divisions of the population into five equal-sized groups (an example of a quantile).

Quota (set by a cartel)   The output that a given member of a cartel is allowed to produce (production quota) or sell (sales quota).

Random walk   Where fluctuations in the value of a share away from its 'correct' value are random: i.e. have no systematic pattern. When charted over time, these share price movements would appear like a 'random walk': like the path of someone staggering along drunk!

Rate of discount   The rate that is used to reduce future values to present values.

Rate of economic growth   The percentage increase in output over a 12-month period.

Rate of inflation   The percentage increase in the level of prices over a 12-month period.

Rate of profit   Total profit (Π) as a proportion of the capital employed (K): $r = \Pi/K$.

Rational choices   Choices that involve weighing up the benefit of any activity against its opportunity cost.

Rational consumer A person who weighs up the costs and benefits to him or her of each additional unit of a good purchased.

Rational consumer behaviour The attempt to maximise total consumer surplus.

Rational decision making Doing more of an activity if its marginal benefit exceeds its marginal cost and doing less if its marginal cost exceeds its marginal benefit.

Rational economic behaviour Doing more of activities whose marginal benefit exceeds their marginal cost and doing less of those activities whose marginal cost exceeds their marginal benefit.

Rational expectations Expectations based on the *current* situation. These expectations are based on the information people have to hand. Whilst this information may be imperfect and therefore people will make errors, these errors will be random.

Rational producer behaviour When a firm weighs up the costs and benefits of alternative courses of action and then seeks to maximise its net benefit.

Rationalisation The reorganising of production (often after a merger) so as to cut out waste and duplication and generally to reduce costs.

Rationing Where the government restricts the amount of a good that people are allowed to buy.

Reaction function (or curve) This shows how a firm's optimal output varies according to the output chosen by its rival (or rivals).

Real balance effect As the price level rises, so the value of people's money balances will fall. They will therefore *spend* less in order to increase their money balances and go some way to protecting their real value.

Real business cycle theory The new classical theory which explains cyclical fluctuations in terms of shifts in aggregate supply, rather than aggregate demand.

Real exchange rate A country's exchange rate adjusted for changes in the domestic currency prices of its exports relative to the foreign currency prices of its imports. If a country's prices rise (fall) relative to those of its trading partners, its real exchange rate will rise (fall) relative to the nominal exchange rate.

Real GDP GDP after allowing for inflation – GDP measured in constant prices: i.e. in terms of the prices ruling in some base year.

Real income Income measured in terms of how much it can buy. If your *money* income rises by 10 per cent, but prices rise by 8 per cent, you can only buy 2 per cent more goods than before. Your *real* income has risen by 2 per cent.

Real national income National income after allowing for inflation: i.e. national income measured in constant prices: i.e. in terms of the prices ruling in some base year.

Real values Money values corrected for inflation.

Real wage unemployment Disequilibrium unemployment caused by real wages being driven up above the market-clearing level.

Recession A period where national output falls for six months or more.

Recessionary (or deflationary) gap The shortfall of national expenditure below national income (and injections below withdrawals) at the full-employment level of national income.

Recognised banks Banks licensed by the Bank of England. All financial institutions using the word 'bank' in their title have to be recognised by the Bank of England. This requires them to have paid-up capital of at least £5 million and to meet other requirements about their asset structure and range of services.

Rediscounting bills of exchange Buying bills before they reach maturity.

Reflationary policy Fiscal or monetary policy designed to increase the rate of growth of aggregate demand.

Regional Development Agencies (RDAs) Nine agencies, based in English regions, which initiate and administer regional policy within their area.

Regional multiplier effects When a change in injections into or withdrawals from a particular region causes a multiplied change in income in that region. The regional multiplier (k_r) is given by $1/mpw_r$, where the import component of *mpw* consists of imports into that region either from abroad or from other regions of the economy.

Regional unemployment Structural unemployment occurring in specific regions of the country.

Regression analysis A statistical technique which allows a functional relationship between two or more variables to be estimated.

Regressive tax A tax whose average rate with respect to income falls as income rises.

Regulatory capture Where the regulator is persuaded to operate in the industry's interests rather than those of the consumer.

Relative price The price of one good compared with another (e.g. good X is twice the price of good Y).

Replacement costs What the firm would have to pay to replace factors it currently owns.

Resale (or retail) price maintenance Where the manufacturer of a product (legally) insists that the product should be sold at a specified retail price.

Reserve averaging The process whereby individual banks manage their average level of overnight reserves between MPC meetings using the Bank of England's operational standing facilities and/or the interbank market.

Restrictive practice Where two or more firms agree to adopt common practices to restrict competition.

Retail banks 'High street banks'. Banks operating extensive branch networks and dealing directly with the general public, with published interest rates and charges.

Retail banking Branch, telephone, postal and Internet banking for individuals and businesses at published rates of interest and charges. Retail banking involves the operation of extensive branch networks.

Retail deposits and loans   Deposits and loans made through bank/building society branches at published interest rates.

Retail price index (RPI)   An index of the prices of goods bought by a typical household.

Revaluation   Where the government re-pegs the exchange rate at a higher level.

Reverse repos   When gilts or other assets are *purchased* under a sale and repurchase agreement. They become an asset to the purchaser.

Risk   When a (desirable) outcome of an action may or may not occur, but the probability of its occurring is known. The lower the probability, the greater the risk involved in taking the action.

Risk averse   Where a person is not prepared to take a gamble even if the odds of gaining are favourable.

Risk loving   Where a person is willing to take a gamble even if the odds of gaining are unfavourable.

Risk neutral   Where a person is willing to take a gamble if the odds are favourable and is unwilling if the odds are unfavourable.

Risk transformation   The process whereby banks can spread the risks of lending by having a large number of borrowers.

Sale and repurchase agreement (repos)   An agreement between two financial institutions whereby one in effect borrows from another by selling it assets, agreeing to buy them back (repurchase them) at a fixed price and on a fixed date.

Sales revenue maximisation   An alternative theory of the firm based on the assumption that managers aim to maximise the firm's short-run total revenue.

Say's law   Supply creates its own demand. In other words, the production of goods will generate sufficient demand to ensure that they are sold.

Scarcity   The excess of human wants over what can actually be produced to fulfil these wants.

Search theory   This examines people's behaviour under conditions of ignorance where it takes time to search for information.

Seasonal unemployment   Unemployment associated with industries or regions where the demand for labour is lower at certain times of the year.

Second best (problem of)   The difficulty of working out the best way of correcting a specific market distortion if distortions in other parts of the market continue to exist.

Second-best solution   The solution to a specific market distortion that recognises distortions elsewhere and seeks to minimise the overall distortionary effects to the economy of tackling this specific distortion.

Second-degree price discrimination   Where a firm charges a consumer so much for the first so many units purchased, a different price for the next so many units purchased, and so on.

Second derivative   The rate of change of the first derivative: found by differentiating the first derivative.

Second-derivative test   If on differentiating an equation a second time the answer is negative (positive), the point is a maximum (minimum).

Secondary action   Industrial action taken against a company not directly involved in a dispute (e.g. a supplier of raw materials to a firm whose employees are on strike).

Secondary labour market   The market for peripheral workers, usually employed on a temporary or part-time basis, or a less secure 'permanent' basis.

Secondary market in capital   Where shareholders sell shares to others. This is thus a market in 'second-hand' shares.

Secondary marketing   Where assets are sold before maturity to another institution or individual. The possibility of secondary marketing encourages people or institutions to buy assets/grant loans in the primary market, knowing that they can sell them if necessary in the secondary market. The sale of existing shares and bonds on the stock market is an example of secondary marketing.

Securitisation   Where future cash flows (e.g. from interest rate or mortgage payments) are turned into marketable securities, such as bonds. The sellers (e.g. banks) get cash now rather than having to wait and can use it to fund loans to customers. The buyers make a profit by buying below the discounted value of the future income. Such bonds can be very risky, however, as the future cash flows may be less than anticipated.

Self-fulfilling speculation   The actions of speculators tend to cause the very effect that they had anticipated.

Semi-strong efficiency (of share markets)   Where share prices adjust quickly, fully and accurately to publicly available information.

Sensitivity analysis   Where a range of possible values of uncertain costs and benefits are given to see whether the project's desirability is sensitive to these different values.

Set-aside   A system in the EU of paying farmers not to use a certain proportion of their land.

Shares (equities)   A part ownership of a company. Companies' distributed profits are paid to shareholders in the form of dividends according to the number of shares held.

Short run (in production)   The period of time over which at least one factor is fixed.

Short run under perfect competition   The period during which there is insufficient time for new firms to enter the industry.

Short-run shut-down point   This is where the *AR* curve is tangential to the *AVC* curve. The firm can only just cover its variable costs. Any fall in revenue below this level will cause a profit-maximising firm to shut down immediately.

Short selling (or shorting)   The practice of borrowing an asset (for a fee) and selling it, hoping that the price will fall so that it can then be purchased and returned to the lender. The difference between the sale and purchase price (minus the fee) is thus profit to the short seller.

Short-termism Where firms and investors take decisions based on the likely short-term performance of a company, rather than on its long-term prospects. Firms may thus sacrifice long-term profits and growth for the sake of a quick return.

Sight deposits Deposits that can be withdrawn on demand without penalty.

Size distribution of income Measurement of the distribution of income according to the levels of income received by individuals (irrespective of source).

Social benefit Private benefit plus externalities in consumption.

Social cost Private cost plus externalities in production.

Social efficiency A situation of Pareto optimality: where all possible Pareto improvements have been made: where, therefore, it is impossible to make anyone better off without making someone else worse off.

Social efficiency (improvement in) A Pareto improvement: where changes in production or consumption can make at least one person better off without making anyone worse off.

Social rate of discount A rate of discount that reflects *society's* preferences for present benefits over future ones.

Social-impact standards Pollution control that focuses on the effects on people (e.g. on health or happiness).

Sole proprietorship A firm owned by one person. That person has unlimited liability.

Sovereign debt crisis The financial and economic problems caused by excessive public-sector debt and by the fear that governments will be unable to raise sufficient finance to repay maturing debt.

Special drawing rights (SDRs) Additional liquidity created by the IMF. SDRs give countries the right to borrow a certain amount of additional funds from the IMF, with no requirement for extra deposits (quotas).

Special purpose vehicle (SPV) Legal entities created by financial institutions for conducting specific financial functions, such as bundling assets together into fixed-interest bonds and selling them.

Specialisation and division of labour Where production is broken down into a number of simpler, more specialised tasks, thus allowing workers to acquire a high degree of efficiency.

Specific tax A tax on a good levied at a fixed amount per unit of the good, irrespective of the price of that unit.

Speculation Where people make buying or selling decisions based on their anticipations of future prices.

Speculators People who buy (or sell) commodities or financial assets with the intention of profiting by selling them (or buying them back) at a later date at a higher (lower) price.

Spot price The current market price.

Spreading risks (for an insurance company) The more policies an insurance company issues and the more independent the risks of claims from these policies are, the more predictable will be the number of claims.

Stabilising speculation Where the actions of speculators tend to reduce the magnitude of price fluctuations.

Stagflation A term used to refer to the combination of stagnation (low growth and high unemployment) and high inflation.

Stakeholders (in a company) People who are affected by a company's activities and/or performance (customers, employees, owners, creditors, people living in the neighbourhood, etc.). They may or may not be in a position to take decisions, or influence decision taking, in the firm.

Standardised unemployment rate The measure of the unemployment rate used by the ILO and OECD. The unemployed are defined as persons of working age who are without work, available to start work within two weeks and either have actively looked for work in the last four weeks or are waiting to take up an appointment.

Steady-state growth path The growth path for a given saving rate (where growth results from technological progress).

Steady-state level of national income The long-run equilibrium level of national income. The level at which all investment is used to maintain the existing capital stock at its current level.

Sterilisation Actions (e.g. open-market operations) taken by a central bank to offset the effects of foreign exchange flows or its own bond transactions so as to leave money supply unchanged.

Stochastic shocks Shocks that are random and hence unpredictable, or predicable only as occurring within a range of values.

Stock An amount of something (inputs, goods, money, etc.) existing at a point of time. (Contrasts with *flow*.)

Stock (or inventory) appreciation The increase in monetary value of stocks due to increased prices. Since this does not represent increased output it is not included in GDP.

Stop–go policies Alternate deflationary and reflationary policies to tackle the currently most pressing of the four problems which fluctuate with the business cycle.

Strategic alliance Where two firms work together, formally or informally, to achieve a mutually desirable goal.

Strategic trade theory The theory that protecting/supporting certain industries can enable them to compete more effectively with large monopolistic rivals abroad. The effect of the protection is to increase long-run competition and may enable the protected firms to exploit a comparative advantage that they could not have done otherwise.

Strong efficiency (of share markets) Where share prices adjust quickly, fully and accurately to all available information, both public and that only available to insiders.

Structural public-sector deficit (or surplus) The public-sector deficit (or surplus) that would occur if the economy were operating at the potential level of national income: i.e. one where there is a zero output gap.

Structural unemployment Unemployment that arises from changes in the pattern of demand or supply in the economy. People made redundant in one part of the economy cannot immediately take up jobs in other parts (even though there are vacancies).

Structuralists Economists who focus on specific barriers to development and how to overcome them.

Subcontracting Where a firm employs another firm to produce part of its output or some of its input(s).

Sub-prime debt Debt where there is a high risk of default by the borrower (e.g. mortgage holders who are on low incomes facing higher interest rates and falling house prices).

Subsistence production Where people produce things for their own consumption.

Substitute goods A pair of goods which are considered by consumers to be alternatives to each other. As the price of one goes up, the demand for the other rises.

Substitutes in supply These are two goods where an increased production of one means diverting resources away from producing the other.

Substitution effect of a price change The effect of a change in price on quantity demanded arising from the consumer switching to or from alternative (substitute) products.

Substitution effect of a rise in wage rates Workers will tend to substitute income for leisure as leisure now has a higher opportunity cost. This effect leads to *more* hours being worked as wage rates rise.

Substitution effect of a tax rise Tax increases reduce the opportunity cost of leisure and thus encourage people to work less.

Substitution effect – international As prices rise, people at home and abroad buy less of this country's products and more of products from abroad.

Sunk costs Costs that cannot be recouped (e.g. by transferring assets to other uses). Examples include specialised machinery or the costs of an advertising campaign.

Supernormal profit (also known as **pure profit, economic profit, abnormal profit,** or simply **profit**). The excess of total profit above normal profit.

Supply curve A graph showing the relationship between the price of a good and the quantity of the good supplied over a given period of time.

Supply schedule A table showing the different quantities of a good that producers are willing and able to supply at various prices over a given time period. A supply schedule can be for an individual producer or group of producers, or for all producers (the market supply schedule).

Supply-side economics An approach which focuses directly on aggregate supply and how to shift the aggregate supply curve outwards.

Supply-side policy Government policy that attempts to alter the level of aggregate supply directly (rather than through changes in aggregate demand).

Surplus on the current budget The amount by which public-sector receipts exceed those expenditures classified as current expenditures.

Sustainability (environmental) The ability of the environment to survive its use for economic activity.

Sustainable output The level of national output corresponding to no excess or deficiency of aggregate demand.

Systemically important banks (SIBs) Banks identified by a series of indicators as being significant players in the global financial system.

Tacit collusion Where oligopolists take care not to engage in price cutting, excessive advertising or other forms of competition. There may be unwritten 'rules' of collusive behaviour such as price leadership.

Takeover bid Where one firm attempts to purchase another by offering to buy the shares of that company from its shareholders.

Takeover constraint The effect that the fear of being taken over has on a firm's willingness to undertake projects that reduce distributed profits.

Target real wage theory The theory that unions bargain for target real wage increases each year irrespective of the level of real growth in the economy.

Tariff escalation The system whereby tariff rates increase the closer a product is to the finished stage of production.

Tariffs (or import levies) Taxes on imported products: i.e. customs duties.

Tax allowance An amount of income that can be earned tax-free. Tax allowances vary according to a person's circumstances.

Tax avoidance The rearrangement of one's affairs so as to reduce one's tax liability.

Tax evasion The illegal non-payment of taxes (e.g. by not declaring income earned).

Taylor rule A rule adopted by a central bank for setting the rate of interest. It will raise the interest rate if (a) inflation is above target or (b) real national income is above the sustainable level (or unemployment is below the natural rate). The rule states how much interest rates will be changed in each case.

Technological unemployment Structural unemployment that occurs as a result of the introduction of labour-saving technology.

Technology-based standards Pollution control that requires firms' emissions to reflect the levels that could be achieved from using the best available pollution control technology.

Terms of trade The price index of exports divided by the price index of imports and then expressed as a percentage. This means that the terms of trade will be 100 in the base year.

Third-degree price discrimination When a firm divides consumers into different groups and charges a different price to consumers in different groups, but the same price to all the consumers within a group.

Tie-in sales Where a firm is only prepared to sell a first product on the condition that its customers by a second product from it.

Time deposits Deposits that require notice of withdrawal or where a penalty is charged for withdrawals on demand.

Time-series data Information depicting how a variable (e.g. the price of eggs) changes over time.

Total consumer expenditure on a product (*TE*) (per period of time) The price of the product multiplied by the quantity purchased: $TE = PQ$.

Total consumer surplus The excess of a person's total utility from the consumption of a good (*TU*) over the amount that person spends on it (*TE*): $TCS = TU - TE$.

Total cost The sum of total fixed costs and total variable costs: $TC = TFC + TVC$.

Total currency flow on the balance of payments The current plus capital plus financial account balance but excluding the reserves.

Total physical product The total output of a product per period of time that is obtained from a given amount of inputs.

Total (private) surplus Total consumer surplus (*TU – TE*) plus total producer surplus (*TR – TVC*).

Total producer surplus (*TPS*) Total revenue minus total variable cost (*TR – TVC*): in other words, total profit plus total fixed cost (*TΠ + TFC*).

Total revenue A firm's total earnings from a specified level of sales within a specified period: $TR = P \times Q$.

Total revenue (*TR*) (per period of time) The total amount received by firms from the sale of a product, before the deduction of taxes or any other costs. The price multiplied by the quantity sold. $TR = P \times Q$.

Total social surplus Total benefits to society from consuming a good minus total costs to society from producing it. In the absence of externalities, total social surplus is the same as total (private) surplus.

Total utility The total satisfaction a consumer gets from the consumption of all the units of a good consumed within a given time period.

Tradable carbon permits Each firm is given a permit to produce a given level of pollution. If less than the permitted amount is produced, the firm is given a credit. This can then be sold to another firm, allowing it to exceed its original limit.

Trade creation Where a customs union leads to greater specialisation according to comparative advantage and thus a shift in production from higher-cost to lower-cost sources.

Trade cycle or **Business cycle** The periodic fluctuations of national output around its long-term trend.

Trade diversion Where a customs union diverts consumption from goods produced at a lower cost outside the union to goods produced at a higher cost (but tariff free) within the union.

Traditional theory of the firm The analysis of pricing and output decisions of the firm under various market conditions, assuming that the firm wishes to maximise profit.

Tragedy of the commons When resources are commonly available at no charge people are likely to overexploit them.

Transfer payments Moneys transferred from one person or group to another (e.g. from the government to individuals) without production taking place.

Transfers (by the government) Transfers of money from taxpayers to recipients of benefits and subsidies. They are not an injection into the circular flow but are the equivalent of a negative tax (i.e. a negative withdrawal).

Treasury bills Bills of exchange issued by the Bank of England on behalf of the government. They are a means whereby the government raises short-term finance.

U-form (unitary form) of corporate organisation Where the managers of the various departments of a firm are directly responsible to head office, normally to a chief executive.

Uncertainty When an outcome may or may not occur and its probability of occurring is not known.

Underemployment Where people who want full-time work are only able to find part-time work.

Underground markets Where people ignore the government's price and/or quantity controls and sell illegally at whatever price equates illegal demand and supply.

Unemployment The number of people who are actively looking for work but are currently without a job. (Note that there is much debate as to who should officially be counted as unemployed.)

Unemployment rate The number unemployed expressed as a percentage of the labour force.

Unit elasticity of demand Where quantity demanded changes by the same percentage as price. Ignoring the negative sign, it will have a value equal to 1.

Universal benefits Benefits paid to everyone in a certain category irrespective of their income or assets.

Util An imaginary unit of satisfaction from the consumption of a good.

Value added tax (VAT) A tax on goods and services, charged at each stage of production as a percentage of the value added at that stage.

Variable costs Total costs that vary with the amount of output produced.

Variable factor An input that can be increased in supply within a given time period.

Velocity of circulation The number of times annually that money on average is spent on goods and services that make up GDP.

Vent for surplus When international trade enables a country to exploit resources that would otherwise be unused.

Vertical equity The redistribution from the better off to the worse off. In the case of taxes, this means the rich paying proportionately more taxes than the poor.

Vertical merger When two firms in the same industry at different stages in the production process merge.

Vertical restraints   Conditions imposed by one firm on another which is either its supplier or its customer.

Wage–price spiral   Wages and prices chasing each other as the aggregate demand curve continually shifts to the right and the aggregate supply curve continually shifts upwards.

Wage taker   An employer or employee who has no power to influence the market wage rate.

Weak efficiency (of share markets)   Where share dealing prevents cyclical movements in shares.

Weighted average   The average of several items where each item is ascribed a weight according to its importance. The weights must add up to 1.

Wholesale banking   Where banks deal in large-scale deposits and loans, mainly with companies and other banks and financial institutions. Interest rates and charges may be negotiable.

Wholesale banks   Banks specialising in large-scale deposits and loans and dealing mainly with companies.

Wholesale deposits and loans   Large-scale deposits and loans made by and to firms at negotiated interest rates.

Withdrawals (W) (or leakages)   Incomes of households or firms that are not passed on round the inner flow. Withdrawals equal net saving (S) plus net taxes (T) plus expenditure on imports (M): $W = S + T + M$.

Working to rule   Workers do the bare minimum they have to, as set out in their job descriptions.

Yield on a share   The dividend received per share expressed as a percentage of the current market price of the share.

Index

Note: emboldened page numbers refer to pages containing definitions

abduction **28**
absolute advantage **709**
accelerationist theory 602–3
accelerator 520
  coefficient **516**
  effect 519, 574
  financial **580**–1
  fiscal policy 635
  instability of investment **516**–18
  principle 810
  theory **516**
  see also multiplier/accelerator
    interaction
acquisitions see mergers and
    acquisitions
acreage controls (set-aside) **93**
Action Plan 737
AD curve derived from IS/LM model
    590
AD/AS diagram and 45° line diagram,
    relationship between 515
Adam Smith Institute 25
adaptive expectations **478**
  expectations-augmented Phillips
    curve 602, 604, 605
  inflation and unemployment: new
    classical school 611, 612
  integrated model of output,
    inflation and expectations 620
  Keynesian position on inflation and
    unemployment 617
  limitations 608–9
ADI/ASI model 582–5, 601
  aggregate demand and supply
    plotted against inflation 582–4
  inflation target line 583
  and IS/MP models, combining 582,
    618, 619, 621
  movement along ADI curve 583
  permanent increase in aggregate
    supply 584–5
  position of ADI curve 583
  response to changes in aggregate
    demand and supply 584–5
  rise in aggregate demand/supply
    584–5

shift in ADI curve 583
slope of ADI curve 583
temporary supply shock 584
adverse selection **124**
advertising 25, 66, 126, 196, 211, 230,
    330
Advisory, Conciliation and Arbitration
    Service (ACAS) 259
Agenda 21 827
aggregate demand 8, 9, **405**, 464,
    466–7
  business cycle 417, 418, 516
  circular flow of income 408
  classical macroeconomics 469
  contraction: Keynesian position on
    inflation and unemployment
    617
  curve 441–3
  diagram and 45° line diagram,
    relationship between 512
  economic growth 424, 425
  and exchange rates 460
  expansion: Keynesian position on
    inflation and unemployment
    616–17
  financial crisis and new consensus
    488
  free-floating exchange rates 764
  globalisation and instability 781
  and inflation 450, 452, 515,
    598–601
  and interest rates 654–5
  Keynesian analysis 686
  Keynesian revolution 474–5
  for labour curve **436**–7
  monetarist analysis 686
  and national income (GDP),
    relationship between 494, 495
  new classical school 479
  output and employment 622
  and prices 622
  and unemployment 438–9, 447, 515
aggregate supply 8, 9, **467**, 594–602
  ADI/ASI model 601
  business cycles 418
  classical macroeconomics 469

curve 441–3, 447, 452
diagram and 45° line diagram,
    relationship between 512
economic growth 420, 424, 425
expectations 596
fiscal policy 631
flexibility 466–7
and inflation 598–601
interdependence of firms 595
investment 595–6
Keynesian analysis 686
of labour curve **436**–7
of labour, effective 597
long-run 595–8
market imperfections 481
monetarist analysis 686
and Phillips curve 610–13
short-run 594–5
see also aggregate supply,
    unemployment and inflation
aggregate supply, unemployment and
    inflation 593–623
  aggregate demand output and
    employment 622
  aggregate demand and prices 622
  expectations and the economy 622
  inflation and unemployment: new
    classical school 609–14
  integrated model of output,
    inflation and expectations
    618–21
  Keynesian position on inflation and
    unemployment 615–18
  longer-term growth, causes of 622–3
  macroeconomic thinking post-crisis
    622–3
  see also expectations-augmented
    Phillips curve
agriculture and agricultural policy
    86–96
  buffer stocks **89**
  butter, grain and beef 'mountains'
    92
  commodity markets 76
  country is a net importer 90
  country is self-sufficient 90–1

agriculture and agricultural policy
        (*continued*)
    declining farm incomes 87–8
    dumping surpluses on world
        markets 92–3
    fallacy of composition 88
    fertilisers and pesticides 92
    food price inflation 94
    Foresight Project 94–5
    government intervention 89–91
    harmful effects on the environment
        92
    high minimum prices 90–1
    import levies 92
    inequity 92
    intervention 86–8
    milk quotas 91
    neglect of agriculture 817–18
    protection in advanced countries
        808–9
    reductions in supply 91
    reforms 22
    rising populations, diminishing
        returns 94
    short-term price fluctuations 87
    structural policies 91
    subsidies 89–90, 726–7
    surpluses (not sold on world
        markets) 92
    tariffs 726–7
    wine 'lakes' 92
    world food prices 94
    yields of selected crops 92
    see also Common Agricultural Policy
airline deregulation in the USA and
        Europe 190–1
allocative efficiency **13**
allocative inefficiency 186
Almunia, J. 384
alternative exchange rates 742–52
    adjustable peg **750**
    adjustment process 749
    balance of payments deficit (UK)
        746–7
    band **751**
    budget surplus and balance of trade
        (UK) 744
    crawling peg **751**
    current account balance of
        payments (UK) 747
    disequilibrium correction 748–9
    expenditure changing (income
        effect) **749**–50
    expenditure reducing **748**
    expenditure switching (substitution
        effect) **748**–9, 750
    external balance **742**–3
    fixed rate, correction under 746–9

foreign exchange intervention
        746–8
    free-floating rates, correction under
        749–50
    intermediate regimes 750–1
    internal balance **742**–3
    joint float **751**
    managed floating **750**–1
    national income, employment and
        prices 749–50
    nominal rates 743–5
    policy objectives 742–3
    public finances and balance of trade
        744
    real rates 743–5
    rise in prices 750
    sterilisation **748**
Alternative Investment Market (AIM)
        276
alternative market structures 171–2
alternative maximising theories
        228–35
    diversification, growth through 231
    Enron and business growth 234
    equilibrium for growth-maximising
        firm **235**
    going global, growth through 234–5
    internal expansion, growth by 231
    managerial utility maximisation
        228–9
    maximisation, growth by **230**
    mergers and acquisitions (M&A) and
        globalisation 236–7
    mergers, growth by 231–3
    profit maximisation **228**
    and the public interest 235–7
    sales revenue maximisation 229–30
    strategic alliances, growth through
        233
    vertical integration, growth through
        231
alternative theories of the firm **133**,
        221–44
    alternative aims 222–3
    behavioural theories 224–7
    comparison with other firms 239
    conservatism 239
    information, lack of 222
    multiple aims 238–40
    multiple goals: predictions and
        behaviour 239
    organisational slack **239**
    pricing in practice 240–4
    profit maximising difficulties 222
    satisficing and the public interest
        239
    satisficing and target-setting 238–9
    stakeholder power 238

time period 222
    traditional theory, problems with
        222–3
    see also alternative maximising
        theories
ambient-based standards **361**
American Recovery and Investment
        Act 632
'animal spirits' (sentiment or
        confidence) 487
appreciation **458**
arbitrage **456**
arc elasticity **65**–7
arc method 65, 70
Ariely, D. 266
AS curve 622
ASI curve 622
ASI/ADI model 659
Asia-Pacific Economic Co-operation
        (APEC) forum 732–3
asset bubbles 277
asset prices and yields 655
asset stripping 232
assets **403**, **529**–31
    fixed 676
    non-financial 502, 503
    paper 268
asymmetric information 224–**5**, 227
asymmetric shocks **791**, 792
austerity measures 786
Austrian School 348
average revenue product (ARP) 327

bailouts 487, 618
balance of payments 402–3, 453–6
    account **402**, 453–5
    assessing figures 455–6
    capital account 454
    current account 453–**4**
    current transfers of money 454
    deficit (UK) 746–7
    direct investment 454–5
    equilibrium *see* external balance
    and exchange rates 458–9
    financial account 454–5
    financial flows 455
    and fixed exchange rates 753–4
    income flows 454
    inflation 446
    long-term 808–10
    portfolio investment 455
    selected industrial countries 454
    short term 810
    trade in goods account 453
    trade in services account 453
    United Kingdom 453, 459, 746–7
    see also balance of payments and
        exchange rates

balance of payments and exchange
        rates 741–76
    adjustable peg system (1945–73)
        765–7
    Bretton Woods system **766**
    disequilibria and adjustment
        problems 766–7
    equilibrium exchange rate
        prediction 768
    fixed exchange rates 452–6
    inflation rates 771
    internal policy conflicts 769
    international liquidity problems and
        collapse of the system 767
    large-scale disruption 767
    managed floating 767–9
    open economy and *ISLM* analysis
        772–6
    real exchange rate indices 768, 770
    speculation 767–9
    sterling fluctuations 768–9
    stop-go policies 767
    volatility of exchange rates 769–71
    see also alternative exchange rates;
        free-floating exchange rate
balance sheet **403**, 404, 527, 538, 551,
        565
balance of trade **9**, **453**
balanced budget principle 471
balances, active **553**
Bali Ministerial Conference (Bali
        package) 727, 728
bandwagon effects 520
Bank Advisory Committee (BAC) 825
bank bills **530**
bank deposits multiplier 545–6, 643
Bank of England 401
    1-week repos 539
    alternative exchange rates 747, 748
    Asset Purchase Facility 539
    balance of payments 455
    balance sheet 538
    Banking Department 538, 539
    borrowing rate 539
    corridor system 539
    cost-push inflation and supply
        shocks 600
    deposit rate 539
    deposit taking and lending assets
        532
    European Economic and Monetary
        Union (EMU) 791
    Exchequer account 538
    expectations-augmented Phillips
        curve 605, 607–8
    Financial Policy Committee 540
    floor system 539
    free-floating exchange rates 763

inflation 402, 445, 449, 451
    Inflation Report 663
    interest rates and financial crisis
        (2007–9) 660–1
    Issue Department 538
    liquidity 539
    managed floating 769
    monetary changes and national
        income 563, 569, 571
    monetary policy 644, 648–9, 654,
        655
    monetary policy and goods market
        576, 578, 579–80
    money market rates 539
    money supply 543, 546–8
    National Loans fund 538
    operational standing facilities 539
    price-setting survey 242–3
    profitability and liquidity 533
    quantitative easing 539, 551
    Ways and Means advances 538
    see also Bank Rate; Monetary Policy
        Committee
Bank of England Act (1998) 660
Bank of England Rule 663
bank lending 275, 655
    net 697
bank levy 531
Bank Rate 289, 529, 538, 539, 540,
        541, 542, 644
    managed floating 769
    monetary policy 649, 652, 655
    policy-making environment 658
banking, money and interest rates
        523–58
    definition and functions of money
        524
    equilibrium 557–8
    money, demand for 553–6
    money as means of establishing
        value of future claims and
        payments 525
    money as means of evaluation 525
    money as means of storing wealth
        524–5
    money as medium of exchange **524**
    money supply, national income and
        national wealth 524
    what counts as money 525
    see also financial system; money
        supply
banking system 526–7
barometric firm price leadership **200**
barriers to entry 173, **181**–2, 184, 188,
        197, 231
barter economy **17**
Basel Committee on Banking
        Supervision 531, 536

Basel II accord 533
Basel II minimum capital requirements
        536
Basel III capital requirements 536, 537
basic needs approach 800–1
'Battle of Seattle' 726
Baumol, W. 229
Becker, G. 114
behavioural economics 29, 100, 125–8
    altruism 129
    bounded rationality **126**
    changing behaviour 127
    choice 126–7
    definition 125
    economic policy 128
    and economic theory 128
    experiments, role of 125
    framing options 126
    herding and groupthink 126, 128
    irrational behaviour 126–8
    relativity 126
    self-interested behaviour 129
    sunk costs 128
Behavioural Insights Team 127
behavioural theories 224–7
    asymmetric information and the
        principal-agent problem **224**–5
    firms use of behavioural economics
        226–7
    rationality of firms 224
    revenge 224
    sub-prime housing crisis (USA)
        226–7
    survival and attitudes towards risk
        225–6
Belobaba, P. 191
Benefit Cost Ratio (BCR) 344–5
benefit principle of taxation **296**
benefits 306–8
    cash benefits 306
    inequality reduction 310
    in kind 296, **306**–8
    means-tested **306**, 308
    pensioner poverty 311
    and redistribution of income 308
    tax credits (UK) 309
    tax/benefit system and problem of
        disincentives: poverty trap **308**
    universal **306**
    see also taxes, benefits and
        redistribution of income
Bernanke, B. 28
Bertrand, J. 206
Bertrand model 206
Big Mac index 759
bills of exchange **529**–30, 649
    rediscounting **541**
biofuels 87, 88, 811, 827

Blair government 310, 687, 688
booms 50, 416, 417, 520, 617
borrowing 275, 471
   flows 403
   fluctuations 519–20
   short 532
bounded rationality **126**, 128
Brady, N. 825
Brady Plan 825
brand loyalty 119, 126, 182
Bretton Woods system **766**
Brewer, N. 263
BRICS 707, 784, 822
British Electricity Trading and
   Transmission Arrangements
   (BETTA) 394–5
broad money (M4) **543**, 544, 549,
   570–1, 648
Brown government 418, 688
bubbles 50, 530
budget balance 744
budget, current 628
budget deficit 496, **626**, 789
budget line 109, **111**–12, 113, 115,
   116, 117, 304
budget surplus 496, **626**, 744
buffer stocks **89**
building societies 527
bureaucracy 726
Bush administration 349, 364, 632,
   689, 815
Bush, G. Snr 349, 689
business cycle 9, 516–21
   accelerator: instability of investment
     516–19
   booms and recessions 520
   borrowing and debt fluctuations
     519–20
   determinants of course of 520
   expansionary phase 416, 516
   international 781–3
   multiplier/accelerator interaction 518
   peaking out, slowdown, recession or
     slump 416, 516
   political 608
   real **479**–80, 482, 613–14
   recession phase 516
   stock fluctuations 518–19
   or trade cycle **416**
   unemployment 435, 438
   upturn phase 516
   see also economic growth,
     short-term and business cycle
business expenses 301
busts 617
   see also recession
'buy-to-let' industry 51
bygones principle 139

Cable, V. 636
cap and trade 359
capital **7**, 147, 148, 150, 151, 419, 529
   heterogeneous 271
   marginal efficiency of capital (MEC)
     273, 419, 673
   physical 268, 273–4, 697
capital account 403, 453, **454**, 502
capital accumulation 673
capital adequacy 536–7
capital adequacy ratio (CAR) **533**, 537
capital balance sheets 408
capital conservation buffer 536
capital equipment 504
capital expenditure **627**
capital and investment 271
capital issue, net 697
capital market **541**
capital market imperfections 696
capital productivity 152
capital and profit 268–78
   business finance 275
   capital 268
   demand for capital: investment
     272–3
   demand for capital services 269–70
   demand for and supply of capital for
     purchase 272–4
   determination of price of capital
     services 271–2
   determination of rate of interest 274
   factor prices versus price of factor
     services 268–9
   financing investment 275
   individual firm's demand 269–70
   land 268
   market demand 270
   market supply 271
   non-human factors of production
     268–9
   profit-maximising employment of
     land and capital 269
   stock market, role of 275–7
   stocks and flows 271
   supply by a single firm 270–1
   supply of capital 273–4
   supply of capital services 270–1
   supply to a single firm 270
capital services price, determination of
   271–2
capital-intensity bias 819–21
capital-intensive technologies 818–19
capital/output ratio, marginal **517**
capitalism 349
Carbon Emissions Trading Scheme
   (ETS)(EU) 366–7
carbon tariffs 721
carbon tax 363

career breaks 263
carry trade 757–9, **758**
cartels **198**, 383, 384, 386
cash benefits 296, 309
cash ratio deposits 529
cash reserves 529, 532
central bank 527, 537–40
   acts as bank to banks 538
   acts as bank to the government 538
   acts as bank to overseas central
     banks 538
   ADI/ASI model 583
   aggregate supply 601
   balance sheet 538
   balances 532
   constrained policy discretion 485–6
   deposit taking and lending assets
     529, 530
   European Economic and Monetary
     Union (EMU) 788
   exchange rates 460
   inflation 452
   inflation targets 662
   integrated model of output,
     inflation and expectations 621
   intervention to maintain fixed
     exchange rate 747
   issue of notes 538
   Keynesian revolution 475
   lending adjustment to banks 643,
     645
   monetary effects of changes in
     goods markets 572–3
   monetary policy and goods market
     577
   and monetary policy in USA 646–7
   money markets 541
   money supply 545
   operates government's exchange
     rate policy 540
   operates government's monetary
     policy 538–9
   oversees activities of banks and
     financial institutions 540
   provision of liquidity 539–40
   remits 605, 607–8, 621
   run on a bank 524
   see also Bank of England; European
     Central Bank; Federal Reserve
central parity 795
centrally planned (or command)
   economy **18**, 20, 22, 348
certificates of deposit (CDs) **528**–9,
   533, 542
certified emissions reductions (CERs)
   364
CET1 ratio 536, 537
ceteris paribus **28**, 103, 125

Chamberlin, E. 194
Chancellor of the Exchequer 537, 539, 660
characteristics theory 119
charitable status 386
Charities Act (2006) 386
Charity Commission 386
Chicago School 114
child poverty reduction (UK) 310
Child Tax Credit (CTC) 309
China 23, 814–15
'China price' effect 449
choice 10–11, 13, 126–7
Churchill, W. 470
Ciolos, D. 95
circular flow of goods 17–18
circular flow of income 17–18, 405–8, 409, 474–5
    equilibrium 408
    export expenditure 407
    government expenditure 407
    import expenditure 406–7
    injections 407, 506
    inner flow 406
    macroeconomic equilibrium 495
    and macroeconomic objectives 407–8
    net saving 406
    net taxes 406
    unemployment 431
    withdrawals 406–7
classical analysis 476
classical macroeconomics 468–73
    crowding-out effect 472
    fiscal policy in the 1930s 471
    free market economy and demand and supply 468–73
    Great Depression 470–2
    output and employment 468–9
    prices and inflation 469–70
    public expenditure 472
    Say's law 469
    Treasury view on public works 471–2
    Treasury view on unemployment 471
classical model of labour markets 596–7
classical school 487, 489
classical theories 421, 464, 477
Clean Development Mechanism (CDM) 364, 366, 367
clearing price 540
climate change 357, 364–5
    see also Kyoto Protocol
Clinton, B. 689
closed shop 259
co-ordination 146
    failure 530

Coalition government:
    alternative exchange rates 746
    banking system 527
    classical macroeconomics 472
    cost-benefit analysis 344
    European Economic and Monetary Union (EMU) 792
    expansionary policies 487
    fiscal policy 633, 636, 637, 639
    government intervention 339
    inequality reduction 310
    interventionist supply-side policy 698, 701, 702
    monetary effects of changes in goods markets 574
    nudge theory 127
    supply side policies 687
    taxes, benefits and redistribution of income 301, 306
Coase theorem 336, 359
Cobb-Douglas production function 148, 149
Cobb-Douglas utility function 113
Coca-Colanisation 809
collateral 540
    effect 503
collateralised debt obligations (CDOs) 534–6
collective bargaining 258–9
collusion 193, 388
    tacit 199, 200–1, 213
    see also oligopolistic collusion
collusive oligopoly 198, 224
collusive tendering 385, 388
command economy 20–1, 22
command-and-control (CAC) systems 360–1, 363
commercial bank loans rescheduling 825
commercial bills 529
Commission on Sustainable Development (CSD) 827
commodity price inflation 450
Common Agricultural Policy (CAP) 91–2, 93–6, 734
    2003 package 93
    acreage controls (set-aside) 93
    'CAP towards 2020, The' 95–6
    criticisms of price support system 92–3
    'Health Check' 93–4
    MacSharry reforms 93
    production quotas 93
    single farm payments 93
common but differentiated responsibilities principle 365
common market 432, 729–30, 733
Communism 22, 23

comparative advantage 708–10
    gains from trade based on 711–13
    Heckscher-Ohlin version 807
    international trade and development 713, 715–17, 726, 806–11, 813
    law of 710
    and terms of trade 714
competition 25, 198
    for corporate control 186
    European Union 736–7
    fair 728
    international 186, 466
    international trade 717–18
    international trade and development 813
    market-oriented supply-side policies 694–5
    preferential trading 731
    see also competition policy
Competition Act (1998) 385, 386
Competition Commission (CC) 208, 385, 387, 388
Competition and Markets Authority (CMA) 183, 337, 385, 386–7, 388, 392–3, 395
competition policy 382–9, 734
    assessment 387–8
    European Union 383–5
        cartels 384
        merger policy 384–5
        monopoly policy 383–4
        restrictive practices policy 383
    merger policy 382–3
    monopoly and the public interest 382
    payday loans 388
    restrictive practices policy 383
    targets of 382–3
    UK 385–7
        merger policy 387
        monopoly policy 386–7
        restrictive practices policy 385–6
        school fees 386
competitive advantage 718–19
complementary goods 37
compliance deficit 738
compounding 272
compromise strategy 210, 212
concentration ratios: measuring degree of competition 173
congestion costs 371–2
conglomerates 237
Connexions 701
conservationist approach 355–6
conservatism 239

Conservative government:
  alternative exchange rates 746
  European Union 734
  interventionist supply-side policy 699, 700
  Keynesian revolution 476
  market-oriented supply-side policies 688, 692
  monetary policy 641
  unemployment 438
  wage determination in imperfect markets 259, 260
  wage determination under perfect competition 249
consolidation, discretionary 633
consortium **233**
constraint equation 152
consumer demand 501, 504, 517
consumer durables **120**, 121
consumer expenditure 427
consumer expenditure on a product (per period of time), total **63**
consumer price index (CPI) 444–5
  inflation 449, 605, 607, 656, 660, 662, 785
consumer sentiment 498
consumer sovereignty **180**
consumer surplus **103**, 329, 335
  marginal **103**
  total **104**
consumer theory 119
consumers' share of a tax on a good **83**
consumption 7, 496–9
  and balance sheets 502–3
  consumer sentiment 498
  determinants 501
  distribution of income 498
  of domestically produced goods and services **405**, 498–9
  durables, age of 498
  economic growth, long-term 422
  expectations of future prices 498
  expected future incomes 497
  financial system and attitudes of lenders 497
  fiscal policy 636
  function **496–8**
  household wealth and household-sector balance sheets 497–8
  injections 505
  marginal propensity to consume **497**
  point, optimal 103–5, 112–13, 115–18
  possibilities and trade 712, 713
  smoothing **497**
  tastes and attitudes 498
  taxation 497

'container principle' 145
contestable markets theory 188–91
  airline deregulation in the USA and Europe 190–1
  assessment of theory 189
  costless exit 188–9
  and natural monopolies 188
  perfectly contestable markets 188
  potential competition or monopoly 188
  and public interest 189
contingent term repo facility (CTRP) 540
contractionary (deflationary) policies **452**, 476, 604–5, 617, 792
convergence of economies **784**
convergence in GDP per head **672**
core workers **259**
corporate social responsibility 365
corruption 726–7
cost:
  average (total) **141**, 142
  average variable **141**, 142
  curve **154**, 155–6, 162
  external **323**, 808
  pricing, average **201**, **240–4**
  total **140–1**, 152
  see also costs in the long-run; costs in the short-run; marginal cost
cost-benefit analysis 314, **340–7**
  direct private monetary costs and benefits 341–2
  discount rate 346
  discounting 346
  dishonesty 342
  distribution of costs and benefits 346–7
  external benefits/costs 341
  Hicks-Kaldor criterion 347
  High Speed Rail (HS2) 344–5
  identifying benefits/costs 341
  ignorance 342
  individual uncertain outcomes 343, 346
  inferences from people's behaviour 342
  measuring costs and benefits 341–3
  monetary costs/externalities 341
  non-monetary costs/externalities 341
  non-monetary private benefits: consumer surplus 342
  price of a human life 343
  private non-monetary benefits 341
  procedure 340–1
  questionnaires 342
  risk and uncertainty 343–6

  specific account of distributional consequences 347
  strict Pareto criterion 346
  traffic congestion economics 373
  uncertain outcomes 346
cost-push inflation **447–8**, 515, 599–600, 601
costless exit 188–9
costs in the long run 154–8
  derivation from isoquant map 157–8
  long-run average costs (LRAC) 154
  long-run cost curves in practice 156
  long-run marginal costs (LRMC) 155
  long-run and short-run average cost curves, relationship between 155–6
  minimum efficient scale (MES): economies of scale 156–7
costs in the short run 139–44
  average cost and marginal cost, relationship between 142
  average fixed cost (AFC) 142
  average and marginal physical product 142
  average variable cost (AVC) 142
  cost curves: fixed factors are divisible 143
  costs and inputs 139–40
  explicit costs 139
  fixed **139**, **141**, 142
  historic costs **139**, 140
  implicit costs (sunk costs) **139**
  marginal cost (MC) 141–2
  measuring costs of production 139
  price of factors 139
  productivity of factors 139
  total costs **140–1**, 144
  total fixed cost (TFC) 140, 144
  total variable cost (TVC) 140–1, 144
  TPP, APP and MPP 139
counter-cyclical buffer 537
countervailing power **207**, 350
Cournot, A. 205
Cournot equilibrium **205**
Cournot model of duopoly **205–6**
crawling peg **751**, 795
credible threat (or promise) **212**
credit bubble 530
credit creation 545–6
credit cycles 550–1
credit items 454, 455
credits (receipts of money from abroad) 453
cross-price elasticity of demand 73–4
cross-subsidise **382**
crowding-out **471–2**, **573–5**, 633–4, 744

cultural costs 812
cumulative causation principle 475, **508**
currency:
  demand and supply curves, shifts in 458
  union **789**
  volatility 783
  see also currency stability
currency stability 793–7
  exchange rate target zones 794–5
  exchange transactions 793–4
  non-interest-bearing deposits 794
  quantitative controls 794
  Tobin tax 794, 796–7
current account 453–4, 528
  balance 10, **785**
  of the balance of payments **453**
  deficit 454, 455–6, 742–3
  surplus 454, 753
current budget surplus **628**
  cyclically-adjusted 639
customer loyalty 190
customs duties *see* tariffs
customs union 729, 731–2, 733
Cyert, R. 224, 239

Darling, A. 301
De Gucht, K. 727
de-mergers, vertical 237
de-trending techniques 415
deadweight loss **302**, 335
deadweight welfare loss **329**
debentures (company bonds) 275
debit item (outflow of money) 453–5
debt 823–30
  attitudes towards 483
  commercial bank loans rescheduling 825
  debt forgiveness 826–9
  debt servicing costs 824
  debt-for-bonds swaps 828
  debt-for-cash swaps 828
  debt-for-equity swaps 828
  debt-for-export swaps 828
  debt-for-nature or debt-for-development swaps 828
  debt-to-local-debt swaps 828
  in developing countries 823
  ecocide (debt and the environment) 826–7
  fluctuations 519–20
  heavily indebted poor countries (HIPC) initiative 827, 829
  national **626**, 645, 789
  official loans rescheduling 825
  oil shocks (1970s) 823–4
  rescheduling 824–5

  secured 503
  structural reform in developing countries 825–6
  subordinated 533
  swapping debt 828
Debt Management Office 541
debt-servicing costs **497**
decision tree (or game tree) **212**
deduction **27**
'deep green' approach 357
deflation 402, 449, 460, 766, 767
deflationary policy *see* contractionary policy
deflationary or recessionary gap **513**, 742
demand 8, 35–42, 100–28
  actual 8
  behavioural economics 125–8
  change in **38**
  declining farm incomes 87
  derived **253**
  determinants 37–8
  elastic **62**, 63, 82
  elasticity for labour 301–2
  estimated demand equations 39
  free-market economy 21
  function **39**
  for good being produced 253
  hospital treatment provision 84–5
  house prices 50
  increase in **38**
  infinitely elastic 64
  kinked demand theory **206**–7
  for labour: marginal productivity theory 252–4
  land and rent 278–9
  law of **35**
  potential 8
  price and output determination 47–8
  and price, relationship between 35–6
  real-world demand function (lamb) 40–1
  response of to increase in supply 75
  schedule for an individual **36**, 39
  schedule (market) 36
  shock and inflation 447
  short-term price fluctuations 87
  simple demand functions 39
  stock market prices 52–3
  and supply of capital for purchase 272–4
  and supply relationship 17
  totally inelastic 64
  unstable 653–4
  see also aggregate demand; indifference analysis; inelastic demand; marginal utility theory

demand curve **36**–7, 38–41
  elasticity 61, 65
  identifying position of 49–54
  price and output determination 46–7, 48
  underground markets 57
demand under conditions of risk and uncertainty 120–5
  attitudes towards 121–2
  diminishing marginal utility of income **122**
  expectations and people's actions 121
  imperfect information 120–1
  insurance: removal of risk 122–4
  pooling of risks **123**
  total utility of income 123
demand-deficient or cyclical unemployment 438–9, 513, 515, 685
demand-for-money curve *see* liquidity preference curve
demand-management policies **476**
demand-pull inflation 446–7, 476, 513, 515, 598–9, 601
demand-side policies **9**, **452**
  and supply-side policies, link between 687
Department of Business, Innovation and Skills (BIS) 259
Department of the Environment and Rural Affairs (DEFRA) 364
Department for Transport 343, 344
Department for Work and Pensions 310
dependency **813**
deposit taking and lending 527–32
  accounts 528
  balance sheets 527
  capital and other funds 529
  certificates of deposit **528**–9
  liabilities 528–9
  sale and repurchase agreements **529**
  sight deposits **528**
  time deposits **528**
  see also deposit taking and lending assets
deposit taking and lending assets **529**–31
  bills of exchange **529**–30
  cash and reserve balances in central bank 529
  long-term loans 531
  market loans **529**
  reverse repos **530**
  short-term loans 529–30
  taxing balance sheets 531–2
  wholesale funding 530–1

depreciation 270, **458**, 782
destabilising speculation **76–7**, 128, 570
devaluation 476, **750**, 817
developed countries:
    economic growth, long-term 422
    inflation 402
    international trade 707, 709–13
    pollution policies 368
developing countries 20, 799–830
    agriculture and agricultural policy
        92–3
    basic needs approach 800–1
    climate change 364–5
    cost-push inflation and supply
        shocks 600
    development (definition) 800–5
    elasticity 72
    exchange rate and purchasing power
        disparities 803
    gross national income (GNY) 801–5
    human development index (HDI) 804
    income distribution issues 803, 805
    international trade 709–13
    market price distortion 803
    maximum (low) price setting 56
    pollution policies 368
    rich/poor divide 800
    selected world statistics 802
    underdevelopment problems 800–5
    see also debt; international trade and
        development; structural
        problems
diamond model (Porter) 718
diamonds-water paradox 107
diminishing marginal rate of
        substitution **110**, 119, 150
diminishing marginal returns 358
    law of **135**, 152
diminishing marginal utility **101**–2,
        358
    of income **122**, 288–9
diminishing returns 270, 420, 443
    law of 150
discount market **529**, **541**
discount rate **272**, 646
discount window facility (DWF) 540,
        644, 647
discounting **272**
discretion, constrained **485**–6
discrimination 263–8
    prevention 259
    racial 265–7
diseconomies of scale **146**, 154, 732
    external **147**, 177
disequilibrium 22, 474
disequilibrium unemployment **437**–9,
        465–6, 467, 473, 690–1
disguised unemployment **819**

disintermediation **647**
disutility of work, marginal **248**
diversification **123**
dividend yield 52
Doha Development Agenda 92, 726–7,
        728, 809, 816
domestic policy 757
dominance 387
dominant firm price leadership **200**–1
dominant-strategy game **209**–10
double counting 425
downward causation **488**
Draghi, M. 565, 651
dualism **818**
Dubner, S.J. 3
dumping 92–3, **720**
duopoly **205**, 206
dynamic stochastic general
        equilibrium (DSGE) models
        484–**5**

e-commerce 178–9, 186
earnings statistics 288–9
echo effects 520
ecocide (debt and the environment)
        826–7
econometrics **39**
economic discrimination **265**, 267
economic efficiency **12**, 818
economic growth 10, 379, 401, 402, 785
    circular flow of income 407
    and inflation 607
    rate **401**
    and supply-side policies 685
    unemployment 431
economic growth, long-term 419–25,
        669–82
    average annual growth rates 671–2
    capital 419
    causes of 419–24, 672–3
    classical theory 421
    comparison of growth performance
        in selected countries 671–2
    costs 422–3
    diminishing returns 420
    effects of actual growth on potential
        growth 424
    increases in quantity of resources
        419–20
    industrialised countries 670–3
    investment, role of 424–5
    labour 419–20
    land and raw materials 420
    new growth theory 421
    output growth 670, 671
    policies to achieve growth 424
    productivity/quantity of factors
        672–3

productivity/quantity of resources
        420
    theories 421
    twin characteristics of growth 670
    see also economic growth, long-term
        without technological progress;
        economic growth with
        technological progress
economic growth, long-term without
        technological progress 673–7
    capital accumulation 673
    capital intensity 676–7
    GDP per head of the population
        675–7
    human capital and education 675
    long-run equilibrium level of
        national income 673–4
    model of economic growth 673–5
    saving rate 674–5
    steady-state output 674
    workforce, increase in 675–7
economic growth, short-term and
        business cycle 414–19
    actual growth, causes of fluctuations
        in 417–18
    actual and potential growth,
        distinction between **414**–16
    fluctuation 418
    growth rates in selected industrial
        economies 417
    length of phases 416
    long-term output trend 416
    magnitude of phases 416–17
    output gaps: measurement of excess
        or deficient demand 414–**15**
    stability/instability 418
economic growth with technological
        progress 678–81
    endogenous growth theory **679**–82
    labour productivity 680–1
    and output 678
    policy implications 682
    saving rate increase 678
economic models **27**–8, 431
economic and monetary union (EMU)
        730, **788**–93
economic objectives, tradeoffs
        between 404
economic policy 128
economic reasoning 27–9
economic rent **251**
economic sentiment and spending
        504–5
economic systems 18–27
    classification 18–20
    command economy 20–1
    free-market economy 21–6
    mixed economies 26–7

economics of the environment 354–9, 379
  conservationist approach 355–6
  environment as a common resource 358
  environmental problem 354–8
  externalities 358
  free-market approach 355
  Gaia approach **356–7**
  ignorance 358
  intergenerational problems 358
  market failures 358
  non-renewable resources, increased price of 355
  optimum use of the environment 355–8
  population pressures and limited resources 354–5
  public opinion 355
  reduction in environmental degradation 355
  social efficiency approach 355
  Stern Report 356–7
  sustainability **355–7**
  technological developments 355
  see also pollution policies
economics as a science 27–9
economies of scale **145–6, 156–7, 173, 188**
  European Union 736
  external **146**, 177, 731
  growth through vertical integration 231
  internal 731
  international trade and development 717, 726, 813
  monopoly 184–5
  and perfect competition 177
  police as a public service 326
economies of scope **146**
efficiency 13, 347
  mechanical 818
  private **315**
  productive **12, 147**
  semi-strong 276–7
  strong **277**
  weak **276**
  see also efficiency under perfect competition; markets, efficiency and public interest; social efficiency
efficiency under perfect competition 315–23
  allocative efficiency 320
  consumer demand 318
  consumption 316, 320–1
  factor demand 318–19

factor market (intermediate analysis) 322
factor supply 319
general equilibrium 317, 318–20, **322**
inefficiency 318
interdependence of goods and factor markets 319
interdependence and the 'invisible hand' 318–20
intermediate analysis in goods market 320–2
marginal benefit and marginal cost 315–16, 320
no externalities 318
private efficiency 316, 317, 320–1
producer supply 318
production 316–17, 321
  see also social efficiency
efficiency wage hypothesis **259–63, 482**
efficiency wage rate **261**
efficiency wages 262, 616
efficient (capital) market hypothesis **276**
elasticity 61–74
  advertising and effect on demand curves 66
  arc elasticity (measurement of elasticity) **65–7**
  cross-price elasticity of demand **73–4**
  and incidence of taxation 82–3
  income elasticity of demand 71–2
  interpretation of figure for 62
  point elasticity (measurement of elasticity) 67–8, 71
  pricing on buses 67
  of a straight-line demand curve 68
  of a variable to a change in a determinant 72
  see also price elasticity
electricity industry: privatisation and competition 394–5
embargoes 720
emissions:
  charge 360
  reduction units (ERUs) 364
  trading 364
employment:
  classical analysis 468–9
  effects in pollution policies 362
  financial crisis and new consensus 487
  fiscal policy 636
  increased, in international trade and development 814

Keynesian revolution 474–6
natural level **597**
endogenous growth theory 679–82
endogenous money supply **551**–2
endogenous variable **495**
Energy Saving Trust 364
Engels, F. 257, 293
Enron 53, 234
Enterprise Act (2002) 385, 387
Enterprise and Regulatory Reform Act 385, 387
Enterprise Zones 702, 703
entrenchment 618
entry barriers 189
entry costs 188
envelope curve **156**
environmental charges **360**
environmental costs 372, 423, 812
environmental ('green') taxes and subsidies 360, 362
environmental issues 374, 422, 720
environmental policy 353–79
  economics of the environment 354–9
  see also traffic congestion economics; urban transport policies
environmental sustainability 806
equal pay for equal work 262–3, 267
equality and inequality under perfect competition 254–5
equation of exchange **470**
equi-marginal principle **106**, 107, 112, 147, 320
equilibrium 21, 557–8
  in circular flow 408
  exchange rate 742
  foreign exchange market 558
  for growth-maximising firm 235
  IS/LM model 587–9
  long-run 176–7, 179, 673–4
  macroeconomic issues and analysis 443
  monetary policy and goods market 578–9
  in the money market 557
  Nash **206**, 210, 211, 213, 727
  open economy and ISLM analysis 773
  partial 47
  price **21**, 46, 50, 55, 57, 182–4, 240–1
  with trade 717
  see also general equilibrium; macroeconomic equilibrium

equilibrium ('natural') unemployment
   437, 465, 513, 615–16, 689–90
   classical macroeconomics 469
   inflation and unemployment: new
      classical school 606
   market-oriented supply-side policies
      685, 690–1
equities **275**
equity **13**, 332, 347, 368, 373
   horizontal **296**
   intergenerational 311
   negative 51
   vertical **296**
errors and omissions item, net 455
Euribor 542
euro 637–8, 789
European Agricultural Guidance and
      Guarantee Fund (EAGGF) 92
European Central Bank (ECB) 449,
      789, 790, 791
   Executive Board 650
   fiscal policy 638
   fixed exchange rates 756
   free-floating exchange rates 762–3
   Governing Council 649, 650, 660
   independence 651
   interest rates and financial crisis
      (2007–9) 660–1
   monetary changes and national
      income 565
   monetary policy 640, 643, 645, 648,
      650, 654
European Coal and Steel Community
      733
European Commission 156–7, 185,
      366–7, 734, 735–6, 789
   competition policy 383, 384, 385
   currency stability 794, 797
   fiscal policy 638
European Council of Ministers 734,
      737, 789, 794
European Court of Justice 383
European Economic and Monetary
      Union (EMU) 788–93
   asymmetric shocks **791**
   competition and efficiency,
      increased 789
   currency conversion costs,
      elimination of 789
   euro 789
   exchange rate mechanism (ERM)
      788
   exchange rate uncertainty,
      elimination of 789–90
   fiscal policy 791–2
   inflation and interest rates, reduced
      790
   investment, inward 790

   loss of separate monetary policies
      791
   Maastricht Treaty and single
      currency 788–9
   monetary policy 791
   national currencies, lack of 790–1
   opposition 790–2
   optimal currency areas 792
   single currency: advantages 789–90
European Monetary Institute (EMI)
      788
European Monetary System (EMS) 751
European Stability Mechanism (ESM)
      639
European System of Central Banks
      650, 789
European Union 733–9
   average transposition deficit 738
   benefits and costs of single market
      735–7
   Common Agricultural Policy (CAP)
      734
   competition policy 734, 736–7
   costs of radical economic change 737
   direct costs of barriers, reduction in
      736
   economies of scale 736
   features of single market 736
   historical background 733
   internal market completion 737–9
   internal market scoreboard 738
   monopoly/oligopoly power 737
   mutual recognition **734–5**
   new member states, effect of 738–9
   regional multiplier effects, adverse
      737
   regional policy 734
   social policy 734
   Stability and Growth Pact (SGP) 638
   taxation harmonisation 734
   trade creation 735–6
   trade diversion 737
Europhiles 792
Eurosceptics 789, 792
eurozone 650–1
excess burden (of a tax on a good) **335**
excess capacity (under monopolistic
      competition) **196**
excess nominal money balances 568
exchange equalisation account **540**
exchange rate **403**, 456–7
   balance of payments 455, 458–9
   band **751**
   borrowing from abroad 460
   controls 720
   currency demand and supply curves,
      shifts in 458
   dealing rooms 459

   deflation 460
   depreciation 558, 764
   determination of in free market
      457–8
   equilibrium 457
   European Economic and Monetary
      Union (EMU) 789
   financial crisis and new consensus
      490
   fundamental equilibrium exchange
      rate (FEER) 795
   import controls and/or foreign
      exchange dealing 460
   index **456**
   injections 506
   and interest rates 460, 654–5
   intermediate **746**
   macroeconomics 402–3
   management of 459–60
   or money supply, choice of 566
   nominal 753, 785
   overshooting **761**
   overvalued 812, 818
   pegged 460
   purchasing power parity (PPP) 410,
      803
   real **745**, 753
   regime **743**
   reserves 460
   short-term fluctuations reduction
      460
   and speculative demand 555
   sterling 456
   supply-side policies 460
   targets 658, 794–5
   transmission mechanism **561**,
      565–7
   undervalued 815
   volatility 796
   weights of foreign currencies in
      sterling exchange rate index 457
   see also alternative exchange rates;
      balance of payments and
      exchange rates; fixed exchange
      rates; floating exchange rates
Exchange Rate Mechanism(ERM) 654,
      751, 767, 768, **788**, 794, 795
Exchange Rate Mechanism 2 (ERM2)
      751, 767, 789
exchange transactions, control of
      793–4
exit costs 188–9
exogenous variable **495**
expansion path **157**
expansionary (or reflationary) policy
      452
   see also fiscal policy; monetary
      policy

expectations 401
  about prices 556
  additional effects 556
  aggregate supply 596, 601
  of changes in prices of securities and
      other assets 555
  and the economy 622
  financial crisis and new consensus
      489
  of future price changes 38, 44, 498
  and inflation 449, 451, 452, 515
  injections 504
  of interest rate levels over the longer
      term 556
  Keynesian position on inflation and
      unemployment 616–17
  of output 598
  and people's actions 121
  rational **479**, 609–10, 611–12, 617
  role of in working of the market 467
  stock market prices 53
  see also adaptive expectations;
      integrated model of output,
      inflation and expectations
expectations-augmented Phillips curve
      602–9
  accelerationist theory 602–**3**
  adaptive expectations 602, 604, 605,
      608–9
  central bank remit 607–8
  clockwise Phillips loops 605
  contractionary policy 604–5
  economic growth and inflation 607
  evidence 605–8
  inflation, elimination of 605
  long-run Phillips curve and natural
      rate of unemployment 604
  policy implications 608
  political business cycle 608
  rightward shifts in long-run Phillips
      curve 605
  RPI inflation, actual and forecast
      606
  stagflation 605
  UK 606
expenditure:
  aggregate **495**
  changing (increasing) from
      depreciation **749**
  changing (reducing) from a
      contraction **748**
  current **627**
  final **627**
  method 409, 427
  switching from a contraction **749**
  switching from depreciation **748**–9
export-orientated industrialisation
      strategy 815–16

exports 408, 506, 813–16
  expenditure 407
  tax 724
external balance **742**–3
external benefits **323**
external costs **323**, 808
externalities **316**, 327, 332, 340, 358
  internalising 335–6
  in privatisation 391–2

factor prices 154, 713–14
  equalisation **807**
  versus price of factor services 268–9
factor quality 152, 154
factors of production **7**, 17–18, 133,
      714
  non-human 268–9
Fair Trade movement 808
fairness 347, 392
fallacy of composition 88, 211, 488,
      489, 530
family behaviour, economic approach
      to 114–15
Fannie Mae and Freddie Mac 647
federal funds rate 646
Federal Open Market Committee
      (FOMC) 646, 655, 660
Federal Reserve Act (1913) 660
Federal Reserve Board 646
Federal Reserve (Fed) 449, 647, 791
  free-floating exchange rates 762–3
  globalisation and instability 781
  interest rates and financial crisis
      (2007–9) 660–1
  monetary changes and national
      income 564
  monetary policy 578, 579–80, 646,
      649, 654, 655
  policy-making environment 664
Field, C. 357
finance:
  availability 505
  long-term 275
  short-term 275
  sources 483
financial account 403, 453, 454–5
  of the balance of payments **454**
  deficit 753
financial capital 268
Financial Conduct Authority 277, 388,
      540
financial crisis (2007–8) 28, 226, 465,
      486–90
  aftermath of crisis 486
  analysis of and subsequent recession
      and recovery 621
  austerity policies 487
  banking system 527

behavioural economics 125
capital and profit 277
debates over policy 487
expansionary policies 486–7
financial sector, importance of 488
interest rate responses 660–1
liquidity 532
long run 488
macroeconomics, debates over state
      of 487
micro foundations, problems with
      relying on 488
monetary changes and national
      income 564
and monetary framework 644
monetary policy 581, 651
new consensus, emergence of 488
paradox of thrift 488, 489
short run 488
unemployment 431
financial deregulation **527**, 694, 780–1
financial flexibility **264**
financial flows 406, 455
financial instability hypothesis 550–**1**
financial instruments **527**
financial interdependence 780–1
financial intermediaries **525**
Financial Services Authority 78, 540
Financial Services (Banking Reform)
      Act (2013) 527
Financial Services Compensation
      Scheme 532
financial stability 404
financial system 525–43
  and attitudes of lenders 497
  banking system 526–7
  capital adequacy **533**, 536–7
  central bank 537–40
  deposit taking and lending 527–32
  expert advice 525
  expertise in channelling funds 525
  liquidity 532, 537
  maturity transformation **526**
  money markets 541–2
  net stable funding ratio (NSFR) 537
  profitability and liquidity, balance
      between 532–3
  risk transformation **526**
  role of financial sector 525–6
  secondary marketing and
      securitisation **533**–6
  transmission of funds 526
financial transactions tax (FTT) 794,
      797
financial wealth 502, 503
fine-tuning operations 644, 651
first-best situation 341, 391
first-best solution **333**–4

first-degree price discrimination **214**
first-mover advantage **213**
Fiscal Compact 638–9, 792
fiscal drag **630**–1
fiscal policy **452**, 464, 626–39
  in the 1930s 471
  adverse supply-side effects 630
  automatic fiscal stabilisers **630**–1
  business cycle 520
  central government deficits and
    surpluses **626**
  current budget 628
  discretionary **631**–2
  European Economic and Monetary
    Union (EMU) 791–2
  evolving frameworks in UK and
    eurozone 637–9
  expansionary 467, 490, 665–6
  fiscal drag **630**–1
  fiscal expansion to fiscal
    consolidation 632
  fiscal rules 636–7
  fixed exchange rates 755, 773–4
  floating exchange rates 775
  free-floating exchange rates 764
  general government 626–7
  government discretion, constraining
    637–9
  government expenditure 633–4, 636
  government finances: terminology
    626–8
  government's fiscal stance 627–30
  high income-related benefits and
    poverty traps 630
  high tax rates and effort and
    initiative discouragement 630
  high unemployment benefits and
    equilibrium unemployment 630
  ISLM analysis 665–7
  key UK fiscal indicators 628
  Keynesian revolution 475
  magnitude, problems of 632–5
  mandate 639
  monetary effects of rise in injections
    634
  national debt **626**
  national income 629, 634–5
  public expenditure, total 627–8
  public-sector deficit or surplus
    627–30
  pure **633**
  random shocks 635
  stabilising or destabilising 635–6
  structural balance 629–30
  taxation 634, 636
  time lags 635–6
  UK fiscal policy during and after
    financial crisis 632

  UK public-sector deficit measures as
    percentage of GDP 629
  US, UK and eurozone general
    government debt 633
  see also policy-making environment
fiscal stabilisers, automatic **630**
fiscal stance **628**–30
fixed costs **139**
  average **141**, 142
fixed exchange rates 460, **745**, 752–6
  advantages 754
  automatic correction of monetary
    errors 754
  balance of payments deficits and
    recession 755
  balance of payments problems,
    causes of 753–4
  certainty 754
  competitive deflations and global
    depression 755–6
  disadvantages 754–6
  external shock 753
  fiscal policy 755, 773–4
  and free markets contradiction 754
  growth rates between countries 754
  income elasticity of demand and
    imports/exports 754
  inflation rates between countries
    754
  internal shock 752–3
  international liquidity problems **756**
  Keynesian view 754–6
  macroeconomic policies 754
  monetary changes and national
    income 566
  monetary policy 754, 755, 774
  new classical view 754
  open economy and *ISLM* analysis
    772–3
  speculation 754, 756
  structural changes, long-term 754
fixed factor **133**
flexible firm **264**–5, 700
floating exchange rate **457**, 458
  classical macroeconomics 469
  fiscal policy 775
  international trade 716
  managed **750**–1, 765
  monetary changes and national
    income 566
  monetary effects of changes in
    goods markets 574
  monetary policy 775–6
flow-of funds equation **549**–51
Food and Agriculture Organisation
  (FAO) 95
foreign exchange market 542, 555,
  558, 812

Foresight Project 94–5
45° line diagram 495–6, 512, 515
forward exchange market **765**
forward guidance 578, 580, 608, 656
franchise/franchising **233**, **396**
free market 25, 468–73
free movement *see* Single European
  Market
free trade areas 468, **729**
  see also in particular European Union
free trade and free capital movements
  694–5
free-floating exchange rate **745**–6,
  757–65, 768, 769, 774
  advantages 761
  automatic correction 761
  carry trade 757–9, **758**
  currency market fluctuations 761
  de-stabilising speculation 760–1
  depreciation of sterling 764
  disadvantages 761–5
  domestic economy and lack of
    discipline 765
  and domestic policy 757, 761
  equilibrium, long-run 760
  external shocks 759
  fiscal policy 764
  insulation from external economic
    events 761
  internal shocks 757–9
  international liquidity and reserves
    761
  monetary policy 764
  purchasing-power parity rate **757**,
    758–9
  speculation 672–3, 760–1
  uncertainty for traders and investors
    763, 765
free-market economy **18**–19, 21–6,
  355
free-rider problem **326**
freedom of entry 172, 179, 194, 247
frictional (search) unemployment
  439–40, 450–1, 468, 470, 513,
  515
frictions 464, 481–2
Friedman, M. 349, 477, 478
Friends of the Earth 328
Fryer, R. 266
FTSE ('footsie') 100 52, 78
functional distribution of income
  285
functional flexibility **264**, 265
fundamental equilibrium exchange
  rate (FEER) 795
funding (in monetary policy) **645**
future price **79**
futures or forward market **79**

Gaia approach/philosophy 356–7
game theory 209–14, 222, 224
  assessment 213
  complex games 210, 212
  decision tree 212, 213
  multiple-move games (repeated/ sequential) 212
  pollution policies 368
  profit possibilities 210
  simple dominant-strategy games 209–10
  single-move games 209–12
  threats and promises 212
  timing 212–13
  see also prisoners' dilemma
Gates, B. 814, 815
gearing or leverage 530
General Agreement on Tariffs and Trade 727
general equilibrium 318–20, 322
  diagrams (in trade theory) 717
  models 485
general government:
  debt 626
  deficit (or surplus) 626, 785
Ghosn, C. 814
Giffen good 118
Giffen, Sir R. 118
gilt repos 529, 532, 649
gilt-edged securities (gilts) 529, 532, 540, 541, 780–1
Gini coefficient 287–8, 289, 293
global systemically important banks (G-SIBs) 537
global warming 356
  see also climate change
globalisation 186, 466, 489–90
globalisation and instability 779–87
  annual growth in world real GDP and volume of world merchandise exports 779
  consumer price inflation 785
  current account balance 785
  economic and financial interdependence 786–7
  economic growth 785
  financial interdependence 780–1
  general government surplus 785
  interdependence through trade 779
  international business cycles 781–3
  international harmonisation of economic policies 784–7
  international macroeconomic indicators 785
  international policy co-ordination 784
  nominal exchange rate index 785

  overseas holdings of British government gilts 781
  short-term nominal interest rate 785
  sterling liabilities of UK banks to non-domestic residents 780
  US trade imbalance 782–3
going rate 249
gold quotas 767
gold reserves 767
gold standard 469, 470, 472
golden-rule 639
golden-rule saving rate 675
Goodhart's law 653, 659
goods market 17–18, 498–9, 611
Gorbachev, M. 22
Gosplan 22
government 626
  bonds (gilts) 531, 532
  budget deficits 467
  debt 789
  deficits 471, 789
  exchange rate policy and central bank 540
  expenditure 407, 427, 473, 500, 600
  general 626, 785
  monetary policy and central bank 538–9
  policy 43, 404, 418, 480, 520
  policy towards business see competition policy; privatisation and regulation services 426
  surplus (from a tax on a good) 335
  see also fiscal policy
government failure and the case for the market 348–51
  advantages of free market 350
  automatic adjustments 350
  bureaucracy and inefficiency 349
  competition even under monopoly/ oligopoly 350
  dynamic advantages of free market 350
  freedom, lack of, for individuals 350
  information, poor 349
  intervention, drawbacks of 348–50
  libertarianism 348–9
  market incentives, lack of 349
  policy, shifts in 350
  shortages and surpluses 348–9
  socialism 348–9
government intervention 19, 323–32, 333–40, 464
  agriculture and agricultural policy 89–91
  behaviour, laws affecting 337
  common resources 326–7, 328

consumption, external benefits of 325
consumption, external costs of 324
deadweight loss from taxes on goods and services 335
deadweight loss under monopoly 329
dependants 330, 338
economic decision-making by individuals on their own behalf 330–1
externalities (side-effects) 323–5
factors, immobility of and time lags in response 330
first-best world 333–4
goods and services, direct provision of 338
health-care provision (NHS) 332
ignorance and uncertainty 330, 338
information provision 338
knowledge, lack of 335–6
laws prohibiting or regulating behaviour that imposes external costs 337
laws to prevent firms from exploiting people's ignorance 337
laws to prevent or regulate monopolies and oligopolies 337
legal restrictions: advantages/ disadvantages 337
lump sum tax 334
macroeconomic issues and analysis 483
market power 327–30
monopolist producing less than the Pareto optimum 329
Pareto optimality, lack of 327, 329
police as a public service 326
positive externalities 338
price controls 338
production: external benefits/costs 324
property rights, changes in 336
protection of people's interests 330–1
public goods 325–6
public ownership 338–9
public provision of healthcare (NHS) 339
regulatory bodies 337
second-best tax and subsidy policies 333, 334
social justice 338
structure, laws affecting 337
taxes and subsidies 333–6
undesirable structures or behaviour, laws prohibiting or regulating 337

Governor of the Bank of England 537
grandfathering **366**, 368
Great Depression 470–2
'great moderation' 486
Green Climate Fund 365
green tax **360**, 362–3
greenhouse gas emissions 356
gross domestic product (GDP) 403,
    408, **426**, 441–2
  actual 415
  annual 543, 544
  at constant prices *see* real GDP
  balance of payments 454
  calculation 425–8
    expenditure method 427
    gross national income 427
    households' disposable income
      428
    income method 426–7
    net national income **428**
    product method 425–6
  classical macroeconomics 470
  constant-price 410
  deflator **441**, 444
  economic growth, long-term 422
  and externalities 412
  figures ignore distribution of income
    412
  growth projections 662
  ignores externalities 412
  injections 502, 505
  measurement **408**–9
  nominal **409**, 410, 470, 569
  per head 409–10, 411
  statistics as indicator of standard of
    living 410–13
  statistics to measure welfare 412
  total 409
  UK 427
  and well-being/happiness
    measurement 413
  see also real gross domestic product
gross fixed capital formation 696
gross national income (GNY) **427**, 800,
    801–5
gross value added (GVA) **425**, 426, 427
growth:
  actual **414**, 415
  annual, in selected countries 787
  average annual 415
  by internal expansion 231
  by merger 231–3
  classical theory 421
  maximisation **230**
  potential 17, **414**
  rate 412
  short-term 420
  steady-state growth path **678**

theory, endogenous **679**–82
through diversification 231
through going global 234–5
through strategic alliances 233
through vertical integration 231
see also economic growth
'guns versus butter' trade-off 11

Halifax Bank of Scotland (HBOS) 78
Hall, R.L. 206
Harford, T. 3
Harmonised Index of Consumer Prices
    (HICP) 444
Hayek, F. von 348–9
heavily indebted poor countries
    (HIPC) initiative 827, 829
Heckscher-Ohlin theory 814, 818
Heckscher-Ohlin version of
    comparative advantage **807**
'Help to Buy' schemes 51
herding and groupthink 126, 128, 277
heterodox economists **487**
heuristics **126**
Hicks, J.R. 347
Hicks-Kaldor criterion 347
Higgins, D. 345
high quality liquid assets (HYQLAs)
    537
High Speed Rail (HS2) 344–5
historic costs **139**
Hitch, C.J. 206
Hoover, W. 182
hostile takeovers 237
Hotelling, H. 280
Hotelling rule 280
House of Commons Public Accounts
    Committee 702
households 17
  circular flow of income 406
  consumption 474–5
  disposable income **428**
  sector balance sheets 502–3
  wealth and household-sector
    balance sheets 497–8
housing equity withdrawal (HEW)
    503
housing market (United Kingdom)
    50–1, 77
human capital **267**–8, 677
  and education 675
  employed 676
  international trade and
    development 805
  investment 697
human development index (HDI) 804,
    805
hyperinflation 446, 570
hysteresis **483**, 598, 615–16, 618

IBOR (interbank offered rate) 542
  see also LIBOR
Iceland: Financial Supervisory
    Authority 786
identification problem **49**
idle balances **554**
ignorance and uncertainty 330, 358
immigration and UK labour market 251
imperfect competition **171**, 327
  see also monopolistic competition;
    oligopoly
imperfect information 120–1, 610, 612
imperfect markets *see* wage
    determination in imperfect
    markets
import:
  controls and/or foreign exchange
    dealing 460
  expenditure 406–7
  levies 92
  licensing 720
  relative quality 501
  substitutes 754
  withdrawals 500–1
import-substituting industrialisation
    (ISI) **806**, 810–13, 818
impulses *see* technology shocks
incentives 21, 49, 54, 225, 303–6, 689
income:
  account 403
  actual and anticipated 50–1
  -consumption curve **113**
  and demand 38
  disposable **497**
  domestic 458
  elasticity of demand **71**–2, 808
  expected future 497
  and expenditure account or profit
    and loss account **403**
  flows 454
  functional distribution **285**
  Keynesian revolution 474–5
  method 409
  method of GDP calculation 426–7
  net national income (NNY) 427, **428**
  real **113**
  redistribution *see* taxes, benefits and
    redistribution of income
  size distribution **285**
  spent on foods, proportion of 62
  stock market prices 53
  and substitution effects 36, 116–18
  support or aid, direct **89**
  tax, negative **308**
  see also circular flow of income;
    diminishing marginal utility of
    income; income distribution;
    income effect

income distribution 38, 246–81, 295, 423
  by class of recipient **285**
  consumption 498
  fiscal policy 631
  international trade and development 814
  issues 803, 805
  land and rent 278–81
  unequal 184, 812
  see also capital and profit; wage determination
income effect 35, 113–14, 304, 306
  aggregate demand curve 442
  inferior good 118
  market-oriented supply-side policies 689
  normal good 117
  of a price change **116**
  of a rise in wage rates **249**
  of a tax rise **303**
independence (of firms in market) **194**
Independent Commission on Banking (ICB) 327
index long-term repos (ILTRS) 540
indifference analysis 100, 109–20
  budget line **111**–12
  characteristics theory 119
  consumer theory 119
  family behaviour, economic approach to 114–15
  Giffen good **118**
  income, change in 111, 113–14
  income elasticity of demand and income-consumption curve 113–14
  income and substitution effects of a price change 116–18
  indifference gap **110**
  indifference map **110**–11, 119
  indifference set **109**
  individual's demand curve: deriving 116
  inferior good **117**–18
  marginal rate of substitution and marginal utility, relationship between 110
  marginal utility approach to demand: limitations 109
  normal good 117
  optimum consumption point 112–13
  price, change in 111–12, 115–16
  usefulness 118
  see also indifference curve
indifference curve **109**–13, 115, 117–19, 250, 304, 322, 717
  social 321–2, 716

indirect taxes 80–4, 286, **297**
  effect of imposing taxes on goods 80–2
  effect of tax on price and quantity 81
  effect of tax on supply curve 81
  elasticity and incidence of taxation 82–3
indivisibility **145**
Indonesia 826
induction **27**
industrial policies **695**, 697
industrial relations 146
industrial reorganisation 699
Industrial Reorganisation Corporation (IRC) 699
industrial tariffs 727
industrialisation 22, 670–3
  see also import-substituting industrialisation
industry costs 177
inelastic demand **64**, 362
  for food 87
  indirect taxes 82
  for loans 652–3
inelastic supply: indirect taxes 82
inequality 331, 391, 808
inequality and poverty 285–95
  analysis of poverty 285–6
  causes of inequality 293–4
  differences by gender 292
  differences in geographical distribution of income 292
  differences in household composition 290–1
  distribution of income 289–90, 295
  distribution of wages and salaries by occupation 290
  distribution of wealth 285, 292–3
  earnings statistics 288–9
  functional distribution of income in UK 289–90
  Gini coefficient **287**–8, 289
  government attitudes towards inequality 294
  Lorenz curve **286**–7, 288
  minimum wage legislation 295
  national income: ratios of shares 287–8
  poverty in the past 293
  size distribution of income 286–9
  types of inequality 285–6
infant industry **720**–1
inferior goods 38, **71**, **117**–18
inflation 9, 10, 402, 411, 444–52
  and aggregate demand and supply 598–601
  balance of payments 446

bias **485**
causes 446–52
circular flow of income 408
classical analysis 469–70
commodity price 450
constrained policy discretion 485–6
consumer price inflation rates for selected countries 445
cost-push **447**–8, 451, 515, 599–600, 601
costs 446
and deflation 449
demand-pull **446**–7, 448, 476, 513, 515, 598–9, 601
demand-shift 448–9, 451
demand-side policies **452**
elimination 605
European Economic and Monetary Union (EMU) 789
and exchange rates 458
and expectations 449, 451, 452
financial crisis and new consensus 489
fiscal policy **452**
house price 50
hyperinflation 446, 570
Keynesian revolution 474–6
and long-term monetary control 641–2
menu costs **446**, 481–2
monetarism 477–8
monetary policy **452**
national income and output measurement 409
Phillips curve: unemployment 450–1
policies 452
rate **9**, 289, **402**, 444, 771
redistribution 446
resources 446
selection of annual UK inflation rates 445
supply-side policies **452**, 685
targets 658, 662–3
temporary 447
uncertainty and lack of investment 446
wage inflation 445
see also ADI/ASI model; non-accelerating-inflation rate of unemployment; unemployment and inflation (Keynesian analysis)
inflation and unemployment: new classical school 609–14
  aggregate supply, Phillips curve and expectations 610–13
  flexible wages and prices 609

inflation and unemployment: new
  classical school (*continued*)
  goods market 611
  labour market 612–13
  policy implications 613
  rational expectations 609–10, 612
  real business cycles 613–14
  short-run Phillips curves 612, 613
  supply-side effects 613
  turning points 613–14
inflationary gap 513–**14**
informal sector 19–**20**
information, imperfect 120–1, 610,
  612
infrastructure **147**, 467, 697, 805
Infrastructure Finance Unit 692
injections **407**, 501–6
  capital equipment, cost and
    efficiency of 504
  consumption and balance sheets
    502–3
  expectations 504
  exports 506
  finance availability 505
  government expenditure 506
  household sector balance sheets
    502–3
  increase 572–3
  increased consumer demand 501,
    504
  interest rate 504
  investment 501–5
  Keynesian revolution 474–5
  monetary changes and national
    income 561
  multiplier **507**
  multiplier formula **509**
  net worth 502
  sentiment and spending 504–5
injections and withdrawals 512
  monetary policy and goods market
    575, 576, 580
  policy-making environment 657
  relationship between 407
innovation 180, 697, 700, 726
input prices 43, 443
input-output analysis **20**
inputs 132, 133, 149
insider dealing 277
insider power 616
insider-outsider theories 482
insiders **259**, 482, 483
instability:
  of investment **516**–18
  see also globalisation and instability
Institute of Economic Affairs 345
insurance: removal of risk 122–4
insurance companies 548

insurance markets failure 124
integrated model of output, inflation
  and expectations 618–21
  analysis of financial crisis (2008–9)
    and subsequent recession and
    recovery 621
  central bank remits, alternative 621
  expectations incorporation 620
  IS/MP and *ADI/ASI* models,
    combining 619
  potential national income 620–1
intellectual property protection 697
interbank lending rate 529
interbank market 542, 644
interbank offered rate (IBOR) 542
  see also LIBOR
interdependence 22–4, **198**, 595, 779
interest rate 401, 402, 411
  and aggregate demand and
    exchange rate 654–5
  on assets 554–5
  balance of payments 455
  classical macroeconomics 469, 471
  determination 274
  differential 580
  equilibrium 557
  European Economic and Monetary
    Union (EMU) 789
  and exchange rates 458, 460
  financial crisis and new consensus
    489
  globalisation and instability 781
  increase 460
  injections 504
  -investment link 563–5
  Keynesian revolution 475
  low 818
  monetary changes and national
    income 566
  monetary policy 648–54
  and money supply, relationship
    between 551–2
  nominal 570
  and portfolio balance 567
  real 570, 811
  responses and financial crisis
    (2007–8) 660–1
  short-term nominal 785
  transmission mechanism **561**–5
  see also banking, money and interest
    rates
Intergovernmental Panel on Climate
  Change (IPCC) 364
  Fifth Assessment Report (ARS) 357
intermediate exchange rate regimes
  746
intermediate goods and services 676
internal balance **742**–3

internal funds 275
Internal Market Scoreboard 737
internal rate of return **273**
international agreements and
  pollution policies 368
international harmonisation of
  economic policies **784**–7
international issues *see* globalisation
  and instability
International Labour Organization
  (ILO) 432–3
international liquidity **756**
  and collapse of the system 767
International Monetary Fund (IMF)
  460, 531, 766, 797
  currency stability 794
  debt 825, 827, 829
  globalisation and instability 74,
    786–7
  quotas 767
International Panel on Climate
  Change (IPCC) 365
international substitution effect **442**,
  446
international trade 25, 706–39
  absolute advantage 708–**9**
  advantages 707–19
  competition, increased 717–18
  competitive advantage 718–19
  constant opportunity costs 712–13
  consumption possibilities and trade
    712, 713
  decreasing costs 717
  demand conditions 717, 718
  determination of price of individual
    trade good 715
  as 'engine of growth' 718
  equilibrium before trade 716
  equilibrium with trade 717
  exports of goods and services 707
  factor prices 713–14
  free trade and cheap labour
    exploitation 713
  gains from trade 717–18
  growth 707
  intermediate analysis of gains from
    trade 716–17
  merchandise trade by destination
    and origin 709
  non-economic advantages 718
  opportunity costs and specialisation
    limits 714
  patterns and trends 708
  pollution policies 362
  pre-trade 712, 716
  preferential trading 729–33
  production and consumption gains
    from trade 713

international trade (*continued*)
  related and supporting industries 718–19
  resources availability 718
  share of world merchandise exports 707, 710
  specialisation 707–9
  strategy, structure and rivalry of firms 718
  terms of trade **714–16**
  top trading countries by value and world share 709
  trade partners 708
  volume of world merchandise exports and GDP 708
  see also comparative advantage; European Union, trade restrictions
international trade and development 805–16
  agricultural protection in advanced countries 808–9
  balance of payments problems 808–10
  Chinese economic miracle 814–15
  comparative advantage 811, 813
  comparative costs change over time 808
  competition, increased 813
  economies of scale 813
  effective access to foreign markets 806
  employment, increased 814
  engine for economic growth 808
  environment sustainability 806
  exchange rates, overvalued 812
  export-orientated industrialisation strategy 815–16
  exporting manufactures 813–16
  exporting primaries – exploiting comparative advantage 806–10
  external costs 808
  financial environment 805
  food exports as percentage of total merchandise exports 807
  foreign exchange 812
  growth rates and export performance of selected outward-looking countries 813
  human capital 805
  import-substituting industrialisation (ISI) 810–13
  income distribution 812, 814
  inequality 808
  institutional quality 806
  investment, increased 814
  inward-looking to outward-looking industrialisation transition 813
  levels of development dimension 806
  low income elasticity of demand for primary products 808
  monopolies 811
  openness to trade 806
  physical infrastructure 805
  primary outward-looking stage 806
  protection, uneven 812
  rapid growth in imports 809
  real interest rates, artificially low 811
  relationship between 805–6
  secondary inward-looking stage 806
  secondary outward-looking policy (benefits) 813–15
  secondary outward-looking stage 806
  social, cultural and environmental costs 812
  structural and institutional dimension 805–6
  tastes 808
  technological developments 809
  terms of trade deterioration 809–10
  trade policies and process dimension 806
  trade strategies 806
  traditional trade theory 808
  urban wages above market-clearing level 811–12
  vent for surplus **807**–8
  world primary commodity prices 809
international trade multiplier **779**
international trading patterns 458
interventionist policies 424, 440
interventionist supply-side policy **686**, 695–703
  advice and persuasion 698
  capital market imperfections 696
  case against 702–3
  direct provision 698
  grants 698
  gross fixed capital formation 696
  industrial policy 697
  industrial reorganisation 699
  information 698
  market, case against 696
  market-based policies, move towards 702–3
  nationalisation 698
  net bank lending and net capital issue 697
  planning 698
  rationalisation 698
  regional and urban policy 699, 702
  research and development (R&D) 698–9
  selective intervention 698–702
  training and education 699, 700–1
  unemployment and supply-side policies 703
inventory *see* stock
investment **16**, **272–3**
  aggregate supply 595–6
  banks 526–7
  business cycle 517
  curve: monetary changes and national income 562
  deposit taking and lending assets 531
  direct 454–5
  discretionary 229
  and economic growth, long-term 424–5
  and exchange rates 458
  expenditure 427
  financing 275
  income 289–90, 455
  induced **516**
  injections 501–5
  international trade and development 814, 815
  physical capital 697
  portfolio 455
  positive externalities 421
  risks 273
  volatility 519
'invisible hand' of the market 24–5, 47, 318–20
irrationality 126–8, 244, 267, 277
IS curve 576–7, 579
IS/LM model 576, 577, **585–91**, 665–7
  demand for money and interest rate changes 587
  demand for money and national income 587
  deriving *AD* curve from 590
  equilibrium 587–9
  goods market, changes in 589
  injections, rise in 589
  IS curve 586
  LM curve 586–7
  money market, changes in 589–90
  money market equilibrium 586
  money supply, rise in 589
  see also open economy and *ISLM* analysis
IS/MP model 579–80
  and *ADI/ASI* model 582, 618, 619, 621
isocost 148–52, **150**, 157
isoquant **148–52**
  map 149, 157–8
  shape 150
issue price 541
Iyengar, S. 126

J-curve effect **766**
Jevons, W.S. 107, 348
jobseeker's allowance (JSA) 432, 693–4
Johnson, A. 339
Johnson, B. 376
joint float **751**
joint implementation 364, 366, 367
joint supply goods **44**
joint venture **233**
Joseph Rowntree Foundation 310
Jubilee Peru 828
'jumping on the bandwagon' 77
just-in-time (JIT) **239**, 265

Kaldor, N. 347
Keynes, J.M. 420, 438, 464, 471, 489,
        562–3
Keynesian analysis 686
    see also business cycle (Keynesian
        analysis); unemployment and
        inflation (Keynesian analysis)
Keynesian approach 665–6, 686–7,
        754–6
Keynesian economics/economists/
        Keynesians 464, 466–7, 487,
        567
    aggregate supply 594
    financial crisis and new consensus
        488
    monetary changes and national
        income 561–3, 570, 571
    monetary effects of changes in
        goods markets 573–4, 575
    monetary policy and goods market
        577
    policy-making environment 664
    unemployment 438
    see also new Keynesians; post-
        Keynesians
Keynesian models:
    alternative exchange rates 742
    injections 506
    labour markets 597–8
Keynesian position on inflation and
        unemployment 615–18
    aggregate demand contraction 617
    aggregate demand expansion
        616–17
    demand-deficient unemployment
        616
    equilibrium unemployment
        615–16
    expectations 616–17
    hysteresis 615–16
    modern developments of Keynesian
        model 615
    non-intervention 617–18
    structural unemployment 615

Keynesian revolution 473–7
    employment and inflation 474–6
    fiscal policy 475
    labour market 473
    loanable funds, market for 473–4
    monetary policy 475–6
    policies of 1950s and 1960s 476
    rejection of classical
        macroeconomics 473–4
    wage cuts and unemployment 474
Keynesian unemployment *see*
        demand-deficient or cyclical
        unemployment
kinked demand theory **206–7**
Kyoto Protocol/Summit/Treaty 359,
        364–5, 366, 368

labour **7**, 147, 148, 150, 151, 157
    economic growth, long-term 419–20
    as a factor of production 248
    homogeneous 247
    mobility **250**–1, 251
labour force **432**
    surveys 433
Labour government:
    central bank 537
    classical macroeconomics 471
    cost-benefit analysis 344
    European Economic and Monetary
        Union (EMU) 792
    European Union 734
    fiscal policy 633, 639
    inequality and poverty 295
    inequality reduction 310
    interventionist supply-side policy
        699, 700, 701, 702
    Keynesian revolution 476
    managed floating 769
    market-oriented supply-side policies
        687, 692, 694
    privatisation and regulation 389
    taxation 334
labour market:
    classical model 596–7
    flexibility 259, 264–5
    inflation and unemployment: new
        classical school 612–13
    Keynesian models 596–7
    Keynesian revolution 473
    primary **264**
    secondary **264**
    supply, growth in 439
    and unemployment 436–7
labour movement/trade unionism in
        the UK 26
labour power, reducing 690–1
labour productivity 152, 680–1, 700
labour supply curve 301

labour theory of value 107, 248
labour-intensive technologies 819
Laffer, A. 303
Laffer curve 303
Lafontaine, O. 795
Lagrangian multipliers 113, 152
laissez-faire or 'hands-off' policy 25,
        348, 467, 468, 617–18
Lamy, P. 726
Lancaster K. 119
land and raw materials **7**, 420
land and rent 278–81
    determination of rent 279
    non-renewable resources 280
    price of land 279
    quantity of assets owned 281
    rent: reward to landowners 278–9
    rental value 281
large numbers, law of **123**
leakages *see* withdrawals
Learndirect 701
Learning and Skills Council (LSC) 700
least-cost method 147, 151, 152, 154
Lehman Brothers 486, 530
Leitch Committee/Review 701
lender of last resort **541**, 643
lending:
    long 532, 534
    patterns and money supply 550
    through the discount window 646
Lenin, V.I. 22
Lepper, M. 126
Levitt, S. 3
liability **403**, **527**
Liberal Democrats 692
libertarians 25, 348–9, 350, **686**
LIBOR (London interbank offered rate)
        529, 542, 649, 652
limit pricing **183**
liquidity 532, **532**
    backstop 643
    Bank of England 539
    central bank 539–40
    coverage ratio (LCR) 537
    international **756**, 767
    preference curve (demand for
        money curve) 555, 557, 562
    preferences **553**
    and profitability, balance between
        532–3
    ratio **532**, 533, 536, 545, 640–1
    strengthening international
        regulation of 536–7
    trap **563**, 654
Listing Agreement 275–6
Lloyds TSB 78
loanable funds market 274, **468**–9,
        473–4

loans 455
  personal 532
  short-term 532
Local Enterprise Partnerships (LEPs)
  699, 703
Logistic Performance Index 822
logistics 167
'London Club' 825
London Stock Exchange 52, 275–6
long-run **133–5**, 152, 153
  average cost curve **154**, 155–6, 158
  equilibrium of the firm 176–7, 179
  equilibrium level of national
    income, growth to 673–4
  free-floating exchange rates 760
  industry supply curve 176–7
  marginal cost **155**
  marginal social cost (LRMSC) 392
  money illusion 598
  neutrality of money **641**
  Phillips curve 613, 621, 622, 686–7
  production function 148
  profit maximisation **228**, 235
  shut-down point **166**
  supply of capital services 271
  under perfect competition **173**
long-run theory of production 144–53
  decision making in different time
    periods 152–3
  isoquant/isocost approach:
    optimum combination of
    factors 148–52
  location 146
  marginal product approach:
    optimum combination of
    factors 147–8
  scale of production 144–6
  size of whole industry 146–7
Lorenz curve **286–7**
loss-minimising point 175
lost-benefit rate 309
low-reserve tranche range 646
Lucas, R. 479, 610

M0 (narrow money) 543, 570, 571
M1 544
M2 544
M3 544, 550, 648, 650
M4 547, 548, 550–1
  see also broad money
Maastricht Treaty 637, 651, 734,
  788–9
macro-prudential regulation **537, 540**
macroeconomic equilibrium, short-
  run 494–521
  aggregate demand and national
    income (GDP), relationship
    between 494, 495

business cycle (Keynesian analysis)
  516–21
circular flow of income model 495
consumption 496–9
45° line diagram (Keynesian) 495–6
injections 501–6
national income determination
  507–12
unemployment and inflation
  (Keynesian analysis) 513–16
withdrawals 499–501
macroeconomic issues and analysis
  430–61
  aggregate demand curve 441–2
  aggregate supply curve 442–3
  balance of payments 453–6
  constrained policy discretion 485–6
  emerging consensus up to financial
    crisis (2007–8) 484–6
  equilibrium 443
  exchange rates 456–7
  financial crisis and search for a new
    consensus 486–90
  government intervention 482
  government policies 480
  hysteresis **483**
  Keynesian revolution 473–7
  market imperfections 481–3
  monetarist counter-revolution
    477–8
  new classical school 479–80
  new orthodoxy 477
  see also exchange rates; inflation;
    unemployment
macroeconomic issues, debates and
  controversies 463–90
  aggregate supply flexibility 466–7
  classical macroeconomics 468–73
  current account 464
  debates 464–5
  expectations, role of in working of
    the market 467
  fiscal deficit 464
  government budget deficits,
    significance of 467
  growth 464
  inflation 464–5
  macroeconomic indicators from
    1900 464
  policy implications 467
  prices and wages flexibility 465–6
  unemployment 464–5
macroeconomics 8, 9–10, 18, 401–5
  balance of payments and exchange
    rate 402–3
  circular flow of income 405–8
  debates 401
  financial stability 404

GDP calculation 425–8
government policy 404
inflation 402
objectives 331
and the production possibility curve
  16–17
sector accounts 403–4
and supply-side policies 685
UK net worth 404
unemployment 401–2
see also economic growth; national
  income and output
  measurement
MacSharry reforms 93
Major government 438, 688
majority voting 735
Malthus, T.R. 134
managed flexibility 767
managed floating **750–1**, 765
managerial utility maximisation
  228–9
March, J. 224, 239
marginal benefit **12**, 13, 25, 129,
  315–16
  ratios 320
marginal capital/output ratio **517**
marginal consumer surplus **103**
marginal cost **12**, 16, 129, **141–2**, 256,
  315–16
  curve 162, 184, 186
  long-run **155**
  ratios 320
marginal disutility of work **248**
marginal efficiency of capital (MEC)
  273, 419, 673
marginal physical product **136**, 137,
  149, 318–19
marginal private cost 324
marginal product approach 147–8
marginal productivity approach 151,
  252–4, 261, 263
marginal propensity to consume **497**,
  511–12
marginal propensity to import **500**,
  773
marginal propensity to save **499**
marginal propensity to withdraw **501**,
  562
marginal rate of factor substitution
  150
marginal rate of substitution (MRS)
  109, 110, 320–1, 716
marginal rate of transformation (MRT)
  321, 716
marginal revenue **159**, 279
  curve 162
  product (MRP) **252**, 279, 318–19,
  327

marginal social benefit of road usage 371

marginal social cost (MSC) 324, 371–2, 392

marginal tax propensity **499**

marginal tax-plus-lost-benefit rate (marginal deduction rate) 308, 309

marginal utility theory 100, **101–8**
  ceteris paribus assumption 103
  demand curve for a good 105–6
  diamonds-water paradox 107
  diminishing marginal utility **101–2**, 104
  function 103
  individual's demand curve 105
  marginal benefit 105
  marginal consumer surplus **103**, 104
  marginal cost 105, 108
  marginal utility **101–3**
  market demand curve 106
  multi-commodity version and demand curve 107–8
  optimum combination of goods consumed 106–7
  optimum level of consumption 103–5
  rational decision making and choices at the margin 105
  time dimension 108
  total consumer surplus **104–5**
  total utility **101–3**
  weaknesses of one-commodity version 106

mark-up pricing, average **240**, 241–4

market **17**, 25

market allocation: government rejection 84–6

market clearing **46**, **479**

market demand 61
  schedule 36

market distortion 302

market equilibrium, determination of 46

market failures 358

market forces 389–90

market imperfections 464, 481–4
  menu costs and nominal price rigidity 481–2
  sources of frictions and imperfections 482–3

market loans **529**

market power 171, 327–30, 722–3

market price distortion 803

market rate of interest 279

market relationships, introduction of into public sector 694

market share 201

market supply 61, 271

market-based policies 359–60, 702–3

market-based systems 364

market-clearing wage 262

market-oriented approach 440

market-oriented policies 424

market-oriented supply-side policies **686**, 687–95
  1980s 687–8
  competition, encouragement of 694–5
  deregulation 694
  employment rises 689–90
  free trade and free capital movements 694–5
  government expenditure, reduction of 688
  labour power, reducing 690–1
  market relationships, introduction of into public sector 694
  more people wishing to work 689
  people work more enthusiastically 689
  people working longer hours 689
  Private Finance Initiative (PFI) 692–3, 694
  privatisation 694
  tax cuts 688–90
  unemployment falls 690
  USA 689
  welfare reduction 691–4

marketing practices 197

markets in action 60–96
  indirect taxes 80–4
  market allocation: government rejection 84–6
  see also agriculture and agricultural policy; elasticity; time dimension

markets, efficiency and the public interest 314–51
  government failure and the case for the market 348–51
  social efficiency 314
  see also cost-benefit analysis; efficiency under perfect competition; government intervention

markets, parallel or complementary 541, 542

Marx, K. 107, 248

mass production 146

mass unemployment 472, 473

maternity pay and leave 263

maturity gap **532**

maturity transformation **526**

maximum price **55**

May Committee 471

means-tested benefits **306**, 309

Measuring National Well-being Programme (MNW) 412

medium of exchange **524**

medium-term finance 275

medium-term financial strategy (Thatcher) 478

Menger, C. 107, 348

menu costs of inflation **446**, 481–2

mergers 182, 199
  and acquisitions (M&A) 232, 236–7, 276
  conglomerate **232**
  due to opportunity 232
  for economies of scale 232
  for growth 232
  horizontal **232**, 237
  for increased market valuation 232
  for monopoly power 232
  policy 382–3
    EU 384–5
    UK 387
  and relationship between growth and profit 233
  to reduce uncertainty 232
  vertical **232**

merit goods **331**, 338

microeconomics 8, **9**, 10–13, 18
  and choice 10
  command economy 20
  objectives 12–13
  and the production possibility curve 15

migration, rural-urban 819–20, 821

Mill, J.S. 379

MINDSPACE acronym 127

minimum efficient plant size (MEPS) 156

minimum efficient scale (MES): economies of scale 156–7

minimum price **55**

minimum reserve ratio **640**

minimum wage legislation 56, 295

minimum wage rate 259

Minsky, H. 550–1

Minsky moment 551, 621

'miracle of the Rhine' 328

Mises, L. von 348–9

mixed economy **19**, 26–7

mixed market economy **26–7**

model building 27–8

monetarists 476, 484
  analysis 686
  counter-revolution 477–8
  financial crisis and new consensus 487
  interventionist supply-side policy 702
  model 742
  monetary changes and national income 566, 571

monetarists (*continued*)
monetary effects of changes in
goods markets 573–4, 575
monetary policy and goods market
577
position 666
monetary base **543**–4
control **646**
monetary changes (elasticity) 62
monetary changes and national
income 561–72
balance sheets 565
domestic currency 565–6
effect on interest rates of fluctuating
demand for money 563
elastic liquidity preference curve 563
exchange rate transmission
mechanism 565–7
exports and imports 565–6
interest rate changes 564
interest rate mechanism 567
interest rate transmission
mechanism **561**–5
investment 563–5
monetary transmission mechanisms
562
money 561, 562–3, 565–6
money-interest link 562–3
national income 565–6
portfolio balance effect 567
quantity theory of money 561
velocity of circulation 567–71
monetary costs and benefits, private 340
monetary effects of changes in goods
markets 572–5
crowding out **573**–5
exchange rates 574
injections 572–3
interest rates: responsiveness
(elasticity) of demand for
money to change in 573
interest rates: responsiveness
(elasticity) of investment to
change in 573–5
money supply: exogeneity or
endogeneity 575
monetary financial institutions (MFIs)
527, 550, 551, 552, 650
monetary flows, short-term 455
monetary policy **452**, 640–56
automatic stabilisers 641
Bank of England 644
broad money supply control 648
central bank lending adjustment to
banks 643, 645
central bank and monetary policy in
USA 646–7
constrained policy discretion 485

European Economic and Monetary
Union (EMU) 791
eurozone 650–1
exchange rate 654–5
expansionary 467, 490, 665–6
financial crisis and monetary
framework 644
fixed exchange rates 755, 774
floating exchange rates 775–6
free-floating exchange rates 764
Goodhart's law 653
inflation 641–2
interest rates 648–55
ISLM analysis 665–7
Keynesian revolution 475–6
liquidity ratio 640–1
monetary base control 645–8
money demand 642
money supply control 640–8
money supply reduction 642
national debt funding 645
normal operation of monetary
framework 644
open-market operations 640
policy setting 640
public-sector deficits 641
quantitative easing 655
short-term 642
use of 654–6
variable minimum reserve ratios
645
see also monetary policy and goods
market; policy-making
environment
Monetary Policy Committee (MPC)
401, 538–9, 640, 644, 649, 655,
658, 660
Inflation Report 579
monetary policy and goods market
575–82
central bank policy 578
equilibrium 578–9
financial accelerator 580–1
goods and money markets 575–6,
579–81
inflation target rate 578
inflationary shock 578
interest rate differential 580
investment and saving responsiveness
to interest rate changes 577
IS curve 576–7, 579, 580–1
IS/MP model 579–80
MP curve 577–8, 579–81
multiplier size 577
national income effects on shifts in
either or both *IS/LM* curves 581
national income, potential 578
monetary surprise model 479

money:
balances, deficit 568
economy 17
illusion 411, **450**, **596**
and income, difference between 406
as indicator of aggregate demand
653
-interest link 562–3
markets **527**, 541–2
in equilibrium 557
parallel 542
multiplier **546**, 558, 647–8
neutrality 479
transfers, current 454
see also banking, money and interest
rates
money, demand for 553–6
precautionary motive 553–4
rate of interest (or rate of return) on
assets 554–5
speculative or assets motive 553–5
total demand for money 555–6
transactions motive 553–4
see also expectations
money and goods markets 560–91
ADI/ASI model 582–5
monetary changes in goods markets
572–5
see also IS/LM model; monetary
changes and national income;
monetary policy and goods
market
money supply 543–53
additional deposit 545
annual rate of growth of M4 548
balance sheet 545
broad money multiplier in the UK
546–8
counterparts to changes in M4 552
credit creation 545–8
credit cycles and financial instability
hypothesis 550–1
curve: exogenous money supply 552
customers may not want to take up
credit on offer 546
definitions 543–5
difficulties in controlling 645–8
effect of changes in 561
endogenous **551**–2, 575
exogenous **551**–2, 575
financial crisis and new consensus
489
flow-of-funds equation **549**–51
increases, causes of 548–9
inflow of funds from abroad 549
and interest rate, relationship
between 551–2
liquidity ratio 546, 548–9

money supply (*continued*)
  multiplier calculation 547
  non-bank private sector chooses to hold less cash 549
  public-sector deficit 549
  rise 477–8
  some of the extra cash may be withdrawn by the public 546
  target 563, 653, 658
  UK and eurozone money aggregates 544
monopolistic competition **171**, 172, 173, 180, 194–7, 337
  aggregate supply 594
  assumptions 194
  equilibrium of the firm 194–5
  government intervention 330
  limitations 195
  market imperfections 482
  and monopoly comparison 197
  non-price competition **196**
  and perfect competition comparison 196–7
  and the public interest 196–7
monopoly 25, **171**, 172, 181–7, 225, 241
  advantages 184–6
  aggregate supply 594
  aggressive tactics 182
  barriers to entry **181**–2
  bilateral **256**, 258
  competition 186–7
  competition policy 382
  contestable 396
  definition 181
  disadvantages 184
  economies of scale 181, 184–5
  economies of scope 181–2
  equilibrium price and output 182–4, 186
  government failure and the case for the market 350
  higher cost curves due to lack of competition 184
  higher price and lower output 184
  innovation and new products 186
  international trade and development 811
  intimidation 182
  legal protection 182
  limit pricing **183**
  lower cost curves due to more R&D and more investment 186
  lower costs for an established firm 182
  market power 327
  mergers and takeovers 182
  natural **181**, 188, 390–1, 396

network economies 181
opening up the market: Sky and football coverage 185
ownership of, or control over, key inputs 182
ownership of, or control over, wholesale or retail outlets 182
police as a public service 326
policy 382
  EU 383–4
  UK 386–7
power 272, 318, 341, 737, 754
  and price discrimination 186
privatisation and regulation 391
product differentiation and brand loyalty 182
profit maximising 182
and public interest 184–7
unequal distribution of income 184
union 257–8
X inefficiency 186
see also monopolistic competition
monopsony **256**–7, 258, 267
  power 269, 270, 272, 295, 327
Mont Pelerin Society 349
moonlighting 301, 412
moral hazard **124**, 227, **534**, 829
moral issues 261
mortgage-backed securities (MBS) 647
mortgages 51, 532, 534
most favoured nations clause 728
MP curve 577–8, 579–81
MPC 500, 541, 661, 663
MPP 279
MRS and *MPP*, relationship between 150
multi-factor case: marginal product approach 147–8
Multilateral Debt Relief Initiative (MDRI) 829
multiplier:
  /accelerator interaction 518
  bank deposits 545–**6**, 643
  deflationary gap 513
  deriving formula (algebraic proof) 511
  effect **475**
  effects, global 725–6
  effects, regional **699**, 702, 737
  fiscal policy 634–5
  income and expenditure approach 510–11
  Lagrangian 113, 152
  normal 631
  numerical illustration 510–11
  qualifications 511–12
  'round' 510
  shift in expenditure function 510

withdrawals and injections approach **507**–10
  see also under national income determination
mutual agreements 232
mutual recognition **734**

narrow money (M0) 543, 570, 571
Nash equilibrium **206**, 210, 211, 213, 727
Nash, J. 206
National Careers Service 701
national debt **626**, 645, 789
national economy 400–28
  circular flow of income 405–8
  GDP calculation 425–8
  macroeconomics 401–5
  short-term economic growth and the business cycle 414–19
  see also national income and output measurement; economic growth, long-term
National Health Service (NHS) 82, 694
national income 524
  business cycle 517
  fiscal policy 636
  full-employment level **513**
  gross **427**, 800, 801–5
  net 427, **428**
  potential 620–1
  statistics comparisons 411
  steady-state **674**
  see also monetary changes and national income
national income determination 507–12
  aggregate expenditure increase 510
  cumulative causation **508**
  equilibrium national income 507
  45° line diagram and aggregate demand and supply diagram 512
  injections and withdrawals 512
  marginal propensity to consume domestic product 511–12
  withdrawals, shift in 509–10
  see also multiplier
national income and output measurement 408–14
  exchange rates: PPP measures 410
  expenditure method 409
  income method 409
  inflation 409
  national income statistics comparisons 411
  national output, problems of measuring 410, 412
  non-marketed items 412

national income and output measurement (*continued*)
    population: per capita measures 409–10
    product method 409
    production of certain 'bads' leads to increase in GDP 412
    production does not equal consumption 412
    production has human costs 412
    real and nominal values, distinction between 411
    'underground' economy 412
    see also gross domestic product
National Infrastructure Plan (NIP) 693
national insurance contributions (NICs) 298
National Investment Plan (NIP) 693
nationalised industries 338–9, 389, **390**, 524, 627, 698
natural (equilibrium) unemployment 478, 630, 690
natural level of employment **597**
natural level of output **597**
natural monopoly **181**, 188, 390–1, 396
natural rate of unemployment 604
    see also non-accelerating-inflation rate of unemployment (NAIRU)
natural resources 268
natural unemployment *see* equilibrium unemployment
natural wastage **258**
nature, random shocks and other unpredictable events 44
near money **546**
negative income tax **308**
negative public-sector net cash requirement (PSNCR) 549, 551
neo-Austrian economists 348, 350, **686**, 702
neo-Marxist economists 813
neoclassical theory 248, 252, 319, 818
net present value of an investment **273**
net stable funding ratio (NSFR) 537
net worth **403**, 502
network **233**
    economies **181**
New Approach to Public Private Partnerships 693
new classical approach **479–80**, 484
    aggregate supply 594
    alternative exchange rates 742
    constrained policy discretion 485
    financial crisis and new consensus 487
    fixed exchange rates 754
    interventionist supply-side policy 702

ISLM analysis 666
    market-oriented supply-side policies 690, 691
    monetary changes and national income 566
    monetary effects of changes in goods markets 574
    supply-side policies 686
    see also inflation and unemployment: new classical school
New Economic Policy 22
New Economics Foundation 379
New Electricity Trading Arrangements (NETA) 394–5
new growth theory 421
new Keynesians **481**, 484, 487, 516, 682
new orthodoxy 477
new realism 260
non-accelerating-inflation rate of unemployment (NAIRU) **483**, **604**, 615–16, 617, 621
non-bank private sector 516
non-discrimination in international trade 728
non-economic discrimination 267
non-excludability **325**, 358
non-interest-bearing deposits 794
non-intervention *see* laissez-faire
non-marketed items 412
non-monetary costs and benefits 340
non-price competition **196**, 198, 208
non-renewable resources 280, 423
non-risk-based leverage ratio 537
non-rivalry **325**
non-wage employment costs 697
normal good 38, **71**, **117**, 249
normal rate of return **274**
normative statement **29**
North American Free Trade Association (NAFTA) 732
Northern Rock 524, 530
nudge theory 126, 127
number unemployed (economist's definition) **432**
numerical flexibility **264**, 265

Obama administration 344, 365, 632
objective function 113, 152
occupational mobility 251
Office for Budget Responsibility 301
Office of Communications (Ofcom) 393
Office of Fair Trading (OFT) 385, 386, 388
Office for Gas and Electricity Markets (Ofgem) 393, 394, 395

Office of Water Services (Ofwat) 393
Official List 276
official loans rescheduling 825
Oil Producing and Exporting Countries (OPEC) 202–3, 754, 768
oil shocks (1970s) 448, 823–4
oligopolistic collusion **198**, 201, 204, 224, 337, 383, 396, 732
oligopoly **171**, 172, 173, 180, 197–209, 225, 241, 257–8, 332
    aggregate supply 594
    barometric firm price leadership 201
    barriers to entry 197
    buying power of grocery sector in UK 208
    competition and collusion 198
    concentration ratios for Innocent Drinks Company 199
    dominant firm price leadership **200–1**
    government failure and the case for the market 350
    government intervention 330, 334
    industry equilibrium under collusive oligopoly 198–200
    interdependence of firms 198
    non-collusive **198**, 204–7, 224
    Oil and Petroleum Exporting Countries (OPEC) cartel 202–3
    power 737
    and the public interest 207–8
    tacit collusion: price leadership **200–1**
    union 257–8
    see also oligopolistic collusion
oligopsony **208**, 256, 257
open economy **453**
open economy and *ISLM* analysis 772–6
    balance of payments equilibrium (BP curve) 772–3
    elasticity of supply of international finance 773
    equilibrium 773
    fiscal policy under fixed exchange rates 773–4
    fiscal policy under floating exchange rates 775
    fixed exchange rate 772–3
    free-floating exchange rates 774–5
    full equilibrium in goods, money and foreign exchange markets 773
    marginal propensity to import 773
    monetary policy under fixed exchange rates 774
    monetary policy under floating exchange rates 775–6
open-market operations (OMOs) **539**, **643**, 644, 646
Operation Twist 647

operational standing facilities **539**
opportunity cost **11**, 12, 15, 108, **139**, 140, 315
  and choice 10–11
  constant 712–13
  increasing 15
  informal sector 19
  international trade and specialisation 714, 716
  of production, increasing **16**
  of studying 14
optimal currency area **791**, 792
optimal position 177
optimum consumption point 103–5, 112–13, 115–16, 118
optimum production point 152
optimum rate of saving 675
optimum tariff **723**
opting in versus opting out 127
ordinary share capital 533
Organisation for Economic Cooperation and Development (OECD) 379, 410, 432–3, 703
  Development Assistance Committee (DAC) 829
Organisation for Economic Cooperation and Development (OECD) Environmental Outlook 355
organisational economies 145
organisational slack **239**
Osborne, G. 487, 692
Ostrom, E. 328
other financial corporations (OFCs) 539, 548, 551, 569
output 132, 149, 152, 157
  actual 17, 415, 417
  classical analysis 468–9
  determination *see* price and output determination
  economic growth with technological progress 678
  financial crisis and new consensus 487
  gap 414–**15**
  for given cost of production 152
  maximising for given total cost 152
  natural level **597**
  potential 17, **414**, 415, 417, 419
  steady-state 674
  see also integrated model of output, inflation and expectations
Outright Monetary Transactions (OMTs) 651
outsiders **259**, **482**, 483
over-confidence/over-optimism 277
overheads 145–**6**
overshooting 762–3, 764
Oxfam 829

Paish, F. 636
paradox of aggregates *see* fallacy of composition
paradox of debt (or paradox of deleveraging) **488**
paradox of thrift 488, 489
parental leave 263
Pareto criterion 346
Pareto improvement **315**, 316, 321
  potential 347, 373
Pareto optimality **315**, 316, 317, 318, 319, 321–2, 323, 331, 391
  lack of 327, 329
Pareto, V. 315
Paris Club 825, 826, 827
Parsley, D. 759
part-time workers 263
participation rate **675**
patents 182
pay-as-you-earn scheme (PAYE) 297
payday loans 388
peak-load pricing 215
peg 566
  adjustable **750**, 765
  crawling **751**, 795
penal rate 643
pension funds 548
pensioner poverty 311
percentage tax 81
perestroika (economic reconstruction) 22
perfect competition **171**, 172–80, 184–5, 186, 329
  assumptions 172
  concentration ratios: measuring degree of competition 173
  constant industry costs 177
  decreasing industry costs: external economies of scale 177
  e-commerce and market structure 178–9
  government intervention 330
  incompatibility and substantial economies of scale 177
  increasing industry costs: external diseconomies of scale 177
  long-run **173**
  long-run equilibrium of the firm 176–7
  long-run industry supply curve 176–7
  loss minimising 175
  and monopolistic competition comparison 196–7
  output 174–5
  preliminary definition **35**
  price 174
  privatisation and regulation 391

  and public interest 177–80
  rate of profit 173–4, 175
  short-run **172**
  short-run equilibrium of the firm 174–5
  short-run supply curve 175–6
  see also efficiency under perfect competition; wage determination under perfect competition
perfect knowledge 172, 178–9, 247
perfect markets 35
perfectly competitive factor market 269
perfectly contestable market **188**
personal income tax 297
personal loans 532
Phillips, B. 450
Phillips curve **450**–1
  aggregate supply 601
  aggregate supply and expectations 610–13
  breakdown 451, 615
  fiscal policy 630
  inflation 515
  integrated model of output, inflation and expectations 619
  Keynesian position on inflation and unemployment 615–16
  Keynesian revolution 476
  long-run 478, 489
  original 450–1
  policy-making environment 659
  short-run 613, 617
  unemployment 450–1, 515
  see also expectations-augmented Phillips curve
Phillips loops 620
physical capital 268, 273–4, 697
physical goods (previously visibles) 453
physical product, average 135–6, 137
picketing **258**
plant economies of scale **145**
plant, machinery and cultivated assets 677
point elasticity **67**–8, 71
point method 65
police as a public service 326
policy:
  discretionary 657
  and economics 29
  family-friendly 263
  ineffectiveness proposition **479**
  objectives, external **742**–3
  objectives, internal **742**–3
  see also policy-making environment

policy-making environment 656–64
  Bank of England Rule 663
  discretion, case for 657, 659–64
  inflation targets 658, 662–3
  interest rate responses and financial
     crisis (2007–8) 660–1
  political behaviour 657
  rules, case for 657
  targets, difficulties with 659, 664
  Taylor rule 659, 662, 663, 664
  time lags with discretionary policy
     657
political behaviour 657
political business cycle 608
political left 486, 487
political right 486, 487
pollution policies 359–69
  Carbon Emissions Trading Scheme
     (ETS)(EU) 366–7
  command-and-control systems
     (laws and regulations) 360–1,
     363
  education 361
  emissions charge 360
  environmental agenda 364–5
  environmental ('green') taxes and
     subsidies 360
  game theory and international
     agreements 368
  government, reliance on 367–8
  green taxes 362–3
  individuals' attitudes and
     behaviours 364–5
  international co-ordination on
     climate change: Kyoto Protocol
     364–5
  market-based policies 359–60
  private property rights 359
  social efficiency approach 360
  tradable permits 362–7
  user charges 360
  voluntary agreements 361
pooling risks (for an insurance
    company) 123
population:
  growth 134, 819
  per capita measures 409–10
Porter, M. 718
portfolio balance 567
portfolio investment 455
positive statement 29
positive sum game 25
post-Keynesians 487, 488
Postal Services Act (2011) 389
potential growth 17, 414
potential output 17, 414, 415, 417,
    419
poverty see inequality and poverty

Poverty Reduction Strategy Paper
    (PRSP) 827
poverty trap 308, 309, 691
Pratten, C.F. 156
precautionary effect 503
precautionary motive 553
predatory pricing 190–1, 217, 387
prediction (models) 27–8
preference shares 533
preferential trading 729–33
  arrangements 729–30
  Asia-Pacific Economic Co-operation
    (APEC) forum 732–3
  common markets 432, 729–30
  customs unions 729, 731–2
  free-trade areas 729
  North American Free Trade
    Association (NAFTA) 732
  in practice 732–3
  trade creation 730
  trade diversion 730–1
prejudice 263
present value approach to appraising
    272–3
price:
  of and/or return on substitutes 52–3
  benchmark 201
  ceiling 55
  changes 467
  classical analysis 469–70
  control 55–7
  and demand, relationship between
    35–6
  effect of changes in 115–16
  equals marginal cost 177–8
  expectations and speculation 75–7
  fiscal policy 636
  flexibility 243
  floor 55
  and income elasticities of demand
    in UK for foodstuffs 87
  inelasticity of demand 482
  leadership 396
  maximum 55
  mechanism 21, 24
  minimum 55
  reform 817
  rigidity, nominal 481–2
  stability 207
  and supply 52
  taker 35, 159, 172
  and wages flexibility 465–6
price discrimination 214–19, 387
  advantages to firm 216
  cinema tickets 218
  competition 217
  conditions necessary for operation
    of 214–16

  distribution 217
  first-degree 214, 216
  and monopoly 186
  peak-load pricing 215
  profit-maximising prices and output
    216–17
  profits 217
  and the public interest 217
  second-degree 214
  third-degree 214, 216–17
  on trains (London) 215
price elasticity of demand 61, 69, 160,
    218
  average (or midpoint) formula 66
  and consumer expenditure 63–5
  determinants 62–3
  formula 61
  measurement 61
price elasticity of supply 69–71
  formula 70
price and output determination 45–54
  demand and supply curves,
    identifying position of 49–54
  equilibrium price and output 45–7
  house prices (UK) 50–1
  incentives 54
  incentives in markets 49
  markets equate demand and supply
    47
  movement to a new equilibrium
    47–8
  stock market prices 52–3
price-cap regulation 393
price-consumption curve 116
price-consumption line 116
price-making firms: straight-line
    demand 'curve' 161
price-taking firms 161
pricing 240–4
  cost-based 240–4
  flexible 609
  irrational consumers and profit
    increases 244
  predatory 190–1, 217, 387
  price-setting by companies 242–3
  strategies 482
primary labour market 264
primary market in capital 275
principal-agent problem 224, 261, 330
Priority Schools Building Programme
    (PSBP) 693
prisoners' dilemma 210, 211, 368, 727,
    785
private efficiency 315
Private Finance 2 (PF2) 692–3
Private Finance Initiative (PFI) 694
private property rights, extension of
    359

privatisation and regulation 328,
          389–96
     accountability to shareholders 390
     advantages of privatisation 389–90
     disadvantages of privatisation 390–1
     electricity industry 394–5
     externalities and inequalities 391–2
     fairness 392
     first-best situation 391
     fiscal policy 627
     government interference, reduced
          390
     greater competition 390, 396
     market forces 389–90
     market-oriented supply-side policies
          694
     nationalisation 389
     natural monopolies 390–1
     planning and co-ordination of
          industry 391
     regulation 392–6
          assessment 393–6
          identification of short-run
               optimum price and output
               391–2
          identifying long-run optimum
               price and output 392
     second best theory 391
     tax cuts, financing 390
     utilities 337
pro-cyclical changes 483
problem of the second best 333
procurement policies 720
producer surplus 329
producers' share of a tax on a good 83
product:
     development 196
     differentiation 182, 194, 208
     method of GDP calculation 409,
          425–6
production 7
     costs 43, 700
     function 135, 137, 415
          Cobb-Douglas 148, 149
     -line processes 146
     mass production 146
     multi-stage 145
     point, optimum 152
     possibility curve 13–17, 321–2, 712,
          714, 716, 717
     quotas 93
     see also factors of production; long-
          run theory of production
productive capacity 231
productive efficiency 12, 147
productivity:
     deal 257
     gap 700

of labour 253
of resources, increase in 420
profit 132
     in Cournot model 205–6
     money supply 545
     normal 165, 175, 254, 274
     rate 173
     supernormal 274
     see also capital and profit
profit maximisation 162–7, 170–92,
          193–219, 252, 267
     alternative market structures 171–2
     average curves 164
     contestable markets theory 188–91
     definition of profit 164–6
     difficulties 222
     driving down costs 167
     driving up profits 167
     driving up revenues 167
     employment of land and capital 269
     finding where MR equals MC 165
     logistics 167
     long-run 164, 166
     long-run shut-down point 167
     loss minimising 166
     marginal curves 163–4
     maximising total profit equation
          165
     maximum profit output calculation
          165
     maximum profit using totals curves
          163
     monopolistic competition 194–7
     price and mark-up 241
     rule 163
     short-run 166
     short-run: average and marginal
          curves 163–4
     short-run: total curves 163
     short-run shut-down point 167
     stock of capital 273
     theory 261
     total revenue, total cost and total
          profit 163
     whether or not to produce at all
          166–7
     see also game theory; monopoly;
          oligopoly; perfect competition;
          price discrimination
profit satisficing 223, 229
profitability 532
     of alternative products (substitutes
          in supply) 44
     of goods in joint supply 44
     and liquidity 532–4
progressive tax 300
property rights, changes in 336
proportional tax 300

proportionate or percentage measures
          62
protection, effective rate of 812
prudential control 540
Prudential Regulation Authority 540
psychological factors 277, 564
public finances and balance of trade
          744
public goods 325–6
public interest:
     and alternative maximising theories
          235–7
     competition policy 382
     and contestable markets theory 189
     and monopolistic competition
          196–7
     and oligopoly 207–8
     and perfect competition 177–80
     and price discrimination 217
     and satisficing 239
     see also markets, efficiency and
          public interest
public limited company 222–3
public works: classical Treasury view
          471–2
public-sector 627–8
     deficits 628, 641
     deficits and surpluses and
          government's fiscal stance
          628–30
public-sector net borrowing (PSNB)
          628, 744
public-sector net cash requirement
          (PSNCR) 549, 573, 628, 641, 643
public-sector net debt 628, 639
purchasing-power parity (PPP) 771
     exchange rate 410
     free-floating exchange rates 757,
          758–9
     GDP figures 411
     theory 757
purchasing-power standard (PPS) GDP
          410
'Purity' EC investigation 384

quantiles 286
quantitative controls 794
quantitative easing 452, 489, 551, 571,
          655
     Bank of England 539
     fiscal policy 636
     monetary policy 644, 654, 655
     QE1 647
     QE2 647
     QE3 647
quantity changes (elasticity) 62
quantity demanded 36
     change in 38

quantity supplied, change in **44**
quantity theory of money **469–70**, 471–2, 474, 477, 489, 561
quintiles **286**
quotas 202–3, 720, 728, 767
  and exchange rates 460
  production 93
  set by a cartel **199**

random shocks 464, 520, 635
random walk **277**
rate of return approach 272, **273**
rational choices **11–12**, 100, 114, 129
rational consumer **101**
  behaviour **104**
rational decision making 11, **12**, 105
rational economic behaviour **315**
rational expectations **179**, 609–10, 611–12, 617
rational forward-looking optimising economic agents 484–5
rational producer behaviour **133**
rationalisation **145**, 698
rationality 125
  bounded 126, 128
rationing **56**
reaction function (or curve) **205**
Reagan administration 349, 687, 688, 689
Reaganomics 689
real balance effect **442**
real business cycle theories **479–80**, 482, 613–14
real gross domestic product (GDP) 409, 417
  business cycle (Keynesian analysis) 519
  or GDP at constant prices **409**
  globalisation and instability 779
  market imperfections 482, 483
  new classical school 480
  in selected countries 787
real income **113**
real and nominal values, distinction between 411
real-wage rigidity 482
real-wage unemployment **437–8**
realignments 795
recession 9, 416, 417, 418, 520
  financial crisis and new consensus 489, 490
  house prices 50
  hysteresis 483
  Keynesian position on inflation and unemployment 615–16
  stock market prices 53
  unemployment 431, 434
reciprocity in international trade 728

redemption price 541
rediscounting bills of exchange **541**
redistribution and inflation 446
redistributive effects in pollution policies 363
reference value (ECB) 648
refinancing operations 650–1
refinancing rate 643
reflation/reflationary policies 476, 616, 766
regional multiplier effects **699**, 702, 737
regional policy 699, 702, 734
regional unemployment **440**
regression analysis **39**
regressive tax **300**
regulatory capture **393**
relative price **26**, 500
rent:
  controls 57
  see also land and rent
replacement costs **139**
repo markets 541
repo rate (discount rate) 529, 649
representative agents 480
  with rational expectations (RARE) 488
resale (or retail) price maintenance **386**
reserve accounts, interest-bearing 543
reserve averaging **539**
reserve requirements 646
reserves 455, 460, 529, 532, 533
resource allocation 20
restrictive practices **383**, 385–6
retail banking **526**
retail deposits 532
  and cash in M4 (previously M2) 544
returns to scale 149
  constant 144, 148, 149, 152
  decreasing 144, 148, 149, 152
  increasing 144, 148, 149, 152
revaluation **750**, 767
revenue 158–62
  average revenue (AR) **159**, 160, 161, 162
  curves, shifts in 162
  curves when price varies with output 160–2
  for firm facing downward-sloping demand curve 160
  marginal revenue (MR) **159**, 160–1
  maximisation 218
  price elasticity of demand 161
  price-making firms 161
  price-taking firm **159**, 160, 161
  total revenue (TR) **158**, 159–60, 161–2

Revenue Incentives Innovation Outputs (RIIO) 393
reverse repos **530**
reverse shocks 614
Ricardo, D. 107
risk **77–80**, 225–6
  aversion 122, 211, 275
  factors 533
  independent **123**
  loving 122, 211
  neutral 121
  and sub-prime market 534
  transformation **526**
  and uncertainty 80, 343–6
  -weighted assets 533
  see also demand under conditions of risk and uncertainty
rivalry 326, 358
Roskill Commission 342
RPI inflation 605–6
RPI minus X formula 393, 394
run on the bank 524
run on the currency 455
Russia 22–3

Sadler, L. 375
sale and repurchase agreements (repos) **529**
sales revenue maximisation **229–30**, 235
Sargent, T. 610
satisficing 238–9
savings 289–90, 469, 489
  accounts 528
  flows 403
  net 406, 499
  rate increase 674–5, 678
Say, J.-B. 469
Say's law **469**, 470, 474
scarcity **7–8**, 9, 11, 16, 358
Schumacher, E.F. 379
Schumacher, U. 815
screening (insurance) 124
seasonal unemployment **440**, 513
second-best solution **333**, 334, 342
second-best theory 391
second-degree price discrimination **214**
secondary action **259**
secondary market in capital **276**
secondary marketing **533–6**
sector accounts 403–4
sector income accounts 408
Securities and Exchange Commission 78
Securities Market Programme (SMP) 651, 791
securitisation 226–7, 530, **533–6**

self-employment 289, 301
self-fulfilling speculation 75
self-interested behaviour 129, 319
semi-strong form of efficiency 276–7
senile industry argument 721
sensitivity analysis 343
sentiment and spending 504–5
Serious Fraud Office 385
set-aside 93
share/shares 275
    capital 529
    new issue 231
    prices 53, 78
    yield 277
shirking 261, 262
shocks:
    exogenous 657
    external 759
    internal 757–9
    random 464, 520, 635
    reverse 614
    stochastic 485
    supply-side 448, 480
    technology 480, 613
short selling (or shorting) 78
short-run 133–5, 152, 153
    average cost curve 155–6
    and long-run analysis, merging of
        484
    shut-down point 166
    supply of capital services 270–1
    supply curve 175–6
    under perfect competition 172–4
short-run theory of production 133–8
    averages and marginals, relationship
        between 138
    diminishing returns 134, 135, 137
    population growth and starvation
        134
    production function: average
        physical product 136–7, 138
    production function: marginal
        physical product 137, 138
    production function: total physical
        product 135–6, 138
    short- and long-run changes 133–5
short-termism 275, 276, 393, 696
shut-down point, short-run 166
sight accounts (checking accounts)
    646
sight deposits 528
Single European Act (1987) 350, 695,
    735
single European market 251
Single Market Directive 737
size distribution of income 285
Skills Funding Agency 701
slowdown 483

Smith, A. 24–5, 47, 107, 225
Smith, I.D. 309
snowballing effect 239
Snowdon, P. 471
social benefit 324
social charter 734
social cost 323, 812
social effects of long-term economic
        growth 423
social efficiency 315, 320, 331
    between consumers 321
    between producers 321
    economics of the environment 355,
        358
    in exchange 321–2
    intermediate analysis 320
    in the market 317–18
    Pareto optimality 315
    pollution policies 360, 361
    road usage 371–3
    tax rates in pollution policies 362
    through the market 316–18
    under perfect competition 321–2
social goals 331
social good 319
social indifference curves 321–2, 716
social mobility 310
Social Mobility and Childhood
        Poverty Commission 310
social objectives 26
social policy 734
social rate of discount 346
social security benefits and pensions
        289–90
social-impact standards 361
socialism 348–9
socially optimum level of road space
        (long run) 373
soft buffers 795
soft paternalism 127
Solow (neoclassical) growth model
        673–4
Solow, R. 673
sovereign debt crisis 487
Spahn, P.B. 796
special purpose vehicles (SPVs) 534–6,
        548, 569
specialisation 145, 707–9, 714, 814
specific tax 80, 299
speculation 51, 75–7, 653–4, 756
    balance of payments and exchange
        rates 767
    destabilising 76–7, 128, 570, 760–1
    free-floating exchange rates 672–3,
        760–1, 764
    house prices 51
    self-fulfilling 75
    stabilising 76, 77

speculative or assets motive 553
speculative demand and the exchange
        rate 555
speculative financial flows 768–9
speculative (or assets) demand for
        money 554–5
speculators 75, 77, 79
Spengler, J. 182
spot price 79
spread 540
stabilisers, automatic 641
stabilising speculation 76, 77
Stability and Growth Pact (SGP) 791–2
stagflation 476, 477, 605, 615
stakeholders (in a company) 238
Stalin, J. 22
Stamp out Poverty 796
standardised unemployment rate
        432–3
standing facilities 644
state of the economy: fiscal stance
        628–9
steady-state growth path 678
steady-state level of national income
        674
steady-state output 674
sterilisation 651, 748
Stern Report 356–7
Stern, Sir N. 356
stickiness in wages 437, 438, 439, 473,
        481–2
stimulus package 632
stochastic shocks 485
stock market 52–3, 275–7
stocks 426
    appreciation 426, 427
    and flows 271
    fluctuations 518–19
    holding 80
stop-go policies 476, 767
strategic alliance 233–4
strategic trade theory 721
strategy, structure and rivalry of firms
        in international trade 718
strong efficiency (of share markets) 277
structural balance 629–30
structural deficit (or surplus) 629
structural operations 651
structural policies 91
structural problems within developing
        countries 817–23
    agriculture, neglect of 817–18
    BRICS 822
    capital-intensity bias 819
    devaluation 817
    education and advice 817
    external influences 820–1
    financial provision 817

structural problems within developing countries (*continued*)
government support for rural infrastructure projects 817
land reform 817
new technologies and practices 817
population growth, rapid 819
price reform 817
rural co-operatives 817–18
technology, inappropriate 818–19
unemployment 819–22
structural reform in developing countries 825–6
structural unemployment **440**, 451, 469, 513, 515, 615
sub-prime debt **536**
sub-prime housing crisis (USA) 226–7, 780–1
sub-prime loans (USA) 51
sub-prime market and risk 534
subcontracting **233**
subordinated debt 533
subsidy 333–6, 725
employment 725
environmental 360, 362
production 725
on products 426, 427
subsistence level 421
subsistence production **20**
substitute goods **37**, 62, 119
substitutes:
in supply **44**
traffic congestion economics 371
substitution effect **35**, 304, 308
aggregate demand curve 442
inferior good 117–18
inter-temporal **442**
international **442**, 446
market-oriented supply-side policies 689
normal good 117
of a price change **116**
of a rise in wage rates **249**
of a tax rise **303**
see also diminishing marginal rate of substitution
sunk costs 128, **189**
Sunstein, C. 127
supernormal profits **166**, 173, 175, 176, 182–3, 184, 188
monopolistic competition 194
wage determination under perfect competition 254
supply 8, 42–5, 132–67
actual 8
of capital 273–4
of capital services 270–1
change in 21–2, **44**, 48

costs in the long run 154–8
curve 42–3, 44, 132
elasticity 61
identifying position of 49–54
price and output determination 46–7, 48
declining farm incomes 87–8
determinants 43–4
elasticity 82, 301–2, 773
equation 45
of finance 273–4
hospital treatment provision (providing goods and services free at point of delivery) 84–5
house prices 50
inelastic 82
of money curve: endogenous money supply 552
potential 8
and price 52
profit and the aims of a firm 133
profit maximisation 162–7
response of to increase in demand 74
revenue 158–62
schedule 42
shocks and cost-push inflation 600
shocks (single shifts in aggregate supply curve) 447
short-term price fluctuations 87
stock market prices 53
see also costs in the short run; long-run theory of production; money supply; short-run theory of production
supply-side economics **466**
supply-side policies 9, **452**, 684–703, **685**
and demand-side policies, link between 687
and economic growth 685
exchange rates 460
financial crisis and new consensus 489
inflation 685
Keynesian approach 686–7
and macroeconomy 685
new classical approach 686
'Third Way' policies 687
unemployment 685, 703
see also interventionist supply-side policies; market-oriented supply-side policies
supply-side shocks 448, 480
surplus on the current budget **628**
surprise models 613
sustainability **355**, 726
Svensson, L. 662
Sweezy, P. 206

tacit collusion 199, **200**–1, 213
takeover bid **206**
takeover constraint **231**
takeovers 182, 199
targets, difficulties with 659, 664
targets and instruments principle 651
tariffs 182, 720, 723–4
ad valorem **720**
binding 728
carbon 721
escalation **810**
and exchange rates 460
external 733
or import levies **90**
industrial 727
internal 733
optimum **723**, 724
protection 726
rates 812
trade restrictions 726
tastes 37, 180, 371, 498, 501, 808
tax 333–6
balance sheets 531–2
carbon 363
classical macroeconomics 471
consumers' share of a tax on a good 83
and consumption 497
cuts 688–90
environmental 360, 362
export 724
financial transactions tax (FTT) 794, 797
green **360**, 362–3
harmonisation 734
incidence of **81**
Keynesian revolution 475
marginal tax propensity **499**
multiplier 631
net 406, 499–500
percentage 81
producers' share of a tax on a good 83
on products 426, 427
tobacco 82–3
Tobin 794, 796–7
windfall 334
see also indirect taxes; taxes, benefits and redistribution of income
taxes, benefits and redistribution of income 296–312, 422
ad valorem tax **81**, 299
allowance (tax) **297**
average rates of income tax 298
balance of taxation 299–300
basic rate of tax **297**
basic tax rate cut 304–5
benefit principle **296**

taxes, benefits and redistribution of
income (*continued*)
  benefits 306–8
  capital gains tax 298
  cheapness of collection 296
  convenience to government 297
  convenience to taxpayer 297
  corporate tax 298, 300
  council tax 299
  credits (tax) 310
  customs duties (tariffs) 299
  cuts and incentives 304–5
  different types of people 304
  different types of tax change 305–6
  difficulty of evasion 297
  direct taxes **297**–9, 427
  economic costs of redistribution
    302–3
  employers' social security
    contributions 298, 300
  evasion and avoidance **297**, 301
  evidence 306
  excise duties 299
  general expenditure taxes 299
  goods and services taxes 301
  higher rate of tax, cut in 305
  horizontal equity **296**
  how to help the very poor 301
  incentives 303–6
  income redistribution 296, 300
  income tax 297, 298, 301, 302, 304,
    308
  indirect tax 299, 302
  individuals' social security
    contributions 298
  Laffer curve 303
  legislation 296
  lump-sum tax 300
  marginal income tax 298
  marginal tax-plus-lost-benefit rate
    (marginal deduction rate) 308–9
  minimal disincentive effects 297
  negative income tax **308**
  no income tax 304
  non-distortion 297
  pay-as-you-earn (PAYE) scheme 301
  payroll taxes 300
  personal allowances 301
  poll taxes (community charge) 299
  problems with using taxes to
    redistribute incomes 300–3
  progressive taxes **300**, 301, 304
  proportional tax **300**
  purchase taxes 299
  raising basic rate of tax 305–6
  raising higher rates of tax 305
  rates of tax 301
  reducing tax allowances 306
  regressive tax **300**
  requirements of a good tax system
    296–7
  specific tax **80**, **299**
  structural policies 296
  subsidies 296
  tax/benefit system and
    disincentives: poverty trap **308**
  threshold rise 305
  types of tax 297–300
  undesired incidence of tax 301–2
  value added tax 297, **299**
  vertical equity **296**
  wealth, taxes on 298–9
Taylor, J. 659
Taylor rule 578, **659**, 661, 662, 663,
  664
team work/collective effort 265
technical inefficiency *see* X
  inefficiency
technological progress/improvement
  208, 421, 504, 731, 809
technological unemployment **440**,
  615
technology:
  inappropriate 818–19
  and market power position 178
  shocks 480, 613
  state of 154
technology-based standards **361**
terms of trade **714**–16, 731
  deterioration 809–10
Thaler, R. 127
Thatcher government 349, 438, 478,
  480
  market-oriented supply-side policies
    687, 688, 691, 692, 694
'Third Way' policies 687, 692–3, 702
third-degree price discrimination **214**,
  216–17
Thurow, L. 722
tie-in sales **387**
Tier 1 capital 532, 533, 537
Tier 2 capital 533, 537
time deposits **528**, 646
time dimension 74–80
  dealing in futures markets 79
  price expectations and speculation
    75–7
  short selling 78
  short-run and long-run adjustment
    74–5
  uncertainty and risk 77–80
time lags 62–3, 70, 520, 635–6, 657
tit-for-tat game 212
tobacco taxes 82–3
Tobin, J. 794, 796
Tobin tax 794, 796–7
total consumer expenditure on a
  product 63
total consumer surplus **104**
total cost **140**–1, 152
  curve 162
  of production 132
total currency flow balance 742
total factor productivity 424, 680
total physical product **135**
total (private) surplus **317**
total producer surplus **316**
total product 135–6
total quality management (TQM) 265
total revenue **158**
  curve 162
  (per period of time) 63
total sales revenue 132
total social surplus **318**
total utility **101**–3
  of income 123
total volume of national output 441
tradable permits **362**–7
trade:
  creation **730**, 735–6
  cycle *see* business cycle
  diversion **730**–1, 737
  in goods account 453
  see also international trade; trade
    restrictions
trade restrictions 182, 719–29
  administrative barriers 720
  arguments in favour of 720–3
  bureaucracy 726
  corruption 726–7
  cost of protection 723
  country with monopoly supply of
    export 723
  country with monopsony demand
    for an export 723
  dumping **720**, 725
  economic arguments having some
    general validity 720–1
  economic arguments having validity
    for specific groups or countries
    722–3
  embargoes 720
  environmental issues and free trade
    720
  exchange controls 720
  import licensing 720
  imports should be reduced since
    they lower the standard of
    living 725
  improvement in balance of
    payments 723
  infant industry argument 720–1
  market power 722–3
  method 720

trade restrictions (*continued*)
non-economic arguments 723
optimum tariff or export tax 724
prevention of dumping and other
unfair trade practices 721
prevention of establishment of
foreign-based monopoly 721
prevention of importation of
harmful goods 721
problems with protection 723–7
procurement policies 720
protection of declining industries 723
protection may allow firms to
remain inefficient 726
protection needed from cheap
foreign labour 725
protection reduces unemployment
725
protection as 'second best' 725
quotas 720
reduction of influence of trade on
consumer tastes 721
reduction of reliance on goods with
little dynamic potential 721
retaliation 726
senile industry argument 721
spread of risks of fluctuating markets
721
strategic trade theory 722
subsidy 725
taking account of externalities 721
tariffs 720, 723–4, 726
why buy goods from abroad and
deny jobs to workers in this
country? 725
world multiplier effects 725–6
World Trade Organization 726–8
trade unions 259
trade-offs 331
traditional theory of the firm **133**
traffic congestion economics 369–73
actual and optimum road usage 372
car ownership increase in European
countries 370
complements, price of 371
congestion costs 371–2
cost-benefit analysis 373
demand for road space (by car users)
369–71
environmental costs 372
existing system of road space
allocation 369–71
income 370
long-run supply of road space 371
marginal social benefit of road usage
371
marginal social cost of road usage
371–2

motoring costs as percentage of
household expenditure 370
passenger transport in UK 369
price 370
road space, supply of 371
short-run supply of road space 371
socially efficient level of road usage
(short run) 371–3
substitutes, price of 371
tastes/utility 371
time taken to travel between 2
points along a given road 372
tragedy of the commons **327**
training and education 267–8, 699,
700–1
Training and Enterprise Councils
(TECs) 700
transactions motive 553
transactions plus precautionary
demand for money 553–4
transfer payments **406**, 427
transfers **627**
transport costs 146, 173, 714
transposition (or implementation)
deficit 737, 738
Treasury 540
bills **529**, 532, 541
market-oriented supply-side policies
693
view of balanced budgets (classical)
476
view on public works 471–2
view on unemployment (classical)
471
Treaty of Amsterdam 794
Treaty of the Functioning of the
European Union 383, 384, 385,
387
Treaty of Rome 91, 733
Troubled Asset Relief Program (TARP)
647
trust 368
Turner, A. 127, 797
'20/20/20' package 366
two factor case: marginal product
approach 147–8

uncertainty 77–80, **78**, 231, 446
see also demand under conditions of
risk and uncertainty
underconsumption 489
underemployment **819**
'underground' markets/economy 22,
56, 57, 412
unemployment 9, 10, 401–2, 431–41
age group differences 435
average duration 439
average unemployment rates 432

business cycle, phase of 434
by duration 433
circular flow of income 408
claimant **432**, 434
classical macroeconomics 471
classical Treasury view 471
composition 435–6
costs 436
definition 432
demand, change in pattern of 440
demand-deficient or cyclical **438**–9,
447, 513, 515, 685
disequilibrium 436, **437**–9, 465–6,
467, 473, 690–1
disguised **819**
duration 433–5
equilibrium (or natural)
unemployment 436, 439–40,
478, 630, 690
ethnic group differences 435–6
financial crisis and new consensus 489
flows into and out of 434
frictional (search) **439**–40
gender differences 435
geographical differences 435
hysteresis 483
and inflation 450–1
interventionist approach 440
Keynesian revolution 476
and the labour market 436–7, 439
market-oriented approach 440
mass 464, 472, 473
monetarism 478
natural rate 604
number employed (size of stock of
unemployment) 433
official measures 432–3
pool 433–4
rate **432**
rate of inflow and outflow from
stock of unemployment 433–4
rate, standardised **432**–3
real-wage **437**–8
regional **440**
seasonal **440**, 513
standardised unemployment rates
431, **432**–3, 435
structural **440**, 451, 469, 513, 515,
615
structural problems within
developing countries 819–22
supply-side policies 685, 703
technological **440**, 615
trap 309
voluntary 606
and wage cuts 474
see also non-accelerating-inflation
rate of unemployment

unemployment and inflation 593–623
  macroeconomic thinking post-crisis 622–3
  modern Keynesian position 615–18
  output, inflation and expectations: integrated model 618–21
  see also aggregate supply; expectations-augmented Phillips curve; inflation and unemployment: new classical school
unemployment and inflation (Keynesian analysis) 513–16
  AD/AS diagram and 45° line diagram, relationship between 515
  at the same time 514–15
  deflationary (recessionary) gap **513**
  full-employment national income 513
  inflationary gap 513–**14**
union monopoly or oligopoly 257–8
unit elasticity:
  of demand **62**, 64–5
  of supply 70
unit trusts 548
United Nations 95, 786, 829
  Conference on Environment and Development (UNCED) 827
  Development Programme (UNDP) 804
United States:
  central bank and monetary policy 646–7
  Department of Justice 190
  Department of Transportation 343
  and Kyoto Protocol 365
  M3 544
  Securities and Exchange Commission 234
  trade imbalance 782–3
  see also Federal Reserve
universal banks 527
universal benefits **306**
Universal Credit 309, 310, 702–3
University for Industry 701
urban policy 699, 702
urban transport policies 373–9
  area charges 376
  area licences 377
  car access restriction 374, 375
  congestion may not be solved 374
  direct provision (supply-side solutions) 373–4
  electronic road pricing (ERP) 377
  environmental impact of new roads 374
  equity objective 373

existing taxes, extending 374–5
government or local authority provision of public transport 374
greener vehicle discount 376
London Congestion Charge 376
market signals, changing 374–8
new taxes, introduction of 375
parking restrictions 374
regulation and legislation 374
road pricing 375–7
road solution 373–4
subsidising alternative means of transport 377–8
variable electronic road pricing 376–7
variable tolls 376
urban wages above market-clearing level 811–12
user charges 360
util **101**
utility function (Cobb-Douglas) 113

value added 425
  domestic 812
  gross **425**, 426, 427
value added tax (VAT) 297, **299**
value, expected **340**
value-in-exchange 107
value-in-use 107
variable costs 139, **140**, 175
variable factor **133**
variable minimum reserve ratios 645
velocity of circulation 406, **470**, 567–71
  causality, direction of 571
  long-run stability 567, 570–1
  money balances in different sectors 568–9
  money and spending, growth in 568
  short-run variability 567, 571
  stability 570–1
Venezuela 826
vent for surplus 807–8
vertical de-mergers 237
vertical equity **296**
vertical merger **232**
vertical price-fixing agreements 385–6
vertical restraints **387**
voluntary agreements 361
voluntary unemployment 606

wage cuts 474
wage determination in imperfect markets 256–68
  behaviour at work and employee motivation 266
  collective bargaining 258–9

discrimination 263–8
efficiency wage hypothesis **259**–63
equal pay for equal work 262–3
firms and labour with market power (bilateral monopoly) 258
firms with market power in employing labour (monopsony) **256**–7
flexible labour markets and flexible firm 264–5
labour market imperfections 263
labour with market power (union monopoly or oligopoly) 257–8
labour movement/trade unionism in the UK 26
labour turnover, reduced 261
marginal productivity theory 261
morale 262
'shirking', reduced 261
wage determination under perfect competition 247–55
  causes of inequality 255
  demand for labour: marginal productivity theory 252–4
  derivation of firm's demand curve for labour 253
  derivation of industry demand curve for labour 253–4
  elasticity of demand for labour 254
  elasticity of market supply of labour 250–1
  equality and inequality 254–5
  immigration and UK labour market 251
  indifference curve analysis to derive individuals' supply curve of labour 250
  labour as a factor of production 248
  labour supply 248–51
  low-paid to high-paid jobs 255
  marginal cost of labour (MCL) 252
  marginal product of labour (MPL) 253
  marginal revenue product of labour (MRPL) 252, 253
  market supply of a given type of labour 249–50
  mythical world of perfect wage equality 254–5
  perfect labour markets 247
  profit-maximising approach 252–3
  supply of hours by an individual worker 248–9
  supply of labour to an individual employer 249
  wages and profits under perfect competition 254

wage rates 253, 443
  above market-clearing level 818
wage setters 256
wage taker **247**, 249
wages:
  flexible 609
  and profits under perfect
      competition 254
  rent and interest 271
  and salaries 289–90
  stickiness 437, 438, 439, 473,
      481–2
Walras, L. 107, 348
War on Want 794, 796
waste elimination 265
weak efficiency (of share markets) **276**
wealth:
  distribution of 285, 289, 292–3
  national 524
  stock market prices 53
Webb, S. 311
Wei, S.-J. 759
welfare reduction 691–4

Welfare to Work Programme 702
White Knight strategy 232
wholesale banking **526**–7
wholesale deposits and loans **526**
wholesale funding 530–1
Wilde, O. 3
Willetts, D. 311
Williamson, J. 794–5
Williamson, O.E. 228–9
win-win situation 25
windfall tax 334
withdrawals 406–7, 499–501
  function, total 501
  imports 500–1
  and injections, relationship between
      407
  Keynesian revolution 474–5
  or leakages **406**–7
  marginal propensity to withdraw
      501
  monetary changes and national
      income 561
  MPC 500

net saving 499
net taxes 499–500
  shift in 509–10
Wolf, A. 701
Wolf report 701
workforce, increase in 675–7
Working Families Tax Credit 309
Working Tax Credit (WTC) 309
working to rule **258**
World Bank 796, 812, 825, 827
  Logistic Performance Index 822
world multiplier effects 725–6
World Trade Organisation 74, 727–8,
      779
  Doha Development Agenda 92,
      726–7, 728, 809, 816

X inefficiency 186, 225

yield on a share **277**

zero price 16
zero-hours contracts 260